AMERICAN LABOR

*FROM CONSPIRACY
TO
COLLECTIVE BARGAINING*

ADVISORY EDITORS

Leon Stein   *Philip Taft*

HOW COLLECTIVE BARGAINING WORKS

Harry A. Millis, editor

ARNO & THE NEW YORK TIMES
NEW YORK   1971

ST. PHILIPS COLLEGE LIBRARY

Reprint Edition 1971 by Arno Press Inc.

LC# 74-156436
ISBN 0-405-02933-0

American Labor: From Conspiracy to Collective Bargaining—Series II
ISBN for complete set: 0-405-02910-1
See last pages for titles.

Manufactured in the United States of America

HOW COLLECTIVE BARGAINING WORKS

A TWENTIETH CENTURY FUND INVESTIGATION

THE TRUSTEES of the Fund choose subjects for Fund investigations, underwrite the expenses of the surveys, and appoint the special committees which have charge of them. The Trustees, however, assume no responsibility for the research findings or the recommendations for action that result.

TRUSTEES

A. A. BERLE, JR.
FRANCIS BIDDLE
BRUCE BLIVEN
PERCY S. BROWN
HENRY S. DENNISON
JOHN H. FAHEY
OSWALD W. KNAUTH

MORRIS E. LEEDS
ROBERT S. LYND
JAMES G. MCDONALD
WILLIAM I. MYERS
CHARLES P. TAFT
HARRISON TWEED
W. W. WAYMACK

OFFICERS

JOHN H. FAHEY, *President*
HENRY S. DENNISON, *Chairman, Executive Committee*
PERCY S. BROWN, *Treasurer*
EVANS CLARK, *Executive Director*
J. FREDERIC DEWHURST, *Economist*

LABOR COMMITTEE OF
THE TWENTIETH CENTURY FUND

THE FOLLOWING committee has been in charge of the investigation by the special research staff, whose findings are summarized in this volume. The staff is responsible for these findings. The committee will be responsible for an analysis of collective bargaining and recommendations for action which are to be incorporated in another volume now in preparation.

WILLIAM H. DAVIS, *Chairman*
Chairman, National War Labor Board; formerly Chairman, New York State Mediation Board

WILLIAM L. CHENERY
Editor, *Collier's Weekly*

HOWARD COONLEY
Chairman of the Board, Walworth Company, Incorporated; Chairman, Finance Committee, formerly President, National Association of Manufacturers

CLINTON S. GOLDEN
Assistant to the President, United Steelworkers of America, affiliated with the Congress of Industrial Organizations

WILLIAM M. LEISERSON
Member, National Labor Relations Board; formerly Chairman, National Mediation Board

FRAZIER MACIVER
Vice President, Phoenix Hosiery Company

SUMNER H. SLICHTER
Lamont University Professor, Harvard University

ROBERT J. WATT
International Representative, American Federation of Labor

EDWIN E. WITTE
Professor and Chairman, Department of Economics, University of Wisconsin; former member, Wisconsin Labor Relations Board

HOW COLLECTIVE BARGAINING WORKS

A Survey of Experience in Leading American Industries

Research Director
HARRY A. MILLIS

Contributing Authors

DONALD ANTHONY
JOSEPH W. BLOCH
EMILY CLARK BROWN
ROBERT K. BURNS
C. LAWRENCE CHRISTENSON
MILTON DERBER
WALDO E. FISHER
WILLIAM HABER

FREDERICK H. HARBISON
ANTHONY LUCHEK
W. H. MCPHERSON
ROBERT J. MYERS
PHILIP TAFT
GEORGE W. TAYLOR
ROBERT WINTERS
HARRY D. WOLF

New York
THE TWENTIETH CENTURY FUND
1942

COPYRIGHT 1942 BY THE TWENTIETH CENTURY FUND, INC.

MANUFACTURED IN THE UNITED STATES OF AMERICA
AMERICAN BOOK–STRATFORD PRESS, INC., NEW YORK

FOREWORD

THIS VOLUME contains full-length sketches of the actual workings of collective bargaining in sixteen United States trades and industries and thumbnail summaries covering thirteen other fields. Each of the broader pictures covers both the growth of organized dealings between employers and labor unions in the industry, and the situation at the time of writing. Although most of the field work was done in 1939, almost all the chapters include developments in 1940 and about half of them cover events in 1941. A survey of the women's clothing industry by Patrick M. Malin was to have been included but, owing to unavoidable delays, this chapter was not completed in time for publication.

Since this report was written the United States has been catapulted into the most gigantic war of all history. Collective bargaining is likely to change its form and procedure under the pressure of war, but the experience of the last war, at least, indicates that the basic problems of industrial relations remain after the end of hostilities. It also showed that during the conflict sound labor policies are essential elements of victory. In wartime both the area of collective bargaining and its importance are increased. All this makes a clear understanding of collective bargaining even more urgent now than in times of peace.

As it has happened, six of the industries here covered in detail are now in the war essentials class—steel, electrical products, bituminous coal, railroads, automobiles, rubber. These, together with the other ten, were originally picked out to show collective bargaining in all the various stages of youth and maturity. In railroads, for example, collective bargaining has long passed the unpredictable and stormy years of youth and adolescence; while in the automobile and steel industries it is still in the formative stages. In railroads an industrial government has been set up on the basis of mutual understanding and confidence; in steel and automobiles the smoke and dust of conflict still hang over scenes of recent struggle. Through the murk each side still measures the other with some suspicion.

Like other surveys of The Twentieth Century Fund this one is the joint product of three parties: the Fund Trustees, who have chosen the subject and financed the undertaking; a special committee appointed by the Trustees, which has had general supervision of the project; and a special research staff, which has provided the factual findings. This volume contains the full text of the reports of the members of the research staff, each of whom has accepted full responsibility for his own text. The committee, however, reviewed the first drafts of the manuscripts of these reports and gave the authors the benefit of their advice and criticism.

On the basis of the information in these pages, and of such other knowledge as they may have, the members of the committee will prepare a report which will contain the committee's analysis of the problems of collective bargaining and a program of action to deal with them. It is hoped that this second volume will suggest policies useful both for the war effort and for the hardly less prodigious task of postwar reconstruction.

This volume is in itself a joint undertaking. The separate industry chapters were written by separate authors—each chosen for special knowledge in the particular field. The survey research director, Dr. Harry A. Millis, assembled this staff, planned the volume and acted as its editor during most of its preparation. His appointment to the chairmanship of the National Labor Relations Board in the Fall of 1940, however, has prevented him from seeing the volume through its final stages. Natalie Pannes, his assistant, has taken on much of this responsibility. She also rewrote or revised some of the manuscripts to bring them up to date. Dr. J. Frederic Dewhurst, the Fund's Economist, reviewed the manuscripts in all their stages of development, and gave the staff the benefit of his advice and criticism. Louise Field assisted him in reviewing the manuscripts and prepared them for publication.

FOREWORD

A large number of organizations and individuals gave valuable assistance to the staff by furnishing them with information and by reviewing the manuscripts of the various chapters before publication. A list of these is given on the following pages. To all those who have cooperated in the undertaking—and especially to Dr. Millis and the contributing authors—the Fund extends its deep appreciation.

> EVANS CLARK
> *Executive Director*
> *The Twentieth Century Fund*

330 WEST 42D STREET
NEW YORK, NEW YORK
MARCH 17, 1942

ACKNOWLEDGMENTS

THE FOLLOWING list of acknowledgments is by no means complete. Scores of union and management officials gave valuable assistance in the preparation of the various chapters. To all of them—too numerous to mention—the staff is deeply indebted.

Allegheny Ludlum Steel Company
Hugh Allen, Director of Publicity, Goodyear Tire and Rubber Company
Amalgamated Clothing Workers of America
American Iron and Steel Institute
American Newspaper Publishers Association
American Steel and Wire Company
Connie Anderson, formerly Assistant Research Director, United Rubber Workers of America
Wilfred Andrew, Manager, Labor Department, Seiberling Rubber Company
T. O. Armstrong, Personnel Director, Westinghouse Electric and Manufacturing Company, East Springfield, Massachusetts
H. J. Arries, Statistician, Brotherhood of Locomotive Firemen and Enginemen
Automobile Manufacturers Association
Automotive Parts and Equipment Manufacturers
Automotive Tool and Die Manufacturers' Association
Claude M. Baker, President, International Typographical Union
Meyer Bernstein, Steel Workers Organizing Committee
George L. Berry, President, International Printing Pressmen and Assistants' Union of North America
Bethlehem Steel Company
Anne Bezanson, University of Pennsylvania
Ferdinand Bindel, President, Pittsburgh Plate Glass Company, Creighton local, Federation of Glass, Ceramic, and Silica Sand Workers of America
Earl Blank, Jones and Laughlin Steel Corporation
Harry Block, General Vice President, United Electrical, Radio and Machine Workers of America
John Boylan, Secretary, Anthracite Board of Conciliation
R. R. R. Brooks, Williams College
Walter Brower, Impartial Chairman for the New York Men's Clothing Industry
Hugh V. Brown, United Mine Workers of America

L. S. Buchmaster, President, Firestone Tire and Rubber Company local, United Rubber Workers of America
Leo J. Buckley, President, International Stereotypers' and Electrotypers' Union
Edward F. Burpee, American Newspaper Publishers Association
L. L. Callahan, President, B. F. Goodrich Company local, United Rubber Workers of America
Matthew Campbell (deceased), General Vice President, United Electrical, Radio and Machine Workers of America
Harry G. Cantrell, Secretary, Franklin Association of Chicago
Claude V. Capers, American Newspaper Publishers Association
Carnegie-Illinois Steel Corporation
Cyrus Ching, Director of Industrial and Public Relations, United States Rubber Company
Earl Constantine, President, National Association of Hosiery Manufacturers
E. M. Craig, Secretary, National Association of Building Trades Employers
Mark Cresap, President, Hart, Schaffner and Marx
George M. Cucich, Research Director, Railway Employees' Department, American Federation of Labor
Sherman H. Dalrymple, President, United Rubber Workers of America
Irwin DeShetler, President, Federation of Glass, Ceramic, and Silica Sand Workers of America
Gladys Dickason, Director of Research, Amalgamated Clothing Workers of America
Paul Dildine, B. F. Goodrich Company
George Dougherty, Assistant Secretary, National Association of Manufacturers of Pressed and Blown Glassware
Corwin Edwards, Chairman, Policy Committee, Anti-Trust Division, U. S. Department of Justice
William Eichelberger, formerly of the Office of the Bituminous Coal Consumers' Counsel
Wayne P. Ellis, Secretary, Bituminous Coal Producers' Board, District No. 8
Charles W. Fair, Reading Coal Company
Fairchild Publications
Firestone Tire and Rubber Company
Phillips L. Garman, formerly Research Director, International Printing Pressmen and Assistants' Union of North America
Clinton S. Golden, Steel Workers Organizing Committee
B. F. Goodrich Company
Goodyear Tire and Rubber Company
T. G. Graham, Vice President, B. F. Goodrich Company
Morris Greenberg, Vice President, Hart, Schaffner and Marx
Frank Grillo, Secretary-Treasurer, United Rubber Workers of America

ACKNOWLEDGMENTS xiii

John B. Haggerty, President, International Brotherhood of Bookbinders
Marion Harper
Ralph Hetzel, Jr., Director, Economic Division, Congress of Industrial Organizations
Sidney Hillman, General President, Amalgamated Clothing Workers of America (on leave)
Alfred Hoffman, First Vice President, American Federation of Hosiery Workers
Phillip A. Hollar, Pennsylvania Railroad Company
Everett G. Holt, Chief, Consumption Materials Unit, U. S. Department of Commerce
Max Holtz, formerly President, Rochester Clothiers' Exchange
John House, formerly President, Goodyear Tire and Rubber Company local, United Rubber Workers of America
Miriam Hussey, University of Pennsylvania
Industrial Relations Section, Princeton University
Inland Steel Company
Charles M. James, University of Pennsylvania
Leo Jandreau, General Vice President, United Electrical, Radio and Machine Workers of America
Harry Jenkins (deceased), formerly Secretary, Glass Bottle Blowers' Association
E. A. Johnson, Secretary, Building and Construction Trades Council of the Metropolitan District of Boston
Jones and Laughlin Steel Corporation
David Kaplan, formerly Research Director, International Association of Machinists
Milton Kaufman, formerly Executive Vice President, American Newspaper Guild
Fred Keightley, Director of Labor Relations, Pittsburgh Plate Glass Company
Harvey J. Kelly, formerly Chairman, Special Standing Committee, American Newspaper Publishers Association
Thomas Kennedy, United Mine Workers of America
George F. Lang, President, Full-Fashioned Hosiery Manufacturers of America
Julius H. Levy, Executive Secretary of the New York Clothing Manufacturers' Exchange
A. D. Lewis, National Chairman, United Construction Workers Organizing Committee
Paul W. Litchfield, President, Goodyear Tire and Rubber Company
Eugene MacKinnon, Chairman, Special Standing Committee, American Newspaper Publishers Association

David McDonald, Steel Workers Organizing Committee
L. L. McDonald, Carrier Representative, National Railroad Adjustment Board
Alexander F. McKeown, President, American Federation of Hosiery Workers
Joseph Mitton, President, RCA Manufacturing Company, Camden local 103, United Electrical, Radio and Machine Workers of America
National Credit Office
Charles Newell, formerly Business Agent, Westinghouse Electric and Manufacturing Company, Pittsburgh local 601, United Electrical, Radio and Machine Workers of America
John Nicholas, President, Libby-Owens-Ford Corporation, Toledo local, Federation of Glass, Ceramic, and Silica Sand Workers of America
Katherine Ormstead, American Newspaper Guild
Joseph C. Orr, Secretary, International Printing Pressmen and Assistants' Union of North America
Victor Pasche, formerly Secretary-Treasurer, American Newspaper Guild
Florence Peterson, Chief, Industrial Relations Division, U. S. Bureau of Labor Statistics
Pittsburgh Steel Company
Lester M. Rachofsky, Director of the Stabilization Department, Amalgamated Clothing Workers of America
Woodruff Randolph, Secretary-Treasurer, International Typographical Union
Donald Reichow, Assistant to the Vice President in Charge of Production, B. F. Goodrich Company
Republic Steel Corporation
Clara Roberts, Statistician, International Stereotypers' and Electrotypers' Union
T. W. Rowe, Owens-Illinois Glass Company
Harold Ruttenberg, Steel Workers Organizing Committee
David J. Saposs, formerly Chief Economist, National Labor Relations Board
William Smith, General Secretary-Treasurer, American Federation of Hosiery Workers
William H. Spencer, Dean, Business School, University of Chicago
Steel Workers Organizing Committee
John A. Stephens, United States Steel Corporation
Peter Stone, Temporary National Economic Committee
Charles A. Sumner, Secretary-Treasurer, International Stereotypers' and Electrotypers' Union
Gladys M. Swanson, American Newspaper Publishers Association
Vincent Sweeney, Steel Workers Organizing Committee

Acknowledgments

Don H. Taylor, Executive Vice President, New York Employing Printers Association
Lazare Teper, International Ladies' Garment Workers' Union
John W. Thomas, Chairman of the Board, Firestone Tire and Rubber Company
Florence Thorne, Director of Research, American Federation of Labor
International Union, United Automobile, Aircraft and Agricultural Implement Workers of America
United Rubber Workers of America
United States Rubber Company
United States Steel Corporation
E. J. Volz, President, International Photo-Engravers' Union of North America
J. A. Voss, Republic Steel Corporation
Gerald A. Walsh, Secretary, Printers' National Association
Robert J. Watt, International Representative, American Federation of Labor
Ruth Weaver, American Newspaper Publishers Association
Weirton Steel Company
Wheeling Steel Corporation
James Wishart, formerly Educational Director, United Rubber Workers of America

CONTENTS

	Page
CHAPTER 1. ORGANIZED LABOR AND THE NEW DEAL by Philip Taft	3
1. Government Encouragement of Labor Organization	4
2. The Collective Bargaining Situation	17
a. Importance of Collective Bargaining in Various Industries	18
b. The Bargaining Unit	23
c. Union Status	24
d. Collective Bargaining Machinery	25
e. The Terms of Employment	27
f. Variations in Collective Bargaining	30
CHAPTER 2. DAILY NEWSPAPERS by Robert K. Burns	31
1. The Industry: Its Economic Status and Characteristics	32
a. Present Size and Relative Position	32
b. Nature and Economic Characteristics	32
2. Union Organizations: Their Status, Jurisdictions and Functions	39
a. Jurisdictions and Employment	40
b. Government and Functions	41
3. Publisher Organizations and Their Functions	43
a. City and Regional Associations	43
b. The American Newspaper Publishers Association	44
4. Development of Collective Bargaining	47
a. Background of Collective Bargaining in the Industry	47
b. Development of Formal Collective Bargaining, 1885–1900	48
c. Industrial Relations Under the International Arbitration Agreements	50
5. Collective Bargaining: Main Issues and Settlements	65
a. Union Status	66
b. Wages and Hours of Work	70
c. Hiring and Discharge	85
d. Other Trade Regulations	94
6. Collective Bargaining: Evaluations and Conclusions	101
a. Results	101
b. Supporting and Limiting Factors	102
c. Unsettled Problems	106
7. Collective Bargaining in Editorial and Commercial Departments	108
a. History of Organization	108

b. Settlement of Disputes	111
c. The "Freedom of the Press" Issue	112
d. Results of Collective Bargaining	113
e. Conclusion	116

CHAPTER 3. BOOK AND JOB PRINTING by *Emily Clark Brown*	118
1. The Industry	118
a. Size, Divisions and Location	118
b. Economics of the Industry	121
2. Development of Organization and Collective Bargaining	125
a. Organization in the Nineteenth Century	126
b. Evolution of Negotiation and Written Agreements	127
c. Organizational Gains in the Late 1930's	133
d. Present Union Strength	136
3. Collective Bargaining Structure and Methods	137
a. Local Autonomy	137
b. Craft Autonomy	139
c. The Agreements	142
4. The Results	148
a. Civil Rights and Democratic Equality	148
b. Peaceful Adjustment of Controversies	150
c. Wages and Hours	154
d. Working Rules	160
e. Union Policies and Their Effects	167
f. Competition	170
5. Experience with Other Methods of Collective Bargaining	172
6. Conclusions	176

CHAPTER 4. BUILDING CONSTRUCTION by *William Haber*	183
1. Introduction	183
2. The Industry	185
a. Size	185
b. Building Markets	185
c. Cost Elements	189
d. Technology and Materials	189
e. The Building Business	192
f. Characteristics of the Industry and Its Labor Problems	195
3. Organization Among Workers	196
a. The Unions	196
b. Dual Unionism	198
c. Amalgamation	199
d. Local Building Trades Councils	200

Contents

	Page
e. Jurisdictional Disputes	200
f. Union Strength	203
4. Employers' Organizations	205
5. The Collective Bargaining Process	207
a. Negotiations	207
b. The Agreements	208
6. Problems and Obstacles	221
CHAPTER 5. BITUMINOUS COAL *by Waldo E. Fisher*	229
1. Introduction	229
2. The Struggle for Collective Bargaining, 1850–1898	230
a. Economic Conditions, 1878–1898	232
b. Working Conditions and Labor Policies	233
c. An Experiment in Interstate Collective Bargaining	234
d. Formation of the United Mine Workers of America	235
e. Efforts to Re-Establish Interstate Collective Bargaining	236
3. Collective Bargaining in the Central Competitive Field	237
a. Basic Theory Underlying the Central Competitive Field Compact	238
b. Organization and Procedures of the Interstate Conference	239
c. State and Local Agreements	241
d. Issues in Collective Bargaining and Content of Agreements	241
e. Procedure for Handling Grievances	244
f. Experience with Arbitration	245
g. Strikes, Lockouts and Suspensions	249
h. Attempts to Extend the Scope of the Central Competitive Field Compact	253
i. Trend of Wages, Hours and Employment Under the Interstate Compact	254
j. Collapse of the Interstate System	257
4. Collective Bargaining in Outlying Producing Fields Before 1927	262
5. Attempts to Organize the Nonunion Areas Before 1927	263
6. Return of Ruthless Competition: 1927 to 1933	264
7. Period of Governmental Intervention: 1933 to Date	268
a. The NRA	269
b. Other UMW Activities	271
c. The New Bituminous Coal Act	272
d. The Agreement of 1939	273
e. The Agreement of 1941	274
8. Major Problems of the Industry	275
9. Conclusion	277

	Page
CHAPTER 6. ANTHRACITE *by Waldo E. Fisher*	280
1. Introduction	280
2. Industrial Relations Under Free Competition, 1842–1900	282
a. A Decade of Collective Bargaining, 1865–1875	282
b. Twenty-five Years of Individual Bargaining	285
3. Industrial Relations in a Sellers' Market, 1900–1927	288
a. The Strike of 1900	288
b. The Strike of 1902	289
c. The Award of 1903	291
d. Labor Relations Under the Award	293
e. Trade Agreements Replace the Award	294
f. War and Postwar Years	295
g. The Strike of 1922	298
h. The Pinchot Settlement of 1923	300
i. The Strike of 1925–1926	300
j. Trend of Hours, Wages and Employment Opportunity, 1902–1926	302
4. Industrial Relations in a Declining Market, 1927–1941	303
a. Reasons for the Decline in Production	304
b. The Agreement of 1930	306
c. The Operators Request a Wage Reduction	306
d. The Miners Obtain the Seven-Hour Day	307
e. The 1939 and 1941 Agreements	307
f. Wage Rates, Hours and Employment After 1926	308
5. Negotiating the Trade Agreement	310
6. Procedure for Handling Grievances	311
7. Summary and Conclusions	314
CHAPTER 7. RAILROADS *by Harry D. Wolf*	318
1. Introduction	318
2. Extent and Nature of Railroad Employment	319
a. Financial Condition of the Railroads	319
b. The Volume of Employment	321
c. Types of Employment	322
3. Development of Collective Bargaining	323
a. The Pre-World War Years	323
b. Government Operation of the Railroads	326
c. The Work of the Railroad Labor Board	328
d. The Railway Labor Act	328
e. Gains of National Organizations at Expense of Company Unions	330
4. The Railroad Labor Organizations	332

	Page
5. Negotiating Agreements	337
a. Bargaining with Single Labor Organizations	338
b. Joint Bargaining on a National Scale	339
6. The Agreements	343
a. Employees Covered by an Agreement	344
b. Wages and Hours	345
c. Seniority	351
d. Absence of the Closed Shop	356
7. Procedure for Handling Disputes	357
a. Disputes over Changes in Agreements	357
b. Disputes Arising Under Agreements	360
8. The Labor Organizations' Broad Program	364
a. Labor's 1931 Program	366
b. Legislative and Bargaining Gains	368
9. Conclusions	373
CHAPTER 8. MEN'S CLOTHING *by Robert J. Myers and Joseph W. Bloch*	381
1. Characteristics of the Industry	382
a. Historical Development	382
b. Location of the Industry	384
c. Economic Characteristics	385
2. Clothing Workers and the Amalgamated	393
a. The Workers	393
b. The Amalgamated	394
3. The Employers	402
a. Characteristics of the Employers	403
b. Employers' Associations	403
4. The Formative Years of Collective Bargaining	405
a. Origin at Hart, Schaffner and Marx	406
b. Extension of Collective Bargaining	409
c. Early Experience	410
5. The Bargaining Organization in Maturity	414
a. Present Significance of the Labor Agreement	414
b. Direct Negotiation	416
c. The Part Played by the Impartial Machinery	417
d. Some Established Principles	420
6. Determination of Wages	422
a. The Amalgamated's Wage Policy	422
b. Complexity of the Wage Structure	423
c. Fixing of Piece Rates	425
d. Adjustment of General Wage Levels	426
e. Trends in Wages	428

7. Union Participation in Management	431
a. Influence of Declining Production on Union Policy	431
b. Union-Management Cooperation	432
c. The Amalgamated and the NRA	435
d. The Amalgamated's Stabilization Plan	436
8. Conclusion	444

CHAPTER 9. HOSIERY *by George W. Taylor* — 450

1. Introduction	450
2. Fundamentals of Collective Bargaining in Hosiery	452
a. The Economics of Rate Setting	452
b. Industry-Wide Collective Bargaining	454
c. Administration of Agreements	457
d. Civil Rights of Employees	460
e. Collective Bargaining and Job Security	462
3. Development of Collective Bargaining	464
a. The Running Battle Prior to 1921	464
b. Turning Point for the Industry—the 1921 Strike	471
c. Rapid Industrial Expansion and Decreasing Union Strength—1922–1928	473
d. Retreat of the Union and "Industry-Wide" Collective Bargaining	480
e. Organizing and Bargaining, 1933–1935	489
f. Lapse of Collective Bargaining, 1936	496
g. The 1937 Drive for Agreements	498
h. The Rehabilitation Program	503

CHAPTER 10. STEEL *by Frederick H. Harbison* — 508

1. Introduction	508
2. Developments Prior to the SWOC Drive	510
a. The Amalgamated Association of Iron, Steel and Tin Workers	510
b. Development of Employee Representation Plans	512
c. The United Mine Workers and the Steel Campaign	515
3. SWOC Organizing Tactics and Strategy	517
a. Early Organization Strategy	517
b. "Capture" of the Carnegie-Illinois Employee Representation Plans	520
c. The U. S. Steel Agreements of 1937	522
d. SWOC Victories: March to May 1937	524
e. "Little Steel"	525
f. Recession and Revival	527

	Page
4. SWOC Structure and Aims	534
a. Structure	534
b. Objectives	538
c. Strength	541
5. The Steel Companies' Policies and Organization	542
a. Development of Collective Bargaining Policies	542
b. Management Organization	547
6. Labor Relations Under the First Contracts: 1937–1941	549
a. The Standard Contracts of 1937	549
b. Interpretation of Contract Provisions	551
c. Procedure for Settlement of Grievances	556
7. The "New Standard Agreement" of 1941	560
8. Conclusions	563
9. Basic Issues Beyond the Scope of Collective Bargaining	566
a. Introduction of New Methods and Machinery	567
b. National Defense	568

CHAPTER 11. AUTOMOBILES *by W. H. McPherson*   571

1. Introduction	571
2. The Industry	572
a. Development	572
b. Size	573
c. Structure	573
d. Location	575
e. Production Methods	576
f. Employment Fluctuations	576
g. Competition and Price	577
3. Labor Organization	578
a. Craft and Industrial Unionism	579
b. Competitive Unionism	580
c. Factionalism in the UAW	584
d. UAW-CIO Victory at Ford	587
4. Attitudes and Tactics	589
a. The Open-Shop Years	589
b. Response to Changing Economic and Political Conditions	590
c. Period of Aggressive Unionism	591
d. Present Situation	594
5. Bargaining Methods	596
a. Negotiation of Agreements	597
b. Settlement of Grievances	602
6. Results of Collective Bargaining	609
a. Hours	609

	Page
b. Methods of Payment	611
c. Wage Rates	613
d. Job Security	617
e. Speed of Operations	623
f. Vacations	624
g. Other Working Conditions	625
7. Current Problems	625
a. Union Problems	626
b. Management Problems	628
c. Joint Problems	629

CHAPTER 12. RUBBER PRODUCTS *by Donald Anthony* — 631

1. Characteristics of the Industry	631
a. Structure and Location	632
b. Instability of the Industry	634
c. The Workers and Their Earnings	635
2. Company Policies and Labor Organization	637
a. Labor Struggles in the 1930's	638
b. Present Union Strength	641
3. A Brief Analysis of the Agreements	644
4. Collective Bargaining in Akron	649
a. The Early Years: From Management Control to Union Domination Through the Sitdown	649
b. Collective Bargaining in a Hostile Atmosphere	652
5. Summary of Problems	676

CHAPTER 13. GLASS *by Milton Derber* — 682

1. Introduction	682
2. The Old Unionism in the Container and Flint Glass Industries	687
a. Effect of the New Deal on Union Membership	687
b. The Joint Conference System	690
c. History	691
d. The Agreements and Their Enforcement	698
e. Settlement of Grievances	701
f. Problems	703
g. Results of Collective Bargaining	713
3. The New Unionism in Flat Glass	718
a. Organization of the Skilled Workers	718
b. Collective Bargaining with the Cutters	722
c. The Federation of Flat Glass Workers	723
4. Summary and Observations	739

Contents

	Page
CHAPTER 14. ELECTRICAL PRODUCTS *by Milton Derber*	744
1. Introduction	744
2. General Electric at Schenectady	747
a. The Metal Trades Council	748
b. The Employee Representation Plan	749
c. Rise of the United Electrical and Radio Workers	750
d. The 1938 Agreement	752
e. Problems and Results	757
3. Westinghouse	760
a. East Pittsburgh	761
b. East Springfield	772
4. The Radio Industry	781
a. Philco	782
b. RCA	790
5. Observations and Conclusions	801
CHAPTER 15. CHICAGO SERVICE TRADES *by C. Lawrence Christenson*	806
1. Introduction	806
2. Chicago's Cleaning and Dyeing Industry	808
a. The Dry Cleaning Business	808
b. Organization for Collective Bargaining	813
c. Current Labor Standards	815
d. The Instruments of Joint Control	816
e. Development of Control of Labor Standards	817
f. Disintegration and Reorganization: 1930–1939	822
g. The Logic of Collective Control	827
3. The Motion Picture Machine Operators of Chicago	830
a. The Motion Picture Industry	830
b. Organization of Employers and Employees	831
c. Current Working Conditions	833
d. The Supply of Labor and Union Control	834
e. The Course of Collective Control: 1920–1940	837
f. Forces Supporting the Bargaining Structure	844
4. The Musicians of Chicago	848
a. The Bargaining Units	848
b. Methods of Collective Bargaining and Union Control	851
c. Employment Standards	856
d. Job Control and Enforcement of Union Standards	858
e. Factors Supporting Collective Bargaining	862
5. Summary	866

APPENDICES

	Page
A. COLLECTIVE BARGAINING BEFORE THE NEW DEAL *by Philip Taft*	871
1. Early History, 1786–1850	871
2. Nationalization of the Labor Movement	873
a. The Iron Industry	875
b. Anthracite Mining	876
c. Bituminous Coal Mining	876
d. Shoemaking	877
e. Other Industries	879
3. The Later Nineties to the World War	880
a. Building Construction	881
b. Shoemaking	883
c. Printing	883
d. Bituminous Coal Mining	885
e. Anthracite Mining	887
f. Railroads	887
g. Water Transportation	888
h. Glass and Pottery	890
i. The Stove Industry	890
j. Steel	893
k. General Foundries	895
l. Metal Trades	897
m. Iron and Steel Construction	898
n. Other Prewar Developments	898
4. World War Period	901
5. A Period of Union Stagnation	904
B. BRIEF REVIEW OF OTHER INDUSTRIES *by Philip Taft*	908
1. Clay, Chemical and Allied Industries	908
a. Pottery	908
b. Brick and Clay, Other Than Pottery	911
c. Cement	912
d. Chemicals	913
2. Clothing	914
a. Boots and Shoes	914
b. Fur	915
c. Hats and Millinery	916
3. Food and Liquor	918
a. Baking	918
b. Brewing	919
c. Flour and Cereal	920
d. Fruit and Vegetable Growing and Processing	921

	Page
e. Meat Processing and Distribution	922
4. Hotels and Restaurants	924
5. Lumber, Pulp and Paper	925
a. Lumber	925
b. Pulp and Paper	927
6. Machinist and Related Trades	928
a. The Machinists	928
b. Pattern Making	930
c. Airplane Manufacture	930
d. Shipbuilding	932
7. Maritime Industry	934
a. On Ship	935
b. On Shore	938
8. Mercantile Establishments	940
9. Metal Mining, Smelting and Fabrication	942
a. Metal Mining and Nonferrous Fabrication (Excluding Aluminum)	942
b. Aluminum	944
10. Office Work	945
11. Petroleum Production	946
12. Public Utilities, Other than Railroads	948
a. Transportation	948
b. Communications	952
c. Electric Light and Power	955
13. Textiles	955
C. 1941 TRADE UNION MEMBERSHIP	958
1. American Federation of Labor Unions	958
2. Congress of Industrial Organizations Unions	962
3. Unaffiliated Nationals and Internationals	964
INDEX	967

TABLES

	Page
1. Estimated Percentage of Workers in Various Industries Covered by Agreements with Outside Unions	19
2. Union Wage Rates Per Week in Competing Centers, for Hand Compositors, Cylinder Pressmen and Cylinder Press Assistants, 1939 and 1929	158
3. Strikes in Building Trades, 1914–1939	219
4. Indexes of Wage Rates in the Central Competitive Field and in Some Seventy Unionized Trades	256
5. Written Grievances in a Large Akron Rubber Plant	675
6. Motion Picture Theatre and Operator Licenses Issued in Chicago, 1915–1937	835

FIGURES

1. Adjustment of a Grievance in Illinois	246
2. Employment, Pay Rolls, and Average Earnings in the Anthracite Industry	309

HOW COLLECTIVE BARGAINING WORKS

Chapter 1

ORGANIZED LABOR AND THE NEW DEAL

PHILIP TAFT

THE AMERICAN LABOR MOVEMENT has a long and multicolored history reaching back to the days of the founding fathers. But not until almost the close of the nineteenth century did it attain a definite form and character. Then, with the triumph of the American Federation of Labor over the huge, sprawling Knights of Labor, it turned away from political and reform movements and settled down to the business of getting better employment and working conditions for its members—mostly skilled craftsmen.

Its achievements were considerable. Notable systems of collective bargaining had their start in the years around 1900, some of them earlier. But they were limited to a small number of industries—the building and printing trades, the railroads, coal mining and a few others. And this remained true up to the first World War, when trade-union membership spurted and many hitherto open-shop areas temporarily yielded recognition. It was true also of the 1920's, a decade whose first three years saw over half the wartime gains swept away and whose last seven prosperous years were a period of almost complete union stagnation.

Still centering nearly all their efforts on improving the material position of the skilled crafts, and handicapped by political and economic developments, the labor unions showed no signs of ability or desire to reach more than a small fraction of American workers. There was no indication that the millions of unorganized employees in the mass production industries, the clerical and service trades, or agriculture would ever be organized. And when depression hit the country, even the old union strongholds received what seemed a mortal blow. Membership fell off and the disintegration and lack of vitality so evident in the twenties became much more pronounced. With little apparent hope for a successful comeback, the labor movement retreated before the gathering economic storm.[1]

1. Government Encouragement of Labor Organization

Not until the spring of 1933, when a new administration took over in Washington, did organized labor come out of its slough of despond. Then, for the first time in the nation's history, unionism and the right to bargain collectively came under strong government protection and encouragement.

Yet this new policy was not so much an innovation as a revival and extension of previously enunciated principles. During the first World War, the War Labor Board upheld collective bargaining and forbade interference with it. That stand was not entirely abandoned even in the twenties, despite organized labor setbacks. On the contrary, what was once a wartime regulatory policy was written into a federal statute and survived the test of the courts.

This was the Railway Labor Act of 1926, which had the blessing of both carriers and rail labor organizations—the first law ever passed by Congress to specify in so many words the right to organize without interference and coercion.[2] It applied to only one, though important, group of organized labor, and even the power of Congress to do this was challenged. But the Supreme Court of the United States upheld that power in the case of *Texas & New Orleans Railroad Co.* v. *Brotherhood of Railway & Steamship Clerks.*[3]

Less than two years after this decision came the Norris-La Guardia Anti-Injunction Act which stated the same principles and, in effect, encouraged their application in wider fields.[4] But

---

1. See Appendix A for details about labor history before the New Deal.
2. Section 2 of the law provided that: "Representatives, for the purposes of this Act, shall be designated by the respective parties in such manner as may be provided in their corporate organization or unincorporated association, or by other means of collective action, without interference, influence, or coercion exercised by either party over the self-organization or designation of representatives by the other." 44 Stat. L. 578, Pt. 2.
3. 281 U. S. 548 (1930).
4. Section 2 defined the public policy of the United States as follows: "Whereas

however encouraging, this legislation was limited. It remained for the National Industrial Recovery Act of 1933 to affirm in explicit terms in the famous Section 7 (a), labor's right in Code industries to organize without employer interference and to bargain collectively.[5]

Effect of Early New Deal Legislation

Although Section 7 (a) and the act of which it was a part were not destined to live more than two years, it served as a catapult for rapid organization of labor. Workers flocked into old unions and set up new ones. From June to October 1933 the American Federation of Labor chartered 584 directly affiliated federal unions with 300,000 members—more than in any other comparable period in the Federation's existence.[6] At the same time, national and international unions affiliated with the AF of L chartered 2,953 locals. Although its convention report showed an average of 2,126,796 members for 1933, the Federation estimated

---

under prevailing economic conditions, developed with the aid of governmental authority for owners of property to organize in the corporate and other forms of ownership association, the individual unorganized worker is commonly helpless to exercise actual liberty to contract and to protect his freedom of labor, and thereby to obtain acceptable terms and conditions of employment, wherefore, though he should be free to decline to associate with his fellows, it is necessary that he have full freedom of association, self-organization, and designation of representatives of his own choosing to negotiate the terms and conditions of his employment, and that he shall be free from the interference, restraint, or coercion of employers of labor, or their agents, in the designation of such representatives or in self-organization or in other concerted activities for the purpose of collective bargaining or other mutual aid or protection." 47 Stat. L. 70, Pt. 1.

5. "(1) . . . employees shall have the right to organize and bargain collectively through representatives of their own choosing, and shall be free from the interference, restraint, or coercion of employers of labor, or their agents, in the designation of such representatives or in self-organization or in other concerted activities for the purpose of collective bargaining or other mutual aid or protection; (2) . . . no employees and no one seeking employment shall be required as a condition of employment to join any company union or to refrain from joining, organizing, or assisting a labor organization of his own choosing." 48 Stat. L. 198, Pt. 1.

For a discussion of Section 7 (a), see Paul Brissenden, "Genesis and Import of the Collective Bargaining Provisions of the Recovery Act," *Economic Essays in Honor of Wesley Clair Mitchell*, Columbia University Press, New York, 1935, pp. 27-62.

6. *Report of the Proceedings of the Fifty-third Annual Convention of the American Federation of Labor . . . 1933*, p. 78.

its membership in October of that year at 3,926,796.[7] Total trade-union membership is estimated to have risen from an average of 3,144,300 during 1932[8] to 4,200,000 by the beginning of 1935.[9]

Even more significant than new charters or increased membership was the wide geographical and industrial spread of union activity. In many mass production industries there were marked gains. In rubber tire manufacturing in 1934 there were seventy-five local unions, almost all of them organized since the enactment of the NRA. In June 1933 no AF of L unions existed in the automobile industry; a little over a year later 106 federal locals were active. Between July 1933 and July 1934 locals in the aluminum industry rose from one to twenty, and in lumbering, from four to 130 in twenty-one states and Canada.[10]

Although designed to protect the code worker's right of self-organization, Section 7 (a) did not prevent company unions. The fact is that it placed a premium upon their establishment. As efforts were made to thwart attempts at independent organization, a race began between outside and company unions. Hundreds of employee representation plans were introduced, and company-union coverage increased from an estimated 1,263,194 employees in 1932[11] to about 2,500,000 in the beginning of 1935,[12] or almost

7. AF of L total membership in October 1933 [a]   3,926,796
    Reported as paying the per capita tax   2,526,796
    Exempt from dues   100,000
    In new federal unions   300,000
    In new international local unions   500,000
    Recruits in old international unions   450,000
    Recruits in old federal locals   50,000

a. *United Mine Workers Journal*, October 15, 1933, p. 9.

8. Leo Wolman, *Ebb and Flow in Trade Unionism*, National Bureau of Economic Research, New York, 1936, p. 16. (In 1933 the average declined to 2,973,000.) Canadian membership of approximately 150,000 at the close of 1932 and 140,000 at the close of 1933 should be subtracted. See the Department of Labour of Canada, *Twenty-Second Annual Report on Labour Organization in Canada*, 1934, p. 80; and *Twenty-Third Annual Report*, 1934, p. 140.

9. *Labor and the Government*, Twentieth Century Fund, New York, 1935, pp. 21-24. This figure does not include Canadian membership.

10. AF of L, *Proceedings*, 1934, pp. 43-55.

11. National Industrial Conference Board, *Collective Bargaining Through Employee Representation*, New York, 1933, p. 16.

12. Twentieth Century Fund, *op. cit.*, p. 79.

60 per cent of the total trade-union membership—an all-time high.[13]

Replies to a Bureau of Labor Statistics questionnaire from 14,725 firms employing 1,935,673 workers showed 30.2 per cent in April 1935 employed in establishments dealing with some or all workers through trade unions, 19.9 per cent in establishments dealing through company unions, 7.4 per cent in establishments with both company and trade unions, and 42.5 per cent in establishments without any recognized labor organization. Company unions were widespread in iron and steel, chemical, and transportation equipment industries and in "miscellaneous manufactures." And while trade-union strength was concentrated in plants employing less than 2,500, the company union was prevalent among firms employing 2,500 or more. Over 60 per cent of the company unions had been organized between 1933 and 1935.[14]

NRA Administrative Machinery

Organized labor's vigorous drive and employers' counteroffensives sharply increased labor disputes in the summer of 1933[15] and threatened the hoped-for industrial revival. The National Recovery Administration lacked machinery to handle these disputes until August 5, when President Roosevelt established the National Labor Board, with Senator Wagner as impartial chairman and three representatives each from labor and industry. This body heard complaints, undertook strike settlements, and held plant elections to determine collective bargaining representatives. A large proportion of the cases filed with it grew out of contests between trade and company unions, or were charges of discrimination against employees engaging in union activity.

13. This comparison is subject to criticism, for the trade-union and company-union figures are not closely comparable. In connection with company union figures, it will be noted that the word "coverage" is used. The figures are for employees in the plants with company unions. Prior to 1937, only a small proportion of the company unions were associations with memberships and dues; the great majority were merely plans for the election of representatives.
14. "Characteristics of Company Unions, 1935," *Bulletin No. 634*, U. S. Bureau of Labor Statistics, 1938, pp. 37-38, 48, 51.
15. Florence Peterson, "Strikes in the United States," *Bulletin No. 651*, U. S. Bureau of Labor Statistics, 1938, p. 45.

Similar duties were undertaken by its successor, the first National Labor Relations Board, which came into being in July 1934, by the National Mediation Board for the railroads, and by special boards handling labor disputes in such industries as automobiles, textiles, steel and coal.[16] Although many elections conducted by these government labor boards were held by consent, their authority in other cases was contested in the courts. Frequently the results of elections held without employer consent were ignored, as were some board decisions in nonelection cases. With such uneven accomplishments the boards' effectiveness diminished rather than increased. Generally speaking, all these bodies were ineffective in getting industry to accept their interpretations of Section 7 (a), and their usefulness steadily declined until May 1935, when the NRA was declared unconstitutional.[17]

The National Labor Relations Act

To meet this situation—to salvage principles laid down by the National Labor Board and the first National Labor Relations Board, and to provide for enforcement of decisions—the Wagner bill was introduced early in 1935. After amendment, it passed in the following July, not many weeks after the NRA died. Not, however, until the Supreme Court upheld its constitutionality and gave it broad coverage in April 1937[18] did the National Labor Relations Act become a powerful instrument for the widespread extension of collective bargaining. Employers were required to meet with the accredited representatives of a majority of their employees and to make an honest effort to reach agreements on issues raised; though actual agreement was not required, collective bargaining became compulsory when requested by an appropriate labor organization (one having as members a majority of the employees and not dominated or assisted by the employer).

16. For a detailed history of the labor boards under the NRA, see Lewis L. Lorwin and Arthur Wubnig, *Labor Relations Boards*, Brookings Institution, Washington, 1935.
17. *A.L.A. Schechter Poultry Corp., et al.* v. *United States*, 295 U.S. 490 (1935).
18. *Associated Press* v. *NLRB*, 301 U.S. 103; *NLRB* v. *Jones & Laughlin Steel Corp.*, 301 U.S. 1; *NLRB* v. *Fruehauf Trailer Co.*, 301 U.S. 49; *NLRB* v. *Friedman-Harry Marks Clothing Co.*, 301 U.S. 58; and *Washington, Virginia & Maryland Coach Co.* v. *NLRB*, 301 U.S. 142.

For workers covered by the national act or by one of the five similar state acts enacted in that year, the right to organize came to be more vigorously protected than almost anywhere else in the world.

Since the spring of 1937 the National Labor Relations Act has had a phenomenal effect upon the labor movement. Union membership has greatly increased while formation of new company unions by employers has almost ceased. The structure and characteristics of old company unions have changed and many of them have become regular trade unions. Between 1935 and the end of 1939 the National Labor Relations Board ordered 340 company unions to be disestablished; in the agricultural machinery, automobile, rubber, oil, steel and other industries there have been dissolutions. Nearly all the survivors have undergone reorganization or modification, so that the typical company union of today is a membership organization with meetings at stated intervals, with financial independence, and with some valid claims to being an agency for collective bargaining.

The Split in the Labor Movement

The forward surge in union membership is one outstanding fact of the New Deal years. It was offset, in part at least, by the split in the labor movement arising in 1935 out of general dissatisfaction and dissent within the American Federation of Labor over the issue of industrial organization.

Although the AF of L sent organizers to many areas, it did not take full advantage of the opportunities presented by the receptive attitude of mass production workers. Its 1933 convention authorized a conference of national and international unions to devise methods of organizing the unorganized. Meeting in January 1934, the conference affirmed that:

> The paramount issue is not what particular form of organization shall be followed in this emergency and this unusual situation. The demand of the moment is to promote organization in whatever form or method is best designed to rally the wage earners to the cause of Organized Labor, bearing in mind that in the pursuit of organization the present structure, rights and

interests of affiliated National and International Unions must be followed, observed and safeguarded.[19]

This resolution posed the Federation's dilemma—to organize the wage earners into the most suitable type of organization without encroaching upon the jurisdictions staked out by its international affiliates in the past. The Federation's inability to solve this problem was the chief cause of the split in the ranks of labor. The AF of L 1934 convention tried to conciliate the divergent groups with a compromise resolution, but a careful reading of the resolution shows that each side could interpret it to suit its own interests. While authorizing industrial charters in a number of mass production industries, it reiterated the Federation's "duty to formulate policies which will fully protect the jurisdictional rights of all trade unions organized upon craft lines. . . ."[20]

Even though they had few members in mass production industries, craft and semi-industrial unions were unwilling to give up their jurisdictional rights. Another obstacle was the AF of L's slowness to provide the organizational and financial support needed for the campaigns in these sectors. As a central body of autonomous unions, the Federation was never intended to assume general responsibility for labor's organizing efforts. It had neither the equipment nor the personnel for such tasks, and the leaders of the internationals were reluctant to risk thousands of dollars of defense funds in attempts to organize groups that had been indifferent to organized labor's appeal.

By the summer of 1935 little doubt remained that union gains of 1933 and 1934 were fast being destroyed, partly because vigorous organization along industrial lines was not being pressed and partly because the NRA guarantee of the right to organize failed to be as effective as anticipated. But despite these clear warnings, a resolution to organize the mass production workers into industrial unions was voted down at the 1935 convention, 18,024 to 10,933, after sharp and bitter debate.[21]

19. AF of L, *Proceedings*, 1934, p. 41.
20. *Ibid.*, pp. 586-587.
21. *Ibid.*, 1935, pp. 521-575.

Rise of the CIO

Less than a month later, officers of eight unions[22] representing 940,000 members met in Washington and formed the Committee for Industrial Organization to promote unionization of the unorganized workers in the mass production industries and elsewhere. The Committee's announced functions were "educational and advisory"; ostensibly it would organize within the framework of the AF of L. But shortly after its formation it was ordered to disband. Rejecting this demand, the CIO taunted the Federation for failing to organize the steel industry and offered to raise $500,000 for a campaign by its own organizers. The AF of L Executive Council spurned this offer, then suspended all but two of the original CIO unions[23] and four others which had later affiliated with it. With the insurgent unions unrepresented, the 1936 convention overwhelmingly upheld the Council's action.[24]

The labor movement was thus divided into two rival groups, although not until two years later did the Committee for Industrial Organization change its name to Congress of Industrial Organizations and become an independent federation. Despite the defection of the Hatters in 1936 and the Ladies' Garment Workers in 1938, the CIO has continued to prosper; it weathered a serious business slump which hit hardest those industries where its strength was concentrated.

Time and conflict widened AF of L–CIO differences and encouraged mutual recriminations and raiding of jurisdictions. The CIO's initial position was that "it is not the purpose to take from any national or international union any part of their present membership, or any part of their potential membership employed in certain types and plants of industry [i.e., where craft distinc-

---

22. Amalgamated Clothing Workers; United Hatters, Cap and Millinery Workers; International Ladies' Garment Workers; Mine, Mill and Smelter Workers; United Mine Workers; Oil Field, Gas Well and Refinery Workers; United Textile Workers; International Typographical Union.

23. The International Typographical Union and the United Hatters, Cap and Millinery Workers were not suspended because their affiliation with the CIO was in doubt.

24. *Ibid.*, 1936, pp. 416-417; Committee for Industrial Organization, "Industrial Unions Mean Unity," Washington, pamphlet (no date), pp. 5-8.

tions are important]."[25] But it later invaded building construction and other industries. The AF of L reciprocated. The differences became more difficult of solution owing to the evolution of the CIO into an independent institution performing functions paralleling those of the AF of L. Moreover, pride and fear of loss of prestige or political influence handicapped all efforts to bring the two organizations together.

Organizational Gains, 1937–1941

This very dissension was partly responsible for the extraordinary organizational efforts and expenditures after 1936. Beginning in the rubber tire and automobile industries, CIO unions won collective bargaining rights by organized pressure or peaceful persuasion on a wide industrial front—in steel, electrical manufacturing, shipbuilding and textiles, among others. It was a cyclonic campaign. In March 1934, a high official of the General Motors Corporation asserted that his company would neither recognize unionism nor agree in advance to an election of bargaining representatives.[26] Three years later both General Motors and Chrysler signed agreements with the CIO automobile union. Perhaps even more important was the peaceful acceptance of collective bargaining by the United States Steel Corporation. Many other basic and fabricating firms in the steel industry followed, and finally, in 1941, "little steel's" resistance collapsed. Earlier in the same year, another antiunion stronghold surrendered when Ford signed a very favorable contract with the CIO.

CIO victories prodded AF of L leadership into more vigorous action. Many international unions increased their organizational staffs and not infrequently extended their jurisdictions. Indeed, many unions that had formerly shied away from the semiskilled and unskilled welcomed them with open arms. Moreover, the Federation decided to take the leadership in campaigns in the unorganized industries. In May 1937 a conference of international

---

25. Committee for Industrial Organization, "Industrial Unionism," Washington, pamphlet (no date), p. 13. The quotation is from a speech by President Howard of the Typographical Union at the 1935 AF of L convention.
26. Lorwin and Wubnig, *op. cit.*, p. 355.

and national unions voted to assess themselves one cent per member a month to support an organization campaign.[27] The organizing staff was enlarged and a division with a director in charge was created to supervise its activities.[28] Organizational expenditures by the Federation increased from $338,576 (a sum larger than usual) in 1935 to $1,174,015 for the twelve months ending on August 31, 1938; in 1940–1941, $1,039,759 was spent.[29] In spite of losses from the expulsion of CIO affiliates, the AF of L enlarged its membership.

Present Union Strength

Between 1933 and 1938 total trade-union membership rose from an annual average of slightly less than 3 million[30] to about 8 million.[31] With business revival in 1939, following the recession of 1937–1938, it continued to expand. By early 1940, between 8.5 and 9 million workers in the United States and Canada[32] were attached to the AF of L, the CIO, or unaffiliated "outside" unions. The following year total membership approached 11 million. Perhaps an additional half million to a million were in "independent" groups more closely connected with management than with the organized labor movement.[33] All wage and salary workers actually at work in 1941 totaled nearly 40 million.

27. AF of L, *Proceedings*, 1937, pp. 110-111. This assessment was abolished at the 1940 New Orleans convention and the per capita tax increased from one cent to two cents a month. *Ibid.*, 1940, pp. 444-446.
28. *Ibid.*, 1937, p. 80.
29. *Ibid.*, 1935, p. 26; 1938, p. 65; *Report of the Executive Council*, 1941, p. 3.
30. See p. 6, note 8.
31. See National Resources Committee, *The Structure of the American Economy*, Pt. 1, Washington, June 1939, p. 118. The "claimed membership" figure given (over 8 million) is stated to be a rough estimate.
32. Canadian membership at the close of 1939 was about 200,000. See Labor Research Association, *Labor Notes*, March 1941, p. 9.
33. The railroad brotherhoods and several other nationals and internationals are unaffiliated with either branch of labor, but their general policies and outlook are not fundamentally different from those of the CIO and the AF of L. The independents, on the other hand, represent an attempt to divert the desire for organization to single plant or company groups. In a sense these groups are hostile, or at least indifferent, to the aspirations of organized labor. Their representatives are not found in legislative halls working for labor or welfare legislation, nor do they make common cause with other labor groups on issues vitally affecting wage earners. They are, at least in attitude, close to their outlawed ancestor, the company union.

The Problem of Estimating Union Membership

These figures are, of course, rough estimates at best, for the division in the ranks of labor and the youth of many unions, together with their location and uncertain status, complicate the problem of estimating union membership. Who is a union member? Traditionally only he who regularly pays dues. But because many leaders of the younger unions fear that revelations of actual dues-paying membership might injure their organizations or cause them a "loss of face," published figures do not always accurately reflect membership as measured on this basis.

However, there are a number of reasons for not rejecting general membership claims. Particularly in newly organized industries without the checkoff, or the closed or preferential shop, many workers obviously will not pay dues regularly. When vital issues are at stake, union supporters are more willing to contribute voluntarily; but at other times moral suasion and indirect pressure do not suffice, and dues payments fall off. Moreover, most of the newer unions are in industries with widely fluctuating employment, where dues payments are a far greater financial burden than in the more stable industries, and dues-paying members are a considerably smaller percentage of the total union membership. Indeed, unemployed members and those with small earnings because of part-time work are frequently "exonerated," or exempted from the payment of dues. This is true also of fresh recruits obtained in organizing campaigns.

One example will illustrate the sometimes wide divergence between dues-paying membership and general membership claims. The Steel Workers Organizing Committee claimed in the summer of 1941 about 600,000 members, but the number paying dues was probably less than 350,000.[34] On the other hand, the discrepancy is sometimes much smaller; in May 1940 the CIO United Auto Workers had a dues-paying membership of 294,428 and, at the convention in July, claimed a "general membership" of 382,000.[35]

In such groups as the SWOC, a count of dues-paying members

---

34. See the "Steel" chapter.
35. R. J. Thomas, *Report to the 1940 UAW–CIO Convention*, p. 7.

does not adequately reveal union strength. Although dues payments are of great importance for membership stability and for long-run organizational strength, those employees who join, work with the union and support its policies, without paying dues regularly, cannot be ignored. Therefore in this chapter and in Appendix C, figures representing both dues-paying members and general membership claims have been used. The AF of L figures are of the former, more conservative type, many of those for the CIO, of the latter.

The Old Unions

Since 1933 only a few national or international unions have decreased in size. The Wood Carvers, the Metal Engravers, the Sleeping Car Conductors, the Rural Letter Carriers, the Plasterers, and the Stonecutters have all lost; so have a few others.[36] Most unions of this group, however, play minor roles in both the labor movement and the national economy. The overwhelming majority of trade unions have increased in size and influence. While some gains were only moderate after 1933—usually because organization was already fairly inclusive—an impressive number had tremendous growth.

Membership in such old and strongly intrenched organizations as the Brotherhood of Railway Carmen, the Photo Engravers' and Pressmen's unions increased rather slowly—from 10 to 30 per cent from 1933 to 1941. The same was true of the International Typographical Union, the Sheet Metal Workers' Union and the National Federation of Post Office Clerks. But unions in coal mining, clothing, baking and other industries grew by leaps and bounds. Between 1933 and 1941 the United Mine Workers' membership rose from 300,000 to 600,000, the Amalgamated Clothing Workers from 125,000 to 275,000, and the Brotherhood of Electrical Workers from 94,000 to 201,000. The Machinists more than tripled—from 65,000 to 222,000. The Bakery Workers, with some 84,000 members in 1941, showed about a fivefold increase, and the Teamsters, with over 400,000, almost a sixfold increase. At

36. AF of L, *Report of the Executive Council, Annual Convention,* 1941, pp. 10-11.

the same time membership of the Meat Cutters and Butcher Workmen jumped nearly eightfold—from 11,000 to 85,000—and that of the Hotel and Restaurant Employees, over ninefold—from 23,000 to 214,000.

The growth of these old unions reflects not only more complete coverage of traditional jurisdictions but also, in many cases, inclusion of related trades and industries or of unskilled and semiskilled workers. Almost half the 1940 members of the Amalgamated Clothing Workers were journeymen tailors, and shirt, neckwear, laundry, and cleaning and dyeing workers.[37] Before the New Deal, members of the Brotherhood of Electrical Workers were largely in the railroad and construction industries, but after 1933, powerhouses and electrical manufacturing plants were organized, which accounted for 105,000 of the union's 203,000 members in November 1939.[38] The Machinists set out to organize the aircraft industry, among others, on an industrial basis, and the Bakery Workers after 1936 sought bargaining rights in mechanized bakeries. These are only a few examples of the greater inclusiveness of long-established unions.

Rise of New Unions

Even more striking than the gains of the old unions has been the appearance of new ones in hitherto unorganized, or practically unorganized, trades and industries. Hundreds of thousands of workers have been drawn into strong industrial unions in such mass production industries as iron and steel, autos, and electrical and radio manufacturing. The Steel Workers Organizing Committee claimed in 1941 roughly 600,000 members; the United Automobile, Aircraft and Agricultural Implement Workers, 600,000; and the United Electrical, Radio and Machine Workers, around 300,000. Additional thousands of union members were in the rubber, aluminum and flat glass industries. Other fields of economic activity, such as office and professional work, agriculture and canning, and editorial and commercial work on newspapers, have also been reached by the organized labor movement.

37. See the "Men's Clothing" chapter.
38. Information submitted by the organization.

2. The Collective Bargaining Situation

Although not all union members have achieved collective bargaining rights, the number of unorganized employees whose employment and working conditions are directly determined by collective agreements is probably large enough to make union control coequal with union membership.[39] Collective labor agreements, therefore, cover roughly 11 million, or more than a quarter of the nearly 40 million wage and salary workers actually employed.

Obviously, such an over-all estimate gives by itself an inadequate picture—the extent of collective bargaining varies widely among industries, which in turn are of unequal significance in the national economy. For this reason a breakdown of collective bargaining coverage by industries is presented in Table 1. The estimates given are, of course, both incomplete and, in many cases, very rough.[40] And no attempt has been made to include in the table employment figures for each industry; they range from a few hundred employees in diamond cutting to nearly two million in construction.

The percentage classification, moreover, is not equally significant for all industries. In the construction trades, where markets are for the most part local, control over employment and working conditions through collective bargaining may be complete in certain areas, even though the whole industry is by no means entirely covered. On the other hand, such control may be severely limited in industries with national markets, unless the coverage is almost complete. The experience of the American Federation of Hosiery Workers in the years after 1927 illustrates the difficulties which have frequently been encountered in the absence of industry-wide control.[41]

39. See p. 24 for reference to the decline in relative importance of closed-shop agreements.
40. To indicate at all accurately the extent of collective bargaining in more than a relatively small number of industries is impossible for various reasons: difficulties in defining industries; lack of acceptable estimates of the number of wage earners employed in them; the multiplicity of unions, each with a separate contract, in many industries; and the difficulty of estimating the proportion of workers not covered by agreements.
41. See the "Hosiery" chapter.

a. IMPORTANCE OF COLLECTIVE BARGAINING IN VARIOUS INDUSTRIES

In 1940 only two giant American industries were almost 100 per cent covered by union agreements—the railroads, with about a million employees, and coal mining, with half a million. But about three fourths of the 500,000 auto workers were under contract; so were over three fifths of the 500,000 steel workers[42] and the 400,000 in electrical manufacturing, together with well over half of the nearly two million in construction. The addition of such industries as rubber, private shipbuilding, men's and women's clothing and meat packing, each employing over a hundred thousand and from half to almost 100 per cent covered by labor agreements, makes clear the vital role that collective bargaining plays in the United States.

Plus these, collective agreements embraced from 50 to over 90 per cent of the workers in other, less important industries—glass, brewing, hosiery and flour milling and cereal manufacturing. Moreover, in a number of otherwise poorly or only moderately well-organized industries, strong craft unions determined the employment and working conditions of certain occupational groups. The International Brotherhood of Blacksmiths, Drop Forgers and Helpers claimed that early in 1940 its agreements covered 100 per cent of the craftsmen within its jurisdiction employed by small hardware and tool manufacturers. In the textile industry, the International Spinners Union bargained for all of the spinners of textile yarns; and agreements of the Metal Polishers, Buffers, Platers and Helpers International Union applied to some 60 per cent of the eligible workers in the chrome furniture industry. The Association of Machinists and the Brotherhood of Electrical Workers had contracts covering maintenance and repair workers in textiles, food products, paper and pulp, and chemicals, and the Pattern Makers' League of North America bargained for skilled pattern makers in the aircraft and other industries.

Collective bargaining has advanced on most fronts. Formerly limited to the building, printing, and needle trades, the railroads

42. About 200,000 union members were in steel processing and fabricating concerns, not classified as part of the iron and steel industry.

and coal mining and a relatively small number of other industries, it is now found in nearly every branch of the American economy. Before 1933, it was in the main confined to urban centers, except in the case of coal mining and the railroads; it appears now in middle-sized and small manufacturing communities as well. No longer limited geographically or industrially, collective bargaining is fast becoming the most important single device for determining wages, hours and working conditions in the United States. Transportation, mining, construction and manufacturing are more and more coming under its sway.

Yet in spite of this rapid progress since 1933, nearly three quarters of American wage and salary workers are not members of trade unions or covered by collective agreements. Collective bargaining has made little headway among the 6.5 million wholesale and retail trade employees, the more than 4 million in the financial and service trades, the 4 million government employees or the 3 million agricultural workers. In addition, hundreds of thousands in textiles, in chemicals and in other important industries are without union agreements.

TABLE 1

ESTIMATED PERCENTAGE OF WORKERS IN VARIOUS INDUSTRIES COVERED BY AGREEMENTS WITH OUTSIDE UNIONS [a]

Industry	90 or more	75 but less than 90	55 but less than 75	45 but less than 55	25 but less than 45	10 but less than 25	less than 10
TRANSPORTATION Air line pilots			X				
Intercity bus			X				
Salt-water transportation: * longshoremen	X						
Salt-water transportation: * ship personnel [b]			X				
Steam railroads [c]	X						
Trucking						X	
* Urban transportation (electric railway, trolley bus and motorbus)				X			

TABLE 1 (*Continued*)

ESTIMATED PERCENTAGE OF WORKERS IN VARIOUS INDUSTRIES COVERED BY AGREEMENTS WITH OUTSIDE UNIONS [a]

Industry	90 or more	75 but less than 90	55 but less than 75	45 but less than 55	25 but less than 45	10 but less than 25	less than 10
MERCANTILE, PROFESSIONAL AND SERVICE TRADES							
Actors (legitimate stage)	X						
Building service						X	
Hotels and restaurants						X	
* Laundries					X		
* Mercantile establishments							X
Motion picture machine operators [d]	X						
Motion picture production (including actors, writers, cameramen, building craftsmen, etc.) [d]	X						
Stagehands [d]	X						
MINING, QUARRYING, ETC.							
Cement					X		
Coal mining	X						
Granite cutting	X						
Lime and gypsum						X	
* Metal mining and nonferrous smelting and fabrication (excluding aluminum)					X		
Quarrying				X			
BUILDING CONSTRUCTION [e]			X				
FOOD, LIQUOR AND TOBACCO							
Baking					X		
Brewing	X						
Cigar making						X	
Fishing				X			
Flour milling and cereal manufacturing					X		
Meat distribution						X	
* Meat packing			X				

TABLE 1 (Continued)

Estimated Percentage of Workers in Various Industries Covered by Agreements with Outside Unions [a]

Industry	90 or more	75 but less than 90	55 but less than 75	45 but less than 55	25 but less than 45	10 but less than 25	less than 10
METALS, MACHINERY AND TRANSPORTATION EQUIPMENT							
*Aircraft					X		
*Aluminum		X					
Automobile		X					
*Electrical manufacturing			X				
*Farm equipment					X		
Iron and steel			X				
Machine tool					X		
*Shipbuilding (private)				X			
PAPER AND PRINTING							
Bookbinding				X			
Lithographing				X			
Newspapers (daily): *editorial and commercial employees						X	
Newspapers (daily): mechanical tasks	X						
Paper and pulp					X		
Printing and publishing: book, magazine and job			X				
TEXTILES AND APPAREL							
*Boot and shoe					X		
Caps and cloth hats		X					
Fur	X						
Gloves							X
Hats: fur and wool-felt, men's straw				X			
Hat and cap materials: men's					X		
Hosiery (full-fashioned)			X				
Men's clothing	X						
Millinery		X					
Neckwear			X				

TABLE 1 (*Continued*)

Estimated Percentage of Workers in Various Industries Covered by Agreements with Outside Unions [a]

Industry	90 or more	75 but less than 90	55 but less than 75	45 but less than 55	25 but less than 45	10 but less than 25	less than 10
Shirts, nightwear and bathrobes			X				
* Textiles					X		
Women's clothing		X					
MISCELLANEOUS MANUFACTURES							
* Chemicals							X
Cooperage			X				
Diamond cutting	X						
Die casting					X		
Furniture						X	
* Glass containers	X						
Glass: flat	X						
* Glass: flint				X			
Leather (tanneries)						X	
* Lumber						X	
* Petroleum refining [f]						X	
Rubber			X				

* Industries where there is substantial competition between two or more unions.

a. Unless otherwise indicated the estimates are those submitted by the union in response to the Twentieth Century Fund inquiry, or those made by the research associates. (See the various industry chapters and Appendix B.) These estimates apply to the period 1939–1940. Because of recent labor advances, e.g., in the automobile industry, a number of them are too low.

b. Preliminary estimate of the Maritime Labor Board as of March 1941; limited to deep-sea merchant vessels of American registry and of 1,000 gross tons and over, "suitable for service" as of September 30, 1939; covers licensed and unlicensed personnel, radio operators, pursers and concessionaires.

c. The extent to which the various unions represented their respective classes of employees in 1940 is shown in the *Sixth Annual Report of the National Mediation Board,* 1940, pp. 21-22. The percentage of mileage covered by the principal national unions varied from 99 in the case of the Brotherhood of Railroad Trainmen to 77 in the case of the International Brotherhood of Blacksmiths.

d. Information furnished by Professor Murray Ross of Brooklyn College.

e. Includes tunnel and street construction. The areas of union control are given in the "Building Construction" chapter.

f. Testimony of H. H. Anderson, Vice President, Shell Oil Company, *Hearings Before the Temporary National Economic Committee,* Pt. 16, "Petroleum Industry," Sec. III, pp. 9002-9005, 9304.

b. THE BARGAINING UNIT

The rise of industrial unionism, already referred to, was partly, if not largely, responsible for the extension of collective bargaining. Today industrial or semi-industrial unions provide the dominant organizational and bargaining patterns.

A second development of recent years has been a tendency for agreements to cover a wider geographical area. The most common agreement is still local, negotiated with single employers or local associations of employers and tending to set standards for the local market. But regional and national agreements are increasing. They are found, for example, in stoves, hosiery, coal, shipping, paper and pulp, clothing, glass containers and pottery. Such agreements usually result in standardization of labor conditions over wider areas—often an important contribution to the stability of collective bargaining. In the face of large wage differences, the standards in any one firm or plant may be subject to severe pressure, and the union's position jeopardized.[43] During the last decade such pressure was intensified; unions were forced to give greater attention to the relationship between wage rates in different plants; and, except in such cases as the building trades and cleaning and dyeing, where the market is local, they have increasingly sought industry-wide agreements or industry-wide uniformity of agreements to make less difficult the problem of enforcement.

Of course enforcement of uniform piece or hourly rates also involves difficulties, since technical and organizational conditions vary from plant to plant. Weak firms may be unable to continue in business unless the uniform rate is set at an extremely low level. Confronted by such a problem, unions may have to make concessions to less efficient establishments, as in the hosiery industry.

However, reduction of inequalities in labor standards promises to continue as a very important trade-union objective. It has been a factor in the tendency toward multiple-plant or company-wide agreements in such branches of industry as motor vehicle pro-

43. See, for example, the "Bituminous Coal," "Men's Clothing" and "Hosiery" chapters.

duction, dominated by a few large concerns. Multiple-unit agreements which equalize labor costs remove reasons for diverting work from one plant to another; they reduce the time allotted to bargaining, leaving national officers free for other activities; and they increase union prestige and so aid organizational effort.

More recently the exigencies of national defense have also encouraged wider agreement coverage. For example, to prevent "labor pirating" and to stabilize industrial relations in shipbuilding, defense officials promoted the negotiation of regional contracts for each of the three coasts.

c. UNION STATUS

The status of the union varies considerably from industry to industry (and within industries), depending, in the main, upon the age of the organization and the length of time collective bargaining has been in effect. Most unions seek a closed, union or preferential shop,[44] but newly organized ones usually have difficulty in winning any one of these from employers traditionally opposed to unionism. Ten years ago most agreements provided for the closed shop. In recent years there have been more exceptions than at any time since the 1880's; unions were willing to take what they could get in order to secure a foothold in areas previously closed to them. For example, many agreements signed in the 1930's with new industrial unions in the mass production industries stated that the union was to bargain for its members only. However, as collective bargaining gained more general acceptance and as unions won National Labor Relations Board elections, these "membership" agreements were generally replaced by contracts designating the union as exclusive representative of all employees, except certain groups such as supervisors and salaried employees. Agreements of this type are prevalent in the rubber and auto industries.

A number of employers have yielded to union demands for

---

44. Under the closed shop only union members can be hired and workers must remain union members to retain employment. Under the union shop nonmembers can be hired, but to retain employment must become union members after a certain period. The preferential shop gives union members preference in hiring or layoff, or both.

greater security. Often this step was taken as a result of employer recognition that a financially secure union can be a more responsible bargaining agent. Sometimes the motive was removal of friction between organized and unorganized workers in a plant; sometimes both employer and union have wanted protection against a rival union.[45] And so an increasing minority of "exclusive bargaining" contracts is being replaced by some form of the closed or preferential shop. However, except for the railroads, where it is illegal, the closed shop is most prevalent in industries where labor organization and collective bargaining have been long accepted—building construction, printing and the needle trades, among others.

The closed shop was an important issue in disputes certified to the National Defense Mediation Board, established early in 1941. This body of union, employer and public representatives was given investigatory and mediatory powers to deal with the problem of strikes in defense industries. The Board never formally announced any general policy on the closed shop, but attempted to decide each case on its merits. It recommended adoption of the closed shop in one case, and in a number of others suggested a union membership maintenance clause, under which all present or future union members must remain in good standing as a condition of continued employment, though no employee has to join the union. But in the captive mines dispute in the fall of 1941,[46] the Board rejected the United Mine Workers' demand for a union shop. This led to the resignation of all CIO members and destroyed the Board's usefulness. With America's formal entrance into the war, steps were taken to reorganize the machinery for dealing with industrial disputes. In January 1942 the Defense Mediation Board was replaced by the National War Labor Board, to which were given greater powers than those of its predecessor.

d. COLLECTIVE BARGAINING MACHINERY

The machinery for negotiating an agreement is usually comparatively simple—formal conferences on a local, regional or

---

45. See, for example, the "Steel" and "Glass" chapters.
46. See the "Bituminous Coal" chapter.

national basis between union representatives and employers or their representatives, sometimes with provision for arbitration when the two sides cannot agree.[47] Such machinery does not, of course, guarantee peaceful settlement of the issues involved. Strikes and lockouts may often be the ultimate deciding factor, their frequency and extent varying with such things as the business cycle and employer resistance to unionism and collective bargaining.

As industrial activity in the United States picked up because of defense spending, strikes naturally increased. In the first seven months of 1941 they numbered almost twice those in the corresponding period of the preceding relatively inactive year; the number of man days lost was more than five times as great. When 1941 is compared with the five-year period 1935–1939, however, the contrast is not so marked. From January through July 1941, there were some 2,500 strikes involving 1.3 million workers, and 15.8 million man days were lost; the figures for the corresponding period in 1935–1939 were 1,800, 0.7 million, and 10.9 million, respectively.[48] Main causes of 1941's strikes were union efforts to get greater recognition, a more secure status and wage increases.[49]

Administration of Agreements

More complex than the procedure for negotiating an agreement is the machinery for administering it—for peacefully settling disputes over its interpretation and application. The procedure followed varies, of course, among industries, but there are certain similarities. First, an attempt must be made to settle a dispute by the worker involved, or his union representative, and the foreman. Then there is a system of appeals to higher union and management officials. In industries where collective bargaining has been

47. See the special studies for detailed descriptions.
48. U. S. Bureau of Labor Statistics figures, as published in *The New York Times,* August 27, 1941.
49. Until the captive mines dispute, the National Defense Mediation Board's efforts to minimize strikes in defense industries had a good deal of success. There were few cases where strikes were called after a dispute was certified to it, and few failures to abide by its recommendations.

long established, such as coal, printing, hosiery and the needle trades, final appeal is often to a standing body composed of an equal number of representatives from each side, plus an impartial third person, or to a permanent impartial chairman alone. Arbitration is less frequent in newly organized industries. Practically every agreement makes it mandatory that the established procedures, rather than strikes or lockouts, be used to settle disputes arising during its life.

Obviously here, too, the machinery alone, no matter how well conceived, is not enough to insure successful relations. More depends on the attitudes, experience and judgment of the persons involved, and consequently on the length of time collective bargaining has been in effect. The process of training union and management officials in handling grievances is a slow one. Wholehearted acceptance of collective bargaining and mutually satisfactory delimitation of its scope come slowly. For these reasons violations of agreements may be rather frequent in newly organized industries. But as collective bargaining becomes more firmly established, little trouble is usually encountered in securing observance, the established machinery is relied on to secure adjustment, and it in turn tends to function more smoothly and expeditiously. More disputes are settled close to the source of trouble, thus preventing delays and the accumulation of discontent.

e. THE TERMS OF EMPLOYMENT

The extent to which the terms and conditions of employment are directly determined by collective bargaining varies. In the newly organized mass production industries, management, jealous of its prerogatives, has frequently opposed joint determination of individual wage rates, for example. It prefers to set the rates itself, with opportunity for union protest through the grievance machinery. On the other hand, many unions have independently developed and enforced their own rules.[50] Thus the scope of collective bargaining may be wide or narrow. Here an attempt is made to indicate very briefly some of the more important de-

50. See the "Daily Newspapers" chapter.

velopments of the last decade in the terms and conditions of employment as they have been affected by the rapid spread of trade unionism and collective bargaining.

Wages

Wage increases in the middle thirties were considerable. And to a large extent trade unions were responsible, as they were for the maintenance of rates in the 1937–1938 recession. According to one estimate,[51] hourly earnings of industrial wage earners were 11 per cent higher in 1938 than in 1928 and 1929; at the same time real hourly earnings were 30 per cent above the 1928–1929 level. More recently, as the defense boom got under way, union pressure has again resulted in substantial increases—in steel, autos, coal, aircraft and shipbuilding, among others—though these have been at least partially offset by the rise in the cost of living.

The increase in wage rates is one result of the greater strength and inclusiveness of unionism and collective bargaining. Another is the reduction in the differences between wage rates for similar jobs,[52] to which earlier reference was made. At the same time has come a narrowing of the spread between the rates for different jobs—in part a result of the rapid growth of industrial unionism and of agreements covering all or a large proportion of the workers in a plant. Hitherto skilled wages in the United States had been much higher—when compared with unskilled and semi-skilled wages—than in countries like England and Australia. Relative scarcity of skilled labor plus concentration of union organization in this group largely accounted for such a situation. In recent years, with an increasing number of agreements written on an industrial basis, the tendency has been to reduce the difference between skilled and unskilled wages by establishing high minimum rates and granting larger relative increases in the lower brackets.[53] Introduction of minimum wage legislation has also contributed to this trend.

---

51. Spurgeon Bell, *Productivity, Wages, and National Income*, Brookings Institution, Washington, 1940, p. 16.
52. Of course, in some cases, these differentials have been increased as a result of only partial organization of an industry. See the "Automobiles" chapter.
53. See, for example, the "Electrical Products" chapter.

Seniority and Work Sharing

An outstanding development of the depression was greater union interest in the problem of layoffs. To provide a measure of job security for the individual and to protect him from discrimination, an increasing proportion of collective agreements provide that layoffs, rehirings and promotions shall be based on seniority. This development has been a controversial matter and a prominent issue in labor disputes during the New Deal years. Union men maintain that seniority is the most equitable criterion on which to base layoffs, rehirings and promotions. But management has been opposed to its use, unless "other things," such as "ability," are equal, claiming that otherwise efficiency would be reduced by removing incentive for self-improvement and by increasing the age of the work force. However, in layoffs and rehirings, seniority is apparently becoming less of a bone of contention. As its administration improved, management has often come to regard the system with toleration, or even approval.[54]

Unions have not always been happy about the way seniority systems have worked out. There are problems of administration in mass production industries. Conflicts frequently arise within the union when seniority is applied on a divisional or plant-wide basis, those laid off protesting strenuously. Even when it is applied only on a departmental basis, it is, of course, a source of dissatisfaction and protest on the part of the younger men against whom it discriminates.

To meet objections to sole reliance on seniority, work sharing has been widely practiced. In highly seasonal industries, such as the needle trades and boots and shoes, equal division of work during slack seasons—not layoffs based on seniority—is usually the rule. In a large number of other cases, work sharing is combined with seniority: sometimes short-service employees are dropped before work is divided; sometimes work is equally shared until average hours fall to a certain level, and thereafter layoffs are made on a seniority basis; sometimes these two methods are combined. Such arrangements are rather common in

54. See the "Electrical Products" chapter.

steel and rubber agreements and in electrical and radio manufacturing.[55]

The share-the-work movement was probably more important in its effect than reductions secured by unions in full-time working hours. These reductions were, of course, considerable—in a large majority of collective agreements, the standard work week is forty hours, spread over five days; in many it is less than forty. But in general during the thirties, actual hours worked were less than the standard number. Part of the reduction was merely an inevitable accompaniment of the depression. Part, however, was due to work sharing instituted by the trade unions.

f. VARIATIONS IN COLLECTIVE BARGAINING

Collective bargaining does not have a uniform pattern. The geographical coverage of the agreement, its scope, the status of the union, machinery for adjusting disputes, and ways of meeting fluctuations in employment are only some of its aspects which vary among industries. Others are policies with regard to technological change and methods of wage payment. Some unions with a high degree of control have promoted unusually restrictive policies and practices; others have undertaken extensive programs for the rehabilitation of a part, or even the whole, of an industry.

These variations, as well as the equally striking similarities and the problems connected with collective bargaining, are brought out in the following chapters, which contain the results of investigations of sixteen trades and industries—some mass production, some not; some organized by the AF of L, some by the CIO. In a majority of them collective bargaining has had a relatively long history; in the rest it is new and still in an experimental stage. Less extensive data on a number of other industries have been assembled in Appendix B, in an effort to round out the picture of trade unionism and collective bargaining in American industry.

---

55. For an analysis of methods of controlling layoffs in unionized industries, see Sumner H. Slichter, *Union Policies and Industrial Management*, Brookings Institution, Washington, 1941, Ch. IV.

Chapter 2

DAILY NEWSPAPERS

Robert K. Burns

FEW INDUSTRIES have had as interesting and meaningful experience with collective bargaining as newspaper publishing. Production and mechanical operations of the daily press are almost entirely under union jurisdiction. In this industry four great craft internationals have achieved a high degree of organization and, in cooperation with publishers, have developed bargaining relationships that in many respects are remarkable.

Some of the earliest American efforts in collective control, antedating union organization itself, were made in the newspaper industry. Here, also, is found the first recorded voluntary arbitration of industrial disputes. Out of this experience publishers and unions developed, almost forty years ago, the first nation-wide system of industrial arbitration. Through the years this system built up a comprehensive body of industrial law and precedent, strong and flexible procedures, and an effective administration and discipline under which generally peaceful relations have been maintained.

There is an opportunity here to study certain specialized economic effects of collective bargaining under highly unionized conditions. In newspaper publishing unique cost conditions and a complex market situation have an important bearing upon production, employment, the level of wages and long-run collective bargaining policy. Since it is within this framework that collective bargaining functions, it will be well at the outset to analyze briefly some of the industry's more important economic characteristics—its size, production requirements and trends, as well as costs and income. Union-publisher organization and the development and operation of collective bargaining can then be examined more profitably.

1. THE INDUSTRY: ITS ECONOMIC STATUS AND CHARACTERISTICS

a. PRESENT SIZE AND RELATIVE POSITION

In 1939 the United States had 2,147 daily newspapers. When compared with all branches of manufacturing, this industry, together with periodical publishing, in 1937 stood thirteenth in number of wage earners, twenty-second in cost of materials used, but first in value added by manufacture. This is one of the best available measures of the productive importance of an industry. Obviously a relatively high ratio of value added by manufacturing has important implications for the determination of wage levels.

The value of products in newspaper publishing amounted to $862 million in 1937. Wages were $186 million. Exclusive of salaried employees, there were some 110,000 workers, whose annual earnings averaged $1,690, in contrast to $1,380 in book, music and job publishing, and $1,180 in general manufacturing.[1]

The total number employed in the daily newspaper industry itself is about 150,000.[2] Of these, 75,000, or slightly more than 50 per cent, are employed in the mechanical departments where collective bargaining has reached its highest development. The remaining nearly 75,000 are in the editorial, advertising and business departments, where labor organization is a recent development.

In the mechanical departments, all except 11,000 miscellaneous workers, or 14 per cent of the total, are employed in craft operations. Those in the composing room are numerically the largest and most important, constituting over 39,000 workers, or 53 per cent; those in the pressroom number nearly 11,000, or 14 per cent; in the stereotyping division, over 5,000, or 7 per cent; in the photoengraving department, 2,000, or 3 per cent, and in the mailing room, 7,000, or 9 per cent.[3]

b. NATURE AND ECONOMIC CHARACTERISTICS

All of this work requires considerable intelligence, training and mechanical proficiency. The printing trades workers were among

1. "Printing, Publishing, and Allied Industries," U. S. Census of Manufactures, 1937, pp. 5, 12; and special tabulation by the U. S. Bureau of the Census.
2. *Editor and Publisher,* October 29, 1938, Sec. II, p. 1.
3. *Ibid.,* including unpublished data.

the first to organize and, through the decades, they have vigorously and effectively extended their organization and control. Employers, for the most part, are men of outstanding ability, organizing skill and experience, who understand the social and economic forces of which collective bargaining is a part.

Production Requirements
Newspaper publication has unusual and rigorous production requirements. Few industries yield a product quite as perishable as the daily newspaper. Speed, timeliness and regularity of issue are vital to the gathering and dissemination of news and, to a somewhat less degree, of advertising.

Daily and periodic changes are much more important in the newspaper industry than the relatively small seasonal variations in production. The volume of news and advertising may vary considerably; a sudden decrease may create surplus men on a shift, while an increase in either or both may involve extra work and overtime. A newspaper cannot stagger its requirements uniformly throughout a twenty-four-hour period; it must have the required labor forces available on call to meet peak production needs within single shifts. These factors, in addition to the costliness and complexity of machines used, have in part determined the type of labor employed and the need for an elastic labor supply.

Trends in Production
After the Civil War, the newspaper industry entered a period of rapid growth. Daily papers increased from 909 in 1880 to an all-time peak of 2,461 in 1916. Much of this growth was due to the great expansion of the evening press. Since 1916 the number has fallen off rather steadily to 2,331 in 1921, 2,248 in 1929 and 2,147 in 1939.[4] During later years the number of dailies in newspaper chains increased, rising from 158 in 1923 to a peak of 328

---

4. N. W. Ayer and Son, *American Newspaper Annual*, 1880–1910; *American Newspaper Annual and Directory*, 1910–1929; *Directory of Newspapers and Periodicals*, 1930–1940. The Ayer figures include trade dailies as well as those of religious, fraternal and other such organizations. It is, however, the only compilation which is reasonably comparable from as far back as 1880. *Editor and Publisher* annual data on English-language dailies of general circulation only, going as far back as 1920, record 2,042 dailies in 1920, 2,008 in 1925, 1,942 in 1930, 1,950 in 1935 and 1,888

in 1935.[5] Then a decline set in; by 1937 sixty chains controlled 318 newspapers.[6] The declining trend in the number of papers has developed despite the fact that between 1910 and 1930 total population increased by more than a third, urban population by almost two thirds and the number of urban centers by over 50 per cent. From a circulation standpoint, however, daily newspaper publishing is still, to a limited degree, an expanding industry. Average daily circulation receded very little throughout the depression, and by 1937 reached an all-time high of 43.3 million. The long-run trend has followed closely the growth of urban population. If the latter curve now tends to flatten out, as population studies indicate, total circulation will probably increase only very slowly, if at all. Other factors, such as the changing market situation for the industry, may well cause circulation declines in the future.

Behind the decline in the number of newspapers and their relative concentration in larger centers [7] is the outstanding trend in the industry today—the growth of one-newspaper cities. Cities with a single daily newspaper numbered only 350 in 1900. By 1920 they had risen to almost 700 [8] and by 1937 to nearly 1,100.[9]

in 1939 (Annual Yearbook issues, 1920–1940). The significance of the decline in the number of newspapers is not fully revealed by these figures. Many of the large established newspapers which were important employers of labor have gone out of existence while the many smaller papers which have begun publication, although important numerically, have not afforded as much employment.

5. Although chain newspapers in 1935 amounted to only 17 per cent of all daily and 25 per cent of all Sunday papers, they represented 42 per cent of total daily and 52 per cent of total Sunday circulation. In many localities chain papers with greater capital reserves have been less opposed to union proposals for wage increases and in other ways have influenced collective bargaining.

6. W. Weinfeld, "Growth of Daily Newspaper Chains in the United States: 1923, 1926–35," *Journalism Quarterly*, December 1935, p. 363.

7. Despite the great growth in the number of cities with less than fifty thousand inhabitants, the number of newspapers in these smaller cities has fallen off markedly. In 1910, there were 1,879 daily and Sunday newspapers in 2,133 such cities, whose population totaled approximately 17.5 million. By 1930, the number of papers had fallen to only 1,628, while the number of such cities had risen to 2,974 and their population to 26 million. In cities of over fifty thousand, whose number and population has also increased greatly, the number of papers has risen, but to a lesser degree.

8. Malcolm M. Willey and Stuart A. Rice in *Recent Social Trends*, McGraw-Hill, 1933, p. 205.

9. Alfred McClung Lee, "Recent Developments in the Newspaper Industry," *Public Opinion Quarterly*, School of Public Affairs, Princeton University, January 1938, p. 129.

If cities having only one newspaper or newspapers under a single ownership are lumped together, about 60 per cent of all daily papers are noncompetitive.[10] This is primarily due to the consolidation and suspension of established papers, and secondarily to the extension of the daily press to cities not having a newspaper previously. Of the 913 one-newspaper cities in 1930, a little over a third were the result of the establishment of newspapers in unserved communities, while nearly two thirds were due to consolidations and suspensions. These latter increased four times faster than new papers during the twenty years from 1910 to 1930.[11] Apparently, the increasing number of suspensions and consolidations, the decline in the number of newspapers and the growth of one-newspaper cities go hand in hand.

These trends have real significance for collective bargaining. Reductions in the number of competitive newspapers may insure greater financial stability for the industry, more stable collective bargaining relationships and higher wage rates. But they may also mean declining employment. Concentration of newspapers in larger centers tends to lessen mechanical man-hour requirements per unit of output. Contributing to these trends are certain cost conditions and a changing market situation.

Costs

In the mechanical departments, with which this study is chiefly concerned, wages are only a minor part of total production costs. It is estimated that out of total expenditures (excluding capital charges and rent) of $600 million made by the newspaper industry in 1936, mechanical wage costs were only $137 million, or 23 per cent.[12] They were, in fact, slightly less than the expenditures

---

10. From a survey by Charles J. Cole cited in *Editor and Publisher*, October 29, 1938, p. 30.

11. W. Carl Masche, *Factors Involved in the Consolidation and Suspension of Daily and Sunday Newspapers in the United States Since 1900: A Statistical Study in Social Change*, unpublished thesis, University of Minnesota, 1933, p. 122.

12. Arthur Robb, *Editor and Publisher*, January 9, 1937, p. 40. Mechanical labor costs as a proportion of total operating costs and expenditures are, of course, even lower. The statements filed by Hearst Publications, Inc., before the Securities and Exchange Commission in Washington, March 20, 1937, showed the cost of mechanical labor to be only 12.5 per cent, 12.9 per cent, and 13.2 per cent of this total in the years 1934, 1935 and 1936, respectively.

for paper, ink and other materials, which amounted to $156 million. Yet the mechanical payroll exceeds that of other departments; it is 45 per cent of total labor costs as compared to 36 per cent for business and advertising and 19 per cent for editorial departments.[13]

Perhaps even more significant than these constituent cost relationships is the essential nature and character of cost in the industry, its relation to changes in total circulation, to the number of newspapers and to the output of each. As we shall see, these inherent cost characteristics, together with a changing market situation for the industry, go far to explain production trends and the limited competitive conditions that prevail.

Newspaper publishing is an industry of decreasing unit costs, enjoying important economies of large-scale production. As a newspaper increases its circulation, man-hour requirements in the mechanical departments do not rise proportionately. Man-hour requirements in the composing room are unaffected by any change in circulation unaccompanied by a corresponding change in lineage; the effect on photoengraving and stereotyping is likewise negligible. While man-hour requirements in the pressroom and in mailing tend to increase as circulation rises, actually they fall relatively because of economies in equipment and technique realized only as scale of operations is increased.[14]

It has been shown that when circulation doubled from 50,000 to 100,000, mechanical man-hour requirements for composition, stereotyping and presswork on each four-page section increased from 164 to 173, or approximately 5 per cent, while the number

13. In 1936, 224 newspapers in forty-four states reported that their mechanical payrolls amounted to $54.3 million, or 45 per cent of total labor cost; editorial $22.5 million or 19 per cent; and general payroll (business and advertising) $43.1 million or 36 per cent. A breakdown of mechanical wage costs shows that more than one half, or 52 per cent, is for the composing room. One sixth, or 17 per cent, covers labor cost in the pressroom, 8 per cent is for stereotyping, 8 per cent for mailing operations, 4 per cent for photoengraving, and 11 per cent for delivery room operations. American Newspaper Publishers Association, *Bulletin B-Special No. 6771*, issued from the New York office, December 10, 1937, p. 635.

14. In the nonmechanical departments, the circulation department will reflect expanding output in increased personnel; the work force in the business department will increase somewhat, and the editorial department least, assuming no changes in bulk size or frequency of issue.

of copies produced per man hour rose from 305 to 580. As circulation jumped fivefold, from 100,000 to 500,000, mechanical man-hour requirements increased from 173 to 239, or only 38 per cent, but the number of copies produced per hour rose from 580 to 2,092. In the first case, mechanical wage cost rose approximately $11, from $208 to $219, but labor cost per ten thousand copies declined from $41.65 to $21.85—revealing the enormous reductions in cost from expansion in output. As circulation rose from 100,000 to 500,000, mechanical wage cost increased from $219 to $301, while the labor cost per ten thousand copies further declined from $21.85 to $6.02.[15]

Obviously, such economies of large-scale production are inconsistent with the maintenance of competitive conditions. They lead to concentration of production in a steadily diminishing number of units. As noted above, actual trends in the industry confirm these theoretical expectations to a surprising extent.

Revenue

Changing market conditions have affected differently the revenue from the industry's two products—news and advertising. Because of the highly inelastic demand for the news product, circulation income has been relatively stable, averaging about one third of total revenue. In fact publishers have successfully raised subscription prices to offset in part increased costs and declining advertising income.[16] This should tend to increase and stabilize total newspaper income and, in the long run, give a firmer financial base for collective bargaining.

15. S. Kjaer, "Productivity of Labor in Newspaper Printing," U. S. Bureau of Labor Statistics, *Bulletin No. 475*, 1929, pp. 20, 25.
16. Between 1900 and 1920, the modal subscription price for daily newspapers was about $5 per year. By 1930 this had risen to $7 (Masche, *op. cit.*, p. 103). More recently, per copy prices have registered increases. Out of 375 daily papers surveyed in 1936, 45, or 12 per cent, increased their price that year (American Newspaper Publishers Association, *Bulletin No. 6776*, issued by the New York office, 1937, pp. 651-652). A later survey showed that in the first nine months of 1938, 194 dailies out of 873 had raised their circulation rates. Temporary losses in circulation of approximately 10 per cent were "in great part regained . . . in the ensuing three to six months." (*Ibid., No. 6891*, 1938, p. 669.) Since the percentage price increases are generally much greater than circulation losses, this indicates that the demand for the news product is rather inelastic.

From advertising, newspapers obtain approximately two thirds of their income. Such revenue has been highly unstable and greatly influenced by changes in business activity. From a peak of $797 million in 1929, newspaper advertising fell in 1933 to $429 million, or 54 per cent of its former high, and in 1937 amounted to $574 million.[17] For this decline there are two main causes: smaller advertising appropriations, and the rise of competitive advertising media.

Total expenditures for advertising in the principal media in 1937 were $968 million, or only 13 per cent below the 1929 peak of $1,115 million.[18] During that time, newspaper advertising declined 28 per cent. The daily newspaper's share of the national-advertising dollar dropped from 47 cents in 1929 to 41 cents in 1937, while radio's share increased from 3.5 to 15 cents.[19] In local advertising, the financial bulwark of the press, the decline in newspaper and rise in radio advertising were even more pronounced. Obviously, these trends in newspaper advertising and the rise of competitive media affect collective bargaining and wage policy in the newspaper field.[20]

Newspaper income has been relatively stable during depressions as compared to periodical publishing, commercial printing and all manufacturing; but it has lagged somewhat in recovery. Up to 1929, newspaper publishing enjoyed a steady growth in total income, reaching a peak of $1 billion that year. During the twenty years before the depression, its products increased in value almost fourfold. With the onset of the depression newspaper income declined considerably. By 1933, it had fallen to $688 million, a decline of 38 per cent; in 1937 it had risen to only $862 million, or about 20 per cent below the 1929 peak. In contrast, manufac-

17. "Printing, Publishing, and Allied Industries," *U. S. Census of Manufactures,* 1937, p. 12.
18. Estimates made by L. D. H. Weld, *Printers' Ink,* June 16, 1938, pp. 19-22.
19. Compiled from reports in: Broadcaster's Yearbook; L. D. H. Weld, *op. cit.;* and American Newspaper Publishers Association, *Reports of the Bureau of Advertising,* Chicago, 1929–1937.
20. There is a substantial degree of integration between newspapers and radio stations in terms of ownership and affiliation. Out of a total of 732 radio stations in operation in April 1939, 229, or almost one third, were newspaper-owned or -affiliated (ANPA *Annual Report,* 1939, p. 41). In 1940, newspapers had a proprietary interest in 269 out of 814 licensed radio stations. *Ibid.,* 1940, p. 302.

turing income declined 55 per cent between 1929 and 1933, but in 1937 was only 13 per cent under its 1929 level. Throughout the years newspaper publishing as a whole has appeared to be a relatively prosperous industry.[21] Earnings of some of the big and well-established papers and chains have been both large and stable.[22] Some of the less well-established and smaller papers have not been so fortunate. A growing number have been unable to meet the higher costs and newer competition of recent years. Fewer newspapers, shifts in production, new competition and declining income—all these affect collective bargaining by posing problems which the parties involved have not fully faced before.

2. UNION ORGANIZATIONS: THEIR STATUS, JURISDICTIONS AND FUNCTIONS

The International Typographical Union, organized in 1852, is the oldest national union in the country. Originally all printing trades were under its jurisdiction. With increasing specialization and division of labor in the industry, however, the pressmen, photoengravers, and stereotypers and electrotypers formed separate national unions. The pressmen seceded in 1889, although jurisdiction was not formally surrendered by the ITU until 1894. The stereotypers' and electrotypers' secession movement began in 1898 and ended with formal recognition in 1901. Photoengravers formed a national union in 1900, which was recognized in 1904. The mailers are organized into a semiautonomous trade district

21. A study of profits of large corporations engaged in manufacturing, covering the period 1919–1928, showed newspaper publishing—as represented by a sample of the larger corporations—had earnings of almost 26 per cent on capital invested, and was the second most profitable industry (Ralph C. Epstein, *Industrial Profits in the United States*, National Bureau of Economic Research, 1934, p. 43). In a subsequent study, bringing the data up to 1932, printing and publishing showed a slight deficit, but it was listed by the National Bureau of Economic Research as one of the relatively profitable industries of the year. Solomon Fabricant, "Profits, Losses, and Business Assets, 1929–1934," National Bureau of Economic Research, *Bulletin No. 55*, April 11, 1935, pp. 4, 12.

22. See, for example, net income data for the Chicago Daily News, Inc., The Gannett Company, Inc., The Copley Press, Inc., The Brush-Moore Newspapers, Inc., and the Scripps-Howard Newspapers, in *Moody's Manual of Investments, Industrials*. For income and other data on the Hearst newspapers, see the *Registrants File*, Securities and Exchange Commission, Washington, 1938.

union within the Typographical Union, under provision made in 1898.

These unions have established a remarkably high degree of organization. The pressmen and stereotypers control about 95 per cent of all "situations" for their crafts in the daily newspaper field. Between 90 and 95 per cent of newspaper photoengravers and about 90 per cent of the typographers on daily papers are members of their respective unions.

a. JURISDICTIONS AND EMPLOYMENT

The Typographical Union claims the exclusive right to organize compositors, machine tenders, mailers and proofreaders who are practical printers. In addition, it requires locals to maintain scales for all copyholders and machine tenders' assistants regardless of whether they are members of the union, and recently it has insisted that vacancies among composing room helpers shall be filled by journeymen or apprentices.[23] The jurisdiction of the Pressmen's Union in newspaper plants covers pressmen, paper handlers and certain other workers whose membership in the union is negligible. The stereotypers and electrotypers, who make duplicate plates for presses, the photoengravers, who make the cuts for illustrations, and the mailers, who perform labeling, wrapping and mailing work, all claim jurisdiction over their crafts as well as over associated miscellaneous help.

Newspapers are important or major employers of members of these unions. Some 56 per cent of the 59,709 union compositors who work at the trade are employed on newspapers; 28 per cent of the 43,700 union pressmen, 49 per cent of the 8,699 union stereotypers and electrotypers, and 21 per cent of the 10,398 members of the Photo-Engravers' Union are in newspaper employment.[24]

23. ITU, *Proceedings*, 1939, p. 138. This action was precipitated by the attempts of the American Newspaper Guild to have itself certified as the bargaining agency for certain unskilled or semiskilled composing room workers. The Typographical Union accordingly reasserted its jurisdiction over and control of all composing room work performed by nonmembers.
24. Typographical journeyman membership, exclusive of mailer and news writer members, was 74,004 on May 1, 1940. The number of typographers working or seeking work at the trade totaled only 59,709—the larger figure including aged, incapacitated and retired members. Mailers numbered 5,164, and news writers 58.

b. GOVERNMENT AND FUNCTIONS

All printing trades unions function through the convention, an executive council or board of directors, and the referendum. All but the pressmen hold annual conventions. Quadrennial conventions of the pressmen were temporarily suspended in 1932 and 1936, but one was held in 1940. Convention delegates are apportioned on a basis that gives smaller unions representation of greater proportion than their membership. Because of the costs involved in sending delegates, however, smaller unions are usually underrepresented at conventions, where union laws are adopted and broad bargaining policies formulated.[25] Only the Pressmen's Union recognizes the division of interest existing between its newspaper and commercial members and allows the newspaper people to act separately upon measures for the regulation and control of their branch.

Referendums on important issues increase the influence of the smaller locals which are usually more conservative in their demands under collective bargaining. Moreover, the referendum has contributed to greater centralization of power in the internationals, since it counteracts the influence of the larger stronger locals who usually oppose encroachment on their autonomy and freedom of action.

ITU, *Officers Reports*, 1940, pp. 118, 147. (Figures compiled from quarterly reports from locals for three months ending April 30, 1940.) Estimate of newspaper employment based on data from their membership survey as reported in their *Bulletin*, Supplement, November 1935.

Pressman membership based on per capita tax payments, as reported to the American Federation of Labor. (AF of L, *Report of the Executive Council*, 1940, p. 11.) Estimate of newspaper employment based on data from the Service Bureau, International Printing Pressmen and Assistants' Union.

Stereotyper and electrotyper membership from ISEU, *Journal*, July 1940, p. 34; photoengraver membership from IPEU, *Officers Reports*, 1940, pp. 4, 31. These figures differ somewhat from those given in AF of L, *Proceedings*, 1940. (See the "Book and Job Printing" chapter.)

From ISEU, *State of Trade Report*, April 1939, it is estimated that about 4,958 of this union's members are stereotypers, of whom 86 per cent work on newspapers. Electrotyper members of the union are employed for the most part in commercial work. The percentage of photoengravers in newspaper work was calculated from reports on 8,576 members.

25. Only in the Pressmen's Union does the International pay the expenses of delegates to the convention.

In all the internationals the executive council has large powers, and its influence on conventions, union policy and collective bargaining is considerable. Between conventions, the council supervises all union matters. The president, who generally controls the council, appoints convention committees, including the important "committee on laws," through which all "proposals" are presented to the conventions.

Subject to the approval of their respective executive councils, international presidents appoint representatives and organizers and supervise their relations with the local unions. These subordinate unions function through general meetings, and their standards are policed through shop organizations, or chapels.

Dominance of Internationals

Subordinate unions in the printing trades pass laws and handle their own affairs within the limits of international union laws. Throughout the history of union organization in the printing trades the trend has been toward greater control by the internationals. At present all but the stereotypers require local unions to submit their constitutions and by-laws to the executive council for approval. While collective bargaining and the negotiation of agreements is a local union responsibility, no stereotyper contract is valid unless approved by the international. The typographers, mailers, pressmen and photoengravers go even further, requiring the international to pass on the terms which a local union proposes to present to an employer, as well as on the completed contract. In the case of all the unions, approved contracts (which constitute the great majority of all contracts) are underwritten or guaranteed by the respective internationals. Finally, the internationals, through their laws, prescribe minimum conditions which must be met in local contracts. These requirements have become more rigorous through the years, particularly those of the Typographical Union, the scope and intricacy of whose laws present problems of interpretation and enforcement.

The internationals also lay down the procedure that must be followed before a strike can be initiated, and all strikes must receive international sanction before locals become eligible for the strike benefits which all of these internationals provide.[26] During negotiations internationals frequently aid the locals in interpreting contracts, analyzing proposals made by the publishers, and drafting counterproposals. Their research and service departments, particularly the Typographers' and the Pressmen's, provide the subordinate unions with data on changing trends in craft wages, cost of living, the volume of advertising and other information of great value in collective bargaining and arbitration. Finally, international officers serve as union representatives on national boards of arbitration, which are long-established institutions in the industry.

3. Publisher Organizations and Their Functions

Publishers are organized for collective bargaining into one or more of the following types of organizations: local publisher associations, usually in the larger cities; state or regional associations; and a national organization, the American Newspaper Publishers Association.

a. CITY AND REGIONAL ASSOCIATIONS

The local or city association was the first form of publisher organization. As early as 1886 a permanent local association was formed in Chicago. About the same time similar organizations sprang up in Washington, Pittsburgh and other cities. Growing union strength and increased complexity of collective bargaining were primary factors in furthering publisher cooperation and organization.

The labor activities of the local association are usually carried on by a paid full-time secretary or labor expert. He negotiates with the local unions, represents the publishers in collective bargaining and arbitration, and through the American Newspaper Publishers Association keeps informed on trends in industrial relations

26. All the internationals also provide mortuary benefits. In addition the Typographical and Pressmen's unions provide old-age pensions and maintain a home and a sanitarium for aged and infirm members; the Stereotypers have a group insurance plan and provide a home for aged members; while the Photo-Engravers have a tuberculosis benefit system and a group insurance plan. In 1939 pension funds paid by the Typographical Union constituted more than one half of all pensions paid out by AF of L unions.

throughout the industry. While local associations are completely independent organizations, they are generally guided in their labor activities by the national association and rely heavily on it for fact-finding and statistical aid and for the broad formulation of collective bargaining policy.

State and regional associations likewise have no formal connection with the ANPA but cooperate with it informally. They are active in collective bargaining and frequently employ a labor relations expert to help their members in negotiations and related matters.[27] Unlike the city associations, they do not negotiate joint agreements for all their members. Since there is no close coordination between these associations and the local and national organizations, they do not always pursue the same policy in collective bargaining and industrial relations. As a result the publishers have been hampered at times in taking a united stand.

b. THE AMERICAN NEWSPAPER PUBLISHERS ASSOCIATION

The importance of the American Newspaper Publishers Association is shown by the fact that in 1935 its members represented about 80 per cent of the circulation of all daily newspapers, employed about the same per cent of the newspaper employees, and used more than 80 per cent of all newsprint paper consumed in the United States.[28]

The Association was organized in 1887 by representatives of fifty-one newspapers [29] for the sole purpose of dealing with trade

27. Membership in the regional associations, as in the national association, is limited to daily newspapers. State associations in general do not so limit their membership. In 1933 the number of members in these associations who published daily papers was as follows: Inland Daily Press Association, 250; Southern Newspaper Publishers Association, 205; California Newspaper Publishers Association, 132; Pennsylvania Newspaper Publishers Association, 111; New York State Publishers Association, 80; New England Daily Newspaper Association, 72; Del-Mar-Va Daily Newspaper Association, 56; and the Pacific Northwest Publishers Association, 35. Figures on membership submitted by Elisha Hanson, attorney for the American Newspaper Publishers Association, in NRA, *Hearings on the Proposed Code of Fair Practices and Competition for the Newspaper Publishing Industry*, 1933, pp. 1210-1211. Files on Newspaper Code, NRA Record Section, U. S. Department of Commerce, Washington.

28. Elisha Hanson before the Committee on Education and Labor, U. S. Senate, 74th Congress, *Hearings* on S. 1958, 1935, Part III, p. 649.

29. E. B. Dietrich, "National Arbitration in the Balance," *Social Forces*, December 1929, p. 286.

activities. Its functions were later expanded to embrace other matters, including labor relations which are now directed by a special standing committee.[30] The ANPA is supported by annual dues based on circulation and by monthly dues fixed according to the number of machines in the mechanical departments. By 1905 membership in the Association had increased to 239. In 1930 it stood at 501. With the decreasing number of newspapers in recent years, membership was 436 in 1935, and 449 in 1940.[31]

The Special Standing Committee

The Special Standing Committee was appointed in 1900 "to take up labor questions affecting generally the members of the American Newspaper Publishers Association," and to negotiate an arbitration agreement with the Typographical Union, which then included all local unions in the printing trades but the pressmen. It has functioned continuously for forty years and has a full-time chairman and staff, with permanent offices in Chicago.

From the date of its creation, the committee has adhered to its original purpose: "not . . . to provoke controversies or to antagonize labor, but on the contrary to promote a better understanding between union members and their employers." [32] Its office is a clearing house for publishers in the interchange of ideas and information related to collective bargaining. Its chairman looks after the interests of member publishers directly or through local associations and stands ready to assist them in their negotiations with local unions. For use in negotiating contracts or in arbitration, the Committee furnishes wage and hour data, analyses of scales and contractual provisions in comparable cities, digests of arbitration awards and precedents, and information on publishers' rights under existing contracts and union laws. Through its confidential bulletin and special memoranda it keeps members informed on

30. The Association maintains separate departments which specialize in advertising, traffic, mechanical and labor problems. In 1939 committees reported to the delegates at the convention on such matters as advertising agents, radio, newsprint prices and production, traffic and transportation problems, journalism and printing trades schools, social security and other legislation, and labor relations.
31. ANPA, *Annual Reports,* 1905–1940.
32. Statement by the Special Standing Committee in 1900. Quoted in George A. Tracy, *History of the Typographical Union,* ITU, Indianapolis, 1913, p. 642.

economic trends, labor relations and developments in collective bargaining throughout the industry. It cooperates with officials of the various internationals in adjusting disputes, settling differences and in furthering collective bargaining and arbitration between local parties.

Although the membership of the American Newspaper Publishers Association represents less than one quarter of all daily newspapers, it employs about 72 per cent of all union news compositors.[33] The Association has estimated that its members employ an even higher percentage of the newspaper craftsmen in the other printing trades unions.[34] In 1935, the composing rooms of 86 per cent of its member papers were union, while only 14 per cent were either nonunion or open shop.[35]

The Open-Shop Department

The small minority of Association members who operate on a nonunion basis was served until recently by the Open-Shop Department, established in 1922 when open-shop sentiment was increasing in almost all industries. Union-shop members opposed the new department, fearing that contractual relations with the unions might be adversely affected. Open-shop members, however, argued that they were entitled to as much service from the Association as union-shop publishers. After prolonged discussion, an Open-Shop Department was established "under such conditions as will enable it to become a substantial aid to members who desire permanently to operate under open-shop conditions, it being definitely understood that this department is under no circumstances to be used as a strikebreaking organization." [36]

Actually, the chief activity of the Open-Shop Department was to furnish nonunion workers to newspapers experiencing or threatened with strikes.[37] During recent years its operations have been

33. ITU, *Bulletin*, Supplement, November 1935, p. 264.
34. ANPA, *Annual Report*, 1933, pp. 541-542.
35. ITU, *Bulletin*, Supplement, November 1935, p. 264.
36. ANPA, *Annual Report*, 1922, p. 351.
37. Enrollment in the Open-Shop Department obligated members to "pledge themselves to furnish one or more men at the call of the Executive Secretary of this division, to work in any office where there was trouble," expenses to be paid by the publisher who was thereby aided. ANPA, *Annual Report*, 1923, pp. 338-339.

greatly curtailed. The Wagner Act and the Byrnes Law, forbidding the transportation of strikebreakers across state lines, contributed to its decline. Now virtually inactive, the department has at no time seriously threatened unionism in the newspaper trades.

4. Development of Collective Bargaining

a. BACKGROUND OF COLLECTIVE BARGAINING IN THE INDUSTRY

Collective bargaining of printers in America in a sense antedates union organization itself. In the late eighteenth century, temporary "general meetings" were occasionally called whenever a matter of general importance arose.[38] When the meeting had decided what the attitude of the trade was to be, those who were willing signed an agreement to stand by each other during the difficulty.

Establishment of a wage scale was responsible for sporadic organization in the last five years of the eighteenth century and in the early nineteenth century. Short-lived though these societies were, they nevertheless developed certain forms of cooperation which led eventually to stable organization on a national scale.[39] When a local society voted a new "price list," or scale of wages, other societies were urged to prevent employers from securing printers from their cities. If a strike resulted, other societies were asked to notify their journeymen. They also cooperated in exchange of names of journeymen transgressing rules of the trade.[40] The more permanent societies organized after 1830 strengthened all these forms of intersociety cooperation. It became apparent, however, that this was not enough. Lack of control over the labor supply, inability to support strikes, and absence of clearly established policies definitely limited the effectiveness of the societies.

Birth of ITU

Although there had been one short-lived attempt to organize a national union some fifteen years previously, a successful move-

---
38. Tracy, *op. cit.*, p. 17.
39. See George E. Barnett, "The Printers," *American Economic Association Quarterly*, October 1909, pp. 16 ff.
40. The "price lists" and other rules of societies at that time were binding upon members, but not upon employers.

ment did not start until 1850, when a convention of printers was called for the purpose of setting up a national organization.[41] At the third convention, held in 1852, the National Typographical Union came into existence, and with a change in name has continued ever since.

For more than thirty years after its organization the national union had little effect on collective bargaining. Its sovereignty over subordinate unions was stated in strong terms but in reality it exercised few powers. Instead, it merely made more effective the forms of cooperation between local unions that already existed. Its main function was to prevent employers from hiring strikebreakers and to prevent printers from violating "scales" set by local unions. National rules were almost without exception stated in terms of "recommendations" to local unions. The National had no way to discipline its locals other than to suspend or expel them. Such local negotiations as there were between publishers and unions continued to be more a matter of "higgling" than collective bargaining.

b. DEVELOPMENT OF FORMAL COLLECTIVE BARGAINING, 1885–1900

Increased power and control of the International Typographical Union, as it had come to be called, came after establishment of a "defense fund" in 1885. Local unions previously had been jealous of their autonomy, and not until they suffered severe reverses were they willing to strengthen the International. The severe depression from 1873 to 1878 was instrumental in changing their attitude, as was the success of certain internationals in other trades, which had begun to centralize controls and establish ways of aiding their subordinate unions. The Typographical Union's defense fund enabled locals to get strike benefits, if the international executive council sanctioned the strike in advance. While local unions thus strengthened their bargaining position with the publishers, the International increased its control over union bargaining policy. By fostering conciliation and arbitration, and by promoting written contracts, the international organization contributed to the extension of

---

41. Barnett, *op. cit.*, pp. 23-25; National Typographical Convention, *Proceedings*, Washington, 1836.

contractual relations between unions and publishers. By 1902, such control had developed to a point where, according to union law, no local union could sign a contract until it was approved by the international president.[42]

Centralization of union control over bargaining policy was also increased in 1884 when the first successful typesetting machine appeared. Obliged to consider very carefully the national problem created by this revolution in the printing process, local unions turned to the International for guidance in developing a common policy. The wisdom and success of this guidance greatly increased the prestige of the International. It refused to oppose introduction of the machines or reduce the scale for hand composition in order to compete with them. Instead, it encouraged printers to learn machine operation and granted wage concessions during the training period. Later events proved the union contention that skilled printers made better machine operators than those inexperienced in composing room work.

Publishers' Associations Stimulated

Concurrent with these developments which increased union strength, and in part stimulated by them, was the establishment of local publishers' associations. Such organizations, as instruments for negotiation, also contributed to the wider use of written agreements, to the formation of definite bargaining procedures and to more centralized and more responsible union organization.

The introduction of arbitration was closely bound up with the coming of publishers' associations and the growing use of written contracts. Although the Typographical Union had, as early as 1871, recommended arbitration of wage disputes, not until 1875 did local unions and publishers, notably in Chicago and later in Washington, resort to it. The Chicago publishers' association and the local typographical union concluded agreements in 1892, and again in 1897, which provided that all disputes arising out of the interpretation of the contracts should be settled by conciliation and

42. ITU, *Proceedings*, 1902, p. 110. As we shall see, the use of internationally approved written agreements received great impetus after 1900 from the system of international arbitration which was established.

arbitration.[43] The procedures established were models for the first national arbitration agreement in the industry.[44]

C. INDUSTRIAL RELATIONS UNDER THE INTERNATIONAL ARBITRATION AGREEMENTS

(1). *Inauguration of the International Agreements*

In the years immediately before 1900, a number of serious strikes spurred some publishers to more serious consideration of their labor problems. Union control of the labor supply had become a power to be reckoned with. In other strongly organized industries, employers' associations were dealing directly with the national unions, and some sort of national agreement in the newspaper industry seemed feasible. Operation uninterrupted by strikes was indeed becoming especially important to newspapers, for the industry was expanding, and advertising revenue—so dependent upon continuous publication—was increasing in relative importance.

These considerations led the American Newspaper Publishers Association in 1900 to set up a Special Standing Committee to deal with labor problems. Important local variations in publishing conditions, requirements and problems precluded national bargaining for scales and working conditions. But the partial success of arbitration agreements in the few cities where they had been tried out suggested that local arbitration might be extended and improved by a national agreement. Accordingly, the Committee presented the idea of a national arbitration agreement to the typographers' convention where it met with a favorable response. The agreement subsequently negotiated, and effective for one year beginning May 1, 1901, was approved unanimously by the convention of the Publishers Association—on condition that acceptance by

---

43. T. H. Robinson, *Chicago Typographical Union No. 16 and Its Relations With the Newspapers*, unpublished thesis, Graduate School of Social Service Administration, University of Chicago, 1924, pp. 162-165.
44. See H. B. Fagan, *Industrial Relations in the Chicago Newspaper Industry*, unpublished dissertation, Department of Economics, University of Chicago, 1930, pp. 89 ff.

individual publishers be made voluntary.[45] The union members accepted the plan by a referendum vote of 12,544 to 3,530.[46] Thus was inaugurated a twenty-one year period of international arbitration agreements and a tradition of arbitration in the industry which survives today.

(2). *Arbitration Agreements Between the ANPA and ITU, 1901–1922*

The first International Arbitration Agreement was limited to disputes arising out of the interpretation of local contracts. A local union and publisher who could not settle such a dispute by conciliation were to set up a local arbitration board, each party to select one arbitrator and the two thus chosen to select a third. The board's decision was binding unless appealed by either party to the International Board of Arbitration, consisting of the president of the international union, the Labor Commissioner of the Publishers Association, and, should they disagree, a third member selected by these two.[47] Although the International Board was designed primarily as an appeal agency, it could also hear disputes directly "if local arbitration or arbitrators [could] not be agreed upon."

Any publisher operating a union shop, and electing to sign the

---

45. The Association at that time numbered among its members some two hundred newspapers. These papers employed a total of about twenty thousand mechanical workers, of whom about 60 per cent were union members. Seventy-five per cent operated union composing rooms. Since some publishers were skeptical of local union responsibility, and since some operated nonunion composing rooms, the members of the Association would endorse the agreement only if acceptance by individual publishers were made voluntary. See statement of the ANPA Labor Commissioner in ITU, *Proceedings*, 1900, p. 41; and ANPA, *Bulletin No. 837*, 1901, p. 162.

46. Tracy, *op. cit.*, p. 647. The favorable vote of the union membership was partly a result of vigorous support by national union executives, who took what they themselves termed "a somewhat unusual course" and campaigned for the agreement through the union journal. The officers viewed the agreement with particular favor at that time as a means of strengthening the union for its contemplated fight for the eight-hour day in the commercial branch of the printing industry. See ITU, *Officers Reports*, 1900, pp. 6-7; ITU, *Proceedings*, 1911, pp. 359-360; E. B. Dietrich, *op. cit.*, p. 288.

47. The Labor Commissioner had been appointed at the time the Special Standing Committee was established. In 1907 the former office was abolished and the Chairman of the Special Standing Committee took over the duties previously allocated to the Commissioner.

agreement, entered into a contract with both the local and the international union, the latter guaranteeing observance of the local contract terms. No strikes or lockouts were allowed during the life of a local contract. Conditions existing at the time an issue was raised were to prevail until settlement by conciliation or arbitration. If either party refused to comply with a majority decision of the National Board, his national organization was to withdraw all support and publicly disavow his acts.

This original agreement, however, provided no protection against strikes which might occur when a contract expired.[48] Nor were sympathetic strikes outlawed, for international union law required that local contracts provide for the suspension of contractual obligations when an affiliated union struck or was locked out after other efforts to settle a dispute had failed. Nevertheless, the Agreement was very successful during its first year of operation. No administrative difficulties were experienced and no strikes took place in shops covered by the Agreement, although seven strikes occurred in composing rooms outside it.[49] In particular, the one case brought before the International Board convinced the publishers' Labor Commissioner that effective protection against stoppages was afforded, for despite a delay of more than one year before final settlement, a threatened strike was averted.[50] The president of the union noted with satisfaction that twenty newspaper offices had been unionized during the year.[51] Both sides agreed to the renewal and extension of the Agreement for a five-year period. Subsequent five-year agreements were negotiated in 1907, 1912 and 1917.

48. The International Agreement provided that a publisher could elect to enter into the Agreement with *"any* or all mechanical departments" which were union departments. Thus a publisher might choose to enter into arbitration with composing room employees, but not with stereotyping, photoengraving or mailing departments. The international union officers were not willing to extend the scope of the agreement to the negotiation of new contracts under these conditions, for without the concerted action of union members in all departments, publishers would have the opportunity of using their economic power to force weaker departments to accept their terms. See statement of President Lynch in ITU, *Officers Reports,* 1901, pp. 6-7. All departments except pressrooms were then under ITU jurisdiction, although they were organized into semiautonomous trade-district unions.
49. Tracy, *op. cit.,* p. 689.
50. ANPA, *Bulletin No. 964,* 1902, p. 367.
51. Tracy, *op. cit.,* p. 689.

Subsequent Arbitration Agreements

In the twenty years from 1902 to 1922, three important types of modifications were incorporated in the arbitration agreement. These included changes in scope, in the constitution of arbitration boards and in procedure. The scope of the second agreement was extended to cover the negotiation of new contracts, so far as their wage and hour provisions were concerned. After 1903, other working conditions and shop practices not regulated by international or local union "laws" were also made arbitrable. The third and subsequent agreements further extended arbitration by providing that rules (or "laws") of local unions "affecting wages, hours and working conditions" were subject to decisions of the boards in cases of dispute. This had the effect of preventing local unions from arbitrarily imposing new shop rules, and thereby helped to eliminate what had hitherto been a source of considerable friction.

In 1907, important changes were made in the constitution of local and international arbitration boards. Local boards were enlarged to four members—two representatives of the union and two of the publisher; and membership of the International Board was increased to six—three executive officers of the international union and three from the Special Standing Committee. But the provision for adding an impartial chairman, either locally or nationally, when these representatives became deadlocked, was eliminated. This radical change was occasioned by the fact that, following the extension of the agreement to the negotiation of new wage scales, some local unions became dissatisfied with the decisions rendered by the arbitrators. Unions complained that "the ... chairman is frequently taken from walks of life where there is little opportunity for the gathering of that knowledge of newspaper management and composing-room conditions that is essential to a fair adjustment of a proposed wage scale in controversy." [52] After the change, however, both local and national deadlocks were such a problem that in 1911 impartial chairmen were restored.

52. Statement of President Lynch of the International Typographical Union, *ibid.,* p. 852.

A Test of the Agreement

A real test of the effectiveness of the arbitration agreement came with the great increase in cases following its extension of scope in 1902. An important weakness was revealed, the failure of the agreement to define arbitration procedure in unequivocal terms. In 1902 and 1903 procedural disputes were, in fact, largely responsible for authorized strikes in two jurisdictions. International union officers believed the local publishers involved had forfeited their right to the protection of the agreement by their unlawful procedure; the publishers, on the other hand, thought the union had violated the no-strike provision.

The difficulties were ironed out by drawing up a Code of Procedure in 1903 which, with modifications, remained a part of the arbitration agreements thereafter. It outlined specific steps to be taken in initiating arbitration proceedings, and definite rules for the conduct of hearings. As an enforcement measure, the International Board was empowered to investigate complaints of "evasion, neglect, collusion or fraud"; and if the complaints proved justified it could either order a rehearing or annul the local arbitration contract.

The code also included this definition of the scope of arbitration with relation to union laws:

Local union laws, not affecting wages and hours, and the laws of the ITU shall not be subject to the provisions of the Arbitration Agreement: Provided ... that International and Local laws enacted subsequent to the execution of an arbitration or a local contract shall not affect either contract during its life.[53]

Local parties were required thereafter to submit points in dispute to the International Board for certification of arbitrability, prior to all arbitration hearings.

The broadened scope and increasing acceptance of arbitration contracts compelled further procedural changes. The International

---

53. *Stipulations, Interpretations, and Code of Procedure Governing the Execution of the Arbitration Agreement between the ANPA and the ITU*, October 1903, Section 2. Some disputes over the exact construction to be placed on this clause later resulted in the drawing up of a more precise clause in the 1917 agreement, providing that the laws exempt from arbitration were those in effect at the time the International Arbitration Agreement was last negotiated.

Board became overloaded with cases upon which local boards deadlocked, or which were brought directly to it without a local hearing. This situation became particularly serious after 1907. As a result, amendments designed to insure more local decisions were added to the Code of Procedure in 1909. A distinction was made between the procedure for settling disputes over interpretation of existing local contracts, and cases relating to negotiation of new contract terms. The former could be taken directly to the international union president and the chairman of the Special Standing Committee, in order to obtain prompt settlement. But those involving new contract terms were to be considered first by a local board, and by the International Board only upon appeal. To reduce local deadlocks, each party was to choose for a local board one direct representative and one member "free from personal connection with, or direct interest in, a newspaper or local union."

The distinction between the two types of cases was retained even after the use of impartial chairmen was again stipulated. The requirement that some local board members be chosen from outside the trade was eliminated in 1917.

When the first arbitration agreement was formulated, acceptance was voluntary for publishers, but not for local unions. In 1907, however, local unions were given the option individually to refuse the new arbitration agreement if a publisher had not elected to come under the previous one. This provision was intended to prevent a publisher from using an agreement as a "storm shelter," or from suddenly signing it when he contemplated a specific change which he knew would be opposed. Union members regarded this practice as a violation of the spirit of arbitration. Finally, in 1912, acceptance was made completely voluntary for both parties. Many local unions at first used their new power to refuse arbitration contracts,[54] but pressure exerted by the inter-

---

54. There was considerable ill-feeling at this particular time, occasioned by a widely circulated letter sent out by New York and Chicago publishers, repudiating the arbitration agreement because of its exemption of international union laws from arbitration, and expressing their determination no longer to be a party to it. This action was construed by many union members as a sort of "declaration of war," although the Association insisted that it did not represent national sentiment and many individual publishers were indignant at the action taken.

national officers soon overcame this attitude. In the meantime, so many publishers without arbitration agreements applied for the assistance of the Special Standing Committee or for the use of international arbitration machinery that, in 1914, the Association ruled they were bound by decisions when arbitration boards were called at their request.[55]

(3). *Arbitration Agreements of the Stereotypers, Photoengravers and Pressmen*

The Pressmen's Union was so impressed with the success of the typographers' experiment with arbitration that it negotiated almost identical agreements in 1902 and 1907. When the stereotypers and photoengravers obtained their independence, they, too, negotiated similar agreements, which remained in force until 1922.

The pressmen declined to renew their international agreement in 1912, and not until 1920 was it re-established. Opposition to renewal was precipitated by a particularly sharp dispute in Chicago just at the time that the 1907-1912 agreement expired.[56] However, the international officers continued to urge arbitration as a policy, and since many individual arbitration contracts continued to be signed in the period 1912-1920, the international machinery was retained informally for the convenience of those who chose to arbitrate. But for this, a more serious effort to renew the agreement might have been made earlier.

(4). *Breakdown of Three Arbitration Agreements*

Despite the great success of the international arbitration agreements in promoting peaceful industrial relations, they were not renewed by the typographers, photoengravers and stereotypers in 1922. The breakdown was the result of a long-standing disagreement between the Publishers Association and the unions over exemption of international union "laws" from arbitration. In 1922 the Association for the first time took a determined stand that any

---

55. ITU, *Officers Reports*, 1915, pp. 14-15.
56. For a detailed discussion of the difficulties, presented from varying points of view, see: *ibid.*, 1912, pp. 119 ff.; U. S. Commission on Industrial Relations, *Report and Testimony*, 1916, Vol. I, pp. 626 ff.; and Fagan, *op. cit.*, pp. 320 ff.

future international agreement must provide for unrestricted arbitration of all issues affecting both employee and publisher interests. That they chose to emphasize this issue in 1922 seems to have been due to three conditions of the time: the widespread open-shop movement in American industry, which gave moral support for opposing unions; the industrial depression of that year; and confidence that lack of an international agreement would not spell the end of arbitration in the industry. The fact that the pressmen's unions continued to use arbitration even without a formal international agreement between 1912 and 1920 was the basis of this confidence.

The unions—and particularly the typographers—were, in their own words, unwilling to "expose to the hazard of arbitration" rules painstakingly established through years of organizational effort. International rules or laws were not arbitrary, they held, but adopted only after long consideration and usually after establishing the conditions through bargaining in many localities.[57]

The pressmen alone agreed to arbitrate all conditions except the union shop and rules relating solely to internal union affairs; and they alone have negotiated formal international arbitration agreements up to the present.[58]

(5). *Arbitration Since 1922*

Despite the breakdown of all but one of the international arbitration agreements, the machinery established under them has been maintained and the use of arbitration to settle disputes has continued almost undiminished.[59] Where local parties agree to arbi-

57. The union position was stated in letters of officers to the arbitration committee of the Publishers Association. See ITU, *Officers Reports,* 1922, pp. 7-10; ANPA, *Annual Report,* 1922, pp. 328-336.

58. Although the other three unions took a united stand in refusing to change their arbitration agreements to permit arbitration of conditions regulated by union law, the issue was of far greater importance to the typographers than to the other unions. Of the photoengravers' laws, only those relating to the forty-four-hour week were then issues of importance. And the only important point of difference between the stereotypers and the Association at that time was the union stipulation of the minimum number of men on machines. The typographers, on the other hand, regulated a larger number of important conditions affecting publishers' interests by this ex parte method.

59. Actually, many individual publishers were willing to make the concession which the Association was unwilling to grant. The president of the Typographical

trate under the rules of the former international agreements, local and international arbitration boards function by mutual consent, and decisions have the same force and effect as if the international agreements had been formally renewed. Local provision for the arbitration of disputes arising out of the interpretation of existing contract terms is still almost universal, with more than 90 per cent of the local contracts of each international on file with the Special Standing Committee containing this type of provision. Local parties may be "arbitrated" into including such a provision in a new contract if either union or publisher proposes it.

Provision for arbitration of the terms of a new contract, on the other hand, must be mutually agreed upon. Although the decline in the number of local agreements stipulating this type of arbitration is marked,[60] arbitration is such a firmly established principle in the industry that it is usually employed by mutual consent when conciliation fails, even though no previous provision for its use has been made. The internationals usually recommend arbitration to their local unions when difficulties in negotiations become acute; and international control of strike funds gives such recommendations almost the force of mandates. Only the photoengravers refuse to support wholeheartedly arbitration of new contracts.

Support of arbitration has continued to be the policy of the

Union reported in 1929 that members of the Association, almost without exception, could be classified into three groups: those with individual arbitration contracts which provided for the exemption of union laws; those who desired such contracts but had not secured them because of local union opposition; and those who waited until a dispute arose and then offered to arbitrate under a code exempting union laws (ITU, *Officers Reports*, 1929, p. 12). Ten years later (July 1939) 90 per cent of the 242 typographical arbitration contracts on file with the Special Standing Committee provided for the exemption of international union laws from arbitration. Only 22 per cent of the stereotypers' contracts provided for exemption of all international laws from arbitration, the issue being of less importance to this union, as had been suggested previously. Local unions of the photoengravers almost without exception now limit the scope of individual arbitration contracts to the interpretation of existing contract terms; and exemption provisions are therefore infrequent and unimportant in this union.

60. In 1922, when most arbitration contracts came under the International Arbitration Agreements, almost all of them provided for arbitration of the terms of a new contract, as well as for arbitration of disputes arising in the interpretation of an existing contract. In April 1939, only 37 per cent of typographical contracts on file with the Special Standing Committee, 2 per cent of photoengraver contracts, and approximately 70 per cent of mailer, stereotyper and pressman contracts so provided.

American Newspaper Publishers Association. Among individual publishers, arbitration contracts have increased in favor through the years. According to the present chairman of the Special Standing Committee, "cases now practically never arise in which the employer rejects arbitration."[61]

Since 1922, the Pressmen's five-year international agreements besides providing for the arbitration of all except internal union matters and the union shop, have called for the selection of the chairmen of the International Board from a permanent panel of not more than ten arbitrators agreed upon by the union and the Special Standing Committee. This provision, designed to prevent delays in the selection of chairmen, has been informally administered. Little difficulty in choosing a chairman has been experienced in recent years.[62]

The average yearly number of arbitration cases heard by the International Boards has decreased since 1922.[63] Since union and publisher sources indicate increasing, rather than decreasing, satisfaction with the arbitration system, this is probably attributable to the growth of conciliatory attitudes, and to the final settlement of a larger proportion of arbitration cases locally.[64] Willingness to

61. Eugene MacKinnon, "Arbitration in the Newspaper Business," *Arbitration Journal*, October 1939, p. 330.

62. Although it is specified that either party may not remove more than two men from the permanent panel, in practice the parties usually are able to agree upon an arbitrator without much regard to the panel, and neither forces the acceptance of an arbitrator to whom the opposing side objects.

63. In the period 1907–1921, the International Board heard 184 typographical cases—an average of 12.3 per year; whereas, in the period 1922–1936, eighty-two cases, an average of 5.5 per year, were heard. Forty-four Pressmen's cases were heard by their International Board during the period 1922–1936—a yearly average of 2.9 cases. From the standpoint of the number of arbitration contracts held by their locals, this represents about an equal use of international arbitration machinery by these two unions. The Stereotypers and Photo-Engravers have averaged about one national arbitration case every two years in the period since 1922, whereas in the period 1907–1921, the annual averages were one and one quarter, and one, respectively. All data on Typographical, Stereotyper and Photo-Engraver arbitration cases, here and immediately following, have been tabulated from records on file with the Special Standing Committee of the Publishers Association. Data on Pressmen's arbitration cases have been supplied by their Service Bureau.

64. A total of one hundred Pressmen's cases were arbitrated locally in the period 1922–1938, as compared to forty-five cases arbitrated nationally. That the tendency in recent years is for a larger percentage of all arbitration cases to be settled locally is revealed by comparing Pressmen's cases in the period before 1930 with the period 1930 and after.

make reasonable concessions in bargaining is indeed one of the virtues of the standing arbitration system.

(6). *Problems Encountered Under the Arbitration System*

Three general sets of problems have been encountered in the history of arbitration in the newspaper industry: eliminating delays in the settlement of cases; obtaining decisions satisfactory to the contending parties; and developing workable arbitration procedures sufficiently definite to prevent abuses, but flexible enough to insure successful operation.

The Problem of Delays

In early years, delays in arbitrating a new contract were numerous and caused considerable difficulty. As the parties became more familiar with the procedures of arbitration, much of this delay was eliminated. In addition, preventive provisions have been incorporated in the Code of Procedure. Time limits within which a conciliation conference must be held, once an issue is raised, have been progressively lowered from a maximum of sixty to as low as twenty days. By raising an issue before the expiration of a contract, arbitration proceedings may be instituted almost immediately after the contract expires.

Prompt settlement of disputes arising under a contract is perhaps even more important. Many disputed points of this type are not of great consequence when they arise, but if settlement is delayed they gradually assume importance, arouse ill-feeling and become "matters of principle" to both sides. By providing after 1909 that the president of the international union and the chairman of the publishers' Special Standing Committee might hear such cases directly without submission to an arbitration board, decisions were expedited. As local parties became more skilled in negotiations, the majority of these cases came to be heard locally by the "joint standing committees." Today this is the usual procedure, with a time limit of about five days ordinarily set for their consideration.

The choice of arbitration board chairmen has recently been described by the chairman of the Special Standing Committee as the most difficult step in local procedure.[65] However, delays extending into months, which were characteristic of the 1902–1907 period, are no longer possible under international arbitration procedure; it has been provided since 1912, if the local parties are unable to agree on a chairman within thirty days the president of the international union and the chairman of the Special Standing Committee can be requested by either side to choose one for them. As arbitration became well established, fewer difficulties were experienced in agreeing on chairmen for the International Boards. Today, this is no longer a serious problem; through the years there has gradually been established what amounts to a "panel" of experienced arbitrators, composed of men who are familiar with newspaper conditions and problems and who are regarded by the unions and publishers as capable of deciding fairly questions in dispute.

Satisfactory Decisions

The problems of choosing arbitrators and of securing satisfactory decisions are closely related. Both publisher and union spokesmen regard decisions reached in conciliation as more satisfactory than rulings of an arbitrator. Consequently arbitrators are not called in until union and publisher representatives have held a conciliation conference. Many original issues are thus settled by union and publisher representatives on a joint arbitration board even in cases where an arbitrator is used to decide certain other points on which no agreement has been reached.

Experience has demonstrated the advantages of *local* arbitration. Local residents have two natural advantages as arbitrators. They are familiar with local economic conditions; they can also investigate personally, if necessary, working conditions in question in the plant. Even if an International Arbitration Board is called upon to review a local decision, it is easier to weigh the evidence as an appeal board and reach a fair decision quickly than to act as a court of original jurisdiction. With the right of appeal any fla-

---

65. MacKinnon, *op. cit.*, pp. 327-328.

grant mistakes of local arbitrators can be rectified by the more experienced International Boards.[66]

Procedural Problems

While it has been necessary to lay down some specific rules for the conduct of arbitration hearings, an effort has been made to keep hearings as informal as possible. It has been found, for instance, that the use of attorneys to represent the parties in arbitration cases tends to emphasize legalism, formalism and technicalities to a degree not conducive to the maintenance of a spirit of good will and compromise. Moreover, cases in which attorneys have been used have sometimes run to interminable lengths.[67] As a result, the International Boards ruled in 1909 that practicing attorneys should not be permitted to serve as representatives on arbitration boards.[68] The internationals have also generally discouraged their locals from using professional labor counsel. If union members prepare and present cases themselves, they develop a greater interest in union affairs and more conciliatory and responsible attitudes toward the solution of joint problems. Both publishers and unions, aided by their international officers and service bureaus, have acquired considerable skill in presenting cases before arbitrators.

Newspaper arbitration has no rigid rules of evidence as in courts of law. The chairman judges the evidence without restric-

66. Relative to this point, a union spokesman comments: "Although there is some natural advantage to having a local person to serve as an arbitrator, there is frequently a great disadvantage involved, particularly in small towns and areas like the South, where the majority of available persons are not likely to be as sympathetic toward the union point of view as they should be. This is one of the most important reasons for our insistence upon use of the appeal procedure—to protect our unions in such not infrequent situations." Letter, June 7, 1940.
67. In a San Francisco Mailers' case of 1908–1909, testimony and cross-examination by attorneys representing the contending parties amounted to more than two thousand pages, yet proved so unsatisfactory that the International Arbitration Board ordered rehearings without attorneys. In a Stereotypers' case of about that same time (1906–1909) the record of testimony and evidence also totaled almost two thousand pages. Cases on file with ANPA Special Standing Committee.
68. Attorneys owning substantial interest in a newspaper or working in the trade have not, however, been barred from participating in arbitration cases. Both parties have, on occasion, waived the right to object to practicing attorneys, according to Harvey Kelly, former chairman of the Special Standing Committee. Letter, May 20, 1940.

tion. Nor is he bound by precedent "established" by former arbitration decisions, although these precedents, often persuasive, are frequently introduced as a basis for arguments. Thus flexibility is assured.

For further flexibility a standing agency rules on questions of procedure as they arise. The chairman of the Special Standing Committee and the respective presidents of the international unions serve as such an agency, and through their Joint Letters have settled a multitude of problems, minor by themselves, but taken together, vastly important for satisfactory operation of the system.[69] A few practices which have never been formally ruled upon are mutually recognized. One of the most important is the general acknowledgment that a publisher's books of account need not be submitted to an arbitration board unless he pleads inability to pay, despite the fact that a section of the Code of Procedure states that "[the local arbitration board] shall have free access to all books and records bearing on the points at issue."

(7). *Important Achievements of the Arbitration System*

The most notable accomplishment of the arbitration system—and the purpose for which it was inaugurated—has been to minimize strikes and lockouts. Harvey Kelly, a member of the Special Standing Committee, and its chairman from 1926 to 1936, recently said: "[The newspaper industry has] one of the most efficient and mutually satisfactory nation-wide arbitration plans in the country. Its record for harmonious relations ranks among the best in the country, if actually it is not the best."[70] Besides the direct prohibition of strikes and lockouts during the term of an arbitration

---

69. A few examples will illustrate the types of decisions they have made. It has been ruled that either party may submit new proposals while unsettled issues are still in arbitration, if difficulty is being experienced in reaching a decision. Strike threats for the purpose of forcing the signing of a local award have been ruled improper; likewise, offers made in conciliation are not admissible in evidence before local or international arbitration boards. Arbitration awards on wage scales have been held to be for a minimum of one year and a maximum of three years. Many decisions have been made specifying points which are arbitrable, when international union laws are exempt from arbitration. For example, the Typographical "reproduction" law is not arbitrable, but the time limit within which material must be reset is arbitrable.

70. Letter, May 20, 1940.

contract, the system has achieved its aims through fostering (1) written contracts; (2) conciliatory attitudes on the part of both employers and employees; and (3) a sense of responsibility for fulfilling contractual obligations.

Arbitration made written contracts almost a necessity.[71] Both the Publishers Association and the internationals issue "form contracts" to guide local negotiators on all important points over which disputes might arise. This service has undoubtedly promoted the drafting of clear, unequivocal, inclusive contracts. The possibility of disputes arising from ambiguities or failure to define obligations has been correspondingly reduced. Ambiguity has been further minimized by the requirement that proposed local contracts be submitted to international union officers for their approval. The latter have placed increasing emphasis on this procedure since the inauguration of the arbitration system.[72]

Workers and employers have been educated by arbitration to an understanding of their joint problems and a realization of the legitimate interests of each other. Unreasonable demands have thereby been discouraged and conciliatory attitudes promoted.

Nonobservance of contracts or repudiation of arbitration decisions has been rare. The international union officers and the publishers' Special Standing Committee realize that a satisfactory arbitration system is based upon the utmost respect for contractual obligations. The firm stand taken by these national representatives has done much to establish the general conviction among union members and among publishers that observance of contracts is essential to harmonious industrial relations. In the few cases where local unions have struck in violation of the terms of an agreement, the internationals have made every effort to fill strikers' places with union men and in some cases have reimbursed publishers for losses. Publishers have rarely violated arbitration awards, and upon those who have the Association has exerted the necessary pressure to bring them into line.

71. In April 1939, out of 731 contracts between ANPA newspapers and the mechanical trades unions, 655 were written. ANPA, *Annual Report*, 1939, p. 25.

72. In the union fiscal year 1938–1939, 411 local typographical unions submitted proposed contracts for review. (These figures do not differentiate between newspaper and commercial contracts.) ITU, *Officers Reports*, 1939, p. 26.

5. Collective Bargaining: Main Issues and Settlements

In the long development and successful operation of collective bargaining in the daily newspaper industry, three types of issues have arisen: those concerned with union recognition and status, the establishment of wage scales, and the regulation of working conditions.

Issues involving union recognition and status have long since ceased to be important matters of negotiation between the parties. The closed shop, regulation of apprenticeship and union rules pertaining to foremen are now widely accepted throughout the industry.

Issues relating to the negotiation of wage rates and hours of work have always been of major concern to the unions. In very early times unions frequently established and enforced scales without negotiation with the publishers. But with the spread of collective bargaining throughout the industry these have come to be settled largely through conciliation and arbitration rather than through any attempt at unilateral settlement by either party.

In the regulation of working conditions, however, there has been divergence of opinion between the unions and publishers as to the method of control. The publishers have frequently argued that in the interests of economy, efficiency and flexibility, they should establish as in preunion days the working arrangements and controls they deem best. The unions, on the other hand, have felt that upon the regulation of working conditions depends not only the welfare of their members but also their ability to raise wages and shorten hours. Confronted with certain abuses and problems, they have sought to make and impose rules in the union office.

In the interest of uniformity and trade-union unity, the internationals have insisted that some of these regulations be recognized in all union contracts. In many cases, however, international "laws" were enacted only after a substantial number of local unions had successfully negotiated with employers for observance of the conditions stipulated; the international action merely helped weaker locals to obtain the same conditions. In other cases, as in the reduction of the work week, the internationals took the initiative in enacting regulations and establishing new conditions.

Only slowly have many of these conditions come to be disposed of by collective bargaining. Arbitrary local union rules affecting employer-employee relations have been largely eliminated, but many international rules have not yet been fully replaced by negotiation or arbitration, although efforts have been made to extend the area of joint settlement.

a. UNION STATUS

(1). *The Closed Shop*

The closed shop is so well established in the industry that publishers usually agree without question to hire only union members and observe union rules.[73] In return, the unions contract to furnish as many competent craftsmen as the publishers need at any time and, with the exception of the photoengravers, at the regular scale provided in the agreement.[74] If the unions cannot supply the extra help needed, their members work overtime at regular rates of pay.[75] Only in a minority of contracts is employment of nonunion workers permitted, and many of these specify that those men must apply for union membership if they wish to keep their jobs.

The importance of the closed shop in the newspaper trades can scarcely be overestimated. It gives the union control of the job and a strong hold over its members. This control is basic to the union in furthering organization, in protecting members against employer discrimination, in the maintenance and advancement of scales, and in the enforcement of rules and regulations.

73. As early as 1807 a closed-shop policy was considered by some of the stronger local typographical societies to prevent the undercutting of their scales. By 1830 it began to be adopted rather widely and by 1850 the closed shop was generally being enforced. It was not until 1899, however, that this requirement became international law.

74. The photoengravers treat the contract rate as a minimum and permit, if not encourage, their members to bargain individually for higher rates of pay.

75. In November 1938, more than 90 per cent of all contracts providing for the five-day, forty-hour week stipulated that straight rates should prevail on the sixth day if the union was unable to furnish competent extra men. Union laws require members to "give out" this overtime work later by "laying off" when extra men are available. For the effect of the Fair Labor Standards Act, see p. 84, note 105.

(2). Control of Foremen

Union rules affecting the foremen, who are the representatives of management in the mechanical departments, have also played an important part in furthering union control. Since 1889 the internationals have required foremen of union departments to be union members. In the printing trades foremen usually acquire the experience necessary for their jobs only by having worked as journeymen; consequently "they have a definite bond of experience and understanding with their fellow craftsmen," as a union spokesman put it. The requirement that they be union members is also attributable to the number and complexity of trade regulations. The unions contend that a foreman who is a union member, while recognized as the representative of management, is at the same time better acquainted with union rules and their enforcement, and thus is able to manage employees with the least friction. They argue that a foreman can better present the employer's side to his fellow workmen without being suspected of hostility to the union. Union foremanship is also important in assuring the unions that no nonmembers will be employed on union work. In the commercial branch of the industry particularly, foremen are frequently "working foremen," or at least take a hand in emergencies.

In early years, many publishers were strongly opposed to having their representatives owe allegiance to the union. As contracts became more inclusive, however, and rights of both employers and unions more clearly defined, publishers in general ceased to object to the foreman law. They are now chiefly concerned lest foremen should be subject to union discipline for differing with the local union in the interpretation of the terms of a contract. The internationals generally recognize the justice of the publishers' position and a method is provided for the joint settlement of such disputes. The unions do not, however, forego their right to discipline foremen for disobeying laws relating to internal union matters, or for deliberately disregarding union rules. Although there is still occasional complaint that some locals attempt, by disciplining foremen, to enforce conditions not provided for in contracts, the practice is not so common as to constitute a major issue.

The foreman represents the employer in dealing with grievances arising in his department. He settles many day-to-day grievances and complaints with the chapel chairman, without recourse to the joint standing committee or to arbitration. A complaint by a union member is taken up by the chapel chairman, who is the administrative agent of the union in each office. If he and the foreman disagree, the issue is considered by the executive committee of the local union. If the union and the foreman or publisher still fail to agree, the matter goes to the joint standing committee, and eventually may be taken to arbitration for final settlement.

(3). *Regulation of Apprenticeship*

Apprentice regulations aim to increase union control over the labor supply—both as to the number and efficiency of craftsmen. The highly skilled nature of the crafts undoubtedly helps unions to control entrance to the trades. However, the limitation of apprentices by prescribed ratios of apprentices to journeymen has been a part of typographical union policy since 1862, and was adopted by the other internationals as they gained independent status. Ratios are set locally, usually by agreement with publishers, largely in accordance with the probable needs of the trade and the facilities available for proper training.

From time to time the Publishers Association has questioned the adequacy of apprentice ratios in maintaining the supply of skilled workers. It has charged that local union policies, especially those of photoengravers and typographers, are restrictive. There has been no concern about a shortage of web pressmen, probably because of the more liberal local policies of this union. However, surveys of composing rooms in 1920 and 1923—the only two ever made in any of the craft departments—showed that publishers were not employing even the full quota of apprentices allowed by local contracts.[76] It is true that the Photo-Engravers' Union, whose members are the highest paid in the newspaper industry, is unwill-

---

76. See ITU, *Officers Reports,* 1920, p. 252; ANPA, *Annual Report,* 1924, pp. 167-169.

ing to guarantee to, and at times cannot, furnish men at contract rates.[77]

Available figures suggest that the number of new journeymen entering the typographical, stereotypers' and photoengravers' unions through apprenticeship channels in recent years has not been large enough even to replace union members lost by death, retirement or other causes.[78] The adequacy of the labor supply, however, depends also on two other factors: (1) the number of craftsmen entering the trades through other than union channels; and (2) the future labor needs of the industry. A large proportion of young compositors, for example, apparently get their training outside the union.[79] As to the needs of the industry, all the

77. Facilities for training newspaper photoengravers through other than union channels are much more limited than for compositors. The smaller papers rarely have photoengraving departments.

78. The exact "mortality" from all these causes, in the printing trades, is not known, but it has been estimated at 5 per cent annually for all skilled trades. (See National Industrial Conference Board, *Wanted: Skilled Labor,* Report No. 216, 1936, p. 4.) Apprentices have been entering the typographical, stereotypers' and photoengravers' unions as new journeymen members at a rate of not more than 2 per cent annually in recent years, according to liberal estimates made from the limited data available. See International Typographical Union, *Bulletin,* October 1938, p. 225; International Stereotypers' and Electrotypers' Union, *Journal,* May 1939, p. 16; International Photo-Engravers' Union, *Officers Reports,* 1938, p. 34; *ibid.,* 1939, p. 31.

79. From 1930 through 1938, new members entering the Typographical Union from apprentice ranks constituted only 26 per cent of all new members. The average age of members entering the union from outside was only 29.8 years. This period may not be typical since in these years organizing work, especially in the commercial printing branch, was extensive. However, Census figures for 1920 and 1930 also suggest that the proportion of all compositors trained by the union is small. Presumably those trained outside the union receive their elementary instruction in printing schools or in nonvocational schools which give some courses in printing, and their practical training in nonunion establishments—particularly in small towns where the union may not be active. The Service Bureau of the Pressmen's Union believes that a larger proportion of its journeymen pressmen enter through apprentice channels than is the case with the compositors.

Since 1923 the Publishers Association has contributed to the support of a number of printing schools. From 1923 through 1938 these contributions amounted to $220,980, or an average of $13,811 per year, which was distributed among six schools. During the same period, a total of 2,221 students, or about 139 per year, were graduated. Obviously, the number graduated has had little significance in terms of a labor supply for the Association, particularly after the activities of the Open-Shop Department began to wane. In 1940 the Association reduced its contributions to the schools. The Chicago Photo-Engraving School, established by the Chicago Newspaper Publishers Association in 1926, graduated an average of twenty students yearly until 1933, when it was closed.

unions have felt that unemployment in their crafts during recent years justified strict limitation of apprentices. If employment in the industry continues to contract as it has in the past few years, it is likely that there will be no need to replace all those currently available for work.

To maintain and increase the union scale and to serve the best interests of the craft the unions are also interested in regulating the training of apprentices. Internationals require local unions to define the class of work upon which apprentices shall be employed from year to year, and to set apprentice scales, expressed as a proportion of journeyman scales, subject to acceptance by the publishers. The internationals specify the apprenticeship period (five to six years), minimum age for beginners and other general conditions. Typographical and pressmen's unions also give fairly complete correspondence courses which apprentices must take to supplement their practical training. In some large cities, unions cooperate with employer groups and educational institutions in apprentice-training programs. Undoubtedly it would be desirable that more entrants to the trades should have the advantages of a union apprenticeship. But until the unions are more confident of the employment opportunities in the industry, they will be reluctant to enter upon any plans to train larger numbers of apprentices.

b. WAGES AND HOURS OF WORK

(1). *Trend of Wages*

In the first half of the nineteenth century the unions were concerned primarily with establishing and maintaining wage scales; they did little to regulate working conditions through agreements with employers. Wage demands were pushed vigorously and strikes were numerous. Unionism was comparatively new, and the right of workmen to formulate demands collectively was denied by many publishers. However, the unions were aided in these difficult years by editors and publishers of the new "penny" papers, whose mass circulation was affected by their attitude toward the laboring man and who therefore found it good business to be on friendly terms with union workmen.[80] Keen competition between daily papers in the larger cities also helped the unions. A uniform scale to equalize competitive conditions was favored by some publishers.

Until the last decade of the nineteenth century, newspaper wages were usually on a piece-rate basis, and data on earnings are meager. Union agreements, however, frequently set a weekly minimum as well as a scale for the few timeworkers employed. Until the late 1830's scales for both compositors and pressmen were seldom over $8 or $9 for a week's work on evening papers, and $9 or $10 on morning papers.[81] From about 1837 to 1850 these scales usually specified $10 to $12 a week for day work. During the next forty years substantial increases were obtained, and by 1890 average full-time weekly earnings of unionists in the newspaper trades were about $22; hourly wage rates averaged 44.8 cents.[82] Their gains appear to have exceeded the average gain of all wage earners in the United States, estimated to have been about 79 per cent between 1850 and 1890.[83]

Between 1890 and 1928, the average hourly wage of newspaper craftsmen rose 172 per cent—an increase considerably less than that of wage earners in a group of union and "nonunion" industries studied by Professor Douglas.[84] However, their wage rates in

80. See Alfred McClung Lee, *The Daily Newspaper in America: The Evolution of a Social Instrument,* Macmillan, New York, 1937, p. 136; George A. Stevens, "New York Typographical Union No. 6," New York Bureau of Labor Statistics, *Annual Report,* Pt. I, 1912.

81. Photoengraving and stereotyping in newspaper publication did not become common until the 1870's. Scales for pressmen and compositors are published in "History of Wages in the United States from Colonial Times to 1928," *Bulletin No. 604,* U. S. Bureau of Labor Statistics, 1934, pp. 120-123, 489-520.

82. Data given here and later on wages from 1890 through 1928 are from Paul H. Douglas, *Real Wages in the United States, 1890–1926,* Houghton Mifflin, Boston, 1930, pp. 96, 97, 101-102, 118-123, 139; and Paul H. Douglas and Florence Jennison, *The Movement of Money and Real Earnings in the United States, 1926–1928,* University of Chicago Studies in Business Administration, 1930, pp. 32-33, 37.

83. See Harry A. Millis and Royal E. Montgomery, *Labor's Progress and Some Basic Labor Problems,* McGraw-Hill, New York, 1938, pp. 81-83.

84. In the union group were the granite and stone industry, planing mills, baking, book and job printing, newspaper printing, building trades and metal trades. The last industry was not included after 1926. The "nonunion" industries, studied by means of payroll data rather than union scales, were: cottons, woolens,

the nineties were so much higher than in the other industries that, in terms of actual money rates, hourly wages on newspapers in 1928 were above those of the union manufacturing industries, although somewhat lower than those of the building trades. The average hourly rate of newspaper craftsmen in 1928 was $1.22.

A similar trend in full-time weekly earnings characterized the period from the nineties to 1928. The newspaper trades received smaller relative increases than the union group as a whole, although the absolute level of their weekly wages in 1928 was from 17 to 21 per cent above the other union industries, excepting stone workers and the building trades.

When considered in terms of purchasing power, the gains in weekly wages in the newspaper industry in this period were largely offset by changes in the cost of living, as was true of other industries. "Real" weekly wages of newspaper craftsmen in 1928 were only 6 per cent above the level of the nineties; the comparable figure for union manufacturing industries was 15 per cent. Up to 1914, while weekly money wages in the newspaper industry increased 25 per cent, the cost of living rose 39 per cent, so that real wages decreased 10 per cent. The next four war years saw a rapid drop in real wages; money wages failed to keep pace with the rapidly rising cost of living. The newspaper trades suffered greater relative losses than any other union group. In 1918 their real wages were 36 per cent below the level of the nineties, as compared to 23 per cent for all union manufacturing industries. In the postwar years, especially from 1918 to 1921, newspaper trades enjoyed greater relative gains than the other industries, but not until 1927 did their real weekly wages reach the level of the nineties.

Trends Since 1929

From 1929 to 1939 average hourly wage rates in the newspaper industry increased every year except 1932 and 1933.[85] At their low

knit goods, men's clothing, boots and shoes, slaughtering, sawmills and iron and steel. In 1928 average hourly wage rates in the union industries were 267 per cent above the level of the nineties, while those in the nonunion group had increased 241 per cent. Of all the union industries, the newspaper trades showed the smallest relative gain.

85. For the period since 1928, indexes of the U. S. Bureau of Labor Statistics have been relied upon for newspaper average wage rates and trends. While not

point in 1933 they were only 5.5 per cent below their 1929 level, and steady increases in the next six years brought them in 1939 to $1.30, a point 11.2 per cent above 1929. Average hourly wage rates in the newspaper industry now stand at the highest level ever attained. By separate crafts the 1939 averages were: mailers, $0.98; stereotypers, $1.24; pressmen, $1.24; machine compositors, $1.36; and photoengravers, $1.70.[86] Because of the reduction in hours of work per week during the 1930's, average full-time weekly wages declined somewhat more up to 1933, and continued to fall even after hourly earnings rose. Weekly wages in 1933 were 8.5 per cent below the 1929 level of $52.25. By 1936 they were 10.5 per cent below. The rise in hourly earnings pulled them up to $49.27, or within 5.7 per cent of the base-year figure in the next three years.

Real weekly wages in the newspaper trades, however, increased markedly during the depression period, because of the great decline in the cost of living. In 1933 real wages were 20.1 per cent

strictly comparable with Professor Douglas' data for the earlier years because of a slightly different system of weighting to obtain the average rates, the general trend is adequately revealed. Because the Bureau's wage indexes in the newspaper industry go back only to 1907, and because the Douglas study makes possible more reliable comparisons with the trends in other industries, it seemed desirable to use his data through 1928. The methods used by Professor Douglas are discussed in his work which has already been cited. Some discussion of the Bureau's methods appears in "Union Scales of Wages and Hours in the Printing Trades, May 15, 1937," *Bulletin No. 655*, 1938, pp. 1-4. For other data used in the discussion that follows, see "Union Scales of Wages and Hours in the Printing Trades," *Monthly Labor Review*, December 1939, p. 1487; "Changes in the Cost of Living," *Serial No. R 1084*, U. S. Bureau of Labor Statistics, December 15, 1939, p. 7.

86. Night workers in the newspaper trades receive on the average 11 cents an hour more than day workers at the same work in the same city. For specific trades, this differential, in 1939, amounted to approximately 7.9 cents for machine compositors, 10.1 cents for mailers, 14.2 cents for stereotypers, 14.9 cents for pressmen, and 21.1 cents for photoengravers.

Other differentials in hourly rates are prevalent as between regions and between cities of varying sizes. Average rates for all crafts are higher in Northwest and Pacific Coast cities than in the South. In all regions there is a uniform decrease as size of city declines. The 1939 average hourly rates for union members in the newspaper trades ranged from $1.42 in cities of more than a million inhabitants to $1.07 in cities of from forty to one hundred thousand inhabitants. These variations by city size, and by region, are much less, however, than in many other industries, according to a National Industrial Conference Board study. See *Monthly Labor Review*, December 1939, pp. 1495-1498, 1500-1505; M. A. Beney, *Differentials in Industrial Wages and Hours in the United States*, National Industrial Conference Board, 1938, pp. 12-31.

higher than in 1929, and by 1936, although they had declined, they were still 9.3 per cent above the 1929 level. These changes may be compared with those in average real weekly wages in manufacturing as a whole, which are estimated to have declined about 18.1 per cent between 1929 and 1933,[87] and then to have risen by 1936 to a point 3.3 per cent below the 1929 level.[88] Thus, in the depression and recovery period of the thirties, the newspaper craftsmen fared well as compared with wage earners in other manufacturing industries. Real average weekly wages on newspapers continued to increase after 1936, and in 1939 were 14.2 per cent above the 1929 level.

(2). *Factors in Wage Determination*

The comparatively high wages in newspaper publishing are a result of many factors already discussed—the nature of the industry, its relative prosperity, the efficiency and productivity of its skilled workers. The discussion which follows will be confined to the more immediate considerations upon which changes in wage rates have been based, especially during the period in which arbitration has been the rule in the industry. The most important of these have been variations in the cost of living, wage differentials between comparable cities and between newspaper crafts, and economic conditions in the industry.

Cost of Living

Frequently changes in the cost of living have been advanced as the primary justification for wage adjustments. So important has this factor been that in hardly a case during forty years of arbitration did one or both sides fail to analyze its changes. Study of arbitration decisions shows that experienced arbitrators also con-

87. The U. S. Bureau of Labor Statistics cost of living index was applied to the estimate of average weekly wages in manufacturing given in Leverett S. Lyon, *et al.*, *The National Recovery Administration*, Brookings Institution, Washington, 1935, p. 778.

88. Changes between 1933 and 1936 are based on Leo Wolman, "The Recovery in Wages and Employment," *Bulletin No. 63*, National Bureau of Economic Research, p. 12. This estimate is assumed to be roughly comparable with the estimate relating to manufacturing previously cited.

sistently agree on the importance of cost of living changes.[89] A few local contracts even have clauses which fix wage changes on the basis of movements of the cost of living index. Usually these contracts have not been entirely satisfactory because the parties have been unwilling to be bound by such terms.[90]

Related to the cost of living argument is the claim of the unions for increased wages to insure an adequate "health and decency" budget. Because of the relatively high earnings of workers in the newspaper trades, such budget claims have not been as important in recent arbitration decisions as in earlier years.

Comparative Wage Criteria

The general trend of skilled wages has frequently been an initiatory force in opening scale negotiations. The high hourly scales of carpenters, plumbers and other skilled craftsmen are often cited by the unions, while publishers emphasize the greater stability of employment in newspaper trades. Although such wage data for other trades are often introduced in negotiations and in arbitration, they are of relatively minor direct influence in fixing wage rates in the industry.

89. But despite the recognized importance of this factor, it will have been noted in the discussion of wage trends that the variations in money wages and in the cost of living have not always taken a parallel course. This was particularly apparent in the war years and in the depression period of the 1930's. In both periods changes in money wages lagged far behind changes in the cost of living, to the disadvantage of workers in the former period and to their advantage in the latter. The relatively great lag in periods when the cost of living was changing rapidly may have been partly, although not entirely, attributable to the longer term contracts of the printers. In the war period, a shortage of labor in many other industries may also have tended to advance the wages of their workers to a greater degree than in the newspaper industry.

90. Union resistance to decreases in wage rates is the greatest stumbling block to successful operation of contracts providing for automatic wage adjustments in accordance with changes in the cost of living. Reference may be made to the 1919 agreement in the Chicago book and job printing industry which provided for wage changes at six-month intervals, whenever the cost of living changed as much as 5 per cent. As long as the cost of living rose, wage adjustments were made without trouble, but when it fell between August 1920 and February 1921, the union resisted and only submitted to a decrease after weeks of argument and arbitration proceedings. Moreover, this particular provision was not included in the agreement when it was renewed. See Francis H. Bird, "The Cost of Living as a Factor in Wage Adjustments in the Book and Job Branch of the Chicago Printing Industry," *American Economic Review*, December 1921, pp. 622-642 and Emily Clark Brown, *Book and Job Printing in Chicago*, The University of Chicago Press, 1931, pp. 166 ff.

Newspaper craft wages in comparable localities are a much more important consideration. These wage comparisons are usually presented in terms of craft wages in cities of approximately the same population, or in a selected sample of cities similarly situated from an economic and industrial standpoint. Sometimes the average craft wage in a given state or region or for all daily newspapers is the basis for comparison.[91]

In arbitration decisions such comparisons are usually one of the controlling considerations,[92] although sometimes arbitrators have held them to be irrelevant for wage determination. Some have reasoned that, since wage rates between comparable cities varied when the original agreement was made, their task is simply the adjustment of wages in the light of changes in conditions in the interim. This reasoning, however, which would tend to perpetuate any existing inequities, is not common.

Differentials between the crafts are frequently emphasized in wage adjustments. For many years compositors enjoyed a higher scale than pressmen, stereotypers, photoengravers and mailers. Only recently have the photoengravers succeeded in pushing their scales above the compositors. The other lesser-paid crafts have also been interested, and to some extent successful, in reducing their adverse differentials. Increased organization, bargaining skill and strength, and more aggressive wage policies have all served to increase relatively the scales of these unions. Most arbitrators, however, hold that craft differentials which have grown up in the industry are an established condition in wage arbitrations, and evidence must be particularly strong before they will be altered.

91. The ITU, in attempting to raise wage rates for the smaller unions, has sought to establish regional scales and zone agreements. Such attempts have not been vigorously pushed, however, nor have their results been important. The internationals have been opposed to the idea of national wage rates, because of the local character of the newspaper industry and the great differences that exist between different localities in terms of what the traffic will bear.

92. In a typographical case before the International Arbitration Board in 1937, for example, President Howard of the ITU argued, ". . . whether it hits one side or whether it hits the other . . . if there is a dominant factor in fixing wages it is comparing the wage that prevails in the city or locality that is under consideration with cities and localities that are properly comparable." *Transcript of Proceedings, Chattanooga Typographical Union v. Chattanooga Newspaper Publishers Association*, 1937, in ANPA, *Bulletin No. 4286*, 1937, p. 525.

Under collective bargaining and arbitration, comparisons of craft wages in comparable cities and prevailing differentials between the crafts have thus become important criteria in wage determination. Their most rigorous application is in decisions of arbitration boards. The rulings and the reasoning of those tribunals tend to establish precedent which gradually is diffused and more or less observed throughout the industry. Emphasis on these considerations in wage determination has given rise to what may conveniently be termed a follow-the-leader wage policy in the industry. When a wage increase is negotiated by one craft, perhaps because of sheer superiority in bargaining power, existing differentials are disturbed. Demands follow for similar or proportionate increases by the other crafts. Moreover, other locals in comparable cities, particularly in nearby jurisdictions, press for similar increases. Even the judicial procedure of arbitration is sometimes led to an impasse by this process. With different local arbitrators establishing wage scales in a given region, the actual operation of the follow-the-leader policy and its implications for wage determination are not always evident in individual cases. But when the same arbitrator, passing on local appeals from the same region, attempts to apply a consistent policy, certain contradictions emerge. As Professor Douglas, Chairman of an International Arbitration Board, observed:

... I don't want to start an argument on this, but I sat on the Knoxville case. The Knoxville union contended we should level the scale up more closely to the Chattanooga scale, and in my award I think you will find a reference to the fact that I thought we ought to eliminate some of these pockets in the South. But now, if Knoxville claims you should level up to Chattanooga, and then the Chattanooga printers say we ought to maintain a differential over Knoxville—I mean, just where do we get off on that? [93]

The comparatively low wage costs in some small mechanical departments at times influence individual publishers to yield to union wage demands and save the time and inconvenience of prolonged negotiations. Along with the follow-the-leader wage

93. *Transcript of Proceedings, Chattanooga Typographical Union v. Chattanooga Newspaper Publishers Association,* 1937, p. 27.

policy, this may contribute to the upward movement of wages throughout the industry, as it seems to have done in recent years.

Economic Conditions

A third set of factors emphasized in wage negotiations consists of changes in general and local business conditions and changes in the volume of national and local advertising. Adverse business conditions and a decline in advertising volume frequently lead publishers to seek wage reductions or oppose increases. However, the effect of these changes on actual wage determination cannot be definitely established. Probably they are more influential in local conciliation and bargaining than in arbitration, particularly before International Arbitration Boards. One reason is the long-standing principle that publishers are not obliged to submit their books of account or profit and loss statements as evidence; ability to pay is therefore, by common consent, taken for granted. The unions have held, moreover, that since wages are paid for skilled services rendered and are not fixed according to profits, they should not be regulated by changes in business conditions or advertising volume. Within the limits imposed by economic conditions, wage scales tend to be based on changes in the cost of living, comparative wage factors and the bargaining strength of the parties.

Tactics and Attitudes

Bargaining tactics play an important part in wage negotiations. For example, the presentation of counterdemands to exact concessions from the other side is common. Although many of these claims cancel out, counterdemands in arbitration may be very effective if an arbitrator tends to "split the difference" in making awards.

Another device is "stalling" to avoid changes in the scale. This charge was frequently leveled against the publishers during the early International Arbitration Agreements, particularly when prices and wage rates were rising. Protective provisions were incorporated in later agreements and are now used in individual arbitration contracts. But apparently it is never possible to eliminate delay entirely. Under pressure from their members, representatives of the publishers and unions have occasionally stalled negotiations, when it has suited their purpose, by failing to issue joint letters determining arbitrable points, by neglecting to appoint proxies, and by other devices.[94] If wage negotiations go to arbitration, a retroactive ruling may be made, particularly if deliberate delay is shown. Such rulings, however, have not been numerous, although arbitrators often take delay into account when fixing wages.

A final and rather intangible factor in wage settlement by arbitration is the probable attitude of the parties toward the particular scale established. This is an important and perhaps controlling consideration in many local and international arbitration proceedings. Of course, the validity of the claims of the respective parties determines the limits within which an arbitral settlement is made. But the exact form of that settlement is unquestionably conditioned by the degree of acceptance it is likely to receive. This is understandable, since the success of arbitration depends upon the long-run approval by the parties in interest of the decisions that are made.

(3). *Trend of Hours*

The shorter work day did not become an important question for newspaper compositors until after the introduction of the linotype in 1884. Before that time, printers were usually employed on a piece basis, and because they were willing to work long hours to increase their earnings, the printing societies and unions made little attempt to shorten working hours.[95] To some extent the production requirements of newspapers set a natural limit on the length of the working day. Time spent in setting type, even before

---

94. As President Howard stated before the 1934 convention of the ITU: "There are times when local unions want haste and there are times when they do not want it. Perhaps the members of the New York union who instructed the delegates have forgotten that in 1929 they had a scale expire in the newspaper branch because they could not arrange a settlement, and placed the matter in the hands of the international president, and he held it, and their settlement was not arranged until December 1932. From the time the scale expired, in 1929, if my memory serves me right, until December 1932, the members of the New York union enjoyed the highest scale they ever had during that entire period of the depression, because of the dilatory tactics of the international president." ITU, *Proceedings*, 1934, pp. 130-131.

95. Barnett, *op. cit.*, p. 143.

the advent of the machine, rarely exceeded seven or eight hours, but about three additional hours were required for distributing the type. By eliminating the process of distributing type, the linotype made transition to the eight- and seven-hour day comparatively easy. As early as 1891 the international recommended that hours on machine work be reduced "to the lowest possible number, eight hours being the maximum." [96] This recommendation was enforced in most localities without much difficulty. Fifteen years later, in 1906, the Typographical Union enacted a law making the eight-hour day mandatory.

In all the other newspaper departments reduction of the work week took a similar course and as technological improvements appeared hours were reduced without much strife. The eight-hour day was made mandatory for newspaper pressmen by an international law of 1910. The photoengravers in 1906 provided that the international officers should not endorse local contracts calling for more than a forty-eight-hour week. A similar resolution was adopted by the stereotypers in 1910.

In 1890 the average number of hours a week for the newspaper trades as a whole was 49.2, as calculated from union scales by Professor Douglas.[97] Between then and 1930 only minor reductions took place. The 8 per cent decrease in weekly hours up to 1928 was relatively smaller than in any other unionized industry which he studied.[98] This was, of course, partly due to the shorter work week enjoyed by the printers in earlier years.

With the depression of the 1930's, and union emphasis on reducing the number of shifts a week to spread employment, weekly hours dropped sharply, especially after 1932. In 1939 the industry's average work week was 37.9 hours, or 15 per cent below 1928.[99]

96. ITU, *Proceedings*, 1891, p. 196.
97. Douglas, *op. cit.*, p. 112.
98. Douglas and Jennison, *op. cit.*, pp. 36-37.
99. In June 1939, 51.6 per cent of the union members in the newspaper trades were on a 37.5-hour week and 25.4 per cent on a 40-hour week. Those working less than 37.5 hours amounted to 17.7 per cent; and those working more than 40 hours constituted only 3.9 per cent. The average weekly hours by crafts were: mailers, 40.1; photoengravers, 38.2; stereotypers, 38.1; pressmen, 37.7; and machine compositors, 37.3. See *Monthly Labor Review*, December 1939, pp. 1505-1507.

Some local typographical unions established the five-day week earlier, but not until 1933 did the ITU require its members, under penalty, to limit their work week to five shifts.[100] Work on the sixth day was to be given to substitutes, or turned into regular "situations" (full-time jobs) and filled in priority order. The union justified the new law as a necessary means of spreading available employment. It also claimed that one of the publishers' objections to the substitute system, namely, the employment of less competent men, could be eliminated by creating more regular situations.

The five-day week was opposed by publishers primarily because of its anticipated effects on output and costs. They believed office efficiency would decrease and costs would rise. Unions would seek six days' pay for five days' work. Production routine would be disrupted—particularly where a local union rotated its unemployed through the composing room to the extent of available employment. Compositors employed in commercial printing, and less efficient on newspaper work, would be encouraged to migrate into the latter field.

Despite these objections, the five-day week came in the great majority of typographical jurisdictions rather quickly and with surprisingly little strife. Opposition from publishers was silenced in many cases by government declarations supporting the shorter work week, and by the passage of the National Industrial Recovery Act.[101] By the end of 1933, out of 30,654 newspaper typogra-

---

100. The movement for the adoption of the mandatory five-day week by the ITU, however, dates back to the depression unemployment of 1922, when the union adopted a law permitting locals to establish the five-day work week for a period of not more than eight weeks per year. Such local laws were mandatory, not on employers, but on union members, who were thus required to take one day off per week and employ substitutes in their places. In the recession of 1927 the limiting period was removed, and a year later all the locals were advised by the International to adopt every possible means to secure the five-day week. The Stereotypers in 1932 adopted a similar course by permitting locals to require their members to work only five days a week.

101. President Howard commented that "had it not been for the adoption of the recovery program the International Union would have been in about the same position in regard to the enforcement of the five-day law last June and July as it was when it attempted to enforce the forty-four-hour law [in commercial shops] in 1921, and . . . we would have been confronted with a very serious situation in a great many jurisdictions. . . ." ITU, *Proceedings*, 1934, p. 88.

phers in the United States, only 1,606, or about 5 per cent, worked more than five days a week.[102]

Effect of Five-Day Week

After the five-day, forty-hour week went into effect, the publishers claimed that it contributed to the trend toward five-day newspaper publication, particularly in the smaller cities. On smaller papers with few editions, there was frequently not enough work for an eight-hour shift, while employment of the extra men which the law necessitated raised costs prohibitively; according to the publishers, production requirements called for a shorter day with six shifts a week. As a result the Stereotypers' Union, which passed a five-day law in 1935, at first permitted six shifts a week on smaller papers, provided the work week was not more than forty hours. In 1938 this concession was eliminated from the five-day law, and, as a consequence, the union has had difficulty in enforcing it in many cities of 100,000 or less. Nor have all of its local unions willingly observed the law; difficulties arise in supplying extra men for publishers who have only one or two days of work a week for "extras." Pressmen have hesitated to enforce their five-day law, enacted in 1933, on the smaller newspapers except with the consent of the publishers.

In composing rooms on the smaller newspapers, the operation of the five-day law is not so much of a problem. Since newspapers employ more compositors than other craftsmen, regular "situations" in the composing room can more easily be created by an all-round reduction of the work week. Nevertheless, varying production requirements led the ITU to amend its forty-hour law in 1935, when the NRA expired; the forty-hour week on either a six- or five-day basis was permitted.[103] Except for some of the

102. ITU, *Officers Reports,* 1933, pp. 2-3. Eighty-one small locals, with a total membership of 2,893 were not included in the survey because of their failure to submit reports. Approximately 10 per cent of the mailer membership was reported to be working more than five days a week.

103. In that year the law was also amended to require that it be given contract recognition. Previously, where the publishers had not created more "situations," but had merely allowed regular employees to take the sixth day off and give their work to substitutes on that day, enforcement of the law was an internal union matter. It was feared that when the support of the Recovery Act was removed, enforcement would prove more difficult unless contract recognition was secured.

larger locals which favored more work spreading, even to the extent of a four-day week, this solution seemed to be satisfactory. In 1939, however, this union voted, by a two to one majority, that the five-day week again be mandatory for all newspaper compositors, beginning in 1942. At the same time, a proposal to allow subordinate unions to enact a four-day law was defeated.

With unemployment still a problem in the industry, the issue of an even shorter work week is by no means settled. The final disposition of this issue probably will come as a result of the operation of economic forces. The conflict between higher weekly earnings and further reductions in hours necessarily must be faced. Local unions are likely to oppose any considerable shortening of the work week in the future where this means an appreciable decline in weekly wages.

(4). *Miscellaneous Regulations Relating to Hours of Work*

As a means of enforcing the union scale of hours, the unions have found it necessary to incorporate provisions in contracts for higher wages on overtime work. Before they became interested in reducing hours, overtime for timeworkers was commonly paid for at the regular hourly rate, and the standard working day merely protected the standard daily or weekly rates which otherwise would have varied from office to office as the length of the work day varied. Since the latter part of the nineteenth century, however, the usual "time and a half" for overtime has been designed to prevent evasion of hours provisions in contracts. That this is its purpose is indicated by the fact that, except in particular situations where the rule is impracticable, all the unions forbid overtime work if competent substitutes are available.[104] The typographers and stereotypers definitely stipulate that overtime is cumulative

---

104. Only the Photo-Engravers have ever been charged with using the overtime law to obtain higher wages. The Chicago Newspaper Publishers Association asserted in arbitration proceedings in 1925 that although the contract since 1920 had specified forty-four hours a week, photoengravers had always worked forty-eight hours, and that the four hours' overtime pay was used to equalize wages as between newspaper and commercial departments. See E. Pancoast, *The International Photo-Engravers' Union*, unpublished dissertation, Department of Economics, University of Chicago, 1927, p. 434, n. 1. The Photo-Engravers' local unions in general do not agree to furnish men at the contract rate. See above, p. 66.

and must be cancelled by "laying off" whenever substitutes become available.[105]

It has long been a union policy that members inconvenienced by working unusual hours should have additional compensation. Higher pay for night work has prevailed since the first union scales were formulated. As early as 1850 the unions also required a bonus when a member was called back to work after having left the office, or for beginning work before the usual starting time.[106] Pay for work on recognized holidays is usually time and a half, often with a guarantee of at least a full day's wage for the four to six hours necessary to get out the paper. The unions of course recognize that inconvenient work schedules cannot be entirely eliminated, and in general the extra-pay provisions are not onerous. Such regulation does, however, provide some incentive for management to plan and stabilize production.

(5). *Vacations with Pay*

The most recent scale issue, and one of growing importance, is the union demand for vacations with pay. For many years these were classed as "gratuities," and the internationals displayed no interest in negotiating such provisions.[107] They took the position that they were selling the skilled labor of their members on a price basis; that their primary objective was to raise wages and lower working hours; and that vacation provisions were unnecessary since the worker might take time off at will if a competent substi-

---

105. The Fair Labor Standards Act requires time and a half for all work in excess of forty hours. However, Section 7(b)(1) allows unions to agree to work up to fifty-six hours per week provided the contract specifies that individuals shall not work more than one thousand hours in any consecutive twenty-six weeks. The Special Standing Committee therefore recommends that the "layoff" provision be worded to cover this requirement.

106. See *Bulletin No. 604,* U. S. Bureau of Labor Statistics, 1934, pp. 501 ff. At the present time the "call back" bonus is usually one dollar, while work done before the regular shift is considered overtime.

107. Joint rulings by the chairman of the Special Standing Committee and the president of the Typographical Union have established that "vacations are a gratuity and, while they are subject to conciliation, are not arbitrable under this procedure which covers only wages, hours, and working conditions." (Joint Letter, International Arbitration Board Proceedings, Columbia Typographical Union No. 101 and the Washington Publishers Association, 1938.) Vacations are arbitrable in the case of the Pressmen's Union, however, since it has, as we have seen, agreed to arbitrate all matters affecting operating costs.

tute was available. Interest of the unions in getting vacations with pay has been aroused by a number of factors: growth of the vacation movement in other industries; success of the American Newspaper Guild in securing contract clauses specifying paid vacations; fear of growing publisher resistance to further wage increases; and desire to reduce unemployment in the newspaper trades by sharing work through paid layoffs.

The Photo-Engravers took the lead in obtaining vacation provisions by enacting a law in 1938 which provided that proposed local contracts would not be approved by the International unless they contained a provision for vacations with pay.[108] The Typographical Union has also made it mandatory, beginning in 1940, for its locals to include vacation provisions in all proposed agreements.[109] The other crafts are actively seeking vacation clauses. Although at the present time only a minority of publishers have accepted them in local contracts, their number is growing rapidly. In November 1939, a survey made by the American Newspaper Publishers Association showed that seventy-six of its member newspapers had granted vacations with pay to composing room employees; ninety-four to pressmen; eighty-six to stereotypers; ninety to mailers; and fifty-three to photoengravers.[110] The vacations are almost always one or two weeks in the year.

C. HIRING AND DISCHARGE

Unions in the printing trades have long maintained that tenure of position and promotion from substitute to regular "situation-holder" should be based upon length of service rather than upon competency. They also believe that to prevent discrimination and favoritism, a union should have the right to challenge discharges which appear to have been made without sufficient cause. Since the 1880's, this policy has been expressed in resolutions, union laws and collective bargaining action.

From the earliest days of the National Typographical Union, the printers have desired to have employment and discharge in the

---

108. International Photo-Engravers' Union, *General Laws*, 1938, Section 41.
109. ITU, *General Laws*, 1940, Article III.
110. ANPA, *Bulletin No. 4400*, 1939, pp. 867-869.

hands of the foreman, in whose fairness and understanding they had more confidence, rather than in the hands of the employer or publisher. Until the 1880's they did not question the foreman's right to employ or discharge at will, so long as there was no discrimination against employees for union membership or activity. However, when foremen began, in the 1880's, to post "sub lists" or to restrict the right of certain union members to "substitute" in an office, a greater interest in hiring and discharge practices became evident. About the same time, local unions began to resist the "favoritism" and personal prejudice some foremen seemed to manifest in employment and discharge practices. Favoritism in filling regular situations was especially resented when it meant passing over "subs" of long service in an office to hire an outsider or a newcomer. In 1888 the convention of the Typographical Union adopted a resolution denying foremen the right to discharge "on purely personal grounds." [111]

(1). *Valid Grounds for Discharge*

All these dissatisfactions culminated in an ITU law of 1890 which stated the grounds on which discharges might validly be made: incompetency, neglect of duty, violation of office or union rules, and reduction of the work force. Foremen were required to give a written statement of the cause if a discharged employee demanded it, and subs were guaranteed a preferential right to vacant situations in an office.[112] Except for the later institution of priority or seniority rules to govern discharges made to reduce the force, the law has remained essentially unchanged. The other international unions also require that discharge be for "sufficient cause" and that, when requested, the cause must be given in writing. Only

---

111. Barnett, *op. cit.*, p. 230.
112. The law was repealed in 1893, but re-enacted in 1894. The repeal was occasioned by the fact that in 1892 an amendment was enacted giving substitutes priority standing, which had to be followed in filling vacant situations from the sub list. But the sentiment for wider distribution of work in order to relieve unemployment was strong; and it was feared that foremen would be more restrictive in their definition of competency for subbing if they knew that subs were acquiring priority rights to future vacant situations. When the law was re-enacted the amendment was left out. The year 1893 was one in which business conditions were depressed, and unemployment occasioned by the introduction of the linotype was aggravated. For later union action on priority, see p. 89.

the stereotypers have followed the example of the typographers in enumerating the valid causes for discharge. The laws of all the unions are similar in expressing the union's right to challenge arbitrary discharges.

Simple and defensible as these regulations appear, they nevertheless caused conflict in application until a method for joint union-publisher decision on discharge cases was worked out. Since the conflict was most acute in composing rooms, the discussion is here centered on the experiences of typographical unions.

For effective enforcement of the new law governing discharges, subordinate typographical unions enacted supplementary local laws providing that the chapel could order immediate reinstatement if it found an employee had been discharged for insufficient cause. International law provided that appeals against a chapel's action could be taken by the foreman to the executive council of the local union, thence to the local union, to the ITU executive council, and ultimately to the International Convention for final decision.[113] But locals required that the reinstated man could retain his job throughout the long process of appeals. Publishers complained that chapels and local unions were frequently injudicious and resisted even valid discharges. They declared that composing room discipline was disrupted, and the foreman's authority impaired because reinstated men often continued in employment for as long as a year, even if the discharge was sustained.

In 1908, the International Arbitration Board, acting without an impartial chairman, recognized the validity of the publishers' complaints. The Board ruled that, pending final settlement, publishers did not have to comply with local reinstatement orders, provided they assumed liability for wages covering the time lost if the local order was sustained.[114] Although the Denver Decision, as it was called, was hailed by publishers as a favorable step, it soon became apparent that not all strife had been eliminated. Publishers disliked to run the risk of having to pay wages for the considerable

---

113. This is the general procedure used by all the international unions when charges are made against a union member. In this case, the discharged man would have made a formal charge against the foreman.

114. For a detailed statement of the decision, made in Denver in 1908, see ITU, *Officers Reports*, 1920, p. 129.

period during which no service was rendered. So numerous were the difficulties that in 1912 the executive council of the Typographical Union recommended to locals an alternative method of settling discharge disputes: their submission to a local joint standing committee of union and publisher representatives, with provision for arbitration in case of the committee's failure to reach an agreement.[115]

This procedure has been increasingly incorporated into local typographical union contracts with members of the Publishers Association.[116] The other international unions followed the example of the Typographical Union in making discharge disputes subject to joint decision. They do not require special contract clauses to specify joint standing committee jurisdiction over discharge disputes, but instead include such disputes in the general category of differences arising in the interpretation of an existing contract. Joint decision is therefore almost universal in pressman, stereotyper and photoengraver disputes.

Since the new procedure has become widely accepted, the seriousness of discharge disputes has been minimized. Cases are settled promptly, and both publishers and unions receive fair consideration of their claims.

(2). Priority

The original discharge law of the Typographical Union, enacted in 1890, allowed the foreman the unrestricted right to

---

115. *Ibid.*, 1912, pp. 31-32. The executive council added that if a union member was, in the opinion of the local union, discharged because of his enforcement of a union law or because of union activity, the case should continue to be one for union consideration and disposition. "Maintenance of existing conditions" pending final decision, as provided for in arbitration procedure, does not apply to discharges made for the purpose of effecting necessary reductions in the working force. Early confusion on this point was cleared up by the rulings of arbitration boards.

116. Whereas in 1915, only 11 contracts provided for joint settlement of discharge cases, by 1928 there were 78, and by 1939, 175 such contracts, representing about 80 per cent of the union compositors employed by ANPA members. Approximately two thirds of the Mailers' contracts include similar provisions. The Association since 1922 has strongly recommended to its members that they include such contract clauses, for in that year the Denver Decision was nullified by a new ITU law. Unless the joint procedure is stipulated in local contracts, discharged employees must now be reinstated on order of the local union, pending final settlement through appeal to the International.

select the worker to be laid off when the force was reduced, provided that the discharged person be re-employed if the force were increased within sixty days. It was found, however, that foremen could evade the purpose of the priority law by weeding out the force in dull times. Successive modifications brought the law to its present form which has been almost unchanged for more than thirty years.

As the typographers' law now stands, reductions in the force must be made according to seniority. The last man hired is the first discharged, and when the force is increased the men are called back in reverse order of discharge before any others are hired. There is no time limit on the reinstatement requirement. Similar regulations have been adopted by the pressmen's and stereotypers' unions, except that the reinstatement provision applies only for ninety days for pressmen and one year for stereotypers. Supplementary regulations of all three unions give persons discharged to reduce the force a prior right to "extra" work in the office.

The seniority principle is also applied by the unions in filling regular situations which fall vacant. Except for one year, this policy was not generally enforced by typographical unions until 1902, when the international president interpreted the law giving subs preference over outsiders to mean that the competent sub oldest in continuous service had a right to the first vacancy.[117] A few years later, his decision was incorporated into international union law. The pressmen and stereotypers have also followed this policy with respect to filling situations. The stability of the working force in photoengraving departments is so great that this union has never had a priority law. Priority regulations are a much

117. The Typographical Union has always left the regulation of the priority of substitutes with respect to "extra" work to local unions. Evidence reveals that this has become a more prominent issue in local bargaining in recent years. In 1931 President Howard stated that of 353 contracts reviewed by the executive council in that year, only eight proposed and eight signed contracts included clauses relating to this point. In 1937, however, all but twenty-two of the 232 contracts on file with the Special Standing Committee of the Publishers Association mentioned this issue. Sixty-four per cent provided for full recognition of priority on extra work; 18 per cent stipulated that only persons laid off held such priority; and 9 per cent provided that there should be no priority on extra work.

more important issue in composing rooms than in other union departments because the working force is much more variable.

Seniority laws survive because they are the most effective assurance that unions have of impartiality in hiring and discharge. The equality of treatment they promote is of great importance to trade union unity. Members are protected against union politics and other forms of favoritism within the union in supplying men for jobs, as well as from foremen's discrimination and favoritism. By promoting job security seniority rules tend to increase the cooperativeness of the working force, and to promote more congenial working relationships.

Publishers hold that seniority impairs their right to employ and to retain the most efficient workers in preference to those of average competency. They maintain further that it encourages mediocrity because workers secure in their jobs will not put forth their best efforts. The latter argument is open to challenge but there is probably some truth in the former.[118] It must be remembered, however, that it is to the unions' advantage in terms of wage scales to maintain a high average standard of competency among members, and that they try to raise standards through apprentice training programs and their requirements for admission to union membership. It is also true that the "burden" of priority regulations depends on the way in which they are administered. In 1911 the president of the Typographical Union reprimanded those local unions which had been administering the law so rigidly as to require that the oldest sub in continuous service be given the first vacancy regardless of his competency; he emphasized that the sub

118. For some time after priority was instituted by the Typographical Union, some union members themselves objected to the law on the grounds that by penalizing moving, it tended to decrease labor mobility and also the competition of employers for workmen, that it was unfair to men of superior efficiency, and that the distribution of work was curtailed because foremen were more rigid in their competency requirements for subbing when they knew that the subs might eventually be promoted to regular situations on the basis of their priority standing (Barnett, op. cit., p. 241). In the main, however, the seniority principle has been supported by union members because the advantages seem to outweigh the disadvantages. It is significant that the Typographical Union has never applied the seniority principle to the hiring of substitutes by regular situation holders, and therefore has been able to combine its desire for a wide distribution of work with its desire to accomplish the aims which the priority law makes possible.

must be competent to meet the requirements of a situation which became available. The definition of competency is indeed an important factor in the effect of priority laws, and some discussion of this matter is therefore in order.

Competency

Many local typographical unions have set up minimum competency standards for machine operators to protect members against what they regard as unjust discharge. Publishers maintain that the standards set by some local unions are so low that they protect incompetent workmen in their jobs. The union position is that the minimum standards are primarily for beginning journeymen and newcomers who cannot turn out the amount of work required until they become accustomed to new machines and office routine. Union spokesmen deny that they contest honest discharges for incompetency, even if the employee is producing more than the minimum standard. In cases of "lying down on the job" discharge may be made for neglect of duty, if not for incompetency. The stereotypers' laws provide that any member discharged for incompetency "may demand a thorough mechanical test under the scrutiny of the union of which he is a member."

For all practical purposes, however, the definition of competency in composing rooms, as in other union departments, is left largely to the foreman. It is naturally assumed that competency requirements do not change suddenly, and therefore if the foreman hires more efficient workers who may be available and discharges employees whose production records had met standards up to then, the union charges this is an evasion of the priority law. To this extent, average competency becomes the standard. Since requirements on different newspapers vary widely, the union makes no attempt to apply a uniform definition of competency on a national basis. The fact that large offices, with many editions and tight schedules, attract and hold the type of workers they need is one indication that union policies do not unduly limit the selection process.

In highly specialized composing rooms it is recognized that an employee may not be competent in all branches of work. By mutual agreement of a local union and publisher, "departments" may be established and priority administered on this basis.

Superannuate Scales

Only the Typographical Union has made distinct provision for its older workers, whose productive capacity has declined but who wish to remain on the job. It recommends that special lower scales be set locally for them. These so-called superannuate clauses have been incorporated in 129 contracts with members of the Publishers Association.[119] In the absence of such provision, the International Executive Council has ruled that length of service shall be no bar to discharge for incompetency.[120]

(3). *Control of Substitutes and Number of Regular Situations*

It has long been the custom in composing rooms that a regular employee may hire a substitute whenever he chooses to take time off. Because newspapers have variable labor requirements in composing rooms on different days of the week, extra men are always attached to the office and then hired by the office as "extras" or by the regular employees as substitutes. Because of the share-the-work feeling within the craft and also because unemployed members are a potential menace to the maintenance of the union scale and other regulations, "regulars" have usually been more generous in their distribution of "subbing" among a large number of men than have the foremen. Foremen have tried from time to time to bring all hiring into their own hands and restrict the subbing privilege. But they have been blocked by union legislation which protects the right of regular employees to choose substitutes.

The first attempt of foremen to control employment of subs was the posting of sub lists designating a comparatively small number of men who would be allowed to substitute in a given plant. But local unions regarded this as discrimination against those who were excluded and in 1883 an international union law was enacted prohibiting sub lists. Foremen then designated the days on which regular employees should not hire substitutes; this

119. ANPA, *Bulletin No. 4380*, 1939, p. 507.
120. *Ibid., No. 3398*, 1928, p. 429; *ibid., No. 4193*, 1936, pp. 424-425.

restriction likewise met with resistance, and was prohibited by international law in 1891. When Sunday newspapers became common and many extra men were needed on the busy last days of the week, foremen sought to keep the more efficient extras in the office by distributing most of the subbing work among them. Consequently they began "phalanxing" or giving out six-day situations on seven-day papers; by rotating the off-day of regular employees, they could give almost full-time work to the substitutes they favored.[121]

When the local unions prohibited phalanxing, some foremen simply stopped giving out any regular situations, and hired all new employees as extras. This practice would gradually have brought the control of all hiring and discharge into the foreman's hands, since extras were hired on a day-to-day basis. In 1901, therefore, the international passed a law against phalanxing and the day-to-day selection of forces, and stipulated that foremen must give out enough regular situations to take care of ordinary office needs.[122] Some local unions enforced the law by providing higher than regular scales for extra work.

While the law requiring a minimum number of situations was retained, foremen after 1906 were allowed to give out six-day situations. The present phalanxing law prohibits giving out situations of less than five days a week. These provisions appear to be necessary for the enforcement of the priority law.[123] Without such requirements, a foreman might give out only a few situations, or hire regulars on a three- or four-day basis, with the result that he could distribute extra days among preferred men. Local unions enforce these national regulations by including in local contracts clauses stating that a "situation" is created when extra help have

---

121. Ordinarily regular employees had been hired for the full week of publication, and if a paper was published seven days a week, the regulars had an extra day to give out to substitutes. All members of the union had been limited to six days of work per week since 1890.

122. ITU, *Proceedings*, 1901, p. 126; *ibid.*, 1902, pp. 136, 140.

123. Another national rule with the same purpose states: "Laying off a situation holder [i.e., on pretense of reducing the force] and employment of another member to perform work to which the situation holder's priority and competency entitle him is prohibited." Violation of either this law or the phalanxing law makes the foreman subject to fine by the union. See ITU, *Book of Laws*, 1939, p. 108.

worked a specified number of consecutive days at the same type of work.[124]

A similar law passed by the stereotypers in 1938 requires the creation of a new situation whenever extra work to the extent of the prevailing work week has been given out. Exceptions are permitted in cases of "special demand," which is defined as "employment not to exceed two consecutive prevailing work weeks." [125] Previously the union had merely required that a vacant situation be permanently filled within a week, but difficulties of enforcement gave rise to the more specific provisions.

d. OTHER TRADE REGULATIONS

(1). *Determination of Manning Requirements*

The determination of the number of men to man presses and stereotyping machines has long been a major issue between the publishers and these unions. The size of crew is important to the publisher because it influences directly the wage bill and to the unions because it affects employment and the working load of members. Publishers have argued that management, in the interests of economical and efficient operation, should have the sole right to determine such questions. The unions, on the other hand, have contended that journeymen, intimately acquainted with the operation of the machines, are in a better position to know how many men are needed. More important, they feel they cannot look to the employer to protect them against oppressive manning practices. For protection against possible abuse, both sides need to have a voice in determining the size of crews. With the development of collective bargaining and arbitration, manning has come to be regarded as largely a matter for joint determination.

The Pressmen's Union has no compulsory national manning provision. Because of wide variations in equipment and publish-

124. Five days has been the international union interpretation of the number of consecutive days after which a situation is created. Where international laws are recognized in full, this is frequently observed unless the contract specifically provides otherwise. According to Special Standing Committee figures, only thirty typographical contracts included specific provisions on this point in June 1939.

125. International Stereotypers' and Electrotypers' Union, *Amendments to Constitution and General Laws: Effective January 1938 and January 1939*, pp. 6, 14.

ing schedules, it is impossible to set a manning standard that would apply to all pressrooms. Two plants with the same type of presses may differ in the number of editions per shift, the size of the editions and general working conditions in the pressrooms. Manning has therefore been a question for local settlement, although national union policy has been expressed since 1910 in recommendations for minimum manning requirements for all sizes of presses.

Local pressmen's unions have been increasingly successful in negotiating definite manning specifications in contracts. In 1911 about 50 per cent of the contracts with members of the Association allowed foremen to determine manning requirements; but in 1938 only 11 per cent of the contracts declared the foreman to be the sole judge, with 28 per cent containing no manning clauses whatsoever. Between 1938 and 1939 the proportion of contracts containing definite manning specifications rose from 61 to 66 per cent.[126] With substantial unemployment among pressmen and stereotypers, contract provisions on manning have become more common because of the union pressure to increase the complement of men on the machines.

Adjustments in manning practice are often necessary as publishing schedules and pressroom equipment change. Arbitration machinery furnishes a means of making such adjustments when settlement by conciliation proves difficult. Some contracts specifically state that the foreman may reduce press crews if laborsaving equipment is installed, provided that the union shall have the right of appeal to an arbitration board if the foreman's decision is deemed unfair. If there is no stipulation of this type, arbitrators sometimes require that contract specifications be observed until a new contract is negotiated, even though new equipment has been installed.

Manning requirements in stereotyping departments also vary with local conditions. Since stereotyper unions are for the most part in the larger cities, the variation between departments is somewhat less than between pressrooms. Stereotypers, unlike the pressmen, have therefore attempted to regulate manning by inter-

---

126. All figures were obtained from ANPA sources.

national law. For many years the general laws of the union have specified the minimum crew for autoplate machines. When the automatic autoplate came into wider use, manning of these machines became an issue but the matter was left to local bargaining and arbitration. Proposals to enact a national law came before the 1929, 1930 and 1931 conventions, but were rejected on advice of the executive board. With the growth of unemployment among the stereotyper membership, however, a manning law was enacted in 1932, and in 1934 additional legislation was adopted stipulating requirements on the double automatic autoplate.

Enforcement of the manning laws on large papers has created no problem since more than the minimum number of men are usually employed on the stereotyping machines. The real burden is on "newspapers of small circulation and modest equipment where the production required does not demand the number of men" the law stipulates.[127] However, the officers of the international have not been inflexible in the enforcement of the national laws on manning where local conditions demand special consideration.

In March 1938, only about 31 per cent of stereotyper contracts on file with the Special Standing Committee included specific manning tables or formally recognized union manning laws. Nineteen per cent specified the foreman as the sole judge, while 50 per cent contained no manning clauses whatsoever. How many contracts with no reference to manning recognized local or national laws informally is not known, but presumably in such cases the issue was not of great importance.

(2). *Transfer of Employees*

One of the laws of the International Pressmen's Union specifies that: "No web press crew or part thereof shall be allowed to work on more than one newspaper web press in any one regular working shift." Justification of the law, in the opinion of the union, rests on the desirability of minimizing health hazards arising out of uninterrupted heavy work on newspaper presses, and accident

---

127. Statement of the Executive Board, International Stereotypers' and Electrotypers' Union, quoted in ANPA, *Bulletin No. 3718,* 1931, pp. 528-529.

hazards arising out of presses left undermanned when a part of a regular press crew is transferred. From the publishers' standpoint, however, it sometimes appears to be an unwarranted interference with efficient and flexible operations. When the work necessary in getting out the regular daily editions is slack it is not unreasonable, they maintain, to transfer some press crews or portions of them to presses turning out Sunday comics or feature pages. Otherwise extra pressmen must be hired while regular employees are idle.

Since the laws of the Pressmen's Union are subject to negotiation, enforcement of the national rule depends on local bargaining and arbitration. In January 1938 only ten pressmen's contracts, out of 142 on file with the Special Standing Committee, prohibited transfers. Seven additional contracts imposed some restrictions on the right to transfer.[128] Thirty-eight allowed transfers at the publishers' option, and the remaining eighty-seven contracts had no transfer provisions. Local union policy evidently has not been particularly restrictive.

Transfers from one class of work to another are also sometimes needed for economical management in composing rooms. Until recently the transfer law of the Typographical Union has not been burdensome. It provided merely that transfers could be made to meet office necessities, but not to evade priority laws or as an excuse for discharging an employee by transferring him to work with which he was not sufficiently familiar to be competent. It was essentially a protective law. Effective in 1939, the law was strengthened by adding that "except to meet bona fide emergencies, transfers for more than one half the regular shift are prohibited." Presumably the amendment was designed to make the protection afforded by the law more effective. If rigidly enforced, it would necessitate hiring so many extra men (while regular men stood idle) that the additional expense to publishers would arouse

---

128. Some stated the maximum number of transfers allowed, i.e., one a day, or one a week. Some allowed transfers only when the union was unable to furnish the necessary extra men. Others limited the transfer privilege to certain editions. Records of the Pressmen's Union for October 1937, covering 350 newspaper contracts, revealed that twenty-three prohibited transfers of press crews except in emergencies, thirty-five permitted them without restriction, and the remainder made no mention of them.

strong opposition. If difficulties arise locally, flexible interpretive rulings by the international executive council may remove some of its potential danger to amicable relations.[129]

(3). *The "Reproduction" or Reset Requirement*

No law in the history of union-publisher relations in the newspaper industry has aroused more articulate opposition than the reset or "reproduction" law of the Typographical Union. This law forbids the exchange of previously used typeset matter, or matrices, between local newspapers, or between a job office and a newspaper office, unless the material exchanged is again composed, proofread and corrected, within a specified time limit, by employees of the newspaper receiving it.[130]

Similar laws were initiated by local unions before the invention of the linotype when the piece rate system of wage payment was common. Under the system then in vogue, all operations performed by compositors, including typesetting and make-up work, were paid for according to measurement of the matter composed. Because of the difficulty of devising fair differential rates for different kinds of copy, that which included large blank spaces, or spaces filled by cuts or plates, was paid for at the same rate as straight news composition. The former, which was called "fat" because it usually took less time to set and make up than did straight news matter, was presumed to be distributed as equally as possible among the composing room workers. As newspaper advertising increased, this type of copy became more and more important, and unions sought to prevent any diversion of "fat"

129. Transfers have not constituted an important issue in other union departments. The Photo-Engravers have something analogous to a transfer law in their general policy of specialization within the craft. Apprentices and journeymen must elect the branch of photoengraving in which they are to work, and no member is allowed to do even temporary work in another branch without permission from the chapel chairman. Permanent transfer to another branch of work requires union consent. However, most contracts specify the right of transfer, and in any case the nature of photoengraving work is such that the law probably affects only the departments of small papers. Apparently chapel chairmen have allowed adjustments to meet local conditions.

130. A related law permitting local unions to regulate the use of plate matter now affects primarily the exchange of magazine sections, syndicated feature material, out-of-city ads and similar copy.

from their respective offices. Many therefore required that matter set outside must be measured and paid for as though it had been set in the receiving office. It was feared that otherwise publishers would have the "fat" set outside and so, in effect, lower the piece rate and earnings. With the introduction of the linotype and the general time rate system of wage payment, "measuring" outside copy and paying for it on a piece basis became impracticable, and publishers were required instead to have the matter reset or "reproduced."

After the papier-mâché method of making matrices or molds from type forms presented a convenient way of transferring matter, the international followed the lead of locals with a resolution "discountenancing the practice in several cities of loaning and borrowing matter between morning and evening newspapers." [131] In 1876 the resolution was incorporated into a law enjoining locals to "put forth every effort" to prevent interchange of matter. And in 1902 the law was amended to prohibit interchange among newspapers not under the same ownership and published in the same plant, unless such matter was reproduced. Since that time, the law has been changed to apply also to exchanges between news and job offices, and to require that previously used matter be proofread and corrected as well as reset.

The national law has affected chiefly the interchange of local advertisements. Since 1902, the executive council of the union has held that the national law does not apply to material coming to a newspaper from outside the city. The international has also urged locals to be liberal in their reproduction requirements with respect to magazine supplements and other feature matter because of the beneficial effect which the use of such material has on circulation and employment.[132]

The expense of reproduction to a newspaper varies largely according to local union policy on the use of feature matter and national advertisements, and the time limit within which matter must be reset. These issues are subject to bargaining and arbitra-

---

131. ITU, *Proceedings*, 1873, pp. 57-66. The use of the papier-mâché method became general around 1870.
132. See ITU, *Officers Reports*, 1905, pp. 22-23.

tion although the minimum requirement of the national reproduction law itself is not negotiable. Records show that local requirements covering feature matter and national ads are generally not burdensome.[133]

The union often argues that the law helps to protect workers from bearing all the burden of technological developments. In addition two other arguments have been advanced: first, that it protects independent papers against unfair competition from chain newspapers;[134] second, that a publisher has an obligation to provide "extras" with "as much opportunity to work as the business of that concern will legitimately afford to them," in return for the flexibility which the reserve of union extras makes possible.[135] Irrespective of the merit of this argument, a more economical plan for meeting the problem might well be devised. The first union argument is not so persuasive, for had the reproduction law helped to protect the independent paper, it would hardly have aroused such general opposition from the publishers.

Publishers contend that union policy on reproduction is self-defeating; that by preventing economies of publication it curtails the bulk size and number of papers published, and hence the amount of employment. However, as long as most unions continue to allow the exchange of almost everything except local ads,

---

133. In January 1939, Association newspapers in 250 cities used without reproduction: (1) printed supplements, syndicate pages and other features; and (2) plates, cuts or matrices of advertisements received from outside the city. In 22 additional cities, only the second type of material was exempt from reproduction. A 1938 survey of 219 cities showed that 38 per cent of the contracts allowed at least 30 days in which to reproduce exchanged matter. Nineteen per cent allowed from two to three weeks; 24 per cent stipulated one week to twelve days; and only 19 per cent allowed less than one week. When a reasonable time limit is allowed, the international law may necessitate the hiring of few, if any, extra men. Ordinarily there is spare time, or "standing time," between peak periods during which much of the reproduction work can be done by the regular force. It should be noted that the time required to reproduce copy which has already been set is always less than the time required to set it originally—sometimes by as much as 50 per cent, according to union members.

134. U. S. Commission on Industrial Relations, *Final Report and Testimony*, Vol. I, 1916, pp. 594-608 (Testimony of James Lynch, former president of the ITU). This argument was also given, in a slightly different form, by President Howard, in 1924. See *Transcript of Proceedings, Anaconda Typographical Union No. 255* v. *Anaconda Standard*, 1924, pp. 113-115.

135. President Howard, *ibid.*

the reproduction requirement will probably become less and less important. Advertising policies are becoming so discriminating that local ads in different papers in the same city are often varied according to type of circulation and the time of the edition. And when ads are not identical their exchange is, of course, impossible. Although the reproduction of any exchanged matter is obviously uneconomic, the net effect on production costs today is probably slight.

6. Collective Bargaining: Evaluations and Conclusions

Having sketched the development and operation of collective bargaining in the newspaper industry, we are now in a position: (1) to summarize its results for those who are parties to the industrial equation—the workers, employers and the public; (2) to single out for brief discussion the supporting and limiting forces affecting collective bargaining; and (3) to indicate some of the more important unsolved problems that are properly of concern in current collective bargaining policy.

a. RESULTS

It is apparent that under collective bargaining one of the most important gains for workers in the newspaper trades has been the establishment of definite democratic rights in industry. The former arbitrary management of labor relations has been replaced by representative management. In part this has been limited by arbitrary application of certain union laws. On the whole, however, the working environment and relationships have both improved. Moreover, the responsibility of participating in self-government in industry has important implications for self-government in a democracy.

The standard of living of the craftsmen in the industry has unquestionably been improved through collective bargaining. Wage rates have risen and annual earnings have increased. Hours have declined to a point where in many instances union members themselves oppose further reductions. Working conditions also have been improved. Health and accident hazards are no longer a serious problem. Job security has been safeguarded to an extent unapproached in most other industries. Through the closed shop and the operation of union rules, workers are protected against discrimination and favoritism in hiring and discharge.

Under collective bargaining, publishers have enjoyed relative freedom from strikes and other interruptions to production. Recognition of the closed shop guarantees the publishers an adequate supply of trained and efficient workers, except in their photoengraving departments. Pressmen, with their engineering service and technical trade school, and photoengravers, with their technical bureau, have made special efforts to raise efficiency; and all unions have contributed to efficiency through their regulation and training of apprentices. In addition, union policies on hiring and discharge have reduced costs of labor turnover. The unions have also assumed responsibility for certain supervisory and disciplinary duties in their departments, the burden of which management would otherwise bear. Finally, through orderly collective bargaining the publishers have won employee good will and a more favorable public opinion.

Publishers have not gained these advantages without paying a price. In the depression years from 1930 to 1940, union organization and wage policies not only blocked wage reductions but brought increases in hourly rates, both of which caused hardships and severe readjustments for some newspapers. In many localities the enforcement of certain union rules has raised costs and prevented needed economies.

For the economy as a whole, collective bargaining in the newspaper industry has contributed to industrial peace. Conciliation and arbitration methods which have been developed are of exemplary significance. Many groups—employers, unions and government—have drawn lessons from the industry's experience.

b. SUPPORTING AND LIMITING FACTORS

There are a number of different factors that have influenced the success and stability of collective bargaining in the industry. These may be classified into three groups: (1) those relating primarily to the economic character of the industry; (2) those pertaining to the nature and degree of organization of workers and employers; and (3) those relating to certain operative aspects of collective bargaining itself.

Economic Characteristics of the Industry

The fact that the newspaper industry has been relatively stable has contributed to stability in collective bargaining relationships. Unlike many industries, newspaper production and employment have not been vitally affected by business cycles, seasonal factors or shifts in demand. Nor, in recent years, have basic methods of production been affected by any fundamental technological or other laborsaving changes.

Technological changes may in the future, however, present problems to some crafts—particularly compositors and stereotypers. Already perfected is the teletypesetter, which operates automatic typecasting machines in an office from a punched tape—or sets type automatically at any number of points by wire transmission. Although such equipment is potentially capable of considerable labor displacement, the typographers have taken steps to control this by extending their jurisdiction over the few machines already introduced, by insisting on union scales for tape punchers, and by manning provisions covering the automatic typesetters. Machines for composition other than linotypes are also being developed. Offset newspaper printing, which eliminates the stereotyping process, is also being introduced on a few small dailies, because reductions can be made in capital and operating costs. If, in the future, offset newspaper production becomes practicable and the equivalent of a composing typewriter is introduced, mechanical operations on daily newspapers may be revolutionized and collective bargaining profoundly affected.

Unlike many industries, newspaper publication is essentially local in character. With more than 60 per cent of all dailies in one-newspaper cities, competition is limited. Where one newspaper monopolizes a local field, it has been easier for unions to get higher wages and improve their situations. The relatively prosperous condition of the industry, particularly in early years, has also provided a stable financial base for collective bargaining.

Certain cost conditions have had an important bearing on the stability of collective bargaining. The fact that for the mechanical trades the proportion of labor costs to total costs is not high has made it possible for unions to secure more substantial wage increases than might otherwise have been the case. During periods of rising revenues, increases in labor costs apparently have not been a heavy burden on the industry, although the higher wage rates in depressions have been burdensome. Relatively heavy capital charges have placed a premium upon continuous operation, particularly since investment is more or less immobile. Organized relations to insure uninterrupted production have been desirable from the publishers' standpoint.

A number of economic factors tend to limit the successful operation of collective bargaining. Most important are the steady decline in the number of daily papers and the shrinkage in employment opportunities, especially since 1930. To meet the unemployment problem, the unions have reduced hours on a share-the-work basis. But work-sharing programs lower per capita weekly earnings and beget demands for higher wages. Wage rates and industry costs have risen during a period when revenues have shown no substantial recovery to the levels of predepression days. The number of newspaper consolidations and suspensions has risen. Production is tending more and more to be concentrated in a declining number of larger papers, whose man-hour labor requirements per unit of output are proportionately less. Obviously, employment opportunities in the industry are adversely affected and in the long run this may seriously weaken collective bargaining.

Characteristics of the Organizations

The character of union and publisher organization has done much to promote successful collective bargaining. Although the publishers are not as highly organized nationally as the unions, a working unity has been obtained through close cooperation in local associations and through employer leadership provided by the American Newspaper Publishers Association. Strong organization has made it possible for the unions and publishers to carry out more effectively their bargaining policies. The relative equality in bargaining power has discouraged them from direct action and has fostered conciliation and arbitration. Finally, able and far-sighted leadership long enjoyed by both sides has contributed greatly to orderly relationships.

Operative Forces in Collective Bargaining

Basic to all bargaining relationships in the industry has been the willingness of unions and publishers to negotiate and to settle peacefully their differences. This attitude has been reflected in the atmosphere under which collective bargaining has functioned. Agreement has been facilitated where negotiations have been carried on in an orderly and businesslike manner, and where use has been made of those techniques which minimize existing differences.

Clearly defined methods and procedures and adequate machinery for settling disputes have contributed to the success of collective bargaining in the newspaper industry. Local written agreements, the use of local and international arbitration, and the emergence of a body of common law have made for stability in industrial relations. For example, local written agreements which are inclusive and specific have reduced disputes arising out of interpretation of contracts. Needed flexibility has been provided through interim "opening" provisions limited to changes in scales. The practice of the internationals and the Publishers Association in approving and underwriting local agreements has been a powerful force for promoting the observance of contractual obligations by the local parties.

Finally, long experience with collective dealings and development of seasoned methods of negotiation are other factors contributing to stable bargaining relationships in the industry. Through this experience unions and publishers have come to think in terms of joint solutions of their problems and possibilities of agreement have thereby been widened. Because orderly procedures have proved advantageous to both unions and publishers, collective bargaining, as it has developed through the years, has come to be an accepted tradition in the industry.

C. UNSETTLED PROBLEMS

One unsolved problem confronting the parties is the relation of union legislation to collective bargaining. This involves the question of how far unions may go in passing laws which affect the scope of collective bargaining and contractual relations. The issue has been long-standing and in 1922 contributed to the breakdown of a formal system of arbitration with all the internationals except the Pressmen's Union. Publishers feel strongly that ex parte union legislation, affecting wages, hours and working conditions, weakens collective bargaining and limits arbitration; that recent union laws establishing the five-day week, union approval of office rules and union regulation of transfers make a solution of this problem urgent. Sooner or later this question must be faced and satisfactorily settled.

Rising Costs and Shrinking Numbers

A second major problem is the relation of the growing number of suspensions of daily newspapers to wage scales and labor costs. Only in the last few years, when important papers have "folded" in increasing numbers, has the problem become a matter of concern to the international unions and the Publishers Association. Rising labor costs in the mechanical departments are cited as a contributory factor. However, there have also been important increases in newsprint prices, in taxes and in labor costs for non-mechanical workers, as well as declines in advertising and an inherent tendency toward concentration of production in the industry. Nevertheless, many publishers and some union officials wonder how long the industry can continue to support a steadily mounting structure of wage rates, and how union sentiment for rising wage and living standards can be reconciled with the stubborn fact that the industry is no longer expanding nor is it as profitable as in former years.

A reasonable wage policy in collective bargaining and arbitration is frequently difficult to establish. Where internationals are democratically governed, union politics often strongly influences wage negotiations and makes it hard to temper wage demands in the light of prevailing economic conditions. Some way must be found: (1) to show the workers how steadily increasing labor and other costs affect newspaper stability, volume of employment and total wage payments; (2) to develop cooperative union-publisher policies which will improve efficiency and reduce costs without necessarily lowering union standards or retarding their improvement. Recently, President George Berry of the Pressmen's Union said:

> the . . . newspaper industry of America is not necessarily a growing institution, but there is evidence of disintegration that must challenge the attention of every member of our unions, and we must give our best . . . in the stabilization and in the making of a profitable enterprise in the business in which we engage, to the end that there should be more for us, more for the management and more for the investor . . . .[136]

President Berry proposed a federation of unions in the printing trades, for offensive and defensive purposes, to further collective bargaining, and to deal with joint problems in the industry. Similar proposals advanced in earlier years were blocked by problems of cooperative financing and control. Today it appears that the internationals are still too much concerned about these matters and their own individual interests to be ready to federate and cooperate in solving the larger problems confronting collective bargaining.[137]

From the standpoint of union-publisher cooperation, federation is desirable. For example, such an organization could sponsor a program for effecting economies, which the officers of the individual internationals could not do. The publishers, in return, might then be willing and better able to grant certain union demands. If, through cooperative effort, the industry could be made more profitable, labor incomes, standards, and perhaps employment would rise.

---

136. Statement before the convention of the Typographical Union. See ITU, *Proceedings*, 1939, p. 27.
137. The recent suspension of the Typographical Union by the American Federation of Labor, for failure to pay an assessment levied in connection with the AF of L-CIO controversy, may tend to create more unity in the printing trades. See *The New York Times*, January 30, 1940.

7. COLLECTIVE BARGAINING IN EDITORIAL AND COMMERCIAL DEPARTMENTS

The years since 1933 have witnessed one of the most interesting developments in the history of the American labor movement—the first widespread unionization of white collar workers in a major industry. In a little more than seven years, the American Newspaper Guild has organized 11,516, or more than 40 per cent of the employees in editorial departments, and 5,694, or about one ninth of those employed in the commercial departments of daily papers.[138] The background, development and results of this remarkable achievement call for a brief examination.

a. HISTORY OF ORGANIZATION

Before the organization of the Guild, both the International Typographical Union and the American Federation of Labor tried without much success to organize news writers. Lack of sustained interest on the part of editorial workers, opposition from publishers and widespread feeling that trade unionism did not apply to this type of work, all played a part in previous failures. Of fifty-nine news writers' unions chartered by the ITU between 1891 and 1919, only six survived more than five years.[139] The AF of L, which assumed jurisdiction over news writers in 1923, chartered

---

138. "Report of the Administrative Officers to the 1940 Convention of the American Newspaper Guild," *Proceedings of the Seventh Annual Convention of the American Newspaper Guild,* July 1940, p. 17. Book membership figures since the organization of the Guild are reported as:

Editorial Departments		Commercial Departments
June 1934......... 4,936............		(Not in Guild jurisdiction)
June 1935......... 5,250............		(Not in Guild jurisdiction)
June 1936......... 5,830............		(Not in Guild jurisdiction)
June 1937......... 11,112............		(Not in Guild jurisdiction)
June 1938......... 13,505............		3,292
June 1939......... 13,727............		5,028

The decrease in membership from the 1938 and 1939 totals is declared by the Guild to be a result of "the first sustained campaign, . . . in connection with the introduction of new forms, to clear deadwood off the books, . . . lump removals of long inactive membership [totaling] 4,635." New members added during the year 1939-1940 are reported to number 3,235.

139. Lee, *op. cit.,* p. 670.

some nine locals in the decade that followed. Only five were in existence in 1936 when they affiliated with the Guild.[140]

(1). *Organization of the American Newspaper Guild*

A combination of economic and political factors contributed to the resurgence of interest in union organization in 1933. During the early years of the depression, editorial workers suffered far heavier wage cuts and unemployment than did the strongly unionized employees in mechanized departments of newspapers. Problems of editorial workers were sufficiently acute to make them take advantage of the chance to improve working conditions which the National Industrial Recovery Act of 1933 appeared to offer, and a number of local associations of reporters sprang up within a few months. They were formed chiefly to give editorial employees representation in the formation of an industrial code for the industry. Leadership and encouragement were given particularly by the New York Guild under Heywood Broun, who called a national convention in December 1933. Delegates from thirty cities met, and the American Newspaper Guild was formed.

The Guild affiliated with the AF of L in 1936. In 1937 affiliation with the CIO was voted. At the same time it was decided to extend jurisdiction to commercial departments, and to promote actively industrial unionism in the industry, so far as compatible with the existing organizations in the mechanical trades. Since that date those eligible for membership include editorial and commercial employees on newspapers and news magazines, as well as those doing similar work for press associations, news syndicates, news photo agencies, newsreel companies, radio news services and broadcasting companies. Most of the organization to date has been on newspapers.

(2). *Development of a Trade-Union Attitude*

During the first year of the new union, the majority of its members were torn between the old conception of newspaper work as a profession and a new desire to improve their economic condi-

---

140. "Collective Bargaining in the Newspaper Industry," *Bulletin No. 3*, National Labor Relations Board, Division of Economic Research, October 1938, pp. 111-112.

tions by collective action. They contemplated an organization which would bargain with publishers, but not in the trade-union sense of employing such traditional labor weapons as strikes, boycotts, picketing and the like. "Its strength . . . will be in the collection, study, and intelligent presentation of facts," declared one leader of the New York Guild, in November 1933.[141]

The original constitution of the American Newspaper Guild gave the national union and national officers virtually no important powers, nor was there to be national intervention in local bargaining except upon request of a local guild. The National Executive Committee was given power to bargain with press associations and syndicates of national scope; but no bargain was binding without a two-thirds endorsement, by referendum, of the employees affected. Individual members could continue to negotiate personally with employers, though without the support of the Guild.

Disillusionment over the effectiveness of this form of organization was soon forthcoming. The Guild obtained under the NRA Newspaper Industrial Code almost no provisions for improving the welfare of editorial workers. Union-publisher antagonisms made the Industrial Board an almost completely ineffective instrument. Only over the opposition of the Publishers Association did the Guild even attain representation on the Board.[142] A few publishers granted wage increases and minor improvements in working conditions, but only one important contract with a publisher was made before September 1934.

The second Guild convention, in June 1934, was in a more favorable mood to adopt trade-union methods. A bargaining program was approved,[143] local guilds were advised to consult more

---

141. *Guild Reporter,* November 23, 1933.

142. Later, the Guild did receive effective support in its drive for recognition from the National Labor Relations Act. From 1935 through September 1938 the Guild brought more than thirty cases to the NLRB. The 1937 decision of the U. S. Supreme Court, upholding a 1936 Board decision in favor of the Guild, and establishing that the Act did not violate the constitutional guarantee of freedom of the press, gave great impetus to the Guild's campaign. *Associated Press* v. *National Labor Relations Board,* 301 U. S. 103 (1937).

143. The most important points were: a graduated scale of minimum wages, maximum hours, the Guild shop (union shop), overtime pay or accumulated time off for overtime, one-year contracts, graded dismissal notices, sick leaves with pay,

frequently with national officers, and individual members were forbidden to negotiate "for a wage or other standard of employment inferior to that secured by the Guild in any collective action." The amended constitution also required the submission of proposed local contracts to the National Executive Committee for recommendations. At later conventions the powers of the national organization were further strengthened until in 1939 the Executive Board was given power to suspend the charter of any local which, without its authorization, signed a contract containing "serious deviations from the Collective Bargaining Program" adopted by the national conventions. The national office of the Guild now compiles information to guide bargaining negotiations, and since 1935 has supplied locals with a standard contract form.

b. SETTLEMENT OF DISPUTES

Unlike the other unions in the newspaper industry, the Guild has never favored advance commitments to arbitrate disputes, but it does not oppose arbitration in certain circumstances. A number of disputes over discharges and contract interpretation have been arbitrated. In at least two cases (Duluth and Wilkes-Barre) wage scales were arbitrated after strikes which brought agreement on all other points. A few agreements which set up standing arbitration machinery for the settlement of disputes arising under a contract have also been made.[144] The Guild constitution allows no agreement to provide for arbitration of contract renewals. The Guild position is that "at this stage" voluntary restrictions on the right to strike are not in its best interests. It argues that arbitration stabilizes existing conditions, that arbitrators tend to be biased in favor of the employer point of view, and that Guild status is not

---

paid vacations, no salary reductions during term of contract, apprenticeships or some system of training and advancement, grievance committees for handling grievances, and staff to perform no duties of employees in other departments. *Editor and Publisher*, June 16, 1934, p. 41.

144. In June 1938 there were nine such agreements and in January 1940, seventeen (ANG, *Survey of Agreements and Bulletin Board Statements in Effect on June 1, 1938;* ANPA, *Bulletin No. 4410*, January 1940, pp. 209-250). A larger number of contracts (sixty-six in January 1940) provide for grievance committees with whom the publisher agrees to meet. In 1939 there were arbitrations with the Guild on three newspapers, two of which were members of the ANPA. *Editor and Publisher*, April 27, 1940, p. 20.

yet secure enough to entrust decisions to an outsider. It is quite probable, however, that if and when the Guild receives the same degree of recognition from publishers that the mechanical trades have long enjoyed, its faith in arbitration will be strengthened. Up to the present, publishers in general have fairly strongly opposed Guild organization, despite their rather satisfactory experience with the other unions.

The relative success of early Guild strikes—a surprise to many persons, including some Guild members—increased the confidence of the union in its ability to gain its ends by militant measures if necessary. Effective use of boycotts and strong support of organized labor at the scene of difficulty have greatly aided Guild strikes.[145]

c. THE "FREEDOM OF THE PRESS" ISSUE

"Freedom of the press" is a phrase which has figured prominently in opposition to the Guild almost since its origin.[146] Partly on the grounds of preserving this freedom, the publishers opposed the inclusion of editorial department employees under the Newspaper Industrial Code, and later contested the jurisdiction of the National Labor Relations Board set up under the NRA. After the National Labor Relations Act was passed, the United States Supreme Court ruled in the Associated Press case that under the law union activity for collective bargaining did not constitute a threat to freedom of the press.[147]

---

145. ANPA sources record one strike begun in 1934, three in 1936, eight in 1937, eight in 1938, and two in 1939. All except one, where the paper permanently suspended publication, resulted in the signing of Guild contracts or (in four cases) unilateral statements in bulletin board notices. Seven were union-shop and seven open-shop agreements. In one case, the seventeen-month strike on the Chicago *Herald-American*, the Guild lost in the final election to determine the bargaining agent for editorial and commercial departments. Nine of the strikes lasted for more than three months, four others for more than one month.

146. As early as 1899, publishers opposed the efforts of the ITU to organize news writers, on the same grounds, and organization was somewhat hampered on that account. Tracy, *op. cit.*, p. 522.

147. The Court stated that "The act . . . does not require that the petitioner retain in its employ an incompetent editor or one who fails faithfully to edit the news to reflect the facts without bias or prejudice. The act permits a discharge for any reason other than union activity or agitation for collective bargaining. . . . The regulation here in question has no relation to the impartial distribution of the news.

Since then, the freedom of the press issue has been raised primarily against the Guild-shop provision. Inclusion of all editorial employees in the Guild, it has been alleged, would result in biased news writing. The Guild, however, stresses that its membership is open to all editorial workers; that publishers may hire new employees who are not Guild members, provided they join the Guild within thirty days after their employment; and finally that sole control and direction of editorial policy rests with the publisher as before.

There seems to have been no complaint from publishers who have recognized the Guild shop that their editorial prerogatives are infringed. Fears of press "censorship" or news bias by Guild members, as expressed by nonpublisher critics in recent months, seem to stem from distrust of the present Guild administration, rather than from fear of the Guild-shop provision itself.

d. RESULTS OF COLLECTIVE BARGAINING

Union Status and Organization

The American Newspaper Guild is recognized by some type of agreement in 132 out of a total of 143 newspapers having union contracts or understandings covering their editorial or commercial departments, or both.[148] Twenty-seven papers have union-shop, seven modified union-shop, and seventy-eight open-shop agreements; twenty operate under "policy notices," or unilateral statements by employers covering wages, hours and working conditions. On 66 newspapers the agreements include only the editorial

---

The order of the Board in nowise circumscribes the full freedom and liberty of the petitioner to publish the news as it desires it published. . . ." *Associated Press* v. *National Labor Relations Board*, 301 U. S. 103 (1937).

148. A labor organization other than the Guild is recognized on sixteen newspapers, of which five, however, recognize the Guild in one department and a different organization in another department. These other organizations are distributed among the sixteen newspapers as follows:

Independent local unions	6
AF of L unions	10
American Federation of Newswriters, Reporters and Editorial Writers	5
News Distributors' and Office Workers' Union	4
American Federation of Newswriters, Reporters and Editorial Writers; Newspaper Commercial Associates	1

departments, on 3 only the commercial, and on 63 both editorial and commercial departments.[149]

Of course the extent of Guild organization is hardly comparable to that of the Publishers Association. Out of 266 cities with Association newspapers in September 1939, the Guild was established in only 79, and was organizing in 7 others. Larger cities have been more successfully organized than the smaller towns.[150] Organization work has been handicapped by lack of money and inability to support more than three field organizers.

Wages and Hours

In the years immediately preceding the depression, wages in the news and commercial departments had not made any advance comparable to the rise in the cost of living or to the increase in wage rates in mechanical departments. Between 1930 and 1934, according to a survey by the Bureau of Labor Statistics, earnings of newspaper editorial workers as a whole had declined about 12 per cent. In the latter year, 46 per cent of the reporters, for example, earned less than $36 a week, while 13 per cent received less than $20.[151] *Editor and Publisher,* commenting on the wage situation at that time, stated: "No one with newspaper experience doubts that editorial pay is scandalously out of line." [152]

149. All the above figures are compiled from ANPA, *Bulletin No. 4428,* July 1, 1940. The 1940 convention of the Guild reported 131 newspapers under contract with the Guild on June 1 of that year. This represented an addition of 19 shops to the 120 of the previous year, 8 papers with Guild contracts having "folded" during the year. The Guild claimed 54 shops to be operating under union-shop or modified union-shop agreements; however, newspapers were not tabulated separately from the 19 wire services, news magazines and radio stations. *Proceedings of the Seventh Annual Convention of the American Newspaper Guild,* July 1940, p. 9.

150. There are Guild locals in 88 per cent of the cities whose populations are in excess of 200,000, in 39 per cent of the cities between 100,000-200,000, in 26 per cent of the cities between 50,000-100,000 and in only 10 per cent of those between 25,000-50,000. Tabulated from ANPA, *Memorandum* of September 15, 1939.

151. The average for deskmen was $51.32; photographers, $34.79; artists, $47.80; and copy, office and errand boys, $13.28 (U. S. Bureau of Labor Statistics, *Monthly Labor Review,* May 1935, pp. 1420-1422). A survey made by the Guild, covering 158 dailies, showed that the average worker had 9.6 years of experience, of which 5.4 were with his present employer *(Wage Survey, American Newspaper Guild,* Records Section, U. S. Department of Commerce). Another survey, covering 821 newspapers, was made by the ANPA, with findings similar to those of the Bureau of Labor Statistics. See ANPA, *Bulletin No. 4050,* 1935, p. 260.

152. October 13, 1934, p. 24.

Since 1934 no survey of actual wages paid has been made. However, some information is available from Guild contracts providing for minimum weekly wages, based on experience or length of service, which are graduated upward, usually over a five-or six-year period. Minimum wages for reporters, for example, commonly range from an average of $25 the first year to $40 or $45 in the fifth or sixth year. Of course, many employees are paid above minimum rates. Because of this fact and the great variety of occupational classifications, particularly in commercial departments, it is difficult to trace the trend of wages under Guild organization. From a study of contract minima, however, the Guild appears to have secured higher wages in the lower paid classifications and on starting jobs, and to a lesser degree for those workers with long years of experience who are in the upper wage brackets. Hours have been reduced in almost all jurisdictions to forty a week on a five-day basis, so that hourly earnings have in effect been increased thereby. The five-day, forty-hour week was made mandatory for all Guild contracts by an amendment to the constitution in 1937. The Guild is currently seeking a thirty-five-hour week in some jurisdictions.

In addition to advancing wages, the Guild succeeded, during the recession of 1938, in preventing reductions in pay.[153] More favorable overtime provisions stipulating payment at a higher wage rate, or specifying equivalent time off, have also been won. Finally, the Guild has helped to obtain such other wage gains as sick leave and vacations with pay. Although these were doubtless granted by the majority of papers before the advent of the union, contract clauses have insured continuance of these practices and given them wider application. They are now provided for in virtually all contracts.

Security of Employment

The Guild has been a pioneer among labor organizations in protecting employment tenure of its members by securing dismis-

---

153. Heywood Broun, *Proceedings* of the American Newspaper Guild, 1938, p. 19. Provisions prohibiting reductions in pay during the life of the contract have helped the higher paid employees especially.

sal or "severance pay."[154] The widespread adoption of such provisions may be traced to several factors. "Capricious firing" had been prevalent in the nonmechanical departments of the industry. Suspensions, consolidations and retrenchments on newspapers had also thrown many workers in the editorial and commercial departments out of their jobs. As a consequence, one of the primary objectives of the Guild in collective bargaining was to establish the principle of dismissal compensation. At present it is guaranteed in almost all agreements, usually with one week's pay for each thirty weeks, eight months, or one year of service. In some agreements the right to dismissal pay is unqualified, but in most contracts it is not paid if discharge is for cause.

Protection against unfair discharge is generally provided by specifying in the agreements the justifiable reasons for discharge. The commonest are gross misconduct, neglect of duty, insubordination, dishonesty, drunkenness and willful provocation of discharge to obtain dismissal pay.

Certain other contract provisions affect promotion and transfer. Almost half of the agreements give first consideration in filling vacancies for higher positions to employees on the staff. To give a chance for employment and promotion by transfer to other newspapers, over 40 per cent of the agreements prohibit arrangements between publishers not to employ members of each other's staffs. Duties of photographers and reporters are separated, except for emergencies, to prevent the elimination of jobs.

e. CONCLUSION

In the few years of its existence the Guild has achieved a rather remarkable success for a white collar union. If organization is extended in the future it will probably be chiefly in the smaller cities and in commercial departments. It is possible that diverse interests of members in the editorial and commercial departments, and of higher and lower paid workers, may become problems. At present there is a deep organizational cleavage in the membership be-

154. The Guild has also feared that layoff of part of the staff might follow the signing of an agreement providing for wage increases, and therefore approximately one half of the contracts specifically prohibit layoffs occasioned by the expense of putting the agreement into effect.

tween those who favor a strict trade-union program and those who support Guild declarations and action on the nation's domestic and foreign policies. As a consequence, growth in membership and effectiveness in collective bargaining have been checked.

Despite its short history, the Guild has helped to raise wages in news and commercial departments and has introduced new issues for collective bargaining in the industry. It has forged a chain of new demands such as sick leave and vacations with pay, guaranteed employment and dismissal compensation. Because many of its members by their very training have a broad grasp of social, economic and political affairs, the Guild, if ably led, may have an important influence on organized labor and collective bargaining in America.

Chapter 3

BOOK AND JOB PRINTING

Emily Clark Brown

THE ROOTS OF COLLECTIVE BARGAINING in the book and job printing industry reach down into the early decades of the nineteenth century, when societies of journeymen printers in many cities presented price lists to their employers.[1] For many decades the International Typographical Union and its sister unions in other printing crafts have played important parts in book and job printing. A rich history is recorded in these unions' minute books and publications, and by the associations of employing printers, shorter though their history is. Union-employer relationships in this industry, with their long experience and their well-established traditions, are a guide post either to point the way or to warn of danger spots.

1. THE INDUSTRY

a. SIZE, DIVISIONS AND LOCATION

Job printing in the early nineteenth century was only a small side line of newspaper shops. By 1880, however, it was a distinct industry which employed 58,506 wage earners in 3,468 book and job shops. In addition 10,612 bookbinders were reported employed in 588 shops.[2] By 1937 the entire book and job industry, as the trade itself draws the lines, employed 192,045 wage earners in 13,948 plants. Of these, 10,587 establishments in book, music and job printing and publishing employed 141,368 wage earners; 2,364 periodical printing and publishing plants employed 25,344

---

1. Ethelbert Stewart, "A Documentary History of the Early Organizations of Printers," U. S. Department of Commerce and Labor, *Bulletin of the Bureau of Labor*, Vol. II, 1905.
2. U. S. Bureau of the Census, *Manufactures, 1905*, Pt. III, p. 713; *1921*, p. 649.

BOOK AND JOB PRINTING

wage earners; and 997 bookbinding and blankbook-making establishments employed 25,333 wage earners. The value of the products of the entire group was $1.4 billion.[3]

The industry includes not only general commercial or job printers and binders, but a number of more or less distinct groups, such as periodical printers, music printers, book manufacturers, edition bookbinders and producers of a great variety of specialized products in the commercial field—labels, catalogues, color printing, law printing and others. Allied industries, photoengraving and electrotyping, except in the case of very large printing plants, are carried on in separate establishments, which sell their products to book and job printers. Collective bargaining for these groups is conducted by separate employers' associations. There is also a separate lithographing industry, but increasing amounts of lithographing or offset printing are produced in general commercial plants.

This industry ranges all the way from the tiny old-fashioned "bedroom shop" to the huge plant with two or three thousand employees, producing mail-order catalogues, telephone directories, or popular periodicals and books, by methods approaching mass production. A large part of the products are the unstandardized, made-to-order, small-run jobs needed by local businesses. The typical printer accordingly is small. In 1937 about 88 per cent of the book, music and job plants had only twenty wage earners or less, and they employed 32 per cent of all the workers.[4] On the other hand, large-scale production has increased on work for big business concerns and for the mass market. In these fields competition is no longer local, and big plants competing on a national basis are of increasing importance.[5]

---

3. *U. S. Census of Manufactures, 1937*, Pt. I, p. 585; memorandum, "Summary for the Periodical Printing and Publishing Industry, 1937 and 1929." Census classifications do not exactly fit the usage of the industry. Census publications include periodical with newspaper printing and publishing and do not separate printing from publishing. The Bureau of the Census has, however, supplied data for periodical printing and publishing separate from newspapers for 1937.

4. U. S. Census of Manufactures, "Wage Earners and Wages in Establishments Classified According to Number of Wage Earners, 1937," release July 7, 1939.

5. In 1937, according to the Census, there were fifteen book, music and job plants employing 500-1,000 wage earners, two in the 1,000-2,500 class, and two with more than 2,500 wage earners. These biggest plants, however, employed only 13 per cent of the workers. To these should be added part of the thirty-two news-

Distribution of Plants

Because of the close relation between the printer and the businessmen whom he serves, the industry is widely distributed. A large part of the printing required in every city is done locally. New York and Chicago, the two biggest centers, each employed in 1937 about 15 per cent of all wage earners in book, music, job and periodical printing and publishing, bookbinding and blankbook making. No other city employed as much as 5 per cent of the total. With the growth of wider competition, came a trend away from the larger cities. This was notably true of New York, and in varying degrees of other cities. The ten leading cities in 1919 employed 53 per cent of the wage earners and produced about 60 per cent of the value of products in book and job printing, while in 1937 they accounted for only 49 per cent of the wage earners and 56 per cent of the value of products.[6] Migration of bookbinding and periodical work away from New York was especially marked. Chicago gained relatively in both fields, and about held its own in the total.[7]

From the standpoint of the big cities, the trend is towards decentralization. On the other hand, substantial amounts of work

paper and periodical plants in the 500-1,000 class and part of the seven with over 1,000 wage earners. Bookbinding and blankbook making had five plants with 500-1,000 wage earners, although most of the plants in that branch of the industry also were small.

6. Computed from U. S. Census of Manufactures, summaries for cities, 1919 and 1937.

7. The number of wage earners in New York and Chicago in 1937 and 1929 is as follows:

	New York 1937	New York 1929	Chicago 1937	Chicago 1929
Book, music and job printing and publishing	20,733	25,922	21,276	24,137
Periodical printing and publishing	2,370	3,023	2,576	2,561
Bookbinding and blankbook making	6,671	8,547	4,725	2,980
Total	29,774	37,492	28,577	29,678
Per cent of total for United States	15.5	18.7	14.8	14.8

U. S. Census of Manufactures, 1937, "Summary for New York and Chicago," and "Memorandum on Periodical Printing and Publishing"; 1929, Vol. III, pp. 158-159, 378-379.

gathered from a wide geographic area are being centralized in large plants in the country or in small towns. The market has widened under the influence of improved transportation and communication. Economies of specialization and large-scale production are possible, as well as relief from the high rents, congestion and transportation difficulties of production in the center of a big city. Economies in wages and other elements of labor cost are important in some cases. Moreover, postal rate zones influence the location of plants printing mass magazines. All of these factors have contributed to shifts of the industry from large cities and from the East, and to the growth of new centers where large plants compete successfully with plants in older areas.

b. ECONOMICS OF THE INDUSTRY

Craftsmanship still rules in this industry. In 1930 the skilled workers—compositors or typesetters, pressmen, bookbinders, photoengravers and electrotypers—were more than twice as numerous as the semiskilled and unskilled assistants in pressroom and bindery and the still smaller numbers of unskilled laborers. Men greatly outnumber women, except in the binderies.[8] Employers also are usually craftsmen up from the ranks, although increasing numbers, especially in the larger plants, have had college or business training rather than technical experience.

Competition and Profits

In an industry characterized by small plants, by easy entrance to and exit from the trade, by employers who are often better craftsmen than businessmen and by unstandardized, made-to-order products, complaints of excessive competition are not surprising. Lack of knowledge of costs is widespread, and leads whenever business is slack to price cutting below levels considered reasonable by the industry. For fifty years or more through their trade associations, employing-printers have tried to educate the industry in business methods and to develop feeling against "spoiling the market." These campaigns assume that volume depends more on

---

8. U. S. Bureau of the Census, *General Report on Occupations, 1930*, Vol V, pp. 512-514.

the general level of business than on printing prices. Accordingly, when the industry is unprofitable it needs higher prices. The large numbers of plant owners who do not know their own costs are urged to follow the experience of others who have such records. The associations publish records of average costs and production and urge their use in determining prices.[9] However, in spite of changes in business policy resulting from these efforts, cutthroat competition remains a problem. Throughout the decades the trade journals complain of the price cutter and his unfortunate effect on profits.[10]

The history of profits in the industry, so far as records are available, does not entirely support these complaints of the employing-printers. A relatively good profit record is indicated by the publications of the national association, the United Typothetae of America, based on reports of its members. The average profit on net worth for the years 1926 through 1929 ran between 11 and 13 per cent. After five depression years, two of them showing a loss, the recovery from 1935 through 1939 brought profits varying between 4 and approximately 7 per cent.[11] On the other hand, even in this selected group, a large proportion of plants made little or nothing, although at the upper end of the scale profits were substantial. For 1938 and 1939, the top 8 or 9 per cent averaged about

9. See, for example, United Typothetae of America, *Production Standards and Economic Cost Values*, Second Edition, Washington, January 1938.

10. A history of these efforts in one locality is given in the author's article, "Price Competition in the Commercial Printing Industry of Chicago," *Journal of Political Economy*, April 1930, pp. 194-212. See also Leona M. Powell, *The History of the United Typothetae of America*, University of Chicago Press, Chicago, 1926.

11. United Typothetae of America, *Ratios for Printing Management, Annual*, 1926 through 1939. The ratios are based on reports of from three to five hundred plants.

See also the relatively good profit record between 1919 and 1928 for printing as compared with other manufacturing, as reported in R. C. Epstein, *Industrial Profits in the United States*, National Bureau of Economic Research in cooperation with the Committee on Recent Economic Changes, New York, 1934, pp. 275, 408. Dun & Bradstreet, however, present data for a small sample of job printers, fifty to seventy in various years, showing an average net profit on tangible net worth for the five years 1933-1937 of 2.5 per cent. Printing was tenth from the bottom in a group of forty-two manufacturing industries. For 1937 the upper fourth of job printers in this group had a profit of 10.1 per cent or better. The lower fourth had a loss of 2.1 per cent or more. Only half of them had profits of 3.5 per cent or more. Roy A. Foulke, *They Said It With Inventories*, Dun & Bradstreet, New York, 1939, pp. 26, 36-47.

35 per cent profit. In each year from 1936 through 1939, however, well over half of the firms had no profit or were classified as poor in profit record.[12] Income tax reports also show large numbers of corporations reporting no net income. In short, the industry is one in which many small plants come and go, making poor livings if any for their proprietors, but in which the successful firms make good profits. In general the average profit ratios rise, according to Typothetae records, from the groups of the smaller plants to the larger ones.[13]

Decline in Output

A decline in volume of output has increased the problems of the industry in the last ten years.[14] Closely associated with general business, commercial printing follows the swings of the business cycle. In addition, the growth of radio advertising has replaced large amounts of direct-mail advertising, as well as of advertising pages in periodicals. Moreover, the decade has seen a marked growth in the use of cheaper substitutes for letterpress printing—such as multigraphing and simple offset processes by which some businesses supply their own needs. Improvements have made offset printing a formidable competitor for much work in which economy is important. Although many commercial printers now meet this challenge by adding offset equipment to their plants, the development has had important effects upon competition and prices.

Decline of volume inevitably brought pressure on prices, and bitter complaints of price cutting. It increased efforts of the associations to strengthen their programs for the stabilization of the industry. It has forced, also, a marked increase in attention to questions of efficiency. Technical improvements which bring down costs have come very rapidly in the past decade. Many printers find

12. United Typothetae of America, *op. cit.*, 1936 through 1939.
13. The class of largest plants includes all with annual sales of $750,000 and over.
14. The number of wage earners in book, music and job printing and publishing declined more than 10,000 between 1929 and 1937, although periodical printing and publishing and bookbinding and blankbook making showed increases of 1,343 and 579, respectively.

that the way to profits is to reduce costs, and thus be able to compete through lower prices. A new emphasis, small but growing, on standards of efficiency has brought a reaction against the old educational campaign with emphasis on average costs, which include the costs of the inefficient. The new line of thought seeks a solution of the problems of the industry not in higher prices, but in low prices and increased volume. It believes that demand for printing is not so inelastic as has been assumed, and that lower prices will inspire more uses of printing and expand the volume of output to the benefit of the whole industry as well as of the consumer.[15]

Technical Changes

The drive for efficiency and lower costs has stimulated technical change. Even before 1929 progress in the pressroom and bindery was increasing mechanization of the industry. Hand-feeding of presses was being eliminated, both by the introduction of automatic feeders on the large presses, and by new, small, fast automatic presses. More recent improvements have increased the speed of both big and small presses. Other developments, such as the standardization of inks, have changed the character of the skills required by the pressmen. The small automatic press tends to eliminate the semiskilled press feeder or assistant. On the other hand, the huge pressrooms which print catalogues or periodicals need more unskilled or semiskilled paper handlers, "fly-boys" and others. In the binderies, machines are taking over much work formerly done by the skilled hand worker. In edition binderies the unskilled men are sometimes as numerous as the skilled machine

---

15. See, for example, W. M. Gordon, "Do You Want to Stay in the Printing Business?" *Typothetae Bulletin,* November 1, 1938, pp. 44-47; and statement of Hugo Dalsheimer, "Production management . . . is successful to the extent that the plant . . . can turn out a product satisfactory to the customers at a cost below the price they are willing to pay for it." (*Ibid.,* June 1, 1939, p. 35.) Indicative of this trend, and contributing to it, is the work of the Production Standards Corporation of Chicago, whose book of production standards, *Par for Printers,* is being used by a small but increasing number of progressive printers. Some of the local associations also have published production standards.

To what extent demand for printing is elastic is a controversial question. There must be considerable elasticity for books especially, and perhaps in other parts of the field as well. There is no doubt that the cheaper substitutes have been developed as a reaction to high printing prices, and that some of the losses could be won back by lower prices.

operators. But in the composing room, though technical improvements have been made, the need for skill continues. Large non-union composing rooms tend to use less skilled workers for much of the routine work, with a few highly skilled "key men." In general, however, the threat to the craftsmen of the composing room is not so much from technical changes there, as from developments which may do away with typesetting entirely. Reproduction of the typewritten page by the offset method has made inroads, and the threat of further progress in photocomposition is serious. Yet more than in most industries, the need for skilled craftsmanship still continues.

2. Development of Organization and Collective Bargaining

Union employing-printers deal with three major craft unions: the International Typographical Union, made up of compositors or typesetters and a smaller group of mailers, with some 79,300 members in 1940; the International Printing Pressmen and Assistants' Union, with 43,700 members, including skilled and semi-skilled pressroom workers, and occasionally unskilled help in the pressroom or other departments; and the International Brotherhood of Bookbinders, with 18,700, including journeymen bookbinders and bindery women, and, to a greater or less extent in various jurisdictions, also unskilled people in binderies. The first two of these unions cover newspaper as well as book and job plants. There are also three smaller unions in allied industries—the International Photo-Engravers' Union, with 10,500 members; the International Stereotypers' and Electrotypers' Union, with 8,300; and the Lithographers' International Protective and Beneficial Association, with 12,400.[16]

16. *Typographical Journal,* Supplement, August 1940, p. 7; AF of L, *Proceedings,* Annual Convention, 1940, pp. 46-47. The ITU figure is the average membership in good standing for the fiscal year ending May 1940. The others are based on per capita tax payments to the AF of L.
A serious jurisdictional dispute exists in the increasingly important field of offset printing, between the Lithographers on the one hand and the IPP&AU and the IPEU on the other; the claims of the latter two are supported by the AF of L, which has ordered a solution by amalgamation. The field is in part unorganized, in

The book and job employing-printers are organized nationally in a series of trade associations: the United Typothetae of America, an organization of commercial printers; the Employing Bookbinders of America; the Book Manufacturers Institute, and other special groups. None of these at present is concerned primarily with labor questions or engages in collective bargaining. Associations which deal with labor are local, in some cases the local Typothetae, affiliated with the United Typothetae, in others a closed-shop branch of the local Typothetae, in still others an independent association of closed-shop printers. Since 1936, also, local closed-shop groups have formed the Printers' National Association for the exchange of information and experience among union-recognizing employers. This association, however, does not itself engage in collective bargaining.

a. ORGANIZATION IN THE NINETEENTH CENTURY

The history of organization in this industry begins with the typographical societies of Philadelphia, New York, Washington, Baltimore and other eastern cities in the first two decades of the nineteenth century. Of present-day unions, only one goes back to that first period, the Columbia Typographical Union of Washington, organized in 1815; the next oldest, in Baltimore, dates from 1831. Since the fifties the typographical unions in most of the larger cities have had a continuous history. National organization was successfully achieved in 1852 in the National Typographical Union,[17] which later became the International Typographical Union.

These unions included not only printers, or compositors, but also pressmen and bookbinders. Later, as technical developments increased the differentiation among the crafts, a desire for craft autonomy led to secession movements. In 1889 the International

part organized by each group. (AF of L, *Report of the Executive Council,* Annual Convention, 1938, pp. 40-41.) The CIO has entered the printing field only in a few local instances, in general limited to related specialty plants or the organization of unskilled groups. See below, pp. 133-134.

17. Stewart, *op. cit.,* pp. 940-941; George E. Barnett, "The Printers," *American Economic Association Quarterly,* October 1909, pp. 13, 14.

Printing Pressmen's Union was organized, and in 1892 the International Brotherhood of Bookbinders.[18]

Organization of employing-printers followed that of the journeymen. Temporary loose organizations of employers came together to discuss the unions' new "scales of prices," and sometimes to resist them, in New York, Chicago and other cities. The first employers' association to achieve some degree of permanence was the Typothetae of New York, organized in 1862.[19] In Chicago, the union employing-printers organized in the middle 1870's.[20] Although interest in problems of competition and price cutting was a second reason for the organization of the master printers, a threat of nation-wide action by the Typographical Union for the nine-hour day was the stimulus for widespread organization. In 1886 and 1887, local Typothetae were started in St. Louis, Louisville, Chicago and other cities. In the fall of 1887, in Chicago, the United Typothetae of America was organized, representing eighteen such local associations.[21] By 1904 fifty-four local societies were associated with the United Typothetae of America, although in smaller cities in many cases the only employers' organization was still the informal one for discussing a union's demand for changes in wages.[22]

b. EVOLUTION OF NEGOTIATION AND WRITTEN AGREEMENTS

By this time collective bargaining had developed in many cities to the stage of formal written agreements between the unions and permanent organizations of employers. Under the earlier system the union adopted a "scale of prices" which it presented to the individual shops for acceptance. Sometimes there was a conference, and occasionally an organized battle over the change. In 1859 a Typographical Union delegate from Philadelphia reported to the convention that employers were always invited to confer with

18. George A. Tracy, *History of the Typographical Union*, International Typographical Union, Indianapolis, 1913, pp. 503-511. See also the "Daily Newspapers" chapter.
19. Powell, *op. cit.*, p. 7.
20. Emily Clark Brown, *Book and Job Printing in Chicago*, University of Chicago Press, Chicago, 1931, pp. 13-20.
21. Powell, *op. cit.*, pp. 10-18.
22. Barnett, *op. cit.*, pp. 334, 352-353.

the union before a scale was adopted, and discussion at the convention indicated approval of formal contracts.[23]

In New York in 1869 a dispute between the Typothetae and the Typographical Union ended in a compromise agreement signed by a joint committee.[24] Through the seventies and eighties there were many conferences on changes in scales, but no more formal written agreements were made in that city until 1897 and 1899, when agreements for the nine-hour day and for overtime regulation were signed. The first general agreement, signed in 1902, covered all composing room work for three years.[25] In Chicago the first written agreement, for linotype work in certain shops, in 1887, led to a similar agreement for all job shops in 1896, and to a general composing room contract for a four-year term in 1898. The first agreement between the Chicago Typothetae and a local union was made in 1901 with the press feeders.[26]

The U. S. Industrial Commission reported in 1901 that agreements in this industry usually consisted of union scales which were conceded and signed by the employers after more or less conference and mutual concession. There was, however, increasing resort to real negotiation and the making of written agreements.[27] Interest in these formal contracts was reflected in discussions at the ITU conventions. In 1900 and 1901 local unions were urged to submit their contracts to the Executive Council for approval before signature; and in 1902 it was made a law of the union that changes in scales must be submitted to all interested employers before becoming effective. In that year also President Lynch urged that contracts, including arbitration provisions, be executed wherever possible. In 1903 he urged the local unions to be tolerant of the employers' organizations, and to try to establish friendly relations with them.[28] By this time the Typothetae looked with favor upon the experiment of collective bargaining, and

23. Tracy, *op. cit.*, p. 181.
24. George A. Stevens, "New York Typographical Union No. 6," New York Bureau of Labor Statistics, *Annual Report*, Pt. 1, 1912, pp. 296-304.
25. *Ibid.*, pp. 340-344, 374.
26. Brown, *op. cit.*, pp. 64, 68, 70, 81.
27. U. S. Industrial Commission, *Reports*, Vol. XVII, pp. 365-369. See also testimony of President S. B. Donnelly of the ITU, Vol. VII, pp. 270-272.
28. Tracy, *op. cit.*, pp. 628, 669, 697-698, 710-711, 723.

many of its locals had written agreements with local typographical and pressmen's unions.[29]

National Agreements and the Fight Over the Eight-Hour Day

Collective bargaining had developed in the main as a local matter. Union interest in a nation-wide reduction of hours, however, led to important developments between the international unions and the United Typothetae of America, which had been formed under the impetus of the nine-hour demand. Typothetae opposition succeeded in postponing reduction in hours. In 1898, however, representatives of the United Typothetae of America and the three international unions—Typographical, Pressmen and Bookbinders—reached an agreement for establishing the nine-hour day. The unions agreed in return to try to remedy competitive inequalities in wage scales in different districts.[30]

The second national agreement made by the Typothetae was an arbitration agreement with the International Printing Pressmen and Assistants' Union, signed in 1902, to be effective until May 1, 1907. It provided for the nine-hour day, the open shop and arbitration of all questions of wages and working conditions. The Typographical Union also proposed an arbitration agreement similar to one which it had recently made with the American Newspaper Publishers Association, but since the Typothetae insisted upon an open-shop clause and the union held that its laws could not be subject to arbitration, no agreement was reached.[31]

Meanwhile the Typographical Union pressed for the eight-hour day. Among Typothetae members, however, antiunion feeling was growing as a result of the frictions of the first years of contractual relations. Accordingly, in 1903, in a Declaration of Policy, the United Typothetae of America upheld the nine-hour day and the open shop and invited uniform action against "encroachments of labor organization upon the rights of employers." [32] Although conferences were held between the Typothetae and the

29. Powell, *op. cit.*, pp. 48-49.
30. Tracy, *op. cit.*, pp. 563-565.
31. Powell, *op. cit.*, pp. 48-49, 57-58. See also the "Daily Newspapers" chapter.
32. UTA, *Proceedings, 1904*, p. 18.

union, agreement was impossible, and the union maintained its decision to inaugurate the reduction of hours on January 1, 1906. Strikes ensued in all Typothetae cities.[33]

The result was general establishment of the shorter work week, considerable loss of strength by the Typothetae in many cities and a sharp division of employing-printers into union and nonunion groups. The eight-hour day was postponed in pressrooms by the agreement running until 1907. A renewal of this agreement, including the fifty-four hour week until January 1, 1909, was negotiated, but later rejected by the convention of the International Printing Pressmen and Assistants' Union. Finally in February 1908, the Typothetae recognized the eight-hour day by removing from its Declaration of Policy its opposition to any reduction of hours below fifty-four.[34]

Development of Local Agreements

After the eight-hour-day fight, and the shift of the Typothetae in most cities to a nonunion position, the need was obvious for another organization to represent employing-printers in dealings with the unions. Under the leadership of Charles Francis, New York employers in 1906 formed the Printers' League, with the avowed purpose of establishing a friendly and cooperative relationship with labor. The unions welcomed the new organization, and during 1907 and 1908 agreements were made between the League and first the press feeders, then the pressmen, and finally the typographical union. Thus began the Printers' League system of contracts, still in existence, with their provision for the settlement of disputes through joint conference committees or arbitration.[35] In Chicago in 1909 an Employing Printers' Association was established, and began its system of union agreements.[36] The New York experience was influential in bringing about similar organ-

---

33. In 1904 there were fifty-four local Typothetae in the chief printing centers. Barnett, *op. cit.*, p. 334.

34. Powell, *op. cit.*, pp. 66-75; Tracy, *op. cit.*, pp. 810-844, 863-879, 892-902.

35. Printers' League of America, *First Convention*, New York, 1909, pp. 68-89, 103-108; Charles Francis, *Printing for Profit*, Bobbs-Merrill, New York, 1917, pp. 315-324.

36. Brown, *op. cit.*, p. 134. As the Franklin Association it has continued to represent the union employing-printers in their relations with the unions.

izations and agreements in other cities.[37] In 1909 a national Printers' League of America was launched, in the hope of promoting League principles on a nation-wide basis. The unions offered their cooperation, but the industry was not yet ready for such activity on a national scale.[38]

Further Attempts at National Action

From this time, because of the division on labor policy among its members, the evolution of the United Typothetae of America was away from its original primary concern with labor matters to a major interest in business problems, costs, prices and related questions. In 1908 it decided to leave all labor matters to its locals and individual members. In 1911, however, it permitted members to form open- or closed-shop divisions.

A national amalgamation movement among employing-printers, which led various groups back into the UTA, now a trade association, made it possible for the Printers' League in New York and similar organizations in other cities after 1913 to become the closed-shop branches of the local Typothetae. In 1916 a national Closed Shop Division of the United Typothetae of America was organized, and promptly followed Printers' League principles in an arbitration agreement with the International Typographical Union. So far as is known, however, only two plants ever signed the individual arbitration agreement necessary to put this agreement into effect.[39]

In 1919, under the stress of postwar adjustments, the 1909 proposal for a national organization representing employing-printers and unions was revived. The International Joint Conference Council of the commercial and periodical branches of the printing industry which resulted included representatives of the Closed Shop Division of the United Typothetae of America, the Printers' League of America, the International Association of

37. Printers' League, *op. cit.*, p. 127; U. S. Commission on Industrial Relations, *Final Report and Testimony*, 1916, Vol. I, pp. 683-684.
38. Printers' League, *op. cit.*; U. S. Commission on Industrial Relations, *Final Report and Testimony*, Vol. I, testimony of Charles Francis, pp. 683-697, and of George L. Berry, President, International Printing Pressmen and Assistants' Union, pp. 755-760.
39. Powell, *op. cit.*, pp. 103, 118, 128-129, 135-137.

Electrotypers and four international unions—Typographical, Pressmen and Assistants, Bookbinders, and Stereotypers and Electrotypers. Action of the Council was to take the form of recommendations, to become effective only after ratification by the constituent bodies. Unfortunately, a question arose as to whether either the Closed Shop Division of the Typothetae or the Printers' League had authority to speak for the closed-shop printers.

The major action of the IJCC was upon the forty-four-hour week which unions in the larger cities actively demanded. The Council recommended postponement of the reduction in hours until May 1, 1921, when it should go into effect nationally. The recommendation was adopted by the constituent bodies, although the New York and Chicago unions voted against it. Ratification by the Closed Shop Division of the Typothetae took place at a convention in New York attended largely by the New York members. May 1, 1921 brought strong resistance against a shorter week. Behind this was a combination of circumstances—the depression, a general campaign for the open shop throughout the industry, and the fact that employing-printers in many areas could claim with some justice that they had not been party to the agreement and were not bound by it. An effort to secure further postponement through the IJCC failed. While employing-printers in New York, Chicago, Washington, Cincinnati and other cities fulfilled their agreement and granted the reduction, in most cities a bitter strike followed, similar to that of 1906. In many areas the power of the unions was broken for the time, and a strong group in the industry was successfully established on a nonunion basis.[40]

The IJCC continued to hold meetings until 1925, but it was unable to arouse interest in employers for action on a national basis. Its recommendations on such things as apprenticeship and a standard form for contracts exerted some influence on practices. It also promoted a health survey of the commercial printing industry, fi-

---

40. "International Joint Conference Council of the Commercial and Periodical Branches of the Printing Industry, Constitution and Activities"; UTA, "Statement of Facts, Forty-Four-Hour Week Situation, Revised as of March 1, 1921"; Powell, *op. cit.*, pp. 144-158; Emily Clark Brown, "Joint Industrial Control in the Book and Job Printing Industry," *Bulletin No. 481,* U. S. Bureau of Labor Statistics, 1928, pp. 7-10.

nanced by unions and employers and conducted with the cooperation of the U. S. Bureau of Labor Statistics. After 1925 the national associations—Closed Shop Division and Printers' League—dropped out of sight. In 1922 the UTA had forbidden its labor divisions to use the name Typothetae in their titles, in an effort to avoid involving the parent association in their activities, and in 1928 all provision for such labor divisions was dropped from the UTA constitution.

During the 1920's and 1930's the nonunion shop predominated in many areas in which previously the local Typothetae or other group had bargained with the unions. The unions nevertheless made some gains and by 1927 the ITU had restored its membership to the prestrike level.

C. ORGANIZATIONAL GAINS IN THE LATE 1930'S

Not until the widespread organization campaigns beginning in 1936, however, did extensive reorganization take place. By 1939 the International Typographical Union and the International Brotherhood of Bookbinders had each added about six thousand to their membership as reported to the American Federation of Labor, while the International Printing Pressmen and Assistants' Union had added seventy-six hundred.[41] These gains resulted in bringing back under union control many areas long nonunion. In addition many of the large plants were unionized, especially in the periodical printing and book printing and binding fields. An increase of union organization took place also in such related specialty fields as the manufacture of envelopes, loose-leaf and blankbooks, paper boxes, paper cups, wax paper and ink.[42] Finally,

41. AF of L, *Report of the Executive Council*, Annual Convention, 1939, pp. 11-12.

42. The IPP&AU has organized successfully on an industrial basis in a number of these fields. Its industrial local in San Francisco has contracts in the paper box and other paper products industries. In New York, Pressmen's Union No. 51 has organized such "auxiliary workers" in separate branches, which in a number of cases have contracts with paper products manufacturers. Throughout the country other locals have agreements covering wax paper, box, envelope and ink workers. Local industrial unions of the CIO have contracts in a number of such plants. In some large specialty plants the International Brotherhood of Bookbinders has contracts, although usually not on an industrial basis. The Pulp, Sulphite and Paper Mill Workers and federal unions of the AF of L also have organizations in this field.

the upsweep of organization reached into the ranks of unskilled workers in bookbinding, periodical and commercial printing plants and brought larger numbers into the unions than ever before.

The Problem of the Unskilled

The craft unions in the past tended to ignore the relatively small numbers of unskilled workers, but their policies are changing. Many old craft unionists, fearing dilution of their strength, hesitate to take in the unskilled, especially when, as in the binderies, there are substantial numbers of them, and insist that the necessary routine work should be done by members of the craft. Others, however, believe that it is impossible to prevent the use of the unskilled or to maintain the strength of the craft organizations unless the conditions of the unskilled, as well as the skilled, are controlled. In addition some fear that an unsatisfied desire for organization will open the way for the CIO or some other group outside the AF of L allied printing trades. In a number of cases the unskilled have been organized by the CIO, by the AF of L in directly affiliated local unions, by the Lithographers or by independent unions. But more often the unskilled, if organized at all, are affiliated with or are members of the craft unions.

The policy of the International Printing Pressmen and Assistants' Union is clear—all the unskilled in the printing plants should be organized, in their own interest and that of the crafts.[43] Sometimes the unskilled in the pressrooms are in the pressmen's union; sometimes these miscellaneous workers and others in other departments have been organized in locals affiliated with the pressmen, and contracts made for them. In other cases efforts of affiliated paper handlers' unions to secure recognition for themselves and for miscellaneous workers have been unsuccessful. The first city-wide agreement covering all miscellaneous workers was signed in February 1940 by the Graphic Arts Association of Washington, D. C. and the Printing Commercial Workers Union, a local of the IPP&AU.[44]

43. See statement of President George L. Berry, *American Pressman*, March 1939, p. 17.
44. *Printers National Association Bulletin*, February 1940, p. 2.

In the binderies, where mechanization has increased the proportion of the unskilled, the problem is more serious. The International Brotherhood of Bookbinders permits their admission on a Class B basis, with lower dues and benefits, but leaves the decision as to their inclusion to the locals.[45] In some cities where there has been less mechanization, all the work is done by journeymen, journeywomen and apprentices. In others, as in Chicago, the local union has made no provision for the unskilled, and they are unorganized. In New York the union in the commercial binderies has a division for the unskilled, and has been recognized in some large binderies, although it has no Printers' League contract for this group. The edition bindery agreement includes rates for the unskilled and semiskilled. So far as the former are organized, they are in a Class B division. The IBB reported only 350 Class B members in a total of 19,300 in May 1940.[46]

The policy of the International Typographical Union is to recognize only apprentices and journeymen in the composing rooms, and to insist upon the union's jurisdiction over all composing room work, except as conceded by agreement to other international unions. Nevertheless, and sometimes with specific provision in contracts, considerable numbers of unskilled workers are employed in large composing rooms. A union survey found unskilled people in about 23 per cent of the commercial composing rooms, numbering more than half as many as the apprentices, and nearly 4 per cent of the commercial members.[47] In 1939 the union adopted a law requiring local unions to reclaim jurisdiction and to provide for the gradual elimination of such miscellaneous workers and the filling by apprentices and journeymen of vacancies as they occur.[48] No provision was made for classification of unskilled workers. In several cases, however, local typographical unions have conceded jurisdiction over certain unskilled work to locals of the International Printing Pressmen and Assistants' Union.

45. *International Bookbinder,* September-October 1940, pp. 3, 41-42.
46. *Ibid.,* March-April 1940, p. 14.
47. *Typographical Journal,* Supplement, August 1939, p. 45.
48. *Ibid.,* Supplement, September 1939, pp. 137-138.

Employers' Attitude Toward Organization of the Unskilled

It cannot be said that employers welcome the extension of collective bargaining to the unskilled. Some are afraid lest their organization outside the allied trades lead to irresponsible action. On the other hand, their inclusion within the craft organizations would be dangerous should the crafts insist upon journeymen's scales for all work in the department, or fail to classify properly and set appropriate rates for different grades of work. To a large extent also, employers point out, the unskilled are a young group, who should not be encouraged to remain in these largely dead-end jobs.[49]

The Printers' National Association

As in the past, the increase in union activity stimulated organization of employers. Some of the newly organized plants as well as local organizations which had dealt with unions since 1921, saw the need for a national organization for the exchange of information. After an initial effort in 1934, the Printers' National Association was successfully launched in the fall of 1936. In 1939 it included the closed-shop groups in the major printing centers, and most of the important large union plants outside the cities.[50] As on previous occasions the international unions welcomed this effort of the employing-printers to organize, and wished them success.[51]

d. PRESENT UNION STRENGTH

It is impossible to estimate accurately either the proportion of the wage earners in the industry who are union members, or the share of the volume of production that is under union control. Census occupational classifications neither distinguish between branches of the printing industry, nor separate "operatives" and "laborers" by departments. Included in the total of all wage earners in book and job printing, therefore, are many who have not been eligible in the past for membership in the printing crafts

---

49. *Printers National Association Bulletin*, November 1939, p. 4.
50. *Ibid.*, 1936–1939; *Printing*, Walden, Sons & Mott, October 1939, p. 52.
51. Cf. p. 131.

unions. In 1940 apparently less than half of all wage earners in the book and job industry were union members, although among compositors, pressmen and assistants and the smaller skilled crafts the proportion must have been larger.[52] The U. S. Bureau of Labor Statistics, however, estimated that more than half of the workers in the book, magazine and job printing and publishing industry in 1938 were covered by union agreements.[53]

To estimate the union share in the volume of production is even more difficult. Many plants which are considered union are so only as to craftsmen in certain departments. However, if plants are counted as union when they recognize unions in their major departments, even though they may employ some nonunion people, there is little doubt that more than half the volume of the entire industry now is union. The extent of union control differs in the various branches. In book and periodical printing and edition bookbinding the union proportion is perhaps 80 per cent or more, according to well-informed estimates in the industry. Commercial or pamphlet binding is considerably less organized. In commercial printing the situation differs greatly in different centers. San Francisco, Washington, Indianapolis and Minneapolis are more than 75 per cent unionized; New York, Chicago and St. Louis well over half. Other cities range from predominantly open shop to largely union.

3. Collective Bargaining Structure and Methods

a. LOCAL AUTONOMY

In an industry so decentralized, it is not surprising that the collective bargaining system remains essentially local. In spite of increased competition on a national basis, a strong preference for

---

52. The number of wage earners in book, music, job and periodical printing and bookbinding and blankbook making in 1937 was 192,045 (see p. 118). Union membership may be estimated in 1940 as around 80,000 (see p. 125 for the total membership of these unions). This includes 33,000 book and job members of the ITU (estimated on the basis of 1938 figures in *Typographical Journal*, Supplement, August 1939, p. 45); 26,000 for the IPP&AU; 18,700 for the IBB, and a few thousand union electrotypers, photoengravers and lithographers in commercial printing plants.
53. *Monthly Labor Review*, March 1939, p. 508.

solving labor problems locally persists among employers. Their fears lest satisfactory situations be upset through action on a national basis find support in the history of the industry, as in the 1921 fight.[54] The Printers' National Association now represents a substantial part of the union employing-printers, but it has not seriously considered, as yet, any functions beyond those of exchange of information and experience. Much the same can be said of the Book Manufacturers Institute for that branch of the industry.

The unions, too, have local autonomy, but only within limits set by the laws and the influence of the strong international unions.[55] Local contracts must conform to international union laws, and be approved by international union presidents. The national offices assist local unions in negotiations in various ways. Standard contract forms are offered as guides. On request, aid is given in preparing material to use in negotiations or arbitration cases. The Typographical and Pressmen's unions publish reports on wages, hours and other conditions in all local union contracts. In addition, monthly bulletins report new contracts, arbitration decisions, executive council decisions and such basic economic data as trends of prices, cost of living and production, from government and other sources. If local negotiations are in danger of breaking down, the international must be notified, and the president or his representative attempts to find a basis of settlement. Strikes may be called only after authorization by the international. A local union which violates union laws or orders of the international officers may be disciplined by fine or suspension or even revocation of its charter. These controls in many cases restrain a local union from militant action which its membership is prepared to take, and especially among the larger locals there is, as a result, a considerable feeling that greater local autonomy would be desirable.[56]

54. See p. 132.
55. See the "Daily Newspapers" chapter.
56. See, for example, the discussion on a proposal to require the Executive Council, after certain procedures have been followed, to grant to a local union power to take such action as the local deems necessary, in *Typographical Journal*, Supplement, September 1939, pp. 94-97.

b. CRAFT AUTONOMY

Craft autonomy is the second dominating characteristic of collective bargaining in book and job printing. Typically, the employers negotiate agreements separately with each craft. In many localities the division among the workers goes so far as separate unions and agreements for compositors, pressmen, press assistants, bookbinders, bindery women, mailers and, in some cases, paper handlers and other less skilled men in the pressrooms. Large plants also may have photoengraving and electrotyping departments, each with separate unions and agreements. These craft agreements differ usually in expiration date, and often on such basic conditions as hours, overtime provisions and Saturday work. In practice, the negotiations of the strongest craft frequently set the stage for the others, which then get approximately the same settlement. The Typographical Union is often the leader, partly because its locals include newspaper members, and so are in a strong position to wage a strike, if necessary, with the aid of members who continue at work.

The Allied Printing Trades Councils

Cooperation among the crafts is promoted by the local Allied Printing Trades Councils, organized wherever there are two or more locals of the unions represented in the International Allied Printing Trades Association. Although the major function of the local councils is to control the allied printing trades label,[57] there are instances of cooperation in collective bargaining through the councils, as well as sometimes through less formal arrangement. The Boston Allied Printing Trades Council for about ten years, beginning in 1912, signed agreements with a number of big plants covering several crafts. In Chicago, from 1919 through 1921, five

---

57. This may be issued to local plants, or withdrawn, only by unanimous consent of the local council. Since a council may be organized while some of the printing crafts in the locality are not yet organized, the existence of the council does not insure the cooperation of all crafts. There have been cases where the label was used and the plant was considered a union plant, although certain groups were unorganized. In other cases it was not possible to secure the unanimous consent necessary to remove a label from a plant, although a newly organized craft was on strike for recognition.

unions negotiated jointly with the Franklin Association, the organization of closed-shop plants, under a supplementary agreement calling for wage adjustments based on changes in the cost of living. This was ended on the insistence of the employers that negotiations for new contracts be conducted with each union separately, since problems of shop conditions were involved.[58] Recently in San Francisco and other cities negotiations were conducted between the entire group of unions and the employers, although final contracts were completed and signed with the separate crafts.

In recent years local unions frequently cooperated in organizing new plants through the Allied Printing Trades Council and sometimes in the name of the council brought cases to the National Labor Relations Board. In several cases, single agreements covering all crafts followed such united campaigns. In Baltimore, long open shop, a joint contract between three major unions and the newly organized Graphic Arts League resulted from an organization campaign by the unions in 1940.[59] The tendency now, however, is for cooperation not to go so far. If local unions keep each other informed of their plans or make agreements on policy before presenting their demands for new contracts, they are engaging in a degree of cooperation rare in this industry of strong craft, rather than industry, loyalties.

The St. Louis System

An exception is St. Louis where representatives of the unions of the composing rooms, pressrooms and binderies and of the union employers have for many years negotiated in a group and signed a single agreement. The Men and Management Conference began in 1922 with a simple agreement asserting a desire to maintain harmonious relations and providing for negotiation of changes in wages or hours or other matters. Since then this group has negotiated changes in wage scales for all crafts at once. In 1934 the written agreement was expanded to include certain basic

---

58. Brown, *Book and Job Printing in Chicago*, pp. 163-192.
59. *American Pressman*, Supplement, September-October 1940, p. 1-14; *Typographical Journal*, Supplement, August 1940, p. 164.

working conditions and provision for a joint standing committee and arbitration. The 1937 and 1939 agreements carried somewhat more of the details of the accepted shop practices. In practice the unions confer and agree on their proposals before entering into negotiations with the employers. New agreements go into effect only after ratification by all the unions.

Factors Making for Independent Action

The more usual system of independent craft action is explained in part by the difficulty of getting unified action from a group of autonomous locals, each under the control of a different international. Moreover, the spirit of craft solidarity is much stronger than any feeling of common interest among the entire group of workers in the industry. Each local tends to use every opportunity to promote its own position. Stronger unions hesitate to give up their special advantage in bargaining by cooperating with the weaker ones, while the weaker sometimes fear inadequate attention to their interests in joint action. The problem of wage differentials, especially, hinders cooperation unless the existing structure is satisfactory.

With some exceptions employers have promoted this craft separateness. The different problems of shop practices in the various departments make separate negotiations with each union seem as desirable to them as to the unions. Moreover, in dealing with the unions one at a time, they, like the unions, can make use of any bargaining advantage which appears. Granting a demand of one craft at a crucial moment may prevent the development of a movement for more unity and militancy. On both sides, the bargaining process involves shrewd tactics and maneuvers—something of a "war of nerves" with the threat of force in the background.

Trends Toward Cooperation

On the whole the existing system of craft bargaining and agreements is accepted in the industry with little open questioning, although the wave of organization in recent years has inevitably brought some breakdown of the separateness of the unions. Occasional signs of discontent with the lack of unity among the crafts have appeared in union ranks, and a feeling that closer cooperation should be developed. President George L. Berry of the IPP&AU has proposed, as he did some years ago, a Federation of Printing Trade Unions which would aim to establish uniform expiration dates for agreements, and cooperation of the crafts for "offensive and defensive purposes." The ITU agreed to confer, in an effort to work out a plan for closer cooperation "without loss of essential autonomy of individual printing trades unions," and the other unions have shown sympathy with the plan. But there has been no result as yet.[60]

Only rarely have employers indicated favorable interest in such tendencies toward joint action by the craft unions. In St. Louis, on the other hand, the system of joint negotiations and a single contract appears to have the approval of both employers and unions. Its present form is the result of a long experience during which an unusually stable leadership on both sides has built up mutual confidence and respect. Harmony and cooperation among the local unions is much greater than is typical in other cities. There is no indication of the suspicion frequently found elsewhere that employers play off one group against another to get an advantage. In general, basic working conditions are uniform in all departments, which is advantageous to mangement and prevents dissatisfaction among the crafts. Most important is the fact that changes in wages or hours are made for the entire industry at once, after consideration of the condition of the industry and the probable effect of the changes. While the unions retain their autonomy, the fact that they work out their demands and present them as a group makes possible considerable moral pressure upon any union attempting to gain advantages for itself at the risk of jeopardizing the interests of the whole group.

C. THE AGREEMENTS

The book and job printing agreements reflect their purpose to standardize and stabilize labor conditions in a highly competitive

60. *American Pressman,* Supplement, September-October, 1940, pp. R-4-5; *Typographical Journal,* Supplement, September 1939, pp. 25-27, 162; Supplement, August 1940, pp. 42-47.

industry. Their very detailed regulation of wages, hours and working conditions aims to be so precise that their application will be clear in a large number of different plants. Wage rates for various classifications, and regulations on hours, shifts, holidays and overtime are always found. The closed shop is general. Considerable detail is usual on the authority of foremen in employment and discharge, with provisions for protection of workers against unreasonable discipline. Priority, the term used in this industry for seniority, is provided in Typographical Union agreements, and sometimes in others. Occasionally there are also provisions for the sharing of work in slack times. Regulations varying in detail determine ratios of men to various machines. Apprenticeship is usually regulated in numbers, type of work and rates of pay.

Settlement of Disputes

Contracts usually are written for specific periods of one to three years and sometimes with provision for continuance if there is no notice of desire to change. Almost universally they include arrangements for the peaceful settlement of differences under the agreements, including arbitration if necessary. The obligation to settle disputes without resort to force is stated or implied in all. Whether arbitration should also be accepted in advance for the settlement of disputes over the terms of a new contract is more controversial. The earliest Printers' League contracts in New York provided for such arbitration. Since then, however, the tendency has been for arbitration agreements to expire with the scale agreement, or at most to extend a short time beyond. In Chicago for many years after 1910 the pressroom unions, and for a time the bookbinders, made continuing arbitration agreements; but by 1939 only the press assistants made such commitment. In many smaller cities, however, arbitration agreements cover the negotiation of new contracts, sometimes with provision that changes in wages shall be retroactive to the date the old agreement expired. The agreements of individual big companies frequently provide for arbitration of new agreements if necessary. About one fourth of the agreements in commercial pressrooms have such clauses.

Opposition to such agreements was shown in proposals at the

1938 and 1939 ITU conventions to prohibit local unions from contracting to arbitrate wage scales, but they were defeated. A strong preference for peaceful settlement of disputes is traditional in these unions. Control by the internationals over strikes exerts a strong influence towards the observance of contractual obligations and towards the exhaustion of all means for peaceful settlement before resort to strikes. Nevertheless in the absence of continuing arbitration agreements, employers do not have complete guarantees against interruptions of operations when agreements expire. The ITU officers refuse to force a local union to arbitrate, but support the use of arbitration when it seems propitious. They go less far than the officers of the IPP&AU who on many occasions have stated their preference for settlement by arbitration rather than warfare.[61]

Coverage

Most prevalent is the market agreement negotiated between an employers' association and a local union for the entire locality, signed by the association, and applying to all members without their individual signatures. In other cases the agreement is negotiated by a committee of employers and the union, but the individual companies are the signers. A different type, of increased importance in recent years, is a separate agreement negotiated with the union by an isolated large plant.

Types of Control

Such agreements set up a government in industry quite different from that in which the control of labor conditions and relations is, within limits, in the hands of the employer alone. There is, however, no uniform type of union-employer control in the industry. At one extreme is a one-sided, almost entirely union-imposed control; at the other a well-developed collective bargaining system with strong organization on both sides.

During many decades when employers were relatively unorgan-

---

61. See statements by President C. M. Baker and Vice President F. G. Barrett, *Typographical Journal*, Supplement, October 1938, pp. 46-47, and by President George L. Berry, *American Pressman*, October 1939, pp. 26-27.

ized, whatever there was of standardization and stabilization was brought about by the union alone, through the enforcement of its price scales. This long history is reflected in many one-sided practices today, especially where employer organization is still weak. Enforcement of association agreements upon nonassociation plants is a holdover from the primitive system of ex parte union control. The tradition that international union laws, even those affecting work in the plants, are not subject to negotiation or arbitration is another reflection of this system. A third is the settlement of disputes in many localities through the machinery for appeals established in the union constitutions, rather than through a system of joint committees and arbitration.[62]

At the other end of the scale is a mature, well-organized, balanced system, based upon strong organization of both employers and labor, expressing the equal interest and responsibility of both for the interpretation and enforcement of the agreements. The Printers' League system in New York is of this sort. The League's membership represents a large proportion of the volume of union printing in the city. Agreements with the unions are negotiated and signed by the League. Under their constitution members are bound to abide by the terms in the case of all the unions which the individual member has recognized by written notice to the League.

The Executive Committee of the League has full power to discipline members who violate agreements. Although an employer may resign at any time, he may be released from his obligations under a union contract only by agreement with the union in question through the office of the League or by the expiration of the agreement. When a dispute arises between an employer and a union, officers of the League and the union try to adjust the matter informally. If settlement in this manner is impossible, the issue goes to the joint standing committee whose decision is final. If necessary the matter goes to arbitration. While the actual policing of the industry must be done by the unions, both sides are

62. The far-reaching control established by the ITU especially has been termed a "union dictatorship." See Selig Perlman, *A Theory of the Labor Movement*, Macmillan, New York, 1928, pp. 262-272. For discussion of the international law question, see below, pp. 160-161; also the "Daily Newspapers" chapter.

equally interested in maintaining the agreements and share responsibility for interpretation and enforcement.

A less highly developed but more typical form of collective bargaining is found in many other cities. Both sides are organized, but the employers' association has less authority than in New York. Sometimes the association has no office, and functions little except at the time of negotiations. Elsewhere, as in Chicago, it serves as a "point of contact" instead of an organization to which the members have delegated power, and in such cases the actual adjustments are generally made between the union and the company. In some areas the joint standing committees provided for in the agreements are seldom or never used.

In Chicago the Franklin Association now has a small membership, although it includes the major large union plants. The agreements are negotiated and signed by the Association, but they do not bind any firm for the stipulated period. Members are free to resign and change their basis of operations, if they can, at any time; only so long as they remain members are they obligated to observe the terms of the contracts. The agreements provide joint machinery for settling disputes. When a difference of opinion arises in a plant between the company and a union, the employer may consult the Association, but usually the settlement is made directly between the employer and the union without conference between association and union officers. When a joint committee gets a dispute, it seldom issues a formal decision, interpreting the obligation of one or the other side. More often the process is moral suasion or bargaining over what should be done. Sometimes the Association allows a discharge dispute to be decided through the union appeal machinery. Employers are disinclined to take the time or the responsibility to make these decisions, and in some cases they prefer to put the final decision up to the international union executive council.

The Union in the Plant

Each union has its own plant organization, traditionally called a "chapel," with an elected chairman who represents the members in any issue with the employer. The foreman, although a union member, represents the employer.[63] When difference of opinion arises between the foreman and the chapel, either over interpretation of rules or the rights of an individual member, a union officer may be called in to attempt to settle the matter. If no agreement is reached, the issue is appealed. If there is no specific provision in the contract for settlement of disputes through joint committees, the issue then goes to the union, whose decision in open meeting is binding upon all parties. Appeal may be made to the international union executive council and from its decision to the union convention. The prevalence of this system of settling issues in the last instance by the authority of the international unions is a commentary upon the employers' lack of organization. The International Typographical Union reported that only 178 of the 494 local book and job and newspaper contracts which it approved in 1938 provided for reference of controversies over discharge to joint committees.[64]

In large isolated plants operating under agreements with well-established unions, the system is a balanced one, with mutual responsibility for interpretation and maintenance of the agreement. Chairmen of the various departments and shifts represent the unions in relations with management. Often the union officers work in the plant and act as chairmen. Any matters of common interest, whether differences of opinion over the meaning of the

63. See the "Daily Newspapers" chapter. In book and job printing the union membership of foremen is so thoroughly established that it does not become an issue except occasionally in a newly organized plant. It is clearly recognized that the foreman's first responsibility is to management. His duty to the union is to administer the agreement fairly in the plant. There are advantages in this system in that the foreman, necessarily a skilled man himself, is thoroughly acquainted with the problems of the men and with the union agreement and rules. He is in good position, therefore, to interpret the union's position to management, and vice versa. However, the fact that he may be disciplined by the union, if the union considers that he has violated the agreement or a union rule, is a source of difficulty in some cases. Fear of union discipline sometimes interferes with a foreman's efficiency, although the strong foreman is little affected. There is in some cases a need for more thorough protection of foremen from union discipline for carrying out office orders, pending determination of an issue through the negotiation or arbitration machinery.

64. *Typographical Journal,* Supplement, August 1938, p. 31; see also discussion, *ibid.,* August 1935, p. 8. The ITU system of control over discharge is discussed below, pp. 162 ff.

agreements, or the rights of individuals, or other matters such as lighting and conveniences in the plant, can be discussed by the union representatives as a matter of right and on a basis of equality.

4. THE RESULTS

a. CIVIL RIGHTS AND DEMOCRATIC EQUALITY

A century-old tradition of labor organization and long collective bargaining experience have firmly established in a large part of this industry the right of wage earners to share in decisions on wages, hours and other vital matters, giving them a voice also in the interpretation and enforcement of agreements. Workers are, in effect, bulwarked by a system of constitutional government, protecting them against arbitrary or discriminatory action by management. The safeguard of the right of appeal of individual members under the democratic constitutions of the locals renders these protections even more effective.

Paralleling this system of rights in relation to the employer, is a system of democratic equality among the members of a union. A strong feeling of common interest exists within each skilled craft. Union rules make clear the rights of each member as to wage rates, tenure and other matters. A union department tends thus to be free from the competition based on insecurity which prevails in nonunion plants. Union men often speak of the better feeling in such a department, where there is no fear of favoritism from the foreman to promote dissension and jealousy. Whatever may be said of it from other angles, the priority system, so thoroughly established in Typographical union practice, is a strong expression of the idea of equal rights based on length of service. On the other hand, during the depression, various arrangements for sharing the available work showed widespread recognition that brotherliness requires more than mere protection of seniority rights.[65]

---

65. The union work-spreading plans are a response also to the tendency of union plants, because of higher wage rates and the availability of a supply of union labor, to lay off employees more promptly when work is slack than do open shops.

Spreading the Work

By 1930 the unemployment among union members inspired discussion of reduction of hours as a work-sharing device. This time, helped by the NRA, the shorter week came gradually and peacefully through local agreements. By the summer of 1933 the forty-hour week was in effect in a number of cities. Two years later average hours in the book and job trades, under union agreements, had dropped to forty.[66]

In addition to cutting down the regular work week, the unions limit by a variety of devices the hours which any member may work, thus giving more work to the unemployed. Typographical union law since 1922 has permitted local unions to enact five-day laws.[67] Members must cancel overtime by taking time off and giving work to substitutes. Thus do many local unions "spread the work." In some cases by special agreements with employers, as in the 1932 pressroom agreements in New York and Chicago, efforts have been made to absorb some of the unemployed by limiting the work of members of the unions to less than the contract hours for certain periods. Furthermore, agreements in some of the newly organized big plants call for equal division of work in slack times among all regular employees.

The fraternal aspects of unionism which these efforts to maintain job security reflect, also show concretely in elaborate systems of financial benefits which likewise increase security. Through the depression years many local unions carried a heavy burden of unemployment by special assessments on their working members to pay out-of-work benefits. Usually, also, local unions keep unemployed members in good standing by paying their per capita taxes to the international unions.[68]

---

66. U. S. Bureau of Labor Statistics, "Union Scales of Wages and Hours in the Printing Trades, May 15, 1936," *Bulletin No. 631,* 1937, p. 7. From January 1, 1935, the ITU prohibited the making of contracts for more than forty hours (*Typographical Journal,* Supplement, October 1934, pp. 82-90). It is the policy of both the IPP&AU and the IBB to refuse to approve contracts for more than forty hours. The IBB by referendum in January 1940 voted to limit hours to forty, from Monday to Friday. *International Bookbinder,* March-April, 1940, p. 2.
67. See the "Daily Newspapers" chapter.
68. Unemployment benefits paid by some of the large local unions, according to reports of their officers, were: New York Typographical Union No. 6, nearly $3.5

Union members thus receive substantial advantages from their well-established system of constitutional government in industry and its accompanying mutual aid. But it must be remembered that a considerable number of unskilled and even semiskilled workers are outside this system.

b. PEACEFUL ADJUSTMENT OF CONTROVERSIES

The long history of collective bargaining in this industry has been marked by several serious large-scale clashes—the nine-hour-day strikes in 1887, the eight-hour-day fight in 1905–1906, and the forty-four-hour fight in 1921. Nevertheless the long-run tendency has been towards the peaceful solution of controversies. Chicago history illustrates this trend. In the early years of the unions in that city there were many strikes for organizing purposes and over changes in scales. Breakdowns also occurred in the first years of contractual relations. But since the present system of contracts between the unions and the Franklin Association there has been far greater stability. Between 1887 and 1907 there were twelve or more strikes important enough to be mentioned in Association records, four of them serious conflicts lasting for weeks and affecting large parts of the industry. From 1909 through 1939, while there were about the same number of strikes as in the earlier twenty-year period, only three affected a large part of the industry and these lasted only a very few days. Although the continuing system of agreements did not entirely eliminate strikes even in Association plants, forceful settlement became far less prevalent.[69]

Much the same story can be told of the relationship beginning in 1907 between the New York Printers' League and the unions. Since the fight of 1919, bitter and costly to both sides, contractual relations of the major unions and the League have not been interrupted. In recent years strikes in Chicago and New York, as elsewhere, have been in large part organizing affairs.[70]

million between 1928 and 1939 to book and job and newspaper members; New York Printing Pressmen's Union No. 51, over $2 million between 1930 and 1937; Chicago Pressmen's Union No. 3, over $2 million between 1930 and 1939.

69. Brown, *Book and Job Printing in Chicago;* Franklin Association, *Minutes,* 1930–1939.

70. In the three years 1931–1933, during which there was pressure for wage

In numerous cities the 1921 strike broke off long-standing systems of agreements. Nevertheless many plants and groups of plants have long records of peaceful relationships. Two of the oldest are in Cincinnati and in Washington. In Cincinnati agreements have been negotiated for more than fifty years between the unions and the group now known as the Printers' League. In Washington since 1901 the relationships were broken only for a few weeks during the eight-hour strike. San Francisco's system of agreements is more than twenty-five years old. Contractual relations in St. Louis have been uninterrupted since the present plan began in 1922. One large plant in a small town has been operating under union agreements for twenty-five years.

Settlement of Disputes Over Changes in Agreements

Except in rare cases, renewals of agreements are accomplished without strikes. When there is no commitment to arbitrate a dispute over the terms of the new contract, there is always a possibility of an interruption of operations, and threats of force by both sides enter into the bargaining process. When crucial points are reached, the unions tend to ask permission of the international union to take a strike vote. New York Typographical Union No. 6 has a large defense fund and has shown signs of irritation at the restraining hand of the international.[71] The New York Printers' League also has an emergency fund, and in such a crucial period as 1932, when the employers insisted upon a wage reduction, the League was prepared to fight if necessary. In Chicago, at that time, Typographical Union No. 16 was operating under a five-year contract. The Chicago employers finally forced the issue by posting notices of a wage reduction and closing some of the

---

reductions, sixteen of eighteen strikes reported in book and job printing involved wages or hours as the major issue. From 1934 through 1936 there were thirty-one strikes, but only nine involved wages and hours primarily; twenty-two had as their major issue questions of recognition or some other matter of union organization. Data are not available on the causes of the twenty-seven strikes reported in 1937 and the nine in 1938, but they were without doubt associated with the organization drive of those years. Only six strikes were reported in 1939. Florence Peterson, "Strikes in the United States, 1880–1936," *Bulletin No. 651*, U. S. Bureau of Labor Statistics, 1938, p. 147; *Monthly Labor Review*, May 1938, p. 1191; May 1939, p. 1115; May 1940, p. 1091.

71. *Typographical Journal*, Supplement, September 1939, pp. 95-97.

plants. Although in both these cases the issue was settled, as usual, at the conference table, the possibility of force was in the background.

Settlement of Disputes Arising Under Agreements

The tradition of strict observance of the terms of the contracts is very strong and a matter of pride to the unions. While there are differences in the success with which the agreements operate, on the whole disputes are adjusted peacefully without interrupted operations and without complaints of union irresponsibility. The great majority of issues are settled by union representatives and management directly in the plants. In Chicago, for example, from 1930 through July 1939, only twenty-four cases reached joint committees. Their wide variety covered disputes over wage scales, the complement of men on presses, overtime pay, discharge, "struck work" and other matters. Typically, after discussion in committee, the issue was finally settled by the original disputants. So far as the records show, formal decisions by the committee were made in only four of these cases.

In New York, where the employers' association takes more responsibility than in Chicago, records show some two hundred questions up for conference between union and League representatives in the five years, July 1, 1934 to July 1, 1939. Discharge cases were the most numerous, numbering about sixty, while financial claims and questions of union jurisdiction each accounted for more than thirty cases. The others involved a wide variety of subjects, including issues over the manning of machines, wages, hours and other matters of individual complaints. The Typographical Union brought the largest number of complaints—more than eighty—and the Press Assistants were second with nearly sixty. The most frequent single issue was discharge or some other question under the Typographical Union priority law, which accounted for one fourth of all cases, one third of all joint committee cases, and four of the nine arbitrations during the period.

Ninety per cent of all cases were settled by informal conference, usually in the plant. Of the twenty-one more difficult issues which finally reached joint committees, nine were agreed upon by the committee, three were settled by concessions by the employers, and nine went to arbitration. Although neither side is entirely satisfied with the operation of the system in cases involving serious differences of opinion, the great majority of questions are settled with little difficulty. Long habits of peaceful adjustment based on common interest in the maintenance of the agreements operate here as in many other localities.[72]

Use of Arbitration

Although the industry has a strong preference for settling issues directly rather than by calling in outsiders, arbitration is used to settle disputes both under the agreements and over the terms of new agreements. While there are no complete statistics on the matter, it is clear that arbitration is less frequent now than twenty years ago. The International Printing Pressmen and Assistants' Union has a record of forty-three arbitration cases in the commercial printing industry from 1920 through 1939.[73] Twenty of these occurred in the first three years, and eight more in the next three years. Only seven occurred in the eight years from 1932 through 1939.

In Chicago the Franklin Association arbitrated questions of wage scales five times between 1918 and 1925, and the interpretation of an agreement once. Since 1925 all issues have been settled by negotiation. New York has made more use of arbitration. Between 1920 and 1929 it had twenty-nine cases, twenty-three of them involving wage scales. Sixteen of these occurred in the year from December 1920 to December 1921. From 1930 through July 1939 New York had thirty-two arbitrations, but only three involved wages, and these related to certain classes, not entire crafts. Sixteen were discharge disputes, four were issues on the complement of men, and nine others questions of the interpretation of agreements.

72. For a detailed analysis of the administration of agreements in New York, see Brown, "Joint Industrial Control in the Book and Job Printing Industry," pp. 103-118.

73. Twenty-four of these, and possibly more, involved the terms of new contracts, but it is not shown in which years these occurred. Forty-one cases involved wage scales. Other of the more important issues involved were hours in fourteen cases, manning of presses in ten, apprentices in six, discharge and layoff in five.

Washington is unusual in the extent to which arbitration is used to settle the terms of new contracts. Since the twenties most of its new agreements have been completed by arbitration of any issues on which the committees deadlocked, both groups finding this a useful way out. In general, however, the trend is in the opposite direction. Extensive use of arbitration from 1918 through 1921 reflected the difficulty of reaching agreement on wages at a time of rapid changes in the cost of living. Union dissatisfaction with the results contributed to the present preference for direct settlement by the parties concerned. But in all except very rare cases the industry still uses arbitration as a last resort instead of fighting out the issue by a strike.

C. WAGES AND HOURS

(1). *Trend of Hours*

Under this system of collective bargaining, there has been steady progress to shorter hours and only less so to higher wage rates. On the question of hours international union policy has been influential. The reduction from the ten-hour to the nine-hour day became general after the agreement between the United Typothetae of America and the international unions in 1898. In 1907, although the International Typographical Union had secured the eight-hour day in the offices with which it had agreements, the average of union rates of hours in book and job shops, for all crafts, was still a little over fifty-four a week. A rapid reduction in the next few years brought the average to about fifty-one, where it stood for a decade. The movement for the forty-four-hour week brought a small decline in 1920, and a sharp drop in 1921 to an average for all crafts of forty-five hours. The level was then stable at a little over forty-four until 1932.

Thereafter the policy of the international unions to bring about the shorter week by local agreements brought the reduction, not suddenly as in 1921, but gradually over a few years. By 1934 the average for all crafts was down to 40.6 hours, and a continuing downward drift brought it to 39.6 for 1939.[74] In this year 87.6

74. See index numbers of changes in union scales of hours and wage rates, U. S. Bureau of Labor Statistics, "Union Scales of Wages and Hours in the Printing

per cent of all union members in book and job printing had a forty-hour regular work week. Only 1.1 per cent in all the crafts had a longer week.[75] The International Typographical Union reported that on December 31, 1938 more than 90 per cent of its book and job members were under five-day-week plans.[76]

(2). Hourly and Weekly Wage Rates

The trend of union hourly wage rates [77] for the book and job printing crafts has been upward through all the years since 1907, with the exception of 1932 when there was a slight drop, and of 1933 when there was a substantial one. Starting with about 31.5 cents as the average for all crafts in 1907, the rates rose rapidly with the reduction of hours to eight, then slowly until the war, and rapidly during the years of rising prices from 1916 through 1920, when the average rate was about 80.5 cents per hour. A further increase in hourly rates to an average of 89 cents accompanied reduction of hours in 1921. Rates continued to rise during the 1920's to a peak of $1.07-1.08 in 1930–1932, and then dropped off in 1933 to $1.01. With the introduction of the forty-hour week, however, the upward trend in hourly wage rates was resumed, and in 1939 the average rate for all crafts stood at $1.135.[78]

Until the forty-hour week and the depression of the 1930's, increases in hourly rates tended to be more than sufficient to compensate for reductions in hours, and union rates per full-time week rose steadily. From an estimated average of $17.07 for all crafts in 1907, they reached $21.43 in 1913, $39.62 in 1920, and $47.58 in 1930, their peak. Depression wage cuts, combined with reduction

---

Trades, June 1, 1939," *Monthly Labor Review,* December 1939, p. 1487. The actual rates given above from 1924 on are from this report, p. 1506, and the earlier reports, "Union Scales of Wages and Hours of Labor." The rates for before 1924 have been computed by the application of the index numbers to the 1929 rates, the base.

75. *Monthly Labor Review,* December 1939, p. 1506.
76. ITU, *Bulletin,* February 1939, p. 27.
77. See *Monthly Labor Review,* December 1939, p. 1487.
78. *Ibid.,* pp. 1487, 1496. See note 74. The average rates given by the Bureau of Labor Statistics reflect changes in membership of the unions affected as well as in actual rates. Increased membership of the less skilled groups results in averages which underestimate slightly the actual changes in wages.

in hours, reduced the average to $41.91 in 1933, but by 1939 it had recovered to $44.94.[79] Comparison of these increases with changes in the cost of living [80] shows that from 1913 to 1920 real full-time wages dropped. The average weekly rates increased only 85 per cent while the cost of living increased more than 110 per cent. Thereafter, however, since living costs declined, the purchasing power of full-time wages increased. In 1930 full-time wages were 122 per cent above 1913, compared with a cost of living increase of 70 per cent. In June 1939 wages stood 109.7 per cent and cost of living 42.3 per cent above the 1913 levels. The union member who had full-time employment gained substantially. But the prevalence of short time, due to lack of work and work-sharing plans, made full-time wage rates mean little to a large number of the workers.[81]

Craft Differentials

In the process of local negotiation through which these wage rates are determined, differentials between the various crafts become firmly established. One craft's negotiation of an increase sets in motion a series of changes, and stability is attained only when "proper" differentials are again in force. An arbitration award or agreement with a single craft which upsets the accustomed structure of rates usually leads to serious unrest. Thus it is not surprising to find that the indexes of changes in wage rates for the separate crafts have moved closely together since 1907.[82] An exception is the more rapid rise of the rates of the lower paid workers, press assistants and bindery women, in the earlier years. The press assistants' rates dropped somewhat more than the others in 1933, but they have risen sharply since. The Typographical Union rates showed a substantial decline only in 1933, a year after average rates dropped in pressroom and bindery. Over the whole period

79. Computed from average rates of hours and hourly wage rates, above.
80. *Ibid.*, January 1940, p. 140.
81. The ITU estimates that for all its members, newspaper as well as book and job, the ratio of actual earnings to the full-time rate in 1939 was 79.5. Their average full-time rate was $46.71, and actual earnings were $37.14. (*Typographical Journal*, Supplement, August 1939, p. 133.) The lowest ratio was 65.7 in 1933, when actual earnings were $31.95.
82. *Monthly Labor Review*, December 1939, pp. 1489-1490.

pressmen gained slightly more than compositors. But these differences do not alter the long-run similarity in trends for all these crafts. Since 1929, only the photoengravers and the electrotypers have had increases in hourly wage rates sharply above those of the other crafts.

Geographical Differentials

Trends of wage rates by cities are significant because competition for large volumes of work, periodical, catalogue, book printing and binding and other large order jobs, is not limited to local markets. The trends for the whole industry are indicated by the union hourly rates for one key craft—hand compositors—in ten important cities.[83] Standing by themselves at the top since the war are the two biggest centers, New York and Chicago, and San Francisco, a strongly unionized city. Through the 1920's, union strength was less in most of the other cities than it had been previously, and the wage differentials between them and New York increased until 1932. The recent increase in union strength is reflected in the narrowing of the differentials.

In 1918 the lowest scales included in this group of cities—those in Baltimore and New Orleans—were 75 per cent of the New York rate. The four highest, New York's, Chicago's, San Francisco's and Denver's, were closely grouped, while the next highest, the St. Louis rate, was 90 per cent of New York's. In 1922 the lowest rate, New Orleans', was only 63 per cent, and in 1932 only 57 per cent, of New York's. In 1922 the St. Louis rate, first below the top three, stood at 82 per cent of New York's; in 1932 Washington's rate, now in fourth place, was only 77 per cent of New York's.

Later increases were less, proportionately, in the top three cities than in the others. So in 1935 Boston's rate, then the lowest, was 69 per cent of New York's and in 1939 the New Orleans rate, which had fallen to last place, was 70 per cent of the top. The

83. New York, Chicago, San Francisco, Washington, Philadelphia, Denver, St. Louis, Boston, Baltimore and New Orleans. Rates for the years 1907–1937 are found in U. S. Bureau of Labor Statistics reports, "Union Scales of Wages and Hours" and "Union Scales of Wages and Hours in the Printing Trades," May of each year; figures for June 1938 and 1939 from union agreements and bulletins.

fourth rate down, Washington's, was 83 per cent of New York's in 1935 and 87 per cent in 1939.

A similar significant trend shows in comparing the rates in a larger group of cities, including some large and many smaller places with large plants, which are strong competitors in national markets. Table 2 compares 1939 with 1929 union wage rates per

TABLE 2

UNION WAGE RATES PER WEEK IN COMPETING CENTERS, FOR HAND COMPOSITORS, CYLINDER PRESSMEN AND CYLINDER PRESS ASSISTANTS, 1939 AND 1929 [a]

City	Hand Compositors June 1939[b]	Hand Compositors June 1929[c]	Cylinder Pressmen January 1939[b]	Cylinder Pressmen January 1929[d]	Cylinder Press Assistants January 1939[b]	Cylinder Press Assistants January 1929[d]
New York	$54.50	$57.00	$54.50	$56.00	$43.00	$45.50
Chicago	54.00	54.00	54.00	51.00	46.25	43.25
Baltimore	40.00	40.00	31.53	37.84	24.26	29.11
Boston	42.40	42.24	42.40	43.50	36.80	39.50
Buffalo	44.00	44.00	42.00	40.00	32.00	30.00
Cincinnati	47.00	51.00	42.25	44.00	33.50	35.25
Cleveland	44.32—46.16[e]	49.00	44.92[e]	47.75	35.36[e]	37.75
Detroit	50.00	52.80	50.00	48.00	37.00	38.40
Philadelphia	46.60	39.45	45.20	40.33	36.00	35.00
St. Louis	44.08	45.32	45.37	46.65	35.52	37.40
Washington	44.25	45.00	42.00	42.00	35.50	35.60
Albany, N. Y.	48.00	48.00	48.00	46.00	35.45	32.00
Binghamton, N. Y.	45.00	43.00	—	35.00	—	24.00
Concord, N. H.	39.80	40.50	39.40	40.00	31.80	30.50
Dayton, Ohio	50.00[f]	46.00	48.00	41.80	36.00	30.00
Dunellen, N. J.	53.00	50.00	49.50	42.00	40.90	40.00
Harrisburg, Pa.	39.80	35.00	39.80	35.00	31.00	15.00
Indianapolis, Ind.	47.00	47.00	46.00	47.00	38.76	39.00
Kingsport, Tenn.	38.00	—	42.00	—	30.00	—
Mount Morris, Ill.	46.00	47.08	46.00	47.00	36.00	36.74
Nashville, Tenn.	36.00	38.00	38.00	38.00	26.00	26.25
New Haven, Conn.	40.00	38.00	40.00	35.00	24.00	22.50
Old Greenwich, Conn.	48.00[f]	38.00	42.00	—	30.00	—
Rahway, N. J.	49.50	46.00	—	46.00	—	37.50
Richmond, Va.	—	39.00	36.00	35.00	29.00	22.00
Rochester, N. Y.	44.00	45.00	44.00	41.00	30.80	30.24
St. Charles, Ill.	50.00[f]	—	51.47	—	43.05	—
Scranton, Pa.	45.20	46.00	42.30	44.00	31.30	30.50
Springfield, Ohio	48.00[f]	38.00	46.00[f]	35.00	34.00[f]	25.00
Stroudsburg, Pa.	43.10	—	43.00	—	32.00	—
York, Pa.	36.00	—	38.80	—	28.00	—

a. ITU, "Minimum Wage Scales of Typographical Unions," June 20, 1929, June 20, 1939; IPP&AU, "Weekly Wages of Local Unions, April 1929"; "Commercial Minimum Wage Scales, Hours and Working Conditions, May 1, 1939"; UTA, "Wage Scales Where Reported, May 15, 1929."
b. 40 hours.
c. 44 hours.
d. Hours not reported.
e. 36 or 37.5 hours.
f. Scale for one big plant.

week in thirty-one such competing centers, for hand compositors, cylinder pressmen and cylinder press assistants. It is clear that competitors outside the biggest centers in most cases have markedly lower scales. But efforts of the unions in the past decade to strengthen their organization and to pull up rates in the low-wage centers have noticeably narrowed the differentials. For each of the crafts in 1929 more than half of the centers had rates $10 or more below New York's. By 1939, however, a substantial upward movement had increased the number of centers with rates within $10 of New York's. For compositors there were only fourteen centers in 1939 with scales $10 or more below the New York scale, compared with twenty-three in 1929. For pressmen, there were eighteen centers in this class in 1939 and twenty-four ten years earlier. For press assistants the ratio was fifteen in 1939 to twenty in 1929.

Further evidence on wage differentials and the current trend towards their reduction is available in the reports of the Bureau of Labor Statistics on rates in seventy-two cities. On June 1, 1939 the average rates for all crafts in book and job printing varied from $1.23 an hour in the cities of over 1,000,000 population, to $.89 in cities between 100,000 and 250,000 in the South and Southwest, and $.92 in smaller cities of those areas.[84] From 1937 to 1939, years of rapid increase in union strength, the differences in the rates of increase in the various groups are significant. The two groups of largest cities, with populations of over 500,000, had only small average increases in rates, 1 and 3 per cent. Three groups of smaller cities had average increases of from 4.6 to nearly 6 per cent. The larger increases occurred chiefly in the North and on the Pacific Coast but in a few small southern cities gains were greater than elsewhere.[85] To sum up, while differentials are still substantial, the unions' efforts to pull up the lower rates have had considerable effect, especially in the medium-sized cities of the North and the Pacific Coast, and in certain very small places.

84. *Monthly Labor Review*, December 1939, p. 1501. The average for the smallest cities in the South does not include any bindery rates.
85. Percentages of increase computed from average rates per hour given by U. S. Bureau of Labor Statistics, *loc. cit.*, and "Union Scales of Wages and Hours in the Printing Trades, May 15, 1937," *Bulletin No. 655*, 1938, p. 21.

d. WORKING RULES

The highly detailed regulation of working conditions by book and job agreements has a twofold purpose: to protect and aid union members, and to protect the union plant by uniform conditions among competitors. Employers recognize the value of such competitive equality, but the "restrictive rules" are to them a more serious problem than wage rates, and are the chief basis of criticism of the unions.

Employers criticize these rules mainly on three grounds: the union-imposed, one-sided character of some of them; competitive inequalities as to rules between different localities; and the uneconomic and restrictive character of some of the rules themselves.

Many of the rules most criticized are embedded in international union law.[86] The International Typographical Union has a considerable number of such laws, with a firmly established policy that they must not be voided by local arbitration or negotiation. Among them are the forty-hour law, overtime regulations, cancellation of overtime by laying off and giving work to extras, a minimum of at least four hours when a man is called to work, apprenticeship regulations, a "struck work" clause and, more controversial, the priority law. The laws of the International Printing Pressmen and Assistants' Union contain less detailed regulation of local affairs, and in practice they are not rigidly exempt from local action; but they do include controversial rules on the manning of presses, the number of presses per foreman and "struck work." The International Brotherhood of Bookbinders has laws providing for the forty-hour, five-day week and relating to "struck work," jurisdiction over machines and the manning of certain machines.

On some of these laws there is no serious controversy. Typical contracts include a blanket provision for the inclusion of international, and sometimes local, union law in effect on the date of

86. The ITU for a time hesitated to legislate on matters affecting the internal affairs of printing offices, but a law to prohibit such legislation, passed in 1903, was repealed in 1904 (Tracy, *op. cit.*, pp. 551, 733, 766-770). Rather frequently in recent conventions, however, proposals for increased restrictions have been voted down on the ground that local unions should have autonomy on these points.

the agreement. In practice there is discussion as to whether certain laws are to be accepted and put into effect. As a matter of principle and backed by strong feeling on the effects of certain laws, employers protest union practice in passing a new law, then expecting it to be enforced in the plants without negotiation. One local employers' association a few years ago was invited to confer with the Laws Committee of the ITU, but rejected the invitation as "a little out of line." On numerous earlier occasions, employers' representatives have spoken at union conventions. Nevertheless, there has been no move as yet towards a solution through national bargaining. A compromise in the recent Chicago typographical agreement, however, provides that local and international union laws enacted after January 1, 1939 are to become effective "only by mutual agreement of both parties."

Inequalities of some of the rules as between competitors in different localities are a second serious grievance, especially to employers in the bigger cities. Local autonomy in bargaining results in lack of uniformity as to night differentials, overtime rates, the minimum day when a man is called to work, the manning of machines and priority. Moreover there is a distinct tendency for less rigid enforcement of rules in smaller jurisdictions, especially in large isolated plants where the common interest of employer and labor in preserving a favorable competitive position is easily seen by both. Employers' complaints against international law seem to be a plea for local autonomy; but the existing local autonomy leads to lack of uniformity of conditions among competitors. The bigger centers are handicapped both by their competitive disadvantages in rules and by the tendency towards more rigid enforcement.

Finally, employers criticize certain rules as definitely uneconomic and restrictive. The inflexibility which accompanies the very detailed regulation in these contracts is frequently a disadvantage. Extreme rigidity of jurisdictional lines between the crafts hampers operation, especially on the border lines of the less skilled work. Limitation on the number of apprentices, rules relating to the manning of presses and particularly the priority law have been sources of controversy.

(1). *The Priority Law*

The Typographical Union's priority law provides, in effect, that foremen may discharge for four reasons only: incompetence, neglect of duty, violation of office rules, and to decrease the force by letting off first the man with lowest priority standing. Reemployment also must be in order of priority. The Pressmen's and Bookbinders' Unions do not by law set up any such control over hiring and firing, although the Pressmen's laws include a provision that in general the last man on should be the first man off, and vice versa. Recently, however, an increased number of pressroom and bindery contracts provide for some form of priority, especially in large plants.[87]

Priority has been the subject of differences of opinion in the Typographical Union for many years. It was first adopted in 1892, but was not enforced in book and job shops until much later.[88] It was included in the contract in Chicago for the first time in 1922, and in New York in 1923. The New York employers accepted priority, with some misgivings, in the belief that it would reduce the bidding up of premium wages by making it less easy for men to change jobs in a time of labor shortage. The union has argued that a strict priority law is essential to prevent partiality or arbitrary action by foremen in filling positions. The law has strong support also as a protection of the jobs of older men who might be displaced by young and faster operators when jobs are scarce. Finally, it is a clear-cut rule which is easily enforceable and thus avoids danger of political influences in the union affecting the job security of members.

On the whole the Pressmen's and Bookbinders' Unions have not been interested in priority. They point out that since the work in pressroom and bindery is more varied than in the composing room, workers are less often interchangeable. The skilled man therefore does not need the protection of priority, nor in most cases would it be feasible to attempt it. The older man has ad-

---

87. The U. S. Bureau of Labor Statistics in 1939 found seniority provisions in 317 of the 484 typographical contracts analyzed, but in only 25 of 172 pressroom agreements, and in only 9 of 54 for bookbinders, 7 of 66 for photoengravers, and 10 of 92 for stereotypers and electrotypers.

88. Tracy, *op. cit.*, pp. 453, 466; Stevens, *op. cit.*, pp. 529-532.

vantages of skill, acquired through his longer experience, which are more than enough to counteract any slowing down because of age. Protection against discriminatory discharge is possible by other means.

Nevertheless, recent developments have made these unions look more favorably upon seniority provisions. Technical changes, which have somewhat reduced the advantage of the old experienced man, plus severe unemployment, make some members envy the security given by the priority law in the composing room. Moreover, in the big pressrooms and binderies, where considerable groups of workers perform the same class of work, it is more feasible to operate, in part at least, on a seniority basis. When these large plants are isolated in small towns there is a strong case for protection of seniority rights, since the only jobs are those in the one plant. Seniority provisions have become very general in these big plants, in contrast to the situation in the older areas with many smaller shops.[89]

Employers in many of the older centers make a strong case against the priority law as enforced in their composing rooms: it interferes with the efficiency of operations by preventing the selection of the best men in the case of either a reduction or an expansion, and it creates a serious problem of the superannuated in a plant with an old force. Moreover, the protection is so complete, and proof of incompetency so difficult, that it lessens the incentive for efficiency. Discharge, they say, is "almost impossible." In addition, the priority law—and at this point many younger men in the union agree—restricts the opportunities of the good man, and makes it more difficult for an unemployed man to find work in other cities.

While not essentially different from that in other cities, the situation in New York brings these problems into high relief. With the age of union members increasing because the industry has decreased in volume, both a heavy unemployment list and an urgent need for increased efficiency appear. Frequent controversies over discharge result.[90]

89. Frequently seniority rights are combined with work-sharing arrangements.
90. See p. 152.

Priority is an issue on which rigid application of international union law fails to meet the needs of either side. The legitimate demand of the union members for security comes into conflict with the necessity for efficient operation; but only efficient plants can compete successfully for jobs, and only the plant or local industry successful in competition can provide security. Sometimes union leaders recognize this problem and apply the priority law with moderation, admitting special cases and permitting selection on the basis of competency. Occasionally provision is made for cooperation to retire old men on a union pension or to provide a reduced scale for superannuated men. But the problem remains a serious one in many areas.

(2). *Manning of Machines*

A second group of controversies concerns the manning of machines. It is generally accepted that the agreements should establish a minimum standard, both for protection of the workers and for uniformity between competitors. Conflicts of interest nevertheless occur, owing to the need of employers for economic operation in a highly competitive industry and the need of the unions for more jobs for their members, especially when machines are displacing men and the industry is depressed. Jurisdictional conflicts between unions over the existing jobs sometimes complicate issues. In many localities these matters are worked out in negotiations without any serious continuing problems, but difficulties have been recurrent especially in the larger cities.

The technical revolution in the pressrooms in the past thirty years has upset old relationships and made the manning of presses one of the most controversial problems in the industry. Not only have hand feeders been eliminated, but the "press assistants," as the feeders are now called, are coming into competition with pressmen for certain jobs, and are losing their position as a distinct group. Press assistants are decreasing in number and pressmen increasing. This displacement of assistants occurred in both union and nonunion shops in New York from 1924 to 1929.[91]

91. Elizabeth Faulkner Baker, *Displacement of Men by Machines*, Columbia University Press, New York, 1933, p. 104.

The traditional complement of men on cylinder presses has been one pressman to two presses, with a press feeder for each press. On the whole the same ratio has been kept on these presses now that they have automatic feeding attachments. But in Washington an agreement permits the operation of two such presses with a single assistant. On big periodical presses, requiring a larger crew, there have been controversies. In New York during the 1920's concessions were made by the unions in some cases, but big periodical jobs were lost to the city because requirements were beyond those in competing plants. In several cases arbitration decisions reduced the complement of men.[92] In two such decisions, one by William M. Leiserson in 1928 and one by Morris L. Cooke in 1930, it was urged that the industry find ways to cooperate to solve the problem of the need of security for the men and of efficient operation for the plants.

The most serious controversies now are over the manning of the small, fast, automatic cylinder presses, already important in the 1920's and increasingly so in the 1930's. In open shops they tend to be operated by a skilled pressman with the aid of some unskilled boys. In union plants the system varies in different localities, depending largely upon the strength and independence of the press assistants' union.[93] Competitive inequalities which result are a substantial grievance to employers in the big cities.

In New York the controversies which began with the introduction of automatic press feeders were accentuated by the development of small automatic presses and the loss of large periodical work from the city. Faced by a serious unemployment problem, the press assistants' union fought every effort to reduce the claims of its members to jobs.[94] The pressmen agreed with the employers to

92. *Ibid.*, pp. 152-160.
93. In some cases these presses have been run by a union pressman with the aid, if needed, of only a nonunion boy. The more usual arrangement is a pressman and a press assistant to two presses. In some cases the employers favor "unit operation," that is, the operation of one press by a pressman without an assistant. The policy of the International Printing Pressmen and Assistants' Union calls for the employment of an assistant if two or more of these presses are used, or in some cases one pressman per press without an assistant.
94. See Baker, *op. cit.*, Chapters 6-8, for a detailed account of these controversies to 1932; also Brown, "Joint Industrial Control in the Book and Job Printing Industry," pp. 95-97.

operate certain presses without an assistant, but their international president ruled that this was an encroachment on the jurisdiction of the assistants and permissible only in the case of an odd press. Bitter controversies have continued between the press assistants and the pressmen and employers. Concessions have been made on certain presses. In the 1937 contract a provision was made for a Pressroom Commission, made up of members of the Printers' League and the various pressroom unions, to study questions of economical press operation, but the effort was without result. Conferences between international officers of the union, local officers and the League also failed to find a solution.

The necessary adjustments to changes in technology in the pressrooms are difficult when there are two or three separate unions, of pressmen, assistants, and even paper handlers, all in the same international union but each attempting to protect jobs for its members. Where there is a single pressroom union it is easier to agree on efficient operating methods and at the same time give the more able assistants a chance to become apprentice pressmen.[95] In New York promotion from press assistants' union to pressmen's union is not easy, since the pressmen are more concerned with their own unemployed than with the need of an outlet for the assistants. The "feeder problem" appears insoluble where the only way out is for the men to fight for their jobs and existence as a union.

(3). *Apprenticeship Regulation*

Limitation of the number of apprentices is another subject of criticism by employers who are concerned over the future supply of skilled labor in the industry. In recent years some employers have encountered great difficulty in inducing unions to indenture apprentices. Nevertheless, the unions have for many years made a real contribution to the industry by establishing training standards, giving correspondence courses and supervising apprentices. In many localities the apprentice system is under the joint control of unions and employers; sometimes, as in New York, with the co-

---

95. The IPP&AU is encouraging such amalgamation. The number of assistants' unions decreased from sixteen in 1929 to ten in 1939.

operation of the Board of Education they maintain a school for apprentices. But it has often been the employers' lack of interest which has hampered union efforts to train an adequate supply of skilled labor.

Union limitation of the number of apprentices has two purposes. The first is to insure adequate all-round training. The unions have been very critical of the open shops, which in many cases use large numbers of so-called apprentices and turn out partly trained men. The second purpose is to limit the numbers so that all will be able to find a place in the industry. During the depression years, therefore, it was not surprising that fewer apprentices were registered.

The apprentice ratios are determined locally and very widely. Seldom, if ever, are they based on a thorough study of the needs of the industry. The constitution of the International Printing Pressmen and Assistants' Union calls for working out ratios after a locality has been surveyed to determine the replacement or expansion needs of the industry, but this is more a pious hope than an actuality. The International Typographical Union at its 1939 convention adopted a new provision establishing a general ratio.[96] Employers point to this as an unemployment-inspired restriction, rather than one based on a long-run view of the needs of the industry. They are worried by the fact that in no year since 1931 has the number of youths admitted to journeyman membership equaled the number of deaths.[97] Although many skilled men are now unemployed, provision for meeting the future needs of the industry for trained workers has not been assured.

e. UNION POLICIES AND THEIR EFFECTS

Unquestionably, individual restriction of output is in the union

96. *Typographical Journal,* Supplement, September 1939, pp. 140-142. The ratio established is one apprentice to two journeymen, one for each additional five until four apprentices are employed, then one to each additional ten journeymen. The locals may limit the total number of apprentices in any office to less than four.

97. From 1930 through 1938 there were 10,492 deaths of union members, while 8,345 apprentices were admitted to journeyman membership (ITU, *Bulletin,* October 1938, p. 225; *Typographical Journal,* Supplement, August 1939, p. 164). In 1931, 16 per cent of the members were sixty years of age or over; in 1939 the percentage was 20. *Ibid.,* Supplement, August 1931, p. 48, August 1939, p. 98.

tradition. Union members feel it contrary to the interest of the whole group to set a pace which others cannot follow without undue strain. The "swift" is unpopular. The Typographical Union's opposition to piece scales stems from this feeling.

On the other hand, the unions have frequently expressed interest in cooperation for efficient production, and showed recognition of the problems of management. A few comments will illustrate:

> If the International Typographical Union cannot improve upon the standard of competency prevailing in the nonunion composing room, what advantage or inducement has the union to offer the nonunion employer to unionize his plant? [98]

> Where we have established satisfactory collective bargaining relations with employers, so that records of operating expenses may be freely discussed in conference between management and union representatives, our members are in position to cooperate to improve efficiency. . . . [99]

> We have proved the genuineness of our intentions through our schools, our correspondence courses and apprenticeship arrangements. . . . We negotiate contracts to increase productivity and to improve quality. In the negotiation of our contracts we accept the fact that we can't take out of industry more than we put into it, that its prosperity is essential to our prosperity.[100]

The constructive work of the unions on apprenticeship gives support to these statements. In addition, the Pressmen's Union is doing outstanding service through its Technical Trade School which gives advanced training on presswork, and makes the results of its technical research available both to employers and union workers. Its periodical, *The American Pressman,* besides being a trade-union organ, is reputed to be the best technical paper in the field of presswork. Through its work for improving methods and for increasing the individual skill of its members, this union is a genuinely progressive force in the industry.

Employers' experience differs widely on the question of whether union workers cooperate for efficiency. In many cases employers

---

98. *Ibid.,* Supplement, August 1930, p. 36; also Supplement, August 1937, p. 12.
99. *International Bookbinder,* January-February 1938, p. 6.
100. *American Pressman,* January 1939, p. 14.

have convinced their men of the common interest in efficient, low-cost production, with good results.[101] On the other hand, many employers feel that they have serious grievances on these points. Sometimes, without doubt, in this industry of many small plants, inefficient employers put upon the union the blame that belongs upon management itself.[102] There are cases, however, where efforts of employers to bring about a real consideration of problems of management by the unions have failed; the Pressroom Commission in New York is an example. In the big city with its many plants and thousands of workers, it is especially difficult to secure active consideration of the common interest of unions and employers in efficient production.

Effects on Costs

Through their shop rules, policies and practices, the unions tend in some ways to increase costs, in others to decrease them. Influences towards increased costs come from improvements in standards for the protection of workers, such as payment for overtime, which are generally regarded as reasonable if all plants are on an equal basis. They come also from less defensible rules which hamper efficiency—rigid jurisdictional lines, excessive complements of men, unreasonably enforced priority rules.

Counteracting these are influences which may even reduce costs. When a nonunion plant is unionized, the result is likely to be an improvement in production methods. While some nonunion plants succeed by their unusual efficiency, it is probably true that on the whole management efficiency is relatively low in such plants. The necessity of paying higher wages on a union basis forces management out of its comfortable rut, induces careful selection of the more efficient workers, better organization of production, more prompt layoff when work is not available,[103] more frequent pur-

101. See, for example, John F. Cuneo, "Getting Along with the Unions," *American Pressman*, August 1940, pp. 30-31.
102. See the bitter complaints of a pressman about a poorly managed pressroom, *ibid.*, January 1937, p. 21.
103. The experience is rather general in this industry that in open shops employees are given more regular work, while in organized plants pay is higher but layoffs are more prompt.

chase of new equipment, and a general increase in the efficiency of operations. In at least some cases, the fact that the unions are recognized promotes good morale in the departments and a cooperative spirit rather than one of jealous individual competition. Cooperation in production is the natural result. But the net effect on costs in any one case cannot be predicted. It depends upon local situations, union leaders, the individual union members, and whether the individual employer exercises the all-important leadership which his position makes possible.

f. COMPETITION

The highly competitive character of this industry brings about what at first glance may seem to be a curious result. Employers, who on some points are highly critical of the unions, look to them for help in the solution of one of their most serious problems—cutthroat competition. Nonunion employers, in accepting unionization, have in many cases hoped for some advantage in the long run from the union influence towards stabilization of the industry.

There is little doubt that the unions help in local competition. Wages are about 30 per cent of sales of job printers.[104] Materials, which average about 35 per cent, are fairly uniform in price. Stabilization of labor costs by equalization of wages and working conditions must therefore have substantial influence in reducing extreme competition. The extent of this influence depends upon whether an open-shop sector can operate at lower labor standards and upon the success of the unions in maintaining their standards in the union section of the local industry.

When the unions are strong enough, as now, to be a threat to the open shops, union standards tend to be followed there. Enforcement in the union shops depends upon the union's activity in policing the industry. Enforcement is more difficult, and therefore less complete, when there are a great many small shops, when there is much unemployment, when the organization is new and both unionists and union employers are inexperienced in living

---

104. UTA, *Ratios for Printing Management for the Year 1938*, p. 51. The ratio varies among branches of the industry. For periodical printers, whose customers supply paper, wages may run to 65 per cent of sales.

under union standards, and when union standards are very high. Some or all of these conditions, in most areas, prevent complete enforcement. Nevertheless, employers usually agree with the unions that the local competitive condition is sounder when the unions are strong.

In the increasingly important wider competition, inequalities between labor costs of union and nonunion areas, and among union areas, are of great consequence. Disparities between the wage rates of the big cities and other localities have been noted. When only union sections of the industry reduce hours, as happened in 1921, union plants are at a serious competitive disadvantage. Add to these inequalities union rules more severe than in competing plants, and the balance is tipped far enough to take substantial amounts of work from the old centers to others where work is produced more cheaply. While high labor costs were not the only reasons for the loss of work from New York, for instance, in the 1920's and 1930's, they contributed to the movement.[105] A large volume of work moves rather easily from one center to another, and competitive inequalities in labor costs stimulate such movements.

Unions as well as employers are fully aware of this fact now. International union efforts are directed towards equalizing competitive conditions in different localities. The desirability of equalizing wages has been discussed ever since the journeymen printers' first convention in 1850, which led to organization of the National Typographical Union. Recently much attention has been given to the possibility of regional scales, and in some areas rates are related to the scales of the near-by big city.[106] Increasing union strength has narrowed wage differentials between large and small cities. So long as the gap remains, however, it tends to help the low wage areas in competition and to hold back the upward movement of standards in the big centers. The conflicts of interest between the two types of areas are as obvious to union members as to employers. Those who benefit competitively from lower stand-

[105]. See pp. 120-121, 157-159.
[106]. For example, San Francisco scales set the standard for much of northern California. Certain towns near New York and Chicago base their rates upon those of the metropolis. See *Typographical Journal*, November 1939, p. 570.

ards wish to preserve their advantage. Neither international unions nor national employers' organizations want to go the whole way towards equalizing conditions. But union influence is strongly towards reduction of extreme disparities in wages and other conditions.

5. Experience with Other Methods of Collective Bargaining

The results of trade-union collective bargaining in book and job printing are emphasized further by comparison with other experience. In three localities the industry has experimented with a new form of employee representation as a solution of the labor problems of a highly competitive industry. A fourth city has an independent industrial union.

Company unions in separate plants have been relatively unimportant in this industry. The Bureau of Labor Statistics in 1935 found only twelve company unions out of 723 book and job plants, five of them connected with the group plans to be discussed below.[107] A number of plans were successful barriers to the attempts of the unions to organize. Others have been replaced by union collective bargaining. In several cases, plans set up while the unions were attempting to organize in 1937 have been ordered disestablished by the National Labor Relations Board.

Employee Representation Plans

The American Guild of the Printing Industry in Baltimore, the Graphic Arts Industrial Federation of Boston, and the Open Shop Council Plan of the Edition Bookbinders of New York were employee representation plans covering local groups of plants. There were thirteen plants under the Baltimore plan, sixty-eight at first and about forty later in Boston, and seventeen larger plants in New York, later reduced to ten by dissolutions, resignations and removals from the city. The plans were alike in that they were organized by employers in 1921 or 1922 at the time of the fight

---

107. "Characteristics of Company Unions, 1935," *Bulletin No. 634*, 1938, pp. 44, 73.

against the forty-four-hour week and for the open shop. These employers attempted to insure the success of their open-shop policies by giving their employees what they hoped would prove an acceptable substitute for unionism. The plans included insurance features to replace union financial benefits and set up standards for wages, hours and working conditions.

Quite to the surprise of most observers, probably also the originators, the plans survived for more than fifteen years. The New York bookbinders' plan ended in 1937, after the Bookbinders' Union won National Labor Relations Board elections by large majorities in several plants. Closed-shop contracts were then made with this union for the men workers and one group of skilled women members. The American Guild in Baltimore ceased operations as a collective bargaining agency after an order of the NLRB in 1938. In 1940 an intensive organization campaign conducted by the allied printing crafts resulted in successful NLRB elections in several plants, and a joint contract between the three major unions and a newly organized employers' association, the Graphic Arts League.[108] The Boston plan became inactive after its last meeting in 1937, although in 1939 it still existed on paper and as a social organization.

Despite differences in detail, all of these plans provided for a plant organization to handle local matters and for a board of representatives of employees and employers to act on general problems and appeals from the plants.[109] In Boston and New York the employee representatives met separately before meeting the employers. The joint meetings were held regularly in those two cities, less regularly in Baltimore. Wage scales, standards of hours and provisions for overtime payment were adopted, and wage adjustments were made at various times. Apprenticeship plans were adopted in Baltimore and New York. Baltimore worked on an elaborate plan for classification and rating of employees, in connection with their wage scale which was a "normal" rather than a

108. *Typographical Journal,* May 1940, p. 656; Supplement, August 1940, p. 164; *American Pressman,* Supplement, September-October 1940, p. 1-14.
109. For the first seven years, those of greatest activity, see Brown, "Joint Industrial Control in the Book and Job Printing Industry," Chapters 2-4.

minimum scale, and finally set up a classification board, which acted on a few cases. Boston had a cooperative buying plan, and its winter bowling programs gave an important opportunity for employee contacts which sustained interest in the Graphic Arts Industrial Federation. The shop organizations to deal with problems within the plants functioned not at all in some plants, more in others, and on the whole still more in the bigger New York plants where there were regular monthly meetings.

These plans all had considerable success in establishing standards for the local market in the early years when employers were interested and anxious to prevent the return of the unions, and workers were willing to try this substitute for unionism. Later, in time of depression, the lack of force behind the organizations made the standards much less effective. A wage cut was finally adopted in New York, while in Baltimore the control of rates lapsed for a time. In Boston a reduction was, in effect, accepted by the Joint Industrial Board. Testimony from all the cities indicates that uniform standards were not effectively maintained from that time.

Whether individual employees dared to raise questions over violations of the standards was a crucial question. In the early years a considerable number of individual grievances were remedied through the organizations. Later much depended upon the courage of the worker, and there can be no doubt that many individuals and employee representatives feared reprisals from foremen if they raised questions. In spite of the good faith of leading employers, these organizations gave only limited protection to employees in the years of depression. Employees on the whole did not use the organizations as much as they might have, had they had more faith in them. The success of the plans depended less upon employee initiative than upon employer interest at first and the threat of union activity later.

Independent Industrial Unionism in Rochester

A different type of experiment is the Rochester Printing Crafts Association, an independent industrial union. Rochester had been for the most part open shop since 1921. In 1933 employees in the book and job shops began an organization movement. Because of the severe unemployment at the time, the unions were hesitant to admit new members. They encouraged the organization of an independent industrial union, which succeeded in getting recognition and a contract from fourteen plants, covering the major part of the industry in the city. This agreement, renewed several times, regulated wages, hours and overtime, but included fewer details on shop practices than is usual in printing trades agreements. It covered all crafts. Grievances were to be adjusted by the shop chairman or officers of the Association and the employer, with resort to arbitration if necessary.

For seven years this Association has set the standards for the Rochester printing industry through its agreements. At the beginning its rates were higher than the existing union rates, which later were raised to this level. It was tolerated if not welcomed by the employers. It has been able to adjust grievances and secure redress in cases of violation of the agreements. The fact that all crafts have worked together has aided the weaker crafts especially. But the membership has recognized that the organization is weak because of nonaffiliation with other organizations and lack of strong financial backing and that it exists because of employer toleration. It has not therefore tried to enforce its conditions rigidly.

When the international unions wished to take over the organization in 1938, the Association was willing to hear their story. The unions proposed that individual members affiliate with their craft organizations, but that the Rochester Association continue to function as a local unit and to make a single contract for all crafts. After considerable discussion, a vote showed 116 to 94 against affiliation with the internationals. Soon after in one of the larger plants, a National Labor Relations Board election resulted in a union victory, but in a smaller one the Association won. In the plant which voted union, a contract was negotiated jointly for all the crafts and signed by the group of unions. To the group as a whole at this time, the value of industrial organization and a local arrangement seemed more important than the advantages of increased strength from affiliation. But the situation still remains unstable.[110]

Employee Representation Plans and the Independent Versus the Trade Unions

The weaknesses of both this independent industrial union and the city-wide employee representation plans are evident from a comparison with the trade unions. Although they have succeeded within limits both in setting standards and in protecting individuals from violations, they are essentially dependent upon the employers. Even the greater independence and greater employee initiative of the Rochester organization do not conceal the fact that it can gain only what employers are willing to concede, that it lacks the stronger collective bargaining weapons of the trade union. As agencies for democratic participation in the making of decisions and for protection of the rights of workers, these organizations are far less effective than the unions. Their lack of strength results in general standards of wages, hours and conditions lower than those in strongly unionized towns, and on the whole less completely enforced. As to working conditions, these systems have the strength of their weakness; they are less inclined to impose rules which are rigid, inflexible or uneconomic from the standpoint of the competitive needs of the local industry. But because of their incomplete enforcement, they are less effective than the unions in stabilizing local competition. They can have no effect upon competitive conditions in a wider market, other than what they themselves, by their lower standards, contribute to competitive inequalities for the country as a whole.

6. Conclusions

The values of trade-union collective bargaining to labor and to employers in the book and job printing industry are implicit in much that has been said, and need only summary. To labor the system means a clearly established status in the industry, protection of individual rights, adjustment of differences by peaceful

---

110. *Typographical Journal*, Supplement, August 1939, pp. 35-38; *International Bookbinder*, September-October 1940, p. 100.

means, and participation in a democratic process through which matters of vital concern are decided. Workers gain a considerable measure of security through protection of their jobs, as well as through union financial benefits and improvements in their wages, hours and working conditions.

To employing-printers collective bargaining means a well-established, functioning system for the adjustment of differences, which promotes a self-respecting, friendly relationship between workers and management. It gives security against interruption of operations, and stability of labor costs for definite periods. By equalizing labor conditions in the local market, it promotes a sound basis for competition in a highly competitive industry. While in the national market the strongly organized centers are put at a disadvantage in some respects by competitive inequalities, recently increased union strength is leveling up the standards in other centers. Further, the unions make available to employers a supply of skilled labor, and make it unnecessary for the plant to maintain its own labor reserve. The union apprenticeship systems contribute to the replenishment of this supply. Finally, union pressure, which forces employers to become more efficient, is a salutary if not an entirely welcome influence in the industry.

Problems Resisting Solution

But there are serious problems for both groups in the industry, which in spite of long experience, collective bargaining has as yet been unable to solve. The first set comprises unemployment and individual insecurity, arising from depression, geographical shifts of the industry and, for some groups, technological change. Union efforts to deal with these problems lead at times to such uneconomic action as unduly rigid application of the priority law and excessive complements of men. Increased costs, competitive inequalities, loss of business and increased local unemployment are inevitable results. Only an expansion of volume in the industry could solve this problem of insecurity. No method of joint attack upon this basic problem has been found.

A second set of problems affects relations among the workers. Traditional craft unionism which binds the common interests of one group, has not solved the problems of how to insure harmony and cooperation between different crafts, or of how to extend the protection of unionism to less skilled workers.[111] Where there are large groups of the unskilled without organization, the situation is unstable.

Finally, there are questions as to the effect of collective bargaining on the economic position of the industry as a whole—on costs, prices, the volume of production and employment, and the incomes of employers and wage earners. We have seen that with rare exceptions, unions in this industry have a good record for observance of their agreements. But is the record as good in regard to economic responsibility, that is, responsibility for the effects of demands and policies? There is some basis for charges of economic irresponsibility in the maintenance of union standards in the larger cities far above those in competing areas while work continued to leave these cities. A disproportionate unemployment burden in New York, for instance, is connected with such policies.[112]

Union Responsibility

There are a number of hindrances to economically responsible collective bargaining on the part of the unions. One lies in craft autonomy. Since each craft sees itself as only a part of the industry, the final effect of increased costs resulting from its demands is not always clear enough to affect its action in negotiations. Moreover, in local typographical unions newspaper members vote on matters affecting job agreements, although there is no basis in their own economic interest for responsibility towards the job industry. Employers in many cities are much concerned over this problem. In contrast, in rare cases where the unions negotiate as a group, as in St. Louis, it is easier to see the problem as a whole, and to take action in the light of the probable effects of changes upon the entire industry.

The fact that agreements usually cover a diverse group of em-

---

111. See discussion, pp. 134 ff., 141-142.
112. Other causes for the migration of the industry, in addition to labor costs, have been mentioned on p. 121.

ployers in the local market, rather than single companies, also creates difficulty. In the case of a single big plant, or a small group of employers, changes in the volume of work are known to every journeyman and influence the character of the union demands. In the big city, on the other hand, the effects of changes in costs upon the ability of employers to compete, and therefore upon the volume of employment in all plants, are far from obvious. The agreement affects a large number of employers with widely differing conditions, some making profits, some not. Which firms should be considered typical? The problem is so complex that often it is avoided; and as a result unions frequently give inadequate attention to the effect of their proposals upon the competitive position of the local industry.

Furthermore union members often lack adequate knowledge of the economics of the industry upon which to base their decisions. Proposals by employers for joint study of the problems of the local industry have had little result. Attempts by employers themselves to put economic information before the rank and file have naturally enough aroused union suspicion and resentment. Union officers usually have a better understanding of local problems than the rank and file, but how to inform the membership adequately of the facts involved is unsolved. Union members, as a result, often underestimate the economic difficulties of their employers.

These are problems of a functioning democracy and its leadership. In a democratically run union, local leadership often has an extremely rapid turnover. A leader has only time to begin to acquire knowledge of the problems involved and to become a good negotiator with real understanding of the economics of the industry as it affects the welfare of his members, when he is displaced by an inexperienced man. Then too, only a man of unusual courage will take the risk of telling his members unpopular facts. This is true especially in the big locals, where the great mass do not attend meetings, and where policy tends to be decided by a small group of the more militant members. The referendum, well established in these unions, is a safeguard, but its use does not solve the problem of the lack of information by members on these complicated questions. In some smaller locals a recent development is a system of fines for nonattendance at meetings. This is useful in insuring that members know what is going on and keep control of their organization.

Employer Responsibility
There are also hindrances to responsible collective bargaining on the side of the employers. Sometimes they fail to accept the unions as a permanent factor in the industry, and therefore miss an opportunity to develop cooperation. Often they promote the separatist tendencies of the craft unions, and so fail to get from the local unions consideration of the problems of the industry as a whole. Frequently employers do not accept their own responsibility for making collective bargaining work, are unwilling to give it the necessary time and energy and fail to take their opportunity for education of the unions in the problems of management. The weakness of the organizations of employers is pertinent here. In many cases they are not prepared as a group to deal with the union organizations on a basis of equality.

Union complaints that they are not given full financial information are largely justified. In the case of a group of competitors, negotiating in a group, this is a difficult but not insoluble problem. In a few cases outside accountants have made studies of the books of a group of companies for use in arbitration cases. But more usually discussion is only in general terms of economic trends and conditions. Among large companies, which negotiate separately, the situation is different; in many cases information on profits and other business conditions is available to the negotiators, or is used in arbitration proceedings.

Encouraging Signs
More could be done advantageously by both sides in thorough studies of the economic needs of the industry, locally or nationally, as a basis for the joint decisions on wages and conditions which are so vital in their effects on both groups. There are encouraging signs. One is the study of the economics of the industry by the international unions. The International Typographical Union through its Statistical Bureau gathers and publishes economic

data, from government and other sources, of interest to local unions in their negotiations. The International Printing Pressmen and Assistants' Union goes further. Its Research Division conducts a continuing economic study of the union's own materials. From government data and other sources it publishes a Bulletin for the local unions, and helps to provide the factual basis necessary for successful collective bargaining.[113]

The international officers of the printing trades unions also exert their influence upon consideration of the needs of the industry. Employers pay tribute to their intelligence, honesty, broad view and cooperation on many problems.[114] Often international officers exert a restraining influence upon locals which are ready to indulge in action that appears unwise to the international, although there is a question as to how far an officer will go in unpopular action.

Another favorable factor is the growth of the employers' associations. Increased union strength plays the traditional role of forcing employers to get together and to give more time to labor problems. Strong organization on both sides, necessary for thorough joint consideration of the problems of the industry, is more common. For the first time, a national organization really representative of the closed-shop part of the industry is in existence— the Printers' National Association. While most of the industry wants to preserve local autonomy, it is beginning to be said that there is a place for national action on some of these problems.

Expansion or Stabilization?

A final issue, an important test of economic responsibility, is whether collective bargaining in the long run will promote expansion or stabilization in the industry. In many cities the employers' associations had hoped that the increase in union strength would help the old stabilization program. But these programs often disregard the fact that much of the industry suffers from in-

113. See Phillips L. Garman, "Why Collective Bargaining Has Become So Effective and Important to Wage Earners," in *Fifty-Third Anniversary Publication, Franklin Union No. 4,* Chicago, 1939.
114. See *American Pressman,* Fiftieth Anniversary Number, October 1939, pp. 37-39.

efficiency and unduly high costs and prices as well as from low profits. A stabilization program that protects the inefficient can only maintain costs and prices at unduly high levels and keep volume unnecessarily low. Such a program, carried on with union help, must result in less employment than would otherwise be possible.

On the other hand, some union leaders see the desirability of increasing efficiency and are ready to cooperate in the interest of lower prices and an expansion of volume. If employers' associations follow a policy of expansion, they should be able to induce the unions to cooperate in promoting the interests of all in the industry through lower prices to increase volume and therefore employment.

The unions in this industry have been pioneers in organization and collective bargaining. The value of collective bargaining to both employers and workers is so great that there is every expectation of its continuance and expansion. Many of the problems are those of a mature system which developed under somewhat different and simpler conditions than today. Local collective bargaining through a series of strong craft unions suited the conditions of a localized, small-scale industry, manned by highly skilled craftsmen. It remains to be seen whether this mature system of industrial government can adjust itself to the different needs of full and successful collective bargaining in an industry still highly competitive, but more efficient, producing by modern large-scale, low cost methods, and selling increasingly in nation-wide markets.

Chapter 4

BUILDING CONSTRUCTION [1]

WILLIAM HABER
Assisted by ROBERT WINTERS as Field Agent

1. INTRODUCTION

COLLECTIVE BARGAINING is a long-established institution in the building industry. Such basic issues as recognition, the trade agreement, and the closed shop have been widely accepted for many years. With certain notable exceptions, union conditions have for over half a century provided the dominant pattern for industrial government. The trade agreement has furnished the terms of employment and procedures for settling hundreds of problems which characterize employer-employee relations in this industry. Hourly wages have been steadily increased, and are now higher than in most trades. A working day of eight hours, or less, is the general rule.

But despite wide union organization and long collective bargaining experience in many localities, industrial relations in the building trades are still disturbed and there is much evidence of discord. Collective bargaining has not always brought industrial peace and stability. Jurisdictional disputes have often provoked needless and expensive strikes—in spite of trade agreements and tested ways and means for settling such disputes. High hourly rates have not brought high annual incomes. On the contrary, it has often been argued that these rates, together with exorbitant

---

1. For a more complete discussion of this industry, see William Haber, *Industrial Relations in the Building Industry,* Harvard University Press, Cambridge, 1930; Royal E. Montgomery, *Industrial Relations in the Chicago Building Trades,* University of Chicago Press, Chicago, 1927; and Frederick L. Ryan, *Industrial Relations in the San Francisco Building Trades,* University of Oklahoma Press, Norman, 1935. See also *Hearings Before the Temporary National Economic Committee,* Pt. 11, "Construction Industry," 1939.

financing costs and frequently pegged prices of materials, are directly responsible for the high building costs which cut down employment and yearly earnings. Such uneconomic and restrictive practices as "collusive agreements," price fixing, and restrictions on and prevention of the use of new materials and improved methods of construction, have been rather common.

Regardless of whether these practices are the exception or the rule, the industry has often been under public displeasure because of them. They have recently been the subject of indictments obtained by the Department of Justice under the antitrust laws.[2] In addition charges of graft and corruption against unions or contractors have occasionally led to legislative and grand jury investigations.[3] Attempts to unseat the unions have provoked costly strikes and produced an aggressive union leadership, suspicious of any proposals which might infringe upon its powers and prestige.

Most of the industry's problems arise from the economic or technological environment in which building construction is carried on. Building operations are highly seasonal. In spite of new methods which make a twelve-month building year practicable except for small operations, winter work is uncommon. Handicraft methods still prevail on dwellings and small buildings, and, even on the largest construction jobs, in important trades like carpentry and bricklaying. High specialization has threatened the position of the skilled worker and has brought craft jealousy and costly jurisdictional disputes. Little capital is needed to enter the industry, which means keen competition and leads to efforts at control. In many areas competition has been effectively killed by organized employers, sometimes supported by the unions. In other cases employers have been poorly organized and the industry has been highly competitive. Lack of organization among employers has often resulted in union control with consequent abuses. All of these conditions affect the industry's collective bargaining.

2. See pp. 224 ff.
3. Particularly revealing were the findings of the so-called Lockwood Committee in New York and the Dailey Committee in Chicago. Haber, *op. cit.*, pp. 212, 321, 365, 368.

2. THE INDUSTRY

a. SIZE

At its peak in August 1928, employment in the construction industry is estimated to have totaled about 2.4 million men,[4] and an additional 500,000 to 1.0 million manufactured or distributed building materials. According to some estimates the industry gave direct employment in 1929 to 5.5 per cent of all gainfully employed nonagricultural workers in the United States—"the largest single employer of labor in America."[5] The percentage declined to 4 per cent in 1938. Building operations affect directly the prosperity of many subsidiary industries, not only building materials but also glass, furniture, rugs, linoleum and the hundreds of accessories used to equip the modern home and office structure; quite properly, building construction has been called "the balance wheel of American industry."

During the peak years of the twenties, from 1925 to 1929, new construction was between $10 billion and $12 billion a year.[6] From this high point it fell to $3.2 billion in 1933. In 1938, when the industry had not fully recovered from the depression, which hit it particularly hard, some $5 billion was invested in new construction. In 1939, it was around $8 billion, still only about two thirds of what it had been during the period from 1925 to 1929.

b. BUILDING MARKETS

The building industry has a number of main "markets."

(1) The *public market* is government-financed construction—federal, state, municipal. Its volume need not depend upon cost factors or even immediate necessity; usually it is determined by public policy. In the short run, however, costs do influence the volume of public construction, since fixed appropriations obvi-

---

4. Testimony of Commissioner Isador Lubin, *Hearings Before the Temporary National Economic Committee*, Pt. 11, "Construction Industry," June 27, 28, and 29, July 6, 7, 11, 12, 13, and 14, 1939, p. 4936. (Based on U. S. Bureau of Labor Statistics data. The term "construction employment" refers to workmen employed on the site of construction and includes "all contract construction, state road maintenance and federal force account.")
5. *Ibid.*, p. 4942.
6. *Ibid.*, pp. 4943-4944.

ously produce more or less construction according to changes in cost. In 1930, expenditures on public construction were about $3 billion. They declined to slightly less than $2 billion in 1933 and rose to nearly $3.7 billion by 1938.[7]

Owing to its many-sided activities in the building industry, government has played a vitally important part since the depression began in 1929. Its policy has been to increase public construction; to stimulate private building by long-term, low-interest loans; to finance directly large-scale public housing projects; to establish minimum wages and specifications for government work, which, of course, also influence those of private projects; and finally, to correct restrictive practices which retard private building.

Early in the depression RFC self-liquidating loans made possible the expenditure of over $954 million, mostly for new, large-scale public works projects.[8] The Home Owners' Loan Corporation, formed in 1933 to stop the wave of foreclosures, refinanced 1,021,818 mortgages in three years. By lowering interest rates and extending loans to fifteen years,[9] it sought to relieve the pressure on the real estate market. The Federal Housing Administration insured $4.4 billion loans for property improvement, home mortgage, and rental and group housing projects in the period 1934–1940.[10]

From June 1933 to March 1, 1938, the Public Works Administration spent $6.1 billion on 34,508 projects. The work was on a contract basis, but wage rates and working conditions were stipulated in the federal act.[11] While primarily a work relief plan, the Works Progress Administration influenced building conditions by paying the "prevailing rate" (in many areas interpreted to mean the "union rate"), and by providing immediate employ-

---

7. *Ibid.*, p. 4944.
8. Jesse H. Jones, Chairman, *Reconstruction Finance Corporation Seven Year Report to the President and Congress of the United States*, February 2, 1932—February 2, 1939, pp. 7, 22.
9. Federal Home Loan Bank Board, "Safeguarding the Nation's Homes," pp. 7-10.
10. Abner H. Ferguson, Administrator, *Seventh Annual Report of the Federal Housing Administration,* year ending December 31, 1940, p. 8.
11. *Principal Acts and Executive Orders Pertaining to Public Works Administration,* Federal Emergency Administration of Public Works, July 1938, p. 5.

ment for skilled building workers either on its relief or non-relief rolls. The "prevailing rate" as a basis of pay was later abolished on WPA relief jobs but continued on other public works projects.[12]

The United States Housing Authority also stimulates building with its loans and subsidies for slum clearance and low-cost housing projects.[13]

Without this wide governmental help the building trades unions would not have kept as much of their predepression membership, wage rates, and standards as they did. Government efforts revived demand and checked unemployment among building trades workers. And without official recognition of "prevailing rates," union wage scales could not have been maintained to the extent that they were.

(2) The *semipublic market* is created by private philanthropy and includes private educational, institutional, hospital, religious, social and recreational buildings. Activity in this market depends not only upon cost of construction but also on business conditions, income and inheritance tax laws, and many intangibles which affect the flow of charitable gifts.

(3) The *industrial and factory market* reflects business growth and outlook. Cost considerations have relatively small influence upon industrial construction, since expansion occurs when business demands warrant it. However, they cannot be entirely disregarded. Current construction costs have some bearing upon long-term investment, and marginal producers cannot overlook them.

(4) The *commercial market* includes hotels, office buildings and amusement centers. Local business outlook more than general business conditions determines demand here; it involves long-term investments, is highly elastic, and strongly influenced by current costs.

---

12. 46 Stats. L., Pt. 1, Ch. 411, p. 1494; 50 Stats. L., Pt. 1, Ch. 896, pp. 888-899. In addition to the federal government, thirty-four states regulate the payment of wages on public works. "Laws Relating to Payment of Wages on Public Works, as of January 1, 1936," U. S. Bureau of Labor Statistics (mimeographed).

13. "The United States Housing Act of 1937 as Amended," United States Housing Authority, pp. 5-10; *Annual Report,* United States Housing Authority, 1938, p. 7.

(5) The *residential market,* next to government spending, is the most important and probably has the most elastic demand. In 1926, one of the most active construction years in the twenties, residential construction amounted to $5.2 billion. By 1933, the amount expended dropped to $392 million; it rose by 1938 to $1.5 billion. (The totals after 1933 include FHA insured loans referred to above.)

Residential building consists of low-cost housing—which may be roughly defined as dwelling units costing $3,000 or less and renting at $35 a month or under; and high-cost housing, costing above $3,000 and renting for more than $35 a month.[14] Because of the great shortage of new low-cost houses, low-income families are largely dependent on the used-house market. The volume of residential building is directly influenced by the cost of construction, income, internal migration, marriage and birth rates, standards of living, job security and labor turnover. Government financing and other help have been increasingly important. Costs are determined by wages, building materials prices and interest rates. Local building codes, union working rules and competitive practices of contractors also affect costs. Prevailing rentals, interest and amortization rates, rent laws, low-cost housing legislation and general business conditions influence the decisions of speculative builders and either stimulate or discourage construction.

(6) In addition, there is the *farm construction market,* where speculative building is virtually unknown and where the volume of building depends directly on current income and prospects.

(7) Finally, the *repair and maintenance market* competes for labor and materials and thus influences costs in the other markets. The more old structures are maintained and renovated, the less the demand for new construction.

All groups in the industry have failed to recognize at all fully the relation between volume of building and costs of construction. In fact, the industry seems to have assumed that the demand for housing is inelastic and that consequently price exercises little

14. The President's Conference on Home Building and Home Ownership, *Home Ownership, Income and Types of Dwellings,* Washington, 1932, pp. 69-75.

effect upon demand.[15] Monopolies and restrictive practices which commonly prevail may in part be explained by this attitude.

c. COST ELEMENTS

Since all building projects represent a long-time investment, the cost of financing has considerable influence on the volume of building demand. Funds generally come from insurance companies, building and loan associations, trust companies, mortgage and surety companies, corporation surpluses, public funds and private savings.[16]

The proportion of labor costs differs with the type of project. The cost of direct labor on a site may be as low as 22 per cent or as high as 40 or 50 per cent. The amount of direct labor costs is determined by the size of the job, the type of building, the builder's organizing skill and the amount of shop fabrication. Mixing of concrete is a direct labor cost if performed on the job, and part of materials costs if mixed elsewhere. Costs of materials may range from less than 30 per cent to about 50 per cent.[17]

d. TECHNOLOGY AND MATERIALS

The building trades have been much less influenced by technological developments than many other American industries. They are still largely on a handicraft basis; some trades retain the methods of fifty or a hundred years ago. Plasterers' or carpenters' work is not much different from that of the past, even though materials and working conditions have greatly changed. The mechanical bricklayer is still no serious competitor of the mason and the spray gun has not displaced the brush, as was predicted in the late twenties.

---

15. A high degree of specialization makes it more difficult to recognize the relationship between prices and wages and demand. The subcontractor and the union leaders in one craft are probably correct in considering the demand for their particular product inelastic. On the other hand, the general contractor or speculative builder, interested in the cost of the whole building, is more concerned with reducing costs than are the various specialized groups.

16. *Hearings Before the Temporary National Economic Committee*, Pt. 11, pp. 5084-5112, 5129-5142; also Haber, *op. cit.*, pp. 62-67.

17. Testimony of L. Seth Schnitman, *Hearings Before the Temporary National Economic Committee*, Pt. 11, pp. 5021-5022.

Changes in Equipment and Methods

Nevertheless, the industry has felt the impact of the machine.[18] The construction of large office buildings, apartment houses, hotels and factories requires large outlays for equipment, tools and machinery, and has stimulated large-scale construction organizations and equipment companies. The skyscraper, structural steel and concrete have brought to the industry advanced methods of production and extensive mechanical and technical equipment, such as excavating machinery, hoisting equipment, diesel engines for power, concrete mixers, and, more recently, transit mixers, which do their work while delivering the concrete from the supply yards to the job location.[19] Through use of the transit mixer, not only are labor costs converted into materials costs, but the contractor can reduce the overhead involved in maintaining mixing equipment.

Methods also have advanced: steel girders are now frequently welded instead of riveted, saving from 3 to 10 per cent in steel; steel forms are used for pouring cement and, by the vacuum mat process, cement poured in the morning will be dry by afternoon. Similar improvements have made possible more rapid construction and lower costs. In house construction, power driven tools are available, and when employed produce a substantial decrease in the time required to build.[20]

Prefabrication

The effect of technology has been even greater upon building materials. More and more, lumber, metal and paints are prepared and fabricated in the mill and delivered to the job ready for use. Glass, steel, hardware, cement, stone and even wooden materials are turned out by highly efficient mechanical means. Prefabrication of wall, floor and roof panels is becoming more common.

Pressure for low-cost housing has led to experimentation, with

18. See Haber, *op. cit.*, pp. 34-38, 120-122, 161-163, for more detailed discussion.
19. Their introduction has, incidentally, created a jurisdictional dispute between the operating engineers and the teamsters.
20. *Construction Methods and Equipment,* May 1939; *Engineering News-Record,* February 4, 1937, p. 163; August 19, 1937, p. 303; July 7, 1938, p. 91; and December 11, 1930, p. 925.

scattered success, in mass production methods effective in other industries. On one project prefabricated fixtures and housing parts, such as stairs, windows, cupboards and trim, were delivered to the job ready for installation, with skilled workers shifting directly from one house to another.[21] This operation needs careful advance planning and transforms much of the construction process into an assembly job.

Most ambitious of all are prefabricated houses which are built in sections at the factory and set upon foundations at the site.[22] They have been assembled in large-scale individual housing operations, but their future in this country is still problematical. Advocates of prefabricated houses claim for them substantial savings in cost. While these claims are generally accepted, some unions have disputed them. One union, for example, maintains that "increased factory prefabrication cuts down labor time on the job but the greater cost of such materials, coupled with freight and other handling costs, seems to increase the cost of the completed structure rather than to lower it."[23] The housing committee of the Congress of Industrial Organizations, on the other hand, in October 1940 issued a statement strongly advocating the use of prefabrication in the building of defense housing and has since continued to advocate the use of industrialized methods that drastically cut across trade lines.[24]

The scale of operations of prefabricated construction is still too small to develop major economies in fabrication, but substantial economies in the purchase of materials have already been made. Expansion will be slow; there is strong opposition from the industry as it is at present organized; serious problems of litigation arise in many cities. As a result, the volume of capital financial institutions are willing to make available for such enterprises is restricted. Nevertheless, the need for low-cost housing is pressing and the quest for economical prefabricated houses will con-

21. *Engineering News-Record,* January 14, 1937; *Architectural Forum,* December 1938, pp. 476-481; *American Builder,* February 1939, pp. 42-46.
22. *Engineering News-Record,* February 18, 1937.
23. "How High is Low-Cost Housing?" *The Journal of the Electrical Workers and Operators,* December 1939, p. 625.
24. Housing Committee of the CIO, *Memoranda* to the Office of Emergency Management, October 14, 1940, January 23, 1941 and April 15, 1941.

tinue. For example, during the last year or so, prefabrication has been given a tremendous impetus by the defense housing program, which has accelerated progress in prefabricating methods over normal expectancy.

New Materials

The search for lower costs and better methods has turned up new materials—glass blocks; plywood substitutes for boards, sheetings and concrete forms; stronger and lighter steel alloys;[25] and such widely used insulating materials as glass fiber, exploded mica and rock wool. Wall and gypsum board have replaced plaster in many types of building. Progress in design has enabled contractors to make greater use of their space with a saving of labor time.

e. THE BUILDING BUSINESS

There is a difference between the "large-scale" and "small-scale" building industry. The first puts up large structures and has at its command modern architectural, engineering and construction techniques. It came into being with the development of steel and reinforced concrete construction. The small-scale industry, which builds one- and two-family houses and other comparatively modest structures, is distinct in personnel, customs, business methods and operations.[26] For the most part, the small producers belong to no national trade association; they have little invested capital and practically no facilities for utilizing laborsaving devices available to larger builders.

25. *The New York Times,* March 7, 1939, p. 1.
26. F. W. Dodge Corporation surveyed the activities of 33,554 builders in thirty-seven states east of the Rockies who, in 1938, produced 110,000 one- and two-family houses. Relatively few of these contractors erected more than one house during the year. Only 279 builders produced more than thirty houses each, or a total of 17,578 buildings, representing less than 16 per cent of the total number of houses constructed. In addition, 1,426 builders constructed eleven to thirty houses each, or a total of 22,982. The top 5 per cent, or 1,705 producers, were responsible for less than 37 per cent of the total output. On the other hand, more than half of the total number of contractors, 17,351, produced just one house each, not quite equal to the total output of the 279 contractors at the top of the list. Thomas H. Holden, "Integration of the Housing Function," address before the American Statistical Association, Philadelphia, December 28, 1939, p. 5.

Subcontracting

With few exceptions, actual construction is not done by one firm but is parceled out to contractors, subcontractors, and perhaps even to sub-subcontractors, who do the carpentry, the plumbing, the wiring and the like. A general contractor may perhaps employ labor directly only for the one or two trades in which he specializes. Often he is only a "broker," hiring no labor at all but dividing the job among subcontractors. Since the building construction industry has more than thirty trades, each with special problems, a uniform system of labor relations is not easy.

Of course, the subcontractors perform a very important function. The general contractor finds it impossible to keep pace with the technological changes taking place in all sectors of the industry. To erect a building alone he would have to deal with a large number of unions and with several types of supply houses. He would have to know the complicated rules in each trade and keep on hand the equipment and labor necessary for all types of work. A well-trained and specialized subcontractor can perform the work with greater speed. But there are indications that subdivision of function has been carried too far, and that better buildings could be erected at lower cost by reducing the number of subcontractors so that the remainder would be able to introduce more efficient business methods, establish purchasing and accounting departments and utilize other aids to efficient business.

In any case, the contracting and subcontracting system is an important factor in the industry's labor relations. Fly-by-night contractors are not concerned with industrial stability and are always ready to cut standards. Since wages are a high percentage of total costs, established rates of pay and hours are constantly threatened. As a protection against such hazards, unions in many trades have rigid "working rules." To obtain at least a minimum of responsibility among employers, the unions frequently require subcontractors, for instance, to have at least an office and a telephone before they may hire union labor. The restriction against union members becoming contractors, enforced by many unions, is partly based on the fear that as self-employed individuals they may work for less than the union scale or "contract for labor only" and connive at reductions in the wage rate.

The Bidding System

The competitive nature of the building business is further heightened by prevailing methods of "bidding." Prospective owners rarely ask for bids from only one construction firm, but from several general contractors, who in turn may ask for bids from several subcontractors for each trade.

The process is full of pitfalls. Most subcontractors keep few records and have wholly inadequate cost accounting systems. "Estimates" are submitted to the general contractor who adds the bids for all trades together, includes an item for his own profit and overhead, and hands the total to the owner. Since the owner usually awards the job to the lowest bidder, subcontractors are under great pressure to make low bids. In addition, the practice of "bid shopping," or putting pressure on the low bidder to get still lower bids, intensifies the downward drive and leads to many evils—inaccurate estimates, shoddy quality, and disregard of labor standards—which in the end may adversely affect the construction worker.

One effort to solve the problem is the "bid depository," under which bids are submitted to one person or to a central organization, opened simultaneously, and once made may not be resubmitted and revised. So-called fair trade practices have long sought to correct the evils of overbidding and bid shopping. The increased experience with public works projects and the development of standard forms for estimates and cost accounting which they require have encouraged more intelligent bidding methods.

Monopolistic Practices

Attempts to correct some of the abuses which result from the business methods employed in the industry have frequently led to rigging of bids and price fixing. Monopolistic practices can thrive because of the local character of the building industry. When local contractors split up the market or fix prices, effective competition may easily be killed. Dealers in building materials have frequently supported such practices by agreeing to sell only to retailers "registered" with the local association, and unions in some instances have refused to permit their members to work for independent contractors even though union wages and working conditions were observed.

Restraints of trade and collusive practices have involved every group in the industry. Investigators working with the Assistant Attorney General in charge of the Anti-Trust Division report that producers of building materials use patents, basing point systems, price formulas, voluntary apportionment arrangements and other devices to limit output, allocate markets and raise prices. Distributors fix markups and boycott those not routing their business through the distributive hierarchy. Contractors divide the work through the use of bid depositories, central estimating bureaus and division of the field. Labor, often in conjunction with contractors and distributors, limits individual performance and restricts the use of laborsaving devices or new materials. In some instances unions have withheld labor from those jobs where the rules of the distributors have been violated.[27]

f. CHARACTERISTICS OF THE INDUSTRY AND ITS LABOR PROBLEMS

Out of their technological and business environment have stemmed the peculiar industrial relations problems of the building trades. The threat of new methods and materials to the security of old skills and jobs has been real, and building trades labor has set up protective devices against this threat. "Working rules" have therefore been devised to restrict the use of laborsaving materials and tools. Factory-prepared products, particularly those made by nonunion labor, have been resisted and often barred from local markets.

Technological changes have also increased the industry's jurisdictional problems. New ways have wiped out or blurred traditional boundaries and led to conflicts between the crafts.

The building industry has a number of distinctive character-

27. *Hearings Before the Temporary National Economic Committee,* Pt. 11, pp. 5148-5150, 5435; testimony of General Robert E. Wood, *ibid.,* pp. 5162-5168; *New York Herald Tribune,* March 30, 1940; *The New York Times,* June 11, 1940.

istics: its business organization and competitive practices; its requirement of finishing a job on a given date; its constant pressure upon wages and labor costs; the absence of economic responsibility on the part of a great majority of employers, many of whom have only recently come from the ranks of labor; and the relatively weak organization of contractors. All of these have created an environment favorable to certain types of unions, union leaders and union policies.

3. ORGANIZATION AMONG WORKERS

a. THE UNIONS

Building trades unions are among the oldest and strongest in the United States. In 1937 the twenty internationals claimed a total membership of over a million, but less than 700,000 were in the construction industry.[28] For the jurisdiction of some of these unions extends over other industries—the Brotherhood of Carpenters, for example, organizes lumber workers and the vast majority of the Teamsters are in general trucking and bread, milk and coal dis-

---

28. Cf. C. R. Daugherty, *Labor Problems in American Industry*, Revised Edition, 1938, pp. 351, 353-354; and Building and Construction Trades Department of the AF of L, *Report of Proceedings of the Thirty-First Convention*, 1937.

The unions and their 1940–1941 average total memberships are: International Association of Heat and Frost Insulators and Asbestos Workers (4,000); International Brotherhood of Boiler Makers, Iron Ship Builders and Helpers (42,600); Bricklayers, Masons and Plasterers' International Union (65,000); International Association of Bridge, Structural and Ornamental Iron Workers (52,000); United Brotherhood of Carpenters and Joiners (300,000); International Brotherhood of Electrical Workers (201,000); International Union of Elevator Constructors (10,200); International Union of Operating Engineers (80,000); Granite Cutters' International Association (5,000); International Hod Carriers, Building and Common Laborers' Union (183,700); International Union of Wood, Wire and Metal Lathers (8,100); International Association of Marble, Stone and Slate Polishers, Rubbers and Sawyers, Tile and Marble Setters' Helpers and Terrazzo Helpers (5,500); Sheet Metal Workers' International Association (20,000); Brotherhood of Painters, Decorators and Paperhangers (104,900); Operative Plasterers' and Cement Finishers' International Association (21,200); United Association of Journeymen Plumbers and Steam Fitters (45,400); United Slate, Tile and Composition Roofers, Damp and Waterproof Workers' Association (4,400); Journeymen Stonecutters' Association (4,100); International Brotherhood of Teamsters, Chauffeurs, Stablemen and Helpers (408,300); Paving Cutters' Union (2,000). Total: 1.6 million. Based on per capita tax payments to the AF of L (*Report of the Executive Council*, 1941, pp. 10-11). Paving Cutters' figure from *Preliminary Report of the Committee on Naval Affairs*, 77th Cong., 2d sess., H. Rept. 1634 (1942), p. 369.

tribution. Increased building activity during the last year or two and government financing of housing for defense workers, together with the closed-shop policy prevailing on these projects, resulted in large increases in union membership. By the end of 1941 the Building and Construction Trades Department of the AF of L claimed nearly 1.6 million construction members—more than double the 1937 membership.

These unions have organized seven state and 441 local councils, all affiliated with the Building and Construction Trades Department.[29] The present organizations replaced or absorbed earlier unions, most of which were local and varied in strength with the waves of prosperity and depression. These early unions were mainly concerned with wages and hours of labor. Not until after the Civil War did they show some stability.

Many of the national unions appeared in the seventies and eighties. Although the building trades organizations operated in local areas and were primarily local in character, several factors called for the creation of national unions. Intercity migration of its workers has always been a characteristic of the building industry. Craftsmen have traveled in search of work, following rumors of building booms and high wage rates. To protect themselves against newcomers, local unions charged high initiation fees to keep the strangers out. "Green hands" entered the trades and endangered the standards of skill as well as wages. In addition, national contracting companies were beginning to operate in several cities beyond the reach of isolated local unions.

The national unions sought to control entrance to the trade by a country-wide apprenticeship system. They negotiated with interstate contracting companies and provided a national "passport," or traveling card, for members. Some national organizations paid strike benefits and established various fraternal features to attract new members.[30] During the past quarter century the national unions have taken on new functions, particularly in relation to strikes and collective bargaining.

29. Building and Construction Trades Department, *Report of Proceedings of the Thirty-First Convention*, 1937, pp. 96-97. Unions pay per capita taxes to a department only on those members engaged in the industry.
30. Haber, *op. cit.*, pp. 277-279.

Despite these national organizations, local autonomy remains strong.[31] For example, while the painters' constitution provides detailed apprenticeship regulations,[32] the really vital decision on the ratio of apprentices to journeymen is left to local unions. Although locals are directed to submit collective bargaining agreements to the national organization for examination and advice[33] (as is also required by other organizations), the local committee has full power to negotiate and settle with an employers' association. A like policy guides the relations of the United Brotherhood of Carpenters and Joiners and their local affiliates.[34]

b. DUAL UNIONISM

Dual unionism was for many years a serious obstacle to interunion peace. The Brotherhood of Carpenters and Joiners and the Amalgamated Woodworkers International Union had been engaged in many contests before they merged in 1912.[35] Dualism split the Electrical Workers from 1908 to 1912. The Brotherhood of Painters and Decorators fought a rival from 1894 to 1901 and dealt with additional stubborn dual groups in New York City. By 1920 the strongest rivalries were settled, and what interunion warfare there has been since has been over two claims to a single jurisdiction.

However, an organizing drive by the Congress of Industrial Organizations in the building industry appears likely to revive dual unionism. Since the CIO is formed along industrial lines, it is a rival or dual union to all national craft unions within the American Federation of Labor. Although its early statements[36] avowed its intention to concentrate on unorganized sections of the building industry, the CIO will doubtless come into conflict with the national craft unions wherever it operates. Some agreements with building contractors have already been signed; and

---

31. The exceptions to this are the national agreements for sprinkler fitters and elevator constructors and a few other national union, national contractor agreements.
32. *Constitution of the Brotherhood of Painters, Decorators and Paperhangers of America*, pp. 26-27.
33. *Ibid.*, p. 54.
34. *Constitution and Laws*, p. 7.
35. Haber, *op. cit.*, pp. 280-308.
36. *C.I.O. News*, September 25, 1939, p. 2.

the activity of established craft unions in the New York City small house construction field, which employs nearly forty thousand workers, mostly unorganized, is partly spurred by recent CIO efforts in that area.[37]

In March 1940, representatives of the United Construction Workers Organizing Committee, a CIO affiliate, met with the board of governors of the New York Building Trades Employers Association and sought to gain recognition. This committee proposed a standard $9 wage for mechanics instead of the prevailing $11 to $14. It also assured employers freedom from jurisdictional disputes, wider latitude for mechanization, and "no interference with the use of materials."[38] It remains to be seen whether these concessions are merely to get a foothold in the industry, or represent a more flexible trade-union policy. Should the CIO succeed in enrolling a substantial number of building craftsmen, the internecine conflicts of the early days of dual unionism may be repeated.[39] An additional source of conflict arises from the fact that building materials installed by AF of L craft unions are sometimes manufactured in shops organized by the CIO. Interunion rivalry was the issue in the famous Currier case in the fall of 1941. This involved an AF of L threat to strike all Michigan defense projects if a defense housing contract for Wayne were awarded to the Currier Company, which had a closed-shop contract with the CIO. Even though this company was the low bidder, the contract was withheld to avoid labor strife.

C. AMALGAMATION

Changes in building technology created areas of conflict between unions in related crafts and after 1900 led to the movement for amalgamation. The painters brought into their union paperhangers, decorators, glaziers and sign painters. Stairmakers, cabinet makers, furniture makers, mill workers and other related trades were absorbed into the United Brotherhood of Carpenters and Joiners. These are only two of numerous amalgamations.

37. *The New York Times,* March 21, 1940, p. 20.
38. *Ibid.,* March 20, 1940, p. 1.
39. In July 1940, the CIO claimed to have more than 150 locals in the construction industry. *United Construction Workers News,* August 1940, p. 3.

As a result, true craft unions are few in the building trades. Both national and local unions are amalgams of related crafts. For a long time there has been a noticeable tendency for the powerful national unions to extend their jurisdiction on the basis of the material or process. Thus the Bricklayers, Masons and Plasterers include the trowel trades; the Brotherhood of Carpenters and Joiners, the wood trades. Complete amalgamation will mean merging unions as closely related as the plasterers and bricklayers, which now have separate national unions. Even if this were done, the structural form of the building trades unions would still fall far short of the CIO proposal for an industrial union.

d. LOCAL BUILDING TRADES COUNCILS

For local collective action by all crafts, the building trades council was developed. The New York Building Trades Council was formed in 1884,[40] the San Francisco Council in 1896,[41] that in Chicago in 1890.[42]

The sympathetic strike, a quick and effective weapon, was made possible on an industry-wide basis by the building trades council. It overcomes some disadvantages of separate craft organizations and often gives to isolated organizations the cohesiveness of an industrial union. By the simple rule that no union member may work where a nonunion man is employed the council can quickly bring a building job to a standstill.

A local building trades council frequently underwrites trade and even industry-wide agreements. It tries, sometimes unsuccessfully, to settle jurisdictional disputes, it strengthens the member union during collective bargaining proceedings, and it supervises strike calls. Capably led, the building trades council may bring order and stability to local labor relations.

e. JURISDICTIONAL DISPUTES

While joint action was being perfected locally, rivalry and friction often characterized relations among national unions. Rival

---

40. Haber, *op. cit.*, p. 347.
41. Ryan, *op. cit.*, pp. 26-27.
42. Montgomery, *op. cit.*, pp. 17-18.

jurisdictional claims have been a prolific cause for disagreement. It has been estimated that nearly 75 per cent of all strikes in larger cities are due to such controversies.

The causes of these disputes are numerous and complicated. Erecting a big building requires more than a score of trades, each protected by jurisdictional boundaries. Machinery, materials, methods, tools—all change. Each change creates a problem, a dispute, perhaps a strike, before which collective bargaining is often impotent. In spite of agreements to the contrary, work frequently stops. Introduction of metal trim to replace wood threatened the jobs of thousands of carpenters, and a long contest followed between them and sheet metal workers. The laying of glass blocks created a conflict between glaziers and bricklayers. Since the blocks were glass, the glaziers' union claimed control; but since the blocks are substitutes for brick or stone and they are laid with a trowel, the bricklayers also claimed them. The arbitrator to whom the dispute was submitted upheld the bricklayers.[43]

Local arbitration of such disputes was formerly successful in many cities, particularly in New York. Because local decisions showed considerable variation and threatened to confuse the jurisdictional claims of the national unions, disputes were later referred to the national organizations which were then becoming influential. If the contending unions disagreed, the American Federation of Labor sought a settlement. As the Federation defined the jurisdiction of national unions in their charters, it was the logical agency to adjust such controversies; but it had no power to enforce its awards, and larger unions frequently disregarded them.

Jurisdictional Awards Difficult to Enforce

As early as 1888, Samuel Gompers suggested an interorganization of national craft unions.[44] In 1897 the National Building Trades Council was formed, primarily to settle jurisdictional disputes. This venture failed and was followed some years later by

43. Decision by Referee John A. Lapp, June 14, 1938.
44. Haber, *op. cit.*, p. 332.

the equally ineffective Structural Building Trades Alliance.[45] In 1908 the American Federation of Labor finally took the initiative and set up the Building Trades Department, which was to be composed only of building trades internationals chartered by the Federation.[46]

Like its predecessors, the principal aim of the Department was to settle jurisdictional disputes. Results have not been outstanding, for while small and weak unions have been kept in line, some large unions have habitually ignored decisions made. The carpenters' union, for example, has seceded or been suspended four times; it has been a member of the Department only nineteen of thirty-two years.[47] This is the largest union in the Department and at one time represented about 40 per cent of its membership. The carpenters' dispute with the sheet metal workers over metal trim was repeatedly decided in favor of the metal workers' union; but the decision could not be enforced and the carpenters continued to control the disputed work whether in or out of the Department.

National Referees Also Fail

In 1918 contractors and architects joined with labor in the National Board for Jurisdictional Awards. After an excellent beginning, the board ran against the same obstacle—inability to enforce its awards. Again the carpenters were the dissenters, and when they withdrew the board's influence waned. In 1927 the Department repudiated the board[48] in an effort to get the carpenters to rejoin, but unity was short-lived. During the next ten years the carpenters were in and out of the Department. Other unions seceded, and for a while the Department was split into two groups, which made settlements impossible.

In 1936, the seceders—the Carpenters, Electricians, and Operating Engineers—re-entered, and a national referee was appointed

45. *Ibid.*, pp. 331-335.
46. Lewis L. Lorwin, *The American Federation of Labor*, Brookings Institution, Washington, 1933, pp. 93-95, 374-385.
47. Haber, *op. cit.*, p. 340; also *Report of the Proceedings of the Building Trades Department, 1935.*
48. Haber, *op. cit.*, pp. 182-190.

with power to hold hearings and make awards.[49] The new program worked effectively until the operating engineers lost two decisions and revolted. After two years, John A. Lapp, the referee, resigned, and later on William Carroll of the Cleveland Building Trades Employers Association succeeded him. In the meantime, the Department had made with the Associated General Contractors of America [50] a national agreement which aimed at buttressing other efforts for settling these disputes. This agreement went the way of its predecessors. In September 1939 eight projects were reported stopped by jurisdictional quarrels.[51] The Department has not succeeded in solving the problem of jurisdictional disputes but it has contributed to the solution of many of these conflicts and has been a means for closer cooperation among the national organizations.

The Anti-Trust Division of the Department of Justice sought to restrain jurisdictional strikes but its action was not supported by the U. S. Supreme Court, which refused to consider such stoppages a violation of the antitrust laws.[52]

f. UNION STRENGTH

Union organization in the industry is not uniform throughout the country or in the several building markets. It is strongest in the larger building centers of the East, North, and Far West. Southern cities are not well organized. Unions are successfully entrenched in commercial, industrial, public, semipublic, apartment and high-cost residential building. Small house construction in many large cities and most work in small towns and rural areas are largely nonunion; repair and maintenance work is frequently nonunion. The closed shop prevails wherever union control is effective. There are few open-shop trade agreements similar to those in the railroad and mass production industries.

49. Building and Construction Trades Department, "Plan for Settling Jurisdictional Disputes Nationally and Locally," 1938, pp. 3-5 (pamphlet).
50. J. P. Coyne, "Jurisdictional Disputes in the Building Construction Industry," *American Federationist*, January 1940, pp. 1298-1301.
51. *The New York Times*, September 18, 1939, p. 21.
52. *United States* v. *William L. Hutcheson, et al.* (1941).

Organization of Related Industries

In the twenties union organization spread rapidly to mills and factories supplying building materials. Here, too, CIO organization of thousands of workers in the lumber, steel, rubber, hardware, glass, electrical and plumbing fixture industries, may create serious jurisdictional conflicts with the American Federation of Labor unions.

For many years the carpenters' union sought to organize the mills by refusing to install nonunion material. The electrical workers' union has until recently been less successful than the carpenters, and the recent organization of electrical supply and manufacturing houses has been due to the general increase in union membership during the period of the National Recovery Administration and the National Labor Relations Act. Where the union controls the construction job and can impose its ban upon nonunion materials, organization of all supply houses and mills seems inevitable.

The Building Trades Unions and the Depression

The depression's effect upon union membership is not easy to measure. New building fell precipitously—from $10.3 billion in 1929 to $3.2 billion in 1933. Despite extensive government construction, federal stimulation of home building and considerable recovery, building construction in 1938 was only $5.3 billion—approximately 53 per cent of the 1929 value. Even after allowance is made for changes in prices, the building industry did not come out of the depression until stimulated by the defense activities of 1940 and 1941.

During the depression many union members were employed on the various government relief and work projects and may have kept their union affiliations. Others left the industry, as in earlier years, when building trades workers sought steadier employment and "regular wages" in the automobile and allied industries. Except for shorter hours and increased public works, the national unions advocated no specific policies to help recovery in the industry or to check falling membership. The locals, however, made some efforts—though not always in the right direction—and took steps to increase or equalize the employment of members through shorter working hours or through rotating work.

The building trades unions have weathered the depression with their power and control in important construction markets unimpaired. It is significant of their strength and their place in the industry that employers' organizations did not use hard times and unemployment in the thirties as a lever to dislodge the unions. Since 1910 they have achieved organizational stability. Membership has fluctuated with business conditions, but such losses as have occurred have not endangered the unions' position, influence or control. Between 1928 and 1933 there was a loss of about 300,000 members, but with improvement in business conditions and employment on public projects the losses were recovered and trade-union membership in the construction industry reached almost 700,000 in 1937, and around 1.6 million in the fall of 1941.[53]

In addition, considerable progress has been made in the consolidation of related trades; about sixty separate skills have been combined in twenty national unions. The increasing control of the national unions over agreements and strikes has tended to reduce the strong localist tendency in the industry and to provide for greater uniformity of conditions throughout the country.

4. EMPLOYERS' ORGANIZATIONS

Building trades employers have been less well organized than building craftsmen. The employers' organizations have a hard time in both getting and keeping their members. The number of contractors in the various trades is large and it is difficult to include a major portion of them in a stable organization. Since it is easy to enter the industry with little or no capital, the turnover is large among contractors, who shift from one branch of

---

53. AF of L membership claims have been disputed by A. D. Lewis, director of the CIO organization campaign in the construction industry. He asserted in 1940 that the total was only around 500,000. (*The New York Times*, March 21, 1940.) He also put the number of unorganized workers at 2.5 million, an obvious exaggeration because even in 1928 the total employed in the industry was only approximately 2.4 million. In October, the peak month in 1938, the number employed was 1.3 million. See *Hearings Before the Temporary National Economic Committee*, Pt. 11, p. 5461.

the industry to another. A contractor's interest in an employers' organization may come from danger of immediate labor trouble or from a desire to regulate competitive practices. When the danger passes, support of the association frequently lags. The owner of the building has only temporary interest in the industry; he wants his building finished. He does not want his property to be a labor battleground, nor is he interested in enforcing any principles of industrial relations.

Since it is so hard to organize the majority of the contractors, some employers' organizations look with favor upon the union—in fact, rely upon it as a policeman to equalize and regulate competition by enforcing uniform labor and wage standards upon nonassociation employers. The industry has some antiunion associations; some, like the Committee to Enforce the Landis Award in Chicago, are temporary, and some permanent ones, like the National Erectors' Association, are devoted to furthering the open shop. But these are by no means typical;[54] contractors' associations have usually not been enthusiastic open-shop advocates.[55]

The structure of employers' associations follows that of trade-union organizations. The local subcontractors' associations are craft groups, such as masonry, carpenter or sheet metal contractors. These are affiliated with national contractors' associations. National associations in turn may be affiliated with a national federation of contractors' organizations, such as the National Building Trades Employers' Association, the Associated General Contractors of America, or the National Association of Builders' Exchanges.

In most localities the local subcontractors' organizations join the local building trades employers' association, whose functions somewhat parallel those of the local building trades council. The building trades employers' association is primarily interested in labor relations and grievances, and gives advice and protection to member employers.[56] The local subcontractors' organizations are, in addition, interested in regulating competitive practices.

54. Haber, *op. cit.*, pp. 453-454.
55. *Ibid.*, pp. 348-362, 447-451.
56. *Ibid.*, pp. 453-454.

The lack of strong employers' associations may have caused many abuses; some unethical or uneconomic practices are possible only when the bargaining power is one-sided and resistance is ineffective. But many collusive arrangements and unethical practices have existed, not only in spite of strong organization on both sides, but even because of it.

5. THE COLLECTIVE BARGAINING PROCESS

The building trades have had nearly a half century's experience with collective bargaining. Occasionally it has broken down, but never for long and seldom because of fundamental differences. In New York City since 1903, in Chicago since 1900, and in other cities for more than thirty years, the organized employers and workers have jointly negotiated labor agreements.

a. NEGOTIATIONS

These agreements are usually negotiated between a local contractors' association and a union local. In the same locality therefore there may be forty or fifty agreements,[57] or one for each trade. Negotiations are usually conducted by a joint bargaining committee, with both sides equally represented. The committee may be empowered to conclude a final agreement, but usually the rank and file of the local union have the right to approve or to reject it. If agreement cannot be reached, the issues may be arbitrated.

In some trades national union officers have participated in trade agreement negotiations, and in some instances local agreements are subject to national organization approval. Some unions have country-wide agreements with large construction organizations. Thus, the Elevator Constructors Union, the Sprinkler Fitters and the Tile Layers have national agreements with employers' associations.

A local building trades council and the employers' association may also make an industry-wide agreement covering general industrial relations for all crafts. This type of contract, existing in

57. Any one international may have a variety of locals based upon a specific occupation. A majority of the internationals are, in fact, compound- or extended-craft organizations.

most organized cities, regulates strikes and lockouts in all trades, methods in settling controversies and interunion disputes, and often includes a statement of "principles for industrial relations." Its chief aim is to provide uniformity in provisions and procedure and general supervision over the collective bargaining process in the local market.

b. THE AGREEMENTS

Agreements vary with the trades. They may outline on a single sheet of paper the understanding as to wages, hours, working conditions and methods of settling disputes. Mostly, however, they are longer, with detailed statements on the issues negotiated. The objectives of the agreement between the New York City carpenters and their employers, for example, are:

> To establish and maintain wages, hours, and working conditions for the work covered by this agreement . . .; to prevent strikes and lockouts; to insure the peaceable adjustment and settlement of any and all grievances, disputes or differences that may arise between the parties as such or between them as employer and employee, and to provide for adjustment of disputes between trades and jurisdictional disputes.

(1). *Wage and Hour Provisions*

Wages and hours, though not the most controversial issues in this industry's collective bargaining, are of basic importance. Pay provisions are covered in great detail. They include the rate per hour; overtime, which is usually from one and a half to twice the standard rate; the method and time of payment; prohibitions of "kickbacks" to employers and hiring bosses, of bonus systems, and frequently of piece work; payment for "readiness to work"; and the rate for out-of-town work.

The hourly rate, although high compared with other skilled trades, must, of course, be considered in relation to annual earnings. Considerable regional differences exist in hourly wage rates, and even within a region variations are wide. Whether the town is primarily urban or rural, its industrial composition and its degree of unionization are important influences. In 1937, hourly wages for asbestos workers ranged from 40 to 60 cents an hour in Knoxville, Tennessee, to $1.50 an hour in Boston, $1.60 in Chicago, and $1.65 in New York City; hourly wages of bricklayers from 60 cents to $1.25 in Knoxville to $1.70 in Chicago, $1.75 in Pittsburgh, and $1.84 in New York City. Hourly wages for carpenters ranged from 40 cents to 80 cents in Knoxville to $1.50 in Butte, Montana, $1.625 in Chicago, and $1.75 in New York. These variations are typical of all building trades.[58] Hourly rates in the industry have continued to move upward; in 1939 a comprehensive sample of contractual rates showed that they averaged 7 per cent higher than in 1929, the increases ranging from 5 per cent for painters to 22.5 per cent for steam and sprinkler fitters' helpers.[59]

The seasonal nature of the industry, which limits working weeks from thirty-six to forty a year, is the weightiest reason for high hourly rates. The cost-plus psychology in the industry has conditioned employers to accept them. Disregarding for the moment the possible effect of high rates upon demand, it is relatively easy to transfer increased costs, uniform for all firms, to the owners. It has been urged that lower hourly rates of pay would increase annual earnings. However, after several experiments, labor remains unconvinced of this. Impatient of the slow working out of economic forces, labor refuses to accept a lower-wage policy unless it shows fairly certain and quick results.

Substantial reductions in wages were conceded by several local unions during 1932 and 1933.[60] But the economic collapse was too heavy; low labor and material costs alone, even when drastically reduced, were not enough to revive demand for building. Consequently, the policy was discarded. As soon as building demand increased—in 1934 and 1935—unions which had accepted wage adjustments in the early years of the depression forced restoration of their old rates.

58. *Wage Rates Per Hour for the Building Trades in the Principal Cities for 1937*, compiled and issued by E. M. Craig, Secretary of the Builders' Association of Chicago.
59. *Hearings Before the Temporary National Economic Committee*, Pt. 11, p. 5588. (Based on BLS data comprising contractual scales in 28 journeymen trades and 9 helper and laborer trades covering 440,000 union members in 72 cities.)
60. "Union Scales of Wages and Hours in the Building Trades, May 15, 1936," *Bulletin No. 626*, U. S. Bureau of Labor Statistics, 1937, pp. 3, 5.

Prevailing Wage Does Not Always Prevail

To what extent the hourly rates stipulated in the agreements have been actually in effect is unknown. Severe unemployment among building workers and the resulting competition for jobs made kickbacks common, with the result that the actual wage paid may have been considerably lower than the scale provided.[61] In less than six years, the Public Works Administration found $644,000 "stolen" from workmen through kickbacks [62] on public works projects costing $6.1 billion.

When the CIO United Construction Workers Organizing Committee proposed to the New York Building Trades Employers' Association a daily wage scale of $9 for journeymen, $6 for helpers and $5 for common labor, its head said that workers had been found getting from $4 to $7 a day [63] instead of the official and contracted-for rate of $11 to $14. A report by the New York Building Trades Employers' Association made for the New York Board of Estimate showed that average wages for carpenters were less than half of the union scale. Nor was this unusual in other parts of the country; only on government contracts and large private jobs did union wage scales generally prevail.[64] Officers of both the Chicago building trades' unions and building employers' associations agree that wide evasions of union rates have been common in their city.[65]

Working hours are no longer a serious controversy. Since 1920, the eight-hour day and the five-day week have been included in virtually all important trade agreements. Since 1935, the seven-hour day has prevailed in many communities, and the six-hour day in some trades in New York City and the Far West. Unemployment during the thirties was responsible for demands for a thirty-hour week. This was designed to spread the work, but it

---

61. *Engineering News-Record,* June 11, 1931, p. 990.
62. *America Builds, the Record of P.W.A.,* Washington, 1939, pp. 87-88. The Public Works Administration states that kickbacks of 25 per cent of the prevailing rate were found.
63. *The New York Times,* March 31, 1940, p. 20.
64. New York Building Trades Employers' Association, *News and Opinion,* April 1935, p. 3; June 1935, p. 1.
65. Oral information secured by Robert Winters.

would not have increased total employment, and might even have decreased it by increasing costs.

(2). Control of the Supply of Labor

Apprenticeship Regulations

Next in importance to wages and hours in the building industry is labor supply. Employer-employee agreements in all crafts provide a steady but restricted supply of skilled craftsmen by regulating apprenticeship and entrance to the trade. The strictly controlled ratio between apprentices and journeymen has been under frequent criticism; unions are accused of creating a shortage of skilled mechanics in the industry.[66] A similar accusation might be made against contractors, for during the twenties the apprenticeship quotas were not fully used. Employers were unwilling to assume responsibility for apprenticeship training when there was no assurance that apprentices they trained would not go to competitors.

The absence of industry-consciousness was an important factor limiting apprentice training. The more progressive elements recognized this, and to meet the problem joint apprenticeship committees, with or without the cooperation of the schools, were organized in many cities. In Cleveland and Niagara Falls there was considerable cooperation among employers, unions and local school committees. Apprentices were enrolled in vocational schools, an efficient training system was devised, and standards and terms of apprenticeship were formulated.[67] The U. S. Department of Labor likewise helped.

66. Haber, *op. cit.*, pp. 133-134.
67. For a typical plan, see William J. Small and Robert H. Rogers, "Cooperative Apprentice Training in the Building Trades at Niagara Falls, New York," *Bulletin No. 797*, University of the State of New York, February 1, 1924; Estelle M. Stewart, "Apprenticeship in Building Construction," *Bulletin No. 459*, U. S. Bureau of Labor Statistics, April 1928, pp. 1-11.
Reference should also be made to the statewide system in Wisconsin, in effect since 1915. Apprentices and their training there have been under supervision of both the Wisconsin Industrial Commission and local advisory committees composed of an equal number of journeymen and employers. Of the more than three thousand apprenticeship contracts carried to completion from 1915 to 1931, nearly five hundred were in the building trades. *Monthly Labor Review*, November 1932, pp. 1104-1106.

After 1930, many training programs were abandoned because unemployment in the industry weakened whatever incentive there was to train apprentices. Yet the large increase in construction in 1940–1941 apparently did not bring any real labor shortage. Temporary and isolated shortages of skilled union labor, however, have occurred. In 1938 the New York local union of electrical workers issued "working permits" to nonmembers for daily or weekly fees. This practice, which was not confined to one local, met a temporary demand for skilled workers yet avoided permanent increase in the union membership.[68] It has been sharply criticized as monopolistic by antiunionists as well as by labor progressives. Likewise condemned are exorbitant initiation fees of which a typical example is the $100 charged by the New York Electrical Workers Local 3. High initiation fees limit entrance to the trade and control the labor supply, yet even willingness to pay them does not mean admission; the union might not be open to new members. Such restrictions are not general. Most unions are "free" and open, fees and dues are not restrictive, and apprenticeship regulations have not caused artificial labor shortages.

The Closed Shop

Successful enforcement of these rules makes a closed shop inevitable. Some responsible employers, in fact, favor it because of conditions prevailing in the industry and they do not oppose cost-increasing practices and regulation of apprentices lest they undermine union aid in equalizing labor costs. Since labor is between 20 and 50 per cent of total construction cost,[69] the pressure to pay less than standard rates is very great. This is especially true for smaller contractors. As a result the larger contractors look to the union to "keep the contractors in line." To do this effectively the union needs the closed shop.

Almost all of the better skilled workers belong to the union, and large employers, who usually operate in the bigger cities, find union headquarters the largest and most dependable employment

68. *Business Week,* March 19, 1938.
69. Testimony of L. Seth Schnitman, *Hearings Before the Temporary National Economic Committee,* Pt. 11, p. 5021; testimony of D. W. Tracy, *ibid.,* p. 5262.

agency. To maintain an open shop an employer must defeat the union and prevent it from again actively influencing his workers. Such a policy leads to strikes, uncertainty and increased costs, and often to guerilla warfare. Higher costs that may come with closed-shop operation affect all in the industry. Therefore, they can be passed on to the buyers. These stabilizing influences have encouraged general acceptance of the closed shop in the building trades.[70]

Even closed-shop agreements do not seriously restrict the employers' right to hire and fire, except insofar as hiring must be done through the union office which, as in New York City, may place 50 per cent of the men needed on a job. In addition, some unions may regulate hiring by requiring the employer to hire older workers. The New York electrical workers, for example, stipulate a certain ratio between older and younger men.[71] Similar rules may in effect restrict hiring and firing, as in the case of the Chicago glaziers, who require each employer to keep at least one glazier steadily employed.

In recent depression years, the unions have sought to impose more equal distribution of work. On the Chicago Post Office job 10 per cent of the men were laid off every day to spread the work.[72] In New York City, the bricklayers set up a central employment bureau, registered all their unemployed and assigned jobs in order of registration,[73] while a joint committee of the Electrical Contractors' Association and the union also agreed to rotation of union workers.[74] On such large jobs as the World's Fair and large public projects, the rotation plan was frequently employed. Lists drawn up in the union employment office were used in hiring, but only men longest unemployed were assigned to jobs. Employers have often objected to the competence of the men employed in this manner, and to the "political power" which it gives the business agent.

70. Haber, *op. cit.*, Ch. 9, pp. 251-265.
71. *Agreement*, 1939, pp. 16-17.
72. Information from P. Sullivan, President of the Chicago Building Trades Council.
73. *Agreement*, 1938-1940, pp. 10-14.
74. See *Amendment to Agreement and Working Rules* between New York City Electrical Contractors' Association and Local Union No. 3 of the International Brotherhood of Electrical Workers, 1939.

(3). *Limitation of Output*

Union regulations and "working rules" affecting efficiency and limiting the use of laborsaving devices have long been controversial subjects in the building trades. It is generally assumed that union workers of any trade where the output is measurable limit the quantity of work during a normal working day. Union agreements and by-laws, however, seldom define or limit a day's work. Although prohibitions against "pace setters" and "hustling" on the job are still found, only in older agreements are there provisions which fix the amount of a day's work.

Even so, architects and contractors insist that restriction of output prevails in most trades. The explanation for restriction often lies in the insecure, highly seasonal nature of the industry, where both organized and unorganized workers believe that work is definitely limited and should be made to last as long as possible.

Very little precise information exists to test the opinion that restriction prevails. The U. S. Bureau of Labor Statistics in 1923 investigated and reported, "notwithstanding the persistence of articles and interviews in newspapers and trade journals about the relative efficiency of labor as compared with former years, this bureau was unable to find a single building contractor, superintendent, or foreman who had a record of work done per man hour on the jobs in progress or upon any former job."[75] In the absence of production records, opinions as to a fair day's work are based upon general experience and observation.

Prohibition of Short Cuts

Rules which restrict methods or machinery may have as great an effect upon output as more direct limitations. New York bricklayers will not allow mortar to be delivered or spread in bulk; it must be spread by a trowel. The Boston plasterers' tenderers' agreement sets the size of the hod and forbids loading mortar boards on wheelbarrows.

Many painters' locals prohibit paint sprays. Other locals allow

---

75. Ethelbert Stewart, "Labor Productivity and Costs in Certain Building Trades," *Monthly Labor Review*, November 1924, p. 1.

them for certain paints or types of work but demand higher pay for their use, which raises costs and cuts part of what the spray method saves. Philadelphia granite cutters proscribe the pneumatic hand harnesses with a tool of over one inch. New York steam-fitters require radiator branches and coil connections to be cut and threaded on the job. The New York plasterers' agreement calls for the same on-the-job placement of all permanent plane moldings. Milwaukee carpenters require that mortising for locks, butting of hinges, and installation of all hardware shall be done on the job. Many glaziers' locals do not allow glass to be installed in the shop.

(4). *Restrictions on Materials and Other Rules*

Many trades impose restrictions upon various building materials. Carpenters, sheet metal workers, electrical workers, plumbers and stone cutters have long tried to force the unionization of mills by refusing to work on materials made by nonunion labor.[76] With less success, iron workers tried to unionize the fabricating plants. Interunion conflict provoked Portland, Oregon, carpenters to reject lumber from CIO mills. Prison-made goods are excluded in most agreements.

Many regulations are not directly related to unionization efforts. Some unions refuse to install materials not supplied by the contractors; in some cities plasterers will not handle gypsum board in place of plaster; bricklayers have long objected to hollow tile. Again, in some places unions have cooperated with contractors to get prohibition of certain competitive materials in local building codes—such as the New York regulations against wall board and hollow tile.[77] Many a municipal regulation is drawn to help friendly contractors and supply men.

A few agreements have full-crew rules, prescribing the number of men for certain types of work. In New York City two electrical workers must be on jobs involving live wires of 440 volts or more. Operating engineers generally stipulate the number of men needed on their machines. Boston sign erectors require three men on any

76. See p. 204.
77. *The Architectural Forum*, October 19, 1939, p. 52.

job. Chicago glaziers have a detailed full-crew rule for all rack wagons.

Working Employers and Foremen

Local contracts often prohibit the employer from doing manual work on the job; a working employer replaces a journeyman and is a potential pace setter. However, bricklayers working on fireproofing in Chicago specifically allow the employer to use tools.

Nearly all unions require foremen to come under their control as union members. Foremen who order violations of union rules or are "slave drivers" can thus be curbed, for suspension from the union automatically ends foremanship. Sometimes detailed rules govern foremen's wages, ratios to journeymen and conditions under which they may use tools.

Limiting Contractors

Employers and labor leaders prefer limited competition. Contractors' associations do not relish increased competition; the union has trouble policing too many small contractors. Some agreements prohibit journeymen from becoming contractors. Chicago painters have elaborate rules governing the transformation of a journeyman into an employer—at least five years in the union and an examination of his ability to read plans and estimate work. Other unions permit the change by the mere stamping of the union card to that effect.

In some crafts, the agreements authorize union participation in some affairs generally regarded as exclusively management's. Contracts of New York pipefitters, Portland plasterers, and Seattle cement finishers contain rules concerning bid depositories. Under agreement between the New York City District Council of Painters and the Master Painters and Decorators, all jobs must be registered with the secretary of the employers' association, who must inform the union secretary daily of new jobs.[78] A paint trade board, established under the agreement, registers all union members and certifies all jobs on which union men are to be employed. The board may summon and question any employer or journey-

78. *Agreement*, 1938-1939, p. 13.

man and may "require the production of books, papers, or other evidence it may deem necessary."[79]

Employers in the New York electrical trade must send the union a summary of their pay rolls each week, because, so runs the agreement, "economic planning is necessary and essential to maintain industrial stability and . . . statistics are vitally important to accomplish such." An employer must also have a "permanent place of business, with a business telephone, and open to the public during normal business hours."

(5). *Effects of the "Working Rules"*

These "working rules" give building workers substantial job control. They guard against relaxed standards of hours and wages, against changes in methods of production, and even against business practices which might imperil health, job security, or union bargaining power.

Although the purpose of most of these regulations is protective and regulatory, in practice they are frequently restrictive. Many well-intentioned rules overstep the bounds of desirable regulation and obstruct the employers' freedom of action and the progress of the industry. While regulation of apprenticeship, for example, is a desirable objective, it is restrictive whenever it causes a reduction in the number of trained workers below the industry's long-time needs. Likewise, the closed shop may be desirable in view of the industry's special problems. But when it is accompanied by a closed union, high initiation fees, "working permits" and similar practices, it may be inimical to the industry and to the consumer.

(6). *Trade Disputes*

In spite of elaborate machinery for peaceful settlements, controversies and disagreements have been frequent. Negotiations and mediation at times fail, and the will to peace is not strong enough to overcome the possible rewards of direct action. Causes of strikes are often found in one-sided organization of the industry. Employers, as has already been indicated, are comparatively poorly organized. Lack of balance of power may lead to

---
79. *Ibid.*, p. 22.

excessive demands and eventual disruption of the negotiatory procedure. Although provisions for arbitration of disputes arising under an agreement are found in most cases, trade-union officials have not always been enthusiastic advocates of arbitration, particularly of disputes over the terms of a new agreement. Strikes, therefore, have been common in connection with the negotiation of a new agreement,[80] less common over differences arising under an existing agreement. In addition, a large number have resulted from jurisdictional conflict, especially in the large cities.[81]

Strike statistics reflect in part the volume of building and the contractors' general attitude toward unionization. During periods of intense building activity strikes tend to increase; unions seek recognition, the closed shop and wage increases or other improvements in working conditions. When building construction declines, fewer strikes occur; unions are more cautious and disagreements are more readily adjusted, though employers' attempts to cut wages, or to re-establish the open shop, are likely to lead to defensive strikes.

Strikes Since the World War

Thus, as shown in Table 3, strikes rose rapidly during the World War when building was active and labor relatively scarce. Economic conditions were less favorable in 1920–1921, but the open-shop drive was being strongly pressed by contractors in many cities, and strikes increased. In spite of active building they fell off during the twenties and reached a low point in 1928. Considerable stability in industrial relations was achieved during this period.

Strikes increased during the early thirties as a result of wage reductions but declined with the increasing severity of the depression. Strikes in 1933 were about half those in 1932, and employees involved were less than half. The decline continued until 1936, though more workers were affected in 1934 than in any other

---

80. Very often employers make no attempt to operate during such strikes. Commonly, the agreements expire at a time when there is very little building construction, so that the strikes are, in many respects, more nominal than real.

81. See p. 201. Unfortunately the data available do not classify strikes according to these three types.

year between 1933 and 1936. When the industry revived in 1937, strikes again increased. The next two years' fluctuation reflects changes in construction activity. The number of workers involved is, of course, influenced by both the number and location of specific strikes. Thus a strike in Chicago or New York usually involves a large number of men because of the importance of building activity in those cities.

TABLE 3

STRIKES IN BUILDING TRADES [a]
1914–1939

Year	Number of Strikes	Number Involved
1914	275	..
1915	259	..
1916	394	..
1917	468	..
1918	434	..
1919	473	..
1920	521	..
1921	583	..
1922	113	..
1923	208	..
1924	270	..
1925	349	..
1926	272	..
1927	189	50,376
1928	141	24,421
1929	198	42,062
1930	163	26,814
1931	193	25,183
1932	182	62,834
1933	99	24,298
1934	87	26,993
1935	76	10,576
1936	111	22,355
1937	192	48,017
1938	152	27,808
1939	162	48,649

a. Florence Peterson, "Strikes in the United States, 1880-1936," *Bulletin No. 651*, U. S. Bureau of Labor Statistics, 1938, pp. 38, 123, 158. The figures for 1937, 1938, and 1939 were compiled from *Monthly Labor Review*, April 1937 to May 1940. From 1933 to 1939, strikes on PWA jobs are excluded. The total is not significantly affected.

Despite numerous strikes, contractors and organized workers have developed procedures for peaceful compromises after over fifty years of experiment with joint relations. The decline in number of strikes between 1914 and 1939 indicates improvement in collective bargaining.

(7). *Administering the Trade Agreement*

The machinery for administering the trade agreement is not uniform. In most cases, relatively simple provisions describe the methods of settling grievances and differences over interpretation. The larger building centers, however, often have more elaborate machinery.

Grievances are usually first considered by representatives of the union and the employer involved. The union business agent, particularly, plays an important role in settling the many issues which constantly arise. He visits the job often, and the men or the employer refer problems or disputes to him. A conference may be adequate to adjust the differences. While most agreements provide for mediation and arbitration, conferences between the union representative, or the union committee, and the employer are sufficient to dispose of the great majority of the day-to-day issues which arise.

Disputes which cannot be settled by the employer and the union may be referred to committees of the employers' association and the building trades council. Because of the importance of the sympathetic strike in this industry, the council can exert a tremendous influence on individual unions. When the council approves a strike, the local union is assured of the sympathetic action of the other unions in the industry, if that should become necessary.

Where the council and the employers' association are not able to agree, the issue may be referred to arbitration. Arbitration awards are not popular with the unions and not always with the employers. Many serious disputes in the building markets of New York, Chicago and San Francisco have, however, been settled by such awards.

Several factors affect the enforcement of agreements and arbitration awards. Where the building trades council exerts a strong influence upon the local union and underwrites the agreement, violation of the no-strike clause is largely eliminated. Similarly, the existence of a strong employers' association leads to greater use of mediation and arbitration and deters the unions from employing direct action. Violations of agreements are at a minimum in those areas where both groups are well organized and the machinery for adjusting disputes is long established.

6. Problems and Obstacles

Successful collective bargaining has opposite meanings to different groups. To the building contractor it is successful if work is not disrupted by strikes or stoppages and if working rules do not interfere with an adequate supply of skilled labor or restrict his "managerial freedom." In principle, he has no objection to collective bargaining and union recognition. On the contrary, his experience may have convinced him that in this industry the union is a necessary and indispensable agency for the employer as well as its members. He fears, however, the effect of union control upon efficiency and output and upon changes in methods of production. The employer, therefore, frequently looks upon collective bargaining negotiations as a contest in which he must protect himself against rules and regulations.

The building trades worker has other problems. Seasonal employment and low annual earnings, technical changes threatening to destroy the bargaining value of his skill, occupational hazards endangering his health—control over these forms of insecurity are to him the significant test of whether collective bargaining is successful.

In the case of large buildings involving big capital investment, the owner may be willing to pay a high—often excessive—price for industrial peace. He has only temporary interest in the building industry and extra costs from uneconomic practices can be passed on or spread over time. Consequently, he is not greatly concerned with the details of employer-employee relations or the restrictive practices and rules which may bring increased costs. He may find such restrictions quite tolerable if they avoid strikes and assure continuous production.

All this differs from the type of stabilization which benefits the public. The public is interested in the general prosperity and peace of the industry, but even more in greater efficiency, higher quality and lower cost. Consequently, stabilization based upon collusive agreements is not socially desirable. Nor can collective bargaining be said to be successful when restrictive practices of contractors and unions are a part of trade agreements. Industrial peace on the basis of such practices may have too high a social cost.

These varying points of view frequently conflict. The solution usually is not arrived at by reasonable compromise among the three interests involved—employers, labor, and the public—but by a test of strength. The consumer's power manifests itself only through refusal or inability to buy. The effect of this has been somewhat offset by large public construction since 1933. The employers have been short-sighted and often themselves parties to restrictive and collusive arrangements. Nor have labor leaders seen the challenge presented by a poorly managed industry. With few exceptions they have been too absorbed in their own disputes and the problems of the separate crafts to give the essential leadership and the broad viewpoint needed if industrial stability is to be realized.

Fluctuations in Employment

Seasonal fluctuations, which play havoc with a worker's annual income, are partly responsible for the many union restrictions. There are, of course, great variations in the seasonal patterns of the different crafts: masons and painters are subject to the greatest ebb and flow; sheet metal workers, steamfitters, and electricians reverse the usual pattern—their steadiest employment is during winter months. Whenever the layoff occurs, however, from 20 to 30 per cent of the worker's time is lost in an average year. In addition to seasonal influences, moreover, the building trades are peculiarly sensitive to general depression or prosperity.

This intermittent employment is basic. It aggravates every other industrial relations problem in the industry, particularly wages, overtime policy and apprenticeship control. High hourly pay is defended as necessary to neutralize seasonal unemployment.

Persistent efforts to establish the five-day week, and now the thirty-hour week, the heavy penalties for overtime, the restrictions on entrance to the trade—all these aim at spreading the work either among more members or over a longer period. Union members and nonunion workers hold that the total volume of building to be done is relatively fixed, and they firmly believe in shorter hours or more "stretching" of the job. So firmly fixed is this belief, that it will be discarded only when unemployment ends. This attitude is partly responsible for accentuating evils it seeks to cure.

Little progress has been made in curing seasonal unemployment. Technical equipment and improved construction methods have made winter work possible and even practicable, except for small operations. However, the prevalence of small contractors with limited managerial efficiency and without technical equipment is a definite drawback to rapid progress.

Among the suggestions for reducing unemployment have been flexible wage rates, to be lower in the slack seasons than in busy months; flexible hours, with a longer work week during the busy season; a guaranteed annual wage with lower hourly rates.[82] All of these have met resistance.

Flexible Wage Rates

Flexible wage rates, it is urged, would help break the custom of summer building, and the price inducement would probably cause postponement of much construction to the slack winter months. A varying work week would also decrease the pressure for more labor in the summer with subsequent unemployment in the winter.

The annual wage might encourage building and revive a depressed market. High hourly rates could probably be reduced if the guaranteed annual wage were higher than the present yearly earnings. Irrespective of the desirability of an annual wage, there

---

82. Testimony of D. W. Tracy, *Hearings Before the Temporary National Economic Committee*, Pt. 11, p. 5276.

is little evidence that the industry can guarantee it. Only a small number of contractors have permanent crews of workers; most contractors do not belong to any association which could underwrite an annual wage.

However, wage rates are only one factor responsible for high costs. General labor efficiency and working rules are additional factors, but finance charges and particularly material prices, when pegged by monopolistic practices, are also elements of excessive costs. These considerations not only suggest the difficulties in solving the construction industry's unemployment problem but also indicate that a joint effort by all elements in the industry, as well as the general public, is required for a successful attack on the problem.

Interunion Conflicts

Jurisdictional disputes and failure of unions to adjust such differences peacefully are major causes of unstable industrial relations in the building trades. Employers and the public are, in the main, innocent bystanders. As these struggles involve the right of a craft to perform a specific type of work, they are apt to become long and bitter.

A solution of the problem has been sought vainly for more than half a century. Until key unions subordinate their interests to the good of the industry, these controversies are likely to continue and even multiply with more technological change.

Should the CIO establish itself in the building trades, AF of L unions may have to find a satisfactory formula very quickly. For, while industrial unionism may not smooth out all jurisdictional quarrels, it could reduce them materially.

Restraint of Trade

Monopolistic restraints which raise costs and restrict the demand for building are another difficult problem in the industry. Antitrust investigations have been made simultaneously in eleven cities, including Chicago, Detroit, Cleveland, St. Louis, Pittsburgh, San Francisco, Los Angeles and Seattle—all leading building centers—to determine responsibility for the present high building costs. Indictments have been returned against contractors, materials dealers and labor union officials in a number of cities.[83]

In considering labor's status under the antitrust acts, the Department of Justice regards five practices as restraints upon trade: efforts to prevent the use of new materials and equipment, compelling the hiring of unnecessary labor, graft and extortion, illegal price-fixing, and attempts to undermine an existing system of collective bargaining.[84]

The prohibition against "illegal price-fixing" is just as applicable to labor unions as to any other economic group. So is that against "graft and corruption," although it may be questioned whether the antitrust laws are the proper method for dealing with this problem. Prosecution of unions for enforcing restrictions on new materials and equipment was directed against the exclusion of such materials, and not against regulation of their introduction and use. Prosecuting "attempts to undermine an existing system of collective bargaining" was intended to avoid jurisdictional strikes or other interruptions of work, particularly when such interruptions occur in spite of the awards of labor boards.

Perhaps the most controversial of the practices which the Department of Justice sought to restrain is that "compelling the hiring of unnecessary labor." Broadly interpreted, government officials could inquire into most union rules and practices which directly or indirectly determine how much labor is to be hired for a job. The Department denied any intention to make such a broad inquiry. It was concerned with "that extreme form of pay roll padding in which the employer is required to hire men who are completely unnecessary." There are local instances involving the Brotherhood of Teamsters, for example, where complaints have been made against hiring extra drivers who have no function to perform.

The building trades unions voiced strong objections to the application of the antitrust laws to union practices. This opposi-

---

83. Corwin D. Edwards, "Can the Antitrust Laws Preserve Competition?" *American Economic Review,* Supplement, March 1940, p. 168.
84. Letter of Thurman Arnold to Indianapolis Central Labor Union, U. S. Department of Justice release, November 20, 1939, p. 3.

tion was in part supported by the U. S. Supreme Court, which held that jurisdictional controversies and restrictions on machinery are not indictable under the antitrust laws.[85] Indictments against price-fixing arrangements and the general activity of the Anti-Trust Division in ferreting out secret understandings designed to fix prices and restrict competition should have desirable results and contribute to protection of the consumer's interest.

The extent to which these practices of contractors and unions result in higher building costs and the savings which would result from their elimination are difficult to determine. If all the restrictions in the building markets—not merely the labor restrictions—were removed, it is claimed that building costs could be reduced "by at least 25 per cent."[86] These claims are not based on detailed studies and there are probably no adequate data on the basis of which they could be tested. Moreover, problems are involved in determining which practices should be eliminated. "Illegal" practices can be defined by law and the courts; "uneconomic" practices, however, are not so clearly designated.

Higher costs cannot be ascribed primarily to union practices. Insofar as restrictive practices affect the building of small homes, the responsibility of the trade unions is quite limited. A union leader estimates that 90 per cent of mechanical work done on houses costing less than $15,000 is nonunion.[87] And high costs particularly retard housing in the lower price field. More than 50 per cent of city families cannot afford to buy or rent a house costing $4,000 or more, yet in 1936 only 15 per cent of the houses built cost less than $4,000.

In localities where union leadership is selfish and power-seeking, local rackets and unwholesome local rules have been permitted to exist. Such leadership has occasionally been encouraged by local contractors. It may be too strong to state, as did one union official, that "the contractors decide more than the rank and file

85. *United States of America* v. *William L. Hutcheson, et al.* and *United States of America* v. *Michael Carrozzo, et al.* (1941).
86. Estimates made by "responsible complainants" and cited by Corwin D. Edwards, U. S. Department of Justice, in an address in Chicago, October 11, 1939.
87. Testimony of D. W. Tracy, *Hearings Before the Temporary National Economic Committee,* Pt. 11, p. 5264.

what sort of labor leaders are elected," but it is generally conceded that the attitude and ethics of the contractors' associations influence the type of union leadership. The competitive struggle, prevailing business ethics, the noninclusive organization of contractors may at times be responsible for "conspiracies against the public."

The unions and the contractors' associations should assume the responsibility of reviewing the industry's practices which bring them in conflict with the antitrust laws and public policy in general. For the persistence of these problems will eventually result in a strong public demand for regulation. And such regulation, under the auspices of an unfavorable administration, might injure the position already achieved by the unions.

No concrete suggestion has been made for relaxing the industry's price policies. The current antitrust prosecutions may upset the more flagrant price-fixing arrangements; a consent decree already won against the Tile Contractors' Association of America and the bricklayers' union[88] may lead to similar action. But that alone would be insufficient. Leadership in the building trades, both labor and employer, could help by experimenting with more flexible price and wage policies. In the more cost-conscious home building market, the unions might try differential rates on a market basis—particularly in residential, repair and maintenance work. For many years such proposals have not been well received.[89]

Similarly, flexible hours might be considered, not on an industry-wide, but a market basis. Finally, working rules might be revised for the fullest use of efficient methods and materials.

Obviously the unions alone can do very little to improve the methods in the industry and to provide more stable conditions. Contractors, materials producers and distributors, finance com-

---

88. *The New York Times,* June 11, 1940.
89. A conference of over two hundred building union officials to stimulate construction of one- and two-family houses and to establish a uniform small house wage scale was held in New York City, March 19, 1940. Rates of $9 and $10 for an eight-hour day were proposed instead of $11 to $14 prevailing in existing contracts. (*The New York Times,* March 20, 1940.) About six months later it was announced that union representatives had agreed to reductions on such construction in the Bronx. *PM,* September 6, 1940.

panies and agencies, also are responsible. Moreover, labor organizations would not relax many of their rules or cut their rates of pay without some guarantee against the hazards and insecurity faced by the workers in the industry.

Chapter 5

BITUMINOUS COAL [1]

WALDO E. FISHER

1. INTRODUCTION

FEW INDUSTRIES offer more fruitful fields for research in collective bargaining than bituminous coal. Unionism has been long established, first appearing about halfway in the nineteenth century. Interstate collective bargaining was introduced in 1886, but failed in 1889 after dissension among operators, union rivalry and the withdrawal of important producing areas from the arrangement. Nine years later came the first of a long series of interstate agreements which affected a large proportion of the tonnage of the northern fields. Similar contracts were later made in the Southwest, West and a few southern areas. Today this industry is almost completely unionized.

The bituminous coal mines are scattered over thirty-odd states in the North, South and West. Ownership is widely decentralized, and except perhaps during the World War, and under the Bituminous Coal Act of 1937, competition has been ruthless. In 1929, 4,612 companies operated 6,057 mines and produced 535 million tons. About 20 per cent of this tonnage was from 221 mines of the 17 largest companies, 23 per cent from 416 mines of 70 other companies, and the rest—about 57 per cent—from 5,420 mines of 4,525 companies. In 1929, 1,581 mines and 553 companies supplied 80 per cent of the total output.[2] In 1938 soft

---

1. Economic conditions and therefore many of the problems of industrial relations in anthracite and bituminous coal mining are essentially different. For this reason, notwithstanding many similarities and the fact that the same union has jurisdiction in both, the story of collective bargaining in these two industries is presented in separate chapters.

2. F. G. Tryon and L. Mann, *Coal in 1929*, U. S. Bureau of Mines, 1930, p. 715. The authors point out that the figures for number of companies do not take into

coal mines employed on the average about 437,000 workers and produced 393 million tons of coal.[3]

Bituminous coal is pre-eminently the fuel of commerce and industry in all parts of the country. In 1929 about 75 per cent of the domestic consumption (exports are about 3 per cent of production) went to railroads, factories, coke ovens, electric utilities and steel works including blast furnaces and rolling mills. Domestic and other uses and the bunker trade accounted for the remaining 25 per cent.[4]

Only about a fourth of 1929's total shipments were intrastate, and because of interstate competition, not a single coal-producing state supplied its entire coal requirements. In that year 93 per cent of the coal used in manufacturing establishments, iron and steel mills, gas plants, railroad shops and coke ovens was consumed east of the Mississippi. States north of the Ohio and Potomac and east of the Mississippi used about 80 per cent. Pennsylvania and Ohio consumed 38 per cent.[5]

2. THE STRUGGLE FOR COLLECTIVE BARGAINING, 1850–1898 [6]

The first bituminous coal union seems to have been formed in the Belleville district of Illinois in the 1850's. In 1861 Illinois and Missouri miners established the American Miners' Association—

account "interlocking ownership of interests." They add, however, that had this been done it "would not alter the essential picture . . . which shows a very large number of producing interests competing for a limited business."

3. *Minerals Yearbook, 1940,* U. S. Bureau of Mines, 1940, p. 779. Data are preliminary.

4. Tryon and Mann, *op. cit.,* pp. 770-771. The term "other uses" includes "heating large buildings other than factories, such as hotels, apartments, stores, offices, theaters, garages, and service stations; also a number of other items that cannot be separated, such as water works, construction industry, threshing, public institutions, central heating plants, laundries, and very small industrial consumers not covered by the Census of Manufactures."

5. These consumption figures do not include coal used by railroads for locomotive fuel and that consumed by electric utilities, coal mines, other mines and quarries, the bunker trade and household and miscellaneous users. Percentages are based on data published in the 1929 *Census of Mines and Quarries.*

6. Much of the material in this section has been drawn from Chris Evans, *History of the United Mine Workers of America,* Indianapolis, 1918 (?), Vols. I and II. Specific footnote references have for the most part been omitted, except where other sources have been used.

the first attempt to form a national union in this industry.[7] Thereafter the movement spread to Ohio and Pennsylvania. Wage cuts during the postwar deflation led to bitter and unsuccessful strikes in 1867 and 1868, and the Association disappeared with many of its locals.

But encouraged by successes of anthracite miners in organizing, the soft coal miners formed local unions in Illinois, Indiana, Pennsylvania, Maryland, Michigan, Kentucky and West Virginia in the next five years. At the same time they sought state legislation for shorter hours and safer working conditions, and were partially successful in Ohio and Pennsylvania.

In 1872 Illinois, Indiana and Missouri miners established the Miners Benevolent and Protective Association. The following year, with the help of union delegates from Ohio, Pennsylvania and West Virginia, they formed the Miners' National Association of the United States. The 1873 depression ushered in wage cuts which led to strikes, discharge of union members and the employment of strikebreakers.[8] Two years later, the Miners' National Association faced prosecution for criminal violation of the conspiracy law. The president was acquitted, but an organizer and several local officers and miners were fined and sentenced to prison. Despite these obstacles, the national union grew "beyond the anticipation of its leaders" [9] and in 1875 counted 35,354 members in 347 local branches in twelve states and the Indian Territory.[10]

Early in 1876 the situation became still worse. Wages were then as much as 80 per cent of total costs, and operators tried to reduce them. Exasperated by the tactics of some operators and by what seemed to be endless wage slashing (as early as 1874 wages had been cut 30 per cent in some mines) many local unions struck, despite the earnest pleading of national officers. Faced

---

7. Eleventh Special Report of the Commissioner of Labor, *Regulation and Restriction of Output*, 1904, p. 385.
8. Letters of the president of the Miners' National Association to local officers and members, and union records published in Evans, *op. cit.*, Vol. I, pp. 50-74.
9. *Ibid.*, p. 53.
10. Arthur E. Suffern, *The Coal Miners Struggle for Industrial Status*, The Institute of Economics, Macmillan, New York, 1926, p. 30.

with debt and little chance of replenishing an empty treasury, the headquarters of the National Association closed. After this collapse, local organizations had hard going and most disbanded.[11] After more than a decade of determined effort, the miners lacked the solidarity, self-discipline and experience to force union recognition and interstate or industry-wide collective bargaining.

a. ECONOMIC CONDITIONS, 1878–1898

The next two decades were especially turbulent. A general decline in wholesale prices accompanying sharp liquidation after the Civil War continued until 1896, except for temporary interruptions in 1879, 1881 and 1887.[12] These twenty years saw the depression of 1883–1885, the recessions of 1888 and 1890, and the four years of business stagnation that followed the panic of 1893, one of the severest in United States history.

During these twenty years the bituminous coal industry, as did manufacturing, mining and trade generally, expanded rapidly. Soft coal production increased by a phenomenal 362 per cent under most adverse conditions. Undeveloped reserves of bituminous coal were plentiful, coal mining was still a small-scale undertaking, and owners of untouched lands were constantly tempted to start production. Inasmuch as coal carrying was a very large proportion of their tonnage and revenue, many railroad companies encouraged expansion of existing mines and new developments. They fixed freight rates to distant markets which in some instances amounted to subsidies. This new competition heightened problems of old-established fields which had expanded to meet the requirements of nearby markets. As F. G. Tryon pointed out, "many of the coal fields were staked out before the railroad net of the country was well defined and the rapid increase in railroad mileage of the seventies and eighties threw into com-

---

11. A survey of labor organizations in Illinois made by the Illinois Bureau of Labor Statistics in 1886 found only one union whose date of origin went back as far as 1876. (*Annual Report,* 1886, p. 181.) A similar survey in Ohio by the Ohio Bureau of Labor Statistics in 1900 uncovered only one union with a continuous history beginning prior to 1880. *Twenty-Fourth Annual Report,* p. 368.

12. Willard L. Thorp, *Business Annals,* National Bureau of Economic Research, New York, 1926, pp. 132-138.

petition mines which might never have been opened had our present railroad facilities been available at the start." [13] This expansion was also encouraged by the system of assigning railroad cars to the mines, which put a premium on high daily capacity.

Since mining equipment cannot be used for other purposes and development costs cannot be recovered except by mining coal, the mines operated as long as bare out-of-pocket costs were forthcoming. When this practice led to bankruptcy, new management took over with greatly reduced capital charges.

b. WORKING CONDITIONS AND LABOR POLICIES

These conditions brought a capacity far in excess of demand and a seemingly endless succession of price wars and wage reductions with irregular operation, much unemployment, low hourly and annual earnings and many abuses by the operators.[14] Between 1881 and 1900 the U. S. Bureau of Labor compiled data on 22,793 strikes involving 117,509 establishments in 40 different industries or groups of industries. Coal mining—both anthracite and bituminous—and coke manufacturing accounted for 11 per cent of the strikes and 31 per cent of the employees thrown out of work.[15] Only 52 per cent of the coal and coke strikes were ordered by labor organizations.

Some idea of the many points of friction may be gained from a breakdown of strike causes. Between 1891 and 1900 there were 2,515 strikes involving 14,575 mines and coke ovens and 1.9 million employees.[16] Alone or in combination with other demands, wages and methods or bases of wage payment were strike causes in 81.6 per cent of the affected establishments; working hours in 2.5 per cent; union recognition in 4.5 per cent; discharges in 3.8 per cent; sympathetic strikes in 3.9 per cent; and working condi-

---

13. "The Effect of Competitive Conditions on Labor Relations in Coal Mining," *Annals of the American Academy of Political and Social Science*, January 1924, p. 84.
14. See the annual reports of the bureaus of labor statistics in the important coal-producing states, especially Ohio and Illinois.
15. *Sixteenth Annual Report of the Commissioner of Labor*, 1901, p. 31.
16. *Ibid.*, pp. 478-483. The 14,575 mines and coke ovens are not necessarily different establishments. An establishment involved ten times in strikes in this period would appear as ten establishments.

tions and company policies and practices in 13.5 per cent. Chief among company practices objected to were: long or irregular pay intervals; high charges for tools, powder and the like; violation of agreements; and overdue wages.

C. AN EXPERIMENT IN INTERSTATE COLLECTIVE BARGAINING

Such conditions inspired much union activity. After the demise of the Miners' National Association in 1876, local unions reappeared but made little progress. The economic setting made aggressive tactics very difficult. Immigrants from Hungary, Bohemia, Poland and Italy entered the industry in large numbers.[17] The Knights of Labor began to organize the coal industry. Unions competed for recognition; and a growing body of immigrants, beset by language difficulties and racial prejudices, undermined the solidarity of the English, Scots and Welsh and made creation of an industry-wide union exceedingly hard.

Despite these difficulties and after many unsuccessful attempts, Illinois, Indiana, Ohio, Pennsylvania, West Virginia, Iowa and Kansas miners organized the National Federation of Miners and Mine Laborers in 1885. Union representatives then invited the operators to a joint conference in October 1885 to make an interstate agreement to adjust "market and mining prices in such a way as to avoid strikes and lockouts and give each party an increased profit from the sale of coal." [18] A committee of operators and miners pointed out that if wages rose uniformly, not only would the relative competitive position of the employers remain the same, but they would benefit through reduction in general labor discontent.

Although only one operator accepted the invitation, others were persuaded to participate. Out of the session came a joint invitation to the operators of competing coal fields to meet with the miners later in the year. This second session led to a joint national convention early in 1886. Encouraged by higher prices for coal—the highest since 1880—the operators adopted an interstate agree-

17. W. J. Ashley, *The Adjustment of Wages,* Longmans, Green, London, 1903, p. 93.
18. From a circular of September 12, 1885 inviting the operators to attend a joint conference, Evans, *op. cit.,* Vol. I, p. 145.

ment which fixed piece rates for tonnage men at selected coal fields in each participating state: Illinois, Indiana, Iowa, Ohio, Pennsylvania and West Virginia. The purpose was to standardize labor costs and to place the competition between fields on a higher wage level. The agreement also provided for a general board of arbitration and conciliation to adjust all interstate disputes.

Dissension and Failure

Dissension arose almost immediately. The Grape Creek operators of Illinois claimed that wages for their mines were too high and locked out their employees. The dispute spread to other Illinois fields. At the second annual conference the West Virginia operators withdrew, and the next year Illinois operators, because of internal dissension, found it impossible to continue the arrangement. Faced with increasing competition from Illinois, Indiana withdrew in 1889, leaving only Ohio and western Pennsylvania, whose operators and miners negotiated separate district agreements.

Causes of the failure of the first attempt to stabilize the industry were: (1) a heavy strain from a 10 per cent decline in the average value per ton of coal in 1888;[19] (2) noncooperation of certain operators, who under the former arrangement had a competitive advantage or who felt that the new order placed them at a disadvantage; (3) intense rivalry between older established unions and the Knights of Labor which weakened labor effectiveness not only at the conference table but in compelling unsympathetic operators to live up to the terms of the agreement; and (4) the failure of important coal-producing fields to participate.

d. FORMATION OF THE UNITED MINE WORKERS OF AMERICA

Realizing that the successful operation of interstate agreements necessitated a solid labor front, some union leaders sought an effective working arrangement between the Knights of Labor and the National Federation of Miners and Mine Laborers. Up to this

---

19. F. G. Tryon, L. Mann and H. O. Rogers, *Coal in 1930*, U. S. Bureau of Mines, 1932, p. 647.

time the Knights of Labor, which as late as 1888 had enrolled the majority of union coal miners, had not been particularly cooperative, and in fact sometimes undercut existing union scales to secure recognition of its own organization. Having lost heavily in membership and influence after the collapse of the interstate agreement, it was now willing to consolidate. The result was establishment of the United Mine Workers of America early in 1890.[20]

The new union was a loose federation which preserved the essential features of both organizations. The same national and district officers served both unions and the same dues and assessments were levied. Some control was also established over the right of locals and districts to call strikes. This dual organization continued until 1898 when the organization representing the Knights of Labor in the bituminous coal industry was dissolved. The United Mine Workers of America reorganized and soon dominated this and the anthracite industry.

e. EFFORTS TO RE-ESTABLISH INTERSTATE COLLECTIVE BARGAINING

The national organization had a difficult time maintaining its existence. In 1891 its efforts to re-establish the interstate agreement failed and so did that year's general strike for a wage increase and the eight-hour day. This setback and the refusal of workers in certain districts to respond to the strike call did much to discredit the national organization with both operators and miners. By 1892 the paid-up membership of the United Mine Workers had fallen to 19,376—approximately 9 per cent of the eligible wage earners in the industry.[21]

Next came the severe depression of 1893 to 1898. Coal prices, which for four years were practically stationary, tobogganed. The average price of all coal at the mine dropped from 99 cents a ton in 1892 to 80 cents in 1898.[22] In some districts the decline was greater; in 1897 the entire output of a commercial mine in the Danville field was sold as mine-run coal for 48 cents a ton and in

20. Suffern, *op. cit.*, pp. 51-54.
21. Data supplied to the U. S. Coal Commission of 1922 by the UMW.
22. Tryon, Mann and Rogers, *op. cit.*, p. 647.

some mines coal sold for as little as 25 cents a ton.[23] Drastic price reductions compelled operators generally to sell their coal for less than cost of production.[24] For three years after 1894 the annual working time dropped to an average of 187 days,[25] and wages fell with prices. In the Hocking Valley, rates dropped from 70 cents a ton in 1892 to 45 cents in 1896.[26]

The national union sought to protect the miners' falling standard of living by a series of strikes. Later it called out miners not primarily to get better terms of employment but to reduce the coal surplus so that with higher prices the operators could pay more wages. In the spring of 1894 approximately 125,000 miners quit work at the request of the national union. Within three weeks this number rose to 180,000, a remarkable achievement for a union with a membership of only 24,000.[27] The suspension led to a joint conference of operators and miners from Indiana, Ohio, western Pennsylvania and West Virginia,[28] which resulted in a partial victory that postponed a pending wage reduction, and brought temporary adoption of the agreed-upon wage scale at some mines.[29] After further attempts to re-establish interstate agreements failed in 1895 and 1896, the miners' union, which now had a membership of only 9,731, ordered a strike in July 1897. To this order 150,000 miners responded.[30]

3. Collective Bargaining in the Central Competitive Field

The twelve weeks' strike seriously affected the economic position of the producing fields involved. It seemed to drive home to

23. Eleventh Special Report of the Commissioner of Labor, pp. 387-388. "Mine-run" coal is coal not yet run over screens for sizing.
24. Ashley, *op. cit.*, pp. 103-104.
25. U. S. Bureau of Mines, *Mineral Resources of the United States, 1917*, Pt. II, p. 932.
26. Tryon, "The Effect of Competitive Conditions on Labor Relations in Coal Mining," p. 84.
27. Evans, *op. cit.*, Vol. II, p. 360.
28. Suffern, *op. cit.*, p. 68.
29. Eleventh Special Report of the Commissioner of Labor, p. 390.
30. Suffern, *op. cit.*, pp. 69-79.

the operators the experience of the last decade that frequent wage cuts usually led to corresponding reductions elsewhere with competition just as ruthless as before.[31] More important was the prospect of relief from competition of nonunion mines south of the Ohio River which the union promised to organize and bring under contract. Through efforts of Ohio, Indiana and Illinois state boards of arbitration, representatives of the miners and operators of Illinois, Indiana, Ohio and western Pennsylvania—commonly referred to as the Central Competitive Field—were brought in joint conference.[32] After considerable negotiation they established, in 1898, the basic eight-hour day, a uniform wage scale for daymen, and tonnage rates at basing points in each area for the men who actually mined the coal.[33] This agreement, with minor modifications, was renewed the following year and subsequent agreements, sometimes involving wage adjustments and other changes, were negotiated or renewed, usually at one- or two-year intervals, until 1927. When the conferees deadlocked, notably in 1910, 1914 and 1922, contracts were negotiated within individual districts.

a. BASIC THEORY UNDERLYING THE CENTRAL COMPETITIVE FIELD COMPACT

The joint declaration of principles of the interstate conference stated, "this movement is founded and . . . it rests upon correct business ideas, competitive equality, and upon well-recognized principles of justice." [34]

Miners and operators attempted to establish tonnage rates with local differentials throughout the four areas so that operators might ship coal to their customary markets. Miners and loaders were not guaranteed "equal pay for equal work." On the contrary, the primary goal sought, at least in theory, was uniform costs in fields with common markets [35] and thus, as one union official

---

31. Evans, *op. cit.*, Vol. I, pp. 148-149.
32. *Report of the Industrial Commission, 1901*, Vol. XVII, p. 326.
33. Evans, *op. cit.*, Vol. II, pp. 550-552.
34. Waldo E. Fisher, "Wage Rates in the Bituminous Coal Industry," *Report of the United States Coal Commission*, 1925, Pt. III, p. 1047.
35. Ashley, *op. cit.*, p. 105.

expressed it, to hold "selling prices up to reasonable rates" or levels.[36]

Actually, competitive equality was not the sole determinant of wages. The rates of pay fixed by the joint conferences also reflected such other factors as the miners' demand for uniform earnings, the bargaining power of operators and miners which varied from time to time and field to field, competition from other fuels and from nonunion and newly developed coal fields, as well as fluctuations in business activity.[37]

The competitive system of wage differentials for tonnage workers that evolved was established partly by the joint conferences of the three states and western Pennsylvania—especially the 1898 conference—and partly by local or state conferences and agreements. Much of this early structure still exists. Differentials in rates to keep the less fortunate mines in business were never applied, save for minor local exceptions, to men paid on a daily basis.[38]

b. ORGANIZATION AND PROCEDURES OF THE INTERSTATE CONFERENCE

Miners and operators of each of the four states sent delegates to a joint conference called by the president of the United Mine Workers acting alone or in conjunction with the chairman of the preceding Joint Interstate Conference. Before 1904 wage agreements were negotiated annually, from 1904 to 1916 biennially, and thereafter until the collapse of the Central Competitive Field Compact in 1927 for periods ranging from seven months to three years.[39]

Delegates' numbers also varied. In 1898 the miners had 278 representatives and the operators 250. In 1906 the miners had 633 and the operators 357 representatives. Experience soon proved

36. *Report of the Industrial Commission,* 1901, Vol. XII, p. 63.
37. Proceedings of various joint conferences of the Central Competitive Field.
38. This group consists of the "inside daymen" who work inside the mine and are responsible for maintenance, haulage, ventilation and repairs, and the "outside daymen" who are an auxiliary force on the surface. They are about 40 per cent of the working force.
39. Louis Bloch, *Labor Agreements in Coal Mines,* Russell Sage Foundation, New York, 1931, p. 85.

that so many participants made the making of a wage scale slow and cumbersome.[40] Beginning with 1912 conferees were generally limited to sixty-four, eight delegates for each group from each of the states of Illinois, Indiana and Ohio, and from western Pennsylvania. These sixty-four did not include national officers of the United Mine Workers or the officers of the conference. Each delegation from each state had four votes, with no allowance made for the fact that certain areas regularly produced much more coal than others. All matters affecting the proposed wage scale and the agreement, however, required unanimous vote for adoption.[41] The miners' interests were looked after by a strong international industrial union, while those of the operators were furthered by district organizations, except in Illinois which had a state association.

After the preliminaries, the miners submitted their demands, formulated ahead of time at the international union convention. The arguments and counterarguments, and sometimes the charges of bad faith, that followed were not taken too seriously. They gave the conferees time to circumvent deadlocks and to some extent served as a warming-up process.

When the oratory was exhausted, the demands were turned over to a Joint Scale Committee—usually thirty-two members, four from each side for each state—and negotiations began in earnest. Sometimes when the Committee deadlocked, a subcommittee of sixteen carried on informal negotiations. Each side tried to get as much as it could and to give as little as possible, the ruling motive being self-interest.[42] When agreement was reached, the Committee's report was placed before the conference for acceptance. The agreement was then generally submitted to the miners for approval by a referendum or at a special convention, decision in this matter resting with the international union convention.

The system was one of conciliation and collective bargaining

---

40. Suffern, *op. cit.*, p. 196.
41. Proceedings of various joint conferences of the Central Competitive Field.
42. John R. Commons, *Trade Unionism and Labor Problems*, Ginn and Company, New York, 1905, p. 2.

and not a system of arbitration. The driving force behind the negotiations was the desire to keep the mines running.[43]

C. STATE AND LOCAL AGREEMENTS

The Joint Interstate Conference handled only matters affecting the competitive position of the four areas and its jurisdiction was limited to a basing point in each. For these points it fixed wages for the different classes of labor and attempted to set up uniform working conditions.[44] How the interstate agreement should be applied to widely different "natural conditions of mining"[45] in local areas, and questions which affected operators and miners of a single state were left to state, district or subdistrict bodies. Ohio negotiations were carried on by six subdistrict conferences of operators and miners. One contract usually covered western Pennsylvania, while Indiana had separate agreements for deep bituminous and block coal mines.[46] The great diversity of seam conditions in Illinois led operators and miners to hold local conferences to adapt state-wide agreements to local conditions. Even under today's new alignments the same machinery for collective bargaining within individual states and districts still prevails.

d. ISSUES IN COLLECTIVE BARGAINING AND CONTENT OF AGREEMENTS

The restriction of its jurisdiction to basing points and to factors that affected the competitive position of the member fields greatly simplified the interstate conference's job of collective bargaining in this highly competitive, overdeveloped industry in which labor costs were from 65 to 70 per cent of total costs. The primary task and by far the greatest achievement was the establishment of a

---

43. *Report of the Industrial Commission*, 1901, Vol. XVII, pp. 327-328.
44. Isador Lubin, *Miners' Wages and the Cost of Coal*, The Institute of Economics, McGraw-Hill, New York, 1924, p. 61.
45. The term "natural conditions" as used in this industry includes the thickness, pitch, faults and irregularities of the seam, purity of the coal (that is, freedom from such foreign bodies as slate, sulphur balls and flinty nodules), roof and floor conditions, drainage and relative hardness of coal. These conditions which affect output, as well as labor and other cost items, vary greatly from district to district, within the same field, and even within the same mine as the work of mining coal progresses.
46. The introduction of strip mines added a third wage contract.

competitive system of wage differentials for tonnage workers which removed some of the gross inequalities in costs. A second accomplishment was standard pay rates for inside daymen.[47]

Hours of work were an important issue in 1898 when the eight-hour day was won and after 1919 when the union demanded the six-hour day and thirty-hour week. In earlier years the question whether pay should be based on run-of-mine or screened coal received considerable attention as did also the size of coal screens. The miners were opposed to the system of paying for coal after it was run over screens for sizing. Because of abuses incident to the use of screens they preferred to base their wages on run-of-mine coal, that is, before it passed over the screens. This issue was a major source of irritation until 1916 when the run-of-mine basis of payment was adopted throughout the Central Competitive Field.

Other issues were wage differentials for machine mining and for yardage and deadwork,[48] the checkoff, hiring lists, violations of agreements, restriction of output, bases for discharge and equalization of turns (number of mine cars delivered to a miner's work place). These were brought up before the joint conference, but usually were referred to state or district conferences for settlement.

Some district contract provisions aimed at operators' practices that "nibbled" at contents of the pay envelope. The usual agreement specified: (1) fines for sending up coal with excessive slate and dirt; (2) charges against the miners for powder, other explo-

[47]. The rates of outside daymen were never standardized. Beginning with 1912, however, the agreements specified the amount of change to be made in the existing rates for outside day occupations. The failure "to bring about uniform rates for outside workers is in a large part due to the lack of complete control by the union." *Ibid.*, p. 145.

[48]. When the working place is narrow, as when the haulage ways are being cut, the miners are paid an additional rate for every linear yard or foot the working place is advanced. Yardage is often paid in addition to the regular tonnage rate for the removal of slate, clay, bone and sulphur occurring in the coal seam. It is also allowed for "taking down" the roof or "taking up" the bottom where the seam is not of sufficient height to mine coal. Extra payment may be allowed for setting props and cribs, for the removal of falls, etc. Payments for developmental and narrow work, as well as for unusual conditions arising as the work of coal mining is carried on, are referred to as yardage and deadwork.

sives and equipment used in mining, blacksmithing, etc.; and (3) deductions for household coal, rent and light in company houses and, in some instances, for medical services, schools, hospitals, etc. The contract also provided for a checkweighman selected and paid by the employees to insure accurate scales and reliable tonnage weights. Other provisions covered payment for deadwork, overtime and extra work, semimonthly (instead of monthly) pay days, and the practice of some operators of withholding wages for the initial pay period.

To make work and protect jobs, the contracts frequently specified the number of loaders to a machine, the ratio of men to work places, the procedure in sharing work during dull seasons and the differentials between machine and pick mining. The contracts also provided for equal distribution of mine cars at work places, review of discharges, and machinery for handling grievances.

The union obtained the checkoff and also elimination of certain abuses connected with scrip and company stores and houses. Some contracts regulated transfers of men from one class of work to another and recognized length of service in assigning work and filling vacancies. As a rule, however, it was not obligatory to transfer or promote on the basis of seniority.

The district agreements also laid down workmanship rules to protect the operators. The miner was required to undercut, drill and shoot his coal so as to produce the greatest percentage of lump coal, to exercise care in sending out "clean" coal free from impurities, to support and "snub" properly his work place (take down portions of the roof) according to standard procedure, and to handle and load cars properly. To enforce these standards, fines, suspensions or discharge were open to operators. Penalties were also established for absence without leave and usually for unauthorized strikes. Moreover, managers, foremen, shot firers, head electricians, boss machinists and men engaged in construction and emergency work, etc., were exempt from the terms of the contract. Management had an unrestricted right to hire and fire, provided there was no discrimination on account of creed, color, nationality or union membership.

e. PROCEDURE FOR HANDLING GRIEVANCES

Although they varied from district to district during the life of the Central Competitive Field Compact, procedures for handling grievances had a number of points in common. All contracts provided for a pit or mine committee elected by union employees. Any grievance which could not be settled by the individual worker and his foreman was passed on to the committee, which, in consultation with the foreman, attempted to iron out the difficulty. If this failed, the problem was taken up by a higher union official such as the subdistrict president (sometimes the district president or the district executive board) and the mine superintendent or a representative from the operators' association for the district.[49]

At this point the machinery varied. In certain Ohio fields cases were sometimes referred to the international officers of the union. Elsewhere in the interstate system, unsettled grievances went to a joint executive board of representatives of operators and miners of the district. In Indiana, western Pennsylvania and a part of Ohio no provision was made for resolving a deadlock.[50] In Illinois, however, when the joint board failed to reach an agreement, the dispute was either submitted to arbitration or to a special joint committee of one operator and one miner, or a full joint executive board of executive officers of operators and miners from the entire state. Should these joint agencies disagree the dispute could be referred to a standing arbitrator or to a board of arbitration. This action was resorted to only with the consent of both parties.[51]

Bituminous coal wage contracts thus established an orderly process by which the rights of both parties could be protected, disputed terms could be interpreted with the minimum of friction, and "continuous bargaining" could "take place on subjects not specifically covered by the agreement." [52]

49. *Report of the United States Coal Commission*, Pt. III, p. 1344.
50. *Ibid.*, p. 1345.
51. Illinois Coal Operators Association, *A Brief Outline of 25 Years History and Experience, with Special Reference to the Unusual Developments of the War Period and Subsequently,* June 1921, pp. 33-34.
52. *Report of the United States Coal Commission*, Pt. III, p. 1345.

Experience in Illinois

Illinois experience shows how this machinery worked and with what success. Probably 85 per cent of the grievances were settled at the mine by the foreman and the pit committee, or by the mine superintendent and the miners' subdistrict president.[53] Most of the remaining disputes were disposed of by an executive board member of the miners' union and a field man representing the operators' association or by the district or state joint boards or their representatives.

Analyzing 17,057 disputes in Illinois mines between April 1915 and January 1927, a statistician of the United Mine Workers found that approximately 62 per cent were won by the miners in whole or in part, and 30 per cent by the operators. About 8 per cent went back for local settlement or to a joint commission, and their disposition not recorded, or were deferred, or withdrawn because the case had little merit or because of desire to avoid an adverse decision which might serve as a precedent.[54]

Of 6,695 cases handled and reported under Illinois grievance machinery between December 1908 and December 1920, about 63 per cent involved extra pay or pay envelope matters; 11 per cent were over discrimination in hiring, assignment of work and cars, union activity, etc.; 16 per cent over discharge; and 14 per cent related to discipline and incompetence. Other issues grew out of supervision of work, loading dirt, absences, complaints against foremen, services to employees and mine conditions. About 6 per cent of the cases involved strikes and 2 per cent lockouts.[55] The strike and lockout figures are not complete since many stoppages were over unrecorded disputes.[56]

f. EXPERIENCE WITH ARBITRATION

Operators and miners have used arbitration only as a last resort. It has taken two forms: (1) arbitration of disputes over

---

53. Illinois Coal Operators Association, *op. cit.*, p. 34.
54. Bloch, *op. cit.*, pp. 131-132.
55. Illinois Coal Operators Association, *Twenty-Five Years History of the Illinois Coal Operators' Association*, p. 45, quoted in Suffern, *op. cit.*, Chap. IX.
56. *Ibid.*, p. 246.

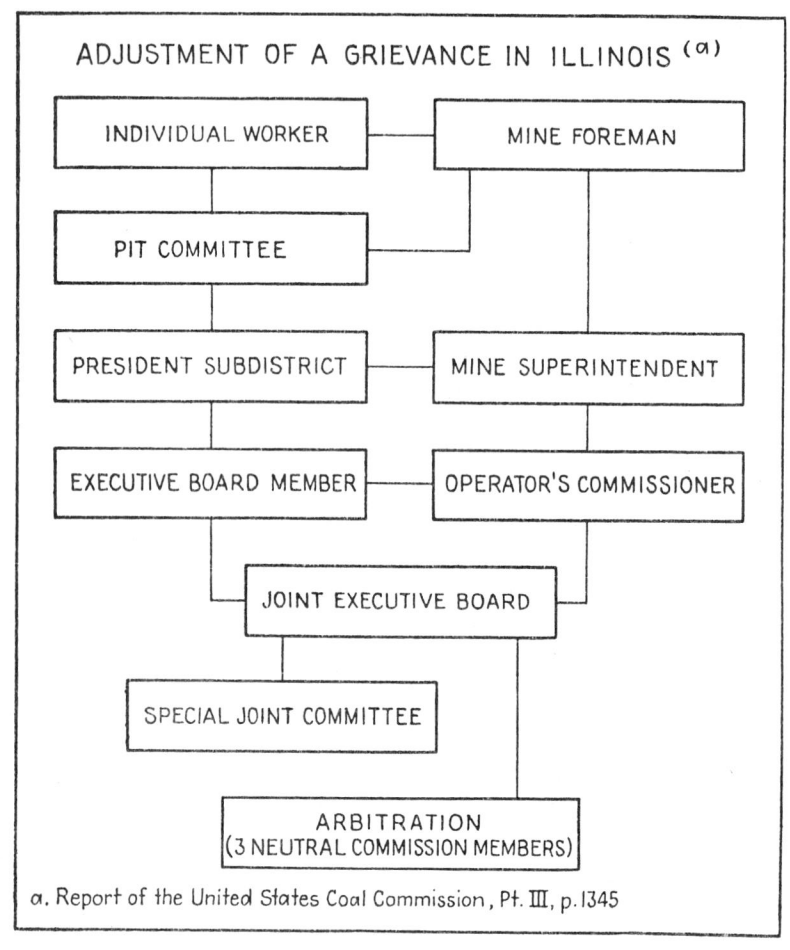

```
┌─────────────────────────────────────────────────────┐
│   ADJUSTMENT OF A GRIEVANCE IN ILLINOIS (a)         │
│                                                     │
│   ┌──────────────────┐      ┌──────────────────┐    │
│   │ INDIVIDUAL WORKER├──────┤   MINE FOREMAN   │    │
│   └────────┬─────────┘      └─────────┬────────┘    │
│            │                          │             │
│   ┌────────┴─────────┐                │             │
│   │  PIT COMMITTEE   ├────────────────┤             │
│   └────────┬─────────┘                │             │
│            │                          │             │
│   ┌────────┴──────────┐    ┌──────────┴──────────┐  │
│   │PRESIDENT SUBDISTRICT───┤  MINE SUPERINTENDENT│  │
│   └────────┬──────────┘    └──────────┬──────────┘  │
│            │                          │             │
│   ┌────────┴──────────┐    ┌──────────┴──────────┐  │
│   │EXECUTIVE BOARD    ├────┤OPERATOR'S           │  │
│   │MEMBER             │    │COMMISSIONER         │  │
│   └────────┬──────────┘    └──────────┬──────────┘  │
│            │                          │             │
│            │   ┌──────────────────┐   │             │
│            └───┤JOINT EXECUTIVE   ├───┘             │
│                │     BOARD        │                 │
│                └─────────┬────────┘                 │
│      ┌──────────────────┐│                          │
│      │SPECIAL JOINT     ││                          │
│      │  COMMITTEE       ││                          │
│      └──────────────────┘│                          │
│              ┌───────────┴──────────┐               │
│              │    ARBITRATION       │               │
│              │(3 NEUTRAL COMMISSION │               │
│              │      MEMBERS)        │               │
│              └──────────────────────┘               │
│  a. Report of the United States Coal Commission,    │
│     Pt. III, p. 1345                                │
└─────────────────────────────────────────────────────┘
```

FIGURE 1

interpretation of the contract or over matters not covered by the agreement; and (2) arbitration of disputes over a new agreement or extension of a contract about to expire.

Arbitration Under the Agreement

Practically all fields at one time or another have made use of arbitration under the agreements when grievances could not be settled by conciliation. Certain areas, notably Illinois, the

Southwestern Interstate Field—Arkansas, Kansas, Missouri and Oklahoma—and central Pennsylvania [57] have long maintained arbitration machinery.

Illinois experience discloses some of the difficulties that arise with this type of arbitration. Early in the history of joint relations union officials adopted the custom of upholding the men in every grievance case "without particular reference to its merits." When the operators rejected a demand, the union frequently called a strike.[58] This practice led the operators to raise a common defense fund. In 1910 the miners reluctantly agreed to submit to one of three previously selected arbitrators disputes which could not be settled by the joint boards. The next year a number of disputes were arbitrated. Subsequently there was a "universal refusal on the part of the miners and their representatives to permit any further cases to be so referred" and there were more strikes.[59]

In 1914 came a second attempt to establish arbitration. Again the miners' representatives were reluctant, pointing out that "our people have a deep-seated prejudice against this proposed arbitration" and "like many other organized workers, are not going to surrender the right to strike if they feel they have a just cause to strike for." [60] The plan finally adopted stipulated that vitally important disputes would be submitted to arbitration "only at the discretion of the Joint Executive Board"; other disputes would automatically be arbitrated.[61] This was more successful. Of 17,057 disputes under the agreement from April 1915 to January 1927, about 3 per cent were arbitrated.[62] Independent action, however, did not disappear.

Arbitration of Disputes Over New Agreements

At its inception the interstate system was one of conciliation and collective bargaining. The miners insisted upon the right to

57. For a short discussion of collective bargaining in outlying producing fields, see pp. 262-263.
58. Illinois Coal Operators Association, *A Brief Outline of 25 Years History and Experience*, p. 38.
59. *Ibid.*, pp. 38-39.
60. *Ibid.*, p. 39.
61. *Ibid.*, p. 43.
62. Bloch, *op. cit.*, pp. 131-132.

strike when the terms and conditions of a contract could not be agreed on and conceded to the operators the right to lock out. The agreements did not provide for arbitration of disputes over terms of a new contract.

When the 1902 joint convention formulated a series of governing principles, arbitration of disputes by a board of referees was rejected.[63] The biennial suspensions which began in 1906 and especially the prolonged one of 1910 led both parties to consider ways of eliminating work stoppages. In 1912 the operators proposed keeping mines in operation during negotiations for new agreements. The miners' 1914 convention approved but referred "further consideration of this subject to the Interstate Joint Conference." [64] At the 1914 joint conference the miners agreed to accept the policy provided the new contract was made retroactive, but the operators would not accept unless the miners would arbitrate all points at issue. The union would not forego its right to strike.[65]

The general strike of 1919, which tied up about 75 per cent of the industry's tonnage, brought agencies of the federal government into the situation. Operators and miners finally agreed to arbitration by the United States Bituminous Commission appointed by President Wilson.[66] The Commission's award was incorporated in the new agreement of March 31, 1920. A prolonged and extensive strike in 1922 again brought federal intervention. President Harding and members of his Cabinet urged the miners and operators to consider the public interest and end the strike. When that appeal failed, the President suggested that, pending arbitration by a commission to be appointed by him, the miners return to work under the terms and conditions existing before the strike. The operators accepted the principle of arbitration but could not agree upon the specific plan suggested by the President. The United Mine Workers approved of a Presidential commission to investigate the industry but refused to permit the wage issue to

63. Suffern, *op. cit.,* pp. 194-195.
64. *Ibid.,* p. 216.
65. *Ibid.,* p. 217.
66. C. F. Stoddard, "The Bituminous Coal Strike," *Monthly Labor Review,* December 1919, pp. 61, 77-78.

be settled in this way on the ground that operators representing 50 per cent of the tonnage in strike fields had not attended the President's conferences, and so far as the union could ascertain had no intention of participating. The strike was eventually settled through joint negotiation.[67]

The record clearly establishes the fact that operators favored both types of arbitration primarily because local stoppages enabled competitors to take over their business, and suspensions enabled nonunion areas to encroach further on their markets. The record also shows that the miners disliked arbitration even as a last resort. In 1923 the miners' representatives told the United States Coal Commission that they had not received just and fair treatment under arbitration; that it was the resort of the "underdog"; that whenever the operators thought they had the upper hand they had refused to arbitrate; and that it was unfair to force the miners to accept arbitration when they now had the bargaining power to obtain wages and working conditions to which they believed themselves entitled.[68]

g. STRIKES, LOCKOUTS AND SUSPENSIONS

In bituminous coal there are three types of strikes: (1) strikes for union recognition and the right to bargain collectively; (2) strikes, usually termed "suspensions" in this industry, called at the expiration of an agreement when the parties, although continuing to bargain collectively, are unable to agree on the terms of renewal; and (3) strikes in violation of an existing wage contract.[69]

Strikes to Win the Right to Bargain Collectively

Strikes for union recognition, particularly in unorganized soft coal fields, have been accompanied by acts of violence on both sides involving loss of property and life. During the interstate agreements in the Central Competitive Field, strikes of this character were for the most part against local operators who would

67. Margaret Gadsby, "The Coal Strikes," *ibid.*, November 1922, pp. 15-16.
68. Letter of the United States Coal Commission to the President and the Congress of the United States, August 23, 1923, mimeographed release, p. 2.
69. *Findings of Fact and Conclusions of Law, Carter v. Carter Coal Co., et al.,* In Equity No. 59,374, Supreme Court of the District of Columbia, 1935, p. 78.

not join or who refused to live up to the wage contracts adopted by the interstate and district joint conventions.

Suspensions

Suspensions have been common occurrences in coal mining. The existence of large nonunion areas, as well as the growing competition of other fuels, made it increasingly difficult for union operators to grant the wage increases and conditions demanded by an unusually aggressive and at times uncompromising union leadership.

From 1899 to 1927 a surprising amount of time was lost through strikes and lockouts, most of which occurred in years when wage contracts expired. Of nineteen such years, suspensions took place in eight—at each of the biennial negotiations from 1906 to 1914, and in 1919, 1922 and 1927. The 1906 and 1910 suspensions spread throughout most of the union areas and involved well over 200,000 men. The 1906 stoppage lasted from two to three months and that of 1910 from 45 to 157 days.[70] In 1910 man days lost because of strikes in Illinois were almost 79 per cent of man days worked; and in 1914 in Ohio time lost by strikes greatly exceeded time worked. The World War years were remarkably free from strikes, but the postwar period was marked by three long, bitterly contested disputes, two of which were practically nation-wide and brought federal intervention. The 1927 strike in the Central Competitive Field was especially severe and its failure led to the abandonment of the Central Competitive Field Compact.

Collective bargaining in the Central Competitive Field did not reduce industrial strife. On the contrary, man days lost on account of strikes and lockouts were much greater in those districts than in the outlying areas, many of which were unorganized. Between 1899 and 1927 the percentage of man days lost through industrial disputes to man days worked in Illinois, Indiana and Ohio combined was 12.7, while the comparable figure for all remaining areas in the United States was 4.2.[71]

---

70. *Ibid.,* p. 39.

71. Based on data compiled by the U. S. Bureau of Mines and published in its annual reports. Disputes in western Pennsylvania could not be included because the data are available only by states.

Strikes Breaching the Agreement

Throughout the history of the interstate movement the operators have repeatedly charged the miners with contract violations, admitting, however, that such stoppages often occurred contrary to the wishes and orders of the union officers. At the 1902 convention of the United Mine Workers, President John Mitchell pointed out that "violations of the letter or spirit of our joint agreements on the part of both operators and miners have been less numerous during the past year than ever before" but "that in some instances individual operators and local unions have sought to obtain temporary advantage by evading, if not deliberately repudiating, some provisions of our joint agreement." He warned that "when the contract is made and signed, if we expect the operators to carry out those provisions that are advantageous to us, we, in turn, must carry out just as explicitly those provisions which are unfavorable to us." [72] Again, at the 1914 convention, John P. White, then president of the union, strongly condemned the numerous local unauthorized strikes—called sometimes in spite of the efforts of district officials to prevent them.[73]

Work stoppages prevailed in every year from 1899 to 1927, even in those in which no contracts were negotiated.

Strikes during the life of an agreement are important not so much because they materially curtail production but because, as pointed out by the United States Coal Commission, they are "a menace to the orderly procedure which is provided for under the agreement." [74]

Causes of this type of strike are varied. Violations or abrogations of wage contracts by operators—sometimes because nonunion competitors slashed wages and prices—have frequently preceded such stoppages. More often they resulted from workers' irritation over matters which should have been taken up under the established grievance machinery. Not infrequently the immediate reason was not the real cause, as in a mine in the Southwestern Inter-

---

[72] UMW, *Proceedings of the Thirteenth Annual Convention*, 1902, quoted by Bloch, *op. cit.*, pp. 307-308.
[73] See *Proceedings of the Twenty-fourth Consecutive and First Biennial Convention*, 1914, Vol. I, pp. 80-81.
[74] *Report of the United States Coal Commission*, 1925, Pt. III, p. 1292.

state Field when the employees stopped work because the foreman kicked a mule. Behind such specific acts and causes is usually a backlog of grievances and a history of recurring friction between men and management. Strikes were also called "by the union to change the terms of the agreement before the agreement expired," and sometimes as "a protest over changes made by the management" which the union believed interfered with its "rights under the agreement." [75]

Penalty Clauses to Discourage Strikes

To discourage such strikes operators and miners in many fields wrote into their contracts penalty clauses which fined employees "guilty of throwing a mine idle or of materially reducing the output of a mine, by failure to continue at work" in accordance with the agreement.[76] A similar penalty was placed on employers who ceased to operate their mines in order to enforce some condition in violation of the contract. That these clauses were frequently not effective is indicated by the resolution incorporated in the Washington Wage Agreement of October 6, 1917, pointing to the seriousness of strikes in violation of the agreement and instructing miners and operators to introduce penalty clauses in districts without them and to strengthen existing clauses where necessary.

Even the modified provisions did not work out to the satisfaction of the operators. At the 1923 joint convention, when the miners demanded "that the automatic penalty clause be eliminated from future agreements," P. H. Penna, chairman of the conference, said:

> We are asking and shall expect to receive something in lieu of that clause that will make a contract with the United Mine Workers worthy and valuable. A contract now with your association has no value because it is not respected by the United Mine Workers. The fining clause, the abolition of which you seek, is helpful to a degree; but it does not secure what believers in collective bargaining desire that it should and we must have something that will do that.[77]

75. *Ibid.*
76. *Agreement* between Illinois Coal Operators Association, etc., and UMW, District 12, August 16, 1920, pp. 63-64.
77. *Joint Conference of Bituminous Coal Operators and Coal Miners of the Central Competitive Field,* New York, 1923, p. 16.

When union officials challenged this statement the chairman declared that it was "susceptible of proof" but that the facts would be "a discredit to the mining industry, the operators as well as the miners."[78] The new contract retained the penalty clause.

h. ATTEMPTS TO EXTEND THE SCOPE OF THE CENTRAL COMPETITIVE FIELD COMPACT

Early in the history of the interstate system the conference was faced with the question of admitting the operators and miners of outlying fields. The issue was raised at the joint conference of 1900 when both the operators and miners of Michigan and Iowa sought admission. The parties to the compact agreed that West Virginia should be included, inasmuch as its mines perpetually menaced the stability of joint relations. West Virginia operators had been invited to participate in the first joint conference but had refused. Moreover, the four-state compact had been established with the understanding that the United Mine Workers "would increase their strength in West Virginia and force the operators of that state to make terms" and come under the interstate arrangement.[79]

Over admission of Iowa, Michigan and other unionized areas the conference deadlocked. Answering the miners' contention that Iowa was "as directly a competitor with Illinois and other states in the present system as West Virginia," the interstate operators argued that "conditions in Iowa are already 'fair' enough, and that there is 'no excessive competition' with the central area." They added that the admission of the western outlying districts would "make the convention unworkable," and that it "was difficult enough" already "to get unanimous consent of all the delegates." They suggested that outlying western areas form a new interstate convention.[80] At the 1901 convention the miners again attempted to extend the movement but the operators remained adamant.

After the World War the growing competition from southern

---

78. *Ibid.*, p. 22.
79. *Report of the Industrial Commission*, 1901, Vol. XVII, p. 329.
80. Ashley, *op. cit.*, p. 107.

areas led the conference to consider enlarging the joint machinery. The 1919 joint conference called by the U. S. Secretary of Labor was asked but refused to invite outlying union areas and establish a general scale committee.

The issue became major in 1922. Two proposals were submitted to the joint conference, and both were rejected. To the first, which provided for a national wage conference to fix base rates for all the districts, the operators offered their usual objections. For their part, the miners would not agree to the arbitration clause included in this proposal. Nor would they agree to the second plan, which would have allowed each district to act independently in fixing wages, as well as providing for arbitration in the event of failure to reach an agreement and for wage adjustments to permit competition between all districts. The conference then returned to the existing machinery to formulate the new agreement.[81]

i. TREND OF WAGES, HOURS AND EMPLOYMENT UNDER THE INTERSTATE COMPACT

In his annual address at the 1899 UMW convention, President Ratchford said of the benefits obtained by the miners under the 1898 interstate agreement:

> The agreement quoted advanced your wages generally about 18 per cent, and reduced the hours of labor almost in the same ratio; it reduced the size of screens to the smallest prevailing standard, and to a very great extent abolished them entirely. It equalized the wages of different classes of labor and made conditions uniform in all the fields covered. It re-established healthy and mutual relations between employers and employees. It gave our organization place and prestige in the business and industrial circles of the country, and banded together in unity and fraternity a greater number of miners, covering a greater number of States, than was ever known at any previous time in our history. Of all the advantages gained, to which only a brief reference is made, the 8-hour day is decidedly the greatest because it is the most lasting.[82]

It should be borne in mind that the contracts were negotiated annually from 1898 to 1904, biennially from 1904 to 1916, and

---

81. See *Minutes of Joint Conferences of Coal Operators' and Coal Miners' Representatives from Western Pennsylvania, Ohio, Indiana, and Illinois*, 1922, pp. 40-41, 44-45; and Suffern, *op. cit.*, p. 211.

82. *Report of the Tenth Annual Convention*, 1899, p. 13.

at irregular intervals—ranging from seven months to three years—in the years that followed. Before a contract expired it was customary to negotiate a new one. At these times it was often union strategy to call a suspension or strike.

Two contracts were modified before their specified expiration dates. One was the contract that had been signed in 1916. Our entry into the World War created new conditions: the cost of living increased, high wages in other industries tended to draw workers away from coal mining, and the large profits of the industry made the operators vulnerable to new demands. Consequently, the wage rates of bituminous coal workers were increased by means of two supplementary agreements in 1917. The other case arose in the summer of 1920 when the miners, dissatisfied with the wage increases granted that April, struck in violation of the contract and forced new increases.

Wages Move Upward

Table 4 shows that from 1898 to 1916, except when the miners took a 5 per cent reduction in 1904, wage rates moved gradually upward. During these eighteen years pick miners, tracklayers and inside common labor received advances which averaged from 55 to 57 per cent, following closely the increases in the hourly rates of union labor in the United States.

After 1916 wages bounded up. But whereas the pick miners after 1919 and machine miners after 1923 lost heavily compared to union workers in general, the tracklayers and inside common labor were much better off throughout these years. Only in 1927 did the rates of organized workers in general begin to approach those of the daymen. For the twenty-nine years that the Central Competitive Field Compact was in existence the pick miners received increases which amounted to 165 per cent, tracklayers to 295 per cent, and inside common labor to 316 per cent. These figures do not include the increases granted on April 1, 1898, which averaged about 18 per cent.

One fact stands out—the skilled tonnage men did not fare as well as the men paid by the day, unskilled as well as skilled, nor were they able to hold their position relative to organized labor

TABLE 4

INDEXES OF WAGE RATES IN THE CENTRAL COMPETITIVE FIELD AND IN SOME SEVENTY UNIONIZED TRADES [a]

1912=100

Figures are for calendar years

Year	Pick Mining	Machine Mining [b]	Tracklayers	Inside Common Labor	Unionized Trades
1898	67	c	68	67	c
1899	67	c	68	67	c
1900	78	c	78	77	c
1901	81	c	81	81	c
1902	81	c	81	81	c
1903	89	c	89	89	c
1904	88	c	87	88	c
1905	86	c	86	86	c
1906	90	c	90	90	87
1907	91	c	91	91	91
1908	91	c	91	91	93
1909	91	c	91	91	94
1910	95	c	95	95	96
1911	96	c	96	96	98
1912	100	100	100	100	100
1913	101	102	101	102	103
1914	101	102	101	102	104
1915	101	101	101	102	105
1916	104	106	105	105	110
1917	117	126	130	131	116
1918	136	150	179	184	136
1919	138	153	180	185	158
1920	168	194	231	240	203
1921	176	202	268	280	210
1922	176	202	268	280	197
1923	176	202	268	280	216
1924	176	202	268	280	233
1925	176	202	268	280	243
1926	176	202	268	280	256
1927	176	202	268	280	265

a. Rates for pick miners, tracklayers and inside common labor taken from the original wage contracts; machine mining rates, from Waldo E. Fisher and Anne Bezanson, *Wage Rates and Working Time in the Bituminous Coal Industry—1912-1922*, University of Pennsylvania Press, Philadelphia, 1932. No bituminous rates go back beyond April 1898. Since rates for machine mining were not available prior to 1912, that year was taken as the base. Rates for unionized trades are those published in the *Monthly Labor Review*, January 1926 and November 1928. All figures except those for the year 1898 are weighted annual averages.

b. Index numbers are of the combined rate for machine cutting and hand loading.

c. No data.

in general. This supports the claim frequently made that industrial unions tend to narrow the differentials between the rates of skilled and unskilled labor.

Wide Fluctuations in Employment

The eight-hour day, established in April 1898, was in effect throughout the entire period. The annual working time of the miners in the Central Competitive Field fluctuated widely. From 1898 to 1913 days worked in Illinois, Indiana and Ohio, the states for which data are available, varied between 175 and 218. In 1914 they dropped to 152. A heavy demand for coal during the war years increased working time considerably but even in the peak year of 1918, the mines operated only 232 days. After 1920 new low levels were reached and the average for the seven years—1921 to 1927—was 141 days. Beginning with 1924, the number of men employed dropped sharply. By 1927 mine employment in these three states fell to 72.1 per cent of 1923, the year of maximum employment. This big decline was due partly to a steady decrease in the demand for coal, partly to expansion in the newer unorganized areas, partly to the very attractive wage rates that prevailed in the industry during these years, and lastly to the fact that both operators and the union failed to deal constructively with the situation.

j. COLLAPSE OF THE INTERSTATE SYSTEM

Central Competitive Field operators were disappointed in their hopes that union recognition would eliminate price wars. As railroad facilities increased, many southern nonunion fields expanded rapidly. In 1898, the union districts of Pittsburgh and Ohio supplied 86 per cent of the coal shipped to the lake trade. By 1913, shipments from these districts had dropped to 67 per cent. Meanwhile southern West Virginia shipments rose from approximately forty thousand to over six million tons.[83] Lake cargo coal supplied by southern West Virginia, eastern Kentucky, Virginia and eastern Tennessee increased from 14 per cent of the total shipments

---

83. Tryon, "The Effect of Competitive Conditions on Labor Relations in Coal Mining," p. 87.

in 1909 to 73 per cent in 1925, and Ohio, Pennsylvania and northern West Virginia shipments fell from 86 to 27 per cent.[84] In the Central Freight Association markets—embracing the territory bounded by Pittsburgh, Erie and Buffalo on the east, Milwaukee and the Mississippi River on the west, the Great Lakes on the north, and the Ohio River on the south—the coal carried by the northern roads declined about 8 per cent between 1919 and 1925, while the shipments of the southern roads doubled. Even the trade to the tidewater markets, New York, Philadelphia, Baltimore and Hampton Roads, underwent a similar adjustment. During the same seven years, New England shipments on northern roads dropped from 71 to 46 per cent, while those of the southern carriers rose from 29 to 54 per cent.[85]

Advantages of Southern Mines

These extraordinary gains were due to a number of causes. Southern coal is lodged in higher seams and on the whole is of better quality than northern. Many mines were opened comparatively recently and were large-scale undertakings with modern machinery and equipment. In addition, the southern mine owners benefited from periodic suspensions in the union areas as well as from flexible nonunion wage scales. For the eleven years from 1912 to 1922 inside daymen in all organized areas in the industry received on an average 10.8 cents, and the outside daymen 13.9 cents, more an hour than corresponding workers in nonunion areas; the rates of tonnage workers were also higher than in the nonunion fields. During the same eleven years, the tipple time of nonunion mines averaged 227 days and that of union mines only 194 days.[86]

Southern competition became increasingly burdensome when the postwar boom collapsed. The overdevelopment which appeared in 1914 but was arrested by the World War, now reappeared in exaggerated form and the resulting competition disrupted the industry. Operating under a flexible wage policy,

84. Charles Reitell, "The Shift in Soft Coal Shipments," *Pennsylvania Industrial Survey, Bulletin No. 1,* 1927, p. 17.
85. *Ibid.,* pp. 13-24.
86. Fisher and Bezanson, *op. cit.,* pp. 87, 140.

nonunion employers ordered general wage reductions in the 1920 depression. Bound by a wage contract, union fields continued to pay the same rates. By 1922 the hourly rates of all daymen in nonunion areas were 40 cents below those in the organized areas.[87]

Refusal of Certain Operators to Continue the Arrangement

When the miners' union invited the operators to a joint conference in January 1922, those of Ohio and western Pennsylvania declined, giving these reasons: (1) inability under union terms to compete with nonunion producers; (2) disruption of the interstate system by strikes breaching the agreement; and (3) liability to legal action, since both parties had been indicted for previous joint activities. In support of their first contention they pointed out that wages in some nonunion areas were now 56 per cent below those in certain union districts.[88]

The operators advanced other reasons. They pointed out that the conferences had become so unwieldy "that the original intent and purpose of collective bargaining is made impossible." [89] They contended further that the original conditions which resulted in the Central Competitive Field arrangement had gradually disappeared, that the competition between western Pennsylvania and southern Ohio, on the one hand, and Illinois and Indiana, on the other, was no longer direct and active as in 1898. They pointed out that owing to freight-rate differentials, the real competitors of western Pennsylvania and southern Ohio were the fields of West Virginia and eastern Kentucky [90]—a claim which subsequent statistical studies have confirmed.[91]

More fundamental, however, was the declining demand for bituminous coal, which resulted in the industry's chronic overcapacity, irregular operation and economic disorganization. The decline in demand was due partly to the completion of the railroad net of North America, to a shift in manufacturing from

87. *Ibid.*, p. 90.
88. Margaret Gadsby, "The Coal Strikes," p. 4.
89. *Coal Age*, March 2, 1922, p. 181.
90. *The Coal Crises, Bulletin No. 1*, 1922, p. 3, published by *Coal Age*.
91. See National Labor Relations Board, "The Effect of Labor Relations in the Bituminous Coal Industry upon Interstate Commerce," *Bulletin No. 2*, June 30, 1938, pp. 9, 57.

crude, heavy products to lighter products requiring less fuel, and to the big rise of the scrap iron industry which definitely retarded virgin pig iron consumption.[92] The growing demand for competing fuels, notably oil and gas, also reduced coal consumption. The largest single factor in the decline of soft coal demand, however, was increasingly efficient fuel consumption encouraged by high postwar coal prices.[93]

Response of the Union

President John L. Lewis had a difficult decision to make. Should he accept a wage reduction and bring North and South rates into closer relationship, or should he hold fast to union gains and conduct a still more vigorous campaign to organize the southern mines? The first course might lead to wage slashing in both areas and a return to the chaotic and turbulent conditions of the nineties. It would also strengthen the more radical elements in the union who could seize upon such a policy to arouse discontent and further their own ends. On the other hand, a standpat policy would undoubtedly mean further curtailment of union production, especially in southern Ohio and western Pennsylvania, and might well disrupt the interstate movement.

President Lewis decided to maintain the existing wage level and to intensify his drive to organize the South. On April 1, 1922, when it became clear that the operators would not negotiate on an interstate basis, he called a general strike of the industry which lasted twenty weeks. The strike was settled on August 17. The agreement to maintain existing rates cannot, however, be regarded as a central competitive one inasmuch as only about 20 per cent of the tonnage was represented at the conference. Yet operators' associations which had remained away soon fell in line and signed contracts.

Efforts to organize the southern fields met with stubborn re-

92. F. G. Tryon, *The Trend of Coal Demand*, Ohio State University Press, Columbus, 1929, pp. 6-7; and *Findings of Fact and Conclusions of Law, Carter* v. *Carter Coal Co., et al.*, pp. 36-37.

93. *Report of the Committee on Prices in the Bituminous Coal Industry*, Conference on Price Research, National Bureau of Economic Research, New York, 1938, pp. 18-19.

sistance and in the spring of 1923 the union's foothold in the South was even more precarious than in 1922. Nevertheless, at the urgent request of the United States Coal Commission, Illinois, Indiana and Ohio operators made a tristate agreement which was later signed by the western Pennsylvania operators. This agreement extended the wage rates and terms of employment for one year.

In 1924 the operators again demanded wage reductions in the union fields. The union stood firm. Finally, as the result of increased demand for coal, pressure from Secretary of Commerce Hoover, and fear of repeating the long strike of 1922, the operators renewed the 1923 contract for another three-year period.[94] This is known as the Jacksonville Agreement and is commonly regarded by the operators as the specific event which broke the interstate compact.

1927 Conference Deadlocks

In February 1927, about six weeks before the Jacksonville Agreement expired, miners and operators met in joint conference. For the union, the time was inopportune because coal prices and wages in important nonunion districts were moving downward. The operators demanded a wage scale which would be "continuously competitive" with southern areas and strongly urged a sliding scale. Instructed not to accept a wage reduction, the union representatives rejected this proposal on the ground that it would only lead to progressive rate cutting and eventually to wage levels and conditions as determined under individual bargaining in the southern areas. Instead they proposed renewal of the present scale for two years and interim meetings at which the Joint Conference could discuss the industry's problems and attempt to obtain stabilizing legislation. When the operators refused the conferees deadlocked.

The conference adjourned on February 22 and the next day the union announced that the outlying fields would be permitted to continue the old wage scale after March 31 without prejudice pending a settlement in the Central Competitive Field. This many

---

94. National Labor Relations Board, *op. cit.*, p. 25.

of the districts agreed to do. The same privilege was extended to the fields and individual operations in the Central Competitive Field on February 28 but except for a limited number of companies little interest was shown. A general strike involving about 175,000 men and affecting mining in Arkansas, Illinois, Indiana, Iowa, Kansas, Missouri, Ohio, Oklahoma and much of Pennsylvania was called on April 1. Despite the efforts of Secretary of Labor Davis and the governors of the coal-producing states involved, no basis for a general settlement was reached. On July 18, 1928, the United Mine Workers cancelled the strike order and instructed district leaders to return to work on the best terms they could get.[95]

4. COLLECTIVE BARGAINING IN OUTLYING PRODUCING FIELDS BEFORE 1927

In the Central Competitive Field the union gained its strongest foothold. From 1898 to 1925 the central compact covered approximately one third of all mine workers and slightly more than a third of the country's output of soft coal. In 1927, production fell to 22.8 per cent of the total.

A second center of unionism for almost twenty-five years was the Southwestern Interstate Field, lying between Iowa and northern Texas and consisting of Arkansas, Kansas, Missouri and Oklahoma. These four states in 1923 produced about 4 per cent of the total tonnage and their collective bargaining system resembled that of the Central Competitive Field. Directly north of the Southwestern Interstate Field are the Iowa mines, which have been union for many years. Other areas in which collective bargaining has had a long history are central Pennsylvania, Montana, Michigan, a large portion of Washington, western Kentucky and Wyoming. Certain sections of West Virginia and much more limited areas in Kentucky and Alabama were also under contract for varying periods.[96]

Although distinct entities, the outlying union fields were largely

95. *Ibid.*, p. 33.
96. For the evolution of contractual relations in these areas, see Suffern, *op. cit.*

governed by events in the Central Competitive Field. Their joint conferences were usually called after the central competitive agreement had been signed. While the separate districts were free to make their own conditions and while wages in some areas varied from those of the central field, basically the district contracts resembled the four-state area's.[97]

5. ATTEMPTS TO ORGANIZE THE NONUNION AREAS BEFORE 1927 [98]

As early as the late nineties, union organizers penetrated Alabama, West Virginia, unorganized sections of Pennsylvania—and subsequently Kentucky and Tennessee. At the beginning of the century, many Alabama coal companies operated under union agreements. After 1902 the union lost strength and practically disappeared after the long strike of 1908. Gains made under wartime conditions were lost in 1921 and thereafter until 1933 unionism was nonexistent.

Northeastern Kentucky operators were able to resist all efforts of the United Mine Workers to compel recognition. In southeastern Kentucky and Tennessee the union's strength increased so steadily that in 1907 and 1908 it could negotiate general wage contracts. After 1910 the union lost ground and though it was stimulated by the wartime situation, it lapsed into insignificance after 1922 and did not revive until the advent of the NRA.

In West Virginia fields the union met with varying successes. Locals that had flourished in the southern areas in 1901 were greatly weakened the following year by an unsuccessful general strike and the region henceforward resisted unionization. In other fields, unionism and collective bargaining thrived longer. Agreements covered most of northern West Virginia, except that state's portion of the Cumberland-Piedmont district, from 1918 through the early 1920's, and a large part of the New River field in eastern West Virginia from 1915 to 1921. In the Kanawha area, col-

---
97. *Report of the United States Coal Commission*, Pt. III, p. 1339.
98. For a more complete statement of the union's efforts to widen the area of collective bargaining, see Fisher and Bezanson, *op. cit.*, pp. 21-26.

lective bargaining was maintained generally for eighteen years, 1902–1920. But by the middle twenties most West Virginia mines were again operating on a nonunion basis.

Union efforts were more successful in Pennsylvania. Operators of the Pittsburgh district had long recognized the unions and were charter members of the Central Competitive Field Compact. As early as 1899 many central Pennsylvania operators negotiated trade agreements; collective bargaining continued there until 1927. However, in the geographically small, though commercially important, producing areas in Somerset, and parts of Greene, Westmoreland and Fayette counties, the union failed completely in its attempts to establish collective bargaining. This nonunion stronghold comprised the well-known Connellsville, Somerset, Ligonier, Latrobe, Greensburg and Irwin Gas districts.

After more than a quarter of a century of almost continuous strife, the southern coal fields were still unorganized. This bitter struggle supplies some of the blackest pages in the history of American industrial relations. Both the operators and the union spent vast sums in the fight for supremacy, and resorted to extreme measures to gain their ends. The union made many gains during the World War, only to lose them during the postwar depression.

In 1919, a year when the union was fast approaching the height of its power, it was estimated that approximately 72 per cent of the total supply of bituminous coal was produced under union contracts.[99] Six years later, at the close of 1925, the percentage had dropped to 40. In that year, nonunion mines accounted for at least 93 per cent of the coal produced in West Virginia, 98 per cent in Kentucky and 90 per cent in Tennessee.[100]

6. RETURN OF RUTHLESS COMPETITION: 1927 TO 1933

The collapse of the interstate movement was the signal for a bitter struggle for markets. The price war began in earnest and,

---

99. "Coal Situation," Natural Resources Production Department, U. S. Chamber of Commerce, Washington, April 1, 1922.

100. F. G. Tryon and H. O. Rogers, "Classification of Mines by Wage-Contract Policy of Coal Operators," *Coal Age,* January 27, 1927.

as John L .Lewis had predicted, wages were slashed drastically in both North and South. In the fall of 1927 temporary agreements extended the Jacksonville scale in Illinois, Indiana, Iowa, Kansas, Michigan, Missouri, Montana and Wyoming. A number of these set up joint agencies to study the demands, claims and counter-claims of both sides and to report to their respective joint scale committees early in 1928, but no agreement was reached on wage policy, and contractual relations were dropped in practically all fields until the fall of 1928.

At that time separate wage contracts with substantial wage reductions were negotiated. In Illinois and Indiana reductions for inside skilled workers amounted to $1.40 a day, $1.70 in Iowa, $2.40 in Kansas, $2.50 in Missouri, $1.63 in Michigan, and $1.20 in Montana and Wyoming. In Ohio, the few companies that had union contracts in 1928 forced wage reductions of $2.50 per day. When the contract expired March 31, 1930, all mines in the state became nonunion. Contracts in the remaining aforenamed fields were renewed and continued without change until the summer and autumn of 1932,[101] when the miners granted further reductions in the union areas except in Iowa, Kansas and Michigan. Reductions for the skilled daymen ranged from $1.10 to $1.52 a day. In April 1933 the Illinois, Indiana, Missouri, Montana and Wyoming contracts were renewed without wage adjustments. But Iowa and Kansas operators, who had not obtained downward revisions in 1932, received wage reductions which for skilled daymen were $1.10 and $1.35 a day respectively.[102]

Throughout the remainder of the industry, except for agreements with individual or small groups of operators, wages and other terms of employment were negotiated through individual bargaining or employee representation plans or company unions. While the rates of skilled daymen in Illinois dropped from $7.50 to $5.00 per day the corresponding scales in the nonunion fields

---

101. An exception was made in the case of Michigan where an additional decrease of 95 cents was granted in September 1931. In Iowa the agreements were extended to March 31, 1933.
102. F. E. Berquist, et al., *Economic Survey of the Bituminous Coal Industry under Free Competition and Code Regulation*, NRA, Division of Review, 1936, pp. 585-612.

showed more drastic reductions. In the spring of 1933, Illinois operators paid a basic $5.00 scale. In Pennsylvania the wages of loaders—the principal piece-work occupation underground—averaged $2.65 a day, in Ohio $2.50, in West Virginia $2.84, and in Kentucky $2.80. The basic scale for the inside daymen was somewhat higher.[103]

Intraunion Dissension

The demise of the interstate system, the disappearance of collective bargaining throughout most of the industry, and particularly the low wages, irregular working time and loss of status led to dissension within the union and much discontent among the workers.

In September 1928, a group of progressive and left-wing workers from eleven states, who favored a more militant policy, formed the National Miners Union. In June 1931 spontaneous local strikes occurred in the Pittsburgh district and spread to southeastern Ohio and northern West Virginia. This insurgent movement involved some twenty thousand miners.[104]

Another insurrection had been brewing for some time in Illinois where district leaders for many years had opposed the Lewis leadership. The feud came to a head in 1929 when the national office, informed that funds were mishandled in one subdistrict, ordered an investigation and on the basis of the findings instructed the subdistrict officers to make a proper accounting and adjustment. With the consent of the district officials, these leaders failed to comply with the national union's order. The subdistrict autonomy was suspended, provisional officers were appointed by the national office, and later the district charter was revoked. The dispute dragged through the courts until a circuit court designated the United Mine Workers as the official organization in Illinois.[105]

In March 1930, the district officials of the Illinois miners held a rival convention at Springfield, Illinois, to reorganize the na-

103. *Findings of Fact and Conclusions of Law, Carter* v. *Carter Coal Co., et al.,* p. 64. Data are those published by the U. S. Bureau of Labor Statistics.
104. Berquist, *et al., op. cit.,* p. 184.
105. David J. McDonald and Edward A. Lynch, *Coal and Unionism,* Cornelius Printing Company, Silver Spring, Maryland, 1939, pp. 183-185, 191-192.

tional union. Asserting that the national officers had abrogated the constitution by not calling a biennial convention in 1929, the convention elected as president Alexander Howat, who earlier had been expelled from the United Mine Workers but was at that time a member of the union. The insurgent movement claimed miners in Illinois, Kansas and the Southwest. After a year of bitter dispute, a reconciliation was effected between the officers of the two organizations. Miners from Illinois and other districts, however, held in April 1931 a "rank-and-file" convention which claimed to represent thirty thousand miners, but it failed to establish a new union.

Out of the confusion in Illinois a number of unions arose, of which the Progressive Mine Workers of America, organized in September 1932, was the only one of any importance. As an affiliate of the AF of L it is the present rival of the United Mine Workers, a CIO affiliate. Its achievements have been inconsequential; in November 1939 its agreements covered fifteen thousand workers.[106]

Decline in Union Strength

By 1932 the once-powerful United Mine Workers had become a mere skeleton. In that year the union reported a total membership, including anthracite workers, of three hundred thousand, but Lewis L. Lorwin estimates that the actual dues-paying membership was probably half of that figure.[107] Since many district unions were bankrupt, the national organization "took over the administration of their business, and appointed such officers as were needed. Only western Pennsylvania, Indiana, Iowa, Wyoming, Michigan, Nova Scotia and Montana, plus the three anthracite districts—10 out of 29—retained their autonomy." [108]

Assuming that the contracts in effect in the union fields in 1932 covered all operating mines, the tonnage involved would have been about 20 per cent of the total soft coal production in that

---

106. Information submitted by the Progressive Mine Workers.
107. *The American Federation of Labor,* The Institute of Economics of the Brookings Institution, 1933, p. 497.
108. McDonald and Lynch, *op. cit.,* p. 190.

year.[109] Since many mines in these areas were nonunion, the figure is unquestionably too high.

7. PERIOD OF GOVERNMENTAL INTERVENTION: 1933 TO DATE

By the spring of 1933 a number of leading operators decided that the demoralizing competitive struggle in which wage cuts followed price reductions in a downward spiral was no solution to the industry's problem.[110] It is true that northern operators had received reductions below the union scales of the early twenties amounting to about 35 per cent in Illinois, 46 per cent in Pennsylvania, and 59 per cent in Ohio; but reductions averaging 50 and 52 per cent in Kentucky and West Virginia had offset most of the gains of the northern nonunion group.[111] As a result, the same ruthless competition continued at a much lower wage level, which the operators admitted hurt the industry and strengthened the influence of left-wingers.[112]

Both operators and miners sought some other remedy. The operators, who since 1925 had given consideration to the creation of central sales agencies, formed Appalachian Coals, Inc.—an organization of voluntary regional selling agencies. The actual establishment was delayed until the summer of 1933, pending the decision of the Supreme Court upon this type of regional collaboration. Two additional central selling organizations were established in Ohio. A few months later, however, the NRA Code became effective and minimum prices were established under it.

The union leaders had become convinced that economic organization of miners was inadequate to protect workers in a decentralized, overdeveloped industry in which many employers fought unionization and refused to bargain when unions were established. As early as 1930 the Davis-Kelly bill to regulate the bituminous coal industry, which had been drafted with the collaboration of the miners' union, had been introduced in Congress but failed to

109. The union fields included Illinois, Indiana, Iowa, Kansas, Michigan, Missouri, Montana and Wyoming.
110. National Labor Relations Board, *op. cit.*, pp. 40, 44-46.
111. *Findings of Fact and Conclusions of Law, Carter* v. *Carter Coal Co.*, p. 64.
112. Berquist, *et al., op. cit.*, pp. 184-185.

reach a vote. The miners then urged President Hoover to convene a joint conference of operators and miners to work out some solution of the industry's problems. A meeting of representative northern and southern operators in July 1930 failed to get anywhere, and so did several other attempts. At the 1932 convention the miners decided to work for the reintroduction of the Davis-Kelly coal bill and for a federal law limiting hours to six a day and thirty a week.[113]

a. THE NRA

On June 16, 1933, Congress passed the National Industrial Recovery Act, which gave great impetus to the campaign to organize the industry which had begun as early as March. Organizers and hundreds of volunteers scurried through the coal fields to carry the news that the United States Government guaranteed all workers the right to join unions of their own choosing. Union membership grew by leaps and bounds even in the strongest nonunion citadels. Union officers met with operators of Illinois, Indiana and certain western union areas and drafted a proposed code for bituminous coal—one of the twenty-five separate codes submitted for this industry.[114]

After months of protracted negotiations, the miners, with the help of the Administration, negotiated wage agreements in most of the coal fields. Minimum wages and maximum hours were written into the Code which President Roosevelt approved on September 18, 1933. This code provided for minimum prices, prohibited certain unfair trade practices, and guaranteed the miners the right to bargain collectively through their own unions, to select checkweighmen, to trade where they wished and to live in other than company houses.

Strikes, which initially had been called in Pennsylvania because the operators delayed in adopting the code, but which later were continued to compel steel companies to recognize the union and grant the checkoff in their captive mines, were terminated after

---
113. McDonald and Lynch, *op. cit.*, pp. 188-192.
114. *Ibid.*, pp. 192-196.

October 30 when the President worked out a basis of settlement.[115]

Union Gains

The NRA had helped John L. Lewis to rebuild his union. It also enabled him to achieve what no other union in this industry had been able to accomplish—acceptance of collective bargaining by the great majority of southern operators. Hourly earnings were increased about 29 per cent.[116] A maximum eight-hour day and forty-hour week were established. The contracts also set up grievance machinery, regulated company stores, abolished scrip payments of wages and provided for a joint conference of operators and miners in six months. Important also was the new Appalachian interstate bargaining machinery to replace the Central Competitive Field Compact.

The new bargaining arrangement, which continued until April 1941, conformed more closely to the competitive situation in the industry. It included the producing fields of Pennsylvania, Ohio, Virginia, West Virginia, northern Tennessee and eastern Kentucky. Illinois and Indiana no longer were represented in this determination of wages, hours and conditions, but like the outlying districts adjusted their terms of employment to those adopted by the new interstate conference. The Appalachian fields alone produce more than 70 per cent of the national tonnage.[117]

On April 1, 1934 the Appalachian fields negotiated new one-year contracts which reduced maximum daily hours from eight to seven and weekly hours from forty to thirty-five. The agreement also raised the basic wage rates for inside skilled daymen to $5.00 in the North including northern West Virginia and $4.60 in the South. Miners paid on a piece-rate basis were given corresponding increases. The provisions of the agreement were approved by the NRA, applied to outlying fields and made effective by administrative orders. For the industry as a whole the increases in hourly

---

115. Berquist, *et al., op. cit.,* p. 189.
116. Based on data published by the Bureau of Labor Statistics in monthly issues of *Employment and Pay Rolls.*
117. Berquist, *et al., op. cit.,* p. 188.

earnings amounted to 13 cents, or about 22 per cent.[118] Hourly earnings were now about 57 per cent above the pre-Code level.

Code Price Structure Begins to Break

Between October 1933 and January 1935, the heavy losses which had plagued the industry for many years were substantially reduced and the financial position of the operators was much improved.[119] At the beginning of 1935, however, the Code price structure began to break. Faced with uncertainty and falling prices, the operators were unwilling to negotiate new contracts with wage increases as demanded by the miners. A general suspension was postponed several times at the request of the President. The Supreme Court's invalidation of the NRA on May 27 added to the miners' and operators' difficulties. In August the Bituminous Coal Conservation Act of 1935 was passed to take the place of the defunct Bituminous Coal Code. The miners were now determined to replace the 1934 agreement, which had been extended four times, by more favorable contracts. In September, when the negotiators found themselves unable to agree, the union finally called a suspension. The new agreement signed on October 2 added approximately 8 per cent to the average hourly earnings of all mine workers.[120]

b. OTHER UMW ACTIVITIES

Having signed wage contracts which covered practically the entire industry, the United Mine Workers turned to new fields of endeavor. In the fall of 1935 John L. Lewis helped to organize and assumed the leadership of the Committee for Industrial Organization. With him went other UMW officers to important executive positions in the new organization. The miners dug deep into their treasury and contributed about $2 million to the drive to organize steel and other industries,[121] and $500,000 to the 1936 campaign of the Democratic Party. The union also continued its fight for social and labor legislation.

118. Based on data in monthly issues of *Employment and Pay Rolls*.
119. *Findings of Fact and Conclusions of Law, Carter v. Carter Coal Co.*, p. 89.
120. Based on data in monthly issues of *Employment and Pay Rolls*.
121. McDonald and Lynch, *op. cit.*, p. 221.

C. THE NEW BITUMINOUS COAL ACT

On May 18, 1936 the Bituminous Coal Conservation Act was declared unconstitutional. Once again the attempt to stabilize the industry through control of minimum prices was frustrated, and collective bargaining threatened. Convinced that some form of governmental participation was essential to insure collective bargaining in this industry, the union helped to draft a new control bill and exerted all its influence to obtain enactment. Meanwhile expiration of the contract drew near. Early in 1937 the union insisted upon a further wage increase. Realizing that a new coal control act was almost certain, the operators under union pressure granted wage advances which increased the hourly earnings of all mine workers about 12 per cent.[122] These contracts, which covered practically the entire industry, remained in effect until March 31, 1939.

The Bituminous Coal Act of 1937, passed April 26, eliminated the labor sections of the 1935 Act which the Supreme Court had declared unconstitutional a year before. The new Act instead of explicitly providing for collective bargaining and guaranteeing the workers certain rights with respect to peaceable assemblage, the selection of checkweighmen, living in company houses and trading at company stores, includes a statement of public policy to the effect that: (1) employees shall have the right to organize and bargain collectively through representatives of their own choosing; (2) employers shall not interfere with this right nor discriminate against employees for exercising it; and (3) employees shall not be required to join an association for collective bargaining in which the employer has a share of direction or control.

The Act also authorizes cooperative marketing agencies, empowers a commission of seven to promulgate a "Bituminous Coal Code" and determine fair and reasonable prices, imposes a general tax of one per cent per ton on sales of coal and establishes a special division to look after consumers' interests. Observance of the provisions of the Code is obtained by exempting producers who

---

122. Earnings figures based on data in monthly issues of *Employment and Pay Rolls*.

arc members of the Code from a 19.5 per cent tax on sales of coal. Percy Tetlow and John C. Lewis, both of whom had long served the United Mine Workers in various capacities, were appointed to the commission as labor representatives.

On July 1, 1939 the functions granted to the commission under the Act were transferred to a newly created Coal Division of the U. S. Department of the Interior. At the same time the new Consumers' Counsel Division of the Department of the Interior took over the duties and responsibilities of the old office of Consumers' Counsel.

d. THE AGREEMENT OF 1939

In March 1939 the miners asked for a six-hour day and thirty-hour week, an increase of 15 cents a ton for piece workers and 50 cents a day for daymen, vacations with pay, a guaranteed 200-working-day year, improved recognition clauses and certain improvements in working conditions. The Appalachian operators insisted that the prevailing wage level was already too high for profitable operation and stood firm against further concessions. Realizing that additional wage increases were out of the question for the time being, the UMW held that it must be protected against attempts of the Progressive Miners of America to establish competing unions and demanded either elimination of the penalty clauses from district agreements or a union (closed) shop. The operators refused both demands. A suspension called in the Appalachian area April 1 extended to the outlying fields fifteen days later.

On May 9 the President intervened and insisted that the two parties reach an agreement. Two days later, after a shutdown ranging from four to six weeks, fifteen operators' associations signed a two-year agreement containing a union-shop clause. The remaining associations, with the exception of the Harlan County Operators Association, signed similar contracts a week or two later. On July 19, after a bitter struggle, the Harlan County operators also accepted the Appalachian agreement, except that instead of a union shop they granted the union exclusive bargaining rights and preferential hiring.

When the United Mine Workers of America celebrated its golden jubilee at Columbus, Ohio, in January 1940 it was at the peak of its power, prestige and influence. It claimed some six hundred thousand anthracite and bituminous coal miners. The union had won for its members a seven-hour day and a thirty-five-hour week, and wage rates which enabled the soft coal miners as a whole to earn approximately 88 cents an hour and $6.16 a day.[123]

This convention proposed to replace regional contracts with a national agreement covering all bituminous coal operations in the country. It called for the six-hour day and thirty-hour week, time and a half for overtime from Monday through Friday and double time on Saturdays and Sundays, and the abolition of discriminatory wage differentials in and between districts. It also urged President Roosevelt to call a conference to formulate "a constructive national program designed to cure the evil of unemployment" and it declared for liberalization of existing social legislation.[124]

e. THE AGREEMENT OF 1941

The next year brought partial realization of one of these aims—abolition of wage differentials. In March 1941 negotiations began over union demands for wage increases, equalization of rates, vacations with pay and elimination of the reject clause, under which pay is deducted for coal containing impurities. Unwillingness of southern operators to eliminate the North-South differential led to their withdrawal from the joint conference early in April. Only after a strike lasting that entire month, intervention of the National Defense Mediation Board on two occasions, followed by a union threat to strike again in July, did the southern operators fall into line. They signed an agreement almost identical with the one northern operators had accepted and signed weeks earlier. Thus came a split in the interstate bargaining machinery, which now consists of the Appalachian Joint Conference—Pennsylvania, Ohio, northern West Virginia, western Maryland and Michigan—and the Southern Wage Conference—southern West

---

123. Earnings figures based on data in monthly issues of *Employment and Pay Rolls*.
124. *United Mine Workers Journal*, February 15, 1940.

Virginia, Virginia, eastern Kentucky and northern Tennessee. Each contract covers approximately 150,000 miners.

These two-year agreements, retroactive to April 1, 1941, set uniform rates for daymen, though not for tonnage men; raised the basic inside day labor rate to $7.00—an increase of $1.00 in the North, $1.40 in the South; granted higher tonnage rates and ten-day vacations with pay; eliminated the reject clause (the southern contract provides machinery for possible adjustments for companies suffering financial hardship because of this); and extended the union shop to Harlan County, so that by the summer of 1941 the union shop prevailed throughout the industry, except for the steel companies' captive mines.

These mines employed some 50,000 of the total 450,000 bituminous coal miners and produced 10 per cent of the total yearly output of 453 million tons. About 95 per cent of their employees were already union members. In the fall of 1941 the United Mine Workers demanded that the steel companies sign a union shop agreement. There was good reason to believe that the union expected and the companies feared that this would be an opening wedge to get the union shop in the steel mills. The companies refused to sign the agreement and the dispute went to the National Defense Mediation Board. The Board's eventual rejection of the union's demand was followed by a strike—the third since the dispute began—and then, after appeals by President Roosevelt, by agreement to arbitrate the issue. Union victory finally came on December 7, when the arbitration board, in a two-to-one decision, ruled that the union shop should prevail in the captive mines.

8. Major Problems of the Industry

Although its labor costs are stabilized, the soft coal industry still faces uncertainties and difficulties. Miners' gains since 1933 have added substantially to prices and production costs. The April 1934 contract which shortened working hours and increased pay rates about 22 per cent, boosted labor costs 18.5 per cent, and total costs 14.5 per cent. With the approval of the Administration the added costs plus an additional charge of 6.8 cents a ton were passed on to the consumer,[125] whereupon sales income per ton of coal at the mine rose 18.3 per cent.

Faced with increased costs as well as a drop in the daily output of their employees (the 1934 hour revisions decreased man output per day 10 per cent) and finding themselves in a better financial position, the operators placed heavy orders for loading machines. By 1937 machine-loaded coal was up 64.2 per cent, and daily output per man about 9 per cent. As production rose, the number of working days fell—193 in 1937, contrasted with 199 in 1933. Man days per million tons of coal produced were now only 1.4 per cent above the 1933 level.[126] In February-March 1937 when production was about 7 per cent above comparable months of 1929, hourly earnings were 20.2 per cent above 1929, but total money pay rolls were 11.0 per cent below and real pay rolls only 15.5 per cent above. Total man hours were 1.2 per cent below those worked in 1929.[127]

These figures indicate that adjustments in wages and hours which add to production costs should be considered in the light of their effect upon total employment and total pay rolls. Undoubtedly unemployment growing out of mechanization will receive increasing attention in future negotiations.

Higher costs and prices also have a bearing on the extent coal is displaced by fuel oil, natural gas and hydroelectric power, also upon more efficient use of coal by public utilities, railroads, manufacturing industries and even domestic consumers.

These three economic forces—mechanization, competitive fuels and more efficient utilization—are a triple threat to the future stability of the industry. The miners' union must decide whether to seek a higher standard of living for a steadily declining number

125. The industry had taken severe losses since 1923. The Bureau of Internal Revenue collected income statistics of coal companies in 1925 and in 1928 and subsequent years. In all these years the deficits of corporations which reported losses far exceeded the net income of those reporting surpluses. See Berquist, *et al.*, *op. cit.*, pp. 59-60.
126. Waldo E. Fisher, *Economic Consequences of the Seven-Hour Day and Wage Changes in the Bituminous Coal Industry*, University of Pennsylvania Press, Philadelphia, 1939, pp. 94-97.
127. Waldo E. Fisher, "Union Wage and Hour Policies and Employment," *American Economic Review*, June 1940, p. 297.

of workers or the economic well-being of all employees attached to the industry. It has bargaining power to raise wages, lower hours and probably to increase annual earnings. In all likelihood such action would encourage mechanization, more efficient consumption and greater substitution of competing fuels—all of which leads to more unemployment and smaller pay rolls. Effective handling of these economic problems demands a high order of industrial statesmanship.

9. Conclusion

The history of labor relations in bituminous coal shows the utter helplessness of the individual employee and employer in the face of economic forces and conditions arising from an overdeveloped industry. Particularly where the establishments are many, widely decentralized and supply the same markets, collective bargaining under capable leadership is necessary not only to protect workers and maintain decent standards of living but also to safeguard employers' investments.

Bituminous coal labor relations also support the contention of labor economists that successful collective bargaining must embrace substantially all producing fields serving common markets. The failure of the Central Competitive Field Compact must be laid largely to union inability to organize the southern fields. No system of collective bargaining can long work if one group of employers must pay rigid wage scales and meet union standards of employment while another group conducts its business under flexible wage scales and working conditions arrived at through individual bargaining. Under such conditions nonunion operators control both costs and prices and can therefore dominate markets.

Adverse economic conditions, while exceedingly difficult to deal with, are by no means the only deterrent to effective collective bargaining. Of great importance is the attitude of the two parties to collective bargaining. While many coal operators, especially in the Midwest, Southwest and Far West, were sympathetic to unionism and accepted its obligations in good faith, the majority merely tolerated labor organizations or refused to deal with them. In the

South and in the nonunion stronghold of Pennsylvania operators were especially antagonistic. Organizers were barred from company towns. Civil liberties were violated. To keep the union out operators not only made their employees sign antiunion contracts, but resorted to armed guards and deputy sheriffs, strikebreakers, wholesale evictions, and not infrequently to tear gas and guns. Sometimes they were helped by state officials and the National Guard.

The miners were also culpable. Sometimes on their own initiative but often incited by union organizers they intimidated and coerced nonunion employees, and engaged in mass picketing, armed marches and riots which resulted in destruction of tipples, tearing up of railroad tracks and killing of company guards and nonunion miners. The record of the struggles in nonunion areas is spotted with intolerance, disregard of personal rights, violations of law and order and destruction of property and life.

Even in union areas the attitude of the two parties towards collective bargaining has left much to be desired. The cooperation of the operators has been characterized by reluctance and confined in the main to the making and enforcement of wage contracts. Undue stress has been placed on the shortcomings of the union and on enforcing the letter of the agreement. The operators have been concerned with curbing the abuses of the union—not with helping its leaders to deal more intelligently with the difficult tasks which confronted them. The union has been recognized as an agency for collective bargaining but has not been regarded altogether as a constructive force in the industry, nor has its aid been sought in solving the many economic conditions which disrupted the mining and delivery of bituminous coal.

The union leaders have frequently been uncompromising and at times unduly arrogant in dealing with union operators. Until the collapse of the interstate movement in 1927 they concentrated chiefly upon building up their organization, improving their bargaining position, and gaining objectives even at the expense of the economic well-being of the operators with whom they had been dealing for many years. More recently they have widened their field of activity and have concerned themselves greatly with governmental regulation of coal, social legislation and the extension of industrial unionism to the mass production industries. The union's theory of bargaining has been based largely on force and on the retention of gains no matter what the cost. Strikes in violation of wage contracts and general suspensions when agreements expired have been of too common occurrence. Arbitration has been unacceptable—the resort of the "underdog."

In defense of militant unionism its apologists point to the economic conditions of the industry and the attitudes of the operators toward unionism and collective bargaining. The lot of the wage earners who have jobs has been greatly improved under collective bargaining, especially since 1933. Materially aided by the Administration and the forces of recovery, the union had—even before the 1941 increases—raised the hourly earnings of all employees on the pay rolls 94 per cent above the pre-Code level. The miners' daily earnings averaged $6.16 in 1940 and their standard working hours now stand at seven per day and thirty-five per week.[128] Moreover, union contracts protect the miners in their jobs, guarantee them improved working conditions, and insure them greater personal freedom—all notable achievements.

128. Earnings figures based on data in monthly issues of *Employment and Pay Rolls*.

Chapter 6

ANTHRACITE

WALDO E. FISHER

1. INTRODUCTION

LIKE THE BITUMINOUS COAL INDUSTRY, anthracite has a long history of labor organization and collective bargaining. Unions were powerful factors as early as the late 1860's and early 1870's. Since the Award of the Anthracite Coal Strike Commission of 1903 they have had contracts with the operators on an industry-wide basis.

In 1939 the anthracite mines employed 93,000 workers and produced 51.5 million tons of coal.[1] Unlike bituminous coal, nearly 80 per cent of the production goes to householders and other nonindustrial users. The anthracite market is mainly the middle Atlantic and New England states.[2]

Also unlike bituminous coal, the anthracite industry is compact, confined to ten counties in Pennsylvania. Within this area, three fields are commonly designated: (1) the Northern or Wyoming Field, fifty miles by six, lying between Forest City and Shickshinny; (2) the Lehigh Field consisting of two fields to the south of the Wyoming—the Eastern Middle Field, twenty-six miles by ten, and the Western Middle Field, thirty-six miles by four or five; and (3) the Southern or Schuylkill Field, seventy miles by eight, lying between Mauch Chunk and Dauphin.[3] This geographic concentration accounts partly for the fact that since 1900 anthracite has frequently been called a monopolistic industry.

1. U. S. Bureau of Mines, *Minerals Yearbook, 1940*, p. 838. Data are preliminary.
2. Mimeographed release of the Anthracite Coal Industry Commission, September 10, 1937, pp. 2-3. The release was based on a report by Richard R. Mead, *Anthracite Marketing Situation*.
3. See Sydney A. Hale's chapter in *What the Coal Commission Found* (ed. E. E. Hunt, F. G. Tryon and J. H. Willits), Williams and Wilkins, Baltimore, 1925, p. 283.

Before then anthracite, like bituminous coal, was overdeveloped and beset with excessive competition, price wars and unemployment. The situation was further complicated by the fight among the coal-carrying railroads to own or control the limited coal resources, and by a struggle between independent operators and the railroads upon which their access to the coal markets depended.

After 1900 anthracite entered the second stage of its development. By consolidating railroads and mining properties, the railroad companies obtained increasing control of the industry. In 1901 the consolidation of the Reading and the Central of New Jersey enabled the management of the former railroad to claim ownership or control of 63 per cent of all unmined anthracite in Pennsylvania.[4] In that year seven large companies were sufficiently united to have common price and tonnage quota policies and through their command of transportation to keep independent companies under their control.[5] Seven years later the Supreme Court pointed out that eight producing companies, affiliated to some extent with the railroads, produced 74 per cent of the total output and controlled 90 per cent of the underground reserves.[6] The "community of interest" during these years enabled the operators to dominate the domestic fuel markets on the eastern seaboard for over two decades; it also gave them a strategic bargaining position with the new miners' union, organized in 1900.

This concentration has continued. Ten anthracite companies, usually associated with the same financial interests as the anthracite-carrying railroads, owned and leased or controlled 94.7 per cent of the total recoverable tonnage in January 1937.[7] But since 1927 concentrated ownership has not played as important a role in the industry's collective bargaining. In that year, anthracite production and consumption, which had a slight downward trend in the late postwar years, began a sharp decline. High market

---

4. W. J. Ashley, *The Adjustment of Wages*, Longmans, Green, London, 1903, pp. 124-125.

5. *Ibid.*, pp. 126-127.

6. David L. Wing, "Corporate Organization of the Anthracite Industry," in *What the Coal Commission Found*, p. 371.

7. Mimeographed release of the Anthracite Coal Industry Commission, September 20, 1937, p. 2. The release was based on a report by C. V. Maudlin, *Anthracite Lands and Deposits*.

prices, business depression, and particularly the mounting competition of substitute fuels brought fewer working days, more unemployment and smaller pay rolls. Such conditions curtailed the ability of the industry to meet higher wage demands, and the miners found it advisable to seek their demands through negotiation rather than strikes and suspensions.

2. Industrial Relations Under Free Competition, 1842–1900

As early as the 1840's there were two anthracite unions. The first, formed after a strike in 1842, was crushed almost immediately.[8] A second was organized six years later, won some concessions from the operators in 1849, and disappeared in the following year in an atmosphere of friction, distrust and employer opposition.[9]

a. A Decade of Collective Bargaining, 1865–1875

During the next fifteen years unionism made little headway. The rebirth of the movement in the 1860's must be attributed in very large measure to economic conditions growing out of the Civil War. During the war years anthracite production shot up,[10] as did prices of both anthracite[11] and other commodities.[12] At the same time labor shortages and big wage advances[13] accounted for the absence of union activity until almost the close of the war.

About 1864 two unions were formed: the Workingmen's Benevolent Society of Carbon County,[14] and the Miners' Benevolent Association in the Lehigh Field.[15] These organizations were unim-

8. See National Labor Relations Board, "Written Trade Agreements in Collective Bargaining," *Bulletin No. 4*, 1939, pp. 95-96.
9. Peter Roberts, *The Anthracite Coal Industry*, Macmillan, New York, 1901, pp. 105, 172-173.
10. F. G. Tryon and Sydney A. Hale, *Coal in 1922*, U. S. Geological Survey, 1924, Appendix table.
11. Roberts, *op. cit.*, p. 174.
12. Frank T. Carlton, *History and Problems of Organized Labor*, D. C. Heath, New York, 1911, p. 55.
13. Roberts, *op. cit.*, p. 110.
14. Chris Evans, *History of the United Mine Workers of America*, Indianapolis, 1918(?), Vol. I, p. 12.
15. Roberts, *op. cit.*, p. 174.

portant until 1867 when the miners were aroused over heavy wage cuts induced by drastic postwar price declines.[16] Making matters worse were large numbers of unemployed miners demobilized from the Union Army. In that year leaders of local unions in the Lehigh and Schuylkill fields formed a new organization, the Workingmen's Benevolent Association.

Union Gains

In July 1868 a strike spread throughout both the Lehigh and Schuylkill fields. Lasting until August 28, it ended in partial victory for the miners, who lost their demand for the eight-hour day, but won a 10 per cent wage increase.[17]

The union leaders, realizing that effective bargaining power required organization of the entire industry, sent organizers into the Northern Field in the fall of 1868. They succeeded, and within a few months about 85 per cent of the anthracite workers belonged to the WBA. In December 1868 the Schuylkill operators who were paying wage rates out of line with those in the northern region demanded a 25 per cent reduction, but could not compel the union to accept it. In May 1869 the miners began a general suspension of work to reduce "the surplus of coal already in the market" so as to afford "the operators and dealers fair interest on their investments" and the miners "a fair day's wages for a fair day's work." [18] Work was resumed five weeks later, after Schuylkill and Lehigh operators met the miners' demand for a sliding scale which related wages to the selling prices of coal.[19] Three months later, violating its agreements, the WBA called another strike for higher wages. Again the operators were forced to accept the union's terms, the latter refusing "all offers of compro-

16. *Ibid.*, p. 110.
17. *Ibid.*, p. 176.
18. Evans, *op. cit.*, Vol. I, pp. 18-19.
19. The agreement established basic rates and selling prices. The miners received specified percentage increases when the price of coal advanced above the base and took corresponding reductions when the price fell, except that no wage reductions were allowed when prices dropped below the agreed-upon base price. Prices were determined monthly by a committee of five operators selected by the president of the Anthracite Board of Trade and the president of the union. See the *Report of the Industrial Commission*, 1901, Vol. XVII, p. 325; and Evans, *op. cit.*, Vol. I, pp. 20-21.

mise."[20] Wages were now some 20 per cent above those during the Civil War.

In January 1870, Schuylkill County operators served notice on their employees that the sliding scale base was too high. The miners went on strike to resist any changes in the scale, but finally accepted a modified proposal known as the "Gowan Compromise."

The strength of the union during these years has been described by Peter Roberts:

> The power of the union was supreme. Its leaders dictated terms and prices [wages] to operators, to which they must comply if they wished to stay in business. The unreasonable and arbitrary demands of the men crushed scores of individual operators, while it added to the strength of corporations by bringing more collieries under their control. Affairs had assumed such a condition in many localities that the operators could not say their property was their own.[21]

Concentration of Ownership and Union Collapse

During these years of union domination several factors were at work to strengthen the bargaining position of the operators. Small-scale mining was passing because easily accessible deposits were exhausted. Extraction of coal from the deeper beds required considerable capital and more systematic and informed mining methods. Individual operators found it increasingly difficult to compete with large companies utilizing machinery and large-scale operations. Moreover, the coal-carrying railroads, reduced in numbers as the result of mergers, now entered the mining business and bought up small companies and large acreages of coal reserves. By 1872, six railroads had sufficient control of the coal fields to attempt to regulate production and to fix transportation rates.[22]

Greatly disturbed by the growing power of the union, the operators decided that the time had come to fight to protect their common interests. Three leading companies in the Northern Field

20. Edgar Sydenstricker, "Collective Bargaining in the Anthracite Coal Industry," *Bulletin No. 191*, U. S. Bureau of Labor Statistics, 1916, p. 14.
21. *Op. cit.*, p. 179.
22. *Ibid.*, p. 66.

—the Delaware, Lackawanna and Western; the Delaware and Hudson; and the Pennsylvania Coal Company—acting in concert ordered a 30 per cent wage reduction. The miners appealed to the WBA and a strike of the entire industry was called in January 1871. After almost six months of idleness, the labor organizations in the Northern and Lehigh fields were defeated and the miners returned to work on the operators' terms.

The union in the Schuylkill region was strong enough to force arbitration of the issue. The resulting award ordered a reduction in the basic rates of the sliding scale. Four years later, in January 1875, the operators announced a 10 per cent reduction. After a five-month strike the union was completely broken and the workers accepted, not a 10, but a 20 per cent wage reduction. Labor organizations as a potent factor disappeared from the industry.[23]

b. TWENTY-FIVE YEARS OF INDIVIDUAL BARGAINING

Between 1876 and 1884 there was little union activity. A secret organization called the Mollie Maguires which appeared in the sixties continued its intimidation, violence and murder in the mining communities. Consisting of an inner ring which controlled the Ancient Order of Hibernians in anthracite regions, this group can hardly be classed as a labor organization. Its reign of terror ended in 1876 when ten ringleaders were executed and fourteen were jailed.[24]

Developments Unfavorable to Unionism

Wages had fallen so low that many anthracite miners entered other industries. These wages, however, were acceptable to the newer immigrants, especially those from central Europe whose immigration was encouraged by anthracite operators. In 1880 central Europeans were less than 2 per cent of the foreign-born population in eight counties of the anthracite region; by 1900 they were over 46 per cent.[25] These widely differing races broke down

---

23. Sydenstricker, *op. cit.*, p. 15.
24. Mary Ritter Beard, *A Short History of the American Labor Movement*, Harcourt, Brace and Howe, New York, 1920, p. 82; also Roberts, *op. cit.*, pp. 71 and 193.
25. Frank Julian Warne and John R. Commons, "Slavs in Coal Mining," *Trade*

the miners' solidarity and made effective unionization of the coal fields impossible for two decades.

Meanwhile consolidation of mining interests continued. Overdevelopment of the industry, the heavy capital outlay needed to open deeper seams, as well as the severe competition and periodic price wars, forced many small companies to sell out to large producers or shut down. The growing consolidation of mining properties and railroads by no means removed rivalry from within the industry. The history of this period was punctuated with broken price agreements and breaches of faith on the part of many carriers. But whenever unionism became threatening, a solid front was effectually maintained.

Sporadic Union Organization

With the demise of the Workingmen's Benevolent Association, wages were reduced and by 1877 reached the lowest level in thirteen years.[26] In that year came the great railroad strike, and miners in the Northern Field took advantage of the enforced suspension of operations to form a union and later to demand a 25 per cent wage increase. The operators rejected this demand. A violent strike followed, ending three months later in a conflict with the city guards of Scranton with four miners killed and over a score wounded. The employees were forced to return to work on the operators' terms and the union "folded up." The next year the operators voluntarily granted a 10 per cent increase, and in 1879 an additional 15 per cent.[27]

Labor unions reappeared in 1884. In the Southern or Schuylkill region the English-speaking miners organized an association which enrolled thirty thousand miners in three years. Meanwhile the Knights of Labor were at work in the Northern and Lehigh fields. These two organizations united late in 1887, and soon after the miners of the Lehigh Field went out on a strike which spread to the Schuylkill region in January 1888. The union, whose bargaining power was far from strong, attempted in vain to get

Unionism and Labor Problems (ed. J. R. Commons), Ginn and Co., Boston, 1905, pp. 337-338.
26. Roberts, *op. cit.*, p. 110.
27. *Ibid.*, pp. 110 and 181-182.

the operators to arbitrate. In March the strike was called off and unions again disappeared from the industry.

For twelve years the operators were free from employee interference. Yet the period was an unprofitable one for the operators. Prices fell, and despite mergers, pools and price agreements, ruthless competition prevailed. Data on days worked by the mines before 1890 are not available, but in the five years following, the mines averaged only 198 working days and in the five years after 1895, they averaged only 169 days.[28] Falling prices, cutthroat competition and irregular operation meant financial losses.

Conditions of the Miners

The miners also suffered. The findings of the Anthracite Coal Strike Commission of 1903 indicate that the daily wages of miners for the years under discussion were not out of line with those prevailing for work of comparable skill and training,[29] but annual earnings were far below normal. Under individual bargaining, wages in the Northern Field continued at the 1879 level until 1900 and in the Middle and Southern fields wages were adjusted to a sliding scale determined by the operators alone.[30]

During these twelve years the miners' grievances were numerous. At thirty-seven mines, companies maintained stores at which trading was compulsory and, according to the miners, prices were double those elsewhere.[31] Powder for shooting down coal had to be bought by the miners at $2.75, although bought wholesale by the companies at from 90 cents to $1.00.[32] Employees complained of living conditions in company houses, of payment in scrip instead of lawful money, of excessive fines for loading impure coal, of deductions from the pay envelope for medical attention, of insufficient cars at the work place, and of favoritism in their distribution, of child labor, of monthly instead of semimonthly pay-

28. Computed from data published in Edward W. Parker, *The Production of Coal in 1900*, U. S. Geological Survey, 1901, pp. 33-35.
29. "Report of the Anthracite Coal Strike Commission," *Bulletin of the Department of Labor*, No. 46, 1903, pp. 468, 477-478.
30. Roberts, *op. cit.*, p. 110.
31. Sydenstricker, *op. cit.*, pp. 16-17.
32. Ashley, *op. cit.*, p. 130.

ments as required by law, of long work hours, and of the denial of the right to hire checkweighmen, a practice common in bituminous coal mining.[33]

While some charges were not substantiated by the Commission and others were shown to be greatly exaggerated, the fact remains that they had sufficient factual basis to create irritation and discontent. The evidence shows that operators, generally speaking, gave little serious attention to the management of labor, and that the terms and conditions of employment reflected the industry's competitive struggle.

3. Industrial Relations in a Sellers' Market, 1900–1927

Under the conditions described, it was to be expected that organizers of the United Mine Workers, who entered the anthracite region in the late nineties, would soon have a substantial following. No one, however, suspected that within four years, "the differences in race, religion, and ideals of the twenty nationalities in the region" would be swept aside.[34] The success of President John Mitchell and his associates was all the more remarkable in view of pronounced racial jealousies, an oversupply of labor and the operators' uncompromising hostility to unions in general and the United Mine Workers in particular.

a. THE STRIKE OF 1900

The union called a convention in August 1900 at which it drafted a long list of demands, including wage increases of from 10 to 20 per cent, and invited the operators to a joint conference.[35] When it became clear that the operators had no intention of meeting with the miners, a strike was called. So popular was the union cause that on September 17 not only the 8,000 union members but between 80,000 and 100,000 other miners stopped work. Two weeks later 90 per cent of the 144,000 workers in the industry had responded to the union's call.

---

33. "Report of the Anthracite Coal Strike Commission," pp. 465-505.
34. John Mitchell, *Organized Labor,* American Book and Bible House, Philadelphia, 1903, p. 362.
35. Parker, *op. cit.,* p. 159.

The operators were in an excellent position to fight unionism. Working agreements had been made not only between the railroad companies but also between the carriers and the independent coal companies. The result was a solid employer front. An additional advantage was a glutted coal market.

Fortunately for the miners, 1900 was a national election year. Republican managers feared spread of the strike to the soft coal industry, and also its effect upon public opinion, especially in the light of the growing sympathy for labor in current papers and periodicals. Sensing public reaction, the Democratic candidate for President, William Jennings Bryan, denounced the anthracite companies as an example of the "inexorable greed of trusts and combinations." Senator Hanna, chairman of the Republican National Committee, had previously attempted to prevent the strike and now made repeated efforts to end it. After much pressure upon the coal companies and the financial interests controlling the large carriers, a settlement was effected. The operators granted a 10 per cent increase in wages, but refused to recognize the union or to negotiate an agreement.[36]

b. THE STRIKE OF 1902

Results of the 1900 strike exceeded the expectations of union officials and enhanced the organization's prestige. To the union leaders it was only a preliminary struggle, since the first essential of collective bargaining—union recognition—had not been achieved. Early in 1901 the United Mine Workers invited operators to a joint conference to negotiate a new wage scale and to discuss conditions of employment. The operators refused to meet the miners. Later, however, certain "outside friends of the labor movement" arranged a meeting of the two groups at which the operators "held out the hope that, if during the present year the mine workers demonstrated their willingness and ability to abstain from engaging in local strikes, full and complete recognition would unquestionably be accorded at a future date." [37] The

---

36. Cf. Ashley, *op. cit.*, p. 132; Mitchell, *op. cit.*, p. 366; and Roberts, *op. cit.*, p. 185.
37. Ashley, *op. cit.*, pp. 134-135.

operators posted notices that the existing terms of employment would continue in effect until April 1, 1902. Meanwhile, according to John Mitchell, some companies built stockades around their mines, established storage depots for coal, and sent agents among the union members to get copies of the records and proceedings of the union.[38] The mine workers also strengthened their organization. By 1902 practically every man and boy was enrolled in the union.

In February 1902, the union asked the operators to meet with them to formulate a wage scale and to consider other terms of employment. The operators refused, saying "there cannot be two masters in the management of business."[39] A convention of miners was then held which decided to send a telegram to the railroad presidents asking them to meet the union's representatives. Through the good offices of the National Civic Federation, a conference was finally arranged, but the operators refused to make any concessions at this or a later conference. The union cut in half its demands for increased wages, but the operators stood firm, disregarding the recommendations of Senators Hanna, Quay and Penrose, Governor Odell, and others, as well as the National Civic Federation. The miners offered to submit their demands to arbitration. Resentful of political and financial pressure and determined to retain the control they had enjoyed for a quarter of a century, the operators refused to arbitrate.

Role of Public Opinion

The union called a suspension on May 12 which was officially declared to be a strike at a convention of miners three days later.[40] Thus began one of the outstanding struggles in the history of American industrial relations. The operators were confident of success, having made careful preparations. They failed, however, to consider two forces. One was the moral and financial assistance

38. *Op. cit.*, p. 369.
39. *Ibid.*, p. 370.
40. The discussion of the 1902 strike is based on the works of Edward W. Parker, *The Production of Coal in 1902*, U. S. Geological Survey, 1904, p. 176; Mitchell, *op. cit.*, pp. 368-373; Sydenstricker, *op. cit.*, pp. 21-23; and particularly the "Report of the Anthracite Coal Strike Commission," pp. 457-463.

(approximately $2.6 million) which the miners received from soft coal workers and from organized labor generally both at home and abroad. The other was an aroused and indignant public opinion. The large railroad companies were already in public disfavor because of general antipathy to big business and the operators' attitude during the strike of 1900. When cold weather came and hard coal was not forthcoming, the public became impatient. Refusal of the operators to arbitrate or to heed the suggestion of public officials and civic organizations turned impatience into irritation. Anthracite prices rose "from $3 and $4 a ton to $20 and $30," and there was considerable distress in some of the larger cities.[41]

Taking advantage of an aroused public opinion, President Theodore Roosevelt invited the parties to a conference at the White House. He called upon both operators and miners to "meet upon the common plane of the necessities of the public" and proposed arbitration. The union representatives promptly accepted the offer, but the operators refused, denounced the union and its leaders, and asked for federal troops to protect the mining property and the employees.

This demonstration of absolute indifference to consumer necessity crystallized public opinion, and the press of the country was practically unanimous in denouncing the coal corporations. Finally, through the elder J. Pierpont Morgan, the operators agreed to submit to arbitration by a commission appointed by the President. The strike ended October 23, 1902.[42]

C. THE AWARD OF 1903

On March 18, 1903, the Anthracite Coal Strike Commission submitted its report. The Award granted certain increases in wages,[43] reduced working hours from ten to nine for the great

---

41. Sydenstricker, *op. cit.*, p. 22.
42. Cf. Ashley, *op. cit.*, pp. 112-113, and 135-141; Mitchell, *op. cit.*; and Sydenstricker, *op. cit.*
43. The contract miners (see p. 295, note 49) and their laborers were given an increase of 10 per cent. The remaining employees, except certain limited groups for which special provision was made, were paid the same rates for a nine-hour day that they had received for a ten-hour day in April 1902.

majority of mine workers, established a sliding scale based on the price of certain prepared sizes of coal at New York Harbor,[44] and created a Board of Conciliation of three representatives each for the miners and operators, as well as an umpire or impartial chairman whose decisions were to be final. The Board was given power to handle disputes arising under the Award, which could not be settled locally. The wage provisions were retroactive to November 1, 1902.[45]

The Award did not change the method of wage payment or the working conditions under which coal was mined. No attempt was made to equalize wages or to remove inequalities. The pay increases were applied equally to all workers in a given occupation. The intricate system of wage payment, together with the many rate differentials and inequalities—determined by individual bargaining under severe competitive conditions—was taken over by the Anthracite Commission and crystallized.

Although the Award in many respects gratified the miners' union, its failure to compel union recognition—the major issue of the 1902 strike—was a disappointment. The Commission claimed that this demand was not within its jurisdiction, but pointed out that the right to join a union, which the operators conceded in their brief, was "a privilege of doubtful value," if the organization was "to be rendered impotent," and its usefulness "nullified by refusing to permit it to perform the functions for which it was created, and for which it alone exists." [46]

---

44. Under this arrangement a base average price of $4.50 per ton f.o.b. at or near New York was established for white ash coal of all sizes above pea coal. For each increase of 5 cents in the average price of these sizes above the base all mine workers were given an increase of one per cent in their compensation. The rates fixed by the increases in the Award, however, were minimum rates and were not to be subject to further decrease by the operation of the sliding scale. To illustrate, when the price of said coal reached $4.55 per ton, the compensation of the workers was increased one per cent, and this increase continued in effect until either the price of coal fell below $4.55 per ton, when the one per cent compensations ceased, or until the price reached $4.60 per ton, when an additional one per cent was added, etc.

45. "Report of the Anthracite Coal Strike Commission," pp. 506-509.
46. *Ibid.*, p. 489.

d. LABOR RELATIONS UNDER THE AWARD

The nine years following the 1903 Award were surprisingly free from strife, except for petty strikes and the suspension of 1906. The operators were in a strategic bargaining position. They were reluctant, however, to force issues because they finally realized that public opinion as well as economic strength determined the outcome of labor disputes in their industry. The union also was willing to compromise, notwithstanding a membership which comprised the great majority of the wage earners. The prices of coal moved to somewhat higher levels, which advanced wages on an average about 4 per cent. Moreover, workers' annual earnings were higher because of increased working days per year. Finally, day-to-day grievances were aired and adjusted by means of the machinery established under the Award. These factors added to the union's prestige and held the loyalty of its members. The union leaders, John Mitchell and John T. Dempsey, whose judgment was tempered by a wide experience, exercised discretion and prudence and held in check the less responsible elements in the union.

The Award expired in March 1906. The operators, fearing that the union's demands might be unreasonable, built up surplus stocks of coal. To compel the operators to consider its demands, the union called a suspension. About five weeks later the Award was renewed for three years.

In 1909 union membership was somewhat depleted. Many miners were opposed to a strike. Their conference committee was instructed to secure the best possible terms and in case no concessions were granted, to appeal for federal arbitration.[47] The operators rejected the union's demands, which included additional wage increases, the eight-hour day and recognition of the United Mine Workers, but offered to extend the Award for another three years. This the union agreed to do after it obtained minor changes in the contract.

47. Sydenstricker, *op. cit.*, p. 53.

e. TRADE AGREEMENTS REPLACE THE AWARD

When the Award expired in 1912, the union's bargaining position was greatly improved. Union membership had been considerably increased, and the workers were dissatisfied because no wage increases or other important concessions had been won since 1903. The union leadership no longer counseled moderation, but advocated the use of force to win the union's demands. Moreover, 1912 was a national election year. The miners asked for a 20 per cent wage increase and a more uniform and convenient procedure for handling grievances. They also demanded the eight-hour day, union recognition, and election of checkweighmen—terms which the soft coal miners had had for more than a decade. To enforce its demands the union called a suspension.

1912 Gains of the Miners

After approximately seven weeks of idleness a new four-year agreement was negotiated which abolished the sliding scale and granted a 10 per cent increase over the rates established by the 1903 Award. Abolition of the sliding scale was by mutual consent. The union was dissatisfied with it because the system was too complex for the rank and file to understand, and because union representatives could not check the operators' price computations on which wages were based. The operators were willing to discontinue the scale because it was cumbersome and required elaborate bookkeeping. Moreover, they were considering raising the prices of certain grades of anthracite which would have automatically raised wages more than the 10 per cent increase.[48]

The new contract also provided for a grievance committee at each mine, specified how complaints would be handled, granted the mine workers the right to elect their own checkweighman, and made other changes in working conditions. Once more, however, the United Mine Workers failed to achieve the goal of union recognition.

Further Wage Increases

The 1912 agreement expired in April 1916 but the mines con-

---
48. *Ibid.,* pp. 34-35.

tinued in operation. On May 5 a new agreement gave a 7 per cent increase to the men on piece work as well as to most of the company men, and gave the bulk of the daymen the same pay for eight hours as they previously had for nine, plus an increase of 3 per cent.[49] The increase to the employees working by the day represented approximately 16 per cent more in hourly rates but only 3 per cent more in daily earnings. The operators still refused to recognize the United Mine Workers.

f. WAR AND POSTWAR YEARS

Upon our entrance into the World War, union leadership was increasingly dissatisfied with the results of moderation and conciliation. It became more aggressive and militant in its demands. It was more reluctant to arbitrate the issues in dispute, and more willing to call suspensions.

The 1916 agreement was to have remained in force until March 31, 1920. However, the rapid increase in the cost of living brought on by the war and the difficulty of maintaining an adequate force of mine workers in the face of higher wages paid in other industries brought increased wages in April 1917, November 1917, and again in November 1918. The contract miners and their laborers now had an advance of 40 per cent over the May 5, 1916 rate, and the principal classes of day and company men received increases ranging from $1.20 to $2.00.[50] These advances were ac-

---

49. The wage earners employed in anthracite fall into two general classes: those whose working places are underground in the mine proper, generally called inside men, and those whose working places are on the surface, commonly referred to as outside men. Of the 102,081 wage earners employed in this industry in 1936 approximately 75 per cent were inside men.

About 69 per cent of the men working inside the mine are engaged in shooting down and loading coal. These workers are classified as (1) contract miners or tonnage men, and (2) company men. The former, who comprise the great majority of these workers, are paid on a piece basis. The company men are paid on an hourly, daily or monthly basis. All other workers are commonly referred to as daymen. Because of the location of the work places which makes supervision practically impossible, as well as the method of wage payment in effect, a record of time worked by the tonnage men is seldom kept by the operators. These workers leave the mine when they have completed what is customarily regarded as a day's task.

50. Waldo E. Fisher, "Wage Rates," in *What the Coal Commission Found*, pp. 306-307.

companied by a larger demand for coal and increased working time.[51]

The supplementary agreement of 1918 expired March 31, 1920. On March 9 the union presented sixteen demands, including (1) a 60 per cent increase in the contract wage scale and $2.00 more a day for daymen, (2) a six-hour day and five-day week, (3) time and a half for overtime and double time for Sundays and holidays, and (4) a closed-shop contract. The first three demands were similar to those made upon the soft coal operators of the Central Competitive Field in the fall of 1919 and then being arbitrated by the United States Bituminous Coal Commission. The major issue was the demand for a closed shop; full recognition of the union had long obtained in most of the union soft coal fields.

Negotiators Deadlocked

When it became apparent that no agreement could be reached by March 31, 1920, when the contract expired, the joint scale committee agreed that mining should continue during the negotiations and that the agreement should be retroactive to April 1. After eight weeks of negotiation the operators offered wage advances which averaged about 15 per cent.[52] The miners rejected them but agreed to modify their original demands. They now insisted on wage advances at least equal to those granted the bituminous miners—31 per cent for tonnage men and 20 per cent for daymen.[53] They also agreed to withdraw the demand for the six-hour day and five-day week provided the eight-hour day was extended to those employees (about 2 per cent) still working longer hours.

51. The days worked averaged 253 in 1916, 285 in 1917, 293 in 1918, 266 in 1919, and 271 in 1920. F. G. Tryon and L. Mann, *Coal in 1923*, U. S. Geological Survey, p. 518.

52. *Reply of the Anthracite Operators to the Demands of the Anthracite Mine Workers before the United States Anthracite Coal Commission*, Scranton, Pa., July 1920, p. 3.

53. *Majority and Minority Reports of the United States Bituminous Coal Commission to the President*, 1920, p. 38. The daymen were given only a 20 per cent increase because their wages were advanced disproportionately under the Washington agreement.

The Commission's Award

The operators rejected the modified demands and offered to arbitrate. This was unacceptable to the miners as was also a compromise submitted by the Secretary of Labor. Finally, after the Administration brought pressure to bear on the union leaders, the issues were submitted to arbitration. The Commission's award was incorporated in a new contract on September 2, 1920, retroactive to April 1. The rates of the contract miners were advanced 65 per cent above the 1916 base. Certain classes of daymen had their 1918 rates increased 17 per cent, while others received an advance of 4 cents an hour.[54] The Commission ordered that the new contract should be signed by the union officials under the designation—"on behalf of the United Mine Workers of America." Recognition of the union was finally achieved.

Miners Dissatisfied

Despite these gains, the award led to a two-week "vacation strike" by the miners, who were dissatisfied with its terms and resentful of the fact that "the final decision of the arbitrator was changed between twilight and dawn," a change which Lewis laid to the "operators' well-known policy of keeping close to an arbitrator." [55] The miners claimed that the Commission's wage increases were based upon advances in cost of living since 1902, rather than since the last wage adjustment. This, they held, took away the net gains made in agreements after 1902.[56] But an examination of Paul H. Douglas' data shows that between 1902 and 1920 hourly earnings increased about 244 per cent and daily average earnings approximately 175 per cent, while cost of living rose only approximately 138 per cent between 1902 and December 1920, and 157 per cent between 1902 and June 1920, the peak of retail prices.[57]

---

54. Fisher, "Wage Rates," in *What the Coal Commission Found*, pp. 306-307.
55. The Anthracite Bureau of Information, *The Anthracite Strike of 1925-1926*, Philadelphia, 1926, pp. 15, 17.
56. *Report, Findings, and Award of the United States Anthracite Coal Commission*, 1920, Minority Report, pp. 40-41.
57. *Real Wages in the United States, 1890-1926*, Houghton Mifflin, Boston, 1930, pp. 60, 154, 161. The Bureau of Labor Statistics cost of living indexes for June and December 1920 are used instead of Professor Douglas' yearly figure for

The miners' representatives also maintained that the daily minimum wage of $4.20 set by the Commission was far below that needed to support an "ordinary family" at a "level of health and decency," which according to exhibits submitted by the miners amounted to $2,242.[58] While annual earnings of men paid at the $4.20 rate are not available, data for important occupational groups are. The United States Coal Commission found that in 1921, a depression year, contract miners earned about $1,922, contract miners' laborers between $1,465 and $1,470, the inside daymen $1,480, and the outside daymen $1,320.[59] The Douglas figures on average annual earnings show that anthracite workers received $664 more than bituminous employees in 1921, and that for the nine years between 1918 and 1926 the anthracite men earned on an average $341 more a year than soft coal workers. Moreover, average annual earnings in anthracite were consistently higher, in some cases much higher, than those of most of the separate industries included in the Douglas study.[60]

g. THE STRIKE OF 1922

The 1920 agreement expired April 1, 1922. On March 15, the union presented nineteen demands, including an increase of 20 per cent in tonnage rates, a $1.00 a day more for day workers, changes in the methods of wage payment and the checkoff. Rejecting these demands the operators pointed out that anthracite workers had not taken a wage decrease in line with the general readjustment in other industries and that consumers' deflated

1920. The increases in hourly and daily earnings were measured between 1902 and 1921. These latter figures reflect the changes resulting from the 1920 Award and, since no further changes were made in 1921, may be considered correct measures. The increases in daily earnings lagged behind those for hourly earnings because of reductions in daily hours from ten to eight. It was not considered wise to compute annual earnings because 1902, the base year, was characterized by a prolonged strike.

58. *Report, Findings, and Award of the United States Anthracite Coal Commission,* Minority Report, pp. 40-41.

59. Anne Bezanson, "Earnings of Coal Miners," *The Annals of the American Academy of Political and Social Science,* January 1924, pp. 6-11. The contract miners and their helpers averaged 250 starts, the inside daymen 290 eight-hour days, and the outside daymen 293 eight-hour days.

60. Douglas, *op. cit.,* pp. 217-400.

pocketbooks were not equal to the then prevailing prices.[61] They objected to further increases because (1) living costs between June 1920 and December 1921 had dropped 19.5 per cent in the country as a whole and 16.6 in Scranton, Pennsylvania;[62] (2) actual weekly earnings were 152 per cent above 1914;[63] and (3) labor costs had risen from $1.60 per ton in 1913 to $4.05 in 1921, an increase of 153 per cent.[64] They also asserted that the miners' demands would add over $3.00 a ton to the price of anthracite, a contention which the author cannot verify.

Union Opposition to Arbitration

After some seven weeks of fruitless efforts at conciliation, the operators proposed that all questions at issue be placed in the hands of a commission appointed by President Harding, but this did not meet with the miners' approval. The union leaders suggested on June 14, that the operators "accept our request for (1) an actual eight-hour day for daymen in the industry" (about 2 per cent of the wage earners were working more than eight hours), (2) for "complete union recognition," that is, a union or closed shop and the checkoff, and (3) that existing rates be accepted as minima and that further negotiations be confined to consideration of an upward revision.[65] The operators refused to accept arbitration under these conditions. On July 2, the suspension which had been called by the union on April 1 was officially declared a strike. At the request of the President, negotiations were resumed and the Administration attempted a settlement. When this failed, the President suggested resumed operations on condition that a commission establish a temporary scale of wages, make an exhaustive study of all phases of the industry, and submit "recommendations

---

61. The Anthracite Bureau of Information, *The Anthracite Strike of 1922*, Philadelphia, 1922, p. 8.
62. The figures quoted are those published in the *Monthly Labor Review*, February 1922, p. 56.
63. The data on weekly earnings published by Paul H. Douglas show an increase of 164.5 per cent. *Op. cit.*, p. 154.
64. The labor costs of thirteen companies producing about 70 per cent of the total output rose from $1.62 to $4.04, an increase of 149.4 per cent. *Report of the United States Coal Commission*, 1925, Pt. II, p. 856.
65. The Anthracite Bureau of Information, *The Anthracite Strike of 1922*, p. 26.

looking to a lasting peace in the industry." This proposal was rejected by the union leaders. Despite continued efforts at intervention, the union insisted upon its original demands. Finally, on September 11, it agreed to extend the contract of 1920 to August 31, 1923, it being understood that the President would appoint a commission which would investigate and report promptly on every phase of the industry.

h. THE PINCHOT SETTLEMENT OF 1923

In the summer of 1923 the union submitted eleven demands, including a 20 per cent advance in contract miners' rates, $2.00 for daymen, and the union shop and checkoff. When the negotiations failed, the United States Coal Commission persuaded the parties to make another effort to reconcile differences. Fearing impaired anthracite markets after another long suspension, the operators proposed arbitration and in that event offered to accept the existing rates of pay as a minimum. The union declined. A second conference was held with the Commission on August 20, but without solution. On September 1, the union ordered a suspension. Sometime later Governor Gifford Pinchot of Pennsylvania intervened and brought the two groups together. A new agreement effective until August 31, 1925 was signed September 17, 1923. It included a general wage increase of 10 per cent, granted the eight-hour day to the 2 per cent of the mine employees who still worked nine hours or longer, and speeded up the handling of grievances.

i. THE STRIKE OF 1925–1926

On July 2, 1925, the miners submitted seven demands and two supplementary recommendations. The rates of tonnage men were to be increased 10 per cent and those of daymen $1.00 a day. Other demands included uniformity and equalization of all day rates, time and a half for overtime and double time for Sundays and holidays, the five-day work week, and the checkoff. The recommendations covered improvements in company houses and equal division of work at all collieries.

The operators rejected these demands and asked for a "substantial reduction in labor costs." They stated that the miners' demands would add at least $2.00 a ton to the price of coal, and pointed out that hourly earnings of anthracite miners had risen 192 per cent since 1914, while those in railroading had increased only 141 per cent, in manufacturing 129 per cent and in building 111 per cent. They called the miners' attention to an estimated loss of five million tons of anthracite consumption to fuel oil, and to the growing competition of electricity and coke, and warned that coal consumers had indicated "in no uncertain terms" that they believed "the price of anthracite [was] already too high." Finally, they urged arbitration of any issues remaining when the contract expired and that existing terms be continued until an award was rendered.[66]

Beginning July 9, the operators and miners held almost continuous sessions. The operators persistently refused to increase costs and prices. The miners refused to arbitrate, pointing out that they had no confidence in this device since the Award of the Anthracite Commission of 1920 and that advance commitment to arbitrate disputed issues tended to preclude the possibility of a settlement through collective bargaining.[67]

The agreement expired on August 31 and the union leaders, refusing "to disarm themselves" by continuing at work while negotiations were in process, called a suspension.[68] Efforts at mediation were made by Governor Pinchot, and by legislators, businessmen and other local groups in the anthracite region. In February 1926, while Congress was giving serious consideration to the advisability of federal intervention, the parties, without outside assistance, agreed upon a settlement.

Terms of the Settlement

On February 17, after 170 days of idleness—the longest shutdown in the history of the industry—a new agreement was signed. It continued the same wages and working conditions until

66. The Anthracite Bureau of Information, *The Anthracite Strike of 1925-1926*, pp. 6-10.
67. Arthur E. Suffern, *The Coal Miners Struggle for Industrial Status*, The Institute of Economics, Macmillan, New York, 1926, pp. 123-124.
68. *Ibid.*, p. 123.

August 31, 1930, but provided that after January 1927 either side might propose modifications. Such proposals could not be made oftener than once a year. The operators and miners obligated themselves to confer within fifteen days after receipt of wage-modification notice and, should no settlement be reached within thirty days, to submit the controversy to a board of two, selected from a panel of six disinterested persons, three named by each party. This board, which was authorized to enlarge its membership to resolve a deadlock, was given full power to make a settlement. Questions about equalization of wages, cooperation and efficiency were referred to the Board of Conciliation created under the 1903 Award and later modified.

j. TREND OF HOURS, WAGES AND EMPLOYMENT OPPORTUNITY, 1902–1926

The condition of anthracite workers was much improved during the second stage of the industry's development. For the men who actually mine the coal, assuming that they could send out as many cars of coal in an eight- or nine-hour day as in the ten-hour day, the dollar of daily earnings of April 1902 was increased to approximately $1.14 by the 1903 Award, $1.21 in May 1912, $1.30 in May 1916, $2.14 in April 1920, and $2.35 in September 1923 and later years. Because daymen's working hours were reduced from ten to nine in 1902 and nine to eight in 1916, they had by 1917 only a 13.3 per cent daily pay increase.[69] Rates per day of all daymen are not available after 1916. Between April 1916 and October 1923 inclusive, the hourly earnings of this group increased between 143 and 158 per cent and those of contract miners about 148 per cent.[70] Average daily earnings of all mine workers fluctuated considerably prior to the World War. In 1916 they were 12.4 per cent above the 1902 rate of $2.25. The large increases during the war and postwar years resulted in a level

---

69. *Report of the United States Coal Commission*, Pt. II, p. 343; and Fisher, "Wage Rates" in *What the Coal Commission Found*, pp. 306-307.
70. *Request of Anthracite Operators for a Modification of the Wage Scale; Reply of Anthracite Operators to Opening Statement of United Mine Workers of America*, a report submitted by the operators to the Board of Reference created under the wage agreement, 1933, p. 14.

which in 1925 was 214.7 per cent, and in the following year 208.0 per cent, above the 1902 base.[71]

More Regular Employment

Employment became more regular during these years. During the five years before 1902, days worked by the mines averaged 161. From 1903 to 1910 inclusive, they rose to 209 days—up about 30 per cent. For the nine years beginning in 1911 the average was 256, or 59 per cent above the five-year base; in the seven years beginning in 1920, it was 237 days, or about 47 per cent above the base period.[72] The decline in the twenties was primarily due to industry-wide stoppages in four of the seven years.

Data on annual earnings in this industry are not available before 1902, and the great strike makes the average for this year unrepresentative. From 1903 to 1908 annual earnings were very unstable, the average for these six years amounting to $526. The next eight years showed an upward trend, the average being $573. In 1917 annual earnings stood at $919. War and postwar advances in wage rates as well as in working time sent annual earnings of all mine workers to new high levels. Except for the strike year of 1922, they ranged from $1,286 in 1918 to $1,841 in 1924. The strikes of 1925–1926 reduced the annual income considerably.

Anthracite miners were relatively well paid in the early twenties. Their annual earnings in 1924 were well above the $1,240 average for all manufacturing, topped bituminous coal by $721, lumber and timber by $873, and iron and steel, marble and stone, petroleum refining and steam railroads by smaller amounts.[73]

4. INDUSTRIAL RELATIONS IN A DECLINING MARKET, 1927–1941

In 1927 anthracite production began a steady decline. By 1938 it was 45.4 per cent, and in value about 62 per cent, below 1926.[74]

---

71. Data on daily earnings here and annual earnings below are from Douglas, *op. cit.*, pp. 154, 350.
72. Averages based on figures compiled annually by the U. S. Bureau of Mines (see annual reports published in *Mineral Resources of the United States*).
73. Douglas, *op. cit.*, pp. 240, 271, 283, 296, 299, 325, 350.
74. Percentages were computed from data compiled by the U. S. Bureau of Mines and published annually in *Minerals Yearbook*.

These drastic changes seriously affected those dependent upon the industry.

The decline in production caused much unemployment, and some unemployed miners and their sons turned to "bootlegging." This illegal mining and sale of anthracite became "a problem of grave consequence" as early as 1932. In 1936–1937, bootleg production amounted to 2.4 million tons for which the final consumers paid roughly $16 million annually.[75] In December 1936, after several requests by the operators for state intervention, George H. Earle, then Governor of Pennsylvania, made a three-day tour of the region to study the situation at first hand. Early in 1937 he appointed the Anthracite Coal Industry Commission, whose task it was to report on conditions in the industry. As yet, no action has been taken by the state legislature on the Commission's final report and recommendations, nor by Congress on a bill proposing to regulate the industry somewhat along the lines of the Bituminous Coal Act of 1937.

a. REASONS FOR THE DECLINE IN PRODUCTION

The major cause of the recession in this industry was the growth of substitute fuels in markets long supplied by anthracite. While anthracite consumption fell from 78.0 million tons in 1926 to 43.8 million in 1938, heating oil sales, when measured by coal equivalents, rose from 5.7 million tons to 29.5 million, and range oil sales, also converted into coal equivalents, from 1.1 million in 1931 to 8.0 million in 1938.[76] Important also were interruptions in anthracite shipments because of long suspensions in 1922 and especially in 1925–1926. These stoppages turned many an anthra-

75. Anthracite Coal Industry Commission, Commonwealth of Pennsylvania, *Bootlegging or Illegal Mining of Anthracite Coal in Pennsylvania,* 1937, p. 1.

76. Data taken from *Minerals Yearbooks,* or their coal chapter supplements. Oil was converted to an anthracite basis at a ratio of four barrels of oil to one ton of coal.

The principal competitors of anthracite used for domestic heating are raw bituminous coal for which no data are available, heating and range oils, and by-product coke, sales of which amounted to 7.1 million tons in 1938. Other competing fuels are manufactured, natural and liquefied gases; fuel briquets; imported anthracite; lignite; and petroleum coke. M. Van Siclen, L. Mann and J. R. Bradley, "Pennsylvania Anthracite," *Minerals Yearbook, 1939,* p. 838.

cite consumer to substitute fuels during the emergency. As a consequence the rate of substitution accelerated.[77] A third factor was the steady increase in the market price of domestic anthracite from 1913 through 1926.[78] These higher prices were caused by higher transportation costs and by advances in hourly earnings which according to the operators amounted to 192 per cent between 1914 and 1925.[79] The 1929 depression generally accelerated the downward trend of production and consumption.[80]

Lastly, the slump in the anthracite industry came partly because the operators were neither prompt nor aggressive in meeting the challenge of competing fuels. Although pioneering work has been done by the Anthracite Institute and Anthracite Industries, Inc. during the last seven years, "unified and sustained action by all concerned" is still needed.[81]

The big decline in the demand for anthracite since 1926 has influenced industrial relations in the industry. There have been no industry-wide strikes, except for a one-day stoppage in 1941. Apparently both parties realize the futility of long stoppages of work and their heavy losses.

77. O. E. Kiessling and H. L. Bennit point out that "during the prolonged interruptions of supply in 1922 and 1925 and 1926 some millions of tons in potential sales of anthracite were lost to competitive fuels." They add that "for the strike years of 1925 and 1926 the Bureau of Mines has accounted for an equivalent of 27,100,000 net tons of substitutes to replace a computed deficit of 25,000,000 net tons of anthracite," and that, although the vast majority of the former customers lost in 1926 were recovered by the operators, substitute fuels retained "a considerable portion of the gains made" by them in 1925 and 1926. "Anthracite in 1927," *Mineral Resources of the United States*, 1927, Pt. II, p. 5.

78. O. E. Kiessling and H. L. Bennit, *Pennsylvania Anthracite in 1928*, U. S. Bureau of Mines, 1929, p. 6.

79. The Anthracite Bureau of Information, *The Anthracite Strike of 1925-1926*, p. 6.

80. The demand for anthracite is less sensitive to the swings of the business cycle than that in many industries. In 1931 the Federal Reserve Board index of production in manufacturing and mining was 19.3 per cent below the level that prevailed in 1929 while that of anthracite showed a drop of only 6 per cent. F. E. Berquist, H. L. Bennit and F. G. Tryon, *Coal in 1931*, U. S. Bureau of Mines, 1933, p. 489.

81. *Report and Final Recommendations of the Anthracite Coal Industry Commission*, Commonwealth of Pennsylvania, Philadelphia, March 31, 1938, p. 14. In 1936 Anthracite Industries, Inc. was established by anthracite producers to promote the greater use of anthracite by various promotional and merchandising devices. Its activities were expanded in 1937 and again in 1938. See annual reports on anthracite in *Minerals Yearbook*, 1937 to 1939 inclusive.

b. THE AGREEMENT OF 1930

Neither the operators nor the miners requested adjustments in the rates of pay after January 1927, permitted by the agreement of February 17, 1926. In June 1930, union and employers met in joint conference and wrote a new contract. Effective for five and one half years, this agreement continued existing wages and hours with a proviso that either side could propose modified wage scales at any time, but not more than once a year. It provided for a permanent joint committee of twelve to deal with "all questions arising under the contract relating to cooperation and efficiency and performance of the parties." It also granted the miners a voluntary checkoff. The absence of even the threat of a strike as well as the unusually short period of negotiations showed a greater understanding between the union and the operators than had ever prevailed in this industry.

c. THE OPERATORS REQUEST A WAGE REDUCTION

In August 1932 the operators asked for a 35 per cent pay cut. They said the output of anthracite in 1932 would be "less than it was forty years ago," that wage rates were 120 per cent, while prices were only 77 per cent, above the 1916 level, and that "operating margins have been wiped out and business is being conducted at a loss." They maintained that "price deflation" was "the only solution to hold and improve the anthracite market" and insisted that since labor costs constituted two thirds of present mine costs, substantial reductions in labor and other costs as well as in freight rates must be obtained.[82]

The miners rejected this request, arguing that the nation's economic condition was due to speculative prices and inflated real estate values, that currency inflation was imminent, and that high wages were a necessary condition to recovery. After four weeks of fruitless negotiation the matter was turned over to a two-man Board of Reference. The Board deadlocked, and, because the

---

82. *Request of Anthracite Operators for a Modification of the Wage Scale*, a statement submitted by the operators to the Board of Reference created under the agreement, 1933, pp. 3-6.

miners' representative would not agree to the addition of a neutral member, no action was taken.[83]

d. THE MINERS OBTAIN THE SEVEN-HOUR DAY

A new wage agreement was concluded without a suspension, on May 7, 1936. This contract, like the bituminous coal contract of 1934, provided for a seven-hour day and thirty-five-hour week. It granted the same daily wage as was previously paid for eight hours, and gave the miners the complete checkoff of union dues. District and international union officers agreed to accept full responsibility for the prevention of strikes in violation of the agreement, which had become more prevalent after 1932.[84] The contract was originally to have expired in April 1938, but in November 1937 it was extended by a joint committee until April 30, 1939.

e. THE 1939 AND 1941 AGREEMENTS

At the 1939 conference the miners demanded a six-hour day and five-day week; the same pay for six hours as they got for seven hours, plus a nominal increase; equal division of working time; establishment of seniority rights; a guarantee of two hundred working days a year; two weeks vacation with pay; time and a half for overtime, and double time for Sundays and holidays; abolition of physical examinations; the union shop; and the elimination of contract mining.[85] The operators submitted a counterproposal suggesting a forty-hour week and wage reductions approximating 20 per cent. After six weeks of negotiation, a new two-year agreement was signed which continued the exist-

---

83. *Report of George Rublee* to the committees representing the operators and the mine workers, March 1, 1933, pp. 3-5. Mr. Rublee was the operators' representative on the Board of Reference.

84. F. G. Tryon, H. L. Bennit and J. R. Bradley, "Pennsylvania Anthracite," *Minerals Yearbook,* 1937, p. 873. The increase in petty strikes may be accounted for in part by the internal dissension which developed in the miners' union as layoffs and reduced working time became progressively more severe. The insurgent movement was especially pronounced in District No. 1. The uprising which for a while materially impaired the prestige and effectiveness of the union was brought under control after several years of persistent efforts on the part of district and national leaders.

85. *Coal Age,* May 1939, p. 78.

ing provisions regarding wages, hours and conditions, but called for a union shop throughout the whole industry.[86]

Two years later when the defense boom was well under way, the miners demanded wage increases of a dollar a day for daymen and 20 per cent for contract miners. The new two-year agreement, signed after a one-day stoppage, gave them, in addition to a vacation payment of $20, a raise of 7.5 per cent to October 1941 and 10 per cent thereafter—about 60 cents more a day for daymen, and 75 cents for contract miners.[87]

f. WAGE RATES, HOURS AND EMPLOYMENT AFTER 1926

From 1926 to 1937 when anthracite production dropped 45.4 per cent and total value 58.3 per cent, the number of men employed declined 40.1 per cent, days worked 22.5 per cent, and man days worked 53.6 per cent. The eight-hour day and forty-eight-hour week continued until 1936, when the seven-hour day and thirty-five-hour week became standard. Rates of pay of all workers also continued at the 1926 level until 1936, when hourly rates were increased 14.3 per cent so as to maintain daily earnings under the seven-hour day.

Figure 2 shows what happened to earnings, employment and pay rolls during the years when the Bureau of Labor Statistics compiled data. Between 1932 and 1939 hourly earnings of all wage earners increased 12.1 per cent but weekly earnings remained about the same. From 1929 to 1939 the number of men dropped 49.4 per cent and total pay rolls 60.5 per cent. Because of a substantial decline in the average number of working days, the per capita income of full-time wage earners dropped from $1,610 in 1929 to $1,368 in 1932, but rose to $1,535 in 1934, the last year for which figures are available.[88]

86. *United Mine Workers Journal,* June 1, 1939, pp. 3-4.
87. *The New York Times,* May 20, 1941.
88. The data on per capita income were computed by Robert R. Nathan of the Division of Economic Research of the Bureau of Foreign and Domestic Commerce. They were obtained by dividing the total income that was received as wages (not including salaries) by the number of full-time wage earners. The employment figures used in this computation were estimates and were converted to their full-time equivalent. The average earnings, therefore, approximate the average earnings of employees engaged throughout the year. See *National Income in the United States, 1929-1935,* U. S. Department of Commerce, 1936, pp. 31-33, 88.

Annual earnings of full-time anthracite wage earners were much higher than those in bituminous coal and in manufacturing industries as a whole in the period 1929–1934, and exceeded those in the profitable petroleum refining industry in 1933 and

EMPLOYMENT, PAY ROLLS, AND AVERAGE EARNINGS IN THE ANTHRACITE INDUSTRY

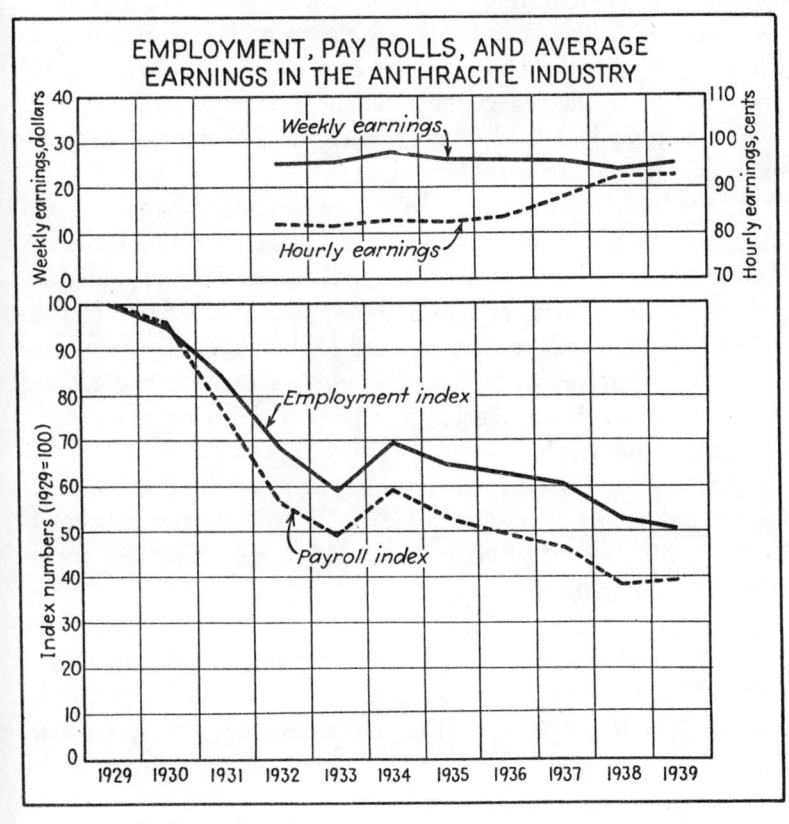

FIGURE 2

Source: Data published by the Bureau of Labor Statistics in monthly issues of *Employment and Pay Rolls*. The index figures have been adjusted to the 1929 and 1935 Censuses.

1934.[89] The average annual earnings of the hard coal miners throughout the thirties, however, were considerably below those prevailing in the years of uninterrupted production in the twenties.

89. This statement is based on data supplied by Robert R. Nathan.

5. Negotiating the Trade Agreement

Since the 1903 Award of the Anthracite Coal Commission, wage agreements have been customarily reached by the industry at joint conferences of miners and operators. Exceptions were in 1917 and 1918 when supplementary agreements were drawn up in conjunction with the United States Fuel Administration, in 1920 and 1922 when the federal government intervened by appointing special commissions, and in 1923 when the Governor of Pennsylvania brought about a settlement.

As a rule the procedure for collective bargaining begins several months before a contract expires. Union officers call a tridistrict convention composed of national and district officers and delegates of local unions, at which the various grievances are considered, the demands to be submitted to the operators are formulated, the measures to be taken in the negotiation process are determined, and the delegates to represent the mine workers on the scale committee are selected. The scale committee consists of forty-three members, of whom thirty-one comprise the district boards and twelve are rank-and-file miners.[90] To facilitate negotiations a subcommittee of six is appointed to meet with the operators' scale committee.

Formerly the operators held meetings to determine their policies and select their delegates. Recently this has fallen to the operators' General Policies Committee, a permanent committee consisting of four independent operators, four representatives of the railroad companies and a chairman. At present six operator delegates constitute the operators' scale committee.

If the scale committees meet with unusual difficulties, a smaller subcommittee of one or two men from each side continues negotiations. When the operators have approved, their representatives initial the new wage agreement. The miners' representatives initial the agreement and then refer it to a miners' referendum or to

90. The districts are given approximate but not equal representation because the number of subdistricts varies in the several districts and representation is on the basis of subdistricts. In the earlier years the scale committee consisted of thirty members, ten from each district.

a special tridistrict convention. When thus ratified, the agreement is signed by representatives of both parties.

6. Procedure for Handling Grievances

Essential features of the system for handling grievances were established by the Anthracite Coal Strike Commission of 1903. Both the Board of Conciliation and the office of Umpire created by the Commission continued to function, but the former has undergone changes in its duties and procedures.

The six-man Board is composed of two members from each of the three anthracite districts, one appointed by the union and the other by the operators. In theory both parties may change representatives at any time except when a controversy is pending. Cases before the Board are decided by majority vote and decisions are final and binding on both parties. When the Board cannot agree, the matter is placed before an umpire, who until 1939 was appointed by a circuit judge of the third judicial district of the United States. The 1939 agreement authorizes the Board to make its own appointments but provides that if it fails to do so the former procedure shall become operative. The umpire's decision is final and binding, and suspensions of work are forbidden while a matter is pending.

Local Settlement

The 1903 Award provided that "all difficulty or disagreement" arising under it, with respect "to its interpretation or application, or in any way growing out of the relations of the employers and the employed," which could not "be settled or adjusted by consultation between the superintendent or manager of the mine or mines, and the miner or miners directly interested," or was of a scope "too large to be so settled or adjusted" should be referred to the Board of Conciliation.

By inference, an attempt should be made to settle grievances locally. To encourage such a practice, the Board of Conciliation ruled in 1903 that every grievance must first be brought to the mine foreman, then to the company superintendent, and then to the two district members of the Board, before it could be brought to the Board itself. This procedure took time, so the agreement of 1909 stipulated that a dispute "must first be taken up with the mine foreman and superintendent by the employee, or committee of employees directly interested, before it can be taken up with the Conciliation Board for final adjustment."

The agreement of 1912 called for a grievance committee of not more than three employees at each mine and authorized this body to "take up for adjustment with the proper officials of the company, all grievances referred to them by employees who have first taken up said grievance with the foreman and failed to effect proper settlement of the same." It was agreed that at this stage the miners' Board member of the district or his representative could assist in the deliberations, and that a deadlock should be referred to the two Board members of the district, and then, in the event of further deadlock, to the Board of Conciliation.

Even this modification did not wholly succeed in forcing the parties to begin their deliberations at the bottom, and the 1916 agreement explicitly stated that grievance committees could consider only questions that discussion between the foreman and employee failed to settle.

After 1912 the conciliation process was complicated by unofficial "general grievance committees." These seem to have arisen because a number of companies having more than one mine found it convenient to hold joint meetings of two or more grievance committees. These unauthorized assemblies undertook to act on their own responsibility and thereby weakened the established procedures.[91] In recent years general grievance committees have been wholly suppressed in District 1, and in Districts 7 and 9 have been brought under union control and are now little more than debating societies.

Time Limits

Beginning with the 1916 agreement, limits were set on the time allowed the Board of Conciliation for consideration of grievances. Unless extended by mutual consent, sixty days was the limit. If a

91. Sydenstricker, *op. cit.*, pp. 76-77.

decision was not handed down in that time, the matter was referred automatically to the umpire. A more elaborate system of limits was established in the 1923 agreement. Grievances referred to the Board had to be answered within fifteen days, heard within thirty days of filing, and decided within thirty days after hearing. Grievances referred to an umpire had to be decided within thirty days.

The Board's Functions

Several new duties were imposed on the Board of Conciliation in 1916 and later. First it was to hear complaints regarding allegedly obsolescent day rates, and in 1920 it was instructed to act as a commission to study the uniformity of day rates for daymen, also it was directed to work out rates for certain pumpmen and hoisting engineers. In 1923 it was authorized to study all wage scales. In 1926 it was given authority to equalize wages and was also instructed to "work out a reciprocal program of cooperation and efficiency." [92] Evidently this last duty was too remote from the Board's regular activities to be conveniently administered, and in 1930 a separate committee of twelve was established for this purpose, as well as to supervise the performance of the contract by the two parties. By two resolutions the 1936 joint conference directed the committee of twelve to study safety and health in mining and make appropriate recommendations, and to consider "the problems of the anthracite industry, the shrinkage of its markets, its competitive position with other fuels, . . . illicit mining, and kindred matters" and to make recommendations concerning these problems.[93]

In 1936 the grievance machinery was further modified so that disputes over equalizing working time between the mines of a single company could be referred directly to the Board of Conciliation through the district president or a designated district officer.

92. This meant, according to John L. Lewis, that the miners were to cooperate by promoting efficiency and the operators were to cooperate by installing the checkoff. This interpretation of the provision was not accepted by the operators and it was not until 1930 that a modified checkoff was granted. *Coal Age*, February 25, 1926, p. 307, and April 28, 1927, p. 609.
93. *Monthly Labor Review*, June 1936, pp. 1581-1582.

The 1939 agreement clarified the relationship of the committee of twelve to the Board of Conciliation. It was provided that by majority vote the committee may refer to the Board any difficulty over terms of the agreement which cannot otherwise be satisfactorily settled.

Nature and Disposition of Cases

Two studies have been made of grievances before the Board of Conciliation.[94] The first covers 1903 to 1913, the second the period between 1913 and 1922. The studies show that grievances over wages predominated in both periods but were a much larger proportion (84.6 per cent) in the later period. Between 1903 and 1913, complaints of discrimination against employees accounted for about one out of every four cases. In the second period, such cases declined materially. Other grievances were over petty strikes in violation of the agreement, conditions of employment, hours of work, classification of workers, discharge, discipline, collection of union dues, and check docking bosses and checkweighmen.

These studies also disclose that the Board decided a smaller proportion of cases between 1913 and 1919 than between 1903 and 1913.[95] Conversely, there was an increase in cases withdrawn or referred to the umpire. Finally, about 53 per cent of the decisions of both Board and umpire were favorable to the employees in the first period, while only 39.4 per cent sustained the employees wholly or in part during the second period.

7. Summary and Conclusions

During the early years, employers had exclusive right to hire and fire and to establish wages and other terms of employment without interference. Economic conditions and the evident indifference of the operators to the needs of their workers, led some wage earners to organize, but the tradition of individualism which

---

94. Sydenstricker, *op. cit.*, pp. 77-82; and Suffern, *op. cit.*, pp. 263-267.

95. From April 1, 1919 to March 31, 1922 the cases settled by the Board and those withdrawn before decision were not reported. See Suffern, *op. cit.*, pp. 265-266.

prevailed in these years, as well as the determined opposition of the employers, prevented workers from securing an effective bargaining position.

When deflation after the Civil War brought drastic wage reductions, irregular operation and heavy unemployment, the workers again attempted to organize. This time, the operators could not maintain a solid front, because of ruinous competition and a bitter struggle between a dozen odd railroads, and the union obtained a preponderance of bargaining power. Ill-advised use of this power caused the operators, whose bargaining position had been improved by mergers and consolidations, to unite and for the time being to destroy unionism in the industry.

Having rid themselves of labor organizations, the operators replaced many Anglo-Saxon employees with immigrants from central Europe, and suppressed every attempt of the workers to improve their conditions through collective action. For a quarter of a century the philosophy of individual enterprise and unrestrained competition held sway. That it failed to stabilize the industry or to achieve anything like satisfactory industrial relations is revealed by the record compiled by the Anthracite Coal Strike Commission as well as by the remarkable achievements of the UMW organizers in 1900 and 1902. The uncompromising attitude of the operators in these years and their rejection in 1902 of the arbitration recommendation of the President gave rise to an unfavorable public opinion which impaired their freedom of action in later years.

The decade following the strike of 1902 was relatively peaceful. Although effectively organized and in a strategic position, the operators did not exert their economic strength to force labor issues through fear of federal or state intervention. Union leadership, having obtained a success greater than anticipated, was in a conciliatory frame of mind. Because rates of pay were tied to slowly rising prices of coal and the average number of days worked by the mines showed a considerable improvement, annual earnings moved to higher levels. The mine workers as a consequence were content to follow a leadership counseling prudence and moderation. During these years the bargaining power of both sides was sufficiently strong to command respect and to cause both parties to exercise self-restraint.

When the United States entered the World War, a shortage of labor, a sharp increase in demand for coal and rapidly rising prices and profits, strengthened labor's bargaining position. A new leadership now insisted upon big advances in the rates of pay. By skillful negotiations, an indifference to public opinion, and a readiness to call industry-wide stoppages, it drove annual earnings to a level higher than that generally prevailing in manufacturing, mining and on the railroads. In a little over two decades the attitudes of the two parties were reversed. The operators were conciliatory and to avoid stoppages were quite willing to arbitrate demands for higher wages and better terms of employment. The union leaders, actively supported by the rank and file, and in a position to close down the industry until their demands were met, were reluctant to compromise, and, as in 1922, 1923 and 1925, unwilling to arbitrate. The United States Coal Commission pointed out that "the conditions which preceded 1903 had so far reversed themselves that the miners' organization was in a position where it was frequently able to dictate terms to many individual operators and the operators' organization was less effective in daily bargaining than the union." [96]

Higher costs and prices and especially prolonged suspensions of work in the 1920's accelerated substitution of oil and other fuels for anthracite. The fuels were also clean and convenient and their use was not aggressively met by the operators. Business depression further curtailed demand. Notwithstanding very substantial declines in the production and consumption of anthracite as well as in total income from coal sales, the miners' drive for shorter hours and higher hourly earnings continued. After 1926, this drive was carried on without interruptions to the movement of anthracite to consuming markets. Since 1926 hourly earnings have increased, but the number of men employed, the number of days worked and total pay rolls have dropped to much lower

---

96. H. S. Dennison, W. E. Hotchkiss and J. H. Willits, "Labor Relations in the Anthracite Industry," *Report of the United States Coal Commission*, Pt. I, p. 119.

levels. Except for strike years, the annual income of the miner in the thirties was considerably below that prevailing in the twenties.

Collective bargaining in this industry suggests that equality of bargaining power is not attained merely by giving workers the right to organize. Bargaining power is the product of many forces which vary with circumstances and changing economic conditions. How bargaining power will be distributed between the union and the employers in a given industry will be determined by general business conditions, the leadership of both sides, the type and degree of organization of the employees, the attitude of the public and of government agencies towards unionism, and particularly by the economic conditions prevailing in the industry. These in turn depend on such factors as the demand for the product, that is, whether elastic or inelastic, the relation of capacity to demand, the presence or absence of competition between producers or from substitute products, and the relative importance of labor costs.

Experience in anthracite shows that a preponderance of bargaining power on either side does not make for satisfactory industrial relations. Under these conditions the party in power tends to forget that rights also carry responsibilities. As a result it is prone to disregard legitimate interests of the other side and not infrequently of the public. Both operators and unions have abused their power. If collective bargaining is to work in the interest of all concerned, rules of the game must be established that will govern the actions of both labor and capital.

Finally, the experience in anthracite substantiates economists' contentions that wage and hour levels must be related to labor productivity, and that attempts to force demands which place too heavy a burden upon the industry or the consumer will ultimately result in lower production, employment and pay rolls.

Chapter 7

RAILROADS

Harry D. Wolf

1. Introduction

Collective bargaining on the railroads has reached a greater maturity and wider acceptance than in almost any other American industry. In no other are there such comprehensive working rules, established procedures and customs governing the relations between management and men. All but a negligible proportion of railway employees are included under one or another of the more than four thousand agreements filed with the National Mediation Board.

Although collective bargaining on the railroads antedates government intervention by a number of years, its present development came, in part at least, from the early and continued interest Congress showed in promoting amicable labor relations by more than half a century of legislation to this end. The present Railway Labor Act is thus the culmination of many years of experimentation. It guarantees employees the right to organize and to be represented in negotiations with management by representatives of their own choosing, imposes upon management and men the duty to exert every reasonable effort to make and maintain agreements, and provides machinery and procedures for the settlement of disputes.

Legislation has a significance in collective bargaining in this industry unparalleled in any other. Because Congress has power under the commerce clause of the Constitution to exercise control over practically every phase of railroad activity, the railroad labor organizations have made increasing use of their political power until now it is scarcely less important than their bargaining power.

These powers supplement each other at every turn. The carriers cannot ignore the possibility that the organizations may turn to Congress if they do not get what they want through collective bargaining, as a growing body of legislation will testify. Thus the legislative policies and programs of railroad labor are important not only in themselves, but as effective strategical factors which strengthen its bargaining position.

Self-organization, recognition, and agreements which cover the day-by-day relationships of management and labor are, of course, essential elements in collective bargaining. Unless collective bargaining goes beyond these essentials, however, it fails to realize its full possibilities. The most significant development in industrial relations on the railroads during the past decade has been the extension of the principle of joint negotiation and collective bargaining to problems common to the whole industry. The outstanding example of accomplishment along these lines is the program jointly worked out by the railroads and the labor organizations for rehabilitation of the industry, which has recently been embodied, in part, in the Transportation Act of 1940. This is collective bargaining in its fullest sense. That it has been hastened by the serious condition of the industry which affects the welfare of both carriers and men adds to its significance.

2. Extent and Nature of Railroad Employment

a. FINANCIAL CONDITION OF THE RAILROADS

Almost a third of the total railroad mileage of the United States was at the end of 1940 in the hands of trustees or receivers.[1] At least another third cannot long avoid bankruptcy unless conditions continue to improve. The remaining third is in fair shape, with some roads showing good earnings.

This situation is largely the result of the drastic decline in the

---

1. Julius H. Parmelee, "A Review of Railway Operations in 1940" (reprinted from *Railway Age* for January 4, 1941 and figures revised to March 25, 1941), Association of American Railroads, Bureau of Railway Economics, Special Series No. 70, Washington, 1941, pp. 9-10.

demand for rail transportation over the last decade.[2] The past several years have been lean ones for the railroad industry, with 1938 one of the worst in its history. Operations improved substantially in 1939 and 1940, but were still far below the predepression years. Revenue car loadings in 1940 were 36 million as against 30 million in 1938 and 46 million in 1930. Revenue ton-miles increased from 290 billion in 1938—the lowest since 1915, except the years 1932–1935—to 373 billion in 1940; but were a good deal short of the peak of 447 billion in 1929. Revenue passenger-miles reached their peak of 46.8 billion in 1920. The 1940 figure was just short of 24 billion, an increase of slightly more than two billion over 1938, which, again excepting the years 1932–1935, was the lowest since 1904.[3]

There is no single cause of this unprecedented decline in traffic volume. After 1929 the depression was the most important. But even before that, other forces were operating. Structural and technological changes in industry, such as the relocation of industrial plants, the development of hydroelectric power, increased use of natural gas as a substitute for coal, and greater efficiency in the use of coal as a fuel have cut down railroad tonnage. Perhaps more important has been the growing competition of other forms of transportation. The railroads doubtless will continue to be the backbone of our transportation system. In 1937 they accounted for approximately 65 per cent of the total inland revenue ton-miles of freight—a drop from 75 per cent of the total in 1926.[4] Meanwhile, other forms of transportation showed increases during the eleven-year period. Pipe lines showed an increase of almost 100 per cent in revenue ton-miles of freight. Their share of the total rose from 3.9 per cent in 1926 to 8.0

2. While considering the decline in demand as the primary cause, the Interstate Commerce Commission lists the great volume of indebtedness with its fixed interest charges as the chief contributory cause. Other contributory causes which it mentions are financial exploitation, failure to modernize equipment and facilities because of lack of credit, and the construction of expensive passenger stations. See *52nd Report*, November 1, 1938, pp. 2-5.

3. *Report of Committee to Submit Recommendations Upon the General Transportation Situation*, December 23, 1938, p. 58; Parmelee, *op. cit.*, pp. 21-22.

4. *Report of Committee to Submit Recommendations Upon the General Transportation Situation*, pp. 67, 69.

in 1937; Great Lakes shipping from 15.2 per cent to 16.6 per cent; other inland waterways from 1.6 per cent to 3.0 per cent; and intercity trucks from 3.9 per cent to 7.7 per cent.

The railroads' share of passenger service declined even more drastically, from 75 per cent of the total revenue passenger-miles in 1926 to 52.5 per cent in 1937. Intercity buses, on the other hand, increased from 9.2 per cent to 41.7 per cent. The situation as a whole, including the slowing down in the normal rate of industrial expansion, is well summed up thus: "In brief, the rate of increase in the grand total of transportation has been declining, and the railroads, because of intensified competition, are getting a smaller part of the smaller total."[5]

b. THE VOLUME OF EMPLOYMENT

The decline in the volume of railroad business has been accompanied by an even greater decline in employment. Railroad employment reached a peak of slightly over 2 million in 1920. The number of employees fell sharply to about 1.6 million in 1921, and remained fairly constant until 1930, when it further declined to about 1.4 million. It fell below a million in 1933 and has fluctuated narrowly around that figure since. Thus the railroads in 1940 had only half the employees of two decades ago.

A part of this decline is a result of technological displacement. This was particularly true during the second half of the 1920's when the roads spent large sums to improve their physical plant and rolling stock.[6] Heavier locomotives, longer and faster trains, extension and consolidation of divisions, automatic train control and improved technique in track laying and maintenance are but a few of the many changes which cut down jobs for all classes of employees. During the last eight or nine years the decline in traffic volume has been a relatively more important cause of reduced employment. Also financial difficulties have retarded

---

5. William James Cunningham, *The Present Railroad Crisis*, University of Pennsylvania Press, Philadelphia, 1931, p. 31. The trend of traffic to competing forms of transportation continued through 1940. See Parmelee, *op. cit.*, p. 12.

6. Federal Coordinator of Transportation, *Employment Attrition in the Industry*, 1935, p. 4.

maintenance and improvements and further reduced employment opportunities.

In addition to the foregoing, railroad employment is subject to seasonal fluctuations. Heavy freight movements from different sections of the country occur in different months, necessitating a considerably larger total number of employees than the monthly average reported by the Interstate Commerce Commission.[7] Some of the individual roads and certain occupational groups, such as maintenance of way employees, experience even greater seasonal fluctuations than is indicated by Commission statistics for all roads combined.

The whole problem is further complicated by the almost universal application of the seniority principle, which distributes the burden of unemployment unequally and tends to eliminate the younger men. Finally, the roads' financial condition forces economies in abandonments and consolidations, ever-present threats to the security of employees.

Yet, the railroad industry is still one of the largest employers in the United States. The average number of workers employed by Class I railroads for the year 1940 was about 1,027,000. The total payroll was slightly in excess of $1.96 billion.[8]

C. TYPES OF EMPLOYMENT

The Interstate Commerce Commission classification gives a rough idea of the occupational distribution of the railroads' one million employees. Of the seven main occupational categories, the maintenance of equipment and stores accounted for 28 per cent in November 1939. The train and engine service group was second, with 22 per cent, closely followed by maintenance of way and structures, with 20 per cent. The professional, clerical, and general group accounted for 16 per cent of the total; and the transportation group, other than train, yard, and engine service, for 12 per cent. Yardmasters, switch-tenders and the like accounted for a little over one per cent and executives another one

---

7. *Official Proceedings,* Ninth Convention, Railway Employees' Department of Labor, 1938, p. 4.
8. Parmelee, *op. cit.,* p. 33.

per cent.[9] The further subdivision of these seven main categories into 128 classifications ranging from common laborers and janitors to the highly skilled train dispatchers, locomotive engineers, and conductors suggests the wide diversity of railroad occupations.

3. Development of Collective Bargaining

Collective bargaining on the railroads began at the latest in the early 1870's, and perhaps earlier.[10] It grew slowly, because of employer hostility and the difficulties of building strong organizations with widely scattered membership; also, because the organizations, unable to cope with the more powerful employers, hesitated to show force and relied on the efficiency and model deportment of their members to win favor.

a. THE PRE-WORLD WAR YEARS

The engineers were the first to organize permanently when they founded the Brotherhood of the Footboard in 1863.[11] The present Order of Railway Conductors was organized in 1868, the Brotherhood of Locomotive Firemen in 1873, and the Brotherhood of Railroad Trainmen in 1883.[12] Many railroad employees, particularly skilled workers in the mechanical trades, as well as other less skilled workers, were members of the Knights of Labor during its heyday. After 1886 and the decline of the Knights, the present national organizations began to

---

9. *Wage Statistics of Steam Railways in the United States,* ICC, Bureau of Statistics, Statement No. M-300, November 1939.
10. John R. Commons, *et al., History of Labour in the United States,* Macmillan, New York, 1921, Vol. II, p. 67.
11. George E. McNeill, *The Labor Movement,* A. M. Bridgman & Co., Boston, 1887, pp. 312 ff.
12. The Brotherhood of the Footboard was organized to resist encroachments of the carriers on what the men considered their rights. It abandoned its militant attitude after one year, and embarked upon what would now be called a policy of appeasement, even changing its name to the Brotherhood of Locomotive Engineers to signify the complete break with the past. The conductors' organization was a benevolent and fraternal order from the beginning, with drastic provisions against participation in strikes by its members until it was reorganized as a bona fide trade union in 1890. Much the same was true of the Brotherhood of Locomotive Firemen. The Brotherhood of Railroad Trainmen was more in the nature of a bargaining organization from the outset. See Edwin Clyde Robbins, *The Railway Conductors,* Columbia University Press, New York, 1914.

appear. During the late eighties and early nineties were formed the shop craft unions, the maintenance of way employees, the telegraphers, the switchmen, and the clerks. By 1900 all but three of the present "standard" railroad labor organizations were in existence.

Despite the chief interest of the early organizations in mutual insurance, improvement of character, and the fraternal aspects of unionism, efforts to secure recognition from the carriers and to improve wages and working conditions were never absent. These frequently led to strikes, some of considerable importance. The country's concern over these led Congress to enact the first law for the promotion of railroad industrial peace.[13] The Act of 1888 provided for voluntary arbitration, which was never used, and for investigation of disputes, but only one investigation was ever made.

Early Organizations Not Brotherly

Overlapping interests, jealousies, and their attitude toward strikes brought frequent conflicts between these early labor organizations. Occasionally members of one organization acted as strikebreakers.[14] This situation prompted Eugene V. Debs, in 1893, to organize the American Railway Union.[15] Built along industrial lines, it was designed to end strife among the several organizations and to present a united front of railroad workers. A promising beginning was cut short by the disastrous Pullman Strike of 1894. Belated investigation of this strike revealed the impotency of the Act of 1888 and led to the Erdman Act which provided for mediation and voluntary arbitration.[16] Also, because some of the bitterest strikes of the period came from the refusal of certain carriers to permit union membership and to recognize

---

13. 25 Stat. 501 (1888). For a discussion of this and later legislation, see *Use of Federal Power in Settlement of Railway Labor Disputes*, Bulletin No. 303, U. S. Bureau of Labor Statistics, 1922.

14. Robbins, *op. cit.*, p. 22; see also Commons, *op. cit.*, p. 474.

15. Testimony of Eugene V. Debs, *Report on the Chicago Strike of June-July, 1894*, by the United States Strike Commission, Ex. Doc. 7, 53d Cong., 3d sess., pp. 129-180.

16. 30 Stat. 424 (1898).

and bargain with the unions, Congress wrote a ban upon yellow-dog contracts into the law.[17]

While bitterly opposed to the American Railway Union, the early organizations sought through federation objectives which Debs had in mind. Both the system plan of federation (the Cedar Rapids Plan of 1893), and the association plan, with the national unions as the participating units, were tried; but neither proved wholly satisfactory. The greatest successes along this line came with the "concerted movements."

"Concerted Movements"

From about 1900 to the World War a number of railroad unions grew fairly steadily, with the transportation brotherhoods leading the way. When the government took over the roads during the war, the transportation brotherhoods had agreements on practically all roads in the country.[18] Of outstanding importance during this period were the "concerted movements" instituted by the conductors, who were shortly joined by the trainmen, in western territory in 1902.[19] In effect, they amounted to collective bargaining on a regional rather than a system basis. They strengthened the bargaining power of the organizations and secured their object—greater uniformity of wages, hours and working conditions throughout the country. Altogether there were eighteen of these movements between 1902 and 1915. The engineers and firemen, the trainmen and conductors, combined forces a number of times. In 1915 all four organizations jointly participated in a drive for the eight-hour day, the outcome of which was the Adamson Eight-Hour Law.[20]

An important by-product of the concerted movements was passage of the Newlands Act.[21] The Erdman Act brought considerable success in settling disputes, but dissatisfaction with the results

17. This provision was nullified by the U. S. Supreme Court in *Adair* v. *U. S.*, 208 U. S. 161 (1908).
18. Walker D. Hines, *War History of American Railroads*, Yale University Press, New Haven, 1928, p. 152.
19. J. Noble Stockett, *The Arbitral Determination of Railway Wages*, Houghton Mifflin, Boston, 1918, pp. 12 ff.
20. 39 Stat. 721 (1916).
21. 38 Stat. 103 (1913).

of arbitration was growing. In the conductors' and trainmen's wage movement in eastern territory in 1912, neither the carriers nor the organizations would agree to arbitrate. To meet this crisis the Newlands Act, passed in 1913, created a permanent board of mediation and provided for arbitration boards of six members instead of three.

The shop crafts also made substantial progress during this period. When the country entered the World War, one or more of these organizations held agreements on about 70 per cent of the roads.[22] Important regional gains were made in 1917, and a nation-wide drive for standardization of wages, hours and working conditions was in preparation when the government took over the roads.[23] Of the other organizations, only the telegraphers, who held agreements on about 74 per cent of the roads, had made any marked progress. Clerks, maintenance of way employees, station employees and similar groups were poorly organized and held a negligible number of agreements.

b. GOVERNMENT OPERATION OF THE RAILROADS

Railroad labor fared well in most respects under government operation, although wages failed to keep pace either with the cost of living or with wages in other industries.[24] The real gains came largely to organizations other than the transportation brotherhoods, which had already secured them. Chief gains were union recognition, the right to bargain collectively and general application of more liberal working rules. Some of the latter increased the earnings of many employees through payment for overtime and reclassification of occupations.

The announcement by the Director-General of Railroads that there would be no discrimination because of union membership was followed by an intensive organizing campaign. The greatest gains were made by the less skilled workers. However, on those roads which theretofore had frowned on all unions, with the pos-

---

22. Hines, *op. cit.*, p. 152.
23. *Ibid.*, p. 153.
24. Paul H. Douglas, *Real Wages in the United States, 1890–1926*, Houghton Mifflin, Boston, 1930, pp. 320 ff.

sible exception of the transportation brotherhoods, the more highly skilled also profited.

Some of the far-reaching changes in working rules became important issues after the roads were returned to private operation. Practically all classes of employees were granted the eight-hour day. Piecework was eliminated from railway shops. The seniority principle was extended to classes which had not before enjoyed it. Nation-wide standardization of hours, wages, and in some cases rules, long a goal of railroad labor, was achieved. Finally, these gains were consolidated in a series of national agreements between the Railway Administration and a number of the organizations, some of which previously had few, if any, agreements on the individual roads.[25]

An important contribution to the technique of settling industrial disputes was the machinery set up by the Railway Administration. A clean-cut distinction was made between controversies growing out of proposed changes in wages, hours and working conditions, and those arising from the interpretation and application of agreements. A Board of Wages and Working Conditions was established to consider the former, and to make recommendations to the Director-General. To decide the latter, along with any individual grievances that might arise, three bipartisan boards of adjustment, each having jurisdiction over certain groups of employees, were set up, with appeal to the Director-General in case of deadlock. This machinery was highly successful, and the distinction between the two kinds of disputes was made in all later legislation, though not until 1934 was it adequately implemented.

Well pleased with government operation of the roads, railroad labor took active steps in an effort to make it permanent.[26] Out-

[25]. Five such agreements were made. The first was with the Federated Shop Crafts. Others were made with the Maintenance of Way Employees and Railway Shop Laborers, the Brotherhood of Railway Clerks, the Brotherhood of Stationary Firemen and Oilers, and the Brotherhood of Railroad Signalmen. See Hines, *op. cit.,* pp. 175 ff.

[26]. The sixteen standard railroad labor organizations organized the Plumb Plan League, the purpose of which was governmental acquisition and operation of the roads. A weekly newspaper, which soon became the current *Labor,* official weekly newspaper of sixteen of the standard organizations, was started to spread the gospel of government ownership along Plumb Plan lines.

side of its own ranks, however, little support for government ownership appeared, and the roads were returned to private operation by the Transportation Act of 1920.[27]

c. THE WORK OF THE RAILROAD LABOR BOARD

To replace the machinery for the settlement of disputes under government operation, Title III of the Transportation Act created the Railroad Labor Board. This was a tripartite body of nine members, the carriers, employees and the public having equal representation. It was given jurisdiction over wage or salary disputes which the parties themselves were unable to settle in conference. It was expected that disputes about grievances, rules and working conditions would be handled by adjustment boards like those set up under government operation. In the absence of such boards, or in the event of their failure to settle a controversy, disputes involving these matters were likewise to be passed on by the Labor Board. The Board was without power to enforce its decisions, but relied on the weight of public opinion; the parties to a dispute not settled in conference, however, were obligated to refer it to the Labor Board, or to the proper adjustment board, for hearing and decision.

The Railroad Labor Board inherited the difficult problem of sharing in readjustment of employer-employee relationships under private operation. Moreover, it was overburdened with work as a result of the failure of the carriers and the organizations to establish adjustment boards, and this undoubtedly contributed to its downfall. It performed some useful services, but certain questionable decisions, its inability to secure compliance from certain carriers, and the bitter hostility it aroused necessitated its replacement. This was done in 1926, when Congress passed the Railway Labor Act,[28] a measure jointly drawn up and supported in Congress by the carriers and the organizations.

d. THE RAILWAY LABOR ACT

Basically, the Act of 1926 shifted the emphasis from adjudication of disputes to mediation. It abolished the Railroad Labor

27. 41 Stat. 456 (1920).
28. 44 Stat. 577 (1926).

Board and in its stead set up a Board of Mediation of five members. It provided for voluntary arbitration of disputes should mediation fail, and for the appointment of emergency boards of investigation should an unsettled dispute threaten serious interruption of interstate commerce. It made mandatory the establishment of adjustment boards to handle grievances and disputes arising out of interpretation and application of agreements, although the Act itself did not establish such boards, nor did it fix penalties for failure of the carriers and employees to do so.

One timely and important provision was a guarantee that each side should have the right to name its representatives for collective bargaining ". . . without interference, influence, or coercion . . . by the other." Its inclusion was prompted by the mushroom growth of company unions which followed an unsuccessful shopmen's strike in 1922. Though collective bargaining was clearly contemplated, the Transportation Act of 1920 failed to include the guarantees of right to union membership and freedom from discrimination enjoyed under government operation. The Railroad Labor Board, however, had specifically ruled that there should be no interference with the right to organize and no discrimination because of union membership; that employees should have the right of representation of their own choice; and that the principle of majority rule should prevail.[29]

In the case of the striking shopmen, these assurances were nullified by the Board itself. Its "outlaw resolution," which declared the strikers no longer employees [30] and suggested formation of new organizations, encouraged company unions on a number of roads. While company unions made some headway with other classes of employees, the shopmen suffered the greatest losses.[31] This was the situation which gave rise to the collective bargaining provision, in which, for the first time, Congress legislated on the question of representation.

29. Decision 119 (2 R. L. B. 87).
30. Decision 1267 (3 R. L. B. 767).
31. Sixteen roads, covering nearly a quarter of the total mileage of the country, formed company unions for their shopmen between July and October 1922. *Characteristics of Company Unions, Bulletin No. 634*, U. S. Bureau of Labor Statistics, 1935, p. 20.

The TEXAS AND NEW ORLEANS *Case and the Amendments of 1934*

The validity of this provision was upheld by the Supreme Court of the United States in 1930 in a decision of far-reaching importance.[32] During a wage dispute between the Brotherhood of Railway Clerks and the Texas and New Orleans Railway, the carrier established a company union. The Brotherhood secured an injunction restraining the carrier on the ground that its action violated the Railway Labor Act. The carrier ignored the injunction and recognized the dominated company union as representing its employees. The District Court then found it guilty of contempt and directed it to disestablish the union. In upholding this ruling, the Supreme Court stated: "collective action would be a mockery if representation were made futile by interferences of choice."

This decision paved the way for the 1934 Amendment to the Act of 1926, and a number of important changes in the law.[33] The new act replaced the five-man National Board of Mediation with the present three-man National Mediation Board and established the National Railroad Adjustment Board. It forbade the yellow-dog contract and invalidated any such contracts in existence at the time. It further forbade any interference with the right of employees to join, organize or help to organize the labor organization of their choice. It made it unlawful for a carrier to use its funds in encouraging any labor organization, or other agency for collective bargaining. Finally, it prohibited carriers from influencing or coercing employees over membership in any labor organization. This last provision makes illegal closed-shop and percentage agreements on the railroads.[34]

e. GAINS OF NATIONAL ORGANIZATIONS AT EXPENSE OF COMPANY UNIONS

After the *Texas and New Orleans* decision, railroad company unions began to decline, particularly because the Federal Coordi-

32. 281 U. S. 548 (1930).
33. 48 Stat. 1185 (1934).
34. Percentage agreements provide that an agreed-upon proportion of the employees of the class represented by the organization making the agreement shall belong to the union. The Brotherhood of Railroad Trainmen had a number of such agreements prior to 1934.

nator of Transportation insisted that employees be given complete freedom in their choice of representatives. With the obstacles to organization and collective bargaining removed by the 1934 Amendment, the employees launched a spirited organizing campaign and demanded elections of representatives. The national organizations made steady gains, as shown by the number of their agreements. In 1935, national unions held 71.1 per cent of all agreements on Class I roads, while system associations, or company unions, held 24.1 per cent. By 1938 the share of national unions had increased to 83 per cent, while that of the system associations had declined to about 14 per cent.[35] Perhaps the greatest gains were made by the shop crafts, in whose jurisdiction company unionism had previously made the greatest inroads. Between 1930 and 1938 these organizations established or re-established representation on 135 roads.[36]

The extent to which each national organization represents its class of employees in bargaining with the carriers is more convincing evidence that company unions are relatively unimportant except in the mechanical trades. The Brotherhood of Railroad Trainmen represents its class of employees on 99 per cent of the total mileage of Class I railroads in the country, as does the Order of Railroad Telegraphers.[37] The other three transportation brotherhoods represent their classes on 98 per cent of the total mileage. Close behind come the Clerks with agreements covering 96 per cent of the total mileage, the Maintenance of Way Employees with 93 per cent, and the Signalmen with 89 per cent. The important shop craft organizations lag somewhat, but are steadily

35. National Mediation Board, *Fourth Annual Report*, 1938, p. 30. The *Fifth Annual Report* of the Board, for the year ending June 30, 1939, does not give the relative percentages of the total number of agreements held by national organizations as over against system associations. It does state, however, that "national organizations continued to increase the proportions of the total mileage on which they represent employees. At the same time there has been a further decrease in the portions of the mileage on which the employees are represented by system associations." (p. 17)

36. *Official Proceedings,* Ninth Convention, Railway Employees' Department, American Federation of Labor, 1938, p. 132. Not all of these are Class I roads, however.

37. National Mediation Board, *Sixth Annual Report*, 1940, p. 21.

displacing the system associations, now less than half a dozen of any importance.[38]

4. THE RAILROAD LABOR ORGANIZATIONS

No fewer than thirty-two organizations, other than system associations, committees and the like, were listed by the National Mediation Board in its annual report for the year ending June 1940 as representing at that time one or more classes of employees on one or more roads.[39] Many of these are of little consequence, representing only a small group of workers on a few roads, in some cases only one. The number remaining, however, is still too large to be examined separately, but the organizations are sufficiently homogeneous in structure, objectives, methods of bargaining and other fundamental characteristics to be considered as a whole.

Jurisdiction

Few railroad labor organizations have the degree of craft purity commonly ascribed to them. The extension of unionism to new areas, the blurring of craft lines as a result of technological change, and the decline in jobs and in the number of actual and potential members have caused many organizations to claim juris-

38. The percentage of Class I mileage represented by the shop craft organizations as shown by the 1940 Report of the National Mediation Board ranges from 77 per cent by the International Brotherhood of Blacksmiths to 83 per cent by the Sheet Metal Workers. (p. 22)

39. *Sixth Annual Report,* 1940, pp. 21-22. The following are the most important railroad labor unions. The approximate number of members in 1939 are given for those organizations for which such data are available. It is contrary to the policy of some organizations to make public such information: Brotherhood of Locomotive Engineers, 60,000; Brotherhood of Locomotive Firemen and Enginemen, 80,000; Brotherhood of Railroad Trainmen, 140,000; Order of Railway Conductors, 35,000; Switchmen's Union of North America, 8,000; International Association of Machinists; Brotherhood of Railway Carmen of America, 65,000; International Brotherhood of Electrical Workers, 10,000; Sheet Metal Workers' International Association; International Brotherhood of Blacksmiths, 3,000; International Brotherhood of Firemen, Oilers, Helpers, Roundhouse and Railway Shop Laborers, 27,000; Order of Railroad Telegraphers, 35,000; Brotherhood of Railway and Steamship Clerks, 185,000; Brotherhood of Railroad Signalmen of America, 9,000; Brotherhood of Maintenance of Way Employees, 65,000; American Train Dispatchers' Association, 2,500.

diction over groups already claimed by others. Consequently, jurisdictional disputes are common. Although the shop crafts occasionally quarrel among themselves, they have been able on the whole to limit their jurisdictions and maintain craft lines.[40]

The clerks and telegraphers, on the other hand, are really amalgamated unions, having absorbed one group after another as they developed. A particularly troublesome area, complicated by promotion and seniority rules, lies within the jurisdiction of the transportation brotherhoods. Amalgamation efforts have failed, and there seems little likelihood of success in the near future, although such action would undoubtedly clear up many problems.

Joint Action

Despite the difficulties inherent in craft unionism, industrial unionism has never succeeded on the railroads. The outstanding example was Debs' ill-fated American Railway Union. The organizations, however, have sought its advantages through joint action, though always jealously guarding the autonomy of the individual unions. After the early federations came the Chicago Joint Agreement between the engineers and firemen and the Cleveland Compact between the conductors and trainmen.[41] The closely related shop crafts have consistently shown greater ability to act together than have the other organizations, and joint federations existed as early as 1892.[42] The Railway Employees' Department of the American Federation of Labor, organized in 1908, and reorganized on a sounder basis in 1912, was built around them and has since been dominated by them. At present they make up the Department, the Maintenance of Way Employees and the Signalmen having withdrawn in 1935 and 1936, respectively. The more inclusive but less compactly organized Railway Labor Executives' Association was established to work toward the same ends.

40. The shop craft organizations have recently adopted a new plan, to which six of the seven crafts are parties; disputes not settled by the chief executives of the organizations involved will be referred to a referee whose decision will be binding. See *Labor*, February 13, 1940.
41. See pp. 353 ff.
42. Testimony of A. O. Wharton, *Final Report and Testimony Submitted to Congress by the Commission on Industrial Relations*, 1916, Vol. 10, p. 9760.

The Association grew out of the Plumb Plan League. It was organized in its present form in 1926 and for the next few years was a clearinghouse for discussion and consideration of matters that jointly concerned the several groups. In 1931 the Association acted as a collective bargaining agency, and in addition to the wage agreements resulting therefrom, it has since negotiated other outstanding agreements with the carriers.

As at present constituted, the Railway Labor Executives' Association comprises the chief executives of twenty of the standard railroad labor organizations. (The Brotherhood of Railroad Trainmen withdrew in 1937.) It is a purely voluntary association. Each member organization maintains complete autonomy over its own affairs and is bound to the Association only to the extent that it wishes. Organized to further mutual interests, particularly to determine policies and promote legislation, its activities have probably far exceeded expectations, especially its activities as a bargaining agency.

Objectives

The railroad labor unions are, in their general outlook, essentially conservative. From the beginning they have been largely dominated by the transportation brotherhoods, long known as the aristocrats of the American labor movement. Primary objectives have always been higher wages, shorter hours and better working conditions, with increasing emphasis on security against the hazards of unemployment and dependent old age. Aware of the need of adequate support for these demands, several of them maintain research departments directed by competent statisticians. Much of their success in recent years comes from able and forceful presentation of their claims to employers, and before arbitration and investigating boards and Congressional committees.

The insurance and benefit features so important in early years have never been abandoned, although with many of the organizations they are of little consequence. The transportation brotherhoods, however, have a well-rounded insurance system. A few of the organizations have built imposing office buildings, but except for these and a few rather unsuccessful business ventures, including labor banks, they have steered clear of cooperative and business undertakings.

Attitude Toward Bargaining Versus Legislation

Like other unions, the railroad labor organizations look upon collective bargaining as the chief means of gaining their objectives. But since the railroads are under greater governmental control than most industries, legislation has never been neglected. It has become increasingly more important in recent years, both in itself and as a means of making collective bargaining more effective. Several organizations have legislative departments, coordinate with their protective (bargaining) and insurance departments, and maintain representatives in the state, provincial, and national capitals of the United States and Canada. One of the chief purposes of the Railway Labor Executives' Association is to look after members' legislative interests, and for this purpose it has permanent headquarters with a full-time secretary in Washington.

Politically, the general policy of the railroad labor organizations has been nonpartisan; they have never favored a labor party. After the Plumb Plan League failed to make much headway in 1919, the idea of government ownership receded, but it was revived in 1935 when the Railway Labor Executives' Association went on record for it. More recently, considerable doubt appears to have arisen as to its advantages for the employees, for it carries the distinct possibility of consolidation of individual properties into a national unified system, with further displacement of large numbers of employees. One prominent organization executive has lately declared that there is less sentiment now for government ownership than for many years.[43] Perhaps the realization that it is likely to come about unless the railroads' condition improves is largely responsible for the initiative taken by the organizations in attempting to work out with management a rehabilitation program.

43. President George M. Harrison, Brotherhood of Railway and Steamship Clerks, Freight Handlers, Express and Station Employees, *Report of Grand Lodge Officers* to the Sixteenth Regular Convention, May 1939, p. 113.

Structure

The observation that ". . . the governments of railway unions, fashioned in the last century to fit that industry, have required but little modification throughout the years,"[44] applies equally well to their internal structure. The basic organic unit is the local lodge or local division. The local's jurisdiction extends over part or all of the division, varying with each organization. The local comes in contact with management through its grievance committee.

Second in importance only to the national or international organization itself, is the system or "general" committee. This body is composed of the several chairmen of the local or divisional grievance committees. It is the bargaining agency of the organizations; subject to the direction and approval of the national organization, it negotiates with management upon hours, wages and other conditions of employment. Grievances that cannot be settled by the local grievance committee are appealed to it. Although the general committee nominally performs these duties, most of the actual work and responsibility fall on the general chairman, usually a full-time, salaried official who ranks next in importance to the officers of the national organization.

Between the system committees and the national organization there may be one or more additional agencies. The brotherhoods, for example, have regional and national associations of general chairmen. These policy determining bodies are called into action, in addition to their regular meetings, when matters of general interest, such as a regional or national wage movement, are being considered or negotiated. Even where matters are negotiated on a national scale, however, the actual agreement is made between the system committee and the individual railroad.

This structure applies to each of the shop crafts as well as to the other organizations. In addition, the local and the district system lodges are paralleled by federations. The local lodges on each road form local federations with joint protective boards to handle grievances which cannot be settled by local grievance committees.

---

44. Harry Henig, *The Brotherhood of Railway Clerks*, Columbia University Press, New York, 1937, p. 250.

Next, a system federation composed of representatives from the district lodges, with a system federated board, is the bargaining agency for the shop crafts. It is made up of representatives from each of the several crafts, and has the same duties as the system committees of the other organizations, except that it bargains for all the shop crafts on each road.

5. Negotiating Agreements

The Railway Labor Act of 1926, as amended in 1934, is the framework within which collective bargaining is now carried on. The existing procedure has been hammered out between the organizations and the carriers for nearly three quarters of a century. In the absence of the Act, negotiations would be carried on much as they are now—as they were before its enactment. To a large extent, the Act is a codification of practices which the stronger organizations had already secured for themselves. By standardizing the procedure and giving it a legal status, however, the Act has made it available to organizations formerly unable to get it by their own efforts.

The Act makes it the duty ". . . of all carriers, their officers, agents, and employees to exert every reasonable effort to make and maintain agreements concerning rates of pay, rules and working conditions. . . ." [45] Either side wishing a change in any of the basic provisions of an agreement must give the other at least thirty days' written notice,[46] and carriers are specifically prohibited from making any change except in the manner prescribed.[47] The date for the beginning of a conference to consider changes must be agreed upon within ten days of receipt of notice, and must fall within the thirty-day period stipulated.[48] Each side, it will be recalled, is guaranteed the right to select its own representatives without interference from the other. Majority rule is established by the provision that "the majority of any craft or class shall have

---

45. Railway Labor Act, 44 Stat. 577 (1926), Sec. 2, First.
46. Sec. 6.
47. Sec. 2, Seventh.
48. Sec. 6.

the right to determine who shall be the representative of the craft or class for the purpose of this Act." [49]

Except for the shop crafts, which act as a unit, collective bargaining on the railroads is ordinarily carried on between a single carrier and a single organization. Yet there have been many exceptions, for example, the concerted movements of the brotherhoods, which are becoming increasingly more common.

Exceptions are of two kinds: first, where a single union presents its demands simultaneously on all or most of the roads in a region or in the country as a whole; and second, where two or more unions jointly present their demands on one or more carriers. Such bargaining alliances are temporary, and a wage movement conducted by one combination of unions may be followed by another wage movement by another combination.

If a change in rules is desired by either side, negotiations are generally confined to a single road, since interpretations of the rules vary more widely from road to road than do wages or hours and are thus less amenable to general consideration. Or if wages on one road are lower than those on other roads, efforts may be confined to this one road in an attempt to level them up. On the other hand, if a general increase in wages is sought by a single organization or by a group of organizations, negotiations must be extended to all roads on which an increase is desired.

a. BARGAINING WITH SINGLE LABOR ORGANIZATIONS

A movement for a general wage increase may originate through the insistence of the membership, meeting in local lodges and petitioning the general officers; with the general officers acting on their own initiative; or by instructions from a convention to the general officers. Regardless of origin, the next step is consideration of the matter by the general chairmen. If they approve, the proposition is formulated and the general strategy worked out. It is then submitted to the membership for approval and for authority to proceed. This having been secured, notices are served on the carriers, individually, asking for conferences in accordance with Section 6 of the Transportation Act.

49. Sec. 2, Fourth.

In conference, the carrier may accede. If so, an agreement is reached, a copy of which must be filed with the National Mediation Board, and the matter is ended. More likely, however, as a first move, the carrier may refuse the demands. Or it may make a counterproposal, agreeing to consider a wage increase if the organization will agree to consider certain changes in rules. Individually, the carriers may refuse any concessions, but may be willing to form a carriers' conference committee with delegated authority to carry negotiations to a conclusion. If they refuse either to accede or to appoint such a committee, the next step is for the organization to take a strike vote.

Armed with authority to call a strike if necessary, the general officers are in a position to push their bargaining more vigorously. Often the carriers will belatedly appoint a conference committee before the strike vote is tabulated. If and when they do, negotiations are resumed and an agreement may be reached, granting the requests in whole or in part. If an agreement is not reached, or if the carriers still refuse to appoint a conference committee, the organization faces the alternative of calling a strike on all or as many of the roads as seems wise, or of letting the whole matter drop. After negotiations are broken off and before a strike is actually called, however, either or both parties may appeal to the National Mediation Board, or the Board may proffer its services.

The procedure followed by the shop crafts is similar, except that all six of the older organizations, and increasingly, a seventh, the Firemen and Oilers, act as a unit. Any proposed course of action must first be approved by the Railway Employees' Department of the American Federation of Labor, and negotiations are carried on by the system federation instead of the system committees of the individual unions.

b. JOINT BARGAINING ON A NATIONAL SCALE

Apart from the wartime national agreements, collective bargaining on the railroads on a nation-wide scale is a recent development. It originated in 1932 when the carriers got the Railway Labor Executives' Association to agree to a 10 per cent wage deduction. Since then, in addition to subsequent wage agreements, two other things of outstanding importance, the Washington Job Protection Agreement and the present Railway Employees' Retirement Act, have come from bargaining on a national scale.

Wage Deduction of 1932

The wage deduction of 1932 grew out of the depression. Late in 1931 the Railway Labor Executives' Association presented to a committee of nine railroad presidents a program for stabilizing employment which called for joint action by the Association and the roads.[50] The carriers' committee proposed instead that the association executives recommend to their membership a voluntary deduction of 10 per cent. Unless it was accepted they threatened to insist on a 15 per cent reduction. The outcome was an agreement for a 10 per cent deduction from the pay of each employee for one year, beginning February 1, 1932. Basic rates were to remain unchanged, with the deduction automatically terminating January 31, 1933. On stabilization of employment, the carriers committed themselves no further than to agree to "make an earnest and sympathetic effort to maintain and increase railroad employment." This was much less than the organizations had hoped for, but a voluntary deduction of 10 per cent in wages was considered preferable to the alternative of carrying the issues to a conclusion on the individual roads, with the likelihood of disrupting the existing wage structure.[51]

The 1932 wage deduction agreement was extended twice. When the carriers sought a third extension in February 1934, the organizations countered with a request for an increase of 10 per cent in wages effective July 1. After prolonged negotiations, and despite President Roosevelt's expressed hope for an extension of the existing agreement, the organizations were successful in restoring wages to the 1931 level. The agreement provided that one fourth of the deduction was to be restored July 1, 1934; a second fourth, January 1, 1935; and the remaining half, April 1, 1935.[52]

50. *Official Proceedings,* Ninth Convention, Railway Employees' Department, American Federation of Labor, 1938, p. 2. The program submitted by the Association is discussed later. See pp. 366 ff.
51. *Ibid.,* p. 8.
52. *Ibid.,* p. 17.

The agreement also carried the recommendation that future general wage changes should be negotiated nationally.

Movements to Secure Wage Increases

With the improvement in business conditions, the rail labor organizations decided, late in 1936, that the time was ripe for a movement to secure a wage increase. On this occasion, however, the five transportation brotherhoods, including the Switchmen's Union, decided to act together, but independently of the other organizations. This new alignment presented demands for a 20 per cent increase to the individual roads in March 1937.

A good deal of jockeying and maneuvering followed. Some roads refused the organizations' demands outright. Others made counterproposals for changes in rules. None showed any sign of agreement. This being apparent, the five union executives jointly asked J. J. Pelley, President of the Association of American Railroads, to appoint a national conference committee representing the roads to meet with them and carry the negotiations to a conclusion.

Despite the fact that all wage negotiations since 1932 had been handled on a national basis and that the final agreement of the series which restored wages in 1935 had recommended that subsequent movements be so handled, Mr. Pelley suggested that the matter be handled on a regional basis. Only after extended correspondence, during which the labor organizations secured authority from their memberships to strike if necessary, did the carriers set up a committee to negotiate on a national scale. Failing to reach an agreement, negotiations ended late in August. The National Mediation Board offered its services, and in early October 1937 an agreement was reached which increased basic rates of pay 44 cents a day.

In the meantime similar negotiations had been carried on by a joint committee representing fourteen of the other sixteen member organizations of the Railway Labor Executives' Association.[53]

53. *Report of Grand Lodge Officers,* to the Sixteenth Regular Convention, Brotherhood of Railway and Steamship Clerks, Freight Handlers, Express and Station Employees, pp. 64 ff.

The developments here paralleled those just outlined at almost every step, culminating in a mediation agreement on August 5. Here the employees were successful in securing an increase of five cents an hour. A significant provision in this agreement stipulated that the share-the-work practices which had been put in effect earlier in the depression should end on request of the general chairmen. "This," it was explained, "is intended to bring about regular employment to such forces as are required by each carrier. Forces will be increased or decreased in conformity with the seniority rules . . . on the individual carriers." [54] Inclusion of this provision was prompted by the organizations' conviction that instead of living up to their 1932 agreement to make every effort to maintain and increase employment, the carriers had, while sharing work, actually decreased the number of employees on the payroll.

Carriers Move for Increased Rates and Reduction in Wages

The business recession beginning in the autumn of 1937 cut deeply into the carriers' revenues. For relief, they petitioned the Interstate Commerce Commission for an increase in rates and they asked the organizations to accept again a voluntary wage reduction. The organizations refused. A number of informal conferences were held by committees representing the two sides, and joint conferences were held with the President. No satisfactory plan was worked out, however, and on May 12, 1938, the carriers served formal notice of a reduction in wages, effective July 1.

Formal conferences were held in accordance with the Railway Labor Act, but without agreement.[55] The carriers then invoked the services of the National Mediation Board which, unable to mediate the dispute successfully, urged arbitration. The carriers were willing, but again the organizations refused and took a strike vote. With a strike called for October 1, 1938, President Roosevelt on September 27 appointed an emergency board to investigate the dispute. This action automatically stayed the strike for thirty

---

54. *Report of Grand Lodge Officers,* to the Sixteenth Regular Convention, Brotherhood of Railway Clerks, 1939, p. 66.

55. The Brotherhood of Railroad Trainmen, having withdrawn from the Railway Labor Executives' Association in 1937, conducted its negotiations separately.

days, during which the Board could make its findings and report, and for thirty days thereafter.

In a report made public on October 29, 1938, the Board found that railway wages had not advanced proportionately more than in other industries, and that their levels were not high as compared with wage levels elsewhere.[56] It concluded that a horizontal reduction of wages, such as the carriers sought, was not justified. The carriers accepted this decision, and dropped their wage reduction plan. As a result of the 1937 increase, railroad wages were some 7.5 or 8 per cent higher than in 1931.[57]

1941 Wage Increases

Larger railroad earnings in the first half of 1941, rising wages in other industries and an advancing cost of living prompted railroad labor again to demand increases in the summer of 1941. The operating brotherhoods asked for a 30 per cent raise, the nonoperating unions for 30 cents more an hour. When negotiations broke down and the organizations voted to strike, the President appointed an emergency board. After more than a month of hearings, the board recommended increases of 7.5 per cent for the first group, and 9 cents an hour for the second—both to be temporary additions and not increases in basic rates. The organizations, however, rejected these recommendations and decided to go on strike. In a final effort to settle the dispute peacefully, the President asked the fact-finding board to act as a mediation board. This time a compromise settlement was forthcoming, and on December 1 both sides agreed to an increase in the basic rate of 9.5 cents an hour, or 76 cents a day, for the operating employees and 10 cents an hour, or 80 cents a day, for the nonoperating ones. Nonoperating employees were also granted paid vacations.

6. THE AGREEMENTS

The oldest known rail labor agreement contains some seven rules which can be reproduced on less than a typewritten page. A

---

56. *Report of the Emergency Board* appointed by the President September 27, 1938.
57. *Ibid.*, p. 6.

single article in the formidable present-day agreement may embrace several times that many rules—the whole agreement filling a score or even over a hundred printed pages.

In their essentials the rail agreements differ little from those in other industries. They provide for classification of work, for the amount and method of payment, working hours, procedures to be followed in hiring, promotion and discharge, for discipline and seniority. The chief differences are that ordinarily they have a larger number of provisions than are found in other agreements, that the provisions are elaborated to a greater extent, and, of course, apply to the peculiar conditions of the railroads.

a. EMPLOYEES COVERED BY AN AGREEMENT

When an organization makes an agreement with a carrier, it tries to include all classes of employees over which it claims jurisdiction. It happens, however, that management will recognize certain classes, but not others. For example, the Brotherhood of Railroad Clerks may get recognition for clerks and station employees, but not for freight handlers.[58] Situations of this sort are becoming fewer and of less importance since the organizations' jurisdictions are becoming more clearly defined and collective bargaining for all classes more generally accepted. One organization, however, may hold an agreement which covers employees generally recognized under the jurisdiction of another. This happens because the Railway Labor Act guarantees employees the right to select their own representatives; and sometimes they choose an organization other than that which they would be expected to select. The 1939 report of the National Mediation Board showed that the Brotherhood of Locomotive Firemen and Enginemen represented the engineers on four roads and that the Brotherhood of Locomotive Engineers represented firemen and hostlers on three roads.[59]

"Excepted" positions offer another example of employees not

---

58. Henig, *op. cit.*, p. 136.
59. *Fifth Annual Report*, 1939, p. 27. In an address made in Cleveland on December 2, 1939, President Robertson of the Brotherhood of Locomotive Firemen and Enginemen stated that his organization represented the engineers on thirty-eight roads. The National Mediation Board reports only on Class I roads.

included in an agreement. Certain jobs, usually supervisory or confidential, are generally excluded from the scope of agreements. Such employees are generally ineligible for union membership, and the union makes no effort to control their positions.[60]

b. WAGES AND HOURS

For groups other than those engaged in road train and engine services, the wage and hours provisions offer little that is unusual. Payment on an hourly basis is the rule. Only the professional, supervisory, and a few miscellaneous groups—less than 10 per cent of all employees—are paid on a daily or monthly basis. Even the shop crafts, except in a few cases where piece rates still prevail, are paid hourly rates. The eight-hour day is general, with time and a half for overtime. Buttressing the basic provisions are many others, relating to such matters as the time of beginning work, lunch periods, Sunday and holiday work, vacations and sick leave.

(1). *Wages of Road Train and Engine Service Employees*

Provisions relating to payments for road train and engine service employees,[61] and to a lesser extent for yard service employees,[62] are far more numerous and more complicated. They have grown up over the years as management and men have tried to work out a satisfactory system of payment for a wide range of services which can be standardized only in part. Train runs vary in length, in attractiveness because of starting time or some other feature, and in the incidental services which train and engine crews must perform. The earliest system of payment, a straight time basis, with wages paid either by the day or month, was not flexible enough to take all these irregularities into account. It was succeeded by a crude piece-rate system of payment by the trip

---

60. Henig, *op. cit.*, p. 136.
61. In discussing this subject the writer has leaned heavily on *A Survey of the Rules Governing Wage Payments in Railroad Train and Engine Service*, published in mimeographed form in 1936 by the Federal Coordinator of Transportation.
62. Employees in yard service are paid on an hourly basis. For engineers and firemen the rates vary with the weight of the locomotive. The basic day is eight hours with overtime at the rate of time and a half. Yard employees may also receive constructive allowances.

which gave way, in turn, to the present system based on a combination of mileage and daily or hourly rates of pay. Superimposed on this are payment for overtime, "arbitraries" or constructive allowances, and daily, and in some cases monthly, guarantees.

The Basic Day and Overtime

For freight train employees, the basic day is eight hours or less, one hundred miles or less. A conductor in through freight, for example, who completes his scheduled run, whether a hundred miles or less, in eight hours or less, gets a full day's pay. The rate of pay may be expressed in terms of day, hour, or mile. A rate of $6.16 a day is the equivalent of 6.16 cents a mile, or 77 cents an hour. Differentials prevail for conductors and trainmen for local freight, through freight, work train, and the like. For engineers and firemen there are differentials for different types of work, and in addition, for different classes and weights of locomotives. In straightaway passenger service, one hundred miles or less, five hours or less is the basic day for engineers and firemen, again with the foregoing differentials. For passenger trainmen and conductors the basic day is one hundred and fifty miles or less, seven and one half hours or less.

Overtime is usually calculated on the minute basis at an hourly rate of three sixteenths of the daily rate in freight service, and one eighth of the daily rate in passenger service. Just when overtime begins, if at all, depends on the length of the run and the number of hours required to make it. In road freight service, overtime begins at the end of eight hours, if the scheduled run is one hundred miles or less; and at the end of five hours for passenger engineers and firemen, and seven and one half hours for conductors and trainmen, if the scheduled runs are one hundred miles or less or one hundred and fifty miles or less. On runs greater than those distances, overtime begins when the normal speed is not maintained. In road freight service the normal speed is twelve and one half miles an hour, i.e., the ratio of miles to hours of the basic day. A conductor who makes one hundred miles in nine hours is entitled to one hour of overtime in addition to his daily rate. If he makes a run of one hundred and twenty-five miles in ten hours, he gets his daily rate, plus an amount equal to twenty-five times the rate per mile, but no overtime in addition. If, however, it requires eleven hours to make the one hundred and twenty-five miles, he receives the daily rate, plus the additional mileage as just calculated, plus one hour of overtime since the normal speed of twelve and one half miles an hour was not achieved.

Most agreements limit the number of miles and thus the earnings of the various classes of employees. For example, the usual maximum mileage for engineers and firemen in passenger service is 4,800 a month and in regular freight service 3,800 a month. The power to establish mileage limitations is vested with the general committees on the individual roads, and is one which they have been reluctant to yield to the national organization.

"Arbitraries" or Constructive Allowances

In addition to these payments, employees in train and engine service also receive "arbitraries" or constructive allowances—payments ". . . for services rendered or for hardships endured which in theory are not necessarily a part of the work to which crews are assigned." [63] Considered historically, they represent payments for services or hardships, once included in the day, month, or trip when such was the basis of payment, but which in the present system of payment are simply added on. They consist of such specific items as switching services performed by the road crews, deadheading—these two items alone accounting for over half the total payments for constructive allowances—hostling, and terminal delay.

Daily and Monthly Guarantees

Over and above all these elements are the daily and monthly guarantees. The guarantee of a day's pay for any part of a day's work is practically universal. In addition, the provision is common that when a passenger service employee's daily earnings from all sources are less than a stated minimum, he nevertheless shall receive that amount for every day that he works. Finally, a monthly

63. William Z. Ripley, "Railway Wage Schedules and Agreements," *Report of the Eight-Hour Commission,* Washington, 1917, p. 340.

guarantee prevails for conductors and trainmen, for which an equivalent amount of work usually must be made up by employees in passenger service.

(2). *Payment for Hours Not Worked*

One of the most frequent criticisms of this system is that it grants pay for hours not worked.[64] The manner in which the Interstate Commerce Commission publishes its monthly and annual data on wages and hours appears to lend support to this criticism. The reports show in parallel columns, "Straight time actually worked," and "Straight time paid for," in terms of both hours and compensation. The latter totals are always the larger. Thus, for 1938, train and engine service employees are shown as having been paid $452 million for 498 million hours.[65] However, they are shown as having actually worked only 403 million hours, payment for which amounted to $366 million. Here is a difference of 95 million hours between those worked and those paid for, involving payments of $86 million. How is this discrepancy to be accounted for, and does it represent payment for which no services were rendered?

Payments included under the caption "straight time paid for" throw some light on these questions. Straight time paid for is an aggregate of three items. The first results from the guarantee of a full day's pay even though an employee works only part of a day. Some of the discrepancy between hours paid for and hours worked appears when a carrier reports payment for a full day but only the number of hours worked that the employee was actually on duty. The second item is closely related and arises from the guarantees given certain classes of employees that they will be paid for every working day in the month, if available for work, whether or not their services are actually used on a given day.

---

64. E.g., Garret Garrett in "Peace on the Rails," in the *Saturday Evening Post* for September 9, 1939, comments, in part: "Thus, the railroads paid for 94,515,996 hours that were not worked, and the amount paid for these hours that were not worked was $85,866,391."

65. *Wage Statistics of Class I Steam Railroads in the United States,* ICC, Statement No. M-300, 1938.

These two items together account for about one fourth of the amount of the discrepancy between time paid for and time actually worked.[66]

To the extent just indicated, train and engine service employees unquestionably receive pay for time not worked. Whether such payments are justified or not is another question. The purpose behind them is to guarantee employees a minimum wage, and to protect them from reporting for work and being sent home without compensation if they are not needed. Similar provisions are commonly found in agreements in other industries and are in no way peculiar to the railroads.

The third and most important factor which explains the discrepancy between hours worked and hours paid for, is to be found in the practice of reporting miles which are run at a rate of speed in excess of the ratio of miles to hours in the basic day as hours paid for, but not as hours worked. A conductor in through freight, for example, who runs one hundred and twenty-five miles in eight hours is reported as having been paid for ten hours, but as having worked only eight. Similarly, if his regular run is, say, ninety miles which he completes in five hours, he is reported as having been paid for a full day of eight hours, but as having worked only five hours. The amount paid out for this "straight-time excess mileage" accounts for the remaining three fourths of the discrepancy between hours worked and hours paid for.[67]

Here again it is literally true that train and engine service employees receive pay for hours which they do not work. However, it must be borne in mind that payment by the mile is essentially a piece-rate system introduced by the carriers to speed up production—in this case the number of miles per hour. If an hour is regarded as the equivalent of twelve and one half miles, which is the ratio of hours to miles in the basic day, it may be argued that service is rendered in return for payment for straight-time excess

66. Federal Coordinator of Transportation, *op. cit.*, pp. 5, 6. This study covered the month of March 1934. Current data published by the ICC cannot be broken down to show this, but it seems reasonable to assume that no significant change has taken place since 1934.
67. *Ibid.*

mileage.[68] Considered in this light, a freight conductor's run of one hundred and twenty-five miles represents ten hours of work rather than eight. Moreover, had the run actually been ten hours instead of eight, the pay would have been the same. Criticism here, if it is in order, should be directed not at the system of wage payment as such, but at retaining as the basis of calculating a day's work a rate of speed which is now obsolete. One result of retaining "100 miles or less" as the day's work has been a tendency for straight-time excess mileage payments to increase during the past several years. Another result, and equally significant, has been a corresponding tendency for overtime payments to decrease.

(3). *The Issue of Constructive Allowances*

Provisions and rules associated with arbitraries and constructive allowances are especially criticized. Why, it may be asked, should a road crew which completes its run in less than the scheduled time be paid extra for performing a few minutes' switching service? Nowhere does the difficulty of working out satisfactory payment for jobs which cannot be standardized show more clearly than at this point. Hauling passengers and freight involves a wide range of incidental services, sacrifices and inconveniences for which employees feel they should have extra pay. Where this is recognized and agreed to by management, a provision is written into the agreement defining the service or inconvenience, and listing the payment for it. Constructive allowances give a flexibility necessary for expeditious handling of unusual situations. But this fact does not justify keeping uneconomical provisions in agreements where such can be shown to exist.

(4). *Earnings*

A final criticism of the system of payment is that it enables some employees to make excessively large earnings. A study of annual earnings of railroad employees by the Coordinator of

---

68. "Money so earned cannot fairly be considered a payment for time not worked. It is a payment for service rendered, and is proportionate thereto. It has grown because the employees' mileage output per hour has increased, and their return in wages has therefore increased also." Federal Coordinator of Transportation, *op. cit.*, p. S-6.

Transportation for the period 1924 to 1933 [69] showed that about one tenth of one per cent of the employees in train and engine service earned an average of $300 a month in 1933. Less than 15 per cent earned $200 per month or more. Average earnings of all employees in this class of service were less than $1,800 or $150 a month. In 1929 less than 5 per cent earned as much as $3,600 a year, while average earnings were slightly less than $2,300. The conclusion of the Coordinator was that ". . . if any train or engine service employee is able to realize excessive earnings under the present system of rules governing wage payments, the number of such employees is insignificant."

C. SENIORITY

The most important provisions in the agreement from the employees' standpoint relate to seniority. While not confined to the railroad industry, it is here that the principle of seniority has been developed most completely and is most widely applied.

A railroad man's seniority begins when he is accepted for employment. It may increase as long as he remains in service and even longer.[70] When forces are reduced, employees are laid off in the reverse order of their seniority; and when they are again increased, senior employees are called first. Should a more desirable position become available, a senior employee has first claim on it. "Fitness and ability being sufficient," promotion is based on seniority, rather than merit—a practice which probably does not make for maximum efficiency. Each class of employment ordinarily has its own seniority roster; and an employee's seniority is limited to his seniority district, which may be a shop, department, office or division.[71]

69. Federal Coordinator of Transportation, *Annual Earnings of Railroad Employees, 1924–1933*, 1935 (mimeographed).

70. E.g., a provision in a current agreement reads as follows: "In case a conductor is employed by his organization, he will be considered in the service of the company as to his rank and rights of promotion and will retain the same rank he would have gained if in actual service." Chicago, Milwaukee, and St. Paul Railway (Western Lines) *Schedule for Conductors*. Under this provision an employee might be out of active service for thirty years and still head the seniority list.

71. E.g., "Road conductors have no seniority rights in yards, or yard conductors on the road." Baltimore and Ohio Railroad Company, *Rules and Rates of Pay for Conductors*.

Sources of Conflict

Seniority has been an important source of conflict within and among rail labor organizations. It is part of a complex of rules, provisions and practices pertaining to such closely related matters as hiring, promotion, demotion, and, in the case of train and engine service especially, mileage limitations, and representation.

Lines of promotion in train and engine service run from fireman to engineer and from trainman to conductor. Upon promotion, a fireman goes on the extra list, and for several years will likely alternate between engineers' and firemen's jobs. His seniority as an engineer dates from the time he enters upon the engineer's work, but he also retains his fireman's seniority. Consequently, when he must return to firing, some fireman his junior has to make way for him. The fireman thus displaced can exercise his seniority over any fireman his junior, and so on down the line until the last fireman has no one to displace and must "take to the woods." As a result of this process, during the early thirties every fireman on some divisions was forced to make way for an engineer.[72]

An employee entering service as a fireman usually joins the Brotherhood of Locomotive Firemen and Enginemen, and takes out one or more forms of insurance that organization has for its members. When he is eligible for promotion to engineer, he has acquired considerable equity in his insurance, which increases in value as long as he retains membership in that organization, even though he works as an engineer. He is therefore reluctant to give up membership in the Brotherhood of Locomotive Firemen and Enginemen. Upon promotion, he may, of course, keep his membership in the firemen's organization, and also join the Brotherhood of Locomotive Engineers. Many firemen do that. Or he may go along with only his membership in the firemen's organization, relying on it to handle his grievances and to look after his interests generally, except in the making of agreements, which is the prerogative of the engineer brotherhood. The latter organization,

---

72. *Brotherhood of Locomotive Firemen and Enginemen Magazine,* April 1930, p. 251. The right of an engineer to displace a fireman his junior is ordinarily confined to those who have been promoted. Hired engineers hold seniority as engineers but not as firemen. See Ripley, *op. cit.,* p. 387.

however, may feel justified in bringing pressure upon him to join, particularly during a time of acute unemployment and declining membership such as we have had over the past several years. Here is a vital point of conflict between two organizations. A similar situation exists between trainmen and conductors.

Closely akin to all this is the issue of hiring of engineers instead of the promoting of firemen when additional engineers are needed. Heavier locomotives, longer trains, as well as the decline in traffic, have displaced many engineers. When it needs more engineers, should a road promote a fireman or hire an engineer who has been displaced? The latter, says the Brotherhood of Locomotive Engineers, with unemployed members. The former, says the Brotherhood of Locomotive Firemen and Enginemen, anxious to secure promotions for its members.

The question of how many miles an engineer shall run a day and each month is also a point at issue. Since their pay is figured according to miles as well as hours, the engineers favor larger mileage. This, however, reduces the number of engineers needed, retards firemen's promotion, and adds to their unemployment. The mileage of an engineer's run thus becomes a moot point between the two brotherhoods.

The Chicago Joint Agreement

Such vexatious questions provoked what has been termed "open warfare" [73] between firemen and engineers almost from the very beginning. Conflict was stilled for a number of years after 1913 by a compact known as the Chicago Joint Agreement between the two organizations. This twice-revised agreement set the maximum and minimum mileage for the several classes of employees; also the conditions under which engineers, failing to average the minimum, might exercise their seniority and return to firing, thus displacing firemen. It also fixed a ratio between the number of engineers to be hired and the number of firemen to be promoted when more engineers were needed. Finally, it affirmed, on the one hand, the right of each organization ". . . to make and interpret contracts,

---

73. *Brotherhood of Locomotive Firemen and Enginemen's Magazine,* May 1939, p. 342.

rules, rates and working agreements. . . ." for members of its craft; and on the other, the right of a member of either organization to have his grievances handled by a regularly constituted committee of his organization, but ". . . under the recognized interpretation of the General Committee making the schedule involved." This meant that the conditions of employment of all engineers would be negotiated by the Engineers. But an engineer holding membership only in the Brotherhood of Firemen and Enginemen would look to that organization to handle his grievance, subject to the interpretation by the engineers' committee making the agreement.

Abrogation of Chicago Agreement and Cleveland Compact

While the Chicago Joint Agreement was in effect, agreements made by each of the brotherhoods with the railroads were in accord with it; and a large number were made jointly. A practically identical situation existed between the Conductors and the Trainmen who made in 1919 the Cleveland Compact, which closely resembled the Chicago Joint Agreement. Both agreements were abrogated, the Cleveland Compact in 1925, the Chicago Joint Agreement in 1927, in each case the senior organization taking the initiative. Efforts to make new agreements failed,[74] and old controversies which had been held in check flared up again. Some of the organizations, in bad shape because of financial difficulties and loss of members through unemployment, began a spirited and frequently competitive campaign for new members.[75] In some cases constitutions were amended to make eligible for membership certain classes of employees previously recognized as belonging to other organizations. Resulting accusations and recriminations, official and personal, aroused violent animosities.[76] Some

74. The Conductors and Trainmen negotiated a new agreement in 1932, but it lasted only a short time.

75. On May 1, 1935 President Whitney of the Brotherhood of Railroad Trainmen issued Circular No. W 93, ". . . classifying the Order of Railway Conductors as a rival and antagonistic organization." *Proceedings,* First Quadrennial Convention, Brotherhood of Railroad Trainmen, 1935, p. 11.

76. "We find in the office of every General Chairman and Legislative Representative, as well as in the Division and Lodge Halls of the four organizations, vast quantities of circulars containing charges and countercharges of the actions of the chief executives relative to jurisdictional matters, the merits or lack of merit of the insurance departments of the Sister Organizations, that tend to confuse and

agreements made with the roads by certain brotherhoods were protested by other organizations, because they violated not only the latters' interests, but also established custom and earlier joint agreements. Some of the resulting controversies became so serious as to require the appointment of emergency boards.[77] The continued existence of this situation leads many to believe that amalgamation of the Engineers and Firemen, on the one hand, and the Conductors and Trainmen, on the other, offers a logical and desirable solution.

Seniority Versus a Share-the-Work Policy

Seniority has also provoked intraorganizational friction in recent years. Under given hour and mileage limitations,[78] it operates in conflict with a share-the-work policy; and when forces must be reduced, the younger men are the first to go. As a consequence, depression unemployment hit the younger men harder than their elders. This brought vigorous demands from the younger men, supported by the national officers of most of the organizations, for a more equal division of work.[79] The Federal Coordinator[80] made similar recommendations, and as a result, hours were voluntarily reduced and mileage reductions accepted, the minimum frequently becoming the maximum on many roads.

On other roads, however, the older men's opposition blocked the reductions. One reason for their opposition was that reduced monthly earnings would mean smaller pensions under the anticipated retirement legislation. Many of the older men also felt that

---

sow the seeds of distrust in the minds and hearts of the men in the train and yard service we are severally and collectively endeavoring to represent." From *Report of the Joint Relations Committee*, BRT, First Quadrennial Convention, p. 279.

77. *Report of the Emergency Board* appointed by the President April 14, 1937. The Board found that agreements had been made between the carrier and the senior organizations relating to the handling of grievances which tended to make membership in the junior organizations less attractive, and which were in conflict with earlier agreements and with established practices.

78. In a sense, any limitation placed on the number of miles that an employee can make per month is a division of work.

79. *Brotherhood of Locomotive Firemen and Enginemen's Magazine*, January 1930, p. 15.

80. *Report of the Federal Coordinator of Transportation*, H. Doc. 89, 74th Cong., 1st sess., 1934, p. 82.

seniority entitled them not only to the better positions and to security of tenure, but also to the maximum hours and mileage permitted by their organizations. In many cases the general committees on the individual roads, which regulate these matters, being composed of, or under the influence of, older men, prevented a division of the work. Bitterness and internal dissension resulted. The opposition of the older men, plus the organizations' growing belief that, while sharing work and reducing working hours, the carriers were also reducing the number of employees on the payroll, led to a general reaction against it. The 1937 wage agreement between the carriers and the organizations other than the brotherhoods stipulated that share-the-work practices should be ended on request of the general chairmen.[81]

Aging of the Work Force

In a period of declining employment seniority is a selective process, tending to eliminate the younger men and to raise the age level. "The average age of railroad employees is higher," declared the Federal Coordinator of Transportation in 1934, "and the proportion of those aged 65 and over is greater, than for any other major industrial group." [82] The average age of all railroad employees, according to his report, increased from 37.1 years in 1925 to 44.2 years in 1934. Other causes, such as the age of the industry itself, have helped to bring this situation about, but seniority has been a major factor.

d. ABSENCE OF THE CLOSED SHOP

The closed shop has never been an issue on the railroads until recent years. The brotherhoods would find it impracticable, because of the practice of their members to alternate between positions of firemen and engineers, or between trainmen and conductors.[83] Until recently, the other organizations have been content to

---

81. See p. 342.
82. *Report of the Federal Coordinator of Transportation*, 1934, p. 80.
83. It will be remembered, however, that prior to 1934 the Trainmen had a number of "percentage agreements," providing that a certain proportion of the class represented by the organization making the agreement should belong to the union. See p. 330, note 34.

secure recognition and collective bargaining. Of late, however, a number of them, including the telegraphers, the clerks and the maintenance of way employees, have gone on record in favor of the closed shop; and it seems likely that soon it will be demanded. A modification of the Railway Labor Act is necessary, however, before the closed shop is legally possible.

7. Procedure for Handling Disputes

a. disputes over changes in agreements

If the parties negotiating a new agreement are unable to adjust their differences, either or both may appeal to the National Mediation Board, or the Board may offer its services. This step taken, no change may be made in the conditions of employment, except by mutual consent, until all succeeding steps required by the Act to adjust the dispute have been taken.[84]

The distinction should be kept in mind between disputes growing out of the making or revising of agreements, and those arising over interpretation and application. This division roughly marks the line between the jurisdiction of the National Mediation Board and that of the National Railroad Adjustment Board.

Constitution and Role of the Mediation Board

The National Mediation Board consists of three members, appointed by the President for three years. Not more than two may be of the same political party, and no one is eligible who has a pecuniary interest in any organization of employees, or any carrier, or is in their employ. The Board's headquarters are in Washington, but it may meet at any other place it sees fit.

The Board's jurisdiction covers not only disputes over changes in rates of pay, rules, or working conditions, but "any other dispute not referable to the National Railroad Adjustment Board and not adjusted in conference." [85] The most important "other dis-

---

84. Railway Labor Act, 44 Stat. 577 (1926) as amended, Sec. 6.
85. *Ibid.*, Sec. 5, First (b).

putes" are between the employees themselves as to the selection of representatives. Of minor importance are some arising from interpretation of agreements reached through mediation.

Its services once asked for, the Board must use its best efforts to effect a settlement through mediation. If unsuccessful, it must try to induce the parties to arbitrate. If arbitration is agreed to, the Board's responsibilities are over, unless the arbitrators selected by the disputants fail to agree upon the remaining arbitrator or arbitrators, in which case the Board must choose.

If either or both parties refuse to submit the matter to arbitration, as is their legal right, the Board notifies them that its mediatory efforts have failed; and that for thirty days thereafter, there shall be no change in rates of pay, rules or working conditions or established practices, unless the parties agree meanwhile to arbitration, or an emergency board is created. If, in the judgment of the Board, the dispute threatens to interrupt interstate commerce to the extent of depriving any section of the country of essential transportation service, it must notify the President. The President may then, in his discretion, appoint a board composed of as many persons as he sees fit. Such a board must investigate and report to the President within thirty days from its creation. After a board has been appointed, and for thirty days after it has made its report, no change may be made except by mutual agreement in the conditions out of which the dispute arose.

Record of Accomplishments

During the five years from July 1, 1935 to June 30, 1940, services of the National Mediation Board were invoked in 1,483 cases.[86] Less than half, 659, were representation cases; 813 were mediation cases; and a negligible number, 11 in all, were cases in which the Board was asked to interpret agreements reached through mediation. The Board disposed of 1,382 cases during this time, leaving 101 pending and unsettled.[87]

86. National Mediation Board, *Sixth Annual Report*, 1940, pp. 10 ff.
87. In 403 of 633 representation cases disposed of, elections were held to determine the proper representatives. In 118 cases representatives were certified after a check of employee authorizations against payroll records of the carriers, making

Railroads

The long period of unbroken peace on the railroads is not fortuitous.[88] Management and men have learned through long experience the superiority of negotiation over force. Legislation has encouraged and strengthened the bargaining process, and the work of the National Mediation Board, and that of its predecessor, the National Board of Mediation, deserve commendation. The only criticism of the Board's work known to the writer is delay in handling cases, which has been emphasized by the Board itself.[89] At present it is about a year behind in its work. One important cause of delay has been the large number of representation cases.[90] With various organizations competing for the right to represent certain crafts or classes of employees, the crux of the Board's problem is to sort employees into their crafts or classes, and to issue rules for electing representatives. This has compelled the Board ". . . to make special investigations, hold formal hearings, prepare findings of fact, and make definite rulings, all of which has proved time-consuming and diverted the efforts of the Board from the mediation of labor disputes . . . its most important duty."[91] These interorganizational disputes unfortunately show only little tendency to decrease.[92]

---

a total of 521 cases in which representatives were certified. In 25 cases representatives were recognized by the roads without formal certification. Forty-seven cases were withdrawn during investigation; 14 were withdrawn before investigation; and 26 were dismissed because no dispute was shown to exist, or because authorizations were incomplete, or for other reasons.

Of 740 mediation cases disposed of, 354 agreements were reached with the Board's help. One hundred and sixty-three cases were withdrawn as a result of mediation; 127 were withdrawn before mediation; and 14 were dismissed after it became apparent that the parties were no longer interested in the dispute. Agreements to arbitrate the points at issue were signed in 11 cases; and 62 were closed by the Board after one or both parties had refused arbitration. In 9 cases in which no settlement was reached, the disputes were serious enough to call for an emergency board of investigation.

88. There have been only about half a dozen strikes since 1926.
89. National Mediation Board, *Fourth Annual Report*, 1938, p. 8.
90. In 1936 the scope of the Railway Labor Act was amended to cover "every common carrier by air engaged in interstate or foreign commerce, and every carrier by air transporting mail for or under contract with the United States Government, and every air pilot or other person who performs any work as an employee or subordinate official of such carrier or carriers. . . ." 49 Stat. 1189 (1936).
91. National Mediation Board, *Fourth Annual Report*, 1938, p. 2.
92. National Mediation Board, *Sixth Annual Report*, 1940, p. 10.

b. DISPUTES ARISING UNDER AGREEMENTS

The procedure and machinery established by the 1934 Amendment to the Railway Labor Act for handling grievances and disputes arising out of the interpretation and application of agreements marked the culmination of years of effort by railway labor organizations. Pleased with the functioning of the national adjustment boards during government operation, labor sought similar boards when the roads were returned to private operation. Their insistence on national rather than regional or system boards came from the belief that they brought greater standardization of working conditions. The carriers opposed national boards for the same reason. They favored system boards, which, they argued, would better meet the peculiar conditions of the individual railroads.

The Transportation Act of 1920, it will be recalled, permitted establishment of adjustment boards by agreement between the carriers and the employees, but said nothing about the kind of boards to be set up. The Act of 1926 made their establishment mandatory, but likewise failed to define them. Though legally sanctioned, adjustment boards under these two acts were far from satisfactory. Both sides believed them desirable, but could not agree upon the type to be created. As a result, only four regional boards were established, those by the transportation brotherhoods and the carriers, and a considerable number of system boards by the carriers and other organizations. Being bipartisan, these boards were deadlocked more frequently than not; and there was no provision for breaking the deadlock. As one careful observer stated, "increasingly . . . the adjustment boards, voting strictly along partisan lines, were merely accumulating controversies and not settling them." [93] Apparently convinced of the futility of leaving this matter longer with the carriers and their employees, Congress complied with the wishes of the labor organizations and established the National Railroad Adjustment Board in the 1934 Amendment to the Railway Labor Act.

---

93. William H. Spencer, *The National Railroad Adjustment Board,* University of Chicago Press, 1938, p. 12.

The Railroad Adjustment Board

This Board is a bipartisan body of thirty-six members, half of whom are selected and paid by the carriers, the other half by the "national" labor organizations. The Board itself seldom meets as a whole, for each of its four divisions adjudicates disputes of specified groups of employees, and each acts independently of the others. The First and Second Divisions, of ten members each, handle disputes involving train and yard service employees,[94] and the shop crafts, respectively. The Third Division, also of ten members, has jurisdiction over a more heterogeneous group, including the clerks, telegraphers, maintenance of way men and signalmen. The Fourth Division, consisting of six members, has jurisdiction over railroad employees who are engaged directly or indirectly in water transportation and all other employees not included in other divisions. Each division, and the Board as a whole, annually elect a chairman and a vice chairman, alternating between representatives of the railroad labor organizations and of the carriers.

Disputes growing out of grievances, or out of the interpretation or application of agreements, are handled ". . . in the usual manner up to and including the chief operating official of the carrier designated to handle such disputes. . . ." If no settlement is reached they ". . . may be referred by petition of the parties or by either party to the appropriate division of the Adjustment Board . . ." [95] The wording of the Act seems to indicate that an individual might petition the Board directly for a redress of grievances and present his case in person.[96] In practice this cannot be done;[97] an individual's case must be presented through an organization. As intended, this is a powerful inducement to join a recognized organization.

Oral hearings may be had before a division if requested by

---

94. The First Division took over the work of the four regional boards. The Switchmen's Union of North America is included among the organizations coming under the jurisdiction of this Division.
95. Railway Labor Act (1934), Sec. 3 (i).
96. Sec. 3 (j) reads, in part, ". . . the parties may be heard either in person, by counsel, or by other representatives, as they may respectively elect."
97. Spencer, *op. cit.*, p. 39.

either party; otherwise, the matter is considered on the basis of the written record and decided by majority vote. Deadlocked cases go before a referee selected by the division. If the division cannot agree upon a referee, which happens frequently, the National Mediation Board must appoint a competent, impartial person to act in that capacity.

Results

During the five years ending June 30, 1939, more than nine thousand cases were filed with the Adjustment Board, of which about fifteen hundred were withdrawn. Awards were made in about forty-five hundred cases, leaving some three thousand pending. Nearly eight thousand, or about 85 per cent of all cases received by the Board, have gone to the First Division, which is a full two years behind in its work.[98] So far as the volume of work is concerned, the other divisions might well be combined.

The several divisions have decided about two thirds of the cases without the help of a referee. About as many awards are made in favor of the claimants in the absence of a referee as when a referee is present—68 per cent and 69 per cent respectively.[99]

Since any rule or provision of an agreement may give rise to a dispute, the subjects coming before the Board extend over the whole range of the collective bargaining agreement. With more than four thousand agreements, each with dozens of rules covering in the aggregate the work conditions of a million men, the variety of misunderstandings and disagreements between management and men is almost infinite. Their general nature is shown in the following classification by Dean Spencer, who has served many times as referee: (1) claims for additional pay for time actually spent in service; (2) claims for time lost either by the employer's disregard of the employee's seniority, or because of the employer's failure to call employees in their turn; (3) requests for removal of discipline, or reinstatement of employees alleged to have been unjustly dismissed; (4) protests against prac-

---

98. *Ibid.,* p. 50.
99. *Ibid.*

tices of carriers alleged to be in violation of agreements; and (5) miscellaneous claims for violations of agreements.[100]

A large majority of the awards require a carrier to make money payments to an employee or a group of employees.[101] In some cases where the award calls for back pay over a period of years, the amount involved runs into large figures. In one case in which Dean Spencer was referee, the estimated back pay was about $250,000.

Awards of the divisions of the Adjustment Board are ". . . final and binding upon both parties to the dispute, except insofar as they shall contain a money award." [102] Responsibility of enforcement rests, not with the Board, but with the courts upon petition of the person granted the award. The organizations, however, have consistently refrained from appealing to the courts, preferring to bring pressure directly on a recalcitrant employer through threat of strike. This in effect deprives the carrier of judicial review of an award, for the Act contains no provision under which it can appeal to the courts.[103]

Appraisal

Most of the criticisms of the Adjustment Board have come from the carriers. They maintain that in many instances the referees have shown a labor bias and that their lack of practical knowledge of railroad operations has resulted in questionable awards. They also allege that discipline has been impaired by reinstating employees discharged for negligence or violation of rules.[104]

While some employee groups have not been entirely satisfied with the work of the Board, they nevertheless rallied to its defense when it was the subject of a somewhat general attack by the carriers in the summer of 1939. There were intimations that the

---

100. *Ibid.*, p. 51. See also Garrison, "The National Railroad Adjustment Board: A Unique Administrative Agency," *Yale Law Journal*, February 1937, pp. 581-586. Dean Garrison has also served as referee on numerous occasions. The Act does not require referees to be lawyers and some have been drawn from other fields.
101. Spencer, *op. cit.*, p. 51.
102. Railway Labor Act (1934), Sec. 3, First (m).
103. Spencer, *op. cit.*, p. 56.
104. *Railway Age*, June 17, 1939, p. 1049.

employees might withdraw their support from the railroad legislation before Congress at the time unless an understanding could be reached, and a joint committee representing carriers and organizations has been considering the problem.

Appraisal of the Adjustment Board's work is difficult. Machinery to handle grievances and to interpret the terms of the agreement is essential, and is found in practically every industry where collective bargaining exists.[105] On the railroads this machinery has been given a semiofficial position, and it operates on a national scale. Before establishment of the Adjustment Board, the belief was expressed that its awards would be regarded as precedents, and would contribute to prompt settlement of disputes on the individual roads. This appears not to have been realized, since an interpretation in a given award frequently brings a large number of additional cases from other roads with a view to getting a similar interpretation.

The need of speeding the work of the First Division and eliminating delay is obvious. The practice which deprives an individual from having his complaint heard without first joining a union appears indefensible. Finally, "blocked cases" rising out of interorganizational conflict work grave injustice to the employee whose case is blocked.[106]

8. THE LABOR ORGANIZATIONS' BROAD PROGRAM

The past decade has seen interesting and significant developments in railroad labor relations. Both the scope and method of

---

105. David A. McCabe, "Machinery for the Adjustment of Disputes under New Collective Agreements," *Law and Contemporary Problems,* Duke University School of Law, 1938, p. 265.

106. ". . . many cases arise where one or another of the labor organizations represented on the Board feels that an award in favor of an employee member of another Organization will react adversely to his [the representative's] Organization. So many cases of this kind have arisen that, keen though their rivalry is, the Brotherhood of Locomotive Engineers and the Brotherhood of Locomotive Firemen and Enginemen have apparently agreed among themselves that no case will be presented to the Board by one Organization without the consent of the other and the Board will not assume jurisdiction unless this consent is given. Consequently, not only in the case of the Carrier involved here, but throughout the whole railway system of the United States, an increasing number of grievances cannot be even

collective bargaining have been expanded. The organizations show an increasing tendency to seek uniform national agreements on matters which previously were negotiated on individual roads. In addition, the organizations have more vigorously sought favorable legislation both from state legislatures and Congress.

During this period, the problem of unemployment has been the most important factor in shaping the policies of the railroad labor organizations. Prior thereto their chief objectives had been higher wages, shorter hours and better working conditions. These they sought mainly through collective bargaining. In certain cases they turned to Congress for some specific measure designed to promote safety and comfort, such as the Hours of Service Act of 1907, the Ash Pan Act, the Boiler Inspection Act, and the Federal Employers' Liability Act. Generally speaking, however, they first endeavored to secure their ends directly from the employers through their own efforts.

As long as the railroad industry was expanding and relatively free from the competition of other forms of transportation, these objectives appeared adequate to the organizations. When they did not get what they wanted, they attributed their failure not to the inability of the carriers to comply, but to their own weakness. Consequently, their problem, as they saw it, was to strengthen their organizations and thus their bargaining power.

When the industry ceased to expand and began to contract, this situation changed. As jobs continued to decline, the unemployment situation forced itself into the foreground. The financial plight of many of the carriers, brought about by the same forces that were eliminating jobs, compelled the organizations to broaden both their objectives and their methods. Collective bargaining along traditional lines was not enough. To safeguard jobs, wages, hours and working conditions, something more had to be done. And any program which failed to include measures to improve the position of the roads could scarcely hope to succeed.

All these facts had already been recognized by the shop crafts.

heard by the Board." *Report of the Emergency Board* appointed by the President April 14, 1937. The Board reported that a similar arrangement appeared to exist between the Order of Railway Conductors and the Brotherhood of Railroad Trainmen.

Early in the twenties these organizations, under the direction of Captain Otto Beyer, now a member of the National Mediation Board, had done some praiseworthy pioneering in union-management cooperation. The idea behind this movement was to improve the quality of service by drawing upon the technical knowledge of the employees, promote better relations between management and men, eliminate waste and stabilize employment—with the resulting gains shared between the two parties.[107] This plan of cooperation, known as the "B. & O. Plan," because it was first tried out on that road, was making some headway when its progress was cut short by the depression and by the removal of Captain Beyer to other fields.[108]

a. LABOR'S 1931 PROGRAM

In the meantime the Railway Labor Executives' Association turned its attention to the unemployment problem.[109] After considering the matter for some years, a program for stabilizing employment, to be undertaken jointly by the organizations and management, was submitted to a committee of railroad presidents late in 1931. The Association's program was far-reaching. It proposed to stabilize employment by budgeting the year's work wherever possible, with assurance of full-time work for an average force, and a certain amount of part-time work for the necessary stand-by force. It called for extensive grade-crossing elimination, financed in part by federal funds. It also included a basic six-hour day without reduction in pay, legislation to regulate competitive forms of transportation, federal retirement insurance, elective workmen's compensation, limitation on length of trains, full crews, the establishment of a system of unemployment reserves, a system of employment offices or placement bureaus for railroad workers, and protection of the rights and interests of railroad employees in consolidations.

107. L. A. Wood, *Union-Management Cooperation on the Railroads*, Yale University Press, 1931.
108. The shop crafts endeavor to have the Cooperative Preamble written into all agreements with the carriers, hoping to establish the Union-Management Cooperative Plan at some future date. *Official Proceedings*, Ninth Convention, Railway Employees' Department, American Federation of Labor, 1938, p. 181.
109. *Ibid.*, p. 2.

The carriers, it will be recalled, countered with their successful demand for a 10 per cent deduction in wages.[110] Little progress was made on the organizations' program for stabilization of employment. On several of the proposed measures no agreement could be reached. Others, it was agreed, should be studied by a joint committee representing the carriers and the organizations. About the only point on which there was complete accord was the proposal to establish regional employment bureaus.

Having failed to secure the carriers' cooperation, the Railway Labor Executives' Association turned to the federal government. Bills embodying a number of its proposals were introduced in the Seventy-third Congress, and reintroduced, along with others, in succeeding Congresses. While the organizations have not been wholly successful, they have been largely so in having their program enacted into law. Moreover, the threat of legislation undoubtedly helped them to get concessions from management through collective bargaining which otherwise might not have been forthcoming.[111]

Little headway has been made in Congress on measures to limit the length of trains, or to fix minimum train crews, although a number of states have enacted such legislation. The proposed six-hour day was studied in 1932 by the Interstate Commerce Commission, which found that while its application would have no material effect on either operation or service, it would increase operating expenses by some $630 million a year, assuming the same volume of traffic and rates of pay as existed in 1930.[112] The organizations challenged these estimates and have continued to

110. See p. 340.
111. Notwithstanding the substantial gains secured through legislation, the political method is regarded as definitely secondary to collective bargaining. "The real significance of our political policy . . . has been the influence it has had on collective bargaining . . . Rather than submit to legislature enactments as a means of settling the problems of the industry, the railroad managements have preferred to negotiate with our organizations on these subjects . . . As a result we have participated in a series of national conferences dealing with job protection in consolidations, wages and pensions which are unique in the Labor Movement." Report of the Executive Council, *Official Proceedings,* Ninth Convention, Railway Employees' Department, American Federation of Labor, 1938, p. 175.
112. *Six-Hour Day Investigation in re the Effect Upon Operation, Service, and Expenses of Applying the Principle of a Six-Hour Day in the Employment of Railway Employees,* ICC, Ex parte No. 106, December 6, 1932.

press their six-hour day bill upon Congress, but with little progress.

b. LEGISLATIVE AND BARGAINING GAINS

As against these failures, substantial gains were secured through legislation and collective bargaining. Outstanding legislation, affecting all railroad employees, were the Amendment to the 1933 Federal Bankruptcy Act, the Amendments to the Emergency Railroad Transportation Act of 1933, the 1934 Amendment to the Railway Labor Act, the Railroad Employees' Retirement Insurance Act of 1937, and the Railroad Unemployment Insurance Act of 1938. Through collective bargaining the organizations, represented by the Railway Labor Executives' Association, negotiated the wage deduction and restoration agreements, the Washington Job Protection Agreement and agreements on the retirement insurance measure.

A number of national agreements have also been negotiated by single unions. Early in 1937 the Brotherhood of Locomotive Firemen and Enginemen concluded an agreement calling for firemen (helpers) on Diesel and electric locomotives.[113] The maintenance of way workers as well as the train dispatchers have concluded national agreements with the carriers covering working conditions.

(1). *Legislative Achievements of 1933*

Labor's first important legislative triumph came in 1933 when the organizations secured an amendment to the Federal Bankruptcy Act of that year, forbidding any judge, trustee or receiver to change wages or working conditions of railroad workers except in accordance with the Railway Labor Act, or with the January 1932 wage agreement. The amendment also forbade interference with the right of railroad employees to belong to unions of their own choice, the use of the yellow-dog contract and the use of funds of the carriers to maintain company unions. These

---

113. *Brotherhood of Locomotive Firemen and Enginemen's Magazine*, March 1937, p. 147. It was estimated that this make-work rule, as it largely is, would give employment to some 700 additional firemen or helpers on locomotives then being operated by one man.

provisions were later embodied in the 1934 Amendment to the Railway Labor Act.

Equally important were the amendments to the Emergency Railroad Transportation Act of June 16, 1933, a measure which was designed to bring about greater economies for the carriers through consolidations of lines, terminals and facilities.[114] The organizations were greatly interested in this measure because most of the economies would come from decreases in the labor force. The most important amendments secured were Section 7 (b) and (d).

Paragraph (b) of Section 7 provided, first, that the number of employees in the service of a carrier should not be reduced as a result of consolidations and mergers below those on the payrolls during May 1933, after deductions had been made for deaths, normal retirements or resignations (but not more in any year than 5 per cent of the number in service during May 1933); and second, that no employee should be deprived of employment he had during May, nor receive less pay for it. Paragraph (d) directed the Coordinator to determine the amount of, and to direct the carriers to compensate employees for, property losses and expenses imposed upon them by reason of transfers of work from one locality to another.

(2). *Washington Job Protection Agreement*

The Emergency Railroad Transportation Act was intended as a temporary measure. It was twice extended and finally terminated June 17, 1936. In the meantime the railroad labor organizations, anxious to make permanent the protection it gave employees in cases of consolidation, made with the carriers the "Washington Job Protection Agreement."

That agreement has the same general purposes and follows much the same lines as Section 7 of the Emergency Railroad Act. Employees who are retained after a consolidation or merger are assured that, for a period not exceeding five years, they will not be transferred to jobs with less favorable pay or working conditions than were enjoyed at the time of the consolidation. An employee ordered elsewhere is reimbursed for the cost of moving and

114. 48 Stat. 211 (1933).

for the traveling expenses of himself and his family. If he owns his own home, the carrier must make up any loss suffered if he sold for less than fair value.

Employees who lose their jobs because of a railroad consolidation receive under the agreement a coordination allowance, based on length of service.[115] Employees of one year's service or more get a monthly payment of 60 per cent of their average monthly wage for a period ranging from six months for one year's service to sixty months for fifteen or more years of service. If he chooses, an employee entitled to a coordination allowance may take a lump sum "separation allowance" of from three to twelve months' pay, depending on his length of service. For employees with less than one year's service, the coordination allowance is a lump sum payment equal to sixty days' pay. Each carrier and each organization is bound to the agreement for five years. After that a carrier or an organization may withdraw upon one year's notice.

Railroad labor organizations regard the Washington Job Protection Agreement as one of their outstanding achievements.[116] Nevertheless, they have not acquiesced in consolidations merely because of this protection. They have consistently opposed consolidations and abandonments of lines where the interests of their members would be adversely affected; they have been responsible, at least in part, for the refusal of a number of applications by the Interstate Commerce Commission. Where blocking a consolidation appeared unlikely, they have sought to have the terms of the Agreement applied and were often successful.

(3). *Transportation Act of 1940*

Meanwhile the organizations sought to strengthen and extend the benefits of the Agreement by re-establishing governmental protection. Largely through their efforts the Interstate Commerce Commission adopted the policy of requiring assurance of protection of employees' interests as a condition of approving consolida-

---

115. If given another job the employee is then entitled to the protection outlined in the preceding paragraph.
116. George M. Harrison, "Protection of Railway Employees in Consolidations," *American Federationist,* November 1936, p. 1150.

tions, an exercise of power which was upheld by the Supreme Court.[117] They were then successful in having this requirement made mandatory by the Transportation Act of 1940.[118] By the terms of this Act the Commission is instructed, in approving consolidations, to ". . . require a fair and equitable arrangement to protect the interests of the railroad employees affected." The protection stipulated is that for a period of four years subsequent to the Commission's approval, no employee involved shall be adversely affected with respect to his employment. The period of protection guaranteed an employee, however, shall not exceed the period of the employee's service to the carrier prior to the approval of the consolidation. The Act also permits voluntary agreements pertaining to the protection of employee interests. Since the provisions of the Washington Job Protection Agreement are more favorable to the employees than are those of the Act, it may be presumed that the labor organizations will endeavor to continue and extend the Washington Agreement, falling back on the Act when and where they are unsuccessful.

(4). *Retirement and Unemployment Insurance Acts*

Shortly after making the Washington Agreement, the organizations and the carriers agreed on two bills—a compensation bill and a tax bill—for railroad employees' retirement insurance. Two previous laws secured by the organizations over the protests of the carriers had been declared unconstitutional. Thereupon, President Roosevelt suggested working out a measure that could be supported by both sides. The resulting two bills were passed by Congress and signed by the President in 1937.[119]

Less harmony developed over legislation for unemployment compensation for railroad employees. The organizations hoped for the same joint sponsorship given the retirement insurance measure. When it became apparent during negotiations that no agreement could be reached before Congress adjourned, the Asso-

---

117. *U. S., et al.* v. *Lowden, et al.*, 60 Sup. Ct. 248 (Dec. 4, 1939).
118. *Public, No. 785*, 76th Cong., 3d sess. (S. 2009).
119. *Railroad Retirement Act of 1937*, 50 Stat. 307; *Carriers' Taxing Act of 1937*, 50 Stat. 435.

ciation of Railway Labor Executives decided to sponsor its bill independently. It passed both Houses without a dissenting vote.[120]

(5). *The Current Rehabilitation Program*

The increasing willingness of both the labor organizations and the carriers in recent years to extend the principle of joint negotiations to broad problems of mutual concern is concrete evidence of growing statesmanship in their field of industrial relations. Nowhere is it more clearly evidenced than in the program of rehabilitation for the railroad industry recently passed by Congress. Fully aware that their own and the carriers' interests are impaired and threatened by the decline of the railroad industry, the organizations have shown greater initiative and aggressiveness than the carriers in seeking a remedy. While the emergency investigation proceedings in the 1938 wage dispute were on, they pressed for a joint committee representing management and employees to study the whole transportation situation and to report findings and recommendations to the President. Reporting in December of that year, this Committee, popularly known as the "Committee of Six," laid down a national policy covering all forms of transportation.[121] Such a policy, the Committee declared, should provide ". . . for fair, impartial regulation of all modes of transportation, so administered as to preserve the inherent advantages of each." Among its specific recommendations were those extending the regulatory powers of the Interstate Commerce Commission over rates, services, valuation and accounting of the various agencies of transportation; repeal of the long-and-short haul clause; tolls for the use of improved waterways; relief from alleged unjust tax burdens on the railroads; loans to carriers by the Reconstruction Finance Corporation; and elimination of grade crossings at government expense. The only recommendation dealing directly with employees was one calling for a fair and equitable arrangement to protect their interests in consolidations.

These recommendations were introduced in the first session of

---

120. *Railroad Unemployment Insurance Act 1938*, 52 Stat. 1094.
121. *Report of Committee to Submit Recommendations Upon the General Transportation Situation*, December 23, 1938, pp. 3 ff.

the Seventy-sixth Congress, and a transportation bill (S. 2009) was passed by the Senate. The House rewrote the Senate bill and passed it in greatly altered form. The two bills were then turned over to a conference committee, and a conference report was adopted by both houses during August 1940. This measure, the Transportation Act of 1940, was signed by the President on September 19. The principal labor provisions of the Act, having to do with employees' interests in connection with consolidations, have already been discussed.[122] A consideration of the other provisions, which embody some but not all of the Committee's recommendations, falls outside the scope of this study.

9. Conclusions

Collective bargaining, like any other institution, must be appraised in the light of its objectives, accomplishments and incidental results. Its fundamental purposes are to promote friendly discussion and to substitute negotiations for the strike and lockout in settling differences between employers and employees. Nowhere is it more important that these purposes be achieved than on the railroads, where a suspension of operations ordinarily affects the public more directly and to a greater degree than do similar interruptions in most other industries.

Achievement of Industrial Peace

If this test be applied to collective bargaining on the railroads, the results must be regarded as highly successful. There has been no major strike since the shopmen's strike of 1922. In nine of the first fourteen years after enactment of the Railway Labor Act there were no strikes at all. In each of three years, 1928, 1929 and 1936, there was one small strike. In 1937 there was one small strike, one that was somewhat more serious, and two minor stoppages.[123] Another small strike occurred in 1940. Upon some nineteen occasions since 1926 existing disputes were sufficiently serious to warrant the appointment of emergency boards of investigation.

---

122. See p. 371.
123. National Mediation Board, *Third Annual Report*, 1937, p. 4.

With two exceptions, the recommendations of the boards were accepted by both sides and the disputes ended, although acceptance is no sense mandatory.[124]

This record of almost complete freedom from strife for nearly a score of years is all the more remarkable, in view of the number of employers and employees in the industry, the trying circumstances under which they have operated, and the experience of other industries during the same period. As the National Mediation Board points out, ". . . there has been no lack of disputes in the railroad industry. It differs from other industries only in that its disputes are amicably adjusted with the aid of agencies set up by the Act." [125]

But the situation on the railroads differs from that elsewhere in other important respects which tend to reduce strikes. Because all sections of the country depend on railroad service, any interruption immediately comes to public attention. And since both the roads and the employees are almost continuously seeking legislative favors from Congress and from the states, they are particularly sensitive to public opinion. The maturity of the industry and that of the organizations also are factors. Like the railroad industry itself, many of its labor organizations are among the oldest in the country. Collective bargaining for them has passed through its period of "growing pains." The two sides have long lived together, and each understands and respects the other pretty thoroughly. Each occasionally blasts away at the other through its official journals and the newspapers, but as often as not the spirit is Pickwickian and the purpose strategical. Although the strike has by no means been abandoned by the organizations, the taking of a strike vote, as has been shown,[126] does not necessarily mean that a

124. The most serious strike during the period under discussion grew out of the refusal of a carrier ". . . to give sympathetic consideration to the recommendations of emergency boards set up by the President in prior cases; to apply awards of the National Railroad Adjustment Board; and to confer jointly with the duly accredited representatives of the employees as contemplated by the Railway Labor Act." (*Ibid.*) The second case, it will be recalled, arose in 1941, when the labor organizations rejected an emergency board's wage recommendations. See above, p. 343.
125. *First Annual Report*, 1935, p. 8.
126. Henig, *op. cit.*, p. 182.

strike is seriously contemplated. Here again strategy may be the key; it may be the carriers' strategy, or it may be the men's.

Compared with employees in other industries, have not railroad employees fared well without having to resort to the inconveniences and expenses of strikes? An even more pertinent question is —have not the policies of the railroad labor unions contributed in some degree to the condition of the roads, and might not some modification of those policies be to their own advantage as well as to that of the carriers? Collective bargaining should surely do more than merely promote peaceful relations, important as this is; it should at the same time work with a fair degree of justice for both sides, and it should be directed at the vital problems of the industry. The railroad industry has been and still is beset with financial difficulties. Railroad employees have seen their numbers cut in half during the past two decades. In what ways, if at all, have the policies of the railroad labor organizations, and those of the carriers, been shaped to meet these problems?

General Wage Level

For an industry that has felt the effects of acute and prolonged depression far more than its competitors, and is actually experiencing a secular decline in demand for its service, the railroad labor organizations have made surprisingly few concessions. They have lost no opportunity to press for higher wages. They accepted, reluctantly, a 10 per cent deduction in 1932. They were successful in having this restored by 1935, and in securing an increase of 7.5 or 8 per cent in 1937. They refused to submit to the 15 per cent reduction sought by the carriers in 1938, and had the satisfaction of seeing their position upheld by the President's Emergency Board which was appointed to look into the controversy. Despite the decline in railroad traffic and employment, hourly earnings of railroad employees at that time were 7.2 per cent higher than they were in 1920, and 15.5 per cent higher than they were in 1929.[127] It will be recalled, however, that the Board concluded that the level of wages of railroad labor was not high when compared

---

127. *Report of the Emergency Board* appointed by the President September 27, 1938, p. 36.

with wage levels in other industries, and that railroad wages had not advanced proportionately more than other wages. Average hourly earnings of employees in twenty-five manufacturing industries were 18 per cent higher in 1938 than in 1920, and 21.2 per cent higher than in 1929.[128]

While maintaining and even bettering their wage structure, the railroad labor organizations have won other gains. The Washington Job Protection Agreement which protects them against unemployment and enforced acceptance of inferior positions because of consolidations, mergers, etc., is a unique and important development in labor relations in this country. Partly through collective bargaining and partly through their legislative efforts, railroad employees enjoy considerably greater protection against unemployment and old age than employees who come under the Social Security Act. In contrast to the share-the-work policy followed in most industries, the seniority principle on the railroads further safeguards the older men in the industry, though at the expense of the younger men and some no longer young. In view of these advantages, not shared by employees in industry generally, would railroad employees make too great a sacrifice if they accepted a somewhat lower level of wages? And inasmuch as wages average something over 60 per cent of total cost of railroad operations, would not a lower level contribute materially to the welfare of the industry and at the same time permit greater employment?

If it were clear that these results would follow from a lower wage level, such a request would seem not unreasonable. Unfortunately it is not clear. If all the savings thus brought about were passed on in the form of lower freight and passenger rates, there would doubtless be some increase in the volume of traffic and employment. Even if there were no significant increase in the volume of traffic, a lower wage level still might lead to some increased employment, especially in maintenance of track and equipment. The employees take the position, however, that such savings might go to pay fixed charges and dividends instead; that a disproportionate share of any benefits which might follow from a general lowering of wages would go to the larger and more

128. *Ibid.*

prosperous roads, which do not need it, rather than to more distressed ones which do. They argue that no small part of the roads' difficulties result from preventable wastes, estimated in some quarters at a million dollars a day; from overcapitalization of railroad property, with its burden of fixed charges; and from mistakes of management. They see no justification for a general reduction in wages until management has set its own house in order.[129]

Problem of Wage Uniformity

However, even granting that wages, taking the railroads as a whole, are not excessively high, there can be no doubt that they are too high for many roads to pay. Such roads, while not free to discontinue operations altogether, are forced to cut down on their services and curtail employment. In other industries, hosiery manufacture for example, where standardization of wages does not prevail, such cases are cared for by adjustments in wages. In the railroad industry the control of adjustments rests with the international officers of the unions who are unwilling to make concessions, even though the workers immediately concerned may be willing, indeed anxious, that they be made. There appear to be two reasons for this attitude: the first is that such action would jeopardize national standardization of wages; the other is the belief that any relief given would probably be siphoned off by the big roads through rentals and division of joint rates, with the result that the distressed carriers would get little if any relief, and the employees no more work.

Management and Labor Must Share Responsibility

The vital importance of the railroads in our national life makes their problems, and those of railroad employees, matters of na-

---

129. These arguments, among others, were advanced before the President's Emergency Board in 1938. See their *Report*, pp. 25 ff. Labor costs have actually declined since the 1920's. ". . . the pay-roll cost per car-mile (all services) was 5.06 cents in 1913, rose to 12.5 cents in 1920, and in 1937 was 6.72 cents. The freight pay-roll cost per ton-mile (not distinguished from passenger expenses before 1920) was 5.93 mills in 1920, 4.25 mills in 1926, 4.14 mills in 1929, and 3.57 mills in 1937. From this it appears that despite the higher railway wages and annual compensation, freight cost per ton-mile in 1937 was very much lower than prior to 1929, subject to qualification as to difference in degree of adequacy of maintenance in the two years." *Statistics of Railways in the United States*, ICC, 1937, p. S-37.

tional concern. Some of the basic causes of the conditions which have plagued the industry during the past two decades, and especially the past ten years, are beyond the control of either management or employees. They are to be found in our lack of a comprehensive transportation policy, in the overdevelopment of facilities, in the technological and structural changes and in the loss of traffic. Part of the responsibility, however, must be shared by management and employees. Management has shown less initiative in meeting its problems than might reasonably have been expected. It has been too ready to call for higher rates as a way out. Somewhat belatedly, it has attempted to meet competition, with considerable success, by lighter, faster trains, and by various trucking and pick-up and delivery services, designed to attract and win back the patronage of passengers and shippers. And it has sought legislation which would place the railroads more nearly on a basis of competitive equality with other forms of transportation.

Commendable as these steps are, it is extremely doubtful if they are enough to meet the problems. Others must be taken. To whatever extent it may exist waste must be eliminated. The capital structure of the industry needs a thoroughgoing readjustment which will bring valuation and earning power more nearly in line. Finally, little progress has been made in bringing about consolidations and coordination of facilities, a requisite, obviously, for any long-run solution of the railroad problem.

The railroad labor organizations likewise must accept their share of the responsibility and must modify some of their policies for genuine rehabilitation of the industry. Because of wide differences in the earning power of the roads, any wholly satisfactory solution of the wage problem will be difficult as long as the roads operate on an individual basis and the unions insist on national standardization of wages. Consolidation of the railroads of the country into a few large systems, proposals for which have been under consideration since 1920, would contribute greatly to a solution. Unless and until this can be achieved, a modification of wage policy which would allow distressed roads some concessions would be to the advantage of the roads and would undoubtedly give more employment. Management and employees could probably work out some arrangement whereby this could be done without jeopardizing wages on more prosperous roads. It would need no great sacrifice on the part of the employees, where, as is true in many cases, railroad wages are high as compared to wages in other industries in the vicinity.

Although railroad management, as a whole, has not shown great zeal in bringing about consolidations,[130] not all blame for failure in this direction can be placed at its door. Despite the protection guaranteed railroad employees by the Washington Job Protection Agreement, the unions have steadily opposed consolidations and mergers, and claim to have blocked them in some cases. While the protection of the Washington Agreement may not be enough, it is much greater than most employees in other industries enjoy. Unreasonable though it is to ask employees to bear the major cost of economies effected by consolidations, where consolidations are clearly in the best interests of the industry and of the public, they should be made.

Obsolete Rules Need Renovation

The purpose of rules in the agreements is to protect the worker on the job against discrimination and hardship. They have developed on the individual roads and many of them have been drawn to meet particular situations. Where efforts are made to make them work universally, as in negotiations between management and union officials, and before the Adjustment Board, they become both inequitable and uneconomical. They have developed by a process of accretion over a long time. Appropriate once, some of them are almost certainly obsolete now. There is little doubt that some of them are "make-work" devices. They fall in the same category with much of the train-length and full-crew legislation, and are not conducive to economy nor always necessary for efficient operation. A thoroughgoing revision and modernization of

[130]. "Railroad executives are wont to say that section 7 (b) has stopped coordination projects. They have not yet, however, shown ability to put through such projects, even if there were no section 7 (b). It is beside the point to talk about labor restrictions when the managements are themselves unable to agree, or for other reasons are unwilling to act constructively...." *Fourth Report of the Federal Coordinator of Transportation,* 74th Cong., 2d sess., H. Doc. 394 (1936), p. 38. This observation would seem to apply equally well to the Washington Agreement.

agreements, which would eliminate all uneconomical and obsolete rules, and bring others into line with technical developments in the industry, is a joint responsibility of both management and employees. That such a revision would result in substantial savings to the carriers has, however, been questioned.[131]

Management and employees have repeatedly and consistently demonstrated their willingness and ability to work together. Joint negotiations have been successfully extended to many problems common to the whole industry. The legislation recently passed by Congress, embodying, in part, the findings and recommendations of the Committee of Six, a joint committee representing the carriers and the organizations, is an outstanding example of cooperative effort to rehabilitate the industry. But that will not be sufficient in itself. Maturity of the railroad industry has brought with it problems which are absent or of less importance in young and expanding industries. If the railroads are to be genuinely rehabilitated, both management and employees will have to make some readjustments and some sacrifices. Collective bargaining has accomplished a great deal on the railroads. Much remains to be done.

131. "The extent of the financial burden imposed on the carriers by the various working rules is not subject to measurement. Informed opinion among the carriers estimates the total savings that might accrue from the elimination of what they consider 'unjustifiable' working rules at a slight fraction of the total operation wage bill." Harold G. Moulton, *et al.*, *The American Transportation Problem*, Brookings Institution, Washington, 1933, p. 193. The findings of the Federal Coordinator of Transportation are much to the same effect: "The impression that labor agreement rules necessarily add to the cost of railroad operation and that if the rules were eliminated, the labor cost of the railroads would be greatly reduced, is erroneous. If there were no jointly agreed-to rules, it would still be necessary for railroad managements to regulate conditions of employment by general orders and instructions in the nature of rules. In such orders and instructions it is probable that most of the provisions of the present rules would still find a place, for it would still be necessary for the management to reimburse their employees for services rendered, in accordance with a suitable system of payments. The mere fact that the rules are jointly agreed-to, that is to say, are the product of collective bargaining, does not inevitably make them more costly to the railroads than if they were simply promulgated by management." *A Survey of the Rules Governing Wage Payments in Railroad Train and Engine Service*, 1936, Vol. I, p. S-10.

Chapter 8

MEN'S CLOTHING[1]

ROBERT J. MYERS and JOSEPH W. BLOCH

LABOR RELATIONS in few American industries have commanded more public interest than those in the production of men's clothing. Once notorious for sweatshops and frequent, bitter strikes, this industry has won during the past quarter-century wide recognition for its effective welfare programs and the peaceful cooperation between its workers and employers. In recent years it has provided one of the best-known American examples of industrial democracy.

Because of its long and rich experience and distinctive features, the industry's system of collective bargaining is a particularly inviting subject of study. During the past thirty years it has developed and tested policies and techniques which are utilized effectively in many industries. Bringing together individual employers or weak, local associations of employers, on the one hand, and on the other a highly centralized union whose membership embraces over 90 per cent of the industry's wage earners, it has helped to answer the question, "What would happen if a union should become strong enough to exercise a predominant influence in an

1. The following are only a few of the many publications dealing with collective bargaining in the men's clothing industry: *The Hart, Schaffner and Marx Labor Agreements*, compiled by Sidney Hillman and Earl Dean Howard, 1914; Charles H. Winslow, "Collective Agreements in the Men's Clothing Industry," *Bulletin No. 198*, U. S. Bureau of Labor Statistics, 1916; *The Clothing Workers of Chicago, 1910–1922*, Chicago Joint Board, Amalgamated Clothing Workers of America, 1922; Francis J. Haas, *Shop Collective Bargaining: A Study of Wage Determination in the Men's Garment Industry*, Charles H. Potter, Washington, 1922; Charles E. Zaretz, *The Amalgamated Clothing Workers of America*, Ancon Publishing Co., New York, 1934; Robert H. Connery, *The Administration of an N.R.A. Code: A Case Study of The Men's Clothing Industry*, Public Administration Service, 1938; George Soule, *Sidney Hillman, Labor Statesman*, Macmillan, New York, 1939. The Research Department of the Amalgamated Clothing Workers issues an excellent bibliography for use in studying labor relations or other aspects of the industry.

industry?" At the same time, it has shown certain limitations of collective action by workers.

Recent developments affecting labor relations in the industry have been as significant as those of the past. The union's current Stabilization Plan promises to write a new chapter in the history of industrial control.

Labor relations in the men's clothing industry have been much influenced by certain factors, such as the geographic location of the industry, the technical processes of clothing production and the industry's capital structure. A full understanding of the industry's bargaining system demands some consideration of these factors.

1. CHARACTERISTICS OF THE INDUSTRY

Men's wearing apparel, including shoes and hats and the various intervening aids to comfort and decency, is manufactured in a dozen or more different industries, most of which are clearly distinguishable in terms of materials used and equipment and processes involved in production. The men's clothing industry produces for both men and boys such outer clothing as suits, topcoats and overcoats, separate pants, vests, coats, uniforms and knickers. Most of its products are of wool. The production of work clothing and of various types of washable outer clothing used chiefly for summer wear and for sports involves different productive processes and is carried on in separate industries, excluded from the present discussion.

a. HISTORICAL DEVELOPMENT

Until about a century ago men's clothing in this country was almost invariably made by women at home, or by itinerant tailors. Even as late as 1880 only 40 per cent was ready-to-wear.[2] This was poorly made, ill-fitting and worn only by those who could afford nothing better.

Ready-made clothing improved greatly in quality and fit toward

[2] *Report of the Committee on Manufactures on the Sweating System,* U. S. House of Representatives, 1893, p. V.

the end of the century and, with the support of effective national advertising, rapidly made its way into general use. By World War days it had overcome all serious competition and was the customary garb of our adult male population. Although Census figures at that time failed to distinguish the men's clothing industry from work clothing and other related industries, it appears that in 1914 over 125,000 wage earners were making men's clothes. By this measure the industry was undoubtedly among the fifteen largest manufacturing industries in the United States.

Clothing production since the World War has been marked by extreme cycles and has failed to show the gains apparent in manufacturing production generally. The industry's highest level of output was achieved during a brief period of riotous expansion in 1919–1920 and in the prosperous year 1923. The value of the product dropped almost without interruption during the following decade, and in 1937, the best recent year, was still approximately 30 per cent below the 1923 level. Probably half the decrease from 1923 to 1937 was caused by lower clothing prices. Influenced somewhat by lower hourly rates and the displacement of labor by machinery, payrolls fell 25 per cent. With shorter hours and spreading of work, the average number of workers employed was still at the 1923 level.[3]

It could not be expected that the industry's early rate of growth would be maintained, once it had achieved complete domination of the men's clothing field. If relative production costs and consumer demand remained unchanged, the general trend of production should have been roughly parallel to the slow growth of the adult population. This would have meant an increase of over 30 per cent during the past twenty years instead of the decrease which actually occurred. But it is evident that the importance of clothing to the consumer has declined. As an item of warmth and comfort it has felt the influence of improved interior heating and the closed car. As an article of conspicuous consumption it appears to have lost ground to the automobile, the radio and other competi-

---

3. Preliminary 1939 figures released by the Census of Manufactures reveal a further slight decline (1.7 per cent) in the value of product from 1937 to 1939, and an increase (1.2 per cent) in the number of wage earners employed.

tors for the consumer's income.[4] Such factors, however, can hardly exercise a controlling influence indefinitely, and it is expected that clothing manufacture will sooner or later resume a definite, though moderate, upward movement.[5]

Still, men's clothing is one of the nation's leading industries. The Census reveals that in 1937 it included approximately 1,300 manufacturing and 900 contract shops, which together employed 138,000 workers and paid out $142 million in wages. The industry turned out 22 million suits, 7 million overcoats and topcoats, and over 25 million separate coats, vests, pants and miscellaneous garments. Their total value was $557 million. The industry is one of the major consumers of wool cloth, using, in a year such as 1937, in the neighborhood of 200 million square yards.

b. LOCATION OF THE INDUSTRY

A marked characteristic of the industry is its concentration in and about a few large cities. In 1937 nine centers employed roughly three fourths of the industry's workers and turned out four fifths of the product. The industrial area about New York City alone accounted for a fourth of the workers and a third of the product. Philadelphia, with fewer than half as many workers, was second, and Chicago a fairly close third. The six remaining centers, in order of number of workers employed, were Rochester, Baltimore, Cleveland, Cincinnati, Boston and St. Louis.[6] Sizable

---

4. The effect of these factors has undoubtedly been offset in part by reductions in the relative cost of clothing production. Unfortunately, however, comparable data on physical output are not available.

5. Recent medium estimates of population growth indicate that the number of men and boys fifteen years of age or older, now about fifty million, will increase about 9 per cent by 1950, and will reach its peak of roughly sixty-two million some two or three decades later.

6. The number of workers and value of products for the nine industrial areas in 1937 were as follows: New York City, 35,800 workers, $224 million; Philadelphia, 15,700 workers, $71 million; Chicago, 13,100 workers, $53 million; Rochester, 8,700 workers, $29 million; Baltimore, 8,300 workers, $34 million; Cleveland, 6,400 workers, $34 million; Cincinnati, 5,600 workers, $22 million; Boston, 4,500 workers, $22 million; St. Louis, 2,300 workers, $10 million. The figures on value of product include the cost of contract work, which involves some duplication; the effect of this is to exaggerate somewhat the importance of the three chief contract markets, New York, Philadelphia and Baltimore. The larger cities—particularly New York—naturally serve as distributing centers for greater amounts of clothing than they manufacture.

amounts of clothing are also produced in Buffalo, Syracuse, Indianapolis, Richmond, Nashville, Milwaukee, New Orleans and various smaller places, chiefly in the East. Only about 3 per cent of the workers in the industry are employed west of St. Louis.

About the beginning of the World War the industry was much more concentrated than it now is. From 1909 to 1929 the proportion of workers employed in the nine chief centers fell off by nearly a third. This outward movement, which has been retarded or stopped only within the past six or seven years, affected first and most severely the Chicago market and later, the New York, Baltimore and Rochester markets. Philadelphia and smaller places known to the trade as "country towns" showed healthy gains.

Although technological changes reducing the importance of skilled labor helped the movement, undoubtedly the chief motivating force was management's wish to avoid unionization. Decentralization began simultaneously with the rise of the Amalgamated; Chicago and other union strongholds were hardest hit, while the open shop market of Philadelphia expanded. Only a policy of union moderation and cooperation finally checked the exodus from the major centers.

C. ECONOMIC CHARACTERISTICS

In the men's clothing industry ownership and management are still generally in the same hands. Concentration of manufacture has made little headway; production, though considerably mechanized, is not highly automatic, and the trade retains numerous other features outgrown by some leading industries more than half a century ago. Those economic characteristics of the industry have probably helped rather than hindered successful collective bargaining.

The Demand for Clothing

Though there are no statistics to prove it, observation and other evidence indicates that purchases of men's clothing are appreciably influenced by the price per garment. Family records, for example, show that the percentage of family expenditures devoted to clothing rises markedly as income increases.[7] Variations in national income appear to be accompanied by more than proportionate variations in clothing production. Elasticity of demand is, of course, to be expected of goods largely for adornment and display. The relatively large outlay for a suit or overcoat also contributes to elasticity of demand since even a small change, say 10 per cent, in the price is important to most consumers.

Clearly the nature of the demand for clothing must be taken into account in the determination of labor policy. An elastic demand means that an increase in wages or a rise in piece goods prices, other conditions remaining the same, will result in some reduction of employment. Conversely, reduction of costs can be expected to bring expanded production and new employment opportunities.[8]

Pronounced seasonal variations in demand result in seasonal production and seasonal employment. Peak production, in contrast with peaks of retail selling, usually comes in midsummer and midwinter. Spring and fall are normally slack periods.

This seasonality undoubtedly increases the cost of clothing, with probably little effect on average profits. The typical worker is unemployed a fifth to a quarter of the time owing to seasonal fluctuations alone. Such unemployment does not appear to be offset by high wage rates.

Productive Processes

The technical processes of clothing manufacture are extremely intricate and familiar in their entirety to few persons in the industry.[9]

The major operations are: (1) designing the models; (2) sponging (shrinking) and examining the fabric; (3) cutting the fabric and trimmings from patterns; (4) sewing fabric and trim-

---

7. National Resources Committee, *Consumer Expenditures in the United States,* 1939, p. 79; see also Table 14A, p. 81.
8. A change in only one item of cost will, of course, result in a much smaller proportionate change in retail price.
9. For a full discussion of manufacturing processes, see M. E. Popkin, *Organization, Management and Technology in the Manufacture of Men's Clothing,* I. Pitman & Sons, New York, 1929.

mings together into garments; and (5) pressing the garments into shape at various stages of production. Designing, sponging and examining require the services of few employees. Sewing operations need the most.

Cutting and trimming rooms are usually in the central establishment, near the executive offices, sales rooms and stock rooms. Assembly of coats, pants and vests, respectively, is carried on in separate shops—frequently near the workers' homes and several miles from the cutting rooms.

Nearly all productive operations can be performed by machine and all grades of men's clothing sold in any quantity involve much machine work. Hand-tailored garments, however, are better fitting, more flexible and retain their shape better than those made entirely by machine. Better grades of clothing, consequently, contain more hand work than poorer grades.

Extensive use of machinery means wide division of labor; in some large concerns more than two hundred and fifty workers participate in the manufacture of a single suit. Two types of cutting machines, several scores of different sewing machines, and more than a dozen kinds of pressing machines are in common use. This equipment is not of a highly automatic type. Each piece requires the full attention of a dexterous worker. The past twenty years have brought few new machines, but many improvements have been introduced and sewing machine speed has been greatly accelerated. These developments, together with some relaxation of consumers' standards of quality, have lowered skill requirements and reduced the man hours of labor for making a suit.

Many Small Producers

The few well-known companies which make clothing in large daylight factories and advertise nationally exercise great influence on the industry, but they are by no means typical. Their output is but a small part of the industry's. In 1935 the eight largest companies employed only 10 per cent of all workers and turned out only 7 per cent of the total product. Of twenty-one manufacturing industries that employed a hundred thousand or more workers, only three showed less concentration of production in the largest concerns.[10] Among the thousand or more separate manufacturers producing men's clothing, a concern with a $1 million output is regarded as a good-sized firm. A big majority of all firms are less than half as large. Almost half the workers in the industry are on payrolls which list less than two hundred and fifty employees.[11] Such prevalence of small concerns makes contact between employers and workers easy and reduces employers' ability to resist unionism, but it does complicate enforcement of uniform labor standards.

The ease with which the industry can be entered accounts in part for the persistence of small concerns. The vital production processes are free from restrictive patents, designs can be "borrowed," woolens can be bought on credit,[12] space and equipment for cutting can be rented cheaply and the fabrication of garments can be turned over to contractors. Scores of small manufacturers begin with a capital of only $25,000, or even less. For the cheaper grades of clothing, the marketing advantages of an established reputation are slight and the economies of large-scale production are modest.

Ownership of the Industry

The typical men's clothing concern is a partnership or a closed corporation, the owners of which personally engage in the business. Much of the operating capital is supplied by the owners, either directly or from reinvested earnings.[13] Long-term borrow-

---

10. These figures are from a special tabulation of 1935 Census data, published in the National Resources Committee's *The Structure of the American Economy*, Pt. 1, "Basic Characteristics," Washington, June 1939, p. 241.

11. Since the typical large manufacturer operates several separate "shops," production units are smaller and more numerous than business units. In 1937, a third of the workers in the industry worked in shops employing one hundred workers or fewer. Eighty-five per cent of all shops were within this size class.

12. Until a few years ago the "easy credit" policy of the woolen mills was notorious. One executive admits that his company's credit recommendation was generally considered to be worthless. This policy was responsible for heavy losses during the depression. In recent years credit has been much more difficult to obtain.

13. The combined liabilities of twenty-nine fairly representative firms, as of the end of the year 1938, amounted to approximately $12 million, distributed as follows: accounts payable, 18 per cent; notes payable, 11 per cent; other liabilities (owed to contractors, wages payable, taxes payable, etc.), 11 per cent; capital stock, 24 per cent; surplus, 36 per cent.

ing is almost unknown in the industry. Consequently, when dealing with labor problems, management enjoys unusual freedom from interference by stockholders or creditors.

Components of Cost in Clothing Manufacture

Almost a third of the total sales revenue of men's clothing manufacturers is paid out for direct labor.[14] The percentage varies, of course, with the quality of the product, being greatest in expensive, hand-tailored garments. On the average, however, labor cost is somewhat higher in men's clothing than in manufactured products generally. This explains the importance of laborsaving devices and of any wage change. A 10 per cent change in hourly rates involves, it is true, only a 3 per cent change in the manufacturer's total cost, but in this industry of narrow margins such a percentage may equal the manufacturer's profit. The labor cost of a medium-grade suit is around $5 or $6, which pays for seven or eight hours of labor.

The largest cost item is materials—more than half of sales revenue. Materials consist chiefly of woolen "piece goods," although the typical suit also includes approximately twenty varieties of trimmings. Piece goods have wide and abrupt price fluctuations, and their purchase for stock involves considerable speculation. Without an organized futures market to permit effective hedging against price changes, clothing manufacturers buy partly on a hand-to-mouth basis. The danger inherent in inventory specula-

14. Profit and loss statements of the twenty-nine firms mentioned reveal aggregate net sales in 1938 amounting to $23 million. This was distributed as follows:

Item	Per Cent
Net Sales	100.0
Labor	33.0
Materials	51.2
Factory overhead	2.5
Cost of goods sold	86.7
General overhead	13.2
Net income	.1

These figures slightly exaggerate labor cost, since accounting practice in the industry includes with direct labor all payments to contractors. Actually only about 75 or 80 per cent of the contractor's income is paid out to manufacturing employees. Several of the twenty-nine manufacturers had garments made up in contract shops.

tion restricts manufacture for stock and is partly responsible for seasonal unemployment.

Since expenditures for factory space and equipment are relatively unimportant items, the full-time use of such property is a secondary consideration. This contributes to irregular production and employment, but also explains the ease with which the short week has been achieved. The more highly specialized machines are economical to operate only when division of labor is great. Even then the advantages are partly offset by increased rigidity and greater problems of supervision. Such operations as sponging cannot be performed economically by the small manufacturer and ordinarily are turned over to a specialist, on a contract basis. Production advantages of large-scale operation, therefore, are extremely limited, and allow small firms doing $500,000 worth of business to compete on fairly even terms with a concern ten times as large.

The Contract System

Under the contract system the manufacturer cuts out materials and trimmings in his own factory or "loft," assembles the pieces in "bundles" and sends them by truck to coat, vest and pants contractors to be made up. The manufacturer, of course, buys the materials, and designs and sells the garments, while the contractor has no expenses except for direct labor and certain factory and general overhead items. Contractors are always specialists, most of them making coats, vests or pants of a given quality. Some contractors specialize still further, making, say, only "coat fronts" or buttonholes. Even large firms frequently contract out the sponging and examining of cloth.

The fact that contract shops in 1937 numbered over nine hundred and employed nearly a third of all workers in the industry shows the importance of the system. Contracting is concentrated, however, largely in New York, Baltimore and Philadelphia; half or more of all men's clothing produced in these markets is made in contract shops.

Relationships between the contractor and the manufacturer are rather complex. A manufacturer making two distinct grades of clothing deals regularly with at least six contractors—two for coats, two for vests, and two for pants—in addition to a sponging house and a coat front shop. Unless the manufacturer has a fairly large business, probably none of these contractors works for him exclusively. Various units of a garment may be produced in different sections of the city, or in different cities, and by workers of different nationality. It is consequently difficult to maintain uniform quality standards under the contract system.

Many of the industry's labor problems come from this system. The contractors, usually poor managers, sometimes ignorant and often on the verge of relief, are extremely weak bargainers. When acting independently they are constantly played against one another by the manufacturers, induced to cut prices to get work and forced to cut wages to stay in business. A half century ago, when contracting was even more common than now, "sweatshop" and "contract shop" were almost synonymous. Even now contract shops pay the lowest wages in the eastern markets.

The contract shops make possible expansion of output in boom times after manufacturers exhaust the capacity of their "inside" shops, and they are the first to suffer when business falls off. Employment in them is more irregular than in any other part of the industry. The smallest shops are hard to find and hard to organize. Fly-by-night contractors have sometimes decamped without meeting payrolls. Nonunion contract shops have offered a ready means of completing strike-bound work. The control of the contract shop has been one of the most challenging tasks the union has faced, and the policies which have been successful in accomplishing this task are of fundamental importance in the study of collective bargaining.

A Competitive Industry

Competition in the men's clothing industry is relentless, no quarter is asked or given. Small capital requirements, ease of obtaining materials and equipment and the extent of the contract system encourage scores of new producers to enter the industry whenever business is good.[15] Competition is on a national basis. The cost of transporting a suit halfway across the country is but a small percentage of the retail price. Hence the larger producers sell garments throughout the United States, and any disturbance of competitive relationships, such as an increase of production cost affecting only one market, alters the location of the industry promptly and appreciably.

The competitive nature of the industry is tremendously important both to owners and workers. Profits are usually modest.[16] None of the country's great fortunes has come from production of men's clothing, nor has monopoly ever threatened. Moreover, the rapid flow of capital in and out gives the industry a remarkable resiliency. Coming after a decade of stagnation, the 1929–1932 depression cut production value to less than half the 1923 level, forced hundreds of producers out of business, and caused heavy losses throughout the industry. By 1933, however, most of the firms still in business were making money, and by 1935 prosperity was general.

The mobility that has characterized capital has, to be sure, been markedly lacking among the workers.[17] This explains in part the prevalence of part-time employment and wide fluctuations in hourly rates.

So footloose is the industry and so significant is any change in labor cost that even a minor wage differential may result in a shift from one market to another. The experience of Chicago and the other union markets during the twenties proved that such a shift may quickly throw thousands out of work and threaten the union's very existence. Faced with resistance to increased wages in some

---

15. The marketing advantages of large producers appear to be relatively unimportant. Clothing is usually sold direct to the retailer, with no jobber intervening. Except for purchases by chain stores and occasional retailers' associations, buying is usually in small lots. A major development in the last fifteen years has been the increase in ownership or control of retail outlets by the large manufacturers.

16. In 1936, the most profitable recent year, twenty-nine firms for which complete figures are available showed net profits equal to 12 per cent of net worth. This is exceptionally high for an average rate and reflects generous gains from inventory appreciation. Profits as a percentage of sales revenue rarely exceed 5 per cent.

17. The effect of the various union devices for work spreading on the number of workers retained in the industry since the early twenties is discussed briefly on pp. 445-446.

markets—particularly the unorganized markets—the union has been forced to adopt a policy of moderation in all. The program worked out under these difficulties is none the less significant because it has been prompted by self-preservation rather than by benevolence.

2. Clothing Workers and the Amalgamated

It is a simple matter today to recognize in the clothing workers the qualities essential to democratic government. Their union, the Amalgamated Clothing Workers of America, among the strongest and most progressive of American labor organizations, is widely accepted as a natural response of determined and intelligent employees to adverse economic conditions. Thirty years ago, however, when the industry was on the threshold of collective bargaining, the picture was far different. It seemed incredible that the wretched clothing workers could demand and attain an influential voice in the conduct of their industry. The characteristics of the workers and their union have played an important part in transforming their industrial relations.

a. THE WORKERS

The clothing industries have depended largely on immigrant labor. Even in 1930 three out of five workers in "suit, coat and overall factories"—the highest percentage for any industry—were foreign-born, and a large proportion of the natives were of foreign parentage. About the same time the Amalgamated was issuing official publications in eight different languages, and 56 per cent of the delegates to the 1938 biennial convention listed foreign countries as place of birth. The Jews, who provide many of the union leaders, are commonly believed to be the most numerous of the various racial and national groups in the industry; actually they are outnumbered by non-Jewish Italians.

Other than foreign background, modern clothing workers have little in common with the poorly assimilated workers of sweatshop days. The typical worker today has at least an elementary education, and his children are in high school or college. He is interested in politics, both European and American, and in social movements of all kinds. He is an orderly and efficient employee, a cooperative fellow worker, and a good citizen.

In part the assimilation of the clothing worker has been due to the curtailment of immigration, the improvement of his economic position and the extension of educational and cultural influences in this country. Most important, however, has been the harmonious and democratic influence of the Amalgamated Clothing Workers.

Sewing operations in making men's clothing draw women employees, who number slightly more than half of the entire working force. Although women have presented serious organization problems, they have been enrolled by the union in large numbers. They have supplied effective organizers and local officers and have been represented on the General Executive Board of the Amalgamated.

The workers' average age is relatively high. This reflects the low level of employment in recent years and the union policy of permanent tenure, which have reduced openings available for new workers. Even in 1930 over a third of all the workers in "suit, coat and overall factories" were forty-five years or older, while nearly half the skilled male workers were in this age group. In some markets, the numerous aged workers constitute a serious problem for employers and union alike.

Division of labor has reduced most jobs to fairly simple operations which can be mastered in a few weeks. The typical clothing worker, therefore, is not a highly skilled worker, but a specialist who performs one or two operations with great speed and dexterity. Except among the cutters and trimmers, whose exacting work on costly materials calls for coolness and deliberate care, payment by the piece is now almost universal.

b. THE AMALGAMATED

The difficulties met by the clothing workers in forming an effective union were unusually formidable. The intensity of competition, the poverty and helplessness of the early workers, their racial differences and the high proportion of women, seemed to doom organizing efforts to failure even before they began. The story of the Amalgamated's rise in face of these difficulties well deserves an important place in American labor history.

(1). *Early Clothing Workers' Unions*

Literally scores of unions lived and died in the men's clothing industry before the rise of the Amalgamated. Down to the eighties the only important unions were among the cutters, whose skill and key position give them an advantage in dealing with employers. The early cutters' unions were usually organized to gain some immediate end. Frequently they achieved it by striking, and thereafter died of sheer ennui, for advantages of continuous organization were insufficient to hold the workers' interest.[18] Progress in the unionization of other workers began with the entry of the Jews into the industry in the eighties. Organization activities were pushed by the newly founded American Federation of Labor, and by the United Hebrew Trades Union, founded in 1881 to unionize immigrant workers.

The United Garment Workers of America, organized in 1891, included both cutters and shop workers and became the first national union of clothing workers. The UGW affiliated with the American Federation of Labor, organized energetically, stressed the union label and agitated against sweatshops. It must be given considerable credit for the improvement in conditions apparent soon after 1890. Its greatest membership of almost 61,000 was attained in 1914, immediately before the secession of the Amalgamated group. Since then the persistent expansion of the Amalgamated has gradually forced the UGW out of the industry. Its members are now employed almost exclusively in work-clothing industries.

---

18. One of these, the Garment Cutters' Association of Philadelphia, was among the pioneers of the American labor movement. This union was organized in 1862, but seven years later was found by a majority of the members to be without purpose. Thereupon the membership divided the $89.79 remaining in the treasury and disbanded. From the ashes of this union sprang the Noble Order of the Knights of Labor. Another early cutters' union, but one with more lasting objectives, was the Boston Clothing Cutters' Union, organized in 1878. Except for a few years of affiliation with the United Garment Workers around the turn of the century, this union remained an independent organization until 1919, when it became Local 181 of the Amalgamated. This local is the oldest workers' organization in the industry.

(2). Rise of the Amalgamated

An important factor in the 1914 split was the controversy over industrial unionism. The insurgents charged that the national officers of the UGW were concentrating their efforts on the support of two protected groups, the cutters and the makers of work clothing, and were failing to extend and strengthen the organization in other parts of the industry. It was also claimed that the administration was autocratic and corrupt. Failing to obtain recognition from the AF of L as the true representatives of the UGW, the secessionists adopted a constitution and began an independent existence as the Amalgamated Clothing Workers of America. Delegates from sixty-eight locals were seated at the first convention, held in December 1914.

The new union claimed 38,000 members in July 1915. Most of them came from New York, Baltimore, Boston and certain smaller eastern markets, while Chicago (except for the firm of Hart, Schaffner and Marx), Rochester and Philadelphia were scarcely represented at all. After the World War the Chicago and Rochester markets were organized and tremendous gains were made throughout most of the industry. By 1920 the Amalgamated's membership, including Canadians and workers in related industries, was 177,000.

Although a number of notable victories were won in the following decade, chief of which was the brilliantly executed organization of the Philadelphia market in 1929, the membership trend was definitely downward. This was due chiefly to the industry's declining labor requirements and its movement away from the union strongholds. At the depth of the depression membership dropped below 70,000.

The National Recovery Administration introduced a new period of rising influence for the Amalgamated. Organizing activities were encouraged and protected by federal legislation. Union prestige was enhanced by its part in framing the men's clothing code, and by its admission in 1933 to the AF of L. At first as a result of shorter working hours, and later in response to expanding production, employment shot upward. The union won one victory after another against remaining nonunion clothing manufacturers, and enrolled thousands of workers in related industries.[19] In 1940 it claimed approximately 260,000, of whom roughly 135,000 were in the men's clothing industry. In the summer of 1941, *The New York Times* reported its membership as 275,000. There are now no more than a half-dozen sizable men's clothing firms with which it has failed to establish bargaining agreements.

Structure

Authority over Amalgamated policies and actions is concentrated largely in the hands of the international officers. The extent of this concentration is not entirely apparent from the constitution, which names the General Convention as the supreme authority and makes the customary provision for the referendum. In practice the General Convention, which has met only thirteen times in twenty-six years, exercises little actual control. The General Executive Board, consisting of the president, secretary-treasurer and fifteen other members, not only determines national policies, approves the admission of locals and represents the union in dealing with outside agencies, but also plans organization campaigns, supervises the major local welfare activities and controls national and local industrial relations.

Within the individual market the most authoritative unit is the Joint Board, which is chartered by the General Executive Board and is designed to represent the interests of the locals. Under the guidance of the international office the Joint Board plans and conducts the general market program. In collective bargaining it represents the union in market-wide negotiations and in dealing with all questions of fundamental importance.

Despite its great emphasis on industrial unionism, the Amalgamated is not organized strictly along industrial lines. The locals, of which there are several in each major market, and which numbered 170 in 1938,[20] are sometimes organized on a craft basis. The

---

19. These included chiefly the journeymen tailors, and shirt, neckwear, laundry, and cleaning and dyeing workers; in a few instances, however, the Amalgamated has opened its doors wide enough to admit isolated groups of button makers, retail clerks, photoengravers and macaroni makers.

20. This number includes only locals in the men's clothing industry. Another 171 locals existed for shirt workers, journeymen tailors, laundry workers and others.

cutters, for example, have a strong craft consciousness, and are always members of craft locals; in New York and Boston the cutters' locals are so powerful as to be almost independent of the Joint Boards. In some markets all the coat shop workers are in one local, and the pants shop and vest shop workers in others. In the larger markets where such groups would be unwieldy, shop workers are usually organized along fairly haphazard lines into more restricted groups. Thus there may be a local of Bohemian coat makers, a pressers' local, a Kuppenheimer's vest shop local and the like. Carrying on as they do social and educational activities, locals are convenient units for discussion, voting and dues collection.

Finances

The Amalgamated's devoted membership has been raised on the tradition of heavy sacrifice for the power that money gives a union. Initiation fees are limited by the constitution to $10, but dues average approximately $2 a month, including a 70-cent per capita tax which goes to the international office. Special assessments by the international office or the various Joint Boards are frequent. The Amalgamated has always had marked success in collecting dues, and its position is reinforced by the checkoff in its agreements in most markets.

The Amalgamated's financial resources have at times appeared prodigious. It has paid liberal strike benefits for months, sometimes, as an indication of its strength, increasing the rate in the middle of a strike. During a general lockout in several eastern markets in 1920 it raised a $2 million defense fund. Such resources explain in part the Amalgamated's effectiveness in industrial disputes. The union has also given hundreds of thousands of dollars to various liberal movements in which its members have been interested. In the two years ending January 31, 1940, the international office took in slightly more than $3 million, of which approximately $600,000 went into surplus. The estimated total income of the union in this period, including the Joint Boards' and the locals', was between $8 million and $9 million.

Leadership

Much of the strength of the Amalgamated unquestionably lies in its leadership. The men who have made decisions for it and directed its activities have been exceptional in their judgment, determination, integrity and absolute devotion to unionism.

Sidney Hillman, who emigrated from Russia in 1907, at the age of twenty, has been president of the Amalgamated ever since its organization in 1914. Working as a cutter at the Hart, Schaffner and Marx factory in Chicago in 1910, he witnessed the birth of the industry's system of collective bargaining; from the outset he played an important role in its development.

An inspiring leader, a good judge of men and a determined and tireless campaigner, Hillman deserves credit for many of the Amalgamated's victories. He is frankly admired and liked by most of the employers in the industry and has negotiated many a peaceful settlement when a strike or lockout seemed inevitable. His success in persuading the federal administration to buy more than $10 million of surplus clothing in 1938 did much to save the industry from chaos.

Hillman, to be sure, could not possibly accomplish all the work for which he is given credit. His lieutenants include half a dozen men of greater caliber than the typical international president, and a score of other key men who excel in some particular line. Moreover, when the proper man is not available from within the ranks, the Amalgamated's policy is to find one and press him into service. Thus, whatever it undertakes, an organizing campaign, a strike, labor banking, unemployment insurance or a difficult piece of research, the person in charge is almost sure to be an expert in his line.

In its early days the Amalgamated was led by youths in their twenties and thirties. From among those early leaders largely came the officers in control today. The union recognizes as one of its problems the development of new leaders capable of assuming responsibility in the future.

Objectives

Soon after its organization, the Amalgamated was named as an outstanding exponent of "the new unionism"—a unionism consciously tending toward a new social order.[21] Considerable basis existed for this claim. The preamble of the union's constitution fairly bristled with class consciousness. When the 1914 New York convention called on union members to support "their own political party" it was not thought necessary to mention that this was the Socialist Party; and a declaration on "Public Control of Industry," drawn up by the General Executive Board in 1918 and unanimously approved by the convention, stated that "the war has demonstrated the complete bankruptcy of private ownership in industry. . . . Conditions are now fully ripe for the public ownership of industries, with the workers in them in control."

Toward the end of the Amalgamated's first decade, however, the visions of a new society began to fade. A number of economic developments, including a gigantic lockout in 1920 and the depression of 1920–1921, had strengthened the convictions of the more practical of the leaders, who were now becoming increasingly articulate and persistent. Expansion of membership among the more conservative groups outside New York City was another influential factor. Anyway, when the constitution was revised in 1922 its stirring preamble was omitted, and soon afterward the discussion of imminent control of industry by the workers was dropped.

Today the Amalgamated must be included among the most farsighted and liberal of labor organizations. Adequate incomes, favorable hours and comfortable working conditions, it is true, constitute more important objectives than in the union's earliest years, but it has frequently shown willingness to sacrifice such obvious and immediate gains for the sake of spreading employment, benefiting the weakest bargainers in its ranks, and maintaining a stable and orderly industry. The union has continued to show a strong interest in the general labor movement. Its enthusiastic support of the CIO led to its suspension from the AF of L in 1936, after only three years of affiliation.

21. J. M. Budish and George Soule, *The New Unionism in the Clothing Industry*, Harcourt, Brace and Howe, New York, 1920.

Program

The Amalgamated's program has touched every field of union activity, but its changing emphasis has clearly reflected the evolution of the union's policy.

In its early days the Amalgamated emphasized adult education, cooperation with the general labor movement and support of the Socialist Party. In 1922 it launched the Russian-American Industrial Corporation "to facilitate and encourage the investment of American capital in Russia." Since the early twenties, however, its program has been somewhat more practical. The workers' education branch, earlier preoccupied with music, literature and other cultural subjects, now emphasizes labor economics and the history of trade unionism. Support of the general labor movement has continued, but along fairly conventional lines,[22] and the Amalgamated's major political activity has been in behalf of candidates of the old line parties. Recently it has shown increasing interest in the union label, and has strongly supported state and federal labor legislation.

Much of the Amalgamated's energy since its first decade has gone to collective bargaining and to the support of other practical devices for stabilizing and increasing the workers' income, such as employment exchanges (introduced in 1922), labor banking (1922), unemployment insurance (1923), credit unions (1923), cooperative housing (1926), the dismissal wage (1926), investment trusts (1926), unemployment relief (1932), sickness benefits (1939) and life insurance (1939).

Each of the union's many activities follows a carefully worked out plan, administered by able executives with full support of the Amalgamated. The employment exchanges, for example, have served both workers and employers effectively for years. The unemployment insurance plan in Chicago paid out approximately $10 million in benefits, before being transformed into a life insurance and sickness benefit system, as a result of the passage of the Social Security Act. Beyond their more direct benefits, such

---

22. In order to promote organization activities of workers in the steel, textile and automobile industries the Amalgamated has contributed generously of its financial resources and the ability of its officers.

activities have had great publicity value and have done much to hold the membership's interest and enthusiasm.

Always the Amalgamated has worked ceaselessly for complete organization of the industry. Because of the strategy of its leaders and the zeal of its organizers, it has been unusually effective. Although it has encountered the yellow-dog contract, the blacklist, spying and violence, it has rarely lost any fight for recognition.

In strikes and lockouts the Amalgamated has been a dreaded foe. Among its famous fights were the 1920 New York lockout and the 1925 International Tailoring Company strike, both of which it won, and the Curlee strike of 1925, which it lost. At times it has responded to calls for strikebreakers by providing its own members, who later led new strikes; and when faced with violence or blocked by injunction it has shown its ability to fight fire with fire.

Sometimes cooperation succeeded where force failed. One important New York firm decisively defeated Amalgamated organizing attempts for years. Then a new firm member, given the task of reorganizing production, convinced the management that he needed the Amalgamated's help; whereupon the firm urged its employees to join the union it once fought.

3. The Employers

Organization and cooperation did not come naturally to the industry's employers. In most markets it has taken real emergencies to bring about any organization at all, and the associations formed have typically been weak and short-lived. This not only delayed the inauguration of collective bargaining but obstructed its successful operation.

The Amalgamated has preferred to deal with associations rather than with individual firms and has strongly supported both market and national organizations. The primitive state of organization among employers is due chiefly to intense competition and rapid turnover among firms, and to characteristics of the employers themselves.

a. CHARACTERISTICS OF THE EMPLOYERS

Employer background is surprisingly similar to the workers'. Most employers are immigrants or sons of immigrants. As late as 1930 fully two thirds of the proprietors, managers and officials [23] in "suit, coat and overall factories" were foreign-born. Practically all of the manufacturers are Jewish. Many were workers in earlier years or come from families long engaged in clothing manufacture.

Although inclined to be a suspicious and obstinate competitor, the typical manufacturer or contractor is a sympathetic employer. Having few workers, he knows them and their problems well.

The level of managerial ability is unquestionably low among the small employers who predominate in the industry. Obsolete equipment and organization remain much longer than is justified by economic considerations. Cost accounting is unknown among hundreds of small firms, pricing is dependent on rule-of-thumb methods and marketing is extremely wasteful. The Committee on Waste in Industry in 1921 rated the industry as the most wasteful among six industries examined, and held management 75 per cent responsible.[24]

In large firms which can afford specialized executives, management is on a respectable level. Yet, in analyzing market situations or in presenting a case to an arbitrator, few manufacturers can match singlehanded the experienced leaders of the Amalgamated.

b. EMPLOYERS' ASSOCIATIONS

Employers' associations existed in the men's clothing industry at least fifty years ago. Most of the early ones were organized to fight unions. They accumulated large war chests, commonly made use of blacklists and espionage, and later, injunctions and yellow-dog contracts. Some associations, like the early unions, were formed to deal with urgent problems, and went out of existence when the problems were solved. Others were designed to function permanently but could not keep going. Probably the oldest

---

23. For proprietors alone the proportion would be somewhat smaller.
24. *Waste in Industry*, Committee on Elimination of Waste in Industry of the Federated American Engineering Societies, Washington, 1921, p. 9.

association active today is the Rochester Clothiers' Exchange, organized about 1890.

With the conquest of the industry by the Amalgamated, associations were revived or were formed to sign agreements in nearly all of the major markets. In Chicago, in 1919, the several associations then in existence in different branches formed a joint organization to deal with the Amalgamated. In Rochester, the same year, the agreement was signed by the Clothiers' Exchange. In New York City a number of market associations were formed and dissolved before the present one came into existence in 1924. When the antiunion association in Philadelphia was defeated in 1929 it perished, and an agreement was made with another association, formed originally for trade promotion and regulation of trade practices.

Most of these, however, are paper organizations; only two maintain full-time executives and are constantly active. The membership of the New York Clothing Manufacturers' Exchange, Inc., includes almost half of the manufacturers in the New York market, employing about two thirds of the workers. The Exchange handles for its members all negotiations on labor questions, but gives little attention to nonlabor matters. Dues range from $250 a year to $1,500, depending on the size of the firm. The Philadelphia Manufacturers' Association, formed in 1922, covers practically every firm in the market. This association negotiates all labor questions for members, and carries on a limited amount of trade promotion work. Dues range from $100 to $375 a year. The Rochester Clothiers' Exchange has complete coverage of the market, but maintains no full-time office and charges nominal dues. The president of the Exchange negotiates with the union the few labor questions which fail to be settled in the shops. The associations in Chicago, Boston and Baltimore have become rather inactive, but in an emergency would probably be revived.[25]

25. Special mention should be made of the flourishing contractors' associations of New York City and Philadelphia. These are strongly supported by the Amalgamated and the employers. The Philadelphia Association is operated by a former Amalgamated officer. Including all contractors in their memberships, these organizations have done much to regulate competition and to improve working conditions in their respective markets, and play an important part in the collective bargaining picture.

Attempts at National Organization

Attempts to organize employers on a national scale began in 1919, when New York, Chicago, Rochester and Buffalo representatives formed the National Industrial Federation of Clothing Manufacturers with the principal object of dealing with labor problems. This organization joined with the Amalgamated to form a National Joint Council, which dissolved after unsuccessful attempts to bargain collectively for the entire industry. No strong national association was formed until 1933, when, under the stimulus of the NRA, two associations—one prounion and the other antiunion—were formed within eleven days. Their chief purposes were to administer and to oppose, respectively, the Code of Fair Competition. The antiunion association was formally disbanded soon after the NRA was invalidated.

The prounion group, the Clothing Manufacturers' Association of the United States of America, voted to continue. Its members pledged themselves to observe the code, though there was no longer any legal requirement to do so. Still in existence, the Association is rather inactive. When an industry-wide wage increase was negotiated in the spring of 1937, the Amalgamated dealt not with it but with a hastily assembled committee, which quit after the increase was granted.

4. The Formative Years of Collective Bargaining

The advanced stage of collective bargaining for which the men's clothing industry is famous is the result of long and painful evolution. If the present system were imposed upon an industry to which bargaining is new, it would probably break down immediately. Establishment of mutual confidence between workers and employers, development of suitable personnel and adaptation of bargaining methods to the changing characteristics of the industry have been indispensable to its success.

The formative period of collective bargaining appears to have ended in the early twenties. The system had just survived two of its most critical tests: the postwar price fluctuations, and in the eastern markets a gigantic lockout designed to smash the union. The early twenties also saw the withdrawal in Chicago of the last of the permanent arbitrators, whose decisions had laid the foundation for the system, and the abandonment of arbitration as a method of adjusting general wage levels. Finally, the decline of the industry, which set in after 1923, brought union and employers close together in joint attacks on the industry's economic problems.

a. ORIGIN AT HART, SCHAFFNER AND MARX

Collective bargaining in the men's clothing industry grew out of the Chicago strike of 1910. This strike was not a carefully planned attack to gain specific objectives, but a spontaneous and unorganized revolt,[26] resulting from an accumulation of grievances and petty persecutions. It started in a pants shop of Hart, Schaffner and Marx in September and spread rapidly throughout the entire market to involve at its peak nearly forty thousand workers. It was marked by bitterness and violence and resulted in several deaths.

The industry's working conditions had been notorious for years, and public opinion strongly supported the strikers. Labor groups, social workers, churches and schools contributed funds, and their leaders served as pickets, speakers and negotiators. Nevertheless, after nineteen weeks, the strike against most concerns was lost, and the beaten workers returned to their jobs with no assurance of better conditions in the future.

The Hart, Schaffner and Marx workers fared better than the others, thanks largely to the intervention of Joseph Schaffner, secretary-treasurer of the company. They had returned to work some weeks earlier, with assurance against discrimination for participating in the strike or for union membership, and with an agreement that other grievances should be adjusted by a three-man board of arbitration. This board, which actually consisted of only two members [27] because these two could not agree on a third, hur-

26. The UGW did not originate the strike and did not call its members out until the strike was well under way. The UGW's handling of negotiations thereafter was unsatisfactory to many workers and was one of the important causes of the split in 1914.

27. Of these two Clarence Darrow represented the workers and Carl Meyer the firm.

riedly surveyed the situation and, on March 13, 1911, handed down a decision. The decision, which was to remain in force until April 1, 1913, called for better wages, hours and working conditions. It required the firm to establish suitable arrangements for handling grievances, and continued the board of arbitration as a permanent board of appeals for workers whose grievances were not satisfactorily adjusted.

In conformity with this decision, the firm established a Labor Complaint Department to adjust grievances. This department, however, proved unable to effect prompt and consistent settlements. Consequently, numerous cases involving highly technical matters were brought to the board of arbitration. Although it met more than fifty times during the first year, the board could not handle these cases promptly. Its decisions, moreover, lost much of their value as a result of being unwritten and, to most workers, unknown. Growing employee dissatisfaction again threatened open strife.

Machinery Improved

Early in 1912 a trade board was established with original jurisdiction and subordinate to the board of arbitration. This new body was composed of five representatives of the firm, five representatives of the workers and an impartial chairman. Its decisions were to be set down in writing. At the same time arrangements were also made for settlements, where possible, by "deputies" of the workers and employers without recourse to the trade board. The workers' deputies represented the major branches of the trade, such as cutting, coat making and so forth. Early in 1913, moreover, trade board decisions recognized the shop chairman of the union as the "fellow worker" [28] who under the arrangement could take up an employee's grievance with the firm's shop representative, usually the foreman. By the spring of 1913, when by another decision of the board of arbitration the arrangement was extended for three years, a grievance could be handled successively by (1) the shop chairman and the foreman, (2) the union and manage-

---

28. Representation by a fellow worker had originally been permitted for the benefit of employees unable to speak English.

ment deputies for the respective branches of work, (3) the trade board, and (4) the board of arbitration. This machinery is basic to the operation of collective bargaining in the industry today.

The revised system functioned so smoothly and effectively that earlier dissatisfaction quickly subsided. Analysis of fourteen hundred grievances adjusted between April 1912 and June 1914 shows that most of the burden had been transferred from the board of arbitration to the newer parts of the machinery. Eighty-four per cent of the adjustments were effected by deputies, 15 per cent by the trade board and only one per cent by the board of arbitration. In addition, of course, unrecorded hundreds of simpler problems were handled by shop chairmen and foremen.

The decision extending the life of the "agreement" after the first two years also attempted to solve several other pressing problems. Among these none was more difficult than that of the union's status. The UGW demanded the closed shop, which the company steadfastly refused. After much fruitless negotiation and the intercession of outside parties, the chairman of the board of arbitration proposed adoption of the "preferential shop" plan previously employed in the New York cloak and suit industry. This proposal assured preference for union members in hiring, temporary layoffs and permanent discharge; it satisfied both sides and became a basic part of the bargaining arrangement.

Another serious problem concerned workers displaced by reorganization or introduction of machinery. The board of arbitration recognized the firm's responsibility to re-employ such workers in suitable jobs, so far as possible. The decision extending the plan also gave the board of arbitration power to adjust general wage levels in certain emergency circumstances.[29] The continuation

29. It is an interesting fact that true collective bargaining did not exist until 1913. In the beginning the adjustment of disputes had been based not on an agreement, but on a decision of the board of arbitration; moreover, there was no recognition of the union, and no opportunity for the firm to appeal any question to the board of arbitration. The arrangement consequently amounted to a device for the protection of otherwise helpless workers. By 1913, however, the decisions establishing and continuing the arrangement were viewed with such general satisfaction that it was no great distortion of fact to refer to them as agreements. A satisfactory degree of union recognition had been granted and most disputes were actually being settled by representatives of the workers and the firm. Provision for appeal by the firm had been made when the trade board was introduced.

of the bargaining relationship in 1916 and thereafter was accomplished by formal agreements, signed by the union [30] and the firm.

Although development of adequate machinery for adjusting disputes contributed greatly to the success after the first year, an equally important factor was the quality of the impartial chairmen. John E. Williams, whose previous experience as an arbitrator was chiefly in the coal mining industry, became chairman of the board of arbitration in 1912 and served until he died, early in 1919. The complete confidence which he inspired, his wisdom and his devotion to the principles of justice and fair play made him one of the greatest industrial arbitrators of all time. James Mullenbach, a former welfare worker, whose experience also included blacksmithing and preaching, was the able and respected chairman of the trade board from its inauguration in 1912 until he died in 1935.

b. EXTENSION OF COLLECTIVE BARGAINING

Although the UGW had agreements with groups of clothing manufacturers in New York City, Rochester and Boston as early as 1913,[31] the Amalgamated had to begin almost at the beginning in extending collective bargaining. A bitter strike in Chicago in 1915 against firms other than Hart, Schaffner and Marx failed. The same year an agreement was signed with an employers' association in New York City, but it proved ineffectual. Some progress was made in Baltimore and Boston, where agreements with important firms were made in 1916.

During the war peaceful settlement of disputes was encouraged by the War Labor Board, and the sudden upsurge of business after the war helped the union. The entire Chicago and Rochester markets came under collective agreements in 1919 and good progress was made in other centers. But although a series of agreements were negotiated in New York City after 1915, no stable

---

30. The Amalgamated had enrolled the employees of Hart, Schaffner and Marx in 1914 and thereafter had represented them in dealing with the firm. It was the Amalgamated that signed the 1916 agreement.

31. For a description of these agreements and the strikes that preceded them, see Winslow, "Collective Agreements in the Men's Clothing Industry."

and lasting market contract was made until 1924. Philadelphia was an open-shop market until 1929.

Most of the new collective bargaining systems followed closely after the Hart, Schaffner and Marx corrected plan, providing for initial negotiation of grievances by the shop representatives and later reference, if necessary, to the deputies, a trade board and a board of arbitration.[32] The larger firms quickly established labor complaint departments and other special machinery was provided when necessary.

C. EARLY EXPERIENCE

Operating in many markets, under highly dissimilar conditions, the industry's collective bargaining system soon proved flexible and efficient. Chicago continued to set the standard. The successful background of the Hart, Schaffner and Marx system, the size and permanence of the Chicago firms, the strength of the union's joint board and the high caliber of the impartial chairmen made the market a logical proving ground for fundamental policy.

Some early decisions of the Chicago chairmen [33] gave in great detail the arguments of both sides and showed how the chairman reached his conclusion. These decisions serve to this day as models throughout the industry. The principle of union preference was dealt with in dozens of cases until apparently every conceivable angle had been covered by thoughtful and consistent decisions. Other cases fully established the workers' rights in the event of the abolition of a section or the introduction of machinery. Application of equal division of work was defined. Soon the number of cases requiring settlement greatly decreased, for many of the problems had already been solved. Thus the written decisions of

32. An interesting exception was the temporary agreement entered into with a group of New York City manufacturers in 1915. This agreement, duplicating in part the machinery established in the New York cloak and suit industry, provided for a "Committee on Immediate Action," a "Committee of Two" and a "Council of Moderators." The first Rochester agreement specifically provided for the open shop; and the agreements in several eastern markets took special account of the contract system.

33. After the first few years the partisan members of the boards became inactive, since it was found that in practice the chairmen almost invariably had to issue the deciding vote. Complete dependence on the chairman became the rule in all markets.

the impartial chairmen appeared to be forming a sort of common law, through which order could be assured.[34]

Compliance With the Agreement

Both the union and the employers' associations, in the early years, had difficulty restraining their members from violating agreements. Industrial conflict, therefore, although greatly reduced, was not altogether eliminated.[35] On the whole, the union was more successful in minimizing violations than were the associations. Nevertheless, lack of discipline among the union members several times threatened to wreck the system. In Rochester, for example, where the union had a mushroom growth, numerous outlaw "stoppages" occurred, and separate bargaining was attempted by favorably situated individuals and groups.

Within the associations were many employers who had been persuaded to adopt collective bargaining by force rather than by logic. These hostile employers, especially numerous in New York, cut wages, sent work to nonunion contractors, moved to other cities on an open-shop basis and in other ways violated their agreements. A number of disciplinary strikes resulted, culminating late in 1920 in a gigantic lockout involving most of the workers in the New York market and intended to break the hold of the union once and for all. Lasting for twenty-six weeks and extending to Boston and Baltimore, this lockout failed and left the union stronger than ever.

One of the severest tests the bargaining system faced came as a result of the sharp price movements at the end of the World War. Prices and sales rose so rapidly in 1919 that manufacturers bid against each other for workers, and to maintain stability the union had to restrain its members from accepting unauthorized wage increases. In 1921 came downward pressure on wages. In both instances, adjustments were eventually made through slow but

34. Cf. Commission on Industrial Relations, *Industrial Relations,* final report and testimony submitted to Congress, 1916, testimony of Earl Dean Howard, Vol. 1, p. 573.
35. This statement applies to that part of the industry covered by bargaining agreements. In the remainder of the industry industrial disputes were numerous. The Amalgamated has recorded 542 strikes and lockouts in which it participated during the six years ending March 31, 1924.

orderly processes of arbitration. Although much uncontrolled individual bargaining also took place, this experience showed the potentialities of collective bargaining as a stabilizer in the industry and won for it new respect.

Improved Position of Labor

During the first decade of the Amalgamated's existence the position of the worker improved remarkably. The forty-four-hour week was established as early as 1919, bringing an average reduction of seven hours a week within five years,[36] and putting men's clothing workers well in advance of industrial workers generally. By the end of the period, provisions for comfort and sanitation were extended and arbitrary discharge and discrimination were eliminated. Equal division of work was made in slack seasons, the interest of the workers was considered in the introduction of new methods or machinery, and in numerous other ways the worker's dignity and importance were recognized.

Hourly wage rates tripled between 1914 and 1924, and in the latter year averaged about 76 cents.[37] Despite reduction in hours, annual earnings doubled. Although part of the increase came from the rise of the general price level, it is estimated that by about 1924 the typical clothing worker could buy a third more with his annual earnings than ten years earlier.[38]

Influence on Efficiency and Labor Cost

Extension of collective bargaining did not preclude a marked advance in efficient production during the war years and the early twenties. In fact, rising wage rates stimulated introduction of im-

36. A work week of fifty-four hours had been typical as late as 1912.
37. U. S. Bureau of Labor Statistics, "Wages and Hours of Labor in the Men's Clothing Industry; 1932," *Bulletin No. 594*, 1933, p. 2. In general the wage rates of the lower paid workers gained more than those of the higher paid. Thus hourly earnings of the prosperous cutters increased by roughly 150 per cent from 1914 to 1924, while those of female basters rose 220 per cent, those of female operators 180 per cent and those of male operators 220 per cent. The reduction of wage differentials in this manner was a definite part of Amalgamated policy.
38. Paul H. Douglas, *Real Wages in the United States, 1890–1926*, Houghton Mifflin, Boston, 1930, pp. 265, 267.

proved equipment [39] and better organization. Furthermore, direct negotiation and arbitrators' decisions extended piece payment, and production standards were adopted for a number of timeworkers.[40]

The result was substantial reduction in the hours of labor required to produce a garment, which offset in part the influence of rising wage rates. Direct labor costs, which were about 28 per cent of the manufacturer's sales revenue in 1914, rose in the next decade only a bit faster than the other cost elements and by the early twenties had gained but slightly in relative importance.[41] To be sure, labor cost very likely had increased more in the organized than in the unorganized markets. At any rate, at the end of the formative period of collective bargaining, about 1923, the decline of the union markets was daily becoming more apparent.

Modification of Bargaining Organization

Collective bargaining had withstood several serious tests and was firmly established throughout much of the industry. A number of changes had come about which reduced the importance of impartial machinery in favor of direct negotiation.

Arrangement for settlement of disputes by shop chairmen and foremen, and by deputies, was so successful that the number of cases calling for further action was already small. With clarification of rights and responsibilities, moreover, even important cases ceased to be carried beyond the trade board, since the board of arbitration almost invariably upheld the lower board's decision.

39. Little new machinery was put on the market during this period or since, but models in use at the beginning of the World War were greatly improved. The use of electric power was extended, sewing machines were made faster and specialized steam pressing machines came into common use.

40. Certain supervisory expenses and other costs were also reduced. The savings resulting from collective bargaining are discussed more fully on pp. 431 ff.

41. The importance of direct labor cost in 1914 is indicated by a special study of sixty-four firms, made by Walter B. Palmer, and published by the U. S. Bureau of Foreign and Domestic Commerce in "The Men's Factory Made Clothing Industry," *Bulletin No. 134,* 1916. Cost data available to the writers for eight substantial firms in 1928 reveal approximately the same ratio of labor cost to net sales revenue as the Palmer study. It is probable, however, that labor cost was relatively less important in 1928, after additional laborsaving changes had taken place in the industry, than four or five years earlier.

When in 1922 the Amalgamated began to modify its agreements, and provided for general wage changes by direct negotiation rather than by arbitration, the last important function of the superior board disappeared. Although provisions for both a trade board and a board of arbitration still exist in Chicago agreements, the latter board has had no permanent personnel since 1925. Most of the other markets never appointed permanent arbitrators, and one by one eliminated from their agreements all reference to a second board.[42]

5. THE BARGAINING ORGANIZATION IN MATURITY

The streamlined and effective system of collective bargaining that emerged from the early twenties contrasts strongly with the earlier system. First, years of harmonious and successful operation have subordinated its formal aspects, and it depends largely on the judgment and good faith of the principals. This characteristic has increased both the system's stability and flexibility. Second, the handling of frequently encountered problems has been reduced to familiar routines. Questions of discipline and of piece-rate adjustments, for example, rarely need the attention of higher officials, who consequently can devote their time to more vital matters. Another important development is the growing appreciation of both parties, but particularly the union, of the limitations of collective bargaining. Finally, an industry-wide point of view has replaced the former emphasis on individual market situations.

a. PRESENT SIGNIFICANCE OF THE LABOR AGREEMENT

Illustrative of the informality of the bargaining relationship in the men's clothing industry is the written agreement, which is a brief and simple document, embodying in nonlegalistic terms a few fundamental principles to which both parties have consented. The typical agreement contains scarcely twenty-five hundred words. It is much shorter than the Amalgamated's agreements in the

---

42. Whereas the trade board was retained in Chicago and the board of arbitration abandoned, other markets retained the board of arbitration and abandoned the trade board. This distinction, so far, is academic, since the functions and authority of the boards have been essentially the same.

laundry industry, and is in marked contrast to the detailed documents in book and job printing, bituminous coal and other industries.

In New York City, Philadelphia, Rochester, Baltimore and Chicago the agreement is negotiated with an employers' association. Unaffiliated concerns in these markets and all concerns elsewhere sign individual agreements similar in most respects to the market agreements.[43] The signatories for the union may represent the joint board, the international office or both; but in any event it is understood that both stand behind the agreement. Agreements usually run for two or three years, subject to renewal by negotiation before the expiration date. A change in general wage rates, hours or conditions of labor, however, may be negotiated any year, to become effective on the anniversary of the agreement.

The agreements cover a wide variety of subjects. A few include a brief preamble, which states the purposes of the bargaining arrangement.[44] Five items are common to nearly all the agreements: (1) stipulation of the classes of workers covered (such as "all workers engaged in manufacturing operations"); (2) union recognition and provision for the closed or preferential shop; (3) prohibition of strikes and lockouts and provision of machinery for settling disputes; (4) specification of maximum weekly hours; and (5) provision for the annual reconsideration of wages, hours and working conditions. Other frequent provisions cover com-

---

43. Even the employers' associations sometimes require members to sign individual agreements.

44. The preamble most frequently used is a condensation of the famous preamble written by John E. Williams for the Hart, Schaffner and Marx agreement of 1916. The condensed version is as follows:

"On the part of the employer it is the expectation and the intention that this agreement will result in the establishment and maintenance of a high order of discipline and efficiency by the willing cooperation of union and workers; that by the exercise of this discipline all stoppages and interruptions shall cease; that good standards of workmanship and conduct will be maintained and a proper quantity, quality, and cost of production will be assured; that cooperation and good will will be established between the parties hereto.

"On the part of the union it is the intention and expectation that this agreement will operate in such a way as to maintain and strengthen its organization so that it may be strong enough to cooperate, as contemplated in this agreement, and to command the respect of the employer; that it will have recourse to a tribunal in the creation of which its vote will have equal weight with that of the employer, in which all of its grievances may be heard and adjusted."

pulsory registration of contractors, responsibility of manufacturers for the wages of their contractors' employees, equal division of work in slack seasons, limitations on overtime, specific limitations on discipline and discharge, the checkoff and methods of renewing the agreement. Agreements with small-scale employers or with employers who have previously violated their agreements sometimes require the posting of a compliance deposit with the union, or specify that the employer's books must be available for inspection.

Specific, or even minimum, wage rates are rarely included in agreements.[45] New machinery and restriction of output are not ordinarily mentioned, nor is seniority, for in men's clothing is found the maximum application of equal division of work.

All in all, the written agreement plays a surprisingly unimportant part in the industry's collective bargaining, and exclusion of an item does not mean it has been neglected. Added to principles in the written agreement are others, equally important, embodied in arbitration decisions, covered by oral agreement or simply traditional in the industry.[46]

b. DIRECT NEGOTIATION

Settlements by direct negotiation are preferred by both the union and employers as quicker, more realistic and more stable than settlements handed down by an outsider. Settlement by negotiation requires not only that representatives of the two parties shall respect each other's integrity and judgment, but that they enjoy the full confidence of their constituents.

Most settlements are made by the union's shop chairman and the foreman. Many cases involve only trivial problems and are

---

45. Specific or minimum rates have at times been given for cutters, trimmers and other week workers. Provisions for general wage changes may, of course, be recorded in the agreement.

46. The slight regard in which the written agreement is held is amusingly illustrated by the experience of the Philadelphia market. In this market the original 1929 agreement was written to cover only one year. Actually collective bargaining was continued by oral agreement throughout an entire decade, during which a number of fundamental changes were made. When in 1939 the able manager of the Philadelphia Joint Board drew up and submitted a new written agreement he explained that persons studying the Amalgamated's plan expected something of the kind and that it seemed desirable to have something to show them.

settled informally after a few minutes of discussion. Yet, these cases are important, for in the absence of collective bargaining an accumulation of petty grievances has often caused poorer work, a stoppage or a strike. The shop chairman and foreman are not expected to hold hearings or produce extensive evidence, but the judgment and personality of these men are of great importance.

Problems which the shop chairman and foreman cannot settle, and certain other matters of considerable importance or affecting more than one shop, are handled by the union deputy (business agent), representing the joint board, and an executive of the firm.[47] These parties hear some evidence in cases settled by negotiation, and play an important part in hearings before the impartial chairman. Disputes which the union deputy and firm representative are unable to solve go to higher executives of the joint board, who deal with the head of the firm or the representative of the employers' association. Such important and general problems as the introduction of machinery, extension of piece rates or changes of contractors, usually come to these parties immediately. The manager of the joint board and the executive of the employers' association present the cases before the impartial chairman. Beyond the joint board, the union is represented by its international officers, who now are concerned with all matters of industry-wide significance and rarely deal with local problems.

Direct negotiation, even between trusted and practiced bargainers, is not a simple matter. It needs a ready background of dependable information regarding the industry involved and other industries as well. For such background, in important cases, the Amalgamated depends heavily on its Research Department. Although diplomacy, timing and compromise are basic essentials, bluffing and maneuvering sometimes play a part.

C. THE PART PLAYED BY THE IMPARTIAL MACHINERY

Still of tremendous importance as the ultimate preserver of industrial peace, the impartial machinery today handles few cases

---

47. With the establishment of basic principles for the determination of most problems the "labor complaint departments" and full-time labor managers, once characteristic of the industry, have been found to be unnecessary and have gradually disappeared.

and is relatively inactive. Permanent chairmen still serve on the single remaining boards in New York City, Philadelphia, Baltimore, Chicago and Boston,[48] but in the last two of these, and in other markets, which have no permanent chairmen, cases rarely arise. In New York City in fifty-four months ending August 1939, only 108 cases were handled by the impartial chairman, and in Philadelphia during approximately the same period only 93 cases were handled.[49] A safe estimate of cases now going to an impartial chairman is less than six a month throughout the entire industry.

The functions of the chairman, now as formerly, include the interpretation of the agreement, its application through specific decisions and, to some extent, the enforcement of these decisions. Problems outside the agreement, or requiring a departure from earlier practice, are sometimes placed before the chairman by common consent. Expenses of the office of an impartial chairman are shared equally by the employers and the union.

The decisions of the impartial chairman continue to point the way to informal settlement in thousands of cases that never reach arbitration. That these accumulated decisions should develop into a body of common law, however, and establish binding precedents for all like cases is now considered undesirable.[50] A chairman's decision today merely indicates the action he will probably take under similar circumstances, and establishes no binding precedent.

Few cases coming before the impartial chairmen in recent years involve far-reaching issues. Of the 93 Philadelphia cases mentioned above, 55 were chiefly concerned with the discharge or re-

48. Of the five present chairmen one is an attorney, one is a rabbi, and three are economists connected with universities. Professional men have been popular with workers and employers alike. A recent Amalgamated agreement in Cleveland provided that the arbitrator, in case of a dispute, was to be selected by William E. Wickenden, President of the Case School of Applied Science, and affirmed in advance that both parties would abide by his award.

49. These figures exclude certain informal hearings resulting in no written decision.

50. Such policy, known in judicial practice as the doctrine of *stare decisis*, is considered too inflexible to apply to a rapidly changing industrial situation, and has been viewed by the union as an obstacle to the progressive improvement of working conditions. A Chicago agreement specifically renounced the policy and it has since been disclaimed by several impartial chairmen.

instatement of individual workers or small groups. Of the 108 New York cases, 33 were of this type. Disputes concerning the contractors to whom an employer should send his work accounted for 10 cases in Philadelphia and 33 in New York. Only 4 cases in each market were chiefly concerned with the setting of piece rates, and the remainder involved a great variety of other matters, including the disciplining of manufacturers and of workers, the setting of production standards for cutters and reductions of staff.

Decisions are enforceable by action of the signatories, by the chairman himself, or by reference to a court of law or equity. In the background public opinion is additional restraint against violation of important decisions. These sanctions have been so effective that outright disobedience of a chairman's decision is rare.

Methods by which the chairman may enforce decisions range from mere warnings to discharge of workers or dissolution of firms. In addition the chairman may authorize the union or the employers' association to apply enforcement measures of their own. In one extreme case a New York manufacturer, although a signer of the union agreement, persistently sent work to nonunion contract shops. After a series of warnings and minor penalties, he was required to post a compliance bond of $1,000. When subsequently, in violation of his agreement, he established a nonunion shop in Baltimore his bond was forfeited, and the Baltimore concern was abruptly closed and put in the hands of receivers. Such cases are very rare.

Many cases which have gone to the industry's impartial chairman have been arbitrated only as the most orderly way of making an unpleasant but obviously unavoidable settlement. Discharge cases, for example, are frequently appealed by the union to show that the worker is not being "railroaded," even though the offense is so flagrant that appeal is certain to be denied. In other cases union officials or the employers' associations may feel the necessity of making concessions which their constituents, selfishly or ignorantly, are sure to oppose. Then it is convenient to have the concessions imposed by an arbitrator, rather than to urge their adoption by a rebellious membership.

d. SOME ESTABLISHED PRINCIPLES

During the three decades of collective bargaining in the men's clothing industry, certain fundamental questions have arisen again and again. Literally hundreds of negotiated settlements and arbitrators' awards have dealt with these questions, and have established basic principles now accepted in all organized markets. Not all of them regularly appear in the written agreements, but they are more important than many subjects which do. Some of leading importance are:

(1) The closed shop is accepted throughout all important markets. Chicago, with its provision for the preferential shop, appears to be an exception, but this exception has only theoretical significance since all but a handful of aged workers are union members.

(2) Discipline and discharge are permissible only for just cause. Workers are protected from impetuous discharge for minor infractions of the rules, generally being disciplined by layoffs or fines. Discharge, however, is usually approved for such flagrant offenses as repeated drunkenness during working hours or unprovoked fighting in the shops. When opinion differs over what just cause means, workers can always appeal through the union to the impartial chairman.

(3) The worker's right to his job is recognized. Workers affected by new machinery or the reorganization of production are to be given new work as similar as possible to what they formerly did.[51]

(4) The burden of seasonal layoffs and other underemployment must be shared through equal division of work. This rule requires that "in so far as is practicable," regular employees (excluding temporary workers, but otherwise without regard to seniority) of a shop shall share equally in all work to which they are accustomed. Effort is made to secure approximately equal dis-

---

51. This right has, at times, been waived in emergency circumstances—for example when a firm's business has dropped off to the point where equal division of work is impracticable, and a reduction of staff is essential to the continuation of production.

tribution of work by large firms to the various shops with which they deal.

(5) The employer is responsible for his contractors' payrolls. If the contractor goes bankrupt or disappears without paying his workers, the manufacturer, not the workers, must bear the loss. The union, in fact, has complete control over the contractor through the manufacturer.[52]

(6) The union is responsible for supplying workers as needed. This means not only that the union shall maintain an employment exchange, but also that the membership of the union shall remain open when a shortage of workers exists or is threatened. If the union cannot furnish suitable labor the employer is free to hire such workers as he can find, providing they are union members or are willing to join the union.

(7) The union is expected to restrain its members from violating the agreement and to cooperate in maintaining discipline. The union takes this responsibility seriously, and ordinarily discipline is good.[53]

(8) Introduction of machinery shall not be opposed and there shall be no restriction on output. New machinery and new methods are installed without serious opposition, although a partial deterrent is the firm's responsibility for placing the workers affected in other jobs. Among the few machines now available which some manufacturers feel restrained from adopting is the electric band saw, designed for cutting trimmings and the fabrics for cheap garments.

Limitation or restriction of output is now of little practical importance since most workers are paid by the piece. Among the

---

52. Interesting evidence of this exists in the New York market, where the manufacturers are required to pay the contractors' social security taxes. These payments, at present amounting to 3.6 per cent of the contractor's charges, do not pass through the contractor's hands at all, but are paid over to a jointly maintained office, which sees that the workers receive proper credit. This device was worked out after it became apparent that many of the contractors were unable to master the complications of the tax system.

53. In one extreme case, in Rochester, when a particular group of workers got out of control, the Amalgamated supported the Clothiers' Exchange in locking the workers out and finally permitting to return only those who agreed to maintain strict discipline.

cutters, however, who are usually paid on a time basis, the number of layers of cloth which may be piled together and cut simultaneously is limited by the union. The limit on the height of "lays" has generally been liberal, and exceeds in most firms the height which the quality of the product allows.[54]

6. Determination of Wages

If industrial peace were the only objective of the bargaining system, it would be easy to claim for it a high degree of success. Strikes and lockouts have ceased to be a problem in concerns observing agreements, and, with the spread of collective bargaining in recent years, have all but disappeared from the industry. Certain other problems, however, have defied routine treatment. Undoubtedly the most complex and delicate of these is determination of wages.

a. THE AMALGAMATED'S WAGE POLICY

The Amalgamated's attitude toward wages is extremely practical. The union's closest approach to marginal productivity theory has been through its insistence that workers changing from time to piece payment should earn more money in return for their greater output. Although the leaders have undoubtedly recognized the relationship between wage levels and the volume of employment, they have tended to disparage its importance,[55] and in times of depression the membership has resisted wage reductions until some obvious and urgent development has shown them to be inescapable.

The first halt in the rise of wage rates after the spread of collective bargaining was a result of the industry's migration from

---

54. The manner in which the height of lays was determined in Philadelphia appeared in a case which came before the impartial chairman in August 1939. In the course of this hearing it was brought out that no limit at all had existed until a year or two earlier, when the union had inquired as to the maximum height recently cut in the respective firms, and set approximately that amount as its limit. It was further brought out that firms wishing to exceed this limit under unusual circumstances had no trouble in obtaining permission to do so.

55. President Hillman's views on this subject were expressed briefly in the Fortune Round Table on "How Can the U. S. Achieve Full Employment?" *Fortune*, October 1939, p. 116.

union centers. This development was felt all the more severely after the early twenties because of the decline in the industry. In explaining why it had not pressed for a wage increase and other concessions in 1928, the General Executive Board pointed to the condition of the industry, and added: "It is also apparent that, unless we could force a similar increase on the nonunion markets, the organized markets would have been placed at a serious disadvantage."[56] Even today it is obvious that the union's wage policy is affected by the actual or potential competition of nonunion firms. This accounts in part for the Amalgamated's support of minimum wages for the industry under the Fair Labor Standards Act; the union could easily enforce such rates in the organized firms.

As the union's control grew, the same disparities which gave an advantage to nonunion operation continued to disturb competitive relations among the organized markets. For at least a dozen years the Amalgamated has pointed to the need for "standardization" among the union markets. With regard to what is to be standardized, it is interesting to note that the Amalgamated aims not at equal earnings or equal wage rates for comparable groups of workers, but at approximately equal labor costs for manufacturers.

Finally the union favors reduction of wage differentials among the workers of various skills, and has often proposed wage increases by which the most poorly paid would gain the most. This policy has been impracticable when wages are maintained at a constant level,[57] and in several wage cuts skilled workers have lost relatively less than the unskilled. Apparently a further reduction of wage differentials must await the advance of average hourly earnings beyond the level of the early twenties.

b. COMPLEXITY OF THE WAGE STRUCTURE

The intricacy of the industry's wage structure makes it difficult to put wage policy into effect. The overwhelming majority of the

---

56. *Documentary History, 1926–1928*, Amalgamated Clothing Workers, p. 18.
57. The policy has also been unpopular with certain of the more highly skilled groups, whose members still display an appreciable degree of craft consciousness.

workers are paid on a piece basis, which has been extended sporadically from the first days of collective bargaining. Because of its association with speeding, wage cutting and the hated "task system," the piece payment method has been bitterly opposed, particularly in New York. The persistent spread of this efficient method, in the face of strong opposition from the rank and file, required the utmost patience and diplomacy of the union officers. It is one of the Amalgamated's outstanding examples of cooperation with management.

Uniform piece rates in the industry are difficult to fix because a "piece" is not the same from one worker to another. Not only are there differences in skill among workers, but also differences in production organization, materials and equipment, and types and quality of the finished goods.

There is no standard way to make a suit of clothes. The processes involved in making an identical garment may be divided among fewer than fifty workers in one factory and among three hundred in another. Moreover clothing is valued not for its uniformity but for its individuality. In addition to those variations in the "piece" that reflect the organization of work in a particular plant, there are a thousand others due to the texture, weight or pattern of the fabric, kind of lining, number and style of pockets, shape of lapels and type of belt loops. Thus the rate to be paid each worker, or each group of workers in a large plant must be determined independently, and as often as the job changes. To check labor costs by comparing the piece rates of workers performing identical operations is impractical, since so few workers perform operations which are really identical.

Average hourly earnings of piece workers are also an inaccurate indication of labor cost. Although one firm may pay an average of 10 cents more an hour than its competitor, this difference does not necessarily imply that its payment for equivalent work is greater. The difference may instead reflect a larger proportion of skilled workers, a smaller proportion of aged workers, or more efficient organization which increases the workers' output.

Incomparability of rates for piece workers has led to many disputes between union and employers and even among union members. Actually, however, in the absence of any standardization of product, the union is in scarcely a better position than the manufacturer to determine minor differences in labor costs. The crude test of equitable rates is a firm's ability to survive competition, which means that sometimes an autopsy takes the place of accurate diagnosis.

C. FIXING OF PIECE RATES

Constant changes in models of garments and fabrics make determination of wages a continuous activity. It involves two distinct processes: fixing piece rates for individual operations, and control of general wage levels. It is sufficiently accurate to state that the first of these processes is intended to make correction for changes in operations performed, without altering the workers' hourly rate of pay; the second is intended to maintain or modify hourly rates, irrespective of changes in operations—as when all piece rates are simultaneously increased 10 per cent.

The fixing of piece rates is not spectacular, but it is the bone and sinew of the industry's wage structure. Each new model introduced into a shop calls for a series of specifications, describing in detail the operations to be performed. The rate to be set for each operation—often only a fraction of a cent per garment—is determined by a two-man "price committee," representing the joint board and the employer. Both representatives must be intimately acquainted with the processes of manufacture. If the two members of the committee fail to agree—which rarely occurs—the price is determined by the impartial chairman. In practice the union representative has great influence, and in small firms he acts almost independently.[58]

There is no test of the accuracy of the committee's determination, other than comparison of the worker's hourly earnings before the changes with his earnings after he is used to the new way. This is a crude test, to be sure, since factors other than the change in specifications may also affect hourly earnings. It does

---

58. Where the total labor cost is fixed in advance, as under the Stabilization Plan described below, the fixing of individual piece rates is, of course, of little concern to the manufacturer.

not appear, however, that serious changes in average hourly earnings have resulted from any consistent bias in the fixing of piece rates.[59]

d. ADJUSTMENT OF GENERAL WAGE LEVELS

Changes in the general wage level before the advent of collective bargaining were sporadic and uncontrolled. The need for an orderly way of wage adjustments was recognized at Hart, Schaffner and Marx as early as 1913, when an "emergency clause" was added to the agreement, empowering the board of arbitration to make whatever changes in wages or hours it deemed proper. This clause served as the basis for an increase in wages in 1917. It was subsequently incorporated, with certain modifications, into several other agreements; arbitration was the accepted method of adjusting general wages until 1922.

The chief examples of wage arbitration were during the remarkably prosperous times following the World War and in the subsequent deflation. In the earlier period decisions requiring substantial wage increases were handed down in several markets and were accepted without protest. In fact, as has been seen, some employers could not be restrained from offering even higher wage rates, in order to attract more workers. Later wage adjustments were not accomplished so smoothly. A decision calling for a market-wide decrease—the only such decision in the history of the industry—was rendered in Chicago, and reductions were accomplished by arbitration in individual firms in Baltimore and Cleveland. In the rest of the industry, however, settlements involved industrial conflict or were made, after delay, by direct negotiation.

Resort to arbitration over wage adjustments was a sign of immature bargaining. Not only did the representatives lack confidence in each other, but they were afraid their own constituents would not support them in making concessions. This was particularly true of the Amalgamated's officers, who had enrolled

---

59. Such changes have resulted from time to time, however, from general changes in the type of product, variations in the frequency of overtime work, and loss of time while waiting for work when business is dull.

thousands of new members only a year or two before the depression.

The first move to abandon arbitration as a means of adjusting wage levels was made in 1922, when renewed Rochester and Chicago agreements omitted the "emergency clause." This action was taken on initiative of the union's General Executive Board which explained later that adjustment by direct negotiation was in line with its general policy in collective bargaining and should result in faster and more satisfactory settlements. Later the clause was dropped from all agreements,[60] and the adjustment of general wage levels became a matter for determination by a direct test of strength between the union and the employers, though not necessarily involving recourse to strikes or lockouts.

Direct negotiation proved its effectiveness in the prosperous year 1923, when increases were achieved peacefully throughout the industry. The remainder of the twenties saw much bargaining and occasional special adjustments for individuals or groups, but no general change.[61] During the depression several general reductions were made, and many firms were saved from bankruptcy by additional, special wage cuts. A number of NRA code regulations brought about substantial increases in wage levels, with the greatest increases coming in those cities where wages were lowest, and to the lowest paid workers in all cities. The Amalgamated played an important part in establishing and enforcing these regulations.

The supreme achievement came in 1937, when representatives of the union and of the employers in the various markets discussed in New York City a general wage increase for the entire industry. Employers conceded a 10 per cent increase, but the union

60. A modified emergency clause is still commonly retained in agreements with firms not affiliated with employers' associations. This is of little importance in the larger markets, however, since, if arbitration were actually required, the arbitrator would undoubtedly be guided by the action of the union and the association. Independent adjustments by arbitration have been made from time to time under special circumstances. Most important of these was the market-wide wage arbitration case in Chicago in 1923. Outstanding among recent cases was the 1940 case of the firm of Friedman-Harry Marks of Richmond, Virginia. Both of these cases resulted in wage increases.

61. However, employers in Chicago, Rochester and New York City agreed to make small contributions for unemployment insurance.

demanded 15 per cent. A compromise on 12 per cent was quickly reached and successful wage bargaining on a national scale had been achieved.[62]

e. TRENDS IN WAGES

Powerful and divergent influences have affected wage rates during the past fifteen or twenty years. The growing strength of the union, extension of collective bargaining and the increasing productivity of labor have tended to raise wages; nonunion competition, however, the depressed condition of the industry, declining skill requirements and the general downward movement of prices have tended to lower them. So that, while hourly earnings in other manufacturing industries have attained new high levels, those in the men's clothing industry appear to be only about as high as they were in the prosperous middle twenties. Throughout the industry as a whole, hourly earnings dropped from 76 cents in 1924 to about 75 in 1938.[63] But since the cost of urban living decreased approximately one sixth during this period, hourly earnings bought more in 1938 than in 1924.

An over-all average rate is, to be sure, a highly artificial concept. Records for thirty thousand individual workers in 1938 showed that 2 per cent earned less than 30 cents an hour, 6 per cent earned from 30 to 40 cents, 16 per cent from 40 to 50 cents, 32 per cent from 50 to 75 cents, 21 per cent from 75 cents to a dollar, and 23 per cent earned a dollar or more.[64] The chief cause of such variation is difference in skill requirements. Cutters ordinarily receive $1.25 or more an hour, while the least skilled workers frequently get no more than the 40 cent minimum gen-

62. Prior to the anniversary of the agreement on May 1, 1940 the union served notice that it might again request an industry-wide wage increase. This request was waived, however, when the anticipated increase in business failed to materialize.

63. This estimate is based on a careful study of the wage rates of over thirty thousand union workers in late 1938 and early 1939. The study was made by the Amalgamated, with the cooperation of the Clothing Manufacturers' Association; preliminary findings were summarized at hearings of the Apparel Industry Committee of the U. S. Wages and Hours Division in December 1939. The estimate is supported by additional material in the possession of the writers.

64. These figures are supplied by courtesy of the Amalgamated's Research Department.

erally required by the union.[65] Among the major markets average hourly rates are highest in Chicago, where the proportion of skilled workers is relatively high, and lowest in Cleveland and St. Louis, each of which is dominated by a large nonunion firm. Although women have the same piece rates as men for identical work, they are concentrated in less-skilled occupations and consequently get much lower average rates. The average hourly rate for all men workers is almost certainly more than half again as high as that for women workers.

At 75 cents an hour for thirty-six hours a week,[66] the typical clothing worker would have a modest annual income of about $1,400. Excessive unemployment reduces the actual average to around $1,000.[67] This is about one sixth below the estimated average in 1923. Since living costs have declined in almost like degree, it appears that clothing workers' real income was about the same in 1937 as in the previous peak year, although hours of work were much shorter.

Annual earnings, like hourly rates, show great variations from the average. The highest amount earned by any appreciable number of workers is $2,300, about the amount a New York cutter would get if employed full-time for forty-two weeks. Many cutters work less than this, and weekly rates for cutters in most markets are lower than in New York City. Examination of the 1938 earnings of more than two hundred Chicago cutters shows an average of $1,280; not one earned above $1,400. Probably a quarter of all workers, counting the less skilled occupations, earn less than $700 per year. Women workers as a group average little more than half as much as men.

65. In July 1940, a 40-cent minimum wage became effective for the industry under the Fair Labor Standards Act.
66. The thirty-six-hour week was established by action of the Code Authority in 1933.
67. Dividing aggregate wage payments in 1937 by the average number employed during that year yields an average annual wage of $1,030; if the maximum number of workers employed in any one month be used as a denominator the resulting average is $960. Actual earnings figures are available for approximately five thousand Rochester workers for the year 1937. These workers were paid an average of $1,054. Approximately the same number of workers averaged $930 in 1936 and $828 in 1935. A small number of Chicago coat shop workers for whom similar data are available averaged $1,037 in 1938.

Wage adjustments have been remarkably orderly, which is no mean accomplishment in so competitive, seasonal and unstable an industry as men's clothing. Workers no longer need fear an abrupt wage cut when work temporarily slackens. Employers do not have to choose between a strike and increased labor cost at the height of the season, when their orders are already in. By eliminating wage adjustments to purely transitory conditions, moreover, collective bargaining has removed one of the important causes of industrial conflict, for changes under such circumstances are always followed by a reaction when normal conditions reappear.

On the other hand, the industry's wage rates have been extremely responsive to protracted changes in economic conditions. This tendency has helped to reduce the fluctuations in employment and output. From its highest recorded level in 1924 to its lowest in 1932, the average hourly rate for men's clothing as a whole dropped 33 per cent; and from 1929 to 1932 it dropped about 29 per cent.[68] Union rates in book and job printing, on the other hand, were only 4 per cent lower in 1933 than in 1929.[69] Comparable figures for newspaper publishing [70] and for the building trades [71] are 5 per cent and 13 per cent respectively. A recent analysis [72] of changes in hourly rates paid (not limited to union rates) in forty-four industries from 1929 to 1932 shows that wage rates in more than half of these industries declined by less than 15 per cent, and that the decline in the men's clothing industry exceeded that in any other. The increase of men's clothing rates from 1932 to 1938 was also very substantial, amounting to over 40 per cent.

68. The competitive nature of the industry has been at least as important as union policy in bringing about flexibility of wage rates. Because of the competition of nonunion concerns the Amalgamated was forced to make much greater wage concessions during the depression than it felt to be justified by other considerations. The union's control over the industry is now greater than it was in 1930, and in another depression drastic wage cuts would be more firmly resisted.

69. *Monthly Labor Review*, December 1939, p. 1487.

70. *Ibid.*

71. *Ibid.*, November 1939, p. 1208.

72. National Resources Committee, *The Structure of the American Economy*, Pt. 1, "Basic Characteristics," June 1939, p. 151.

7. Union Participation in Management

For a union dedicated to a new social order, the Amalgamated displayed a remarkable degree of cooperation with friendly management from the beginning. Many of its leaders, including President Hillman, had worked in the peaceful and orderly atmosphere of Hart, Schaffner and Marx. Quite early they recognized the competitive nature of the industry and the seriousness of inequality of labor costs.

As evidence of this, the union left management a relatively free hand in the introduction of machinery and new methods, provided only that the workers should not suffer unduly from the change. President Hillman pleaded eloquently with a shortsighted membership for acceptance of the piece-rate system. In some areas where this was delayed, as in Rochester, production standards were adopted in numerous houses. In Chicago, in 1921, market-wide production standards were established for cutters, whose work does not ordinarily allow piece payment. Although some of these policies originated in arbitrators' decisions, they soon won the support of union officials.

Management's savings [73] through collective bargaining were not limited to "direct labor" alone. The piece-payment system and the discipline maintained through the union appreciably reduced the cost of shop supervision. Union employment exchanges reduced labor turnover and almost eliminated the manufacturer's expenditures for hiring and training workers. The union cooperated in many reorganizations designed to increase efficiency. Such developments have brought a modest decline in the cost of production since the early twenties. The ratio of labor cost to the total has risen little if any.

a. INFLUENCE OF DECLINING PRODUCTION ON UNION POLICY

The decline of the industry after 1923, especially heavy in unionized markets, had a profound effect on the Amalgamated's program. Between 1920 and 1925 its membership dropped almost

---

73. By "savings" is meant reductions in labor costs from what they would otherwise have been, wage rates being what they were. Cf. pp. 412-413.

a third. The union faced the alternatives of organizing the entire industry or of adopting an even more cooperative policy toward employers with whom it had agreements.

Its attempt to realize the first alternative was not immediately successful. The threat of unemployment hampered membership drives. Several strikes to win recognition failed—notably the Curlee strike in St. Louis in 1925—and the great International Tailoring Company strike of the same year cost the union over $500,000 before it finally won.

Membership continued to drop. A policy of increased moderation was inescapable; the union suddenly relaxed pressure on wages and hours and began a campaign of cooperation and good will which seldom, if ever, has been equaled in an important American industry.

b. UNION-MANAGEMENT COOPERATION

It is doubtful whether the General Executive Board dreamed at the time of the extremes to which this program would lead, but there is no doubt whatever it was aware of a fundamental change of policy. Commenting on the manufacturers' demands for wage decreases in 1924, it wrote that the business situation "imposed on the industry conditions which it is the function of the union to assist in solving." Then it added this significant statement:

> Because of this attitude of the union, the wage negotiations of 1924 were rapidly converted into a survey of the industry, with a view to discovering all possible sources of saving and means of increasing employment. Prolonged conferences were had with individual firms in which labor costs, overhead, sales methods, shop organization were all discussed and analyzed. The union made suggestions and took under consideration proposals from the employers. The technically trained deputies of the union worked with the management in devising more economical methods of production; whole new shops, with this effective cooperation of the union, were quickly organized and put into operation without friction and high expense of promotion. This process of readjustment was carried on without any change in the general level of wages; only occasionally an abnormally high rate was adjusted or a particularly expensive practice modified. Throughout its history the Amalgamated had opposed restric-

tion of output and at its Boston convention in 1920 went on record with reference to the question of measured production. But these steps of 1924 and 1925 were considerably more radical departures in the methods and policies of a labor organization. Through them the Amalgamated was assuming in practice, as well as in theory, a large share in the actual management and responsibility of the industry. The significance of these steps in terms of the power and influence of the union cannot easily be exaggerated.[74]

Assistance in Securing Supervisory Personnel

One noteworthy example of the Amalgamated's new cooperative venture was the securing of capable supervisory personnel. Many foremen and executives holding over from pre-union days had been chosen largely for their effectiveness in fighting the union; they could not be expected to excel in production efficiency as well. Through union help scores of capable men were appointed to appropriate jobs, from foremen in small shops to production managers of some of the industry's largest concerns. As reported by an observer in the industry's trade journal: "While they rarely become public, instances of the union's recommending executive personnel changes to the houses which work most harmoniously with it, are by no means rare. Indeed . . . one of its most constructive contributions to the industry consists in just this, and the ACW may without partiality be credited with being the very best executive personnel agency the industry has."[75]

Reorganization of Firms

Another example of cooperation was the help of the Amalgamated's production men, bankers and other experts in the reorganization of firms on the verge of dissolution. Recently, a large Rochester concern which had bitterly fought the Amalgamated for many years and operated under an agreement with the United Garment Workers, drifted toward the rocks. Its business had declined, and when the old management withdrew in February 1938, it was uncertain whether the firm would continue. When the company decided to keep on, the Amalgamated's General Execu-

---

74. ACW, *Documentary History*, 1924–1926, p. 13.
75. George J. Hexter, in the *Daily News Record*, Fairchild Publications, October 22, 1930.

tive Board members Chatman and Blumberg took part in one of the most thoroughgoing reorganizations the industry has ever seen. The firm has operated on a healthy basis ever since and a competent and unbiased observer close to the scene has declared that the Amalgamated should receive chief credit. The union was amply rewarded when the firm, enthusiastically supported by its employees, signed an Amalgamated agreement.

Special Production Arrangements

The union has often made special production and cost arrangements to help firms adversely affected by changing conditions. Although such cases were common after 1930, they originated in the development of the famous "X brand" line which Hart, Schaffner and Marx put out in 1926 in response to the growing demand for cheaper clothing. Working together, the firm and the union arranged for a more minute subdivision of labor than formerly, the substitution of machine work for many hand operations, a reduction in the number of styles and increased efficiency in routing material through the plant. With these changes effected, the union could guarantee a remarkably low over-all labor cost per garment. The plan soon accounted for a large proportion of the firm's entire output, but has since been discontinued.[76]

Other Special Assistance

In a few cases the Amalgamated has given direct financial aid to important firms temporarily embarrassed, whose dissolution would leave many workers without jobs. At the time of the rapid price decline in 1920–1921, a Baltimore concern, one of the largest manufacturers in the industry, was caught with large inventories and suffered such serious losses that abrupt liquidation threatened. Convinced that the firm was operating on a sound basis and aware that its failure would demoralize the entire Baltimore market, the Amalgamated underwrote securities for several hundred

76. Some competent observers, including at least one union official, believe the Amalgamated went too far in its special production arrangements and, in a desperate effort to avoid general wage reductions, made changes adversely affecting the quality of the product. The reputation of some markets for products of superior quality was for a time seriously injured.

thousand dollars, made concessions in labor cost and participated for years in the firm's financing and business operations.

Union-management cooperation has even extended to retail prices. A nationally known retailer who wished to install a line of $22.50 suits asked the manager of the Philadelphia Joint Board in 1939 to put him in touch with a suitable manufacturer. The manager not only made satisfactory arrangements, but also persuaded the retailer to reduce his markup from the customary "42 + 10" per cent to 37 per cent, thus enabling him to offer a better suit for the money—and incidentally giving more work to Philadelphia workers. This reduced markup is understood to have brought such favorable results that it was later extended to other men's clothing lines.

C. THE AMALGAMATED AND THE NRA

Labor's importance in policy formation and in the control of the industry received ample recognition under the NRA. The men's clothing Code of Fair Competition was not only one of the first to be put into operation but one of the most successful. The Amalgamated was represented on the Code Authority by three members [77] with full voting privileges and played an important part in the Code's administration from beginning to end.

Notable for its liberal labor provisions, the Code was considerably more favorable to labor than proposals by either of the employers' associations, and it testified to the persuasiveness of the Amalgamated's representatives.

The provisions of the Code were unusually well observed. One reason was the effectiveness of the label system which facilitated the detection and punishment of violators. Another was that the Amalgamated threw all its industrial power behind enforcement of the labor provisions. The Code may be credited with reducing maximum hours from forty-four to thirty-six a week, increasing hourly wage rates by one third, eliminating very low rates and providing employment for twenty-three thousand additional work-

---

77. Two others were chosen from the UGW, which at that time still had agreements with a number of firms. The total membership of the Code Authority was twenty-three.

ers. Market-to-market variations in average wage rates were greatly reduced. Home work and the trifling amount of child labor left were eliminated.

Many of these gains were retained even after the invalidation of the National Industrial Recovery Act. The greatest significance of the NRA experience to collective bargaining, however, lay in its demonstration of the possibilities of joint industrial control.

d. THE AMALGAMATED'S STABILIZATION PLAN

Most comprehensive and intrepid of all the Amalgamated's undertakings in the field of management is its "Stabilization Plan," launched in 1939.[78] Designed primarily to equalize labor costs among competing manufacturers, but involving a large amount of control over production and competition, this program compares with the NRA itself in its implications for the industry.

Inequality in labor costs has troubled the Amalgamated from the first. Competitive relationships were particularly disturbed by the sporadic wage adjustments during the early years of the depression and in the post-NRA period. The irregularity of these adjustments after 1935 was partly due to the relaxation of control by the international office. Hillman and his lieutenants, who at one time studied and approved every wage change, became absorbed with other pressing matters—extension of the Amalgamated's membership in other industries, Labor's Non-Partisan League, the CIO, and the Textile Workers' Organizing Committee—and control over wages fell into the hands of the joint board managers.

Hillman had preached "cooperation with management" to these officials for a decade without completely convincing many of them; but in the mad scramble for business after 1932—particularly after invalidation of the NRA—they were converted heart and soul. At first to bring more work into the market, then to protect themselves against the other markets, they made individual wage concessions to firm after firm. The deputies and

---

78. Attempts had been made to put certain features of this plan into operation in the New York and Philadelphia markets as early as 1933. Owing to the neglect of important details, inadequate provision for enforcement and competition from outside markets, these early attempts met with little success.

workers supported these concessions, and sometimes made concessions of their own, of which the joint board managers knew nothing. This competition for work was keenest in the East, where the 12 per cent wage increase of 1937 was largely whittled away. By 1938 conditions were so serious that many manufacturers were protesting vigorously, and resolutions calling for equalization of labor costs were submitted at Amalgamated conventions.

(1). Features of the Plan

It was clear that there could be no equalization of labor costs without some standardization of production. Moreover, it was recognized that determination of wage costs for contractors would be futile unless the contractors' prices could cover such costs. Accepting the challenge in the spring of 1939, the Amalgamated's international office took up its gigantic task. After weeks of study and conferences with employers' representatives, who, in general, strongly supported the union's move, it announced its Stabilization Plan in May 1939. It called for:

1. Classification of all production within six defined "grades," and prohibition of changes in grade without consent of the union. The establishment of grades was designed to accomplish the standardization of production needed before labor costs could be equalized.[79]

It should be noted that the classification of production was limited to the so-called tailoring processes and did not include sponging, cutting and other miscellaneous activities. There was no attempt to standardize the specific operations involved in production. Any firm was free to use as much or as little division of

---

79. In the production of coats, for example, the cheapest classification (Grade 1) included garments considered by the trade to be entirely machine-made. These coats were also assembled with a minimum of basting and underpressing, and were limited in other ways to the simplest of necessary operations. With the addition of a limited amount of hand work in the collar and edge of the coat and with certain other improvements designed to improve its quality, a coat was classed as Grade 2. Still other improvements, including handmade buttonholes, appeared in Grade 3, etc.

Any brief statement is sure to oversimplify somewhat the actual organization of the grading system. The number of grades, for example, is subject to change; although six grades were contemplated when the Stabilization Plan was first adopted, some of the higher grades originally planned have not yet been defined, and already, in late 1940, the establishment of a grade lower than Grade 1 was being considered.

labor as it wished. Arbitrary changes of grade were opposed, as contributing to the instability of employment.

2. Fixing a standard labor cost for each grade. This cost was to cover all productive processes included in the classification system, and to be uniform throughout the industry. The specific amount fixed depended on current actual costs in typical concerns, and was not intended to cause much change in general wage levels. In this manner, the labor cost involved in coat making for a Grade 1 suit was fixed at $1.70, while the costs for pants and vest making were set at $.45 and $.44 respectively; the labor cost in making a Grade 2 coat was fixed at $2.14, and so on. These amounts, of course, are divided among all the workers participating in production, regardless of number.

3. Tightening up the registration of contractors. This registration, which amounted to the recording and approval by the union of the contractor's arrangements with the manufacturer and with his workers, had always been important in limiting cutthroat competition, stabilizing employment, and preventing the production of clothing in nonunion contract shops. Under the Stabilization Plan the limitation of cutthroat competition was particularly important for attaining standardization of labor cost [80] and avoiding wage cuts. The Amalgamated also wished to avoid unauthorized changes in grades of production by switching contractors.[81]

4. Fixing of contractors' prices. This step, actually put into effect by the contractors' associations, but strongly supported by the union, was also designed to assure the equalization of labor cost to the manufacturer and to relieve pressure on wages. Experience, moreover, had shown the necessity of preventing overoptimistic contractors from making too moderate an allowance for overhead and going bankrupt. Closely following NRA Code Authority methods, the contractors' associations fixed standard percentages to be added to labor cost to cover overhead and profit. In making coats the allowance for overhead was 25 per cent, and

---

80. It is common practice in the industry to consider the whole price paid to the contractor as direct labor cost.
81. Whereas manufacturers were sometimes permitted to produce two or more grades of clothing, contractors were restricted to one.

for pants and vests, somewhat higher. Consequently the contracting price for Grade 1 coats was set at $2.12, and similar prices were scheduled for other garments.

5. Concentration of all authority over general wage adjustments in the hands of a Stabilization Department, a separate administrative unit directly responsible to President Hillman. This provision was made to end competition between markets and assure a uniform policy throughout the industry.

6. Employment, as members of the Stabilization Department, of full-time inspectors to police the industry and prevent chiseling.

(2). *Operation of the Plan*

The Stabilization Plan was launched auspiciously in July 1939. A former manufacturing executive was engaged as Director of the Stabilization Department, and the Amalgamated's customary effective publicity prepared manufacturers and workers for the beginning of the program. In order not to tackle too big a job at once, the plan was first applied only to Grades 1 and 2 clothing, produced almost exclusively in the East, where it constituted a substantial proportion of the total output.

As an initial step, the appropriate grade of production for each manufacturer and each contractor was agreed upon, and the total labor cost fixed. Piece rates were then determined for each occupational group.[82] President Hillman asked union members to help enforcement by reporting any violations they saw.

Certain modifications, some temporary, were made to obviate undue hardships. A few manufacturers producing in their own shops were allowed minor liberties with the grading system with appropriate cost allowances. Some variations in contractors' prices and other small concessions in the various markets were also permitted. Nevertheless, hundreds of firms whose labor costs were previously suspected of being different are now operating on an equal basis. Both workers and employers support the plan and beyond question a big step has been taken towards equalized costs.

[82]. Among the contractors this process was carried on in connection with the annual registration. It is interesting to note that in this registration the union does not send a representative to the employer (contractor) but the employer comes to the union office.

Problems

The Stabilization Plan faces serious problems. Production standardization in the higher grades will be particularly hard since the qualities which distinguish the best clothing from cheap or medium grades are difficult of exact description. It is simple enough to say whether an operation shall or shall not be performed, or whether it shall be performed by hand or machine; but to lay down the degree of perfection which a hand operation must attain is not only difficult but provocative of dispute.

Enforcement will also be a problem. Some chiseling, with the connivance of the workers, has already been uncovered. A contributory factor will be the gradual realization by certain manufacturers, or whole markets, that the Stabilization Plan has taken away their competitive advantage. At present, what with the prevailing confusion on labor costs, the persuasiveness of the Amalgamated's publicity and each employer's tendency to suspect that his labor cost exceeds that of his competitors, everyone expects to benefit.

Finally the legal status of the plan is uncertain. Equalization of labor cost is a common result of payment on a piece basis and does not appear open to serious question; but other provisions of the plan impose restrictions on freedom of competition whose "reasonableness" is yet to be finally determined. These are: (1) the "registration of contractors," through which the union largely controls business relationships between manufacturers and contractors; (2) the specification of the grade (or grades) of clothing which a manufacturer or contractor may produce; and (3) the determination of the price which a contractor may charge for his work.[83]

A review of decisions under the Sherman Act leaves much uncertainty about what attitude the courts would take toward these features of the Stabilization Plan. Proponents of the plan should be able to establish that their objectives are to maintain decent living standards and to eliminate "wasteful" and "destructive" competition, and that there is no evidence of intent to restrain or

---

83. Prices are actually established by the contractors' associations, which, however, are greatly influenced by the union.

monopolize interstate commerce. Secondly, in the absence of any attempt to limit production and in view of the ease with which new producers may enter the industry,[84] there should not be the remotest possibility that the plan will result in monopoly or materially affect the price of clothing.[85] Finally, it may be claimed that some restraint of trade is justified to accomplish the legitimate purpose of protecting wages, hours and conditions of work. Because of the sweatshop background of the industry, the recognized lack of managerial ability among the contractors, and the union's past moderation with regard to wages, this claim could be strongly supported.[86]

Implications

From the employee's point of view, the plan, while tending to decrease the difference in earnings of comparable workers, is unlikely to bring about uniform hourly earnings. One worker may still earn more an hour than another of the same skill and efficiency in a different shop. This may be because he receives a more liberal share in the division of the total labor cost among the various operatives, because of the superior machine equipment

---

84. This is not true of contractors; that is to say, a contractor opening up a shop against the wishes of the union would have little chance of finding a manufacturer who would send him work. Since it has not been established that manufacture in contract shops is more efficient than manufacture in inside shops, however, freedom of manufacturers alone to enter the industry should assure the maintenance of a competitive price.

85. The proponents of the Stabilization Plan take comfort in the U. S. Supreme Court opinion in the *Appalachian Coals* case, which held, among other things, that the Sherman Act does not prevent those engaged in interstate commerce from adopting "reasonable measures to protect it from injurious and destructive practices and to promote competition upon a sound basis." *Appalachian Coals, Inc., et al.* v. *United States,* 288 U. S. 360 (1933). Also relevant is the decision in the more recent *Apex* case. The Court held in this case that intent or effort to form a monopoly, influence prices or discriminate among purchasers must be established to prove violation of the Sherman Act, and that it is not enough to demonstrate some incidental interference with the flow of interstate commerce resulting from an attempt to gain some legitimate end. *Apex Hosiery Co.* v. *Leader, et al.* (May 1940).

86. At the time of this writing, the "rule of reason" had never been applied specifically and directly to labor cases, although there is some basis for predicting that such application will be made in the future. The Anti-Trust Division of the U. S. Department of Justice has announced (through Thurman Arnold) its intention of observing this rule in prosecuting labor cases.

of his shop or because of the shop's more efficient organization of production.

If a manufacturer's labor cost depends solely on the grade of clothing he produces, what incentive has he to maintain the highest standards of efficiency in production?[87] The union's energetic support of efficient organization should, to be sure, prevent notorious lapses in efficiency. At best, however, the union can insist only on the most efficient *known* organization; it cannot require experimentation to discover superior methods. On the other hand, it is clear that discounts or penalties for variations in efficiency might again introduce estimate and opinion into the determination of labor cost and threaten to defeat the Stabilization Plan's purpose.

Effect on the Consumer

Can the Stabilization Plan help the consumer by providing accurate quality standards for garments? This question may be answered in a qualified affirmative. Amalgamated specifications for each grade are not minimum but maximum requirements; they are designed to assure that for a given labor cost the workers shall not be required to do more than a given amount of work. But, having paid for the operations specified, the manufacturer can be expected to insist that they be performed and thus the minimum and maximum will ordinarily coincide. Buyers for retailers already know the grades of clothing and consequently can buy more wisely.[88] Consumers would also have an appreciable advantage if they could identify garments by grade. They could not, for example, be misled into paying a high price for a suit "hand-tailored throughout" if they knew it was Grade 2.

The advantage of the grading system to the consumer, however, may be easily exaggerated. The present system ignores the quality

---

87. It is recognized that the manufacturer would still profit from a reduction of waste of materials, and from certain economies in overhead costs.

88. A few small manufacturers have complained, in fact, that the grading system enables the buyer to calculate cost of production very closely, and thereby gives him a bargaining advantage. Large manufacturers who produce the same quality of product year after year seem indifferent to this fact, claiming that the buyer can usually estimate their costs very closely, even without the grading system.

of the fabric or the trimmings used in a garment; nor does it affect the thoroughness and care of sponging or cutting. An additional disturbing factor exists when the union permits on occasion some deviation from grade specifications, with appropriate adjustment in labor cost. Such deviations also intensify competition between garments of different grades and threaten to disturb the standardization of production which is essential to equalization of costs.

Other questions center about the sanctity of established grades. Assuming that he observes the grade specifications and pays the appropriate labor cost, why cannot a manufacturer change at will from one grade to another? In case of a sudden shift in consumer demand from one quality of clothing to another, how will the Stabilization Plan permit adjustment? Only change to a *lower* grade is seriously opposed. Such a shift reduces the work to be done and the money to be divided among the workers. Changes to a *higher* grade increase the work and the money to be apportioned and are usually approved with little delay.[89] Of course, shifts involving a change of contractors may throw some workers out of work and thereby raise special problems. Those grade changes which the union allows, together with those which may come about through the ordinary turnover of firms, should provide enough adjustment for changes in consumer demand under ordinary circumstances. However, an abrupt and radical change in demand would probably require a relaxation of the union's present regulations.

Finally, may not the equalization of labor cost itself result in instability? In a competitive industry high labor cost often counterbalances advantages of other types and helps to maintain equilibrium. Is there danger that with the extension of the Stabilization Plan advantages of location, reputation for high quality products or other factors may cause new shifts in the industry? The final answer to this as to other questions must await the fuller development of the plan itself. In the great game of stabilizing the industry the Amalgamated has not yet played its last ace.

---

89. The union's attitude in this matter, of course, rests upon the assumption that the shift in grade results in no change in the quantity produced.

8. Conclusion

The transformation of labor relations in the men's clothing industry has been made in a comparatively short time. Some of the same workers who toiled in wretched sweatshops around the turn of the century today take part in fixing their own wages and working conditions. Some of the same employers whose production schedules were time and again upset by strikes now operate without fear of strikes. Collective bargaining is not responsible for all gains, but its role has been important.

The dominant factor in collective bargaining has been the Amalgamated. Far surpassing the employers, whose inability to form a strong national organization has limited their effectiveness, the union now determines the industry's major policies. Its chief adversary is the stubborn nature of the trade. Under other circumstances, it might be seriously questioned whether a union's possession of such power is consistent with wise public policy. The secret of the Amalgamated's strength, however, lies in the moderation, impartiality and good judgment with which it has been used. The employers have, to a large extent, voluntarily accepted the Amalgamated's control because they are convinced of its prudence. It is almost unthinkable that this competitive and mobile industry could be so controlled by a union which, unlike the Amalgamated, was arbitrary and oppressive.

What Collective Bargaining Has Meant to the Worker

Considering the strength of his union, the gains of the clothing worker under collective bargaining have been surprisingly moderate. Moreover, the most notable of them are of the intangible quality which an accountant calls "good will."

Probably his greatest achievement of all is increased security. The clothing worker need fear neither discrimination nor arbitrary discharge. He is protected against loss of time through strikes and lockouts. If he works for a contractor, a manufacturer guarantees the payment of his wages. If new machinery reduces employment in his shop, he knows that the loss will be shared by all workers and that he is unlikely to be displaced.

The clothing worker of today possesses a feeling of dignity and importance. He has a voice in his own destiny. He participates in determining the policies of his industry, plays an important part in local and national politics, and is a respected citizen in his community.

Collective bargaining has been an important factor in establishing the thirty-six-hour week in the industry, and in improving working conditions. Besides, the worker has had gains in real income. The unemployed worker no longer trudges from factory to factory seeking a job; he depends on the employment exchange to look after his interests. Thousands have benefited from housing projects, unemployment insurance, investment service, dental care, study groups and other activities which their union, strengthened by collective bargaining, has been able to provide.

Wage achievements have not been spectacular. Hourly earnings almost tripled during the prosperous early years of the system; since about 1923, however, while the wages of other industrial workers climbed irregularly to new peaks, the clothing workers' wage rates and earnings decreased slightly. For the unimpressive behavior of wage rates collective bargaining cannot be held responsible. The adverse position of the industry as a whole, together with technological and other changes, weighed irresistibly on the workers' wages. Without the protection of collective bargaining the decline might have gone further, and its effects would certainly have been more violent.

The decline in earnings, however, if not wage rates, resulted in part from union policy. For the Amalgamated's policy of job security, and its various devices to spread the available work—short hours, opposition to overtime, and equal division of work—tended to retain in the industry more workers than it was well able to support. In fact, not only were those already in the industry at its peak protected, but thousands of additional workers, who otherwise would be in other industries or unemployed, have been drawn in.

Without replenishment from the outside, the number of workers in the industry should have decreased by many thousands since 1923, because of transfers to other industries, disablement, death and other causes. Actually, in spite of the decline in production and in payrolls, the average number of workers is again at about the 1923 level, indicating that newcomers replaced all those who have left.

Although some of these additional workers have been added because of the growth of the industry in new centers and because of actual shortages of certain skilled operatives, many others have been brought in as a means of handling peak production. The expansion which the industry can achieve by employing each worker full-time has been limited by the shortening of the work week; the union's opposition to overtime, though occasionally relaxed, has frequently led to adding new workers as an alternative means of expansion. The Amalgamated's policy has not seriously affected the employer, since most workers are paid on a piece basis. The resulting depression of earnings, however, has been unfortunate, and suggests the desirability of moderating the restriction on overtime in peak periods. This would permit a substantial expansion of production without drawing in new workers.

What Collective Bargaining Has Meant to the Employer

To the employer, collective bargaining has meant many gains and few losses. Among the important gains is freedom from strikes, for the union has been remarkably successful in holding its members to their agreements. The orderly control of wages has also been especially helpful, because the manufacturer can determine his labor costs accurately and with confidence that they will not be abruptly changed.

Collective bargaining has brought no serious restriction of output or interference with improved equipment or methods. The union has cooperated in the extension of the piece payment system and application of production standards. In consequence, the relative importance of labor as a cost item has not increased appreciably over a quarter of a century, in spite of the rise of hourly earnings. Moreover, collective bargaining has made possible real savings in items other than direct labor—particularly in supervision, recruitment and labor training.

Employer dissatisfaction frequently results from suspicion of discrimination or persecution. Some employers regret the loss of their former dictatorial power. Some dislike collective bargaining because they have lost personal contact with their employees, and because the union rather than the company is the object of workers' loyalty. Most employers, nevertheless, strongly support collective bargaining and would not willingly return to the old methods of industrial conflict.

Public Gains

The public has probably gained as much from the industry's collective bargaining as either the worker or employer.

Great cities have been rid of the industrial warfare which once raged periodically in their streets. As the National Labor Relations Board observed, in the Friedman-Harry Marks case in 1936: "Today the Amalgamated has collective agreements with clothing manufacturers and contractors employing the greater number of the clothing workers in the United States. These collective agreements have brought peace to that portion of the industry that has entered [into] such agreement." [90] Less spectacular but equally valuable has been the testing and development of machinery and procedures that are of general and permanent usefulness in maintaining industrial peace and security. Again and again, as in the defense emergency, workers and employers cooperated with public officials to speed up production or otherwise modify normal industrial activity for the public good.

The industry's unusual efforts to safeguard the welfare of its workers, moreover, have lightened considerably the problems of public and private welfare organizations. Improvement of working conditions has removed a public health hazard. The consumer has benefited from efficient production. For an equal proportion of his income he can buy a better suit today than in 1910 or 1914.

Obstacles

In early years probably the most disturbing obstacle to collective bargaining was the contract system, which tested the strength

---

90. *In the Matter of Friedman-Harry Marks Clothing Company, Inc. and Amalgamated Clothing Workers of America;* 1 NLRB 421 (1936).

of the agreement on innumerable occasions. Frequently inefficient and irresponsible, the contractors have continually depressed prices, and consequently wages, through desperate and imprudent competition for business. However, recent contractors' associations have—with strong union support—exercised effective control over their members and greatly reduced the threat to the bargaining system.

The decline of the industry since the early twenties has also interfered with successful bargaining, because of its pressure on profits, wage rates and employment. The economic instability of the industry has at all times constituted a problem; the turnover of firms has hindered the development of stable industrial relations, and seasonal changes, shifts in consumer demand and so on, have resulted in unemployment and wage problems. Other obstacles have been the late development of employers' associations, employers' traditional opposition to unionism, and the inevitable chiseling of individual employers and workers.

Factors Conducive to Collective Bargaining

High in the list of favorable factors is an excellent bargaining machinery. Its vital characteristics are *permanence, rapidity of action* and *assurance of a settlement for every question.* The shop organization, though informal, is indispensable and has settled most of the disputes. Little used now, but still essential as a guarantee against excesses or bad faith, is the office of impartial chairman. The ready availability of arbitration is a final safeguard of the bargaining structure.

Of almost equal importance has been the quality of the system's administrators. Many union leaders and a number of individual employers have displayed unusual wisdom and patience in dealing with the industry's formidable problems. The impartial chairmen have included the best in the field—men with an ideal combination of training, experience, reputation and personality—who were unwilling to admit the existence of a problem which could not be settled peacefully. Specially important is the fact that the turnover among key persons has been exceptionally low, many of them working together in the industry for a decade, and a few for a quarter of a century.

The prevalence of small concerns and of individual ownership, characteristic of the industry, has made contact easier between workers and employers. The industry's geographic concentration has favored the organization of the workers. Specialized processes and materials have helped to minimize jurisdictional problems.

The broad authority of the union's international office has been of vital significance, for bargaining on a strictly local basis could never achieve stability. Credit also goes to the strong public interest in activities of the clothing workers, and to the exceptional organizing ability of the Jewish workers. Finally, the trust with which the union and employers regard each other and the proficiency of their leaders as bargainers have been strengthened immeasurably by a quarter century of experience. Collective bargaining in the men's clothing industry is a convincing demonstration of the expediency and effectiveness of self-rule. It is one of the best sanctions of the American form of government.

Chapter 9

HOSIERY

GEORGE W. TAYLOR

1. INTRODUCTION

THE "TEXTILE INDUSTRY" is actually composed of a number of separate and distinct industries, fundamentally unlike in products, processes, raw materials and a host of other economic factors. This means that the industry can be thoroughly analyzed only in terms of these individual industries, of which the full-fashioned hosiery branch employing nearly ninety thousand is of major importance.[1] The four hundred full-fashioned hosiery plants are distributed through sixteen states, but principally they cluster in Pennsylvania and North Carolina, with other concentrations in the Midwest, New Jersey and Tennessee. Within recent years, these plants have turned out annually over forty million dozen pairs of hosiery. Their yearly wage bill is about $90 million.[2]

Full-fashioned hosiery, however, is more than a major textile industry; it is one of the few industries in this country in which collective bargaining, keyed to meet changing conditions, has been conducted on a large scale for any length of time.

The Golden Age in Hosiery

Until 1927, full-fashioned hosiery workers could readily accept the official doctrine of the all-sufficiency of the collective agreement. They had fared well with the American Federation of

---

1. In 1937, nearly two million wage earners were employed in manufacturing textiles and their products and received total wages of approximately $1.5 billion. *U. S. Census of Manufactures, 1937.*
2. Monthly reports on production published by the National Association of Hosiery Manufacturers.

Hosiery Workers as their bargaining agent.[3] In the early 1900's, the relatively few knitters in the small industry worked sixty hours a week for a $16 wage that was subject to fines for any work designated as "bad" by management. For forty-eight hours of work in 1927, good knitters in the greatly expanded industry were frequently paid $125 a week and more. Payroll records for 1928 show that some individual knitters earned from $6,000 to $7,000 a year. Nor did employers have any real complaint about high wages. The 1920's were a golden age of profits in which annual returns of 100 per cent or more on capital investment were not unusual.

It was not difficult to satisfy both parties to the collective bargain when the demand for full-fashioned hosiery increased much faster than the industry could produce. Prices paid by the consumer were large enough to give both employer and employee big returns. This was the situation through most of the twenties, despite a steady increase in annual production. An output of 6.3 million dozen pairs of full-fashioned hosiery in 1919 expanded to 19.8 million in 1927.[4] Skilled knitters were scarce during the period of rapid growth; their services were at a premium. Orders for machines were accepted for delivery two years later. These were the "golden days."

The utmost possibilities of collective bargaining were tasted by full-fashioned hosiery workers in all their sweetness in the 1920's; its bitter limitations were experienced in the 1930's. In the early days, most knitters were unionized and the industry was principally in Philadelphia, with the only other major producing areas in New Jersey and the Midwest. New capital flowing into the industry in the 1920's first explored various places in the country where unionism lacked strength and then built formidable defenses against union penetration. As manufacturing expanded, union control steadily decreased from almost 90 per cent of the

---

3. The American Federation of Full-Fashioned Hosiery Workers was formed in 1913 by local hosiery unions that had previously been affiliated directly with the United Textile Workers. The name of the hosiery union was changed, in 1933, to the American Federation of Hosiery Workers in recognition of an extension of jurisdiction over seamless hosiery workers.

4. U. S. *Census of Manufactures, 1919* and *1927.*

equipment of the industry in 1921 to 25 per cent by 1930.[5] The union mills, moreover, kept their old machines and did not share substantially in the influx of modern and more productive equipment.

When drastic deflation of profits and wages came in the 1930's, the union simply could not maintain its standards. The retreat from 1927 to 1933 brought an approximate 60 per cent reduction in rates. But the "defensive action" was not a rout.

2. Fundamentals of Collective Bargaining in Hosiery

Adversity brought refinements to the industry's collective bargaining and adaptation to the more exacting requirements of a maturing, highly competitive industry.[6] Attention centered on the economics of wage-rate determination and the development of negotiations on a factual basis through a form of industry-wide collective bargaining. In addition, provisions were made for an improved administration of the agreements and for building a common law defining civil rights and obligations of employees as citizens of the industry.

a. THE ECONOMICS OF RATE SETTING

Officials of the hosiery union know from experience that in a highly competitive industry where labor is a large percentage of total costs,[7] an industrial union is limited in the wages it can secure if its members are to be employed. This has especial force when the union bargains for employees in relatively few plants,

---

5. Unpublished studies of the Industrial Research Department, University of Pennsylvania.
6. The full-fashioned hosiery industry may be classed as highly competitive. The influx of new capital, in a period of alluring profits, was rapid. The outflow of capital because of low profits or obsolete machines was halting. A full-fashioned hosiery knitting machine is single-purpose equipment, representing a capital investment of from $10,000 to $18,000. The large overhead cost of idle machinery induces operation even though revenue does not cover total costs. In addition, the cost of transportation represents such a small part of the total value of the product that the hosiery market is nation-wide.
7. Typical cost calculations of representative mills show that the direct labor costs of manufacturing full-fashioned hosiery represent from 30 to 40 per cent of total manufacturing costs.

and when the predominating nonunion plants ordinarily have more flexible wage rates.

A Factual Approach to Collective Bargaining

The hosiery union's participation in labor-rate determination has been accompanied by a repeated underestimation, especially by rank-and-file members, of the significance of the economic forces at work. This is understandable in view of the abrupt deflation of wages which transformed the employees' task from "an occupation that approached a profession" to just another job in the textile industry. Most union members insisted upon maintaining work standards as long as possible, and this attitude often restricted their leaders' negotiations. Wage setting was not solely an economic problem but one in psychological reactions as well. With the industry's migration and the resulting unemployment, the union and its members came to realize the necessity of considering economic factors as over against sheer pressure. This realization is perhaps the most significant aspect of collective bargaining in the hosiery industry. It comes from experience.

Successive wage increases and the maintenance of rates above those paid in nonunion shops were workable union wage policies only as long as added costs absorbed a part of excess profits or could be passed along to the consumer. In the newer and highly competitive hosiery industry, in which the union cannot secure complete control of the labor supply, survival of the union and of the jobs of union members demands a competitive wage policy.

Collective bargaining has, therefore, finally centered about the task of establishing economically sound wage rates that will provide employment, profits and a flow of new and modern equipment to union mills. A "factual approach to collective bargaining" is now taken by the parties as their guide. Negotiations for a new agreement have become more and more a joint appraisal of a host of facts bearing upon the state of the industry and the wages that can be paid. In recent years, this approach has narrowed the differences between the parties enough to bring either mutual understanding or agreement to arbitrate.

Although the hosiery industry has been torn almost continually by bitter organization strikes, not a single strike since 1929 has been over the terms of a future wage agreement.[8] This record was achieved during a period of drastic deflation of wage rates.

b. INDUSTRY-WIDE COLLECTIVE BARGAINING

The union manufacturers organized nationally in 1929 as the Full-Fashioned Hosiery Manufacturers of America, Inc.[9] The major purpose of this association is to deal collectively with the American Federation of Hosiery Workers in establishing a wage policy for the industry. Such joint dealing was preceded by twenty years of hit-or-miss relations, at first without agreements, and then through individual plant agreements. The former amounted to nothing more than guerilla warfare on the industrial front; the plant agreements, though marking the end of guerilla warfare, continued unstable labor relations because they varied widely in rates and conditions of work. On an upswing, the local unions pressed constantly for uniformity at the highest prevailing level; on a downswing employers demanded uniformity at the lowest prevailing level. In 1929, both parties foresaw an impending deflation and favored a definite and uniform wage policy in place of the uncertainty of setting wages by continuous skirmishes.

Acceptance of industry-wide bargaining was based upon employer recognition of the union as a permanent and essential part of the industry. To encourage development of sound union policies, they granted the closed shop and checkoff.[10]

8. A few short-lived insurgent strikes have resulted from drastic wage cuts agreed to by the union or ordered by an arbitrator's decision. It is not unfair to classify them principally as protests against a union policy rather than strikes to secure the granting of demands made against an employer.

9. It is significant that the idea of a manufacturers' association was urged and encouraged by the union which, like the employers, wanted more orderly collective bargaining.

10. It is of interest to note that the only major problem connected with these terms has developed out of the checkoff. Within the past two years, a few employers have failed to pay checkoff deductions promptly to the union, using the funds as current capital. One or two concerns have liquidated while owing substantial payments to the union. In consequence, it has become necessary for the Federation to check the credit ratings of some concerns to determine whether the checkoff can safely be used. Several concerns have protested withdrawal by the union of the "checkoff privilege" on the ground that alternative systems of collecting dues inevitably interfere with efficient plant operation.

Standardization of Piece Rates

Each year from 1929 to 1937, the employers' association and the Federation made national labor agreements,[11] which fixed a uniform, piece-rate scale of wages for all member mills. The previous wage program had been termed the "army-game policy" of playing on variations between plants to get increases or decreases. Now the parties agreed that labor cost should be "eliminated as a competitive factor." All mills, irrespective of individual situations, were to pay the same wages for similar styles made on identical machines, and were "to compete solely on efficiency of management."

Adoption of this wage policy placed union mills at a uniform competitive disadvantage with the nonunion mills. Moreover, the establishment of uniform rates for identical equipment could not make 18- or 20-section, slow-speed machines competitive with 24-section, high-speed equipment.[12] Less productive machines were principally in the older union mills; modern equipment was largely in newer nonunion plants.

The new wage policy required both extension of union organization and influence and the installation of new and modern equipment in union mills. Neither requisite was realized in time. The payment of high rates on less productive machines by a relatively small number of union mills could provide neither profits nor new machinery. Operation under the national labor agreements was characterized by failure, liquidation and migration of many union mills—as well as extremely rapid decrease in wage rates.

Except in 1933, it was not until after the 1937 wave of CIO

---

11. Except in 1936, when relations continued as previously but without an agreement, the agreements have been national in the sense that they applied uniformly to all association members. They have, however, represented only from 20 to 35 per cent of the equipment of the industry. The Federation also deals with nonmember mills through agreements that are identical with, or similar to, the National Labor Agreement. In addition, depending upon the threat of union organization, nonunion mills have "voluntarily" adopted the rates and conditions of the National Labor Agreement. The effect of the uniform policy has been widespread, but its extent has varied from year to year.

12. The full-fashioned knitting machine is composed of a varying number of sections, each operating simultaneously and each capable of producing the leg or foot of a stocking.

strikes that the Federation could enforce the standards of the National Labor Agreement in the larger part of the industry. But by this time, though a uniform schedule of wage rates applied throughout the North, most union mills were almost hopelessly noncompetitive because of the high costs of their old, and often obsolete, machines. The South had become a major producing area, accounting for almost 35 per cent of the industry's output as compared with 7 per cent in 1929.[13] And the South was not organized by the union.

The old-line union mills, especially in Philadelphia, were ready in 1938 for a new wage policy. So was the union. Modern machines were desperately needed to insure continued jobs at "decent" wages. Besides, both parties were impressed with the extreme inflexibility of the National Labor Agreement. Rigidly uniform wage rates made impossible even slight variations to meet peculiar conditions in one plant, for fear that a change of rates would undermine the standard. The uniform piece-rate scale as a technique of industry-wide collective bargaining was deemed too inflexible and impractical for continued use.

The New Wage Policy

The outcome of the matter in 1938 was a new three-year National Labor Agreement that embodied the fundamental principles of the relationship between the parties and provided for supplementary agreements in which labor rates would be set for each member mill. The uniform piece rates could be modified for individual plants to the extent needed to maintain hourly wages or job security, or to assist plant modernization. By January 1, 1939, wide variations existed in the piece-rate scales of member mills, each of which had negotiated its own supplementary agreement.[14]

13. Special tabulation of production data made by the National Association of Hosiery Manufacturers.
14. The significance of this experience of the hosiery industry should not be overlooked in the current enthusiasm for industry-wide collective bargaining, as a solution for most collective bargaining problems. No technique is a cure-all and it may be well for proponents of industry-wide collective bargaining to define more precisely the policies that will be followed. The hosiery experience indicates the importance of policies rather than techniques.

In negotiating supplementary agreements, the parties worked first on a policy of providing, through piece rates, relatively uniform hourly wages for an occupation, rather than uniform piece rates. They soon discovered that this imposed proportionately high labor costs upon the least efficient plants, which would be placed so far out of line in competition that they would be unable to operate. This was acceptable neither to the employers affected nor to their employees, and the idea of uniform hourly earnings was short-lived. Next, an effort was made to keep total direct labor costs of manufacturing approximately equal between plants while apportioning the cost differently among various operations. Such a program was more workable, because departmental efficiency varies from mill to mill. But the present wage policy is an opportunistic effort by the union to get from each plant the highest wage rates that are compatible with its continued operation.

From the varied experiences of hosiery collective bargaining—army-game policy, uniform piece rates and supplementary agreements—it appears that determination of a wage policy is the cornerstone of effective collective bargaining. Nor is there any ready formula to apply. The meeting of any situation requires a clear understanding of objectives and an ability to adjust promptly and effectively to changing economic conditions. This is not easy in view of the lack of understanding of wages as an economic phenomenon, and in the face of the political factors always encountered in running a union and a manufacturers' association.

C. ADMINISTRATION OF AGREEMENTS

Like most labor agreements, those in the hosiery industry have a no-strike and no-lockout clause.[15] It was recognized by the parties to the National Labor Agreement that there must be some means for settling disputes over application of the agreement if

---

15. "The contracting parties, for themselves, their successors or assigns and for their respective members, officers and agents, agree that for the full period of this agreement, there shall be no strikes, stoppages, boycotts or lockouts, nor picketing of any kind or form whatsoever, however peaceable, nor demonstrations, displays or advertisements tending to excite sympathy or protests, and that neither of the contracting parties will authorize, permit, countenance or suffer the existence or continuance of any of the acts hereby prohibited." Article D, Section I, 1938–1941 National Labor Agreement.

the use of economic power was to be effectively eliminated. Otherwise, they wisely reasoned, accumulated grievances and the no-strike, no-lockout clause would start a crucial battle when the agreements ended.

Grievance Procedure

Under the National Labor Agreement an "Impartial Chairman" hears and decides all questions not settled by the parties involved.[16] Most issues which arise will, however, be settled in the shop if collective bargaining is really a joint determination of working problems. The fate of the agreement lies with the union shop committees and the local plant management. They make it a live or a dead document in the use they make of it. Many years of experience with joint dealings are often required before shop committees are ready to accept such responsibilities as telling employees they are wrong. Many management representatives develop slowly to the point of saying an unqualified "yes" to legitimate requests of the shop committee.

Sometimes the shop committee and management well know the right answer to a dispute, but for varied reasons, cannot admit it. Either may then look to the impartial chairman to bear the

16. "All grievances arising in any shop shall be adjusted by the Union and the Association and/or Member involved; in the first instance such grievances shall be submitted to the Shop Committee and the Shop Foreman or Superintendent representing the Member, and in the event that they cannot adjust such grievances, the matter shall then be submitted to the Officials of the Union and the Officials of the Association and/or Member. In the event the Union and the Association and/or Member cannot agree, the grievances shall be referred to the Impartial Chairman for settlement, who shall give his decision not later than ten (10) days after the case has been referred to him. His decision shall be final." *Ibid.*, Article D, Section II.

In recent years, the agreements in hosiery have been long and complicated. The parties have desired the disposition of cases "in line with the contract" and there has been a danger of developing a strict legalistic approach. Yet it is obvious that a labor relations problem arising six months after consummation of an agreement may not be satisfactorily met in terms of a clause previously agreed upon under a different set of circumstances. The Impartial Chairman has consistently ruled that he could not change a "clear and unmistakable term of the agreement," but that if such terms are no longer desirable they should be changed by negotiation of the parties. On the other hand, gross inequities can be avoided by the Impartial Chairman under the clause which states "neither party shall exercise its rights, powers or functions oppressively in dealing with each other." This is a vital clause in a complicated agreement.

brunt of a decision or to "save face." Such cases may be frequent in early stages of collective bargaining. As both sides get experience, this type of case becomes less frequent, and the impartial chairman is called upon principally to adjudicate real differences over the application of the agreement or to decide new issues that it does not clearly cover. Essentially, however, the workability of the agreement in handling grievances depends upon its day-to-day administration in the plant.

In order to prevent a dangerous accumulation of real or imaginary grievances, the jurisdiction of the impartial chairman in the hosiery industry has been broad enough for prompt arbitration of any question arising in administration or application of the agreement.[17] Moreover, it is easy to get a hearing before him.[18] In this connection it is important to realize that arbitration of issues under an existing agreement is essentially different from arbitration of the terms of a future wage contract. The former interprets; the latter promulgates. The distinction is emphasized in hosiery by giving the title of "Impartial Chairman" to the administrator and interpreter, and reserving the term "Arbitrator" for one engaged in agreement-making.[19] It has been found quite desirable to name different persons for the separate arbitration tasks. The impartial chairman must serve as a friend and adviser to both parties to the agreement, a position that could readily be jeopardized if he were required to rule upon issues over general wage or contract changes.

Results

During ten years, some fifteen hundred cases have been ruled

17. "The Impartial Chairman shall have jurisdiction of and the duty and power to decide and adjudicate all matters in dispute between the Union and the Association and/or Member involved, and the Union and the Association and/or Member agree to be bound by and abide by the decisions of the Impartial Chairman." *Ibid.*, Article D, Section III.
18. It is interesting to contrast this attitude with that taken toward arbitration under the terms of existing agreements by many employers in newly organized shops. In such cases, the jurisdiction of the Impartial Chairman or of the Board of Arbitration is frequently challenged even though grievances unconsidered under the arbitration machinery must remain unsettled.
19. The National Agreement does not include provision for either voluntary or mandatory arbitration of disputes over the terms of a new agreement.

upon by the impartial chairman under the National Labor Agreements in the full-fashioned hosiery industry. There is not a single instance of noncompliance or nonacceptance. Cases have covered almost every conceivable type of industrial dispute, although two general types have been most in evidence.

The first is establishment of rates on new styles not provided for in the agreement. Such rates are to be "in balance" with others agreed upon by both parties. Time studies and production studies are jointly carried out and extensively used in such cases. The second is determination of the civil rights and obligations of employees in their industry. A system of industrial common law has been built up principally by the impartial chairman's decisions, by which employee rights and status are prescribed through definite rules and principles.

The impartial chairman not only settles individual problems but also lays down principles of settlement which can be applied by shop committees and plant management when similar questions arise in the future. No case is unimportant, therefore, and ranking officials of the Association and Federation take part in every hearing.

There is a vast difference between the all-too-general running fight over administration of a collective bargaining agreement and the well-defined procedure prevailing in the hosiery industry. The administration of the agreements, however, as an essential phase of collective bargaining has little direct effect upon the economic soundness of the agreements themselves. The terms of agreements essentially determine such fundamental questions as whether orders can be secured, whether people will work, or whether an industry will migrate. The method of administration determines primarily how people shall live together when they work.

d. CIVIL RIGHTS OF EMPLOYEES

In the absence of collective bargaining, the employer may discharge for any reason or for no reason. When this is done by a foreman or by a minor executive abuses frequently develop. Under the hosiery agreement, discharge is considered not an arbitrary privilege of the employer, but an unfortunate responsibility that must occasionally be undertaken as the only way to preserve efficient operation of a plant. Discharges "to maintain discipline," and to secure "respect for management," are not recognized since indiscriminate firings cannot be accepted as a substitute for inept management or for a proper personnel program. Nevertheless, employers are guaranteed by agreement the "free exercise of the right to employ or discharge any worker in accordance with the necessity of his or its business"; and any discharged employee is guaranteed the right of appeal to the impartial chairman. Inefficiency has always been recognized as a valid reason for discharge. On the other hand, a single act of inefficiency may not merit discharge any more than a single error of judgment will ordinarily cause boards of directors to remove executives. When an employee is unable or unwilling to do his job properly, however, there is no alternative but to let him go. The union refuses "to support inefficiency." It is unusual for more than two or three discharge cases a year to be brought to the impartial chairman, yet more than twenty-five thousand employees are subject to the National Labor Agreement.

Promotions and Layoffs

The selection of employees for promotions or layoffs is also typical of decisions determining the civil rights of employees. Under the common law of the industry, ability entitles an employee to preference in promotion and layoff. Seniority is the determining factor only when other things are equal.

In many plants the shop committee has worked out with management an ability rating system. In the matter of promotions, the five or ten employees in line for advancement who have the best records are jointly chosen. Seniority then determines who shall be promoted. Neither employers nor employees question the advantages of this system.

Employees in unionized hosiery mills also have common law obligations. Employees, for instance, must follow management orders pending the disposition of any dispute. Also, employers have the free right to determine how work is to be performed, and employees must cooperate in any change of system. Collective bargaining, in such cases, is confined to the question of whether the interests of workers require a change of rates under new systems.

The experience in the hosiery industry shows that "rules of reason" can be established to govern the civil rights and obligations of employees and employers in industry.

e. COLLECTIVE BARGAINING AND JOB SECURITY

A fair appraisal of the results of collective bargaining in the full-fashioned hosiery industry cannot be restricted to the philosophy of negotiation and the administration of agreements. Of even more compelling importance is the question whether jobs have been made more secure and relatively full-time employment given on a basis profitable to management. The movement of the industry from the North to the South during the past ten years has cast some doubt on the efficacy of collective bargaining in providing relatively full employment for those already in the industry in particular localities.

Southern Competition for the North

The competitive pressure of merchandise from low-cost plants, either because of greater productivity or lower labor rates, has forced many northern mills to liquidate and induced others to move South. Philadelphia, the oldest producing area, has felt the major shock of this relocation since manufacturers in that area, especially, have been unable or unwilling to modernize their plants. In 1929 Philadelphia mills operated one third of the equipment of the industry, but in 1939 they had no more than one fifth, of which a considerable proportion was high-cost, low-production machinery.

The Federation and the Full-Fashioned Hosiery Manufacturers Association realize that survival of the northern industry, especially in Philadelphia, depends upon attracting new capital to the northern union mills. The plan of rehabilitation of equipment undertaken in 1938 has already resulted in a substantial modernization of some union mills—especially in the Midwest producing area. It has not altered the chance of survival for many mills, financially weak as they are and equipped with obsolete machines. Some of these concerns have already found it impossible to install the new machines required by their agreements. All indications point to a northern industry relatively smaller than at present, but one that will be competitive.

It would be a mistake to attribute the liquidation of union mills and the loss of union jobs principally to the effects of collective bargaining. This statement is made in full recognition of the fact that the terms of the union agreement have generally resulted in relatively high and often noncompetitive costs. Such a condition could scarcely have been avoided, however, in view of the almost unbridled inflation of the "golden days," in which both employee and employer participated. Moreover, the failure of the companies to modernize equipment while profits were large resulted in their inability to compete when profits were small and realized only by the more efficient units.

Strength of Collective Bargaining

One may well question whether the position of the North would have been much improved in the total absence of collective bargaining. There is a limit, after all, to the percentage reduction in wages that can be exacted even in nonunion mills. From 1929 to 1933 union rates were reduced 60 per cent. From the new basic wage rates established in 1933, when weekly hours were reduced from forty-eight to forty, piece rates had been subjected by 1939 to a further net decrease of 25 per cent. Certain questions will always remain unanswered. Could union members have been induced to accept even greater reductions? Would they have accepted lower rates in the absence of collective bargaining? Would an even greater deflation of wage rates have induced installation of new equipment, or was the older producing area drying up through failure to change production and merchandising policies? Can it be said that the problems were beyond correction through collective bargaining?

Because of the recent sweeping economic changes in the full-fashioned hosiery industry, it is not possible to appraise convincingly the effectiveness of collective bargaining in maintaining long-time job security for union members and in making manufacturing processes sufficiently profitable to support necessary plant modernization. It is evident from the hosiery experience, however, that negotiations for a collective agreement can be conducted on a factual plan, and can be flexible in the face of changing economic requirements. Moreover, the history of the national labor agreements in the hosiery industry throws light on the peculiar problems of industry-wide collective bargaining and on the working of a carefully thought-out plan for the administration of agreements. The survival, on an amicable basis, of a collective bargaining relationship between the American Federation of Hosiery Workers and the Full-Fashioned Hosiery Manufacturers of America, Inc., is good evidence of the strength and practicality of its principles.

3. Development of Collective Bargaining

The foregoing discussion has emphasized certain of the more fundamental aspects of collective bargaining in the full-fashioned hosiery industry. To understand how and why they came into being requires some attention to history. This delving into the past is not an attempt at mere historical narrative but an effort to discern the episodes of the past that constitute the background of present and future problems.

a. THE RUNNING BATTLE PRIOR TO 1921

About the year 1910, the full-fashioned hosiery industry was composed of a few mills located principally in Philadelphia.[20] A union of a few boarders[21] and knitters in Philadelphia, established

---

20. The American industry started in New England in the early 1880's and spread to Philadelphia in 1887. Many of the English knitters came from Nottinghamshire. Behind them was a history of organization that went back to the introduction of the hosiery frame in 1780 and the consequent Luddite riots in which three hundred frames were destroyed. Besides the English knitters, skilled workers from Germany and Poland early came to the American industry, the latter settling principally in the Midwest. There were numerous efforts to organize the workers almost from the very beginning of the industry, but the earliest attempts were sporadic and lacked definite results.

21. Boarding is the operation for finishing or pressing the hosiery and at this time was performed mainly by men working on wooden forms.

in 1909, was the ancestor of the present organization. As knitters "travelled with the trade" to such scattered producing areas as Fort Wayne and Northampton, they organized local unions directly affiliated with the United Textile Workers of America. Strong craft unions of knitters were soon created in each district, with the exception of Reading, which was to prove a bulwark of antiunion forces. The activity of the local unions served to provide "improved conditions," although relations between management and the shop committees were informal.

Start of the Federation

The local unions retained their affiliation with the United Textile Workers when they combined in 1913 to form the American Federation of Full-Fashioned Hosiery Workers.[22] The objectives of the early Federation included the exchange of wage-rate information and the centralized organization of the few nonunion plants where standards were below those prevailing in union shops.

One of the first policies adopted by the Federation was the retention of the single-machine system of operation,[23] deemed essential for preventing a surplus of knitters. Although outside of Philadelphia the single-machine system prevailed generally in shops which specialized in ingrain work, the double-machine system was

---

22. The locals and the Federation were chartered by the United Textile Workers, but the Federation also chartered the same branches. This unique charter arrangement has carried over to the present. The Federation and its locals are now affiliated, however, with the Textile Workers Union of America. This is a CIO organization stemming from the United Textile Workers as transformed by the Textile Workers Organizing Committee.

23. An understanding of the importance of this question requires some reference to technical operations. In knitting a full-fashioned stocking, the leg is made on one machine and transferred to another narrower machine which adds the foot. Each machine represents such a substantial capital investment that idle machine time is expensive. On the legger, idle machine time reaches appreciable proportions at certain phases of the production cycle, such as turning the welt at the top of the stocking to make the usual double fold of fabric. A knitter can operate two legging machines on an efficient basis only if he is assisted by a helper or apprentice knitter so that two are working together at certain points to minimize the idle machine time. The double versus single machine issue has not been important on footing machines. With the construction of leggers with more sections than formerly, the issue is less important since the newer machines can best be operated on a single-job basis.

followed in Philadelphia, which made mostly gum-silk hosiery.[24] Philadelphia rates were also found to be relatively low; plants in other places customarily offered higher pay to get skilled Philadelphia knitters.

A Split in the Ranks

The difference between union standards in Philadelphia and the rest of the industry created a wide breach in the new Federation. Opinion also differed over affiliation with the United Textile Workers. The Philadelphia union, Local 706, credited the United Textile Workers with having created a union in hosiery and resisted any suggestion of going "independent" outside of the American Federation of Labor. Other locals insisted that the textile workers' union could not help hosiery workers and that it was mismanaged anyway. The inevitable strong clash of personalities was all that was necessary, especially in this time of dual unionism in textiles, to split the hosiery ranks.

The strong Philadelphia local withdrew from the Federation and retained its membership in the United Textile Workers. Other locals were expelled from the United Textile Workers but retained an "independent" Federation. A new Federation local, Branch 14, was chartered in Philadelphia and the typical jurisdictional battle that ensued was limited only by the weakness of the Federation in Philadelphia. The old-line Philadelphia union controlled all but four shops in its district and was about as strong in membership as all the Federation locals. The split in the ranks was not healed until after the big strike of 1921 in Philadelphia had threatened the union with extinction. Until then the two hosiery unions followed divergent collective bargaining policies.

Collective Bargaining on a Hit-or-Miss Basis

Apart from a temporary setback in 1914, the hosiery business was good in the decade before 1920. Increasing consumer demand

---

24. Ingrain hosiery is knit with dyed silk; gum-silk hosiery is knit with undyed silk, or "in the gray," the stocking itself being dyed after knitting. It is recognized that more careful handling of ingrain work is necessary and wage rates were higher for such operations. Today practically all production is gum-silk hosiery.

and a scarcity of skilled knitters caused a continuance of double-machine operation in Philadelphia and a consequent demand on the Federation by out-of-town shops for a similar system. Collective bargaining was a running battle between the shop committee and individual plant management. This existed not only in Philadelphia but also in other sections; the locals had not given negotiating power to the Federation.

Shop committees dominated collective bargaining. Since skilled knitters were scarce and manufacturing was profitable, the organized employees had considerable economic power which they did not hesitate to use. There were constant demands for increased rates, especially on new styles, and frequent and unpredictable stoppages over such issues as the weather, insufficient ice water, and holidays for fishing. Excesses of the shop committees were aggravated by the anxiety of employers to get and to hold knitters; they had no time to train employees to man their new equipment. One employer in Philadelphia induced knitters to leave a competitor and "work for me" by paying a higher rate and promising to serve ice cream to all hands on hot summer afternoons. Even when these employers discovered that they had overshot the mark, they could not venture any corrective measures. They remembered the 1913 Minura strike in Philadelphia. That company had sought to decrease boarding rates by one cent a dozen on new rayon styles. The proposed wage cut was resisted by a two-year strike which "the union won because the company was forced out of business." A similar result occurred in 1914 when the Peerless Hosiery Company attempted to reduce rates by a cent a dozen on footing machines.

The extraordinary power of shop committees and the informal collective bargaining without agreements resulted in unnecessary strikes, a wide difference between shop rules and some variations in piece rates. But the wage level steadily rose under this army-game policy. The union made new demands at plants where it was strongest and at times when the employer could ill afford to risk a stoppage. Then rates would be gradually increased in other shops to conform to the new standard. There was frequent use of the "strike on the job." The assignment of a new style to one or several machines invariably led to a demand for an extra rate. Pending agreement, the jobs in question were not run although the factory operated normally otherwise.

Legacies of Early Bargaining Procedure

The bending of the twigs in the early days has given form to the boughs of the present. The strict internal discipline necessary to enforce early shop rules habituated union members to hard-and-fast adherence to more formal agreements later. The union levied frequent fines against members who violated shop rules by refusing to attend union meetings, failing to pay assessments, working overtime at regular rates or "paying the helper too much." The penalties reached a ridiculous stage when one man was fined for not dropping a bar precisely at quitting time while he was talking with a foreman. Thereafter shop rules were made subject to approval of the local union.

Army-game collective bargaining set up a complicated scale of piece rates with "extras" rampant.[25] It required the lapse of many years, economic depression and a new form of collective bargaining to eliminate or revise many of the "out-of-line" extras.

The shop rules established through the informal collective bargaining developed into lasting customs. Even now, for instance, "toppers' helping money"[26] is part of the wage scale in Philadelphia. In that district, footers formerly followed the practice of giving each topper a "tip" as an incentive. When the footers stopped their tips after wages went down, the toppers demanded and got "helping money" payment from the Philadelphia companies. Other practices were established more generally, such as the

---

25. The emphasis on extras for anything new can be illustrated by the episode concerning welt-turning extras. A 2.5- to 3-inch welt was considered standard and an extra rate secured for the "more difficult" turning of a "long" or 4.5-inch welt. The "long" welt then became standard and when shorter welts "came back" again, there was a demand for an extra rate because it was now "more difficult" to turn a short welt.

26. The leg portion of a full-fashioned stocking is made on a specialized machine. It is transferred to needle bars by toppers or transfer-bar toppers for insertion into a second specialized machine on which the foot is knit. Several toppers work under the supervision of each operator of a footing machine. The footer's production is dependent upon the ability of the toppers to have ample bars ready and upon the speed with which they are inserted into the footing machine.

right of an employee to a particular machine and equal division of work.

Rights and customs once established in the hosiery industry were not readily given up by either side, even though they came from the hit-or-miss practice of informal collective bargaining. They have influenced the entire course of collective bargaining in the industry.

Beginning of Formal Dealings

Although the "running battle" was exciting, the Philadelphia local union and the manufacturers soon wished to avoid the economic losses borne by both sides under the prevailing relations. The power to call a strike was transferred from the shop committee to the local union, and the union created a price list committee to approve uniform minimum rates. In 1916, thirteen of the twenty-six manufacturers in Philadelphia formed the Philadelphia Full-Fashioned Hosiery Manufacturers Association to present a united front in collective bargaining.[27] The Philadelphia Association sought to establish uniform rates and conditions in its member mills. When a strike on the job occurred, the employer refused to discuss a rate until work was resumed and, to enforce his position, threatened to discontinue the disputed style. Within a year, the Association and Local 706 were supervising signed agreements with individual plants that resulted in a comparative equalization of costs and earnings.

The Philadelphia manufacturers found the agreements more to their liking than did the union. Local 706 had agreed to a wage scale that was inflexible in a rising market. In contrast, the Federation operated without agreements and by the army-game process got wage increases, while Philadelphia rates remained constant. A wide gap soon existed between earnings in Philadelphia and those in outside Federation shops. The Federation felt, nevertheless, that its progress was retarded by the Philadelphia situation. Employers continually pressed for the "Philadelphia plan" of

---

27. In other areas manufacturers consulted together as to policy but were not sufficiently numerous to form an association. It was logical that a more formal type of collective bargaining developed first in Philadelphia.

double-machine operation, especially when they shifted from in-grain to gum-silk work.

The 1919 Strike

The Philadelphia union continually asked the manufacturers for increases to the Federation level. Slight concessions were occasionally made but the formal agreements prevented the union from moving very far. The union then considered striking to enforce its demands. Added impetus to such action was given when the 1918 convention of the United Textile Workers approved a general strike for February 1, 1919 to secure a forty-eight-hour work week. Members of Local 706 were working fifty-four hours a week at the time, and felt that the United Textile Workers' demand for a forty-eight-hour work week could be coupled with their own program for proportionate increases in wages.[28] The Manufacturers Association refused the union demand for a 20 per cent wage increase, and a strike on the wage issue was called on January 1, 1919. On February 1, the demand for a forty-eight-hour week was made an issue in conformity with the United Textile Workers' convention decision.

The strike call was effective and practically all Philadelphia plants were closed. After thirteen weeks the union won a complete victory[29]—a forty-eight-hour week, a 15 to 20 per cent wage advance, and an increase in the apprentice training period from two and a half to four years. In addition the Association members agreed not to double up any more machines, thus laying the ground for eventual single-machine operation throughout union mills. The 1919 strike brought wages in Philadelphia to about the same level as in Federation shops.

In general the Philadelphia union established its strength be-

---

28. The United Textile Workers had decided to make its general strike issue on hours alone, feeling that a demand for a proportionate increase in wages would beget an adverse public opinion. In any event, the general textile strike had but a spotty response and was not successful.

29. The boarders had their own local, 696 of the UTW, which also participated in the 1919 strike. The settlement of their claims involved an agreed-upon increase and the submission of a demand for further rate increases to arbitration. The award upheld the boarders' request for a total 18 per cent wage increase and their concept of what constituted "fair production."

tween 1910 and 1919 when twenty major strikes were conducted and won. This activity gave it an unchallenged position in the leading producing area where about two thirds of the equipment of the industry was located. The Philadelphia union had, moreover, placed collective bargaining relationships on a more formal basis, although it had reason to doubt the efficacy of that policy in securing the fullest possible gains. In contrast to the Philadelphia experience, the outside strikes of the Federation were not successful. But they were fought to extend union territory, and not for wage increases in organized mills. Nevertheless, union standards did not prevail in nonunion shops, which, however, did not operate much more than 10 per cent of the machines in use. The largest nonunion producing area was Reading, Pennsylvania. While the lower labor standards in that market represented a potential threat, the situation was not immediately crucial since business was good enough to yield both ample profits and increasing wages in union mills.

b. TURNING POINT FOR THE INDUSTRY—THE 1921 STRIKE

The 1921 strike in Philadelphia was more than an incident in collective bargaining relationships. It marked a turning point in the development of the industry. In seeking the support of public opinion for its demands, the union told the story of the large profits available to hosiery manufacturers. Not only did the union thus assist new capital to discover the hosiery industry, but it kept most of the older mills out of production long enough to induce a rapid flow of new capital to new centers. For the next ten years the industry experienced a mushroom growth that was accelerated by an increasing consumer demand for form-fitting, full-fashioned hosiery to wear with shorter skirts.

Reasons For the 1921 Strike

Full-fashioned hosiery manufacturers met their first major business catastrophe in the 1920 depression. Raw silk fell from $20 a pound in January to $5 a pound in August. All manufacturers took large inventory losses in raw materials and finished goods.

Following these adjustments, the Philadelphia Association members closed their plants on June 20 to enforce a demand for a 15 to 25 per cent wage cut. The union finally called a strike on January 2, 1921 when Association shops attempted to resume operations as open shops with a 15 per cent reduction in rates.

The lockout must also be considered a maneuver to break the union in Philadelphia once and for all. The manufacturers' program was undoubtedly influenced by the current national effort of employers to introduce the open shop or American plan of conducting labor relations. Association shops in Philadelphia were fortified with strike insurance and each posted a bond that individual settlements would not be made. Other companies in the industry had offered assistance. The various contemplated forms of protection proved to be illusory. No more than one or two plants received strike benefits before the insurance and bonding company was unable to meet its obligations. The fighting manufacturers also learned, to their sorrow, that dependence upon competitors for help is apt to be disappointing.

Results of the Strike

All Philadelphia shops were closed for more than a year, with the exception of two which operated at the old wage scale. The relatively few union members who remained at work assessed themselves 25 per cent of their wages to support the strike. This assessment gradually provided a fund, augmented by Federation contributions, to provide strike pay.[30] When it became clear that Local 706 was battling for survival, differences were forgotten and the Federation threw its support to the Philadelphia union. With this united front and with funds for strike pay, it was evident that the union would win.

Settlements with individual companies began in October and continued in the following months, through the intervention of the local Chamber of Commerce. Once again the union demonstrated its economic power. Deeply engraved on the minds of em-

---

30. Strike pay was started some ten months after the stoppage occurred, at the following rates: $11 a week for married men, $7 for single men and $4 for boys. Later on these allowances were doubled.

ployers and of prospective employers was the lesson that it is difficult to dislodge an established union. The strike was also costly to the union, despite restoration of the previous wage scale and its subsequent increase by 10 per cent. A number of hitherto union shops were lost, and many new nonunion shops came into existence to break the standard scale.[31]

The challenge of the employers accomplished what the unions had been unable to do of their own initiative. Local 706 agreed to rejoin the Federation, and the Federation agreed to reaffiliate with the United Textile Workers. The actual merger was accomplished in May 1922.

C. RAPID INDUSTRIAL EXPANSION AND DECREASING UNION STRENGTH—1922–1928

With the reaffiliation of Local 706, the Federation had over three thousand knitter members[32] and the collective bargaining of its locals determined the conditions of operating for over 75 per cent of the industry's equipment. The principal nonunion area was Reading, although the Federation was seriously set back through loss of organization in Fort Wayne and Brooklyn. Employers in those cities had been more successful in 1920 than the Philadelphia employers in eliminating the hosiery union. Nevertheless, the full-fashioned hosiery industry could be classed as well unionized.

31. Major losses were borne by the boarders' union, Local 696, as a result of the 1921 strike. This union did not settle until May 1922, after a number of plants had eliminated their finishing departments by establishing contacts with commercial finishing plants. Others hired female operators to replace men, while the union's policy respecting the improved stationary forms remained unsettled. The union refused to permit greater production or lower rates on metal forms, and tried to prevent the employment of girls on the metal forms at less than wooden-form rates. These policies virtually wrecked the boarders' union, which was not revived until 1927 when a differential on metal forms was accepted and women were admitted to membership.
32. The union remained essentially a craft organization of knitters although there were a few "lady members." Men were employed only in the knitting and boarding operations, whereas all of the numerous auxiliary ones were performed by women. This situation prevails today, except that women have substantially displaced men in boarding. The Federation expanded its membership greatly in later years by taking in women workers, who outnumber the men four to one.

Expansion in Nonunion Territories

In believing that things were under pretty good control, union officials reckoned without the vast expansion that lay just ahead. Reading had shown it could withstand union organization efforts, so new machines poured into that territory because wages were lower and profits were greater. Smaller Pennsylvania towns also vied with each other in offering various inducements, including assurance that the union would not come in. The Middle West also shared in the expansion and, representing the vanguard of a vast development, the first southern full-fashioned hosiery mill started operation.

The industry was spreading out. In 1922 it had 146 mills; by 1929 the number had increased to 263. During the same time the number of machines in place rose from about 4,000 to over 14,000. New mills avoided the union, not only because of the strength shown in the Philadelphia strikes, but also that they might operate their machines on the lower cost, double-machine basis. While all union mills were restricted to single-machine operation after 1921, new mills invariably started with double jobs.[33]

Collective Bargaining Policy

Although the industry was developing away from the union, the hosiery market expanded so rapidly that in the twenties the Federation could continue its former program of increasing rates. The trend to chiffon styles afforded a good vehicle.[34] After its experience with the inflexibility of rates set by agreement, the Philadelphia local was ready to return to a "rough and tumble" form of collective bargaining.

Negotiations were still carried on by the locals, but district

33. Double jobs limited the number of skilled knitters required and enabled the nonunion mill to provide earnings in excess of those received by union knitters while securing lower labor costs. Naturally the piece rate per dozen could be less when one man operated two machines, and a cost saving resulted even though the helper had to be paid. In many instances, the knitter paid the helper.
34. As contrasted with durable service-weight hosiery, chiffon is a sheer product made with a lighter thread. Beginning with the 1920's the consumer demand has been for sheerer hosiery. Whereas 10- and 12-thread merchandise was formerly demanded, 2-, 3- and 4-thread now constitutes the bulk of production.

councils were set up to achieve some measure of rate uniformity within the same region. Rates and earnings in New England and New Jersey were considerably above those of Philadelphia because of a recent specialization on ingrain work at a higher wage. But because of lack of union strength, rates in the Midwest were substantially below those of Philadelphia. Nor did uniform rates prevail in each area, for in getting what the traffic would bear, substantial variations in rates developed within each unionized producing area.

On the upswing from 1922 to 1927, the Federation boosted the earnings of its members to a level that has seldom been attained in American industry. Wage increases were granted by employers without much ado as long as the added costs, compared with those of nonunion competitors, merely affected the size of profits. But before long the difference in costs of production between union and nonunion mills forced the latter to short-time operations. Union employers demanded the two-machine system. The union insisted that deviation from the single-machine principle would merely meet a temporary problem at the cost of a long-time deterioration of standards.

But the Federation policy was not entirely negative. Along with jacking up union rates, it adopted a vigorous threefold policy: (1) organize the unorganized, (2) develop efficiency on the single-machine basis, and (3) create a national uniform scale of wage rates.

Organizing the Unorganized

High wages enabled union members to contribute large sums for an extensive organizing drive. By 1925 the Federation could boast that it was spending more money per capita for organization purposes than any other union in the country.

Yet almost without exception strikes called were failures. One major difficulty was union adherence to the single-machine proposition. New mills offered as much as $200 a week to skilled knitters for operating two long-section, high-speed machines with a boy helper. Should these knitters join the union, they would have to accept a single-machine job, which many claimed was more difficult to operate, and a lower weekly wage. Union organizers could persuade few of these men that sacrifice then might save jobs later. The same nonunion employees also failed to see any reason for keeping union hours when extra hours meant, say, a Packard car instead of a Chevrolet.

The union seemed to be butting its head against a stone wall. New mills started even in Philadelphia and ran almost unmolested under nonunion conditions. Sometimes the standards were lowered most by former knitters, now manufacturers, who had been the most vocal unionists and the readiest to strike upon the slightest threat to their conditions of work.

The failure of the organization drives of the 1920's can also be attributed to the aggressive antiunion tactics of nonunion employers. Individual contracts of employment, known as "yellow-dog contracts," were extensively used. Often the Federation and its members were prevented by sweeping injunctions from seeking recruits among the signers of yellow-dog contracts on the grounds that such action would induce a breach of contract.[35] Counterclaims that these contracts were signed under duress were not allowed. In one attempted strike, called despite the existence of yellow-dog contracts, the court enjoined all third parties as well as the union from willfully taking any step that would cause signers of contracts to break them. The company retaliated by drawing up a new contract under which the employee agreed not to join the union and also not to work in any hosiery mill within a hundred miles of the plant within one year after severance of employment. On occasion, a company union would be installed along with the individual contracts of employment.

Many small Pennsylvania towns passed ordinances, directed especially against the hosiery union, which prohibited or regulated picketing, forestalled distribution of union literature and, in some

35. Of the many cases, a typical one in Philadelphia was *Brownhill and Kramer, Inc. v. the American Federation of Full-Fashioned Hosiery Workers*, cited as CP 4 June Term 1926. The case that attracted national attention was *Kraemer Hosiery Co. v. the American Federation of Full-Fashioned Hosiery Workers*, 305 Pa. 206, in which not only the union but third parties were enjoined from acting to secure union members from the employees who had signed yellow-dog contracts.

cases, forbade union meetings. In the absence of restrictive ordinances, mayors or sheriffs sometimes issued proclamations that were even more drastic than court injunctions.

Labor spies and strikebreaking agencies were widely employed by hosiery manufacturers. At one time, six such agencies operated in nonunion mills in Philadelphia. There is no need to detail the well-known tactics used by such agencies except to state that in one or two instances they bored right into the heart of the hosiery union.

Although the Federation failed to organize additional plants, its membership rose from three thousand in 1922 to over twelve thousand in 1927. This apparently phenomenal growth, however, resulted from the increase in equipment in certain old-line mills and from the organizing of so-called "auxiliary" workers. In this period the Federation was transformed from a craft union of knitters to an industrial union composed of employees in all hosiery operations.[36]

But in the 1920's, the 75 per cent union control steadily decreased until by 1927 collective bargaining was practiced in only about 40 per cent of the industry. At the same time Philadelphia was losing her dominant position. Of the total of approximately ten thousand knitting machines in the industry in 1927, only about one third were in Philadelphia. On the other hand, twenty-two hundred machines were now operated in Reading of which less than two hundred were run by union members. At the same time the industry was gradually growing in the South.

Developing Efficiency in Union Mills

As the union sought to establish its standards abroad, their soundness was defended at home. Union officials asserted that relatively high piece rates were justified for union members because they were the most efficient workers in the industry. They adhered to the single-machine system with the argument that it was more efficient and gave lower long-run costs than double jobs; only by a system of one man operating one machine could quality work

---

36. Occupations incident to mill operation but not typical of the hosiery industry were not organized. They included watchmen, millwrights, engineers, etc.

be produced and the expensive machinery be given the care and attention necessary to insure long life.

Such contentions are not novel in American labor history. It is notable, however, that the Federation officials made a valiant effort to put theory into practice. They undertook an intensive drive for increased efficiency and for the elimination of waste and sloppy work. For example, Local 706 expelled a worker for throwing away bad work and another time endorsed the action of a shop committee in penalizing a knitter for failing to show the foreman a bad set. At the 1925 convention of the Federation, the secretary reported, "The union, for some time past, has through a series of developments come to recognize the need for assuming more efficient operation in the mills where union members are employed. . . . In one instance, the president of the Philadelphia branch spent several weeks in a local mill as a sort of production manager. After painstaking efforts in the plant and a series of conferences with the men, the union president succeeded in effecting considerable reduction in wastage of work and in increasing the output of perfect work."

Without at all detracting from the success of the union in actually decreasing costs, the results did not adequately support the single-machine system. The union faced natural limitations in its efforts since there was no association of manufacturers with which to cooperate on a large scale. Moreover, it was not easy to change overnight the work habits of thousands of employees.

A National Uniform Wage Scale

The organizers for the Federation in the 1920's were frequently asked "What is the union scale of wages?" Since there was no such scale, the organizers had nothing definite to sell. In addition, Federation officials soon realized the serious shortcomings of a wage policy that resulted in such large increases on extras as to make it impossible for union mills to make certain styles.

Strong efforts were made within the Federation and at conventions to secure adoption of a uniform wage scale. At the 1926 convention, the secretary of the Federation stated, "Again I mention our mistake in not having a uniform minimum price list. I believe, however, that we are gradually working toward that end. The prices in New England are practically uniform, as is true of the Midwest, New York and New Jersey . . . and in Philadelphia a uniform minimum price has been in effect for years." Some progress toward uniformity was made to place union plants on a more nearly equal basis. But to union manufacturers, beset by outside competition, such a program was wholly inadequate.

While the union program did not achieve its objective, the three policies adopted by the Federation caused a greater centralization of union authority. Federation officers had superseded the shop committees as the seat of authority for collective bargaining on the union side. It was this shift of power that made possible the later developments in bargaining.

Another Turning Point—1927

The handwriting on the wall was quite plain. Union mills were less and less able to compete with nonunion mills, and every union attempt to meet the situation and still to maintain existing standards had failed. The only way now open was revision of standards.

To the 1927 convention President Geiges reported: "We have reached the peak. What is the use of kidding ourselves that we haven't? . . . We imagine we are much stronger than we really are. We are not taking the competitive market into consideration. If the manufacturer can't manufacture goods in a Union shop, we don't work. It is not merely a strike proposition any longer. It is a question of living and working. Too often, men who join the labor movement imagine that it is merely an organization through which they can use their power, if they care to, to force certain conditions on the employer. . . . I don't approve of that. . . . It is organization and understanding of our own situation that makes for success. That is the thing that builds real organization and that is the policy that we must accept."

These were prophetic words. Years of retreat lay ahead of the Federation, for higher costs now meant not merely a difference between large and reasonable profits, but the difference between profit and loss.

d. RETREAT OF THE UNION AND "INDUSTRY-WIDE" COLLECTIVE BARGAINING

Hosiery prices declined materially in 1927 and the trade papers forecast a 25 per cent reduction in labor costs if union mills were to continue operation. The pressure for lower rates was particularly marked in Philadelphia, where an employers' negotiating committee had been set up. Seeing the inevitability of retreat, the union took steps to do so in an orderly way; a Uniform Price List Committee was appointed.

Trial Retreat

A uniform wage-rate scale, with certain reductions in extras, was established in February 1928 by an agreement for the Philadelphia area. The employers in the New York-New Jersey district immediately demanded the Philadelphia rates. A scale giving them virtual equality of total costs with Philadelphia was adopted although rates for different occupations[37] varied in the two districts. A somewhat similar readjustment of rates also followed in Milwaukee. Two aspects of the revisions are notable: a relatively small adjustment in costs, about 7 to 8 per cent, was effected and the single-machine system was continued.

In explanation of the retreat taken, the president of the Federation reported to the 1928 convention, ". . . it must be understood that this action was taken so we could retreat in an orderly manner, rather than be placed in a position where we would have faced the necessity of accepting unreasonable demands. We demonstrated that we are quite aware of the necessity of having the full-fashioned business profitable for both the employer and the employee. . . ."

The union was not at all convinced of the futility of organization drives to make union standards effective. Actually the need for taking a wage cut, "because of the failure of previous organization drives," spurred the union to increase efforts to extend its influence. A particularly bitter strike occurred in 1928 at Kenosha,

---

37. While the earnings of knitters in New Jersey were above the Philadelphia level, the wages of auxiliary employees were lower. The nonknitting occupations in the West were paid at an even lower scale.

Wisconsin, over the double-job program of the Allen-A Company. In spite of spending about $2 million, the Federation lost, but the company never regained its former position in the industry. Numerous other strikes of the period, less spectacular, were equally ineffective in extending organization or in eliminating double jobs. But the very vigor of the union program made it seem desirable to manufacturers to be free of union influence. Mills started a new movement away from Philadelphia.

With a further failure of intensive organizational drives, and the continued inability of union mills to compete, both employers and workers in these plants finally recognized the need for a carefully devised, long-time wage policy and for a form of bargaining that would contribute to industrial stabilization.

Collective Bargaining on a New Basis

The keynote for scrapping the old wage policy was voiced at the 1928 convention when Vice President Holderman stated: "During the years when the industry was expanding, when wages were increasing and conditions were being bettered, the policy of the Federation as a whole was that each branch should negotiate for its own prices and conditions, with the result that when any particular branch received an increase that increase was always used by some other branch to secure an increase for themselves. . . . It was a system which benefited all of us and, under the circumstances, was the proper one to follow. However, during the past year and a half or two years, we are placed on the defensive . . . and the manufacturer was able to use the lower wage to bring down the wage of those that were paid a little higher."

Many of the manufacturers who dealt with the Federation reasoned that a disorderly deflation of wage rates would demoralize inventory values and the price structure. Yet relatively high union standards could not be maintained in a collective bargaining arrangement that now affected only about a third of the total production.[38]

38. There were about 12,500 machines in operation in the industry in 1928. The union membership included 6,000 knitters who operated on single jobs and on a single-shift basis. Most of the nonunion machinery operated two shifts so that the union mills accounted for only a third of the production. In addition to

Union officials and representatives of a tentative manufacturers' association met in April 1929 to explore the situation. The employers desired recognition of competitive rates and conditions in a uniform national agreement. The Federation accepted the idea of a national agreement, also that union labor costs should be reduced—but not to nonunion levels. The hope of increasing union organization would not be downed, and Federation officials felt that such efforts would have a better chance of success if a national agreement would settle all problems in union mills for a year and permit a concentration of energy upon outside organization.

The first National Labor Agreement was signed in 1929 by fifty-two individual mills operating 4,000 of the 12,500 machines in the industry.[39] Since much of the equipment was of the shorter type and operated on a single shift, about 25 per cent of the industry's capacity was covered by the agreement. Uniform rates were specified. Although the rates were above the northern nonunion level, both parties hoped that the union mills would at least break even. Even this required diverting business from nonunion plants, which the Federation felt would not cut their wage rates because of fear of organization.

The 1929 agreement effected many major changes in collective bargaining terms and procedures. None appeared to be more significant than the union's departure from its cornerstone policy of single-machine operation to agree to a partial doubling up of legging machines.[40] In addition to savings in costs possible through double-machine operation, there was a sizable revision of extra rates. Uniform piece rates were fixed for all departments, but only

a disadvantage through operating single jobs, most union mills carried a further disadvantage in being unable to operate two shifts because of the machinery balance of four leggers for one footer. The latter are operated by a male knitter and two or three female toppers; state laws restricting the hours of work for women limit footers to a single shift. Newer mills had discovered that by installing one footer to every two leggers, the legging machines could be operated on two shifts. This, along with the two-machine system, gave them a decided advantage in costs.

39. In the article on "Policy and Scope" the parties agreed "that it is mutually beneficial and advantageous to arrange and maintain fair, equitable and uniform labor standards and rates throughout the full-fashioned industry. . . . This agreement shall apply uniformly to all the contracting parties hereto. . . ."

40. It was permissible to "double up" 25 per cent of the shorter machines, provided there was no resulting displacement of knitters.

the knitting departments fell under the closed-shop provisions. Along with added membership among auxiliary occupations, the closed-shop clause increased union membership from twelve thousand in 1928 to nearly sixteen thousand in 1930, despite the liquidation or migration of many plants.

The 1929 agreement called for an impartial chairman. He was given broad jurisdictional powers; but substitution of a rule of reason for the well-established pressure methods was naturally a slow development. Some fifty cases were referred to the impartial chairman during the first year[41] and their disposition established many of the fundamental principles that now support the system. It is evident that an impartial chairman cannot "call out the marines" to enforce a decision. The system rather requires the development of a willingness to lose. Such an atmosphere was created in the early years.

The first National Labor Agreement clearly marked the turning point in collective bargaining relationships in the hosiery industry. Both employer and employee representatives displayed courage and foresight in completely changing the nature of their relationship. The new basic principles were (1) a uniform wage scale and agreement to be negotiated by the Association and the Federation, and (2) administration of the agreement by a rule of reason. If the phrase had not been so commonly misapplied, it could be said that the parties displayed "industrial statesmanship" of the highest order.[42]

Rapid Deflation of Wage Rates

The new kind of collective bargaining received an acid test from 1929 to 1933 when the industry encountered a cyclical deflation superimposed upon a downward trend in costs and prices. Union organizing efforts were still unsuccessful. In addition to previous obstacles the fear of unemployment was now added to

41. Paul Abelson acted as impartial chairman from 1929 to 1931.
42. The parties believed they were creating an additional fundamental change in setting up a Joint Time Study and Effort Committee to fix base rates and extras in balance on a scientific basis. Extensive time studies were jointly made at a considerable cost, but the results were not usable. They were too complex for general understanding and a complete analysis was beyond the resources of the parties. This committee's work ceased after 1930.

keep employees away from the union. In these years they often had to choose between wage cuts and unemployment. They chose to work.

The Federation debated two possible programs—a general strike or further wage cuts. It decided that a general strike would be impractical; since only the employees in union mills would respond, a strike would not change the competitive position between union and nonunion mills. Further wage cuts were inevitable. Union labor costs had become so far out of line that some union mills shut down to buy gray goods[43] from nonunion mills at less than they could produce them in their own plants. Other union mills became suppliers of gray goods to nonunion mills which lacked sufficient capacity to meet their peak requirements. The development of a gray goods market was crucial in fashioning later developments.[44]

In 1930, the union labor cost was $3.30 a dozen on a "bread and butter" number. It was estimated that nonunion northern labor costs on a similar style averaged $2.14 while southern direct labor costs were $1.60 a dozen. The Federation, therefore, yielded to the manufacturers' request for further development of the two-machine system and made additional reductions which cut labor costs by 18 per cent. These adjustments were made in the 1930 agreement, which was a contract between the Association for all its members and the Federation for all its locals and members.[45] It had no sooner been signed than a group of employers, presum-

---

43. Knitted and seamed work, not yet dyed or finished.

44. In turning to gray goods business, some union mills saw an opportunity of working with less current capital because goods would not be held so long and merchandising expenses could be avoided. Moreover, speculative losses on the downswing were minimized. They further limited their potential liabilities by engaging in commission knitting, the purchaser supplying the silk. But the giving up of these risk-taking functions also limited the possibility of profits. Moreover, in dealing in a standardized type of work, competition became exceedingly keen and it soon became impossible to secure full overhead costs. The pressure for reduced rates was strongest in commission and gray goods mills; less in mills selling finished goods. By 1937 almost 35 per cent of the production of knitting mills was made on commission or sold in the gray and most of this work was done by union mills. This tendency strongly influenced wage-rate policies under the collective agreements.

45. The closed-shop provision was extended by this agreement to all hosiery-producing departments.

ably bound by the Association action, refused to accept the agreement or to enter into any contractual relations with the union. Nonunion territories and mills, especially in Reading, had undercut the new rates before the ink of the signatures had dried.

Nor did the new agreement solve the union problem. With doubling up of jobs and the demand for hosiery falling off, almost half the Federation members were jobless. The union faced a struggle for survival amidst a wholesale disintegration of standards. Within a few months after its effective date, the 1930 agreement was modified to reinstate the single-machine system. A further sacrifice of rates was necessary to return to the single jobs so essential to provide work for union members.

This policy, effected by the so-called "18th Amendment" to the 1930 agreement, was exceedingly unpopular with employees in the shops where work was relatively steady. As in later years, union policy ran a gauntlet of conflicting interests of employees working steadily and those on short time or unemployed. The differences were more marked when gray goods or commission business increased in many shops, and brought seasonal operations.

When the 1930 agreement neared its expiration date, union mills were working 45 per cent of capacity while Reading mills operated at 80 per cent. The South was at 90 per cent of capacity, but was not a major threat as it was still a relatively small producer. At a special convention of the Federation the Reading workers were warned to join the union and maintain union standards in their shops, or bear the consequences of such a deep cut in union rates as would jeopardize their jobs. The union was determined to place its manufacturers in a competitive position. When the Reading workers would not accept the role assigned to them, the convention worked out a detailed program for a wage cut drastic enough to complete deflation at once.

The 1931–1932 agreement reduced wages 30 to 45 per cent for various occupations, or an average of 60 to 65 per cent below the 1927 peak level. It also brought genuine employer acceptance of a long-sought union objective: the closed shop and the checkoff. For adopting such a wage policy, the criticism of a large part of the labor movement was heaped upon the Federation. The rank and file, moreover, were far from unanimous over it. Only after many years was there general approval of the union's courageous step in 1931, which meant its surviving to build up industry standards.

In the meantime, many employees and locals would not go along with this new National Labor Agreement. Insurgent strikes occurred, especially in the New Jersey district and in Milwaukee. The rank-and-file protest then suddenly focused upon Reading as the cause of the collapse of union standards. There was a dramatic and spontaneous march of five thousand hosiery workers upon Reading. They came in automobile caravans and pitched their camps to stay until the district was organized. But the Reading workers did not respond, and work soon began in all union shops.

For a while, the 1931 agreement improved the condition of union mills. Data collected by a Profits Commission[46] showed that up to January 1, 1932, union mills operated 82 per cent of capacity in comparison with 73 per cent for nonunion mills. But with the deepening of the depression in 1932 this situation did not long exist. Early that year old trends were resumed, union mills moved, closed or liquidated. Moreover, as nonunion manufacturers went on short time they explained to their employees that this novel experience had been caused by the union, which was diverting their established orders to Philadelphia shops. Not only did the nonunion workers accept the wage cuts necessary to get their just share of the business, but they often placed the blame for their cuts upon the union.

Neither the Federation nor the Association had the heart to suggest further cuts and the 1931–1932 agreement was renewed without change for another year. The depths were reached early in 1933, when mills signatory to the National Labor Agreement represented but 22 per cent of the equipment of the industry and accounted for about 15 per cent of the production.

The Federation and Association mills were caught in what ap-

46. A committee of five was composed of two employer representatives, two union representatives, and an impartial fifth member to analyze the profits of union employers in order to determine when a wage increase could equitably be made. The Commission made one report recommending no change of rates and was then disbanded.

peared to be a fatal whirlpool of economic problems. Under the collective agreements, relatively high wages were paid for operating the less productive machines of the industry. The union plants had failed to modernize their equipment when earnings were large and they were, besides, unschooled in the highly competitive business that had evolved. Lacking profits for the past five years, many union mills could not endure further losses without liquidation; and this very situation prevented them from getting credit for the new and more productive equipment necessary to support higher wages and profitable operation.

Smaller union mills, lacking both financial resources and the means of meeting the new distribution problem, turned more and more to selling in the gray to converters, or to meet the peak requirements of nonunion mills. The highly competitive nature of this business and the difficulty of earning a profit created new pressure on wage rates. With an increasing volume of sales in the gray, union mills had less employment in their finishing departments and increased their overhead. A commercial dyeing and finishing industry had developed with advantages in overhead costs and wages. This induced further selling in the gray. In the face of these interrelated questions many a plant manager felt that he was simply going around in circles.

By the early months of 1933, there seemed little hope for the union mills or for the Federation. Their brave attempt to meet their problems appeared wasted effort.

Organization During the Deflation Period

Although the sweeping wage decreases in the years 1929–1931 brought no demand for organization from nonunion employees in the crucial Reading district, demand did arise elsewhere, and in a furious fashion in Philadelphia nonunion mills.

A strike against wage cuts by fourteen hundred employees of H. C. Aberle Company late in 1929 resulted finally in a closed-shop agreement.[47] That was merely the forerunner of troubles to

47. This was a violent strike in which workers from other industries in the Kensington district participated. A striking knitter, Carl Makley, was killed. Later when the Federation developed its nationally known cooperative housing project, it was called "The Carl Makley Apartments."

come. Late in 1930 and early in 1931, employees of eight Philadelphia firms struck against wage decreases and immediately joined the union. A general strike of forty-two Philadelphia nonunion mills was soon in progress under Federation auspices. The union objective was "stabilization of the industry" through uniform labor rates in all mills.

The strikes were bitterly contested. Mass picketing was accompanied by mass arrests—during the strike more than twelve hundred pickets were arrested. Rioting was prevalent and the general public demanded action to stop the conflict. The Mayor of Philadelphia then appointed a committee of citizens to act as a fact-finding commission—which made an inept report.

In the meantime many mills settled with the union. Sweeping injunctions forbade picketing at the larger Philadelphia mills, such as Apex, Artcraft and Brownhill & Kramer, all of which were to experience sitdown strikes in 1937. But from about nineteen mills the union secured agreements to pay the union scale and to adopt union conditions. The results were far from salutary. Most of the newly signed plants liquidated, closed down, migrated or operated on short time. Some did so to protect capital investment; others found it more difficult to operate under union rates, especially since market contacts had been lost during the strike. This experience convinced union officials that extension of union influence could not be successfully accomplished in a piecemeal manner; there had to be either mass organization or no organization.

To be sure, northern hosiery manufacturers outside the Association were not satisfied with conditions. They did not relish the unstabilizing effect of continuous reductions in union wage rates on prices and profits. The Philadelphia strikes had shown that wage cuts in nonunion mills would make their plants vulnerable to unionization. These considerations led the nonunion manufacturers in the Philadelphia area (including many in Reading) to form the Full-Fashioned Hosiery Association, Inc., in order to adopt a wage policy of their own. Many members of this Association believed sincerely in a uniform piece-rate scale, even to the extent of adopting the rates of the National Labor Agreement.

Hosiery

But they were also unanimous in the belief that collective bargaining with the American Federation of Hosiery Workers was to be avoided if mills were to continue to give full-time employment on a profitable basis. This Association of nonunion manufacturers claimed in 1933 to represent 60 per cent of the industry's production capacity. That was undoubtedly an inflated figure; probably only about 40 per cent was represented by the membership of the group.

e. ORGANIZING AND BARGAINING, 1933–1935

The apparent hopelessness of conditions just before 1933 made the New Deal a godsend. The Federation used Section 7(a) of the National Industrial Recovery Act as impetus for a more powerful organization drive. Employers, union and nonunion,[48] promptly moved for a code to eliminate unfair competition and the Federation dreamed of achieving industry-wide standards by the code route.

The 1933 Strikes

Purchasers of full-fashioned hosiery increased their commitments from March to July of 1933 in anticipation of the greatly increased prices the Hosiery Code was expected to bring.[49] The employers were anxious to avoid strikes which would interfere with the first really profitable business that had come along in several years. Almost immediately upon the passage of the National Industrial Recovery Act employees in four Reading hosiery mills struck. The stoppage spread until every one of the thirty mills in the Berks County area was closed. Even at the Berkshire Knitting Mills, the largest full-fashioned hosiery mill in the world, the strike was effective. The Reading hosiery strike became case number one on the docket of the National Labor Board

---

48. Most of them were members of the National Association of Hosiery Manufacturers which was not directly concerned with labor policies but which was otherwise the trade association of the industry. The Full-Fashioned Hosiery Manufacturers of America, Inc. represents the union manufacturers in their relations with the union.

49. This purchasing in the early months of the year resulted in a reversal of the usual seasonal pattern of purchasing. Shipments from the mills decreased in the ordinarily active last three months of the year.

which had been created, under the chairmanship of Senator Wagner, to assist in the amicable settlement of labor disputes.[50]

The Reading strike settlement forecast the way in which national labor policy was to move. An industrial election was held [51] to decide whether the employees wanted two officers of the Federation, listed solely as individuals on the ballot, to represent them in collective bargaining. In twenty-nine mills out of thirty-one that was their wish.

As the Reading strike gathered momentum, a strike was called against all nonunion mills in the Philadelphia area. The call was cancelled upon advice from government officials that all "unnecessary interference with recovery" should be avoided, and the union was urged to make full use of the NRA provisions for settlement of labor disputes. While the projected Philadelphia strike was avoided, numerous stoppages occurred in other parts of the industry, even in certain southern territories. Organization activity was especially strong in Fort Wayne and Indianapolis, as well as in numerous small Pennsylvania towns.

Nonunion Employers' Wage Policy

After five or six years of retreat, the hosiery union was definitely on the march. This was fully realized by nonunion manufacturers in the North. It was certain that under the NRA, the industry would soon reduce operating schedules to forty hours a week for each shift. It was virtually certain that to avoid a reduced weekly wage union pressure would raise existing wage rates by at least 20 per cent.

The nonunion manufacturers' association decided upon a spectacular move. It announced a forty-hour week and adoption of the 1932 National Labor Agreement's scale with a 25 per cent general wage increase. The program was clearly conceived as insur-

50. It will be recalled that this Board was technically empowered to act only under Section 7(a) of the "President's Re-employment Agreements"—the so-called "blanket" agreements. Nevertheless, its services were widely utilized and its actions later approved by Executive Order of the President.

51. The agreement to settle the strike through election for designation of a bargaining agency is of interest in revealing the signs of the time. The officers of the Federation and the Berks County employers "agreed with the Labor Board, but not with each other," to the terms of an election.

ance against unionization. Nonunion manufacturers had to absorb the large increases in labor cost,[52] which were not covered by the slight advances that occurred in hosiery prices or by the prospective decrease in overhead due to full-time operations.

For a short time the National Labor Agreement rates were below the nonunion rates of the North. Such an anomalous relationship could not long persist, and the 1932 National Agreement was adjusted by the union manufacturers to the new level established by the nonunion mills. Uniformity of rates now applied to well over two thirds of the industry or throughout most of the northern producing area.

Code Making

The NRA Code for the hosiery industry was the sixteenth to be approved. Federation representatives participated fully in its preparation. It became effective on September 4, 1933.[53]

Here was really industry-wide collective bargaining. Labor standards were set for the entire industry. Terms that years of collective bargaining had not won were quickly put into a code. A series of minimum wages, for example, was set with occupational classifications.[54] Recognizing the impracticability of eliminating the two-machine system, but still adhering to the single-machine idea, the Federation secured the manufacturers' promise that present double jobs would be operated with two helpers instead of one, and that no more doubling of machines would be allowed. Apparently this increased the possibility of training too many knitters, but actually it became more expensive to operate double jobs.[55] The operation of footing machines on a double shift, more-

---

52. In some instances, nonunion manufacturers increased their wage rates from 50 to 100 per cent to conform to this program.

53. A temporary code embodying the labor provisions had been made effective July 26, 1933.

54. The minima for skilled employees ranged from $13.00 a week for the simple tasks to $27.50 a week for 51-gauge knitters. A wage approximately 10 per cent lower was specified for the South.

55. This particular regulatory device was necessary to meet the argument of employers that double jobs were necessary to train knitters. It was finally agreed that if such training was really essential, the employer should be willing to assume an added cost burden. The issue was no longer so crucial, since longer machines were becoming more usual in nonunion shops which normally operated them as single jobs.

over, was restricted by requiring the payment of bonus wages to the operators. The Federation was also in the forefront in securing labor representation on Industry Code Authorities, two of its representatives being placed on the hosiery governing board.

Negotiating a New National Labor Agreement

In the midst of all the rapid-fire changes in 1933, negotiations were undertaken for a new National Labor Agreement to replace the one expiring August 31, 1933. Negotiations for a new agreement proceeded haltingly. When the Hosiery Code became effective, the pre-Code boom in production and shipments ceased. An already satiated market decreased its buying. Employers were reluctant to make any further concessions to the union. A one-day strike was ordered by the Executive Board of the Federation; the National Labor Agreement was then renewed with the addition of Article E, a flexibility clause,[56] and an agreement to refer the union demand for a 20 per cent increase to arbitration by the National Labor Board set up under the NRA.[57]

The resulting "Wolman Award" of the National Labor Board came December 16, 1933. It ordered an increase in labor costs of 10 cents a dozen [58] and called upon the parties to distribute such a cost increase over the various occupations so as to iron out inequalities in earnings. The award had certain novel and sound aspects. It properly recognized that the real issue was how far added costs could be borne by manufacturers; and it was based upon the premise that a slight addition could best be used to eliminate certain inequalities of earnings rather than as a flat percentage in-

56. The flexibility clause read: "If during the term of this agreement, or any renewal thereof, there shall be any significant change in the factors upon which wages depend, either in cost of production, competitive conditions, cost of living, or other factors of similar importance, either party may demand a change in existing rates. If the parties, within 15 days from such demand, are not able to agree upon a scale of rates, all differences or disputes shall be determined by arbitration before a Wage Rate Tribunal. . . ."

57. A number of other matters respecting the wording of certain clauses of the agreement were submitted to arbitration.

58. The adjustment, which represented a 5 per cent increase in labor costs, was ordered effective retroactively to November 15, 1933, which was designated as the date of the new agreement. This agreement was in force until September 1, 1935.

crease in all rates. The rates of the Wolman Award, as applied by the parties to the National Labor Agreement, were adopted by most nonunion manufacturers in the North, although they did not increase the rates retroactively to November 15, as was required of signatories to the National Labor Agreement.

The year 1933 seemed to bring realization of many fond hopes of the parties to the National Labor Agreement. Industry-wide minimum labor standards had been set to catch the "chiseling fringe" of employers. The union had, at last, extended its organization and exerted sufficient influence to have the union scale of rates and standards effective throughout the North. Moreover, gains during the year seemed to signify the end of deflation and to justify previous retreats that had kept the Federation in business. In general, manufacturers were satisfied with their profit showing for 1933. Happy days seemed really to be here again.

Post-Code Depression

The situation was too good to be true. Early in 1934, it was evident that the Code boom was over; the bottom had dropped out of the hosiery market. Not only did all the old headaches return, but after such blighted hopes the outlook appeared doubly dismal. Union mills resumed their migration to the South, to rural Pennsylvania, and now also to South Jersey, which became the latest rate-cutting territory. In addition, a difference between Code terms applying to inside finishing plants and to commercial dyeing and finishing plants [59] induced union mills to discontinue their finishing operations. This resulted in loss of jobs by union workers and put more union mills in the gray goods business.

The new depression was felt throughout the hosiery industry, which demanded stabilizing action from its Code Authority. The response was: (1) vain and inglorious efforts to effectuate the Code provision that made selling below production cost an unfair trade practice; (2) a mandatory curtailment of shift operation of

---

59. The terms related to overtime operations and Saturday work which were permissible under the Finishers Code, but not under the Hosiery Code. While Code minimum wages were identical for the two businesses, the commercial shops customarily paid the minimum wages while the "inside shops" were required by collective agreement to pay in excess of the minima.

machines under NRA authority to twenty-four hours a week for a five-week period beginning December 18, 1933; (3) a price-fixing venture that aroused the ire of NRA authorities and others and died aborning.

A New Pattern for Organization

The Federation was no more successful than the manufacturers in coping with the unexpected difficulties. It turned again to organization drives now based upon new concepts. "Organization from the top" was attempted, with the union trying to convince the employer of the benefits of a uniform wage policy. Employers were now more willing to accept equality of labor rates as a desirable stabilizing force. They were willing to admit that an industry wage policy required the policing services of the union.[60] Numerous agreements on such a basis were signed at this time, especially in the commercial dyeing and finishing industry. In some instances, preferential or closed shops were secured even though the union membership was a negligible percentage of the employees in a plant.

In most cases, however, the union had to win recognition through organizing employees. The industrial election offered a new and promising technique as a substitute for the organizing strike. The Federation had won an election in Reading after all other tactics had failed; it is not surprising, therefore, that it was an early and frequent user of this technique.

The situation in 1934, however, was different from that of 1933. It was learned that elections could be lost and that victory did not assure genuine collective bargaining. The Federation cancelled all the Reading agreements when employers continued to resist its participation with management in fixing rates and conditions of employment. The system of arbitration that had been introduced under Reading agreements broke down when the employers refused to abide by a decision—the only instance of this sort in the history of the industry. In addition to the loss of Reading a number of important elections were lost in 1934 and in

---

60. Many nonunion manufacturers who had supported northern wage-rate equality found themselves "holding the bag" as their fellows slashed the wage rates they had solemnly accepted for the "good of the industry."

several instances union victory was followed by liquidation or migration. Since 1934 Federation officials have known that there is no royal road to organizing employees.

Reconsideration of Wage Policy

Undermining of union standards was accelerated after the invalidation of the NRA in 1935, despite an effort of the leaders of the hosiery industry to maintain standards by adherence to a "Voluntary Code." The nonunion manufacturers' association sought to maintain the accepted wage scale in nonunion plants and thus preserve the union standards that were still effective in over half of the industry. Some nonunion manufacturers even showed a disposition to cooperate with the union in securing observance of the standards.

Voluntary standards were difficult to maintain. When a company had the choice of hewing to the line or continuing to operate, the standards meant little. The union again subjected its wage policy to scrutiny. President Rieve came out strongly for district agreements as the only way to deal realistically with widely different local and plant problems. The oldest producing area, Philadelphia, had especially the problems of old machines and migration of companies. A national wage policy which would have helped Philadelphia would have been ill-adapted to the Midwest where, for the most part, the equipment was more modern. There was also the question as to whether the same piece-rate scale should be applied to both gray-goods and finished-goods mills.

While these were moot questions, other difficulties with the rigid uniformity of rates appeared. Although piece rates, and hence direct labor costs, were the same for the mills under the National Labor Agreement, wide variations in hourly, weekly and annual wages resulted from such factors as different quality requirements, flow of work, upkeep of equipment, standardization of raw material. It was found that the mills with higher earnings attracted the better workers, thus accentuating the differences between plants. What should be uniform about wages—piece rates or hourly wages? Were wages dependent upon an equality of total manufacturing costs? The comprehensive discussions on the subject were interesting but held forth no promise of resolving the question.

The 1935 Agreement

Much of the discussion over wage policy appeared academic when the manufacturers' association made it unmistakably clear, after extended negotiations, that it would deny the union claim for a 20 per cent wage increase and insist upon a 20 per cent decrease. Nor were the manufacturers willing to bargain on a district or individual plant basis. To avoid the strike or lockout that would probably result from any fundamental change of bargaining policy, the National Labor Agreement was renewed. After scores of "demands" had been made by each party, two points still remained at issue, and it was agreed that they would be arbitrated by Lessing J. Rosenwald. The arbitration covered (1) the employers' claim that an 11 per cent extra bonus to operators on two-shift footers should be eliminated, and (2) the claim of each party for a 20 per cent adjustment in labor rates. All claims were disallowed and the agreement continued as heretofore.

The recent years had emphasized the rapidity with which economic factors could change and make any wage policy ineffective. Moreover, the task faced by the Federation and the Full-Fashioned Hosiery Manufacturers in agreeing upon any wage policy for the whole industry was becoming more and more difficult. An increasing dependence upon arbitration showed that formidable obstacles stood in the way of a clear wage policy.

f. LAPSE OF COLLECTIVE BARGAINING, 1936

During the 1935–1936 agreement, Federation locals continued at sixes and sevens over what constituted a proper wage policy. Some branches bitterly decried arbitration, even insisting upon elimination of the "flexibility" clause of the National Labor Agreement. Strangely enough, these groups favored a uniform piece-rate scale under the agreement. They had been working with relative steadiness and they feared that further wage reductions might be accepted through the pressure of unemployment in other areas, especially in Philadelphia. An equally vocal group insisted upon district or individual plant agreements, either to allow adjustments to meet local problems, or to have another try at the old army game. The formula of renewing agreements and arbitrating all unsettled issues had its adherents. Because of these wide differences, there was little belief that any problems could be solved by a strike.

No single program for collective bargaining policy could receive majority support in the Federation. The National Labor Agreement expired on October 23, 1936 and the Federation cancelled all of its individual agreements.

Paradoxically the breakdown of collective bargaining relations showed the vital strength of the collective bargaining program that had been built up. In the absence of an agreement and with union realization of the futility of a strike, the parties met their day-to-day problems as in the past. Wage rates were not changed, and the industrial common law that had been so laboriously built up solved most of the questions that arose. When it appeared that the momentum of the past relationship could easily carry the parties through a year without formal collective bargaining, a status quo understanding was tacitly reached. Again the parties had an object lesson to show that sound collective bargaining relationships are not dependent upon what is written in an agreement but upon a state of mind which accepts joint participation in meeting all problems of industrial relations. Things were really not much different during the status quo year without agreements than in the previous year when an involved agreement was signed with pomp and ceremony.

Absence of a wage policy and agreements brought no moratorium on organizing efforts. During the year of no agreements, a special organization assessment equivalent to 3 per cent of dues was levied. The officers of the American Federation of Hosiery Workers were active in the formation of the CIO, not only because of their affiliation with the United Textile Workers, but because, like other original members of the CIO group, they had experienced the limitation of pure and simple collective bargaining and sought a wider objective.

g. THE 1937 DRIVE FOR AGREEMENTS

The officials of the hosiery union participated actively in the wave of CIO strikes that began early in 1937. Organization strikes were being won again by the union.

Resumption of a National Labor Agreement

In the atmosphere of "labor on the march" negotiations for a new contract were resumed in June 1937 between the Full-Fashioned Hosiery Manufacturers of America and the Federation. Business was good. Much of the buying was speculative, however, to insure a certainty of supply in the event of strikes. The apparently favorable business conditions resolved for the time being the union's dilemma over a wage policy, for association members were now willing to grant increased wage rates in a revived National Labor Agreement. Since the northern nonunion manufacturers' association had worked for wage rate uniformity and acknowledged the need of a wage policy for the industry, the negotiators sought to write an agreement in which the nonunion group would join. The attempt failed and when the 1937–1938 National Labor Agreement was signed, as of June 15, 1937, it applied only to the members of the Full-Fashioned Hosiery Manufacturers of America, Inc.

The new agreement increased most base rates from 6 to 9 per cent and set a minimum wage of $15.00 a week for skilled employees not specifically covered by higher minima. It also accepted the principle that all employees of hosiery plants involved should be subject to the closed-shop provision with the exception of those in clerical and supervisory positions.[61]

Organization in 1937

Even before the signing of the new agreement, however, strikes

---

61. Most of the employers were not averse to going along with this extension of the closed shop. Already, in a few instances, strikes had been called or pressure applied by other unions claiming jurisdiction over a few truckers or a few machinists employed by a hosiery mill. It was possible that such disputes would result in picket lines through which hosiery workers would not pass, thereby violating the no-strike understanding. There were many advantages to both sides in extending the coverage of the closed-shop provision.

occurred in those nonunion shops which had been urged to go along voluntarily with the agreement. A sitdown strike at the Apex Hosiery Company began in May 1937. After the signing of the National Labor Agreement, the wave of strikes for union recognition that was sweeping the country had its counterpart in the hosiery industry. A drive was started by Branch One [62] to make Philadelphia completely closed shop. Most nonunion mills capitulated to the tremendous pressure of the drive. Besides the Apex affair, a number of other sitdowns were conducted, the most important being at the Artcraft Silk Hosiery Company and the Brownhill-Kramer Company plants.

When Philadelphia mills countered by moving equipment, riots and violence developed. It was now realized that Philadelphia was drying up as the principal hosiery center, and that loss of machines meant permanent loss of jobs. When the drive was over, all but two hosiery plants in Philadelphia had standard, closed-shop union agreements. More machines and plants, however, had been lost in the process. And the union assumed a heavy liability, in terms of adverse public opinion and potential legal damages, for the manner in which the strikes were conducted.[63]

Many of the old type machines moved from Philadelphia were placed in small plants, some of them family shops, where the absence of union standards made it possible to operate them. The old type machines had now reached the stage of obsolescence in which their production had a value but slightly in excess of prime cost, and would not carry any "regular" wages prevailing in industrial centers.[64]

62. When the status of the UTW was obscured by the setting up of the Textile Workers Organizing Committee, Local 706 in Philadelphia, which had also been Branch One of the Federation, discontinued the use of the 706 designation.
63. Some mention should perhaps be made of the *Apex* case. It will be recalled that on November 29, 1939 a United States Circuit Court of Appeals overruled a Federal District Court judgment levying a penalty of over $700,000 against Branch One, on the grounds that jurisdiction lay with the state courts and not with the federal courts. In May 1940 the Supreme Court upheld the Circuit Court decision.
64. The hosiery industry experience shows the reluctance of obsolete machines to leave an industry. To meet their relative disadvantages, they are revalued and change hands. But they will be sold and not scrapped as long as their production has a value in excess of standard prime cost. When machine value computed on

The 1937 organizing effort in hosiery was by no means confined to Philadelphia. As early as March 1937, there were sixteen sit-down strikes in Reading. Finally a number of Reading manufacturers settled with the union and formed the Keystone Manufacturers Association as their bargaining agent.[65] Before the 1937 National Labor Agreement had been signed, the Keystone group made a joint agreement with the union which embodied the rates of the 1935 National Labor Agreement. As compared with mills signing the new agreement, the Keystone group thus had an advantage in rates equivalent to the wage increases of the 1937 National Agreement.

After the organization drives were over, the Federation had more contracts with employers than at any time in its history. Most of them had closed-shop provisions.[66] Besides the 40 mills covered by the National Labor Agreement, 113 individual agreements had been signed in the full-fashioned branch of the industry. The addition of agreements in the seamless branch, in the commercial dyeing and finishing industry and in other related branches [67] brought the total up to 208. In the full-fashioned section of the industry, the union had effective control of the labor standards under which the bulk of the northern production was made.

Business Reaction

The market crash in October 1937 brought an especially drastic falling off in hosiery activity, since anticipatory buying had re-

---

this basis has disappeared, a new value is created through the decrease of the labor cost element of prime cost. These relationships will undoubtedly be affected by the establishment of minimum wages under the Fair Labor Standards Act.

65. The largest mills in Reading, with one exception, were not members of the Keystone group. Each of the nonassociation mills signed individual agreements with the Federation. The Reading strikes in 1937 did not seriously affect the large Berkshire Knitting Mills which, the Federation claimed, had violated the unfair labor practice provisions of the National Labor Relations Act. A prolonged hearing was held on the claim and the decision of the Board, substantially upholding union claims, was appealed by the company.

66. The Reading agreements, with one exception, did not include the closed shop.

67. While the organization drive was under way, the Federation signed an agreement with a company manufacturing knitting machine needles and secured other contracts for silk-throwing departments and mills. Thus the jurisdiction of the union was extended.

sulted in the purchase of fall requirements in earlier months. Curtailed operations were more general in union mills, especially in Reading and Philadelphia, which were at 50 per cent of capacity. On the other hand, the growing number of southern mills continued at or near capacity. Expansion in the South now had the proportion of a little boom. Philadelphia steadily decreased in importance; only 12 per cent of the equipment there was running full time in December.

The union mills, especially those in Philadelphia, bore the full force of the downswing and a few more plants were lost to the Federation. In 1934 there were 3,890 machines in Philadelphia; early in 1937 the number had fallen to 2,814. During the last three months of 1937, 4,500 Philadelphia employees lost their jobs through plant liquidations. Of the machines that moved from Philadelphia, 26 per cent had gone to rural Pennsylvania, 59 per cent to the South, 7 per cent to Maryland, 2 per cent to Delaware and 6 per cent to upper New York State.

So divergent had become the interests of employed and unemployed workers in Philadelphia that Branch One anticipated that its regulations and policies would be determined solely by the needs of the increasing number of the jobless. It seemed likely that "make-work" programs would be demanded and wage rates would be reduced in a vain effort to save obsolete machines that were doomed anyway. Branch One requested the executive committee of the Federation for a ruling to permit the dropping of unemployed members from the union rolls when they failed to register for three consecutive months. This was on the assumption that such failure indicated they had left the trade.

In the face of the new crisis, the officials of the Philadelphia local proposed a 6 per cent wage cut. While the proposal was turned down by the membership, unemployed members showed disposition to work for what they could get. The employees in one shop in New Jersey ignored the terms of their agreement and chose to accept reduced rates rather than to maintain the union standard in idleness. Nor was the Federation successful in having the local courts restrain the company from deviating from its agreement terms.

Arbitration Under the Flexibility Clause

The Full-Fashioned Hosiery Manufacturers explored the possibilities for lowering costs and finally invoked Article E, the flexibility clause of the National Labor Agreement. The manufacturers' claim for reduced rates was arbitrated by William M. Leiserson. A substantial revision of "extras" was ordered in a decision which effected an average reduction of about 14 per cent in labor costs. This decision was followed by a four-day insurgent strike in Philadelphia and New Jersey, principally in shops that had been working relatively "steady" and whose employees saw no need for rate revision. At the same time the Keystone Manufacturers Association invoked their flexibility clause. After arbitration by Alfred H. Williams, the wage rates for the Keystone group were made identical with those in the Leiserson decision.

The Old Machinery Problem

Even the revised rates of the Leiserson decision did not meet the major problems of the union mills. It had become obvious to manufacturers and to union officials that the unfortunate plight of many older union mills did not arise solely from the wages they paid. Already the hourly earnings of employees in many union shops approached earnings in the southern mills, and annual earnings in the latter undoubtedly averaged higher because of their steadier operations. But costs on the older machines were competitively out of line. Nor was there any way to make these machines competitive for the long pull simply by rate reductions.

The mill with 39- and 42-gauge equipment, of 18- and 20-section types,[68] was badly squeezed between competition from small shops operating similar machines without regard to standards, and newer machines making quality merchandise at lower costs. Many concerns with the old equipment could get only gray goods business from other mills.

To be sure, not all union mills produced gray goods on obsolete equipment. Most nationally advertised brands of full-fashioned

---

68. Gauge indicates the fineness of stitch; the newer machines were 45-gauge types. The number of sections determines the number of stockings knit simultaneously. The newer machines were of 24 sections.

hosiery come from union mills which have notable distribution systems and high quality standards. While these mills also faced the necessity of improving their equipment, they were in a better position than others by having retained control over the sale of their goods in finished form. But even these mills showed losses and insisted upon the need for competitive labor costs.

The union could not take direct steps to meet the merchandising problems of the gray goods mill, which caused a constant pressure on wages. It appeared, however, that the sine qua non for improved merchandising was the production of better quality hosiery at a lower cost on modern machines. Insofar as all union mills were concerned, further adjustments on the old machines would merely result in a continuance of severe competition at a lower level, and would only slightly defer the date when the old machines would no longer be usable. A negative or standpat policy could not be followed, however, since that would merely keep all mills in a noncompetitive position.

The various aspects of the situation were thoroughly explored by the joint negotiating committee for the Federation and the manufacturers' association. Many manufacturers agreed with the union that just to take additional wage cuts would not help very long. Wage cuts as incident to a plan for rehabilitation of equipment of union mills, however, were another matter. Both sides joined in working out a "Rehabilitation Program."

h. THE REHABILITATION PROGRAM

The time was opportune in 1938. Inventive efforts of the past decade had created marked improvements in knitting equipment.[69] If this equipment were installed only in the South, then the days of the North as an important producing area were numbered. But if new capital could be attracted to union mills, then

---

69. Legging machines of 26 and 28 sections and footing machines of 30 sections were now available to operate more than 76 courses per minute as compared with 52 courses on the old machines and 60 courses on the 24-section types. A "course" is a row of loops across the stocking. In addition, the newest machines had many automatic features that tended to increase production. The so-called single-unit machine had neared perfection; it was capable of making the leg and the foot on the same machine in a single operation.

high wages could be compatible with low labor costs. The Federation and the manufacturers' association were equally anxious to induce the installation of the newest machines in union plants.

Rehabilitation Formula

After long negotiations, the manufacturers' group was ready to install new machines if the Federation would revise rates on the older equipment to a competitive basis until the rehabilitation program had been completed. This meant, in some plants, acceptance of hourly earnings on a par with, or even below, those of southern mills paying "good" wages for that district.

Two requisites of the program soon became apparent: (1) the agreement must run longer than a year if new capital was to be freely invested; and (2) adjustment of rates involved the scrapping of the uniform scale. Uniform piece rates had resulted in wide variations in hourly earnings. Hourly wages could now be reduced by only a limited amount in mills where wages were low. This was of practical importance because of the virtual certainty that a relatively high minimum wage would be set for the hosiery industry under the Fair Labor Standards Act. On the other hand, cost savings might be made more readily in mills or departments where hourly earnings were still comparatively high. By the very nature of the problem wage-rate negotiation to support rehabilitation had to be conducted on an individual plant basis. For these adjustments were supposed to induce new machinery installations, and those depended upon whether individual concerns could get capital.

On July 15, 1938, the Federation and the manufacturers' association agreed to a three-year renewal of the National Labor Agreement in the form of a master contract defining the fundamental relations between the parties. Article C provided, in part, ". . . the present rates of pay, hours, working conditions, and decisions of the Impartial Chairman heretofore rendered, shall remain in full force and effect . . . provided, however, that with a view toward achieving uniformity of earnings for the various operations and stabilization of the industry, the union may modify rates of pay, hours, working conditions and/or decisions of the

Impartial Chairman heretofore rendered, in any mill, with its consent, by direct negotiations with such member."

Acting under this clause, supplementary agreements were signed by January 1939 between the Federation and each member mill. The pattern of negotiations was unusual for the hosiery industry. An employer gave the shop committee and union officials his minimum program of machinery installation and an estimate of the revision in costs on present equipment necessary to provide continuity of employment. After bargaining on both points, an agreed-upon reduction in total labor costs would be allocated to the various occupations on the basis of a comprehensive wage analysis, prepared by the office of the impartial chairman for each signatory mill. An effort was made to apportion the cost saving over the various occupations so as to maintain reasonable hourly earnings for each. The employer and union officials then presented at a meeting of all plant employees the new program, which had to be approved by a majority of employees concerned and then by officers of the Federation. Although the exact rates for an occupation differed widely among plants, union mills as a group agreed to install new machinery equal to 10 per cent of the equipment in place, in return for a 15 per cent reduction in labor costs.

Without a supplementary agreement, obsolete plants unable to buy new machines were bound by the National Labor Agreement to pay such relatively high wage rates that they would be forced out of business immediately. Even though their days were numbered, neither the managements nor their employees were willing to "fold up" when some work might be had. Most of such plants signed supplementary agreements with new machinery commitments about which both management and union kept their fingers crossed and hoped for the best.

Increase of Silk Prices

The full-fashioned hosiery industry had no unanimous opinion about the practicability of the rehabilitation program. Some employers held that new capital could not be induced to come to union centers and that financing of new machinery should come from profits on old equipment. Many employees felt that they were buying machines for the employers and that their cut in wages should not be "passed along to the buyer."

Most opinions had to be revised when a sharp rise in raw silk prices greatly increased production costs. When the supplementary agreements were being drawn silk was $1.70 a pound; within a few months it was $2.70 a pound. Material costs thus rose 75 cents a dozen while labor costs fell 25 cents a dozen, and market prices for hosiery remained virtually the same.[70]

The impact of the change in raw material prices fell mainly upon the gray goods mills and the commission knitters, as well as companies operating on a narrow margin of working capital. It was soon apparent that many of them could not install the new machines required by their supplementary agreements. Of sheer necessity those contracts were revised.

Despite this unforeseen hindrance to the program, union mills received their first good-sized batch of new machines since 1930. The plans of some companies give promise that their equipment will be entirely modern and fully competitive by the end of the three-year program. There is no doubt that through the rehabilitation project, continued operation of a substantial northern industry is assured for some years to come.

On the other hand, the new type machines have been installed in large numbers in southern territory. The Full-Fashioned Hosiery Manufacturers and the Federation have determined that a weekly wage of $50 shall be maintained for knitters on these new machines. They agree that such a wage is reasonable because of the skill, judgment and steadiness needed to operate a $14,000 piece of intricate machinery. It is likely, however, that a somewhat lower wage will be paid southern knitters on the same equipment, especially if short-time operations are a threat.

Outlook for the Future

After one year's experience with the rehabilitation program two

---

70. A sufficient number of plants were long on silk and maintained hosiery prices. This placed a substantial added cost burden on mills that were short on silk. Buying of hosiery became hand to mouth in the expectation of a decrease in silk prices, and commission knitting contracts were not freely given.

questions loom large: (1) will union mills generally be able to meet their minimum machinery program and, more important, will they be able to rehabilitate their entire plants; and (2) will the new equipment installed in union mills remain competitive with the southern area? Past experience indicates that problems of nonunion competition will be met first by intensive organization efforts by the Federation. Then, if the organization drive fails to protect union standards, further adjustments will be inevitable.

Any organization drives undertaken to maintain union standards on the new machines will undoubtedly develop into a vigorous battle. The Federation feels it has much at stake with the new machines. Southern workers in the full-fashioned hosiery industry, on the other hand, are among the highest paid workers in their areas and have not yet been ready to participate in solving the union or industry problem. It seems certain that even though the Association and the Federation have sought for many years to adjust collective bargaining to changing economic conditions, they have not yet finished their work. Meanwhile, an accolade for bargaining with courage and imagination cannot be denied them.

Chapter 10

STEEL

Frederick H. Harbison

1. Introduction

STEEL IS THE keystone of American industry. With over five hundred thousand employees and as many stockholders, it is our largest manufacturing industry. One out of every four persons in the United States lives in a community where a steel mill is located, and is, therefore, affected in some way by the condition of the steel companies. Indirectly, developments in steel have a far-reaching influence on a great variety of allied fabricating and processing industries for which steel is the principal raw material. The basic iron and steel industry is therefore an economic barometer for many other groups of American employers.[1]

Out of every dollar of gross sales received by the steel industry in 1939 thirty cents was paid to plant workers (exclusive of salaried employees) in the form of wages. Labor relations, consequently, should be of primary concern to employers. Since the turn of the century, steel had been famous as an impregnable antiunion stronghold. The unexpected announcement in March 1937 that the U. S. Steel Corporation had, without a struggle, entered into contractual relations with a CIO affiliate surprised not only the public, but also organized labor and a large majority of steel makers themselves. Had the traditional antiunion policy been abandoned? Would the steel industry engage in collective bargaining with outside labor organizations?

   1. The term "iron and steel industry" as used in this study includes all companies, no matter what their finished product, which by reason of integrated operations produce their own steel or iron as a raw material for further processing. Nearly all such companies are members of the American Iron and Steel Institute. Cf. Carroll R. Daugherty, Melvin G. de Chazeau and Samuel S. Stratton, *The Economics of the Iron and Steel Industry,* McGraw-Hill, New York, 1937, Vol. I, pp. 9-10.

Answers to these questions are found in the development of labor policies in the industry, the origin and growth of the Steel Workers Organizing Committee, the background of the famous "Taylor–Lewis" agreement,[2] and the nature of relations with the SWOC. In the years between 1933 and 1941, the impact of unionization on a nonunion industry, the change in management outlook and the struggle of organized labor for recognition overshadow the techniques and procedures of collective bargaining which by 1941 were still in process of evolution.

Economies of mass production methods and the tremendous investment required in plants and machinery (about $10,000 per worker) naturally resulted in the predominance of a number of large companies. The ten largest producers have over 80 per cent of the nation's steel making capacity, of which the two largest, U. S. Steel and Bethlehem, share more than half. In addition there are more than two hundred small concerns which may compete with the large integrated companies in the sale of finished products, but, at the same time, are dependent on them for raw materials. The study of labor relations, therefore, logically concentrates on significant developments in the large companies.

The ten largest steel companies are: U. S. Steel, Jones and Laughlin, Wheeling, Crucible, Bethlehem, Republic, Youngstown Sheet and Tube, Inland, National, and American Rolling Mill. U. S. Steel employs over two hundred thousand workers in scores of plants scattered throughout the nation. All of the companies just mentioned employ over ten thousand workers each.

Geographically the industry is concentrated in a few steel producing centers, easily accessible to both coal and iron ore: Bethlehem, Pittsburgh, and Johnstown, Pennsylvania; Sparrows Point, Maryland; Wheeling and Weirton, West Virginia; Youngstown, Warren, Cleveland, Canton, and Middletown, Ohio; Gary, Indiana; Chicago, Illinois; Buffalo, New York; and Birmingham, Alabama. The larger companies usually have plants in several of these districts, while the small concerns are more generally confined to a single locality.

In the past steel, in common with other industries, was notable

2. See p. 523.

for long hours and low wages. Today hours are shorter and wages relatively high. The increases of 1936 and 1937, which were granted in response to organized labor pressure, established the highest hourly rates in the history of the industry. In 1939 plant workers' earnings averaged about 83 cents an hour, approximately 27 per cent above the average for all manufacturing industries. An additional general increase of 10 cents an hour in April 1941, together with premium pay for overtime, brought average hourly earnings to about 97 cents in the spring of 1941.

In normal times, the fluctuating level of operations makes employment in the steel industry rather unstable. From 1935 to 1939 employment became more unstable because of the rapid pace of technological improvements. The new continuous rolling mills made obsolete scores of bar, sheet and tin mills. Other laborsaving devices were introduced in various branches of steel manufacture. Consequently, technological displacement very materially aggravated the unemployment problem created by the slump of 1938 and 1939.

The war boom, of course, has eliminated the problem of technological unemployment for the "duration." The steel industry has been working at maximum capacity since the latter part of 1940. Expansion of existing capacity seems necessary to supply even a part of civilian needs after direct and indirect defense requirements have been met. Basically then, there is a steel shortage today. Employment has reached new heights, work is steady, and weekly and monthly earnings of steel workers have shattered all previous records.

2. Developments Prior to the SWOC Drive

a. THE AMALGAMATED ASSOCIATION OF IRON, STEEL AND TIN WORKERS

Present labor relations in the basic iron and steel industry go far beyond any achievements of the old Amalgamated Association of Iron, Steel and Tin Workers, and have little of their origin in the efforts of that organization. Beginning with a decisive blow from the Carnegie Steel Company in the Homestead strike of 1892, the history of the Amalgamated since that time has been one of defeat after defeat. Failure of a general strike against the U. S. Steel Corporation in 1901 was followed shortly afterwards by elimination of the union from most of the plants of large independent steel companies. Although an organization campaign in 1918 and 1919 enrolled over a quarter of a million union members, the industry-wide strike of 1919 failed. From 1920 to 1933 the Amalgamated never represented as much as 10 per cent of the nation's steel workers.

Furthermore, the Amalgamated failed to conduct a successful organizing campaign under the National Industrial Recovery Act. Either the international officers were not alive to the opportunities provided by that act, or they felt that their resources were too limited to challenge the power of the steel companies, which had set up employee representation plans to stave off unionization. Most organizers sent into the field lacked initiative, force and experience. The international officers, moreover, refused to sanction efforts to capture company unions in the larger plants, and urged all members to boycott them completely.

To add to its weakness, the Amalgamated in 1934 and 1935 was split by internal dissension and factionalism. For a while it looked as if an insurgent rank-and-file group might make some progress. This movement was spectacular for a few months, then faded out. Finally, what little strength the Amalgamated ever had was concentrated among skilled and semiskilled workers in small bar, sheet and tin mills, which technological advance was rapidly putting out of business.[3]

With its craft outlook and outmoded constitution, its uninspired leadership and its history of accumulated defeats, the Amalgamated Association of Iron, Steel and Tin Workers has not been an important factor in labor relations in the steel industry since the turn of the century. The recent growth of unionization springs from other roots.

3. For detailed analysis of the Amalgamated during the Code period, see Daugherty, de Chazeau and Stratton, *op. cit.*, Vol. II, Ch. XIX.

b. DEVELOPMENT OF EMPLOYEE REPRESENTATION PLANS

As predecessors to collective bargaining with outside unions, employee representation plans had a dual importance. First, the representation plans necessitated a complete and almost revolutionary change in management's attitude on industrial relations. Second, while to some extent staving off the inroads of independent labor organizations, they ultimately made employees more conscious of the possible advantages of collective bargaining and gave training to future labor union leaders.

A few companies, notably American Rolling Mill and Bethlehem, set up employee representation plans long before the advent of the NRA. These plans worked well as a "management technique" by restoring to some extent the personal relationship that existed between employer and employee when enterprises were small. Through a continuous "two-way channel of communication between management and men" these companies were anxious to show both their own supervisory forces and their workers that this modern means of "collective cooperation" could forestall the clash of conflicting interests implied by the term "collective bargaining."

Most large companies, however, neglected to set up representation plans until forced by the National Industrial Recovery Act to recognize representatives of their employees for purposes of collective bargaining. They hastily introduced such plans in 1933 as ready-made formulae for compliance with the law and as bulwarks against inroads of outside labor unions. Yet it was difficult for these companies, lacking experience in the handling of group relations, to develop in a few months the spirit and technique which such companies as American Rolling Mill and Bethlehem had been working out for years. Many foremen rebelled against this new policy of settling grievances over their heads as usurping their powers and undermining their authority. Superintendents were forced to set aside other duties to listen to hundreds of requests and petty grievances. Some of the "old line" operating executives were skeptical of the plans at the outset. The establishment of industrial relations departments, the appointment of management representatives, the education of superintendents and foremen in administration of the new policies, and the discipline or even discharge of those who would not, or could not, make the necessary changes, effected something like a minor revolution in the domain of management.

Advantages

The representation plans were effective in bringing to the attention of top management thousands of grievances. From 1934 to 1936, settlements numbered 36,709, of which 70 per cent were decided in favor of the employees.[4] Most executives interviewed indicated that the great majority of such cases involved minor grievances which could be adjusted through the regular channels of management. Most corporation officials interviewed agreed that during this period the companies were very liberal in granting hundreds of small individual and group wage increases. As one executive put it: "We seldom refused such requests; we usually made some slight concession wherever possible." Finally, many hazardous working conditions were brought to light which management was willing to remedy to improve plant safety record.

Some accomplishments under employee representation plans were quite impressive. Arbitrary actions by foremen were checked to some degree. The wage cuts of 1931 and 1932 were restored by two increases granted by the major companies in 1933 and 1934. The 1933 raise was granted in anticipation of the increases that would be required under the Code. The 1934 increases originated with a request by employee representatives of the National Steel Company. At that time this company was counting heavily on the support of the representatives in its defense against legal proceedings brought by the United States Government, charging the company with defiance of the National Labor Board. The company, whose operating rate during the depression had been quite satisfactory, was willing to grant a 10 per cent increase. The whole industry was forced to follow suit. Vacations with pay for wage earners were introduced in 1935 by the Inland and Youngs-

4. The statistics on employee representation questions were supplied by the American Iron and Steel Institute on request of the writer.

town Sheet and Tube companies, and granted the next year by the other large corporations.

Disadvantages

In other respects, however, employee representation was not so successful. Some company officials pointed out that the plans lowered the morale of the foremen. Many foremen never heard of grievances in their departments until they were presented by the committees to the general superintendent. An executive of a large corporation gave this reason for difficulties encountered: "We leaned over backwards to sell the plans to the employees and the representatives, but in the process we overlooked the foremen."

From the employees' standpoint the plans had obvious shortcomings. The unit of collective dealing was the individual plant, yet local management was without authority to give answers to requests requiring company-wide action. Cognizant of this drawback the more aggressive representatives organized "central committees," composed of delegates from different plants of a single company, to deal directly with corporation executives on basic issues. Through such central committees the representatives demanded general wage increases, more liberal pensions, vacations with pay and changes in the plans to provide for appointment of an umpire to arbitrate unsettled differences. Some companies recognized these central bodies, but others frowned upon them as "outlaw" committees. Most of the demands were refused.

The drive for central committees indicated the weakness of the bargaining power of isolated plant representation plans with no membership organization behind them to take concerted action. Lacking a clear conception of their ultimate goal, the representatives were using all means at their disposal to make the plans effective bargaining agencies. It was evident, therefore, that these plans, or so-called company unions, carried at least the seeds of independent unionism.

It was apparent that most employee representatives were not mere tools and "stooges" of management. Many were eager to become identified with "a progressive labor movement." The significance of the representation plans in the strategy of the subsequent unionization campaign has been well set forth by Philip Murray, Chairman of the Steel Workers Organizing Committee:

> It was apparent to us that to make any progress in steel we had to first "capture" these company unions. We realized that a great many of the employee representatives, perhaps the majority, were men honestly interested in doing a good job under The Plan which had been imposed upon them and their fellow employees. Our job was to show these men what real unionism meant. To denounce them all as company agents or stooges would be both untruthful and poor strategy.
>
> Therefore we set out to win these employee representatives to the cause of the SWOC and industrial unionism.[5]

C. THE UNITED MINE WORKERS AND THE STEEL CAMPAIGN

The United Mine Workers of America, under the leadership of John L. Lewis, took advantage of the National Recovery Act to recoup their losses in the bituminous coal mines. Not only did they organize the Central Competitive Field (Illinois, Indiana, Ohio and Pennsylvania), but they also penetrated traditional non-union strongholds in Kentucky and West Virginia. In the fall of 1933, however, the miners met stern resistance from the steel companies who owned the so-called "captive mines." Refusal of the steel companies to sign agreements came from the fear that union contracts in the captive mines might be opening wedges for a concerted unionization drive on the basic steel industry. Strikes in the western Pennsylvania mines were followed by the intervention of President Roosevelt and the Recovery Administration. In 1934, following Labor Board elections, the H. C. Frick Company, a subsidiary of U. S. Steel, finally signed an agreement outlining the general terms of employment with the officers of the United Mine Workers as representatives of the company's employees. But it refused to name the union as such in the contract. Several other steel companies soon followed the lead of "big steel" with similar agreements. It was evident that the corporations were not pleased by unionization of the captive mines.

5. SWOC, *Reports of the Officers to the Wage and Policy Convention in Pittsburgh*, December 14, 15, 16, 1937, p. 9.

Although the 1934 convention of the American Federation of Labor was ostensibly in favor of a unionization campaign in steel, the Executive Council during the ensuing year did nothing to organize steel workers. In the 1935 convention the platform of the industrial unionists was defeated, and on November 10 of that year the Committee for Industrial Organization was formed within the AF of L. The United Mine Workers were dominant in this new committee, and their particular interest in steel had just been reiterated by Lewis:

> We are anxious to have collective bargaining established in the steel industry, and our interest in that is . . . selfish, because our people know that if the workers were organized in the steel industry, and collective bargaining there was an actuality, it would remove the incentive of the great captains of the steel industry to destroy and punish and harass our people who work in the captive mines throughout the country. . . .[6]

Lewis and other leaders in the CIO were disgusted with the craft unions' destruction of newly formed industrial organizations in mass production industries. The failure of the insurgent rank-and-file movement in 1934 and 1935 within the Amalgamated Association of Iron, Steel and Tin Workers showed that steel workers could not be organized except with outside assistance. The action of employee representatives in setting up central committees indicated that many steel workers were not satisfied with the company unions. The United Mine Workers alone had sufficient resources and leadership to build a union in steel.

Lewis Moves On Steel

In February 1936, the CIO sent to the Executive Council of the AF of L a conditional offer of $500,000 toward a $1.5 million fund for the organization of the steel workers. In May, the Executive Council announced its own plan to organize steel, in accordance with an agreement to be made with the Amalgamated, which was to have "due regard and proper respect for the jurisdictional rights of all national and international Unions." [7]

6. *Proceedings,* Annual Convention of the AF of L, 1935, p. 539.
7. "Organization Plan for Steel Industry Outlined by Green," *AF of L Weekly News Service,* May 16, 1936.

After the AF of L Executive Council refused to accept money for a campaign in the steel industry along lines to be prescribed by the CIO, Lewis put pressure directly on the Amalgamated. The convention in the spring of 1936 forced the officers of the Amalgamated to accept the CIO proposal for organizing the industry. An agreement made early in June between the CIO and the Amalgamated contained these provisions:

1. Appointment by Lewis of the Steel Workers Organizing Committee, which would have complete charge of the campaign to organize the unorganized workers in the steel industry.
2. Jurisdiction by the SWOC over all newly organized workers.
3. Jurisdiction by the Amalgamated over its existing membership and contracts already in force.
4. Contribution by the CIO up to $500,000 to finance the new membership drive.
5. Termination of the organizing campaign by joint discretion of the officers of the SWOC and the CIO.

Lewis appointed Philip Murray, Vice President of the United Mine Workers, as Chairman of the SWOC. Backed largely by UMWA money, Murray picked his staff for the most part from the ranks of the Mine Workers' organization. The Amalgamated, though nominally represented in the SWOC, withdrew from the scene. The task of unionizing steel was the coal miners' job.

3. SWOC Organizing Tactics and Strategy

a. EARLY ORGANIZATION STRATEGY

The task of organizing steel was one of mobilizing job-conscious workmen who were afraid of unions. With authority concentrated in the hands of veteran strategists, experienced outsiders as organizers, and strong financial backing, the Steel Workers Organizing Committee launched a drive wholly different from previous uncorrelated, sporadic attempts at self-organization by the rank and file.

A favorable economic and political environment helped the early campaign of the SWOC. At the beginning of the drive, in

June 1936, steel was operating at about 70 per cent of capacity. By the time the SWOC had won its major victories in May of the next year, operations were up to nearly 90 per cent, workers employed had increased by fifty thousand, and pay rolls showed a 50 per cent rise. There was a boom in steel.

Politically the SWOC was triumphant. The Wagner Act had been passed in 1935 and the union was quick to press charges with the National Labor Relations Board of unfair labor practices by the employers. The La Follette Civil Liberties Committee was uncovering evidence of industrial espionage and other measures to combat outside unions. In Pennsylvania the Lieutenant-Governor was an official of the miners' union and was instrumental in securing state police protection in the "very tough towns." Moreover, in the national elections of 1936 the New Deal, with which the SWOC had identified its cause, was victorious. Following the election, a feeling of political freedom, the SWOC claimed, impelled steel workers to join the CIO in "droves."

The favorable economic and political factors, however, should not eclipse the clever strategy of the SWOC leaders during the first nine months of their drive. Remembering that national and racial animosities helped to balk earlier attempts at unionization, the SWOC followed the policy of the United Mine Workers in welcoming the support of Negroes and groups of foreign-born workers, thus promoting the ideals of fraternity and unity among workers of every creed, color and nationality.

Expecting the employers to fight the drive through coercion and discharge of workers for union activity, the SWOC legal department retained local counsel in important steel communities to assist the organizers when necessary, and arranged for bail bonds in case of arrest by local authorities. Developments in steel were headline news, and the publicity department sent to nearly a thousand leading newspapers and press associations almost daily reports of SWOC progress. The research department cooperated with outsiders and the SWOC staff in supplying useful factual information. In short, the SWOC launched a "streamlined" unionization campaign.

Organization Methods

The methods used in recruiting members avoided the mistakes of previous efforts. The first few months were devoted to advertising the campaign. To attract attention, mass meetings were staged and addressed by SWOC staff members, ministers, professors and Congressmen. Speakers took pains to emphasize that President Roosevelt and the New Dealers hoped that the workers would organize. "Flying squadrons" of automobiles invaded the steel towns, and from sound trucks the union message was broadcast in several languages. "Our first problem," said Chairman Philip Murray, "was to banish fear from the steel workers' minds."

For many months the signing up of members was carried on under cover. After an organizer had established a connection with a few union sympathizers, he set up a "mill organizing committee." The committee members approached the workers in the mills, in their homes, in fraternal clubs. The function of the organizer was to direct activities and to keep the SWOC national headquarters informed of problems and progress. The strategy of the SWOC dictated that the identity of all who joined should be secret until the union became so strong that discrimination by employers would be difficult. Signed membership application cards were mailed each week to the national offices, the names on them being kept confidential.

By February 1937 scores of lodges were set up. The companies had discharged very few union members; the national elections had gone against the "bosses"; "progressive" employee representatives were openly flaunting the representation plans; fear was disappearing.

By the time the Taylor–Lewis agreement was announced on March 2, the SWOC claimed one hundred and fifty thousand signed membership cards. Although no dues were collected from most members,[8] there was apparently strong moral support of the CIO, particularly following the victories won in General Motors plants in January. The SWOC had created a labor movement in the steel industry.

8. Collection of dues was suspended in November 1936 and resumed in April 1937.

b. "CAPTURE" OF THE CARNEGIE-ILLINOIS EMPLOYEE REPRESENTATION PLANS

Important as was the strength of the SWOC movement, the "revolution" which developed under and in the representation plans of the Carnegie-Illinois Steel Corporation, the principal subsidiary of U. S. Steel, was no less important. Before the advent of the SWOC several plant bodies had requested sizable wage increases and establishment of the forty-hour week with time and a half for overtime. The representatives also pressed, apparently unsuccessfully, for recognition of "central committees" in the Pittsburgh and Chicago areas. At once, therefore, the SWOC set out to assist these representatives and keep them constantly "biting at the heels" of management with all sorts of demands. Although the SWOC openly planned and financed meetings of the central committees, the union was at first careful to conceal the identity of pro–CIO representatives because "their effectiveness as leaders and their contacts with fellow workers in the mills would be lessened by such action." By September, however, the so-called "progressive" representatives were openly favorable to the SWOC, while the "conservatives" continued to bolster the plans actively.

Demands for Wage Increases

In July 1936 the U. S. Steel subsidiaries, followed by the principal independents, announced that overtime would be paid for work in excess of forty-eight hours per week.[9] To representatives who had demanded a forty-hour week, this was a blow. To the SWOC it was a boon. "One hundred organizers for John L. Lewis could not have done as much good for an outside union as this did," remarked an anti–CIO representative.[10] By September 1 nearly all of the plant bodies as well as the central delegate committees—conservative and progressive alike—were demanding wage increases of 10 to 25 per cent, establishment of a $5 minimum

---

9. *The New York Times,* July 24, 1936. This was the first time the principle of overtime was introduced in the industry. Since most employees were working under forty hours, it was of no immediate advantage to steel workers.

10. Statement of Fred Bohne, "Minutes of General Joint Conference," August 12, 1936. Bohne, an ardent opponent of the SWOC, was at that time leading the movement for recognition of the "central committee."

daily rate for common labor, and time and a half for all work in excess of forty hours per week. On September 8 President B. F. Fairless of Carnegie-Illinois announced that wage increases could not be granted at that time.[11] Answering Fairless a week later, Philip Murray retorted: "The growing tide of SWOC's campaign compels a wage raise, and the steel industry, with U. S. Steel leading, will grant it." Murray was right, for after the national election in November, U. S. Steel announced a wage increase of about 10 per cent.

Many representatives were infuriated at U. S. Steel for delaying wage increases until after the election. The corporation, furthermore, had proposed that the various plant bodies should *sign an agreement* for one year providing that further wage adjustments within that period would be governed by the cost-of-living index. Some of these bodies did so; others, where CIO influence was strong, refused, and passed resolutions (based on public statements made by John L. Lewis) declaring they had no authority to negotiate a signed contract and that they rejected the cost-of-living feature as a measure of arriving at just compensation for labor. This gesture by U. S. Steel, as publicly admitted later by the chairman of the board, "served further to activate the Steel Workers Organizing Committee." [12]

Meanwhile, early in November, the Carnegie-Illinois management had recognized a central delegate body of representatives from all sheet and tin as well as steel mills in the Pittsburgh-Youngstown area. Known as the "Pittsburgh District General Council," this body elected as chairman a steel worker from Duquesne, who was one of several employee representatives on the pay roll of the SWOC!

Having "captured" one main bulwark of employee representation, the SWOC set out to destroy the rest. Charges were filed with the National Labor Relations Board accusing the Carnegie-

---

11. Letter to Employee Representatives of the Youngstown District, September 8, 1936. Similar letters were addressed to the employees of other Carnegie-Illinois plants.

12. Myron C. Taylor, "Ten Years of Steel," extension of remarks at the annual meeting of stockholders of the United States Steel Corporation in Hoboken, New Jersey, April 4, 1938, p. 40.

Illinois management of dominating and financing the plans. Formal pro–CIO representatives' councils were set up which openly denounced the plans as a "snare, delusion and an insult to the intelligence of the American working men." Meanwhile, the "conservative" representatives launched a counteroffensive and ousted the pro–CIO chairman of the Pittsburgh District General Council. Some of them set up a "defense committee" to back the representation plans, while others organized independent unions.

Throughout January and February 1937, individual plant bodies, central committees, pro–CIO representative councils, defense committees and independent unions were united in pressing for wage and hour concessions. These were the original SWOC-inspired demands for the $5 minimum daily rate for common labor, an additional 10 cents an hour increase for all others, and a basic forty-hour week. By the end of February many Carnegie-Illinois representation plans were in a state of collapse. Caught between two fires, management knew not which way to turn. The constant demands and internal warfare within the framework of the plans tried the patience of superintendents and operating officials. Many of them thought that the company would support the conservative employee representatives by granting the wage and hour demands. Few of them dreamed that U. S. Steel would make a bargain with the CIO.

C. THE U. S. STEEL AGREEMENTS OF 1937

In a statement prepared for the stockholders of the United States Steel Corporation in 1938, Myron C. Taylor revealed in part the events which led up to the signing of the peace pact with the SWOC in March 1937.[13] In the course of private conversations, Taylor showed John L. Lewis this formula:

> The Company recognizes the right of its employees to bargain collectively through representatives freely chosen by them without dictation, coercion or intimidation in any form or from any source. It will negotiate *and contract* with the representatives of any group of its employees so chosen and with any organization as the representative of its members, subject to the recognition of the principle that the right to work is not dependent on membership or non-membership in any organization and

---

13. Myron C. Taylor, *op. cit.,* pp. 23-45.

subject to the right of every employee freely to bargain in such manner and through such representatives, if any, as he chooses.[14]

On February 28, Lewis and Murray, representing the CIO, and Taylor, representing the corporation, accepted the formula in principle. It was then agreed that, with the approval of the board of directors of the corporation, Murray would negotiate within the terms of the formula an agreement with President Fairless of the Carnegie-Illinois Steel Corporation. On March 2, 1937, Fairless and Murray signed a preliminary contract recognizing the SWOC as *the collective bargaining agent for those employees who were its members*. The full demands of the SWOC and employee representatives for wage increases and the forty-hour week, which were also announced at this time by the principal independents, were incorporated in the agreement. A formal contract between the SWOC and Carnegie-Illinois was signed on March 17.[15] The other principal U. S. Steel subsidiaries signed similar agreements: American Steel and Wire Company, National Tube Company, Columbia Steel Company, Tennessee Coal, Iron and Railroad Company. A similar contract was later signed by the American Bridge Company and the Virginia Bridge Company.

Why U. S. Steel Settled With the CIO

Addressing the stockholders Taylor emphasized two basic reasons for the signing of the SWOC contract. He wished to avoid a strike, and he was able to make an "honorable settlement" with Lewis "that would ensure a continuance of work, wages and profits." [16]

The reasons why Taylor and the Board of U. S. Steel were unwilling to risk a strike can only be suggested. It was apparent that the union movement was strong, and undoubtedly there were enough sympathizers to close down a good many plants. The SWOC, ably led and adequately financed, had strong political alliances in some states. The Earle administration in Pennsylvania had already expressed sympathy with the unionization drive, and

---

14. *Ibid.*, pp. 41-42. (*Italics inserted.*)
15. For discussion of this agreement, see pp. 549 ff.
16. Myron C. Taylor, *op. cit.*, p. 40.

the importance to the union of a friendly state administration had been shown in the General Motors strikes. Domestic and potential foreign demand [17] for steel was strong, and U. S. Steel plants were operating at well over 80 per cent of capacity.[18] Furthermore, the defenses of U. S. Steel were weak, for the disruptive tactics of the SWOC had wrecked the representation plans in many Carnegie-Illinois plants.[19] In the event of a strike, therefore, the SWOC would be in a strategic position. Finally, Mr. Taylor was able to lay down the principal term of the contract: the union was to be recognized as the bargaining agent only for those employees who were its members.[20]

The Taylor–Lewis agreement is significant in the following respects. It grew out of negotiations between a single officer of U. S. Steel and a single officer of the CIO. U. S. Steel, although adhering to its stated policy of representation, ended its former practice of sponsoring representation plans and opposing outside unions, implying an endorsement of the SWOC. Finally, it caused the SWOC to deviate from its original objective of collective bargaining on an industry-wide basis.

d. SWOC VICTORIES: MARCH TO MAY 1937

For three months after the signing of the U. S. Steel agreements, the unionization drive had the momentum of a tidal wave. By May 1 the SWOC claimed over 300,000 members, 600 lodges and 114 signed agreements in various steel and allied fabricating companies.[21] But despite the fact that the Supreme Court, by declaring the Wagner Act constitutional, sounded the death-knell of most employee representation plans in the industry, none of the large independent companies, with the exception of Wheeling Steel, had signed contracts.

17. It was rumored that the British government was about to place large orders for armaments in America.
18. *Iron Age*, April 15, 1937, p. 77.
19. The plans were still strongly entrenched in most of the large independent steel corporations at this time. SWOC had concentrated its attack on Carnegie-Illinois.
20. This principle of representation had been set forth in the captive mines agreements. Myron C. Taylor, *op. cit.*, p. 43.
21. SWOC, *Steel Labor*, May 1, 1937.

In May the spotlight focused on the Jones and Laughlin Steel Corporation. In negotiations with the SWOC that company had offered to sign the standard Carnegie-Illinois contract, *provided* management retained the right to make similar contracts with other groups of employees. Fearful that management might promote a company union, the SWOC rejected this proposal. Feeling that the SWOC did not have a majority, the company then offered to agree to an NLRB election within a few weeks and to concede the SWOC exclusive bargaining rights if the majority of employees so voted. The SWOC countered with a demand for a preliminary agreement that the terms of the Carnegie-Illinois contract would be in effect pending results of the election. The company refused. The local unions then effectively closed down the company's plants for thirty-six hours. The company, in poor financial position to withstand a prolonged strike, gave in. The strikers claimed a complete victory for the SWOC. Furthermore, the strike sentiment contributed to the success of the SWOC in winning the subsequent NLRB election by better than a two-to-one vote. The company signed an agreement recognizing the SWOC as the exclusive bargaining agency for its employees.

Several smaller companies followed the precedent of Jones and Laughlin. Crucible Steel, a large corporation employing fourteen thousand workers, signed a straight Carnegie-Illinois agreement when threatened with strikes in its principal plants.

e. "LITTLE STEEL"

The principal companies which were determined to resist the SWOC in 1937 were American Rolling Mill, National, Bethlehem, Inland, Republic, and Youngstown Sheet and Tube. Up to that time these "little steel" companies were more prosperous as a group than the big four which had SWOC contracts.[22]

Although complying with standards of wages and working con-

---

22. From 1934 to 1936 the four largest contract companies, U. S. Steel, Jones and Laughlin, Wheeling, and Crucible, having about 44 per cent of the industry's ingot capacity, had a total net profit from operations of $95 million, while the "little steel" group, having less than 40 per cent ingot capacity, reported profits of $180 million. This fact is partially explained by the greater proportionate output of "light products" of most of the "little steel" companies.

ditions set forth in the Carnegie-Illinois contract, the "little steel" companies were unwilling to make an agreement with the SWOC, either oral or written. The SWOC felt strong enough to force the issue in only three of these companies—Inland, Republic, and Youngstown Sheet and Tube. Following a conference of local unions, a strike was called May 26, 1937, against these three concerns. Inland and Youngstown Sheet and Tube closed down completely; Republic operated several plants. On June 10 the Brotherhood of Railroad Trainmen and the Brotherhood of Locomotive Engineers called a strike of Bethlehem's railway employees in the vicinity of Johnstown, demanding a signed contract. Steel workers of the Johnstown plant were drawn in to support the Brotherhoods. That this strike was neither planned nor welcomed by the top command of SWOC seems evident, for the Johnstown plant was only one of ten mills operated by the Bethlehem Steel Company.

Resistance of "Little Steel"

The President appointed a three man "Federal Steel Mediation Board" on June 17 to attempt a settlement of the strikes. Appearing before the board, the heads of the four companies involved stated that they would make no agreements, oral or written, with the SWOC, nor would they meet personally with the top officials of the CIO. They argued that the Wagner Act did not compel an agreement, that a signed contract would eventually lead to a closed shop, and that, in any case, the SWOC was an irresponsible body. The board proposed that the companies make and sign an agreement with the SWOC, to become effective only if the SWOC won an NLRB election. Although the SWOC indicated willingness to negotiate on this basis, the companies refused. Failing to get a settlement, the Federal Steel Mediation Board disbanded, censuring the heads of the companies for refusing to enter into a "man-to-man" discussion with CIO leaders, and for refusing to make an agreement with the SWOC regardless of the number of employees it actually represented.[23]

23. For further discussion of these points, see *Report of Federal Steel Mediation Board to Secretary of Labor, Frances Perkins*, July 2, 1937.

The industrial warfare, which lasted for over a month, was marked by outrages by local police, violence by strikers and vigilante committees, company-inspired back-to-work movements, and suppression of civil rights. The strikes were actually broken as a result of the intervention of state police and National Guardsmen who limited picketing and gave the necessary protection for a successful back-to-work movement. The union's failure was complete except possibly at Inland Steel.[24]

Reasons for Failure of the Strikes

Causes for this failure seem clear. First, the SWOC made a tactical error in calling strikes on such a far-flung front; the success of previous months perhaps misled it into premature action. Secondly, though strong as a surging movement, pro–CIO workers were weak as an organization. Unlike the hardy miners, who had learned the value of a strong permanent organization, most of the steel workers were raw recruits, who became restless as the struggle deepened. Finally, the SWOC underestimated the tremendous financial strength of the "little steel" companies and their consequent influence and control in communities where their mills were located.

The only course left open immediately after the strikes was to press charges of unfair labor practices with the NLRB against Republic, Inland, Bethlehem, and Youngstown, as well as against American Rolling Mill and National, in whose plants the SWOC never had more than a small following.

f. RECESSION AND REVIVAL

The sharpest and widest drop in steel production ever experienced by the industry was recorded in the last four months of 1937. By December output was 70 per cent below August's, pay rolls were cut almost in half, and employment fell rapidly.[25] Not

---

24. The strike was terminated at the Indiana Harbor plant of this company following an agreement made between the company and the Governor of Indiana providing that the company's stated labor policy would be carried out and that any unsettled grievances relating to such stated policy would be subject to arbitration by the Indiana Commissioner of Labor.

25. Computed from data supplied by the American Iron and Steel Institute.

until the summer of 1938 was there any revival. The recession was even a greater blow to the SWOC than the defeat in "little steel." Widespread unemployment discouraged union membership. Dues payments dropped sharply, and some lodges in the large mills almost dwindled away. Faced with these conditions, the SWOC tried to bolster its membership and lodges in the large mills, to extend organization in the smaller steel concerns and fabricating firms, and to prevent general wage reductions.

SWOC policy had always been to exonerate unemployed workers from the payment of dues. But that was not all. Staff organizers were ordered to help the local lodges in setting up unemployment and relief committees. Such committees served a twofold purpose. By registering all unemployed union members, the SWOC could use its political influence to have them put on WPA jobs or relief, and also could insist that seniority provisions of the contracts be enforced both in reduction of forces, and again, when operations picked up, in restoration of all former employees to their jobs before new employees were hired. By thus demonstrating to the workers that the union could serve them in depressed as well as in prosperous times, the SWOC built up solidarity and unity among its members which later bore fruit in the emergence of a stronger and more loyal organization. Nevertheless, during this period a lack of interest in the union was evident in many U. S. Steel plants, in part, perhaps, because the contracts were originally handed to the workers on a silver platter.

Throughout this recession, the SWOC obtained contracts with smaller steel and fabricating concerns, which in general were easier to organize than the larger steel producers. Practically all of the previously organized companies renewed their contracts in 1938; in addition, the SWOC increased its agreements about 30 per cent. The number of lodges was correspondingly greater, and revenue from new members helped to defray the large overhead costs of the unionization campaign.

Wage Rates Preserved During Recession

From the SWOC point of view, the greatest achievement of the recession period was preservation of existing wage rates. The fate of unionization in the entire industry hinged on the negotiations for a new contract with U. S. Steel in February 1938, when the original 1937 agreements were to expire. In conference with a committee of executives of U. S. Steel subsidiaries, SWOC leaders asked for a year's contract, more liberal vacations, and official recognition of dues committeemen. U. S. Steel countered with a demand for a general wage reduction. The SWOC refused. Company spokesmen then offered to extend the existing contract indefinitely, with a proviso that either party might give the other ten days' notice for a conference to change the terms of the agreement, and, if there were failure to agree within twenty days of such notice, the 1937 agreements would be terminated. This "escape clause" was necessary, U. S. Steel argued, to meet economic conditions which might necessitate wage reductions and to safeguard "big steel" in the event that "little steel" should decide to reduce wages. The SWOC accepted this proposal. The independent contract concerns and most of the allied steel fabricating and processing companies followed the lead of "big steel." Realizing its precarious position, the SWOC avoided taking the initiative in opening up existing contracts for changes or revisions, lest the companies take advantage of such action to reduce wages.

In the spring of 1938 U. S. Steel informally asked the SWOC to take a wage cut because of the competitive situation in the steel industry and because of impending price cuts. The SWOC spokesmen refused. They advised the steel makers not to cut prices, and hinted that a wage reduction would result in a strike. Nevertheless, price cuts were made in June 1938. Officials of "big steel" and the SWOC continued to discuss wage reductions all through the summer, and at one time the former were thought ready to invoke the termination clause of the agreement.

Revival Forestalled Cuts

By November the situation had eased somewhat, but U. S. Steel still tried to persuade the SWOC to acquiesce in a wage cut because costs were out of line with prices. The SWOC contended, however, that increased productivity from technological improvements enabled the industry to maintain wages at a high level.

Philip Murray, nevertheless, publicly condemned the cutthroat price-cutting practices of the industry and suggested that the federal administration should offer help to remedy such an uneconomic situation. "If the steel corporations cannot put their own house in order," he said, "it is the avowed purpose of the organized steel workers of this nation to promote a constructive legislative program that will adequately protect the interests of the industry and its workers."[26] By the spring of 1939 business had so far revived that wage cuts were no longer a vital issue. The SWOC had forestalled general wage reductions during a major business depression.

The revival, which began in the fall of 1938 and lasted until the summer of 1939, was followed by the "war boom." Beginning in January 1939, the SWOC began to strengthen its lodges in the large steel mills, with new officers, establishment of dues committeeman systems (not recognized by management), and organized membership reinstatement drives. Many lodges were revived and some became stronger than ever. Grievances were pressed with more vigor, and certain concessions in procedure were won from management. The most spectacular progress was made in the smaller fabricating and steel companies, where management resistance to intensive unionization was weakest. With the aid of membership certifications and elections by the NLRB, the SWOC was generally successful in securing exclusive bargaining rights in these companies. By the fall of 1939 probably fifty or more of these concerns, among them several small but well-known steel companies, had granted complete recognition either through informal understandings or outright union-shop agreements. In short, the business boom strengthened the SWOC position in these companies with which it already had contracts.

Intensified Drive for Unionization: 1939–1940

The difficult task of unionizing "little steel" still remained. By the end of 1939 the SWOC had succeeded in establishing active grievance committees in many Republic, Bethlehem, Youngstown

---

26. Statement of Philip Murray in Cleveland, "SWOC Press Release," October 13, 1938.

Sheet and Tube, and Inland plants. Some of the local unions in the "little steel" plants, moreover, were much stronger than many of the lodges in the large companies under contract.

A new organization drive began early in 1939 in Bethlehem, which as second largest producer in the country, is considered the "backbone of little steel." The former weak, poorly led lodges were replaced by "organizing committees" composed of the most active unionists in each plant. The procedure was to organize slowly, enlist the support of as many employee representatives as possible, and set up permanent grievance committees to deal regularly with management. This drive departed from early organizing tactics in that a full-time staff was appointed whose sole activities were concentrated on unionizing the scattered plants of a single large corporation. Yet 1940 passed with Bethlehem still refusing to recognize the union.

By May 1940 organization in the Republic mills appeared to be very strong. Grievance committees functioned at most of the large plants. Militant leaders in the Canton and Youngstown districts apparently had a strong following of active unionists. The United States Supreme Court had refused to review the decision of the Third Circuit Court of Appeals which upheld the decision of the NLRB finding the Republic Steel Corporation guilty of unfair labor practices in connection with the 1937 strikes in Ohio.[27] By this decision the company was ordered to reinstate with back pay several thousand strikers who were not rehired at the time of the NLRB ruling in 1938 and to disestablish relations with its "independent" unions. The psychological effect of this decision, placing the blame for the 1937 strikes on the company, was a boon to SWOC organizers.

The SWOC success at the Indiana Harbor plant of the Inland Steel Company was even more noteworthy. Management had shown a willingness to cooperate with the SWOC grievance committee. With competent grievancemen and an effective dues committeeman system, the SWOC had built one of the strongest and most effective lodges in the industry at the main plant of this company. The leaders of this lodge claimed that the relation-

27. *Republic Steel Corp.* v. *NLRB*, 107 Fed. (2d), 472 (1939).

ship with management was in many respects more satisfactory than in nearby U. S. Steel plants, for there was no contract limiting union action if satisfactory understandings could not be reached. Although apparently making a determined effort to establish permanent and constructive relations with the union, the company was unwilling to sign a contract until such time as the courts should hand down a final ruling.[28]

Collapse of "Little Steel" Resistance: 1941

At the end of 1940 SWOC grievance committees had "de facto" recognition in most "little steel" plants, except American Rolling Mill and National. The upward trend of employment in 1940 and 1941, together with effective organizing work, resulted in a tremendous growth of union membership in most of the large steel mills. Coincident with the increasing pressure of union organization, the defensive position of the "little steel" companies was weakened. After the Supreme Court decision in the *Heinz* case, early in 1941, the companies could no longer obstruct union recognition merely by refusing to sign a contract. Henry Ford's startling decision to "go the whole way" with the CIO following NLRB elections in the spring of 1941 made it virtually impossible for the "little steel" companies to refuse to sign contracts after certification of appropriate bargaining agencies. If the "Myron Taylor peace pact" of 1937 started the industry on the road to unionization, the Ford agreement undoubtedly contributed to completion of the process.

Inland Steel was the first to make known its willingness to sign an agreement with the Steel Workers Organizing Committee, if the union could demonstrate that it represented the majority of the workers in appropriate bargaining units. This action will merely formalize a bargaining relationship which has existed for nearly four years.

In March 1941 the SWOC called a strike at the Lackawanna plant of Bethlehem Steel. After four days the strike was settled

28. The obligation of the employer to incorporate in a signed contract the understandings reached as a result of collective bargaining was the main issue in an NLRB case involving this company. The issue was settled in *H. J. Heinz Co.* v. *NLRB*, U. S. Sup. Ct., 1941.

with the understanding that the NLRB would hold an election to determine the bargaining agent. The SWOC won in May 1941 with a vote of almost four to one. In June it won similar landslide elections in five more Bethlehem plants, and was strengthening its organization looking forward to elections in the remaining plants. In a stipulation signed by the company, the union and the NLRB, Bethlehem agreed to enter into negotiations for a signed contract with the SWOC, covering any or all plants in which the union was certified by the NLRB as representing the majority of the plant's employees.

In a somewhat similar stipulation in July 1941, the Republic Steel Corporation agreed to negotiate and sign an agreement covering all plants where a cross-check of union membership with pay roll records showed an SWOC majority. All NLRB cases filed by the SWOC were settled, providing for the reinstatement with back pay of workers discharged during or after the 1937 strike, and the dissolution of the "independent" unions in the various plants of the company. Youngstown Sheet and Tube followed the same course as Republic.

In July 1941 the SWOC secured a signed agreement covering eight thousand employees of the Great Lakes Steel unit of the National Steel Company. There was still, however, no agreement in prospect with the other National subsidiary, the Weirton Steel Company. Likewise, there was no mention of proposed agreements for plants of the American Rolling Mill Company.

By the summer of 1941 the four-year "little steel" battle had been won by the SWOC. It was certain that within a short while nearly all the major plants in the steel industry would be under contract with the union. Independent unions were no longer a significant factor. The Steel Workers Organizing Committee was the dominant and unchallenged labor organization in the steel industry.

Wages Increased

The boom in steel resulting from the national defense program enabled the SWOC to activate organization in the large steel plants. The steel corporations had substantial profits in 1940, and the union was quick to make general wage increases a leading demand.[29]

U. S. Steel, although agreeable to some small concession on wages, opposed the 10 cent increase demanded, claiming it would start an upward spiral of wages and prices. The union contended that the increases would only diminish profits and that no increase in steel prices would be necessary to offset wage raises. After a strike vote was taken, it looked as if the wage issue might be compromised by an 8 cent increase. The issue was settled, however, by another surprise move, reminiscent of the dramatic pronouncement of Myron Taylor in 1937. E. T. Weir, head of National Steel, announced a general wage increase of 10 cents an hour in the midst of the SWOC–U. S. Steel negotiations in April. "Big Steel" soon agreed to the full 10 cent increase, as well as more liberal vacations. As in the past, the other large companies followed the lead of U. S. Steel.

SWOC Position Summarized

By the summer of 1941 the first stage of the unionization campaign in steel—securing recognition from all the major producers—was almost completed. SWOC success in this respect was the result of many factors: ability to secure tangible concessions, such as wage increases; existence of a political environment favorable to organized labor; and the enlightened leadership of the top command of the SWOC. Nevertheless, although unionization was extensive in 1941, it had yet to become intensive. The SWOC could not claim 100 per cent membership in any of the large steel plants. No large company had conceded the union shop or checkoff. The issue of union status throughout the industry was still unsettled.

4. SWOC Structure and Aims

a. STRUCTURE

The Steel Workers Organizing Committee is not an autonomous international union. It is a temporary administrative organi-

---

29. See pp. 560 ff. for other union demands and the resulting agreement.

zation which, with the aid of a large staff of appointed directors and organizers, has undertaken the far-flung task of unionizing the steel and allied industries. Its main objective is to build a steel workers' industrial union. In the interim, it has been neither controlled nor led by steel workers. Its centralized financial and administrative structure stems from the conviction of the United Mine Workers that loosely governed finances and uncoordinated rank-and-file activity cause many incipient unions to decline and disappear. The UMWA not only furnished most of the SWOC leadership but also advanced the necessary financial support.

Much of the stability, strength and unity of the SWOC comes from this centralization of authority in the hands of experienced and capable leaders. Intraunion factional disputes have been almost nonexistent. Delegates to the first Wage and Policy Convention in 1937 gave unanimous approval to the actions of the SWOC officers and authorized them to continue as collective bargaining agents with full discretionary powers. At the second Wage and Policy Convention in 1940 there was some discussion of immediate "autonomy." The Convention voted overwhelmingly, however, to accept the recommendation of the SWOC top command that the existing regime be continued until 1942. In their report the officers said: "Only by the extension of democratic practices to industry can our political democracy and freedom be fortified and made secure. While our lodges and their membership, by their cooperation with the international officers, have demonstrated their capacity for the assumption of responsibility, the real test of their capacity for self-government will come when a single union in the industry is established, functioning under a constitution approved by the membership." [30]

SWOC To Be Supplanted

In 1942 a constitutional convention will be held to supplant the SWOC with an autonomous union. Before that time the Amalgamated Association of Iron, Steel and Tin Workers will have united with the SWOC; the way should be paved for the

---

30. SWOC, *Report of Officers to the Wage and Policy Convention in Chicago,* May 14, 15, 16, 17, 1940, p. 56.

formal establishment of a single industrial union of steel workers. In the meantime the present officers of the SWOC have secured approval to press the organization drive to completion and to use their best judgment in negotiating general wage and other improvements in the collective bargaining agreements.

The SWOC international office is at Pittsburgh. The two international officers are the Chairman and the Secretary-Treasurer, both of whom are officials of the United Mine Workers and paid by that organization. The administrative staff consists of about 250 directors, field representatives, auditors, publicity, research and office employees. Four regional offices in Pittsburgh, Chicago, Birmingham and Toronto are each in the charge of a director. The first two jurisdictions cover over 90 per cent of the steel industry on the continent. In addition, thirty-six district or subregional offices and twenty-four field offices make a total of sixty-five directing centers located in the important steel producing and fabricating regions in the United States and Canada. The majority of subregional or district directors have been lent to the SWOC by the UMWA, but a recent tendency is to appoint steel workers to these positions as capable leaders develop from the ranks.

Function of SWOC Staff

The job of the SWOC staff is to organize and supervise the affairs of the steel workers' lodges. In the early stages of the organization campaign, the staff representatives exerted considerable influence on election of officers of the newly formed lodges. Sometimes the officers were actually appointed by the district directors; in other places "uncooperative" local leaders were removed. A more usual procedure was for the staff representatives to pick out a promising leader, encourage him to speak in meetings, and thus make him the naturally recognized leader of the group.[31] In some respects, therefore, the lodges might be described

---

31. In this respect, the comments of district directors were significant:
"I have found that in most cases you must appoint the local officers. If a man won't assume responsibility, and won't work under the contract, you must replace him. The rank and file will always back you up on this."

"In the early stages of organization, you have got to develop local leadership.

as "hot house plants" under the watchful care of the SWOC staff.

Primary responsibility for negotiation with the large steel companies rests upon the SWOC directors and their staffs. Several lodges sent resolutions to the 1940 Wage and Policy Convention calling for ratification by the membership of all contracts negotiated by the international officers. The Wage and Policy Committee contended, however, that until the union could negotiate agreements on an industry-wide basis, such procedure would be unduly cumbersome. It was pointed out, nevertheless, that local lodge committees elected by the membership were being given "increasing participation" in contract negotiations.

Centralized Financial Control

Financial administration is likewise centrally controlled. Initiation fees are $3 and dues $1 a month. The lodges are required to remit to the secretary-treasurer of the SWOC all money collected from these sources. They are then entitled to a per capita refund of 25 per cent of dues and 33.3 per cent of initiation fees. Out of these funds the lodges must rent their halls, hire clerical help and compensate grievance committeemen for time spent on union business.

The reason for retention of such a large percentage of members' contributions by the international office is that the SWOC executives believe themselves better fitted than lodge officers to determine long-range objectives. To attain such objectives they hold that experienced organizers, competent lawyers and well-staffed research and publicity departments are needed. These are expensive. A second reason is that the SWOC owes about $1.5 million to the United Mine Workers and the CIO for financing the first ten months of the organization campaign and the 1937 "little steel" strikes. A further point, more effective control over uncooperative lodges can be maintained by making it difficult for them to build up large independent treasuries. And finally, centralized purchasing, accounting and auditing make for economy and more

Now if you left it to the members of the lodge, they wouldn't elect competent men; they would elect their friends. Therefore, in my area I practically appointed many of the key officers."

careful guardianship of the funds collected. The collection and expenditure of funds is further safeguarded by the bonding of local financial officers and the periodic audit of lodge accounts by the international office. The accounting and auditing system of the Steel Workers Organizing Committee has been a model for other unions.

The local lodges established by the SWOC are the main foundations of the evolving steel workers' union. With aid and guidance of the SWOC staff, local lodge officers administer routine affairs. They are primarily concerned with such matters as collection of dues, local membership drives, settlement of grievances with the companies, and in many cases the negotiation of supplementary agreements interpreting the provisions of the contracts. Many of the local leaders have already shown themselves capable of handling their own affairs with little help from the SWOC staff.

Most of the lodges comprise workers from a single plant. There is a tendency to subdivide the larger lodges into departmental groups and thus bring together employees with common interests and closely related problems. An industrial union must recognize different group interests and at the same time integrate all groups. Departmental ties among steel workers are generally stronger than craft ties. Through departmental organization greater pressure can be put on nonunion workers to join up. The policy, therefore, has been to organize plants department by department. As far as possible the SWOC has sought to parallel the structure of management—one dues committeeman for every foreman, and one chief steward or grievance committeeman for each superintendent. In this way the lodge has a permanent group of "watch dogs" in the plants, and the workers are continually reminded of the existence of the union.

b. OBJECTIVES

As stated by Chairman Philip Murray, the main objective of the SWOC has been to carry into effect the right of collective bargaining which steel workers have under the law, and to establish a permanent industrial union in the iron and steel industry for the exercise of that right.[32] More specifically, the ultimate goal has been to establish collective bargaining *on an industry-wide basis* between a steel workers' union and an organization composed of the principal steel producers. Having in mind a grandiose "Appalachian Agreement" [33] for the iron and steel industry, the miners originally set out to build a strong industrial labor organization to match the massed strength represented by the American Iron and Steel Institute.

Original Objectives Modified

In two respects the original objective was later modified. First, having at the outset organized steel processing and fabricating companies only "in response to requests of their employees," the SWOC has devoted more attention to them as time went on. Located near large steel centers, these companies are too small to resist unionization effectively, and are consequently quite easy to organize. Also the SWOC leaders were quick to recognize the strategic advantages in organizing certain steel-consumer groups. Added dues helped to pay overhead costs, and the potential membership has been raised from five hundred thousand steel workers to over a million factory employees. "Should we unionize all these workers," remarked one official, "think of the political and economic power of our organization."

The other important deviation from the original course resulted from the Taylor–Lewis agreement. Industry-wide collective bargaining was abandoned temporarily, and dealing with independents individually in attempts to secure their signatures to a "standard contract" was substituted. Until "little steel" was under contract, there could be no hope of bargaining with an employers' organization representing the industry. Although the resistance of "little steel" is now broken, the goal of industry-wide bargaining and industry-wide agreements is still far away.

Problems in Organizing Steel Workers

In most instances, steel workers did not organize spontaneously.

32. SWOC, *Steel Labor*, August 20, 1936.
33. See the "Bituminous Coal" chapter.

In spite of concessions won for the whole plant by the union, many workers are still indifferent to organization or even resent it. Others may vote for the SWOC in NLRB elections without becoming active union members.[34] To build 100 per cent lodges, therefore, the SWOC has sought management cooperation either through preferential treatment of union members or through the union shop.[35] The union shop, or its equivalent, has been the most important immediate objective of the SWOC. "As collective bargaining develops," say SWOC leaders, "there must be a more cooperative attitude on the part of employers, and they should be willing to insure the responsibility and discipline of the union by giving it complete recognition."

Lacking spontaneous enthusiasm for unionization, many steel workers have even less inclination to pay dues, particularly if they must go to the union office to do so. Sometimes, unionists formed picket lines to collect dues as the workers approached the mill gates. This practice, annoying to workers and objectionable to management, has been abandoned wherever possible in favor of collections within the plant by dues committeemen. Occasionally, the employer has cooperated by reminding union members of their "moral obligation" to support their organization. Finally, the SWOC has urged the "simplest and most effective means" of dues collection: that employers check off dues "as a demonstration of their good faith and of their desire to cooperate with the union." But they have not considered the checkoff as essential as the union shop, for when they get the latter, dues collection is greatly facilitated if not completely assured.

Problem of Leadership

A major task has been development of competent leadership. As one subregional director pointed out, "Outsiders cannot run the steel union forever. Soon the miners will step out of the picture, and, consequently, responsible, effective leadership must be

---

34. Up to October 1939, the SWOC participated in 131 NLRB elections, of which it won 88. Out of 86,560 votes, 55,179 were cast in its favor.

35. Under a "union shop," as the term is used in this study, membership in the union would be a condition of employment once a worker was hired by the company.

developed among steel workers." But executives of the SWOC interviewed felt that years would be needed to fill the "leadership vacuum" left by a background of antiunionism and company-controlled employee representation plans.

The building of an industrial union on the basis of peaceful acceptance of collective bargaining calls for the training of "administrators" rather than "agitators." Although the "fighting type" of union leader has been useful to the SWOC in certain situations, the "negotiator type" appears to have built the lodges which will be most stable in the long run. "Agitation may create excitement," said one SWOC executive, "but only education can build a union." The miners, with years of experience in collective bargaining, train the lodge leaders under their jurisdiction by helping them to cope with each situation as it arises. The Northeastern Regional Director has experimented with summer training camps for lodge officers, which have gone beyond the discussion of immediate problems and touched upon the broader aims of the labor movement and the history of collective bargaining, as well as political and economic theories. Most SWOC leaders seem to think that the type of leadership developed in a union is influenced by the attitude of management at all levels. They say that an antagonistic management strengthens agitators, while a cooperative spirit encourages more sensible and responsible persons to assume leadership. "A serious obstacle to the development of better union leaders," said an SWOC official, "is the lack of proper training by management of its own rank and file."

c. STRENGTH

In active union membership and aggressive local leadership the SWOC lodges are probably not as strong as locals of the CIO union in the automobile industry. On the other hand, the top leadership of the SWOC is more stable and experienced. Although its evolution has been relatively slow, unionism in steel has nonetheless been built upon firm foundations. The SWOC has established a labor organization which will not vanish into thin air.

Of the 600,000 members it claims, perhaps 400,000 are in the basic iron and steel industry, which employs about 500,000 workers eligible for union membership. The remaining 200,000 members work in metal processing and fabricating plants, closely related to the steel industry.

With the exception of one month since it began collecting dues in April 1937, the SWOC has met ordinary operating expenses from current receipts of dues and initiation fees. The initial outlay for the first ten months of the campaign, as well as the expenses of the "little steel" strikes, however, came largely from the treasury of the United Mine Workers. The total dues-paying membership of the SWOC has fluctuated greatly. In the spring of 1937 it was close to 200,000. It dwindled to "very low levels" in 1938 and 1939, but had come back to about 170,000 at the time of the second Wage and Policy Convention in May 1940. Since that time, it is estimated that dues-paying membership has doubled as a result of the boom in steel coupled with more intensive organizing activity. It is certain that the SWOC is in a very strong financial position at the present time (August 1941).

In the spring of 1941 the SWOC had over seven hundred signed agreements. Of these, the great majority provide for exclusive bargaining rights. About a hundred, mostly with small fabricating concerns, provide for either the union shop or checkoff. About seventy-five of the seven hundred agreements are with companies in the iron and steel industry, and of these, less than ten cover over 90 per cent of the membership in the industry. The strength of the SWOC, therefore, is best judged by the nature of its contracts with the large companies, rather than by the total number of agreements with employers who more or less follow the lead of the big concerns.

5. The Steel Companies' Policies and Organization

a. Development of Collective Bargaining Policies

Management constantly strives for more efficient, low-cost operations. In recent years steel has made striking technological progress. The introduction of continuous mills not only lowered the production cost of flat-rolled steel but so improved its quality that it is adaptable to many more uses. Metallurgical research has developed new stainless, alloy, and lightweight steels. Countless other changes in open hearths, blooming mills and wire mills have reduced the cost or improved the quality of steel products.

But improved techniques of management have lagged. With the exception of the American Rolling Mill Company, which undertook a comprehensive program of job study and wage classification as early as 1929, the major companies gave little thought to "scientific management" until price control broke down and competition became increasingly acute during depression years. Long-delayed programs for formulation of systematic job evaluations, work standards, incentive rates, employment policies and ability rating plans were just getting under way when collective bargaining became an important factor in the industry. At once it was necessary to examine the effects of these changes not only on profits but also on the workers who, through organization, were becoming more powerful and articulate.

Before 1933 the term "collective bargaining" was seldom used by the managements of the large steel corporations. A few companies had set up employee representation plans to enlist the "collective cooperation" of employees by providing a means of discussion of mutual problems.[36] In some others an official so bold as to suggest any form of employee representation might be threatened with discharge. Having unchallenged control over employment, wages and working conditions, many corporation executives were unmindful of the tactics used by their supervisors and neglected to examine the effect of their policies on the working forces.

After 1933 the general establishment of employee representation plans throughout the industry brought to light many shortcomings of management. The companies then developed a management technique of group relations which enabled them to reap the benefits of meeting with representatives of their employees without surrendering much of their traditional unilateral control over employment policies. During the NRA period, moreover, most companies were willing to "meet with" representatives of

36. See p. 512.

organized labor. At a White House conference in December 1934 the heads of several large steel corporations, faced by the President, members of the National Steel Labor Relations Board and representatives of the Amalgamated and the AF of L, said that they would agree "to meet, negotiate, and treat with" the bargaining committee of any labor organization, as such, as the representative of employees who were its rightful members. They refused to sign contracts or to recognize any organization as the sole bargaining agency. This conference broke up because the labor spokesmen would not yield their demand for the majority rule principle in representation.[37]

The strong opposition of the steel corporations to the Wagner bill was a clear indication of their antagonism to outside unions. They fought this legislation because it would legalize majority rule and outlaw company dominated employee representation plans and thus "drive a wedge between employer and employee." They argued, further, that the bill would encourage domination of steel workers by outside unions and would legalize the closed shop.[38]

Under the Taylor-Lewis agreement of March 1937 U. S. Steel accepted neither the closed shop nor majority rule; it merely agreed to incorporate in a written contract what had been since 1934 the *stated policy* of the industry with respect to bargaining with representatives of employees. Yet a signed contract implied some degree of acceptance of the SWOC and the abandonment of the practice of opposing outside unions. Many steel executives felt that Taylor had "sold the industry down the river."

After 1937 there was no such thing as an industry-wide policy of collective bargaining. The large union companies followed one course, the smaller concerns another, and the "little steel" groups a third policy.

Attitude of the Large Contract Companies

The large corporations that signed contracts with the SWOC,

---

37. For a full discussion of this conference, see Daugherty, *et al., op. cit.,* Vol. II, pp. 1040-1046.
38. American Iron and Steel Institute, *Steel Facts,* April 1935.

although still unconditionally opposed to the closed or union shop, have either formally or in practice recognized the principle of majority rule. Even where the contracts specify recognition for members only, most companies have dealt with the SWOC as if it were the exclusive bargaining agent, and in some cases have suppressed the activities of other groups. In general, management has preferred to deal with a single organization as the representative of all plant employees. Nevertheless, the concept of "collective cooperation," which was thought to underlie employee representation has been in large measure discarded. Because the SWOC is a militant organization which has challenged the power of management, it has been looked upon by the larger companies as a negative force in industrial relations. Company executives have resisted the attempt of the union to secure a measure of control over such vital matters as the setting of individual wage rates and layoff and promotion policies. Management has attempted, in so far as possible, to limit collective bargaining to redress of grievances.

Looking upon labor relations only as part of a broader program of industrial relations, the large companies have taken the position that they should neither encourage nor discourage workers to belong to the union. At the same time company executives have tried to eliminate causes of grievances, establish a reputation for square dealing with employees, and maintain in fact as well as in theory an "open door" policy on hearing of complaints. Some have thought that if management by its own action could develop sound industrial relations programs, there might no longer be any necessity for outside labor unions. The proponents of this theory hold that after conditions which provoke employee dissatisfaction have been eliminated, organizing issues will disappear and the union may become a "white elephant."

The Small Contract Companies

A few smaller companies have agreed to make union membership a condition of employment. Several others "as a matter of policy" have persuaded their workers to join the SWOC and pay dues. In such cases, wage and employment policies have usually been determined jointly by union and management representatives through collective bargaining. Thus the united front of the industry against the closed shop has broken at the fringes. There are several reasons for this development. First, the smaller companies were forced to grant the SWOC complete recognition to prevent serious labor troubles; they had neither resources nor inclination to fight the battles of the industry. Also, an expedient means of eliminating conflict between organized and unorganized workers in a plant is to force all employees to join the union. Finally, demonstrations by the SWOC that union-management cooperation programs [39] can follow as a result of complete recognition led executives of smaller companies to look upon the union as a constructive rather than a purely negative force in the industry. More important, perhaps, is the possibility that the small producers' interests might be safeguarded by an alliance with the SWOC. In October 1938 Philip Murray indicated that the SWOC might propose a federal legislative program to eliminate "the terror-stricken condition of the steel industry brought about by a system of cutthroat competition and resulting destroyed earnings." [40] It has not been uncommon for executives of the very small steel companies to meet privately with the SWOC to discuss a solution of this mutual problem.

Attitude of "Little Steel"

Until 1941 the "little steel" companies made no secret of their opposition to outside unions in general and the SWOC in particular. They attempted to stave off the CIO by dealing with "independent" unions or employee representation associations. These unaffiliated organizations were in many cases truly independent of company influence, and their leaders did not hesitate to take advantage of the outside pressure created by the SWOC to bargain for concessions from management. But Bethlehem, Republic and Youngstown Sheet and Tube were forced by the NLRB to dises-

39. This union-management cooperation program has been outlined in an SWOC pamphlet called "Production Problems." In 1939 this program was in effect in about ten fabricating companies and was being started in a few small steel corporations.

40. Statement of Philip Murray in Cleveland, SWOC press release, October 13, 1938.

tablish relations with these groups. In the meantime SWOC grievance committees grew in strength and prestige in the "little steel" plants.

In 1941 most of these companies abandoned their original stand of refusing to make written agreements with the SWOC. They are now willing to negotiate and sign agreements for all plants where the union claims a majority of workers in the appropriate bargaining unit. In short, they have agreed to comply with the spirit and intent of the National Labor Relations Act.

In general, the present collective bargaining policy of "little steel" companies is quite similar to that of U. S. Steel, Jones and Laughlin, and other companies which have had union contracts for the past four years. A "hands off" policy is followed regarding encouragement of union membership. Collective bargaining is looked upon largely as a negative process, and the companies are increasingly apprehensive of union encroachments in the field of management prerogatives.

b. MANAGEMENT ORGANIZATION

The advent of collective bargaining has focused the attention of company executives on problems of "human engineering," so that today industrial relations make up a large part of the science of effective business management. The formulation of industrial relations policies has become a major function of top management, and administration of such policies is a primary responsibility of every operating official from the vice presidents down to the foremen. Company-wide understanding of policies as formulated is essential to their satisfactory administration. For foremen and superintendents, who have been accustomed to fighting organized labor, it has been difficult to make adjustment to the new environment of the collective bargaining relationship. The practices of the supervisory forces therefore have often been at variance with stated company policies. Corporation executives, often disagreeing among themselves on the interpretation of policies, have been confronted with the problem of developing a consistent management attitude at all levels of supervision towards collective bargaining.

In large companies today policies are generally formulated by an executive committee composed of the president and other high officers. The top industrial relations officer, whether a vice president or director of industrial relations, usually sits with this committee as a consulting expert. He must be familiar with the details of the industrial relations program and advise management in the formulation of proper policies. Once formulated, policies are transmitted through the line organization to the operating departments, and the office of the director of industrial relations then serves as a clearing house of information on the administration and interpretation of policies. The chief role of the head industrial relations officer is that of staff adviser to the line organization. His other duties may be to supervise and coordinate training programs, safety work and employment policies, to oversee the administration of insurance, annuity and welfare plans, and to handle fourth-stage grievances [41] for the executives of the corporation. In some cases the industrial relations director reports to the vice president of operations. Because of the increasing importance of industrial relations, however, the trend is toward giving him the rank of vice president directly under the chief executive officer.

The same division of line and staff functions characterizes the plants of each corporation. A general works manager reporting to the vice president of operations is usually in charge of each plant. Reporting to the works manager are the various operating department superintendents, as well as the heads of the local staff departments. The plant supervisor or manager of industrial relations consults with the works manager, department superintendents and foremen on industrial relations matters. Under his direction are usually placed employment, training, safety and first aid. One of his many duties is to meet with the union grievance committees and to advise foremen and superintendents, when necessary, on procedures for dealing with committeemen. The main responsibility for administration of industrial relations policy is usually placed on the shoulders of the operating officers, with the supervisor of industrial relations advising them upon coordination of

41. See pp. 556-557.

activities and development of uniform procedures. Although reporting directly to the works manager, the local supervisor is usually in continuous touch with the corporation vice president or director of industrial relations from whom he receives detailed interpretations of policy and advice on problems arising.

Contracts with the SWOC or other labor organizations are generally negotiated by designated executives of the corporation for all plants. Interpretative rulings on matters of general application, basic wage rates, hours of work, or recognition of the union, are generally determined by corporation executives upon the advice of the chief industrial relations officer. The application of seniority rights, division of working time, adjustment of individual wage rates, and adaptation of grievance machinery are more generally left for local plant negotiation. The settlement of grievances is in so far as possible a plant responsibility, but unsettled cases are appealed to company officials.

6. Labor Relations under the First Contracts: 1937–1941

a. THE STANDARD CONTRACTS OF 1937

The Carnegie–Illinois (U. S. Steel) agreement of 1937, which grew out of the "Taylor–Lewis" negotiations, was the standard labor contract in the steel industry until April 1941. The general wage increases and the forty-hour week, which were announced at the same time by the other principal producers, were part of this agreement. A procedure for settlement of grievances was outlined and a broad seniority clause included. Former company policies with respect to vacations, safety and management rights were confirmed. Other companies which recognized the SWOC signed contracts similar in most respects to "big steel's." The discussion which follows, therefore, applies to other steel companies which signed the standard contract as well as to U. S. Steel subsidiaries.

"Big Steel" Points the Way

The SWOC always looked upon the basic labor contracts as "letters of introduction" rather than agreements upon such matters as wages, hours and working conditions. In other words, the union was constantly seeking to broaden the scope of collective bargaining relationships by requesting understandings that went beyond the language of the contracts, in order to secure more complete recognition and greater control over major wage and employment policies. Labor relations, consequently, depended on the degree of acceptance of collective bargaining resulting from the interpretation rather than the substance of the contracts. Written interpretations were few. Oral understandings and alleged statements of policy, sometimes publicly denied, in large measure determined the development of the collective bargaining relationship. In this respect the smaller companies which recognized the SWOC were inclined to follow the leadership of "big steel." As one company official explained, "When U. S. Steel puts on its straw hat in the springtime, the independents do likewise; when 'big steel' takes it off in the fall, they reach for their fedoras."

The SWOC hoped that the U. S. Steel agreement would soon become the basis for wholehearted collective bargaining through complete acceptance of the union. Such a relationship, however, did not develop. U. S. Steel regarded the contract as defining and limiting the scope of collective bargaining. Management was willing to cooperate with the union on matters specifically in the contract, such as the settlement of grievances, but consistently refused to extend the relationship by encouraging union membership or by consulting with union leaders on matters outside the scope of the agreement. Furthermore, local unions in many U. S. Steel plants were weak and handicapped by inexperienced leaders. Thus collective bargaining relations developed more slowly in "big steel" plants than in the smaller companies where there was less opposition to unionization. It is not surprising that during this period local unions in the smaller companies were, for the most part, stronger and better organized than in the large plants.

In 1937 the U. S. Steel agreement was the opening wedge for collective bargaining in the industry. The best contract obtainable at the time, it later became an impediment to the SWOC. Since the smaller companies could be organized more easily, the strategy of the SWOC up to 1940 was to "encircle big steel" by securing, wherever possible, a more wholehearted acceptance of collective bargaining in the other contract companies. This was the easiest, if not the only possible, course to follow at a time when depressed business and strong opposition by "little steel" put the SWOC on the defensive.

b. INTERPRETATION OF CONTRACT PROVISIONS

(1). *Wages*

The 1937 agreements set the basic labor rate at 62.5 cents an hour.[42] Because of the multiplicity of individual and group hourly and tonnage rates in steel plants it is impossible to set forth in a contract the wage scale above the minimum. The standard agreement, therefore, provided for an increase of 10 cents an hour in all hourly rates above the minimum and an equivalent raise in tonnage and piecework rates which would normally yield a net increase of not less than 80 cents an eight-hour day. It was further provided that alleged inequalities in such rates could be adjusted on a mutually satisfactory basis. Interpretative agreements supplementary to the 1938 contract renewals provided that rate cases could not be appealed to an umpire under the grievance machinery.

Wage Rate Structure

Most production employees in the steel industry work under tonnage or piece rates, but maintenance and mechanical workers are usually compensated on an hourly basis. The tendency in recent years has been to extend the incentive or piece rate system to many groups of workers who were formerly "hourly men." The wage structure of the steel industry is a maze of individual or group tonnage, piece and hourly rates, in many cases not uniform for similar work in a single plant, let alone the various mills of

---

42. These rates applied in the large steel producing districts of the North: Pittsburgh, Youngstown, Cleveland, Chicago and the Ohio River Valley. Slightly lower common labor rates were set in Johnstown, Buffalo, Bethlehem, Baltimore, parts of Ohio, Indiana and Illinois in accord with pre-existing differentials. In the South the Tennessee Coal, Iron and Railroad Company contract established an hourly rate of 45 cents for common labor.

The SWOC brought action through the Public Contracts Board to eliminate the differentials in the North. Recognizing the existence, but not the desirability, of the North-South differential, it suggested that this differential might some day be eliminated through collective bargaining.

different companies. One large wire mill, for example, was reported in 1939 to have over one hundred thousand different rates! The complicated wage structure is a result of the wide variety of operations in a steel mill, the multiplicity of products manufactured, the granting of "personal rates" to favorites by foremen and superintendents, and failure of management until recent years to undertake any systematic study of job classifications and rate setting.

As competition increased in the depression years, several large companies undertook systematic studies of job evaluation, rate setting and production methods. The job evaluations were used only as a guide or standard in rate setting. In order to attract and retain highly skilled workers, it was necessary to pay higher than the evaluated rate. For "personal reasons" it was necessary to leave untouched certain rates which were "out of line." The greatest problem, however, was the negotiation of changes in existing rates, and proposed new rates, with employee representatives.

Irrespective of the determining methods, tonnage and piece rates were common in steel mills long before the recent unionization drive. The SWOC has never opposed the principle of incentive rates. Union officers, however, were skeptical of the new methods used by management in setting rates. This skepticism stemmed from the fact that the large companies looked upon job evaluation and rate determination as lying exclusively within the realm of management prerogatives. The SWOC contended that all rates should be subject to joint determination by the company and the union. In 1940 the Wage Scale Policy Committee recommended to the convention that "efforts be directed to establish as far as humanly possible in contract negotiations simplification of classifications and rates, together with provisions for uniform minimum rates for comparable tasks and work."[43] This committee, however, had apparently little interest in the few resolutions submitted to it by local lodges asking for the abolition of piecework, bonus and merit systems.

43. *Report of the Wage Scale Policy Committee*, at the Wage and Policy Convention in Chicago, May 15, 1940, p. 5.

Adjustment of Individual and Group Rates

The adjustment of rates was from the outset a major issue. The union committees pressed for individual increases wherever they thought wages were unduly low, and, during the first year at least, won scores of raises. On the other hand, they opposed cuts in rates which management considered too high, unless only non-union workers were cut, a proviso which most companies rejected. In some plants, therefore, management refused to raise an inequitably low rate, unless the union would agree to lower an inequitably high one. The net result was that after the companies gave as many increases as they thought desirable, the wage rate structure tended to become "frozen."

Of greater consequence, however, was adjustment of rates affected by changes in equipment, processes, materials, routine duties or production requirements. At first, management argued that it had exclusive authority to set the new rates without negotiations with the SWOC committees, on the grounds that Section 8 of the standard contract affirmed their right to manage the works and direct the working forces. With the consolidation of mills, installation of new equipment, and introduction of better production methods, the tendency at first was to set the new rates and let the union protest, if it chose to do so. In strenuous objection, the SWOC held this practice a violation of the contract. Although consenting to the lowering of piece or tonnage rates in accord with technological improvements on a mutually satisfactory basis, the SWOC argued that an employee's former daily or hourly earnings must not be reduced thereby. Management's "arbitrary action" in setting such rates without negotiation was looked upon by the SWOC as a determined effort to break the union.

Subsequently the general practice of most of the large contract companies was to discuss proposed new rates with SWOC committeemen as well as all employees affected. Then the new rates were put in for a two or three months' trial, after which, if necessary, discussions might be resumed. Nevertheless, management did not abandon the claim that it had the exclusive right without negotiation to set rates in connection with changes in equipment, processes or materials, providing the hourly or daily earnings of the employees were not lowered. Although recognizing the wisdom of discussing proposed rate changes, which might, of course, involve negotiation, the large companies on several occasions established new rates in the absence of mutual agreement. From the standpoint of both sides, the procedure for rate adjustment was complicated and unsatisfactory.

(2). *Problems of Job Security*

No less important than wages is job security. In outlining the factors which were to be considered in promotion, layoff, and restoration of working forces, the 1937 contracts stated that where such factors as skill, efficiency, physical fitness, family status and place of residence were relatively equal, length of service should govern. The application and interpretation of this clause was generally a local matter.

In some plants where most union members were younger workers, the committees preferred instead of layoffs the sharing of work even down to one or two days a week. In others, where older workers controlled the union, there were strong demands for layoffs according to seniority. In most cases local agreements were reached providing for a combination of the two.

Another perplexing problem was whether length of service should apply in a department, a plant, or some combination of the two. Although in most cases seniority was applied on a modified department basis, no system could be devised which would satisfy all union members; job security for one group meant insecurity for another. Consequently, union officers were compelled to press for any plan which would satisfy the strongest groups in the lodge, and changes in local union policy were frequent. As in other mass production industries, seniority was a "headache" to men and management.

Ability Rating

Another problem involved weighting of the so-called merit factors. For the most part, unions insist that seniority should govern in layoffs unless an employee's deficiencies in other matters are basic and outstanding. Management, on the other hand, wants to retain the most efficient workers, and believes that seniority should govern only among employees of *equal merit.* Yet in the absence of precise methods of measuring relative competency, length of service is usually the principal factor governing layoff and re-employment of forces in plants where seniority systems have been established. Recognizing this shortcoming, some steel producers installed formal "ability rating" plans to measure competency and improve individual efficiency.

In the absence of 100 per cent recognition, the SWOC insisted on close adherence to seniority as a protection from favoritism and discrimination against union members. The objective was to limit management's discretion in selecting employees for layoff by substituting a clear-cut, definite formula giving preference to those employees of longest service. In developing ability rating programs, management sought to base its employment policies on a more objective merit system and thus to regain control over promotions and layoffs. The issue was squarely a battle for control over layoffs and, to a lesser extent, promotions. Union leaders could not organize steel workers by telling them that job security depended on management's discretion regarding ability. Therefore, many local unions insisted that union and management *jointly determine in advance,* on the basis of both competency and length of service, who should be laid off, re-employed or promoted. In a few plants, management agreed to such a procedure.

(3). *Union Status*

The fundamental dispute between the SWOC and the companies centered, of course, on the issue of recognition. The U. S. Steel agreement recognized the SWOC as the collective bargaining agency only for those employees who were its members. In most of the contract plants, however, the SWOC was the only active labor organization. Since questions of working conditions, wages and seniority rights affected everyone in the plant, the companies usually dealt with the SWOC as the sole bargaining agency. As one company official put it: "In the absence of activity by any other group, we consider the SWOC as the bargaining agency for all employees, for we have no means of knowing, and do not care to know, which of our employees belong to the union and which do not."

The SWOC was continually seeking to build up the prestige of the union so as to induce workers, directly or indirectly, to become members. For this reason it was anxious to have dues committeemen in the plants. An active dues committeeman for every twenty or thirty workers in a department not only could collect dues but also serve as a constant reminder to the workers of the existence of the union. Formal recognition by management of a dues committeeman system was usually construed by workers as company endorsement of the union. The large companies did not try to prevent collection of dues inside the plants as long as work was not interrupted, but management was unwilling, in most cases, to encourage unionization by openly authorizing such procedure.

The SWOC sought to induce the companies to persuade their employees, by one means or another, to join the union. An attitude of indifference on the part of the employer, so SWOC spokesmen claim, is not enough to convince employees that the company has abandoned its antiunion position. The SWOC asked some employers to agree that, if the union furnished a list of nonmembers, the company would urge such employees to join the union. The union also asked company officials to impress upon delinquent union members the necessity of paying their dues. To this end the SWOC was willing to accept an oral understanding in lieu of a written agreement.[44] By the end of 1940 a substantial number of fabricating concerns and small steel companies had made some sort of agreement of this kind. The large companies, however, were still opposed to any such encouragement.

C. PROCEDURE FOR SETTLEMENT OF GRIEVANCES

Both labor leaders and company officials were anxious to perfect a prompt and orderly method of settlement of secondary disputes. In general, the procedure set forth in the 1937 contracts provided that grievances should be taken up in the following sequence:

---

44. The smaller companies were unwilling to make a formal union-shop agreement because of fear of retaliation by open-shop customers and competitors.

Step one: the employee and the foreman of his department.
Step two: a member or members of the grievance committee and the foreman and superintendent of the department.
Step three: a member or members of the grievance committee and the general works manager (or general superintendent) or his designated representative.
Step four: a representative of the national office of the SWOC and the representatives of the company.

Failing settlement in step four, there was provision for appeal to an impartial umpire to be appointed by mutual agreement of the parties.

The union grievance committees generally had from three to ten members— all plant employees. They were allowed time off without pay to transact union business, for which they were generally compensated by the local lodge. In most plants the grievance committee met regularly with the general works manager and the plant industrial relations supervisor to discuss matters which were not settled with the foremen and department superintendents. The head industrial relations officer of the company and the international representative of the union took up only those grievances which could not be adjusted satisfactorily at the plants.

Success or failure of the grievance machinery really depended more on personalities than on procedures laid down in contracts. In fact, sometimes a better relationship existed between the SWOC and companies which refused to sign contracts than with many corporations which granted formal recognition.

Factors in Grievance Settlement

Company executives invariably pointed to the methods and tactics of "hot-heads" and "radicals" as the main cause of unsatisfactory union-management relations. In other cases, management praised the "intelligent and reasonable" attitude of certain union leaders as responsible for building up excellent relations. From the union standpoint, the attitude of superintendents and foremen was of primary concern. As one SWOC executive explained, "It has been our general experience that we can usually come to fair terms with the upper strata of management officials. The trouble encountered usually grows out of the subordinate officials —foremen, supervisors, etc.—going out of their way to indicate to the men that it will be to their disadvantage to be identified with the union. It seems to take a good deal of time for company policy formulated at the top to filter down to these lower officials." It was not unusual for grievance committees to put uncooperative foremen "on the spot" by appealing a large number of grievances over their heads to company executives.

Closely allied with personalities of union and management leaders was the problem of the insecure recognition status of the union. As long as the companies continued to protect the interests of nonunion workers while the SWOC was attempting to persuade them to join the union, each side was bound to distrust the motives for action of the other. This feeling of continual conflict was intensified by a company attitude which regarded a union contract as fixing the bounds of collective bargaining, and a union attitude which looked upon it as "a letter of introduction" or opening wedge for broadening the scope of the relationship.

Results

Although SWOC grievance committees settled thousands of complaints successfully with foremen, they were less fortunate in appealing cases to higher management officials. Such a situation was the reverse of that prevailing under the former employee representation plans where in the great majority of cases the representatives secured some concession. One reason was that employee representation cases generally involved a larger proportion of minor questions concerning working conditions, whereas the SWOC cases, although less in number, dealt primarily with such basic issues as wages or layoff and re-employment of working forces. Under the union system, foremen settled more minor cases informally because the companies insisted that they assume greater responsibility for labor relations in their departments. A second reason was that, faced with the problem of holding membership in an organization whose recognized status was insecure, local unions took up many grievances which had little merit.

As one local union officer pointed out, there were three types of grievance cases. The first included cases not covered by contract. Management sometimes made concessions on these in the first three steps but never in step four. The second comprised those covered by contract but not supported by proper evidence. Such cases were seldom won beyond the first step. The third group included those covered by contract and supported by evidence. Management usually settled these before they went to step four unless company-wide principles were at stake.

About three quarters of the grievances taken up by the union from 1937 to 1939 dealt with adjustment of wage rates and matters concerning distribution of work, seniority, layoffs and re-employment. Discharge cases, although important individually, were relatively few.

Not many cases went to arbitration. The larger companies preferred to settle their differences directly without resort to arbitrators who "know nothing about the steel industry." The SWOC, on the other hand, favored prompt arbitration of all unsettled fourth-step cases. The failure of the company and the union to agree on an arbitrator has led some SWOC officials to recommend a permanent umpire.

Because of the SWOC's powerful centralized control, breakdowns in grievance machinery resulted in extremely few unauthorized strikes. The SWOC executives successfully "kept the lid down" on "indignation committees" which came almost daily to the regional offices with sweeping complaints of management practices and criticism of the SWOC in delaying settlement of fourth-step grievances. It was apparent from interviews that most of this difficulty arose from the conflict between inexperienced local union leaders and an uncooperative management rank and file.

The grievance machinery had certain structural weaknesses. First, there were no time limits on the disposition of cases in the various steps, and delays in final settlement were common. Second, in many cases, there were no adequate written records setting forth the disposition of cases in the various steps. It was not uncommon for grievances to remain pending in the fourth step for several months, only to be referred back to the plant on the ground that they should never have gone beyond the third step. Finally, there was the possibility of ultimate deadlock in the choice of an umpire. Up to the end of 1940, most large corporations avoided arbitration, either by reaching agreement with the union on a basis of settlement after long delay, or by "stalling" on the appointment of an arbitrator.

7. THE "NEW STANDARD AGREEMENT" OF 1941

Realizing that the rest of the industry would take its cue from "big steel," the SWOC set out as early as November 1940 to secure improvements in the Carnegie-Illinois (U. S. Steel) agreement of 1937. From the point of view of the union, the defects in the first contract were several: inadequate recognition status, shortcomings in the grievance machinery, unsatisfactory procedure for adjusting individual and group wage rates, a weak seniority system, and disagreement concerning calculation of the working week for payment of overtime. In addition to eliminating these defects, the SWOC decided to press for a 10 cents an hour wage increase, more liberal vacations with pay, and protection of job rights of employees inducted into military service. In March 1941, when the SWOC announced its determination to end the existing contract, all of these demands were set forth in a nine-point program.[45] This program was the basis of negotiations with U. S. Steel, which ended in a new standard contract.

Wages and Vacations

The SWOC won its main demands for general pay increases and improvements in working conditions and schedules. The 10 cents an hour increase, granted after National Steel had pointed the way, raised average hourly earnings of steel workers to 97 cents. The corporation also made concessions on vacations. Under the 1937 agreements all employees with five or more years' service were entitled to one week's vacation with pay. In the new agreement, all employees with three or more years' service get one

---

45. See *Steel Labor*, March 20, 1941. For the text of the 1941 agreement, *ibid.*, April 18, 1941.

week's vacation and those with fifteen years' service are entitled to two weeks. In addition, the corporation agreed to pay time and a half for noncontinuous operations on July 4, Labor Day and Christmas.

The SWOC also won its demand for a forty-eight-hour rest period in each calendar week for every employee. The corporation accepted the principle that at least 85 per cent of all employees should be scheduled on a five-day week with a forty-eight-hour continuous rest period. Deviations from this principle are made the subject of negotiations on a local plant basis.

Adjustment of Individual and Group Rates

In its nine-point program the SWOC proposed the creation of "a joint commission of representatives of the Corporation and the Union for the purpose of giving consideration to and establishing equalization of rates in various classifications of labor." [46] But the corporation made few concessions on this score, except to spell out in detail the procedures which had evolved under the 1937 agreement.

Thus inequalities in existing rates are still to be adjusted through steps one to four of the grievance machinery. Rates for new jobs, or new rates management proposes because of changes in equipment, methods, materials or products, must be fully discussed by the union committee and local plant management before being put into effect for a reasonable trial period. After this, the union may protest through the regular grievance channels. However, if no agreement is reached, such cases are now subject to arbitration. In all other respects the new contract confirms the position which management took under the 1937 agreement. Although obligated to discuss all proposed new rates with the union and to attempt to secure union approval of its actions, management is ultimately limited only by the possibility of arbitration.

The fact that, under the contract, the corporation still retains control over the setting of new wage rates does not preclude establishment of such rates by a joint commission, if management is willing to agree to such procedure. In fact, there is every indi-

46. *Steel Labor,* March 20, 1941, p. 1.

cation that management may consent to the creation of joint commissions in some plants as an experiment. In the period of production expansion and rising living costs lying ahead, the rate adjustment issue will tend to be more vital and important in the industrial relations picture as a whole.

Job Security

In its nine-point program the SWOC demanded the elimination of "reference to factors other than length of continuous service" in determining layoffs and promotions. The union was anxious to prevent management from controlling layoffs through ability and merit-rating schemes. The 1941 contract, however, contains no important changes in seniority provisions, though, as in the case of rate adjustment, it spells out more fully practices which had developed under the 1937 contract. The corporation made no concession regarding protection of drafted employees' jobs.

Grievance Procedure

The changes the new contract makes in the grievance machinery are advantageous to both parties. First, the procedure is outlined clearly and in detail. Second, to prevent delays, a maximum time limit is set for the disposition of grievances at each step. There is still, however, no provision for resolving deadlocks when the parties are unable to agree on an arbitrator. From the standpoint of the union this remains a major defect in the grievance machinery.

Discharge procedure was amended favorably to the union. No employee can be discharged before a hearing of his case. The only immediate disciplinary action the company may take is to suspend an employee for five days. Within this period, he is entitled to a hearing. If suspension becomes discharge, the employee may have his case appealed through the grievance procedure to arbitration. When the arbitrator finds the discharge unjustified, he is empowered to order payment for lost time.

Union Status

U. S. Steel turned down the union's demand for "adequate machinery to permit the Union to collect dues from all employees who are receiving the benefits of the basic agreement." Proposals for the "voluntary checkoff" and open recognition of the dues committeeman system were unacceptable to management. The union demand for recognition as exclusive bargaining agent as soon as evidence indicates an SWOC majority was not formally agreed to by the corporation. Nevertheless, in view of the recent understandings reached between the SWOC and "little steel" companies, "big steel" will probably formally recognize the SWOC as exclusive bargaining agent when it offers proof that the majority of workers are union members.

Summary

The 1941 agreement with "big steel" again set the pattern of collective bargaining for the industry. In the main the SWOC exerted pressure to secure financial concessions and to improve its recognition status with the large steel companies. "Big steel" was more anxious to prevent encroachment on management prerogatives than to avoid the higher operating costs which would result from wage increases. In a sense, both parties were temporarily victorious. The SWOC increased the pay envelopes of the steel workers, while the large steel corporations still held the union "at arm's length." The present high wage level probably cannot be maintained in a postdefense recession, and collective bargaining cannot become stabilized as long as the union must continue to battle for complete recognition. The 1941 agreement, therefore, is an expedient compromise which postpones a permanent and lasting solution of more basic problems.

8. Conclusions

Three stages have marked the evolution of industrial relations in the steel industry. The first covered the thirty years before 1933, when steel makers were free to formulate labor policies with very little concern for their impact upon the working forces. A few companies, which set up employee representation plans, demonstrated that a systematic procedure for airing grievances and discussing management problems with workers could increase organizational efficiency. Most companies, however, neglected to adopt industrial relations policies to cope with the human problems that developed from the unwieldiness of mass production operations.

Forced acceptance of group relations brought about by the passage of the National Industrial Recovery Act in 1933 ushered in the second phase. As a bulwark against outside unions all the large steel companies set up employee representation plans, which they soon found effective in exposing many arbitrary and shortsighted practices on the part of the supervisory forces. It was found that education of foremen and workers through company-sponsored "collective cooperation" could be consistent with sound business practice. Yet under these conditions, group relations as a "management technique" proved to be unstable and transitional, for some of the plans were "captured" by opposing outside forces, and the representatives became conscious of the bargaining weakness of others.

The SWOC contracts with "big steel" and the established validity of the Wagner Act in 1937 marked the beginning of a third stage, that of unionization of workers on their own initiative for purposes of collective bargaining. Management was henceforth obliged to determine labor policies in the light of their impact on articulate, perhaps strongly organized, groups of workers having the power to question and possibly obstruct company actions.

SWOC's Work Reviewed

Steel workers had neither the leadership nor rank-and-file enthusiasm to organize spontaneously. The organization campaign, therefore, was led and financed largely by the United Mine Workers, who had a vital interest in unionizing steel. In the first year of its existence, the SWOC created a "union movement" in this traditional antiunion industry. At a time when political and economic factors were unusually favorable the SWOC reached an agreement with "big steel." Having provided the pressure to raise wage rates in the steel industry to unprecedented heights, the SWOC handed U. S. Steel employees a signed contract before they had built a cohesive labor organization. Capitalizing on the "big steel" contract, the union was able to induce several of the independent companies, which did not choose to fight, to make similar agreements. Yet the task of developing local unions with competent leadership was hardly begun. The failure of the "little steel" strikes showed that more than a mere movement was necessary to cope with a combination of the most prosperous producers in the industry.

After the strikes the movement languished, but the seeds of organization had been planted deeply enough to withstand a severe business recession. With the revival of operations in 1939 it became apparent that the SWOC had consolidated its earlier gains by developing a more stable and permanent labor organization. In 1940 and 1941, aided by the defense boom, it grew in numbers and in strength. Negotiations with "big steel" resulted in further industry-wide wage increases. "Little steel" capitulated and prepared to bargain on a formal basis with the SWOC. The new and autonomous steel workers' union, to be established in 1942, will probably be recognized by every steel corporation of major importance in the land.

During this period the steel industry has made great forward strides both in improved technology and increased organizational efficiency. The impact of unionization on management has resulted in more effective "human engineering." Whether in response to formal demands by union committees, or upon their own initiative to improve relations with their employees, the companies have eliminated many of the conditions which led to employee dissatisfaction. Management, in general, feels that collective bargaining has come to stay, but remains apprehensive of the growing desire of labor to share in the formulation of major industrial relations policies.

Labor Relations Not Yet Mature

Labor relations in steel have not yet reached the stage of factual collective bargaining characteristic of long-unionized industries. The main problem has been establishment of a collective bargaining relationship rather than settlement of basic issues by collective bargaining procedures. Joint discussions of such matters as wages, seniority, or union-management cooperation have been dominated by the continual struggle of the union to secure 100 per cent membership, and the determination of the larger companies not to encourage unionization in any way and to safeguard what they consider "management prerogatives."

Wages have been raised, hours reduced, qualified seniority rights recognized, and grievance machinery established. But where changes in process or equipment are involved, management still insists on its exclusive right to set new rates without union agreement. The adjustment of individual and group wage rates is rapidly becoming a major problem of collective bargaining, and it is likely that sharp differences of opinion will arise on this score between management and the union. Although recognizing that in general the seniority principle shall prevail in layoffs and promotion, other factors being relatively equal, the larger companies have not abandoned the stand that employment policies are matters within the ultimate exclusive control of management. To the large steel companies, in short, collective bargaining revolves mainly about the settlement of grievances.

The last five years of labor relations in steel have marked only the beginning of collective bargaining in this great industry. The signing of the first U. S. Steel contract may have begun a new era of industrial relations in the industry. It did not thereby establish collective bargaining with one bold stroke; on the contrary, developments in steel strengthen the conclusion that collective bargaining is built up by a slow process of evolution in employer-employee relationships.

9. Basic Issues Beyond the Scope of Collective Bargaining

The SWOC bargains with each steel company separately. At the outset, its aim was to establish collective bargaining on an industry-wide basis, for the major economic problems in steel are common to the industry as a whole and beyond the scope of the existing type of collective bargaining. But even the most "perfect" type of collective bargaining would have definite limitations in an industry which is subject more and more to government edict.

a. INTRODUCTION OF NEW METHODS AND MACHINERY

Recent managerial and technological advances have enabled the steel industry to offset higher wage rates by economies in the use of labor. In 1940, the major steel companies produced a 10 per cent larger tonnage than in 1937, yet the total number of man hours worked was 7 per cent less.[47] Total pay rolls were 3 per cent less. In 1939 the labor cost of producing steel was approximately the same (for comparable periods of operations) as it was in 1936, although wage rates were nearly 25 per cent higher.[48]

The most significant technological improvement has been the introduction of automatic continuous strip mills. In addition to a tremendous saving in labor cost in the manufacture of flat rolled products, these new mills produce steel of finer surfaces and deeper drawing qualities than were hitherto possible. Furthermore, continuous drawing machines have eliminated many former jobs in wire mills, and substantial savings in labor costs have resulted from the introduction of continuous butt-weld pipe mills. The size of open hearths has been increased, making possible a much larger output with very little additional labor. These and countless other mechanical improvements have contributed to the modernization of the country's steel plants since 1935.

Less spectacular, though equally important, are far-reaching improvements in industrial management, just beginning to bear fruit. Industrial engineering departments have studied and recommended better production methods which have eliminated the need for one or two workers here and there over a wide range of operations. Job analysis and classification have proceeded at a rapid rate in recent years. Personnel departments have been developing more careful procedures of selection and training of employees. To what extent savings in labor are attributable to these measures

---

47. *Steel Facts,* March 1941.
48. In August 1936, when the rate of ingot production was 72.1 per cent of capacity, wage earners in companies reporting to the American Iron and Steel Institute received $52.3 million. In September 1939 the ingot rate was 72.4 per cent, and wage earners received $52.9 million. Average hourly earnings in August 1936 were 66.8 cents as compared with 85.1 cents in September 1939. (Calculated from figures supplied by American Iron and Steel Institute.)

is problematical, but steel executives apparently agree that such managerial improvements have perhaps been as important as technological changes.

Until quite recently the SWOC was alarmed by the extent of technological unemployment. Though not opposing the installation of new machinery and equipment, the union wanted to compel the industry to minimize labor displacement by careful scheduling of new technological improvements and to force employers to bear the "social costs" of job elimination. In brief, the union program called for transfer of displaced workers to other jobs in the same mill, special compensation for employees who suffered reductions in earnings as a result of transfer, and "dismissal wages" for all employees dropped from the pay roll.[49]

Yet the union never attempted to press its demands through collective bargaining. On the contrary, Philip Murray made it clear that "in the absence of universal collective bargaining, Congressional regulation of the introduction of large technological changes is necessary."[50] Only through government action could new methods and machinery be planned and introduced so as to minimize displacement of regularly employed workers. New Deal officials, however, politely sidetracked SWOC pleas on this score, as well as CIO proposals for a conference of industry, labor and government to work out a solution to the general unemployment problem. The defense boom has since made the issue of technological unemployment a "dead letter" for the time being.

b. NATIONAL DEFENSE

The present critical shortage of steel calls for both increased production from existing facilities and expansion in productive capacity. Early in 1941 the SWOC gave wide publicity to the "Murray Plan" to achieve maximum steel output.[51] Paralleling the "Reuther Plan" for the automobile industry, the steel plan

---

49. Philip Murray, *Technological Unemployment*, SWOC Publication No. 3, 1940.
50. *Ibid.*, p. 39.
51. Philip Murray, *How to Speed Up Steel Production*, SWOC Publication No. 6, 1941.

calls for the organization of the entire iron and steel industry into one great production unit. Military and civilian steel needs would be met "first, through the most efficient coordination and use of present steel production facilities, and second, through a well-reasoned, responsible program to expand steel melting and finishing capacities where necessary." [52] The required coordination would be achieved through an "industry council" of an equal number of union and management representatives with a government representative as chairman. This council would serve as a "top scheduling clerk" for the entire steel industry. It would thus have power to formulate policies governing the use of existing facilities, as well as the creation of new capacity, and presumably would also assume responsibility for administering such policies.

The industry-council plan in steel would automatically establish industry-wide collective bargaining on matters of wages and working conditions. It would go further than collective bargaining in giving the union an equal voice with management in the determination of prices, production and allocation of steel orders.

Management, of course, has opposed the plan from the outset. The government has been unwilling to delegate such sweeping authority to any industry group, whether a joint association of employers and labor, or not. In fact, the Office of Production Management has assumed the function of "scheduling clerk" in planning expansion, allocating orders, and placing the industry under priority control, while the Office of Price Administration has taken over control of steel prices.

There is, however, provision for a steel industry advisory committee and a steel labor advisory committee. These committees have the right to give advice and make suggestions to the OPM but have no power to approve or disapprove any actions taken. Throughout, the SWOC has been lukewarm to the advisory committee setup, feeling that it is a very unsatisfactory substitute for the industry-council plan.

Now that the steel industry is virtually under government control, the effectiveness of the SWOC will depend in large measure on its ability to influence, directly or indirectly, governmental pol-

52. *Ibid.*, p. 9.

icy. The OPM now directs the flow of pig iron under an allocation system and has power of life and death over the steel companies themselves, as well as the thousands of concerns which are consumers of iron and steel products. Because of shortages of pig iron and steel ingots, thousands of union workers in nondefense plants are being displaced from their regular employment. In many plants forced to curtail production of "nonessential" goods, the problem of union recognition may be eclipsed by joint union-management efforts to secure defense contracts from the government. Wage rate structures and seniority rules may be completely upset by the transfer of workers from nondefense to defense plants. In short, the national defense program may substantially alter the issues in union-management relations at the same time that it creates new problems which are wholly outside the scope of collective bargaining.

The seeds of the present system of labor relations in steel were planted in a governmental environment which encouraged the organization and growth of unions. The collective bargaining pattern of the future will in large measure be determined by a government committed to all-out defense and total war. Both the corporations and the SWOC now face the issue of representation and status in the broad organization of federal defense agencies.

Chapter 11

AUTOMOBILES

W. H. McPherson

Assisted by Anthony Luchek [1]

1. Introduction

THE AUTOMOBILE assembly line has become the popular symbol of American manufacturing genius. Although this industry, with its highly organized mass production, has profoundly affected our industrial techniques and our living habits, not until recently did it contribute to improved labor relations. Before then its labor management was an industrial autocracy with wages, hours and working conditions decided through "individual bargaining."

Collective bargaining began to make headway in the industry in 1933, but three years later union recognition was still almost unknown. In 1937 came a great upheaval; sitdown strikes deluged the industry, and within a year union recognition became the rule rather than the exception. Developments, which in other industries frequently required several decades, were in this case telescoped into a few years. During the last four years the attitudes and policies of many managers and union leaders have drastically changed. Most managers have come to accept collective bargaining as an inescapable—and, in some cases, not undesirable—fact; many union officers have acquired an increasing sense of responsibility.

[1]. Mr. Luchek has contributed many valuable criticisms and suggestions. He has also made available several chapters of a manuscript on *Unionism in the Automobile Industry*, which he is preparing for publication. With the consent of the Brookings Institution, a few passages in the present chapter closely parallel statements in W. H. McPherson, *Labor Relations in the Automobile Industry*, Brookings Institution, Washington, 1940, which contains additional details on some of the topics discussed here.

2. The Industry

The characteristics of the industry have considerable influence on the forms and problems of collective bargaining. The most important of these are the industry's size, structure, location, production methods, rapidity of development, susceptibility to seasonal and cyclical forces, and methods of price determination.

a. DEVELOPMENT

The auto industry came into being during the last five years of the nineteenth century. Car registrations increased from four at the end of 1895 to thirty-two hundred at the turn of the century. Factory sales rose from seven thousand vehicles in 1901 to almost one million in 1915. They exceeded two million in 1920, four million in 1923, and five million in 1929.[2]

The phenomenal growth of the industry during its first three decades caused a chronic labor shortage, and almost constant efforts were needed to attract sufficient workers to the auto manufacturing centers. This scarcity of labor, together with high productivity and high profits, explains the relatively high wage levels long prevailing in the industry. It also accounts for the small employee interest at that time in job security. With new positions readily available, discharge was typically a mild penalty.

Auto production has not again reached its 1929 peak, but before then every year but four saw an increase over any preceding year. In 1930 for the first time came a reduction in passenger car registrations. Our thirty million vehicles so nearly meet the demand at existing prices that any decline in national income at once creates a saturated market.[3]

Though employment in 1937 exceeded that of 1929, the termination of market expansion during the 1930's made unnecessary any further efforts to attract new workers. The original impetus of the defense program during the last half of 1940 and the first half of 1941 revived the search, but this was ended by the sharp

---

2. Automobile Manufacturers Association, *Automobile Facts and Figures*, 1940, pp. 5, 8, 11.
3. See General Motors Corporation, *The Dynamics of Automobile Demand*, 1939, pp. 36-37.

curtailment of auto production later in 1941. When employment was not expanding, employee interest in job security and work sharing increased.

b. SIZE

Steel and automobiles are the giants of American manufacturing, each employing about half a million wage earners when production is active, as in 1937. The auto industry in 1939 had an average employment of 397,537 wage earners, to whom it paid over $645.1 million, while the value added to its product by manufacture was $1.3 billion.[4] Factory sales in that year approximated 3.6 million vehicles with a wholesale value of $2.3 billion.[5] The land, buildings, and equipment used in the industry were valued in 1937 at over $1.0 billion.[6]

c. STRUCTURE

The auto industry comprises four main types of producers—the manufacturers of motor vehicles, bodies, parts, and tools and dies—differing in their degree of integration and concentration and consequently, in certain aspects of their labor relations. Motor vehicles include passenger cars, trucks, busses and more specialized types. Most of the parts products are used as original equipment on new cars, but many are sold for replacements or accessories.

While manufacturers of bodies, parts, or tools and dies confine themselves typically to a single branch of the industry, most motor vehicle companies themselves turn out quantities of these products for their own use. Some produce much more of their requirements than others. The Ford Motor Company, the most highly integrated producer in the industry, greatly expanded its body production during 1939. It operates lumber, steel, glass and

---

4. *Census of Manufactures, 1939*, Preliminary Report, November 13, 1940. These figures do not give a true picture of the size of the industry, since they exclude many of the plants engaged chiefly or entirely in the production of auto parts. The inclusion of these plants would probably increase the figures by at least 20 per cent.
5. Automobile Manufacturers Association, *op. cit.*, 1940, pp. 5, 8.
6. U. S. Bureau of Internal Revenue, *Statistics of Income for 1937*, Pt. 2, p. 76. The Bureau of Internal Revenue and the Bureau of the Census differ somewhat in their delimitation of the industry.

tire plants, and owns transportation equipment, ore fields and a rubber plantation. As a result of this great self-sufficiency, Ford had at least 50 per cent more employees than Chrysler when producing about the same number of cars. Under a policy of maintaining multiple sources, all motor vehicle manufacturers buy parts from other companies, even while producing some themselves.

The varying degree of integration causes wide differences in the relative importance of labor cost. According to Census data, wages for the entire industry usually amount to about a sixth of the value of the product and about half of the value added by manufacture.

Concentration of Production

Passenger car production is now centralized in twelve corporations, three of which produce about nine tenths of the units sold in this country. Truck production is almost as highly concentrated. The small number of competing firms is due chiefly to the economies of large-scale operations[7] and consumer preference for makes having far-flung dealer service stations. The annual model policy is also a contributing factor. A small manufacturer who hurts his reputation by an unsuccessful model may not regain his former market.

While the body branch of the industry has more plants than any other, there are only three large independent manufacturers. Several large body plants are subsidiaries of motor vehicle corporations. Other plants are small, making chiefly custom bodies for trucks or passenger cars. As in the case of motor vehicles, efficient body production must be large scale.

7. The following are average annual percentage returns on investment in the motor vehicle business (before provision for income taxes), for 1936 and 1937:

Chrysler	66.7	Hudson	9.1
General Motors	37.1	Nash	3.1
Packard	20.4	Ford	2.5
Studebaker	9.8		

These figures suggest that efficiency increases with size, but may be adversely affected if expansion is carried beyond a certain point. Derived from data in Federal Trade Commission, *Report on Motor Vehicle Industry*, 76th Cong., 1st sess., H. Doc. 468 (1939), pp. 491, 493, 567, 671, 680, 703, 753, 809.

The parts branch of the industry as a whole shows much less concentration than vehicles, although many single items, e.g., frames, wheels, spark plugs and steering wheels, are produced by only very few companies in quantities large enough to make them potential suppliers for vehicle manufacturers. This part of the industry has two-and-a-half times as many plants as the vehicle branch, and multiple plant ownership is much less common. Since employment in the two branches is nearly equal, the parts plants are obviously smaller. The average number of wage earners per plant in 1937 was 1,485 in the vehicle branch and 593 in the parts branch.[8]

High concentration gives vehicle producers a strong bargaining power over their body and parts suppliers. The latter have few potential customers, and these may decide at any time to manufacture a larger proportion of their requirements. Consequently, body and parts producers must operate at high efficiency to keep their business. While keeping costs at a minimum, they must also forestall labor dissatisfaction which might cause stoppages and interrupt deliveries.

d. LOCATION

Detroit is the center of the industry. In its industrial area alone, nearly half of the nation's auto workers are employed. Many other Michigan cities, especially Flint, Pontiac and Lansing, depend largely on the industry, more than 60 per cent of which (measured in terms of employment or of value added by manufacture) is in Michigan. Another 15 per cent is in Ohio and Indiana, while the rest is widely scattered. Vehicle and body plants are chiefly in the larger cities. Many parts factories are in the smaller communities, mostly within three hundred miles of Detroit.

This high geographical concentration makes it impossible for an auto labor union to be effective unless it is strong in the Detroit area, while the existence of some few plants in widely separated districts forces the union to cover almost the whole nation if it is to protect its organized plants from unequal competition.

[8]. Derived from *Census of Manufactures, 1937*, Pt. I, pp. 1203, 1210.

e. PRODUCTION METHODS

Mass production is an outstanding characteristic of the auto industry, yet the dramatic process of the assembly line uses less than one fifth of the motor vehicle employees.[9] The tasks of the others are no less specialized or less carefully planned. This close coordination of jobs necessitates centralized determination of production standards, which is largely responsible for the charges of "speed-up."

Because of specialization of work and the high degree of mechanization, most jobs are semiskilled and can be learned quickly by those with the necessary aptitudes. Over a fourth of the occupations in the industry require no experience, while less than a tenth need more than a year of training.[10] Elderly employees are not suitable for the assembly lines but they can perform satisfactorily many other jobs. Only a few women are employed in the vehicle and body plants, but approximately a fifth of the parts workers are women, since they are adept at assembly of light units.

f. EMPLOYMENT FLUCTUATIONS

The auto industry is widely known as one of unstable employment. Though the industry is not as unique in this respect as is commonly supposed, it is subject to marked fluctuations, which make incomes of most auto workers irregular and uncertain.

Seasonal Variations

Since automobiles are not stored very extensively, production does not deviate far from current demand. Variations in dealer inventories provide the only leeway. The weather is one cause of fluctuations in retail sales. In the spring public fancy turns to motoring. Even with the popularity of the closed car, sales are more than twice as high in April and May as in January or Feb-

---

9. Automobile Manufacturers Association, memorandum on "Older Workers in Automobile Plants," April 18, 1939, p. 10.
10. Computed by Automobile Manufacturers Association from data in U. S. Employment Service, *Job Specifications for the Automobile-Manufacturing Industry*, 1935.

ruary.[11] A second influence is the annual model policy. Auto manufacturers believe that constant improvement of the product and annual changes in style are necessary to maintain the volume of replacement sales. The chief effect of this policy on demand is to cause a sharp contraction of sales during the two months preceding new model introduction and a marked increase during the following two months.[12]

Advancing the new model date from winter to autumn was one of the important steps the industry took in 1935 to reduce seasonal fluctuation.[13] This permits the building up of dealer inventories during the winter, between the peaks of new model demand and spring sales. Employment slack now comes in July and August instead of October and November, which dovetails well with Michigan's agricultural and summer resort peaks. Seasonal layoffs are now appreciably fewer and shorter than formerly.

Cyclical Variations

Since the auto is an expensive and relatively durable product, sales are greatly influenced by business conditions. Most buyers of new cars normally replace their old ones long before they are worn out. Thus replacement can easily be postponed. Since such postponement appreciably lightens the family budget (at least temporarily), it is one of the first economies when times are hard or uncertain. Auto sales therefore fall sharply in the early stages of depression and rise rapidly at first indications of recovery. Their fluctuations are about twice as great as those in the general level of industrial production.[14] The extent of the business cycle influence is shown by the fact that employment in each month from May through August 1938 was less than half as high as in the corresponding months of 1937.[15]

g. COMPETITION AND PRICE

In the early years of the industry the auto was built as a luxury

11. General Motors Corporation, *op. cit.*, pp. 73-75.
12. *Ibid.*, pp. 75-76.
13. The other was the advance production of subassemblies.
14. Automobile Manufacturers Association, *op. cit.*, 1939, p. 6.
15. U. S. Bureau of Labor Statistics, employment index.

product. Originally the Ford was a relatively high-priced car. In 1907 Ford entered the low-price field without reducing the quality of his product and won a wide market, which made possible the economies of mass production. Several other companies hesitatingly followed his lead. Each price reduction tapped a new level of demand until, during the 1920's, used cars began to meet the transportation needs of lower-income families. Thereafter producers aimed more directly at the replacement market, and style became an important competitive factor.

It has become increasingly risky to attempt to find additional new car buyers by reducing prices. It is doubtful that even sales so expanded would appreciably reduce costs, for production is already on so large a scale that further increases can yield only minor economies. Fixed costs per car can be reduced by an increase in output, but these are already a small part of total unit cost. Estimated unit overhead cost of one of the larger motor vehicle companies in 1937 (with production close to practical capacity) was only slightly more than 7 per cent of total unit cost.[16]

Hence, big price reductions appear unlikely in an industry dominated by a few large concerns. Competition among vehicle producers now takes the form of quality improvement more than of price reduction. Because of this and because overhead costs are low, "cut-throat" competition can scarcely occur—all of which reduces the incentive that auto makers might otherwise have to cut wages.[17]

3. Labor Organization

One striking feature of collective bargaining in the auto industry is the startlingly rapid evolution in labor organization forms. In the few years since 1933 the industry has experienced almost every type of labor representation—company unions, unaffiliated unions, federal unions, and international industrial and

---

16. General Motors Corporation, *op. cit.*, p. 126.
17. This section takes no account of the great effect that government action under the defense program will have on competition and price determination, nor of the effect of possible economies through the use of such new materials as plastics.

craft unions. Only in 1939 did the tempo of change subside with the development of a relatively stabilized condition.

This variety of experience meant unstable bargaining relationships, but it gave automobile workers, most of whom until recently had no first-hand knowledge of unionism, a chance to test various types of organization. They now have a basis for judgment which has apparently made them more ardent unionists than workers in some other recently organized industries where the variety of experience has been more limited.

a. CRAFT AND INDUSTRIAL UNIONISM

While one industrial union is now dominant in the industry, two other industrial unions and several craft unions also have a significant membership. The leading craft unions affiliated with the AF of L are the International Association of Machinists, the Pattern Makers' League, and the International Molders' Union. They have members in a number of auto plants and have won a few Labor Board elections. There are two other small craft unions. The Society of Designing Engineers is affiliated with the CIO through membership in the Federation of Architects, Engineers, Chemists and Technicians. The Society of Tool and Die Craftsmen is an unaffiliated union, which has at times been accused of management domination.

Aside from these instances of craft organization, unionism in the industry has almost from its inception followed industrial lines. The International Union of Carriage and Wagon Workers, affiliated with the AF of L since 1891, early entered the infant auto industry. Its insistence upon industry-wide jurisdiction caused constant conflict with craft unions and led to its suspension from the Federation in 1918. The union then changed its name to the United Automobile, Aircraft and Vehicle Workers of America, and increased its organizing activities. At its peak in 1920 it had about forty thousand members, chiefly in the small eastern custom body plants and in the paint shops of the Detroit body factories.

The depression of 1920–1921, together with introduction of lacquer, reduced employment in the paint shops by perhaps 80 per cent. Union membership consequently fell sharply and failed to rise again. Toward the end of the twenties the remnants of the organization were gathered into the Auto Workers Union (affiliated with the Trade Union Unity League)—a left-wing organization with a very unstable membership, which gradually dwindled away.

The next important union to enter the field began as a craft organization, but soon broadened to industrial jurisdiction. The Mechanics Educational Society of America was organized in February 1933 among automotive tool and die workers. By the following autumn it had some seventeen thousand members. In October it called a general tool and die strike in an effort to take advantage of the key position of its members, but the strikers won concessions in only a few small plants. The MESA subsequently extended its jurisdiction to include all employees in the "fabricated metal" industry, but its membership still consists chiefly of automotive tool and die workers.

The MESA differs from other unions in the industry. It is an independent, unaffiliated organization with an unusual degree of local democratic control. Its leaders advocate a collectivized or socialized economic system and are consequently interested in gaining employee participation in the determination of managerial policies. Though the MESA competes with the other auto unions, its relations with them have occasionally been harmonious and cooperative. It has often been asked to merge with other unions, but shows little interest in doing so.

The other two important unions in the industry are also industrial. Products of internal factionalism, one is affiliated with the CIO and the other with the AF of L. The former is now known as the United Automobile, Aircraft and Agricultural Implement Workers of America (UAW-CIO); the latter is called the United Automobile Workers of America (UAW-AF of L).

b. COMPETITIVE UNIONISM

This pervading factionalism took root during the period from 1933 to 1936, when many types of labor representation vied for supremacy.

Although joint attempts of AF of L craft unions to organize

the auto workers in 1914 and 1926 failed, the National Industrial Recovery Act in 1933 created an atmosphere favorable for organization. The AF of L was quick to use this opportunity. In its new organizing campaign the problem of jurisdiction was temporarily disregarded. Federal locals were established, affiliated directly with the AF of L, with the membership in each local usually restricted to employees in a single plant, regardless of occupation. There was no organic interrelationship between these locals except for common supervision by a single AF of L representative. By the spring of 1934 the campaign had enrolled approximately sixty thousand members.

These federal locals had to face the competition of company unions which most vehicle manufacturers and many of the larger parts producers introduced during the last half of 1933 to counteract the growing demand for unionism. Although these plants seldom dealt with wages, hours, discipline and production speeds, they helped for a time to raise the morale of many workers through their social and recreational activities and through elimination of annoying working conditions. They could do more for the employees than outside unions at this time, because they had recognition and because management made some substantial concessions to keep them successful competitors of the unions.[18]

Between 1933 and 1935 there was a mushroom growth of short-lived, local, unaffiliated organizations. Some were craft unions, others were industrial, and all added to the complexity of the situation.

Plant Bargaining Agencies

The Automobile Labor Board developed a unique form of labor representation. Creation of this board in the spring of 1934 followed a strike threat by AF of L locals for recognition in the motor vehicle branch of the industry. The strike was averted March 25 by an agreement President Roosevelt obtained with the unions and management. The settlement laid down policies governing layoff and rehiring, granted all labor groups a part in col-

18. See A. Luchek, "Company Unions, F.O.B. Detroit," *The Nation,* January 15, 1936, pp. 74-77.

lective bargaining on the basis of proportional representation, and set up the Automobile Labor Board to administer the agreement. Under these terms, management had to deal with any union which presented grievances, but no detailed plan for a bargaining organization was included.

In December the Automobile Labor Board provided for plant bargaining agencies and prescribed rules for their election.[19] These agencies proved relatively ineffective. Since they included unorganized workers together with members of the various outside unions, rivalry and hostility between these groups usually precluded successful cooperation. Moreover, no contact was provided between representatives and their constituents. Bargaining was in most instances limited to a plant basis, and efforts of some employee representatives to establish an interagency organization met with slight success. Without the backing of strong unions, the agencies were little more than glorified employee representation plans, though had the unions first been well established, the agencies might have been successful negotiating bodies.

After the Supreme Court in May 1935 declared the NRA unconstitutional, the Automobile Labor Board disbanded and the bargaining agencies lost their official position. Most of them soon disappeared, but a few continued to handle grievances for nearly two years. Since many motor vehicle workers saw no need for unions under the agency form of bargaining, membership in the AF of L locals declined appreciably during the existence of the Board.

Union Crystallization

While the membership of the AF of L locals was declining from the summer of 1934 to the spring of 1936, many new independent unions appeared. Two achieved considerable importance in the large vehicle plants, where the AF of L locals had few members. The Associated Automobile Workers of America was organized in the summer of 1934 by two federal locals which withdrew from the AF of L when the Federation refused to

19. For a debate on the wisdom of this action, see *The Nation,* March 13, 1935, pp. 297-301.

charter an international auto union. This example subsequently led to frequent threats of secession by other groups whenever factional strife became acute. The Associated Automobile Workers organized five additional locals and reached a peak membership of about fifteen thousand early in 1935.

The Automotive Industrial Workers' Association was organized in the Dodge plant in the spring of 1935 because of general dissatisfaction with the ineffectiveness of the Automobile Labor Board bargaining agency. This union spread to several other plants and eventually attained a membership of about twenty thousand. The chaotic condition of competitive unionism was accentuated by strife within AF of L locals. The insistent demand of these locals for an autonomous international organization led the Federation to combine them in August 1935 into the newly chartered United Automobile Workers of America. This move reduced discontent only slightly, however, because the Federation retained the right to appoint UAW officers. The demand for autonomy gained force with the mounting rank-and-file protest against the conservative policies of the appointed president. Disagreement between this officer and the others became so acute that separate offices were established.

Finally in April 1936, when UAW membership had fallen to about twenty-seven thousand, the AF of L granted autonomy. The competing unions were then ready to merge. On June 1 the largest local of the Associated Automobile Workers joined the UAW, the entire Automotive Industrial Workers' Association followed a month later, and three locals of the Mechanics Educational Society also joined. By midsummer there was no longer the slightest doubt as to which union was outstanding in the industry.

The chief remaining source of discontent with AF of L policies was union jurisdiction; the UAW charter actually granted a less extensive field for organization than that which had been appropriated in practice. The auto workers wanted a broad industrial union, and consequently had a common interest with the Committee for Industrial Organization. In July 1936 the UAW joined the CIO, where it has acquired jurisdiction over both auto and aircraft employees and competes with the Farm Equipment Workers Organizing Committee for members in that industry.

C. FACTIONALISM IN THE UAW

After affiliation with the CIO, factionalism temporarily subsided, and all efforts centered on a vigorous membership drive, which paved the way for the widespread strikes of early 1937. By July the union had approximately three hundred and seventy thousand members. Only Ford and many parts plants—chiefly in outlying regions—remained unorganized.

As the union grew in size and strength, the problem of maintaining satisfactory relations among its leaders became as serious as that of maintaining satisfactory relations with employers. Now that it had become a powerful organization, individuals and groups with various political and economic philosophies fought for control. There ensued a struggle which at times threatened to destroy the union.

Controversial Issues

Dissension centered chiefly around union policies and administration. The Progressive Caucus, headed by President Homer Martin, felt that the union had established itself in the industry and should now attend primarily to administrative problems. It therefore advocated moderation, caution in calling strikes, strict observance of contracts, and extensive control by the international union over its locals.

The chief opposition to Martin's administration came from the Unity Caucus, led by Walter Reuther, which held that the union was still in the organizing stage and should continue an aggressive policy. Members of this group supported the "quickie," or brief strike on the job, as an organizing weapon and sharply criticized the dismissal of effective organizers. Perhaps because they were in a minority, they advocated greater autonomy for the locals. Their criticism was particularly directed at Martin's qualifications and at the moderation of his policies.

The Unity Caucus contained the Communists and Socialists in the union, together with many others. Members of these two parties were probably only a fraction of one per cent of the union membership, but their constant and adroit activity gave them an influence far beyond their numbers. Martin found Communist opposition so bitter and annoying that he finally introduced into the union a counterirritant. He allied with Jay Lovestone, a Communist deprived of the Moscow seal of approval, who had organized the Independent Communist Labor League. Several Lovestone followers were given prominent union positions and the interfactional conflict increasingly became reciprocal public red-baiting.

The Widening Rift

During the last half of 1937 and the spring of 1938 the depression forced sharp curtailment in auto employment. This and rank-and-file disgust over internal strife reduced the UAW dues-paying membership by about three quarters[20] and compelled drastic retrenchment. Bitter wrangling broke out over who should be dropped from the union pay roll. Opposition to Martin gradually increased. Vice President Richard Frankensteen, who had been Martin's leading supporter, broke with him in April 1938 and joined his opponents.

In May, Martin submitted to the executive board a harmony program which included union objectives on which all were agreed,[21] but even unanimous adoption failed to get the officers pulling together. When, in the following month, it appeared possible that the opposition might gain control of the union, Martin suspended the secretary-treasurer and four vice presidents for violating the harmony program. The suspended officers were then tried by the remaining members of the executive board and four were expelled, while the fifth was suspended.[22]

---

20. Members employed less than forty hours a month retain full rights without payment of dues.

21. Among the policies listed were the following: guarantee of democratic rights to the locals, opposition to wage cuts, observance of union contracts, elimination of unauthorized stoppages, attainment of the closed shop, vigorous organizing activity, economy in union expenditure, resistance to war propaganda, and assumption by all union officers of full responsibility for the execution of these policies.

22. For a more detailed discussion of the causes and development of the factional strife up to this time, see W. H. McPherson, "Can Lewis Save the U.A.W.?" *The Nation,* September 17, 1938, pp. 260-263.

Martin opponents refused to let the issue drop. There were threats of mass secession and dual unionism. John L. Lewis sent Sidney Hillman and Philip Murray to Detroit as mediators, and as a result the expelled officers were later reinstated and a committee was established to recommend decisions on any future factional disputes. Since the CIO had generally sided with the Martin opponents, acceptance of its "peace plan" indicated a further decrease in Martin's support on the executive board.

The Final Break

Friction between Martin and a majority of the executive board became even more pronounced in subsequent months. One factor accentuating the internal conflict was Martin's negotiations with the Ford Motor Company. Although a special committee had been placed in charge of the Ford organizing campaign, Martin during December 1938 conducted direct personal negotiations with Ford executives. In January he reported to the executive board that he was on the point of a tentative oral agreement. The board authorized him to conclude an understanding on the basis of the reported terms, but the company soon discontinued negotiations. Mystery and conflicting reports still surround the details of these negotiations and the motives of the parties involved, and Martin's part in them roused suspicion and accentuated the internal conflict.

In the meantime Martin's authority was increasingly curtailed by board action. In some instances he disputed the right of the board to take action and refused to abide by its decisions. At his request the board in January called a special national convention to decide the issues. It refused, however, to follow his wishes regarding the convention's date and location and the eligibility of local unions for representation. Martin then suspended fifteen of the twenty-four members of the board. These and three other board members retaliated by declaring the suspensions unconstitutional and in turn suspending him. They appointed R. J. Thomas to serve as acting president until the convention, at which he was elected president. Martin issued a call for a separate national convention.

The UAW was now irrevocably split. At the two conventions

held early in 1939, each group established a complete union organization. The anti-Martin group was officially recognized by the CIO, while Martin's group in June joined the AF of L.

At the time of the conventions the Martin forces probably were supported by less than one fourth of the dues-paying members. His group subsequently lost many locals—especially the larger ones— to the rival organization. On the basis of its voting strength in the November 1940 AF of L convention, it had only 19,100 members. It is certain that most of its membership lies outside the main auto centers. In April 1940, Martin resigned the presidency and was replaced by Vice President Irvan Cary.

Since the split the UAW-CIO has conducted a strong organizing campaign and has had marked success in the numerous Labor Board elections.[23] Its dues-paying membership reached a seasonal peak of 458,413 in April 1941.[24] The following August the union changed its name to International Union, United Automobile, Aircraft and Agricultural Implement Workers of America, but retained its old initials.

d. UAW-CIO VICTORY AT FORD

The UAW-CIO's most dramatic victory was winning complete recognition from Ford after a lengthy struggle. Ford organizing activities prior to 1941 were seriously hampered by management's use of antiunion discrimination and even violence and by the Dearborn ordinance forbidding distributon of union literature near the plant. This "traffic" ordinance was finally held unconstitutional, and the National Labor Relations Board ruled the company guilty of unfair labor practices in cases involving plants in Dearborn and seven other cities. When on February 10, 1941, the U. S. Supreme Court refused to review a decision upholding on most points the Board's ruling in the Dearborn case, it was evi-

---

23. See R. J. Thomas, *Report to the 1940 Convention*, UAW-CIO, pp. 85-92; and *idem, Report to the 1941 Convention*, pp. 113-123.

For a discussion of the present factionalism in the UAW-CIO, see below, pp. 626-627. Since this union is so much larger than the UAW-AF of L and the MESA, it alone will be considered in the remaining discussion, when referring to conditions since the split.

24. This figure includes many aircraft and some agricultural implement workers, but does not reflect the predicted gain of 70,000 from the Ford closed shop.

dent that the company could not long continue to disregard the National Labor Relations Act.

Under the impetus of these rulings union membership increased rapidly. After March 1, informal grievance negotiations with Ford employees representing the union were held regularly in many buildings of the River Rouge plant, and eventually a plant-wide committee was recognized. On April 1 the management terminated these negotiations (or at least refused to continue to pay its employees for time spent in negotiation) and discharged eight union committeemen. Work stopped in many parts of the plant and at midnight union officials, after vain attempts to reach company officers, authorized a strike and withdrew the men from the plants. The company agreed not to attempt operation, and there was little violence after the first day.

Governor Van Wagoner was instrumental in ending the strike after ten days with an agreement to reinstate all strikers and five of the discharged committeemen, arbitrate the dismissal of the other three representatives, reinstitute the grievance procedure with the addition of a new tripartite appeal board, and expedite the holding of an NLRB election. The union's claim that it was reluctant to call the strike receives support from the fact that it insisted only upon removal of the conditions immediately responsible for the strike and dropped its demands for recognition, seniority, establishment of a shop steward system, abolition of the Ford Service Department, and an increase in wages to equal those paid by General Motors and Chrysler—leaving these matters to be decided by the election and subsequent negotiations.

The success and brevity of the strike greatly increased the union's popularity among Ford employees. The election held on May 21 in the River Rouge and Lincoln plants resulted in a complete victory for the CIO. In these plants where the workers were supposed to be so well satisfied and so hostile to unions, less than 4 per cent voted against union representation.

Although the personnel manager, Harry Bennett, had reportedly said that union recognition would bring no other concessions, the agreement signed on June 20 covering every Ford plant granted all major UAW demands, including those the union had withdrawn at the time of the strike. Ford thus became the first vehicle producer to grant the closed shop and the checkoff, or to use the union label. All former employees whose discharge had been listed in NLRB complaints were reinstated.

4. Attitudes and Tactics

The rapid evolution of unionism has been accompanied by equally striking change in the attitudes and tactics of both management and union. Auto managers, long known for their uncompromising resistance to labor organization, are now for the most part sincerely attempting to develop working relationships with the union, while union policy, which was sharply belligerent three years ago, is now marked by a more definite acceptance of responsibility.

a. THE OPEN-SHOP YEARS

During its first three decades the auto industry granted almost no formal recognition to unionism. Management strongly opposed labor organization, and wage earners showed little interest in it. Managers were technical experts concerned chiefly with meeting production schedules to satisfy an ever-expanding market. They paid relatively high wages to attract sufficient workers, and set their production rates high enough to get their money's worth.

Unionism to them was a threat to production and reliability of employee performance. Most managers, therefore, did everything they could to discourage trade unions. Such organizations as the Employers Association of Detroit and the National Metal Trades Association led campaigns for keeping the "open" (or nonunion) shop. Discharge and discriminatory layoff were common penalties for organizing activity, and blacklisting was apparently widely practiced. A number of manufacturers developed employee welfare programs, but employee representation plans were almost unknown.

Employees were apparently not too dissatisfied with a situation in which they could have no influence on employment conditions. Wages were high enough to compensate for seasonal layoffs.

Since the auto centers were boom towns, the worker who lost or disliked his job had little difficulty in finding another. This labor mobility checked accumulated employee discontent, which might otherwise have focused management attention upon labor relations.

b. RESPONSE TO CHANGING ECONOMIC AND POLITICAL CONDITIONS

In its fourth decade, the industry reached adulthood. It no longer gave promise of the rapid expansion that had been an outstanding characteristic. Opportunity for promotion diminished; difficulty of finding a new job in case of discharge increased. Discipline consequently became more onerous and job security assumed new importance in the worker's mind.

The depression of the early 1930's made the impact of these changes more violent. Employment not only ceased to expand, but contracted as never before in the history of the industry. Unemployed from other industries made the situation worse; those who lost a job in an auto town had little hope of finding one elsewhere. The foreman's power of disciplinary discharge became a constant threat, and management's efforts to reduce costs to the minimum made the "speed-up" more of a problem than ever. Growing dissatisfaction expressed itself in several unorganized strikes in Detroit auto plants during the first months of 1933. Job security and control of production rates became the workers' idea of Utopia.

The National Industrial Recovery Act in 1933 also gave new stimulus to organization. Its promise of freedom to organize and bargain collectively advertised unionism. Psychologically it removed the implications of radicalism and unrespectability surrounding unionism in the minds of many auto workers.

Increasing employee unrest spurred most auto managers to give more attention to the human problems of production. High wages, they realized, were not enough to insure uninterrupted output, and consequently they took a new interest in employment stabilization, systematic layoff procedure and wage-determination methods. Many company unions and employee representation plans were established at this time.

Simultaneously most large companies increased their espionage work. The La Follette "Civil Liberties" Committee[25] found that some of them paid large sums to detective agencies. The presence of industrial spies created ruinous suspicion and dissension in many young unions. Agents who gained official union positions frequently disrupted their locals.

These activities contributed to the decline in UAW membership between the springs of 1934 and 1936. Additional factors were the Automobile Labor Board, rank-and-file disapproval of AF of L policies, and rising wage rates.

C. PERIOD OF AGGRESSIVE UNIONISM

When the UAW joined the CIO in the summer of 1936, union policy became increasingly aggressive. AF of L leaders had favored gradual increase of a well-assimilated membership. Through moderation and internal discipline they sought to gain the confidence of management, but failed to realize that management's antipathy to unionism would not allow recognition without a bitter struggle. Their long experience in the labor movement led them to formulate union policy in terms of a well-established bargaining agency.

When the UAW gained autonomy, its leaders were young and inexperienced in union activity. But their observation as auto workers had convinced them that they must fight for recognition and that only a rapid, militant organizing campaign could succeed. And during the last half of 1936, notwithstanding expanding employment, bonuses and increased wages, their campaign did succeed.

"Quickies" and "Sitdowns"

The eagerness of the local unions to show their strength was displayed by numerous minor labor disturbances toward the end of 1936. The first local demonstrations were "quickies" or brief, localized stoppages, employees in some section of the plant remaining idle in their places while an immediate adjustment of their grievances was sought.

The auto industry is especially susceptible to such pressure be-

25. 75th Cong., 2d sess., S. Rept. 46, Pt. 3.

cause a stoppage in one department soon forces the suspension of production throughout the entire plant and frequently in other plants. Vehicle companies strove to meet production schedules because of the relatively narrow margin of dealer inventories, and parts manufacturers feared their customers would turn to other suppliers if they failed to make deliveries. The alacrity with which management usually granted demands when faced with a "quickie" encouraged greater use of this weapon.

In addition to grievance settlement, the locals wanted management recognition, and late in 1936 several of them struck to get it. These strikes marked the introduction of the "sitdown" in the auto industry. It differed from the quickie in that it embraced the entire plant, was of longer duration, and involved a refusal to vacate the premises. While the sitdown was adopted from the rubber industry and elsewhere, it was also a natural development of the quickie.

The most decisive contest in the struggle between management and the UAW was that which resulted in the winning of recognition from General Motors in February 1937, after several weeks of the most amazing and dramatic strike maneuvers ever witnessed in this country.[26]

Sitdowns swept through the auto industry. Employees in one plant after another refused to leave their shops and barricaded themselves behind closed doors. Small auto parts were used as ammunition when attempts were made to dislodge the trespassers. Improvised blackjacks and clubs were also used. Auto seats and upholstery materials were turned into mattresses. In some instances steel doors were welded shut. Deliberate sabotage, however, was apparently not a factor.

Results of the Sitdowns

These strikes were of course costly to the companies. Aside

26. Detailed descriptions of this strike and those that followed are presented in several publications: Automobile Manufacturers Association, *Sit-Down*, privately printed, Detroit, 1939; Herbert Harris, *American Labor*, Yale University Press, New Haven, 1939, pp. 288-304; Edward Levinson, *Labor on the March*, Harpers, New York, 1938, Chs. VII, VIII; Mary H. Vorse, *Labor's New Millions*, Modern Age, New York, 1938, Chs. V-IX; J. Raymond Walsh, *C.I.O.*, W. W. Norton, New York, 1937, Ch. IV.

from the costs of fighting them, there were the expenses of taking inventories, replacing upholstery materials and cleaning the plants. The lost business, so widely publicized whenever a strike occurs, is, however, largely fictitious as far as the motor vehicle companies are concerned, provided the stoppage is brief. The seasonal nature of the industry and the durable character of the product enable customers to postpone their replacement purchases. The chief result of a short shutdown is that inactivity comes at a different time than otherwise, since production is shifted to a later date. In the case of a prolonged shutdown, however, some purchasers may turn to other makes, some net loss may occur in sales, and general business may be adversely affected by the curtailment in the purchasing power of the idle employees. This analysis applies also to parts and body producers in the case of a single strike, though repeated strikes may lead to a serious permanent loss of business.

It is doubtful whether the UAW could have won widespread recognition without the sitdown. This effective device prevented the operation of a plant by strikebreakers or nonunionists and the removal of dies or machinery to transfer production to other plants. Since it could be started by a relatively small proportion of the employees, it was also an effective organizing device. In larger plants it was safer than a walkout, since any company that sells to the public must hesitate to employ the violence necessary to evict the strikers. Not a life was lost in all the Michigan auto strikes of early 1937. The chief disadvantage of the sitdown from the union point of view was the unfavorable public attitude it produced. Also, it was impractical in the smaller plants because of the relative ease of eviction.

Managers found the sitdown much more obnoxious than the walkout. They could not weaken the strikers' confidence by announcing plans to move or to resume operations. They were alarmed at the strikers' apparent lack of respect for law and order. The workers were not particularly concerned about the possible illegality of the sitdown, since they believed that most managers had shown no respect for the National Labor Relations Act, prohibiting discrimination against union members. Since February

27, 1939, when the Supreme Court definitely outlawed the sit-down,[27] UAW members have sometimes stopped work in the midst of a shift, but have left company property when so ordered by management.

Long after they were over, the bitter strikes of 1937 affected union and management attitudes. The unionists had discovered forceful weapons, and "war" psychology led them to continue their use. For several months production was often held up by local stoppages, which the international was sometimes unwilling and sometimes unable to control. Factionalism within the union made it difficult to enforce discipline, and management's reluctance to grant concessions led most union executives to rely upon force. On the other hand, union failure to maintain discipline reinforced management's unwillingness to deal with the organization, particularly when the outcome of the factional strife was uncertain.

d. PRESENT SITUATION

This vicious circle of mutual distrust and condemnation has been greatly narrowed in a brief three years. The union has achieved at least a moderate degree of internal stability. Its leaders now recognize the importance of demonstrating responsibility and have dealt promptly with the few instances of local breach of contract during the last few years.[28] They realize that the union is now established in the industry and has passed from the organizing stage into the negotiating stage.

Most managers have accepted collective bargaining as permanent. Although union factionalism for years encouraged them to hope for disruption of the organization, they now know they must deal with the union throughout the predictable future. Many now

---

27. NLRB v. *Fansteel Metallurgical Corp.*, 306 U.S. 240.
28. In December 1939 the executive board passed a strong resolution which said in part: "The international union is unalterably opposed to any unauthorized action and will not tolerate any . . . members condoning or participating in any unauthorized strike or labor holiday, deliberate slowdown or arbitrary reduction below established and accepted standards of production. Where small groups threaten to shut down an entire plant by unauthorized action, it is the duty of the local union to support the temporary placing of other workers on the job to avoid a general shutdown."

strive constructively for harmonious working relations with the union. Since they have concluded that industrial peace is impossible so long as they resist the union on every point, they now expedite the bargaining and grievance procedures.

Union Status

This growing managerial acceptance is also shown by the evolution of the union's status. The first collective agreements typically granted the union recognition only for its members. Under the influence of the National Labor Relations Act this right of representation was gradually extended to cover the entire working force, regardless of union membership. The union has now received "sole bargaining rights" in nearly all plants where it is recognized. Any individual worker or group of workers can present grievances to management officials, but can be represented only by the union in the negotiation of a collective agreement. Management opposition to sole bargaining was minimized by the realization that it was impractical to have more than one agreement governing the terms of employment of the same group of employees.

An increasing minority of the agreements gives the union a still stronger position by providing for some form of the closed shop. Almost all of these require that employees in occupations covered by the agreement must join the union within a specified period (usually thirty days) after their employment. Such a provision is generally called a "union shop," but is technically known as a "closed shop with an open union."

Some agreements go further and establish a "preferential shop," giving union members first chance in hiring. Several grant almost the equivalent of a union shop by requiring those who join to remain members in good standing in order to retain their jobs. In a few instances the agreement makes no mention of the obligation of the employees to maintain union membership, but grants to union members some advantage (such as preference in layoff and rehiring), which in practice assures that all eligible employees will join the organization and pay their dues regularly. Ford was the first large company to grant an unqualified closed shop. The

Murray Corporation has already followed suit. Both these companies also granted the checkoff.

The union shop exists in some plants where the agreement contains no relevant provision. This situation arises where managers feel it necessary or desirable to grant the union shop, but are reluctant to make this concession openly because of fear of criticism from other managers in the industry. Under such circumstances a separate secret agreement—written or oral—sometimes covers this point. More frequently the condition rests only upon a general understanding, with the manager indicating to the workers his desire that they join the union. He may do this by giving some evidence of the closeness of his relations with union officials (such as escorting them through the plant) or by the use of personal conferences to advise union membership to any employees who cannot be won over by the union agents.

Union analysis of 563 of its 1941 agreements showed that 40 per cent required union membership of all covered employees.[29] In granting the union shop the employer strengthens the position of the union. The financial income of the union is increased through larger membership, and union agents no longer have to devote much of their energies to the problem of dues collection. Consequently the bargaining power of the union is increased. The authority of the union over its own members is also strengthened. The fear of losing members no longer makes it expedient for union officers to press unjustified grievances or allow employee violation of the agreement to go unpunished. The threat of revoking union membership becomes equivalent to a threat of dismissal. As a result the union tends to become a more responsible party in the administration and enforcement of the collective agreement.

5. Bargaining Methods

Considerable difference exists between bargaining to negotiate agreements and bargaining to settle grievances. An agreement involves negotiation of the terms of the labor contract and specifica-

29. R. J. Thomas, *Report to the 1941 Convention*, p. 55.

tion of the management-union relationship. The objectives of the two parties are often opposed, and there are few tangible guides to a reasonable solution. Grievance settlement, on the other hand, is largely a matter of interpretation, and the terms of the agreement are an approximate, though not always precise, guide to solution.

a. NEGOTIATION OF AGREEMENTS

Most agreements are negotiated annually, though the tendency is growing to allow them to run indefinitely, provided neither side requests a change at specified times. A few permit either party to ask revision of some provisions upon thirty-day notice any time during the life of the agreement.

The agreement usually covers all the plants of a single company, sometimes supplemented on certain points by local plant contracts. Where some plants of a corporation are nonunion, only the organized plants are covered. When different internationals are the bargaining agents in different plants, each union has a contract for the plants it represents.

Since most local unions include only the employees of a single plant, negotiations with one-plant companies are conducted by the top managers and usually the local's chief officers and plant bargaining committee. A district field representative or international executive board member may also be present to advise. In negotiations with companies having several plants, the union often is represented by an intracorporation council of local delegates. The General Motors and Chrysler negotiations are usually conducted by a committee selected by the locals together with some officers of the international. Occasionally a CIO representative deals with special difficulties.

The local union membership participates in the conclusion of an agreement to the extent of (1) exercising a voice in the formulation of the original demands and (2) passing upon the terms tentatively accepted by the negotiators. Many managers protest against the inability of union representatives to make commitments during negotiations, feeling that the latter thus gain an advantage in bargaining power.

(1). *Group Negotiations*

In two instances joint negotiations have been held for several firms in the same branch of the industry, but only one agreement now covers more than a single company. Such negotiations were held by a group of molding manufacturers in 1937, but the method was abandoned after the first agreement expired. The employers found the method unduly time-consuming, because there were many employee representatives and it was especially hard to devise provisions to which all would agree. Had the union had a smaller bargaining committee and taken more pains to unify its demands, the plan might have been more successful.

The other group negotiation is more satisfactory and is still in operation. In May 1937 a master agreement was concluded with the UAW by twenty tool and die producers in the Detroit area. These companies were members of the Automotive Tool and Die Manufacturers' Association, and represented a majority of the production in that branch of the industry. Twenty-three shops participated in the second agreement. Sixteen took part in the 1940 negotiations, but about fifteen more accepted the agreement. The union is represented by four or five shop stewards and the presidents of its two Detroit tool and die locals. It and the participating managements both favor group negotiation because the resulting uniformity places competition on a more even basis.

The union seeks to extend this form of negotiation to other branches of the industry, where it is establishing regional and national Wage-Hour Councils. Regional councils are composed of delegates from plants producing similar products, while the national councils normally consist of delegates from the regional organizations. There are now councils in such branches as bearing, fiber, molding, spring, truck and wheel divisions. They are directed by the union's Competitive Shops Department, whose tasks are organization of nonunion shops and promotion of uniform agreements. As yet they have not had much success. Most employers prefer individual negotiations; under this method, they can refuse certain concessions which competitors may have granted.

(2). *Outside Influences Upon Bargaining*

The local's negotiations are influenced by the international, which usually presses it to make certain demands. In addition to the ever-present demand for wage increases, it emphasized sole bargaining rights in 1938 and vacations with pay in 1939. In 1941 it stressed improved bargaining machinery and extension of the union shop. When certain goals are widely gained, it shifts to other requests less important to the union or harder to win.

Sometimes the CIO influences the negotiations. Hillman and Murray are highly respected by the union leaders and by many auto managers. Their advice carries great weight, and they may be partly responsible for relaxing the drive to abolish piece rates.

Before collective bargaining some associations had considerable influence upon the labor policies of many companies. Since the battle to keep unionism out of the industry was lost, the Employers Association of Detroit and the National Metal Trades Association have had less influence on personnel problems. The Employers Association has modified its policies. It now furnishes information and advice to its members upon request, familiarizing companies in one branch of the industry with labor policies in other branches. Since the hearings before the La Follette "Civil Liberties" Committee in January 1937, the Metal Trades Association claims to have discontinued its strikebreaking and espionage activities.[30]

The Automobile Manufacturers Association and the Automotive Parts and Equipment Manufacturers, Inc., do not make any concerted effort to influence the labor policies of their members. They inform members of the practices of their competitors, keep a close watch on the provisions of new agreements, and compile monthly wage reports, so that each company knows how its rates compare with those paid by others. Also, exchange of opinion at their regular conferences of personnel managers helps to harmonize labor policies.

---

30. The Committee, however, reported that the Association "did not discontinue its strikebreaking services in the early part of 1937." See *Violation of Free Speech and Rights of Labor,* 76th Cong., 1st sess., S. Rept. 6, Pt. 4, "Labor Policies of Employers' Associations," 1939, p. 115.

Influence of Corporate Customers

The vehicle manufacturers are relatively independent of influence by customer-companies upon their labor negotiations. They sell to the general public through their own dealers, so that no one company is a large customer. On the other hand, most body, parts, or tool and die makers are dependent on one or a few vehicle manufacturers for most of their sales and cannot risk their displeasure. Vehicle manufacturers are thus in a position to shape the labor policies of their suppliers. If they wish to check union power, suppliers will resist union demands with greater determination. If they wish above all to maintain steady production, their suppliers will more readily make concessions to the union to avoid threatened stoppage of output and deliveries.

While this influence weighs heavily on the minds of parts and body manufacturers, it is usually more potential than actual. Existence of at least a *passive* influence is borne out by the prevailing opinion in the industry that a parts producer would be unwise to place the union label on his product, though this may be changed by Ford's recent adoption of the label. Another sign is that closed-shop provisions and the right to refuse to work on parts ordered from struck plants are frequently covered by verbal understandings or separate secret agreements and not by the formal contract.

There is little evidence of *active* influence except by Ford officials. Before union recognition became widespread, Ford influence reinforced antiunion policies. More recently Ford influence has occasionally led a supplier to grant certain concessions to the union in order to avoid interruption of operations. Long before Ford recognized the union, union officers sometimes successfully sought the help of Ford officials in persuading a supplier to yield.

Influence of Competitors

Company managers in all branches of the industry are considerably influenced by their immediate competitors. Often a manager rejects a union demand because otherwise his competitors might be embarrassed in their efforts to refuse a similar demand, leading perhaps to retaliation. "If we embarrass our competitors, they may soon embarrass us."

Another influence is more psychological than economic—the pressure of group disapproval. Through conferences held by the employers' associations, personnel directors of competing companies have become well acquainted. Each naturally hesitates to grant changes in his agreement which would displease his associates in other companies. This attitude might be summarized thus: "It is ethical to embarrass competitors as much as possible in, say, an energetic sales campaign, but it is unethical to embarrass them by granting union demands which are distasteful to other producers in the industry." It is interesting to note the similarity between this form of group pressure and the technique of social ostracism often used by unionists to induce others to become members.

(3). *Factors Affecting Bargaining Power*

Although the bargaining power of both union and management is affected by the skill of the negotiators, fundamentally it rests upon the ability successfully to conduct or resist a strike. The temper of public opinion is a major concern to both parties. It is of more concern to vehicle producers than to their suppliers, for they sell more directly to the public. They must therefore hesitate to provoke a situation which might lead to violence. This may explain why they have never in recent years hired professional strikebreakers.

Public opinion is also important to unions because of its influence upon the success of a strike. During the Chrysler strike in November 1939, a CIO foremen's union requested a conference with management. The company's protest that foremen are management representatives and that their organization was a union attempt to sit on both sides of the bargaining table was widely accepted by the public as logical and valid. Embarrassed by this development, the union has since had no interest in organizing foremen.

The union may at times, because of public opinion, find it almost impossible to call a strike. It cannot afford the reputation of being constantly at war. The public will lose patience with a union which is always striking. Because the union conducted several prominent strikes during the last half of 1939, there was almost a certainty that its new agreement with General Motors in the spring of 1940 would be negotiated without resort to any stoppage.

Vulnerability of Industry to Strikes

Specialization and closely interrelated operations make management in this industry unusually vulnerable to strike pressure by a few employees. A strike in one plant will usually cause a reduction or cessation of operations in other plants. Meticulously organized production makes it possible for a small number of employees to conduct a successful strike. A motor vehicle plant cannot operate effectively with a skeleton working force, and strikebreakers, untrained in specialized tasks, could not carry on. This gives to small groups of workers a power which is dangerous to management when the union is too weak to enforce discipline. Its importance diminishes as the union develops and acquires greater influence over its members.

A stoppage in one company almost inevitably throws some union members out of work in other branches of the industry. The severe strain upon the loyalty of the union members indirectly affected is only partially mitigated by the receipt of unemployment compensation.

Seasonal production also affects the bargaining power of the union. A strike's effectiveness varies directly with the volume of output. Consequently strikes in this industry are not called in the summer unless they involve chiefly tool and die workers, who are busiest at this time. Sometimes when an agreement expired during the summer the union continued to work under the old contract and postponed negotiations until autumn, after production had started on the new model.

b. SETTLEMENT OF GRIEVANCES

Successful handling of grievances is a first essential to sound labor relations. Neglected, latent dissatisfaction is the chief threat to employee morale, and one of the most important services a union can render is to bring complaints to light and obtain mutually satisfactory solutions.

Representatives

The negotiation of grievances, unlike that of agreements, is conducted by a great variety of union and management representatives. A system of appeals is provided from minor to major agents. Many grievances are due to misunderstanding, and can be settled by a simple explanation. Others are covered so directly by agreement provisions that there is little doubt of the proper solution. These grievances can be disposed of by minor executives. Consequently grievance procedure always starts at the bottom. When agreement is not reached there, the dispute can then be carried up through various stages of appeal.

The usual organization of employee representation within an auto plant involves stewards, chief stewards and a shop committee. The stewards are the union's "precinct committeemen." They maintain the local contacts between the organization and individual members. They seek new union members, collect dues and are expected to protect union interests in their jurisdiction. For every foreman there is usually one steward, elected by his constituents.

The chief stewards are the "ward leaders." They have more authority than the stewards and a larger jurisdiction. Generally, small plants have one chief steward and larger plants one for each department.

Though the union has stewards in all organized plants, a few large companies—notably General Motors—do not recognize them; they merely organize and collect dues, while grievances are handled by "committeemen." Under the General Motors 1940 agreement there was one committeeman for approximately each 250 employees, with limited exceptions for the smaller plants. As a result, grievance work was centralized, making it easier to control the representatives' absence from shop work. In some other companies not recognizing stewards, grievances are in the hands of the chief stewards. A sample of 103 union contracts [31] in force during the spring of 1940 contains twelve with this provision.

A committee is usually the highest form of employee representation within the plant. It is generally known as the shop committee, but many agreements refer to it as the executive shop committee, the grievance committee, the bargaining committee or the plant committee. Its members are usually elected from among the chief stewards, but several agreements also provide that one or more officers of the local union shall be ex officio committee members.

Representatives of the local or international union, though not employees of the company or members of the shop committee, frequently take a hand in the settlement of more serious complaints.

In most plants management is represented at some stage in the grievance procedure by nearly everyone connected with supervision. Those most commonly involved are the foreman, the superintendent, the plant or factory manager, the personnel director, a labor relations committee, the general manager and the president.

Grievance Procedure

An employee representative does not always present a complaint at the start. Many managers prefer that the grievance be first presented to the foreman by the dissatisfied worker. In this way less working time is lost, for the union representative is not disturbed in cases where the complaint is promptly settled. Also this method reduces the distinction between union members and unorganized employees, since the latter seldom use the union's grievance channels. Union officials, on the other hand, prefer that all complaints be handled only through union representatives. This procedure makes it more certain that the settlement will be consistent with union policy and gives the worker better protection against antagonizing his supervisor. In spite of this union attitude, an appreciable proportion of agreements require that the original complaint shall be first made by the dissatisfied em-

31. These contracts were analyzed by the author.

ployee. Of the 103 contracts recently analyzed, 15 contain this provision, while 12 allow the worker choice of presenting the grievance directly or through a union agent. In 42 of the remaining 76, the representative is the steward, in 12 it is the chief steward, in 17 it is the shop committee, and in 5 it is a member of the shop committee. It is only in the smaller shops that the grievance is originally handled by the committee or one of its members.

In 94 of the 103 agreements the original presentation, whether by the worker or a representative, is made to a foreman. In the other 9, involving small plants, the complaint goes directly to higher officials. At Packard minor grievances are referred by the chief steward to the department foreman, while grievances concerning company policy are taken directly by the district steward [32] to the personnel department representative assigned to that district. Major complaints involve such issues as wages, hours, seniority, transfer or discharge, and are handled more expeditiously and tactfully by labor relations specialists.

Unsettled complaints originally presented by the worker are often discussed next by the steward and the foreman. Those originally referred by the steward or chief steward to the foreman are frequently next taken by the chief steward to the superintendent. Usually, however—especially in smaller plants—the first appeal is handled by the shop committee and the "management." Most agreements fail to specify just which executives shall represent the company, though there is occasional reference to a labor relations committee. In cases where the shop committee and management do not handle the first appeal, they usually handle the second. In the third stage of appeal there is no uniformity, though a field representative or executive board member of the international union often enters at this point.

Steps through which a grievance may pass vary from two to seven. Generally the larger companies, with a more extensive hierarchy of management and union representatives, provide more opportunities for settlement. Of the 103 agreements analyzed, 26 provide for two stages of discussion, 30 for three stages, 30 for

32. There is one district steward in each of the five districts of the plant.

four stages, 13 for five stages, 3 for six stages, and one for seven stages.

While the final stage of appeal takes a variety of forms, over 60 per cent of the agreements analyzed end with a conference between the shop committee and high management officials. In about half of these cases one or both of the parties may call in outside representatives to participate in the discussion.

Arbitration

Of course any unsettled grievance may be referred by mutual consent to an impartial third party, but only five of the agreements studied mention this possibility. The author, however, knows of no case outside General Motors in which this step has been taken on grievance problems.[33]

While provision for voluntary arbitration is practically meaningless, a requirement of compulsory arbitration of unsettled grievances is significant. Ten of the 103 agreements contain such a provision. Six of these call for a board of arbitration—one member to be selected by each party, these two to select a third—whenever the two parties fail to adjust a grievance. Four require the appointment of an individual umpire. An innovation in the 1940 General Motors agreement was provision for a *permanent* umpire. This was an important forward step in grievance procedure in the auto industry and applied to the great majority of General Motors plants, namely those where the UAW-CIO was the bargaining agent. Four major limitations were placed on the authority of this umpire. He could not rule on any dispute over speed of operations. If the worker was found guilty in protested cases of disciplinary layoff and discharge, the umpire could not request the management to modify the penalty it had imposed. He could not order a change in wage payment plans or in any wage rate which was consistent with the agreement.[34] Finally, he

33. One other case of voluntary arbitration involved an amendment to an agreement. This concerned a reduction of wage rates in one plant of the Eaton Manufacturing Company in order to reduce the price so that the customer would not begin making the part himself.

34. The 1941 agreement gives him the right to rule on established wage rates and classifications and also the right to reduce penalties imposed by management.

could not by interpretation add to the terms of the agreement. It is particularly because of this last limitation that he was called an umpire rather than an arbitrator.

General Regulations

Shop committee meetings are usually held at regular intervals. In most instances where this is specified in the agreement, weekly meetings are stipulated. Meetings in smaller plants are generally biweekly or monthly, but special emergency sessions may be called. Although some meetings are held during working hours, most are at the end of the main shift.

The company usually pays stewards and chief stewards at their regular wage rates for time spent on grievances. They are less likely to remunerate shop committee members for meetings held after hours, and when they do, they often set a limit beyond which they will not pay.

The dilemma is to keep representatives from abusing their freedom to leave their work and still grant them enough time with pay to handle all grievances promptly. Some agreements attempt to solve this problem by requiring that they must notify the foreman before leaving their work, or obtain his approval, or that they cannot leave their particular jurisdictions.

In a few plants grievances must be written before presentation. Managers favor this because it closely defines the nature of the complaint and keeps discussion within bounds. Union officials differ. Some believe that this requirement deters many workers from bringing grievances to light; others hold that it clarifies issues and reduces unfounded complaints which the union cannot endorse. Putting disputes in writing before their first appeal might prevent later misunderstandings. But only 7 of the 103 agreements studied call for the written form in the original presentation. Another 28 require it at the first appeal, and 17 at later stages.

Success of Grievance Procedure

Successful handling of grievances rests partly upon method, but still more upon the underlying spirit. If both sides have good will, ways and means can be worked out; but the best of techniques may fail in an unfavorable atmosphere.

The first goal is prompt settlement. Managers are finding that streamlining is as important to grievances as to cars. Both the 1940 and 1941 General Motors agreements, for example, speeded up settlements because they increased the number of committeemen and widened their freedom of action.

It is difficult to define the attitude surest to bring results. Most important is a sincere wish to do the job well. Little good can come if stewards are more interested in unearthing grievances than in settling them, or if the management is more anxious to restrict union prestige by rejecting every possible complaint than to maintain employee morale by disposing of them. Mutual confidence is another requisite. The outcome of negotiations should not depend upon debating skill, with each side trying to trap the other into some statement that will weaken its position regardless of merit.

Any policy suggestive of paternalism is likely to fail. Employee recreation and athletic programs of some auto companies have contributed little to successful labor relations. One company, which has been reluctant to permit union administration of recreational activities and whose personnel manager takes pride in the number of holiday food baskets distributed, has had notably poor labor relations.

Managers of most unionized plants are now making sincere efforts at harmonious relations with the union. One problem has been to change their foremen's antiunion attitudes. This is difficult because the foremen are so immediately involved in the personal frictions of industrial relations. On the whole, companies with the best labor relations have the closest contacts between the foremen and the higher supervisory officials and have tried hardest to train their foremen to the new requirements of their position.[35]

35. For a discussion of grievance settlement in certain motor vehicle companies, see Emily Clark Brown, "The New Collective Bargaining in Mass Production: Methods, Results, Problems," *Journal of Political Economy*, February 1939, pp. 45-54.

6. RESULTS OF COLLECTIVE BARGAINING

Establishment of collective bargaining in the auto industry has affected not only methods of grievance settlement, but hours, wages, methods of payment, vacations, job security, discipline and the timing of operations. Some changes have a significant bearing upon important problems such as employment, efficiency and the migration of the industry.

Present conditions of employment may be contrasted with those preceding union recognition, but what changes would have occurred without union intervention cannot be determined. There would have been some evolution in management policy; and legislation, as well as business conditions, has also affected the terms of employment.

a. HOURS

Seasonal variations in production cause fluctuations in the working week. Because tasks are minutely specialized, managers prefer to alter the hours within certain limits rather than change the size of the working force. The union also prefers fluctuations in hours rather than employment, at least within certain limits.

Before 1930, a sixty-hour week was not unusual during peak production, and normal employment for most employees exceeded forty-eight hours.[36] The depression caused sharp curtailment after 1929. When recovery began in 1933, NRA codes limited hours. Under the auto codes production workers were usually restricted to forty-eight hours, with a long-term average of forty. Union recognition in 1937 resulted in the removal of hour flexibility. The forty-hour week became the almost universal maximum in the industry, with no exceptions for the peak seasons. Consequently, the Wage-Hour Act of 1938 with its present forty-hour restriction affected only a very few auto companies.

Both the Act and the union allow work above the maximum hours if overtime rates are paid, though some agreements limit

---

36. For data on normal employment, see *Census of Manufactures, 1929*, Vol. I, p. 54.

additional work. Union agreements in this industry usually require "time and a half" for all work exceeding eight hours a day and forty hours a week. This bonus usually applies to all Saturday work.[37] "Double time" is almost universal on Sundays or holidays.

Union leaders have sought shorter hours to reduce unemployment, and they also hold that greater leisure should be one of the benefits of increasing technological efficiency, at least so long as appreciable unemployment exists.

While managers are satisfied with the forty-hour week during most of the year, they wish to operate forty-five or forty-eight hours a week without overtime pay during peak production seasons. Under present regulations it is more economical to bring in supplementary employees and add extra shifts than to pay overtime rates; but management would prefer longer hours during seasonal peaks because regular employees are more efficient and would then have higher annual earnings.

Effect of Hours on Employment

The length of the working week is one factor directly influencing volume of employment. During the past decade labor-saving devices and reduced output cut down employment, but counteracting influences were product improvement and hour reduction. Some innovations mean less labor for certain operations, while others introduce new mechanisms which complicate the construction of cars and call for additional labor. During the last decade these two technological influences have roughly offset each other, since man-hour productivity was almost identical in 1929 and 1938.[38] Reduced hours caused a decline in output per employee, and are largely responsible for the fact that, while pro-

---

37. The General Motors and Chrysler agreements are important exceptions. These companies do not pay overtime for Saturday work unless weekly hours exceed forty, but employees shall not be laid off during the week in order to avoid payment of overtime for Saturday work.
38. Spurgeon Bell, *Productivity, Wages, and National Income*, Brookings Institution, Washington, 1940, p. 289. Another factor affecting man-hour productivity —labor efficiency or speed of operations—will be discussed in a subsequent section. Changes in volume of production also exert an influence. If production had been as great in 1938 as in 1929, man-hour productivity would have been somewhat higher.

duction was 33 per cent less in 1939 than in 1929, employment was only 12 per cent lower.[39]

During a somewhat longer period, both employment and leisure increased. Dr. Spurgeon Bell, in contrasting conditions in 1923 and 1924 with those in 1936 and 1937 (just as the union was beginning to win recognition), concluded:

> ... the increase in productivity in the automobile industry was matched by a corresponding increase in the total volume of output. As a result, the volume of employment [in man-hours] remained practically unchanged, though thanks to the decrease in the scheduled hours of work the number of wage earners increased as much as 25 per cent.[40]

b. METHODS OF PAYMENT

Methods of wage payment have undergone considerable change. During the 1920's there was a variety of incentive systems. Vehicle plants had group bonus plans which stimulated mutual supervision and pressure by the members of the group. Workers generally disliked them because of the difficulty of determining the wage and because individual effort had little bearing upon the wage.

As a concession to these objections, individual piece rates were introduced in many plants early in the 1930's; and in 1934 some vehicle manufacturers began to replace both group bonuses and piece rates with hourly rates. The speed of many operations in these plants is regulated by the flow of work or the movement of the conveyors, with the result that individual output of many workers is practically predetermined. In 1936 many parts managers also shifted from piece work, which had been prevalent in that branch, to day work.

These changes in the method of wage payment were probably motivated largely by a desire to reduce employee dissatisfaction, which was partly responsible for growing interest in unionism. Thus the unions were in large part responsible for the introduction of the hourly rate, even when this took place in plants where they were not recognized.

39. U. S. Department of Labor, *Labor Information Bulletin*, March 1940, p. 7.
40. *Op. cit.*, p. 107.

When the UAW gained widespread recognition in 1937, the shift to hourly rates was greatly accelerated. One of the first major demands of the union was for the abandonment of incentive wages. Union leaders have long claimed that the speed of operations was injurious to the health and nervous stability of many employees. They felt that the "speed-up" could be controlled only through the attainment of job security and the abolition of incentive rates.

Piece work still predominates in many plants outside the Detroit area and is used at least to some extent in most plants. Its use is of course better suited to some operations than to others. Also some workers prefer it. A few union leaders, realizing the importance of maintaining labor efficiency, have moderated their opposition.

While many managers are well satisfied with hourly rates, many others—especially in the parts plants, where speed of operations is less frequently predetermined by the machine or the conveyor—prefer piece rates. This method would undoubtedly be more general but for union opposition. Acquiescence of some union leaders permitted restoration of piece work in a few plants during 1940. The Automotive Parts and Equipment Manufacturers found that 60 per cent of 195 plants made some use of incentive wage methods in the spring of 1939, while in February of the next year 64 per cent of 156 plants had at least some piece workers.

Methods of wage payment have affected production costs diversely. The only uniformity lies in the fact that nearly all plants changing from piece to hourly rates experienced a drop in output soon after. Many plants eventually got their production back to standard, while others even now find difficulty in averaging 90 per cent of standard. Cost of supervision has increased in some plants, but not in others. Inspection costs have in some cases risen and in others declined. Some managers say that quality of work has improved, while others report that it has deteriorated. Obviously the effect of wage methods upon production costs is largely dependent upon other personnel policies and the general atmosphere of industrial relations.

C. WAGE RATES

Hourly pay has long been relatively high because of the high labor productivity and the former need for attracting additional workers to the rapidly growing industry. Except during 1922, average hourly earnings were around 70 cents from 1920 until the middle of 1932.[41] During the last half of 1932 they dropped to 55 cents. Largely because of the National Industrial Recovery Act, they jumped from 55.5 cents in July 1933 to 64 cents in September. In the spring of 1934, when a general strike of the motor vehicle branch was threatened, average earnings for the industry again advanced sharply to 70 cents. During the following two and a half years a gradual and irregular increase carried them to 80 cents. During the sweep of union recognition in the first half of 1937 average earnings climbed to 93 cents. In November 1940 they stood at 95.5 cents, and by May 1941 they were up to $1.01.

Some of the increase since the 1933 low came from recovery and some of it was caused by governmental policy; but it is likely that much of it was brought about at first by management's desire to forestall unionism and later by union pressure. The conclusion that the union has substantially influenced wages receives some support from the contrast of pay in the auto and airplane industries. While aircraft workers received in March 1941 average hourly earnings of only 78.3 cents, auto workers averaged 98.4 cents an hour.[42] Since the aircraft industry probably requires as high an average skill and since its rapid growth has necessitated the continual attraction of new employees, its markedly lower wage rates are probably due partly to the fact that until recently it has been much less thoroughly unionized.

Rates are probably somewhat lower in the parts branch than in the motor vehicle and body branches. Tool and die workers are

---

41. Estimates for 1920 to 1931 derived from data in Spurgeon Bell, *op. cit.*, pp. 287-289. (Wages paid in 1924 divided by total wage-earner man hours, and applied to index of hourly earnings.) Estimates for 1932 to 1939 from W. H. McPherson, *op. cit.*, pp. 77, 168-169.

42. *Monthly Labor Review*, June 1941, p. 1563.

by far the highest paid because of exceptional skill requirements and decidedly seasonal employment.

Few industries, regardless of their skill requirement, have as high wages as auto workers. In March 1941 only three industries —newspaper and periodical publishing, tires and tubes, and building construction—had higher average hourly earnings.[43]

Contrary to the widespread impression that the high wage rates in the auto industry are largely nullified by a greater amount of seasonal unemployment, the average annual earnings of employed auto workers compare favorably with other fields. In 1937 only six industries of any appreciable size showed higher average annual earnings than did the auto factories.[44]

Usually only agreements with small companies specify wage rates for each type of work. In most other cases only minimum rates for men and women are given. In the Michigan auto centers these are generally at least 75 and 65 cents respectively; elsewhere they are often lower. The Ford agreement omits even a minimum rate, providing merely that wages shall be at least as high as those of the major competitor, to be named by the union. A new agreement calling for a wage increase usually specifies a blanket raise or stipulates a higher minimum rate and leaves to management (subject to grievance protest) the changes in the other classifications, for managers want to maintain considerable wage differentials between jobs with different skill requirements.

Many agreements call for 5 cents or 5 per cent more an hour for work on the second and third shifts than on the first shift. Apparently this came entirely from union influence, for it had not been the practice in the industry since 1921. Probably most of the companies without such a clause have no extra shifts.

Geographical Wage Differentials

Differences have long existed in auto workers' pay in various parts of the country. In 1937 parts employees earned 38.9 per

43. *Ibid.*, pp. 1562-1566.
44. See W. H. McPherson, *op. cit.*, pp. 98-103. Since the nature of the product makes the industry especially responsive to the business cycle, the rank of the industry might be slightly less favorable in depression years.

cent less an hour in New England than in the East North Central district and 31.5 per cent less in Illinois than in Michigan.[45] Similar differences exist between plants in different parts of the same state; pay is higher in large cities than in smaller communities.[46]

The union opposes these geographical differentials, and has tried to reduce them. A principal object of its national and district Wage-Hour Councils is to standardize wage rates of competing companies.

Union influence has apparently decreased wage differences in the motor vehicle branch and increased them in the parts branch. Motor vehicle plants in various parts of the country are often operated by one corporation, so that the union, as a result of multiplant (or even company-wide) negotiations, has decreased the disparity in wage rates.

Few parts manufacturers have plants in more than one city and most agreements are negotiated locally. Since in 1937 the union was generally much stronger in high-wage centers than in the lower-wage communities, its early effect was to increase the parts wage differentials. No data are yet available to indicate whether this disparity has increased or decreased since 1937. While union leaders strive to raise the lower wage rates, they also continue to demand increases in the high-wage cities.

Effect on Industrial Migration

In the early days, vehicle manufacture was much less localized in the Detroit area than it is today. Gradual centralization came as some companies moved to Detroit and others went out of business. With vehicle production largely concentrated in southeastern Michigan, plants in the other branches of the industry also clustered there.

Toward the end of the 1920's—before the development of the union—Chrysler and General Motors checked the centralization trend with a policy of spreading their plants when they expanded operations. This was said to have been primarily to halt the in-

---

45. Bureau of the Census and Bureau of Labor Statistics, "Man-Hour Statistics for 105 Selected Industries," December 1939 (processed), pp. 73-74.
46. *Ibid.*, p. 74.

dustrial specialization of the chief car-producing cities, rather than to take advantage of lower wages.

It is claimed that the union is responsible for a recent migration of the industry away from the strongly organized, high-wage Michigan auto centers, whose industrial future may thus be seriously threatened. Migration of vehicle plants cannot result from union wage influence, since differentials in this branch have been reduced. But union influence on continuity of production once had a part in it; managers sought alternative sources of supply so that labor trouble in a single plant would not necessitate shutting down all assembly lines. Now that the employees in the vehicle plants are so widely organized, this motive no longer exists.

In the parts branch, however, the situation is quite different. Some plants in well-organized cities have lost business to non-union plants; some companies have moved a portion of their production from Detroit to smaller communities; and a few have shifted all of their operations elsewhere. Most parts companies operate on a small enough scale to be able to move to other cities with ease. But such migration has not been extensive. The Detroit Board of Commerce reports that the number of new businesses opening in Detroit between 1937 and 1939 was more than six times greater than the number of companies that moved part or all of their business away, and that $150 million was spent for the expansion of existing plants.[47] While these figures include other than auto plants, they at least show that Detroit has not yet suffered from migration.

The ability of Detroit to hold its own despite a considerable wage differential arises chiefly from its labor supply and the ability of its plants to make prompt and economical delivery. It appears doubtful, however, whether Detroit could long continue its present dominance in the parts field if the differential should be still further increased. While the increasing unionization of remote plants tends to check the dispersion of parts production, this effect has thus far been largely offset by further wage increases in the main production areas.

47. *Detroit News,* March 26, 1940, pp. 1, 4.

d. JOB SECURITY

Union leaders believe that security of employment is one of the most important benefits that auto workers have received from organization—security involving protection against arbitrary layoff and rehiring, against retirement at an unreasonably early age, and against disciplinary suspension and discharge.

Seniority

Through seniority the union seeks to gain security in layoff and rehiring. Application of seniority prevents certain types of anti-union discrimination, checks attempts by foremen to obtain unreasonable production, and gives each employee an assurance of his relative position when the working force is either cut or expanded.

While employers did not disregard length of service when determining who should be laid off, such other factors as skill, versatility, financial need and friendship with the foreman entered the situation. Under the influence of the Automobile Labor Board, much greater emphasis was placed on seniority, though it was by no means the sole determinant, as it has largely become since union recognition.

Modifications of Straight Seniority

There are only two exceptions to application of strict seniority in the industry. Most agreements give special protection to union representatives who work in the plant. As a rule, stewards and shop committeemen are placed at the top of seniority lists. This assures the union of agents available to handle grievances and collect dues even with a sharply reduced working force, strengthens the bargaining position of these representatives, and in a sense compensates them for their duties.

A few agreements, particularly in the motor vehicle and body plants, make some allowance for skill and versatility. They permit management to compile a preferential list of employees who may be retained during extensive layoffs regardless of their length of service. This is to assure that a plant operating below normal shall have enough versatile employees to keep going and enough specially skilled employees for readjustments when production is begun on new models. The length of the preferential list is usually limited. If union agents believe that favoritism rather than merit is responsible for some names on the list, they may protest the case through the grievance machinery. Preferential lists are becoming fewer. Union leaders generally oppose them on the ground that the employees with the longest service are certain to have the necessary skill and versatility. Many managers, on the other hand, favor them because they are extra incentives for outstanding workmanship.

A new employee does not get seniority status until after a probationary or trial period. These "temporary" employees are laid off in any order management pleases and they may be dismissed without union protest. Most of the vehicle plants have a six-month probationary period. In the parts companies the most frequent duration is thirty days, but sometimes it is sixty or ninety days. The six months' service may usually be cumulative, regardless of intervening layoff, while the thirty-day period generally must be continuous.

In layoffs, probationary employees are first to go. Most agreements provide that hours shall then be reduced before furloughing workers with one year's seniority. The usual hour reduction is to thirty-two hours—sometimes to thirty. After the week has been shortened, layoffs in order of seniority come next. Under some agreements, the order of procedure depends upon the anticipated duration of the curtailment, as in the General Motors agreement, which provides that "for temporary reductions in production, the work week may be reduced before any employees are laid off." In such cases even the probationary employees may be retained.

Rehiring is usually in the reverse order of layoff, but some agreements permit a partial or complete resumption of normal hours before all on the seniority list have been re-employed.

Scope of Seniority

The larger plants have more than one seniority list. Most of their agreements call for a separate list for each department, while some restrict it to an occupational group. Under a few agreements, the scope of seniority varies with the anticipated length of layoff or the extensiveness of the reduction in the working force, while under the Packard agreement and some others the scope of seniority increases with the length of service. In the case of the broader forms of seniority, a worker can displace another only if he is capable of doing the job. In disputed cases, he is often granted a three-day trial to show his ability.

The agreements of some multiplant companies permit interplant seniority under certain conditions. This is most frequently allowed when an operation is shifted to another plant or when technological change has eliminated jobs.

As a rule the union prefers the broader forms of seniority, though some leaders believe that departmental lists are the most practical in larger plants. Most managers prefer narrow limitations upon seniority. They object to plant-wide seniority because elimination of one job held by a long-service employee may shift many workers about and cause substandard production while they are becoming used to new tasks. Thus unit labor costs are temporarily increased during change in the size of the force.

Loss of Seniority

An employee loses his seniority status under almost all agreements when he quits his job, is discharged, is absent without leave or fails to return promptly when recalled from layoff. Under most agreements—Ford's is an exception—seniority is also terminated by layoff of specified duration, usually one or two years. Several companies have recently permitted unlimited retention of seniority so long as the employee notifies the company at least quarterly of his desire to remain on the list. Seventy-seven per cent of the 1941 agreements analyzed by the union safeguard drafted workers against loss of seniority.[48]

Union leaders advocate that employees should retain their seniority regardless of length of layoff. As a result of their efforts, new agreements show a trend toward the liberalizing or removal of this limitation. Most managers, however, prefer to retain the

48. R. J. Thomas, *Report to the 1941 Convention*, p. 56.

one-year limit. They like to keep seniority lists as small as possible, for the most skillful and ambitious employees laid off may find other jobs, leaving only the less desirable ones available for recall.

Consequences of Seniority

While seniority gives the worker more security in his present job, it lessens his chances of obtaining one elsewhere in the industry. If he should lose his job through discharge, or the permanent reduction of operations or the bankruptcy of his employer, he finds that other managers cannot employ him until their regular men are at work. And if he does not lose his job, but finds a more attractive one elsewhere, he may not leave because he would lose his established security.

Thus in periods of unemployment the tie that binds the worker to his job cannot be unfastened any more easily by him than by management. It is important to him that he begin with a company where he will wish to stay and where he will have lasting employment. If the company should fail, he will find it harder than before to get another place and he thus has new interest in the efficiency and financial stability of his employer.

These considerations, however, lose much of their influence whenever there is approximately full employment of workers who have acquired seniority rights. Expansion of employment in the industry under the defense program led in many plants to the re-employment of all persons on the seniority lists. As these lists were exhausted it became increasingly easy for auto workers to change employers. The operation of the seniority system did not prevent an increase in "voluntary quits" as unemployment in the industry dwindled during the first part of 1941, though it did offer a check to any efforts of managers to entice workers away from other unionized companies. The enforced curtailment of auto production since August 1941 has revived the problem of unemployment and intensified union interest in seniority.

Since seniority tends to increase the continuity of employment of the long-service workers, it must correspondingly reduce that of the newer ones. When the union entered the industry, auto executives were surprised to note that older employees were often as much interested in labor organization as the younger ones. This interest of the older workers resulted presumably from fear of job insecurity. The younger men show no signs of open hostility to the seniority system, except that they usually prefer that it have a narrow scope.

Sudden introduction of the seniority system into an industry which has just ceased to expand leaves little room for new employees until the average age of the workers has increased enough to raise the retirement rate. Consequently, young men in auto centers had until recently fewer chances than formerly, primarily because of the leveling off of the industry, but aggravated considerably by the application of seniority.

Retirement

Retirement formerly took place by refusal to rehire after layoff. It comes now in essentially the same manner, but only when all the jobs that the employee is capable of performing (within the scope of his seniority) are already held by workers of longer service. When age decreases an employee's capacities, fewer jobs are open to him through transfer in times of layoff. Thus he may be laid off longer and longer each time until eventually he cannot be rehired.

The seniority system may eventually make it difficult for managers to retire workers whose efficiency has deteriorated with age, but this problem has not yet arisen to any significant extent. Like any rapidly expanding industry, automobile work attracted during its rapid growth chiefly the more independent and adventurous young men. The industry is still relatively a young man's field. During the last decade, however, when employment expanded only slightly, average age increased markedly. Many jobs can be satisfactorily performed by elderly employees, and many companies have long made a special effort to retain these workers. The retirement problem will not become acute until more employees are in the high-age group and most jobs suitable for the elderly are held by long-service men.

Some managers fear that when more workers are near the verge of retirement, the union may possibly seek to reduce the speed of operations, so that its elderly workers can maintain standard production. There would be less likelihood of this should the union amend its constitutional provision permitting unemployed members to retain voting rights without dues payment, regardless of the duration of their layoff.

Discharge

Shop rules rather than agreements generally specify grounds for discharge. These rules are usually promulgated by management, but many agreements provide that no changes shall become effective until they have been discussed with the shop committee, and in some cases approved by it. A few agreements require a joint hearing before discharge or disciplinary layoff, though it is much more usual to impose the penalty and then await protest. An employee who feels that his penalty is unwarranted or unreasonable may appeal to his union representative. The issue is handled as a regular grievance, except that stricter time limits are set for protest, appeal and decision. Also it is customary to skip the lowest stages of settlement and refer the case immediately to a conference of the shop committee and the management, which the employee is frequently required to attend.

If a discharge is declared unwarranted, the employee is generally reinstated with back pay. To forestall such proceedings, most plants now deprive foremen of their former power of summary discharge.

Since the rise of the union, frequency of dismissal has sharply declined. In the vehicle and body plants the rate of discharge per hundred employees decreased from 3.08 in 1936 to 0.86 in 1939, while in the parts plants it dropped from 5.17 to 1.91.[49]

49. Figures for 1936 from H. B. Byer and J. Anker, "A Review of Factory Labor Turnover, 1930 to 1936," *Monthly Labor Review,* July 1937, pp. 160-161. Figures for 1939 from current issues of *Monthly Labor Review.* As a result of the introduction of seniority and unemployment compensation, managers may have classified their separations somewhat differently in these two years, since, prior to these innovations, they were under no obligation to distinguish sharply between layoff and discharge.

e. SPEED OF OPERATIONS

One of the union's strongest indictments of preunion conditions was that speed of operations often impaired health and nerves. It is not alleged that the speed-up was a universal practice but that, because of improper timing, change in materials, or the failure to provide enough relief workers, it was true, at least temporarily, of many individual jobs.

Most tasks in the auto factories are subjected to time study. Standard rates of production are set even where wages are paid by the hour, for the flow of work requires close interrelationship of various jobs.

During the Chrysler negotiations in the autumn of 1939 the union at first demanded joint determination of production standards, but became convinced that such collaboration would be impracticable. Its leaders prefer that management set the standards, provided the employees have an effective means of protest against unreasonable decisions. Most agreements which touch on this subject provide that management will retime any protested job, and some call for participation of a union representative. If this restudy fails to bring agreement, the case is then treated as a regular grievance and may be appealed through the usual stages. As a result, there is little current complaint of overspeeding.

There are numerous complaints by managers that it is harder to get reasonable production from employees, though many say that these difficulties have been temporary. Managers who complain of general underproduction charge the union with removing incentive for efficient operation. Some blame the replacement of piece work by day work, others emphasize the union's check on disciplinary measures or the fact that managers no longer can make merit the chief consideration in determining the order of layoff. The increasing tendency to require seniority to be considered in promotions further weakens the incentive for outstanding performance.

Special aggravated cases of underproduction are temporary, concerted slowdowns by small groups of employees complaining of speed-ups. Opposition of the international union has greatly diminished this protest technique.

f. VACATIONS

Paid vacations to wage earners were practically unknown before union recognition in 1937. Since then they have spread rapidly. Of the 501 agreements analyzed in 1938 by the UAW, 19 per cent provided for paid vacations, while an analysis of 563 agreements by the UAW-CIO in the spring of 1941 showed that 58 per cent of them made such provision.[50]

Vacations are more frequent in the parts factories than in the vehicle plants. Of 275 parts plants, 47 per cent gave vacations in 1939 and 66 per cent in 1940,[51] indicating the success of union pressure.

Vacation plans are amazingly diverse: among 182 parts companies giving vacations were ninety-eight different plans. They follow three main types: those which give vacation (1) in terms of regular pay for specified periods, (2) in terms of a percentage of annual earnings, and (3) in terms of a lump sum payment. About two thirds of the parts plants having vacations use the first form, though there is a sharp trend toward the second type, which figures vacation pay according to the regularity of past employment as well as to wage rate.

While it seems unusual to measure a vacation in terms of a financial payment, often without any reference to free time, this is not illogical in an industry where most wage earners have an annual layoff of two weeks or more. This actually grants remuneration for part of what is otherwise a payless vacation.

Three quarters of the plans of the parts companies base eligibility upon length of service; a seventh base it upon regularity of employment during the past year. The others combine these two standards or grant vacations to all employees. A few companies use the vacation plan as a highly modified incentive system by

---

50. R. J. Thomas, *Report to the 1941 Convention*, p. 57.
51. Automotive Parts and Equipment Manufacturers, *Bulletin No. 295*, June 26, 1940. These figures include nonunion plants.

making the payment dependent upon company earnings or plant efficiency.

g. OTHER WORKING CONDITIONS

In a number of less important respects the union has obtained gains in employment conditions. Many companies are now under obligation to provide a specified amount of work or pay if they fail to notify an employee not to report for work at the regular time. A sample of 103 agreements in effect during the spring of 1940 included 70 that contained this provision for "call-in pay." Nearly all of these required remuneration for a minimum of two hours, though in five instances pay for three or four hours was specified. The union estimates that provision for call-in pay was included in 36 per cent of its 1938 agreements and in 80 per cent of its 1941 contracts.[52]

Many agreements obligate management to notify employees one or two days in advance of layoff. A few also require advance notice of overtime, while in exceptional instances the performance of overtime work is optional with the employee. The agreements of some of the companies which make extensive use of piece work provide for at least limited payments to the workers in cases of temporary, enforced idleness. Finally, since the signing of the Ford agreement, the regular weekly payment of wages is the rule throughout the industry.

While these provisions are not of great significance in that they require actions which would usually be taken by management without compulsion, their inclusion in many agreements is an indication that in the absence of unionism some managers have through thoughtlessness or inefficiency given cause for resentment on the part of their employees.

7. CURRENT PROBLEMS

Although great strides have been made during the last three years, much can still be done to improve the operation of collective bargaining. Some of these remaining problems are prima-

52. R. J. Thomas, *Report to the 1941 Convention*, p. 57.

rily the concern of the union, or of management, while others will require joint efforts.

a. UNION PROBLEMS

The union's outstanding problem of wider organization has now been almost solved by recognition in all Ford plants. This gain without a serious strike is a tribute to the influence of the National Labor Relations Act on industrial peace and evidence of the benefits accruing under the Act to unions which have the patience to await its orderly procedures. Now that the citadel of antiunionism in this industry has fallen, many of the still-numerous unorganized parts plants [53] will probably soon grant union recognition. The problem of competition between organized and unorganized plants is likely to be of diminishing importance.

Avoidance of factional strife is a problem still facing the union. Although the chief source of internal dissension has been eliminated with the separation of the UAW into two groups, the CIO branch is so large that it still contains many divergent elements. The divergency arises partly from personal ambitions, partly from conflicts on policy. It is revealed to a considerable extent in allegiance of union executives to one or another of the leading personalities in the CIO. Many of the officers are disciples of John L. Lewis, while some are followers of Philip Murray, others of Sidney Hillman. Though most of Lewis' supporters repudiated his endorsement of the Republican presidential candidate in 1940, they remain no less loyal to his views on union policy.

The divergency is seen also in the attitudes toward the defense program and OPM officials. The Russo-German War does not appear as yet to have brought the Communist element in the UAW to unqualified support of the program. This group and the Lewis following constitute a strong contingent which is highly critical of Hillman and the OPM because of government action in the Allis-Chalmers and North American Aviation strikes. The other group urges extensive cooperation with defense efforts.

During most of the last two years the executive board has

---

53. Most of these are small.

operated without serious open conflict. But on many major questions there was a close split, with the "left-wing" group, led by Secretary-Treasurer George Addes, generally having the upper hand. There have also been occasional indications of antipathy between two of the most prominent board members—Richard Frankensteen and Walter Reuther. After the 1940 convention, for example, Frankensteen obtained a striking increase in the importance of his duties, partially at Reuther's expense.

Since that time, however, the union has been presenting to the public a united front, except for conflict between the international and some of its locals on the question of defense strikes. Frankensteen and Reuther assumed joint leadership of opposition to "left-wing" elements. They entered the 1941 convention with majority support for their program. Although the CIO representative at the convention apparently induced Frankensteen to modify his opposition to the "left-wing" group, a majority of the delegates continued to support the Reuther program in most respects. The "left-wing" group has at least for the time being lost control of the new executive board. The maintenance of a reasonable degree of harmony within the organization will require great skill and some sacrifice of personal ambition by union officers.

A third problem confronting the unions is that of avoiding jurisdictional disputes. Considering the bitterness of the early factionalism, the presence of three unions in the industry would probably have resulted in disruption to production schedules during 1939 and 1940 had it not been for the National Labor Relations Act. As it is, there were only minor disturbances. The issue has been settled by elections conducted in companies employing at least three fourths of the wage earners in the industry.

Another major union problem is maintenance of the internal discipline essential to the enforcement of union responsibility. The wave of strikes in 1937 caused such antagonism between wage earners and supervisors and such rapid expansion of union membership that discipline was inadequate to prevent innumerable local stoppages. Since then, however, the international officers have taken so strong a stand on this issue that stoppages in breach of contract have become rare. Continued exercise of this discipline requires able leadership, since there is a high degree of rank-and-file control in the union.

b. MANAGEMENT PROBLEMS

Management has a problem in its lesser officials. In general, top executives have made a more rapid adjustment to unionized conditions than their subordinates, who are more directly involved in the disputes. The union claims, with some justification, that many of the unauthorized stoppages of 1937 and 1938 resulted from the provocative actions of foremen. Managers with the most successful records in labor relations are those who gave the most attention to educating foremen in this field.

Another outstanding problem of management is maintenance of labor efficiency. Several of the changes introduced at the insistence of the union—seniority, reduced use of piece rates, lower differentials between skilled and unskilled, uniformity of wage rates on any particular job in a plant, and control of discharge—have increased the security of the wage earners at the expense of efficiency incentives.

To say that these changes have removed some of the chief incentives for efficient work is not necessarily to condemn them, for they have in most instances done away with certain opportunities for employee favoritism and discrimination that many managers have in the past seriously abused. Nevertheless, attainment of these union goals has raised the question—of fundamental importance to management and also, in the long run, to employees—as to whether sufficient incentive remains to maintain reasonably high labor efficiency.

Some incentives do remain. Piece rates are still widely used for tasks whose speed is not set by the timing of machines or the flow of materials. Some companies may still exempt a few of their more efficient and more versatile employees from the seniority system. And every manager has complete freedom in rewarding competence by promotion to supervisory positions. While seniority has in some respects an adverse effect upon incentive, it also has in one respect a favorable influence, at least in the case of marginal plants during periods of prevailing unemployment. By reducing the worker's chances of employment in other companies it should encourage him to protect his job by helping to maintain the competitive position of his employer.

Many employers report that they no longer get such exceptional production from their outstanding employees as they did before the advent of union contracts. Some state that they now find it impossible to get average standard output from their labor force, while others say that they have restored production which fell below normal in any department by using time studies to persuade employees of the reasonableness of the standard. This diversity of experience leads to the conclusion that labor efficiency depends not only upon the method of wage payment and other specific incentives, but also upon the effect of local labor relations on employee morale.

C. JOINT PROBLEMS

All knotty points in industrial relations are to some extent "joint" problems. Efficiency, for example, concerns both parties. But how to devise the best methods for joint consultation is peculiarly a mutual responsibility.

Sound labor relations and high morale can be maintained only when grievances are promptly handled. Auto agreements detail elaborate procedures, but their success depends not only on the machinery but also on the spirit of those who jointly operate it. More and more, managers are expediting grievance settlement and union officials are preventing direct action as a substitute for the grievance procedure. However, a few instances still remain in which local managers unnecessarily await the lapse of the maximum time allowed by the agreement before replying to a submitted grievance.

Relations in the auto industry are now becoming stabilized, and the point may be reached where arbitration can be more widely used as a last resort in grievance settlement. Arbitration is not normally useful for deciding the disputed terms of a new contract, for few standards exist as guides. But for grievances, the contract itself generally indicates the proper settlement, and an arbitrator may be useful in obtaining a just decision without the danger of a mutually undesirable stoppage or of impaired morale.

A contract provision for the compulsory arbitration of unsettled grievances might succeed in cases where management has wholeheartedly accepted the union and where the union officers have the confidence of the rank and file. Unfortunately—though not surprisingly for an industry so recently organized—these conditions are not always present. Since 1940, however, the General Motors agreement has pioneered with provision for a permanent umpire.

The outcome of this experiment remains to be seen, but it is being given a sympathetic trial which promises success.[54] Most other companies and some union officials have viewed it with suspicion and skepticism. If the step succeeds, other companies and their local unions may adopt it. In that case a few years may see the grievance machinery of all the vehicle plants headed by a single umpire, with another arbitrator for the parts manufacturers and their unions.

Such a development would not only insure continuity of production, but might also arrest an alarming trend in agreements in this industry. Early contracts were relatively brief, with broad and general provisions. The more recent ones are increasingly long and detailed, attempting to advance solutions for every possible contingency. If this trend continues, a relatively young and dynamic industry will be saddled with minute, rigid regulations. Such regulations, while preventing certain abuses, would sometimes lead to unjust or unreasonable settlements to the detriment of management, employees and the public. If disagreements can be entrusted to an impartial chairman having reasonably broad powers of interpretation, negotiators of agreements could limit themselves to drawing up more general provisions, knowing that these would be applied fairly to individual cases.

54. There have been important developments in the handling of cases. Attitudes toward arbitration have improved as the umpire has moved from coast to coast, hearing cases with local leaders and rank and file present. The company prints all decisions and distributes them widely. Plant meetings are held to discuss decisions and problems and to instruct supervisors in policies. The union will probably follow a similar program. All this attests to a feeling that arbitration is more than a necessary evil.

Chapter 12

RUBBER PRODUCTS

WITH SPECIAL REFERENCE TO THE AKRON AREA

DONALD ANTHONY [1]

EXCEPT FOR A FEW short-lived and ineffective attempts at organization, unionism was practically unknown in the rubber industry before 1933. The chief reasons were employer opposition, an unsympathetic or indifferent public opinion, an organized labor movement concerned primarily with the skilled worker and an employee group incapable of self-organization in an unfavorable environment. With the great depression and coming of the New Deal, however, all but the first of these factors were radically changed. After years of discouragement and struggle, a unionism emerged which has invaded and entrenched itself in a large portion of the industry. Because the total life of rubber unionism is less than a decade, and its effective recognition by management only about three or four years old, collective bargaining in the industry has not yet reached maturity. It therefore affords a chance to study collective bargaining in process of development.

1. CHARACTERISTICS OF THE INDUSTRY

During the nineteenth century, rubber was a small-scale industry producing boots and shoes, waterproof fabrics, bicycle and carriage tires and mechanical goods. With the phenomenal rise of the automobile industry, however, it too entered the mass production stage. The gross value of all rubber products increased from about $100 million in 1899 to $197 million in 1909, and then to

---

[1]. The author gladly acknowledges valuable assistance from Milton Derber and Frederick Harbison in preparing this manuscript.

$1.1 billion in 1919. This latter figure was of course greatly affected by the high level of prices at the end of the World War, yet, after lower prices and industrial depression reduced totals in the early twenties, a peak gross value of $1.3 billion was reached in 1925. This high level was fairly well maintained through the later twenties. With deep depression again, the value of output fell to $473 million in 1933. By 1937 the industry had recovered much of its losses and the figure for that relatively good year was $883 million. The value of tires and tubes was then some $576 million, or about 65 per cent of the total.[2]

a. STRUCTURE AND LOCATION

Tire production has been carried on in a steadily decreasing number of plants. In 1921 there were 178 in the country, and in 1937, only 46. In contrast, plants manufacturing products other than tires, tubes and boots and shoes increased from 294 in 1921 to 420 in 1937. Yet the 46 tire and tube establishments employed 63,290 wage earners, while the 420 plants making "other products" employed only 48,172.

Another important difference is the location of manufacturing units. In 1937, seventeen tire and tube plants, employing 38,719 workers, or more than 60 per cent of the total,[3] were located in one state, Ohio, and the great bulk of these in one city, Akron. The other products branch, however, was widely scattered through the country with 72 establishments in Ohio, 60 in Massachusetts, 48 in New Jersey, 42 in New York and 38 in California.

Akron has long been the great center of the industry,[4] both for

2. The U. S. Bureau of the Census divides rubber products into three groups: tires and inner tubes, boots and shoes, and other rubber goods. This last category covers over thirty thousand distinct items, including rubber heels and soles, rubberized fabrics, mechanical rubber goods (belting, hose, tubing, etc.), hard-rubber goods, druggists' and medical sundries, rubber erasers, rubber bands, etc. In 1937 the value of boots and shoes was about $64 million while "other products" were worth about $243 million.

3. The Census unfortunately includes other rubber products with the tire and tube figures when an establishment produces both classes of goods. In Akron the three largest plants produce considerable quantities of mechanical goods in addition to tires and tubes. But, while several thousand workers are improperly classified, the general picture remains undistorted.

4. It was almost by accident that Akron became the rubber center. In 1870 Benjamin F. Goodrich was persuaded by Akron businessmen to move his small rubber

tires and other rubber products. It has been estimated [5] that before and up to about 1930 it held approximately half of the entire rubber manufacturing industry of the country. Decentralization, however, in progress even in the twenties, has made considerable headway during the past decade: in 1937 Ohio consumed 41.5 per cent of the crude rubber in the country, whereas in 1935 the percentage was 53.2. This decentralization was due partly to market and distribution demands; branches of large companies now exist in New England, in the Middle Atlantic states, in the southern and Gulf states, in Michigan near the automobile towns and on the Pacific Coast. Akron's high cost of living compared to that of smaller rubber towns, higher Akron wage rates and the "union question" were also factors in the change.

The "Big Four"

The industry is largely dominated by four companies. In 1938 it was reported that three fourths of all tires and tubes were produced by Goodyear, Goodrich, Firestone, and United States Rubber and that not a single new producer had gained a foothold in the preceding fifteen years.[6] Of the forty-six tire plants, the "Big Four" own or control sixteen, including the largest four. Notwithstanding the multitude of small competitors in the other products branch, they are also equally important in this field. It is estimated that they are responsible for between 70 and 75 per cent of the gross value of all rubber products manufactured in the United States.[7] Goodyear operates six establishments; Goodrich, six; Firestone, five; and United States Rubber, eleven.

---

factory to the city from Hastings-on-Hudson, New York. The success of his venture persuaded others to follow suit. Then with the great automobile boom, Akron proved to be in a favorable location to meet the demand for tires and auto accessories. Tires alone consume about 75 per cent of the total amount of crude rubber used by the industry, while other automobile parts such as rubber settings for motors, rubber mats and rubber weather stripping, require an additional fifty pounds per car.

5. P. W. Barker, *Rubber Industry of the United States, 1839–1939*, U. S. Bureau of Foreign and Domestic Commerce, 1939, p. 14.

6. Lloyd G. Reynolds, "Competition in the Rubber Tire Industry," *American Economic Review*, September 1938, p. 459.

7. Accurate figures are unavailable because their public financial statements do not list separately the activities of their foreign branches and subsidiaries.

b. INSTABILITY OF THE INDUSTRY

In spite of the close corporate control, the tire branch has been highly unstable in terms of profits, prices and employment—a factor of great importance in collective bargaining. Before and during the World War the industry made large profits. During the twenties, however, bitter price competition developed, with the result that the tire and tube industry was reported by the Bureau of Foreign and Domestic Commerce to be the least profitable in the country for the year 1928. Nevertheless, despite this chaotic state, the year's combined net profits (before dividends) of Goodyear, Firestone and Goodrich were $23 million, or 4.4 per cent of net sales.[8]

Much of the competitive problem rises out of excess capacity[9] and out of the marketing arrangements in the industry. Tires are sold either to automobile manufacturers or to automobile owners for replacements. Auto manufacturers operate in a buyers' market and can make their purchases at much lower prices than are paid by most dealers. The same is also more or less true of the large chain distributors, so important among dealers. Incentive to competitive underbidding among the rubber companies is therefore very strong.

Another reason for this severe competition is the widely fluctuating price of crude rubber.[10] The importance of cost of materials

---

8. United States Rubber, which subsequently passed under the control of the du Pont interests and received a complete reorganization, suffered large losses in 1928. During the general depression years 1930–1932 when no fewer than forty-seven tire plants went bankrupt, Goodrich as well as United States Rubber reported deficits but Goodyear and Firestone continued to operate profitably.

9. Accurate figures on capacity are not available because no definition has been generally accepted. L. E. Carlsmith, in his doctoral dissertation, *The Economic Characteristics of Rubber Tire Production,* Columbia University, New York, 1934, arrived at an estimate of 78 million tires for 1929 (p. 144). There have been more recent estimates as high as 100 million tire units for a year, but they seem too high.

The actual output of pneumatic casings in 1939 was about 57 million, according to the Rubber Manufacturers Association. Tire capacity has probably increased in past years and the life of tires is much longer, owing to better quality and improved highways.

10. The New York annual low and high spot rubber prices for plantation ribbed smoked sheets (as reported by *India Rubber World*) were 18⅜ and 39⅝ cents per pound in 1924, 34¼ and 123 cents per pound in 1925, 16¾ and 41¼ cents per pound in 1928, 2⅝ and 4¾ cents per pound in 1932, and 14 and 26⅞ cents

varies considerably with different types of rubber products, but in the experience of one large Akron company, which produces all types, it is 59.8 per cent of total cost as against 26.2 per cent for direct labor cost, 7.9 per cent for salaries and 6.1 per cent for overhead. Thus, in the absence of hedging in the crude rubber market, large speculative losses and profits are sustained or realized.[11] The manufacturers of rubber are perforce speculators in rubber as well as manufacturers.

The employment curve in rubber is almost as variable as the price curve. The manufacture of rubber products (particularly those related to the automobile industry) undergoes great rises and falls with swings of the business cycle.[12] Production and employment also vary considerably from one part of a year to another, again owing largely to the automobile business. Finally, volume of employment has been greatly affected by technological change. New machinery and new processes largely explain the fact that the index number of man-hour employment in tires and tubes fell from 100 in 1929 to 50.1 in 1936, while production dropped only from 100 to 91.3. The other rubber products branch was less mechanized, but even here man-hour employment fell from 100 in 1929 to 63.2 in 1935, while production fell from 100 to 77.3.[13]

C. THE WORKERS AND THEIR EARNINGS

Most of the direct labor in a rubber factory is either semiskilled or unskilled, and its training varies from a few weeks to a year. Good calender men and good tire builders, however, are not

per pound in 1937. See P. W. Barker, *Rubber Statistics 1900-1937, Production, Absorption, Stocks, and Prices,* U. S. Bureau of Foreign and Domestic Commerce, 1938, p. 43, Table 13.

11. Inasmuch as the Big Four use most of the crude rubber marketed in the United States, the market does not permit large scale hedging. In this respect rubber differs from a commodity like wheat.

12. The U. S. Bureau of Labor Statistics index number of employment (number of employees) for the rubber industry (average 1923–1925=100) was 111.0 in 1929, 85.9 in 1930, 73.9 in 1931, 67.6 in 1932, 79.1 in 1933, 88.4 in 1934, 85.6 in 1935, 90.4 in 1936, 97.3 in 1937, 75.0 in 1938, and 84.6 in 1939. See various *Annual Review* issues of *Survey of Current Business,* U. S. Department of Commerce.

13. *Production, Employment, and Productivity in 59 Manufacturing Industries, 1919-1936,* National Research Project, Works Progress Administration, Philadelphia, May 1939, Pt. 2, p. 198.

usually developed in a short time.[14] Strength, endurance and good coordination are the basic requirements. A grade school education is sufficient for the typical worker although management regards high school graduates with increasing favor.

Earnings of rubber workers, especially in the Akron area, compare favorably with those in other industries. Average hourly earnings in tire and tube plants from 1934 to 1939 were, by years, 78, 84, 87, 95, 95 and 96 cents, while the comparable figures for plants manufacturing other rubber products were 51, 53, 54, 59, 60 and 61 cents. For all manufacturing industries, the average ranged from 54 in 1934 to 64 cents in 1939.[15] The average annual earnings of rubber workers in Summit County, Ohio (where Akron is located) were $1,504 in 1930, $1,046 in 1932, and $1,328 in 1934.[16] Earnings of rubber workers in the entire state of Ohio.

14. There are three main stages in the production of finished rubber products. First the crude rubber must be processed. This stage consists of plasticating the crude rubber (cutting it into small pieces, washing and grinding it), compounding it (mixing the rubber with various chemicals according to formula) and calendering it (sheeting the compounded rubber either alone or in combination with cotton cord or fabric). This work is all done by men, is mostly mechanized and except for the calendering phase requires little skill. The rubber is then ready to be turned into a commercial product. In the case of tires, various departments of the plant produce the different parts—the plies (which are strips of rubber cut from the calenderized sheet and spliced together), the beads (formerly of pressed rubber but now of wire, which support the tire on the rim of the wheel), the tread (that part of the tire which comes in contact with the road) and the various strips, chafers and cushions (which protect the tire against unexpected jars and give it resiliency). Most of this work is done by women and machines. The tire is then generally assembled by individual tire builders, that is, the various parts are put together by hand on a drum, although in a few plants some tires are built on the assembly line principle. In the case of the large number of miscellaneous rubber products, most of the work is done by women with the aid of presses and molds which determine the final shape of the article. The last stage in rubber manufacture is curing, finishing and inspection. Curing is the all-important process of heating the product under pressure, or "vulcanizing," so that it will not be affected by changes in temperature or humidity. Formerly the curing of tires required great strength and stamina and the men worked in what was realistically called the "pit." Mechanization has eliminated most of the physical discomfort. Finishing (painting, branding, etc.) and inspecting are still largely nonmechanized jobs. See Boris Stern, "Labor Productivity in the Automobile Tire Industry," *Bulletin No. 585*, U. S. Bureau of Labor Statistics, July 1933.

15. *Statistical Abstract of the United States, 1939*, U. S. Department of Commerce, pp. 329-330; *1940*, pp. 336-337.

16. *Findings and Recommendations and Supporting Report* of the Fact-Finding Board appointed by the U. S. Secretary of Labor on November 15, 1935 to investigate a dispute at the Goodyear Tire and Rubber Company, Akron, Ohio, p. 5. Report submitted December 16, 1935.

were slightly less than in Summit County, but reached $1,498 in 1937.[17]

2. Company Policies and Labor Organization

Unionism in the rubber industry would probably have been completely unsuccessful without the support of federal policy and legislation. Apart from an attempt to organize around 1903, swiftly crushed by management, and an unsuccessful IWW strike in 1913, Akron rubber plants were kept free of union activities until 1933. During the war, AF of L locals were set up in a number of eastern plants but after the Armistice, they and their gains were quickly destroyed. Although company policies varied, hostility to unionism appears generally to have dominated the industry.

The large Akron companies not only vigorously combated any attempt at independent labor organization, but also adopted elaborate welfare programs to win employee loyalty. The Goodyear Company, for example, established a labor department in 1910, developed a life insurance plan in 1915, organized a hospital association, and set up a noninterest loan fund, a welfare fund for needy employee families, and a pension plan. It erected a building for classrooms, gave courses in Americanization, in advanced technical and cultural subjects, and provided a library, club rooms and recreation facilities. It also maintained baseball and soccer fields and tennis courts. Goodrich and Firestone were equally active in promoting this type of program.

In 1919 Goodyear, following a policy endorsed by the War Labor Board, established an employee representation plan, which was more or less favorably received by most of the workers. The plan was not simply a device to forestall unionism, as was the case in many rubber plants after 1933, but a genuine attempt by management to learn what was on the worker's mind. The Goodyear Industrial Assembly was modeled after the federal Congress with forty representatives and twenty senators. Bills passed by the two houses were subject to approval or veto by the factory man-

17. Derived from *U. S. Census of Manufactures, 1937*. For estimates of real as well as money earnings no satisfactory data are available. Akron has a relatively high cost of living.

ager. A veto could be overridden by a two-thirds vote of the two houses. But, unlike federal measures, bills enacted were subject to approval or rejection by the company's board of directors. Board action was final. In spite of the Goodyear example, few employee representation plans were established in the rubber industry before the enactment of Section 7(a) of the NRA.

a. LABOR STRUGGLES IN THE 1930'S

The great depression of 1929–1933 destroyed employee faith in welfare capitalism, while the prounion policy of the federal government stimulated a dramatic rush of the workers into their own unions. In the late summer of 1935, the Executive Council of the American Federation of Labor reported that during the preceding two years sixty-nine locals had been established in the rubber industry.[18] In Akron alone more than twenty thousand union members had been enrolled by the spring of 1934. Nevertheless, because of employer opposition and internal union dissension and because the NRA lacked teeth, the initial impetus was almost destroyed, and was not revived until 1936.

With certain exceptions, notably the United States Rubber Company among the Big Four, employers throughout the industry met the union threat with a variety of tactics: espionage, delay before the Labor Boards, litigation, employee representation plans, and many concessions to workers, such as wage increases, recognition of seniority in layoffs and rehiring, and more favorable settlement of grievances. Between June 1933 and February 1937 the Big Three Companies of Akron (Goodrich, Firestone and Goodyear)[19] granted no fewer than six general wage increases ranging from 6 to 10 per cent, most of them unasked for by any employee organization. Goodrich, Firestone and other companies set up company unions in the summer and fall of 1933. Labor Board hearings and investigations revealed that management had invariably suggested these plans and usually had a hand in drafting the constitution and by-laws; that the plans drafted were made effective without the approval of the workers concerned; that the

---

18. AF of L, *Proceedings*, Annual Convention, 1935, p. 95.
19. The U. S. Rubber Company has no plants in the Akron area.

costs of operation were borne by the companies; that worker representatives were paid monthly stipends in addition to reimbursements for working time lost; and that the plans could not be changed without company consent.[20]

The antiunion drive almost succeeded. A survey by the Bureau of Labor Statistics as of April 1935 showed that of fifty-two establishments engaged in the manufacture of mechanical rubber goods, forty-two dealt with individual employees only, four with some or all workers through trade unions, and six through employee representation plans. Whereas the four establishments dealing with trade unions employed only 8 per cent of the 11,644 workers covered by the survey, the six establishments with representation plans employed 50 per cent of them. Of eighteen concerns manufacturing tires and tubes, nine dealt with their employees individually, four dealt with some or all of them through trade unions, while five had company unions. The percentage of the 41,465 workers employed in plants dealing with trade unions at all was only 8.3.[21]

Internal union difficulties helped employers to forestall collective bargaining. Immediately after the first sign of self-organization the AF of L stepped into the picture, enrolling the rubber workers in federal labor unions. William Green sent a well-seasoned organizer to lead the new and inexperienced unionists. However, the demands of the rank-and-file members for a national industrial union and for strike action to overcome employer resistance were not heeded. In June 1934 a national United Rubber Workers' Council was set up, but the craft workers were given separate representation so that although they formed only a small proportion of the total membership they could outvote the production locals.[22] Ten months later great (although probably ill-advised) sentiment for a general strike in Akron developed,

---

20. See *In the Matter of B. F. Goodrich Co., Goodrich Cooperative Plan and the United Rubber Workers Federal Labor Union, Local No. 18319, Decisions of the [First] National Labor Relations Board*, Vol. I, 1934, p. 181; and Firestone cases, *ibid.*, p. 173 and Vol. II, 1935, p. 291.

21. "Characteristics of Company Unions, 1935," *Bulletin No. 634*, U. S. Bureau of Labor Statistics, 1938, p. 44.

22. More than a dozen craft organizations were represented in the Council.

only to be nullified in Washington by an agreement negotiated with the advice of President Green, in which the union was not formally recognized and reference was made only to "representatives of employees." Not even the granting of a national charter by the AF of L Executive Council and the triumph of the rank-and-file leadership over Green and the organizer (whom he tried to make union president at the September 1935 constitutional convention), restored much support. By this time, union membership had fallen to about three thousand.

The Goodyear strike of February 1936 at Akron was probably the turning point of unionism in the rubber industry. During the winter of 1935–1936, the companies, especially Goodyear, contending that costs were too high, had increased hours, lowered wages and, according to the charges of union leaders, replaced older employees by younger men. At Goodyear, where return to the basic eight-hour day was proposed, both the independent union and the Industrial Assembly protested sharply. A fact-finding board appointed by the U. S. Secretary of Labor, with the consent of the company, reported that the proposed change was not warranted by conditions.[23] A series of sitdowns in all of the major plants followed, with mixed success. The Goodyear strike developed out of a protest against the layoff of some seventy tire builders. It was not started by the few union members in the plant, although the union immediately assumed leadership. The works were closed for five weeks. CIO leaders, who saw here a crucial test for industrial unionism, gave valuable aid. The final settlement of the strike on March 22 did not provide for union recognition or abolition of the company union, but it restored all the workers to their jobs, preserved the thirty-six-hour work week in the tire division, and contained management's promise to meet with elected representatives of the employees for negotiation on all questions of mutual interest. What the strike made clear was that the largest corporation in the rubber industry was unable to destroy the weakest of the local unions in Akron's Big Three plants during a dull production period. In July the national union formally joined the

23. *Report* of the Fact-Finding Board appointed by the U. S. Secretary of Labor on November 15, 1935.

Committee for Industrial Organization as the United Rubber Workers of America.

The Goodyear settlement revitalized rubber unionism, not only in the Akron area, but also in the outside plants. The inconclusive nature of the agreement, however, continued the open warfare until April 12, 1937, when the Supreme Court upheld the constitutionality of the National Labor Relations Act. During 1936 and the early months of 1937 the local unions took advantage of improved business conditions to assume aggressive roles. The newly discovered sitdown strike proved an amazingly effective weapon of attack, which for a time confounded the employers, though later it developed into a serious threat to stable union organization and aroused bitter public sentiment. The struggle for recognition reached a new climax in the eight weeks' Firestone dispute, which began on March 5, 1937. The agreement of April 28, owing largely to the Supreme Court's Wagner Act decisions, was far more definite than the Goodyear settlement. The company agreed to bargain collectively with the union and to withdraw all support from its employee representation plan. On the same day, Goodyear and Goodrich similarly announced the withdrawal of financial support from their company unions.

b. PRESENT UNION STRENGTH

After the spring of 1937 the United Rubber Workers of America made further advance. Although the dues-paying membership slumped badly during the 1937–1938 depression, the number of workers covered by written contracts has steadily increased, as shown by the following table compiled by the union:

Year	Number of Contracts	Workers Covered by Contract	Union Members in Industry
1935	5	507	3,080
1936	10	2,213	33,526
1937	36	21,141	70,000
1938	50	34,187	59,466
1939	87	62,238	57,504
1940	91	75,000	63,704

Of the ninety-one contracts in 1940, fifty-five provided for the union shop or covered plants which were 100 per cent organized. In a number of plants without written agreements, local unions dealt with management with varying degrees of success. While collective bargaining was thus extended, strikes in the industry sharply declined. The sitdown period had practically run its course by the end of 1937. A tabulation of U. S. Bureau of Labor Statistics data, not counting sitdowns, shows the steady decline in the number of strikes and the workers involved: [24]

Year	Number of Strikes	Workers Involved	Man-days Lost
1935	7	1,308	18,982
1936	43	76,699	477,286
1937	39	53,829	673,719
1938	29	25,612	165,507
1939	19	9,694	73,868
1940	18	8,526	97,228

Notwithstanding this favorable development, unionism and collective bargaining have a long way to go before they become an integral part of the rubber industry. Of the more than 140,000 rubber workers in the United States and Canada,[25] only 63,704, or about 45 per cent, were claimed as dues-paying members by the URWA at its annual convention in September 1940. Of the more than 500 rubber plants only 127 were partly or completely organized by the URWA. In addition, the American Federation of Labor has organized federal locals in several plants, as well as craft locals of such skilled workers as pattern makers and electricians in a few others. A rough estimate indicates that AF of L contracts cover over 10,000 rubber workers. Most of these workers are in plant-wide unions while the rest are in craft units.

Goodyear, the largest corporation in the industry, has bitterly fought the URWA at Akron, Gadsden [26] and other of its sites,

---

24. *Monthly Labor Review*, data published in May issue of each succeeding year.
25. The *U. S. Census of Manufactures, 1937* reported a total of 129,818 wage earners in the rubber industry in the United States. The *Canadian Annual Review of Public Affairs, 1937 and 1938* (Canadian Review Co., Ltd., Toronto, 1940) reported 13,035 employees in the rubber industry of Canada for 1937.
26. See p. 656.

and until June 1941 none of its plants were under agreement. In that month it signed a wage contract for the Akron works. The Firestone plant at Fall River has not been organized, while the company refused until recently to sign any agreement at Los Angeles.[27] The AF of L won an NLRB election at its Memphis plant in 1940. Goodrich has successfully avoided the union in its small plants at Cadillac, Michigan, Clarksville, Tennessee, and Oaks, Pennsylvania, while its large subsidiary, the Hood Rubber Company, is organized by the AF of L. Even the United States Rubber Company, the only major concern with a noncombative attitude toward unionism, is not wholly unionized.[28] Its Providence plant was won by the AF of L in a Labor Board election held in March 1940.

In the Akron area, where the union first firmly established itself, sixteen contracts covering about twenty-two thousand workers have been signed. In addition, the huge Goodyear plant now operates under a wage agreement. Several small companies, including the important General and Seiberling tire works, are almost completely organized. Of the Big Three plants, Goodrich is strongly unionized, Firestone not so strongly, and Goodyear still less so. Thus, even in Akron, the stronghold of the union, the job of organization is by no means finished.

The situation is much worse outside of Akron, although Los Angeles, where each Big Four company has a small tire plant, is fairly well organized. Most of the plants are small and scattered from Ontario, Canada, to the deep South, and from Vermont to California. Many turning out rubber products other than tires and

27. On March 30, 1940 the National Labor Relations Board, after investigation and hearing, ordered the Los Angeles Firestone management to cease discrimination against the United Rubber Workers of America, Local 100, and to end its domination and support of the Independent Rubber Workers Union, Inc., a rival union in the plant. The Board also ordered an election which Local 100 won, 617 votes to 337. In August 1940 the Board reported that the company had agreed to settle all the issues raised in the Board's decision and was negotiating a contract with the United Rubber Workers.

28. United States Rubber did not sign any agreements with the URWA until August 1938 but it dealt with the union earlier. Only one strike in 1936 is reported at the numerous plants of the company. See "Written Trade Agreements in Collective Bargaining," *Bulletin No. 4,* National Labor Relations Board, November 1939, p. 180.

tubes are of the sweatshop variety. Even were the companies sympathetic toward unionism, the physical task of unionization would still have been difficult; actually management has been hostile and placed numerous obstacles in the path of the URWA. Many of the rural communities have publicly warned union organizers to stay out. The policy of the large companies is to pay the highest wages in the vicinity, and workers are not convinced of the gains which a union might bring. Company unions, independent unions and management discrimination against union membership have all had their effect. The major problem of the URWA is extending organization into these plants.

3. A Brief Analysis of the Agreements [29]

All agreements in the rubber industry cover either an individual plant or the plants of a single company in the same city. The union petitioned the National Labor Relations Board to establish company-wide units for the Goodrich and United States Rubber companies, but the Board denied the requests on the ground that management policies and working conditions differed considerably from one plant to another. Because they are negotiated locally and reflect local conditions, the agreements vary greatly in details.

With few exceptions, the agreements are of the administrative rather than legislative type; they set forth the general framework and leave the details to be filled in by daily negotiation within the shop. Frequently, during the year, supplementary agreements or "interpretations" have been made without incorporation in the main contract. A few contracts, such as one at the Goodrich Company's Akron plant, do include a number of detailed shop rules and practices, but they are not typical.

Duration

Practically all agreements run for a term of one year. About two fifths contain provisions for indefinite continuation unless either side gives a thirty-day notice of wish to change or terminate.

29. Based on a study of contracts in effect in 1939.

Several agreements also provide for their indefinite continuance unless changed before the date they expire. Although a majority of the agreements do not contain a specific renewal provision, some do state that the discussion of a new or changed agreement should start at least one month before the termination date. This type of agreement usually provides also for a thirty-day extension if negotiations are still going on when the agreement ends. The union claims that every agreement has been renewed, although few have remained unchanged.

Union Status

While only one agreement provides for a strictly closed shop, twenty-two provide for a union shop, i.e., union members must remain members or be discharged and new employees must join the union within a specified period. In a number of plants where unionization is practically complete, the union or preferential shop exists as a verbal understanding without mention in the contract. All but a few of the agreements make the union the exclusive bargaining agency for all employees, whether union members or not. Seven agreements contain checkoff provisions; but the individual employee must authorize the deduction of union dues from his check and he may revoke this authorization.

Wages

The piece-rate system of wage payment is widely used in the rubber industry. Hence the thousands of different rates for all the various operations in a typical plant cannot conveniently be included in an agreement of ten or twelve printed pages. These individual rates are constantly adjusted by negotiation between management and union. Wage sections of the agreements are quite short and rates quoted are minimum rather than those actually paid. Almost half of the agreements provide that wage rates paid when the contract took effect cannot be reduced while the agreement is in force. Others provide for changes if competitors in the vicinity alter their wages. One calls for revision of wages should there be a 20 per cent change in the cost of living.

Minimum hourly rates for men vary from 42.5 cents to 85 cents, while the range for women is from 37 to 60 cents, with a considerable difference between rates in tire plants and those making other rubber products. The higher rates in tire plants must be attributed mainly to the higher proportion of male workers, to the financial strength of the large tire companies as compared to the small "other products" companies, and to the concentration of the bulk of tire workers in a few cities like Akron, Detroit and Los Angeles, where cost of living is higher than in small towns and rural communities. Much more important differentials exist between companies and between plants of a single company manufacturing similar products. This is the "Akron-outside-Akron differential problem," which has already played an important role in collective bargaining.[30]

Hours and Holidays

Most of the agreements with large companies provide for a flexible six-hour day,[31] the normal work day being recognized as six hours, but overtime pay at increased rates under certain conditions does not begin until after an eight-hour day or a forty-hour week has been exceeded. Agreements with smaller companies (mostly mechanical goods) generally provide for an eight-hour day, with longer hours in an emergency. The rubber industry is a seasonal one and therefore must have the advantage of flexible work days and weeks if it is not to be greatly embarrassed during a peak load. As would be expected, practically all the agreements provide a penalty rate for overtime work as well as for Sundays and holidays; in most cases this rate is time and a half, though in a number of others it is double time.

Christmas, Thanksgiving, Memorial Day, Labor Day, New Year's Day and July Fourth are usually regarded as holidays.

---

30. See pp. 663-665.
31. About half of the employees who are under an agreement work a six-hour day and a thirty-six-hour week. See Harry Cannon, *Collective Bargaining by Rubber Workers*, U. S. Department of Labor, 1939, p. 16. It should be realized, however, that the standard six-hour day does not guarantee every worker a thirty-six-hour week in actual practice. One of the large Akron companies reported that during 1939, a relatively good production period, male employees averaged 30.5 hours per week and female employees, 28.7 hours per week.

About a fifth of the agreements provide that employees must not be required to work on Sundays and holidays unless an emergency exists.

A large majority of the agreements provide for paid vacations. For most of the small companies, this was an important innovation for the plant and a major gain for the union. Before unionization, some of the large companies granted their factory employees vacations with pay, but with the depression pay allowances were either temporarily reduced or abolished. The vacation provisions in the union agreements are generally more liberal than those previously granted by the companies. Most of the Akron agreements now authorize a week's vacation with pay for workers with two to five years of service and two weeks for those with five or more years to their credit. A week's vacation pay is usually 2 per cent of earnings for the preceding year. Some agreements provide for minimum vacation pay. Goodrich, for instance, pays a minimum of $20 a week to men and $12 to women.

Seniority

Detailed seniority clauses are common in the agreements. Rubber managements are not entirely opposed to seniority, but if they had their own way they would, of course, make merit the primary consideration.[32] The union favors strict seniority because it sees in that system a method of avoiding personal favoritism or discrimination against union men by management and because it offers a measure of added job security to regularly employed workers.

Many agreements provide for departmental seniority; but divisional and plant-wide seniority are also followed in some plants. Seniority is used as the basis for transfer, rehiring, promotion and laying off. Each agreement that provides for departmental seniority gives the conditions under which a man transferred from one department to another acquires seniority in the new department.

32. See *Violations of Free Speech and Rights of Labor, Hearings Before a Subcommittee of the Committee on Education and Labor, United States Senate,* Pursuant to S. Res. 266, 74th Cong., Pt. 45, 1939, pp. 16659-16660, for Goodyear practice in 1935 before the union became a significant force.

An employee does not usually get seniority rights in a new department until he has worked in that department for six months or a year. After he has acquired seniority privileges in a new department, he loses them in his old one, but he may carry over his service record. As a rule, if two employees have equal seniority, their privileges are based on ability. It is often agreed that seniority may be waived in the case of an employee on highly specialized work which men with greater seniority would not be able to do without long training. One type of clause provides that a laid-off employee of less than five years' service retains his seniority for one year, one with more than five but less than ten years' service retains his seniority for two years, and one with ten years' service enjoys the privilege of permanent seniority.

Most agreements make it possible for a workman who becomes an officer of the union to get leave for union work without loss of seniority. Many agreements also provide for leaves of absence without a break in seniority in case of illness, death in the family, and for wartime military service.

Few agreements fail to combine seniority with a work-sharing plan. Most provide that no employee shall be laid off in slack times until working hours have been reduced to an average of twenty-four or less a week for three or more weeks. Thereafter, employees of least seniority are transferred or laid off until the hours of the remaining workers in the department average thirty a week. Many agreements require that management give advance notice of layoffs, usually about three days, if possible.

Grievance Procedure

Shop committee systems are generally used in the settlement of grievances. Grievances, according to most contracts, must first be discussed by the employee or his union representative and the foreman, then by the committeeman and the department superintendent, next by the union business agent or grievance committee and the company labor relations director, finally by the grievance committee and top management. In some cases there is provision for mediation or for voluntary or compulsory arbitration.

4. Collective Bargaining in Akron

The author's field work was limited chiefly to the Akron district, and his analysis of collective bargaining in the rubber industry is largely confined to plants of this area, particularly the five larger ones—Goodrich, Firestone, Goodyear, General and Seiberling. There are twelve other plants in the area, all organized and under contract, but they are small, of not more than a few hundred employees each. Emphasis on Akron, however, need not give a distorted picture. Generally speaking, the basic patterns of collective bargaining are about the same everywhere.

Time prevented an intensive study of some of the plants of the United States Rubber Corporation. This company, the writer has been informed, has approached its labor problems in a manner somewhat different from the others of the Big Four. It has discussed policies with union representatives before their execution, whereas most other companies have preferred to take action first and let the union bring up grievances afterward.

Variation is common between one Akron plant and another, in attitudes, methods of negotiation and the subject matter of collective bargaining. Although the executives of the different companies in Akron have at times cooperated to fight the union, personal and business rivalry among them has been intense from early days and they have generally followed individual courses. Local unions, similarly, have exhibited a strong degree of autonomy and self-direction in spite of the proximity of the offices of the International. In striking contrast to a sister union, the Steel Workers Organizing Committee, control has not been centralized at the top, and outside CIO leaders have played no important roles since the 1936 strike at Goodyear.[33]

a. THE EARLY YEARS: FROM MANAGEMENT CONTROL TO UNION DOMINATION THROUGH THE SITDOWN

The Akron rubber industry has had to date three chief phases in union-management relations. The first began with the emergence

---

33. At the height of the sitdown period in 1936, the CIO sent one of its able representatives to Akron to advise the local union leaders in problems of union discipline and responsibility, but he was withdrawn during the following year.

of unionism and ended with the Goodyear settlement of March 1936. During this period management was completely dominant and collective bargaining was practically nonexistent, even though company officials listened to union complaints and demands. Nevertheless, management conceded through the employee representation plans a number of union-sponsored principles later elaborated into important policies. For example, seniority was recognized as a significant factor in transfers, layoffs and rehiring, although it was applied with great laxity and management made exceptions at will. A formal procedure for grievance adjustment was set up for the first time, though it was generally boycotted by union members.

The second phase was the sitdown period which attracted nation-wide attention. Following the Goodyear settlement, the Akron plants were deluged with sitdowns, most of them lasting only a few hours, others for several shifts, and even days. No one has endeavored to make a compete tabulation,[34] but there were scores of them and they arose over innumerable issues—the presence of nonunion employees, unequal distribution of work, wage rate adjustments, layoffs, discrimination by management, poor working conditions, etc. The significance of the sitdowns was that management was repeatedly compelled to turn to the union officials to restore the normal functioning of the plant. The balance of power for a time had definitely shifted. The company could not discharge a union member or introduce a new machine which might displace workers, or lower earnings.

At first, therefore, the local union leaders welcomed the new technique as the most effective weapon they had yet discovered to win their demands. A small group of men could easily obstruct the operations of an entire division without the expense or the danger of an outside strike. By September 1936, however, the inherent weakness of sitdown strikes became evident. They promoted departmental anarchy and disrupted central union control. An increasing number came without official approval or knowledge. Sitdowns controlled by the union and carefully used only at

34. Goodyear, which was hardest hit, has estimated that out of the 275 working days from March 21 to December 31, 1936, production was interrupted on 94.

strategic times and on important issues might serve the union; but outlaw sitdowns in which an individual or group sought to remedy a petty grievance without giving the grievance machinery a fair chance to work were disastrous. For a while, too, they became a form of hysteria. Many were started simply because somebody wanted to let off steam.

The flood of stoppages slackened toward the end of 1936, although sporadic sitdowns continued until early 1938. The more intelligent union members saw the ultimate consequences of such action and pressed for more discipline and order. The unfavorable reaction of the public and the courts and the companies' charge of union irresponsibility undoubtedly had some effect. The novelty of sitting down also wore off and the men began to appreciate that their earnings were suffering. This realization was strengthened when management decided to change its policy of treating sitdowns as an emergency and simply closed the whole division or the whole works for the remainder of the day. Many workers resented the stoppages, and some potential members were strongly antagonized.

While the sitdowns admittedly got out of hand and in the end were destructive not only to company but to union interests, two facts should be noted. First, there were relatively few or no sitdowns in those plants which signed a contract with the local union and engaged in collective bargaining with it. After April 1937 production at the Firestone plant, for example, was uninterrupted although in plants without a contract and a no-strike clause, stoppages continued. The Goodyear Company, which fought the union most bitterly, was by far the oftenest and the longest affected by these stoppages. A substantial antiunion group among Goodyear workers was, of course, also a factor in the sitdowns, directly fomenting strife between the rival employee groups and indirectly strengthening management's determination to fight. In the second place, the sitdown period impressed most of the companies with the fact that, regardless of their sentiments on unionism, it was preferable to deal with the union leaders than to have departmental anarchy. During the heat of this period the union was frequently assailed as being dominated by Communists, but whatever influence certain Communists may have had in the early organizational years was completely dissipated by 1937. Insofar as is known, no Communist has ever been elected to a national office in the organization.

b. COLLECTIVE BARGAINING IN A HOSTILE ATMOSPHERE

The third and present phase of union-management relations in Akron has witnessed the evolution of varying degrees of collective bargaining under either a signed agreement or "verbal" recognition of the local union. The mere signing of an agreement is not, of course, a sufficient reflection of the progress of collective bargaining in any plant. The human relationship is far more fundamental, since an agreement is obviously but a scrap of paper until interpreted and administered. At Akron management antagonism to the union principle has continued almost unchanged even where collective bargaining has been practiced in good faith. Top company officials have often publicly expressed their opinion that the union is a restrictive and uneconomic institution. As a result whatever gains the unions have achieved were mainly the product of two factors: the strength of the local organization in terms of membership and finance, and the extent of concessions management was willing to make to obtain uninterrupted production.

Where, as at Goodrich, General and Seiberling, for example, union membership has reached high proportions, the gains have been considerable. On the other hand, where the union has been weak, collective bargaining has been limited. At Firestone, the management is definitely dominant, while at Goodyear a contract was not even signed until very recently. In May 1941, hearings begun in the spring of 1939 were still being conducted by the National Labor Relations Board on the charges (denied by the corporation) that the Goodyear Company consistently refused to bargain collectively, sponsored a company union and coerced and discriminated against union members.

All this does not mean that managements which have engaged in collective bargaining and have signed agreements have displayed bad faith and violated their word whenever feasible. On the contrary, most of the companies have been careful to live up to the letter of their agreements. But management's approach to collective bargaining has generally been the negative one of yielding as little as possible in return for peace in the plant and unhampered direction of production. The initiative has been left to the local union.

(1). *Firestone*

The Firestone plant was the first large company to make a union agreement. When the 1937 strike ended, the local claimed about eight thousand members of the plant's ten thousand employees. Nevertheless, within a few weeks the tables turned and the company regained control. What happened is important because the same process occurred in scores of newly unionized plants throughout the mass production industries. First of all, after an agreement was reached many workers lost interest in the union. Many of them saw no reason for paying a dollar a month dues as long as a grievance was not won for them directly or a wage increase was not immediately forthcoming. Then in the late summer of 1937 came the sudden and sharp business depression. Dues collections slumped badly even among the loyal members and many of the most aggressive unionists were laid off according to seniority. Since a large number of the shop committeemen were in this group, the grievance machinery of the union was badly disrupted, in some departments completely destroyed. Many of those laid off blamed the union for their plight. Union leadership was unable to cope adequately with the problem, which was greatly aggravated by Firestone's transference of a larger proportion of its production to branches outside Akron than any other company.

In December 1937 appeared the Firestone Employees Protective Association, an independent labor organization. It claimed that it was not supported by management in any way and it bitterly attacked the URWA local for its CIO and "outside" affiliations and its "high dues" policy.[35] It appealed to the regional office of the

---

35. Whereas the URWA charged $2.00 for initiation and $1.00 a month dues, the Protective Association had no initiation fee and dues of only 25 cents a month. Since the latter was a purely local organization with no organizational or legislative interests outside of the plant, it could, of course, afford a lower dues policy, but it is highly doubtful whether 25 cents a month per member is sufficient to finance a strike or any other of the major functions of a union.

National Labor Relations Board for an election to determine which union had the support of a majority of the employees. The March 1938 election revealed the serious losses of the Firestone URWA local, for it won only 3,696 votes out of an eligible 7,543. With its 2,564 votes, the Protective Association claimed a moral victory. Although this close call further strengthened management's bargaining position, the contract was renewed in 1938 and again in 1939 and 1940. The rival union continued to maintain an office near the plant and tried to win more members but apparently it had shot its bolt. Its appeal to the Labor Board in 1939 was meaningless, as the company decided to continue relations with the URWA.

Since 1937, Firestone management has expressed satisfaction with its labor relations for the simple reason that it has guided their course. It is agreed that the letter of the agreement has been lived up to and that working conditions are comparatively good.

(2). *Goodrich*

The story at Goodrich was quite different. Here local union leaders were developed who could both draw a large proportion of the employees into the organization and negotiate for them skillfully and reasonably. In spite of wide fluctuations in business conditions, the local has retained a high membership and has consistently been the largest and most prosperous union in the International. An anti-CIO organization which suddenly emerged in the plant early in 1938 was laughed out of existence. Even at the bottom of the depression late in 1937, union leaders reported that relations with the company were better than at any previous time, although differences of opinion over policy existed.

Although Goodrich was willing by April 1937 to come to an agreement, the first contract was not signed until May 27, 1938. The union was confident of its strength and its inexperienced leaders felt that unless all demands were won, an agreement would so restrict freedom of action that it would not be worth while. In August 1937 at an NLRB election, the union received 8,212 of the 12,403 possible votes, while only 834 votes were cast against it. Nevertheless the depression in 1937–1938, a rapid decline in union dues, and a company attempt to cut wages reemphasized the desirability of a contract. Negotiations were reopened in March 1938. Management offered to sign an agreement in return for a considerable wage decrease and threatened to remove a large part of its production from Akron if the proposal was rejected. The URWA suggested a joint conference upon wages and related issues with all the important rubber companies of the area, but the companies rejected the idea as impracticable. In spite of caustic criticism from continually hostile business groups of the community, the union refused to yield to management's demand. For several weeks discussions between top management and the union lapsed. Then in May, after the outbreak of a departmental stoppage over a relatively minor matter, the union decided to strike for a contract. After a week-long "labor holiday" a satisfactory agreement was gained. The wage cut was not taken. But negotiation of the contract did not mean a marked change in labor relations; collective bargaining had been in effect for some time before. According to one unionist, the contract was "just an incident" in the progress of the organization.

(3). *Goodyear*

At Goodyear for a brief period in 1937 some form of peaceful collective bargaining seemed about to emerge from the chaos of sitdowns, but that hope was unrealized. While a complete analysis of the situation is here impossible, still it can be pointed out why basic disagreement rather than a measure of harmony prevailed.

In the first place the union was never able to establish itself as firmly as in the other plants. A Labor Board election in August 1937, when the local was at its peak, revealed 8,464 votes for the URWA as against 3,193 for the opposition—a substantial majority for the union but at the same time a dangerous opposition, particularly in view of management hostility to unionism. There were several reasons for the size of this nonunion group. Many workers, including some of the most capable leaders, had acquired a stake in and loyalty to the Industrial Assembly and rejected "outside" affiliation. During the 1936 strike many of them participated in efforts to start a back-to-work movement. Had the company not attempted to cut wages and increase hours in 1935, this group would possibly have maintained the majority position it then held.

The failure of the union leadership to control the sitdowns and to prevent coercion of men into joining the union undoubtedly alienated many other workers. The loss in jobs during the depression, the company threat to move out of Akron, and the failure to win a contract likewise had their effect. As a result, when in December 1937 the anti-CIO faction organized an "independent" union, it made rapid headway so that by a year later it felt ready to petition the Labor Board for an election. The URWA charge that it was a company union and the resultant hearings on that charge have thus far prevented an election from being held.[36]

Management attitude was another significant factor. The company had taken a good deal of pride in its reputation for progressiveness during the twenties. The reaction of the workers, therefore, was a double blow. It not only meant an undesired encroachment upon managerial authority, but also that previous efforts of the company had been found wanting. Management appears, as a result, to have been willing to combat the union even if production was seriously affected. It consistently claimed that it was bargaining collectively with the union, but it repeatedly displayed either bad faith or poor judgment in its dealings. Thus it permitted some of its supervisors and "flying squadron"[37] men to form the antiunion Stahl-Mate club, and did not publicly repudiate the organization until the spring of 1937.[38] When the URWA president and other union officials went to Gadsden, Alabama, to organize the Goodyear plant there, the former was badly beaten by a mob in which plant supervisors were included.[39] In October 1937 management agreed that future bulletins con-

36. While they deny having sponsored or financed the "independent" union, company officials have spoken of it in the most favorable terms.
37. A group of specially-trained men sent to various departments in time of emergency or when an increase in production is desired. Many supervisors are drawn from them.
38. Akron *Beacon-Journal*, February 8, 1937.
39. NLRB, *Release R-2738*, March 11, 1940.

cerning changes in working conditions would be signed jointly by the company and the union, but the next month it announced the immediate layoff of sixteen hundred men despite the union request for a postponement until January 1.[40] A series of sitdowns followed. An agreement was made with the union in November on the handling of layoffs and rehiring; but so many unsettled grievances regarding layoffs and related matters accumulated that another strike broke out on May 26, 1938. When mass picket lines formed to keep the factory closed, they were, according to newspaper accounts, brutally attacked by city and company police with clubs and tear gas, in what was Akron's bloodiest labor dispute.[41] The strike was called off after four days and negotiations were resumed. In June the Goodyear president was quoted in an interview as saying that Goodyear was willing to sign a contract with the union "so long as that contract is one under which the company can live."[42] Yet more than fifty days of negotiation proved futile, because management insisted that the wage clause should remain subject to change at short notice and that daily hours should be increased to eight.[43] These demands were regarded by the union as wholly unacceptable in view of the contracts that it had signed with Goodrich and Firestone.

The third main factor in this disharmonious relationship was that both sides so distrusted each other that each assumed a very stiff attitude in negotiations. Each party hesitated to compromise, fearing that concession would be regarded as a sign of weakness. Thus the insistence of the union first on "share the work" to an undue degree and then on plant-wide rather than departmental seniority was unquestionably a mistake.

The current outlook, however, is brighter. While harmony has, at least until recently, been conspicuously absent, there have been no stoppages at Goodyear since the outbreak of May 1938. And

40. There is no question that the decline in orders justified a mass layoff, and the insistence of the union upon plant-wide seniority was probably an unwise policy in this case, since it would have necessitated considerable transfer and readjustment of men. Yet trouble might have been avoided if the company had agreed to a brief postponement of the layoff.
41. Akron *Beacon-Journal*, May 27, 1938; Akron *Times-Press*, May 27, 1938.
42. Akron *Beacon-Journal*, June 9, 1938; December 15, 1938.
43. *Ibid.*, October 10, 1938; November 14, 1938; December 17, 1938.

with the signing of a wage agreement in June 1941, the company and the union took the first major step toward establishment of contractual relations. This agreement gave a 7 cent increase to men paid more than a dollar an hour, 8 cents to those below. Wage increases at Firestone followed. Goodrich and U. S. Rubber had led the way a month earlier, the latter with only a 5 cent increase.

(4). *Achievements of the Akron Locals*

Although management has felt that the union should act primarily as a grievance machine, an analysis of the contracts and the demands of the Akron locals shows a much more basic function. Their primary job, recognized by the leadership, has been to enable labor to adjust itself to steadily shrinking job opportunities with a minimum of human suffering, and on an equitable basis, free from discrimination or favoritism. With decentralization and rapid technological change, the number of jobs available in Akron's rubber plants has decreased.[44]

The URWA locals are generally recognized as speaking for all hourly and piece-work factory employees, although there are slight variations from plant to plant in regard to the coverage of certain groups. Thus at the Goodrich plant a small number of pattern makers persuaded the Labor Board to hold an election, which they won, for a separate bargaining unit. At Firestone, timekeepers and plant protection employees are specifically excluded from the union sphere. Technically, nonconfidential office employees are eligible to join the union, but neither the URWA nor the clerical staffs have been seriously interested.

---

44. A. F. Hinrichs, in his *Memorandum* to John Steelman, Director of the U. S. Conciliation Service, regarding the Goodrich wage rate controversy of 1938, estimated that employment in Ohio tire and tube establishments, including the departments engaged in making mechanical goods, had declined from 55,307 in 1929 to 43,550 in February 1937, a good business period. In February 1938, when depression was in full swing, only 29,750 were employed. Akron plants were producing 52.9 per cent of all pneumatic casings in 1935 and only 35.2 per cent in 1937. Hinrichs also stressed the importance of technological change in the tire industry, citing U. S. Bureau of Labor Statistics index numbers which indicated a 46 per cent increase in tires produced per man hour from 1929 to 1935. See also evidence of the National Research Project cited earlier on p. 635. The war boom starting in 1940 must, of course, be regarded merely as a temporary phenomenon.

Work Sharing

Wherever possible, work in the department must be equally shared down to a certain limit. For a while the companies maintained a high proportion of their regular forces on the payroll by transfers and by allowing the men to rotate and share work to as low as two days a week. But this policy of *unlimited* sharing was eventually abandoned because it lowered the general morale (the union called it "sharing of misery" since one could earn more on WPA) and because it deprived the organizations of a stable, dues-paying membership. As a result, a series of crises arose in the fall of 1937 in the Goodyear plant, where union sentiment on the share-the-work policy was especially confused and divided.

By the end of the 1937–1938 depression a fairly uniform policy for meeting slack periods had been worked out. At Goodrich, for example, work is shared until hours fall to an average of less than twenty-four a pay-week for three consecutive weeks. After that employees with the least seniority are laid off or transferred until the hours in the department average thirty a week. At Seiberling no layoffs are allowed until a department's work hours have been reduced to an average of twenty-four a week for six weeks, except that employees of less than four months' service may be released when hours have fallen to thirty. At Firestone work sharing continues until hours have been reduced to twenty-four or less for eight consecutive weeks. Thus the policy of equal division of work has continued in effect, but a check has been placed on the degree of sharing.

Seniority

Combined with work sharing is the much advertised and much debated principle of seniority. It was a recognized factor in layoffs, transfers and rehiring during the days of employee representation plans, but not until the sitdown period was the ability factor definitely subordinated. Only one generalization about seniority in the Akron rubber plants is safe: the unions want it applied strictly, while management would prefer to make it a secondary factor. The locals see in it the most effective method of protecting the older workers and of preventing discrimination, while the companies maintain that it reduces efficiency, prevents able young men from getting ahead, and by reducing labor turnover to practically zero makes for an unduly old labor force. In spite of these employer arguments, which the unions do not accept, it has generally been agreed that in times of layoff, the oldest man in terms of service will be retained provided he can do the work or learn the job within a few days. Competency has always been a troublesome question in borderline cases where a worker, anxious to hold a job, claims he has had some experience on similar work. But in general, careful examination of the record and, in some cases, a brief trial have prevented abuses.

The question of what form of seniority to apply has not been decided with the same degree of uniformity. A seniority program which fitted a plant with considerable homogeneity of occupations and a relatively small number of products might be unsuitable for a plant with many types of work and skill requirements. Thus, at Seiberling, a company employing about a thousand employees and producing mainly a high grade tire, plant-wide seniority has operated effectively. At Firestone seniority is applied on a departmental basis. The union request for a wider unit is opposed by management because of expense involved in retraining and the effect it would have on the age composition of the employees.

Seniority at Goodrich

Evolution of seniority at the Goodrich plant illustrates the trial and error pattern of collective bargaining in the newly organized plants. Management holds that seniority is essentially the union's problem as long as efficiency of production is not unduly affected. However, it has declared that in the interest of efficiency no man displacing ("bumping") another has a "right" to a specific job. Management insists on the prerogative of placing the retained employee on whatever job he appears to be best fitted for. The union has not strongly opposed this position as long as there has been no evidence of discrimination.

To the local union leaders, seniority limited to a job or occupational basis is objectionable because it symbolizes the craft unionism which they violently oppose. Believing that the wider seniority is applied the better it is for industrial unionism, they preferred plant-wide seniority to divisional, and divisional to departmental. Experience is causing them to reconsider this position.

The first use of seniority in the reduction and increase of forces at Goodrich was by departments. After work had been shared to the minimum number of hours, employees with the least seniority in a department were either transferred to another department which needed extra help or were laid off. One objection to this practice was that in some divisions with numerous products having different seasonal peaks, such as mechanical goods, many employees were transferred from one department to another during the year and failed to establish the necessary one year's "residence" in any department, entitling them to full seniority rights. When the lay-off period came they were the first to go, even though they might have had considerable plant service. Another complaint was that long service people were laid off in some slack departments while shorter service employees continued to work full time in other departments. The result was that in the 1938 contract departmental seniority was modified by the provision that an employee with five years' or more company service credit could displace any employee with less than two years' service in his *division,* provided he could qualify for the work. The following year, after large numbers of five- to ten-year men continued to be laid off owing to the depression, the rule was further changed to permit five-year men to displace employees with less than five years' service in the *division.*

The extension has had repercussions. Only a few hundred men were affected by the new provisions, but they and their friends protested vigorously at the union meetings. Moreover, the five-year rule meant that some young and aggressive committeemen, who were indispensable to the union grievance machine, could not get back to their departments for a long time. The feeling in favor of wide seniority has therefore cooled.

Hours of Work; "Speed-Up"

With jobs scarce for its members, the length of the normal work day and work week has been of special importance to the union. Hours of work have been carefully regulated everywhere so that the earlier practice of foremen favoring friends at the expense of others has been eliminated. Employees are not to enter their department before the regular starting time and must leave at the close of their regular shift except in case of authorized overtime.

All of the important Akron rubber companies went on the flexible six-hour day, thirty-six-hour week in the early years of the depression. Production being intermittent, two extra hours of work a day two days a week were allowed during busy seasons without payment of penalty overtime rates. But local unions have been quick to protest whenever management has tried to exceed the normal work period at any other time. Since 1935 the companies have sought restoration of the eight-hour day, claiming that they cannot compete efficiently with outside firms, particularly in the mechanical goods field, which have such a schedule. The unions have rejected the argument on the ground that locality and skill favor Akron. Goodrich is the only Akron local to place further limitation on hours by incorporating in the contract a clause forbidding any employee to work more than eighteen hundred hours in a single calendar year.

For the same reason, the locals combated any speed-up in production—whether through new machines and new processes or through "pace-setters," "tightening" of job standards, or other devices to make employees work faster or produce more for the same or less pay. During 1936 and most of 1937 it was impossible for any company to introduce a new laborsaving machine. But union officials realized that in the end this was a disastrous policy which would drive production away from Akron.[45] Present contracts therefore generally state that the union will cooperate fully

45. In June 1940 the vice president of the Rubber Workers presented a brief before the Temporary National Economic Committee in which he stressed the disastrous effects of technological change and decentralization in rubber, claimed that the union policy of a shorter work day at "a decent wage" saved 32,000 jobs, and admitted that the problem was national in scope and required federal action. "Statement of Thomas F. Burns, Vice President of the United Rubber Workers of America, Before the Temporary National Economic Committee of the Congress of the United States" (mimeographed), p. 5.

in the effective use of the machinery provided. The Seiberling contract specifies that the remaining employees must be assured the same average hourly and weekly earnings as in the past. Management has thus been able to modernize its equipment, even where the union is strongly organized; but the union has closely studied each change and protested if the company has neglected to provide for the displaced men or failed to readjust the wage rates adequately. The union contention that the workers should share in the benefits of technological change has not made much headway.

In some cases production speed has been brought under joint control. Without attempting to explain the modified Bedaux system of wage payment used by the Goodrich Company, it should be noted that management has agreed not to demand more than a certain average rate of production. When production speed exceeds the given rate, the union may request an investigation of the time-study standards. In departments of all the plants, union members have agreed among themselves to keep production down to what they consider a reasonable pace—an age-old practice common to nonunion as well as union plants where job opportunities are scarce or diminishing.

Wage Differentials

With the possible exception of seniority and job scarcity, no question in these few years of collective bargaining has needed more attention than that of wages—both the general wage level and individual wage rates. Except for U. S. Rubber at Detroit,[46] the average hourly wage of Akron plants was in 1940 about 20 per cent higher than the wage of out-of-Akron plants. The differential was slightly less in the case of tire production, somewhat more in the case of mechanical and other rubber goods.[47] The in-

---

46. See Hinrichs, *Memorandum*, p. 11.
47. One of the major rubber companies of Akron submitted the following figures to show how it was affected in its various plants by the differential problem. In 1930 the hourly rate for direct labor in the Akron plants of the company was 82 cents while its plants outside of Akron paid an average of 61 cents, making a differential of 21 cents. The differential fell during the next three years until it was about 15 cents in 1933, but after that it rose rapidly and in 1937 reached a high of 37 cents. It should be observed that these figures are biased upward by the fact that tire and other products are combined, and most of the tire production (which

teresting feature of the problem is that management itself raised wages largely without formal union demand. From 1933 to February 1937 the Akron companies granted six general wage increases ranging from 6 to 10 per cent. Without doubt their intent was to forestall the union if possible.

The Goodrich wage controversy of the spring of 1938 was the climax of the issue. The Goodrich Company was most seriously affected by the differential because mechanical and rubber goods other than tires and tubes formed a considerably higher proportion of its production than in the other major Akron concerns. If the union would accept a lower rate and the eight-hour day the company promised to negotiate a written contract, to spend $1.5 million on modernization of equipment and processes, and to undertake no manufacturing operations in new locations for a period of six months. As has been stated, the union refused to give way. It pointed out that the situation was of management's own making and noted that there was no guarantee that a wage cut in Akron would not result in a cut throughout the industry with no change in the competitive situation. It observed that since the companies would guarantee to refrain from decentralizing for six months, but no more, there was nothing to prevent them from doing so later even if a wage reduction was taken. It emphasized finally the skill, experience and high productivity of Akron workers as well as Akron's proximity to the auto market.[48]

During the past three or four years, the large Akron concerns have established additional plants outside of Akron. Firestone has probably gone farthest by building a tire and tube plant in Memphis, transferring part of its steel rim division to Wyandotte, Michigan, starting the manufacture of mechanical goods in

pays higher than other products everywhere) is in Akron while most of the other rubber products are manufactured outside of Akron.

In the Hinrichs' *Memorandum* (pp. 24-25), it is stated that "from May 1936 to January 1937 the percentage difference between the high-wage and low-wage areas declined steadily." However, in February 1937 and in the spring and summer of 1941 wage increases in Akron again increased the differential.

48. As a government investigator of the case wrote: "The presence of a large skilled labor force assures the possibility of an output per man-hour that justifies a higher wage per hour than is paid in most other parts of the country . . . though the data are not detailed enough to determine precisely what differentials can be supported." *Ibid.,* p. 22.

Noblesville, Indiana, and opening a new plastics and mechanical goods division in Fall River, Massachusetts. Goodrich has opened a small mechanical goods plant at Cadillac, Michigan, a heels and soles plant at Clarksville, Tennessee, and a tire plant at Oaks, Pennsylvania. Goodyear has started tire production at Jackson, Michigan, and heels and soles production at Windsor, Vermont; it is now building another plant at St. Mary's, Ohio. General Tire and Rubber located its new mechanical goods plant in Wabash, Indiana. In addition, a certain amount of production appears to have been transferred from the main plant to other old plants of these companies, such as the Goodyear plant at Gadsden, Alabama.

On the other hand, during 1939 and 1940 Goodyear announced it would spend $3 million on modernization of its Akron plant; Goodrich was to construct another Akron factory to manufacture a new product, koroseal; and General planned a five-story addition to its Akron plant.[49] The URWA has not ignored the outward movement, but it believes that to a certain extent it was an extension of the early trend to set up outside plants for marketing reasons. At the same time the leadership holds that one of the best answers to decentralization to evade the union is increased organization in the hinterland, which it has not been strong enough to do successfully.

Wage Adjustments Under a Contract

Most of the contracts provide for the "freezing" of wage rates during their duration, unless "conditions in the industry" warrant a change. In a verbal understanding made at Goodrich the phrase "conditions in the industry" is interpreted as referring either to wage changes by any of the Big Three in Akron or to a 3 per cent change in the Bureau of Labor Statistics and National Industrial Conference Board indexes for the rubber industry as a whole. The Seiberling contract forbids a reduction in wage rates, but allows

49. A statement made by the president of the General Tire and Rubber Company in a full-page paid advertisement in the Akron *Beacon-Journal* (June 26, 1940) announced both the conclusion of a long strike and the proposed erection of the building: "The new building is not the dream of a Ghost Writer in a Ghost Town. It will consist of bricks and mortar built upon the foundation of our firm resolve to continue to have our tires made by the best workers in the world—the rubber workers of Akron."

negotiations for higher wages at any time. And in return for concessions in working conditions and what amounts to a preferential union shop, the Seiberling local accepted a wage level somewhat below that of the Big Three and General.

The question of individual wage rate adjustment is one of the most active sources of discussion and irritation. In 1940 a strike of nearly three months at the General plant had as one of its three major issues the charge that management had "chiseled" on individual rates. Whether incorporated specifically in the agreement or not, it is understood in all rubber plants that the union may question the labor standards of any job and request a new time study. Moreover, every change in the method of production, materials, equipment or the product requires new time studies and the establishment of new rates. When it is realized that Goodrich manufactures an estimated thirty thousand different products while Goodyear has over forty thousand different active rates, and that small technical changes in the rubber industry are of almost daily occurrence, the intricacy of wage adjustments becomes apparent.

The union at General Tire and Rubber has probably been most concerned with the wage rate question and has made gains other locals have not yet achieved. The leaders' goal has been for union and management to determine new rates jointly before they are posted, but the company has insisted on the right to fix rates as in the past, with the union retaining the privilege of bringing up a grievance if it is dissatisfied. If a change has been shown to be necessary, the settlement has been retroactive to the time of protest. In the fall of 1939, for example, the union claimed a new tire rate was too "tight" and demanded a recheck of standards. The time study resulted in a 7 per cent increase in the rate, and 110 tire builders received $55 each in back pay. Management offered to have its time-study expert teach the technique of time study to a number of union committeemen, but the offer was refused because the committeemen felt the workers might be suspicious. Later, the president of the local and the chairman of the grievance committee took a time-study course.

The General contract provides that a time study shall give due consideration to fatigue, speed, machine limitation, lunch period, etc. What "due consideration" means is, of course, undefinable, and the bulk of the time spent in discussing wage rates centers on this issue. Whenever there are delays of more than three minutes owing to power interruption, to waiting for materials or inspection, or to accidents, or whenever the employee is handicapped by mechanical or stock abnormalities not included in the job standards, the employee is guaranteed his day work rate, which is usually about 90 per cent of his average earnings. These are significant provisions because they obviate grievances which otherwise arise almost daily in a rubber plant.

Discharge

With considerable success the Akron local unions have attempted to establish a personal "bill of rights" for their members. The contracts clearly leave to management the direction of plant operations and the right to hire, suspend or discharge for proper cause. But all cases of discipline are subject to appeal, and if joint investigation shows that a suspension or discharge was undeserved, the employee is reinstated to full rights and compensated at his average rate of pay for time lost. Before a reprimand can be written on his record card, an employee must be allowed to state his objections. As a result, wherever the union has a strong organization it has been virtually impossible for the company to discharge a man unless he has been guilty of such serious offenses as repeated drunkenness or theft within the plant. While the union has unquestionably protected some who merited discharge for inefficiency or misbehavior, the check it has placed on foreman autocracy and discrimination is important.

During the 1938 layoffs, Goodrich attempted to remove from the recall list about one hundred men considered undesirable for various reasons—inefficiency, physical disqualifications, poor conduct. Union officials insisted that if these people deserved discharge they should have been removed before the layoffs. Each case was negotiated with management as an individual problem. As a result a majority were returned to their old positions on the recall lists, many with the understanding that their rehire was on a probationary basis. Results of the probationary plan were reported as satisfactory to all.

(5). *Negotiation of the Agreements*

Negotiation of the foregoing policies is carried on for the local unions by a plant bargaining or negotiating committee consisting of the president and four to six other officials. In Goodrich, for example, the grievance chairmen of the six plant divisions automatically serve on the committee. In most plants committeemen are selected by the membership. In crucial cases, such as the Goodrich wage dispute of 1938, the president of the international union has acted as adviser to the local officers. Generally when the negotiations involve revision or renewal of the contract an international representative or organizer is on hand to advise. Otherwise, no outsiders attend local negotiations.

For the companies, contract negotiation has been carried on by top executives assisted by staff officials. At Goodrich the vice president in charge of production has handled all policy meetings with the union leaders. At Firestone the superintendent of the labor department and a company vice president have assumed the burden of discussion. Among the smaller companies, like General and Seiberling, the plant managers and the labor relations directors have represented the companies.

Most of the Akron agreements provide that negotiations for renewal or alteration should begin a month before the contracts run out. With few exceptions the contracts are yearly, the date of expiration coming usually in the spring. There are two main types of termination clauses. One, like the Firestone, states that any provision of the agreement may be reopened for negotiation after ten days' written notice from either side. If no settlement is concluded within thirty days, the clause is terminated although the rest of the contract continues unchanged. As for the contract as a whole, if no agreement is reached before the terminal date, it automatically expires. Since in none of the past three years has the discussion on the whole agreement been completed on time, the old contract was extended for short periods; in 1939 three such extensions were required.

This type of termination clause introduces an element of uncertainty and instability undesirable for satisfactory collective bargaining. Most of the contracts have termination clauses along the lines of the Goodrich model. Except for wages, no alterations may be made in the contract during its duration. If at the end of the year the negotiations for revision or renewal are unsuccessful, the agreement continues in effect until cancelled by either party on thirty days' written notice. The 1939 agreement at Goodrich was not signed until four months after negotiations had started and three months after the terminal date of the old contract.

(6). *Administration of the Agreements*

The final results of collective bargaining depend, of course, on the administration, interpretation and enforcement of the agreement. Most of the Akron rubber contracts provide the same general method of adjusting grievances, as described earlier in this chapter. But variations from this pattern exist in several plants. In some establishments certain of the steps are eliminated; in a number of plants, the president of the local participates in the case at an early stage.

The Firestone contract provides that if a settlement cannot be reached on any grievance, recourse may be had to an umpire satisfactory to both parties. Only one case, however, has actually been submitted to arbitration. The first Goodrich contract provided, upon mutual agreement, for an outside consultant to study a grievance and submit his findings. This form of arbitration was used on two occasions but the local was dissatisfied with the results and the cost. The 1939 contract therefore eliminated the "consultant" clause. It is the general sentiment of most management and union representatives in the rubber industry that arbitration by an outsider is not desirable because no outsider understands the problems of a particular concern as well as the local management and employees.

Union Machinery

Employee representation plans gave employees their first opportunity to learn how to adjust individual or group grievances. Their value to the union as a training school, however, must not be overemphasized because after a brief attempt to capture control, union members were invariably urged not to make use of them. During 1934 and 1935 the local unions had little formal organization in the Akron plants; the few grievances settled were adjusted chiefly over the telephone or in joint conference by the union president or the plant bargaining committee and top management. In the 1936 period of union recovery and sitdowns, the departments elected shop committeemen and the present system gradually evolved.

Committeemen and subcommitteemen were elected in every department and on each shift. The number varied with the size and location of the department, the number of employees, the variety of occupations and (an important detail) the availability of active and capable union members. For instance, at the Goodrich plant about three hundred committeemen and subcommitteemen were elected. The average was one committeeman for thirty men, but some represented as few as six workers and others as many as one hundred and fifty. A rough attempt was made to parallel management's structure. Each department elected a chairman, whose duty it was to conduct department committee and general meetings and to settle grievances with the general foreman. Similarly, each of the six divisions elected a chairman who had analogous duties on the division level. These department and division meetings have been of major importance to the union because they handle the bulk of the business. Frequently more members attend a meeting of a large department or a division than the general membership meeting held twice monthly.

Although the anarchy of the sitdown period no longer exists, departmental and divisional autonomy, as opposed to centralization of authority, is still strong in the rubber plants. At Goodrich uniformity of action has been secured through several agencies. Once a month and on special occasions, all committeemen meet to discuss plant and local problems of a particularly knotty nature. The plant bargaining committee, consisting of division chairmen and the president, carries all unsettled grievances to plant management and negotiates plant policies. Finally the president, who has acted as full-time representative since May 1937, handles a large number of cases.

Perhaps 75 per cent of the Goodrich disputes are settled orally between the employee or the shift committeeman and foreman. Before going beyond this stage, a case must be written up and submitted to the president or the division chairman for approval or rejection. Since committeemen are paid by the union for time lost from work, most cases are turned in to the union office for review. Before returning it to the departmental and divisional committeemen for further attempts at settlement, the president himself may attempt to settle a case by telephone with the industrial relations office of the company. In 1937, about four hundred grievances were adjusted in this fashion. The president approved six hundred additional cases for adjustment in the plant.[50]

The activities of the president have been criticized from two sides. Management charges that he has rejected too few unmerited grievances for fear of antagonizing members. Some department committeemen, on the other hand, feel that he has taken too much responsibility, that fewer cases should be settled over the phone and more returned to the department for adjustment near the source of the dispute. Recently increasing encouragement has been given to the handling of all departmental problems by the foreman and the departmental committeeman. Most problems, according to a company official, require simply a careful collection and interpretation of the facts for their satisfactory adjustment. Most of the telephone contacts between the union president and the industrial relations officer of the company have come to involve the securing of information rather than the actual disposition of grievances.

The other large Akron locals have not been as successful as Goodrich in building so complete a grievance machine, mainly because of less union strength. But even though organization in most of the smaller unions is virtually 100 per cent, willing and efficient departmental committeemen are few and the burden of

50. Management has computed that of 669 grievance petitions written and approved by the union during 1937, 82.9 per cent were settled in the department, 8.1 per cent by the division superintendents, 5.2 per cent by the office of the vice president, and 3.8 per cent were never presented for final negotiation.

grievance adjustment falls mainly upon the half dozen or so members of the plant bargaining committee. The contracts provide that all grievances beyond the employee-foreman stage must be written up, but this is seldom done because the workers do not yet appreciate the value of records. The plant bargaining committee usually holds a meeting once a week in the union hall, just before the conference with management, to receive and consider any unsettled grievances of members.

At General, union leaders experimented with methods of improving settlement of grievances within the shop. At first there was a committeeman on each shift with a head committeeman on each of the three floors in the plant. This system worked badly because there was no coordination by department. It was then decided to refer a case which a shift committeeman could not settle to a departmental committeeman. If he was unable to make an adjustment, the case was to go to the Representatives Council, the entire body of union committeemen. This method likewise failed to speed up and improve grievance settlements. Now, most cases are completed by the five-man bargaining committee or by one of its members. In rate adjustment cases, the union has attained some success with a special rates committee, although a recent strike grew out of wage rate grievances.

Company Machinery

During the "fighting period" top management not only decided on basic policies but also debated the merits of many individual grievances which subordinate officials were either forbidden or afraid to settle. However, after the unions received exclusive recognition by contract, memorandum or orally, and some measure of real collective bargaining was obtained, the high officials slowly gave up their burden and turned back to their own production problems. At Firestone and Goodyear, where the labor departments were highly developed, the superintendent or director took over the responsibility. At Goodrich the assistant to the vice president relieved him of most of his labor functions; at General and Seiberling, new officials were chosen to represent the companies in administering the contract. Top management, while frequently consulted on knotty problems or in case of a deadlock, remains in the background.

Management has followed two main approaches to the settling of disputes within the plant. One group believes that grievances should be settled, as far as possible, by the production men—the foremen and the superintendents—and that only plant-wide and the more important individual cases should be appealed to the labor relations department and top executive officers. The other group holds that the chief function of production men is to supervise production and not to be personnel agencies. They therefore leave most grievance adjustment to the labor relations department.

Goodrich is a good example of the first category. In the early period of conflict top management was hesitant to delegate powers to subordinates, fearing mistakes. The foremen were discouraged from settling all but the most petty complaints. The inexperience and emotionalism of both foremen and union committeemen made grievance adjustment exceedingly difficult. The company's foreman training program was on a divisional basis and did not stress collective bargaining. In 1935 it unified its training program on a plant-wide basis, and in succeeding years foremen were instructed in methods of adjusting grievances, while the contract with the union was interpreted by top management. Management now credits the program with being a primary factor in the efficient operation of the grievance procedure. Classes are held once weekly for twenty-six weeks in the fall and winter. Attendance is said to be voluntary, but since records are kept, examinations given and graded, and general performance noted for future promotions, few foremen are absent.

In Firestone and some smaller companies, the industrial relations department carries on most of the negotiations for management. The advantage to the company of this procedure is that it assures a uniform policy throughout the plant. At General the industrial relations director confers almost daily with the superintendents of the three major divisions. The main disadvantage in centralization of grievance adjustment is delay. The farther away from the job the grievance is settled, the longer it takes to find the facts and to settle it. A few agreements specify that grievances must be answered within a given period by the foreman (three days in one case) or must be settled within a normal time (ten days in another case), but these clauses have not done much good. Many complaints drag on for weeks.

Types of Grievances

The problem of handling grievances varies greatly from one section of a plant to another. Issues of slight importance in one department may be of great consequence in others because of the occupations or the personalities involved. For example, Goodrich's mechanical goods division has many wage adjustment complaints because it has about three times as many job classifications as the rest of the plant. It has more seasonal changes in production, more transfers, more layoffs than any other division. In addition, it has the bulk of the women employees, who bring up many petty personal grievances, and large numbers of foreign-born who speak poor English, cannot make their complaints clear and often misunderstand the foreman. In contrast, the processing division contains only about a dozen women and most of the workers are American-born, with high school education. Here, a large proportion of the disputes are settled orally on the department floor.

Individual personality underlies the entire grievance question. A general foreman friendly to the union and recognized by the workers as fair and understanding can settle the most complex complaints with a minimum of strife. A hard-boiled foreman unwilling to lose any of his former authority can turn a petty issue into a minor crisis. A few independent nonunionists in a department dominated by union members may mean constant trouble.

Statistics on the subject of grievances are of small importance without a multitude of related factors. Comparisons are useless because plants differ in product, personalities and economic condition. A large number of grievances might come from poor working conditions, high level of production or an unusually active union organization. Conversely, few grievances might reflect good conditions, slack times or a weak union. Therefore, the chief value of the accompanying table is to show the types of complaints. The table was compiled by a company which, like the local union, maintains a complete file of written grievances. It should be borne in mind that the period under examination was a time of low employment *after* the bottom of the 1937–1938 depression had been passed, and that wage grievances form a considerably smaller proportion than in more prosperous times.

TABLE 5

Written Grievances in a Large Akron Rubber Plant
(June 1, 1938 to November 16, 1938)

Grievance	Total	Warehouse	Engineering	Processing	Tires & Tubes	Mechanical	Miller
Total of All Problems	161[a]	9	12	22	28	48	42
Wage Problems	51	1	2	9	12	19	8
Standards questioned, found "O.K."	20		2	3	3	9	3
Standards questioned, increased	8				3	2	2
Standards questioned, pending	7			3		3	1
Standards questioned, solution found in improving conditions	9	1		2	3	2	1
Special rate problems	7			1	3	3	
Working Conditions	70	6	6	7	12	15	24
Supervisor doing direct work	5			1	1	1	2
Protesting reprimands	7		1	1	1	2	2
Protesting work hour distribution	13		1		1	2	9
Change in shift hours	5			1		3	1
Complaint against poor machine arrangement and working conditions	6	1			4	1	
Requests for better ventilation	4				1	3	
Unsafe conditions	3	2		1			
Protesting change in production methods	4			1	2	1	
Complaint against employee reporting to work too early	3				1	1	1
Discrimination by management	2		1				1
Requests for additional services, postings, etc.	4					1	3
Requests that certain work be done in certain departments	13	3	3	2			5
Discharge protest (denied)	1					1	
Seniority	40	2	4	6	4	14	10
Concerning layoffs	11	1	1	3	2	1	3
Concerning shift assignment	4		1			3	
Concerning rehiring	6		1			1	4
Concerning transfers	7				1	4	2
Concerning service restoration	5	1				4	
Concerning job assignment where rights have been claimed on basis of seniority	7		1	3	1	1	1

a. Twenty-eight other union problems were drawn up, numbered and approved in the regular way but were not presented to management for negotiation.

(7). Strikes and Stoppages

Between 1933 and 1937 Akron had the reputation of a city of strikes and the public became increasingly embittered against unionism, which it feared, rightly or wrongly, would drive industry away. In the few years since the unions have become more firmly established there has been little trouble except for the internal strife at Goodyear. Goodrich had a week-long "labor holiday" in 1938. In 1939 a small company had a strike of several weeks and in 1940 the General local was out on strike for over eleven weeks. But the tenseness of the past was conspicuously absent. There have been minor flurries and tense moments in many plants, but no other serious outbreaks.

5. Summary of Problems

Attitude of Employers

The conclusion seems inevitable that most employers in the rubber industry, large or small, have little liking for the principle of unionism and would welcome an opportunity to get rid of it. The chief exception is the United States Rubber Company whose director of labor relations has publicly stated that he is not opposed to unionism and that management and organized labor must learn to live together harmoniously.[51] Some companies, like Goodrich and Seiberling, whose employees have been strongly unionized, have decided that at least for the present unionism is the order of the day and have generally shown good faith in their dealings. A number of others have accepted the union only to be sure of uninterrupted production and, where the union is weak, have run things pretty much their own way. A still considerable group of companies has consistently fought the union even at the expense of production.

To management, the union represents a definite limitation of its authority. If the union were to confine itself to serving as a grievance machine, most of the companies would probably be

---

51. See *The New York Times,* May 4, 1938; October 18, 1938; November 29, 1938.

content to see it survive. But unions are also interested in job security and the allocation of job opportunities. Hence they restrict and hamper management's former freedom to choose whatever workers it desires, to introduce whatever labor-displacing machines and processes it wishes, and to formulate whatever plant rules it thinks most suitable. Most managements either ignore this as a basic function of unionism and are irritated, or realize it and do not like it.

Part of management's hostility comes from the belief that unionism results in increased cost of operations which possibly cannot be easily or completely passed on to the consumer. The Akron companies feel that seniority is a burden which will be still more serious later by creating a static and aging working force. They note the differential in hours and wages between the Akron plants and the plants outside of Akron, and hold that the union injured their competitive position. Of course, management was itself chiefly responsible for the increase in the differential, since the six-hour day was introduced before the emergence of unionism and the wage increases were mainly voluntary moves to ward off the unions. However, the central fact to the companies was that a change in hours and wages was prevented only by the union.

Still a third explanation of company attitude is that management is not getting anything from the union in return for its concessions. The mine workers' union has prevented ruinous cutthroat competition in the bituminous coal industry. Clothing unions have stabilized costs and improved production efficiency in the garment industries. Rubber companies see no like help from unions in their industry—only additional costs. Hence, except to keep the peace, there is no incentive for them to "play ball" with the URWA.

It is plain that collective bargaining is still in its initial stage in the rubber industry and that the future is not yet clear. Management is adjusting itself to the reality of the union, foremen are learning how to deal with or fight against an organized labor force, new industrial relations departments are springing up, hiring procedures and disciplinary policies are gradually being reworked. On the union side, there is the arduous task of consolidation and expansion, of developing skilled and mature leaders, of training the membership to be content with slow gains, of clarifying ideas and policies. Owing to the strong spirit of local autonomy, these tasks of the union have been attacked with varying success in different plants.

Problems of Organization

Because of management's attitude and because collective bargaining is in the first instance the union's project, the main burden has fallen upon the URWA. Whether it continues to survive or not, whether it remains a fighting institution or eventually sells itself to management depends first of all upon organization. It is a truism that collective bargaining cannot come into its own until the union principle is recognized and established throughout the industry. The incompleteness and difficulties of organization are apparent even in Akron. Although all the plants are under contract,[52] a substantial number of workers are not dues-paying union members. The union is partially to blame. It failed to exert the proper amount of discipline during the sitdown period, and its frequently unwise attempts to force nonunion workers into the organization have made the task of "selling the union" more difficult. The task of organizing workers in a high-wage, traditionally nonunion industry needs great skill and much time. Quite as difficult is the education of members to pay dues in bad times as well as good, to take an active part in the affairs of the union, and to remain loyal to the union even though gains are slow in coming. This problem of education and of breaking down the natural inertia of the workers has been characteristic of most American labor unions. In Akron it is especially complex because of the declining number of available jobs. Some individuals are bound to benefit at the expense of others, and friction will inevitably result.

But the great challenge to the union leaders is organization outside of Akron. The job, only about a third done, is twofold. First, a considerable proportion of Big Four plants remain to be unionized. Even five of the relatively friendly United States Rubber establishments are without a local union. The main obstacle is

---

52. Goodyear, it will be recalled, has only a wage contract.

that many of these plants are located either in the South or in small rural communities where public sentiment is not favorable to the URWA or any other union. The large companies follow the policy of paying the highest wages in the community as well as providing the best working conditions, and the workers are not disposed to be swayed by union organizers. Nevertheless, the union has made some progress in organization. The National Labor Relations Board on March 11, 1940 ordered the Goodyear Company to disestablish its company union at Gadsden, Alabama, and to reinstate with back pay a number of employees discharged for union activities.

The second aspect of the "outside-Akron" problem is organization of the small independent establishments, of which many are near-sweatshops and some are "fly-by-nights." These concerns are in the mechanical and other rubber goods field. The extent of competition which they offer to the products of the Big Four has not been revealed. That the URWA has made relatively little headway among these plants is not surprising. It was many years before the powerful and mature garment unions got a real grip on a similar type of plant, and there is little reason why the rubber union should find the process any easier.

Within the past few years, the American Federation of Labor's activities have also presented a problem to the URWA. AF of L federal labor unions recently won elections at the United States Rubber plant in Providence, R. I., the large Hood Rubber Company (now owned by Goodrich) at Watertown, Massachusetts, and the Firestone plant at Memphis. In addition, AF of L unions control the Brown Rubber Company of Indiana, the Goodyear Footwear plant in Providence, and craft units in a few other plants. How much of a threat to the CIO organization this will be in the future is hard to say.

The leaders of the URWA are keenly aware of the organizational problem. Almost every national convention brings a request for an increased per capita tax to expand organizing work by the international office. In 1937 the tax was raised by 2.5 cents a month. In 1939 it was decided to initiate an organizing campaign, with the locals contributing as much money and supporting as many organizers in their district as they thought advisable. The results, however, were slight. During the first six months of 1940, nine new locals were organized, but the important elections noted above were lost. The 1940 international convention then voted a 5 cent increase in the per capita tax.

Differential Problem

The war and the defense boom have, of course, drastically changed the economic picture. There is no differential problem in rubber today. But with postwar deflation, it will probably recur and again make necessary extensive organization of plants outside Akron and adjustment of their rates to Akron's. Otherwise the large companies may shift more of their production outside Akron and introduce more laborsaving devices to cut down their wage bill. On the other hand, it may well be, as union leaders have contended, that the problem was exaggerated, that many of the outside concerns with old equipment could not grant substantial wage increases without encountering financial difficulty and thus threatening the jobs of their employees and strengthening the position of the large corporations.[53] In any event, the problem will be eased if a detailed and impartial study of costs throughout the industry is made.

Problem of Adjustment

In plants where collective bargaining has gained a foothold, management and union now face a fundamental problem of learning to live together, whether they like each other or not. That would not be an easy problem even if management fully accepted unionism. Considerable adjustment is necessary on both sides. As long as the union is uncertain of its position and distrusts employ-

---

53. No study was made public which conclusively proved the gravity of the problem for the Akron plants. It is the author's opinion that it was not as crucial or immediate as the public was led to believe. Neither did the companies suffer as much as their protests would indicate. The annual financial statements of the Big Three companies with Akron plants show that the years 1935–1937 (during the union's existence) netted substantial returns. If 1938 was slower than 1937, high production in 1939 amply compensated for it.

Since no figures by plant are available, it is necessary to rely on company-wide data. That, of course, detracts considerably from their value as far as the point in

ers' intentions, however, management cannot expect it to adopt a cooperative attitude. The failure of management representatives to give speedy answers to grievances is always a source of future trouble. In refusing to discuss a new policy or an important step with the union leaders before putting it into effect, management has often made for difficult situations. Unwillingness to yield on minor issues, such as union use of the company bulletin board, has made for unnecessary friction. On the other hand, where the union has gained a strong hold and is no longer fighting for its life, it is evident that it cannot expect endless concessions from the company without contributing something in return. The union has often taken an unduly rigid position on seniority, fearing to give way on an occasional exception or demanding a wider application than is desirable for the plant. Disposal of trivial membership grievances is also a delicate problem for union leaders to solve. The indispensable first step in satisfactory collective bargaining is unqualified recognition of unionism by management and then a willingness on both sides to "play ball" under fair rules.

question is concerned. But at least it may be noted that the existence of the union hardly jeopardized the financial position of the firms. The following data on net operating profit or net income from sales (including subsidiaries) came from *Moody's Manual of Investments*, Moody's Investors Service, New York.

Year	Goodrich	Goodyear	Firestone
1929	$ 9,428,490	$22,313,015	$11,184,880
1930	—5,209,133	13,152,659	2,736,478
1931	—5,834,605 [a]	8,637,663 [c]	6,754,354
1932	—4,032,773 [b]	439,733 [d]	6,164,888
1933	2,475,870	6,180,969	4,058,522
1934	4,004,613	6,392,414	6,235,774
1935	5,680,668	8,861,783	8,093,009
1936	10,099,321	14,907,942	11,531,131
1937	5,948,486	21,884,555	11,839,383
1938	3,663,785	10,179,095	6,954,404
1939	8,893,525	12,850,701	12,149,067

a. Includes inventory write-off of $1,125,807.
b. Includes inventory write-off of $4,426,195.
c. Includes inventory write-off of $5,301,104.
d. Includes inventory write-off of $6,475,327.

Chapter 13

GLASS

Milton Derber

1. Introduction

MEASURED BY CAPITAL invested, value of output and number employed, the glass industry is of secondary importance in the national economy. In the sphere of collective bargaining, however, its record of more than fifty years of successful union-management relations in some of its branches, despite tremendous obstacles introduced by the mechanical revolution, is almost unique in the mass production field. Nevertheless, like most others, the glass industry was radically affected by current social changes. The "old unionism" was transformed, while a "new unionism" emerged to rival it. In this chapter both old and new forms of unionism and collective bargaining will be analyzed. The main emphasis will be placed on today's problems but because of its significance considerable attention will also be given the experience of the past.

The United States Bureau of the Census reports that in 1937 there were 232 glass manufacturing establishments of all types, employing an annual average of 79,000 wage earners, paying out nearly $102 million in wages, and producing goods worth $388 million. One hundred and fifty-three of these plants are scattered through West Virginia, Pennsylvania, Ohio and Indiana near the cheap natural gas supply, their chief fuel. Strictly speaking, however, glass is not one but several industries which differ from each other in structure and production methods, and are related chiefly by the basic raw materials—silica sand, soda ash, and lime —they all use. Three major subdivisions—container, pressed and blown ware (flint glass), and flat (window and plate) glass— produced over 90 per cent of the total product.

Container plants make bottles for food products, beverages, and medicinal and toilet preparations, as well as general-purpose containers; pressed and blown ware plants produce tableware, lamps, lamp chimneys, lantern globes, bulbs for electric lamps, opal ware, tubing and a great variety of novelties; flat glass plants produce chiefly window, plate and laminated glass in addition to smaller supplies of rolled, wire and structural glass. It was purely through accident that the pressed and blown ware branches of the glass industry developed under the same roof, although some products like tumblers and sherbets are produced by both methods. In the case of pressed ware, the molten glass is plunged into a mold either by hand or machine pressure, and, when removed, the article is physically completed, at least so far as its shape is concerned. In the case of blown ware, before the introduction of the machine, the molten glass after being "blown" through an iron pipe by the blower looked more like a bottle with a broken neck than the object it was intended to be, and had to go through a series of cutting and smoothing operations before attaining final shape.[1]

Census figures do not give the number of wage earners in each division, but a rough computation shows that although the container plants are responsible for approximately 42 per cent of the total value of output and the flat glass plants for about 26 per cent, they employ only some 26,000 and 18,000 respectively; pressed and blown ware establishments, responsible for only 22 per cent of the output, employ about 33,000.[2]

The glass industry of today is radically different technically and economically from the industry in existence when collective bargaining got under way. Changes in demand—a result of the growth of large cities, the dynamic rise of the auto industry and

1. Unless otherwise noted, the technical information in this section has been taken from Boris Stern, "Productivity of Labor in the Glass Industry," *Bulletin No. 441*, U. S. Bureau of Labor Statistics, 1927.

2. The value of output percentages are derived from U. S. Bureau of the Census data. Estimates of wage earners come from several sources: the container figure from the Glass Container Association of America; the flat glass figure from the report, *Flat Glass and Related Glass Products* (1937), of the U. S. Tariff Commission; and the pressed and blown ware figure from estimates by the American Flint Glass Workers' Union and the National Association of Manufacturers of Pressed and Blown Glassware.

development of the electric light bulb—had a part in this transformation. But even more important were the tremendous technological advances in all phases of the industry excepting certain branches of pressed ware. Before 1900, glassmaking was still practically in a handicraft stage, although molding machines for pressed ware were invented as early as 1827. The skilled artisan was the backbone of the industry while boys performed the bulk of the unskilled work.[3] The average plant was small; and investment was so slight that there was considerable mobility of labor and capital.

The plate glass branch of the industry was from its beginning, however, essentially a nonskilled industry. Plate glass was made by first casting the rough or rolled plate and then grinding and polishing it on both sides—work which on the one hand was simple and repetitive in nature and on the other dealt with heavy and large sizes of glass. Machines for grinding and polishing were invented and improved during the nineteenth century and overhead cranes were installed with the development of electric power. Thus, while bottles, blown ware and window glass were still on the old hand process basis, plate glass had reached a considerable degree of mechanization. The plate glass branch remained largely unchanged until the 1920's when, with the closed auto and construction booms as a great incentive, it passed through an amazing period of technological change.

Mechanical Revolution

In the latter half of the nineteenth century, two revolutionary European inventions, the Siemens' regenerative furnace and the continuous melting tank[4] set the stage for mechanization. By the

---

3. In 1899, of the total of 40,916 wage earners employed in making bottles and pressed and blown ware, 7,035, or 17.2 per cent, were children under the age of sixteen years. Stern, *op. cit.*, p. 22.

4. The Siemens' regenerative furnace permitted the use of natural gas instead of the former fuel—wood or coal—and saved nearly 50 per cent in fuel costs. Moreover, the heat it produced was more intense and uniform—conditions absolutely necessary for the proper melting of glass. The continuous tanks generally took the place of open or closed pots in which the raw materials were melted to form molten glass. The principal advantage lay in the opportunity it offered for uninterrupted production. The plate glass branch was unable to take advantage of the continuous tank technique until the 1920's.

end of the century, semiautomatic bottle machinery did away with the blower's job but retained the gatherer and the finisher. Complete transformation began in 1904 with the appearance of the automatic Owens bottle machine. In 1905 the Lubber cylinder machine displaced two of the four skilled artisans making window glass. A steady succession of improvements and new inventions followed, including the automatic "gob" feeder, which enabled older semiautomatic bottle machines to compete with the Owens machine; the Westlake machine for bulb making; the Danner machine for automatic manufacture of glass tubing; the Colburn and Fourcault processes for drawing a sheet of glass from a tank; the conveyor technique for grinding and polishing plate glass, and others.

The consequences of these technological advances were enormous. The old hand shop of three skilled workers and four helpers produced under normal conditions 30 gross of four-ounce prescription bottles in an eight-hour shift. But the Owens automatic ten-arm machine, with conveyor, attended by two machine operators and one machine foreman for each machine and one chief foreman for six machines, could average nearly 70 gross an hour of the same type of bottle. The increase in productivity per man hour made possible by the machine ranged from 642 to about 4010 per cent in bottles and jars, from 391 to 1128 per cent in pressed ware, and from 42 to 3043 per cent in blown ware. In the flat glass industry, the increase in productivity was 128 per cent in window glass of single strength and 161 per cent in window glass of double strength; it was 45 per cent for rough plate glass and almost 61 per cent for polished plate glass. The decrease in labor cost varied from 25 per cent (for rough plate glass) to 97 per cent (for four-ounce prescription oval bottles).

This mechanical revolution has eliminated child labor and left very few skilled workers; labor represents only about 30 to 40 per cent of the total cost instead of 60 to 70 per cent. The average plant has grown considerably, and capital investment has become prohibitive to the small manufacturer who once played an active role. The effect upon various branches of glassmaking has depended upon the extent of mechanization [5] and changed demand. But in the entire industry from 1904 to 1939 the number of factories dropped 42 per cent, employment increased only about 20 per cent, while the value of output rose more than 600 per cent.[6] Despite this concentration, glass manufacturing plants are not as large as those of other mass production industries. The biggest does not employ more than four thousand in peak periods and the average unit operated by even a major company employs less than a thousand.

Concentrated Ownership

Ownership, on the other hand, is highly concentrated. The Owens-Illinois Company (1938 assets, $85 million) makes 38 per cent of the glass containers; the Pittsburgh Plate Glass and Libbey-Owens-Ford Companies (assets of $118 million and $45 million respectively) turn out 95 per cent of the plate glass, 60 per cent of the laminated glass, and with the American Window Glass Company (assets $19 million), about 75 per cent of the window glass; and about a dozen concerns, including the Corning Glass Works, produce the bulk of the pressed and blown ware.[7] The industry's four largest producers in 1935 had nearly 37 per cent of the wage earners, paid 41 per cent of the wages, accounted for almost 45 per cent of the value of output, and owned 18 per cent of the establishments. The eight largest corporations gave

5. The pressed ware branch, for example, has been only partly mechanized. One reason is that there are literally thousands of different articles which are pressed in molds. A few of these, like tumblers, are staple commodities produced in sufficiently large quantities to justify the use of expensive machinery. But the bulk of pressed glass articles fall into the "novelties" class which is characterized by frequent change of style, great variety of detail and generally small quantities of production.

6. Derived from data of the U. S. Bureau of the Census. Using 1914 instead of 1904 as the base, the value of product increased about 315 per cent, while the number of employees increased 14 per cent and the number of establishments declined 38 per cent.

7. Production percentages taken from (a) *Hearings Before the Temporary National Economic Committee,* Pursuant to Public Res. 113, 75th Cong., 3d sess., Pt. 2, 1939; (b) U. S. Tariff Commission, *Flat Glass and Related Products,* Report No. 123, 2d Series, 1937; (c) estimate of National Association of Manufacturers of Pressed and Blown Glassware. Asset data taken from *Moody's Manual of Investments, American and Foreign, Industrial Securities,* Moody's Investors Service, New York, 1939.

about 49 per cent of the employment, paid 53 per cent of the wages, accounted for 61 per cent of the value of output, and owned 23 per cent of the plants.[8]

By 1929 the mechanical transformation was almost complete, although inventions and improvements continue. Some glass unions (notably in the window glass branch) could not stand the successive shocks which robbed them of the chief source of their bargaining power and deprived their members of jobs. But others, in the container and flint glass industries,[9] thanks to the foresight and tenacity of their leaders, held on until more favorable conditions prevailed.

2. The Old Unionism in the Container and Flint Glass Industries

a. EFFECT OF THE NEW DEAL ON UNION MEMBERSHIP

To the old unionism of the glass industry, the New Deal gave new life, new form and new problems. On May 31, 1933, the American Flint Glass Workers' Union reported its lowest membership in forty years, 5,636, of whom only 3,616 were employed at the trade. Six years later it reported 21,505 members—more than twice the previous peak reached in 1918. Similarly the Glass Bottle Blowers' Association grew from 3,612 in February 1932 to 21,143 in May 1939. Except for "miscellaneous" workers of the Owens-Illinois Company and a few small plants, the container industry was almost completely unionized. Among the "Flints," Corning Glass and several other companies had evaded the union nets, but over 60 per cent of the eligible membership was enrolled.

The revolution was in structure and outlook as well as in number. Of 15,869 new members in the American Flint Glass Workers' Union, 14,577 came from the so-called "miscellaneous" category. The proportion was somewhat smaller for the Glass Bottle Blowers' Association because repeal of Prohibition in 1933 brought jobs for many former members. From unionism's incep-

---

8. National Resources Committee, *The Structure of the American Economy*, Pt. 1, "Basic Characteristics," Washington, June 1939, pp. 240-241.

9. See pp. 691-692 for description of container and flint glass unions; pp. 718 ff. for flat glass unions.

tion, the glass industry had recognized two types of workers: the employees who "made" the product and the "miscellaneous" employees who helped them or performed such auxiliary tasks as packing, shipping and sweeping. The blower, the gatherer, the finisher, the presser and the mold maker were the aristocrats of the trade, highly craft-conscious, apprentice-trained hand workers. They created the unions. For the more numerous semiskilled and unskilled workers, they showed little concern. Even after the hand worker had been replaced by the machine operator and skill distinctions had been largely obliterated, the miscellaneous group received slight attention or help in organization.[10] This situation was radically altered with the New Deal.

CIO Appears on the Scene

Section 7(a) of the National Industrial Recovery Act aroused a desire for organization among the unskilled and made leaders of the old unions realize that the time had come for expansion. As the spirit and administration of the Recovery Act grew confused, however, the spurt in union activity died out, except for the machine operators. Most of the miscellaneous locals organized by the Flint Glass Workers' Union and the Bottle Blowers' Association either floundered about or became inactive. In 1935 the Flint Glass Workers complained that the miscellaneous members would not pay their dues and voted to relinquish its jurisdiction over them to the AF of L, but the next year it decided upon a fresh start.[11]

The enforcement machinery of the National Labor Relations

---

10. In 1914 the GBBA had obtained an industrial union charter from the AF of L in order to meet the challenge of the machine and to prevent dual unions from arising in the container plants. By 1917 twenty-five packer branches had been organized. Two years later the American Bottle Company agreed to the unionization of all its miscellaneous workers, but when the workers refused to accept the conference agreement of 1920, relations were disrupted and the company would deal only with the machine operators. The GBBA was helpless and the "miscellaneous" campaign collapsed.

11. The miscellaneous workers are organized in locals separate from the craftsmen and machine operators. Sometimes all of the miscellaneous group are joined in one local but more often they are segregated into smaller units, e.g., packers, decorating workers, box shop workers, etc. It is not uncommon in a large plant to find half a dozen local branches.

Act and aggressive tactics of the new CIO Federation of Flat Glass Workers determined the outcome. The National Labor Relations Act convinced employers that unionism was the order of the day. CIO activities among the miscellaneous workers of the container and flint industries served notice upon the older unions that if they did not get busy they would not survive. As a result, more than a dozen times the CIO was blocked by closed- or preferential-union shop agreements between the manufacturers and either the Flint Glass Workers or the Bottle Blowers' Association.

Charges have been made that this procedure marked the AF of L glass unions as "company unions in disguise." Agreements, it was said, were frequently signed before the organizations had more than a handful of adherents, and the employers often assisted, or even requested, the organizing campaign. Though the facts are correct, the accusation of "company unionism" is unjustified. With the choice no longer between unionism and nonunionism, but between two brands of unionism, the employers' action was to be expected. It was natural for those who had dealt harmoniously with the flint and bottle unions to prefer these organizations when collective bargaining was extended to the miscellaneous divisions. To employers who had not previously recognized any union, it was simply a question of choosing what appeared to them the lesser of two evils. The AF of L unions had a long record of relatively peaceful negotiation in the industry; their leaders were reputed to be conciliatory and willing to move slowly. The CIO, on the other hand, was feared for its aggressiveness.

Signing an agreement or obtaining recognition before a substantial union membership had been gained were not uncommon in the industry. Although they used the strike weapon when necessary, union officials found that the technique of selling the union to employers was safer and less expensive. In 1933, for example, after beer returned and Owens-Illinois agreed to unionization of all machine operators, the industrial relations expert of the corporation accompanied the president of the Glass Bottle Blowers' Association to several of the plants to help organization work.

Moreover, the closed- or preferential-union shop contract is a tradition of the industry, not a new device to ward off the rival CIO. Unions regard it as essential to their successful functioning, and the history of collective bargaining in glass bears them out. From the beginning, the AFGWU and the GBBA attempted to equalize wage and working conditions among competing concerns and to regulate entrance into the skilled occupations. Since plants were then small and of high mortality, and labor moved rapidly in and out of the industry's plants, the burden of achieving these goals fell upon the national officers. The closed shop was the mechanism of control. It made possible strict discipline over individual workers and affiliated locals.

b. THE JOINT CONFERENCE SYSTEM

Although expansion of collective bargaining in the glass container and flint glass industries brought new complications for unions and management, the fundamental relationship built up through more than fifty years of earnest give and take remained unshaken. The joint industry-wide bargaining conferences held annually in July or August at Atlantic City show the spirit and method which first took root several decades ago. Meetings are held in alternate hotels—first the manufacturers' and then the union's. On one side of the room sit more than twenty-five employers, on the other about the same number of labor delegates and observers. Each party, which votes and acts as a unit, has a chief spokesman, usually a leading employer and the union president, who take turns as chairman. Notes are written up and distributed throughout the industry.

The conference invariably opens with expressions of mutual confidence. The demands of the workers and the employers, which have already been debated in separate caucuses, are taken up one by one and answers given. If the subject involves a change in wages or something regarded by either faction as of great significance, there is extended discussion without mincing of words, a steady flow of facts and counterfacts. Frequently a point is stated so persuasively that the opposition holds a brief caucus and then decides to concede it. The conference ends with final statements by the spokesmen. If concessions have been made and each group is satisfied, mutual compliments are exchanged. If one side is left discontented, it says so in positive terms, but reaffirms its good feelings, stresses its faith in the soundness of the procedure, and serves notice that it will bring up the subject with renewed emphasis the following year.

Harmony comes from the underlying character and philosophy of the leading negotiators. Because most plants are still relatively small, the relation between management and labor is on a highly personal basis. A number of the managers who rose from the ranks were once union members. A few large corporations have hired former union officials to represent them in the labor field, and employers often speak at union conventions. The labor relations expert of the Owens-Illinois Corporation was for thirteen years president of the Flint Glass Workers' Union, and has been an important force in convincing his superiors and colleagues of the value of dealing with unions. His predecessors as AFGWU presidents have served as secretaries of the National Association of Manufacturers of Pressed and Blown Glassware for thirty years and twenty-four years, respectively. Some unionists are resentful when one of their officials transfers to the employer side of the conference table, but the general attitude is "a man has a right to better himself." In turn, the recently deceased president of the AFGWU was once manager of a glass plant. Consequently there is mutual understanding of production and labor problems. Employer representatives know the dangers of sending the union delegates back empty-handed to their constituents; union leaders know that wage cuts are sometimes essential, and that demands involving increased costs must be pushed cautiously.

C. HISTORY

Such harmonious collective bargaining did not develop overnight. It is the product of conflict, experimentation and constant adjustment to rapidly changing situations. A glass blowers' union existed in Philadelphia as early as 1833. In the next few decades, local unions emerged in all sections of the industry but few survived unsuccessful strikes and internal financial strains. In 1868 the Independent Druggist Ware Glass Blowers League was formed as a national organization, although most of its membership was in the Pittsburgh or "Western" area. The union soon split into two divisions, the Eastern and Western Leagues, which affiliated in 1886 with the Knights of Labor as district assemblies 149 and 143. In 1889 the two groups, with a thousand members between them, again merged after a factional fight threatened the Eastern district with extinction, and the more powerful Western assembly realized that its standards were being undermined. Two years later the national glass assembly withdrew from the Knights of Labor and became the Green Glass Bottle Blowers' Association of the United States and Canada. In 1895 its jurisdiction widened to include all bottle blowers, whether they worked on green or flint glass. Removing the limiting term "green" from its name, it affiliated with the American Federation of Labor in 1899.

While the Glass Bottle Blowers' Association had a homogeneous membership of skilled workers making bottles and jars, flint glass workers were scattered through many departments: press,[12] cutting, lamp chimney, paste-mold, to name but a few. Most of these trades had been organized as local assemblies of the Knights of Labor. In 1878 and the years immediately following, they were grouped into the American Flint Glass Workers' Union, but retained identity as separate departments [13] for collective bargaining. The AFGWU remained independent until 1897 when it came under the AF of L.

Demarcation Between the Unions

The original demarcation between the two unions in the bottle and flint glass industries was the variety of glass used rather than

12. The names of the departments are largely self-descriptive although they may appear meaningless to the outsider. The number of departments has been about fifteen for many years, although some new ones have been added while old ones have been dissolved, owing to the changes in technology and demand for the products.
13. These departments elect their own officers by referendum but do not hold separate conventions. All of the department executives sit on the AFGWU executive board, which consists of about sixty members. While departmental autonomy is still strong (much more so than in the Bottle Union), national officers have gradually extended their power and influence.

the type of product. The Flint Glass Workers worked with flint glass (a heavy, brilliant crystal-like glass, composed of lead potash and sand)[14] while the Glass Bottle Blowers worked with ordinary green glass. Flint glass was then made in covered pots, whereas green glass could be satisfactorily produced in open pots. Since open-pot production cost less than closed, most jars and bottles were green glass. Flint glass, on the other hand, was almost always used in making pressed ware as well as high-grade containers such as prescription bottles.

With the coming in the 1890's of the continuous tank, which could make good quality flint glass, differences between the trades became obscured. Green glass workers, with lower price lists than the "Flints" for similar articles, won control of the entire unionized bottle and jar production, though not without serious interunion strife. The change in name of the Bottle Blowers' Association symbolized these events. Attempts in 1896 and 1897 to amalgamate the Association, the Flint Glass Workers' Union and District Assembly 300 of the Knights of Labor (the window glass workers), so as to check the spread of nonunionism throughout the entire glass industry, failed because of the opposition of certain GBBA leaders. The Bottle Blowers' Association took over some of the pressers and other flint workers, and in 1901 the entire prescription bottle department of some twenty-one hundred members withdrew from the Flint Glass Workers' Union and joined its rival.

In 1903 the Flints withdrew from the AF of L as a result of a decision by the Federation's Executive Council favoring the Bottle Blowers. Not until 1912 was harmony re-established when the two unions agreed upon clearly defined jurisdictions. The Glass Bottle Blowers' Association was given exclusive rights over bottles and jars, while the Flint Glass Workers' Union was granted sole jurisdiction over all pressed and blown ware outside of containers, in addition to the occupations of mold maker and mold repairer.[15]

14. Powdered flints happened to be used at first instead of sand, hence the name.
15. See George E. Barnett, *Chapters on Machinery and Labor,* Harvard University Press, Cambridge, 1926, pp. 72-73.

Employers' Organizations

Employers' organizations in the glass industry developed in response to union demands for equalized wage lists and standardized working conditions. Although single employers opposed unionism, employer organizations were formed to bargain rather than to fight. Employers in the container industry were first loosely united on a sectional basis to deal with the Eastern and Western Leagues of green glass bottle blowers. Manufacturers in the two areas were antagonistic to each other and unwilling to bargain on a national basis; but with the amalgamation of the unions and the GBBA's insistence on a national scale, the National Glass Vial and Bottle Manufacturers Association was formed.[16] This organization conferred with the union until 1924 when it dissolved voluntarily after Attorney-General Daugherty charged that it was a price-fixing agency in violation of the Sherman Anti-Trust Act. There was no question of the legality of its collective bargaining, but the plea of union officials that the Manufacturers Association should be reformed was not heeded. Since then, the employers in the container industry have cooperated informally in their negotiations with the unions. In 1937 they set up a labor committee of twelve, which meets monthly to discuss labor problems. At present a strong movement exists for a more formal association in the container industry.

In the pressed and blown ware industry, collective bargaining was carried on before 1888 with employers singly or in informal groups. The first association, the Associated Manufacturers of Pressed Glassware, grew out of a strike settlement in that year in the Pittsburgh district. This organization met with the Flint Union until 1893 when the annual wage conference failed to agree. The largest concern, the United States Glass Company, locked out its workers in an effort to break certain of the union's controls, but the other companies formed another association and met most of the union's terms.

The National Association of Manufacturers of Pressed and Blown Glassware, as the new group was named, is still in exist-

---

16. Prior to 1902 the covered-pot manufacturers met separately with the union but in that year they were admitted to the Association.

ence. In October 1939, it comprised forty-seven glassware and glass mold manufacturers, who employed sixteen thousand of the AFGWU's members.[17] Its chief duties are to negotiate annual wage scales, adopt and interpret factory rules and working conditions and act as a clearing house for its members in matters of employment and the interpretation and application of labor laws. Its own and the national union officers mediate disputes between management and labor in the plants of member-employers. Two other trade organizations in the flint glass and container industries, the American Glassware Association and the Glass Container Association of America, do not engage in collective bargaining.

Collective Bargaining in the Container Industry

Advent of the machine brought the union tremendous problems of adjustment and shifted the scales of bargaining power to management's side. But the basic pattern of collective bargaining as it was set up in the days of the skilled craftsmen was modified, not radically changed. The bottle makers' first national wage conference was held in 1890 after what the union calls the "great lockout of 1889–1890." Although agreements could not be reached in 1891, 1894, 1906, 1909 and 1921, conferences were held each year without a break. When no new agreement was made, it was customary to continue the old one. However, the 1921 disagreement over a wage reduction came so close to destroying the conference system that union leaders decided not to run the risk again and some agreement has invariably been worked out since then.

17. For a while the prescription bottle manufacturers and the lamp chimney manufacturers held separate conferences with the AFGWU. The Association, however, became the sole organization to deal with the union after it had assumed the negotiating function for the chimney manufacturers in 1909; the prescription department had transferred to the jurisdiction of the GBBA in 1901. Following the 1912 agreement in which the GBBA surrendered to the AFGWU jurisdiction over all mold makers and repairers and certain machine press workers in container plants, it was found necessary for the AFGWU to meet separately with the container manufacturers for these men. From the beginning a few union manufacturers have remained outside of the Association for financial or personal reasons, but they accept the general scale and rules agreed to by the conference. David A. McCabe, *Trade Agreements in the Flint Glass Industry*, typewritten report to the U. S. Commission on Industrial Relations, December 15, 1914. Available at University of Wisconsin Library.

Before 1899 the conferences were held annually, either in July or August, several weeks after the union and the employers' association had held their conventions.[18] But since wages were paid by the piece and each type of bottle had to receive a price, a preliminary conference was held in May to submit demands and settle questions over which there was no disagreement. Debatable matters could then be rediscussed at conventions and finally settled at the main conference. This expensive procedure was justified only by the time saved for discussion of major issues. Because automatic machine operators are paid on an hourly basis, the need for the preliminary conference passed with the extension of the machine and in 1928 it was abandoned for the few hand plants as well.

Introduction of bottle-making machines complicated the conference system. For many years old and new methods of production were carried on side by side, and each required separate collective bargaining. Instead, therefore, of a single conference, the Atlantic City meetings were a series of conferences—the handblown (glass from tanks and covered-pot ware), the stopper-grinding, the semiautomatic machine (narrow-mouth and wide-mouth ware), and the automatic feed and flow—at each of which an agreement was drawn up.

At present only the automatic feed and flow meeting involves any considerable number of workers and manufacturers. Although representatives of the Owens-Illinois Glass Company attend the Atlantic City discussions, a separate conference is held annually with that company in Columbus, Ohio. Some union members have protested against this, but the corporation insists that its Owens machines are sufficiently different from other bottle-making models (like the Lynch and the Hartford-Empire) and so important in the industry as to warrant exception. This separate

18. By 1925 the union was holding its conventions every two years. Recently, officials of the GBBA have discussed the possibility of also holding the wage conference every two years to coincide with their biennial convention, thus permitting the convention to consider the management proposals and to debate proposals from all of the branches. At present in the nonconvention year the burden is placed on the national officers. For financial reasons no conventions were called in the years from 1929 to 1934 but the wage conferences were not interrupted.

conference was first held in 1915 with the American Bottle Company when the Owens was still the only completely automatic machine in the field. It was continued after the American Bottle Company was absorbed by the Owens Bottle Company in 1927 and after the latter merged with the Illinois Glass Company two years later.

In 1937 the GBBA asked the manufacturers to negotiate a uniform agreement for miscellaneous workers. Meetings were held at Atlantic City and Columbus without success. A difference of ten cents an hour in the minimum wage was one obstacle, but the main stumbling block was the employers' refusal to sanction the closed shop, although virtually every local contract provided for it. As a result, collective bargaining for the miscellaneous workers has continued on a company rather than an industry basis, though an industry-wide agreement is likely to come soon.

Collective Bargaining in Flint Glass

The first attempt at a national scale for pressed and blown ware (flint glass) was made in the fall of 1887. Disagreement over wages and an unlimited piece-work system proposed by the employers led to the closing of thirty-eight plants—chiefly tableware —from January 2 to April 28, 1888. As a result, uniform wage lists were established in the press ware, mold, and shade departments, and procedure for settlement of grievances was formally outlined. The following year annual collective bargaining conferences of the departments began.[19] Because a large number of different agreements must be negotiated, wage conferences of the "Flints" last several weeks, whereas container meetings end in

19. In addition to the annual wage conferences, there were formerly a variety of joint meetings during the year. For example, in 1913–1914 there were ten "representative" meetings at which rules and wage lists were negotiated for a small number of plants making a certain line of ware; seven "disputes" meetings at which disputes that could not be settled locally were adjusted instead of being appealed to the main conference; two conferences to consider the "summer stop" for the coming year; and three "special" conferences to consider agreements made at the wage conference which were received in the trade with dissatisfaction. (McCabe, *op. cit.*) Within recent years these extra joint meetings have been reduced in number, except in the case of the miscellaneous department.

about one week. Occasionally some discussions have continued beyond Labor Day when the new agreement normally begins [20] and final determinations have been made retroactive.

In contrast to the Bottle Association, the Flint Union has been successful in placing its miscellaneous workers on the same bargaining basis as machine operators and skilled craftsmen. Union representatives and employers met in Pittsburgh on January 5, 1937, and negotiated an industry-wide agreement for miscellaneous workers. Since then conferences have been held each year at Atlantic City together with the other departments.

From 1888 to the middle nineties preliminary wage conferences were held annually in most departments of the pressed and blown ware industry. In 1897, however, the national president of the Flint Glass Workers' Union recommended giving them up because results did not warrant the expense. After 1902, with one brief exception, no preliminary conferences have been held. Before each union convention, every local sends to the AFGWU office the demands it wishes negotiated. These are discussed at the convention by the entire body if the question is general, and by the representatives of the department if it is of narrower scope. Meeting at the headquarters of their national association, the manufacturers do the same. The union and management proposals must be exchanged at least sixty days before the Atlantic City conference to be thoroughly examined before beginning negotiations.

d. THE AGREEMENTS AND THEIR ENFORCEMENT

Agreements covering the automatic machine divisions in both the flint and container industries are much less detailed than in the old hand or semiautomatic machine divisions. The wages and regulations list for the press ware department, for example, fills fifty-nine pages, whereas the automatic feed and flow bottle agreements need less than ten.[21] Nevertheless, despite the trend toward

20. The agreements in the container departments commence on September 1. Traditionally the glass industry has figured September 1 as the beginning of the new season.
21. This difference is easily explained: (1) the functions of the machine operator are relatively simple so that there is no longer need of the many technical rules

simplification, most agreements (the main exceptions being the local miscellaneous contracts in the container industry) are legislative rather than administrative. The legislative type of contract is one which contains most of the rules of procedure and policy, leaving little to the discretion of the parties within the plants. The administrative contract, on the other hand, is brief and general in nature, leaving the specific rules to be determined by the local parties.

All decisions of joint conferences, as recorded in the minutes, are integral parts of the agreements even though they may not be completely detailed in the little rules booklets distributed through the industry. Invariably a clause [22] declares that no rule or changes may be made outside of the annual conference, and that in the plant no step contrary to the rules may be taken. Local management and local union officials are left little discretion, except in problems obviously local or specifically turned over to them by the conference. For example, container manufacturers have rejected both seniority and the checkoff as national rules, with the understanding that employers may make individual arrangements if they wish. In an emergency, an employer usually gets a temporary suspension of the rules, unless the union officers are suspicious of his objective.

Given capable negotiators and the will to negotiate, success of the joint conference system rests upon (1) the freedom granted the representatives in negotiation by their constituents and (2) the ability of these representatives to insure enforcement of the rules they have made. In both cases the position of the unions has been the controlling factor. For in spite of their willingness to cooperate with one another, whether in formal association or in informal joint action, the employers are not a complete unit. Nothing except union strength prevents a corporation from repudiating the conference agreement or from violating its provi-

(unintelligible to the outsider) once required to safeguard the skilled glass worker from exploitation and to provide a measure of equality between union members of varying ability; (2) the machine eliminated the apprenticeship system, the regulation of which required extensive provisions in the agreements; (3) the machine permitted the substitution of the hourly wage for the complex piece-wage lists.

22. In the case of the Flint Union, only since July 1922.

sions. Employer associations, past and present, have not wished to devise any system of discipline, such as fines, over their membership. Nor have threats and expulsion been wholly effective.

The unions, on the other hand, have maintained a strong and centralized discipline over their members and relentlessly fought employers who occasionally tried to undermine the standards of the joint conferences. In 1910 and again in 1919, for example, when GBBA locals in San Francisco struck in protest against conference agreements on wages, the national officers immediately suspended the branches and stood ready to furnish men to work the plants until the strikers yielded. In 1908, when a container manufacturer withdrew from the conference, the union fought him for three years until he submitted.

Union Representatives' Power to Negotiate

Some employers in the pressed and blown ware industry complained, however, that although the management committee had complete authority in negotiation, the union conferees had to submit all important matters, such as wages and hours, to a membership referendum. Few conference decisions were reversed in this way, yet employers contended that the referendum created uncertainty and inconvenience. The national officers of the union also urged the change so that conferees could bargain more effectively, but the feeling for departmental autonomy was too strong. In March 1904 the Executive Committee of the National Association of Manufacturers of Pressed and Blown Glassware notified the AFGWU that after July 1904 they would not negotiate unless labor delegates had full power to settle the wage list. The threat was not carried out, but in 1906 union officers prevailed upon all the departments except the press, paste mold, and shade to give conferees more power. Since then, most union departments have gradually agreed to delegate full powers to their representatives. Some departments grant final powers in all cases to the conferees while others still except proposals for a *general* increase or reduction in wages or change in working conditions. Departments which still retain the referendum are being strongly influenced to make the change. The GBBA has avoided this problem because almost from the start of the conference system its representatives were given a free hand in negotiation.

Importance of the Human Factor

Apart from more forceful tactics, the unions and employers have found that responsibility in negotiation and compliance with agreements, particularly among the recently organized, have improved when the conferences are attended by more delegates on both sides. Formerly, at all but the most important conferences, it was customary for the employers to be represented by their small executive committees plus three or four officials, and for unions to send to Atlantic City a few delegates from each department to help the national officers. Any employer had the right to attend and, if he wished, to vote, except on a dispute directly affecting him; but few took advantage of this. In 1939, however, the automatic bottle machine conferences included employer and worker representatives from eighteen of the most important companies; a departmental conference of the pressed and blown ware industry, like the caster place or tumbler, had representatives from fifteen.

The top leadership, of both union and management, has been decisive in achieving stability and peace. Since 1896, six years after nation-wide bargaining began in the container industry, there have been only three GBBA presidents. Except for three years, when there were two presidents, the AFGWU has had only four presidents since 1884. The recently retired chairman of the National Association of Manufacturers of Pressed and Blown Glassware served for more than thirty years. This long-term leadership has meant experience and mutual understanding on both sides of the bargaining table, a restraining hand on new and impetuous representatives, trust in the word and intent of the other party, an understanding of the rules of the game and a willingness to abide by them.

e. SETTLEMENT OF GRIEVANCES

Negotiation of policy is primarily on a national level; adjustment of grievances is basically a local problem. Only complaints which cannot be settled elsewhere are discussed at the joint wage conferences.

Star Island Agreement in Flint Glass

The formula for adjustment in the pressed and blown ware industry was worked out in an agreement drawn up at Star Island, Michigan, in July 1903 at a special conference of the Flint Glass Workers' Union and the employers' association. Actually, the same principles were enunciated in the settlement of the 1888 dispute, but they were universally disregarded and local cessations occurred almost weekly. After much employer protest, the Star Island meeting was held. In the same year the union convention adopted its president's recommendation that any local union or factory committee which violated the strike law should be either fined $100, suspended or expelled. So effective were these measures that during the next ten years only six unauthorized local stoppages of more than a day's duration were reported by the secretary of the employers' association. The Star Island agreement calls for attempts to settle disputes through the following steps: (1) the employee and his foreman, (2) the union business committee and the department head, (3) the business committee and the plant superintendent, (4) a local union committee and the plant superintendent and his superior, (5) the national president of the AFGWU or his representative and the proper officials of the company, and (6) the national joint conference whose decision is final and binding. The executive secretary of the employers' association also plays an active role in step five and preceding the conference. Pending discussion and final decision, working conditions are to remain unchanged, and there is to be no lockout or strike. The AFGWU agrees to help the manufacturers to hire competent workmen for the places of employees who refuse to abide by the rulings. If wages are involved, the decision is usually made retroactive to the date of complaint, unless the complainant can be shown as partly at fault.

There are no statistics showing the frequency of grievances or the levels at which they are adjusted. But leaders on both sides are satisfied that the procedure not only lessens strife but also diminishes the number of serious complaints. In recent years the newly organized workers and employers have caused the most difficulty. National officials frequently found it wise to intercede at an early stage in a dispute, but it is recognized that traditions of fifty years cannot be absorbed in two or three.

Procedure in the Container Industry

Although the container industry has no "Star Island Agreement," its settlement of disputes and grievances is much the same. The chief, and a unique difference since 1902,[23] is that complaints not adjusted within a plant are referred to the president of the Bottle Blowers' Association, whose decision is binding unless overruled by the joint conference. One reason for this procedure, which was suggested by the employers, was that most appeal cases at the time involved piece rates. The president was not only a rate expert and greatly respected throughout the industry, but was also unlikely to fix a rate out of line with other plants. He assumed the responsibility with considerable caution, but the method proved notably successful. Between 1902 and 1925 only about 120 of the president's decisions were appealed to the joint conference and of those only 29 were reversed. Since 1925 there have been no reversals. While records are not available, it is known that the cases appealed to the conference are but a small proportion of the number decided by the president.

f. PROBLEMS

(1). *Equalization of Wage Rates*

The major question of the early years of the joint conference system was the equalization of wage rates. In 1878, for example, the thirteen tableware factories of the Pittsburgh area had thirteen different wage lists; after a nine months' strike, a single list was drawn up. In 1883 a ten months' strike in the Ohio Valley glass

---

23. Before 1902 disagreements which could not be adjusted in the plant were left first to the president of the union and the chairman of the manufacturers' committee, then to a joint committee of six, and finally to an outsider whose decision was final. It was never found necessary to resort to an arbitrator.

houses resulted in equalization with Pittsburgh rates and conditions. National joint conferences in both industries were concerned with extending the uniformity of wage lists and breaking down sectional claims for preferential treatment. By 1900 the principle of uniform wage rates was firmly established. Nonunionism is still, in some departments, a threat to that principle. Introduction of machines against which hand methods had to compete brought serious complications. But the union employers recognized in the principle a stabilizing factor which would limit cutthroat competition. And unions sponsored it because it equalized competitive conditions among the workers as well. In some industries, like bituminous coal, uniformity of wage rates on a national scale has proved impracticable but it has been possible in glass because few plants are so situated in terms of market, raw materials, fuel and labor as to operate with substantial handicaps.

(2). *Basis of Wage Payment*

Closely allied to wage rate equalization was the basis of wage payment. A vital issue in the Ohio Valley strike was the fact that the Pittsburgh glass companies paid on a straight piece-work basis, whereas the Ohio concerns paid by the "move" on a "limited turn" basis. The "move" referred to the specified number of an article which the average worker was expected to produce in a turn or half-day shift. Under the "limited turn," an employee, regardless of his speed and efficiency, was allowed to produce no more than the "move" during the turn. The rest of the time he was idle in the plant. Employers resented this system because it was costly and they accused the unions of restricting output; but the unions held it to be the fairest way of dividing available work and of preventing unemployment.

Competition from nonunion and newly mechanized plants, whether union or not, slowly forced labor to abandon the "limited turn" system for payment by either the "move" on an "unlimited turn" basis, or by unlimited piece work. Both systems allowed a man to produce as much as he could within the turn; the "unlimited turn" guarantees him the "move" whether he produces it or not, while under unlimited piece work he is paid only for what he makes.

In departments where hand or semiautomatic methods of production are still dominant, as they are particularly in the pressed and blown ware industry, the "move" system on an "unlimited turn" basis or the piece-work system buttressed by a minimum wage prevails and is unlikely to be altered soon. In the departments using automatic machinery, notably in the container industry, payment by the piece or move has been replaced by the hourly wage, frequently supplemented by a bonus. No longer are the tables at joint conferences of these departments strewn with bottles and jars, while the conferees debate the wage rate for each "move" or the number of articles to be produced in every "move." Most miscellaneous workers are also paid by the hour, and the annual conferences are concerned only with negotiating a minimum hourly rate for each of the many occupations.

(3). *The "Summer Stop" Rule*

Another important problem troubled joint conferences of the early period: the "summer stop" rule required all union glass blowers to discontinue work from July 1 to September 1. The unions contended that health demanded this rest. But since nonunion blowers labored through the summer heat without apparent ill effects, this contention cannot be accepted as the basic reason. More probably, as a study of the United States Commissioner of Labor in 1904 showed, the main object was to give work to a larger number of union members during the remaining months of the industry's year. Like the "limited turn," this form of restriction was broken down by the competition of nonunion plants and by machine techniques. During the 1893 depression, the United States Glass Company demanded of the AFGWU removal of the "summer stop" rule and the limit on "moves" on tumblers, jellies and beer mugs in the press ware department. When the demand was rejected, the company locked out 1,344 men. The lockout lasted nearly four years, cost the union about $1.2 million in benefit payments and deprived the members of about $3 million in wages. Although it ended with a raise in wage rates and abolition of restrictive rules, the company did not return to the conference system until 1913. So that union manufacturers could meet the competition of the United States Glass Company and other nonunion establishments, the union departments were forced to relax their restrictive rules. However, as late as 1918, the bottle blowers throughout the industry were out one month each summer.

The substitute for the "summer stop" in the container and flint glass industries has been for many years simply an optional two weeks' vacation, without pay. The agreement usually provides that a worker may take this vacation any time he wishes, provided production is not disturbed and not more than 15-25 per cent of the regular employees are already on vacation leave. Since 1933 the demand for vacations with pay has been strong. Several of the largest glass corporations recently established paid vacation plans, and this goal of the unions, in spite of management refusals on grounds of expense, may soon be fully realized.

(4). *Apprenticeship*

Since one of their main objects is to limit the labor supply, it was natural for the national unions to be concerned with apprentices. The Eastern League of green glass bottle blowers was almost destroyed because employers could fill their plants with apprentices and force working standards down. The ratio of apprentices to skilled craftsmen, as well as term of service, was argued heatedly. During the 1893 depression, union employers saw the labor point of view and agreed temporarily to ask for no new apprentices until business improved. A brief dispute arose when automatic machines were introduced, but thereafter the apprentice and child labor problem was of slight consequence. In departments where apprenticeship is still a requirement, regulation is recognized and causes no difficulty.

(5). *Union Policies Relative to the Machine*

Although the pattern of collective bargaining remained the same, the mechanical revolution changed the material out of which the pattern was woven. The joint conference spirit and procedure were not basically altered, but the subject matter was radically affected. Union rules limiting production were eliminated [24] and other rules, owing to simplification of jobs, became less complex. The most notable feature was the ability of the union leaders to hold their organizations intact in spite of the widespread dislocations. Leaders of window glass unions pursued a different type of policy and their unions collapsed.

Leaders of the container and flint glass unions were always more farsighted than their following. When the Owens bottle machine was introduced in 1904, President Dennis Hayes of the GBBA warned that old methods were doomed and that the union must adapt itself to the new trend rather than fight it. Although many union members rejected this counsel and refused to work on the machines until years afterwards, a policy of adaptation to the machine was formulated by 1909. Union efforts were helped by the decision of the Owens patent owners not to sell but to lease the machine on a royalty basis to other manufacturers, who were required to specialize in certain lines of bottles. This policy, added to the heavy expenses of installing the apparatus, permitted the plants using semiautomatic machines to continue and even expand their operations.[25] In 1917 the semiautomatic machines were equipped with automatic feeders which eliminated the last of the skilled workers. But between 1904 and 1917 the union had time to make an adjustment, although in spite of a 50 per cent increase in the demand for the product, the number of skilled glass bottle workers fell from eight thousand to about four thousand.

The union leaders attacked the problem from three angles. First, they tried strenuously to keep the hand and semiautomatic plants on a competitive level with the Owens plants. In 1909 they accepted a 20 per cent wage cut, the first since 1894, and three years later they agreed to another 20 per cent decrease. In 1911

24. The container agreements specifically give management the right to determine the number of men to a machine.
25. George E. Barnett has computed that the number of semiautomatic machines in use grew from 20 in 1897 to 250 in 1905. From 1904 to 1917, 200 Owens automatic machines were installed, but the number of semiautomatic machines continued to increase to 428. *Op. cit.*, pp. 69, 89, 92.

the old two-shift system of eight and a half hours a shift was changed to three eight-hour shifts, thus increasing production by seven hours a day and reducing the manufacturers' overhead cost. Next, they sought to retain as many jobs for their members as possible. Under the rules, an apprentice served fifty months of working time (about five years in all) for which he was paid one half the piece price for journeymen. It was recognized, however, that after a year's service the apprentice turned out almost as much ware as a journeyman and was therefore profitable to the employer.[26] The usual apprentice allowance had been one to fifteen journeymen but now the union asked employers to take no new apprentices. This request was agreed to in return for wage decreases. In 1913 the union demanded a radical change in the apprenticeship rule—a forty-month working term and pay equal to 75 per cent of the journeyman's piece price. This left the employer very little advantage in taking on apprentices. At the same time the unions pressed for the placement of old glass craftsmen as attendants, first on the semiautomatic machines and later on the automatics, instead of "green hands." Not until the 1920's were the automatic machine employers completely convinced of the validity of the union argument.

Finally, the union leaders took steps to preserve the organization itself. In 1912, as already noted, the jurisdictional dispute with the Flint Glass Workers ended. In 1914, after President Hayes of the Bottle Blowers' Association had informed his membership that complete reorganization of the industry was essential, they requested and received an industrial union charter from the American Federation of Labor. This charter extended GBBA jurisdiction to all glass bottle workers—miscellaneous employees and semiskilled machine operators as well as craftsmen.

The next year the American Bottle Company, one of the major manufacturers in the Owens group, accepted unionization of its plants. An attempt to draw the packers and others of the miscellaneous group into the joint conference scheme failed, but union-

26. *Report of the Industrial Commission on the Relations and Conditions of Capital and Labor Employed in Manufactures and General Business*, Washington, 1901, Vol. VII, p. 110.

ization of machine operators assured continuance of collective bargaining in the industry. In 1918 the first conference of feed and flow plants was held. The next year the Hartford-Fairmont Corporation people (later the Hartford-Empire Corporation), who controlled the automatic glass feeding patents, agreed that when they leased or sold a machine they would ask their client to cooperate with the union. The Eighteenth Amendment and the refusal of such large corporations as Owens-Illinois and Hazel-Atlas to recognize the union, left the Glass Bottle Blowers' Association in a weak position during the 1920's. But by 1926 the problems of the technological revolution had been met, insofar as the union could meet them.

The AFGWU was not as completely or as swiftly affected by technological change as its sister union. But the blown ware departments, producing such articles as electric light bulbs, tumblers and glass tubing, have been as highly mechanized as the container industry for the past two decades. It is noteworthy that the national officers of the Flint Workers' Union consistently opposed blindly restrictive rules [27] as early as the beginning of the century and that supporters of the rules were largely the local officers and members of the departments, who worked on the job and consequently were less able to take a long-time view. In general, after an initial period of restriction,[28] the union's problem has been met by adaptation rather than blind hostility, except in the case of a few departments, notably the lamp chimney.

Before 1907 the lamp chimney department was the largest in the Flint Workers' Union and the most independent. Then it steadily lost strength until by 1917 it was down from 1,603 to 1,025 members and in 1930 it could report only 105 of its 375 members employed at the trade. At the 1917 convention the international president of the union strongly attacked the department for its policies. He pointed out that it kept a six-week "summer stop" while all others had agreed to a two-week stop. He strongly recommended that the hand division abandon the limited-turn

27. The word blindly is used advisedly. Most rules in a labor ‿agreement are restrictive upon the employer, but it does not follow that they are thereby harmful or not well founded.
28. See pp. 705-706.

system of wage payment so that the hand plants could compete better with the machine plants. He noted that from 1904 to 1916 the department had defeated by referendum sixteen out of thirty-seven questions which had been negotiated at the annual wage conferences. In the 1930 convention the union president declared that with only two out of ten important lamp chimney plants unionized, a wage cut was vital to the union's existence. Yet the members of the department still refused to grant full powers to their conferees at the annual wage conference and rejected by referendum vote the conference agreement allowing for an increase in the size of the move. Of course, a tremendous problem was the decline in the chimney market caused by the growth of the electric light, but there can be no doubt that had the department taken the advice of the national officers, what remained of the industry (both in the hand and machine plants) would have been retained by the union.

(6). *Situation of the Newly Organized Workers*

In recent years the most important collective bargaining problem in the two industries has been absorption of the miscellaneous workers. Machine operators and skilled craftsmen continue to bring up grievances before management, and negotiators at the joint conferences hold strenuous debates,[29] but the lines of action have been laid down during the past fifty years. The miscellaneous workers, however, have struggled with the subtle processes of collective bargaining for little more than three years. The basic factors involved are: (1) except for a brief period (1914 to 1918) neither unions nor manufacturers were eager to see the miscellaneous workers organized; (2) unionization of these workers resulted from outside pressure—stimulus toward self-organization generated by the NRA and the Wagner Act and the campaign of the CIO Federation of Flat Glass Workers' Union; (3) the miscellaneous workers had little of the tradition and loyalty that tied the old unionists to the glass industry; (4) they

---

29. Gains by the GBBA at recent conferences include, for example, (1) a guarantee of three hours' work or pay to men ordered to report for work, (2) inclusion of the "machine upkeep men" in the agreement.

outnumbered the machine operators and skilled craftsmen more than five to one.

The problem has been twofold. Union leaders have had to safeguard their positions because the newcomers, if unified, could easily outvote them. Also they have had to educate a young and energetic group of workers, impressed by the rapid gains of new unions in other mass production industries, to appreciate the conservative nature and practices of the old unionism. A partial solution was for the Bottle Blowers' Association to group its miscellaneous workers in separate plant locals, similar to those of the operators. Dues for miscellaneous members are $1.00 a month for men and $.50 a month for women, as compared to $2.00 per month for the better paid operators. Representation and voting at the union's biennial convention are based on dues payment so that an operator's branch gets twice as many votes as a miscellaneous branch of the same number of men. Nevertheless, the miscellaneous workers have a substantial voting majority. But at the 1938 convention, the officers of the GBBA won their full support and appear, at least temporarily, to have satisfied the more aggressive critics.

The AFGWU has organized its miscellaneous workers as a separate department, which unlike the other departments of the union holds a convention of its own under the supervision of the national officers. This department sends to the Flint Glass Workers' convention only sixteen delegates with one vote each, in contrast to the 190 votes the other departments commanded at the 1939 convention. The old leadership has insisted that the miscellaneous workers cannot expect full privileges without a period of transition. With the CIO alert and willing to take them over, the miscellaneous group has vigorously demanded a total representation and vote equal to the other departments combined. It is probable that such a solution will be worked out. The old organization will not tolerate subordination to a group which it unionized, but a large and aggressive majority, even if inexperienced, cannot be denied an active role for long.

Although the miscellaneous workers of the AFGWU have a national agreement while those of the GBBA have not reached this goal, the gains and difficulties of both unions are similar. The principles of the Star Island Agreement have not stopped impulsive local leaders from calling "sitdowns" or walkouts when management refused to yield on complaints. Leaders of the national organizations, however, have warned of the dangers in these tactics, and few disputes have not been settled peaceably. In striking contrast to other new unions of the mass production industries, dues collection is only a slight problem; active members have been free to concentrate on learning the art of negotiation. The closed or preferential shop is almost universally in effect and the checkoff is common. In many plants without checkoffs, management impresses upon delinquents the advisability of paying their dues.

(7). *Seniority*

The main source of local difficulty has been seniority, particularly in regard to promotions. Old unionists do not favor its use either for promotions or layoffs. One reason is that the closed shop has been so long in existence, seniority has been unnecessary to combat employer discrimination against men for organization activity. Another reason is that glass plants are usually in small towns where there is no other employment, and it was felt that all should share alike in slack times. Furthermore, it was felt that when layoffs were necessary, the employer should keep the men he thought were best, provided he did not undermine the union.

It was agreed at the 1919 conferences of the flint glass industry that when a permanent reduction of forces appeared necessary, management had the right to dismiss whatever employees it desired after a week's notice with the understanding that if the forces were subsequently increased, preference would be given the men laid off, if they were competent to do the work. When there was a temporary slack in work, however, time was to be divided equally and no one discharged. Despite this precedent, seniority was so popularized throughout the country during the thirties that many glass corporations voluntarily granted it in some form to the miscellaneous workers, even before they had been unionized. The result was that the miscellaneous local branches have vigorously fought for extension of seniority. Employers have objected that promotions and layoffs based on seniority without regard for ability are costly and interfere with management's rights. In general, therefore, seniority is applied departmentally, with considerable leeway for exceptions. At the flint glass industry's miscellaneous joint conference employers refused to incorporate any seniority clause in the 1939 agreement.

In recently unionized plants employers have the same difficulties of adjustment to collective bargaining as their employees. It was not easy for many of them to accept curtailment of authority over their workers. In the flint glass industry, the officials of the employers' association have been almost as active as the national union leaders in advising their members upon proper tactics when bargaining with labor organizations. While the employers are relatively few and easily reached, the association has a task requiring great diplomacy, since it lacks the control which the union holds over its members.

g. RESULTS OF COLLECTIVE BARGAINING

No one has seriously questioned the social and economic benefits of unionism to employees of the container and flint glass industries. The Glass Container Association of America reported that factory employees in container plants averaged 38.7 hours of work a week in 1939, compared to 50.1 hours in 1929. The average weekly wage in 1939 was $27.48; in 1929 it was $25.02. The AFGWU has estimated that its skilled members earned an average of over $30 a week in every year except one during the 1920's, and while earnings slumped badly during the depression, they reached an average of $34.83 a week during 1938. Similarly the miscellaneous workers have benefited; those in the handmade glassware plants, for example, averaged $18 a week in 1937, or about 50 per cent more than in 1929.

Experienced employers agree with union leaders that unionism and collective bargaining in their more than fifty years of trial have helped the industry. They make the following claims: (1) the unions have helped to stabilize economic conditions by equalizing wages and thus limiting price competition, and by displaying a readiness to adjust wages downward when serious depressions occurred; (2) union officials have cooperated actively and effectively with employers in combating legislation injurious to the container and flint glass industries and in supporting movements of economic and political value to them; (3) collective bargaining has prevented serious strife between employers and workers during a period when labor disputes were common in American industry.

Unions and Price Stability

Without involved calculations, the first claim is least susceptible to specific proof because labor cost is only one of many in determination of prices and profits. Some general observations, however, may be made. Among smaller companies, particularly in the pressed ware industry, where capital investment is relatively low and wages form a correspondingly high proportion of costs, the unions have had a valuable policing function preventing price warfare. This was apparent in the period between the 1929 business crash and the NRA, when unionism was at lowest ebb, when wage agreements were widely ignored, and when price competition ran to disastrous extremes. Among the large companies union influence on economic issues appears to have been slight. Until the New Deal, companies like Owens-Illinois, Hazel-Atlas, and Ball Brothers had refused to accept unionism, and the labor organizations were powerless to force them. How much they were affected by union scales is difficult to say, and the importance of the unions' effect on cost stabilization must not be stressed too strongly.

On the other hand, the unions have escaped for many years the charge of being responsible for uneconomic and unsound cost rigidity. This has been true of the container union at least since 1909 and of the flint union (except for a few departments) for almost as long. In the depression years of 1921 and 1932, wage reductions of from 10 to 20 per cent were accepted to help the companies meet reduced demand. The unions do not like wage cuts. They took them only when the need for them was unquestioned and subject to the understanding that restoration and additional advances would be made as soon as possible. As a result of this policy, minimum wages for operators on the automatic bottle machines rose from 55 cents an hour in 1921 to 90 cents in 1939. The press ware department had two wage reductions after 1901 and eleven increases, although the postwar net gain was only 14 per cent.

The difficulties of wage regulation by unions are currently illustrated in the handmade tumbler and stemware department, a small division of the flint glass industry. Because of European competition before the outbreak of the present war in 1939, American companies were forced to lay off a number of their skilled workmen. Rather than go on relief rolls, these men used their last savings to form some ten small cooperative establishments in West Virginia. Since their sole aim was to earn a living, the owners of these cooperatives sold below market price. As a result at the 1939 joint conference in Atlantic City, three manufacturers demanded a reduction in wages. When this was refused, they withdrew from the negotiations. At this writing, two are operating nonunion and the third is involved in a strike. The miscellaneous workers of two of the cooperatives are also on strike for the union scale and the ex-union proprietors are using their own wives and children as strikebreakers.

Such a situation could not occur in the machine departments where the capital investment is large, but the general problem facing the unions on the wage issue is obvious. Fortunately for the unions, employers in the glass industry seem strongly disinclined to strain competition. The flint glass policy, for example, is that an employer avoids not only undercutting the national wage scale but also paying above it. Both the union and the employers frown upon special advantages granted in one place because of the pressure which would follow everywhere else.

Unions Help Employers in Lobbying

Upon legislation affecting the glass industry, unions and employers have cooperated closely. For several decades, joint efforts were made to persuade Congress and the State Department to raise the tariffs on glass products against competition from Belgium and Czechoslovakia. Union and management leaders have testified at numerous tariff hearings and submitted many briefs, but their united effort failed to get foreign products excluded. The GBBA, to whom Prohibition meant a 40 per cent decrease in membership, also fought energetically for repeal of the Eighteenth Amendment.

In the states, union officials have proved expert lobbyists, collaborating with employer representatives to promote desired local legislation and to fight hostile bills. In recent years, for example, the glass container industry has had intense competition from tin cans for beer and paper containers for milk. When a number of states passed laws requiring a deposit of two cents on every glass beer bottle, union leaders made active protest to liquor commissions. When a lightweight beer bottle was manufactured so cheaply that it could be discarded after use, GBBA officials revisited state capitols for repeal of the deposit regulation and called upon brewers to reject the can. They have also helped employers to sell to the public the idea that glass containers for preserved food are preferable to cans because the consumer may see the product she is purchasing. For this cooperation, the unions have won considerable praise and good will from glass manufacturers.

Collective Bargaining Has Prevented Strikes

That collective bargaining has prevented much strife in the industry is proved by the record. No large-scale labor dispute has occurred in the container industry since 1890, or in flint glass since 1895. In a brief submitted December 5, 1938 to the Temporary National Economic Committee, the Glass Container Association of America reported that since 1929 strikes not authorized by the GBBA had closed two plants for one week and an authorized strike had closed one plant for approximately three days. The flint glass industry's record is much the same. A few stoppages have occurred in violation or in enforcement of the joint conference agreements, but these were generally short-lived.

A number of strikes outside of the conference system have been invariably due to the manufacturers' refusal to recognize unionism. Among the more important was the unsuccessful Corning strike of 1889. This corporation remains the most powerful large concern not engaging in collective bargaining. There is a strong possibility that one of its affiliates, the MacBeth-Evans plant at Charleroi, Pennsylvania, may soon succumb, not to either the GBBA or the AFGWU, but to the aggressive Federation of Flat Glass Workers. More recent disputes include a fourteen months' strike by the AFGWU at all the mold shops of the Hazel-Atlas Glass Company in 1927-1928, an unsuccessful CIO strike in 1936 at the Toledo closure plant of the Owens-Illinois Company where the GBBA had an agreement, and a half-dozen flint glass strikes in small nonunion shops.

Summary

To summarize: while forces of the New Deal period gave unexpected vitality to collective bargaining in the glass container and pressed and blown ware industries, the basic elements are the product of fifty years of give and take. The threat from the new unionism continues but the old unionism has shown a powerful will to survive and a strong adaptability to social changes. There is little fundamental difference between the container and flint branches. The leadership of the former was apparently more alive to the problem and significance of the miscellaneous workers. The Flint leaders, however, have been faced by a considerably more complicated jurisdiction and correspondingly more involved responsibilities. In their conservative philosophy leaders of the two unions are alike.

Future prospects rest upon the ability of the old unionism and the joint conference system to absorb completely the miscellaneous workers. Organization and assimilation of the machine operators and the skilled craftsmen are practically 100 per cent, but a large number of miscellaneous workers still await unionism. In the container industry the Owens-Illinois Company has refused to bargain with its miscellaneous employees but this refusal is probably temporary. By 1938 the GBBA leaders decided to invade wider fields and to extend jurisdiction over the allied glass industries, such as the "raw products" plants which produce sand, soda, lime, and silica, and the concerns which make closures or bottle tops and bottle packages.[30]

3. THE NEW UNIONISM IN FLAT GLASS

Unionism in the window glass branch of the flat glass industry is as old as that in the container and flint glass industries. The story, however, is not one of stability and peace but of disruption and conflict. It offers a noteworthy picture of a once powerful unionism which refused to adjust itself to the inevitable triumph of mechanization over craft skill and thereby caused its own downfall. In the plate glass branch, on the other hand, collective bargaining is new. As we have seen,[31] plate glass production required little skilled labor from its inception, and a unionism based on the unskilled and semiskilled workers was not forthcoming until the New Deal.[32]

a. ORGANIZATION OF THE SKILLED WORKERS

Before 1880 skilled workers of the flat glass industry were organized on the basis of four crafts—gatherers who took the molten glass from the pot or tank, blowers who shaped the glass into long "rollers," flatteners who smoothed out these rollers into sheets after the ends had been cut off to form cylinders, and cutters who cut the sheets into the desired sizes.[33] These unions

30. In 1927 shortly after neon signs came into use, the GBBA set out to organize the neon sign workers. Within a brief period considerable progress was reported and standards in the industry were raised substantially. Other unions, however, notably the AFGWU and the International Brotherhood of Electrical Workers, claimed jurisdiction. In 1936 the latter, which is a powerful organization, forcibly took over the neon branches and then, as is not uncommon, won authority from the Executive Council of the AF of L.

31. See p. 684.

32. Apart from differences in chemical composition, the chief difference between plate and window glass is that the former is ground and polished on both sides while the latter remains exactly the same as when it is drawn from the tank. As late as 1914 the production of window glass was worth $17.5 million as compared to $14.8 million for plate glass. By 1925, however, the value of window glass output was $37.5 million while that of plate glass was $57.2 million. In 1935 the values were only $18.2 million for window glass and $41.8 million for plate glass. U. S. Tariff Commission, *Flat Glass and Related Glass Products*, 1937, p. 15.

33. This and the two following paragraphs are based chiefly on an excellent account in the Eleventh Special Report of the U. S. Commissioner of Labor entitled *Regulation and Restriction of Output*, 1904.

had bargained with their employers on a local scale, but the problem of unifying wages and working conditions did not arise until it became evident in 1877 that the manufacturers could not prevent the disruptive competition coming from overcapacity and inelasticity of demand for window glass. The unions therefore set out to achieve this end by restricting work first to ten, and later to fewer, months in the year and requiring all plants to take a uniform "summer stop"; by restricting each blower's output, but giving a differential to places where coal was most expensive; and by restricting their membership through apprentice regulations so that about fifteen hundred pots were idle. The twenty-five hundred pots in use were sufficient to supply the country's needs. In 1880 and 1881 the crafts were consolidated into the Knights of Labor Trade Assembly 300, probably the strongest labor organization of the time.

From 1880 to 1896 collective bargaining of this restrictive type was carried on successfully under a national agreement. Then it began to crumble. Essentially the factors in the disintegration were three: conflict within the union, a futile attempt to limit output permanently, and a stubborn belief that mechanical progress could be checked.

Collapse of the Old Unionism

The internal conflict began in 1894 with the election of Simon Burns, a gatherer, as president of Assembly 300. The cutters and flatteners charged that Burns favored the majority trades (blowers and gatherers) at their expense. A large group seceded, but attempts to maintain separate organizations and get recognition from employers were crushed in 1899 and again in 1907. Strife also resulted from union leadership's effort to help the employers to restrict production and raise prices. In 1899 Assembly 300 and the newly formed American Window Glass Company agreed that in return for a block of stock worth $500,000 at par and a seat on the board of directors, the union would furnish enough skilled workmen to run the company's plants at full capacity, even though this would deprive other concerns of labor. A faction of the blowers and gatherers in the independent plants protested and formed a dual organization, the Window Glass Workers' Association of America. The rival manufacturers finally agreed to share the market, but labor committed hara-kiri by private undercutting of wage scales. The new union opposed further limitation of output while Assembly 300 insisted on its traditional policy. In 1905 came the Lubber cylinder blowing machine—the first successful attempt to make window glass by machinery. It gradually eliminated the blower and the gatherer, and the scarcity of skilled labor ended. Machine plants increased the industry's already excess production capacity. In a few chaotic years, wages fell about 60 per cent, the summer stop was abolished and national unionism was disrupted.

By 1910 the industry regained stability through an informal share-the-market agreement between the hand plants and the American Window Glass Company, which controlled the Lubber machine—the only one then capable of producing a good grade of window glass. Skilled workers in the hand plants were able to reorganize under the capable leadership of Joseph M. Neenan (later plant manager for the Libbey-Owens Company) into the National Window Glass Workers' Union.

Although there was no industry-wide contract, an industry-wide wage scale was reinstituted with National's as a model. The number of hand glass workers was restricted and the output of each was closely regulated. But the National refused to recognize the fact that sooner or later new machines would supplant the Lubber process and that the share-the-market agreement would be disrupted. Its members were forbidden to work in any machine plant under penalty of expulsion. Neenan favored one organization for all glass workers, but his overtures to the machine plant workers were rejected because of past animosities. In 1917 the Libbey-Owens Company installed the Colburn process which automatically drew flat sheets of glass directly from the tank of molten glass. Six years later the Fourcault machine was introduced into the United States. By 1926 only 2 per cent of the window glass produced in the country was handmade. The last acts of the National Window Glass Workers' Union before its dissolution in

1927 were, significantly, to abolish the rule forbidding its members to work in machine plants and to set aside ten thousand dollars for organizing the industry's miscellaneous workers. But it was too late and the campaign failed.

Organization in the Machine Plants

While short-sighted policies drove the hand workers' organization toward destruction, the skilled workers (not the miscellaneous employees) in the machine plants followed several lines of organization. The cutters and flatteners, who seceded from Assembly 300 of the Knights of Labor in 1896 and were badly defeated in efforts to hold their jobs in the Assembly's jurisdiction, got a footing among some independent cylinder-machine plants under the name of the Window Glass Cutters' and Flatteners' Association of America, Incorporated. In 1910 the American Window Glass Company formed a "company union" for its machine plants and a few years later the Pittsburgh Plate Glass Company had its cutters and flatteners organized in the same fashion. So strong was the tradition of unionism in the industry that some form of organization was thought necessary to attract capable workmen. The field was completely covered in 1917 with the creation of the Window Glass Cutters' League at the Libbey-Owens plant in Charleston, West Virginia. Miscellaneous workers, however, remained unorganized, as did plate glass workers, few of whom were skilled.

Between the end of the World War and the second year of the Roosevelt administration, consolidation of union forces as well as a steady equalization of wages and working conditions took place throughout the window glass industry. The continuous sheet process outdated the cylinder machine and abolished the flattener, the third of the four original crafts. The leaders of the Window Glass Cutters' League first rejected offers of the Cutters' and Flatteners' Association for an amalgamation, then absorbed the association. Cutters of the Pittsburgh Plate Glass Company were persuaded to affiliate with the League in 1928 and those of the American Window Glass organization were taken over early in 1934.

Effect of the New Deal

The New Deal had the same effect upon the leaders of the Cutters' League as upon container and flint glass union officials. It awoke them to the possibility and desirability of organizing the miscellaneous workers, while simultaneously arousing in this group an awareness of the union idea. Within a year of enactment of the NRA and its Section 7(a), the League's fifteen hundred cutters were augmented by over ten thousand unskilled and semi-skilled window glass and plate glass workers. This inflation, however, was short-lived. Although the two groups were segregated in autonomous divisions, the rank and file of the cutters were in an uncomfortable minority. They voted to end the venture by separating from the newcomers. The flat glass industry was peaceably divided between the Window Glass Cutters' League and the new Federation of Flat Glass Workers, the jurisdiction of the former being again restricted to the cutters of the window glass industry. The latter assumed responsibility for the miscellaneous workers of the window glass plants and for all plate glass labor. The secretary of the League, who had served both divisions, withdrew with his fellow-cutters. But Glen McCabe, the president of the League from 1927 and the chief figure in the organization of the miscellaneous workers, after being defeated for re-election, threw in his lot with the larger and potentially much more important Federation of Flat Glass Workers.

b. COLLECTIVE BARGAINING WITH THE CUTTERS

In collective bargaining between the cutters and the window glass manufacturers, relations are harmonious and uneventful. Instead of an industry-wide joint conference, the union executive board draws up separate agreements with the Libbey-Owens-Ford Company, the Pittsburgh Plate Glass Company, and independent manufacturers who use the Fourcault process and are grouped in an association for sales and collective bargaining purposes. The American Window Glass Company formerly negotiated agreements separately but now meets with other Fourcault concerns. The practically identical contracts each contain a clause that nullifies its binding power if less favorable wages and working conditions are accepted by the union in another agreement.

The most significant feature of this collective bargaining is the control which the union has gained over the job because skilled cutters have been indispensable to manufacturers. Only "known practical window glass cutters who are members in good standing" of the League may be hired. No apprentice may be taken on without League consent, and the two hundred and fifty who have been apprenticed since December 9, 1930 are either sons or close relatives of members. All union dues, fines and assessments are deducted by the employer from wages and sent to the League's office. Except where there is a question of competency, strict seniority applies in layoffs and rehiring. Work must be distributed without favoritism as equally as possible.

Technological Advance Still Threatens

Nevertheless the League is not wholly secure. The technology which has already forced the blower, the gatherer, and the flattener out of the window glass industry is still evolving. A cutting machine with which three men can do the work of twenty-five on certain types of glass was introduced experimentally during the 1929–1933 depression. Union leaders expressed no fear of it, asserting that cutting glass before inspection is exceedingly wasteful and that only skilled workmen can eliminate defects before glass is cut. But in an agreement made with the Libbey-Owens-Ford Company on February 15, 1935 and renewed in 1937 and in 1939, the company guaranteed not to use the machine if there was insufficient work for a minimum of ninety hand cutters at the Shreveport plant and one hundred and fifty hand cutters at the Charleston factory. Provided the demand for window glass does not boom, it appears likely that hand cutters will eventually diminish or disappear.

C. THE FEDERATION OF FLAT GLASS WORKERS

While the Cutters' League retreated to its niche as a small craft union, its offshoot, the Federation of Flat Glass Workers, became a full-blown "going concern." Its stimulating effect upon the old unionism of the container and flint glass industries has already been noted. In the flat glass industry it has established a system of collective bargaining equal to the best of those of the past decade. Reference to the Federation as "new unionism" is not simply because it is less than eight years old and an early affiliate of the CIO, but because its unskilled members, inexperienced in the art of collective bargaining, are aggressively conscious of their importance to industry.

Size and Organization

In the summer of 1940, the Federation of Flat Glass Workers changed its name to the Federation of Glass, Ceramic, and Silica Sand Workers of America. Its roots are mainly in the window and plate glass industries. Some of the approximately twenty-two thousand members of the organization are distributed among mirror, sand, tile, and wire glass factories, but the great majority are in the plants of the Libbey-Owens-Ford Company, the Pittsburgh Plate Glass Company, the American Window Glass Company, and the Independent Fourcault Window Glass Manufacturers.[34] Over ten thousand of the members are in the fourteen plate and window glass plants of the first two companies.

Although both branches of the flat glass industry are treated as a unit for collective bargaining, their outlook on unionism and their labor problems have been quite different. In the window glass branch, where a number of smaller companies compete successfully with the two giants, the union has been regarded as a useful agency in equalizing labor costs and in limiting the tendency toward "harmful" competition.[35] In the plate glass division, however, where the two giants are completely dominant, the

34. As of June 1939, the Federation reported contracts with three rolled and wire glass establishments, eight silica sand plants, one electrical insulator plant, two tile companies, one milk bottle company, and five glass specialty (mainly mirror) companies, in addition to the plate and window glass corporations named. One small window glass and two small wire glass establishments were on the union's unfair list. The Ford Motor Company also manufactures plate glass but only for its own use, and no attempt to organize it has been made.

35. This has been somewhat less valid since the formation in 1935 of the Fourco Glass Company, which acts as selling agent for the Adamston, Harding, and Rolland Companies. Besides this group there are only Libbey-Owens-Ford, Pittsburgh Plate, and American Window Glass.

union has no price function. Management believes its purpose is only to share in profits and limit the corporation's authority over employees and production. It is difficult to say how important this difference in outlook has been, but it is noteworthy that most labor troubles in the flat glass industry have originated in the plate glass branch.

Organization of the miscellaneous workers in the window glass factories was accomplished by Glen McCabe, president of the Cutters' League, in the months following adoption of the NRA. Well-known to employers and labor, and free because of his position to enter any window glass plant, McCabe worked rapidly and with little opposition.[36] The Pittsburgh Plate management set up employee representation plans but was forced to withdraw them immediately from its window glass plants. In plate glass factories, however, where organized employees got charters as AF of L federal labor unions before joining the League, transition to collective bargaining was more involved, though equally successful. At Toledo, for example, the Libbey-Owens-Ford Company discharged some union leaders and almost precipitated a strike. The corporation's top management was forced to reinstate the men and recognize the union. At Creighton, Pennsylvania, the Pittsburgh Plate company union temporarily subsided after a similar strike threat, but was revived only to be finally eliminated during a ten-day strike for a wage increase in January 1935. The company-supported union at Crystal City, Missouri, alone survived.

(1). *Developments in Relations with Management*
Employer Adjustment

Inclusion of miscellaneous workers in collective bargaining required no serious readjustments by executives in the window glass plants. Mainly it was necessary to extend the practices and customs developed in the cutting department. Management in the plate glass plants, lacking this experience, needed advice and

---

36. Before McCabe was able to win over the cutters of the American Window Glass Company to the League in January 1934, the miscellaneous workers had organized themselves. However, he was instrumental in obtaining contract rights for the latter.

assistance. The Libbey-Owens-Ford concern hired a former president of the American Flint Glass Workers' Union as its industrial relations director. He has advised the executive vice president in charge of production on labor policy, trained plant officials in methods of dealing with union members, and smoothed out grievances which could not be adjusted where they originated. Pittsburgh Plate did not follow suit until after the 1935 strike. Then it too selected a man who had been a labor official for many years and in addition had been a government conciliator. These industrial relations directors have had prominent parts in annual negotiations as well as in daily relationships between management and the union.

Evolution of the Agreements

The collective bargaining system has passed through a period of steady expansion. The first agreements were local. The Shreveport and Charleston window plants of the Libbey-Owens-Ford Company came under contract in November 1933, and a brief agreement for the three Toledo works was signed in May 1934. That spring unions at the Creighton and Ford City plants of the Pittsburgh Plate Glass Company were recognized. Six months later, on November 8, a single agreement covered all Libbey-Owens-Ford window and plate plants with the revealing provision that in the event of an industry- or branch-wide compact, this contract would become part of it.

In January 1935 a similar contract was made with Fourcault manufacturers, and the next month Pittsburgh Plate, after adjustment of its strike, agreed likewise to a company-wide contract. Then, following a notable strike, it was decided that the termination date of all three contracts would be February 1, 1938, but that they would continue from year to year, unless notice of cancellation or modification was sent out at least thirty days before the termination date. A joint conference in January 1938 between the Pittsburgh Plate Glass Company, the Libbey-Owens-Ford Company, and the Federation, failed to make a joint agreement and the old ones were renewed. Difficulties with the Pittsburgh corporation prevented another joint conference in 1939, but the system was continued in 1940. Instead of a joint contract two separate but practically identical agreements were again negotiated.

Out of these expanded negotiations has come progressive elaboration of contract terms. The compilation of rules (twelve pages of small type) applying to the settlement of grievances, seniority, promotion schedules, transfers, re-employment, wages, hours, etc., in itself would cause no special comment. It is not unlike the agreement obtained by the Cutters' League and is considerably less complicated than many of the Flint Glass Workers' contracts. But since all parties concerned have expressed a preference for the simple administrative agreement, the current type of contract must be attributed to mutual distrust.

This distrust is reflected in clauses like the following: "The company will not reclassify employees or duties or occupations or engage in any subterfuge for the purpose of defeating or evading the provisions of this agreement." Absence of basically friendly and cooperative relations between management of the larger companies and the union is a significant contrast between the new unionism and the old unionism in the glass industry. It results from a combination of factors: the aggressiveness of Federation leaders and their unwillingness to adopt the conservative philosophy of the old unionism; the pressure exerted on the leaders by rank-and-file members who insist on rapid and continuous gains without which they lose interest and refuse to pay dues; the employers' fear and dislike of the Congress of Industrial Organizations with which the Federation is affiliated; and the fact that the large companies regard the union as a nuisance and of no benefit to themselves.

Terms of the Agreements

Of the three major contracts in the flat glass industry, the one between the Federation of Flat Glass Workers and the Association of Independent Fourcault Window Glass Manufacturers is the most satisfactory to the union. Its greater concessions are partly due to the bargaining superiority which the Federation wields over the handful of small manufacturers and partly to the fact that stabilization through the union means more to small producers than to large companies. A comparison of the January 1935 and the February 1939 agreements shows striking union gains over a brief period. In the prevailing contract the Federation is conceded the preferential shop which, in practice, is the closed shop. Hiring is carried on in close cooperation with the local union president. The first agreement had recognized the union as bargaining agent for its members only. Departmental seniority is the determining factor in promotion, layoff, and rehiring, provided that the eligible employee is capable of performing the work. In contrast, the original contract placed seniority on a footing with skill, efficiency and family status. The first agreement affirmed the southern wage differential as established in the NRA Code, whereas the 1939 agreement made no geographical distinction. Management promised in the early contracts to study with the union committee the proper number of employees necessary for the various operations. The 1939 agreement supplemented this by a schedule of wage increases corresponding to increases in machine speed.

Contracts with the larger corporations are somewhat the same, although these powerful companies have been less willing to share control over the job. The Federation was recognized as sole collective bargaining agency only after certification by the NLRB in January 1939. The preferential or closed union shop has been steadily resisted on the grounds that it is undemocratic and union leadership has not proved its responsibility. For a short time in 1934 some Pittsburgh Plate locals were granted the checkoff, but this was subsequently withdrawn. In several plants, however, where union organization is almost complete, dues delinquency and nonmembership have been limited by the sheer pressure of numbers and the refusal of union members to work with those outside the fold. Seniority prevails both in layoffs and promotions, but exceptions are not uncommon when ability is questioned, particularly in plate glass factories. Management has agreed to add extra men when faster speed is ordered on the production lines, but it will consider an increase in piece rates only when more employees cannot be added or cannot alleviate the situation.

Negotiation of the Agreements

Negotiations on this company-wide or intercompany scale are simple. Meeting places are centrally located cities or the homes of the larger corporations, like Pittsburgh, Toledo, Cincinnati and Cleveland. The Federation's wage committee consists of the national officers and representatives from each local. The companies are represented by high national executives, industrial relations men and sometimes plant managers. The union president speaks for the Federation while the executive vice president or the industrial relations director is management's spokesman. Discussion is usually limited to proposals mentioned in the conference notices, although additional issues may be introduced the first day. Local issues frequently interrupt, and deviations from the topic under consideration are not uncommon. As a result, there has been talk of decreasing the representation on both sides.

Wage conference agreements must be approved by each local union concerned—a rule indicative of the Federation's extreme local autonomy. That negotiations have not been obstructed by the rule is attributable to the presence of the local leaders at the conferences. Upon these men rests the burden first of submitting to the other delegates the proposals of their memberships, and then of "selling" the final compromises to their locals. If the conference has been called by either side expressly for modification and no agreement results, the old contract continues in effect. If the conference notice announces cancellation, then failure to agree leaves the parties without a contract, and a strike or lockout becomes the only means of gaining demands. There is no provision for arbitration nor any apparent desire for it.

Between annual conferences, special meetings may explore certain subjects, interpret newly enacted rules and settle grievances. It is not unusual for the national union president, either alone or with a few wage committeemen, to meet with company representatives. Grievances which cannot be adjusted in the plant are not allowed to take up time at the wage conferences. They are left to the Federation president and high company officials. That few of these grievances come from the larger plants is again a result of the jealously guarded local autonomy.

Leadership of the Union

In early stages of collective bargaining, personalities often exert great influence. From the Federation's founding until the summer of 1937, when he was forced out, the dominant figure was President Glen McCabe, an aggressive leader and a skilled negotiator, unwilling to share either power or responsibility. His bargaining philosophy was that the union could gain greater concessions in wages and working conditions by dealing with each company separately and playing one against the other. He opposed the industry-wide wage conference which other executive board members advocated. His method meant considerable secret maneuvering from which he attempted to exclude the local union representatives. Thus, he alone frequently met with company officials and made agreements about which the wage committeemen remained ignorant until after their execution.

In the first few years, while local conditions were still unsettled, McCabe had no serious opposition. Whether because of his method or not, working conditions did improve. For noncontinuous operations, the six-hour day, thirty-six-hour week replaced a working week of forty-eight hours or more. Wage increases of 1935 and 1937 gave unskilled and semiskilled flat glass workers a basic hourly rate that compared favorably with the best in mass production industry. Minimum wages for women were raised to 55 cents an hour, for men in window plants to 61, and for men in plate and safety glass plants to 63—rates which were more than 10 per cent above those in 1929. But in 1937 opposition to McCabe became sufficiently strong to force him out of the Federation of Flat Glass Workers.[37]

After McCabe's resignation, internal political conditions in the Federation were unfavorable. While local union strength prevented serious undermining of standards, absence of a strong unifying leadership obstructed further progress. In 1937, when

---

37. After his resignation, McCabe turned to the AF of L and tried to organize a rival flat glass union, but his efforts were wholly unsuccessful except for the small vitrolite plant of the Libbey-Owens-Ford Company in Parkersburg, West Virginia. There is now a case before the courts appealing a decision of the NLRB which has placed this plant in the bargaining unit controlled by the Federation of Flat Glass Workers.

the local factions could not agree on a candidate to fill McCabe's place, the CIO appointed a temporary president (not a glass worker) who failed to hold the support of several of the larger locals and in 1939 was likewise forced out. In November 1939 one of the original local leaders who had been general secretary-treasurer was elected president after a hotly contested campaign. Whether he can maintain harmony and give the necessary leadership remains to be seen.

(2). *Sources of Controversy*

The Great Strike

A number of disputes have disturbed negotiations between the Federation and the manufacturers. Some have been economic—demands for more wages; some have involved the fundamental question of control over the job; some came from union efforts to widen jurisdiction. Only one seriously interrupted operations. In November 1936 negotiations between the Federation and the Pittsburgh Plate Glass Company were deadlocked and three days before the contract expired union leaders called a strike. In early December the seven thousand workers of the Libbey-Owens-Ford Company also struck when the Toledo Corporation attempted to fill an order which the Chrysler Motor Company originally placed with Pittsburgh Plate.[38] Neither company seriously attempted to operate any of its plants except Crystal City, where the Federation was weak.

Real causes of the dispute, which ran until the last week of January 1937, are clouded by conflicting stories. Least satisfactory is the suggestion that the strike represented the first step in the CIO campaign to organize the automobile industry. CIO leaders of the steel industry were opposed to the strike because they had used the Federation's gains as a potent talking point in their organizing campaign. The preferential shop, the checkoff and higher wages were the issues most discussed in the conferences. The companies refused to recognize the Federation as sole collective bargaining agent, let alone grant the preferential shop, but offered a

---

38. It will be recalled that these two companies produce about 95 per cent of the plate glass and over 50 per cent of the window glass in the industry.

5 per cent wage raise. Only intervention by CIO officials and pressure from Washington brought the dispute to a semisuccessful conclusion for the Federation. Management won on the issue of representation. The union, however, gained an eight cents an hour increase in wages, although bonuses were to be computed on the old wage base. The seniority system was extended and wage equalization between the two companies was submitted to a joint commission of union and management representatives headed by an impartial chairman.

The Crystal City Affair

Less serious but equally disruptive have been issues at the Crystal City plant. The Pittsburgh Plate Glass Company has refused to permit Federation representatives from this plant to participate in the annual wage conference, contending that their local does not have a majority. The CIO holds that all of the company's plants should be treated as a single unit and that it has a clear majority of the total, although not at Crystal City. In May 1938 it accused the rival union in the plant of being company-supported; and at an NLRB hearing, the corporation admitted the relationship. The company union was ordered disestablished. On January 13, 1939 the Labor Board certified the Federation of Flat Glass Workers as exclusive collective bargaining agent for *all* of the company's plate and window glass plants.

The company refused to accept the certification for Crystal City, the annual wage conference was cut short and the agreement of 1937 was continued pending a final settlement. The Board reconsidered and on September 19, 1939 the bargaining unit was again, by a two to one decision, defined to include Crystal City. In an important minority report William M. Leiserson opposed imposition "on the largest single plant of the company of a representative for collective bargaining whom the employees of that plant have not chosen . . . ." The company then turned to the courts, the case remaining unsettled at this writing.[39] In the meantime strife arose at Crystal City between the CIO and members

---

39. On July 23, 1940, the Eighth District Circuit Court upheld the decision of the Board.

of the former company union which has been re-established, presumably without company help. The company and the union, however, agreed at their 1940 conference that if the courts decided for the Federation, or if it gets a majority of Crystal City employees, the plant would be included automatically in the contract.

Other issues symptomatic of the adolescence of collective bargaining have caused heated debate and occasionally strained relations, but no open warfare. Letters exchanged before the 1939 conferences listed for consideration: from the union—the preferential shop, speed of operation in the plant, the bonus and incentive systems and elimination of wage differentials within each company and between the two large companies; from the management—the status of a worker's employment record after a layoff, seniority problems and the promotion schedule, the representation of certain groups (men who refuse to join the union or members who will not pay dues) and clearer provisions about interruption of work before the settlement of grievances.

Seniority

Of all questions seniority has taken the most time and proved the most complicated. Should seniority be computed from the beginning of operations or from some date in 1933 when unionism went into effect? Should separate seniority lists be made for men and women or, because technological changes have replaced men with women in a large number of jobs, should they be combined? Should seniority be departmental, or plant-wide or interplant in its application? What should happen to a man's seniority in case of a temporary layoff, an indefinite layoff, illness, absence from work due to union business, transfers from one department to another?

These and similar problems have racked the negotiations. Both sides realize that there is no ideal seniority program, that many cases must be solved according to local conditions, that complete uniformity throughout the industry cannot be attained. Management recognizes that seniority as far as layoffs and rehiring are concerned is essentially a union problem. It has therefore protested against union demands only when it believed serious expense would be involved. It has refused to apply seniority outside of the department because "bumping" of employees from different departments means considerable and expensive retraining. It has opposed a combined list of men and women on the ground that women's jobs are easier than men's and pay less. On the other hand, labor has realized from experience some of the limitations of strict and wide seniority and has moderated its demands. The result is a steady trend toward ultimate agreement.

Seniority in promotion still provokes argument. At both the plate and window glass plants it is possible to draw up schedules of promotion within a department and from one department to another based on skill required and wages paid. Usually, though not always, it is possible for a man in a lower level to step into the next higher occupation. The Federation of Flat Glass Workers has won a stipulation that mutually satisfactory promotion schedules must be drawn up and that departmental seniority shall be the first consideration for promotion, provided the man is competent. Management has protested in vain that this clause deprives it of the right to manage its plant, that able young men have no chance for rapid advancement and that incompetent workers get undeserved promotions. The question of incompetency has been raised particularly in the plate glass plants, where the line of progression has been complicated by a steady stream of minor technological improvements. The Federation leaders have replied that seniority is the only fair way to avoid discrimination, and that they do not support a promotion if an employee proves to be incompetent after a trial.

Wage Problems

The wage equalization issue has been of paramount importance to the union. At one time similar jobs in the same and different plants of a company were often paid widely different rates. This has been virtually eliminated with substantial benefits to many workers. The intercompany problem proved a harder nut to crack. For some occupations the Libbey-Owens-Ford Company paid a higher rate than the Pittsburgh Plate; for others the reverse was true. The Fourcault plants paid, in general, somewhat less than the two larger corporations in their window factories. Under the 1937 contract, a five-man commission, including two representatives from the union, one from each of the large companies, and an impartial chairman, was to try to level inequalities. The union compiled through its membership a detailed list of rates. Several meetings got nowhere. The main obstacle apparently was that labor opposed any lowering of rates, while the companies objected to additional raises after the strike settlement. After the 1940 conferences, however, the differential problem disappeared. The two large companies granted a general two cents an hour increase while the Fourcault plants conceded slightly more. The minimum wage for common labor is now 64 cents for the Fourcault plants as compared to 63 cents for the window glass factories and 65.5 cents for the plate glass factories of Pittsburgh Plate and Libbey-Owens-Ford.

Machine Speed

The union has contended for the right to decide, in cooperation with management, the rate at which the lines should move. Management has shown its willingness to listen to complaints and to add extra men when the lines are speeded up, but it will not surrender the right of running production as it sees fit. The problem was met in the Fourcault contract, as has been seen, by higher pay for higher speeds. Management can determine the speed of operation but must pay for the privilege of working the employees at a pace considered above normal, which is somewhat analogous to the payment of extra rates for hours beyond the normal week. The Libbey-Owens-Ford and Pittsburgh Plate executives have thus far rejected such an arrangement, although they agreed to pay more when extra employees on the operation are impractical or cannot lessen the burden.

Nonunion Employees

Nonunion employees are a troublesome problem in plants of the larger corporations. Management has been adamant upon the closed or the preferential-union shop, and the union has had to attempt other methods to gain the same end. Recently, it has contended that since nonunionists do not pay for the benefits of the contract they have no seniority rights or similar privileges under it. Employers have not accepted this interpretation. The Federation has also encouraged more forceful means, such as refusing to work with nonmembers.[40] No clause in the contract adequately covers such a situation.

Administration of the Agreements

Regardless of the degree of collective bargaining by top officials, the agreements must be administered within the individual plants. It is therefore not uncommon, particularly in newly unionized industries, that the administration and interpretation of an agreement differ radically from the legislation both in spirit and subject. Among unions in which local autonomy is a dominating force, this appears the rule rather than the exception. Yet, in the flat glass industry such differences have not occurred; contracts are followed as literally as is possible. Deviations appear only where required by local conditions. To appreciate this anomaly, the following facts must be recalled: (1) each contract is negotiated by and in the presence of leaders from each plant so there is no question of what occurred at the wage conferences; (2) the industrial relations directors of the two large companies attend most meetings held between the plant management and the local industrial relations committee, and therefore can see to it that policy is uniformly executed; (3) written minutes are taken of every local and national industrial relations meeting so that it is possible to keep a check on previous actions.

The company-wide agreements specify in detail the local machinery. The union has an industrial relations committee of the president, vice president, and four members selected by the general membership. This committee is supposed to meet once a month with the plant management, usually the manager, some of his superintendents and the industrial relations director, to discuss

---

40. For example, in March 1939 the Federation local at the Fort Smith, Arkansas, plant of the Harding Glass Company went out on a one-day strike to compel the discharge of a foreman who had refused to join the union and was accused of constantly violating the agreement. The strike was successful.

single or group complaints which cannot be settled in the departments, or to consider ways and means of preventing future disputes. A grievance must first be discussed by the employee or his department representative and the foreman. Should it remain unsettled, it must be placed in writing and submitted to the head of the department. Then it goes to the industrial relations committee. Failure to reach a satisfactory settlement at this stage leads to the intervention of the Federation president and the vice president in charge of production and labor for the company. Any agreement may be reached which does not conflict with the contract; then it is written up as a guide for future use.

Improvement in Adjustments

Adjustment of grievances has steadily improved both in the window glass plants where difficulties were always few and in the plate glass plants where relationships frequently were strained. More complaints are being settled by department representatives and foremen. Industrial relations meetings are calmer and more efficiently run. Instead of lasting for hours and sometimes for days, some plants now find it unnecessary to hold meetings for months at a time. Many meetings are held to promote greater mutual understanding rather than to adjust grievances. The Federation president is called upon only in the most important cases since the industrial relations director, who is present at these meetings, speaks for the company with an authority that is not often reversed. But in the smaller companies, the Federation president takes a more active part in carrying grievances to the highest management authority.

Reasons for more harmonious relationships are: (1) the mere passage of time during which the management has been forced to deal with union representatives and the latter have been forced to bear the responsibilities of the negotiator instead of acting with the freedom of the organizer; (2) the influence of the two industrial relations directors upon the lower officialdom of their companies. One of the first steps of these labor relations men was to impress upon foremen and superintendents that collective bargaining was here to stay. This had a notable influence in the Pittsburgh Plate Glass Company where the status of unionism was shrouded in doubt for at least a year and a half.

In a collective bargaining system like the foregoing, the company-wide wage conferences accurately reflect problems arising in the plants. The annual conference does not normally consider specific cases but discusses the principles under which practically all local cases are settled. Seniority, promotion, wage adjustment in times of technological change, leave of absence, the division of working time prior to layoffs—these are the issues debated. Discharge cases are rare. One of the more difficult problems is the determination of whether a man is "competent" to fill a job. No one has attempted a statistical analysis of grievances in the flat glass industry but it is certain that grievances as a whole have sharply diminished.

Role of "Outside" Factors

Two major industrial forces have seriously affected collective bargaining in the flat glass industry. One is the displacement of jobs by technological changes which rival those in the glass container industry. The United States Tariff Commission has estimated that the productivity of the average plate glass employee was 22,548 square feet in 1935 as compared to 17,723 in 1929. This differential has increased since 1935 and is destined to increase still more. At present in American plants each side of the plate glass must be ground and polished separately. An English patent, however, makes it possible to polish and then grind both sides of the glass at the same time, and thus eliminates about half of the workers on the lines. Union membership can do little to prevent this menace to jobs. Glass manufacturers have been exceedingly ingenious in discovering new uses for their products and it is not likely that total employment will fall much, if at all, in the long run; but the temporary dislocations have complicated the problems of negotiation.

The other major industrial factor affecting collective bargaining in this industry is the severe fluctuation in production caused by the fact that the demand for glass rests upon other industries with irregular production. As is well known, the flat glass industry is almost completely dependent upon the automobile and construction industries. Fewer autos and buildings mean fewer jobs in the glass factory. The decline in these industries during the depression often forced more than half of the union members and most of their officials onto the WPA and the relief rolls. Yet the union did not disappear, as it served a useful function outside of the plant as well as within it. Prosperity in the industries represents, of course, a boon to both the Federation and the glass corporations.

4. Summary and Observations

Collective bargaining is now a vital force in the entire glass industry. Few industries have been so completely unionized. The most notable fact of the pre-New Deal period was the unions' ability to survive the technological revolution. The most notable fact of the New Deal period has been extension of collective bargaining to the unskilled and semiskilled workers. Management did not like this extension but has not been sufficiently antagonistic to combat it actively. The only serious strike of the past decade, that carried on by the Federation of Flat Glass Workers against both the Pittsburgh Plate Glass Company and the Libbey-Owens-Ford Glass Company, merely proved the strength of both sides. The aggressiveness of the new unionism was a strong challenge to the old unionism of the container and flint glass industries, but the latter demonstrated that it was sufficiently flexible to meet the test.

Unless there is a reaction against unionism throughout the United States, the immediate future points to further extension of it in glass. The flint glass union has perhaps the most difficult task, since it faces both considerable technological change and unorganized corporations like Corning, whose wage scale and working conditions compare favorably with, and in some respects surpass, union standards. The union, which still bears the misleading name of the Glass Bottle Blowers' Association, already seeks new worlds to conquer. In the flat glass industry, numerous small mirror plants alone remain unorganized, and the union must decide whether the ultimate benefit is worth the expense and effort.

Threat to Unions Lies Within

The only serious threat to collective bargaining comes not from hostile employers or from disagreement over specific problems pertaining to procedure or substance, but from the unions themselves. As long as the breach between the AF of L and the CIO exists, the threat of a destructive clash remains strong. The miscellaneous workers in the old unions have not yet wholly accepted the "move slowly" doctrine. The flat glass workers often regretted the limiting word "flat" in their title and repeatedly showed a desire to merge all glass workers into one union. The recent change of name and jurisdiction indicates a move in this direction. Should the rival labor groups make peace, there are vast new jurisdictions for all to enter—sand, tile, limestone, closure, glass packaging and other industries which still remain outside the collective bargaining sphere.

Lessons of Fifty Years

What lessons can be drawn from fifty years of collective bargaining experience in the glass industry? Perhaps the most important is the demonstration that with intelligent leadership, good faith and mutual trust between management and union, few problems cannot be amicably and successfully met. There were times when the old unions were at a low ebb owing to circumstances beyond their control—such as the rapid technological changes, the decline in demand for containers during Prohibition, the great depression; yet the collective bargaining system was never allowed to disappear in the flint and container industries. Major credit for this belongs to leaders of the unions. They had the foresight not to resist mechanization for long but to make adjustments to it. They had the skill to "sell" unionism to management so that even when it would have been easy to destroy labor organizations, no such attempt was made. They had the patience and tenacity to suffer reverses and then slowly recover their losses. Where leadership was short-sighted, as in the window glass industry, collective bargaining was disrupted and the union destroyed.

Management, with a few notable exceptions like Corning, has accepted unionism. It has usually granted the closed or preferential shop without indulging in accusations of un-Americanism, and the like, because it realized that the unions were responsible organizations and that a divided shop meant dissension rather than peace. As a result, the disputes which have arisen in the long-organized sections of the glass industry have concerned legitimate economic problems, and not matters of union structure or status. Both sides have been able to devote most of their attention to the procedures and to the questions to be negotiated rather than to dues collection or conflict over union membership.

Nevertheless, stability in collective bargaining relations did not come overnight. In the early days of unionism in the flint, container and window glass industries, there was much strife. Several decades passed before the parties learned that collective bargaining is a process of compromise and give and take, and not a steady line of gains or losses. But as a consequence of this experience, the unskilled or miscellaneous workers in glass have been assimilated into the collective bargaining scheme with little difficulty, in striking contrast to the newly unionized workers of industries like steel, rubber and automobiles.

Employment by the major companies of former union officials to help them handle labor relations deserves special mention. These men have played a double role. They have communicated to top management the union psychology and the union way of viewing problems, thereby eliminating many potential disputes arising from misunderstanding. Also they have strengthened collective bargaining by showing management that unionism could benefit industry as well as employees.

The value of collective bargaining on an industry-wide scale is also shown by experience in the glass trades. The annual wage conferences have enabled the best talent and brains in the industry to focus their attention upon union-management problems. The less intelligent company and union leaders are guided by the wiser; men new to the system are acclimated by the experienced. At the same time, young blood has prevented stagnation. By centralizing collective bargaining, a plentiful exchange of ideas and practices has been attained, allowing the more backward plants to benefit from the more advanced.

Industry-wide collective bargaining has been significant on the economic front as well. One of unionism's major goals is uniform labor standards throughout the competitive market—with due exceptions, of course, for peculiar local conditions. In this way standards are not undermined by competitive undercutting. The joint industry conferences have supplied this uniformity far more effectively than would be possible through local or company negotiations. They have also made collective bargaining more open, honest and efficient. Both sides can marshal and present all of the facts at their command; neither side can easily play one member of the opposition off against another; there is little likelihood of important points being omitted or overlooked. The primary danger in the system is that individual concerns or local unions may be inadvertently injured in the concentration upon industry policy. This appears, however, to have been overcome satisfactorily by the fact that all manufacturers attend the meetings to defend their cases and that, likewise, union delegates are present from almost every company either as spokesmen or as watchers.

No system of collective bargaining can long survive without means of enforcing standards. Invariably some manufacturers would like to gain advantage by evading the rules, and occasionally some locals refuse to accept national decisions. As has been seen, the companies, whether in association or not, have generally left policing to the union leaders, who with their centralized power, have adequately lived up to the responsibility.

It is evident that the manufacturers' associations can play an important, constructive role in collective bargaining and that such associations with full-time paid officials are desirable both from the company and union points of view. They can assemble facts for their members; they can educate new members in the art of collective bargaining; they can speed the settlement of grievances which cannot be adjusted in the plant; they can provide the basis for cooperation with the union in meeting problems of joint concern. It appears to be advisable that industry spokesmen analogous to the national union leaders be available during the periods between conferences.

The history of labor relations in the glass industry clearly shows that the settlement of grievances is chiefly a matter of personality and attitude rather than of formal procedure or written rules. It is the "will to peace" that counts, but this "will" must be mutual and cannot be one-sided. A strong conviction exists throughout the industry that no problem need remain unsettled and that no outsider settles it as well as those intimately connected with the industry. The unique system of union president arbitration in the container industry is merely a reflection of the trust and responsibility on both sides. The system of conciliation or joint conference, which has worked so effectively in the flint glass industry and which is becoming increasingly successful in the newly organized flat glass industry, is further evidence that these factors are fundamental. It is obvious, however, that unionism and collective bargaining must be sincerely accepted and recognized by management.

Finally, the experience of glass shows that unionism can be a positive force of value to the industry as well as to its worker-members. It can stabilize or help to stabilize competitive conditions; it can eliminate strife and lessen discontent; it can be a valuable political agent. Those unions in the window glass branch which opposed technological changes without qualification eventually succumbed. The unions which survived, the American Flint Glass Workers' Union and the Glass Bottle Blowers' Association, did not fight mechanization but they did try, with considerable success, to cushion the blow for their membership. The cooperation of management was of great importance here. Moreover, the unions have been willing to accept wage reductions when really needed, and both parties always understood that any reductions were to be restored as soon as practicable. The fair application of this policy has cemented the relationship.

Chapter 14

ELECTRICAL PRODUCTS

LOCAL SURVEYS OF FOUR LEADING COMPANIES

MILTON DERBER

1. INTRODUCTION

IN THE MASS PRODUCTION industries—steel, automobile, rubber, flat glass, electrical products—collective bargaining is still in an embryonic stage. Unionism in most plants has existed only since the summer of 1933 and in some only since 1936. The first four of these industries were examined in preceding chapters on an industry-wide basis. In this chapter some of the specific problems of collective bargaining in the mass production field will be examined at closer range by case studies of five establishments manufacturing electrical goods.

The electrical manufacturing industry covers about 170 major subdivisions and over 300,000 distinguishable products. Because of its complexity it can be defined in many ways. The Census of Manufactures excludes from it a number of products which require electrical equipment—such as washing machines.[1] But from a labor point of view the industry has wider limits. The jurisdiction of the United Electrical, Radio and Machine Workers of America, the main labor union in the field, covers not only what the Census specifically includes and excludes but radio sets and parts as well. Nine states east of the Mississippi and north of the

---

1. The Census of Manufactures includes all "establishments engaged primarily in the manufacture of machinery, apparatus, and supplies for employment directly in the generation, storage, transmission, or utilization of electrical energy"; but it excludes producers of "electric-lighting fixtures, electric signs, or motor-driven tools, mechanical refrigerators, washing machines, and other machines and appliances with built-in motors or other electrical equipment."

Mason and Dixon Line account for about 87 per cent of total production. In 1937 output value was roughly $2.3 billion.

Peaceful Adoption of Collective Bargaining
Collective bargaining in electrical manufacture has been notable for its relatively wide and peaceful adoption. This has been due partly to the conclusion of some of the larger corporations that legally protected, independent unionism is here to stay and that it is useless to fight it, and partly to the determination, skill and resourcefulness of local and national union leaders. The UER&MWA, which was formed in March 1936 out of an amalgamation of rebelling AF of L federal labor unions and a loosely tied group of independent local unions, ranks high among the newer units of the Congress of Industrial Organizations.

The union reported at its convention in September 1940 that it had signed contracts covering 154,744 workers in 387 establishments and had reached working agreements which covered another 76,385 workers in 37 establishments.[2] Part of these workers are not union members, but the wages, hours and working conditions of all of them are negotiated through the union machinery. Since the electrical manufacturing industry includes perhaps 1,600 establishments and 400,000 employees, and since part of the union's jurisdiction extends over shops which are outside of the electrical field, it may be roughly estimated that between 50 and 60 per cent of the electrical workers are under UER&MWA agreements. The bulk of them work for the 125 major companies which account for about two thirds of the industry's sales and from 75 to 80 per cent of all employees.

Though a large majority of its members are employed in building construction, public utilities and elsewhere, the International Brotherhood of Electrical Workers also has been active in electrical manufacturing. It reported in November 1939 that its membership in manufacturing plants was 40,000. The list of "cooperating manufacturers" published in its monthly journal of

2. It also reported that 5.6 per cent of the workers were covered by agreements of the closed-shop variety, 7.6 came under union-shop agreements, 84.2 were under a sole collective bargaining clause, while the remainder were under agreements for members only.

February 1940 included more than 300 companies. No fewer than 181 of them manufactured lighting fixtures, lighting equipment, portable lamps and lamp shades, and 171 were located in New York City. Most of the companies are small, averaging around fifty workers. The Brotherhood has, however, won a position in some of the larger manufacturing plants, notably those of the National Electric Products Company of Ambridge, Pennsylvania, and of the Crosley Corporation of Cincinnati. Among its other contracts is one with RCA at Indianapolis.

Great Centers of the Industry

The plants studied are not "typical" cases. They were selected primarily for their importance in the industry and to the national union. The Schenectady works of the General Electric Corporation and the East Pittsburgh division of the Westinghouse Electric and Manufacturing Company are the largest plants in the industry and the mainsprings of the great systems which spread about them. Since General Electric and Westinghouse jointly account for about 25 per cent of the industry's annual sales,[3] represent about a third of the industry's capital, and employ on the average well over a hundred thousand men and women, their experiences with collective bargaining are of wide significance. The East Springfield branch of Westinghouse was included because it provides an interesting example of union-management cooperation.

The central plants of the RCA Manufacturing Company and the Philadelphia Storage Battery Company have the same relation to the twenty-year old radio branch that General Electric and Westinghouse have to the electrical manufacturing industry as a whole. In spite of spirited competition from establishments like Zenith, Emerson, Colonial, Crosley and Stromberg-Carlson, as well as General Electric and Westinghouse, they produced about 28 per cent of the eight million radio sets sold in 1937,[4] and em-

3. In 1937, a peak year, General Electric's sales were $350 million and its rival's totaled $206 million *(Moody's Manual of Investments, American and Foreign, Industrial Securities,* Moody's Investors Service, New York, 1938). Total value for the entire industry, including the radio and refrigerator branches, was $2.3 billion. "Machinery, Not Including Transportation Equipment," *U.S. Census of Manufactures, 1937,* Pt. I.

4. "Radio III: A $537,000,000 Set Business," *Fortune,* May 1938, p. 120.

ployed about a third of the forty-eight thousand at work for some hundred and sixty sets' manufacturers. During recent years the Philadelphia Storage Battery Company has lost ground, but RCA appears to have held, if not improved, its relative position. The former company was not only the first major concern in the electrical manufacturing industry to go union shop, but its labor organizations were for several years the bulwark of the union movement in the industry.[5]

2. GENERAL ELECTRIC AT SCHENECTADY

On December 15, 1936, Local 301 of the United Electrical and Radio Workers union won exclusive collective bargaining rights in a National Labor Relations Board election at the General Electric Schenectady works. This important victory was the go-ahead sign to unionism throughout the industry. For the Schenectady plant is not merely the largest of General Electric's twenty-three units; it is also the mother plant, the seat of the general offices and employer of over one fifth of the company's working force. Here are manufactured the "heavy current" products—generators, turbines and marine apparatus—which call for a high proportion of skilled male labor and months of slow, careful, precise work. Here too is the refrigerator department, which operates on a mass production basis, with a large number of semiskilled women employees.

5. Preliminary work was undertaken at two plants where the International Brotherhood of Electrical Workers has contracts, but was discontinued because detailed study would add little that was of value for present purposes. Hence the several local studies are of plants where the bargaining agency is a CIO organization. The field research for this chapter was carried out for the most part during 1939. Since then the industry has been profoundly affected by the defense program and collective bargaining problems in each plant have been altered. Nevertheless, it is felt that the material presented provides a significant and basically unchanged picture of the union-employer relationship in mass production.

None of the cases is examined completely and exhaustively in this chapter; emphasis is placed on significant features in each local situation. If little or no attention is paid to changes in management's structure and psychology in dealing with labor, or to the evolution of the system of laying off and rehiring employees, it is not that they are nonexistent or unimportant, but because they have been dealt with in detail elsewhere.

a. THE METAL TRADES COUNCIL

Unions and collective bargaining were not new to Schenectady. Before the World War, AF of L craft unions found the expanding establishment a fertile recruiting field. In 1911 more than thirty locals in the Schenectady area, largely representing the fourteen thousand workers in the General Electric plant,[6] formed the Electrical Industry Trades Alliance. Three years later the Alliance was chartered by the Metal Trades Department of the AF of L and became known as the Metal Trades Council, with avowed aims to complete organization, prevent isolated strikes, win the eight-hour day and abolish discrimination against workers. During the World War the Council and its constituent unions bargained for their members aggressively and with considerable success. Hours were reduced, wages raised and conditions improved. There were no written agreements, and the right to strike at any time was unquestioned.

Post-World War Collapse

Although the Council brought some cohesiveness to the crafts and lessened jurisdictional disputes, it had a double weakness. It could not stop its autonomous locals from taking individual action that might harm the entire body. This resulted in nonuniformity of procedure for settling grievances, differences in working rules and isolated craft stoppages. Also it could not extend what unifying power it had to other plants of the company.

The war put the unions in a strategic position. Booming production, a sympathetic city administration and the plant manager's favorable attitude contributed to the success of the Council. The end of the war, however, marked the beginning of disaster. In 1918 and 1920 strikes in support of unions in other General Electric plants were lost. The depression of 1920–1921 accelerated the decline in prestige. Where formerly the unions had unofficially limited an individual worker's production, the bars were now let down and competition for bonuses spread. In 1921, wage

---

[6] Only a relatively small group of unskilled, miscellaneous laborers seem to have lacked organization.

cuts of 10 per cent and of 10 cents an hour were made at six-month intervals without much opposition. Although some organizations did not crumble until the late 1920's, only the pattern makers and the steam fitters survived the decade and a half from the end of the war to the New Deal.

Nevertheless, interest in unionism was not immediately extinguished. The War Labor Board persuaded employees of the Lynn plant to accept an employee representation plan in 1918, and a strike against the imposition of a similar plan at the Erie plant failed in the same year. But not until 1924 could the scheme be introduced at the Schenectady plant without disturbance.[7]

b. THE EMPLOYEE REPRESENTATION PLAN

The Works Council plan, as the plant's weekly newspaper explained, was intended to afford workers and management an opportunity to discuss matters of mutual concern. Employees were not asked to approve it but simply to elect more than a hundred councilmen from designated districts to meet once a month with the works manager, the general superintendent and their assistants. It was not a mechanism for handling either individual or group grievances, nor was it intended to be an agency for collective bargaining. There was no provision for a vote on any issue. A "question committee" of five men elected by the Council was responsible for all matters coming before the group, and it was limited by the brief constitution to "any subject of general interest to all the workers." The plan was simply a sounding board for management policy.

Steps Toward Collective Bargaining

That employee expression required greater scope was clearly shown by the gradual transformation of the Works Council. The first employee reaction was ridicule and resignation. But as realization grew that no more effective means of representation was

---

7. In May 1919 the older employees, members of the Quarter Century Club, did establish an employee representation plan to cover themselves, but they were few in number and the younger men were not affected. When an attempt was made by management in 1922 to institute a representation plan for all the workers, it was voted down by 5,704 votes to 3,549.

near, efforts were made to utilize and extend the plan. Presumably with company approval, although the constitution remained unchanged, the councilmen were given the privilege of handling grievances in their districts with both the foremen and the superintendent. The pension system was expanded and a relief and loan plan, though considerably altered by management, was adopted upon employee initiative. Still there was no genuine collective bargaining. The final voice was the company's. Such fundamentals as wages and hours were barely mentioned.

Section 7(a) of the NRA, however, had a profound effect at Schenectady. In the summer of 1933, a new constitution was drawn up under a new name—the Workers Council. It set up grievance machinery and set forth the aim of the Council as "the arriving at settlement of all questions affecting the welfare of employees, either general or individual," in addition to the original purpose of giving "an opportunity for the interchange of ideas between the management and employees." The "question committee" was replaced by a seven-man executive committee, all serving full-time and getting their customary pay from the company. Though management continued to make all final decisions, it was clear that labor was reasserting itself.

c. RISE OF THE UNITED ELECTRICAL AND RADIO WORKERS

While this "controlled reassertion" of the workers was coming about an independent movement also arose. In the spring of 1932 a small group of toolmakers met secretly to reorganize a union. They were disturbed by reduced earnings, decreased work and depression layoffs. Most of them had been members of the old craft locals and, remembering their experiences, now favored industrial unionism. The NRA gave them a chance to come out into the open as the Electrical Industry Employees' Union. Its leaders met with the plant management but settled few grievances and made no important gains.

Yet the existence of this union was significant. For in order to strengthen the Workers Council, as well as its own standing among the employees, the company granted increasing concessions. Grievance settlement was speeded, seniority was given greater weight in layoffs, and a new profit-sharing plan was adopted in April 1934 to replace one discontinued two years earlier. Also a 10 per cent raise in wages was granted. In August 1935, when the company returned to the forty-hour week after the NRA was invalidated by the Supreme Court, the Schenectady management agreed to pay time and a half for Saturday work in all but a few departments. Vacations with pay, eliminated in 1932, were resumed in 1936, and that October a scheme was announced for adjusting wages according to the United States Department of Labor cost of living index. The Workers Council claimed credit for most of these achievements.

Victory of the Independent Union

The turning point came in 1936. Late in 1934 workers of every faction had called for pay increases, to offset mounting living costs and shorter hours of work. The requests of the Workers Council were refused with the others. The leaders of the independent union began to stress the issue. In the spring of 1936, they affiliated with the United Electrical and Radio Workers, as Local 301. They abandoned their policy of boycotting Council elections and tried to elect a majority of the committeemen. Although they failed, their representatives repeatedly embarrassed management and the heads of the Council by the questions they asked and the proposals they submitted. The wage demand, in particular, was used to impress the employees with the ineffectiveness of the Workers Council.

So great an interest was stimulated in its activities, that Local 301 decided to force the issue, although its dues-paying membership was only a few hundred. September 30 it filed a petition for an election with the National Labor Relations Board to determine the sole collective bargaining agency. The campaign was notably peaceful; the company cooperated fully with the Board and assumed a generally neutral position. Both management and labor leaders expected a Council victory, and the final vote on December 15, of 5,111 to 4,033 in favor of Local 301 surprised almost everybody.

Whether the company could have saved the Council by raising

wages at this time, in addition to its cost of living adjustment, is a doubtful point. That an increase was not unreasonable is indicated by the fact that in February 1937 and again in May, wage increases amounting to about 12 per cent were conceded. At any rate, the Workers Council was officially disbanded three days after the NLRB election; many of its committeemen and a large proportion of the employees rushed to join Local 301. The plant manager assured the local's leaders that he would abide by the results. A shop steward system was set up, and the union made one of its most active members its first full-time business agent.

d. THE 1938 AGREEMENT

The most significant development at this time was the decision of the top management of the corporation to accept independent unionism and deal with it on a *company-wide* basis. In January 1937 representatives of seven General Electric locals drew up a ten-point program in Schenectady. March 15 the first meeting was held in New York City between the union negotiating committee and a company vice president. Negotiations dragged on for almost a year. One agreement accepted by the union officials was nullified when two locals refused to approve it. The contract finally drawn up in February 1938 and effective April 1, changed specific company policies little; but it established a flexible framework within which collective bargaining could work and expand.[8] Thus the opening clause provides that as soon as a local is designated by the NLRB as sole collective bargaining agency either through election, certification or "other appropriate means satisfactory to both parties," it automatically falls within the agreement.[9]

8. The main immediate value of the contract to the union was the prestige it brought.
9. In addition to Schenectady and Lynn, where the local had been recognized as exclusive bargaining agent in March 1934, the Bridgeport, New Kensington, Cleveland and Fort Wayne works were thereby covered. The small York, Pa., plant was excluded when the union was defeated in 1937 by a vote of 102 to 45. Since April 1938, the list of General Electric plants under the agreement has been increased by the Bloomfield works, the Newark warehouse, the Detroit and Pittsburgh service shops, the Erie works, the Newark lamp works, the Pittsfield works and the Philadelphia switchgear plant, which in 1938 had lost out to an inde-

Provisions of the Contract

Most of the contract deals with laws of procedure—the rules of the game. Discrimination by management because of union membership and union coercion of nonunion workers are forbidden. The company is not to support any labor organization, financially or otherwise, but both sides may exchange information which will further agreeable relations. The union may use company bulletin boards but all notices must have the manager's approval. Grievances may be taken up by the employee or his representative with the foreman, who will generally give an answer within twenty-four hours. If no settlement is reached, the union's Executive Board may then submit the complaint to plant management. Grievances which cannot be settled locally *may* be referred to the national officers and from them *may* be placed before an impartial umpire or board.[10] Sitdowns, stoppages and lockouts are forbidden during the life of the agreement; the company will not transfer any job under dispute, but the union may not object to transfer of jobs from one machine to another if a change in manufacturing method is involved. Should an unauthorized action take place, the union and the company will confer over including a specific penalty clause in the agreement. This has not been found necessary to date.

The contract also includes a body of substantive law—policies which the corporation first concretely defined in November 1935, when the pressure of employee organization was making itself felt. These were slightly revised in March 1937 when independent unionism achieved an established position. Here are incorporated the vacation plan, the profit-sharing system, the methods for taking on and laying off men, the community wage principle, working hours and provision for payment of time and a half for overtime. Until its abandonment in 1941 the cost of living adjustment

---

pendent union but later reversed the situation. At its 1940 convention the union reported that a total of nineteen plants and service shops were covered by the national agreement and that fewer than five thousand employees working in about two dozen widely scattered small establishments remained unorganized.

10. The umpire is to be named by mutual agreement, but there is no provision for breaking a deadlock if one should occur. Thus far, no disposition to call in an arbitrator for any purpose has been indicated.

plan was also part of the contract. In the early summer of 1939, the company held that vacation rules were not subject to collective bargaining, but the union successfully resisted that contention.

Bargaining Machinery

Revision of the contract requires thirty days' notice whereas cancellation can take effect only after ninety days' notice. An umpire may be called in if no agreement can be reached. The union bargaining committee consists of at least one national officer and one delegate from each of the General Electric locals; an alternate delegate from each local may attend the conferences as observer. The negotiating group for the corporation, called the Manufacturing Committee, comprises plant managers, the vice president in charge of labor and his assistant, the company comptroller, the vice president in charge of engineering and the president of the company. The only time the two groups have met jointly was for a friendly "get-acquainted" session. The vice president in charge of labor relations has carried on all the discussion for the company. Sometimes he has met with the entire union committee. But since negotiations may run for months, expense and convenience have made it necessary for the union to send either a small subcommittee or its national officers to meet with him in preliminary talks.

The machinery does not encourage speed. The Manufacturing Committee, which convenes monthly, assumes responsiblity for the corporation, although the Board of Directors is ever in the background. The union subcommittee, in turn, must submit every move first to the whole committee and then to the locals for approval; if there is a single dissenting local, the measure must be renegotiated. Yet there has been progress, in spite of delays and difficulties union officials have had in selling gradual gains to a membership geared to rapid advances.

Administration of the Agreement

The Labor Board election automatically made Local 301 sole collective bargaining agent for the Schenectady works, but it did not automatically make all of the ten thousand workers enthusiastic unionists, or all of the supervisory force willing to cooperate in the new order. While the handling of grievances was not a novelty for many union committeemen and foremen, there were sources of discord: employees afraid to report grievances, committeemen hesitant or unable to push a case individually, foremen resentful of invasion of their customary authority and ignorant of new company rules, and departments having large proportions of nonunion members.

The year 1937 was an extremely favorable one for a start; production boomed and the plant pay roll jumped to more than twelve thousand. Yet out of the 2,500 grievances reported by union committeemen, about 700 had to be referred to the Executive Board and plant management for solution. During the depression year that followed, of some 1,200 grievances reported, over 300 could not be settled within the departments.[11] Two and a half years after the agreement became effective, the Executive Board of Local 301 complained about "confusion" over the contract and its function, and "lack of knowledge" of the method of taking up grievances.

Procedural Problems

Both union and management agree that complaints should be settled as close to the seat of trouble as possible. During the 1938 depression, with many of the ablest union committeemen laid off because of low seniority, union efficiency was seriously affected. As a result, the union pressed for and obtained seniority preference for its committeemen. The local has also experimented with section grievance committees, i.e., several committeemen to handle a grievance jointly, in the hope that a group will act more aggressively and intelligently. It also favors extending the route

11. The data on grievances submitted by management and the union differ slightly. For 1938 management reported that 389 cases had been discussed with the union negotiating committee. Of these, 88 were for "information only." Of the remaining, 55 pertained to wage rates and job classifications, 46 to scheduling and equalization of hours, 98 to layoffs, 24 to rehiring, 30 to transfers, 6 to service records, 9 to working conditions and 33 to miscellaneous matters. As to the outcome of these cases, management states that 80 were won by the union and 221 were not, but this is an ambiguous picture because many cases are compromised. The union reports a total of 354 cases but does not state in whose favor they were settled.

a grievance may follow. At present, a case goes from the committeeman-foreman level directly to the Executive Board-top management stage. Local officers contend that an additional step (committee-superintendent or general foreman) would bring more settlements within the shop. Management, however, opposes change on the grounds that speed would be sacrificed and expense increased, and that the foreman confers with his superiors anyhow. This is an interesting situation, since in many large plants the union and the company have taken the contrary positions.

Because of slow progress in developing departmental grievance machinery, many cases involving a single worker or a small group, as well as all plant-wide problems, are discussed at the top. Many minor cases are disposed of over the telephone by the union's business agent and the assistant to the plant manager. All others are handled for the local by the union Executive Board, or, more frequently, by a subcommittee named by the business agent who is its sole permanent member. The management committee is composed of the plant manager, his assistant, the works accountant, the general superintendent and two investigators. Meetings are held whenever necessary.

The outcome of these meetings has varied greatly. During prosperous months, with union bargaining strength at its peak, management has granted many concessions. During slack periods when the union has been weak, its gains have been few, and grievances less readily and less satisfactorily settled. Management admits that the leaders of Local 301 are "reasonable" in their demands, and "capable" in their dealings, but asserts that they are often unwilling to reject unworthy grievances for fear of alienating their members. Union leadership does not deny this, but claims that this tendency would disappear if a union or preferential shop were established. On the other hand, there have been times when management allowed such minor grievances as the equalization of hours within a department to be appealed to the national level. Although these appealed cases have numbered only around a dozen a year in Schenectady, they are relatively more numerous than in other General Electric plants and cause unnecessary irritation. A minor discordant note is management's refusal to sign any agreements on grievance cases, although the union has the privilege of keeping whatever records of the meetings it wishes.

e. PROBLEMS AND RESULTS

Since December 1936, changes of a substantive nature at Schenectady have pointed toward a tightening of union demands. During layoffs, first equalization of working hours, then seniority, have been applied with growing strictness. Formerly all other factors had to be equal before seniority was the determinant; now the burden of proving that ability outweighs length of service falls increasingly upon management. Still, the union has not placed obstacles in the way of men of special ability. Although the seniority grievance has been especially prominent during periods of large-scale layoffs and rehiring, it has not provoked much argument. The only dissension came when local management was unwilling to give the union detailed lists of those laid off and rehired, but this was eliminated by national negotiation in the summer of 1939.

Wages share major attention with seniority and division of work. In busy times, such as the spring and summer of 1937, they have headed the list of problems discussed and negotiated. The officers of Local 301 have pointed out that after their recognition as sole bargaining agent the wage for common labor rose from 40 to 59 cents an hour, the differential between skilled and unskilled rates was diminished, and the number of day rate job classifications reduced from seventy-five to twenty-three. The 1941 contract included an additional 10 cents an hour increase for all workers, an added 5 per cent bonus for second shift employees and double time for Sunday and holiday work.

The Community Wage

For many years General Electric has upheld the community wage as against the industry-wide wage. It promises to pay wages equal to or above those in nearby industries for comparable work. Surveys are made every three months. While the UER&MWA has been unable to attain either a company- or industry-wide wage, it has attacked the basis on which the community wage is figured. It has asked why "community" should be defined to include cities and towns two hundred miles west of Schenectady and to exclude others equally distant east and south, such as Springfield and New York City. It has asked also why plants employing only a few thousand men and paying abnormally low rates should be included in the survey, which covers between forty and fifty establishments and some twenty-four occupations. The company has answered that its rates compare favorably with any electrical manufacturing plant in the country and, moreover, that the community survey comparisons exclude overtime, night bonus, profit sharing and cost of living (now abandoned) adjustments from which the employees benefit. The significant point of all this is that the community wage has become a vital part of collective bargaining.

Working conditions are a secondary problem at the Schenectady plant. The question of speed-up is not of great moment. Except for the refrigerator department, which operates on the conveyor system, the major divisions of the establishment—turbine, generator, marine apparatus—do not belong to the mass production category. Work in these departments is highly skilled, products are carefully tested by the purchasers, and the emphasis is on quality rather than speed. Such factors ease collective bargaining problems.

Union Organization Problems

Mature collective bargaining needs strong organization of both management and labor. Much of Local 301's energy, however, is still expended upon consolidating and increasing its forces. Organizing has not been easy, despite management's decision to accept independent unionism. During the early months of 1937 the local's membership rose from a few hundred to several thousand. For the entire year an increase of 6,357 members was reported, and the Schenectady group was temporarily the largest in the international union. But absorbing these members was a tremendous administrative task. As rapidly as new ones were initiated in the fall of that year old ones fell away. The 1938 depression stripped the organization of the bulk of its following. Many of the most capable shop committeemen were laid off. Since the late months of 1938, however, membership rolls have risen slowly but steadily.

The decline in employment and the failure to develop and retain a large body of efficient committeemen were not the only obstacles. During its early campaigns, the union "promised the world" to the workers. Many were rudely disillusioned when they found that the road of collective bargaining is one of compromise and slow movement. Some refused to pay the dollar a month dues unless grievances were settled satisfactorily to them, or wage increases were negotiated. A small group of pattern makers and steam fitters remain attached to their craft unions, which alone survived the twenties.

Company Welfare Work a Factor

Not the least important factor is employee loyalty to the company. General Electric ranks high among corporations in its treatment of workers. Wages compare favorably with the best in the industry. Sanitary and safety conditions are good. The General Electric Employees Securities Corporation has sold employees over $35 million worth of bonds paying 5 per cent interest. More than $175 million of life insurance covers the sixty thousand employees, the premiums for over $70 million of which are paid by the company. The profit-sharing plan added $9.9 million to wages from 1935 to 1938. The cost of living adjustment gave employees additional earnings of $8.3 million in 1937 and 1938. As early as 1917, some thirty-three hundred workers at Schenectady with ten years of continuous service were getting a week's vacation with pay. During the 1929–1933 depression, the corporation adopted an unemployment loan benefit plan which disbursed more than $3.7 million, of which 50 per cent came from management. In addition, the company gave out relief in the form of coal, groceries and cash. This welfare activity, performed with a minimum of paternalistic spirit and combined with a variety of social and recreational facilities, has made unusually difficult the union task of binding its membership into a cohesive unit.

Summary

For General Electric's Schenectady employees, collective bargaining has thus far meant an opportunity to present demands and adjust grievances through a strong independent organization. It has also been responsible for the fact that for the first time during a major depression, the wage rates of the factory workers escaped a reduction in spite of two raises the preceding year. Unorganized salaried employees were not so fortunate.

For the company, acceptance of collective bargaining has meant freedom from strikes, at a time when strikes swept large-scale industry. Before the NLRB election there had been a few departmental sitdowns; one in June 1936 lasted over a week and necessitated the services of a state conciliator. Since the election, production has run without disturbance, although occasionally the negotiating machinery has been severely strained.

3. WESTINGHOUSE

Like General Electric, the Westinghouse Electric and Manufacturing Company has stood in the front rank of "progressive" corporations. Its welfare activities and relatively high wages have won from its employees the feeling that "if you have to work there's no better place." When the company was founded in Pittsburgh by George Westinghouse in 1886, it was announced that Saturday would be a half holiday and that salaried employees would have vacations with pay, at that time an innovation for manufacturing concerns. Unlike their major rival, however, the top executives of Westinghouse were for some time unconvinced of the expediency of dealing with a union on a company-wide basis. Moreover, until recently they refused to sign union agreements either on a company or plant basis.[12] In spite of this attitude, by September 1940 local union aggressiveness and persistence

---

12. March 29, 1940 the NLRB held that the Westinghouse Company was not bargaining in good faith in view of its refusal to sign a contract with the union. See *In the Matter of Westinghouse Electric and Manufacturing Company and its Subsidiaries, Westinghouse X-Ray Company, Inc. and The Bryant Electric Company* and *United Electrical, Radio, and Machine Workers of America and Its Locals Nos. 601, 202, 1207, 107, 111, 130, 1105, 1412, and 209,* Case C-1241. The decision

had brought recognition of the UER&MWA as sole collective bargaining agency in eleven Westinghouse units, including nineteen different plants. In May 1941 the company and the union finally signed a contract resembling General Electric's, and covering forty-five thousand employees in twenty-four plants.

a. EAST PITTSBURGH

The East Pittsburgh works and the five small plants clustering about it [13] are to the Westinghouse Company what Schenectady is to General Electric—the center of the system. A fifth of the corporation's more than forty-five thousand workers are employed here. As at Schenectady, much of the work (generators, motors, switchgear) is made to order and emphasis is on quality of product. The proportion of skilled male workers is therefore higher than in most manufacturing establishments. Management has placed particular stress upon developing men capable of operating a variety of machines.

(1). *From Company Union to Trade Union*

The first signs of unionism appeared in 1914 when a spontaneous month-long strike led by left-wingers was waged. Although the strike failed, it caused management to establish a joint six-man committee to adjust grievances. This committee, which was doubled the next year, settled a number of minor complaints but was not permitted to consider major issues. It was abolished in 1916, after another strike for shorter hours of work had been defeated. In 1919 when the Pittsburgh area was agitated by the AF of L drive to organize steel, Westinghouse executives decided to revive and elaborate the grievance system. A Works Joint Conference Committee plan was prepared "to promote a more direct mutual relationship between the employees and the management

---

was immediately appealed to the Federal Circuit Court of Appeals. After the Supreme Court decision in the *Heinz* case early in 1941, the company agreed to sign local agreements but not a company-wide agreement. Since the union wished to establish collective bargaining on the same basis as in General Electric, a temporary impasse was reached.

13. The company regards them as a single administrative unit with one general manager.

on all matters of joint interest." Joint departmental committees were set up to adjust local grievances, while the Executive Committee had the responsibility of "making recommendations to the management" on general policy. It was patently not intended to serve as a collective bargaining agency.

Until the great depression the plan worked with little friction. During the 1921 economic slump it assisted management in cuting wages 10 per cent. And during the rest of the decade, when company profits were over $150 million and employment was high, it served as a satisfactory means of expression for the bulk of the employees. Only the ill effects of marked unemployment and reduced earnings, aggravated by cases of straw-boss favoritism in distributing work, evoked serious dissatisfaction in 1931 and 1932. Nevertheless, in spite of the NRA stimulus to unionism, attempts at organization, first by the AF of L and then by a smaller, radical group affiliated with the Steel and Metal Workers Industrial Union, failed completely. Not until the spring of 1935 did a handful of men, including four members of the employee representation plan's executive committee, launch a successful campaign and affiliate with the Electrical and Radio Workers Union, a predecessor of the UER&MWA.

Unionism Finally Won

In order to avoid strife which might divide the employees, many of whom were of long service and intensely loyal to the company, the new organization pursued the strategy of boring from within the employee representation plan. Management at first offered no opposition. Later it tried to forestall the union by a variety of means—a 5 per cent wage increase in September 1935, foremen conversations with individual workers, speedier settlement of grievances and an adjusted compensation plan which, for the first eight months of its existence, provided a 10.8 per cent bonus. Nevertheless, union success was forecast in October 1936 when all employee representatives of the Joint Conference Committee joined in a demand for a 20 per cent wage increase. In the November election for the executive committee, five of the victorious candidates—one half of the employee members of the committee—belonged to the union. A sixth was won over in March 1937 after the corporation agreed to simplification of the wage payment system, increases of 8 and 6 cents an hour for men and women respectively, and guaranteed minimum rates of 63 cents an hour for men and 44 cents for women. On April 26 the union filed a petition [14] for certification as exclusive collective bargaining agency with the regional director of the NLRB, and was so certified after hearings in June revealed a union membership of 7,156 out of the 11,521 employees. The company agreed to comply with the decision.[15]

(2). *Evolution of Collective Bargaining*

Early in July, negotiations officially began between the East Pittsburgh management and Local 601. It was necessary to start from scratch in the establishment of procedures and policies, because, until certification, the local had concentrated on organizational work. But the union was at this time in a favorable position. Business was booming at a rate surpassed only in 1929. Employment had risen gradually from a low of 6,472 in June 1933 to 11,974 in July 1937. It was to reach a peak of 12,186 in September, before recession set in. The local failed, nevertheless, to achieve its foremost aim—a signed agreement.

From the first, there was dispute over the meaning of collective bargaining. Management contended that it was simply an opportunity for representatives of the employees to bring up and discuss

14. The original petition included salaried clerks in the unit but this was amended on May 6 to involve only hourly rated employees. Few of the clerks, either in the office or in the plant, were in the organization, although the president of the union belongs to the latter category. Since 1938 there has been active an Association of Westinghouse Salaried Employees. Antagonism exists between the Association and the UER&MWA. When the Association petitioned the NLRB for certification as a bargaining agency, the UER&MWA was successful in persuading the Board to exclude from the Association unit 335 salaried "production" workers consisting of employees doing clerical work on the manufacturing floors, 135 salaried inspectors and their stenographers, and 23 salaried power house workers.

15. The executive committee of the employee representation plan, since it was union-controlled, voted not to oppose the certification of Local 601. The plan was repudiated by the company after the Supreme Court decisions on the Wagner Act in April 1937. The International Brotherhood of Electrical Workers, which had shortly before opened a membership drive in the plant, did not participate in the hearings because it had a negligible membership.

problems affecting the working force, with the final decision reserved to the company. It rejected the notion of a signed agreement because business conditions were too uncertain and a contract "was not to the best interest of all concerned." It refused to permit joint signatures to any statement on a specific issue which was to be posted on the bulletin board. It would not assent to the local's suggestion of arbitration to break deadlocks.

Negotiators for Local 601 maintained that this was not collective bargaining. They pointed out that under the employee representation plan statements were signed by both management and members of the executive committee. They charged the company with delay and evasion, but they took no aggressive action.[16] By the late fall, their opportunity was gone, for with the depression union membership went into a decline. In January 1938, 10,359 men and women were averaging thirty hours of work a week; by October employment fell to 7,751.

Instead of a signed contract, each clause of the union's proposed agreement was discussed separately, beginning with policy and grievance procedure. When an issue was decided, and approved by the union membership, management posted a notice over the signature of the plant industrial relations manager to the effect that the question had been a subject of collective bargaining between the company and Local 601 and the company was now explaining its decision.

Progress in Collective Bargaining

In spite of continuous union claims that genuine collective bargaining was not in operation, policies and procedures in the Westinghouse plant were marked by increasing participation of organized labor. Perhaps the chief of many reasons for this change was management's desire for uninterrupted production and its realization that trouble would be inevitable if the union could not make good on some of its program. Personalities also played an important part. In the spring of 1938 a new plant manager

---

16. The leaders of the union averaged well over forty years of age, a fact which may partially explain their cautious attitude. On January 1, 1939, the average total service of the employees was almost seventeen years.

won the respect of the union leaders by his fair dealings. A few months later factional difficulties in Local 601 were smoothed out by the selection of the first full-time business agent, a young, capable UER&MWA organizer. The gradual recovery of employment and union strength in the late months of 1938 were other reasons for the change. Symptomatic was the tone of the announcements after negotiations. Although still bearing only the company's signature, they no longer gave the impression that the decision had been made by one side alone.

Trial and error characterized this evolution. At first the union's entire negotiating committee (the members of the executive board, the officers and a district organizer) met with a management committee composed of the plant, industrial relations and employment managers. There was much waste of time and talk. Later the union vested discussion of all but the most important questions of policy in a subcommittee of three to five members, with the local president and the business agent serving ex officio. This subcommittee is chosen by the executive board from among the full negotiating committee. A different subcommittee is named according to the subjects considered. Minutes, once customary, are no longer taken in these meetings because they seemed to act as a check upon frank discussion. Helping also to eliminate confusion and to speed negotiations was the insistence of the plant industrial relations manager upon a clear distinction between an individual or group grievance and a plant policy. Management showed a relatively ready disposition to grant individual claims, provided no precedent was established for the plant as a whole.

Layoff and Rehiring Policies

Wages excepted, the most important question under negotiation has been that of layoffs and rehiring. To the union, the problem has meant equitable distribution of work among its members and an end of discrimination by supervisors. To the company, the problem has been essentially one of maintaining the most skilled, efficient force. Before the 1937–1938 depression, reduction of forces at East Pittsburgh rested in the hands of the foremen and superintendents in the various sections, although the employment office had the final word. Ability and attitude were the criteria. Seniority was relied on only when all other factors were equal—which rarely proved to be the case. Family connections and personal friendship had occasionally played important roles in determining who was to work and for how long. It had likewise been not uncommon for salaried men, both clerks and supervisors (particularly those who had risen from the ranks), to "bump" or share hours with regular production workers. In 1931 and 1932 this situation was qualified somewhat by a ruling that no men with ten or more years of service should be laid off, although hours might be drastically reduced. When layoffs were necessary in the years following 1933, this general procedure was continued except that men and women hired after the low point, July 1, 1933, were usually furloughed first.

Leaders of Local 601 were determined to extend the seniority principle. On the details of seniority they are still undecided, but some form of it they regard as essential. Under the first plan, negotiated in December 1937, when employment had to be cut, layoffs based on efficiency affected those hired since January 1, 1937. If work continued to decline, time was to be equally distributed until an average of thirty hours a week over a four-week period was reached. Then transfers to other sections and divisions on the basis of seniority and ability to do the work were to be carried out, if feasible. If not feasible, collective bargaining within the section or department would determine what policy to follow. Rehiring would be in reverse order of layoffs.

July 1938 brought important alterations. It was agreed that when work was to be shared, group leaders,[17] who are appointed by management in spite of the union's desire to have a voice, would not get favored treatment. Much more significant was the declaration that layoffs would be based on total rather than continuous service. This question first came up after the World War.

17. To make production flow more smoothly, most of the workers are divided into small groups or teams which are responsible for specific operations. Each worker is paid on the basis of the total output of the group. The group leader is usually one of the more experienced workers who keeps the group functioning efficiently and thus relieves the foremen of a considerable burden.

The men who had worked at the plant during the war objected when others who had taken leave of absence to get better jobs elsewhere received credit for previous service when they returned. The company then adopted the continuous service system based on the last hiring date, which remained in effect until 1938. The union strenuously objected to it because long layoffs during the years 1929–1935 nullified the considerable total service which many of its members had built up.

In August 1939, after considering more than two score proposals, still a third set of modifications appeared for the benefit of numerous ten- and fifteen-year service men who were idle in some departments while in others short service men were working. Seniority application was widened. When the average hours in a group or section fell for four weeks below thirty-six a week, employees with less than a year's service would be dropped from the division. When average hours fell to thirty-four, employees with one- to five-years' service would be transferred or released. When average hours fell to thirty-two, employees with five- to seven-years' service would be similarly affected. Further reductions would be worked out by collective bargaining within the division. Thus seniority on a divisional rather than departmental basis decided layoffs and transfers, provided always that a man could handle the work. Rehiring also was altered. First, vacancies were to go to transferred employees, next to laid-off employees according to *plant* seniority. Applying to all employees as of July 1, 1937, the new procedure safeguarded the greatest number of union members, for that date was not only the employment peak since 1930, but the peak in union dues.

The end of these changes is not in sight because neither management nor union leaders believe that the ideal solution has been found. Although the local was genuinely desirous of a system free of discrimination, it also took advantage of the opportunity to increase its strength. Thus, it early demanded seniority preference for its shop stewards, pointing out that under the employee representation plan committeemen were similarly given preferential treatment. Management claimed, somewhat facetiously, that the National Labor Relations Act forbade this favoritism. But it did promise that before a steward was laid off, consideration would be given his case by the two negotiating committees in the light of his work as steward, which amounted in practice to the union request. When management claimed that the seniority scheme excluded young people from the plant and might endanger efficiency, the union replied that it would approve the employment of a certain percentage of younger men, provided they automatically became union members. The offer was not accepted. Where nonunionists could be eliminated without setting a precedent, the local has sometimes allowed ability to outweigh seniority.

The Wage System

When in March 1937 the wage system was altered and wages raised by joint negotiation, a step as significant as the seniority program was taken. It emphasized that the entire wage question lay in the realm of collective bargaining—not simply general wage levels, but complex problems of wage computation and administration as well. During the Joint Conference Committee plan the representatives did discuss wages and the wage system, but no fundamental changes were made.

In 1918 the Westinghouse Company introduced an incentive system for hourly paid workers, which soon covered 90 per cent of the force. All jobs were time-studied and classified into five major groups for men and three for women, according to skill, effort, desirability; pay rates were fixed for each. The classifications and their maximum and minimum rates were listed on a key sheet for guidance of the employment department when hiring and of department heads when revising wages. The incentive scheme called for two base rates: a day work rate which was the going rate in the district for the particular job, and a standard time rate which was about 12 per cent higher. If the time taken on a job was greater than the time allowed, the operator received the day rate times his efficiency percentage; if it was equal to or less than the time allowed, he received the higher standard rate times his efficiency percentage. Employees disliked the system. It was complicated, susceptible to manipulation and penalized for "off-days."

New Adjustments Increase Wages

In the negotiations of March 1937 with the then union-controlled executive committee of the employee representation plan, the company agreed to eliminate the "high-low" wage scale. The day work rate was increased to the level of the former standard rate; if a man failed to "make out" in the time allowed, he was guaranteed this as a minimum. In other words, his earnings could not fall below the 100 per cent mark of the time study, but increased effort might bring him 125 per cent or more. As a result, the average hourly "take-out" at East Pittsburgh (including bonus and overtime) increased 18.9 per cent for men and 27.6 per cent for women from July 1936 to July 1937, while increases for the whole electrical manufacturing industry were respectively 15.3 per cent and 17.2 per cent. According to company figures, average hourly earnings of East Pittsburgh men workers in July 1937 were $1.05 as compared to 81 cents for the electrical manufacturing industry, and of women 64 cents as compared to 55 cents. In line with its policy to simplify the wage structure and to diminish wage differentials between the skilled and the unskilled, the union has tried to decrease the number of major classifications and the many wage levels within them.

Union surveillance of the wage system has proved as important as adjustment of the key sheets. In a large plant, top management is ignorant of much that goes on within the shops, and policy legislated at the top is frequently administered in a considerably different spirit. The East Pittsburgh management had carried on reviews of wage rates for many years, but not until February 1938 could labor check these reviews effectively. It was agreed that supervisors of each operating division should make up review sheets semiannually, which would be carefully scrutinized by the divisional, subdivisional and sectional shop stewards. A central rate review committee of three representatives from Local 601 and three from management was appointed to make a general over-all review. These reviews have taken some time, but they have corrected many injustices. In certain divisions many workers were found to be below their appropriate classifications, in others supervisors had ignored the key sheet and set their own rates, while in still others service cards revealed that men "of excellent ability" were rated "low in attitude." Aside from these periodic reviews, shop stewards have the continuing duty of examining job classifications, requesting new time studies and negotiating changes due to new methods or new equipment, or some irregularity.

Grievance Procedure

Grievance adjustment has gone through equally marked changes. Until the meetings of the spring of 1937, when Local 601's recognition was assured, the union had concerned itself simply with problems of organization. Shortly before the NLRB certification, it gave some attention to a shop committee system, which was approved July 16, 1937. Under the system, sectional, subdivisional and divisional grievance men handled complaints in their jurisdictions with their supervisors. Grievances which could not be settled by the employee concerned and his foreman were to be written up in triplicate form and signed by the employee.[18] Questions that could not be settled in the shop would be forwarded to the executive board, which decided whether they were worthy of discussion with the management.

The machinery worked badly for more than a year. Even before the depression had set in, it operated fitfully. Grievances were not written up, many of those brought up were not justified, many that were justified were unreasonably delayed. With the depression and the great decline in union membership and dues, many departments were left without committeemen, and employees in most of the remainder were too concerned with keeping their jobs to bring up complaints. In May 1938 the local tried to revitalize the procedure. It changed the name of grievance committeemen to shop stewards, called for monthly meetings of the Grievance and Shop Stewards Council to discuss complaints and methods, and decided that a subcommittee rather than the entire negotiating committee would carry unsettled cases to management. An agreement was reached with management for quarterly meetings between the division manager, and whatever supervisors he might

18. The signature of the employee was a precaution against the not uncommon occurrence of his taking fright and deserting his committeeman.

designate, and the division stewards to discuss all local problems and thereby prevent individual and group grievances from arising.

Considerable credit for improvement in the grievance procedure appears to be due the man who was plant manager from April 1938 to May 1939, and the local's business agent, who assumed office in June 1938. When the union claimed that some employees were afraid to sign what they felt to be just complaints because such action might be considered a black mark on their records, the manager publicly stated that "the company will not tolerate giving any man a 'bum' deal because he signed a grievance, even if that grievance were not supported on investigation."

The union found that almost as many grievances were settled in the first three months of 1939 as throughout all 1938.[19] Better business and larger union membership were, of course, partly responsible. In May 1939 the procedure was more clearly defined and time limits set for the answers of the supervisors to complaints. Neither side is wholly content yet. Union officers believe that the foremen's attitude has improved markedly, but they hold that two types need tutoring: those who promise the worker that the matter will be taken up without putting it in writing, and those who avoid responsibility by running immediately to their superiors. Management, in turn, contends that too often the steward encourages employees to make complaints which they otherwise would have ignored. It also alleges that, for political reasons, the union fails to reject many poor grievances.

Significance of the Failure to Sign an Agreement

Absence of a signed contract during these years was mainly of psychological import to the East Pittsburgh local. A signed con-

---

19. Since hundreds of grievances are still not officially recorded, the statistics on grievances are not satisfactory. During the last half of 1937, a total of 363 grievances were written up for the union files. Of these 86 involved wages; 25, working conditions; 28, discrimination and intimidation of union members and shop stewards; and 224, rehiring. Fifty-two of the 363 were adjusted by the section steward and foreman, 19 by the steward and general foreman, 33 by the division steward and superintendent, 9 by the executive board and the industrial relations department of the company, 137 by the union office and the employment office. Fifteen grievances were withdrawn, 4 rejected as unsatisfactory, and 94, regarding laid-off employees who have not been rehired, are pending.

tract may persuade some employees to join the union, but it will not affect either policy or procedure. Whatever gains the union may make, whatever new responsibilities it may share, will come, not from a signed agreement, but from its leaders' ingenuity in the art of collective bargaining and from strong organization.

b. EAST SPRINGFIELD

Collective bargaining at the Westinghouse East Springfield, Massachusetts, plant has worked more smoothly and effectively than at East Pittsburgh. East Springfield employed close to six thousand men and women at the peak, but the number usually fluctuates between twenty-five and thirty-five hundred. It makes refrigerators, beverage coolers and such appliances as fans and vacuum cleaners. Until recently small motors were an important department. Air-conditioning equipment is also turned out on a small scale. Most of the jobs require little or no skill.[20] Thus problems arising from the structure of the works are relatively simple. A further contribution to the success of collective bargaining was the absence of a firmly established employee representation plan. When the stimulus of independent unionism was finally felt, there were no vested interests to make for serious disunity in the working force. The obstacles to organization and the possibilities of disturbance in the shops were thereby lessened.

But the central factors have been: (1) ability of the union leadership to develop an organization comprising almost 100 per cent of a working force to whom unionism was previously unknown, and to maintain it intact, in spite of depression and the transfer of the major department to another plant; (2) realization by leaders of the need for tempering aggression with patience and compromise; and (3) management's recognition that the union was a going concern and its consequent decision not merely to "play ball" with it but to get the greatest possible value from its existence.

20. According to management, 25 per cent of the workers are skilled. The union leaders contend that about 50 per cent of the jobs take six or more months to master.

(1). *The Agreement of 1933*

The start was not auspicious. When the NRA came in the early summer of 1933, the Westinghouse Company decided to extend its Joint Conference Committee plan to all plants. At East Springfield, however, the American Federation of Labor was already on the scene; when the manager met with the employee representatives on July 28 to discuss the plan, several were already members of Federal Labor Union No. 18,476.[21] During August the company announced that in accordance with the Electrical Manufacturing Industry Code, it was reducing work hours from forty-three and three quarters a week to thirty-six, and increasing wages approximately 6 per cent in addition to the 5 per cent increase given on July 1. By this time, however, seven of the thirteen committeemen and a large percentage of the employees had joined the AF of L union.

On September 15 the union made nine proposals calling for recognition, further wage increases to compensate for the shortened work period, abolition of the group payment system, time and a half for overtime and double time for Sunday and holiday work. After management denied recognition and refused another wage increase, a strike was called on September 22 and mass picketing closed the plant.

The strike was ended by an agreement reached in Washington, October 20, after national officials of the Westinghouse Company and the National Labor Board had been called in. Wording of the settlement seemed to uphold management's original contentions. Its application signified a union victory.

The careful phrasing of the one-page document indicates the maneuvers necessary to grant the union the recognition it wanted without contravening the corporation's unwillingness to sign a union contract. No termination date was set and nothing was said about hours, working conditions or adjustment of grievances, as is customary in labor agreements. The word "union" was not even mentioned but the corporation agreed to "bargain collectively

---

21. In March 1936 it helped form the UER&MWA of which it became Local 202.

with the representatives of the employees selected in accordance with the provisions of section 7(a) of the National Recovery Act." The Joint Conference Committee idea disappeared. Although a general wage increase was not granted, jobs were to be jointly reclassified and revalued. The number of rates for each classification was to be reduced to not more than three insofar as practicable. The rates themselves were to be readjusted in line with what other manufacturers in the industrial area paid for similar work, and readjustments made within six months were to be retroactive to October 23, 1933. These terms for the first time made occupational structure a subject for joint discussion and were the basis for ending favoritism and discrimination by minor supervisors. Finally, while stating that its policy was "to consider seniority in the retention of its employees when seniority and merit do not conflict," the company reserved full right to deal with layoffs as it saw fit. But from this base, the bargaining process developed a layoff and rehiring system in which seniority was the practice and merit a burden for management to prove.

(2). *Management Attitudes and Policies*

The plant manager did not get along well with the union. It is agreed by many who knew the situation that he could not adjust himself to day-to-day negotiation with organized labor. The job of reclassifying occupations and fixing rates, a difficult one in any event, was dragged out for weeks and created much irritation. A major argument rose over definition of "industrial area"; the union insisted unsuccessfully that wage rates should be compared over an area covering several New England cities, while the manager maintained that only Greater Springfield had been intended. The union set up a shop steward system for settlement of grievances, but many petty cases could not be handled in the departments because foremen were uncertain of what policy to follow. An appeal by the manager to union representatives to help eliminate waste brought no perceptible results. In turn, union requests for a wider application of seniority brought the response that merit came first and that family responsibility would receive great weight in layoffs.

Management Reorganized to Improve Relations

In December 1934 the plant management was thoroughly reorganized and a new manager appointed. How far the labor situation was responsible is difficult to say. Undoubtedly an important element was East Springfield's rank as one of the two poorest divisions in the corporation for labor cost and production waste. But the significance of this reorganization for collective bargaining was the creation of an industrial relations department to coordinate such labor activities as employment, medical care and safety, to centralize responsibility in dealing with the union and to act in a staff or advisory capacity to the works manager.

Until 1934 labor relations were a direct responsibility of foremen and superintendents. Now for the first time labor was regarded as a plant-wide problem. Employment and dismissal became subject to the approval of the industrial relations director and all unsettled grievances went to him. Ultimate responsibility for the company, of course, rested with the works manager, who met once a month with the union committee. But a manager is concerned with many things. As the relationship with the union improved, an increasing proportion of the negotiations was placed under the industrial relations director, who conferred daily with the union's business agent and president in his office.

The new plant manager and supervisors [22] of the new department were not hampered by the psychology of the old manager. Once convinced that unionism was a reality which had to be faced, they set out to make the most of it. They discovered that a direct refusal suited employees better than weeks of delay and hedging. They realized that advance information of a decrease of work enabled union leaders to formulate a program agreeable to most of their members. When the Pittsburgh main office sent out to its plants requests for bids on a flat iron castings order, the East

---

22. The first director of the industrial relations department served only a few months before becoming superintendent of the new air-conditioning department. His successor came into the personnel field fresh from the company's purchasing division. When in May 1939 the manager was promoted to a higher post, the first industrial relations director succeeded him. He immediately announced that there would be no changes in labor policy.

Springfield management placed the case before the union members in the foundry, who agreed to handle the job so that the best bid could be met without any wage cut. In his first meeting with the union committee, the manager declared that in the future incentive workers guilty of defective workmanship would be required to correct the product but would not be charged for the material spoiled. Shortly after, he announced creation of shop regulation committees in the merchandising and small motor divisions to inspect the plant periodically for cleanliness and "good housekeeping," and he asked the union to appoint two employee representatives to serve with two management representatives on each committee. He agreed also to have employees help management select group leaders.

(3). *Union Policy and Jurisdiction*

The union leaders, notably the business agent and the local president, who carry on the bulk of the administrative work and negotiation, responded to the new management attitude in the same spirit. They have repeatedly shown that they have no ambition to usurp management's function of "running the plant." They usually prefer to be critics rather than assume the initiative in protecting employees' interests. Thus in the setting of a new rate, or in discharges, transfers or layoffs, they believe that management should act first. Then, if there is complaint, it can be brought up in the form of a grievance. The union thus avoids the danger of being charged with discriminating between employees. At the same time, union leaders have not hesitated to be aggressive when they deemed the issue sufficiently important.

Jurisdiction has never been a serious question. While a few office workers hold union membership, the union has not tried to organize them. All other employees, including group leaders, instructors and lunchroom employees, but excluding anyone with the right to hire or discharge, are represented. In practice, the union has been the exclusive bargaining agency since the strike, although it was not certified by the NLRB until the spring of 1939.

(4). *Bargaining Procedures and Policies*

Policy negotiation and handling of grievances have rested on a flexible and informal basis. Stenographic minutes of monthly meetings—ten or more typed pages are not uncommon—are distributed to all workers. At first many small complaints were carried to these meetings, but this was soon discouraged and only broad questions, like a general wage increase, payment for overtime, vacations and mass layoffs are normally considered. For the union six elected representatives, including the business agent attend, plus four other members chosen and changed by the local president at frequent intervals, so that an appreciation of the problems of collective bargaining can be gained by many. For the same purpose, the works manager will bring in the section superintendents as well as general foremen.

While an increasing number of grievances are settled by shop stewards and foremen, the bulk are adjusted from day to day in the industrial relations director's office with the business agent and the union president. No records are kept; talk is frank and invariably effective. In these discussions the groundwork for administration of labor policy has been laid.

Application of the Seniority Principle

Under the new regime, seniority received increasing consideration in layoffs and rehiring until, by 1938, it was the predominant factor. For layoffs it applies on a divisional basis; in rehiring, on a plant-wide basis. The only condition is that the worker must be competent. The question of competency at first created difficulties and caused the company much unnecessary expense because men, anxious to hold a job, frequently claimed ability to do work of which a trial soon showed them incapable. Education in the futility of this course, irritation of other members of the group with which the individual worked, and closer examination of previous occupational records ended this phase. A distinction between male and female jobs was sharply drawn and seniority applied by sex. The union did not seek seniority preference for shop stewards; members viewed such a plan with suspicion. Because of the plant's relatively small size, the handling of complaints was not affected when some stewards were laid off during the 1937–1938 depression.[23]

The general approval given this seniority program has enabled the plant to effect the transfer of its major division—the small motors department—with a minimum of discontent. It is true that the move occurred mainly in the fall of 1937, when production was at an all-time peak and the eleven hundred displaced workers could be transferred to refrigerator, fan and feeder departments. But soon after came another depression and employment fell from over fifty-one hundred production workers to below three thousand.

Union-Management Cooperation

One of the first moves of the works manager was to stress the defective work or "scraps" problem which his predecessor had repeatedly and unavailingly brought up. His declaration in December 1934 that the old policy of charging employees for spoiled material would be discontinued won immediate approval of the workers, and some progress was noted. At that same meeting a union committeeman recommended appointing joint committees in various departments to investigate cases of defective workmanship. In 1937 the management initiated a sustained and effective campaign with this proposal as its basis.

First, individual union representatives in the shop had to be convinced that a scraps campaign would benefit the workmen [24]

23. A rather unique scheme for administering layoffs has been devised by the industrial relations director and the union officials. A small office in the industrial relations department to which the union members have free access is reserved exclusively for this purpose. On the walls are two boards, one for men, the other for women, on which are fixed, in order of seniority by divisions or major departments, small cards bearing the name of every worker, his service date and his occupation. At a glance it is possible for the least intelligent employee to see how he stands in his division, and with a little study he can gather a picture of the plant as a whole. In the employment office there is a similar arrangement, except that the cards are those of laid-off workers and the seniority listing is plant-wide.

24. Union officials have explained that they accepted and have supported the program for the following reasons: (1) a reduction in scrap means higher wages since the workmen have to spend less time replacing this defective work; (2) the men can no longer be blamed for defective tooling and defective material; and (3) the foremen can no longer refuse to remedy defective tooling by claiming that higher management refuses to furnish the necessary funds.

as well as show management and the public that a responsible labor organization could make constructive contribution to the welfare of the plant. Joint committees were established in each department to meet once a week or more frequently to discuss local problems and to educate the workers in "quality production." Each scrap case underwent intensive analysis, and methods of avoiding a repetition were outlined. Minutes of these meetings were written up and distributed. Once a month all local committees met in divisional conference to report progress and to study interdepartmental problems. Occasionally a plant meeting was called to describe the course of the campaign.

A colorful, many-sided publicity program was initiated with posters hung in every department. The union's weekly newspaper, *The United Front,* reprinted the posters and slogans in addition to publishing editorials and articles urging cooperation. A periodical "news letter," bearing both the Westinghouse trademark and the official seal of Local 202, was issued under joint editorship. Percentages of scrap reductions were posted to stimulate competition between departments.

The management emphasized the relationship between the campaign and the Westinghouse wage adjustment plan inaugurated in May 1936. Under the plan, when the average monthly income of the corporation for three months is above $600,000 and the average pay roll is less than $5 million, the employees (salaried as well as hourly paid) get a one per cent increase in pay the next month for each $60,000 gain over the $600,000.[25] Thus during the remainder of 1936 the employees earned an average monthly bonus of 10.8 per cent; in 1937 the figure was 13.8 per cent; in 1938, a depression year, it was about 3 per cent. However, since all Westinghouse divisions participate in the adjusted compensation plan, and since scraps savings at East Springfield would affect the total only slightly, the relation is more symbolic than significant. It is doubtful whether many workers were influenced by it.

25. If the average base pay roll is more than $5 million then "the amount of the average net income (above $600,000) which will result in a one per cent increase of base wage or salary for the succeeding month is the figure which bears the same relation to $60,000 which the average base pay roll of the company for the preceding three months bears to $5 million."

Nevertheless, the campaign for elimination of waste and defective workmanship is an integral part of plant policy. It appears to have effected definite economy.[26] In March 1937 losses from waste and defective workmanship were about 12 per cent of productive labor, in 1938 the percentage was 9.1, and in the first eight months of 1939, 6.1. The significant contrast is that between 1938 and 1939, because though production and employment increased in the latter year, the scraps curve continued its downward trend. Only the results over several years of varying conditions will offer proof. However, even if its economic value is slight, the scraps campaign would be worth while for its influence on labor relations. Through the joint departmental and interdepartmental committee meetings, it has given employees and the supervisory officials clearer appreciation of each other's problems and has destroyed many bases of misunderstanding and antagonism.

Problems and Limitations

Notwithstanding its success, collective bargaining at East Springfield still must solve many problems. Job classification is one of the hardest which intrudes weekly in every department. The industrial area over which job comparisons are made and the types of factories they include have caused heated debates from the start. Re-education of foremen in dealing with employees as union members is a troublesome and subtle matter of concern, particularly to the industrial relations department. Many older foremen have not yet learned the advisability of giving reasons with their orders for nonroutine work. The scheduling of production to eliminate acute seasonal fluctuations and to minimize necessary layoffs is likely to attract increasing attention in the future.

To some extent, company-wide policy has limited local negotiations. While plant managers have great discretionary powers they cannot go against main office policies. The basic work week can-

26. This is not easy to ascertain accurately because the extent of plant activity has an important independent effect on efficiency. Waste tends to be proportionally higher during busy periods than during slack periods for many reasons—the greater tendency for men and supervisors to be careless and to ignore petty inefficiencies, the stress on speed to meet orders, the hiring of new, untrained people, etc.

not be changed locally. Neither is the adjusted compensation plan or the vacation policy alterable without national approval. By and large, however, these limitations have not been important at East Springfield.

4. THE RADIO INDUSTRY

In the radio branch of the electrical manufacturing industry, collective bargaining has been greatly affected by price competition. The 1937 *Census of Manufactures* reported 162 firms making radio sets, tubes and phonographs, and employing 48,345. In addition there were over 600 parts manufacturers, employing about 15,000. A few of the leading concerns turning out finished sets—like RCA, the Philadelphia Storage Battery Company (Philco) and General Electric—make the bulk of their own parts. The rest, including important competitors, like Emerson and Zenith, rely upon small parts manufacturers and specialize in assembly.

A Bureau of Labor Statistics study in August 1937 showed that average hourly earnings of all employees in the parts plants were 48 cents as compared to 61 cents for the sets plants. While hourly earnings in plants of "two of the largest producers" together averaged 73 cents, no other establishment in the industry averaged more than 61 cents and two major firms reported average earnings from 50 to 55 cents. Some smaller establishments averaged less than 40 cents.

The failure of the UER&MWA to organize the small parts manufacturers and the manufacturers which depend upon them for their material has obviously jeopardized the standards of the union establishments. In the spring of 1939 the union reported seventeen signed contracts involving about 16,690 workers. About two thirds of these employees were covered by the three agreements with Philco, RCA and the General Electric plant at Bridgeport, Connecticut. At its 1940 convention, the union noted considerable progress in other radio plants but did not announce any general statistics on the number of contracts or their coverage. The International Brotherhood of Electrical Workers, the AF of L union, claimed in February 1940 that it had agreements with thirty radio manufacturing companies, including Crosley,

Detrola and Wells-Gardner. Most of these were small parts producers and the total number of workers covered was less than in the case of its rival. During 1940 several of the International Brotherhood of Electrical Workers' radio plants were won over by the CIO organization. Like the UER&MWA establishments, those controlled by the Brotherhood are organized on an industrial union basis.

a. PHILCO

(1). *Overnight Development of Unionism and Collective Bargaining*

In its twenty-four years of making storage batteries and its first five years as a manufacturer of radios,[27] the Philadelphia Storage Battery Company was not concerned with unionism. A "closed corporation" (until April 1940) in which the stock was held by the executive officers, it had steadily extended sales and manufacturing operations, so that by 1930 it led the radio field as it had previously led in storage batteries. The NRA made unionism an issue. In June 1933 company officials established an employee representation plan, apparently not to forestall independent organization, but because it seemed at the time a popular measure. It did not live long. A company order requiring employees to work ten hours a day temporarily to make up for a July 4 holiday was followed by a spontaneous strike of some 350 assemblers, testers and repairmen in two sections, and tied up the work of over 2,000 more because of the highly mechanized conveyor belt system. It is not clear whether the order alone was responsible or whether discontent stimulated by the general resurgence of unionism was the main factor. At any rate the strikers appealed to the experienced American Federation of Full-Fashioned Hosiery Workers for help and proceeded to organize a union.

Three days later, on July 15, the company signed an agreement providing for the eight-hour day, forty-hour week (instead of forty-seven or more), time and a half for overtime instead of

27. Although Philco continued to produce storage batteries after it began to manufacture radios, the former has been of minor importance.

straight time for all work, abolition of penalties for errors and bad work, payment for waiting time between jobs, shop committees to handle grievances, and minimum hourly wages of 45 cents for men and 36 cents for women. In addition, the company verbally agreed to recognize the new union, the American Federation of Radio Workers, which was chartered by the AF of L on August 3 as the Radio and Television Workers Federal Labor Union No. 18,368.[28] It was further provided that a union "rate committee" would negotiate future wage questions with the management.

These were great gains. But a month later, on August 17, was signed still another agreement with two significant clauses. One provided for the union shop; all new employees were obligated to become union members within two weeks after their hiring. The other affirmed that no other Radio and Television local chartered by the AF of L would accept wage rates lower than those paid at Philco; furthermore, that Philco unions would not demand any increase unless the rates were incorporated in the NRA code for the radio industry or were paid by a competitive company in the radio industry. A letter signed by William Green, president of the AF of L, was appended in support of the wage clause. Such complete acceptance of unionism came from the desire of company officials not to be bothered by "labor problems" and, in part, at least, from ignorance of the significance of their concessions. After the decline in 1933, business was again improving and the sales-conscious executives were preoccupied with maintaining Philco's position as the leading radio manufacturing firm.

The union leaders, up from the assembly lines, were youthful, inexperienced, alert and ambitious. There were actually three locals in the plant—a small body of battery workers, a larger group of machinists who in peak periods numbered well over a thousand, and the main force of radio workers. Attention will be centered on the latter, both because of their numerical importance and the leading role they played.

28. The union left the AF of L when it helped form the UER&MWA in March 1936.

(2). *Labor Relations in a Period of Prosperity*

Boom years followed for the company. Under the NRA Code's thirty-six-hour week, the number of employees increased from 3,700 on July 1, 1933, to 6,100 in late August. The first quarter of 1934 was the best sales period in the company's history. The first three months of 1935 surpassed the 1934 sales record by 28 per cent and found 8,200 at work with a factory pay roll of $2 million. That Christmas the company distributed $250,000 in employee bonuses and declared that the hourly wage rate of its Philadelphia factory workers was 19 per cent higher than the average for all industry, 8 per cent higher than the average for the entire electrical industry, and 25 per cent higher than the radio industry's average. It boasted that the public bought three times as many Philco radios as any other make and almost half as many as all other makes combined. In 1936 more than 10,000 workers were being employed.

Union Advances

It was a favorable setting for furthering union aims, and the agreement of April 7, 1936 strikingly reflected the advance. Local union jurisdiction was extended to wage earners transferred to executive positions on salaries under $35 per week. The normal work week for employees in processing divisions was fixed at thirty-six hours from Monday through Friday. Each shift was given a specific starting and finishing time and work outside of these hours was paid for as overtime. Employees told to report for work by a supervisor were guaranteed three and a half consecutive hours of work. In slack times, work was to be equally divided down to twenty-eight hours a week, after which layoffs would be made according to strict departmental seniority.

Where a seniority question could not be settled by foremen and stewards, a Seniority Board of three foremen and three stewards would decide. Union stewards received seniority preference. The union was to get a copy of every hiring card not later than one day after date of hiring. Jobs were to be classified by joint department committees. If the Rates Committee disagreed, the disagreement went to an umpire. The starting rate for women was set at 36 cents per hour and at the end of six weeks raised to a guaranteed minimum of 44 cents. Respective rates for men were 44 and 56 cents. The company could not buy any part from the outside if one of its departments could make it, unless both management and the union decided the department was running at peak. A shop committee system was set up to handle grievances, and cases it failed to adjust were to go to an impartial chairman named by the U. S. Secretary of Labor.

All this was a far cry from pre-NRA days when hiring was normally by foremen in the employment yard, when men were not infrequently told to report and then kept waiting without pay for several hours or given a few hours' work and then dismissed, when unjustly laid-off employees had no recourse, when fines and penalties were imposed for poor work, and when job rates and classifications were poorly defined and irregularly administered.

Sources of Irritation

These advances did not come easily or without dissatisfaction. The forty to fifty shop stewards,[29] who handled grievances, checked up on delinquent dues payers and helped form union policy, suddenly found that they had great powers. They displaced foremen as key figures in the shop and some treated foremen with slight respect. Employees who objected to union decisions or methods were dealt with harshly. Failure to carry a dues-book or to pay dues would often cause a man to be sent home. While highhandedness was not universal, top management regarded it with increasing irritation. Administration of seniority also created ill feeling. The transfer of employees from one occupation to another according to seniority, without regard for competency, meant undue, expensive retraining. On its side, management made few concessions which added to costs without strenuous opposition.

In spite of these rough spots, production moved smoothly.

29. For the first three years the stewards were appointed by the local president. After that they were elected by the members in their departments. They also became the members of the executive board of the union.

Relations between the three union officers (president, vice president and treasurer) who served as business agents, and the vice president in charge of production, who handled labor relations for the company, were generally harmonious. Apart from a one-day "holiday" called by the union in 1935 to demonstrate its strength during wage negotiations, there were no plant-wide stoppages. Only one wage rate grievance was appealed to an impartial chairman. The employees gained a clearer appreciation of production problems. To promote more capable leadership and make the steward system work more effectively, the union sponsored a time-study course given by the expert who had taught the company foremen.

(3). *The Difficult Years*

But peace could not continue. The union had pushed too far ahead of the rest of the industry, not only in wages but also in other standards and in the functions it had assumed. The union-shop trend which the company thought the NRA foreshadowed had not materialized, especially in the radio branch of the electrical manufacturing industry.[30]

On the economic side was a triple-edged obstacle. The radio market boom reached its peak during 1936 and was leveling out during 1937 preliminary to next year's great slump. Further, Philco was challenged by the growth of RCA, Zenith and other firms. Finally, the union's promise in 1933 that wages in the industry would be equalized was not kept. Neither the AF of L nor the CIO could achieve this end. The Philco management said that because of the efficiency of its production and sales organization, it could compete successfully with a 10 to 15 per cent wage handicap against all other concerns except RCA. During 1935 and 1936 it did compete with striking success in face of even greater differentials, for its organization was geared to huge volume. When business declined, absence of unionism in a large part of the industry and sweatshop conditions in many of the

---

30. It has been suggested, although it is difficult to prove, that many large purchasers of Philco products, notably the automobile corporations, who were antagonistic to the spread of unionism, had expressed dissatisfaction at the concessions granted by the company.

parts plants were a greater threat. Advantages of bigness turned to disadvantages of overhead costs.

End of Peace

On April 30, 1937 the eighty-five hundred workers in the plant were called out on strike. The unions demanded a 10 cents an hour increase for production workers and 5 cents an hour extra pay for night work. The company countered with a demand for modification of the thirty-six-hour basic work week to forty hours during busy seasons, although hours during the slack period would be reduced to keep a thirty-six-hour average for the entire year. An agreement concluding the dispute May 28 was a compromise; hours were not altered, and only a 5 cent hourly raise was granted. All other conditions were unchanged except that seniority in layoffs was broadened from a departmental to a plant-wide basis.

Business at this time was still good. Had the unions asked for a 5 cent increase, they might have had it without any trouble. Immediately after the Philco settlement, RCA gave a similar raise. But in the remaining months of 1937, relationships in the plant were unsettled. The new seniority program brought more irritation because transfers based solely on seniority necessitated an unusual amount of retraining. During December, there was a short sitdown in the parts division over the purchase of parts from the outside.

It is not certain when the company first determined to check the power of the unions. Nor is it certain whether the intent was to smash unionism completely or simply to balance the scales. Nor, again, is it certain whether the orders lost because of the May strike and the worst slump in the company's history beginning that fall were the impelling cause or provided the strategic time.

Negotiations for a new agreement with the UER&MWA began February 21, 1938. Employment, which a year before was over eight thousand and in the early autumn was around five thousand, had fallen below two thousand. Management firmly asserted that under the union agreements of the preceding four and a half years, increasing restrictions had been imposed which its competitors had escaped, that the radio business was heading toward small sets, cheaper prices and low profits, that unless the unions agreed to certain concessions to improve Philco's competitive position and restore employment, the Philco Radio and Television Company [31] (selling agent for the Philadelphia Storage Battery Company) would place its orders elsewhere. The demands included: an hourly base rate of 50 cents for men and 40 cents for women; a forty-hour week, with a forty-four-hour schedule during ten weeks of the rush season; abolition of the restriction on the purchase of materials made more cheaply outside; alteration of the seniority system; and reclassification of certain jobs.

A Four Months' Strike

Union representatives refused these demands, but requested that the expired contract be extended while negotiations continued. Management rejected this proposal and ordered about fifteen hundred employees to report for work at reduced wages. Charging that the company was not bargaining in good faith and was in reality attempting to destroy them, the unions threw picket lines in front of every factory gate. The plant was closed for four months and eight days.

If the primary intent of the corporation was destruction of unionism, the settlement of September 7 was a failure. The unions were not crushed. Indeed, the difficulty union leaders had in persuading the rank and file to accept the agreement, in spite of cessation of state unemployment compensation payments,[32] indicates the strength of union morale.

If modification was the only intent, the company gained most of its objectives. Base rates were reduced from 61 to 52 cents

31. The Philco Radio and Television Company was formed in 1932 primarily to avoid royalty payments to RCA. For every radio built, RCA receives roughly 5 per cent of the manufacturer's selling price to the first middleman. If a corporation owns the first middleman, it can sell to him at cost of production and thus pay the royalty on a smaller figure. RCA attacked this procedure in the courts but was unsuccessful.
32. The State Unemployment Insurance Board had considered the dispute a lockout, rather than a strike, but the period for payments was now ended.

for men and from 49 to 42 cents for women. Above these base rates, however, were to be three classifications under which, according to skill, a man might earn up to 65 cents an hour and a woman up to 52.5 cents. The 25 per cent incentive was removed, but the company agreed to a bonus of one cent an hour if production passed 20,000 sets a week, 2 cents if over 25,000, 3 cents after 30,000, 4 cents after 35,000, and 5 cents after 40,000. The thirty-six-hour week was replaced by the forty-hour week. The union agreed not to discipline members for "any cause relating to production," that is, for exceeding normal production. The company was given freedom to buy materials from outside, but it promised to make all parts that it could even if costs were slightly higher.

To allow for stabilization, the new contract was to run for two and a half years. The union was recognized as sole collective bargaining agent but the union-shop clause was eliminated. However, it was understood under a gentlemen's agreement that the company would require union members to pay their dues; and since no new workers were to be rehired until all the old ones were re-employed, the former union-shop status continued in practice. A seniority board of two union officers and two company representatives was to supervise rehiring and layoff in accordance with seniority and skill. The board was not to nullify the seniority principle, but to prevent poorly trained men from being transferred to new jobs merely on the basis of length of service. The central feature of the agreement was that it gave management a free hand in production problems, subject only to union complaint. What the company had charged were "restrictions" on production were eliminated. In the narrower field of employee-management relations, the position of the union was not affected.

(4). *The New Situation*

Thereafter labor relations at Philco entered a new phase. It was recognized that until a boom in employment recurred,[33] only a small proportion of all workers attached to the plant during the 1935–1936 period could be re-employed. The cabinet factory

33. Television is looked forward to as the panacea.

was dismantled, resulting in the permanent loss of several hundred jobs. The trend toward manufacture of small sets and the reclassification of jobs changed the composition of the working group. Where the company had previously employed mostly men (an exceptional state for the radio industry) it now had a majority of women on the pay roll. With a working membership fluctuating between two thousand and four thousand, and with many of their most active adherents (excluding the stewards) on the street, the unions found themselves badly off. For the first time since collective bargaining was instituted management enjoyed the upper hand, but the shift in power was not so great as to lead to one-sided negotiations or an inequitable interpretation of the agreement. Notwithstanding radical changes, the new contract continues to be one of the most satisfactory, from the labor point of view, in the electrical manufacturing industry.

The outstanding characteristic of labor relations since the signing of the agreement has been their centralization. With the hiring of an industrial relations director during the "lockout," and with the contraction of employment, the responsibilities of minor supervisors in the collective bargaining field were reduced. Foremen were forbidden to adjust all but the pettiest grievances and ordered to refrain from attempting any interpretation of the clauses of the agreement. The bulk of the work of negotiation and settlement of complaints was transferred to the union officers and the office of the industrial relations director. This gives a flexibility formerly absent. In hiring and discharge, for example, discussions are held beforehand so that protests later have been virtually eliminated.

b. RCA

The RCA Manufacturing Company appears to have been unaware that it had a "labor problem" until the tool and die makers of its huge Camden, New Jersey, works spontaneously threatened to strike in the spring of 1933 if a new wage system were put into effect. The hectic, dynamic rise of the radio industry, with its emphasis on production and sales, was responsible for this "oversight," just as at Philco. RCA did not enter the manufacturing field until 1930, after buying the old Victor Talking Machine properties at Camden for $154 million. In spite of the 1929 market crash and the already inflated condition of the radio field, the corporation spent over $5.5 million in renovating, reorganizing and expanding the plant. In an amazing demonstration of "boom" psychology, employment rose from some seven thousand employees to approximately twenty thousand during 1930. Retrenchment was inevitable when management realized the depression trend. Cuts in wages and salaries were made and employment was reduced to a low of slightly more than five thousand by the summer of 1932.

(1). *Labor Relations in a Dual Union Situation*

The tool and die makers' threat was so effective that the men decided to form a union. In March 1933, the RCA Victor Shop Association was established with the purpose of first uniting all tool, die and instrument makers and then organizing all other employees, except those on salary. With the passage of the NRA, however, management decided upon an employee representation plan. Each division of the manufacturing department was "invited to elect representatives who, with representation appointed by the company, would constitute a Joint Conference to discuss and to settle—subject to review by the management—all matters of mutual interest pertaining to working conditions." Employees were not asked whether they approved of this plan. Leaders of the Shop Association tried but failed to gain control of the new organization. In October 1933 they withdrew, charging that the employee representation plan was a company-dominated organization and contrary to the spirit of Section 7(a). They also changed the name of the Association to "The Radio and Metal Workers Industrial Union." However, they remained independent of the Philco unions because the AF of L refused to grant an industry-wide charter. In turn, the leaders of the employee representation plan modified its constitution, altered its name to the Employees Committee Union, asked Administrator Hugh S. Johnson of the NRA to rule that it was not a "company union," and had its leaflets printed outside of the plant by union printers.

Their president even attended a few early conferences of independent unions at Schenectady, Lynn and Springfield, which were considering a national organization, although the ECU, in contrast to its rival, engaged almost entirely in local activities. Still a third union appeared when the men in the "trouble shooters" department, the skilled testers and repairmen, affiliated with the AF of L. This group, however, never succeeded in expanding and was finally absorbed in 1936 by the independents.

Management, represented usually by the assistant to the vice president in charge of manufacture and the personnel director, met with all groups. It disclaimed partiality and expressed willingness to discuss problems with any properly elected representatives of its employees. Once a month it held separate conferences with the delegates of each organization to adjust grievances that could not be settled within the departments and to discuss more general matters. Since as many as seventy to eighty members attended, these meetings gave opportunity not so much for collective bargaining as for individual criticism of management procedure and policy. Too much time and talk were devoted to minor matters, and little was done. The superintendent of the personnel relations division occasionally conferred with a few leaders of the labor groups but without much result. In almost every department were partisans of the two factions and consequent friction.

This uncomfortable situation continued without change for more than two years. Had the company been neutral, it would still have had an enormous advantage in the scales of collective bargaining. But there is ample evidence [34] that it strongly favored, if it did not completely finance and dominate, the Employees Committee Union. The ECU was allowed to claim credit for whatever concessions were granted—10 per cent hourly wage increases in July 1933 and April 1934, time and a half for overtime, a guarantee of four hours' pay when told to report for work, a four weeks' limit on the learning period.

By the spring of 1936, when it became affiliated with the

---

34. See *Hearings before United States Senate Sub-Committee of the Committee on Education and Labor*, Pt. 8, Sec. 2, March 11, 1937, pp. 2909-2920.

United Electrical and Radio Workers union as Local 103, the independent union, in spite of the upsurge of business and employment, was in a precarious position. Its requests for wage increases, holiday pay and equal rates for men and women doing similar work were summarily rejected, although vacations with pay, which had been supported by all labor factions, were finally granted.

(2). Victory of the UER&MWA

The two-union system at the plant was fundamentally unstable. Sooner or later one group had to triumph and, in view of the company attitude, the Employees Committee seemed likely to gain the upper hand. The United Electrical and Radio Workers union, however, regarded organization of the RCA plant as essential to its further progress in the radio industry. The Philco works across the Delaware river were the stronghold of the International and a nonunion RCA was a potential threat to its standards. It was decided to force the issue while business was good. Local 103 on May 20, 1936 asked for a signed contract and got quick refusal. Instead of retiring as in the past, however, the officers pressed their demands—abolition of the ECU, a closed-shop contract similar to the Philco agreement, and a 20 per cent wage increase. On June 8 the first of a series of fruitless negotiations was begun with the president of the RCA Manufacturing Company. As the likelihood of a labor outbreak grew strong, the highest officials of the corporation and the national union stepped into the picture. The company hired Hugh S. Johnson as its special labor adviser, but all discussions were futile.

The 1936 Strike

The four-week strike which began June 23 was accompanied by bloodshed and repeated arrests of union officials and members. The corporation attempted throughout to continue its manufacturing operations, although at a reduced rate, with the active assistance of the ECU leader, the use of over a thousand strikebreakers, the hiring of professional guards and the full cooperation of local police and judges. It expended at least $244,932 to fight the strike in addition to $586,093 which it estimated was the extra cost of getting its orders made elsewhere. How many of the nine thousand production employees joined the strikers is still not clear, although it is known that at the end of the strike, forty-three hundred men and women, including the newly hired strikebreakers, were in the factory.

In spite of bitterness negotiations continued during the dispute. John L. Lewis played a quiet but prominent role in advising the union leaders and in discussing the issues with General Johnson. The forces for compromise were powerful. The union was under a terrific financial strain. Philco Local 101 was particularly interested in the outcome and supplied, in addition to bail for arrested strikers, more than $50,000, but its members were concerned over the expense. The company, on the other hand, not only lost desirable business, but it had an increasing amount of unfavorable publicity from the riots, the suppression of civil liberties and the NLRB complaint that it sponsored a "company union." An agreement was therefore finally signed on July 21.

Terms of the Settlement

The Bellevue-Stratford agreement (from the name of the Philadelphia hotel where it was negotiated) called for the immediate end of the strike and re-employment "as rapidly as work for them becomes available and without discrimination" of all employees whether on strike or not. No new employees were to be hired before March 31, 1937, while those on the pay roll as of June 23, 1936 were available and competent to fill vacancies. The company further agreed to "maintain the policy of paying as high wages under as favorable hours and working conditions as prevail in Camden-Philadelphia manufacturing establishments engaged in similar classes of work," thus insuring equal standards with Philco.

But clauses of an agreement may be mere words unless a strong organization sees that they are enforced. The significant provision of the Bellevue-Stratford agreement was the one declaring for an election under NLRB auspices to determine majority representation. It was agreed, moreover, "that the sole collective bargaining agency shall be the candidate receiving a majority of the votes of all those eligible to vote in such election." [35] The election was set for August 16. The International Brotherhood of Electrical Workers, which asked for protection during the strike for some of its members, advised the Board that it did not wish to be placed on the ballot. The Employees Committee Union was on the ballot, but this organization, after agreeing orally to it, boycotted the election and carried on an aggressive campaign to keep the workers from the polls. The result was a final count of 3,016 votes for Local 103, 51 votes for the ECU—a preponderant majority for the UER&MWA of those voting, but a decided minority of the 9,752 eligible to vote. November 9, 1936 the Board, after considering the strenuous protests of the company, in a precedent-setting decision which stressed the ECU tactics, certified the United Electrical and Radio Workers as the sole bargaining agency of the hourly paid employees in the production department and elsewhere.

Continued Strife

Upon the advice of General Johnson, the corporation refused to accept the decision. It contended that a major proportion of the employees would be deprived of their constitutional rights. It accepted Local 103 as bargaining agent for its members, but also continued to deal with the Employees Committee Union. The prestrike status of collective bargaining was perpetuated. The previous bitterness was now accentuated by aftermaths of the strike and by friction from remanning the factory. Though all but sixty-four strikebreakers were released within three weeks, the company was employing 1,654 fewer people on October 1, 1936 than on June 23 owing to a production decline. Within the shops, where both factions worked side by side, discord was inevitable. At first it found expression in brief stoppages, but for the most part it arose in the many ways that people have to make others uncomfortable. Management pleaded a headache

35. Chairman J. Warren Madden of the NLRB pointed out a few days after the agreement was announced that this clause was probably not in accord with the Wagner Act.

from the strife, claiming that it was a victim of a struggle between hostile unions; the UER&MWA charged that the company was attempting to destroy it. A wage increase in October and adjustments in the job classification system did not alleviate the difficulties. In the early months of 1937 the local charged that the company was discriminating against its alien members who had participated in the strike, that Section 4 of the Bellevue-Stratford agreement was not being lived up to, since not all the strikers had been returned to their jobs by March 31, 1937, and that work which could be handled within the plant was being let out. The president of the company replied that Section 4 did not mean that the workers would be rehired if there were no jobs for them. He denied the remaining charges.

The Exclusive Contract with the UER&MWA

The decision of the Supreme Court in April 1937, validating the Wagner Act, marked the turning point in labor relations at Camden. The union immediately asked for a signed contract, but was informed that a similar agreement would have to be negotiated by the company with the Employees Committee Union. Thereupon it complained to the NLRB regional office that about five hundred persons had not been returned to the positions they had held before the strike, although most of the departments where they formerly had worked were on overtime schedules. It demanded back pay for them.

But the complaint was never carried to a conclusion. For in August Edward F. McGrady, former Assistant Secretary of Labor, was made vice president in charge of labor for the Radio Corporation of America. On October 8, the RCA Manufacturing Company entered into a collective bargaining agreement with the United Electrical, Radio and Machine Workers union in which the latter was recognized as exclusive bargaining agent. Supplemental memoranda called for joint review of the approximately five hundred cases in which discrimination was claimed, and for the prompt payment of vacation pay to those who had fulfilled work requirements but took part in the strike. The company specifically promised not to deal with any other labor organization, including the Employees Committee Union.

The agreement, which was renewed in 1938 and only partly altered in 1939 and again in 1941,[36] continued the policy of paying the wages and maintaining the working conditions prevailing in the Camden-Philadelphia area. Union jurisdiction was limited to the unit established at the time of the election and such workers as watchmen, cafeteria employees and group leaders are still without a bargaining agent. Seniority was recognized as one of the determining factors in layoffs, transfers and rehirings, together with ability and other qualifications. Sharing of work was to precede layoffs, but work weeks were not to be reduced to less than three days during slack times. Any employee dismissed for cause was given the right to a hearing within forty-eight hours. Strikes or other stoppages were forbidden and the local agreed not to ask for a closed shop during the life of the agreement. Formal grievance procedure provided for arbitration by a three-man board if a settlement was not made within the plant. The agreement was to be in full force for a year and, thereafter, from year to year, unless notice for either modification or termination is given sixty days before it runs out.

Genuine collective bargaining did not automatically erase the bitterness of the past. A week after the agreement, the Employees Committee Union was granted a charter by the International Brotherhood of Electrical Workers and immediately distributed leaflets attacking the United Electrical, Radio and Machine Workers union. In October 1939, the NLRB accepted a Brotherhood of Electrical Workers' petition for another election. The 6,294 to 1,035 vote in favor of the UER&MWA vindicated the claims of Local 103 to act as spokesman for the employees. Apart from

---

36. There were only two alterations in the agreement of October 1939. (1) The five-day, forty-hour week replaced a thirty-six-hour week (forty hours in peak seasons). All Saturday work was to be considered as overtime and to be paid for as such, regardless of the number of hours worked during the regular work week. Previously, Saturday morning work was not considered overtime if the full quota of hours had not been filled. (2) The business agent was granted the right to tour any part of the plant during working hours to check on working conditions.

Wages were raised in June 1941, when the contract was renewed four months ahead of time at the union's suggestion.

this outside activity, which was primarily a product of AF of L-CIO antagonisms, some departments in the plant have seen minor but unpleasant entanglements—revenge, pressure to force workers to join the union or to pay dues, and efforts to embarrass the union. Riots, the stripping of women's clothing from their bodies, beatings, scabbing are not easily forgotten or forgiven.

(3). Recent Developments

With the signing of the contract, steps were taken to put collective bargaining on a more efficient basis. The monthly conference was given up. The local formed a new general negotiating committee consisting of the Executive Board and the division chairmen (several of whom are Executive Board members) to determine important policies and procedures. This body almost never meets with management; instead, a subcommittee of three, including the business agent, carries on actual negotiations.

The business agent, who is now also president of the local, is the key union figure, with unusual authority and responsibility. Together with the personnel director he adjusts many minor grievances such as layoffs not in line with seniority. He may enter a case at any level of the grievance procedure to advise and guide shop stewards, or to settle the case by himself. He has the right to tour any part of the plant during working hours to see that working conditions conform to the contract. He sees to it that union members are rehired in the proper order and, wherever possible, before nonunionists; in the hiring of new workers, his aid is sought by job seekers. This increasing centralization is noteworthy since in the earlier days of unionism at Camden, each division was like an independent unit of a loosely bound federation. The need for greater efficiency had a part in the change, but most of it came from the administrative ability of the business agent and the failure of other capable leaders to develop.

For management the industrial relations director is the center of the labor sphere. Before the emergence of the unions, the company had set up an employment office to record hirings and discharges and a personnel office to supervise the welfare activities of the plant. But the power to hire, transfer, fire, fix wages and adjust complaints lay in the shops with the foremen and superintendents. During the years when the ECU was an important factor, however, top management was afraid to allow the supervisors to adjust all but the most petty of grievances lest someone should make a false move or set an undesired precedent. Not only was this demoralizing to minor supervision, but it also delayed the settlement of complaints and fostered irritation. A further weakness of this early centralization lay in the undue burden placed on the executives who were concerned primarily with production. With the appointment of a director of industrial relations in 1935, a new policy was initiated. Responsibility in the labor field was gradually shifted from executive officers of the company to the new official. All discharged workers were guaranteed a hearing by him. His office began to supervise rehiring and transfers. All unsettled grievances were appealed to him. He remains, of course, responsible to the plant manager and the company president, and subject to the general policies laid down by the board of directors as recommended by the Vice President in Charge of Labor, Mr. McGrady. His decisions on specific issues may also be and occasionally are appealed to the vice president. But in his administration and adjustment of the numerous daily problems incidental to collective bargaining, much of the success or failure of the system lies.

Early in 1936 the company opened a weekly management training course to which it attributes great importance. Round table discussions cover all aspects of labor relations, from contract interpretation and grievance adjustment to the significance of federal labor laws. The industrial relations director has paid special attention to the straw bosses and has tried, with the approval of the union, to get more complaints settled in the shop. Probably 15 to 20 per cent more cases are adjusted in the departments, but there is no sign that the number of complaints has declined.

The new relationship between management and labor after the signing of the contract was made clear in December 1937. For some months before, the union and the company had been discussing the question of married couples employed at the plant. It was felt that more than one hundred jobs would be involved.

Union officials were opposed to the indiscriminate discharge of all married women. When the industrial relations director publicly announced the company's program without notice to the union, the latter protested sharply, both through the newspapers and to Mr. McGrady. As a result further negotiations arrived at a satisfactory program.

(4). *Results*

Problems at the RCA Camden plant differ in detail but not in kind from those of other radio and electrical manufacturers. Concessions gained by the union have been gradual and piecemeal. Layoffs and rehiring, once dictated by the supervisor or superintendent, then regulated by such factors as ability and size of family, are now based on strict seniority. Only if management can demonstrate the need for retaining a man because of his special ability, is seniority likely not to be controlling. Lists of those to be laid off are given to union officials in advance, and in some cases the shop steward rather than the foreman breaks the news. Shop stewards get preferential treatment unless a department membership votes to the contrary. As long as any one has work in a department, the steward must also be employed. Thus he need not rotate with the others when work is being shared. A substeward is given top seniority in his section, but he is not exempt from rotation in slack times. Job classifications have been steadily improved. Where once there were a dozen or more different rates for some skilled jobs there are now three or four. The scheduling of production in departments has been made more accurate as a result of the provision that any worker ordered to come to work is guaranteed four hours' pay.

Like Philco, the RCA Manufacturing Company has been one of the high-wage-paying establishments in the industry, but it has not yet strongly suggested that the policies of the UER&MWA have interfered with its general competitive position. Behind this striking difference are the following facts: (1) the patent control of RCA which brings it several millions of dollars in royalties from its competitors each year; (2) its enormous reserve power and prestige, and the fact that it has, at least till recently, regarded manufacturing as second to radio broadcasting; (3) the preeminence which the Camden plant enjoys in some of its other production departments; and (4) the absence of a restrictive union program in regard to seniority or technological changes. What the economic effects of collective bargaining will be in the long run, it is too early to estimate.

5. Observations and Conclusions

Collective bargaining in the electrical manufacturing industry, as in most of the recently unionized industries, is still in its beginnings. Its stability, its form, its procedures and its effects are by no means definitely established. Yet they lead to certain observations.

First, it is apparent that recognition of a union by management, whether through a signed or a "verbal" agreement, is the mere beginning of collective bargaining. Difficult problems are still to be faced. First agreements have been little more than letters of introduction. There has been no disposition to interpret their clauses strictly, and the subsequent union-management relationship has therefore been a product highly colored by the personalities involved. Industrial government must be regarded as a government of men as well as of laws.

In each of the five cases studied in this chapter events which followed management's acceptance of unionism varied with local forces. In general, however, three factors seem to have been of primary importance—the background before collective bargaining, the sincerity with which management accepted unionism, and the strength developed by the union organization.

The prior existence of a long-established employee representation plan, as at the General Electric plant in Schenectady and the Westinghouse plant in East Pittsburgh, helped collective bargaining by familiarizing employees with the techniques and procedures for adjusting grievances and negotiating with management. When it created vested interests among certain worker groups and thereby split employee sentiment over unionism, it had a more important obstructive effect. The example of the RCA plant at Camden shows that where management has encouraged or sanctioned competing employee factions, the ensuing period of collective bargaining with a single union becomes more difficult.

The attitude in which top management accepted unionism was another important factor. In each case the union entered collective bargaining deeply suspicious of the intentions of the company. Considerable time passed before confidence developed and, in at least three cases, that feeling is still lacking. At the Westinghouse plant in East Springfield, progress was limited until the original plant manager had been replaced by one who won the union's respect and trust. Refusal of Westinghouse to sign a contract did not affect relationships at the East Springfield plant because it was understood that local management could not act differently. But at East Pittsburgh, the mother plant, it was an important cause of distrust. At RCA a working arrangement between the company and the union was not even approximated until Edward McGrady became Vice President in Charge of Labor, and the United Electrical, Radio and Machine Workers of America was recognized as the sole bargaining agency.

Union strength is another basic factor. Management is not likely to make important concessions to a weak union. On the other hand, where organization has been almost complete, as at East Springfield, collective bargaining has been most advanced. Significant also is the fact that in three of the five plants the problem of organization was almost as difficult after union recognition as before. As long as a union must give most of its time and energy to winning new members and holding its old ones, collective bargaining suffers.

Philco, however, is a striking illustration of the complexity of collective bargaining. Although management accepted unionism without reservation at the start and the union was firmly established, the system broke down at the first economic depression. The breakdown was partly due to the union's unwillingness to lower its standards even temporarily. Also it came partly from the company's failure to recognize labor as worthy of equal attention with production and sales. But perhaps most of all it was due to the inexperience of both sides in the art of collective bargaining and a failure to recognize that it is a two-sided, give-and-take process.

Management in newly organized industries faces problems of readjustment as complex as those of its employees. The question is not simply, as is commonly thought, a matter of top management's being willing to sit down at the table with union representatives, though this is an indispensable first step. In one plant the manager could not adjust himself to the new conditions and had to be removed. In two other plants labor experts were called in to restore peace after violent conflict had disrupted production. In three of the five plants the companies found it essential to set up new industrial relations departments. Labor became a plant-wide problem rather than a subject of purely departmental concern. The industrial relations director became an important figure in the plant.

Chief among specific issues which arose were distribution of work in slack periods, wage adjustments and methods for settling grievances. An unusual amount of experimentation with methods of dividing work brought solutions with many aspects in common. In spite of all the publicity and concern, seniority was never the sole consideration in slack times. Invariably work in a department was equally divided before transfers and layoffs were made. In contrast to the practice in many of the older unionized industries, like clothing or flint glass, work sharing was not carried to an unlimited degree, but rather to a minimum of twenty-four or thirty hours of work a week, after which came layoffs. The limit was established partly because of the availability of WPA work, partly because the older men with families resented a "sharing of misery," and partly because unlimited sharing would have affected union income in depression periods. Layoff systems vary greatly but one important feature common to almost all is that seniority is the first consideration in a given case, unless management can prove the superior importance of such other factors as ability. In only one of the five plants has management charged that the seniority program was an economic liability.

The general wage level in the plants studied has not been seriously debated except in the unusual case of Philco. Inasmuch as the companies are the largest and most prosperous in the electrical manufacturing industry, they have paid relatively high wages. Union policy was to combat wage cuts unless company need was evident. As a result, for the first time in a depression, the wage increases of the preceding business upturn were not wiped out. The unions fought successfully for a reduction in job classifications and the equalization of pay for similar work. However, they failed to make the industry rather than the community the basis for comparable rate standards.

The experience of the five plants indicates clearly that the method of adjusting grievances is relatively secondary; the personalities involved determine in the end whether many grievances will arise and how serious they will become. An accumulation of minor complaints may create as much difficulty as some of the so-called major issues. The main problem has been the training of foremen and shop stewards in the techniques of grievance settlement. Slow progress in this has led to increased centralization of responsibility and authority. Thus far, top union and company officials spend too much time on minor cases. All agree that men in the departments should solve as many of their own problems as possible. Although the agreements contain arbitration provisions, outside parties are almost never called in.

The unions have indicated that they have no desire to usurp management's function, but wish rather to be intelligent critics of management's policies. For example, they have normally left wage rates to the skilled time-study divisions of the companies, but they have carefully scrutinized the results and brought complaints whenever they believed injustice done to any member. They have been interested in both production and marketing problems as affecting jobs of their members. They have not opposed new machinery, but they have fought strenuously to prevent displacement of union workers. Wherever management consults beforehand with union leaders about production problems, as at East Springfield, difficulties are notably eased.

What are the prospects for the near future? The experience

at the East Springfield plant of Westinghouse gives a clue as to how far union-management relations can advance in a relatively short period. The immediate trend in the plants studied, however, does not seem to point in that direction. The companies consider themselves largely self-sufficient in managing their plants and are unwilling to entrust the unions with any responsibilities. They see in the unions no positive functions which might help them. They deal with the union primarily because they wish to avoid strife and because collective bargaining is the law of the land. The initiative in collective bargaining has consequently been left to the unions. The latter are, however, still primarily concerned with establishing themselves. Until they feel firmly entrenched and convinced that management no longer seeks to undermine them, they cannot be expected to give extensive cooperation.

Chapter 15

CHICAGO SERVICE TRADES

CLEANING AND DYEING, MOTION PICTURE MACHINE
OPERATORS AND MUSICIANS

C. LAWRENCE CHRISTENSON

1. INTRODUCTION

ALTHOUGH THE DEFINITION of any industry must necessarily be arbitrary, there is an identifiable range of economic activity which we commonly refer to as "the service trades." With growing specialization and urbanization, these trades have assumed increasing importance, and within them has developed a substantial tradition of collective bargaining. Because these service trades are, on the whole, somewhat new, union organization does not reach as far back with them as, for example, in printing and building construction. Yet in many metropolitan areas the practice of collective dealing is firmly established in such activities as elevator operation in office buildings, janitor service and building maintenance, cleaning, dyeing, laundry and linen service, various amusements, retail distribution of milk, as well as storage warehouse operation and trucking. To this group might also be added the barbers, whose union organization goes back at least to Knights of Labor days. Despite this wide variety, the service trades have received little attention in the literature of collective bargaining.

Broadly speaking, these groups are identified by the fact that their members create no physical product. Most of their work is either moving goods or operating or repairing existing equipment. Any tangible end-product of their activities appears as a very slight change in the form of goods already made. Consequently, time is an especially significant element for almost all of these occupations. What is wanted is not simply "service," but service at a particular time and place.

This absence of physical product has far-reaching consequences for industrial control within these groups. Since time and place of performance are fixed, the market for the labor of groups within the service trades is almost always identical with the producing area, and the producing area in turn becomes definitely localized. To illustrate, the product of the activity of janitors is disposed of in exactly the same city where the activity takes place, and, therefore, janitors working within a given city are insulated from the competition of janitors elsewhere. The significance of the time factor, particularly in its relation to the absence of physical product, is emphasized by the fact that there can be no "storage" of service in any real sense.

Largely as a result of these factors, service industries have closer contacts with ultimate consumers than do manufacturing plants. Collective control will affect the consumers, but, on the other hand, the nearness of the consumers to service operations affects collective bargaining practices much more directly than in manufacturing industries.

The highly localized operation of these trades means that their collective bargaining activities must be studied on a local basis. Only local investigation will yield enough detail to give an understanding of the actual operation of collective bargaining in this sphere. On the other hand, the results of an investigation in one area may not be typical of collective activity in other markets. The bargaining patterns in Chicago are not identical with those in other sections of the country. Wherever possible, similarities in bargaining procedure in other cities are indicated. However, even though this is not possible in every instance, it is believed that a study of a specific local area may at least lay the groundwork for an answer to the question as to the characteristics of collective bargaining in the same trades elsewhere.

Three Chicago service trades offer sharply varying patterns of collective bargaining. The first of these is the cleaning and dyeing industry, which includes several small crafts that make up a minor segment of the economic system. Second are the motion picture machine operators, a small craft operating within an important and well-defined industry. Finally, we shall turn to a review of the bargaining procedure and practices of the professional musicians, a highly developed craft whose operations cut across several different industries.

2. Chicago's Cleaning and Dyeing Industry [1]

a. THE DRY CLEANING BUSINESS

Units of the Industry

Chicago's cleaning and dyeing industry is made up of three types of business units—"wholesale plants," "branch store plants" and "synthetic shops" (in the trade sometimes called "synthetic plants"). The wholesale plants are the original units of the industry as it developed around the turn of the century. Judged by factory standards, they were not large establishments and even today few have more than fifty employees, the majority of whom are relatively unskilled. These plants get their business mainly from the city's numerous independent tailor shops.[2]

The branch store plant operates its own outlets. These plant-owned stores are likely to be even smaller than the independent tailor shops. Operated usually by a single employee, they receive articles to be cleaned and temporarily store finished work until it is called for. Usually they do no cleaning or finishing. Branch store operation was confined to one firm before 1910. Since 1915, and particularly since 1930, branch store operation has spread considerably.

1. The material in this section is drawn largely from an unpublished University of Chicago doctoral dissertation, Morrison Handsaker, *The Chicago Cleaning and Dyeing Industry; A Case Study in "Controlled" Competition,* 1939. Without the valuable assistance of the Handsaker manuscript it would have been impossible to gather the necessary information in the time available.
2. Many of these shops serve merely as middlemen between the customer and the plant by collecting soiled garments and distributing them after cleaning. Others perform minor alterations and repairs as well as finishing and pressing, but only a small minority are tailor shops in the sense that they do custom tailoring. The tailor shops are frequently referred to as "stops" in the trade because each shop is a stop for the deliveryman.

A still newer unit than the branch store plant, with no apparent existence prior to 1930, is the "synthetic shop," created by the installation of recently developed cleaning equipment in the ordinary small tailor shop. In the conversion of tailor shops to synthetic shops, three requirements appear to have been significant. First and foremost, cleaning fluids had to be safe for use in buildings constructed without special fire precautions and located in congested business districts. Second, equipment for using such materials had to be compact. Finally, the cost of this equipment had to be low enough so that the business of a single shop could justify the investment. Such equipment was advertised in trade journals in 1939 for as low as $850 installed.[3] These machines originally used synthetic solvents, and the name has persisted in the trade even after modifications in equipment permitted other types of solvents to be used and also after some of the large wholesale plants adopted synthetic solvents.

Market Structure

Census data cover wholesale and branch store plants, no distinction being made between them and no recognition being given to the fact that some tailor shops are also synthetic cleaners (Chicago has about a hundred synthetic shops). Most of the plants today do both wholesale and retail business. While only about 20 per cent of them can be classified as branch store plants, almost all the older wholesale plants now have direct contact with individual customers through truck collection and delivery service at dwellings. But for the most part, the plants without branch stores, some eighty in 1939, rely on the three thousand independent tailor shops. The branch store plants tend to confine themselves to their own outlets, numbering roughly three hundred, although some business comes to them by direct collection from customers.[4]

3. See *National Cleaner and Dyer,* June 1939, p. 61.
4. In the absence of a separate Census count of the branch store plants, a check with the Chicago telephone directory in 1939 indicated that there were at least eighteen such plants operating a total of 270 branch stores. Even less satisfying information is available as to the number of synthetic shops. One plant owner, however, told the writer that in 1939 there were more than a hundred synthetic shops operating then. "Most of these," he explained, "are actually financed by the big chemical companies, Midland and Dow, from whom they buy supplies."

Typically they specialize in "cash and carry" service, which means that customers bring the garments to the branch store, call and pay for the work as soon as it is finished. Bureau of the Census data show that in 1935 Chicago's 103 wholesale and branch store cleaning plants employed 2,814 wage earners and 486 salaried workers and officials, and had a gross total business of $7.3 million. Although not classifying types of plants separately, the Bureau does report that 32 per cent of this business was wholesale. If allowance is made for additional retail delivery cost and possible profit, then it appears that more than half the physical volume was still handled on a wholesale basis through the independent tailor shop outlets. Since most of this work is done by wholesale plants operating no branch stores, it seems safe to conclude that even in 1935 these plants still handled the bulk of the business, although the almost exclusive position which they held early in the century had been lost.

Business is usually confined to the metropolitan area. A few plants do some business with customers outside this area, but it represents an insignificant part of the whole. Much more important for understanding economic issues developed later is the fact that rarely do customers within the metropolitan area send garments to outside firms. Either because of limited wardrobes, or for other reasons, customers' demand tends to be insistent. Time allowed for cleaning service limits the market area unless a substantial difference in price between local and out-of-town service makes inconvenience seem worth while. During the depressed conditions of 1930–1932, shrunken incomes of some economy-conscious customers led to temporary resort to mail-order service with out-of-town plants. Also for a time during this period, some out-of-town plants found it worth while to maintain agencies in downtown office buildings (known in the trade as "loop stores"). These functioned as branch stores for the out-of-town plants. Service was slow and somewhat less reliable than local service, however, and only during the depths of the depression did any substantial number of customers put up with this inconvenience. Hence most of these agencies disappeared by 1936.

Internal Plant Structure

The synthetic shop is so small that it rarely uses much hired labor. Often operated by the proprietor alone or with the aid of members of his family, it has really no part in the industry's collective bargaining. The synthetic shops, however, do have repercussions on other sections of the industry.

The plants using significant amounts of hired labor, wholesale and branch store plants, appear to have changed little in size in recent years. Thus the average Chicago plant in 1925 had twenty-three wage earners and five salaried employees, while ten years later the Census figures showed an average of twenty-seven wage earners and four salaried employees. Moreover, although some improvement has been made in technique, especially in the development of more effective chemicals, these basic units of the industry operate about as they did in the years following 1910 when unionism was gaining its first foothold. The general discontinuance of dyeing materials for domestic customers has almost eliminated the use of the expert dyer. The principal service the industry renders today is the chemical cleaning of garments and household goods.

Cleaning Operations

After the collection of soiled goods, either directly from homes, or from tailor shops and branch stores, the internal plant operations involve several rather well-defined processes. These begin with "marking in" the garments for identification, and proceed through "sorting" (by color and character of material according to type of chemical treatment required), "washing" usually with a petroleum solvent, i.e., "dry" cleaning, repairing where needed, "finishing" (mainly pressing), and finally end with resorting and wrapping for delivery. Sometimes in the wholesale plants partial service may be rendered, leaving the repairing and finishing to the tailor shop from which the work was collected. In such cases, of course, the wholesale price to the tailor is adjusted accordingly.

These operations, all largely household crafts, were gradually withdrawn from the home in the years before 1920, not merely for reasons of economy but for safety as well. With the older types of solvents, the danger of fire or explosion was great, especially under uncontrolled household conditions. Although a substantial health hazard is associated with the use of noninflammable synthetic solvents, the expense item probably has been the most important discouragement to home dry cleaning with these newer chemicals.

Dry cleaning proper, or chemical washing, is done in revolving drums similar to some types of domestic washing machines save that they are much larger and have more elaborate control devices. Doors must be solvent-tight, and the equipment must permit drainage and renewal of solvent, either continuously as on some machines, or at intervals during the washing of a single batch of goods. Supplementary to this basic unit are two other essential pieces of equipment. One of these, the "extractor," is a cylinder which by rotating at high speeds extracts solvents from washed material. The other is a filtering device by which solvents are cleaned for re-use. Chemicals used in cleaning plants, even the cheapest of them, are costly enough to justify considerable expenditure in salvaging. Less important equipment, but essential for some types of garments, are steam dryers and hot rooms for removal of remnants of solvent and for deodorizing.

Importance of Wages in Costs

Apart from washing and the supplementary drying processes, where a large number of garments or pieces of material can be treated in a machine at one time, almost all the remaining plant operations require individual handling. This is the basic fact which determines plant organization and the structure of employers' costs. It means that the largest single element in plant expenses will be the wage bill. Although few cost records are available, Chicago plant owners report that wages represent over 60 per cent of total expenses.[5]

5. For six Chicago plants the cost items for 1929, stated as a percentage of aggregate net sales, were as follows:

Inside labor, direct and indirect	38.86	Materials	6.81
Delivery expense, largely labor	17.99	Overhead	6.78
Administrative salaries	13.85	Rent	1.99
		Taxes	0.99

See Handsaker MS, Appendix, p. 382.

Even less specific data are available on investment in Chicago plants, but a suggestion as to capital requirements is given by claims made during the NRA Code hearings. There it was stated that in the United States as a whole, cleaning plant investments ranged from $3,000 to over $1 million, the average per plant being $29,000. In view of the fact that in 1919, the last year for which the Census reported separate capital figures, the average cleaning plant investment in Chicago was $22,000, it seems probable that the national average of the NRA days was not far from being typical of Chicago as well.

b. ORGANIZATION FOR COLLECTIVE BARGAINING

Since 1910 the cleaning plant owners of the Chicago area have maintained some form of organization, although there has never been unanimous support of collective action. Undergoing no less than four changes of name, the organization which started in 1910 as the Chicago Master Cleaners' and Dyers' Association finally, in October 1933, became the Cleaning and Dyeing Plant Owners' Association of Chicago.

Whatever its name and outward appearance, the Chicago organization of cleaning plant owners has been during most of its life the central representative of the industry in collective bargaining.[6] Its principal negotiations have been with two separate unions,[7] one of deliverymen, the other of workers actually employed inside the plants in cleaning, dyeing and pressing customers' garments.

6. The exact representation in the Association has varied from time to time. In the decision in *Cleaning and Dyeing Plant Owners' Association of Chicago* v. *Sterling Cleaners et al.*, 285 Ill. App. 336 (1936), it was stated that "out of 104-105 power plants in the cleaning and dyeing business, 97 are members of the plaintiff association," while another source reported 78 cleaning plants as members of the Association in September 1934. [Records of Clerk, Superior Court of Cook County, Case 36S-1734 (1939).] An official of the Association told the writer in 1939 that there were "about eighty plants" in the organization, in fact "almost all except the chain store outfits," i.e., the branch store plants. The Association, of course, does not include any synthetic shops.

7. For a decade following 1924 the third branch of the industry, the tailor shops, although made up almost entirely of proprietors, was organized into a Federal Union (No. 17,792) affiliated with the AF of L. For details on the operation of this organization, see Handsaker MS, pp. 29, 115-120.

The Deliverymen's Union

The deliverymen have had a continuously effective organization since 1915—the Laundry and Dye House Drivers' Local Union No. 712 of the International Brotherhood of Teamsters, Chauffeurs, Warehousemen and Helpers. Although the Local was organized as early as 1903, its original activity was confined almost entirely to the employees of power laundries, and not until twelve years later did it get any sizable membership among the drivers of cleaning and dyeing plants. Since 1915, its control over the delivery force of these plants appears to have been almost complete. In the summer of 1939 it claimed that six hundred drivers in its membership of thirty-five hundred represented all the deliverymen employed by the cleaning and dyeing plants in the city.[8]

The Inside Plant Employees

Organization of the inside plant employees has been of shorter duration. Not until after a brief strike in 1919 was there a permanent union of these workers. Then for ten years the Cleaners, Dyers, and Pressers Union (Federal Labor Union 17,742) maintained a tight grip on the labor supply of the industry. The trials subsequent to the discontinuance of the NRA, however, and the aspersions cast upon its officials at various times were more than the organization could stand. Although it remained the bargaining agent for some inside employees through 1936, its position was challenged in March 1937 by Local 3 of the newly organized International Association of Cleaning and Dye House Workers. The conflicting jurisdictional claims of these two organizations were not settled until the older union withdrew from the field under AF of L pressure.[9] By the summer of 1939, Local

8. Interview with union official, July 28, 1939.
9. For a time during the period 1935–1937 there were actually three unions in Chicago that claimed jurisdiction over the plant workers of the cleaning industry—the old Federal Local No. 17,742, Local 3 of the International Association of Cleaning and Dye House Workers, and Local 46 of the Laundry Workers' International Union. The organizing activities of Local 46 were checked by an injunction obtained in the Superior Court of Cook County, and later it appears to have made a working agreement with Local 3. Exactly what occurred is not entirely clear, but in any case one official formerly associated with the Laundry Workers became the International Supervisor for Local 3. In January 1937, when the AF of L chartered the International Association of Cleaning and Dye House Workers, an

3 had absorbed the assets and membership of the older union and claimed to have reached a stable position with about twenty-seven hundred members—all the inside workers in the industry except those of one plant operating eleven branch stores.

c. CURRENT LABOR STANDARDS

The agreement of the Laundry Drivers' Union (Local 712) with the Cleaning and Dyeing Plant Owners' Association of Chicago fixes weekly rates and commissions for three classes of drivers—wholesale, retail and branch office. The first two receive a basic wage of $30 a week; branch office drivers are paid $35. However, to these basic rates are added supplementary commissions. Drivers on wholesale routes get commissions of 9 per cent on all business above $100 a week. Commissions on retail routes are 6 per cent on all weekly business from $100 to $300, and 7 per cent on business above $300. The branch office drivers get an extra $3 a week for each branch store over five serviced by the driver. The number of hours in the drivers' working week is not specified.

Except in the pressing and finishing of garments, most inside plant employees are on week work. The 1939 agreement provides both time and piece rates for pressing operations and leaves the

order was given for all formerly existing federal local unions of cleaning plant employees to affiliate with the new International. Local No. 17,742 refused to do so and obtained the support of the Chicago Federation of Labor. After some delay, the AF of L adopted a resolution on April 28, 1938 specifically directed against Local No. 17,742, requiring it to disband and transfer its membership and assets to the new Local Union 3 of the International Association. Following this action Local 3 grew more rapidly, and an election in the fall of 1938 indicated that it had attracted a majority of the membership of Local 17,742, even though the officials of the latter still continued to hope for its survival. The decisive step, which apparently brought most of the market under the new union's control, was a strike at the Birck-Fellinger Company plant during the busy Easter season of 1939. However, its position is by no means as secure as that held by the old union prior to 1929. (Data on the amalgamation of these organizations from Handsaker MS, Ch. 1, interviews with union and management officials during the summer of 1939, and *Federation News*, June 4, 1938, p. 1.) Evidence of the difficulties of the old plant employees' union during the years since 1935 will be found in the records of the following cases: *Cleaners, Dyers and Pressers Union* v. *John Newberry*, Superior Court of Cook County, Case 36S-1734 (1939); *Albert* v. *Ruby Dry Cleaners*, Circuit Court of Cook County, Case 38C-8452 (1938); *Cleaners, Dyers and Pressers Union* v. *North End Cleaners*, Circuit Court of Cook County, Case 38C-8451 (1939).

matter optional with the individual plant management as to which method of payment will be followed.

This first agreement of the newly organized union of inside workers (Local 3) lists thirteen scales ranging from $15 for women apprentices to $45 for head fancy-goods spotters [10] for a forty-four-hour week. While no exact measure is possible, it is certain that most employees get $30 a week or less. These include second dry cleaners ($28), rough spotters ($26), women pressers ($22), and seamstresses and tumbler [11] tenders ($20). The $15 rate applies not only to women apprentices but also to large groups of line girls and checkers who mark-in, sort and package garments. Store girls in the firms' branches are also paid $15 and they comprise the one group of inside employees whose work week is not limited by the agreement. Except for one firm, formal recognition of union standard rates of pay was complete for the entire market in July 1939.

There is some evidence, however, that the union has at times been forced to tolerate departures from the standard wage scales. During the summer of 1939 one union official insisted that he knew some employees were making refunds to employers of part of their pay checks, but the state of the labor market was such that the workers did not dare to protest and the union could therefore do nothing.

d. THE INSTRUMENTS OF JOINT CONTROL

Joint control of standards is provided for in the current (1939) agreements of both the delivery employees and the inside plant workers. The checkoff and the closed shop are accepted practices for both groups. The agreement for the plant employees (Local 3) requires the employer to deduct union dues from wages when presented with "a waiver signed by the employee," [12] while the arrangement covering the delivery employees goes still farther and guarantees that "employers shall honor all orders given by

---
10. These are the most skilled workers of the industry who specialize in the removal of spots from delicate and fine fabrics.
11. "Tumblers" are rotating steam cylinders in which cleaned goods are dried and deodorized before pressing.
12. Agreement of Local 3, Art. 4, p. 2.

the officers of the union for payment of initiation fees and dues."[13]

For both unions, the closed shop is buttressed by the requirement that employers seeking new workers must first requisition the union before generally advertising vacancies. Significantly enough, this is true for all workers except the store girls in the branch offices. The girls who "meet the public" are considered so important in the creation and maintenance of good will that employers insist on unrestricted right of hiring. However, their position for the union is equally important, and hence one of the first acts of the newly created Local 3 was a strike during the Easter season in 1939 to force the employing plants to agree to the inclusion of store girls within the union ranks. Article One of the 1939 agreement is apparently the compromise resulting from this strike. By its terms the store girls must join the union after a two weeks' trial, but the employer need not hire them through the union office.

The control devices in the agreements do not all operate in one direction. The agreements of Local 712 (delivery) and of Local 3 (inside plant) both provide that no firm shall operate a union shop with lower wages than those established in the Association plants. Additional protection for union firms is furnished by a provision that no deliveryman shall solicit business from the customers of his former employer within a year after leaving.

e. DEVELOPMENT OF CONTROL OF LABOR STANDARDS

The quarter century of collective bargaining in Chicago's cleaning and dyeing industry divides sharply into two periods. The year 1930 marks a line between a decade and a half of continuous, and on the whole, smooth functioning of the machinery of collective bargaining, and the beginning of a decade of readjustments which barely stopped short of disintegration.

Role of the Drivers' Union
When the Chicago Master Cleaners' and Dyers' Association

13. Agreement of Local 712 with Cleaning and Dyeing Plant Owners' Association, effective September 1938–March 1940, Art. 4, p. 2.

was formed in 1910, almost all cleaning business came through the small independent tailor shops. The wholesale price for dry cleaning a man's suit was 45 cents, while the tailor's usual charge to his retail customer was $1.50.[14] In this situation there developed a "price war" in which some new plants offered wholesale prices as low as 25 cents a suit. Out of this came the new Association, and the "closed solicitation rule" which forbade a plant owner to engage in "stop-stealing," the trade's term for soliciting business from tailors who were customers of some other plant.

Some plants continued to defy the "closed solicitation" rule, and it was under such conditions, only five years after the formation of the Chicago Master Cleaners' and Dyers' Association, that the Laundry Drivers' Union (Local 712) began to organize the dye house and cleaning plant drivers, apparently with employer support.[15] Out of this attempt developed a relationship which relieved the Association of much of its worry in enforcement of the "closed solicitation" rule. Since commissions based on business secured from the tailor are part of the driver's income, he suffers if he loses a stop or if the tailor pays less than the standard price. Consequently it was in the union's interest to enforce rules forbidding a driver to pick up work from another's stop or from a cut-price tailor. This collaboration brought to the drivers standardized conditions of employment throughout the market, and wage increases which finally reached a peak in 1928 with a basic rate of $41 and a 5 per cent commission on business over $250 a week.

Relationships with the Plant Employees

Not until the acute labor shortage during the first postwar business peak in 1919 was there any appreciable organization among the plant workers.[16] A short strike in August 1919 over union

14. Handsaker MS, pp. 106-107.
15. Handsaker states that one employer reported contributing $200 to the formation of the drivers' union, but is uncertain which side made the initial move. According to one cleaner, employers were actively opposed to organization of their drivers until the union's head pointed out the advantages they could derive from it. For this and the text material immediately following, see Handsaker MS, pp. 110-112.
16. Earlier attempts had been made by the Journeymen Tailors Union.

recognition, wage increases, and the eight-hour day was followed by a lockout which ended in a compromise. The trial of strength, however, brought nine hundred of the two thousand plant workers into the newly organized Federal Union 17,742. Through a second strike in the busy spring season of 1920, the union won recognition from most of the remaining plants, and from then on it negotiated trade agreements with the Cleaners' Association. There is some evidence that plant owners were behind the organization of this union as well as that of the drivers; a representative of the Association later emerged as a prominent officer of the new federal local.[17]

In an industry where labor costs are as important as in cleaning, unwillingness to observe union standards tends to be associated with sharp competition. No doubt exceptions may be found, but it is clear that among Chicago cleaning plants the prominent price cutters and "stop-stealers" have also been outstanding nonunion firms. It is not accidental, therefore, that violence against price cutters [18] has often been a joint venture where agents interested in the preservation of labor standards in union plants have acted with, or for, employers interested in maintaining prices. Frequently during the years before 1930, the unions were called upon to act directly in support of the Association's policy of price maintenance through "controlled competition." To insure such main-

17. One plant owner reported that during the negotiations following the first of these strikes it was pointed out that a new union of plant employees could be a "powerful weapon for price control," but he was not certain whether this played any part in the settlement of the second strike. "Whether or not such was the case, it is abundantly clear that once organized, the inside workers' union was used in that fashion. After the difficulties associated with the organization of the inside workers, there were no strikes called because of ·genuine labor troubles, according to one cleaner. All subsequent strikes were called, he stated, at the behest of the Association, in the interest of enforcing some one of its rules." Handsaker MS, p. 115; see also C. Lawrence Christenson, *Collective Bargaining in Chicago*, University of Chicago Press, Chicago, 1933, p. 331.

18. For an account of numerous instances of violence, including wrecking of delivery trucks, use of acids in destroying customers' garments, and the beating up of drivers, see Gordon Hostetter and Thomas Beesley, *It's a Racket*, Les Quin, Chicago, 1929, pp. 30 ff. In spite of claims that violence has often been due to the activity of persons outside the industry, it is clear that Handsaker is correct in the observation that originally "the development of collusive control came largely from within the industry, and was not imposed by gangsters from the outside." Handsaker MS, p. 120.

tenance fines were levied by the Association, and strikes were called against price-cutting firms.[19]

Results of Joint Control

Under surveillance of the Association the retail price in Chicago for cleaning a man's three-piece suit was kept at $1.50, except for occasional departures, from 1910 to 1917. Then began an upward movement which brought the price to $1.75 in 1920. The postwar depression of 1921 forced a return to the $1.50 level until 1926, when the $1.75 price was restored and observed until well into 1929. Throughout most of this time one outstanding firm, Becker Cleaner, maintained prices below the Association level. Significantly enough, this firm was the only one in the industry which as early as 1910 established direct access to customers through branch stores. No "closed solicitation" rule could directly control the opening of branches. The most that the drivers' union could do to discourage the branch store was to maintain substantial wage scales which prevented direct marketing from spreading to other firms.

For a time the joint action of the union and the Cleaners' Association, sometimes marked by violence, protected the existing price structure. Even before the 1926 advance in prices, Becker's stores had been bombed, but criminal prosecution had resulted in no conviction. Becker reported that he paid $3,000 to the Association in 1927 to get a strike called off. In April 1928, he announced that he was forming a new organization, the Sanitary Cleaning Shops, Inc., with Al Capone as a partner. Although the plans were never completed, the mere announcement appears to have assured Becker's firm freedom from further interference.[20] Pressure on the price structure became increasingly severe as more firms turned to "cash and carry" branch stores.[21]

19. Handsaker MS, pp. 123-124.
20. *Ibid.,* pp. 125 ff.
21. From another quarter there arose a somewhat different threat to the Association position after 1926 when about a hundred north-side tailor shops withdrew their patronage from Association plants and started a cooperative plant under the title of Central Cleaning Company. This company, with one Kornick as president,

These threats to price maintenance and the notoriety which the employers' organization acquired by its actions in fighting them led to a change of front. Unfortunately many important details concerning this abrupt shift in policy are not known. With encouragement from the Chicago Chamber of Commerce, a new executive director of the Master Cleaners' and Dyers' Association was chosen in February 1929 from out of town.

The new executive was an avowed "open shopper" and union officials may have been suspicious of the new regime from the start. Anyway, by the middle of 1929, officials of the inside workers' union had decided upon a vigorous and dramatic gesture to insure favorable renewal of the trade agreement which expired the next August. Through sale of stock to union workers, both within the industry and in other trades, and appropriations from the Cleaners' union, they began construction of a "million-dollar union-owned" cleaning plant.

The termination date of the trade agreement passed without a renewal; Association officials insisted that construction must be abandoned before they would discuss employment relations. Failing in negotiations on this question, the Association began a lockout in all its plants November 4, 1929. After the longest stoppage that the industry had seen in years, there finally emerged a new period, one of appeal for help from outside the industry, of disintegration and decay of the old controls, and attempts to create new patterns of industrial operation.

appears to have operated on a nonunion basis under an arrangement by which the "Moran Gang" (Capone's then north-side rival) received $1,800 weekly for "protection." Kornick, however, seemed to regret this alliance when he found two Moran men installed as vice presidents and contemplated making peace with the Association and changing to a union-shop basis. Moran's men anticipated Kornick's intention and approached John Clay, then Secretary-Treasurer of Local 712, with a proposal to unionize Central. Suspecting an indirect raid on the union treasury, then supposed to contain between $200,000 and $300,000, Clay is reported to have shown the men out of his office after insisting that they had no authority to speak for Kornick. Some days later (November 16, 1928), while holding a meeting of union stewards, Clay met his death from bullets fired through his office window. See Fred D. Pasley, *Al Capone; The Biography of a Self-Made Man,* Ives Washburn, New York, 1930, pp. 249-251.

f. DISINTEGRATION AND REORGANIZATION: 1930–1939

First Attempt to Restore Control

Appointment of an industrial arbitrator [22] December 29, 1929, termination of the lockout and abandonment of the union's competitive venture,[23] and modification of the administration of the Association [24]—these were moves by which the industry hoped to restore stability. But delay in the formulation of the terms of the new collective agreements encouraged nibbling at the existing wage structure and in February 1930 resulted in a joint threat of a renewed stoppage by the drivers and the plant employees. The breach was healed temporarily by arbitration. The arbitrator's decision restored sections of the 1928 scale, but introduced piece rates for the first time on finishing operations; it abolished the 1928 agreement's guarantee of seven months' employment a year, but continued the employers' 2 per cent pay roll contribution to an unemployment reserve fund, and it increased the probation period for new employees from two to four weeks.

The subsequent evolution of the position of the arbitrator serves to emphasize both the critical position of the industry and the intimate relation between labor standards and the industrial price structure. During the weeks preceding the first arbitration decision (February–March 1930), an attempt was made to restore the "closed solicitation rule," and although it proved abortive, a complete allocation of "stops" was planned.[25] In spite of this failure at a fresh redistribution of the field, the Squires' arbitra-

22. The arbitrator appointed was the late Dr. B. M. Squires, then Chairman of the Trade Board of the Chicago Men's Clothing Industry and lecturer in the Department of Economics at the University of Chicago.
23. Exactly what happened to the union's plant is not clear. Some reports indicate that the plant was simply left uncompleted and the stockholders and mechanic's lien holders were permitted to assume the loss. Other evidence suggests that the union abandoned the half-built plant only after the Association had agreed to assume the construction cost. Handsaker, even with his close contact with the industry, was unable to determine the exact disposition of the matter. See Handsaker MS, pp. 168-170.
24. Mr. Patterson, the executive of the Association, who had been installed in February 1929 and was known to have "open-shop" sympathies, left office in the spring of 1930.
25. Handsaker MS, p. 171.

tion decision was followed the next month by a general increase in the basic garment cleaning price from $1 to $1.50. But the relatively new phenomenon of competition from out-of-town plants had not been reckoned with; after four weeks of shrinking business the local plants returned to the dollar price.

Rise and Fall of the Cleaners and Dyers Institute

Groping about for more effective industrial control, the local plant leaders in the midsummer weeks of 1930 worked out plans for a new organization with a powerful central administration. The arbitrator on labor questions was made "sales manager" for each firm joining the new organization. Contract forms were signed by firms in the suburbs as well as by ninety Chicago plants, and in March 1931 emerged The Cleaners and Dyers Institute of Chicago. Although the effective power lay in the hands of the sales manager, he in turn created an administrative six-member board of trustees of which he was chairman. The arbitrator, therefore, under this new arrangement, really served in three capacities: judge of labor standards, director of sales policy for each firm, and administrative chief of the Institute.

The Institute was maintained by a 2 per cent tax on the gross income of member plants. Its funds were periodically used to finance strikes and to picket price-cutting plants. In 1931 it is reported to have turned over between $4,000 and $5,000 to the plant employees' union to finance a strike against the Michigan Cleaners, which was cutting prices on a "cash and carry" basis. Strikes were declared against several plants to force affiliation with the Institute. In some cases plants were told that nonmembers would be subject to premium wage scales 40 per cent above the Institute level. A "labor commissioner" was appointed to "police" the industry and between June 1931 and May 1932 received about $30,000 in salary and expense allowances. Apparently by arrangements made through Al Capone, the commissioner paid one price-cutting firm $3,750 to observe Institute prices during the summer and fall of 1931.

In spite of these methods, the Institute lasted less than two years.[26] Competition from the out-of-town plants, as well as from the local independents who refused to affiliate, proved too much for it. Two more organized attempts likewise failed to achieve the Institute's objectives before government help came under the National Recovery Administration. Twenty-six plants, which had combined in June 1932 to secure the resignation of Dr. Squires as chairman of the Institute, formed the nucleus of a new Chicago Association of Cleaners and Dyers. For a time this Association functioned through union cooperation in strikes against plants refusing to join, "whip" stores against price cutters and outright violence. Eleven months after its formation, it in turn was reorganized as the Cleaners and Dyers Association of Metropolitan Chicago, whose leadership one of the Cook County judges was asked to assume. For a scant two months he served as price fixer for the organization and then withdrew, saying he was "no longer needed," but his price fixing too appears to have met with failure.[27]

Reorganization of the Employers' Association Under the NRA

The final change of the associated employers of Chicago's cleaning industry was the formation of the Cleaning and Dyeing Plant Owners' Association, just one month before the approval of the NRA code for the industry.

The National Code, approved by the Recovery Administration November 8, 1933, authorized the Code Authority to fix minimum prices by local areas. For Chicago, the schedule approved by the Code Authority fixed the basic garment cleaning price at 95

26. Dr. Squires, as chairman, claimed to have no knowledge of some of these activities and made pleas for a "clean" program. His refusal to continue payments to the labor commissioner for "policing" appears to have contributed to the disintegration of the Institute. The aftermath of the Institute era was the trial under Illinois law of twenty-four men, including the Institute chairman, several union officials, a city alderman, and Al Capone, for alleged "restraint of trade in the cleaning industry through price fixing, the latter being promoted by violence and threat of withdrawal of labor supply." Begun in January 1934, when the NRA was still in high favor, the trial continued through several months until finally on May 5 the jury returned a verdict of "not guilty." See *Cleaning and Dyeing Plant Owners* v. *Sterling, et al.*, 285 Ill. App. 336 (1936); also Handsaker MS, pp. 179-273.
27. See Handsaker MS, pp. 282-293.

cents retail. In the weeks preceding the approval of this basic price, the Association price was only 54 cents, while nonmembers charged as low as 29 cents. Widespread departures from the code price naturally continued.[28]

Supplementary to the National Code Authority, the NRA code for the dry cleaning industry called for the setting up of local joint industrial relations boards. Accordingly, the Chicago Joint Industrial Relations Board was established in January 1934, with Dr. Squires, the former arbitrator and sales manager under the Institute, as chairman. When competition forced a revision of the basic garment cleaning price from 95 to 75 cents on December 22, the plant owners at once petitioned for reduction in union wage scales. The National Code standards set a minimum weekly wage of $14, but this had little effect in Chicago because union scales were higher.

No sooner was the Joint Board created in Chicago, therefore, than it was confronted with an insistent demand for wage reduction. The chairman reduced the scales for some of the highest skilled groups from $45 to $40 and lowered the piece rates on finishing from 14 to 9 cents on women's plain dresses, and from 12 to 7.5 cents on men's suits. With these reductions, however, came restoration of the checkoff and, more important still, extension of the new rates to all firms in the Chicago area regardless of whether or not they had formerly observed union rates.

This blanket extension to the entire market spelled the death of the Board, for the central Recovery Administration ruled [29] that the chairman had exceeded his authority. Exactly sixty days later, when violations of the price schedules established in the different market areas under the code had become widespread, orders came from Washington to suspend all trade practice provisions and to keep in effect only the labor provisions. For practical purposes, this was the end of the NRA in the dry cleaning industry.

28. Roos reports that "fifteen per cent of all NRA compliance work" during January, February and March 1934 related to the Cleaning and Dyeing Code. Charles F. Roos, *NRA Economic Planning,* Principia Press, Bloomington, Indiana, 1937, p. 341.
29. February 26, 1934.

Post-NRA Efforts at Market Control

Having failed to get price stability under the NRA, the Chicago plants renewed their complaints against the existing wage structure, but no positive action was taken until September 1934. After the unions refused to consider wage revision, a lockout followed in all plants except those operating branch stores. To remove the Association's cause for complaint the unions then undertook to organize the firms with branch outlets, most of which hitherto had been nonunion. Some minor violence occurred during the picketing, and the struggle was described as "a spectacle of a group of employers locking out union employees apparently in order to induce them to persuade their employers' competitors to charge a higher price."[30] While this resulted in negotiations, the plants outside the Association operating branch stores would accept no price structure without a "cash and carry" differential.

Although the Association failed to make the independents agree on price policy, partial success came with the end of the lockout on September 19, when all independent plants signed trade-union agreements. Hence, without a formal price agreement, union recognition and adoption of union scales brought the cost structure of independent plants more nearly in line with that of Association members. For some weeks after the lockout there seems to have been a tacit understanding that basic garment cleaning prices were to be 85 cents on "call and deliver" work and 69 cents for "cash and carry" work.

It was an ephemeral stability. Hardly a month had passed when the Association resorted to the novel course of applying for an injunction to defend the price structure. In its bill of complaint, filed against twenty-two firms operating branch stores and doing business on a "cash and carry" basis, it claimed that by charging less than 69 cents the defendants were engaging in unfair competition with intent to destroy the business of Association members.

This campaign for "price fixing by injunction," beginning in October 1934, brought a long judicial investigation of the indus-

30. Handsaker MS, p. 306.

trial cost structure which did not end until the Illinois Court of Appeals in May 1936 ruled that no injunction was justified.[31]

The pressure which continued upon the old form of operation probably contributed to the reorganization of the plant employees' union early in 1939 [32] under an announced change in policy. Summarized, the new union program was: "We have nothing to do with the prices the employers charge but are concerned solely with the protection of wage rates and labor standards." Even in the summer of 1939, however, there were indications that union standards were being subjected to severe pressure because of low "chain store" prices and that the union might have great difficulty in adhering to its new position.[33]

g. THE LOGIC OF COLLECTIVE CONTROL

A review of collective bargaining in Chicago's cleaning and dyeing industry makes clear the extent to which trade-union action has been used to control competitive practices. Indeed some writers have been tempted to dispose of the entire matter of collective relations in the industry simply by saying, "It's not collective bargaining; it's a racket!" [34] The fact remains, however, that some aspects of working conditions and wage rates have been the product of collective action for a quarter of a century. It adds little to our understanding of this development to cover up the forces that have contributed to it by dismissing the matter in this fashion.

Traditionally, customers' garments were collected and delivered by the employees of the plant. From the standpoint of the

31. Injunction orders issued in lower courts were twice reversed on reaching the Illinois Appellate Court. The first time [*Cleaning and Dyeing Plant Owners* v. *Sterling*, 278 Ill. App. 70 (1934)] refusal was on technical grounds, but in the second case the issue was met squarely [*Cleaning and Dyeing Plant Owners* v. *Sterling, et al.*, 285 Ill. App. 336 (1936)].

32. See p. 814, note 9.

33. The official who outlined the new union policy for the writer later remarked that he had interviewed the manager of one of the newer plants with branch stores after that plant had begun to solicit business in a territory worked by one of the oldest firms in the city. He added, "I told him, 'You shouldn't have gone in there.'"

34. See Hostetter and Beesley, *op. cit.*

power of trade unions to contribute to the control of competition, this fact is of primary significance. The channels through which business is secured and service rendered are exposed to attack. Moreover, drivers familiar with routes and customers are not easily replaced. It was no accident that organization of the delivery employees preceded unionization of the inside plant employees. Before 1910 drivers were the exclusive contact with the market, except for one firm. Through organization of this group, definitely encouraged by some employers, "closed solicitation" could be enforced and each plant allocated its share of the market. A dispute with the drivers' union was almost certain to result in denying the plant operator concerned access to his customers. It is this which employers have had in mind when they have remarked, "If the drivers weren't in the union, organized labor would have no power."

Organization of the inside plant employees came later at the peak of a wartime labor shortage, but also after development of the branch store had begun to weaken the effectiveness of the "closed solicitation rule" as a control device. Standardization of labor costs through such a union was important to price control for a number of reasons: the normally localized market; the importance of wages in costs; the consequent absence of marked advantage to the large firm; and the intensive competition which could arise partly from this and partly from the maintenance of equipment necessary for seasonal peaks in business.[35]

The rising demand for the industry's services in the two decades following 1910 contributed greatly to the functioning of joint industrial control by employers and union officials. This rising demand was associated with the growth of the city, but was also doubtless augmented by occupational shifts then taking place. The increasing proportion of women in commercial pursuits and the rise in the number of white collar workers generally, both spelled increased volume for the cleaning industry.

35. Records for two Chicago plants showed the pre-Easter peak between 1927 and 1930 to be 160 per cent of the average weekly volume for the year. Seasonal variation is not uniform from one city to another, but there is abundant evidence of marked seasonal swings in almost all city markets in the United States. See Handsaker MS, pp. 34-37.

Effect of New Methods of Operation

During the twenties, with incomes rising and the demand for cleaning services growing, joint action by the employers' association and the union maintained a substantial degree of stability. The weakening of this joint control has been associated with the growth of new operating methods since 1930.[36]

While separate figures on the business of branch store plants and synthetic shops are not available, there is no question that both have made inroads on the trade of the older wholesale plants. Wholesale plant operators have indicated that this has been particularly true in garment cleaning, although they still appear to retain an advantage in cleaning larger pieces of household goods, such as curtains, rugs and draperies. The complete elimination of delivery employees in the synthetic shop, and the shift in the relative significance of delivery service in the branch store plants, makes the old controls largely inapplicable to them. Moreover, since they often operate without any hired labor, union standards which fix minimum wages for internal plant labor can have no effect on synthetic shops. The amount of work that can be done by one man with the aid of family labor is, of course, limited, and this tends to limit their size. But in 1940 the operators of union plants, watching the increase in the number of synthetic shops, were deeply concerned about how far this newest threat to their position would go.

The collective bargaining practices of the dry cleaning industry of Chicago, even during the years since 1930, impressively show the contribution which unionism has been asked to make to price control. This was, indeed, a most important reason for its existence. Whether the new policy that was taking form in 1939 means that collective bargaining in this service industry can divorce itself from direct support of price control is a critical question for the future.

36. *Ibid.*, pp. 106-107; see also *Bill of Complaint in Cleaners, Dyers and Pressers Union* v. *John Newberry, et al.* (Case 368-1734, filed February 1936, dismissed March 1939, Records of Clerk, Superior Court of Cook County, p. 30) where the claim is made that prior to 1930 "business was almost exclusively 'call and deliver.'"

3. THE MOTION PICTURE MACHINE OPERATORS OF CHICAGO

a. THE MOTION PICTURE INDUSTRY

The invention of the motion picture projector at the close of the nineteenth century led in a few decades to a giant new industry. Still in the nickelodeon stage in 1910, it had become by 1925 the "motion picture industry," an industry of "palatial, de luxe" theatres. Early in its history it acquired its three main existing divisions: *production* of motion picture films, *operation* of theatres for the exhibition of these films, and *distribution* of films. The distribution branch, which now operates film exchanges in thirty-two of the principal American cities, makes contracts for film rentals and supervises shipment of film from one theatre to another.

Two aspects of the industry which call for special attention are the theatre box office and the division in the ranks of the theatre owners. Control, originally vested in the production branch, has gradually passed through distribution to the exhibition section. Today the pulse of this industry can be felt most easily at the box offices. Production of new pictures could cease for weeks without serious injury, but were the box offices to close, income would dry up, and all branches would at once feel the drought. A groping realization of this fact led during the decade of the twenties to what one writer, long familiar with the industry, calls "the battle of the theatres."[37]

The swift transformation of the industry raised the average cost of picture production to levels earlier considered fantastic. This also brought classification of theatres and made control of the first-run houses almost imperative for the production branch of the industry.[38] An outgrowth of the battle, at times ruthlessly

37. See Benjamin B. Hampton, *History of the Movies*, Covici Friede, New York, 1931, especially pp. 250-366.
38. Hampton describes the conditions immediately prior to 1920 thus: "Everyone was so busy with his own efforts to gather his share—and possibly his neighbor's—of the industry's increasing profits that no one had time to realize the growing influence of a few first-run theatres. No one knew that the public had concentrated, in less than two hundred houses, sufficient power to dominate all the theatres in the United States—a total then of fourteen thousand or more—and eventually to dominate the screens of the world and to eliminate from business all

violent, was the division of theatre owners into two groups, each with special interests. By 1930 most of the large first-run theatres had become units in producer-controlled chains. A few first-run houses remained outside the chains. These together with the numerous smaller theatres operated by independent exhibitors are known in the trade as "the indies."

While the box office is the commercial pulse beat of the industry, the mechanical pulse beat of the individual theatre is in the projection booth. Theatre income depends upon the smooth operation of this small unit. From one angle a motion picture theatre might be defined as a large investment built around a little machine—the projector. The projector, now usually operated in batteries of two in a booth, may represent a capital expenditure of only a few thousand dollars, but the total investment in even a comparatively small theatre can run to several hundred thousand.

Literally, the man in charge of the booth controls the operation of a motion picture theatre. In many of the smaller theatres one man has entire charge of the booth, and even the largest motion picture "palaces" rarely employ more than six projectionists, two or three in a shift. For any one theatre, therefore, the operation of the motion picture machine requires a relatively small labor force.[39]

b. ORGANIZATION OF EMPLOYERS AND EMPLOYEES

For collective bargaining with this small specialized group of workmen, the exhibitors or theatre owners in most metropolitan areas have been split since the middle twenties into two more or less opposing camps. Chicago is no exception. While this division was not originally due to labor problems, differences on labor matters have widened the gulf, which in turn has made its own contribution to labor policy.

Chicago has two separate employers' associations. One of these, the Exhibitors' Association, dates from a time when there was

---

manufacturers and exchanges except those favored with its patronage." (*Ibid.*, p. 175.) In the face of this concentrated market, to justify higher cost features the producers had to assure themselves of outlet control.

39. In 1937 there were 385 theatres and 660 licensed operators in Chicago proper. See Table 6.

considerable unity among theatre owners. At present it represents almost exclusively two of the larger groups of producer-chain theatres in the city. As such it is the bargaining representative of between fifty and sixty theatres.[40]

The second employers' organization is the Allied Theatre Owners of Illinois, a state-wide affiliate of a national organization. It has an extensive membership outside the city and includes about one hundred and eighty "independent" Chicago theatres. Not all of the city's independent theatres are members, but the organization is wide enough to make it clearly the articulate representative of the "indies."

While there are several trade-union organizations among Chicago theatre employees, the most powerful is that of the motion picture machine operators, Local 110 of the International Alliance of Theatrical Stage Employees and Moving Picture Machine Operators. Local 110 is among the strongest and oldest unions of projectionists in the Alliance. Since its charter was issued in 1915,[41] it has retained almost complete control of the labor force of the theatre booths in the city. In the summer of 1939 it reported an active and associate membership of about seven hundred and fifty. In view of the fact that the number of licensed operators in the city could not be much in excess of seven hundred, it is apparent that the local union controls the entire booth labor force.[42]

40. Interview with Association official, August 8, 1939.
41. This charter followed closely the settlement of the bitterly contested jurisdictional dispute between the Brotherhood of Electrical Workers and the Alliance. On a national scale the formal settlement occurred in 1914 with the award of jurisdiction over the operators to the Alliance by the AF of L convention. The Alliance had its origin as an organization of stage employees in the legitimate theatres long before the motion picture industry had come into existence. The new industry presented the problem of conflicting jurisdictional claims. The date of settlement by the Federation of Labor also roughly marks the time when the conviction became general that the new industry was a permanent institution and not simply a passing fad. See Robert Osborne Baker, *International Alliance of Theatrical Stage Employees and Moving Picture Machine Operators of the United States and Canada,* Lawrence, Kansas, 1933, pp. 40-41.
42. As will be seen later, all motion picture machine operators in theatres are licensed and, assuming strict enforcement of local ordinances, a complete check on the number of operators in the city is possible. It should be pointed out that Local 110 claims jurisdiction over employment in suburban theatres as well as over those in Chicago proper. Hence Chicago license regulations do not strictly parallel the sphere of union influence.

c. CURRENT WORKING CONDITIONS

The agreements [43] governing the terms of employment for Chicago moving picture machine operators cover only such matters as wages and hours. They usually run for a year, and end the last of August. Although most theatres operate throughout the year, a few close down during the summer, and their reopening marks the customary time for revision of the union contract. No standing provision is made for arbitration, either to settle disputes under an agreement or as a final resort to facilitate renewals. Yet arbitrators were called in at least twice during the last decade.[44]

The hourly scales in Chicago for 1939 [45] were fixed at $2 in the neighborhood houses and $3 in the first class downtown establishments. Within this range the actual rates for any particular theatre depended upon the union's classification of the house.[46] Three specific criteria enter into this classification: location of the

43. A copy of the agreement terminating in September 1931 was checked, clause by clause, with a union official to determine the changes since that date. Copies of subsequent agreements have not been available.
44. In 1927 the mayor of Chicago was asked to help settle a dispute involving the number of men to be employed in a booth. (*Monthly Labor Review*, October 1927, pp. 119-120.) In 1931 a controversy over the same question resulted in the creation of a five-man arbitration board. When this board failed to reach a settlement the dispute broke out afresh and the mayor was again asked to intervene. *Variety*, August 25, 1931, p. 7, and October 27, 1931, p. 7.
45. The scales quoted were those of the agreement terminating September 1. In September 1939, the union asked for an increase of approximately 15 per cent. *Variety*, September 6, 1939, p. 4.
46. A similar type of wage structure based on classification of theatres will be found in many other cities. By courtesy of the Bureau of Labor Statistics it is possible to present the skeleton of the rate structures for unionized motion picture machine operators in ten selected cities.

1938 Recorded Scales for Regular Operators, Converted to an Hourly Basis

City	Highest	Lowest
Pittsburgh, Pa.	$3.90	$1.00
San Francisco, Cal.	3.10	1.70
St. Paul, Minn.	2.03	1.36
Washington, D. C.	2.02	0.79
Omaha, Neb.	2.01	1.44
New Orleans, La.	1.92	1.25
Indianapolis, Ind.	1.81	1.40
Rochester, N. Y.	1.16	0.88
Jacksonville, Fla.	1.01	0.81
Charleston, S. C.	0.833	0.635

theatre, seating capacity and ticket prices. But no standard is applied automatically. In the words of one union official, all of these items are considered, but in the final analysis "the particular scale at each house is whatever we can get." [47]

Working hours vary from thirty-five a week in so-called continuous-shift houses, to forty-two a week in smaller neighborhood houses which normally operate only during evening hours. Relief operators, or "swing men," who substitute for regularly employed operators, often work less than full time. Strict observance of the standard hourly scales would mean weekly earnings from $84 in the smallest neighborhood houses to $105 in first-run theatres. Actually, there is evidence that smaller and financially weak theatres are sometimes allowed to undercut the scales so long as the closed shop is strictly observed.[48]

The closed shop is recognized in all Chicago motion picture theatres. Operators are assigned to jobs through the union office, and thus complete control of membership is exercised without resort to the checkoff.

d. THE SUPPLY OF LABOR AND UNION CONTROL

Foremost in union control of the labor market is guarding the entrance to the trade. The degree of skill required for work in the projection booth depends on the extent of the division of labor. Repair and servicing of projection equipment may involve extensive knowledge of electricity as well as rare mechanical ability, but ordinary day-to-day operation when compared with other technical trades is hardly more than a semiskilled occupation. The customary theatre contracts with equipment companies or service engineering firms mean that by and large the work of the regular booth men is confined to the operation of machines and perhaps occasional minor repairs. Hence a relatively short time is needed for training normally intelligent persons to become operators. Theatre owners probably exaggerate when they say that motion

47. Interview, July 20, 1939.
48. The concessions referred to are in addition to the general deductions sometimes effective for the summer season. Through negotiations with the international president, a "ten per cent slice in the summer scale" for the period July 4 to August 31 was arranged in July 1938. *Variety,* July 6, 1938, p. 19.

picture machine operation is so simple anyone could learn the trade in a few weeks. Yet no move has been made to increase the apprenticeship beyond one year, as provided by municipal ordinance. A year, therefore, may be taken as the outside limit of a reasonable training period.

For a trade having limited skill requirements, such a high level of earnings suggests that the length of the apprenticeship period can hardly be the real barrier to entrance to the trade. This is more clearly revealed by the proportion of apprentice certificates issued to total number of operators' licenses, as shown in the accompanying table.

TABLE 6

Motion Picture Theatre and Operator Licenses Issued in Chicago 1915–1937 [a]

Year	Theatre Licenses	Total [b]	Apprentice Licenses Number	Per Cent of Total
1915	576	1,583	425	27
1916	491	1,374	370	27
1917	393	1,208	218	18
1918	349	817	120	15
1919	410	853	57	7
1920	411	832	35	4
1921	419	809	18	2
1922	422	725	22	3
1923	374	720	8	1
1924	334	685	18	3
1925	362	661	8	1
1926	359	692	8	1
1927	385	711	6	c
1928	386	712	6	c
1929	388	833	3	c
1930	379	834	4	c
1931	370	979	22	2
1932	368	643	3	c
1933	372	672	3	c
1934	378	568	4	c
1935	382	693	3	c
1936	385	672	0	c
1937	385	660	1	c

a. Data from *Annual Reports*, Department of Gas and Electricity of the City of Chicago.
b. The total of operators' licenses includes: new licenses to full-fledged operators, renewal of licenses to full-fledged operators, and apprentice certificates.
c. Less than one per cent.

Except for recent years, for which the data have not yet been published, the table gives the complete record of new entrants to the trade while Local 110 has been in existence. It will be noticed that only for the first four years of the union's history were the apprentice certificates more than 10 per cent of all operators' licenses issued. By 1923 the number of apprentices had fallen to only one per cent of the total number in the trade, and while the figure rose to 3 per cent in 1924 it was a bare one per cent again in 1925 and 1926. Since then, except for the year 1931, apprentice certificates have been negligible, never amounting to as much as one per cent of the total licenses. The trade entrance has apparently been carefully guarded.

The high proportion of apprentices in the trade between 1915 and 1916 cannot be regarded as the "normal" expectancy for the later years. In 1915 the motion picture industry was barely under way, and its rate of growth during the early years could hardly be maintained after it had once become established.[49] However, the almost complete stoppage of fresh entrants to the trade since 1923 points clearly to effective artificial restriction.

Devices to Limit Entrants

Several devices have limited the number of eligible job seekers. The union assumes with some foundation that exhibitors' short-run demand for projection machine operators is almost entirely inelastic. Hence, there is no justification for training apprentices unless actual jobs are in prospect. This appears to account for the provision in the municipal licensing ordinance which requires that an apprentice certificate shall be issued only when the application is accompanied by a letter from a prospective employer and from a full-fledged licensed operator stating that the applicant will be regularly employed by the theatre owner and under the supervision of the operator if the certificate is granted.[50] Supplementing

---

49. There were 576 licensed motion picture theatres in Chicago in 1915. In spite of the enormous profits of the industry in later years, that figure has never been reached again. See Table 6.

50. This feature of the license requirements goes back to 1912. (City of Chicago *Council Proceedings*, 1912, p. 2787; 1913, p. 3099; and *Revised Chicago Code*, 1931, Art. XX, Secs. 3541 and 3542.) A large number of cities require operators

this provision of the municipal ordinance is Section Sixteen of the local union *By-Laws,* which reads, "no member of the union shall sign any city apprentice application without first submitting to the body under penalty of fine." [51] An even tighter control over the issuance of licenses comes from the relationship between the union and the city Examiner of Motion Picture Machine Operators. The position of examiner is not subject to Civil Service and has been referred to as a "perquisite of the movie operator's union" since the "examiner is always selected from the rolls of the union." [52] The closed-shop policy and the union entrance requirements, which include an initiation fee of $200, are the remaining links of the chain which controls the gateway to the trade.

e. THE COURSE OF COLLECTIVE CONTROL: 1920–1940

To a large extent, an account of collective bargaining by Chicago's moving picture machine operators during the two decades before 1940 is also a record of the use of power to control the labor supply. In addition to other broad powers, the business manager, who is the principal administrative official of the union, is vested with complete control over jobs and is authorized to make all assignments to positions.[53]

Principal developments of union policy during the twenties were the closing of the union to new members, the union's attempt following the coming of "sound" movies to compel a minimum of two men to a booth, and, closely associated with this attempt, the extension of "permit cards" to nonmembers.

Union Membership Policy
Exactly when the union all but closed its doors to new members

---

to be licensed. Thus in a review of 186 cities the U. S. Bureau of Labor Statistics found that 117 provide for such licensing. *International Projectionist,* April 1938, p. 16.

51. A copy of the local *Union Constitution and By-Laws* will be found in the records of the case of *Britsk* v. *Maloy,* Records of Clerk, Circuit Court of Cook County, Case B261,163 (1932).

52. Confidential letter to writer, April 20, 1940.

53. The practice of requiring theatres to hire operators through the union office is apparently not limited to Chicago. Letter to writer from an Alliance member of long standing, October 14, 1939.

has not been established, but it is clear that it was an accomplished fact by 1925.[54] This action may have come with the decline in the number of movie theatres in the city after 1922. Although the theatre business was profitable in the early twenties, this was not a period of growth in number of theatres,[55] but was marked rather by the increase of large, "de luxe" first-run houses partly at the expense of the older smaller units. In the middle of the decade, between 1924 and 1926, control of these first-run houses in Chicago shifted from the independent exhibitors to the producer-chains.[56]

It was during this time that the union decided not to increase its membership rolls and to issue working permits to nonmembers when called upon to furnish additional operators. But the permit system was not long in effect before introduction of sound movies brought a chance for placing a substantial number of additional operators.

54. *Employers' News,* the official organ of the open-shop employers' association of Chicago, asserts that the union had in fact closed its doors to new members as early as 1918 (see issue of October 1928). While no other authority has been found in support of this claim, it is admitted that, except for replacement of members dropping out, no new members have been accepted since 1925.
55. See Table 6.
56. Just what date should be taken to mark the advent of the de luxe theatre may be a matter of opinion. It is clear that the building of the Central Park, the first of the Balaban and Katz chain, in 1917, set a new standard in motion picture entertainment. This was the first summer-refrigerated theatre in the city, and it boasted an eighteen-piece orchestra at a time when a single pianist was the rule. This was followed by the construction of the Riviera in 1918 and the Tivoli and Chicago in 1921. (*Chicago Daily News,* October 7, 1939.) The Balaban and Katz firm was one of the outstanding "independent" exhibitors supporting First National Pictures, the theatre owners' cooperative venture in film distribution. Producer control, therefore, did not make much headway in Chicago until after 1925. "Then in 1925–1926 Paramount bought control of the Balaban and Katz theatres, and organized the 'Publix Theaters Corporation,' placing the stock of Publix in the treasury of the Paramount-Famous-Lasky Company, and transferring the theatre holdings of Paramount to Publix." (Benjamin B. Hampton, *op. cit.,* pp. 258, 263.) A leveling off or even a decline in the growth curve was apparently a general phenomenon, for Hampton writes, "The only cloud in the sky of 1926 was a tendency toward recession in the profits of many theatres. Even large houses in leading cities were not maintaining the speed that the industry had come to regard as normal, and in several cities neighborhood theatres were having a hard fight to keep income ahead of outgo. Business was spotty, some theatres were doing well, but too many were barely making expenses. There were various reasons for this general slackening in attendance." *Ibid.,* p. 369.

The Two-Man Rule

Theatres began changing from "silent" to "sound" in the fall of 1926 and proceeded feverishly until, by the close of 1929, most Chicago motion picture houses were equipped for the new method of exhibition. The first installations were "sound-on-disk," by which a phonograph turntable mounted in the booth was operated by the same motor as the projection machine. The use of such equipment made the union demand that at least two men be employed in each booth a plausible one, since attention to the phonograph attachment on the part of the operator was an additional responsibility.

Perhaps less than half of the theatres had been converted to sound, however, when the process which was to "revolutionize" the movie industry was itself revolutionized by the introduction of "sound-on-film," made possible with the aid of the photoelectric cell.[57] A significant feature of the new process was that, apart from the simple operation of the volume control switch (sometimes called the "fader"), the projectionists' work now was almost identical with the operations of the old silent days. While the use of porous sound screens on the stage necessitated higher powered lamps in the projectors, somewhat increasing the fire hazard, the union's case for a minimum of two men to a booth was materially weakened even before it had gained general acceptance in the industry.

Through strikes or threats to strike, early attempts at enforcement of the two-man rule after the introduction of sound in 1926 met with at least partial success. The major dispute between the

---

57. So rapidly did these changes occur that members within the industry were skeptical of their permanence and regarded the changes, in which they were themselves participants, as comparable to "fads" or style changes. In 1926 only twenty theatres in the United States were wired for sound. All of them originally used the "sound-on-disk" method. By the end of 1930 about fourteen thousand theatres had been converted to sound, and *Variety* (August 13, 1930, p. 27) reported that the "saturation point is almost reached." (See also Baker, *op. cit.*, p. 67.) Even within this short space of four years, however, the industry became convinced that its original moves were in the wrong direction. By the middle of 1929 all the large film producers, save the one who had started the "revolution" (Warner Brothers), had become convinced that sound-on-film was better than sound-on-disk, owing largely to the problems of storing and shipping as well as the difficulty of cutting dialogue when using records.

theatre owners and the operators during the twenties was over this issue. The outcome was certainly not an employers' victory.[58] The ratio of licensed operators to theatres grew after the introduction of sound movies. For 1925, the last year before sound, this ratio is computed at 1.8, while the corresponding calculation for 1930 yields a figure of 2.2, or approximately 20 per cent more than the 1925 ratio.

Extension of the Permit System

During this expansion of the job market, the union did not modify its closed-membership policy. The new workers required under the two-man rule were furnished to the theatres through an extension of the permit system. Taxed 10 per cent of earnings,[59] permit men became an important source of union income and by a curious anomaly contributed to serious internal weakness in the organization. For although the local union constitution provided that regular members should be given preference in assignment to jobs, it was perhaps too much to expect union officials to observe such a provision when its violation not only meant more income —since dues of regular members were less than the 10 per cent charge on permit men—but was a device to control some of the recalcitrant voting members. There were charges of systematic discrimination against regular members in job assignments, of the use of thugs in elections, and of failure to account for the levy on permit men.[60]

58. For an account of this dispute and settlement, see Christenson, *op. cit.*, pp. 219-221.

59. This 10 per cent assessment was provided by Section Fifty of the local union *By-Laws*. (See also Christenson, *op. cit.*, p. 237.) As will be seen a little later, the 1935 reorganization of the union eliminated many of these permit men, but those who remained were still subject to the 10 per cent assessment in 1939. Interview with union official, July 3, 1939.

60. In the case of *Britsk* v. *Maloy*, in which five union members asked for court assistance in the reorganization of the local union. Specifically, they requested an order declaring invalid the union elections in 1925, 1927 and 1932, and restraining the officials in the disposition of organization funds. The bill in this case was filed December 21, 1932. The case was later dismissed for want of prosecution. (See Records of Clerk, Circuit Court of Cook County, Case B261,163.) A somewhat similar bill asking for the appointment of a receiver for the union was filed almost simultaneously in the Federal Court. This latter request was dismissed December 31, 1932 for want of federal jurisdiction. *Britsk* v. *Maloy*, Records of Clerk, Federal District Court, Northern District of Illinois, Case 12,570 (1932).

Abandonment of the Two-Man Rule

In spite of swelling protests against the two-man rule, especially from smaller theatre managers, and in spite of growing internal dissension over administration of the permit system, union officials refused to yield on either of these issues until late in 1931. By this time the business recession had produced such box-office shrinkages, particularly in the smaller neighborhood houses, that many theatres preferred to close rather than continue with an extra man in a booth. Accordingly, after some weeks of negotiation, 108 independent theatres locked out their Alliance operators early in August 1931. Although the producer-chain exhibitors were drawn into the controversy after some weeks, when stench bombing had spread to their properties,[61] the lockout began with members of the Allied Association and was formally confined to them.

Late in October, after many Chicago theatres had been closed for ten weeks, a settlement was made. About twenty of the smaller theatres were to be permitted to operate with only one projectionist, and there was to be a general reduction of 20 per cent in the hourly scales. Actually this agreement appears to have been only the first step in a union retreat from the two-man rule.[62]

61. The language used in the account of this dispute appearing in Christenson, *op. cit.*, p. 229, may be misleading in carrying the implication that as they were not parties to the lockout, the chain theatres played no part in the controversy. The lockout continued for at least eight weeks without involving the chain houses, but the spread of violence to the larger theatres was a factor which contributed to the final settlement. However, there is no doubt as to the comparative positions of the "indies" and the chain theatres in the controversy. With the aid of counsel from officials of the national organization of independent theatres, the Allied group initiated the lockout, organized a small migration of operators from other cities, and financed the undertaking by means of a special assessment on the participating theatres. No less than sixteen theatres were bombed during the course of the lockout. It was the bombing of the McVickers Theatre, a large downtown house under lease to one of the chains, which marked the spread of the dispute beyond the sphere of the "indies." For a record of charges and countercharges of responsibility for this violence and a week-by-week account of developments in the dispute, see the issues of *Variety* from August 11 to November 3, 1931, and the *Federation News* of June 6, as well as issues for the period from August to December 1931.

62. The settlement originally provided that theatres with "less than four hundred seats" would be permitted to operate with the owner or manager acting as relief man in the booth. Some houses having slightly more than four hundred seats immediately "ripped out extras" in order to take advantage of this concession. By April 1932, there were no less than eighty small theatres using only one booth

For although the ratio of licensed operators to theatres reached a new high in 1931,[63] by 1934 it was lower than at any time during the era of silent movies.[64] These developments failed to bring about any significant change in the union administration. With jobs now scarcer, extensive use of permit men together with favoritism in job assignments, caused still more internal friction than before.

Union Reorganization

In this situation membership resentment against the union administration led to violent action several times before internal reorganization came about. During the period 1930–1935 no less than three protesting members of the union were shot, one of them in the union office. The union official responsible was later exonerated on the grounds of self-defense. In February 1935 the business manager, who had administered the affairs of the union during its entire history, was killed by machine gun bullets which riddled his automobile on Lake Shore Drive. At this point the International Alliance stepped in.[65]

man. Even then, however, another "wholesale shutdown" was threatened; it was reported that "while not generally known . . . more than two hundred operators are behind in their pay envelopes." (*Variety*, April 5, 1932, p. 25.) A fresh outbreak, with the "indies" again threatening to lead, was avoided only when the union consented to take off one operator "in all houses, independent and circuit, formerly employing two men in a booth if deemed in dire need of relief." *Ibid.*, April 26, 1932, p. 21.

63. The high figure (2.64) during this year was clearly the result of the "importation" of many operators from other cities to carry on the lockout.

64. The average ratio of licensed operators (including apprentices) to theatres for the three years 1935–1937 was about 14 per cent lower than the ratio for the three years before the great lockout, 1928–1930, and 8 per cent lower than the average ratio for the last three years of silent movies, 1923–1925. By 1935, therefore, it seems clear that nothing remained of the effort to increase employment through the two-man rule. Perhaps because the International Alliance continued to work in various states for legislation which would require a minimum of two men in a booth, the retreat has not been openly recognized. The facts seem to be, for Chicago at least, that there are actually fewer operators in proportion to the number of theatres than there were during the silent days. Data for these computations will be found in Table 6.

65. See *Variety*, March 27, 1935, p. 7; July 24, 1935, p. 7. Neither the use of permit men nor discrimination in assignments has been confined to Chicago. Exact details vary from one situation to another, but there are also some notable uniformities. In 1933, permit men of the New York City Local 306 sued unsuccessfully in court for full membership. In commenting on the trial the editor of the *International*

Having assumed direct control of the Chicago local, the international officers began at once to audit the accounts and to remove the "favored sons" from the ranks of the permit men. So far as can be learned, the reorganization of 1935 ended use of the permit system as a disciplinary device. Moreover, it seems to have made the constitutional principle of preference to full-fledged members on job assignments a reality. In sharp contrast to former conditions, reports obtained during the summer of 1939 showed that a member without a job could always get another one by "bumping" a permit man.[66] This preference being market-wide, a member might thus assert his claim to the job held by a permit man in any theatre in the area under the jurisdiction of Local 110.

Under the new and allegedly more democratic administration,[67] wages have been kept at about the level established after the concessions of 1931 and 1932. Some employer representatives have complained bitterly about the "exorbitant scales." Such criticism has been met to some extent by allowing temporary deviations from basic scales during slack summer months. In spite of such compromises, the organization remains in its bargaining relations an example of "hard-hitting, here and now" unionism.

Projectionist reported, "since all but a few projectionists' locals of the Alliance practice the permit system, the decision is expected to assert a profound influence among Alliance units throughout the United States." (The New York City case is *Max Alterman* v. *Harry Sherman*, Supreme Court, Kings County, July 11, 1933. The decision will be found reprinted in full, with comments, in the *International Projectionist*, April 1933, p. 12, and July-August 1933, pp. 10-11, 27, 30.) Other cases revealing aspects of the internal operation of the New York union are: *People* v. *Kaplan*, Supreme Court Appellate Division, 269 N. Y. S. 161 (1934); *Kaplan Manufacturing and Supply Company* v. *Motorized Talking Picture Service*, Supreme Court Appellate Division, 268 N. Y. S. 644 (1934); *Polin* v. *Kaplan*, Court of Appeals, 257 N. Y. S. 277 (1931); *Agostina* v. *Parkshire Ridge Amusements*, 278 N. Y. S. 622 (1935).

66. The international president reported that there were 213 permit men in Chicago when the Alliance took control. From interviews with local union officials it appears that about 110 of these were removed and their jobs filled either by regular members or by members of the Chicago sister local of stage hands. Since 1935 a union member when unemployed may displace, i.e., "bump," a permit man from a job. (*International Projectionist*, February 1935, pp. 21, 23, and June 1936, p. 20.) According to Baker, in spite of departures in Chicago and elsewhere, member preference has been the common rule followed by most locals. *Op. cit.*, p. 75.

67. New officers were elected in November 1935, after the International Alliance had supervised the local affairs about nine months. *International Projectionist*, December 1935, p. 30.

f. FORCES SUPPORTING THE BARGAINING STRUCTURE

A small group of homogeneous semiskilled technicians in Chicago theatres has established employment conditions seldom enjoyed by similar craftsmen in other trades. Their pay is high when compared with that of other strongly organized trades; their work week is one of the shortest recognized in industry; and for the regular union membership, unemployment is virtually nonexistent. What forces support this bargaining structure?

Continuous Operation

The motion picture theatre industry during the two decades immediately before 1931 was a thriving, expanding and extremely profitable industry. But theatres, like newspaper printing plants, are absolutely dependent on continuous operation. The service which the motion picture theatre sells to its customers is highly perishable; if a theatre doesn't sell a particular theatre ticket today, it doesn't sell *that* ticket at all. The theatre is not like a manufacturing establishment, which may postpone the filling of orders or perhaps even transfer them to other plants. Its absolute dependence upon continuity of operation at a specific location has made the theatre manager unwilling to risk any labor dispute except over extremely serious issues.

Another aspect of the theatre manager's dependence upon continuous operation is his heavy fixed capital charge. The complete loss of income resulting from any interruption in operation is not offset appreciably by a reduction in expenditures while the theatre is closed. Contracts for film rentals are usually made for a year in advance, and these rentals, together with the fixed capital charges, may well represent more than half of theatre expenses. Such a distribution of costs converts the somewhat romantic motto that "the show must go on" from a sentimental trade cliche into an economic command.

With these heavy fixed charges, only a small percentage of total expenses is represented by the direct labor cost of projectionists' wages. A wage increase may mean a relatively small increase in the exhibitor's total costs. This means that it is frequently less profitable for an exhibitor to resist demands for more wages than to yield without even attempting a compromise.

Differences in Theatre Cost Patterns

But distribution of expenditures is not uniform for all types of theatres. In the smaller, modest neighborhood houses projectionists' wages may amount to 20 per cent or more of gross expenses. To such establishments the pay roll item, although less important than in many industries, is by no means insignificant. In the large de luxe theatres, on the other hand, rentals for premium locations and first-run films, carrying charges on elaborately appointed buildings, and expenditures for "extra" attractions bulk so large that the pay roll item is dwarfed by comparison. In these houses wages paid to machine operators often represent less than 5 per cent of gross expenses.[68]

These differences in the distribution pattern of exhibitors' expenditures must be considered together with the nature of theatre ownership. Although it now extends beyond the de luxe theatres, expansion of the film producers into the exhibition branch of the industry had as its original objective acquisition of control over the first-run theatres.[69] The accomplishment of this objective in the twenties meant that, generally speaking, the booth pay rolls in producer-controlled theatres were a less significant operating expense item.

In a service industry of specifically localized operation, multi-unit control brings bargaining weakness, for it subjects the organization to attack at different points. Unlike a manufacturing trust, a chain theatre corporation cannot shift business from one unit to another; and yet failure to arrive at an agreement covering workers in one particular community may bring on sympathetic action against its theatres in other cities. When this possibility is combined with the fact that concessions on projectionists' wages

---

68. No specific data showing costs for different classes of theatres in Chicago are available, but information from trade literature as well as from personal interviews definitely reveals that the general outline of expense distribution follows this pattern. See Will Hays, *Annual Report to the Motion Picture Producers and Distributors of America, Inc.*, 1938, p. 22; also Christenson, *op. cit.*, pp. 244-247.

69. Hampton, *op. cit.*, pp. 172 ff.

are of relatively minor importance to management in the large theatres anyway, it is clear why, as one independent exhibitor expressed the matter, "the big circuits are forced to yield." [70]

Industry a "House Divided"

Although other factors [71] contribute to the split in the ranks of the theatre owners, the peculiar vulnerability of chain operations and the wide difference in importance of booth pay rolls have certainly helped to draw a sharp line between the "indies" and the chains. It was no accident, therefore, that the "indies" led the fight in the 1931 lockout to abolish the two-man rule. Not until the struggle was well under way did the large downtown units join the rest of the theatre managers. For some of the large theatres, the two-man rule was of no significance whatever; for others it meant a slight addition in percentage terms to their total expenses; but for the small neighborhood theatre, faced with the shrinking business of 1931, the difference between one and two men in a booth meant either profit or loss.

With a growing volume of business, division in the ranks of the theatre managers is covered up because it may not seem worth while for any of them to adopt a firm personnel policy. Business readjustments which force economies, however, show what cost distribution may mean in determining an employer's labor policy. The theatre industry, from management's standpoint, is a "house divided," and, oddly enough, the portion of the "house" with the greater financial strength is the less aggressive bargainer in labor negotiations.

70. The vulnerability of motion picture producers with theatre affiliations was nicely illustrated in the Alliance campaign for the organization of the west coast studios in 1935. When negotiations in Hollywood reached a stalemate, the international president of the Alliance ordered a walkout of the motion picture machine operators in all Paramount theatres in Illinois. A conference was immediately arranged in Chicago, and the theatres were reopened after being closed only a few hours. Graphically, and perhaps with the exaggeration of theatrical language, *Variety* reported, "The I. A. [International Alliance] won hands down and left the meeting with everything but the office furniture." For a full account of the settlement, see *International Projectionist*, December 1935, pp. 7-11.

71. Perhaps the most important single factor separating the "indies" and the chains is the controversy over the question of film rentals.

Sources of Union Strength

Union strength, on the other hand, comes largely from control over the labor supply. A motion picture machine operator's trade can be learned only in a projection booth. The existing craftsmen in a very direct way, therefore, control the number of fresh additions to the trade. In Chicago this control is supported by license requirements, but it would probably be strong enough to stand alone without assistance. Such absolute control over entrance to the trade makes it extremely difficult for employers to lower union standards by hiring substitutes from outside. Practically, there are no "substitutes," and union policy aims at making this permanent.

The size of the "labor force" in a motion picture booth also contributes to union strength. For the small theatre with one operator, a strike means a strike of one man. Such an action can be supported by a trade union more easily than a strike in a large manufacturing plant involving several thousand workmen. Not only is control over an individual strike against a particular theatre a relatively simple matter, but control and discipline of union membership are relatively easy when the total number of competing workmen in a trade is only a few hundred. The motion picture machine operators' union, even in our largest cities, is small and compactly organized.

All of these features taken together account for the operation of the motion picture machine workers' organization as a pure "here and now trade union." There can be no claim that it has *directly* affected theatre ticket prices.[72] Maintenance of union standards may have contributed to the decrease in the number of theatres in Chicago since 1915, but familiarity with the industry certainly leads to the conviction that other factors bear most of the responsibility. The small, poorly ventilated, modestly equipped theatres, using the relatively inexpensive silent films of 1915, could never have maintained their numbers in the extravagant era of the twenties, even though the motion picture machine operators

---

72. To some extent the determination of theatre prices clearly represents a form of what economists describe as a "discriminating monopoly." See A. C. Pigou, *Economics of Welfare*, 3d ed., Macmillan, 1929, Book II, Ch. XVII; also Christenson, *op. cit.*, pp. 242-245.

had worked for nothing. There is no evidence of direct "class collaboration" in any real sense. The case is rather that of a small group of strategically located technicians, able to bargain effectively because of the ease with which the labor supply can be controlled and the absolute dependence of the divided ranks of the employers upon continuity of operation.

4. THE MUSICIANS OF CHICAGO [73]

a. THE BARGAINING UNITS

The difficulty of defining the boundary lines of an industry arises in its most acute form when one attempts a definition of the "Musical Industry." Strictly, there is no such industry. Employers and jobs for musicians are scattered through at least half a dozen well-defined industrial settings. The musicians' union makes a fairly sharp natural division between "steady engagements" and "jobbing," but both types of employment may be found in several different industries. Among the more stable employers who hire musicians more or less continuously are radio stations, theatres, hotels and ballrooms. At the other extreme are the small cabarets, steamboats, carnivals, and political organizations furnishing only occasional, but nevertheless numerous, job opportunities.

That employers and jobs are so widely scattered is an important factor which influences the operation of collective bargaining. To begin with, Chicago has no central organization of employers. Some of the smaller employing groups, however, have associations which act as bargaining agents. During the silent movie days the Exhibitors' Association, which then represented most of the Chicago motion picture theatres, made agreements for its membership with the Chicago Federation of Musicians. Since then, al-

---

[73]. For an early review of collective bargaining among musicians which contains much sharp analysis that is still pertinent, see J. R. Commons, "The Musicians of St. Louis and New York," *Quarterly Journal of Economics,* 1906, pp. 419-442, reprinted with minor revisions in Commons, *Labor and Administration,* Ch. XVI, Macmillan, New York, 1913. A recent thorough study of employment of musicians in symphony orchestras will be found in Margaret Grant and Herman Hettinger, *America's Symphony Orchestras and How They Are Supported,* W. W. Norton, New York, 1940.

though the Exhibitors' Association has remained in existence, so few theatres hire instrumental musicians that each management negotiates separately.[74]

With the shift from silent to sound movies and with the parallel growth of radio broadcasting, the old position of the Exhibitors' Association as the main employers' representative dealing with the musicians' union has been taken by the Chicago Broadcasters' Association. This Association, which appeared in the late 1920's, functions only sporadically and is not a strong, centralized organization. There is also an association of hotels, but it no longer functions as a bargaining unit in dealing with the musicians' union. Apart from the radio industry, then, bargaining is usually between each individual hotel, café, restaurant, or ballroom on the one hand, and the musicians' union on the other.

Musicians' Union Powerful

In sharp contrast to the employers, organization of the musicians has long been nearly complete. The Chicago Federation of Musicians (Local 10, American Federation of Musicians) includes well over 90 per cent of the professional instrumental musicians in Chicago.[75] It is not concerned with the city's many teachers of music, unless they compete for public commercial performances.

Control of the Chicago Federation over its own members is strong and centralized. At the head of the union stands the president,[76] whose elective term is now five years. Consistent with the

74. The union reported that it had agreements with four of the large downtown motion picture houses in January 1938. *Intermezzo,* January 1938, p. 1. (*The Intermezzo* is the official monthly publication of the Chicago Federation of Musicians.)

75. An official of the union made this claim in an interview with the writer on July 17, 1930. It has not been disputed by any Chicago employer of musicians. Since 1930 there is clear evidence that there has been some increase in membership. One radio station operator told the writer in August 1939 that it would not be possible to procure enough nonunion talent in Chicago to maintain the local studios. There is also a small local union (No. 208 of the American Federation of Musicians) of colored musicians in Chicago.

76. The higher officialdom of the Chicago Federation of Musicians has remained practically unchanged since 1922. However much some union members and employers may be irritated by the policy of the union administration, there is also substantial admiration for it. One employer stated, "They can say what they will about

nature of the market in which he must function, he has much broader powers than officials of most other local unions. He may order members to appear for trial before the board of directors and may appoint personal assistants who investigate the observance of union standards.

The Board of Directors of the union consists of five elected members in addition to the president and vice president of the local, and in its weekly meetings, it has the power to act in all matters concerning the local which are not specifically provided for in the by-laws. It examines claims against the union, orders payment of bills, and fixes the salaries of appointed officials. It has the power to "remit dues, call for papers and witnesses, and adjudicate appeals properly brought before it," and ". . . to impose fines and penalties, reduce, remit or stay fines, and render judgment against non-members for unpaid services." It also has the power to make agreements, "levy assessments and amend the By-laws and wage scale."

The Trial Board is the lower court of the local, with nine members elected for five-year terms. It has original jurisdiction over all cases involving members of the union and hence hears all charges of violations of wage scales or local union by-laws. If the president, one of his four assistants, or any other member of the

the president's tactics; he is rude, he is crude, he is shrewd and he drives a hard bargain. But if he makes a promise, you don't need it in writing." Interview, August 1939.

Internal criticism of the Chicago administration has, however, reached the open on at least two occasions. In a bill for an accounting, certain members of the Chicago local charged misuse of union funds and alleged that in June 1933, $100,000 was paid from the union treasury for the release of the president in a prearranged "friendly" kidnapping. The case was brought on December 1, 1933 and it was further charged that during the then current campaign for re-election the officers of the union were using the local's $40,000 relief fund to influence votes. Whatever the merits of the controversy, the administration won the election, polling slightly more than 2,000 out of 2,700 votes. On December 19, the case was dismissed "for want of prosecution." *Rizzo, Belcaster* v. *Petrillo*, Records of Clerk, Circuit Court of Cook County, **Case B281,594.**

A second occasion occurred when the local president, proceeding independently in his attempt to control recordings, found himself working at cross-purposes with the national officers. This procedure brought forth public criticism by the international president in the official journal. See *International Musician*, May 1938, p. 1, and more particularly "Minutes of the International Executive Board," March 29, 1938, published in *International Musician*, April 1938, p. 15.

board of directors believes some member of the union guilty of violation of union rules, a charge is filed against him and he is brought before the trial board. After judgment by the trial board there may be an appeal to the board of directors, and in some cases to the executive board of the American Federation of Musicians. In cases where the original penalty fixed by the trial board for the alleged offense is a fine of $500 or more, appeal may be carried to the floor of the annual convention of the American Federation of Musicians.

b. METHODS OF COLLECTIVE BARGAINING AND UNION CONTROL

Negotiations and Rule Making

Collective bargaining by the musicians' union has two forms. The union may negotiate the usual agreements with employing units, but it also proceeds more simply and directly by unilateral legislative and administrative action, resembling the operation of a medieval guild in governing the charges for the services of its membership. It illustrates how closely a "trade union" may copy a "trade association," providing the industrial setting is favorable.[77]

Because of this twofold bargaining activity, only part of the terms governing the employment of unionized musicians will be found in trade agreements made by the union. An equally significant part will be found in the various working rules adopted through the more or less democractic functioning of the union without consultation with employers.[78] These working rules, or "union law," alone may define the employment relation with most of the smaller or occasional employers in the city. In such cases bargaining is extremely one-sided and approaches dictation. The limits on the enforcement of union rules under these circumstances

77. The Chicago Federation of Musicians accepted an offer of membership in the Chicago Association of Commerce. *Minutes of Board of Directors,* April 18, 1930.

78. Union rules, adopted by the membership directly or arising out of authorized administrative action, make up the code which is commonly referred to as "the union law." That part of "the law" made by the annual conventions of the American Federation of Musicians or by action of that federation's executive board is known as "the International Law." In defining some of the terms of the collective bargain by such working rules, the musicians are of course not unique among trade unionists.

are the same as those governing any other monopoly, namely, "what the traffic will bear."

Perhaps the most regular sources of employment for the instrumental musicians of the city are the thirteen radio stations [79] affiliated with the Chicago Broadcasters' Association. When the union first undertook to control employment in this new industry during the late twenties, it laid down working conditions for musicians without negotiation with employers. Later, radio station managers became more articulate, and also employment became more regular. Today the stations operate under formally negotiated agreements instead of simply under union rules.

Agreements are also made with the theatres, some hotels [80] and the Chicago Orchestral Association. To the wide range of employment in cafes and cabarets [81] and to almost all the "jobbing engagements," however, the union rules are applied directly without special negotiations.

Trade Agreements, Contracts and Contractors

The term "contractor" designates musicians who engage the individual members of orchestras or bands. The term "employer" is reserved for managers of radio stations or theatres, hotel and restaurant proprietors, or others who secure the services of individual musicians indirectly by dealing with union contractors.

"Trade agreement" refers to a negotiated understanding between union and employer, concerning the general terms under which musicians may be hired. "Contracts," on the other hand, are

---

[79]. In 1939 there were seven strictly local stations, two stations (WCFL and WLS) which were classed as local but which had network affiliations, and four network system stations (WENR and WMAQ, National Broadcasting Company stations; WBBM, Columbia; and WGN, leader of Mutual Network).

[80]. Twenty-eight hotels were listed by *Intermezzo* as having signed agreements with the union in May 1937.

[81]. The union practice classifies the "night spots" into four groups. All the downtown ("loop" and vicinity) cabarets and thirteen of the fashionable night clubs outside the "loop" are in the first class. A group of twenty-one smaller but "swanky" clubs, most of them located on the near north side, are in the second class. Another group of ninety-nine using orchestras more or less continuously constitute the third class. About three hundred and fifty of the smallest taverns and restaurants that employ musicians (often only a pianist or pianist and drummer, and sometimes only for one or two days a week) are in the fourth class. *Intermezzo*, May 1937, p. 5; November 1937, p. 7; January 1938, p. 7.

CHICAGO SERVICE TRADES 853

the instruments drawn between "contractors" and "employers" which provide for actual employment at union rates of a certain number of musicians during a stated period. The musicians' union is concerned not merely with the formulation of trade regulations through agreements and by-laws as are other trade unions, but also it exercises direct control over individual employment contracts. In part this is done by regulations governing the contractors and in part by regulations contained in the contracts covering the employment of union members.

Role of the Contractor

The position of the contractor in the bargaining structure of the musicians' union has a peculiar significance. Usually the musical director or leader of an orchestra is also the contractor for his troupe; he must then have definite political and commercial ability as well as musical talent. Because this combination may not always exist in the same person, it sometimes happens that the contractor is one of the subordinate musicians of the orchestra. In rarer cases, he may not even play with the orchestra for which he books contracts. Always, however, he is the commercial representative of the group as well as a quasi-official representative of the union.

Except for solo performers, the by-laws of the Chicago Federation of Musicians, as well as of the national parent body, explicitly forbid individual members to enter into direct employment relations without the intervention of contractors.[82] In turn, contractors engaging union members are always union members

---

82. *Constitution, By-Laws and Price List, Chicago Federation of Musicians*, 1938, Sec. XII, Art. 5, p. 27. (Hereafter abbreviated *Con. C. F. of M*. All references are to the revised 1938 edition.) For the International Law, see *Constitution, American Federation of Musicians*, 1938 ed., Art. X, Sec. 29, p. 80. (Hereafter abbreviated *Con. A. F. of M*.) Only in the case of the permanent organization of "name bands" will the union regard the leader as an *independent* contractor and hence a subemployer charged with liability for Social Security taxes. In other cases, the "contractor" is considered an employer's "agent" and hence not "independent." The original interpretation by the board of directors of the Chicago Musicians' Local 10 did not distinguish between contractors for permanent "name bands" and other contractors. (*Intermezzo*, April 1937, p. 1.) For analysis of the subsequent ruling of the Bureau of Internal Revenue, see *Variety Radio Directory*, 1938–1939, pp. 517-524.

themselves and subject to union rules, including special contractors' scales.[83] Employers rarely select individual orchestra members and in some circumstances they may not even choose their contractor. Often, especially if there is any doubt about observance of union rules, the union office will assign contractors to specific engagements.

To make insulation between the individual musician and employer complete, and to insure that negotiation shall be through contractors, it is specified that:

members receiving remuneration for services rendered shall not be permitted to state the price of engagement on report slips to employer or his agent. This information must be computed by the contractor who shall pay all musicians no less than the scale for the class of engagement played.[84]

The obvious effect of the enforcement of this rule is to remove all higgling between the individual employee and his employer, and to make certain that the contractor will always be the official business spokesman for the group. To strengthen the contractor's hand it also is provided that no member may appeal "to an employer or to anyone in authority, or to anyone having power or influence to reinstate him on an engagement after having received notice of dismissal from the contractor by whom he was engaged." [85] Appeal by an individual member contrary to this law merely confirms his discharge and may bring him to trial before the union administration.

Regulation of Employment Contracts

In addition to these regulations concerning the position of the contractor, specific rules apply to the employment contract itself. If the union's standard form is not used, the contract must in any case include certain standard clauses which provide for: (a) nullification of the contract if the employer hires any other band or orchestra made up of nonunion players, or if the contractor ceases to be a member of the American Federation of Musicians; (b) blanket recognition of all laws of the union; (c) specification

---

83. See footnote 92.
84. *Con. C. F. of M.*, Sec. XII, Art. B-20.
85. *Ibid.*, Sec. XII, G-4, p. 24.

that the employer may not advertise a larger number of musicians than is contracted for; (d) a guarantee that the employer will cover all orchestra members under the Illinois Compensation Act.[86]

On beyond these rules governing the substance of employment contracts are the provisions for filing copies of the contracts at the union office. Originally restricted to certain classes of contracts,[87] the rule has been broadened until now it demands that "on ALL engagements, whether single or steady, contracts must be filed with the office of the Local." [88] This means that literally hundreds of employment contracts are filed with the secretary and therefore become subject to direct scrutiny and enforcement by union officials.[89]

These provisions governing the nature of contracts and the role of contractors must be interpreted in the light of the general character of musical employment. Because of the numerous short engagements and the movements of players from one place to another, one of the union's most important functions is that of a placement agency for its members. Sometimes this is delegated to booking agencies licensed by the union.[90] By careful definition of the contractor's position and of the nature of the employment contract, by provision for the actual filing of contracts, by denial of licenses to booking agencies refusing to observe union regulations, and by directing placement either through the union office or through licensed agencies, employment and working conditions are controlled in a market where, without such devices, the maintenance of standards would be a nearly impossible task. Even

---

86. *Con. C. F. of M.*, Sec. XII, C-5, D, pp. 21-22.
87. Christenson, *op. cit.*, p. 205.
88. *Con. C. F. of M.*, Rule 28, p. 53.
89. For the thirty-month period beginning January 1937 and ending July 1939, an actual count of all contracts filed was made from the minutes of the board of directors. This showed that 1,240 contracts had been filed. *Intermezzo*, February 1937 to and including September 1939.
90. Licenses to all booking agencies as well as to companies making various types of recordings are issued directly by the International, although such licenses must in all cases conform to the regulations of the local unions in the territories in which they operate. As of April 1939, there were forty-nine booking agencies and ten recording companies with union licenses in Chicago. *Intermezzo*, August 1939, pp. 14, 16.

then, it appears that compromises must be made in certain quarters.

C. EMPLOYMENT STANDARDS

Wage Scales

The wage structure of Chicago musicians is not peculiar to that city. It results not only from the many different types of employment but from a union policy designed to fit those conditions. Not only are musicians employed in all sorts of establishments, but within the same places the engagements differ. For example, radio stations employ studio or staff orchestras continuously throughout most of the year. From time to time they also hire orchestras and instrumental soloists for short special engagements. Sometimes musicians who perform before the microphone irregularly may be engaged by advertising agencies or commercial sponsors without direct employment relationship with the radio station. Similarly, theatres may have permanent orchestras and also hire extra orchestras for shorter periods at irregular intervals.

Such a wide variety of employment gives a complexity seldom found in the wage structure of other organized crafts.[91] There is no single "union scale." The 1939 union rate for steady engagements in Chicago's second class cabarets was $1.14 an hour, while on the same basis the broadcasting studio rate on commercial network programs was $5.60.[92] The actual range in scales, however,

91. Data for ten other cities furnished by the U. S. Bureau of Labor Statistics show conclusively that the wide range in scales for unionized musicians is not peculiar to Chicago.

92. While comparison necessitates reducing rates to hourly terms, it should be pointed out that the union practice is to define the rates for steady engagements on a weekly basis. Thus the 1938–1940 radio agreement provides two different sets of rates, one for the "local" stations and the other for the "network" stations. Basic rates for players on the "local" stations were fixed at $80, $90, and $115 weekly, depending on the time of day performances occurred. Basic weekly rates for chain broadcasting were fixed at $110 on sustaining programs and $140 on commercial programs for 1938 and 1939. The agreement automatically raised these rates for chain stations to $120 and $150, respectively, in 1940. The scales quoted are the basic ones for journeymen musicians only. Weekly rates for orchestra leaders in some radio studios reached $250 in 1940. In almost all circumstances contractors are governed by scales considerably higher than those applicable to journeymen. For example, a common provision for many different types of single engagements is that the contractor must charge the full journeyman's scale for his own services, plus $1 for each additional man in his organization. See *Con. C. F. of M.*, pp. 54 ff.

is even greater than these figures suggest, for no standard scale is provided for some kinds of engagements either by trade agreement or union by-laws. In these cases the board of directors has power to set the wage rate for each individual engagement.[93] This applies to the so-called third and fourth class cabarets and night clubs where the pay may be down to 50 or 60 cents an hour. Some musicians have been found in establishments of these classes working the regular six-night week for as little as $10 a week.[94] Thus, there is no standardization in these "small time" establishments; the practice is simply to charge no more than the "traffic will bear" as long as union members are hired and the closed shop is observed.[95]

Pay for single engagements varies similarly. In first class hotels and cabarets it is $10 for three hours. In the second class "night spots" it is $8 for three and one half consecutive hours, but in the radio scale the pay for two hours is $16 on local stations and $24 on networks.

Standard Work Periods

No more uniformity exists in hours than in pay. The single engagement is ordinarily a performance of three or three and one half hours, except on the radio stations, where it must be completed within two hours. On steady engagements the week varies in length from one type of performance to another. Before 1937 the full-time week called for performances on seven days, except in radio studios. As early as 1932 the union laid down the six-day week for radio work, but not until five years later did it proceed to make the six-day week apply to all the better type engagements.[96]

93. *Con. C. F. of M.*, p. 48.
94. Various interviews during July 1939.
95. That it is the type of "engagement" and not the type of "work" or degree of "skill" that is really controlling is shown by the fact that phonograph operators on network stations get $90 weekly, and on strictly local stations, $60. On the network stations the union sometimes spreads these jobs for "pancake turners." Letter from a radio program director, July 28, 1939.
96. The six-day week was established in hotels and first class cabarets in September 1937 and in the vaudeville houses and second and third class cabarets during the months immediately following. (*Variety*, August 11, 1937, p. 49; October 27, 1937, p. 47; November 10, 1937, p. 47; November 17, 1937, p. 67.) Just as the

The next year (1938) the five-day week became standard in radio studios.[97] This does not mean that there is a single standard "full-time" week for Chicago's radio musicians. On *local* broadcasting stations the daytime staff orchestra members, who get $80 a week, are on duty for twenty-five hours within which time they are required to do twenty hours of actual playing. The evening session rate of $90 weekly calls for twenty-five hours of playing time. Performers hired for local broadcasting during both afternoon and evening sessions, and all the network studio musicians, work twenty-five hours but at still different pay.

d. JOB CONTROL AND ENFORCEMENT OF UNION STANDARDS

Students of trade unionism understand that organization standards, whether incorporated in trade agreements or in union by-laws, are not enforced automatically. More important, therefore, than what the standards are is how they are observed and how they are enforced.

The Closed Shop

Enforcement of the closed shop appears to be uniformly vigorous. When the board of directors allows union members to appear with nonunion players, it is usually for noncommercial engagements, in a school, club or church orchestra. On the better commercial programs union job control is so complete that nonunion players may appear only upon paying "stand-by" fees to the union.[98] Sometimes union members are actually hired to stand by even though they do not perform. More often, however, an employer of union musicians who wishes to hire nonunion musical

attempt to establish uniform wage scales breaks down for the lower classes of establishments, so too no effort is made at enforcement of rigid work periods for these. In this connection *Variety* (November 17, 1937, p. 67) uses the following significant language: "Bottom rung, the fourth class spots, will not be touched at all at this time but will be permitted to go along on the present basis."
97. *Intermezzo*, November 1937, p. 1.
98. The exact amounts of such fees paid during the first six months of 1939 have been available for two radio broadcasting companies in Chicago. In each of these cases the expenditures on stand-by fees amounted to less than one per cent of the total expenditures for musicians' services during the period. It will be observed, of course, that since stand-by fees are designed to keep down the number of nonunion performers, they would serve this purpose most effectively if they yielded no revenue at all to the union.

talent for a particular program gets a waiver of the union claim by paying the stand-by fee directly to the union treasury. The fee equals what union members would have earned had they performed. Such fees are most prevalent for radio broadcasts by celebrated foreign musicians who are not union members.[99]

Mobility of Membership and Transfer Rules

Closely related to the regulations designed to guarantee closed-shop conditions are the rules governing employment of traveling members. Under the rules of the American Federation of Musicians, no local union may deny admission to the member of any other local union who presents a properly acquired "transfer card." On the other hand, any member who accepts a traveling engagement within the jurisdiction of another local union must deposit a "transfer card" if he remains more than one week. Acceptance of a "transfer card" admits the member to "full" membership only after six months' residence and payment of the regular initiation fee.[100] In the interval, however, he pays union dues both at home and in Chicago.

In 1938, Chicago's Local 10 had between nine and eleven thousand members.[101] Transfer members from other locals, reinstated former members and new members form an incoming stream of

---

99. Stand-by fees may also be charged in cases where a traveling union orchestra plays an engagement of a type that is reserved for local union members. Thus the Paul Whiteman orchestra, playing at the RKO Palace Theatre, was allowed to broadcast by remote control only after arranging for payment of a stand-by fee. In this case the fee amounted to $323, which was the payment of the single engagement price for nineteen men at the then prevailing union rate of $17 per man. In 1935 an attempt by the Philadelphia local union to prevent the appearance of a traveling conductor on station WCAU brought forth the pronouncement from the international president that local unions could not bar traveling conductors from appearing as long as stand-by fees were paid. *Variety*, September 25, 1935, p. 49.

100. *Con. A. F. of M.*, Art. VIII, Sec. 5, p. 48. The Chicago local initiation fee is $100.

101. In 1937, after the absorption of two smaller unions (The American Musicians' Union and the Polish-American Musicians' Union) the Chicago Federation of Musicians reported a total membership of 10,254. (*Intermezzo*, October 1937, p. 1.) A count from published records, however, showed that during the decade 1929–1938 the largest number of deaths occurring within the membership in any one year was seventy-seven. Unless the death rate for musicians was substantially lower than for the population of the city as a whole, this death record suggests that a fair estimate would place the membership even below nine thousand.

membership. There is also a constant outflow as a result of the issuance of transfer cards, resignations, deaths and the annulments of membership for violation of union rules. For the ten years 1929–1938 a count of the membership changes [102] showed that, apart from the absorption of the members of two small unions in a body in 1937, these two streams have about offset each other. On the other hand, both have risen, showing that movement within the union membership has been increasing. Moreover, if one compares the incoming with the outgoing transfers, it appears that Chicago consistently sends out more members than it gets from other cities.

Only about 25 per cent of the out of town transfer members become fully privileged members of the Chicago local. The continuing stream of transfer members [103] and of traveling members who stay less than a week, means that there are always a large number of union musicians within the Chicago jurisdiction who never take out full membership in the local organization. They are guaranteed restricted working privileges at special costs—such as double local dues, the minor charge of 25 cents per month for the Traveling Card, and payment of special taxes as fixed by the national organization.

Among the regulations designed to protect local markets are those forbidding traveling orchestras to supplant studio staff musicians or to take part in any strictly local broadcasting engagements.[104] Beyond these absolute prohibitions are various International engagement taxes.[105] While they differ somewhat for different types of engagements, their practical effect is comparable to protective tariffs in that they assure local unions that traveling union orchestras will always cost employers considerably more than the "domestic" product. The objective of "revenue," therefore, is mixed with a large measure of the objective of "control."

102. This count was made from the "Local Reports" as published in the *International Musician*.
103. By actual count transfers deposited averaged twenty-seven per month in 1932 and sixty per month in 1938. These represented the minimum and maximum averages for the ten-year period 1929–1938. "Local Reports," *International Musician*, 1929–1939.
104. Con. A. F. of M., Art. X, Sec. D, p. 65.
105. For details, *ibid.*, Art. X and XIII.

Penalties

For violation of some phase of the national or local law of the musicians' union, there are two common penalties—fines and expulsion. The Trial Board handled 359 cases of alleged violations in the four and a half years ending September 1939.[106] Almost nine tenths of these cases involved one of three charges: violation of wage scale, "practicing an imposition on, or imperiling the interests of the Local or members thereof," and breach of the closed-shop rule, either by contractors hiring nonunion musicians, or by union members playing in organizations with nonunionists.

For nine months of this period the records include enough detail to permit analysis not only of the offenses involved, but also of judgments made in each case. The total of assessed fines for this period was $6,290. Sixty-one cases arose but convictions occurred in only fifty, and in forty-one of these cases fines were assessed. In each of the other nine cases members were expelled. Over 60 per cent of the convictions where fines were assessed (twenty-five cases) involved wage scale violations, for which the average fine was $180.

The same formal offense will be accorded different treatment in differing situations. Violation of the wage scale in second class cabarets is one thing; a similar breach on a radio station engagement or in a downtown first class cabaret is quite different. Few violations of union rules are tolerated in radio and "the loop." In the swank Palmer House Empire Room a fine of $500 may be assessed for an offense which might be overlooked in a small southside cabaret, or in any case penalized by a modest fine of $10 or $25. Theatre engagements are also scrutinized carefully, and rarely will any open violation of union law be permitted there with impunity.[107]

---

106. This analysis was made from the records as published in *Intermezzo*, May 1935, to and including September 1939. Specific fines were not included in the reports after March 1936.

107. A contractor paying less than the wage scale on engagements on one of the smaller local radio stations was fined $2,000. *Board of Directors* v. *John Swierczynski*, "Minutes of Trial Board," April 10, 1930, *Intermezzo*, May 1930, p. 9.

"For paying less than the wage scale on engagements at the Morrison Hotel and Palmer House and in and out of the downtown district," Dave Cunningham was fined $1,000. ("Minutes of Trial Board," July 25, 1935, *Intermezzo*, August 1935,

To appreciate the effectiveness of the assessment of fines one must recall the universality of the closed shop. Figures are unobtainable on how generally these fines are paid. However, members who are in default are not allowed to work with union men in any city in the country. Because of the shifting nature of musical employment, members seeking the better jobs can rarely afford the risk of being ruled out of competition. The boycott inflicted upon defaulters has an effectiveness not often found in other organized labor markets. It is not only imposed upon contractors and individual musicians violating union rules, but it also serves as an effective instrument in assisting members in collecting wages due from employers.[108]

e. FACTORS SUPPORTING COLLECTIVE BARGAINING

The numerous short engagements, the variety of employers, the circulation of musicians within a city market and between different communities, these are features which both condition the character of collective bargaining and contribute to its maintenance.

Mobility and Union Strength

With a large mobile proportion of working musicians, the union can perform two functions more effectively than other agencies. Contacts which individual musicians lose with specific

p. 6.) Four months later Cunningham's name still appeared on the "Defaulters List" (*Intermezzo*, November 1935, p. 16), and seven months after his trial it was announced that he had been "reinstated in the Local." *Intermezzo*, February 1936, p. 13.

On the same day of Cunningham's trial the Board heard the case of William Kaufman on charges of contracting "for less than the wage scale on engagement at Riverview Park . . . for the Independent Sick Benefit Association of America." Kaufman was found guilty and fined $25. "Minutes of Trial Board," July 25, 1935, *Intermezzo*, August 1935, p. 6.

The largest fine in Chicago of which any record was found was one for $10,000 levied against E. A. Rivkin in 1929 for paying less than the wage scale on engagements with the Shubert Theatre chain. The writer now has clear evidence that this fine was never paid. For data on other early cases where fines were assessed for wage scale violations, see Christenson, *op. cit.*, p. 20.

108. Cases involving claims against employers for unpaid amounts due on contracts are brought before the board of directors. In the two-and-one-half-year period ending July 1939 the board considered seventy-seven cases involving unpaid amounts due members for services. It approved the claims in all save four cases. After approval by the board such claims must be settled or the defaulting employer cannot contract for services of union members. "Minutes of Board of Directors," *Intermezzo*, 1937–1939.

employers through shifting from job to job can be maintained by the union. Thus placement naturally becomes a union job. The union also serves as a collection agency; employers in default in payment of wages cannot hire any other union musicians. For the Federation, therefore, placement and collection of claims stand high among the justifications for its existence.

Viewed from the standpoint of control over membership, mobility would appear to be a definite handicap. Its weakening influence, however, has been converted into an actual source of power through the institution of the contractor. By guaranteeing contractors a monopoly over job opportunities, it is possible, through the contractors and rules governing them, to solve the problem of control over a large floating membership.

It must be remembered that the contracting musician is a subemployer selling the services of his orchestra. By far the most important item in his operating expenses are the wages of his orchestra. Price stability will be greatly enhanced if a uniform scale for individual musicians is effective throughout the entire market for the same classes of engagements. The musicians' union, in one way, operates as the cleaners', dyers' and pressers' union would if the master cleaners were also members of the union.

The Influence of Broadcasting

One important factor strengthening the bargaining position of instrumental musicians was the rapid rise of radio broadcasting. From an industry which operated with almost no income and in a rather fantastic noncommercial fashion in 1925, it rose in little more than a decade into one of the leading commercial advertising media.[109] This growing and profitable industry found

109. The following two statements taken from a book on the industry published fifteen years ago throw light on its rapid growth and development:

"Only a few of the broadcasters are making any payment for the services of the artists and performers. Home talent is used but the demand for compensation is increasing. A few pay regularly, others only occasionally.

"Up to a recent date, the American Telephone and Telegraph Company was the only one which charged for advertising. For example, its station will permit any concern to broadcast a program and announce its name and position in connection with the rendition. For such advertising WEAF charges $10 a minute or $400 an

that in hiring musicians it had to deal with an already established organization in the Chicago market. The managers knew little about personnel problems, and the prosperity of the industry made it possible to accede easily to already established practices.

It was fortunate for the union that this thriving industry developed just when another technical improvement, sound movies, almost entirely destroyed musicians' opportunities in theatres. Radio employment falls far short of the lost employment in movie houses, but it has compensated somewhat for the loss.

The Chicago Federation of Musicians has benefited from the city's strategic position, which has attracted many broadcasting stations, thus widening the market for the services of musicians within the city. With this has come a simultaneous increase in demand for specific musical names. The "name band" has today a much larger audience than before 1925, when the size of the audience was limited by the largest theatre. With radio, the audience may be nation-wide, and name bands therefore command the attention of advertising sponsors. Another result of radio transmission is the diminution in the significance of the wage bill for orchestral musicians.

Of course, enlargement of the audience of one specific orchestra may mean fewer orchestras. But while radio has reduced the volume of employment, it has increased the bargaining position of those employed. Fortunately for the select few,[110] loss of skill while out of a job soon converts the unemployed into the unemployable.[111]

hour. But even the American Telephone and Telegraph Company has stated that its broadcasting is unprofitable, receiving a revenue of less than half the operating expenses in 1923." Hiram L. Jome, *The Economics of the Radio Industry*, A. W. Shaw, Chicago and New York, 1925, pp. 176-177.

In 1935, total revenue from time sales was more than $52 million, total radio station employment 14,561, and the gross pay roll for the year was just under $27 million. Census of Business: 1935, *Radio Broadcasting*, pp. 24, 25.

110. An estimate based on application of union rules to different classes of radio stations indicates that the regularly employed members in Chicago studios did not exceed three hundred in 1939. Interviews have confirmed this estimate as being generous.

111. A long-standing member of the Chicago Federation writes: "The unemployed musician quickly ceases to be an employable musician. This statement has

Networks Versus Local Stations

Comparison of the radio network with the local broadcasting station shows a repetition of the "chain-theatre-independent-exhibitor" situation. The radio industry is another "house divided." For the local station, talent costs are an important element in operating expenses, but they are relatively unimportant on the networks. The larger and more profitable networks, therefore, give way more freely to union demands and leave the local stations standing alone. When the American Federation of Musicians threatened a strike in 1937 the large networks were the first to make an agreement.[112] The independent local stations followed soon after.

It should be borne in mind that radio broadcasting is continuous. Clock time production is even more necessary than in the case of a metropolitan newspaper or a movie theatre; an interruption is something station managers contemplate with fear. So far no demands have been severe enough to justify risking the losses which a strike might bring.

Adjustment of Union Policy to the Market

Equilibrium has been maintained because union policy has been shrewdly adapted to all aspects of a varied market. Certainly less than half of Chicago's unionized musicians approach continuous employment.[113] Some who work at other occupations regard their music as a sideline, but many are simply unemployed through a large part of the year.

Under these circumstances union policy, supported by the rapid deterioration of skill among the unemployed, has created job classification and maintained noncompeting groups at different wage levels. The market has been sifted to place the more competent and, generally, younger musicians in the better jobs. Those who remain after the sifting work on union jobs where standards

some exceptions, but is general enough to be a legitimate contributory element. The deterioration of skill is not to be compared with that of followers of a 'trade.' It is phenomenally swift." Note to the writer, January 27, 1940.

112. For details of this important national settlement between the AF of M and the networks, see *Variety Radio Directory, 1938–1939*, pp. 1170-1181.

113. A well-informed employer estimated that "not over 2,500 of the Chicago union members get anything like regular employment." Interview, July 1939.

are relatively unregulated.[114] Individual competition is thus concentrated at lower levels.

Supplementary to this classification of jobs is a union financial structure which encourages continued membership by even unemployed musicians. When allowance is made for insurance benefits the ordinary dues of the union are relatively low, but they are combined with a series of engagement taxes which tend to apportion the cost of union maintenance roughly in accordance with "ability to pay."[115] Even the burden of the initiation fee works out in accordance with this principle since it is likely to fall on the younger and more nearly fully employed musicians.

5. SUMMARY

This review of the collective determination of labor standards for three groups of Chicago's workers thrusts into sharp relief an

---

114. There is no question about price cutting on the least desirable jobs in the market, and it is even permitted to extend upward into some of the grades where there are supposedly clearly defined union standards. Thus one member writes:
"Gossip persists that only the unlucky minority of price cutters reach the Trial Board. Price cutting is said to operate continually here and there as a practical modification of rigid price scales. A most persistent evil is the 'kickback' from the individual member to the contractor. A complaint is difficult to present effectively, and the contractor on a steady engagement is a person of real political power in the union internal affairs. That's how he got to be a contractor in the first place." Note to writer, January 1940.

115. Regular annual dues to which all members are subject are $20, payable in quarterly installments (*Con. C. F. of M.*, Sec. XII i 1, p. 25). The initiation fee is $100. It seems reasonable to suppose that members join only when there are definite jobs in prospect. The engagement taxes in 1939 were fixed at 4 per cent on all steady engagements of a local nature. Only on the radio are single engagements taxed; the rate is also 4 per cent. Hence, members who are on the better jobs contribute substantially more to union maintenance than those who have only irregular employment. On the other hand, all members, on payment of regular dues, receive life insurance policies graded upwards from $250 to $1,000, based on length of membership. Supplementing this the union treasury has also made substantial contributions at various times to public concerts, which benefit the normally unemployed musicians more than the employed members. The annual expenditure for Christmas baskets for the indigent members is another item in which the unemployed share disproportionately.

It may be noted that movement among the membership substantially increases the number of initiation fees. For the ten-year period 1929–1938, union income from initiation fees never fell below $43,300 (1932) and reached $69,000 in 1937. Estimate based on membership count, see pp. 859-860.

observation made years ago by an early student of trade unionism: "there is unionism and unionism." [116] All three of the groups examined in this chapter are affiliated with the American Federation of Labor. There are some similarities in their policies; yet their control devices are distinctly different.

Union organization in the Chicago cleaning and dyeing industry is set up along mixed industrial and craft lines; one union claims all employees inside the plants, while the other asserts control over a single occupation, collection and delivery service. So far as these two unions are concerned, there is no direct limitation on the number of workers that may enter. It is true that substantial initiation fees are levied, but paying by installments keeps them from being burdensome. The real limitations on the number of workers in the industry are indirect and operate through joint control designed to limit the number of business units. There is a closed shop but no really closed union. Standards have often been enforced by violence, but resort to force in the cleaning industry has rarely been instigated by workers alone. Rather it has been a joint instrument of employers and unions in attempts to guarantee stability in a highly competitive market. As was pointed out earlier, to some extent these attempts were futile. The dominant characteristic of collective bargaining in the cleaning and dyeing industry, however, is clearly "joint price control."

Contrasted with the cleaners and dyers, the motion picture machine operators are a small group of technicians organized strictly along craft lines in an industry of comparatively high overhead costs. The strategy of their union is to limit the number of eligible workers and take full advantage of the employers' necessity for continuous operation. There is almost no element of joint price control. The force resorted to in protection of standards has been directed against employers or against the union administration. Its use is almost never a venture in which responsibility is shared jointly by the employers and the union organization. The picture this union presents is bold and perhaps a bit garish; this is "here and now unionism" par excellence.

116. R. F. Hoxie, *Trade Unionism in the United States*, D. Appleton, New York, 1917, p. 36.

Collective bargaining procedure for the highly specialized craft of musicians has some elements in common with each of the other two and some distinctive features of its own. The result is a composite unique in the panorama of collective activity. The development of numerous amateur musicians, without reference to union policy or to employers' training programs, means that if the union is to protect its membership against external competition it must at all times keep its doors open to newcomers as do unions in the cleaning and dyeing industry. But limited job opportunities serve to maintain an unduly large reserve of musical talent. Here the musicians' union goes beyond the cleaners and dyers, for it requires union membership of the contractors, who are subemployers, and thus retains control over the jobs of the individual musicians. But from another angle, musicians' union policy parallels the projectionists' in seeking to segregate the locations, such as radio studios, where employers' demand for musical service is relatively inelastic. Here it achieves its most impressive effects. Then by more detailed job classification and by selective protection at different levels, it seeks to minimize the weakness which the economic force of excess numbers imposes upon it. Ingenious construction and judicious use of enforcement agencies, financial machinery and the benefit system strengthen the structure at its most delicate points. Regulation of employment conditions for musicians by collective action becomes "controlled movement and classification of job opportunities."

For all three groups practices and activities appear in the nature of adjustments to the specific economic and industrial forces surrounding them. Any rational recommendations concerning a public program for regulation of collective bargaining, therefore, ought to begin with an appreciation of trade-union action as a product of the market and industry in which it is found.

APPENDICES

Appendix A

COLLECTIVE BARGAINING BEFORE THE NEW DEAL

PHILIP TAFT

1. EARLY HISTORY, 1786–1850

IN 1786, a year before the Constitution of the United States was drafted in the same City of Brotherly Love, some Philadelphia printers struck for a $6-a-week wage. With that strike begins the known story of the American labor movement for collective bargaining. Five years later Philadelphia carpenters laid down their tools to demand a working day from six a.m. to six p.m. with an hour off for breakfast and another for dinner—a ten-hour day, which they failed to get.[1]

Nearly a generation later, in 1822 and again in Philadelphia, the ten-hour day was urged once more, this time by machinists and millwrights. The occupations behind the resolution, which likewise got nowhere, were representative of labor's expansion. With the spread of manufacturing and new industries, new occupations had come into being and older ones had more work to do, and more hands to do it. By the 1820's, a vocal, though confused, working class had shown itself in this country.

It showed itself by organization. The first great strides were around 1825 with the sprouting of craft unions of printers, shoemakers, hatters, tailors, weavers and others.[2] Numerous strikes for higher wages occurred, also attempts to shorten the working day. But labor's grievances were more than against employers over wages and hours. Men could still be imprisoned for debt. Workers had no recourse to liens against employers who failed to pay them. In some states their children were condemned to charity schools. Strikers were liable to be clapped into jail for violation of ancient conspiracy laws. And, indicative of its still middle-class mentality, labor saw in monopolies, particularly the banks, one of the greatest threats to progress.

No wonder, then, that the early American labor movement was part

---

1. See David J. Saposs, "Colonial and Federal Beginnings," in John R. Commons and Associates, *History of Labour in the United States*, Macmillan, New York, 1926, Vol. I, pp. 25, 110.
2. Ethelbert Stewart, "Two Forgotten Decades in the History of Labor Organizations—1820 to 1840," *American Federationist*, July 1913, pp. 518-519.

trade union, part political and part panacea-seeking. Periods of union organization and activity alternated with periods dominated by reform movements. Workingmen's political parties appeared in the later twenties, as more and more states liberalized their voting qualifications. Labor in politics had repercussions. It met with vigorous opposition, which helped split its parties wide open. By 1834, the older parties had accepted much of labor's program, inflation was lowering real wages, and the workers began in earnest to seek purely economic advances. Union membership soared to 300,000.[3] Locals appeared in a number of midwestern communities; city centrals sprang up in such major cities as New York, Philadelphia, Boston, Baltimore, Cincinnati and Louisville;[4] and, as locals mushroomed and interregional competition increased, five national unions were created.

Birth of Collective Bargaining

Up to that time, strikes had been the chief means of improving wages and working conditions; rarely did unions succeed in persuading an employer to negotiate.[5] They continued to present demands, circulate union scales, and then threaten to call out their men unless their demands were accepted. But in the 1830's collective bargaining through joint conferences became more frequent. In Philadelphia, New York, Baltimore, Washington and Newark, parleys between employers and organized craftsmen over wages were not uncommon. However, as labor's demands for higher pay and better treatment became increasingly aggressive, hostile employers sought either to oppose unions by banding together [6] or to destroy them by enlisting aid of the courts. The passing years left judges still rather inclined to throttle trade unionism with the intricacies of judicial interpretation.[7] Yet labor literally was on the march. There were mass meetings and processions, speechmaking and circulation of petitions, strikes and riots. It was a turbulent era, and it brought the ten-hour day for many city mechanics.

3. Edward B. Mittelman, "Trade Unionism," in Commons and Associates, *op. cit.*, Vol. I, p. 424.
4. The first city central was established in Philadelphia in 1827.
5. Employers in printing and shoemaking had in some instances negotiated with representatives of their employees before 1830.
6. Though employers' associations were frequently organized during this period for these express purposes, earlier associations had sought primarily to regulate quality and fix prices, dealing with or fighting labor organizations as seemed called for in their normal functions as manufacturers', merchants' and employers' associations.
7. By prescribing with whom their members would or would not work the unions were still exposed to prosecution for conspiracy. The conspiracy charge had been used against the shoemakers in six prosecutions dating from 1806 to 1815, and against the hatters, tailors, spinners and weavers, as well as the shoemakers, in six cases during the 1820's.

In 1837 business went into another collapse; a disastrous depression followed, bringing low wages and prolonged unemployment. Labor lost most of its recent organization gains. New unions died, new members drifted away. Strikes gained nothing; too many unemployed filled strikers' places, and ship after ship came into New York harbor bearing hundreds of husky immigrants. Discouraged from further economic activity during the forties, labor resorted to panaceas. Except for a brief resurgence during a sudden business revival in 1843, it devoted itself largely to Associationism, Cooperation, land reform, and legislation to secure the ten-hour day for those still without it.

Within a decade gold was found in California, and prices rose. Up with them went organized labor zeal. Interest revived in trade unionism and in higher wages. The practice of drawing up price lists was resumed, and these wage scales were submitted in increasing number to individual employers for their approval. Few approved, however, and strikes were common. Those who did accept the union price list found that the advantage rested with those who did not. To protect these "fair" employers, the unions widened their collective bargaining ambitions; they began to insist on dealing with employers as a body so as to eliminate competition from the "unfair" ones. Wherever they could, trade unions in eastern cities signed up groups of organized employers to wage agreements, then sought to force these terms on employers who still held off. Labor's aspirations, if not its growth, were in evidence during the fifties with no fewer than twenty-six national unions established to carry on organization work and protect locals. Labor had begun to branch out.

2. NATIONALIZATION OF THE LABOR MOVEMENT

Trade unionism was again badly crippled by the depression of the late fifties, unemployment in early Civil War years, and the growing number of union men in the Army. All save four of the new national unions were destroyed. A boom in the later stages of the war, with wages lagging behind rapidly rising commodity prices, reversed the process and encouraged labor organization. Particularly in Massachusetts, New York and Pennsylvania, working men anxious to maintain their real incomes flocked into trade unions. Local trades associations, or city centrals, were formed in many communities and some national unions were revived. In the twenty-odd years which followed, the general trend in union membership was upward; interest in national organization persisted.

In the last half of the nineteenth century American industrial capitalism came of age. More railroads and better communications steadily expanded markets. Served by a host of technological improvements, factories mushroomed in new areas. Stimulated by these developments and stirred by the growing inclusiveness of employers' associations, new national labor unions strove with varying success to coordinate local action and to organize entire markets. By the middle eighties some had become strong organizations with firm control over their affiliated locals—shaping their policies and upon necessity disciplining them.[8]

Among the ten national unions established between 1863 and 1865 were the Plasterers, Cigar Makers, Carpenters and Joiners, Locomotive Engineers, Bricklayers, and Tailors. Despite a two-year depression, seven more nationals appeared in the next four years—among them the shoeworkers' Knights of St. Crispin (1868) and the Order of Railway Conductors (1869). Nine were organized in the relatively prosperous years from 1870 to 1873, including the Telegraphers, Coopers, Steel Heaters and Rollers, and Locomotive Firemen.

Growth of the Knights of Labor and AF of L

Between 1869 and 1872 union membership nearly doubled from 170,000 to about 300,000.[9] But this growth soon not only halted but largely disappeared. For during the severe depression of 1873–1879 many hurriedly formed unions resting on weak foundations collapsed. Not until the depression was spent did growth resume. Nevertheless, several national unions sprang up during the hard times of the seventies—the Amalgamated Association of Iron and Steel Workers in 1876, the Granite Cutters in 1877, the Lake Seamen and the Cotton Spinners in 1878, and the Shoe Lasters in 1879. By 1880 national unions numbered thirty, and a few years later total membership probably reached the 1872 total of 300,000. By 1886 there were almost a million members, most of whom held cards in the fast-growing Knights of Labor.

The Knights combined a reform with a would-be dominant labor federation—and met trouble in both. Since its interest was in all labor, not just the skilled, and since many of its leaders were advocates of all kinds of panaceas, whereas the crafts' concern was chiefly wages, hours and jobs, or "business unionism," the central body frequently came in conflict with some of its affiliates. By 1886 "business unionism" led to the formation of the American Federation of Labor—organized first in 1881 as the Federation of Organized Trades and Labor Unions—which was to be primarily a league of autonomous affiliates. The question of which would be su-

8. While there was an increasing tendency to favor "pure and simple" trade unionism, with its emphasis on job control and collective bargaining, at the same time the history of American labor during this period is shot through with agitation for reform. Cooperation, greenbackism, eight-hour day legislation and socialism, all came in for their share of attention from one or more of the multifarious labor organizations—the labor congresses, the National Labor Union, the socialist organizations, and the Knights of Labor which, combining reformism with "pure and simple" trade-union activity, is typical of this period of transition.

9. John B. Andrews, "Nationalization," in Commons and Associates, *op. cit.*, Vol. II, p. 47.

preme in the trade-union field was soon settled. Internal dissension, the Haymarket riot, and hostile public opinion arising out of violent strikes caused disintegration of the Knights and left the AF of L as the dominant central organization.

With the decline of the Knights and widespread public reaction against organized labor, union membership by 1890 was perhaps half of what it was four years before. The depression of 1893–1896 and a string of labor defeats on many fronts—notably, steel, railroads and mining—kept membership down. The estimate for 1897 was 447,000.[10]

For the most part between the Civil and the Spanish wars, union labor continued to seek control of working conditions through scales and rules—a policy which frequently provoked hostile counterassociations among employers, and strikes, lockouts and guerilla warfare. At the same time, however, there were a number of experiments with collective bargaining. Of these, the most significant were in iron, coal, shoemaking, printing, building and railroads.

a. THE IRON INDUSTRY

After the Civil War American industry faced expansion of output with a downward trend in wholesale prices. Severe competition in many industries put pressure on wages, which stimulated not only labor's resistance but also attempts at a mutually satisfactory solution. A number of participants in collective bargaining sought a "fair" wage policy that would satisfy employees and at the same time solve the cost-price problem, or at least limit competition.

Experiments With the Sliding Scale

One of the earliest of these attempts was in the iron industry. Sharp fluctuations in iron prices during the war caused employer resistance to the rigid union scales of the Sons of Vulcan, an organization of skilled iron puddlers founded in 1858 in the Pittsburgh area. For several years the conflict remained unresolved. In 1865 puddlers and iron manufacturers in the Pittsburgh area established what was perhaps the first sliding scale of wages in the United States. Wages for boiling pig iron were set at $4 a day when iron was 2.5 cents a pound and varied upward to $9 a day when the price was 8.5 cents.[11] This assurance that costs would change with prices made it easier for employers to plan for the future, while labor would have automatic wage increases with each rise in the price of iron. Either side could end the agreement upon ninety days' notice.

Iron fell from 7.5 cents a pound in February 1865, to 4 cents five

10. Leo Wolman, *The Growth of American Trade Unions, 1880–1923*, National Bureau of Economic Research, New York, 1924, p. 33.
11. Massachusetts, *Twelfth Annual Report of the Bureau of Statistics of Labor*, 1881, pp. 8-10.

months later and put the system to a severe and almost immediate test. Unwilling to take less wages, the union gave notice of its wish to terminate the agreement. Temporary peace was kept by abandoning the sliding scale and granting two increases in boiling rates—one when the notice expired and another near the close of 1866. That December, the manufacturers tried to force wage reductions and began a five-month lockout. Eventually, a new sliding scale was worked out. This agreement lasted seven years and again broke down when the union refused to accept a downward revision of wages. A strike followed. When work was resumed on the basis of an earlier union proposal, each producer signed the amended scale for himself, though it was uniform throughout the area.

A sliding wage scale also covered other skilled workers in the iron industry such as plate guide rollers, bar and nail rollers and heaters; and when the unions merged as the Amalgamated Association of Iron, Steel and Tin Workers in 1876, it was continued for most skilled occupations.[12]

Despite difficulties, collective bargaining in the iron industry had some success. But, though minor adjustments could be made easily, sharp price fluctuations made a flexible wage policy hard to enforce and put a strain upon collective bargaining. When reductions were called for, workers were apt to violate the agreement, especially when discipline was not strong.

b. ANTHRACITE MINING [13]

A collectively determined sliding scale did not last long in anthracite. Its abandonment was due partly to the union's high-handed action, and partly to growing concentrated ownership which made the operators strong enough to drive collective bargaining out of the industry for the rest of the century.

The Civil War was largely responsible for rapid expansion of anthracite output. Sharp wage reductions following a shrinking postwar market led to a miners' union, the Workingmen's Benevolent Association. Strikes and wage increases followed and finally, in 1869, the union demanded and got a sliding scale in two of the three anthracite fields. Three months later the union forced an increase by striking in violation of its agreements. After two years of strife, however, the union was completely defeated in the Northern and Lehigh fields, and four years later it was crushed in the Schuylkill field after a long strike against wage reduction. Not until the rise of the United Mine Workers was collective bargaining re-established.

c. BITUMINOUS COAL MINING [14]

The bituminous coal industry was likewise beset after the Civil War by

12. *Ibid.*, pp. 13-15.
13. See the "Anthracite" chapter.
14. See the "Bituminous Coal" chapter.

severe competition and changing markets, but the problems were met by a somewhat different line of attack. In the 1860's and 1870's, the miners who tried to get collective bargaining rights and improve working conditions were crushed by the operators' militant opposition. By the middle eighties, however, many operators had come to hope that collective bargaining with the newly organized National Federation of Miners and Mine Laborers might limit price competition. Accordingly in 1886 they signed an interstate agreement standardizing mine labor costs and calling for arbitration of disputes. No provision was made for an automatic sliding scale. However, largely because the agreement never covered many advantageously situated operators, important coal producing fields gradually withdrew. By 1889, this regional attempt to stabilize an industry was over.

d. SHOEMAKING

Similar problems were faced by the shoemakers. They too failed to bring competing producers under a standard agreement. But they had nothing like the three-year interstate agreement in bituminous coal mining; although wide markets prevailed, what collective bargaining there was between 1870 and the end of the century was entirely local.

The power pegging machine appeared in the late 1850's, the McKay stitcher in 1862, and factories employing machinery rapidly increased. During the Civil War, when manufacturers were extremely busy, these changes were not serious, but demand dropped after demobilization, and severe competition, price-cutting and unemployment followed.[15]

The Knights of St. Crispin was founded in 1867 in protest against the depressed conditions of the journeymen, and soon had fifty thousand shoemakers.[16] Attributing the shoemakers' plight to the wide use of "green hands," the Crispins sought restrictions on their employment.

The Struggle of the Crispins

The organization succeeded in imposing on shoe manufacturers its rules relating to newcomers until 1870, when dissatisfaction among the Lynn, Massachusetts, manufacturers reached a breaking point; whereupon the Crispins submitted their price lists to collective bargaining and an agreement was reached. Before a similar agreement for the next year expired, however, the employers again became dissatisfied. They claimed that many Crispins had entered into secret arrangements to work at less than established prices; Crispins charged that employers failed to cooperate in ad-

---

15. Don D. Lescohier, "The Knights of St. Crispin, 1867-74," *Bulletin of the University of Wisconsin*, No. 365, Madison, 1910, pp. 13-22; Massachusetts, *Third Annual Report of the Bureau of Statistics of Labor*, 1872, p. 271.

16. Frank K. Foster, "Shoemakers in the Movement" in George E. McNeill, *The Labor Movement*, A. M. Bridgman, Boston, 1887, p. 202.

APPENDIX A

justing grievances.[17] Taking the offensive, the employers refused to renew the agreement. Soon after, they reduced wages and a strike followed. But this was only a skirmish; the real battle came over another but related issue—different wage rates between organized Lynn and nonunionized areas elsewhere.

In August 1872, a number of Lynn manufacturers threatened to move to more favorable communities, unless nonmembership in the Crispins was a condition of employment. Rather than accept such terms two thousand went on strike. The strike failed, the Crispin movement in Lynn disintegrated, and at the beginning of 1873 the last charter was surrendered. Thus the first important effort at collective bargaining in the shoe industry was broken[18] and by 1874 the Knights of St. Crispin were few in number.

But some Lynn manufacturers soon had doubts as to whether absence of labor organization was an unmixed blessing. Undercutting prevailed in the local market. To avoid this, a number of employers supported a new union, the Shoemakers' League. It failed to gain a large following and disbanded in December 1875, when its members joined the revived Knights of St. Crispin as Unity Lodge.

Like the national organization, Unity Lodge favored conciliation and arbitration of industrial disputes. A board of eleven workers, each from a different part of the trade, was set up. No strike could be called except by a vote of the board and the unanimous approval of employees in the shop involved. In its first thirteen months, this board settled approximately one hundred disputes.[19] Since most of these disputes arose from attempts to pay wages below the scale, many manufacturers favored the union because it tended to standardize and stabilize wages.

Unity Lodge flourished in Lynn until 1878, when the employers again decided to break it because it handicapped them in the general market. After a two months' struggle, the union succumbed to superior force and never recovered.[20]

These were only two of a series of attempts during more than twenty years to establish collective bargaining in the shoe industry. The eighties and nineties saw occasional employer-labor negotiations in Lynn, Boston and Haverhill, and in Cincinnati and Philadelphia. These efforts failed because the union could not bring competing manufacturers in other shoe centers into line and collective bargaining became unbearable to employ-

17. Under the Crispin constitution, when a grievance arose the lodge involved had to call upon the two nearest lodges, and a committee from the three would then seek a settlement.
18. *Ibid.*, p. 30.
19. Massachusetts, *Eighth Annual Report of the Bureau of Statistics of Labor*, 1877, pp. 42-43.
20. T. A. Carroll, "Conciliation and Arbitration in the Boot and Shoe Industry," *Bulletin of the Department of Labor*, January 1897, pp. 6-7.

ers who had signed up. Manufacturers were willing to subscribe to a program that promised a certain amount of peace and stability, but only if it did not place them at a serious competitive disadvantage. This situation accounts for their volatile attitude—accepting collective bargaining one year, rejecting it the next. These early experiences, however, led to the adoption of the arbitration type of agreement—the "stamp" policy—by the Boot and Shoe Workers' Union at the end of the century.[21]

e. OTHER INDUSTRIES

In the latter half of the nineteenth century there were, then, some significant, though generally short-lived attempts to develop techniques and procedures for settling labor problems; the sliding wage scale in iron and anthracite, the interstate agreement in bituminous coal, and the conciliation machinery in shoemaking are evidence of this fact. These examples were not unique. Elsewhere unionism and collective bargaining made certain advances.

Printing [22]

Nowhere were conciliation and arbitration further developed than in the printing industry. In both the newspaper and book and job branches, the years after the Civil War witnessed, in a number of localities, an evolution from imposing union scales to definite procedures for negotiating agreements and settling disputes. Before the end of the century collective bargaining between the printing trades unions and local publishers' associations was well established in the larger cities; arbitration was increasingly used as a last resort.

Railroads

Because of the opposition of the carriers, collective bargaining was won by railroad workers only after a long and bitter struggle.[23] By the 1890's, however, the train service unions had been recognized as bargaining agents for their members on a majority of the roads. Beginning with the Locomotive Engineers, the seniority principle was established and pay was no longer graded according to length of service.[24] Inequalities of pay between divisions on the same system were eliminated, and an elaborate procedure for settling disputes was created.

21. See p. 883.
22. See the "Daily Newspapers" and "Book and Job Printing" chapters.
23. Difficulties in organizing, the character of the unions themselves, and inter-union conflicts also retarded the development of collective bargaining. See the "Railroads" chapter.
24. William J. Cunningham, "The Locomotive Engineers Arbitration: Its Antecedents and Outcome," *Quarterly Journal of Economics,* February 1913, p. 268. The objection of the engineers to gradations in pay according to length of service was due to the excessive retardation of advances in individual rates.

The nonservice railroad crafts, in a less strategic position, had an even harder time to get recognition. By the late nineties they had made some progress. To avoid competition among divisions, they set up district organizations, and to each district was delegated authority to conduct negotiations over an entire system.[25] At the same time came first attempts at intercraft cooperation for collective bargaining.

Building Construction

Unlike its delayed progress on the railroads, intercraft cooperation made rapid advances in the building trades during the 1880's and 1890's in New York, Chicago, San Francisco and other large cities. Local building trades councils were a significant development. For while some problems were national, the important task facing the building trades workers was achievement of a united local front in this highly competitive industry. Nationalization was achieved in many trades in the 1880's, with national strike and fraternal benefits and regulation of migrant journeymen by traveling cards. But the councils representing the various craft locals and designed to prevent employers from playing one group against another, as well as to reduce jurisdictional disputes, were the chief feature.

3. The Later Nineties to the World War

During the twenty years beginning with 1897 American trade unions grew enormously. Prosperity returned after 1896 and brought rapid industrial expansion. Union membership was less than 450,000 in 1897; by 1912 it was 1,125,000 and 2,022,000 in 1904. Then for some years it remained about the same, but rose to 2,452,000 in 1912, to 2,687,000 in 1914 and 2,773,000 in 1916.[26] In two decades union membership multiplied sixfold.

Multiplied also were the new internationals. They drew together, protected and strengthened many local unions. By this time many older internationals had become centralized organizations. They more or less controlled the calling, conduct and financing of strikes; they adopted policies for the trade or industry, and sometimes imposed laws or rules. Then, too, the American Federation of Labor, with its growing city centrals and state federations of labor, and, later, its industrial departments, came into its own. Except for the railroad brotherhoods, few really important internationals remained unaffiliated with it. While the IWW and other left-wing organizations at times engaged in vigorous propaganda, the AF of L

25. Testimony of Arthur O. Wharton, *Final Report and Testimony Submitted to Congress by the Commission on Industrial Relations Created by the Act of August 23, 1912*, Washington, 1916, Vol. X, p. 9760.

26. Cf. Leo Wolman, *Ebb and Flow in Trade Unionism*, National Bureau of Economic Research, New York, 1936, p. 16.

led and dominated the labor movement. It had cast off some of its earlier ideas and stood for a "pure and simple" or business unionism, relying upon collective bargaining and collective agreements to further its members' interests.

Building upon foundations already laid, unionism was recognized in many new areas and industries. In some trades individual employers were still signed up to union-made scales, but conferences with employer associations became more general. Local agreements still played the major role in the unionized trades and industries, but regional and national conferences and agreements became more numerous. Beyond this, collective agreements were increasingly of the arbitration type; they called for amicable adjustment of disputes arising under their provisions and not infrequently of disputes over terms of a new contract to replace the old. Though stoutly resisted in certain sectors, collective bargaining was widely regarded and publicized as a method of industrial peace. It and unionism probably never were more favorably received by the American public than during the five or six years around 1900. Those were the honeymoon years of collective bargaining.[27]

a. BUILDING CONSTRUCTION

Outstanding among industries where collective bargaining was on a local basis during the first two decades of the twentieth century were the building trades. Local councils increased more rapidly than before, and the AF of L created a Building Trades Department. By 1908 about two hundred councils could be found in large and medium-sized American cities; by 1917 they had increased to 267.

Some in the larger cities fell prey to abuses. Typical of those was the Chicago Building Trades Council, whose leaders levied tribute upon the industry for their own pockets. The unions were confident of their power and frequently violated their contracts; few trades had taken steps to avoid such violations or to settle grievances by arbitration.[28] Finally, the contractors reached the end of their patience. Uniting into the Building Contractors' Council so as to meet labor on even terms, they served an ultimatum on the unions. Its rejection led in 1900 to a lockout in which the unions were defeated.[29]

But employer domination did not effectively eliminate abuses. As the

27. As will be noted shortly, the honeymoon period was anticipated in the glass and stove industries as early as about 1890. Obviously the limits set for any of these "periods" are arbitrary and do not preclude considerable overlapping.

28. *Report of the Industrial Commission on the Chicago Labor Disputes of 1900 with Especial Reference to the Disputes in the Building and Machinery Trades*, Washington, 1901, Vol. VIII, pp. 392-393, 379.

29. Royal E. Montgomery, *Industrial Relations in the Chicago Building Trades*, University of Chicago Press, Chicago, 1927, pp. 25-26.

historian of Chicago building trades unionism has emphasized, employer control "ended in chaos not unlike that of the days just preceding the big lockout." [30] Whenever the scales tilted too sharply, whether for labor or the employers, collective bargaining either broke down or failed to work satisfactorily. Stable relations could only be achieved through power being in balance.

Such a balance did exist most of the time from 1911 to 1921. A strong Building Trades Council and an equally strong Building Construction Employers' Association functioned with sufficient authority to produce relatively satisfactory results for both sides. A "standard agreement" aimed to prevent strikes and lockouts and to promote peaceful adjustment of disputes was negotiated, and a set of "cardinal principles" agreed upon.[31] A Joint Conference Board was organized for the entire industry and boards of arbitration were set up in each trade. Disputes were settled by these arbitration boards, but unsatisfactory decisions could be submitted to the Conference Board. Finally, an impartial umpire, whose decision was final, could decide a deadlocked issue.[32]

The experience of the Chicago building industry was by no means unique. In New York a strong building trades council subjected the industry to the same abuses practiced by its Chicago counterpart. But in 1903 the New York Building Trades Employers' Association was organized and an arbitration plan to avoid strikes and lockouts adopted. An arbitration board was set up in each craft to handle all questions affecting that particular craft. In addition, a General Arbitration Board, consisting of two employer and two employee representatives from each trade, was established to settle jurisdictional disputes and to deal with cases of non-observance of trade board decisions and with cases in which the members of the trade board were unable to agree upon an umpire.[33] The plan broke down in 1910, partly because of the opposition of the union business agents, who were not given any role in the program, and the antagonism of the international union officers who objected to the settlement of jurisdictional issues without their consent.[34]

San Francisco's experience was not unlike New York's and Chicago's. The Council, under P. H. McCarthy, ruled the industry with an iron hand. Restrictive and uneconomic practices became common. A day of reckoning

30. *Ibid.*, p. 33.
31. *Ibid.*, p. 25.
32. *Ibid.*, pp. 67-95.
33. An executive committee was empowered to act as a board of conciliation between regular meetings of the General Arbitration Board. Later, this committee was authorized to act on all complaints before they were submitted to the full board. William Haber, *Industrial Relations in the Building Industry*, Harvard University Press, Cambridge, 1930, pp. 353, 357.
34. *Ibid.*, pp. 358-361.

came in 1921, when the Council's refusal to accept an arbitration award led to a long struggle. The entire business community united to crush the unions and open-shop conditions were established.[35]

Most building trades councils, however, operated without notorious abuses and scandals. They strengthened the weaker crafts and by promoting labor cost standardization and peaceful adjustment of controversies helped to stabilize the industry. Yet serious problems remained—the problem of jurisdictional disputes, the problem of maintaining unity among the crafts in cities where councils existed and the problem of forming new councils elsewhere. It was in an effort to meet these that the Building Trades Department of the AF of L was formed.[36]

b. SHOEMAKING

In the shoe industry, also, local bargaining continued—under a most interesting type of agreement. The Boot and Shoe Workers'. Union, an amalgamation of the three leading labor organizations, in 1899 devised the "stamp contract," under which an employer was granted the right to use the union stamp (label) on his products on condition that he employ only members of the union in good standing. The union would first secure recognition and the closed shop, then hold in abeyance demands for changes in wages, hours and general working conditions until a firm had tested the label's presumed advantage. Any differences over standards and grievances not settled in conference were submitted to state boards, as in Massachusetts, or to ad hoc arbitration boards. This conservative approach and the emphasis upon arbitration, most often used in seasonal or yearly wage demands, appealed to many shoe manufacturers and was relatively successful for many years.

c. PRINTING

Daily Newspapers

The new century brought an important forward step in collective bargaining in the newspaper branch of the printing industry. Impressed with the success of conciliation and arbitration on a local scale, the American Newspaper Publishers' Association and the International Typographical Union signed an international arbitration agreement in 1900, which was renewed, with modifications, until 1922. Only disputes arising under a contract were arbitrated at first, but gradually the agreement was widened to include everything save international union laws.[37]

Exemption of these laws from arbitration was, however, a long-standing source of friction between the publishers and the union. Influenced by the

---

35. Frederick L. Ryan, *Industrial Relations in the San Francisco Building Trades*, University of Oklahoma Press, Norman, 1935, pp. 111-166.
36. See pp. 900-901.
37. See the "Daily Newspapers" chapter.

open-shop movement of the time, the publishers in 1922 made arbitration of all international laws a condition of renewal of the agreement. The union refused, a deadlock developed, and the series of international arbitration agreements between the publishers and the Typographical Union officially came to an end.

The Typographical agreements were models for the other mechanical trades—in pressrooms, photoengraving departments and stereotyping offices of unionized newspaper plants. Save for the pressmen's contract which ended in 1912 after a bitter strike, these agreements worked as effectively as the one covering the composing rooms. They were not renewed in 1922 only because the ITU parent agreement was not continued.

Failure to renew brought strain but otherwise made little difference. So accustomed to arbitrating differences were publishers and unions that in the absence of provision for it, international arbitration has been only somewhat less used than before 1923. International arbitration for pressmen was reinstated in 1920. In 1922, all of its laws having been made arbitrable, except the union-shop requirement and those relating solely to the internal affairs of the organization, this union and the publishers made a five-year agreement which has been renewed three times and is still in effect.[38]

Book and Job Printing

National agreements also became important in book and job printing near the close of the nineteenth century. The employing printers had already organized both local associations and a national association, the United Typothetae, primarily to oppose the growing power of the printers' union. Although the United Typothetae had been formed in 1886 to fight the union's demand for the nine-hour day, in 1898 it made an agreement with the typographers, the pressmen and the bookbinders reducing working hours to nine; at the same time the unions agreed to attempt to equalize wages in competitive districts.

With this as a beginning and influenced by arbitration in the newspaper industry, the United Typothetae and the International Pressmen's Union signed an arbitration agreement in 1902. It was not renewed in 1907 because the pressmen opposed continuing the nine-hour day. Membership in the union was not a condition of employment. Conferences on a similar agreement with the ITU failed, partly because that union had in 1899 adopted a closed-shop law and would not accept the open shop. Failure of the ITU and the Typothetae to agree was followed by a great strike over the eight-hour day in 1906. Finally the shorter day was established in all union offices, but at a great price. The ITU spent over $4

---

38. For a detailed discussion of the international arbitration agreements and of the situation since 1922, see the "Daily Newspapers" chapter.

million, exclusive of local funds. Many of the smaller locals could not stand the grueling battle and surrendered their charters. In addition a number of large printing offices established the open shop,[39] and many local Typothetae became antiunion. The United Typothetae itself, in the years immediately following, acted chiefly as a trade association.

In this situation union-shop employers formed printers' leagues in eastern cities and Franklin associations in the Middle West. The outcome, in 1913, was a reorganized United Typothetae, combining all types of publishers' organizations into a joint national trade association and employers' association. Open-shop and closed-shop divisions were established. In 1917 the latter made an international arbitration agreement with the ITU similar to the newspaper one, effective only when accepted by the individual employers. Although actually incorporated in only two contracts, it encouraged including arbitration clauses in local agreements.

Important also was the International Joint Conference Council established in 1919, by the craft organizations which had made headway during the war and the Closed Shop Division and other organizations of union-shop employers. This council adopted a policy that wage adjustments should be determined by the cost of living and the condition of the industry. The policy was soon discarded, for labor agreed to cost of living readjustments that meant increases, but objected strongly when they meant decreases, as during the 1921 deflation. The forty-four-hour week was also agreed upon in 1919, to become effective in 1921. By 1921, however, deep depression had changed costs, prices and profits, some employers questioned whether they were bound by the agreement, and a long and widespread strike followed.

In both branches of printing there was, then, some collective action on a national scale during the first two decades of the century. Generally, however, wages and working conditions in unionized plants were fixed through local bargaining. This procedure resulted in considerable contract variation, limited, of course, by the enforcement of international union laws and the action of international officers.

d. BITUMINOUS COAL MINING

The contracts with individual employers or with local employers' associations that prevailed in such industries as building construction, shoe manufacturing and printing were not, however, typical of a growing number of other cases. In coal mining, on the railroads, in the maritime indus-

---

39. George E. Barnett, "The Printers," *American Economic Association Quarterly*, October 1909, p. 157; Leona M. Powell, *History of the United Typothetae of America*, University of Chicago Press, Chicago, 1926, pp. 54-75; Selig Perlman and Philip Taft, "Labor Movements" in John R. Commons and Associates, *History of Labor in the United States, 1896–1932*, Macmillan, New York, 1935, pp. 55-60.

try, in glass and stove manufacturing, among others, collective bargaining was carried out on a more inclusive basis.

Earlier efforts to establish a regional system of collective bargaining in bituminous coal failed, as has been seen, because most producers refused to put a floor under wages and adhere to mutually agreeable rules and practices. Organized miners tried a number of times to control conditions. But only after the 1897 strike was an interstate agreement re-established.

Under that agreement representatives of the operators and miners in Pennsylvania, Ohio, Indiana and Illinois met "to so regulate the scale of mining as to make the cost of production practically the same in one district that it [was] in another . . ." [40] The Interstate Joint Conference set rates and working conditions for all classes of mine labor at the basing points in the four states. After this conference, operators and miners held joint district meetings to determine "mining rates based on basic rates theretofore agreed upon in the interstate convention, and to agree upon such wages and mining conditions not common alike to all four states, but peculiar to and necessary for each state." [41] As expressed by one of the leading architects of the system, John Mitchell, "in a rough way an attempt [was] made to establish our mining scales, based upon the comparative opportunities of the different mining fields and perhaps upon the opportunities of the miners in the different fields to earn their wages." [42]

The agreements were renewed and modified from time to time. They eased unequal costs and did away with evils involved in measurement of output and in charges and fines imposed on the miners. But industrial strife was not reduced; suspensions frequently accompanied contract renewals, and strikes in violation of agreements were not uncommon.

Still the conference system did not break down until a generation later. John Mitchell saw what would happen, for in 1901 he declared, "The principal disturbing feature of the coal industry which . . . threatens the perpetuity of the peaceful relationship between operators and miners is the absence of organization or mutual understanding between the operators and the miners of the State of West Virginia." [43] Failure to solve the problem of competition from nonunion areas caused the system's collapse in 1927.

40. Statement of John Mitchell in *Report of the Industrial Commission on the Relations and Conditions of Capital and Labor Employed in the Mining Industry,* 1901, Vol. XII, p. 698.
41. Herman Justi, "Conciliation and Arbitration in the Coal Mining Industry," *Papers and Proceedings of the Fourteenth Annual Meeting of the American Economic Association,* February 1902, pp. 278-279.
42. *Final Report and Testimony . . . Commission on Industrial Relations,* Vol. I, p. 411.
43. *Report of the Industrial Commission on the Relations and Conditions of Capital and Labor Employed in the Mining Industry,* Vol. XII, p. 699.

e. ANTHRACITE MINING

Having captured the bituminous fields in 1897, the United Mine Workers next turned to anthracite, which had been disorganized since the defeat of the Workingmen's Benevolent Association in 1875. Backed by public opinion and political pressure, it won favorable settlement of two industry-wide strikes in 1900 and 1902. The Award of the Anthracite Coal Strike Commission which ended the 1902 dispute provided for joint grievance machinery, among other things, but did not compel recognition of the United Mine Workers. Recognition was not, in fact, secured until 1920. Nevertheless, collective bargaining gradually became firmly established in the years following 1902.

There have been strikes, for even under the most effective collective bargaining, sometimes the demands of one party are impossible, or the obstinacy of the other can be broken only by a show of strength. Yet these contests were not accompanied by the violence of early struggles, when unionism was fighting for its life.

In pre-World War years the possibility of passing on higher mining costs to the consumers made it easier for operators to accept the new regime. As Dr. Sydenstricker pointed out, they were "able to reap from the agreements . . . a return considerably beyond what was necessary to cover the increased cost of labor." [44] After the early twenties the situation changed; as transportation and labor costs rose, so did anthracite's price, until hard coal fell more and more behind competing and cheaper fuels.[45]

f. RAILROADS

From the first the railway labor unions aimed to standardize wages and working conditions, and by 1900 this objective had been attained on the roads west of Chicago. But individual roads rejected further changes in schedules on the ground that they had met standard conditions and that the changes demanded would put them at competitive disadvantage. Consequently in 1902 the conductors and trainmen organized a regional association. Simultaneous demands were then made upon all of the western roads although bargaining was still on a system basis.[46] This step was only a beginning; five years later the organized conductors and trainmen dealt with the thirty-two western roads as one group for their forty-five thousand members. Division on issues involved eventually led to arbitration.[47]

---

44. Edgar Sydenstricker, "Collective Bargaining in the Anthracite Coal Industry," *Bulletin No. 191*, U.S. Bureau of Labor Statistics, 1916, p. 120.
45. See the "Anthracite" chapter.
46. E. C. Robbins, *Railway Conductors*, Columbia University Press, New York, 1914, pp. 63-64.
47. Cunningham, *op. cit.*, pp. 263-274.

Similar techniques were successful in other sections of the country, and for other service groups. But as the years passed and companies faced increased operating costs and government-regulated rates and service, collective bargaining was increasingly strained. Major controversies were usually settled only with the aid of federal mediators or by arbitration. From 1912, however, the unions were greatly dissatisfied with some of the most important decisions. The aggrieved brotherhoods rejected arbitration when management refused their concerted demand for an eight-hour day. Only the Adamson Law, in 1916, prevented a nation-wide strike.

Shop employees made great strides in intercraft cooperation during this period. As carriers played one craft against another, or insisted that former standards in an area prevail, the railway shop unions formed system federations for collective bargaining—covering machinists, boilermakers, blacksmiths, carmen, sheet metal workers and electricians. Next the crafts would notify a company of their wish to reopen their agreements, which usually had thirty-day reopening clauses. Bargaining then began on a new schedule with a set of general rules applicable to all trades, and also embodying special craft rules. This method helped to standardize rules, and assured all shop employees equal treatment. Different interpretations of certain rules, moreover, due to the strength or weakness of the craft, were eliminated.[48]

Despite the opposition of some carriers, the system federations were the collective bargaining agencies in most railway shops before the World War.

g. WATER TRANSPORTATION

In the absence of collective bargaining, the conditions under which sailors have been hired for voyages have been accompanied by evils of one kind or another; on their voyages, especially before passage of the La Follette Act in 1915, they did not have the usual rights of workers in industry; all too frequently their living conditions and personal treatment were bad.

The Sailors' Union of the Pacific was organized in 1885 to protect the welfare of those who shipped from the Pacific ports.[49] After a long strike in 1902, involving the entire membership of the City Front Federation of San Francisco, it won an agreement with the Shipowners' Association. Wages and hours were set; the Association agreed to maintain a shipping office in San Francisco; a committee for the adjustment of grievances was established; agents of the union were to furnish crews in

---

48. Testimony of Arthur O. Wharton, *Final Report and Testimony* . . . Commission on Industrial Relations, Vol. X, pp. 9759-9770.

49. About the same time organizations were founded on the Great Lakes and Atlantic and Gulf Coasts. Representatives from the three districts launched the National Seamen's Union of America in 1892.

ports outside San Francisco; and the sympathetic strike was banned. A similar agreement was made in 1903 with the Steam Schooner Managers' Association, engaged in coastwise shipping. The two associations combined in 1906 with relations with the union unchanged. The agreements were renewed from time to time and harmony reigned until 1921, when a vigorous open-shop campaign began on the Pacific Coast.[50]

On the Great Lakes, around the turn of the century, nearly every class of employees engaged in shipping, from captains down, was organized.[51] By 1903 practically all their unions had agreements with the Lake Carriers' Association or its members. Wages were substantially increased, tenure was protected, all strikes and desertions were prohibited, and provision was made for arbitration.

Perhaps the Lake Carriers recognized the unions only from necessity. In any case, the owners expected stabilized wages, a better class of men and better discipline. Wages were duly stabilized, and the occasional increases were usually less than in both union and nonunion industries ashore. But discipline and order were not realized. This was particularly true of firemen and only less so of deck hands. Both the men and carriers frequently violated their contract, and arbitration was seldom resorted to because of a generally weak union official class and the attitudes of the rank and file. The multiplicity of unions and the struggle between the longshoremen and the seamen for control of organized groups added to the difficulty. So did the hostile attitude of many of the owners, especially after the United States Steel Corporation and certain other owners of ore-carrying vessels became the most important shippers and dominant members of the association. Such owners considered union contracts a makeshift truce and not the foundation of a permanent peace—attitudes doubtless influenced by the open-shop movement and by steel industrialists' hostility to unionism and collective bargaining.

As the years passed the unions were undermined by the stratagems of the owners, and by interunion conflicts. In 1908, the Great Lake Carriers' Association inaugurated its "Welfare Plan," also revocable certificates and continuous discharge books, which effectively weeded out "trouble makers." Unionism was defeated, and not until the World War shortage of labor did it again get a temporary foothold in Great Lakes shipping.

On the Atlantic coast, labor organization was weak and collective bargaining sporadic. After an unsuccessful strike in 1912, the Seamen's

---

50. For an excellent account of the old order and the new under collective bargaining, see Paul S. Taylor, *The Sailors' Union of the Pacific,* Ronald Press, New York, 1923, pp. 46-109.

51. Most of the facts in this section are drawn from H. E. Hoagland, *Wage Bargaining on the Vessels of the Great Lakes,* University of Illinois Studies in the Social Sciences, Vol. VI, No. 3, Urbana, 1917.

Union was torn by one of its periodic dissensions, and a large body of firemen went over to the IWW.

h. GLASS [52] AND POTTERY

Nation-wide collective bargaining was firmly established in the strongly organized container and flint glass industries before the end of the nineteenth century; annual wage conferences in flint glass began in 1889 and a year later in the container industry. In both, effective conciliation machinery for the settlement of grievances was soon developed. In the window glass industry, a strong union of skilled workers successfully engaged in national bargaining throughout the eighties and the first five years of the nineties.

National agreements in the pottery industry came later and only after some years of turmoil.[53] Early pottery unions were ineffective; even the National Brotherhood of Operative Potters, the present union, had difficulty. In 1900, ten years after its formation, the brotherhood signed a national wage scale with the United States Potters Association for the general ware division (vitreous and semivitreous ware). Immediately the eastern workers were dissatisfied with the rates, and bargaining then reverted to a sectional basis. Not until 1905 was the East brought under the uniform list. But from then on national agreements were effective in that branch of the industry.[54] In the sanitary division, a nation-wide contract, which had been successful since 1903, broke down in 1922 over a proposed wage cut.

i. THE STOVE INDUSTRY

Three turbulent, discontented decades preceded peaceful collective bargaining in the stove industry. In this highly charged atmosphere almost any issue might become a cause for war, but wages, apprentice ratios and the use of "bucks" or "berkshires" (helpers) were the most troublesome.

Wages varied between areas and between plants, and the higher paying employers were constantly forced to press for reductions. Moreover, different piece rates often prevailed for the same work in the same shop, and disputes over pay for "dull" (cold) and "dirty" (impure) iron were frequent. Employers' plans to engage an unlimited number of apprentices were fought by the union through fear that this meant a dilution of the trade by cheap boy labor and eventually low wages and unemployment. By doing part of the molders' work, the berkshires could learn the trade,

---

52. See the "Glass" chapter.

53. For an exhaustive discussion of the history and techniques of collective bargaining in this industry, see David A. McCabe, *National Collective Bargaining in the Pottery Industry*, The Johns Hopkins Press, Baltimore, 1932.

54. **For a brief** description of collective bargaining procedures, see **Appendix B.**

and threatened the journeymen's position during labor controversies. Other grievances were absence of standard starting and quitting times and constant pressure on piece rates, the earnings of the most efficient being used as an example of what the average worker could earn.

From the day of its formation in 1859, the National Union of Iron Molders waged a constant fight against these conditions. It tried to be more conciliatory in the 1870's, with less success.[55] Finally the employers in 1886 launched the Stove Founders' National Defense Association "to combine its members for resistance against unjust demands of workmen." The country was divided into four districts. In the event of a labor dispute the district committee might supply its members with workmen, compensate for loss of production, or have other members take care of unfilled orders.[56] Association members were to furnish "molders in case of a strike, or in default, reasonable payment for each man not furnished" and to support those who were boycotted.

Both sides were now organized nationally. In February 1887, the Association and the union were locked in a bitter struggle resulting from wage disputes at the Bridge and Beach Manufacturing Company of St. Louis. When the Association distributed the patterns of the struck plant among other foundries, the union immediately instructed its members to withdraw from those shops. Eventually the dispute involved shops employing five thousand workers. The controversy continued until June, when work was resumed at Bridge and Beach on an open-shop basis, and in the other plants under conditions prevailing before the strike. It was costly, but each side believed it was worth while.[57]

The First National Agreement

Unofficially, each side then strove for peace. One great stimulus was arbitration of the Pittsburgh strike in the summer of 1890. How to bring about general adoption of peaceful methods was explored at frequent conferences.

The first step towards a national agreement was openly taken in 1890 by the Molders' Union convention, which instructed its "incoming executive board to communicate with the representatives of the Stove Manufacturers' Association with a view to holding a conference with them to discuss the points of difference . . . ."[58] This communication was favorably received by the Association.[59] In Chicago in March 1891 the two groups

55. John P. Frey and John R. Commons, "Conciliation in the Stove Industry," *Bulletin of the Bureau of Labor*, January 1906, pp. 138-140.
56. *The Stove Founders' National Defense Association*, New Era Book and Print, Lancaster, Pennsylvania, 1893, p. 2.
57. *Ibid.*, p. 8; Frey and Commons, *op. cit.*, p. 144.
58. Quoted in Frey and Commons, *op. cit.*, p. 146.
59. *Ibid.*, p. 147.

met and resolved to "adopt the principle of arbitration in the settlement of any dispute . . ." [60]

Differences over methods arose at the conference. The manufacturers feared arbitration would invite demands and place a premium on litigation, and they were reluctant to entrust the final word to persons unfamiliar with the industry's problems. They placed their hopes in committees, composed of an equal number of representatives of molders and manufacturers. Their view finally prevailed.[61]

A conference committee of six members, three from each side, was set up. Disputes that could not be settled directly were submitted to the presidents of the two associations. Their failure to agree placed the question before the entire conference committee whose majority decision was binding upon both parties for twelve months. No change in status quo was permitted while a dispute was pending.[62]

Accomplishments

With this beginning, old and new problems were worked out in conference. Between 1891 and 1898 a technique of eliminating inequalities between prices paid for the same type of work in different shops was devised, which largely ended unfair competition. Whenever price disputes arose, representatives from the two organizations visited a foundry in the district and examined prices paid for similar work. These would be used as a guide on a new line of stoves on the principle of equal pay for equal effort.[63] Now and then "board prices"—wages as a whole—were advanced or reduced according to changes in the cost of living and what the industry could afford to pay.

In 1895 the Association shops were threatened seriously by the lower price policy of an independent plant. The union intervened, and informed the independent that it would permit a reduction in the wage scale allowing Association shops to compete, unless the independent ended its "unfair competition." The threat was successful.

Disinclination of the union to adopt a more favorable apprentice ratio put the conciliation program to a severe test. However, the patience of the foundrymen was eventually rewarded by an increase in the ratio of apprentices to journeymen.[64] Peaceful settlement of this thorny question was a major contribution of the system of collective bargaining. The closely related question of the use of berkshires was solved in the same

60. Stove Founders' National Defense Association, *Agreement*, 1891.
61. Chauncey H. Castle, President of the Stove Founders' National Defense Association, "Conciliation, Not Arbitration," *Industrial Conciliation*, Putnam, New York, 1902, pp. 176-182.
62. Stove Founders' National Defense Association, *Agreements*.
63. Frey and Commons, *op. cit.*, pp. 157-158.
64. *Ibid.*, pp. 158-176.

way. The system was discontinued by agreement in 1905. Similarly, the standardization of hours, allowances for "dirty" and "dull" iron, the introduction of molding machines, the regulation of output, and still other problems, old and new, were acceptably solved.[65]

Of course not all problems were solved easily or at once, but the road to negotiation, compromise and understanding was opened. The closed shop, a thorny question, solved itself. Once convinced that its members would not be exposed to discrimination, the demand for it was dropped by the union. Most manufacturers soon began to prefer union men.

The stove manufacturers were for many years about as well satisfied with the agreement as was the union. Management was not "interfered with," wage rates were standardized and made certain, labor costs were more or less equalized, piece rates helped manufacturers to figure their costs closely. The industry had an efficient and a generally adequate labor supply and for many years organization on both sides was so complete that the standards adopted in conference could be successfully imposed upon practically every plant in the industry.

The Situation in the 1920's and 1930's

After the World War came technological changes, severe competition from factory-made central heating systems, and loss of membership by the Association, so that it no longer represented three quarters or more of the industry. But even then, in spite of strain, the conference method was continued, though with fewer producers. The agreement contains some twenty-eight clauses added to the original three adopted in 1891, together with some later resolutions.[66]

Similar agreements were made by the Stove Founders' National Defense Association with the Metal Polishers and Stove Mounters. They were in operation only a few years, however, for the rank and file of these unions doubted the advantages of the peace and stability they imposed.[67]

j. STEEL

The substantial advance of collective bargaining was accompanied during this period by a number of severe setbacks. Nowhere were repercussions more serious than in steel. In its earlier years the Amalgamated Association of Iron and Steel Workers, the dominant union in the iron and

---
65. For an excellent, sympathetic account of the experience, see John P. Frey, "A Thirty-Year Experiment in Industrial Democracy," *International Labour Review*, April 1922, pp. 539-552.
66. See International Molders' Union of North America, *Conference Agreements*, 1937. For the various clauses as they stood at the end of the World War, with notes on their amendments from time to time, see Clarence E. Bonnett, *Employers' Associations in the United States*, Macmillan, 1922, pp. 50-59.
67. See Frederick T. Stockton, *The International Molders' Union*, The Johns Hopkins Press, Baltimore, 1921.

steel industry from 1876, made considerable progress. Virtually all skilled workers in iron mills of western Pennsylvania, Ohio, Indiana and Illinois were unionized. In the seventies and early eighties, the wage rates the union negotiated with Pittsburgh manufacturers were generally accepted by the "western" producers.

At that time the steel industry was just beginning its spectacular career, but by 1885 it had attained a dominant position over iron on the market.[68] Early leaders of the union had all been trained in the iron mills where the men worked under the "heat system," under which a day's work was divided into five heats, or charges.[69] They neither knew nor appreciated the dynamic steel industry. Union rules, which were effective in the rather static iron trade, were transferred to the highly progressive steel industry. Unaware of the importance of the new developments,[70] the union continued to limit the amount of work that could be performed in a turn, or shift. Completion of a turn's work in the sheet mills had required about twelve hours, but with the introduction of improvements less time was required. When the manufacturers attempted to establish eight-hour shifts, so as to have twenty-four-hour operation, the union, fearing a reduction in earnings, resisted for a time and actually revoked the charters of several locals which agreed to a shorter work day.[71] Naturally this policy aroused the opposition of many steel producers. Another sore point with employers was the union's weak discipline. In the iron trades indiscipline, while highly objectionable, was overlooked. In the growing steel industry, failure to live up to agreements was intolerable to aggressive steel makers.

In some steel plants union control was highly vexatious. According to one of the officials of the Carnegie Steel plant at Homestead, Pennsylvania, "the foreman had little authority. . . . Incompetent men had to be retained in the employ of the company, and changes for the improvement of the mill could not be made without the consent of the mill committee."[72]

Moreover, the union was weakened by its policy of limiting membership to skilled workmen. They were losing importance in an increasingly mechanized industry, and because they were predominantly of Anglo-Saxon stock and the unskilled men largely southern Europeans, nationalistic

68. John A. Fitch, "Unionism in the Iron and Steel Industry," *Political Science Quarterly*, March 1909, p. 58.
69. *Report of the Committee of the Senate Upon the Relations Between Labor and Capital and Testimony Taken by the Committee,* Washington, 1885, Vol. II, p. 14.
70. *Report on Conditions of Employment in the Iron and Steel Industry in the United States,* Government Printing Office, Washington, 1913, Vol. III, p. 14.
71. Fitch, "Unionism in the Iron and Steel Industry," p. 67. More than eight hours was necessary to complete a full turn's work.
72. John A. Fitch, *The Steel Workers,* Charities Publication Committee, Russell Sage Foundation, New York, 1911, p. 102.

differences, together with this exclusive policy, caused dissension and suspicion in the working force.[73]

Union defeat in the struggle with H. C. Frick in 1892 was a severe blow to collective bargaining. Frick was forced to grant recognition in 1889, but when the contract expired in 1892, difficulties over wages, which shaded ultimately into the right to organize, came to the fore. The Carnegie Company's mills in other communities became involved in a sympathetic and unsuccessful strike. Gradually additional union plants were lost.[74]

When business recovery came in the later nineties, union fortunes improved. Its membership rose slowly but satisfactorily until the United States Steel Corporation was formed in 1901. Fearing that this combination presaged an attack on its position, the Amalgamated demanded that the American Tin Plate Company, a subsidiary, sign the scale for all of its mills. This proposal was rejected and a strike followed. The union sought to stem defeat by a general strike in all United States Steel Corporation plants, which only made defeat the greater. From 1902, union influence in the steel industry gradually faded and thereafter its control was largely confined to the iron plants.

This serious setback was due largely to failure of the craft-conscious leaders to recognize that their restrictive policies would impede the evolution and growth of a basic industry. Although the "will to power" of the "self-made" steel makers was important, the same financial group was also dominant in anthracite. Unionism could win a place for itself in one field, but it was ousted, after long tenure, in the other.

k. GENERAL FOUNDRIES

The machine foundry and metal trades, which had tried a system of conciliation patterned after the stove industry's, also met with reverses.

In 1898 was organized the National Founders' Association, composed of "persons, firms and corporations engaged as principals in and operators of foundries where castings in iron, steel, brass or other metals [were] made."[75] Its declared aim was a uniform basis of just and equitable dealings between its members and their employees. If a district committee of the Association failed to settle a labor dispute, the Association agreed either to compensate its members for loss of production, transfer work to other member shops for completion, or supply a member with workers up

---

73. *Senate Committee on the Relations Between Labor and Capital*, Vol. I, pp. 1119, 1139; *Report on Conditions of Employment in the Iron and Steel Industry*, Vol. III, pp. 90-93.
74. Fitch, "Unionism in the Iron and Steel Industry," pp. 73-74, 77-78.
75. National Founders' Association, *Officers, Administrative Council, District Committees, Members, Constitution and By Laws*, Detroit, 1899.

to 70 per cent of the normal force. The Association also would bear the expenses of police protection.

Despite its rather bellicose preparations, the Association concluded the "New York agreement" with the Molders' Union in 1899. This provided that when direct methods failed, disputes were to be referred to a committee of the presidents and two other representatives of each organization. A majority vote was to decide the issue.[76] Pending settlement no stoppage by either party was permitted.

Even the first years brought disappointment. Primarily the difficulties encountered were due to the diversity of the general foundry trade, as compared to the homogeneity in the stove industry. The foundry business by its variety impeded standardization. Moreover, it was only partially unionized. Standardization of wages and working conditions on a basis satisfactory to the union would have meant unequal competition between organized and unorganized shops. Unlike the Stove Founders' Defense Association, the National Founders' Association had little to offer the molders in exchange for modification of their rules. And it was largely over these rules that the clashes in conferences and in the molding rooms occurred.

The two groups came into open conflict in 1900. At the Detroit conference that year the Founders' Association proclaimed its right to hire nonunion men, to install molding machines, and to determine the method of compensation. Naturally, such "principles" were rejected by the union. An attempt to put them into effect in Cleveland led to a strike. Each group rallied to the defense of its members,[77] but finally the issues were compromised. There were other similar occurrences during the life of the agreement.

Another serious difference arose over the founders' insistence upon employing and training as many apprentices as they wished.[78] Actually the machine issue was the crux of the difficulty. To raise production and lower costs, the employers sought to utilize molding machines to the full and to man them by union journeymen or others as they saw fit. Although the national union officers were not hostile to the molding machine, they were anxious to regularize its use on the basis agreed upon for manning the linotype, i.e., manning the machines by journeymen, not by helpers, at the standard rate. But they could not control rank-and-file hostility to the new devices. In some cases journeymen did not give the machines a

76. *Reports of the Industrial Commission on Labor Organizations, Labor Disputes, and Arbitration, and on Railway Labor*, 1901, Vol. XVII, pp. 350-351.
77. *Ibid.*, p. 352; Margaret L. Stecker, "The National Founders' Association," *Quarterly Journal of Economics*, February 1916, pp. 359-360.
78. Testimony of Joseph P. Valentine, President of the International Molders' Union, *Final Report and Testimony . . . Commission on Industrial Relations*, Vol. I, pp. 481-516.

fair trial. A break was inevitable.[79] After a strike over a company-announced [80] wage reduction at Troy, New York, the National Founders' Association abrogated the agreement in November 1904 and for more than three decades it occupied, with the National Metal Trades Association, a central position in the open-shop movement.

1. METAL TRADES

Following the examples of the closely related stove and foundry trades, the National Metal Trades Association was organized in 1899 to secure peaceful adjustment of labor disputes on national lines.

An agreement with the International Association of Machinists in 1900 set up machinery for settlement of disputes. Inasmuch as many of its members operated both foundries and machine shops, this Association and the National Founders had overlapping memberships, with the result that most of the procedures and policies of the two organizations were very similar.

The agreement did not last long. In 1901 the machinists demanded a nine-hour day on a nation-wide basis, with wage adjustment to compensate for the reduced hours. The National Metal Trades Association insisted, however, that wages were a local matter and should not be handled nationally. Each side refused to yield. The Association charged that the union had sometimes encouraged restriction of output and had interfered with shop management. It also charged that the union had refused to follow the arbitration procedure required by the agreement and had instead "called a strike against shops of our members which did not accede to certain arbitrary demands by a specified date." [81] The union denied the latter charge. It asserted its willingness to accept arbitration provided it was on a national basis, which the employers had rejected. The one-year agreement expired and collective bargaining between the two national organizations was never resumed. The Association became militantly anti-union, with an arsenal of "union busting" weapons to prevent employee organization.[82]

In retrospect it does not appear that the issue of setting a national standard of working hours warranted the disruption in this industrial sector of a promising beginning in collective relations. The collapse was probably due to over-aggressiveness, inexperience, and the unwillingness

---

79. Margaret L. Stecker, "The Founders, the Molders and the Molding Machine," *Quarterly Journal of Economics*, February 1918, pp. 295-296.

80. The union insisted that differences over wages must be arbitrated before reductions were placed in effect, while management insisted that arbitration should follow the changes made.

81. *Reports of the Industrial Commission on Labor Organizations, Labor Disputes, and Arbitration, and on Railway Labor*, Vol. XVII, p. 359.

82. *Ibid.*, pp. 360-361.

of both sides to yield. Metal trades employers, like the founders, were on the eve of great opportunities; many feared union restrictions, which would hamper the introduction of laborsaving devices and prevent them from employing the most competent or the cheaper men.[83] It was widely believed that the unions would block the most efficient utilization of plant and labor, a belief basic to the opposition that finally led to the disruption of collective bargaining.

m. IRON AND STEEL CONSTRUCTION

The National Erectors' Association was the spearhead of an open-shop drive in another important sector. Originally formed in 1903 to deal with the International Association of Bridge and Structural Iron Workers on wages and hours of labor, it aimed to establish uniform hours and working conditions and to allow each locality to fix its own wage scale. When the national contract expired in January 1905, neither side sought to renew it. The local unions desired to retain their autonomy, while the employers felt that local bargaining gave them an advantage.

Instead of bargaining on a national basis, local contracts were then devised. Leading employers followed a policy of dealing with the union in its strongholds and of avoiding collective bargaining where it was weak. A clash soon came between the union and the American Bridge Company, the most powerful member of the Erectors' Association. Later the strike was extended to all firms holding subcontracts from the company. In January 1906, the iron workers of New York City struck for a wage increase. This action involved firms not in conflict with the union, and gave the Association a chance to transform its nominal negotiatory policy into one of open hostility to unionism. As expressed in Article III of its revised constitution: "The object of this Association shall be the institution and maintenance of the open shop principle in the employment of labor in the erection of steel and iron bridges and buildings and other structural steel and iron work." [84]

The Association now became an active opponent of unionism, considerable open-shop printed matter was issued, and agents were sent into the union to ferret out its plans. In retaliation, officers of the union started a wide campaign of violence which culminated in the bombing of the Los Angeles Times Building.

n. OTHER PREWAR DEVELOPMENTS

The Open-Shop Campaign
Unionism's defeats in the steel, metal trades, general foundry and iron

---

83. Testimony of W. J. Chalmers, *ibid.*, Vol. VIII, pp. 5-13.
84. Luke Grant, *The National Erectors' Association and the International Association of Bridge and Structural Ironworkers*, U.S. Commission on Industrial Relations, Washington, 1915, p. 14.

and steel construction industries were evidence that the collective bargaining honeymoon was over. Throughout the late 1890's and the first years of the new century, organized labor had been favorably regarded by important sections of public opinion. Humanitarians and public-spirited citizens had seen in the labor movement a way by which many of the workingmen's wrongs might be righted. But the large increases in union membership between 1897 and 1904, from 447,000 to 2,022,000, along with unsatisfactory relations with the unions, aroused employers to active opposition. The subsequent campaign against organized labor was forecast in 1902, in a denunciation of unionism by the National Association of Manufacturers. Under the militant leadership of D. M. Parry and John T. Kirby, the NAM aroused employers to resist still more the demands of organized labor on the economic and legislative fronts; it mobilized public opinion against union policies, and helped to launch an open-shop campaign, very effective for a time. Citizens' alliances and employers' associations were organized in many communities to combat unionism. The Citizens' Industrial Association, a coalition of regional and local open-shop associations formed under Parry's leadership, frankly tried to break the hold of unions upon industry, to eliminate collective bargaining, and to foster the employment of nonunion men and the purchase of nonunion-made goods.[85]

By 1904 the tide of unionism began to ebb. Many labor groups succumbed to attacks. Particularly significant for collective bargaining was the extinction of unionism in the mass production industries, just then getting into stride. For all this organized labor was, to some extent, responsible. Its leaders lacked the foresight to recognize that restrictive rules founded upon craftsmanship and limited markets could no longer be applied in mechanized industries with expanding opportunities. In fixing their minds on the immediate loss or diminution of jobs for members, they failed to realize that mass production industries would not stand rules hampering their flexibility and progress. True, many employers were opposed to collective bargaining, but they were joined by moderates largely because of unionism's restrictive policies. Soon opposition to union recognition, originally based on expediency, became a matter of "principle"; and the aggressive antiunionist could now appeal to both interest and principle. Once mastery was won, the mass production industries gave the unions no chance for new footholds. Consequently, practically the only union strongholds were industries technologically static or without cohesion or financial power to defeat organized labor. A few, like coal, found unions a stabilizing force in highly competitive markets. Unionism did hold and even strengthen its position in railway transportation, but this was due not only to its power but to government intervention.

85. Perlman and Taft, *op. cit.*, pp. 129-137.

Yet, the open-shop campaign did more to retard and limit unions than to destroy them. A firm foundation had been laid in many industries, and total union membership was not greatly affected; the lowest after 1902 was in 1906 when it was 1,907,300. The American Federation of Labor showed its solidity and permanence in certain sectors and its power to survive concerted attack as well as depression.

The open-shop movement was challenged through these years by the National Civic Federation, which promoted collective bargaining and trade agreements. Originally the Chicago Civic Federation, it organized nationally in 1900. Composed of capitalists, labor leaders and representatives of the public, the Federation sought to destroy the influence of the Socialists in the labor movement and of the open-shop employer in the world of business. It urged conciliation and arbitration of labor disputes in place of industrial warfare. Among its leaders were Senator Mark Hanna, August Belmont and former President Grover Cleveland, and for a time it exercised considerable influence upon public opinion.

Organization of the Needle Trades

During the first few years of this century the men's and women's clothing industries appeared organization-proof. Severe competition, low wages, miserable standards and stubborn resistance to unionization characterized these industries. But the spell was broken in 1910, when the first successes in both sections of the trade were achieved. The "new unionism," as the labor movement in the clothing trades has been called,[86] has not only held its position, but has pioneered in many phases of industrial relations, union-management cooperation, and cultural activities. Moreover, it has had powerful influence upon other fields of collective bargaining.[87]

The AF of L Departments

Need for greater cooperation among the crafts and elimination of jurisdictional disputes were the chief motives for the AF of L to set up four industrial departments. Each was a central body for international unions in building construction, the metal trades, railway work and mining.

Forerunners of the Federation departments were local trades councils formed in the building and metal trades industries in the eighties and on the railroads in the early 1900's. Especially in the building industry, these trades councils frequently disregarded the internationals, permitted dual groups to become members, made conflicting decisions, and were often biased and unfair. To avoid such actions, efforts independent of the AF of L were made to organize national councils in the building and metal

---

86. J. N. Budish and George Soule, *The New Unionism in the Clothing Industry*, Harcourt Brace and Howe, New York, 1920.
87. See the "Men's Clothing" chapter.

industries in the late nineties. These were unsuccessful, but departments affiliated with the AF of L were organized in the building and metal trades and in railway shops and mining between 1908 and 1912. They were designed to extend organization, to determine policies and perhaps to initiate "concerted movements," to iron out jurisdictional disputes, to guide and control local situations and present a united front on "bargain day."

They have been only mildly effective. The most important department—building trades—has only partial control over local councils, and its record in settling and preventing jurisdictional disputes is not impressive. The locals are expected to bargain through the local council and usually, but not invariably, have done so. The Railway Employees' Department played an important role in the war and postwar periods, but the shopmen's strike of 1922 and rise of the Railway Labor Executives' Association have reduced its importance as a policy-forming and a bargaining agency. Effectiveness of the Metal Trades Department has varied from time to time. The Mining Department, never very active, was dissolved in 1922.

4. WORLD WAR PERIOD

When the United States entered the World War the federal government's attitude toward the trade-union movement changed from apathy to concern—a change which inspired rapid progress. Steps to eliminate labor difficulties in key industries were taken by such bodies as the Shipbuilding Adjustment Board and the Cantonment Adjustment Commission.[88] The imperative need for labor peace in time of war led to appointment of the National War Labor Board to mediate labor disputes.[89] It settled many specific issues and formulated and applied principles, most of which were reaffirmed in Section 7(a) of the National Industrial Recovery Act, and in the National Labor Relations Act. Those adopted at the beginning of the Board's work were:

1. The right of workers to organize in trade unions and to bargain collectively, through chosen representatives, is recognized and affirmed. This right shall not be denied, abridged, or interfered with by the employers in any manner whatsoever.
2. The right of employers to organize in associations or groups and to bargain collectively, through chosen representatives, is recognized

---

88. Alexander M. Bing, *War-Time Strikes and Their Adjustment*, Dutton, New York, 1921, pp. 116-117.
89. U.S. Bureau of Labor Statistics, "National War Labor Board," *Bulletin No. 287*, 1922, pp. 30-34. The Board was composed of twelve men—five representatives of management, five of labor and two of the public. Former President Taft and Frank Walsh were the public members, and served as co-chairmen.

and affirmed. This right shall not be denied, abridged, or interfered with by the workers in any manner whatsoever.
3. Employers should not discharge workers for membership in trade unions, nor for legitimate trade union activities.
4. The workers, in the exercise of their right to organize, shall not use coercive measures of any kind to induce persons to join their organization, nor to induce employers to deal therewith.[90]

In unorganized plants, the Board encouraged the election of shop committees. It forbade interference with union activity, and ordered a number of reinstatements with back pay. Employers were forbidden to compel their employees to sign pledges not to join a labor union, or to force them to join a "beneficial organization conducted by the company." [91] Protecting the right to organize and bargain collectively, the Board held that "discharges for legitimate union activities, . . . espionage by agents or representatives of the company, . . . and like actions the intent of which is to discourage and prevent men from exercising this right of organization, must be deemed an interference with their rights as laid down in the principles of the board." [92]

Union Gains During the War

Such conditions—and a shortage of labor—were favorable for rapid advances in trade-union organization. Total membership increased from 3,061,000 in 1917 to 5,047,800 in 1920.[93] The increases were shared by many unions. Between 1917 and 1920 the railway clerks' membership leaped from 6,800 to 186,000; railway carmen from 39,000 to 182,100; carpenters from 247,200 to 371,900; electricians from 41,500 to 139,200; machinists from 112,500 to 330,800; boilermakers from 31,200 to 103,000; blacksmiths from 12,000 to 48,300; packinghouse workers and butchers from 9,600 to 65,300; textile workers from 37,100 to 104,900; maintenance of way employees from 9,700 to 50,100; teamsters from 70,300 to 110,800; coal miners from 352,000 to 393,600; and seamen from 32,200 to 103,300 in 1921.[94]

Almost all these unions had fairly long prewar histories, but not until the World War could some of them get firm footholds. Then, with government pressure, they won places hitherto closed to them—in large packing plants, some parts of the railroad industry, and many branches of the metal and machinery trades.

Campaigns were launched to regain positions lost in the early open-

90. *Ibid.,* p. 32.
91. *Ibid.,* p. 55.
92. *Ibid.*
93. Wolman, *Ebb and Flow in Trade Unionism,* p. 26.
94. Wolman, *The Growth of American Trade Unions, 1880–1923,* Appendix.

shop drives. The most spectacular was a joint attempt by twenty-four internationals to organize the steel industry. A National Committee for the Organizing of the Iron and Steel Industry was set up, with President Gompers of the AF of L as chairman. First organizing efforts were successful, but after a strike of some 400,000 steel workers in 1919 was broken, the campaign collapsed. However, because of labor shortage, or the wish to avoid labor trouble, or for patriotic motives, many employers in other industries temporarily at least abandoned their opposition to bargaining with "outside" unions.

The Industrial Conferences

Labor continued its gains in the first two postwar years largely under wartime momentum and enthusiasm and because employment was high. Yet signs of a change appeared during the First Industrial Conference called by President Wilson in October 1919. The public, organized labor and employers were represented. On the tenth day, the Chairman of the Board of Directors of the United States Steel Corporation, attending as a representative of the public, openly attacked organized labor and defended his version of the open shop. The labor group withdrew after failing to get approval of its resolution endorsing collective bargaining by trade unions.[95]

A second conference, held early in 1920, drew up an elaborate plan for settling labor disputes through regional and national boards of inquiry, adjustment and voluntary arbitration.[96] It accepted the principle of collective bargaining, but did not clearly meet the trade-union issue which disrupted the first conference. The conference found merit in both company and trade unions and saw complementary advantages in them.[97]

These conferences were not favorable omens for industrial peace. The steel industry's refusal to bargain collectively with its workers was a warning that the basic, large-scale industries would not deal with "outside" labor organizations now that the war emergency had passed.

Postwar Losses

A number of other factors contributed to the postwar deflation of trade-union membership. Under the impetus of "labor revivalism" many workers joined unions but soon cooled off and dropped out. The depression of 1920–1921, withdrawal of government aid, and the vigorous open-shop campaign all contributed. Most strikes the unions called to salvage their positions not only failed but caused more membership losses.

Still the losses did not cancel the wartime gains. Membership increased

95. U.S. Department of Labor, *Proceedings of the First Industrial Conference*, Washington, 1920, pp. 269-275.
96. *Monthly Labor Review*, April 1920, pp. 33-36.
97. *Ibid.*, pp. 37-38.

by 2,465,200 between 1915 and 1920, but between 1920 and 1923 it declined by only 1,425,800. Eighty per cent of the loss was in building construction, the metal trades, machinery and shipbuilding, transportation and communication, and clothing, which had shared 75 per cent of the gain realized between 1917 and 1920; the other 20 per cent was distributed over a large number of unions.

Building construction, which had gained 355,200 members during the war, lost 98,400 or 28 per cent, largely owing to Chicago and San Francisco open-shop movements. Unions in the metal trades, machinery and shipbuilding gained 634,600 and lost 601,700 or 98.8 per cent, reflecting open-shop drives inspired by the Founders' and the National Metal Trades Associations and the closing of government shipyards. Unions in transportation and communication gained 680,100, then lost 348,800 or 51.3 per cent. Return of the railroads to private management, contracting-out of work, hostility to unionism—especially in the nonservice divisions—and the disastrous shopmen's strike were factors in these losses. Unions in the clothing industries lost 79,300 or 39.5 per cent of the 200,800 they had gained; and their losses were largely due to less work and migration of plants from old union centers to the South and rural northern communities.[98]

5. A Period of Union Stagnation

After the losses of the early 1920's, inertia and disillusionment swept through organized labor; many trade unions were content to coast along without trying to organize new workers. Leadership deteriorated; old officers marked time, and few young leaders were energetic enough to challenge their quiescent policies. The labor movement stopped in its tracks.

Postwar conditions did not favor extension of collective bargaining. In 1920 a national administration unfavorable to labor came into office, and its views dominated until the early 1930's. Restrictive labor laws, unfavorable court decisions, and yellow-dog contracts impeded union activity. The open-shop campaign had helped to make large sections of the public suspicious of organized labor. Also, fear of radicalism generated by the Russian revolution made the public more susceptible to antilabor propaganda. Despite its history and its efforts, the American Federation of Labor sometimes failed to free itself from charges of radicalism, and the big postwar strikes convinced many people that the charges were well founded. Labor's wartime wage demands were also used as evidence of its selfishness and lack of patriotism.

There were still other factors. Rapid technological change took its toll.

98. Wolman, *Ebb and Flow in Trade Unionism*, p. 28.

The twenties brought wide shifts in employment; some industries expanded, others employed relatively fewer workers, and some absolutely less. A swing of employment from manufacturing to the service trades handicapped the unions. Moreover, those branches of manufacture which did expand were mainly in the mass production sector, where organized labor had found little place. The open-shop trend was helped by factory migration to less industrially mature sections of the country. This was particularly true of textiles, shoes and clothing.

Membership Losses

As a result, between 1923 and 1929 union membership fell from 3,622,000 to 3,442,600. The chief victims were the United Mine Workers, the railway shop crafts, and the Ladies' Garment Workers.

Mine union membership declined from 492,900 in 1923 to 245,100 in 1929.[99] This was due to employment shrinking from 862,536 to 654,494, and to the loss of union control in much of the bituminous coal industry. The northern soft coal industry, which had bargained collectively since 1898, could not meet the competition of the expanding nonunion southern fields. The operators demanded wage adjustments, but under the influence of the "No Backward Step" policy of John L. Lewis, the union refused, a stand which led in 1927 to a breakdown of bargaining relations. Still, it is doubtful whether a more flexible wage policy would have saved the day for the union, for the southern operators were capable of following the wage cutting example of their northern competitors—even of improving upon it.

The railway shop crafts did not recover from the severe defeat of 1922, largely because many roads organized company unions. The garment unions faced new problems they could not wholly solve. In both the men's and women's branches, collective bargaining was undermined by the removal of plants to nonunion centers.

In addition, the strongest New York locals of the International Ladies' Garment Workers were captured by an aggressive Communist faction. In 1926 came a needless and ill-advised strike, which wasted the union's resources and reduced its control to the lowest point since 1910. Membership shrank from 74,500 in 1923 to 30,800 in 1929.

Impact of Nonunionized Mass Production Industries

Losses in unionized industries were not offset by gains elsewhere, except in building construction where a boom sent membership from 789,500 in 1923 to 919,000 in 1929.[100] Those growing giants, the mass production industries, were not receptive to collective bargaining along the

---

99. *Ibid.*, p. 229.
100. *Ibid.*, p. 40.

craft union lines favored by the AF of L. These industries blunted organized labor's appeal by accepting the widely advocated doctrine of high wages during the 1920's. Employing many thousands who had recently left the farms or small rural communities and were without union traditions, they held a great advantage in any showdown with organized labor. True, these workers were not without grievances even in the "golden twenties," but their complaints were not serious enough to encourage union organization.

Barriers against "outside" unions were strengthened by pension plans, profit sharing and other welfare devices, as well as such antiunion weapons as yellow-dog contracts. Two innovations flourished in the twenties: scientific personnel management and company unionism. Personnel work undertook to reduce labor turnover through central hiring and applied testing and rating techniques to transfers and promotions in a plant. To correct shortcomings of straight time and piece work, new methods of wage payment were introduced. The personnel officer was a combination disciplinarian and father confessor; in a sense, he was modern industry's substitute for the personal relationship between employer and employee which large-scale production had largely wiped out.

Company unions handled minor complaints; they had the form, though scarcely the substance of collective bargaining. First appearing more than a generation ago, the company-union movement was encouraged by government agencies during the World War and made considerable progress. The American Federation of Labor at first welcomed it in the expectation that it would be an entering wedge for trade unionism; later the AF of L recognized it as a dangerous rival.

Throughout most of the 1920's company unions prospered. Between 1919 and 1926 their number—representation plans and associations included—rose from 196 to 913 and then fell to 767 in 1932. The number of workers covered increased from 403,765 in 1919 to 1,547,766 in 1928, then declined to 1,263,194 in 1932. Company-union coverage was 9.8 per cent the size of total trade-union membership in 1919; 40.1 per cent in 1932.[101]

Enjoying automobiles, radios, moving pictures, and what seemed to be permanent, though spotty, prosperity, few workers were in a mood to listen to labor leaders. With real wages generally rising, organized labor's most effective argument was spiked. Moreover, management generally made no frontal attack upon the principles of collective action. It largely omitted the appeal to individualism, the staple of open-shop argument in the early part of the century. Instead, the principle of collective bargaining was frequently accepted, though its real purpose was largely evaded.

---

101. The data were taken from a forthcoming book by H. A. Millis and R. E. Montgomery, *Organized Labor* (Vol. III of *The Economics of Labor*).

Under the company union, it was argued, collective bargaining is carried on between workers and their employers who have a common interest, without the intervention of "dues-hungry outsiders."

Faced with disintegration and diminished hope and confidence, union leaders tried a different attack—organization drives with the backing of management, which, of course, was not forthcoming. Union-management cooperation in improving efficiency was also tried, originally between the shop crafts and the Baltimore and Ohio Railroad, then with microscopic success elsewhere.

More serious setbacks followed the collapse of 1929. Unemployment rose steadily until it reached an estimated 16 million early in 1933.[102] In some industries the volume of work shrank by more than half. As estimated by Wolman, total trade-union membership fell from 3,442,600 in 1929 to 2,973,000 in 1933. Between 1930 and 1933 the year-to-year losses were 49,800, 34,700, 213,800, and 171,300, or a total of 469,-600.[103] By the beginning of 1933 organized labor feared that it might be scraping the bottom of the barrel.

102. H. A. Millis and R. E. Montgomery, *Labor's Risks and Social Insurance* (Vol. II of *The Economics of Labor*), McGraw-Hill, New York, 1938, p. 18.
103. Wolman, *Ebb and Flow in Trade Unionism*, p. 34.

Appendix B

BRIEF REVIEW OF OTHER INDUSTRIES *

PHILIP TAFT

1. CLAY, CHEMICAL AND ALLIED INDUSTRIES

a. POTTERY

With 251 establishments, 33,000 wage earners, and manufactured products valued at $95 million in 1937, pottery is a small and relatively unimportant industry.[1] But it has considerable importance in the union-management relations field because nation-wide collective bargaining has been notably successful since 1905 in its major division, general ware—subdivided into white earthenware (semi-vitreous table and kitchen articles) and hotel china (vitreous china table- and kitchenware for hotel and restaurant use). Between 1903 and 1922 a national agreement likewise prevailed in the sanitary ware (bathroom and toilet fixtures) division of the industry.[2] White earthenware is produced chiefly in East Liverpool, Ohio and near-by Chester and Newell, West Virginia; most hotel china comes from Syracuse and Buffalo, New York; and sanitary ware manufacture is centered in the Trenton, New Jersey area.

Bargaining Procedures in General Ware

Local collective bargaining was carried on in the industry during the 1880's by Knights of Labor assemblies. Because East Liverpool employers would not recognize the Knights, a group of the assemblies seceded and formed the National Brotherhood of Operative Potters in 1890. By the end of 1899, the Brotherhood was the only important union in the field. The employers in the general ware division had been organized since 1875

---

* This appendix was already in type by the time 1941 union membership figures became available. The 1941 figures, insofar as they have been made public, will be found in Appendix C.

1. Unless otherwise indicated, the statistics in this appendix on employment, number of establishments, product value, etc., are derived from the *Biennial Census of Manufactures* or the *Annual Statistical Abstract* of the U. S. Department of Commerce.

2. For a comprehensive study of collective bargaining procedures in this industry, see David A. McCabe, *National Collective Bargaining in the Pottery Industry*, Johns Hopkins Press, Baltimore, 1932.

as the United States Potters Association, primarily a trade association and unconcerned with labor problems until 1894. Attempts at a national agreement in 1897 and in 1900 failed because of discord between western and eastern locals. In 1905, after several years of sectional bargaining, harmony in the union was established and the present national system went into effect.

Severe competition both from foreign potteries (notably the Japanese) and domestic glassware producers reduced the industry's whiteware business from $32.8 million in 1925 to $25.7 million in 1937, and the great depression cut employment from 35,000 in 1929 to 24,000 in 1933. Despite these setbacks national collective bargaining has continued on a stable basis. Except for an abortive strike in 1917 and an eleven weeks' general stoppage in 1922, peace has been interrupted only by a number of local outlaw strikes which were swiftly repressed through the joint action of the Brotherhood and the Association. Symbolic of the cooperative spirit was the union's contribution of $30,000 to help finance an industry exhibit at the New York World's Fair.

Joint collective bargaining conferences are held biennially. The representatives of each side have full and final authority to negotiate, including power to modify proposals adopted beforehand at the union's annual convention. A referendum is held only when the conferees cannot agree and the union must then decide whether to strike or to continue on the employers' terms for two more years. Arbitration in the renewal of agreements is not regarded with favor. The bulk of the contract consists of the wage scale, with piece prices listed in detail. An unusual feature is the "Square Deal" clause, which in effect promises that both sides will show a "true spirit of cooperation," avoiding insistence on technicalities or other petty acts. Although the employers have always refused the closed or all-union shop, they have often indicated to their workers that union membership is desirable.

The contract carefully outlines steps for settlement of disputes—mainly over piece rates. First the employee and his local representative must attempt to adjust the dispute in the shop, but such settlements are not to be definite precedents in other shops. If local settlement is impossible, a national representative of the union discusses the case with the employer and the secretary of the employers' association. The next stage is appeal to the monthly meeting of the national standing committee of three employers and three union representatives. Pending committee decision, work must not be interrupted. If the standing committee cannot agree, the case may be referred to the national executive board of the union and the labor committee of the association, and finally to the biennial joint conference. More often, however, the standing committee refers the case back to the interested parties. In any event, the standing committee may not deliberate on the case for more than ninety days. An arbitration clause was incorporated in the 1905 agreement but remained practically inoperative. A strike cannot be called until approved by a majority of the Brotherhood's executive board and two thirds of the members of the local or locals involved.

It was reported in 1938[3] that the wage contract covered about 95 per cent of the earthenware and about 75 per cent of the hotel china branches. The first estimate seems too high, since the Mt. Clemens Pottery in Michigan, which supplies the Kresge chain, was then nonunion. The country's largest china producer, the Onondaga Pottery Company of Syracuse, has never recognized the Brotherhood, although it is a member of the United States Potters Association. The 1940 dues-paying membership of the Brotherhood in general ware was between 8,000 and 9,000, or nearly twice what it was in 1933. Increased employment was partly responsible, but the main reason for this doubled membership was the greater attention paid by the once craft-conscious union leaders to unskilled workers comprising about 60 per cent of this division of the industry.

Organization in Other Pottery Branches

The Brotherhood's national agreement with the Sanitary Potters Association lasted nineteen years, then ended in 1922 with a long strike over a proposed wage cut. Refusal of the sanitary ware unionists to heed the advice of their national officers to accept some reduction was the immediate cause of the system's breakdown. Back of this was the union's failure either to organize new shops which used the unskilled casting process as a substitute for pressing, or to adjust rates so that the pressing establishments (which used considerable skilled labor) could successfully compete. After the NRA, and particularly after the Supreme Court decisions on the Wagner Act, the Brotherhood regained much of its former strength in the sanitary division. It has organized nearly all of the casters ("key" craft workers who number about half of all production workers in the branch) and a large proportion of the other skilled and unskilled groups in many shops. Of the "Big Three" plants producing sanitary ware—American Radiator and Standard Sanitary, Crane and Kohler—only one is still nonunion. Although relations are good, the union has been unable to persuade manufacturers to negotiate a national agreement.

The second largest division of the pottery industry, the porcelain electrical supplies branch, has never been organized on a general scale, though the Brotherhood has conducted a vigorous campaign. It unionized a number of small shops specializing in porcelain supplies but made no headway

3. *Labor Relations Reporter,* March 14, 1938, p. 8, published by The Bureau of National Affairs, Inc., Washington.

in large plants, like General Electric, which make electrical supplies of other materials as well as of porcelain. The CIO has been more active here.

In 1940 the National Brotherhood of Operative Potters paid dues to the AF of L on 14,000 members. (Its depression membership was 4,500 in 1933 and its peak of the 1920's was 9,200.) About 8,000 to 9,000 of its 1940 members were in general ware, 2,000 in sanitary ware, and the remainder in porcelain electrical supplies and miscellaneous pottery branches. In the summer of 1940 the CIO Federation of Glass, Ceramic and Silica Sand Workers of America announced plans to unionize the unorganized sections of pottery manufacture. There are also a few local CIO industrial unions in the industry, the most important being that at the Mt. Clemens Pottery in Michigan.

b. BRICK AND CLAY, OTHER THAN POTTERY

Brick and clay manufacturing is an industry of small units; its 1,200 establishments in 1937 employed only 60,000 and turned out goods worth $163 million. Manufacturing is usually carried on near clay deposits, which are found in every section of the country. Collective bargaining was slight before 1930, and almost completely absent during the depression of the early 1930's. The United Brick and Clay Workers of America, an AF of L affiliate since 1894 (but under its present name only since 1915), paid dues to the Federation on 5,000 members in 1929; in 1933 it paid on less than a hundred.

The revived union activity in NRA days met with considerable employer opposition, and there were strikes at Endicott, Nebraska, Haldeman, Hayward and Clearfield, Kentucky, Lebanon, New Hampshire, and Daisy, Tennessee. Not until after the Supreme Court upheld the Wagner Act in 1937 were union-shop agreements negotiated. In 1940 the union had 10,000 members.

Since 1937 the United Brick and Clay Workers has signed agreements with the most important clay producers in the United States, including the National Fireproofing Corporation, the largest company of its kind, and the Belden Brick Company, one of the major face brick concerns. Contracts are also held with about 80 per cent of the sewer pipe manufacturers east of the Mississippi River and with approximately 150 small producers of burned clay products.[4] Union agreements cover plants from Pomona, California to Cliffwood, New Jersey, and many are for the closed shop. Because the market for brick and clay products is mainly local, the agreements are normally made for a single plant, or, as in Chicago, for all establishments organized into a local association.

4. Information in files of Technical Service Division of the NLRB.

APPENDIX B

C. CEMENT

In 1937 there were only 94 companies and 158 plants in the cement manufacturing industry. Their year's product was valued at $183 million. Plants are highly mechanized—rotary cement kilns are among the largest pieces of moving machinery in all industry. In 1937 these plants had only 26,000 employees, mostly unskilled; in 1939, only 24,000.[5] Cement is frequently considered an extractive rather than a manufacturing industry because the plants usually extract their own principal raw materials—limestone and clay. About 25 per cent of the labor is in quarry work.[6] Despite a productive capacity more than twice the actual output, prices have been relatively stable during the past decade.[7] U. S. Steel, with 12 plants, is the largest single cement producer and, together with its two closest rivals, accounts for about 35 per cent of the industry's capacity.

In October 1934, the AF of L convention ordered the executive council to establish a special cement workers' organizing committee for this hitherto ununionized industry. Within a year a number of locals had been formed and 10 agreements had been obtained. In the summer of 1936 these locals were combined into the National Council of United Cement Workers. By September 1937, 44 cement worker locals affiliated with the AF of L had 30 agreements with 21 companies in 14 states.[8]

At this time the National Council entered the lime and gypsum field, thus increasing its potential membership by about 15,000 workers in nearly 300 establishments. Two years later, despite protests from some craft unions in the Building Trades Department of the Federation, the AF of L Executive Council authorized formation of the United Cement, Lime and Gypsum Workers' International Union with jurisdiction over all workers in the manufacture, production and processing of cement, lime and gypsum. The new union reported 14,500 dues-paying members in 96 locals, about 85 per cent of whom were covered by the 94 agreements.[9] Approximately a dozen of these agreements, covering 2,500 members, were with lime and gypsum plants, including the United States Gypsum Company. Sixty per cent of the agreements granted the union shop, 30 per cent sole bargaining rights and 10 per cent covered members

---

5. Employment figures for 1939 are from "Wage Earners, By Months," U. S. Census of Manufactures, 1939.
6. *Production, Employment, and Productivity in 59 Manufacturing Industries,* Pt. 2, National Research Project, WPA, Philadelphia, May 1939, p. 30.
7. *Cement and Concrete Reference Book, 1939,* Portland Cement Association, Chicago, p. 9.
8. National Council of United Cement Workers, *First Annual Report,* 1937, p. 23.
9. AF of L, *Proceedings,* Annual Convention, 1939, pp. 46-47; also see *Voice of the Union Cement Workers,* June 1939.

only.[10] In 1940 the union paid dues to the AF of L on 13,200 members. Although the CIO has made some attempt to recruit cement and gypsum workers and has organized a small number into either local industrial unions or locals affiliated with one of its internationals, jurisdictional conflicts have not seriously affected the industry. Collective bargaining has been achieved with little difficulty and without spectacular incident.

d. CHEMICALS

Only within recent years has unionism reached the chemical industry. The 1937 Census of Manufactures lists 27 major groupings of establishments manufacturing chemicals and allied products, with a total of 6,800 plants, employing almost 300,000, and producing goods worth $3.3 billion. Some 600 of these establishments, with about 80,000 employees and a product valued at $933 million, were in what may be called the chemical industry proper, concerned with such items as acids, alcohols, nitrates, dyes, plastics. The remainder of this gigantic and steadily expanding industry covered a multitude of products ranging from drugs and cosmetics to fertilizers, paints and explosives. In the field are great multi-product corporations, like du Pont de Nemours, Allied Chemical and Dye, and Union Carbide and Carbon, as well as numerous small firms specializing in one or a few articles.

The main labor organization in the industry is the Gas, By-Products, Coke, and Chemical Workers, District 50 of the United Mine Workers of America. In 1935 a number of AF of L federal locals, organized in gas and coke plants during the early years of the NRA, formed the National Council of Gas and By-Product Workers. The next September the United Mine Workers set up District 50 as a separate division and absorbed them. In June 1937, the jurisdiction of District 50 was extended to chemical workers. At its second biennial convention in January 1940, District 50 reported 150 contracts, 68 of which provided for the closed shop and 47 for the checkoff. While union membership was given as 22,000, the contracts covered about 20,000 workers. Thirty-four contracts were in gas and coke, the rest in chemicals.[11] Since the 1940 convention, District 50 has taken advantage of the defense boom to make substantial gains. One of its major achievements was winning an NLRB election at the largest single chemical plant in the country, the Dow Chemical plant at Midland, Michigan.

After the split with the CIO, the AF of L also sought a foothold in the chemical industry. On September 7, 1940, a National Council of

---
10. Questionnaire answered by the union.
11. "Officers Report to Convention," *United Mine Workers Journal*, February 15, 1940, p. 19; *C.I.O. News*, January 29, 1940, p. 2; questionnaire answered by the union.

Chemical Workers was formed at Akron, Ohio, and at the 1940 AF of L convention 151 locals representing approximately 20,000 dues-paying members were reported as affiliated with it. Nevertheless, union organization in this basic industry is still of small proportions.

2. CLOTHING

a. BOOTS AND SHOES

Collective bargaining in the boot and shoe industry goes back to the eighteenth century, but except for brief outstanding successes after the Civil War, its career has been checkered by interunion conflict, and stable contractual relations have been narrowly limited. Within recent decades, union organization has been hampered both by the shift of a large portion of the industry from such Massachusetts centers as Lynn and Haverhill to rural New England, the Middle West and the South, and by the welfare activities of some large, long-established concerns. Plants can move easily because about 90 per cent of the machinery in use is not owned by shoe manufacturers but rented—chiefly from the United Shoe Machinery Company.[12]

Among the 1,100 manufacturers are a score of fairly large companies, like International Shoe, Endicott Johnson, and Brown Shoe, but the bulk of the more than 200,000 employees are in small establishments. Sweatshops and fly-by-night concerns, ready to take advantage of municipal subsidies and community protection against unions, have been common throughout the industry. Once a highly skilled handicraft industry, it now employs largely unskilled and semiskilled machine workers, each performing a few minutely subdivided tasks. The product value in 1937 was over $800 million and wages were $211.7 million.

Labor Organization and Agreements

Both the AF of L and the CIO have organizations in the industry. After some earlier mergers, two "independent" unions with a combined membership of 16,000 amalgamated in March 1937 as the United Shoe Workers of America, under the wing of the CIO. The new union launched an intensive campaign which within several months resulted in more than 50,000 members and agreements with 149 firms employing about 22,000 workers.[13] Opposition from a number of shoe manufacturers in Maine led to a bitter strike in 1937 and the imprisonment of several union leaders for conspiracy. In June 1937, 14,000 AF of L members withdrew from the Federation and joined the CIO.[14]

12. National Research Project, *op. cit.,* p. 10.
13. *Monthly Labor Review,* November 1938, pp. 1001-1008.
14. Robert R. R. Brooks, *When Labor Organizes,* Yale University Press, New Haven, 1937, p. 194.

With the depression beginning in the latter part of 1937, the United's progress was temporarily checked. Many plants suspended operations in 1938, partly because the union refused to accept employer appeals for wage cuts. At the same time, the CIO group lost its hold upon many of its members, and when operations were resumed was supplanted in some factories by independent unions, occasionally sponsored by local chambers of commerce.[15]

The union, however, soon recovered most of the lost ground. In the midsummer of 1939, it claimed about 50,000 members, of whom some 28,000 to 30,000 were covered by collective agreements in three branches of the industry—component parts manufacture, shoe manufacture and repair shops. Contracts had been signed with 157 firms mainly in New York and Massachusetts, but also in the Middle West and California.[16] Many contracts are signed by groups of firms in a given locality, and most provide for the closed shop and arbitration of unsettled grievances.

The major rival of the United, the Boot and Shoe Workers Union (an AF of L affiliate since 1895), had serious reverses during the depression. Membership fell from 35,000 in 1927 to 13,400 in 1933, then it made gradual advances and in 1938–1940 reported 30,800 members, of whom about 80 per cent were under collective bargaining agreements in 1939. Ninety-five per cent of the contracts held by the AF of L organization granted the closed shop in return for the use of the union label. In addition to the AF of L and CIO unions, a number of local and regional "outside" unions have been bargaining collectively, so that in 1939 slightly more than 30 per cent of the workers in the shoe industry were under labor agreements.

b. FUR

The fur-goods, fur-dressing and dyeing industry is made up of small shops, needing little capital and meeting intense competition. Of the 1,600 fur-goods establishments in 1937, 1,300 were in New York, together with 9,000 of the 13,000 fur workers in that branch of the industry. Similarly, 95 of the 121 fur-dressing and dyeing shops and 5,300 of the 6,300 wage earners were in New York and New Jersey.

Collective bargaining was widespread in the industry for a number of years before 1933, but the International Fur Workers Union of the United States and Canada (now the International Fur and Leather Workers, a CIO affiliate) was beset by factionalism and serious internal disputes. For a time, two unions were in the field but they merged in 1935, with the Communist faction in control.

15. Information from an employee of the Regional Office of the NLRB in New England.
16. United Shoe Workers of America, *Shoes,* April 1939; also information secured from the Research Director of the union.

The outstanding achievement of recent years was an agreement with the previously antiunion A. Hollander and Son concern, which operates three plants and is the largest firm in the industry. Collective bargaining also prevails for the first time in a number of cities outside of New York. Since nearly all fur establishments are now under union control, the organization is turning to the leather field.[17] The New York City market is regulated by joint agreements with four employers' associations.[18]

In February 1938, a lockout, which eventually became a general strike, tied up the entire industry in New York for fifteen weeks. Among the union gains were increased minimum wages, a more satisfactory system of dividing work in slack periods, prohibition of more than one firm partner from acting as a production worker, establishment of a bureau under joint control to adjust wages and secure employment for elderly workers, and a ban upon use of furs or skins processed in Germany.[19]

C. HATS AND MILLINERY

The headwear industry is divided into two general branches—millinery and hats and caps.[20] In 1937 the 755 millinery manufacturing establishments had less than 22,000 workers (64 per cent of whom were women), and produced goods worth $88 million. The number of workers increased to 24,000 in 1939. In the hat and cap division in 1937, there were fewer establishments, 528; a greater product value, $120 million; and more wageworkers, almost 29,000. In 1939 the number employed was nearly the same—28,000. About 50 per cent of the millinery industry was in New York, but the establishments in the men's division were not so concentrated.

During the thirties, millinery manufacture was a "sick" industry. A Department of Labor survey made at the request of the Millinery Stabilization Commission[21] showed that only about a third of the firms in existence in 1937 and 1938 had been established before 1930, and that

---

17. The Fur Workers amalgamated with the National Leather Workers Union in 1939.

18. International Fur Workers Union of the United States and Canada, *Report of the 12th Biennial Convention*, 1937, p. 71.

19. International Fur Workers Union, *Report of the General Executive Board*, 1939, pp. 37-38.

20. The latter division of the industry includes fur-felt hats and bodies for men, women and children; wool-felt bodies for men's, women's and children's hats and hats finished from these bodies in the same factories; men's straw hats and cloth hats and caps; and men's hat and cap materials.

21. "Conditions in the Millinery Industry in the United States," *Bulletin No. 169*, Women's Bureau, U. S. Department of Labor, 1939. The Millinery Stabilization Commission is an unofficial, impartial body, composed of people agreed upon by representatives of employers and workers, whose purpose is to investigate the problems of the industry and to initiate a campaign of stabilization.

one out of four firms went out of business each year.[22] Only 8 per cent of the firms had sales above $300,000 in 1937 while 60 per cent did a business of under $100,000. The industry has thus been marked by small production units, which suffered from excessive competition and a lack of bargaining power both in the purchase of hat materials (supplied by a few well-established houses) and in the sale of the finished product (disposed of to syndicates, chain stores and individual retailers).

Because of the style factor, production and employment are highly irregular or "seasonal"—the greatest number of workers employed in any week in 1938 was 84 per cent higher than the minimum. But even more workers are attached to the industry than style changes demand. Although the average number employed per firm in the peak week of employment was 35, the number of names on all pay rolls during the year averaged 71 per firm.[23]

Collective Bargaining in Millinery

Collective bargaining was well established in the New York market before the passage of the National Labor Relations Act, and amicable relations between the Cloth Hat, Cap and Millinery Workers' International Union (now part of the United Hatters, Cap and Millinery Workers' International Union) and the Eastern Women's Headwear Association existed for many years. Only during the New Deal, however, has unionism become entrenched in such outlying millinery centers as Chicago, St. Louis, Philadelphia, Cleveland and San Francisco.[24] The union reported an average paid-up millinery membership of some 16,000 for 1940 and claimed that approximately 80 per cent of the employees were under agreements. Contrasted with this, most employers were distributed among 12 associations.[25]

Union and employers have cooperated closely in attempts to cure the industry's ills in the New York market. The Millinery Stabilization Commission has issued a "code of fair practices" and seeks to aid in solving production, style and price problems. But the multiplicity of firms, their relatively high mobility, and a declining dollar volume of business have made stabilization difficult.

In 1940 the New York agreement was renewed for three years without major changes. Most employers appear to favor the union effort to remove wages from the competitive sphere by establishing uniform wage standards. To check violations, each employer submits his weekly pay roll and a work statement to the impartial chairman.

22. *Ibid.*, pp. 13, 20.
23. *Ibid.*, p. 4.
24. *Report* of the General Executive Board to the Third Convention of the United Hatters, Cap and Millinery Workers' International Union, 1939, pp. 73-119.
25. U. S. Department of Labor, *Bulletin No. 169*, p. 13.

Appendix B

Unionism in the Hat and Cap Division

Local union organization in hats and caps goes back to 1810. As early as 1854 there were two international unions which merged in 1896 as the United Hatters of North America. The decision in the famous Danbury Hatters case of 1908,[26] however, was a serious blow to the union's progress. Unions in the hat and cap and millinery divisions of the headwear industry were not amalgamated into the United Hatters, Cap and Millinery Workers' International Union until 1934, largely because the members of the former, who were mainly native-born, remained aloof from the predominantly foreign-born membership of the latter.[27] The hat and cap division has been less extensively organized than the millinery trade. Of 28,000 workers, some 9,000 in hat manufacture, 2,200 in cloth hat and cap plants, and 700 in hat and cap materials were reported as paid-up union members in 1940.[28] Advances have been made in the last few years, the most important being the establishment of collective bargaining relations with the John B. Stetson Company in 1936.

3. Food and Liquor

a. baking

In 1937, the baking industry had about 240,000 wage earners and a product valued at $1.4 billion. A few large firms lead the bread and specialty baking fields, but because of the product's perishable nature and consequent small radius of distribution, and the high costs of advertising, they meet considerable competition from the more than 16,500 local bakeries. The tendency of food chain stores to feature bread and other baked goods as loss leaders in order to attract customers is also partly responsible for the narrow margin of profit in the industry. In the cracker and biscuit branch, where perishability is a secondary factor, the few large concerns, like National Biscuit and Loose-Wiles, more nearly approximate the position of manufacturing giants in other industries.[29]

Since 1886 an AF of L union, now known as the Bakery and Confectionery Workers' International Union of America, has been active in the baking and, less extensively, the confectionery field. The determined antiunion attitude of the large concerns until recently compelled the organization to limit its activity to smaller bakeries, notably those specializing in

---

26. *Loewe* v. *Lawler*, 208 U.S. 274, in which a boycott of hats manufactured by a nonunion Danbury, Connecticut firm was held a violation of the Sherman Act and hence made the union subject to triple damages.
27. "The Hatters, Cap and Millinery Workers," *Labor Information Bulletin*, January 1940.
28. Information from the union.
29. See "Food Products, Basic Survey, Part 1," *Standard Trades and Securities*, Standard Statistics Corporation, New York, March 29, 1940.

fancy cakes and bread. Its membership during the 1920's was only around 22,000. With the depression, membership declined to some 16,000 in 1933, but by 1936 it was up to 25,000.[30]

Organization of the Larger Bakeries
In 1937, partly because of CIO rivalry and partly because the Supreme Court upheld the Wagner Act, the Bakery and Confectionery Workers finally invaded the larger bakeries. Because the employees in these plants earned much less than the fancy cake and bread bakers who were then a majority in the union, their dues were lowered, though they had full union privileges except death and strike benefits. As a result of this new policy, the union signed up several of the largest establishments—A. & P. Tea Company, Continental Baking, Cushman's, General, Ward, Purity, and Interstate Baking Company. Contracts also were made with master bakers' associations in many cities.

Bargaining over wages and working conditions is usually local. The international union, however, requires a work week of between forty and forty-four hours, one week's vacation with pay, and the submission of unsettled disputes under an agreement to arbitration. In November 1939 the union reported 221 locals with 66,000 members in bakeries, 28 locals with over 7,000 members in confectionery plants and stores, 11 locals with some 700 members in macaroni plants, and 22 locals with about 9,000 members in biscuit and cracker establishments. The baking industry was then less than one third, and confectionery less than 15 per cent organized. The following year average total union membership was 81,100.

b. BREWING

The brewing industry consists of relatively highly mechanized small plants producing chiefly for regional consumption. In 1937, 653 establishments with 47,000 employees produced beverages worth $537 million. Because beer demand since repeal of Prohibition has not come up to expectations, overcapacity exists in the industry and the weaker firms are gradually disappearing.[31] By 1939 the number of employees had declined to 36,000.

Collective Bargaining Well Established
Collective bargaining and the union tradition have been firmly entrenched in the breweries for years. An international union has existed since 1886. With Prohibition, the National Union of the United Brewery

---
30. Bakery and Confectionery Workers' International Union, *Official Proceedings*, 1936, p. 50.
31. "Beverages, Basic Survey, Part 1," *Standard Trades and Securities*, January 3, 1940.

Workmen of the United States extended its jurisdiction first to soft drink manufacture and then to flour and cereal milling, and took the new name of the International Union of United Brewery, Flour, Cereal and Soft Drink Workers of America. The flour and cereal jurisdiction was abandoned when the AF of L refused to grant the organization control over craftworkers in the milling industry. Repeal, however, restored the brewing industry and gave new life to the Brewery Workers Union as well.

Breweries are again almost 100 per cent under contract. Employers recognize the union as an effective ally in warding off attacks of reformers and prohibitionists. Strikes are exceptional. Agreements are local but in wages, hours, overtime pay and Sunday work conform to the international union's standards. All contracts have arbitration clauses.

While the union has had few conflicts with employers, it has been continually harried in the last twenty-five years by jurisdictional disputes with the Teamsters and other craft unions which object to its industrial form of organization. In 1941 a fierce fight was still being waged between the Teamsters and the Brewery Workers, despite a decision by the AF of L Executive Council awarding jurisdiction over brewery truck drivers to the Teamsters' union. Appeal to the courts by the Brewery Workers failed. These jurisdictional struggles have also often burdened employers. In the Pacific Northwest, the brewers have been forced either to release their own truck drivers and make contracts with general draying companies or to bargain directly with the Teamsters' union.

Approximately 42,000 United Brewery Workers members are regularly employed in the various industries in which it has jurisdiction, while an additional 8,000 temporary workers get union permits during busy seasons.[32] The union claimed in November 1939 some 37,000 members in brewing, 1,000 in malt, 800 in yeast and 3,000 in soft drink establishments.[33] No attempts have been made by the brewery union to organize either the wine or distillery industries. Some distillery plants, however, have been organized by the CIO Distillery Workers Organizing Committee and by AF of L locals affiliated with a Distillery Workers Council. The latter claimed 44 affiliated locals in 1940.

C. FLOUR AND CEREAL

The flour and cereal manufacturing industry included in 1937 more than 2,000 flour mills with some 26,000 workers, and 112 cereal plants (chiefly breakfast foods) employing about 8,000. The product value of the flour branch was $856 million and that of the highly profitable cereal branch was $164 million. Wages paid in both divisions of the industry

32. Letter from Joseph Obergfell, Secretary-Treasurer of the union, August 22, 1939.
33. Questionnaire answered by the union.

were $41 million. A few major corporations, such as General Mills, Pillsbury Flour Milling, Quaker Oats and Kellogg, dominate the industry.

When craft jurisdictional conflicts forced the brewery union out of this field, about 38,000 mill workers had been successfully unionized in the flour and cereal industry.[34] Thereafter, organization was negligible until 1933 when a number of AF of L federal locals were formed. In 1936 these set up the National Council of Grain Processors and Allied Industries. Strikes were conducted against Minneapolis and Buffalo millers, but in general union progress was peaceful.

Company-wide agreements exist with General Mills and Pillsbury, and a regional contract binds mills of the Northwest Association although local wage arrangements are still made. In addition, there are a number of local agreements, including one with Quaker Oats. In November 1940 it was reported at the AF of L convention that 107 unions were affiliated with the Council and that the total dues-paying membership approximated 12,900. More than 50 per cent of the industry was covered by collective bargaining agreements, though corn milling and cereal manufacture were rather weakly organized. However, in 1941 the AF of L made important advances in the Battle Creek, Michigan plants. The same year CIO local industrial unions also became active in the flour and cereal industry, one winning an NLRB election at the Quaker Oats plant in Cedar Rapids, Iowa.

d. FRUIT AND VEGETABLE GROWING AND PROCESSING

Because fruits and vegetables are highly perishable, agricultural and canning operations are closely related, and a large part of the working force is employed in both branches. Employment is highly seasonal and uncertain and most of the shifting labor supply is migratory, following the crops. The Census reported that in 1937 there were about 2,800 fruit and vegetable canneries with products worth almost $800 million, but warned that its estimate of an annual average of 137,000 workers was probably excessive. The figure given for 1939 was 98,000. California, with an estimated 406 establishments, 34,000 wage earners, and $219 million product value in 1937, has been the leading growing and canning state. Many Pacific Coast establishments are dominated by powerful financial and shipping interests, which have supported the Associated Farmers —theoretically an organization of farmers and canners—in combating unionism.

Collective bargaining in the industry has been featured by sudden and violent strikes. After considerable strife in 1933 and 1934 a number of local unions were organized in California vegetable-growing areas. These

---

34. "Handbook of American Trade Unions," *Bulletin No. 618*, U. S. Bureau of Labor Statistics, 1936, p. 152.

locals joined the CIO in 1937 as the United Cannery, Agricultural, Packing and Allied Workers of America, which has agreements with fruit and vegetable growers and processors in Illinois, Ohio, Michigan, Pennsylvania, New York and California, as well as with the crab-meat packers in Maryland and the pecan shellers in Texas. Perhaps its main accomplishment, although not in the agricultural field, has been a joint agreement for the entire Alaska salmon packing industry. At the end of 1938 the union reported 130 contracts covering about 40,000 workers.[35] At the end of 1939 it claimed over 100,000 members, but only some 17,000 were covered by agreements.[36]

The AF of L has strenuously competed with the CIO in this field. It reported at its 1938 convention 64 federal locals with more than 21,000 members. By 1939 these locals had increased to more than a hundred, mostly in California. The California Federation of Labor has negotiated a single contract with the California Processors and Growers, Inc., covering several thousand workers.

Although the vast majority of the workers are not covered by labor contracts, collective bargaining never has been as extensive in agriculture and canning as it is today. In fact, the movement since 1933 represents the first real attempt at organization of these workers outside of IWW and purely left-wing campaigns.

e. MEAT PROCESSING AND DISTRIBUTION

Four companies—Swift, Armour, Wilson and Cudahy—account for over 60 per cent of the $1.1 billion capital investment, and for about 40 per cent of sales in the meat slaughtering and packing industry. Small packers can compete with the giants only because of lower transportation and overhead expense. Profits, however, are seldom over 2 per cent of sales because of the competition in the purchase of livestock.[37] The Census in 1937 reported some 1,100 wholesale meat packing plants with 127,000 wage earners, and products worth $2.8 billion. Chicago is the leading center and policy for the industry is usually determined there, but its some 70 establishments do not employ more than one fifth of the total working force.

Union Organization and Agreements

Collective bargaining in the meat packing industry met with little sustained success until recently. In 1896 the Amalgamated Meat Cutters

---

35. NLRB, "Written Trade Agreements in Collective Bargaining," *Bulletin No. 4,* November 1939, p. 233.
36. Questionnaire answered by the union.
37. "Food Products, Basic Survey, Part 1," *Standard Trades and Securities,* January 31, 1940.

and Butcher Workmen of North America was established with the aid of the AF of L, but it was badly defeated in 1904 by the major companies after a two months' strike affecting 50,000 workers in nine cities. During the World War government pressure compelled the leading manufacturers to sign with the Amalgamated and ten craft unions and to agree to a labor administrator. In 1921, with government influence removed, the large packers abrogated the agreement and established company unions. A strike of 45,000 AF of L workers in thirteen cities was crushed. After that the open shop prevailed in meat packing while the Amalgamated restricted its activity largely to meat distribution, where it had about 12,000 members during the 1920's.[38]

With the rise of the militant CIO Packinghouse Workers Organizing Committee, however, unionism and collective bargaining made rapid progress. The CIO in July 1938 signed its first contract in the Chicago stockyards district with the "Little Five," employing about 2,000 workers. One feature of the contract was a guarantee of thirty-two hours of work in any week to those employees who worked beyond the first working day. In weeks with a holiday the guarantee was twenty-seven hours. Still more important was an agreement, won only after a strike, with the United Stockyards Transit Company, through whose yards all cattle coming to the Chicago market are cleared. In 1940, one of the "Big Four," Armour, accepted collective bargaining on a plant basis, and more than a dozen of its plants, including two in Chicago, are now under contract with the CIO. Negotiations are being carried on with the other large companies. The PWOC reported in 1940 an additional 40 contracts covering about 18,000 workers employed by the "independent" packers. In all, more than 80,000 members were claimed.[39]

Since the rise of the CIO packing union, the Amalgamated Meat Cutters and Butcher Workmen of North America has also made phenomenal gains. At its fifteenth general convention in July 1940, it reported almost 118,000 members, of whom approximately 85,000 were fully paid up.[40] At its previous convention in 1936, it claimed only 19,000. Over a third of the members were in some 400 packing houses. The union stated that its locals had exclusive bargaining rights in 14 Armour plants in addition to the first agreement ever signed by Swift in California. The bulk of the union's strength, however, was in meat distribution, with national agreements covering nearly 3,000 employees of the Safeway chain and the 20,000 independent stores of the National Association of Retail Meat Dealers. Six thousand of the 9,300 A. & P. meat cutters, 5,000 of the

38. Selig Perlman and Philip Taft, *History of Labor in the United States, 1896-1932*, Macmillan, New York, 1935, pp. 406-499.
39. Letter from the Secretary of the PWOC; also questionnaire answered by the union.
40. Its membership as reported in the 1940 AF of L *Proceedings* was 70,900.

employees of Kingan and Company, and 80 per cent of the Kroger chain employees were under union agreements.[41]

4. Hotels and Restaurants

Before the upsurge of union organization after 1933, collective bargaining in hotels, restaurants and taverns was largely limited to establishments catering to a union clientele. In 1932 the Hotel and Restaurant Employees' International Alliance and Bartenders' International League of America had only 27,500 members. By 1940, however, it reported over 215,000, which made it one of the five largest unions within the AF of L.[42] It is a semi-industrial union, covering all hotel and restaurant occupations except the mechanical trades, with a potential membership of around a million.

Several factors caused this phenomenal growth. The repeal of the Eighteenth Amendment reopened a large jurisdiction in which the union was once strong. The Census reported that "drinking places" employed more than 200,000 workers in 1939. New Deal legislation and the general increase in union sentiment also played an important part. Finally, the depression itself had a twofold effect. Declining hotel patronage and poor restaurant business brought pressure upon wages and working standards, thereby encouraging unionization. On the other hand, the overcrowded labor market created a more stable and more easily organized working force. Previously, many hotel and restaurant workers regarded their jobs as temporary, to tide them over until they got better ones. With the depression and unemployment, even the humblest dishwashing and pantryman's job could not be lightly cast aside.

Nature of Agreements

Because competition in the business is largely local, agreements have been limited to the community area. However, there has been a striking trend toward negotiating contracts with groups of employers rather than with a single establishment. Perhaps the most important contract is that first signed in 1939 by the Hotel Association of New York, covering 22,000 employees in 85 hotels. Six AF of L unions, of which the Hotel and Restaurant Employees' Alliance is the dominant one, represented the workers. The contract included the closed shop, the checkoff, vacations with pay, the furnishing and laundering of uniforms by management, and a permanent impartial chairman to adjust unsettled grievances.

Similar agreements have been negotiated, frequently after strikes and

---

41. *The Butcher Workman,* July 1, 1940, p. 1; August 1, 1940, p. 4. For a brief account of the union, see also *Labor Information Bulletin,* August 1940.

42. *Labor Information Bulletin,* April 1940. In the 1940 AF of L *Proceedings* its membership was given as 202,500.

lockouts, with the Pittsburgh Hotelmen's Association, covering 2,300 workers; the Kansas City Hotelmen's Association, covering 3,000 workers in 16 hotels; the San Francisco Hotel Employers' Association, covering 6,000 workers; the Washington, D. C. Hotel Association, covering 4,000 workers; the San Francisco Tea Room Guild, covering about 20 tearooms; and with several other associations. Since 1938, when the union convention abolished an unwritten law forbidding membership to Negroes and Asiatics, the organization has attempted to unionize railroad dining-car employees and has set up a separate joint council of railroad employees. In 1940 it held agreements with about 30 large companies controlling nearly 60 per cent of all railway mileage.[43]

The national officers of the union act only as advisers in negotiation of local agreements, although they encourage certain minimum conditions everywhere—a six-day week, a nine-hour day for men and an eight-hour day for women, and regulation of the working period to save employees from frequent and unnecessary layoffs in between rush periods in a day's work. Actually many agreements grant conditions far superior to the minimum. The CIO has also organized a number of hotel, restaurant and tavern local unions, but the great bulk of the union men and women in the industry are affiliated with the AF of L.

5. Lumber, Pulp and Paper

a. LUMBER

As classified by the Census of Manufactures, the lumber industry has three main branches: logging camps, merchant sawmills, and combined sawmills and planing mills. In 1937 the 7,600 establishments in the industry had 324,000 workers, and produced goods worth $848 million. Wages were a third of the product value, indicating the great importance of the labor factor. Employment in 1939 was 288,000. Control in the industry is considerably decentralized, with the eight largest producers in 1935 accounting for only 6.4 per cent of the persons employed and for only 7.6 per cent of the product value.[44] The Northwest and the South account for almost two thirds of the country's lumber production.[45]

Union Organization Since 1933

During the World War, left-wing union groups were active on the Pacific Coast but were generally defeated by the Loyal Legion of Loggers and Lumbermen, an intercompany union. Independent unionism was not

---
43. *Labor Information Bulletin*, April 1940.
44. National Resources Committee, *The Structure of the American Economy*, Pt. 1, Washington, June 1939, p. 241.
45. National Research Project, *op. cit.*, p. 120.

revived until 1933, when several federal locals of the AF of L were formed. Within a year approximately 130 locals operated throughout the United States and Canada in spite of the opposition of the companies and the resurrection of the Four L's. In 1935 the locals were united into the Sawmill and Timber Workers' Union, as a department of the United Brotherhood of Carpenters and Joiners of America, which claims jurisdiction over all woodwork except cooperage. When the Pacific Coast lumber operators ignored union demands for a written contract, a strike of 32,000 logging camp and lumber workers was called in May 1935 and lasted at various points until the following August. Settlements on the basis of full or limited union recognition were granted throughout the Northwest.

This promising start in collective bargaining was badly handicapped by internal union conflict over the limited representation in conventions of the lumber workers, who paid lower dues than the skilled members of the Brotherhood of Carpenters and Joiners. In September 1937 representatives of lumber worker locals, with a majority of the 90,000 men then organized, revolted against the Brotherhood, established the International Woodworkers of America, and affiliated with the CIO. A bitter jurisdictional fight developed, with cross-picketing of rival plants and boycotting by carpenters of products made in CIO establishments. Probably no other industry has suffered more from labor's civil war.

Nevertheless, collective bargaining has advanced. In 1940 the International Woodworkers claimed about 70,000 members and the AF of L about 50,000, although both figures appear unduly high. The IWA had one agreement with the Columbia Basin Loggers' Association and the Columbia Basin Sawmill Operators' Association, covering 31 companies and about 5,000 workers, and negotiated another, subject to ratification by individual employers and local unions, with an employers' committee representing 60 logging and 10 sawmill operations in western Washington. The AF of L has a city-wide agreement covering about 2,000 workers in Seattle and a closed-shop contract with the largest lumber mill in Bellingham, Washington. In 1939 the CIO signed a contract with the Conner Lumber and Land Company of Laona, Wisconsin, but neither union has made much headway in the lumber regions outside the Pacific Coast. The CIO has its strongest hold in the logging camps, while the AF of L is best established in the sawmill and plywood operations.

In the spring of 1940, the two unions and the Lumbermen's Industrial Relations Committee, representing 112 companies and about 90 per cent of the production in the Northwest, negotiated for a model agreement to be adopted by individual employers or groups,[46] but the negotiations broke down.

46. *Business Week*, April 6, 1940, p. 32.

b. PULP AND PAPER

The pulp and paper industry, a $1.2 billion product industry, is a major outlet for forest products. In 1937 the 194 pulp establishments (all but seven using wood) employed some 27,000 wage earners; 111,000 more were employed by 647 establishments producing paper and paperboard (newsprint, book paper, wrapping paper, tissue paper and cardboard, but not converted products like bags and stationery). The greater part of pulp produced is consumed in paper mills operated by the same concerns. Washington, Wisconsin, Michigan, Maine, Massachusetts and New York are the leading states in the industry although there has been a definite trend in recent years toward the South, which has large timber supplies and lower costs. The eight major paper producers in 1935 employed 19.2 per cent of the wage earners and accounted for 20.2 per cent of the product value.[47] Attempts at further consolidation have not been successful.

Two AF of L unions, the International Brotherhood of Paper Makers, a skilled craft organization, and the International Brotherhood of Pulp, Sulphite, and Paper Mill Workers, a semi-industrial organization covering the semiskilled and unskilled workers, have been in the industry since the 1890's. Before the New Deal, however, union organization covered only a few workers. The craft union paid dues to the AF of L on 4,000 members during the 1920's but this number fell to 2,300 in 1933. Its sister union claimed only 5,000 members in its much greater jurisdiction throughout the same period.

Regional Bargaining on the Pacific Coast

The most significant development after 1933 was organization of the previously nonunion Pacific Coast mills and establishment of a regional system of collective bargaining. At the suggestion of a union official, the employers formed the Pacific Coast Association of Pulp and Paper Manufacturers. The first contract, signed in 1934, covered 18 companies; now 34 out of 37 West Coast plants and some 15,000 workers are included. A joint bargaining committee negotiates the agreement for the two AF of L unions, after which it is submitted to the general membership for approval.

Grievance machinery has been set up, with the Joint Relations Board of the Pulp and Paper Industry of the Pacific Coast as the final and binding source of appeal. If the Board deadlocks, it must request a United States district court judge to select an impartial person to sit with one representative of the employers and one of the two unions. The decision of two of the three men is final.

47. National Resources Committee, *op. cit.*, p. 241.

In the first contract the unions were recognized as representing their members only; in 1935 the employers agreed not to recognize any other union; and in 1936 the Association agreed upon union membership as a condition of employment. The agreement has been renewed annually. Noteworthy features of the 1940 agreement were clauses granting paid vacations and recognizing the principle of seniority in promotion, layoffs and re-employment of seasonal employees, when other things were equal.[48]

Current Union Membership

Substantial gains have also been made in other sections of the industry. In 1940 the Paper Makers had 24,300 members, and the Pulp, Sulphite, and Paper Mill Workers 40,000.[49] In addition to the AF of L unions, CIO locals have been organized in a few paper mills, notably in New England and the South. There are also a number of independent groups, the most important being the employee representation plan at the Kimberly-Clark Corporation in Wisconsin, which was first organized in 1920 and reorganized in 1933 to meet NRA requirements.[50] The secretary of the American Paper and Pulp Association estimated that in 1939 between 35 and 40 per cent of paper and pulp employees were union members.[51]

6. MACHINIST AND RELATED TRADES

a. THE MACHINISTS

According to the International Association of Machinists' charter, machinist and related work includes "the making, erecting, assembling, installing, maintaining, repairing, or dismantling of all or any parts thereof of all machinery, engines, motors, pumps, and all other metal power devices." A rough estimate of workers in this jurisdiction would be over a million, including approximately 650,000 in the manufacture of machinery and machine tools (excluding electrical equipment), 40,000 in railroad shops, the steadily mounting total in the aircraft industry, and large groups in shipbuilding, construction and iron and steel fabrication. Almost every industry requires mechanics and machinists for maintenance, repair and other work.

History of Organization and Agreements

The International Association of Machinists, formed in 1888, did well

48. *Collective Bargaining in the West Coast Paper Industry,* Industrial Relations Section, Princeton University, Princeton, 1941.
49. AF of L, *Proceedings,* 1940.
50. S. F. Shattuck, "An Introductory Statement," *Personnel Series,* No. 30, American Management Association, 1937.
51. Letter from Secretary Charles F. Boyce, August 31, 1939.

in its early years when it was still almost exclusively confined to highly skilled machine work. In 1900, claiming 60,000 members, it negotiated a national contract with the powerful National Metal Trades Association. After this agreement was abrogated in 1901, conflict and persistent antiunion activity followed.[52] Although all of the plants of the American Locomotive Company had been organized by 1910 and big advances were made among machinists in railroad shops and shipbuilding concerns during the World War, the IAM could not withstand the concerted openshop drive of the 1920's.[53] In 1929 the union claimed only 77,000 workers and in 1933, only 65,000.

After 1933 and stimulated by CIO competition, the International Association of Machinists made striking gains. In 1940 it paid dues to the AF of L on 190,000 members.[54] It held well over 4,000 written and about 100 "verbal" agreements in more than 25 major industry classifications. Roughly 130 contracts covered 11,000 workers in the iron and steel fabricating industry, 55 covered 3,500 workers in nonferrous metal plants, 250 covered 28,000 workers in machinery and tool manufacturing establishments (excluding transportation equipment), 78 covered 10,000 workers in railway car and automobile manufacturing plants, 144 covered 3,000 workers in machine shops, and 2,000 covered 15,000 workers in auto repair shops.[55] The largest single group in the IAM is composed of the approximately 40,000 machinists in the railroad industry, under agreements with 120 Class I carriers. Five large firms comprising the entire newspaper printing press industry have accepted collective bargaining with the machinists' organization, in addition to such diverse corporations as Anaconda Copper, Sinclair Oil and the Underwood Elliott Fisher Typewriter Company.

Bargaining Unit

In many industries, including food products, textiles, pulp and paper, and printing, IAM agreements usually cover only skilled maintenance and repair workers. In other industries, notably iron and steel fabrication, nonferrous metal fabrication, machinery and tool, and transportation equipment, contracts are frequently plant-wide. Whether the bargaining unit is craft, semi-industrial or industrial depends on many circumstances—other AF of L unions in the plant, the threat of CIO encroachment, and ease of organization. Many agreements, as on the railroads, are signed jointly with other AF of L craft unions, while, especially in big cities, a large number are negotiated with groups of small employers such as garage owners.

52. Perlman and Taft, *op. cit.*, p. 115.
53. NLRB, *op. cit.*, Ch. 10.
54. AF of L, *Proceedings*, 1940.
55. Information from the union.

Because of its wide jurisdiction claims, the machinists' union has frequently conflicted with other unions which limited their organizing activities to a single industry or a group of closely related industries. This problem has been particularly acute since the AF of L–CIO split, although it existed many years previously.

b. PATTERN MAKING

Closely allied to the IAM is the Pattern Makers' League of North America, an AF of L affiliate since 1887. Unlike its sister union, the League never tried to extend jurisdiction beyond its craft lines. The approximately 30,000 pattern makers in the country are divided about evenly between small contract shops which work on orders for many firms and large manufacturing establishments which have permanent pattern making departments. With an apprentice-trained, highly skilled, highly paid membership, whose specialized ability is of great strategic importance in collective bargaining, the League has often not even found it necessary to request a written contract. During the 1920's, it was thus in a position to win and maintain recognition in manufacturing establishments like the General Electric plant at Schenectady, New York, in which independent unionism was virtually extinct. But the bulk of its membership has always been in contract shops.

With the decline in employment during the great depression, the League's membership slumped, but regained its strength with recovery in business. It had in 1940 over 7,000 members under written and verbal agreements. In many CIO-controlled plants, the League has succeeded in winning the right to bargain for pattern makers, although those employed by the large automobile manufacturers are generally covered by the agreements of the industrial union. One of the League's chief concerns is regulation of apprenticeship.

c. AIRPLANE MANUFACTURE

It has been estimated that to provide the United States with a capacity of 50,000 military planes a year, about 600,000 production and maintenance workers will be needed [56] instead of the 166,000 employed in April 1941. In this increasingly important industry, the International Association of Machinists and the United Automobile, Aircraft and Agricultural Implement Workers of America, affiliated with the CIO, have carried on a vigorous competition. The IAM reported in 1940 that between 16,000 and 20,000 employees in airplane, aircraft motor, propeller and instrument manufacture were covered by its agreements, including those of the Boeing Aircraft Company. One of the union's chief aims in

---

56. *Aviation*, McGraw-Hill, New York, July 1940, p. 27.

this industry has been to reduce the number of job classifications and to equalize rates for the same work.

The United Automobile Workers' initial drive to organize aircraft hit a snag at the California plant of the great Douglas Aircraft Company, and its early progress was limited to three or four of the smaller concerns —Bell, Lycoming, Brewster and the engine plant of Packard Motor. In July 1940, CIO and UAW leaders announced a renewed determination to overcome employer as well as IAM opposition. Early in 1941 the UAW won a significant victory at the Vultee Aircraft Corporation, leading to its recognition at a number of other southern California aviation plants. The expansion of automobile manufacturers into the aviation field has placed it in an advantageous position. In the fall of 1941 the union claimed 50,000 aircraft members. Its chief, and as yet unrealized goal, is to raise wage rates in airplane manufacture to the high level of the auto industry.

Perhaps the most notorious series of events in this industry took place at the North American plant in Inglewood, California. In March 1941 the CIO won an NLRB election by a small margin. Then weeks passed with the company and the union deadlocked on the union's demand for a general wage increase of 10 cents an hour and a minimum hourly rate of 75 cents. Finally the dispute was certified to the National Defense Mediation Board, the union agreeing not to strike until three days after the Board made public its recommendations and the company agreeing to make any increases retroactive to May 1.

However, after union negotiators reported that the Board was stalling, a strike was called on June 5, shutting down the plant completely. Efforts of international union officials to get the strike called off failed, and on June 9 the Army took over the plant, an action which quickly broke the strike. On the following day the strikers voted to return. The dispute then went back to the Mediation Board, which recommended terms highly favorable to the union—a wage increase of 10 cents an hour retroactive to May 1, an increase in the minimum hourly rate from 50 to 60 cents, with a raise of 5 cents every four weeks until 75 cents is reached, and a union membership maintenance clause. Company acceptance of these terms on July 1 ended Army occupation of the plant.

Indications of future wage uniformity in the aircraft industry came in August when three other California companies (Douglas, Northrop and Vultee) increased the minimum hourly rate to 60 cents. About the same time in Seattle, Boeing announced wage increases—no change in the base of 62.5 cents, but an increase to 70 cents after three months (instead of six months) and to 78 cents after six months.

In addition to the AF of L and the CIO, the industry has a number of employee representation plans or independent unions. Some of the largest plants, including those of the Glenn Martin Corporation, are not unionized at all. Probably about a third of the workers in aircraft and parts manufacture in the first half of 1941 were covered by trade-union agreements.

d. SHIPBUILDING

Like all "war" industries, shipbuilding greatly increased after Europe went to war again. Expansion is so rapid that figures of employment and product value in private and government yards are understatements within a few months after they are recorded. In November 1940 private shipbuilding and ship-repairing yards employed approximately 111,000 workers. A somewhat larger number—almost 124,000—were employed in navy yards.[57]

During the World War, the shipping industry was largely dominated by the Metal Trades Department of the AF of L, comprising the International Brotherhood of Boilermakers, Iron Ship Builders and Helpers of America and several other international unions. During the 1920's shipbuilding practically ceased, but with the revival of commercial and warship construction during the past decade, affiliates of the department again became active. The International Association of Machinists alone reports about 13,000 members in federal navy yards (including the naval gun factory at Washington, D. C.), and well over 1,500 in private shipyards.[58] However, these unions now face serious competition from the Industrial Union of Marine and Shipbuilding Workers of America, organized in September 1934 as an independent national union, and since November 1936 a member of the CIO.

The Industrial Union got its chief impetus from a seven weeks' strike which started in March 1934 at the Camden, New Jersey yards of the New York Shipbuilding Corporation, and resulted in local union recognition as well as a 15 per cent increase in wages for about 6,000 employees. Since then locals have appeared in most private and government shipyards on the Atlantic Coast and agreements have been signed with about half the major private companies, as well as with some smaller ones. In June 1940 the union signed its fourth contract with the Federal Shipbuilding and Drydock Corporation of Kearny, New Jersey after a brief strike terminated at the urgent request of government officials in the interest of national defense. The following year, however, company refusal to grant a union membership maintenance clause, as recommended by the National Defense Mediation Board, forced the government to take over the yard temporarily.

In May 1941 the union ended a long and vigorous campaign by ob-

---

57. *Monthly Labor Review,* March 1941, p. 573. The navy yard figure includes workers engaged in the manufacture of torpedoes, guns, etc.
58. Information from union, September 18, 1940.

taining a contract covering the Hoboken shipyard of the Bethlehem Steel Company, the first union contract signed by the giant corporation. It was followed the next month by an agreement to recognize the union wherever it won NLRB elections. In February 1940, the Industrial Union of Marine and Shipbuilding Workers claimed 31,000 members, of whom about 20,000 were under agreements. Both of these figures have since increased substantially.

On the Pacific Coast, CIO locals have generally been compelled to take a back seat to the AF of L unions; only the San Pedro and Long Beach yards deal with the former. The AF of L unions formed a Pacific Coast District Council to maintain uniform wages and working conditions throughout the shipyards to reduce mobility and dissatisfaction of shipyard workers. Agreements are negotiated by a joint committee of the Metal Trades Department representing all of the crafts. Until 1941 contracts in the Seattle shipyards were not for a specified period but for the duration of construction on a ship.

In the Gulf shipyards, competition between the AF of L and the CIO is keen. The former is reported to hold a majority of the agreements, but the largest concern, the Alabama Dry Dock and Shipbuilding Corporation, has signed with the Industrial Union. AF of L unions also have agreements with most of the Great Lakes companies, although the Defoe Boat and Motor Works is under contract with the CIO's United Automobile Workers, and the Great Lakes Engineering Company was in July 1941 the scene of strenuous rivalry between several unions—AF of L, CIO and independent.

Workers in federal shipyards are under civil service and not under written labor contracts. Nevertheless, the unions are well established and represent their members in the adjustment of grievances. Basic wages are set by a national Navy Wage Review Board, although in each shipbuilding center local wage boards make necessary individual and group adjustments. The unions have contended that both the national and local boards have failed to set wages on a par with private industry.

Regional Contracts

To eliminate strife in the private shipbuilding industry, national defense officials suggested in 1941 the negotiation of regional contracts setting up uniform wage rates and working conditions and banning strikes and lockouts. In April 1941, a Shipbuilding Stabilization Conference of union, employer and government representatives drew up a master contract for 39 Pacific Coast shipyards. Important clauses granted the closed shop, prohibited strikes and lockouts, set a uniform hourly rate of $1.12 for first class mechanics, and provided for arbitration of all unsettled grievances. In June a similar two-year master contract became effective for some 50 Atlantic Coast shipyards. Gulf Coast and Great Lakes shipbuilding came under a master contract about two months later.

Relations under the Pacific Coast agreement were not immediately satisfactory. Early in May, 1,200 AF of L and 700 CIO machinists in 11 San Francisco area shipyards struck in protest against the $1.12 wage scale and payment of only time and a half for overtime. Other machinists in the area were receiving $1.15 an hour and double time for overtime. The main target of the strikers, however, was Bethlehem, which had failed to sign the master contract.

In spite of efforts of government and AF of L officials, the strike continued through most of June, supported for a time by other AF of L metal trades workers. On June 23 Bethlehem finally accepted the National Defense Mediation Board's recommendation and agreed to sign the coastwide agreement for its San Francisco shipyard with the AF of L Bay City Metal Trades Council. Though the AF of L machinists had withdrawn from the Council when other workers went through their picket lines, they voted a few days later to return to work under the terms of the master contract. CIO machinists followed suit.

7. Maritime Industry [59]

The maritime industry is one of the great life lines of the country. Some 300,000 workers in 1937 handled almost 600 million tons of waterborne commerce, valued at nearly $21 billion. Yet the working status of the average maritime wage earner until recent years has been comparable to the lowest in manufacturing industry. In part, the nature of the industry has been responsible. Uncontrollable weather conditions and continual fluctuations in demand for water transportation made for great employment irregularity, an unstable and excessive working force and low average annual earnings. More important, however, was the absence of strong labor organizations to insist upon improved conditions and a system of stabilization. Maritime union-employer relations have a long history of conflict behind them.

The picture is highly complex. Maritime work has a host of distinct and differing occupations—the licensed ship personnel consisting of masters, mates, pilots and engine-room officers, who are required by law to possess licenses issued by the Bureau of Marine Inspection and Navigation of the U. S. Department of Commerce; radio operators, whose status is much the same as the officers although they are not licensed by the Bureau; the unlicensed ship personnel consisting of sailors, firemen, cooks and stewards, and pursers' help; longshoremen, checkers and warehousemen, who load and unload the cargo; and inland boatmen, who

---

59. This section is based almost entirely upon the Maritime Labor Board's authoritative *Report to the President and to the Congress*, March 1, 1940.

work on tugboats, lighters, barges, dredges, ferryboats and similar craft on bays, harbors, lakes, rivers and canals.

Four unions represent the licensed personnel, two compete for radio operator members, four operate in the unlicensed personnel field, two cover the waterfront occupations, and several of those already noted, as well as a smaller craft union, bargain for inland boatmen. By far the most important are the rival AF of L and CIO organizations representing the 140,000 unlicensed seamen and the almost equal number of longshore workers.

The employers too are largely organized into associations either to deal with unions or to fight them. The Maritime Labor Board report listed 42 different associations of employers, most of them on a port basis, but with several representing companies scattered over large regions, such as the Pacific and Atlantic Coasts. Most shipping and stevedoring companies are small, but several, like the Grace Line, Matson, American-Hawaiian, Dollar and the great oil tanker concerns, are powerful enough to counteract the strategic bargaining position of maritime workers ashore or afloat.

a. ON SHIP

(1). *Unlicensed Personnel*

For many years after its organization in 1892, the International Seamen's Union was a federation of district and local AF of L crafts which spoke for the unlicensed personnel of the entire country. During and immediately after the World War it was a force of great power, with a reported membership of more than 100,000 in 1921. But unsuccessful strikes and unrelenting employer opposition resulted in a tremendous decline in strength during the 1920's. In the early years of the New Deal, maritime unions everywhere re-established themselves, and ship unions joined longshoremen in the successful 1934 strike on the Pacific Coast.

Internal dissension, however, disrupted the International Seamen's Union. Craft affiliates on the West Coast became independent units. The Sailors' Union of the Pacific, which had taken the initiative in organizing the ISU and was its strongest member until its separation in 1921, claimed in 1939 some 8,000 members, covering all unlicensed deck hands sailing from West Coast ports, except those engaged in the tanker trade, who were either unorganized or covered by employee representation plans. The Pacific Coast Marine Firemen, Oilers, Watertenders and Wipers' Association controlled all of the 4,000 unlicensed engine-room personnel sailing from West Coast ports, with the exception of the oil tanker men. Similarly, the National Marine Cooks' and Stewards' Association claimed 4,000 members, or all West Coast employees in its jurisdiction except those on the tankers.

With the final dissolution of the International Seamen's Union in 1938, the Sailors' Union of the Pacific rejoined the AF of L and was responsible for the formation of the Seafarers' International Union of North America, which in 1940 had 18,700 members, concentrated on the Pacific Coast and the Great Lakes. The Cooks' and Stewards' Association has joined the CIO, while the Firemen have remained independent.

Bargaining on the Three Coasts and the Great Lakes

These three Pacific Coast unions all bargained collectively with the Pacific American Shipowners' Association (for offshore, intercoastal, and Alaska lines) and the Shipowners' Association of the Pacific Coast (for coastwise lumber and general cargo operators), on the basis of the arbitration awards which concluded the great 1934 strike. In April 1935 they joined with other offshore maritime unions and the longshoremen to form the Maritime Federation of the Pacific to coordinate their activities against possible employer opposition. But personal rivalry between the sailors' and longshoremen's unions led to the defection of the former after the second coast-wide strike in 1936-1937.

On the East and Gulf Coasts and the Great Lakes the dominant union of unlicensed personnel is the National Maritime Union, an outgrowth of a revolt within the ranks of the International Seamen's Union and since 1937 an affiliate of the CIO. In 1938 it obtained a coast-wide agreement, granting union control of hiring through the rotation system, with the American Merchant Marine Institute, which represents the large majority of passenger, freighter and combination carriers on the Atlantic Coast.[60] This agreement was renewed with some change in January 1940 after a three-month deadlock over the rotary hiring system. In contrast to the West Coast situation, the National Maritime Union represents all unlicensed personnel in five occupational divisions—deck, engine, stewards and pursers, and inland boatmen. In 1939 its reported membership was slightly more than 63,000, with about 51,000 seagoing and the rest in the inland-boatmen division. As of June 1939, the National Maritime Union represented men employed on 76 per cent of the merchant ship tonnage operating from Atlantic and Gulf ports.[61]

Unlike salt-water shipping, the Great Lakes are poorly unionized, owing in no small measure to the opposition of the bulk cargo operators who are members of the Lake Carriers Association and own about nine tenths

60. A committee of the Institute negotiated the standard agreement, but since it had no authority to sign for the companies, the latter were required to sign individually.

61. On June 17, 1939, a coast-wide strike by the National Maritime Union against the operators of Atlantic and Gulf tankers terminated unsuccessfully for the union and ended the contractual relationship existing up until that time between the NMU and some of the leading operators of tanker fleets.

of the total shipping capacity. In 1939 the National Maritime Union had agreements covering only 4.3 per cent of merchant ship tonnage on the Great Lakes, while the Seafarers' Union of North America covered only 3.6 per cent.

Hiring Procedures and Grievance Settlement

The coast-wide agreements for unlicensed ship personnel cover wages, hours, overtime, watches, hiring procedures and settlement of grievances. Two issues have been of prime importance under the agreement systems: control of hiring and peaceful adjustment of grievances. In the past, seamen were hired "off the dock" through private "shipping masters," or company offices, or a governmental employment agency, or employer-controlled hiring halls. The unions successfully contended that to prevent discrimination against union members and equalize employment opportunities, the men should be hired in strict rotation through a union hall —the equivalent of the closed shop in manufacturing industry. In the spring of 1938, however, the U. S. Maritime Commission inaugurated the policy of recruiting personnel for government-owned merchant vessels through registers kept by the shipping commissioners stationed in every port. The unions vigorously opposed this policy but without much effect.

Peaceful grievance adjustment has been a serious problem because of frequent "quickies" or "sitdowns" which individual seamen deemed more effective than the slower grievance machinery. In 1940 the National Maritime Union introduced a system of penalties to maintain discipline. Workers who fail to report for duty, or who leave ship without giving the master adequate time to make a replacement, will be shifted to the bottom of the hiring list for a first offense, suspended thirty days for a second offense, and expelled for a third offense.[62] Most agreements contain some provision for arbitration by a neutral agency. Arbitration, however, is not generally resorted to willingly because it is expensive and the union feels that arbitrators have been biased.

(2). *Licensed Personnel and Radio Operators*

The unions representing the deck officers, the engine-room officers and the radio operators are national organizations, many of which were originally benevolent and fraternal associations. In 1939 the National Organization Masters, Mates, and Pilots, affiliated with the AF of L, reported 3,000 members in 34 locals on the three coasts, the Great Lakes and the Canal Zone. The National Marine Engineers' Beneficial Association, a CIO affiliate, had in the same year about 8,000 engine-room members. Both of these craft organizations meet with competition from the United Licensed Officers of the United States of America, an independent union

62. *Pilot*, January 12, 1940.

formed in New York in 1933 as an amalgamation of two older unions, and claiming in 1936 some 2,000 members. In recent years, the International Longshoremen's Association has also organized some officers' locals. Radio operators are divided between the CIO American Communications Association and the AF of L Commercial Telegraphers' Union. Membership in the marine division of the former was estimated in 1939 at 1,950, while that in the latter was about 500. Employee representation plans have been notably widespread among licensed personnel employed on oil tankers.

On the Pacific Coast, agreements with the officers' unions are coast-wide but in the East they are negotiated by individual employers. Whereas unlicensed personnel on approximately two thirds of the salt-water merchant shipping tonnage were covered by union agreements in 1939, the comparable figures were for deck officers 38.3 per cent, for engine-room officers 47.7 per cent and for radio operators 45.5 per cent. On oil tankers alone, however, 38.1 per cent of the tonnage dealt through employee representation plans and only 5.2 per cent with independent unions for licensed personnel.

Preliminary estimates of the Maritime Labor Board indicate that in March 1941, 68 per cent of the total deep-sea vessel personnel [63] were under union agreements; an additional 6 per cent were covered by agreements negotiated under employee representation plans. Excluding tankers, the percentages were 82 and 2, respectively. For tankers alone, 24 per cent were under union agreements, 17 per cent under employee representation plan agreements.

b. ON SHORE

Practically 100 per cent of the longshore work done in the 74 major salt-water ports of the United States and in most small ports is covered by collective agreements. The Atlantic and Gulf ports are controlled by the AF of L International Longshoremen's Association, organized in 1892; the Pacific ports, with few minor exceptions, are controlled by the International Longshoremen's and Warehousemen's Union, once a part of the ILA but since 1937 a member of the CIO. Like the merchant ship personnel, the longshore workers in the Great Lakes ports are not widely unionized.

Pacific Coast Agreement

Pacific Coast ports are covered by a single agreement negotiated between the CIO union and the Waterfront Employers Association of the Pacific

---

63. Limited to deep-sea merchant vessels of American registry and of 1,000 gross tons and over, "suitable for service" as of September 30, 1939. Licensed and unlicensed personnel, radio operators, pursers and concessionaires are included.

Coast, representing 149 steamship, stevedore and terminal companies.[64] However, as a result of an NLRB decision in 1941 that AF of L locals in three minor ports may vote whether or not to withdraw from the coast-wide unit, it appears that these may shortly be under a separate agreement. For freight handlers, clerks, weighers and allied workers, the International Longshoremen's and Warehousemen's Union signs separate regional agreements for the four major districts—Seattle, Portland, San Francisco and Los Angeles. This agreement system developed from the awards of the National Longshoremen's Board which terminated the bitter Pacific Coast maritime dispute in 1934.

The award for the longshore industry provided for a wage increase to 95 cents an hour, a six-hour day, hiring halls controlled jointly by the employers' association and union in each port, a joint labor relations committee in each port to adjust disputes, and temporary impartial umpires to arbitrate each case which could not be settled by the parties. A ninety-eight-day coast-wide strike in 1936–1937 resulted in the preferential union shop and a standing arbitrator for the Pacific Coast and also one for each major port.

Despite the elaborate and mature collective bargaining framework, unions and employers were so distrustful and antagonistic that strife was continual for several years and work stoppages and port lockouts were frequent. Bitter controversies developed over the size and rotation of gangs, the size of sling loads, introduction of laborsaving devices, crossing of picket lines and the handling of "hot cargo." That chaos was averted was due in no small part to the wise decisions of the Coast arbitrator, Dean Wayne Morse of the University of Oregon Law School (now a member of the National War Labor Board).

A new phase in Pacific Coast relations emerged in November 1940 with the signing of a new contract, to run until September 30, 1942. Among the more significant changes were: creation of a coast-wide labor relations committee to act as a court of appeals from decisions of present port committees; appointment of "arbitrator's agents" in each port; and provisions for semiannual review of wages and for the introduction of laborsaving devices, including lift boards, with the understanding that the union may ask for a wage review whenever it feels that these methods are injuring the earnings of the men.

Perhaps the most outstanding achievement of the ILWU has been stabilizing employment in what was formerly a highly irregular labor market. Employment has been "decasualized" by dividing work equally among a limited regular labor force and distributing extra work in peak periods to so-called "permit" men.

64. The Shipowners Association of the Pacific Coast, representing companies concerned only with coastwise trade, sits in on the negotiations and signs the agreement also.

Port Agreements on Atlantic and Gulf Coasts

The Atlantic and Gulf agreements between the International Longshoremen's Association and associations or informal groups of employers are usually confined to single ports. Nevertheless, basic pay and hours are practically uniform for all longshore workers north of Hampton Roads, Virginia, with the New York City agreement as the model. South of Hampton Roads labor standards vary from port to port and are inferior to North Atlantic ones. While the union has firm control over the job in all ports, no effort, such as on the West Coast, has been made to regularize and stabilize employment opportunities for the individual gang or worker. There is more harmony between employer groups and the ILA, strife is less common than on the Pacific Coast, and arbitration is rarely needed.

Union Membership

In 1940 the International Longshoremen's Association reported 62,100 members in 45 locals, covering all types of longshoremen, dock and harbor workers, inland boatmen, fishermen and some licensed and unlicensed seamen. Its rival, the International Longshoremen's and Warehousemen's Union, reported for 1939 a membership of 32,000, also covering longshoremen and allied workers. Together the two unions account for over 95 per cent of the men engaged in longshore work proper (loading and unloading vessels) in salt-water ports. Organization in warehouses and other allied longshore trades is less complete and cannot be accurately estimated.

8. MERCANTILE ESTABLISHMENTS

The U. S. Census of Business in 1939 reported some 200,500 wholesale establishments and 1.5 million retail stores (exclusive of eating and drinking places and service garages). Net sales of the former were $55.2 billion; the latter's were $38.5 billion. Wholesalers employed nearly 1.6 million full- and part-time workers, retailers almost 4.0 million.

Until recently unionism was negligible in this great industry. The Retail Clerks International Protective Association had a voting strength of only 10,000 members at the AF of L conventions of the 1920's, and in 1933 of only 5,000. Beginning in 1935, however, unionism and collective bargaining increased, partly because of continued low wages, no overtime payments and other grievances; partly because union activity was a trend of the times; and partly because of a rival union, the United Retail and Wholesale Employees Association, which affiliated with the CIO in May 1937. Competing unionism had a stimulating influence on organizational activities, but it was not an unmixed blessing, for it led to frequent rival picketing and scabbing, which imposed hardships upon innocent employers and alienated public opinion.

AF of L and CIO Agreements

By the 1940 AF of L convention, the Protective Association could claim 73,700 dues-paying members. At Tacoma, Washington, where leading stores formed an association to deal with the union, a combination strike and lockout was waged in five department and four variety stores during the summer of 1937. This resulted in a contract which fixed wages, hours and overtime payments and set up grievance machinery. The contract covered all types of employees working in the stores (clerks, maintenance workers, janitors, etc.) and was negotiated with several AF of L unions. During 1938 and 1939, important agreements were also signed with the American Stores (a chain with outlets in Philadelphia, Baltimore and Washington, D. C.), the Safeway Stores (one of the largest grocery chains), and the Great Atlantic and Pacific Tea Company for its stores in Milwaukee, Wisconsin and Georgia.[65] In San Francisco the union deals with the Retailers' Council, made up of 43 department and large variety stores. A fifty-five-day strike, which started in the fall of 1938 and was ended by arbitration, won sole collective bargaining rights for the union.[66]

The gains of the CIO affiliate have also been substantial, although in a more restricted area. In New York City the United Retail and Wholesale Employees Association signed its first major agreement in December 1938 with Bloomingdale's department store, covering 3,000 employees. Subsequently, contracts were signed with Macy's, the world's largest department store, covering 2,700 nonselling employees; with Gimbel's; with Cushman Sons, Inc., the largest retail bakery chain in the metropolitan area, operating some 200 outlets; and with a chain of luncheonettes and drug stores. Outside of New York, the United has made most of its progress in Philadelphia, Pittsburgh and other Pennsylvania cities. At the end of 1939 it claimed 70,000 members, of whom 80 per cent were covered by closed- or preferential-shop agreements.[67]

The growth of unionism among retail employees has stimulated employers to organize for collective bargaining and to hire trained labor relations experts. In Pittsburgh, for example, the labor standards committee of the employers, with a permanent secretary as a staff adviser, takes part in the negotiation of both single- and group-store agreements. Contracts have been negotiated by both the United and the Protective Associations, as well as by more than a dozen other AF of L craft organi-

---

65. *Retail Clerks International Advocate*, July-August 1938, pp. 1-7; March-April 1939, p. 12.
66. American Retail Federation, *San Francisco Retail Strike*, January 20, 1939.
67. Questionnaire answered by the union.

zations representing truck drivers, maintenance men, etc. Grievances that cannot be settled within the store are turned over to a joint committee for settlement. The one-store agreements usually stipulate that the same terms will be granted as are given to competitors.

9. METAL MINING, SMELTING AND FABRICATION

Mining, smelting, refining and fabricating of metals is one of the country's major industry groups. Value of the raw metal alone (exclusive of pig iron) reached about $1.5 billion in 1937. The industry is dominated by giant corporations with branches covering every phase from extraction of ore from the earth to ultimate conversion into finished manufactured products. In the important copper division, for example, three companies, Anaconda Copper, Kennecott Copper and Phelps-Dodge, control about 75 per cent of the mining and smelting capacity. Together with the American Smelting and Refining Company, the "Big Three" produce, in addition, more than 50 per cent of fabricated copper and brass articles, in spite of intense competition from 150 smaller concerns.

Yet because of high mechanization, the metal mining and smelting industry employed only 107,000 men in the peak year, 1929, and only about 75,000 in 1935, of whom a quarter worked with iron ore and the remainder with the nonferrous metals, chiefly copper, lead, zinc and aluminum. In the fabricating field, more than 225,000 worked in the nonferrous plants alone.

a. METAL MINING AND NONFERROUS FABRICATION (EXCLUDING ALUMINUM)

The International Union of Mine, Mill and Smelter Workers, a charter member of the CIO, is a descendant of the Western Federation of Miners, which for nearly two decades after its origin in 1893 had a tempestuous history in the Rocky Mountain gold, copper and silver regions. The Western Federation joined the AF of L in 1911 through the influence of the United Mine Workers, and took its present name in 1916. Internal friction and the loss of bargaining rights at the Anaconda Company's Butte mines brought disintegration between 1914 and 1919. In 1933 its membership was only 1,500 in 7 locals.

The National Industrial Recovery Act, however, revived the organization. A five-month strike in 1934 at the Anaconda mines and smelters ended with a written agreement, the closed shop, regulated wages, hours and working conditions, and a procedure for settling grievances. By the 1934 convention, 15,000 members were reported in 96 locals.[68]

68. International Union of Mine, Mill and Smelter Workers, *Official Proceedings*, 1934, p. 23.

BRIEF REVIEW OF OTHER INDUSTRIES 943

Although the Mine, Mill and Smelter Workers' union claims all workers in and around the metal mines, craft unions have had members in a number of localities for many years. During the Anaconda strike, the Building and Metal Trades Departments of the AF of L negotiated contracts with the company for 14 of the skilled crafts covering about 600 of the 5,300 workers.[69] The jurisdictional conflict has been accentuated since the AF of L–CIO split, and the Federation has also tried to organize noncraft workers into federal unions.

An estimated 25 to 35 per cent of metal mining, smelting and nonferrous fabrication in 1939 was covered by either CIO or AF of L collective agreements.[70] At its annual convention in August 1940, the CIO union reported that its 153 contracts covered about 70,000. Of these, some 60,000 were in the basic metal mining and refining industry, representing between 75 and 80 per cent of the potential coverage. This aggressive union has paralleled the far-flung activities of the giant concerns with which it deals and has negotiated agreements not only in mining and smelting but also in metal fabrication, quarrying, cement, clay and tunneling.

Iron workers in Tennessee and Alabama, brass workers in Connecticut, bronze workers in New Jersey and zinc workers in Illinois have been organized. An agreement with the Utah copper producers covers all but one mining company in that state. For the first time in four decades a Coeur d'Alene, Idaho operator has accepted collective bargaining. And in June 1940 the first written contract in Arizona mining history was signed. In addition to these CIO agreements, there are a number of AF of L craft and federal local agreements, notably in the Tri-State (Kansas, Missouri and Oklahoma) lead region. In 1940 the AF of L reported 5,000 dues-paying members represented by locals affiliated with the Fabricated Metal Council. Some major companies, including Phelps-Dodge, have refused to accept either union, while others, including American Smelting, agreed to sign only for individual plants.

Nature of Contracts

The contracts vary, particularly between the various branches of the industry. In the mines, the closed shop is quite common, and wages are generally based on the price of the metal mined. Thus at Anaconda the basic wage in 1934 was set at $4.25 a day (in 1939 it was increased to $5.25) whenever the price of electrolytic copper quoted in the standard trade journal was below 9 cents a pound. When the price exceeded 9.75 cents for thirty consecutive days, miners' basic wages were to be increased 50 cents a day. Additional increases of 25 cents a day were allowed for

69. See AF of L, *Proceedings*, 1935, pp. 615-665.
70. Letter from the Research Director of the IUMM&SW, July 24, 1939.

each 1.5 cent rise in the copper price. Decreases were on the same basis. In manufacturing establishments, the union generally has sole collective bargaining rights. In contrast with coal, layoffs and rehiring in accordance with seniority are in force in all sections of the industry.

b. ALUMINUM

American bauxite mines (producing aluminum ore) have only about 500 workers, but some 30,000 are employed in the manufacture of primary aluminum (the raw refined metal produced from bauxite) and finished aluminum products. One company, the Aluminum Company of America, until 1941 produced all the primary aluminum, more than 90 per cent of aluminum sheet, and almost 100 per cent of such structural items as wire, cable and tubing made from aluminum, as well as large proportions of kitchen and household ware. Prior to the defense boom, it had two refining plants, four smelting plants, and fourteen fabricating plants in the United States, employing more than 18,000 hourly rated workers.[71] The relatively large amount of secondary or reclaimed aluminum, as well as a smaller import supply of aluminum, prevented a completely monopolistic situation in the fabricating division. The 1937 Census reported 153 fabricating establishments employing some 24,000 wage earners. In 1941, as a result of defense requirements and government stimulus, the Aluminum Company greatly increased its smelting and refining capacity and at least one other company was preparing to manufacture primary aluminum.

History of Organization

Until the organization in 1933 of a number of AF of L federal locals, unionism was an insignificant factor in the aluminum industry. In 1934 the locals were united into a National Council of Aluminum Workers. The Aluminum Company's reluctance to engage in collective bargaining precipitated in 1936 a month-long strike in six plants, with eventual union recognition. On December 3, 1936, the company entered into its first agreement with the National Council for the six plants.

In April 1937, a number of locals left the AF of L, formed the Aluminum Workers of America and joined the CIO. The AF of L responded with an intensive organizing campaign throughout the industry and the situation was further complicated by independent unions which appeared in several plants. At the large Alcoa works in Tennessee, for example, four NLRB elections were held during 1938 and 1939 before the CIO organization was finally designated as the exclusive bargaining agent. In November 1939, the company signed a contract covering about 14,000 workers in five of its divisions with the Aluminum Workers of America

71. See *United States of America* v. *Aluminum Co. of America, et al.*, 19 Fed. Supp. 374 (1937).

and the National Association of Die Casting Workers, another CIO affiliate. The first-named CIO union claimed 31,000 members, of which a portion were not in the aluminum industry proper.

In the spring of 1941 the die casters' union won an NLRB election giving it the right to represent the 5,500 hourly production workers of Alcoa's five Cleveland plants. But no agreement was reached until some six weeks later, after the union had called a strike while negotiations on its demands for wage increases were in process before the National Defense Mediation Board. On June 10, the day after the strike started, company and union officials agreed on a compromise settlement proposed by the Mediation Board, and this was ratified locally the next day. Wages were increased, but less than the union had demanded. The contract was to be the same as CIO contracts in other Alcoa plants.

A few plants, like those of the Bohn Aluminum and Brass Company in Detroit with their more than 3,000 workers, have been organized and brought under contract by the CIO United Automobile Workers.

The AF of L has maintained control of the important Massena, New York and East St. Louis, Illinois works of the Aluminum Company, covering some 3,500 workers. In addition, its federal locals have contracts with four plants of the Reynolds Metal Company, the Wisconsin Aluminum Company and a few other concerns. It was reported at the 1940 AF of L convention that 25 locals were affiliated with the Aluminum Workers Council, representing a dues-paying membership of about 6,000.

10. Office Work

Office and professional workers, even in plants in which production employees are unionized, have not usually engaged in collective bargaining. Federal locals of stenographers, typists, bookkeepers and assistants were chartered by the AF of L as early as 1910, but their small membership was limited largely to the offices of trade unions and organizations sympathetic with the labor movement. The great wave of unionism throughout the country during the early years of the New Deal, together with extensive unemployment and depressed wages, led to a partial breakdown in the antiunion attitude of this section of the salaried white-collar class. In June 1937 delegates representing 8,600 workers organized the United Office and Professional Workers of America and joined the CIO.[72]

The CIO affiliate has grown considerably since its formation, particularly in the New York City area, where it claims almost 500 agreements. One contract with the New York Credit Clearing House, the second largest organization of its kind in the United States, covers several hundred workers and grants the closed shop. Most of the agreements,

72. *The Ledger*, June 1937.

which feature paid vacation and sick leave clauses, cover either small offices or social service agencies. Such agencies as the New York Federation for the Support of Jewish Philanthropic Societies, the Brooklyn Bureau of Charities and the Chicago Relief Administration have been unionized.[73] By the fall of 1937, 15 contracts had also been negotiated in the book and magazine publishing business.[74]

The union has also made some headway among insurance agents. Its most important agreement was with the John Hancock Mutual Life Insurance Company, covering more than a thousand industrial insurance agents in the New York metropolitan area. Although it has won an election conducted by the New York State Labor Relations Board at the offices of the important Metropolitan Life Insurance Company, it has, to date, failed to win a contract.

At the end of 1939, the United Office and Professional Workers claimed 46,600 members. In 1937 the AF of L formed an Office Employees International Council and reported at subsequent conventions 68 locals established in 1938 and 39 more in 1939, but the total membership was small. In some factories the office workers are also organized into independent unions. However, unionism still plays only a small part in a field which contains a potential membership of several million.

11. Petroleum Production

In capital investment, the petroleum industry ranks below only agriculture, railroads and public utilities. Value of petroleum refined in 1937 was $2.5 billion. Twenty large, highly integrated companies, with establishments in every branch from oil drilling to gasoline filling stations, produced about 53 per cent of the crude oil, controlled 72 per cent of the crude oil pipe-line mileage, owned 85 per cent of the daily oil-cracking capacity, and sold more than 80 per cent of the gasoline.[75] The industry employs close to 1.0 million workers—121,000 in drilling and oil production, 9,000 in natural gasoline plants, 27,000 in the petroleum pipe-lines division, 12,000 in marine transport, 83,000 in refining plants, and 710,000 in marketing.[76]

Labor Organization and Agreements

Except for a short while during and immediately after the World War,

73. "Collective Bargaining in Social Work," Social Service Division, United Office and Professional Workers, New York, 1938 (pamphlet).
74. *The Ledger,* January 1938.
75. *Hearings Before the Temporary National Economic Committee,* Pt. 14, "Petroleum Industry," September 25-30, 1939, p. 7104.
76. *Petroleum Facts and Figures, 1939,* American Petroleum Institute, New York, p. 146.

collective bargaining with outside unions found no place in the major sections of this gigantic industry until recently. In 1932 the membership of the International Oil Field, Gas Well, and Refinery Workers of America (chartered by the AF of L in 1918, but since 1935 a member of the CIO) had fallen from its postwar peak of 35,000[77] to the insignificant figure of 400. On the other hand, company unions were common, the first one having been formed in the Bayonne plant of the Standard Oil Company of New Jersey in 1916. The U. S. Bureau of Labor Statistics reported in 1935 that of 54 petroleum refineries employing 32,450 workers, 17 dealt with 22,000 employees through company unions, 23 dealt with 1,460 employees individually, 8 dealt with 4,770 employees through both company unions and trade unions, and only 6 dealt with some or all of their 4,220 employees through trade unions alone.[78]

As in other industries, the NRA gave impetus to union recovery, but company opposition resulted in so many disputes that the Petroleum Labor Policy Board—similar in function to the Steel, Auto and Textile Labor Boards—was set up during the Code period. An outstanding gain in collective bargaining was a national agreement in May 1934 between the oil workers' union and several metal trades unions and the Sinclair companies. It covered workers in the producing, refining and marketing divisions, and granted vacations with pay, time and a half for overtime, a wage increase, seniority in layoffs and rehiring, and the checkoff of dues when authorized by the individual worker. Other large companies have since made agreements for single plants or for an entire district, but they have refused to sign on a national basis.[79]

In February 1937 the union, which subsequently changed its name to the Oil Workers International Union, held agreements with 72 companies, including Sinclair, 6 plants of the Cities Service Corporation, 7 of the Texas Company, 2 Standard Oil subsidiaries, 3 Pure Oil plants and 5 Shell Oil plants. Some 75,000 workers were under these agreements.[80] On March 1, 1939, an agreement covering about 3,500 production and refinery workers was signed with the Shell Oil Company in California. Significant clauses provided for a joint labor committee to supervise rotation of shifts, and an impartial umpire to settle disputes which the parties at interest could not adjust.

Even before the AF of L–CIO split, craft internationals of the Federation disputed the industrial union's jurisdiction and organized workers in some oil fields and refineries. This jurisdictional conflict increased after the schism. The Wood River refinery of the Shell Oil Company, for

77. AF of L, *Proceedings,* 1920, p. 224.
78. "Characteristics of Company Unions, 1935," *Bulletin No. 634,* 1938.
79. *Monthly Labor Review,* February 1937, pp. 419-425.
80. *Ibid.*

example, is covered by an agreement with the Metal Trades Department and 13 international unions of the AF of L. In Michigan the International Union of Operating Engineers was seeking in 1941 to organize all oil production workers. In addition, gasoline filling station workers have been organized in some localities by federal labor locals and in other places by the Teamsters' union since the 1920's.

Independent unions also continue to play important roles. At the hearings on the Petroleum Industry before the Temporary National Economic Committee it was reported that 53 per cent of the employees in the 128 refineries of the industry in 1939 were covered by agreements with independent unions. Most of these independents arose during 1937 and were chiefly reorganizations of former employee representation plans.[81] A number of them have been challenged as company-dominated before the NLRB.

12. PUBLIC UTILITIES, OTHER THAN RAILROADS

a. TRANSPORTATION

(1). *Trucking*

Since the World War, motor trucking has taken an increasingly important place in the vast distribution network of the United States. In 1920, the country had about a million registered trucks; in 1939 it had over 4 million.[82] The estimated 3.7 million nonfarm truckers[83] are in two general categories: those employed directly by manufacturing and service establishments and those employed by general local and intercity draying and trucking firms. Counting only fleets of eight or more, some 1,200 public utilities and railroads in 1938 operated 74,000 trucks; 1,600 bakery, confectionery and florist establishments had 62,000; 1,800 dairy firms operated 63,000; 1,300 oil and gas companies operated 92,000; 3,000 builders and contractors operated 49,000; and 5,400 express and hauling companies operated 162,000.[84]

The specialized over-the-road hauling companies have generally been highly competitive and of limited size. A trend toward concentration, however, was revealed in July 1940 with tne request before the Interstate Commerce Commission by the Transport Company of New York for permission to acquire control of 48 other trucking concerns and to recapitalize at $25 million. This request was not approved. Had it been, the organization, the first to be supported by a Wall Street firm, would

---

81. Pt. 16, Sec. 3, October 9-13, 16, 1939, pp. 9005, 9009-9012.
82. *Commercial Car Journal*, Philadelphia, April 1940, p. 24.
83. *Automobile Facts and Figures, 1940*, Automobile Manufacturers Association, Detroit, p. 37.
84. *Ibid.*, 1939, p. 71.

have been the largest trucker in the country, with about 14,000 trucks, and in territory covered would have rivalled some major railroads.[85] In 1941 the group renewed its efforts to get ICC approval.

Union Organization and Agreements

In common with virtually all other unions, the International Brotherhood of Teamsters, Chauffeurs, Warehousemen and Helpers of America lost members during the 1920's and early 1930's. In 1933 total enrollment was only about 70,000,[86] but in the following years an extensive organizational campaign was launched. By 1940 it was the largest union in the AF of L, with 390,000 members in more than 1,800 locals. Locals, both of general truckers and of drivers attached to specific industries, are chartered, but whenever membership in a single industry is small, a mixed local of drivers in several trades is formed. Contracts are customarily on a trade basis, but generally require approval of the Joint Teamsters Council, a delegate body for a given community. In some manufacturing industries, such as brewing, the production union has represented many of the truck drivers, but the powerful Brotherhood of Teamsters has frequently been granted a free hand. Apart from general trucking, its greatest success has been gained in local milk, bread and coal distribution.

For many years the Teamsters' union has dealt with such local employer groups as the Chicago Cartage Association, the Draymen's Association of New York, the Master Truckmen of Boston and vicinity, and the Truckmen's Bureau of New York City. When trucking areas grew wider, the union signed with state truckmen's groups like the Illinois Motor Truck Owners' Association. More recently collective bargaining has been extended to a regional basis to eliminate wage differentials between operators who compete in the same area but have their headquarters in different states. Because they are strongly organized in the large cities, the teamster locals have won control of intercity or over-the-road trucking with little difficulty. Realizing the growing importance of labor relations in their industry, the American Trucking Association, made up of local, state and regional trucking associations, appointed its first labor relations committee in 1938.

One of the first regional agreements was in 1936 between joint councils of the Teamsters' union and the Pacific Northwest Rate Coordinating Bureau, representing truck lines in Oregon, Washington, Idaho and Montana. In the fall of 1937, the union announced an interstate picketing campaign in several states to bring additional over-the-road truck drivers

---

85. *Transport Topics,* American Trading Association, Inc., Washington, July 22, 1940.

86. Daniel Tobin, "The International Brotherhood of Teamsters," *Labor Information Bulletin,* January 1939.

into the organization. Partly as a result of this campaign and partly because employers wished to rid themselves of local interference, an eleven-state agreement covering 2,000 firms and 175 locals was signed in August 1938 with motor freight operators in the Midwest.[87] The agreement, which was renewed in 1940, granted the preferential union shop, limited the drivers' work week to sixty hours, provided for a joint area committee to adjust disputes, and forbade employers to order workers to pass through strike picket lines. In the spring of 1939, the New England Truckers Association, comprising truckmen in Connecticut, Rhode Island and Massachusetts, signed with the union after a month's strike.

(2). *Street Railway and Bus Transportation*

Urban

Municipal public transportation in the United States is furnished largely by about 475 electric railway companies, 36 trolley bus companies, and over 700 motorbus lines, mostly controlled by street railway groups. In 1937 approximately 130,000 wage earners were employed in the electric railway division and about 33,000 more in motor and trolley bus transportation. Slightly more than half of these workers were conductors, motormen and drivers, while the remainder were chiefly ticket agents and maintenance men. Like all public utilities, the municipal transportation industry is closely regulated and the scope of collective bargaining is correspondingly limited. Where municipal ownership prevails, limitations are even greater.

The Amalgamated Association of Street, Electric Railway and Motor Coach Employees of America, founded in 1892, until recently was the only labor union in the field. Just after the World War its membership was over 100,000, but company unions in several large cities, notably Philadelphia, New York and Buffalo, and the depression of 1929–1933 caused a fall to 65,400 in 1932. Under the initiative of business recovery and New Deal legislation, the membership rose to 73,400 in 1935.[88] During the next two years the union reported 84 new locals, with some 24,000 new members, largely, however, in the interstate motorbus field. The voting strength of the organization at the 1940 AF of L convention was based on 80,000 members.

Amalgamated membership would have been much larger in 1940 had it not lost its New York City jurisdiction to the Transport Workers

---

87. The territory covered was Michigan, Ohio, Indiana, Illinois, Wisconsin, Minnesota, Iowa, Missouri, North Dakota, South Dakota, Nebraska, Kansas City, Kansas, and the south bank of the Ohio River between Portsmouth, Ohio and Paducah, Kentucky.

88. Emerson P. Schmidt, *Industrial Relations in Urban Transportation*, University of Minnesota Press, Minneapolis, 1937, p. 157.

Union of America. This CIO affiliate was formed in 1937 by rebellious members of the Amalgamated, the Machinists' and the Teamsters' unions, with a program of organizing all passenger transportation except steam railroads. In a series of powerful drives during 1937, the Transport Workers compelled the two largest companies, the Interborough Rapid Transit Company and the Brooklyn-Manhattan Transportation Company, to sign agreements. The Fifth Avenue Coach Company, the New York City Omnibus Corporation, the Comprehensive Omnibus Corporation and East Side Omnibus Corporation quickly followed suit.

About 38,000 subway, elevated, trolley and bus employees were covered by contracts which provided for the closed shop, hour reductions, wage increases, seniority in time of layoffs, vacations with pay and machinery for the settlement of grievances. Only the Independent Subway System, controlled by the city, remained unorganized. When in the spring of 1940 the city took over all of the subways and elevated railways, the old contracts were continued, although strife was near when the mayor asserted that the 27,000 workers of the IRT and the BMT would become civil service employees with no right to strike and no closed shop.

Trouble arose again the following year from the refusal of the mayor and the Board of Transportation to negotiate new contracts. The city and the Board had brought a declaratory judgment suit to determine whether the latter had the power to bargain collectively. On June 26, a few days before the old contracts were to expire, the Transport Workers voted to strike unless the Board agreed to begin negotiations for a new contract. The issue was temporarily settled by an agreement to continue the old contracts until the courts handed down a decision.

Outside of New York, except for Akron, Ohio and a few other cities, the Transport Workers Union has not broken the hold of either the Amalgamated or the few remaining employee representation plans. The Transport Workers claimed a 1939 membership of 95,000. A segment of these, however, were taxicab drivers and mechanics in New York and other cities as far-flung as Honolulu and Ketchikan, Alaska. Agreements were won with most major New York City taxi companies in 1937 and 1938 but were lost in 1940 after a strike against two of the larger concerns, despite union victory in elections conducted by the State Labor Relations Board.[89]

Intercity

Beginning in 1934, the Brotherhood of Railroad Trainmen, the Brotherhood of Locomotive Firemen and Enginemen, and the Amalgamated Association of Street, Electric Railway and Motor Coach Employees all sought to organize the intercity or over-the-road bus transportation field.

89. *The New York Times*, May 29, 1940.

Only the Amalgamated has had any notable success. This industry is dominated by a few concerns (largely controlled by the railroads), although throughout the country there are about 3,000 companies. A census in 1939 showed about 52,000 revenue-operating busses,[90] of which over a third were estimated to be in the intercity and interstate business. About 60 per cent of these busses are now covered by union agreements.

By 1937 the Amalgamated had contracts with the Interstate Transit Lines and the Union Pacific, both subsidiaries of the Union Pacific Railroad, as well as with the Washington Motor Coach System. These covered nearly all bus employees in the Northwest. Agreements have also been negotiated with the Northland Greyhound System, operating from Chicago to Butte, Montana; the Atlantic Greyhound Lines operating in West Virginia; the Central Greyhound Lines operating in sixteen midwestern states; the Illinois, New England and Pennsylvania Greyhound Lines; and several of the smaller bus companies. The Greyhound agreements grant sole collective bargaining rights, regulate length of runs, wages and hours, and provide for seniority in layoffs. One clause establishes a monthly guarantee of $100 to any extra operators who are available, i.e., promptly accessible by telephone, for service twenty-six days in any calendar month.

b. COMMUNICATIONS

(1). *Telephone*

Telephones are the third largest public utility industry in the country (after electric power and transportation) in terms of capital investment. The Bell System, an affiliate of the American Telephone and Telegraph Company, operates more than 80 per cent of the telephones in the United States, has an annual gross revenue of more than $1.0 billion, and estimates its plant investment at $4.5 billion. There are about 6,500 independent companies (mostly rural) in the industry, but the largest operates only slightly more than 500,000 telephones as compared to Bell's almost 20 million, and the total employment in all is approximately 85,000 as compared to Bell's 257,000. Because of the large amount of direct service and a liberal wage policy, labor costs are about 45 per cent of gross revenues.[91]

Before and during the World War, the International Brotherhood of Electrical Workers had a substantial organization among operators, linesmen, maintenance men and other skilled craftsmen in the industry. Unsuccessful strikes and internal union conflicts, however, led to disintegration. On the Pacific Coast, for example, defeat in a system-wide strike

90. *Automobile Facts and Figures, 1940*, p. 47.
91. "Telephone and Telegraph, Basic Survey, Part 1," *Standard Trades and Securities*, February 2, 1940.

in 1919 resulted in an "independent" organization of toll maintenance men.[92] A New England group of Bell employees withdrew in 1920 from the IBEW in a jurisdictional dispute and formed a separate organization.[93] Three years later an IBEW strike of telephone operators in New England failed.[94]

Employee representation plans and "independent" unions became the dominant form of organization in the industry. A Bureau of Labor Statistics study in 1935 revealed that of some 300,000 workers (about 90 per cent of the telephone and telegraph industry at that time) covered by replies, 78.5 per cent were in company unions. Only three telephone companies, employing 16.2 per cent of the workers, reported dealing with both trade unions and employee representation plans.[95]

Organization in the industry is generally regional and by departments, e.g., maintenance men and telephone operators. In 1939 most groups unaffiliated with the recognized trade-union movement and representing about 100,000 workers were linked into the National Federation of Telephone Workers. Agreements are held with a large proportion of the Bell subsidiaries. In July 1940 the New York Telephone Company, after more than eight months of negotiations, announced its first labor agreement with 4 locals comprising some 10,000 installation men, construction workers and repair men who belonged to the United Telephone Organization, an affiliate of the National Federation.[96] The IBEW, however, still controls telephone wiring in construction projects in large metropolitan areas.

Until the Supreme Court decision of 1937 upholding the National Labor Relations Act, the Western Electric Company, subsidiary of American Telephone and Telegraph and sole producer of equipment for them—as well as for many of the small independents—had an employee representation plan. Since then the Company has dealt with six unions: one for each of its four manufacturing plants, one for its entire sales force, and one for all the installation workers. These six organizations are joined together in a National Committee of Communication Equipment Workers for company-wide bargaining on such matters as vacations and overtime. All but one are affiliated with the National Federation of Telephone Workers.

(2). *Telegraph*

Unlike the telephone, the $500 million telegraph industry seems to have passed its peak, and is meeting considerable competition from the long distance telephone, the Bell System teletype, and the United States air mail. The gross operating revenue of its major corporation was only $92 million in 1938 as compared to $146 million in 1929. The Western Union Telegraph Company, which does about 76 per cent of the business, and the Postal Telegraph Cable Company, which does about 21 per cent, dominate the industry. In 1938, they employed nearly 73,000 of the 77,000 nonrailroad telegraph workers. The Federal Communications Com-

92. NLRB, Cases No. R-1691 and R-1692, decided April 27, 1940.
93. "Handbook of American Trade Unions," p. 283.
94. *The American Labor Year Book, 1923–24*, Rand School of Social Science, New York, 1924, p. 111.
95. "Characteristics of Company Unions, 1935," *Bulletin No. 634*, p. 57.
96. *Chicago Tribune*, July 20, 1940, p. 20.

mission recommended a merger of the two systems in 1939 but the labor unions strongly protested because jobs would be lost. Labor costs form 60 to 65 per cent of the industry's gross operating revenue.[97]

As in the telephone industry, employee representation plans have flourished in the telegraph field, although organizations affiliated with the AF of L and the CIO have recently made considerable inroads. In November 1939 the National Labor Relations Board ordered Western Union to disestablish its twenty-one year old company union—an order which was subsequently upheld by the Second Circuit Court of Appeals, on August 9, 1940.

The Order of Railroad Telegraphers, a member of the AF of L since 1909, has gained almost complete control over telegraphy work on the railroads. In 1939 only 12 of the 148 Class I carriers were not covered by its agreements.[98] Its voting strength at the 1940 AF of L convention was based on 35,000 dues-paying members. The Commercial Telegraphers' Union of North America, the AF of L unit with jurisdiction over all telegraphers outside of the railroads, has had less success. Its 1940 membership was only 3,500. It had agreements with the Associated Press, United Press and International News Service, as well as a local agreement with Western Union, covering some 800 employees in Washington, D. C.[99] In 1940, in an effort to win control over Western Union offices, the AF of L entered into a joint campaign with the Commercial Telegraphers' Union. At the annual convention in November 1940, the AF of L reported the organization of 30 or more federal locals, while other workers were directly joining the Commercial Telegraphers' Union. Currently, a series of NLRB elections are being conducted to determine whether the AF of L or its CIO rival shall dominate the telegraph industry.

The young CIO American Communications Association gained a firm foothold in the telegraph industry by winning a nation-wide election in January 1939 in the offices of the Postal Telegraph Company and subsequently securing a company-wide agreement covering 13,000 of the company's 14,500 workers in 44 states.[100] In addition, it holds agreements with the Mackay Radio Company, covering about 450 workers, the Globe Wireless Company and RCA Communications, Inc. The Association, as well as its AF of L opponent, has waged a vigorous campaign to win Western Union. In February 1939 it reported a membership of about 17,000, including 1,500 in the marine division.[101]

97. "Telephone and Telegraph, Basic Survey, Part 1."
98. National Mediation Board, *Fifth Annual Report*, June 30, 1939, p. 27.
99. *The New York Times*, November 8, 1939.
100. *PM*, September 13, 1940, p. 12.
101. American Communications Association, *Minutes of Fourth Convention*, 1938, pp. 5-6; *RCA News*, March 18, 1939.

C. ELECTRIC LIGHT AND POWER

The electric light and power industry with its $2.2 billion investment in 1938 represented one of the major industries in the country. The revenue from electric service in 1937 was $2.4 billion, yet the total number of employees on June 30, 1937 in some 1,800 generating establishments and 1,700 distributing plants was only 281,000. Most of the labor force is composed of essential workers, clerical and maintenance help and meter readers, so that there is little opportunity for curtailing total pay rolls, even in slack periods.

Collective bargaining in the industry was practically nonexistent in the 1920's, although the International Brotherhood of Electrical Workers had a few contracts covering outside linesmen and some inside workers. With the enactment of the NRA the Brotherhood began an intensive organizing campaign in the utility field. In recent years the CIO has attempted to compete with the AF of L, first through its affiliate, the United Electrical, Radio and Machine Workers union, and then by a separate Utility Workers Organizing Committee; but in general, the IBEW has maintained the upper hand.

In addition to verbal arrangements with municipal, state and federal utility systems (such as the Tennessee Valley Project and the Bonneville Project), the Brotherhood held agreements with 82 utility companies in 28 states in March 1939. Later it announced the negotiation during April 1939 of 20 new agreements with utility companies in New York and Massachusetts, covering 10,000 workers. It claimed during 1939 a membership of 65,000 in utilities, the bulk of whom were covered by agreements. In 1940 the IBEW defeated the CIO in a run-off election held by the NLRB and thereby won a contract with the important Consumers Power Company of Michigan.

In 1937 the Brotherhood had signed an agreement with the large Consolidated Edison Company of New York covering about 30,000 workers. Charges of collusion and unfair labor practices against the company by the CIO led to an NLRB order to cancel the agreement, but the U. S. Supreme Court disallowed the Board's decision. In a 1940 election, however, a large body of the workers at the Consolidated plant repudiated the Brotherhood, rejected the CIO, and formed an independent union.

13. TEXTILES

Textile and related industries are one of the major sources of employment in the United States. Even excluding establishments engaged in the manufacture of wearing apparel (discussed in two of the special studies in this volume), they employed in 1937 more than 800,000. Cotton manufacture, with its 1,200 establishments, 435,000 workers, and products valued at $1.3 billion, is by far the most important; but also of great significance are the wool and hair manufacturing division, with 159,000 wage earners in 704 establishments and a product value of $827 million; and the rayon and silk manufacturing division (excluding hosiery), with 117,000 employed in 848 plants and a product value of $405 million.

The different branches of the textile industry vary in corporate structure, production methods, type of worker and geographic location. In general, however, the major divisions are characterized by intense competition, overcapacity and somewhat inefficient distribution methods. Only a few larger concerns have coordinated their manufacturing and selling activities; in most cases their products pass through many selling agents before reaching the consumer.[102] No single company or group dominates the industry. The eight largest producers of cotton goods accounted for only 15 per cent of the wage earners and 14 per cent of the product value in 1935. The other branches were somewhat more concentrated. The eight largest wool and hair manufacturers constituted around 30 per cent of the industry, in terms of wage earners and product value; in rayon manufacture the comparable figure was 27 per cent.[103] Perhaps the most significant economic fact has been the shift of textile mills from New England to other sections, notably the South, where costs are lower.

Progress of Unionism

Unionism has sought a foothold in textiles for many years, but until recently with limited success. The United Textile Workers of America (organized in 1901) made some gains under the NRA but a national strike of more than 300,000 cotton mill workers in September 1934 won nothing and was a severe blow to the organization. In March 1937, when it held but 25 contracts, exclusive of hosiery and dyeing, it agreed to turn over its affairs to the CIO-sponsored Textile Workers Organizing Committee.

Between March 23, 1937 and March 31, 1939, the TWOC spent $1.8 million in organization work. Although considerable progress was made in the North, it did not achieve its major aim of establishing collective bargaining in the southern cotton mills. Obstacles to organization were inability of the leaders to sell the union idea to the manufacturers, the unreceptiveness of the workers, many of whom had only recently come from farms, and AF of L opposition. In the fall of 1938 the former president of the United Textile Workers left the CIO and rejoined the Federation.[104]

102. "Textiles, Basic Survey, Part 1," *Standard Trades and Securities*, May 19, 1939.
103. National Resources Committee, *op. cit.*, p. 241.
104. *Daily News Record* (the trade paper), April 13, 14, 1939.

Greater success has been attained in other branches—silk, carpet, rayon, wool and worsted goods—particularly after the union decided to concentrate upon limited instead of widely diffused organizational objectives. Early in 1940 a contract covering 5 plants and 28,000 workers and embodying a 7 to 10 per cent wage increase was negotiated with the American Woolen Company. Other large woolen and worsted mills, employing 24,000 workers, immediately made the same concessions. The reasonable attitude of the union negotiators led a writer in the industry's trade paper, the *Daily News Record,* to observe that "the current situation has developed mutual esteem never before apparent in the relations between employer and employee, at least in the woolen textile industry, outside of company unions."[105]

The CIO union, now the Textile Workers Union of America, reported that during the last quarter of 1939 it signed 285 agreements. In all, it claimed agreements with 1,100 employers covering about 300,000 workers. Of this number, however, between 80,000 and 90,000 were in hosiery mills. An independent union in the textile center of Woonsocket, Rhode Island claimed agreements covering approximately 7,000 members. In addition, the United Textile Workers, which was reaffiliated with the AF of L, had in 1939 about 11,500 members, half of them covered by union agreements. The following year, however, it paid dues to the Federation on only 3,600.

105. December 27, 1939.

Appendix C

1941 TRADE UNION MEMBERSHIP

1. American Federation of Labor Unions [a]

Name of Organization	Membership
Actors and Artistes of America, Associated.............	14,800
Air Line Pilots Association, International..............	1,100
Asbestos Workers, International Association of Heat and Frost Insulators and.............................	4,000
Automobile Workers of America, International Union United	26,100
Bakery and Confectionery Workers' International Union of America	84,400
Barbers' International Union, Journeymen..............	49,000
Bill Posters, Billers and Distributors of United States and Canada, International Alliance of...................	3,000
Blacksmiths, Drop Forgers and Helpers, International Brotherhood of	5,000
Boiler Makers, Iron Ship Builders and Helpers of America, International Brotherhood of.....................	42,600
Bookbinders, International Brotherhood of............	21,900
Boot and Shoe Workers Union.......................	30,800
Brewery, Flour, Cereal and Soft Drink Workers of America, International Union of United................	42,000
Brick and Clay Workers of America, United...........	11,500
Bricklayers, Masons and Plasterers' International Union of America	65,000
Bridge, Structural and Ornamental Iron Workers, International Association of...........................	52,000
Broom and Whisk Makers Union, International.........	300
Building Service Employees International Union.........	70,000
Carmen of America, Brotherhood of Railway...........	65,000

a. Figures based on per capita tax payments to the AF of L for the fiscal year August 31, 1940–August 31, 1941. *Report of the Executive Council,* 1941, pp. 7, 10-11.

958

1. AMERICAN FEDERATION OF LABOR UNIONS [a] *(continued)*

Name of Organization	Membership
Carpenters and Joiners of America, United Brotherhood of	300,000
Cement, Lime and Gypsum Workers International Union, United	16,800
Cigar Makers International Union of America	8,700
Circus, Carnival, Fairs and Rodeo Workers International Union	1,100
Cleaning and Dye House Workers, International Association of	16,400
Clerks, National Federation of Post Office	40,000
Clerks, Brotherhood of Railway and Steamship	110,000
Clerks' International Protective Association, Retail	85,400
Conductors, Order of Sleeping Car	1,400
Coopers' International Union of North America	4,500
Diamond Workers Protective Union of America	400
Distillery, Rectifying and Wine Workers International Union	3,300
Draftsmen's Unions, International Federation of Technical Engineers, Architects and	2,200
Electrical Workers, International Brotherhood of	201,000
Elevator Constructors, International Union of	10,200
Engineers, International Union of Operating	80,000
Engravers Union, International Metal	300
Engravers' Union of North America, International Photo-	10,500
Fire Fighters, International Association of	37,100
Firemen and Oilers, International Brotherhood of	34,300
Garment Workers of America, United	40,000
Garment Workers' Union, International Ladies'	225,000
Glass Bottle Blowers' Association of the United States and Canada	20,000
Glass Cutters' League of America, Window	1,600
Glass Workers' Union, American Flint	20,300
Glove Workers Union of America, International	1,900
Government Employees, American Federation of	24,000

1. AMERICAN FEDERATION OF LABOR UNIONS [a] *(continued)*

Name of Organization	Membership
Granite Cutters' International Association of America....	5,000
Hatters, Cap and Millinery Workers International Union, United	32,000
Hod Carriers, Building and Common Laborers' Union of America, International	183,700
Horseshoers of the United States and Canada, International Union of Journeymen	200
Hotel and Restaurant Employees' International Alliance and Bartenders' International League of America	214,100
Jewelry Workers' Union, International	5,500
Lathers, International Union of Wood, Wire and Metal..	8,100
Laundry Workers' International Union	40,400
Leather Workers International Union, United	2,900
Letter Carriers, Federated Rural	500
Letter Carriers, National Association of	60,000
Lithographers International Protective and Beneficial Association	12,900
Longshoremen's Association, International	61,500
Machinists, International Association of	221,800
Maintenance of Way Employees, Brotherhood of	65,700
Marble, Stone and Slate Polishers, Rubbers and Sawyers, Tile and Marble Setters' Helpers and Terrazzo Helpers, International Association of	5,500
Master Mechanics and Foremen of Navy Yards and Naval Stations, National Association of	200
Masters, Mates and Pilots of America, National Organization	3,000
Meat Cutters and Butcher Workmen of North America, Amalgamated	84,900
Metal Workers' International Association, Sheet	20,000
Mine Workers of America, International Union Progressive	35,000
Molders' Union of North America, International	42,100
Musicians, American Federation of	100,000
Painters, Decorators and Paperhangers of America, Brotherhood of	104,900
Paper Makers, International Brotherhood of	25,800

1. AMERICAN FEDERATION OF LABOR UNIONS [a] *(continued)*

Name of Organization	Membership
Pattern Makers' League of North America.............	8,000
Plasterers' and Cement Finishers' International Association of the United States and Canada, Operative..........	21,200
Plumbers and Steam Fitters of the United States and Canada, United Association of Journeymen.............	45,400
Pocketbook and Novelty Workers Union, International Ladies' Handbag	10,000
Polishers, Buffers, Platers and Helpers International Union, Metal	7,000
Porters, Brotherhood of Sleeping Car................	7,200
Post Office and Railway Mail Laborers, National Association of	1,500
Potters, National Brotherhood of Operative............	16,000
Powder and High Explosive Workers of America, United	100
Printers, Die Stampers and Engravers' Union of North America, International Plate......................	1,000
Printing Pressmen and Assistants' Union of North America, International	45,700
Pulp, Sulphite and Paper Mill Workers, International Brotherhood of	44,200
Railway and Motor Coach Employees of America, Amalgamated Association of Street, Electric..............	80,700
Railway Mail Association..........................	22,700
Roofers, Damp and Waterproof Workers' Association, United Slate, Tile and Composition................	4,400
Seafarers' International Union of North America........	20,000
Sheep Shearers' Union of North America..............	600
Siderographers, International Association of...........	100
Special Delivery Messengers, National Association of....	900
Spinners Union, International......................	500
Stage Employees and Moving Picture Machine Operators of the United States and Canada, International Alliance of Theatrical	42,000
State, County and Municipal Employees, American Federation of	33,700

1. AMERICAN FEDERATION OF LABOR UNIONS [a] (continued)

Name of Organization	Membership
Stereotypers' and Electrotypers' Union, International	8,600
Stonecutters' Association of North America, Journeymen	4,100
Stove Mounters International Union	5,300
Switchmen's Union of North America	8,000
Teachers, American Federation of	26,700
Teamsters, Chauffeurs, Warehousemen and Helpers of America, International Brotherhood of	408,300
Telegraphers' Union, Commercial	4,000
Telegraphers, Order of Railroad	33,300
Textile Workers of America, United	15,200
Tobacco Workers' International Union	17,800
Upholsterers' International Union of North America	16,000
Wall Paper Craftsmen and Workers of North America, United	3,100
Weavers' Protective Association, American Wire	400
Wood Carvers' Association of North America, International	300
Local Trade and Federal Labor Unions	198,600

2. CONGRESS OF INDUSTRIAL ORGANIZATIONS UNIONS [b]

Aluminum Workers of America	31,000 [c]
Architects, Engineers, Chemists and Technicians, Federation of	8,500
Automobile, Aircraft and Agricultural Implement Workers of America, International Union, United	600,000
Barbers and Beauty Culturists of America, National Organizing Committee of	3,500
Cannery, Agricultural, Packing and Allied Workers of America, United	102,000 [c]

b. Unless otherwise indicated, the CIO figures are the latest obtainable for 1941. They were submitted by the individual unions or taken from official union publications or from the *Preliminary Report of the Committee on Naval Affairs . . . Investigating the Naval Defense Program*, 77th Cong., 2d sess., H. Rept. 1634 (1942). The figures are not necessarily based on dues payments.

c. 1939.

1941 TRADE UNION MEMBERSHIP

2. CONGRESS OF INDUSTRIAL ORGANIZATIONS UNIONS [b] *(continued)*

Name of Organization	Membership
Clothing Workers of America, Amalgamated...........	300,000 [d]
Communications Association, American...............	20,000
Construction Workers Organizing Committee, United....	44,000
Die Casting Workers, National Association of..........	10,000 [e]
Distillery Workers Organizing Committee.............	3,000 [e]
Electrical, Radio and Machine Workers of America, United	302,000
Farm Equipment Workers Organizing Committee.......	25,000 [e]
Federal Workers of America, United..................	28,000
Fishermen and Allied Workers of America, International Union of	18,000
Fur and Leather Workers Union, International.........	75,000
Furniture Workers of America, United................	44,500
Gas, By-Products, Coke and Chemical Workers, District 50, United Mine Workers.............................	52,000 [d]
Glass, Ceramic, and Silica Sand Workers of America, Federation of	22,000
Inland Boatmen's Union of the Pacific.................	2,000
Iron, Steel and Tin Workers, Amalgamated Association of	[f]
Longshoremen's and Warehousemen's Union, International	40,000
Marine Cooks' and Stewards' Association, National......	4,000
Marine Engineers' Beneficial Association, National......	8,000
Marine and Shipbuilding Workers of America, Industrial Union of	50,000
Maritime Union of America, National.................	50,000
Mine, Mill and Smelter Workers, International Union of..	60,000
Mine Workers of America, United...................	600,000
Newspaper Guild, American.........................	17,000
Office and Professional Workers of America, United.....	30,000
Oil Workers International Union.....................	27,000 [e]

d. January 1942.
e. 1940. The Die Casting Workers' figure is from *PM*, October 6, 1940.
f. Included in figure for Steel Workers Organizing Committee.

2. Congress of Industrial Organizations Unions [b] *(continued)*

Name of Organization	Membership
Optical Workers Coordinating Committee.............	2,000 [c]
Packinghouse Workers Organizing Committee..........	80,000 [e]
Paper, Novelty and Toy Workers International Union, United	52,000
Retail, Wholesale and Department Store Employees of America, United	100,000
Rubber Workers of America, United..................	75,000
Shoe Workers of America, United....................	30,000
State, County and Municipal Workers of America.......	56,000
Steel Workers Organizing Committee.................	600,000
Stone and Allied Products Workers of America, United..	3,600
Textile Workers Union of America...................	450,000
Transport Workers Union of America.................	95,000
Utility Workers Organizing Committee...............	6,000 [c]
Woodworkers of America, International..............	65,000
Local Industrial Unions............................	65,000 [c]

3. Unaffiliated Nationals and Internationals [g]

Conductors of America, Order of Railway.............	35,500
Engineers, Brotherhood of Locomotive................	61,500
Federal Employees, National Federation of............	70,000
Firemen and Enginemen, Brotherhood of Locomotive....	95,600
Letter Carriers' Association, National Rural...........	32,300 [e]
Marine Firemen, Oilers, Watertenders and Wipers' Association, Pacific Coast......................................	4,500
Paving Cutters' Union of the United States of America and Canada	2,000
Postmasters of the United States, National Association of..	24,300
Post Office Clerks, United National Association of.......	35,000
Postal Employees, National Alliance of................	10,200

g. Includes something less than half the total nationals and internationals unaffiliated with either the AF of L or the CIO. Figures submitted in the late summer or fall of 1941 by the unions, or taken from official union publications or from the *Preliminary Report of the Committee on Naval Affairs.*

3. Unaffiliated Nationals and Internationals [g] *(continued)*

Name of Organization	Membership
Postal Supervisors, National Association of	8,100
Railroad Signalmen of America, Brotherhood of	10,000
Railroad Trainmen, Brotherhood of	158,800
Telephone Workers, National Federation of	140,000 [d]
Train Dispatchers' Association, American	2,500 [c]
Typographical Union, International	83,500

INDEX

NOTE: In general the material is indexed under the heading of the industry to which it refers. See Industries for a listing of the principal industries covered in the survey. The unions, employers' associations, and general references are indexed separately.

ABILITY RATING PLANS, 461, 554-55
Actors, 20
Actors and Artistes of America, Associated, 958
Adamson Eight-Hour Law, 325, 888
Agreements (contracts), administration of (grievance settlement), 26-27; arbitration of, *see* Arbitration; company-wide and multiple-plant, 23-24; coverage by, 17-18, table 1, 19-22, total, 17; industry-wide, 23; local, 23; national, 23; negotiation of, 25-26; regional, 23, 24; *see also* separate industries
Agricultural machinery industry, 9, 21
Agricultural workers, 19
Air Line Pilots Association, International, 958
Aircraft, 16, 18, 930-32; agreements, coverage by, 19, 21, 930-31; strikes, North American Aviation, 626, 931; wages, 613, 913
Aircraft and Agricultural Implement Workers of America, *see* Automobile, Aircraft and Agricultural Implement Workers of America
Allied Printing Trades Councils, 139-40
Aluminum, 6, 16, 21, 944-45
Aluminum Workers, National Council of, 944, 945
Aluminum Workers of America, 944-45, 962
American Federation of Labor (AF of L), business unionism, 874, 881; vs. CIO, 9 ff., 107, 109, 134, 198-99, 267, 400, 579-87, 640-41, 745, Appendix B, *passim;* departments: 880, 900-1, Building and Construction Trades, 197, 202-3, 881, 883, 912, 943, Metal Trades, 748, 900-1, 932, 933, 943, 948, Mining, 901, Railway Employees', 333, 339, 366, 367, 901; membership, 6, Appendix C, 958-62; organizing activities, 3 ff., 9-13, 905-6, 944; rise of, 874-75; *see also* separate industries
American Rolling Mill Company, 509, 543

Anthracite, 280-317, 876, 879, 887; agreements, 294-308, *passim;* industry-wide, 280, (1923), 300, (1926), 301-2, (1930), 306, (1939 and 1941), 307-8; arbitration, under agreements, *see* grievances, following, Awards, 285, (1903), 291, Anthracite Coal Commission of 1920, 297, opposition to, by operators, 290, 291, by union, 297, 299-300, 301, 316; "bootlegging," 304; checkoff, 298, 299, 300, 306, 307, 313; checkweighmen, 288, 294, 314; closed shop, 296, 299, 300; competition, 281, 282, 287, 315, 316; employment, 302-3, 308-9; grievances, Board of Conciliation, 292, 311-14, settlement, 292, 293, 311 ff.; hours, 291, 296-300, 302-3, 307-10, 316; individual bargaining, 285-88; location, 280; negotiation, 296-97, 310-11; overtime, 296, 307; ownership, 281, 315; production, 280-82, 284, decline in, 303-5, 308, 316; seniority, 307; strikes, 305, 314, 876, 887, early, 282, 283-84, 285, 286, 288-91, 297, (1922), 298-300, 304, (1925-26), 300-2, 304; summary, 314-17; unemployment, 304, 315; union shop, 299, 300, 307-8; vacations, 307, 308; wages, in declining market (1927-41), 303-9, early settlements, 283-84, 285, 287, 289, sliding scale, 283-85, 287, 292, 294, 876, 879, trends (1902-26), 302-3, under 1903 Award, 291-95, (1920-30), 296-302; workers, 295, conditions of, 287-88; *see also* Anthracite Coal Strike Commission; Mine Workers of America, United
Anthracite Coal Commission, United States (1920), 296-98
Anthracite Coal Industry Commission, Pennsylvania, 304
Anthracite Coal Strike Commission (1903), 280, 287; Award, 291-94, 302, 310, 311 ff., 887
Anti-Trust Division, Department of Justice, 203, 225 ff.; investigations,

967

224 ff.; laws, 184, 203, 225 ff.; see *also* Sherman Anti-Trust Act
Apex Hosiery Company, 488; case, 441, 499; strike, 499
Appalachian Coals, Inc., 268
Apprenticeship, *see* separate industries
Arbitration, 26, 27, 881; *see also* separate industries
Architects, Engineers, Chemists and Technicians, Federation of, 579, 962
Asbestos Workers, International Association of Heat and Frost Insulators and, 196, 958
Associated General Contractors of America, 206
Associated Press, 954; case, 8, 112
Automobile, Aircraft and Agricultural Implement Workers of America, United (UAW-CIO), 583-630, 930-31; in aircraft, 930-31; attitudes and tactics, 589-96; demands, 599, 612; factionalism, 584-87, 626-27; Ford recognition, 587-89, 626; General Motors recognition, 592; history, 583-87; membership, 14, 16, 587, 626, 962; Wage-Hour Councils, 598
Automobile Labor Board, 581-82, 583, 591
Automobile Manufacturers Association, 599
Automobile Workers of America, Associated, 582-83
Automobile Workers of America, International Union, United (UAW-AF of L), membership, 958
Automobiles, 6, 8, 9, 12, 16, 204, 569, 571-630, 633, 683; agreements, 23, 595 ff., 609 ff., coverage by, 18, 21; arbitration, 606-7, 629-30; checkoff, 589, 596; closed shop, 585, 589, 595; company unions, 578, 581, 590; competition, 577-78; costs, labor, 574, production, 578; and defense program, 572, 620, 626; development of industry, 572-73; discharge, 589, 622, 628; dues payment, 596, employment fluctuations, 576-77; grievance settlement, 602-8, 629-30; hours, 609-11, 618; jurisdictional disputes, *see* unions, following; layoffs, 581, 589, 618 ff., *see also* seniority, following; location, 575; management attitude toward unions, 589; negotiation, 596-602; open shop, 589-90; overtime, 609-10, 625; preferential shop, 595; prices, 577-78; problems, union, 626-28, management, 628-29, joint, 629-30; production, 572 ff., assembly line, 576, concentration of, 574-75, methods, mass production, 576, 578, speed of operations, 576, 623; retirement, 621-22; seniority, 581, 617 ff., 628; size, 573; strikes, 580, 584, 591 ff., 601, 626, 628, Ford, 588-89, sitdowns and quickies, 571, 584, 591-94; structure, 573-74; unemployment, 610, 614, 620 ff., compensation, 602; union label, 589, 600; union shop, 595-96; unions, history, 578 ff., craft vs. industrial, 579-87, 627; vacations, 624-25; wages, differentials, 614-16, 628, methods of payment, 611-12, rates, 613-16, 628; workers, nonunion, 582, 598, 604, semiskilled, 576, women, 576; *see also* Automobile, Aircraft and Agricultural Implement Workers (UAW-CIO); Automobile Workers of America (UAW-AF of L)
Automotive Industrial Workers' Association, 583
Automotive Parts and Equipment Manufacturers, 599, 612
Automotive Tool and Die Manufacturers' Association, 598

BAKERY AND CONFECTIONERY WORKERS' INTERNATIONAL UNION OF AMERICA, 15, 16, 918-19, 958
Baking industry, 16, 20, 918-19
Baltimore and Ohio Railroad, 351, 907; Plan, 366
Barbers and Beauty Culturists of America, National Organizing Committee of, 962
Barbers' International Union, Journeymen, 958
Becker Cleaner, 820
Bell, Spurgeon, cited, 28, 610-11
Berry, George L., 107, 131, 142, 144
Bethlehem Steel Corporation, 509, 525 ff.; contract, 533
"Big steel," *see* United States Steel Corporation
Bill Posters, Billers and Distributors of United States and Canada, International Alliance of, 958
Bituminous coal, 229-79, 876-77, 885-86; agreements, coverage by, 272, 274, Central Competitive Field Compact (interstate), 238 ff., 250 ff., 277, 886, early interstate, 234-35, in outlying fields, 262-63, (1939), 273-74, (1941), 274-75; Appalachian Joint Conference, 270-75; arbitration, *see* Joint Conference System, following; checkoff, 242, 243, 269; checkweighmen, 243, 269, 272; company unions, 265; competition, 229-30, 238, 239, 259-60, 264-66; costs, labor, 231, 235, 241, 275-76; production, 275-76; employment trends, 254-57; hours, 242, 269, 270,

Index

273, 274, 279, under Interstate Compact, 254 ff.; Joint Conference System (Central Competitive Field Compact), 238-62, 886, arbitration, under the agreement, 246-47, of new agreements, 247-49, attempts to extend scope of, 253-54, collapse of, 257-62, grievance procedure, 244-47, negotiation, 239 ff.; nonunion fields, 238, 249, 260-61, 263-64, 277-78, 886, 905; NRA Code, 269 ff.; overdevelopment, 232-33, 277; prices, 236-37, 264, 269, 272, 275; problems, 275-77; production, 276; Southern Wage Conference, 274-75; strikes, 231, 237, 245, 249 ff., 260, 262, 266, 269, 273, 279, (1941), 274, breaching agreement, 251-52, 259, causes, 233-34, 251-52, penalty clauses, 252-53, for recognition, 249-50; union shop, 273, 275; unions, early, 230-32, membership, 274, 275, organizing efforts, 260, 263-64, 271, *see also* Mine Workers, United; vacations, 273, 274, 275; wages, differentials, 239, 242, 274, early, 234 ff., earnings (1940), 274, 275, under: agreements, (1939), 274, (1941), 275, Interstate Compact, 238-39, 242, 254-57, 886, government intervention, 269, 270-71, 279, ruthless competition, 265-66, 268; work sharing, 243; workers, unskilled, 255, 257; working conditions, 233-34, 273, 886
Bituminous Coal Act (1937), 229, 304; statement of policy, 272-73
Bituminous Coal Commission, United States (1919), 248-49, 296
Bituminous Coal Conservation Act, 271, 272
Blacksmiths, Drop Forgers and Helpers, International Brotherhood of, 18, 332, 958
Blankbook making, 119, 120, 137
Boiler Makers, Iron Ship Builders and Helpers of America, International Brotherhood of, 196, 932, 958
Book and job printing, 118-82, 879, 884-85; agreements, 142-48, administration of, 144 ff., coverage by, 21, 137, 144, early, 127-32; apprenticeship, 135, 143, regulation, 166-67; arbitration, 128 ff., 143-44, 153-54, 879, 884, 885; closed shop, 25, 126, 131-33, 140, 143, 173, 181, 884-85; company unions, 172-74, 176; competition, 121 ff., 170-72, 177; cooperation, intercraft, 139-40, 141-42; costs, 121-22, 169-70, 171, 177, 182, labor, 170, 171; discharge, 152, 153, 162 ff.; disputes, adjustment of, 143-44, 150-54, 175; employers, 122-23, 136, associations, 126, responsibility, 180, *see also* Printers' National Association; Typothetae of America, United; hours, 154 ff., 884-85, fight for eight-hour day, 129-30; location, 118-21; manning requirements, 160, 164-66; negotiation, evolution of, 127-33, methods: 137-42, autonomy, craft, 139-42, 178, local, 137-38, 178-80; open shop, 129 ff., 167, 170 ff., 884-85; overtime, 149, 160; prices (and profits), 121-24, 182; priority (seniority), 143, 148, 152, 162-64, 177; problems, 177 ff.; production methods, 119-25, 182; restriction of output, 160-61, 167-69; size, 118-21; strikes, 130, 132, 144, 150-51; technological changes, 124-25, 166; unemployment, 149, 163, 165, 177; unions, 125, independent industrial (Rochester), 174-76, membership, 136-37, organization, 125-27, in the plant, 146-48, policies, 167-70, responsibility, 178-80, *see also* company unions, preceding; Printing Pressmen and Assistants' Union; Stereotypers' and Electrotypers' Union; Typographical Union; wages, differentials, 156-59, 171-72, 884, rates, 155-59, 430, 884-85; work sharing, 143, 148-50; workers, 118-20, 121, skilled, 121, 124-25, unskilled, 121, problem of, 134-36, 178; working rules, 160 ff.
Book Manufacturers' Institute, 126, 138
Bookbinders, International Brotherhood of, membership, 125, 958
Bookbinding, 118 ff., 137
Boot and Shoe Workers Union, 879, 883, 915, 958
Brewery, Flour, Cereal and Soft Drink Workers of America, International Union of United, 920, 958
Brewing, 20, 919-20
Brick and clay products, 911
Brick and Clay Workers of America, United, 911, 958
Bricklayers, Masons and Plasterers' International Union of America, 196, 958
Bridge, Structural and Ornamental Iron Workers, International Association of, 196, 898, 958
Broadcasters' Association, Chicago, 849, 852
Broadcasting, *see* Radio
Broom and Whisk Makers Union, International, 958
Broun, Heywood, 109, 115
Building construction, 12, 17, 18, 183-228, 880, 881-83; agreements, 208 ff., coverage by, 20; antitrust investigations, 195, 224-27; apprenticeship, 197, 198, 211-12, 217; arbitration, 207,

218, 220-21, 882; bidding system, 194-95; closed shop, 25, 183, 197, 199, 203, 212-13, 217, 218; competition, 184, 194; costs, labor, 189, 212, materials, 189, production, 188-90, 224 ff.; discharge and hiring, 213, 225, see also seniority, following; dues, 212; employers, organizations, 205-7, working, 216; employment fluctuations, 204, 221, 222-23; government-financed construction, 185-87, 204; grievance procedure, 220-21; hours, 183, 208-11, 227; jurisdictional disputes, 183-84, 195 ff., 200-3, 224, 880, 882, 883; lay-offs, 222, see also seniority, following; limitation, of contractors, 216-17, of output, 214 ff., see also restrictive practices, following; markets, 185-89; materials, 185, 189-92, 194, 195, nonunion, 204, 215; monopolistic practices, 194-95, 212, 224-28; negotiation, 207-8, 217-18; open shop, 203, 206, 218; overtime, 208, 223; prefabrication, 190-92; price-fixing, 184, 194, 195, 225, 227; problems, 221-28; production, 185, scale of, 184, 190-92; restrictive practices, 184, 189, 195, 214-16, 221-22; size, 185; strikes, 183, 184, 200, 217-20, 881-82, jurisdictional, 217-18, 224; subcontracting, 193 ff., 206; technological changes, 189-92, 195, 199, 224; unemployment, 210, 212, 222-23; unions, 196-205, amalgamation, 199-200, control of labor supply, 211-13, and depression, 204-5, jurisdiction, 196-97, 203-4, see also jurisdictional disputes, preceding, local councils, 200, 880, 881-83, membership, 196-97, organizing activities, CIO, 198-99, 204, 224; wages, rates, 183, 199, 208-10, flexible wage rates, 223-24, 227, "kickbacks," 208, 210; work sharing, 205, 210, 213, 223; workers, nonunion, 199, 203-4, 223, 226; working rules, 193, 195, 214 ff., 227

Building and Construction Trades Department, AF of L, 197, 202-3, 881, 883, 912, 943

Building service, 20

Building Service Employees International Union, 958

Building Trades Council, Chicago, 881, 882

Building Trades Employers' Association, National, 206; New York, 199, 210, 882

Bus transportation, 19, 950-52

Byrnes Law, 47

CANNERY, AGRICULTURAL, PACKING AND ALLIED WORKERS OF AMERICA, UNITED, 922, 962

Capone, Al, 820-21, 823-24

Captive mines, dispute, 25, 26, 269, 275, 515-16

Carmen of America, Brotherhood of Railway, 15, 332, 958

Carnegie-Illinois Steel Corporation, 511, 894, 895; employee representation plans, capture of, 520 ff.; see also Steel

Carpenters and Joiners of America, United Brotherhood of, 196, 926, 959

Cement, Lime and Gypsum Workers International Union, United, 912, 959

Cement industry, 20, 912-13

Central Cleaning Company, 820-21

Central Competitive Field, 257 ff., 296, 515; Compact, 238 ff., 250 ff., 277, 886; collapse of system, 257 ff., 277; employment fluctuation in, 257; see also Bituminous coal

Checkoff, 14, 645, 816, 825, 924, 947; anthracite, 298, 299, 300, 306, 307, 313; bituminous coal, 242, 243, 269; Ford Company, 589, 596; glass, 699, 712, 731; hosiery, 454, 485; men's clothing, 398, 416; steel, 534, 540, 542, 563

Checkweighmen, 243, 269, 272, 288, 294, 314

Chemicals, 7, 18, 19, 22, 913-14

Chicago Joint Agreement, see Railroads

Chicago Orchestral Association, 852

Chicago service trades, see Cleaning and dyeing; Motion picture machine operators; Musicians

Chrysler Motor Company, 574, 588, 597, 601, 610, 623, 731

Cigar Makers International Union of America, 959

Circus, Carnival, Fairs and Rodeo Workers International Union, 959

Civil liberties, 278, 518, 591, 599, 794; Civil Liberties Committee (La Follette), 518, 591, 599

Clay industry, 908-11

Cleaners and Dyers Institute of Chicago, 823-24

Cleaners, Dyers, and Pressers Union (Federal Labor Union 17,742), 814-15

Cleaning and Dye House Workers, International Association of, 959; Local 3, 814-17

Cleaning and dyeing (Chicago), 806-7, 808-29, 867; agreements, see price control, joint, following; arbitration, 822 ff.; branch store plants, 808-10, 826, 829; checkoff, 816, 825; cleaning operations, 811-12; closed shop, 816-

Index

17, 867; "closed solicitation" rule, 818, 822, 828; costs, labor, 812-13, 819, standardization of, 828; employers' organizations, 813, 824-25; hours, 815-16; price control, joint, 817-29, logic of, 827-29; size, 813; strikes (and lockouts), 815, 818-19, 821-22, 826; structure, 808 ff., units, 808-9, market, 808-10, internal plant, 811; synthetic shops, 808-9, 811, 829; unemployment reserve fund, 822; unions, 813-15; wages, 812, 815-16, 818, 822, under NRA, 825, pressure on, 827, uniformity, 817; wholesale plants, 808-9, 810, 829; workers, drivers, 814, 817-18, 827-28, inside plant, 814-15, 818-20, 828, nonunion, 826, number, 810, women, 816, 817
Cleaning and Dyeing Plant Owners' Association of Chicago, (Chicago Master Cleaners' and Dyers' Association), 813, 815, 817 ff., 824
Clerks, Brotherhood of Railway and Steamship, 330, 331, 332, 335, 344, 959
Clerks, National Federation of Post Office, 15, 959
Clerks' International Protective Association, Retail, 940-41, 959
Closed shop, 14, 17, defined, 24-25; anthracite, 296, 299, 300; automobiles, 585, 589, 595; book and job printing, 25, 126, 131-33, 140, 143, 173, 181, 884-85; brick and clay products, 911; building construction, 25, 183, 197, 199, 203, 212-13, 217, 218; chemicals, 913; cleaning and dyeing, 816-17, 867; electrical products, 745, 793; glass, 689, 690, 697, 712, 728, 735, 740; hosiery, 454, 483, 484, 485, 487, 494, 498-500; hotels, 924; lumber, 926; maritime industry, 936, 937; men's clothing, 408, 415, 420; mercantile, 941; metal mining, 942, 943; motion picture operators, 834-38; musicians, 857, 858-59, 861, 862, 867; newspapers, 65 ff., 102; office work, 945; pulp and paper, 928; railroads, illegal on, 25, 330, 356-57; rubber, 645; shipbuilding, 933; shoes, 883, 915; steel, opposition to, 25, 545-46, 563; stoves, 893; transportation, 951
Clothiers' Exchange, Rochester, 404
Clothing, see Fur; Hats and millinery; Men's clothing; Shoes; Women's clothing
Clothing Manufacturers' Association of the United States, 405
Clothing Manufacturers' Exchange, New York, 404
Clothing Workers of America, Amalgamated, 11, 15-16, 393-449, 963; finances, 398; leadership, 399, 448; management, participation in, 431-43; and NRA, 435-36; objectives, 399-400; program, 401-2; Research Department, 417; rise, 396-97; Stabilization Plan, 382, 436-43; structure, 397-98, Joint Boards, 397-98; wage policy, 422 ff.
Coal Commission, United States, 238, 244, 249, 251, 261, 298, 300, 302, 316
Coal mining, 3, 8, 19, 23; agreements, coverage by, 18, 20; see also Anthracite; Bituminous coal
Collective bargaining, agreements: administration of, 26-27, coverage by, 17-22, table 1, 19-22, negotiation of, 25-26; bargaining units, 23-24; government encouragement of, 4 ff., 901-2, see also New Deal, NIRA, NRA; history: before New Deal, 871-907, early, 871-80, late nineties to World War, 880-901, postwar, 904-7; World War, 901-4; variation in pattern, 30; see also separate industries
Columbia Broadcasting System, 852
Committee for Industrial Organization, 11; see also Congress of Industrial Organizations
Communications, 952-54; telegraph, 953-54; telephone, 952-53; see also Radio, broadcasting
Communications Association, American, 938, 954, 963
Communist Labor League, 585
Communists, 584-85, 626, 651-52, 905, 915
Company houses and stores, 243, 270, 272, 287
Company unions (employee representation plans), 6 ff., 13, 906; see also separate industries
Competency, 90 ff., 112, 164, 168, 554-55, 660, 738, 777; see also separate industries, ability rating, seniority
Compositors, 32, 121; wage rates, 158
Conductors, Order of Sleeping Car, 15, 959
Conductors of America, Order of Railway, 323, 332, 354-55, 365, 874, 964
Congress of Industrial Organizations (CIO), 11 ff., 25, 30, 911-57, *passim;* automobiles: AF of L-CIO conflict, 579-87, 626-27, sitdowns, 591-94, victory at Ford, 587-89; bituminous coal, 267; book and job printing, 134; building trades campaign, 198 ff., 224; electrical products, 745 ff.; glass, 688 ff., 711, 724, 731 ff.; hosiery, 455, 465, 497-98; men's clothing, 436;

INDEX

newspapers, 109; radio, 782; rise of, 11; rubber, 640-41, 649, 653 ff.; steel, 508, SWOC, 515 ff.; unions, 962-64; *see also* American Federation of Labor; separate industries
Construction Workers Organizing Committee, United, 199, 963
Contractors, *see* Building construction, limitation of contractors, subcontracting; Men's clothing, contract system; Musicians
Coopers' International Union of North America, 959
Corning Glass Works, 686, 687, 717, 739, 740
Cost of living, wage adjustment plans, 74-75, 78, 114, 297, 751, 753, 759
Craft vs. industrial unionism, 9 ff., 23; in automobiles, 579 ff.; *see also* AF of L vs. CIO; separate industries
Crucible Steel Company, 509, 525

DAILY NEWSPAPERS, *see* Newspapers
Danbury Hatters case, 918
Davis-Kelly coal bill, 268-69
Debs, Eugene V., 324, 325, 333
Diamond cutting, 17, 22
Diamond Workers Protective Union of America, 959
Die casting, 22
Die Casting Workers, National Association of, 945, 963
Discharge, *see* Seniority; separate industries
Discrimination and coercion, 4-5; *see also* Civil liberties; Espionage, industrial; Open-shop campaigns; separate industries; Strikebreakers
Dismissal wage, 115-16, 401, 568
Distillery, Rectifying and Wine Workers International Union, 959
Distillery Workers Organizing Committee, 920, 963
Douglas, Paul H., cited, 71-73, 77, 80, 297-99, 303, 326, 412
Draftsmen's Unions, International Federation of Technical Engineers, Architects and, 959
Dry cleaning, *see* Cleaning and dyeing industry
Dues, union, 14-15; *see also* Checkoff; separate industries and unions

EIGHT-HOUR DAY, 80, 129-30, 154, 183, 210, 646, 782, 884, 925
Eighteenth Amendment, 716, 924
Electric light and power, 955
Electrical, Radio and Machine Workers of America, United, 16, 744-805, 955, 963; dues, 759, 785, 789; jurisdiction, 18, 745, 776, 797; Local 103, 793 ff.; Local 301, 747, 751 ff.; Local 601, 763 ff.; in radio industry, 781-801; union-management cooperation, 746, 778-80; *United Front,* 779
Electrical Contractors' Association, New York, 213
Electrical Industry Employees' Union, 750
Electrical Manufacturing Industry Code, 773
Electrical products, 744-805; agreements: coverage by, 18, 21, 745, 781, General Electric (1938), 752 ff., Philco, 782 ff., RCA, Bellevue-Stratford, 794-95, 796, exclusive contract with UER&MWA, 796-98, Westinghouse, unsigned agreements, 763-74, (1933), 773-74, (1941), 761; closed shop, 745, 793; company unions (employee representation plans), 749 ff., 761 ff., 782, 791 ff., 801; discharge, 775, 776, 790, 800, *see also* seniority, following; employers: General Electric (GE), 746-60, 781, 801, policy, 750, 752, welfare work, 759, Philco, 746-47, 781, 782-90, 802 ff., policy, 783, RCA, 746-47, 781, 786, 787, 788, 790-802, policy, 791 ff., Westinghouse, 760-81, 801 ff., policy, 760, 763-65, 772, 774-76, 778 ff., welfare work, 760; exclusive bargaining clause, 745, 794-95; grievance settlement, 753, 755-57, 761-62, 770-71, 775, 777, 785, 790, 792, 797 ff., 804; hours, 748, 773, 782-83, 784, 787, 797, equalization at GE, 755, 756, 757; layoffs, 765 ff., *see also* seniority, following; location of industry, 746-47; negotiation, GE, 754, Philco, 790, RCA, 798, Westinghouse, 763-65; overtime, 753, 757, 769, 773, 777, 782-83, 784, 792, 797; profit-sharing, GE, 751, 753, 758, 759, Westinghouse, 779; rehiring, 765-68, *see also* seniority, following; seniority, 757, 765-68, 774, 777-78, 784, 785, 787, 788, 789, 797-800, 803; size, 744-46; speed-up, 758; strikes: GE, 748, 753, 760, Philco, 782, 786, 787, 788-89, RCA, 793 ff., sit-downs, 753, 760, 787, Westinghouse, 761, 773; time studies, use of, 768, 769, 786, 804; transfers, 753, 755, 766, 767, 776, 785, 789, 797, 799; union-management cooperation, 746, 778-80, scraps saving campaign, 779-80; union shop, 745, 747, 783, 786, 789; unemployment, 762, 789-90, 791, insurance, 759 (state), 788, loan benefit plan, 759; vacations, 751, 753, 754, 759, 760, 777, 781, 793, 796; wages: 804, GE, community wage, 753, 757-58,

INDEX

cost-of-living adjustment, 751, 753-54, 758, 759, Philco, 783, 784-85, 788-89, radio industry, earnings, 781, Westinghouse, 762-63, earnings, 769, 773, 779, incentive system, 768, wage adjustment plan, 779; work sharing, 766, 797, 803; workers, nonunion, 745, 753, 755, 768, 798, semi-skilled, 747, skilled, 747, 772, unskilled, 748, 769, 772, women, 747, 768, 769, 777-78, 783, 785, 788, 789, 790, 799-800; working conditions, 758, 759; *see also* Electrical, Radio and Machine Workers of America, United; General Electric; Philco; RCA; Westinghouse
Electrical Workers, International Brotherhood of, 15, 16, 18, 196, 332, 718, 832, 952, 953, 955, 959; in electrical products industry, 745, 747, 781-82, 795; Local 3, 212, 213
Electrotypers, 39, 40, 121; *see also* Stereotypers' and Electrotypers' Union, International
Elevator Constructors, International Union of, 196, 959
Employee representation plans, *see* Company unions
Employees Committee Union, 791-99
Employers Association of Detroit, 589, 599
Employers' associations, attitudes toward collective bargaining, 177, 180, 221, 323, 405, 631, 637-39, 652, 655 ff., 676 ff., 872-73, 875, 935; open-shop campaign, 898-900; *see also* separate industries
Employers' Liability Act, Federal, 365
Employing Bookbinders of America, 126
Employment, terms of, 27 ff.; total, 17; *see also* separate industries
Engineers, Brotherhood of Locomotive, 332, 352-53, 364, 526, 879, 964
Engineers, International Union of Operating, 196, 959
Engravers, photo-, 32-107, *passim,* 119, 121, 139, 157, 162; *see also* Engravers' Union, Photo-
Engravers Union, International Metal, 15, 959
Engravers' Union, International Photo-, 15, 40 ff., 68 ff., 83, 85, 125, 959; arbitration agreements, 56 ff.
Erdman Act, 324, 325
Erectors' Association, National, 206, 898
Espionage, industrial, 518, 591, 599, 638, 902; *see also* Civil liberties; Open-shop campaigns; Strikebreakers
Exhibitors' Association, 831-32, 848-49

FABRICATED METAL COUNCIL, 943

Fair Labor Standards Act, 66, 84, 423, 429, 500, 504, 609
Fairless, B. F., 521, 523
Farm equipment, 21
Farm Equipment Workers Organizing Committee, 584, 963
Farmers, Associated, 921
Federal Communications Commission, 953-54
Federal Employees, National Federation of, 964
Federal Housing Administration, 186, 188
Federal Workers of America, United, 963
Federation of Organized Trades and Labor Unions, becomes American Federation of Labor, 874
Fire Fighters, International Association of, 959
Firemen and Enginemen, Brotherhood of Locomotive, 323, 332, 344, 352-55, 364, 368, 964
Firemen and Oilers, International Brotherhood of, 332, 959
Firestone Tire Company, 633 ff., 637 ff., 643, 649 ff., 658, 659, 660, 668, 669; agreement, 653, 654; decentralization, 664-65; grievance machinery, 672, 673; profits, 634, 681; strike, 641; *see also* Rubber products
Fishermen and Allied Workers of America, International Union of, 963
Five-day week, 30, 81 ff., 106, 155, 210, 561, 858
Flat Glass Workers' Union, Federation of, *see* Glass, Ceramic, and Silica Sand Workers
Flint Glass Workers' Union, American, *see* Glass Workers' Union, American Flint
Flour and cereal, 18, 20, 920-21
Food industries, 18, 20, 918-24
Ford Motor Company, 573-74, 578, 584, 586, 587, 600, 626, 724; agreement, 12, 532, 587-89, 614, 619, 625; closed shop, 595; UAW-CIO victory, 587-89
Foremen, attitude toward unions, 513-14, 547, 557-58, 564, 628, 780; control of, 67-68, 216, 736; grievance adjustment by, 244-45, 311-12, 407, 413, 416-17, 458, 604, 673-74, 750, 770-71, 784, 790, 799, 804; hiring and discharge by, 86 ff., 89-90, 91, 92-93, 95-96, 143, 162, 590, 667, 799; organizing of, 601
Forty-four-hour week, 132, 150, 154, 412, 816
Forty-hour week, 30, 66, 155, 160, 270, 520, 523, 549, 609-10, 751, 782, 797; *see also* Fair Labor Standards Act

Founders' Association, National, 895-97, 904; machine issue, 896-97
Foundries, 895-97
Foucault Window Glass Manufacturers, Association of Independent, 724, 727, 734-35
Frankensteen, Richard, 585, 627
Franklin Association, 130, 140, 146, 150, 153, 885
Frick (H. C.) Company, 515, 895
Friedman-Harry Marks case, 8, 427, 447
Fruit growing and processing, 921-22
Fur industry, 21, 915-16
Fur and Leather Workers Union, International, 915, 916, 963
Furniture Workers of America, United, 963

GARMENT WORKERS OF AMERICA, UNITED, 395-96, 406 ff., 435, 959
Garment Workers' Union, International Ladies', 11, 905, 959
Gas, By-Products, Coke and Chemical Workers, District 50, UMW, 913, 963
General Electric Company, 746-60, 781, 801; community wage, 757-58; welfare work, 759; Works Council plan, 749-50; *see also* Electrical products
General Motors Corporation, 12, 519, 524, 574, 588, 592, 610; agreements, negotiation of, 597; grievance settlement, 603 ff., 630
Glass Bottle Blowers' Association of the United States and Canada, 687-718, *passim*, 739, 743; membership, 687, 959
Glass, Ceramic, and Silica Sand Workers of America, Federation of (Federation of Flat Glass Workers' Union), 722, 723-39, 911, 963; change of name, 724; leadership, 730 ff.; size and organization, 724-25
Glass Container Association of America, 713, 716
Glass cooperatives, 715
Glass Cutters' League of America, Window, 721 ff., 959
Glass industry, 18, 22, 190, 682-743, 890; costs, labor, 685; summary, 739-43; *flat glass:* 16, 682-87, 718-43, 890; agreements, administration of, 736-37, coverage by, 22, 727-28, evolution of 726-27, negotiation, 729, with cutters, 722-23; checkoff, 731; closed shop, 728, 735, 740; company unions, 721, 725, 732-33; costs, labor, 685; employer readjustment, 725-26, 741; grievances, 729, 737-38, 743; hours, 730; machine speed, 735; ownership, 686-87; preferential shop, 728, 731, 735, 740; seniority, 723, 728, 733-34; strikes, 725, 726, 731-32, 739; technological changes, 684-86, 720, 723, 743; unions, early, 718-21, leadership, 730-31, 740, New Deal, effect of, 722, *see also* Glass Cutters' League, Window; Glass, Ceramic, and Silica Sand Workers, Federation of; wages, rates, 730, equalization of, 732, 734-35, settlement, 729; workers, miscellaneous (unskilled), 718, 721, 722, 730, 739, 741, nonunion, 735-36, semi-skilled, 718, 722, 730, 739, skilled, 721, women, 730;
flint and container glass: 682 ff., 687-718, 890; agreements, coverage by, 22, 23, 698 ff., grievance settlement, 701-3, 890, negotiation, joint conference system, 690-91, 695-701, Star Island Agreement, 702-3, 712; apprenticeship, 706, 708; checkoff, 699, 712; closed shop, 689, 690, 697, 712, 740; costs, labor, 714; employers' associations, 694-95, 742; ownership, 686-87; preferential shop, 689, 712, 740; restrictive practices, 704 ff., 709, "limited turn," 704-5, "summer stop" rule, 705-6; seniority, 699, 712-13; strikes (and lockouts), 700, 705-6, 715, prevention of, 716-17; technological changes, 684-86, 706 ff., 743, Owens bottle machine, 707-9; union-management cooperation, on legislation, 715-16; unions, 687-90, 692-93, attitude toward machines, 706-10, early, 691-92, jurisdiction, 687-88, *see also* Glass Workers' Union, American Flint; Glass Bottle Blowers' Association; vacations, 706; wages, early settlement of, 697-98, 890, basis of payment, 704-5, earnings, 713, and price stability, 714-15, rates, equalization of, 703-4; work sharing, 704 ff.; workers, 687-88, miscellaneous, 687, 697, 698, 705, 710-12, 717
Glass Workers' Union, American Flint, 687-717, *passim*, 739, 743; membership, 687, 959
Glove Workers Union of America, International, 959
Gompers, Samuel, 201, 903
Goodrich Company, B. F., 633-81, *passim;* agreements, 654, 655; attitude, 638, 654-55, 673, 676; grievance machinery, 672-73; profits, 634, 681; seniority, 660-61; *see also* Rubber products
Goodyear Tire and Rubber Company, 633-81, *passim;* agreement, 658; attitude, 638, 655-58, 676 ff.; decentralization, 665; employee representation

plan, 637-38; profits, 634, 681; welfare activities, 637; *see also* Rubber products
Government employees, 19
Government Employees, American Federation of, 959
Grain Processors and Allied Industries, National Council of, 921
Granite Cutters' International Association of America, 196, 874, 960
Granite cutting, 20
Graphic Arts League, 140, 173
Great Lake Carriers Association, 889, 936
Green, William, 639-40, 783
Grievances, settlement of, 26-27; types, in rubber industry, table 5, 675; *see also* separate industries

HANDSAKER, MORRISON, cited, 808 ff.
Harding, Warren G., 248-49, 299-300
Harlan County Operators Association, 273
Hart, Schaffner and Marx, 381, 396, 410, 434; agreement, 406 ff., emergency clause, 426 ff., preamble, 415; arbitration board, 406 ff.; and Sidney Hillman, 399, 431
Hats and millinery, 21, 916-18
Hatters, Cap and Millinery Workers' International Union, United, 917-18, 960
Hayes, Dennis, 707-8
Hazel-Atlas Glass Company, 714, 717
Heinz case, 532
Hillman, Sidney, 399, 422, 431, 436, 439, 586, 599, 626
Hiring (rehiring), 29; *see also* separate industries, discharge, hiring, seniority
Hod Carriers, Building and Common Laborers' Union of America, International, 196, 960
Home Owners' Loan Corporation, 186
Horseshoers of the United States and Canada, International Union of Journeymen, 960
Hosiery, 450-507; ability rating system, 461; agreements: 23, coverage by, 21, 500, industry-wide, 18, 454 ff., National Labor Agreements (1929-37), 455 ff., 482 ff., 490 ff., 495-96, 504-5, flexibility clause, 492, 496, 502, lapse in 1936, 496-97, resumption, 498-500, supplementary agreements, 456-57; checkoff, 454, 485; closed shop, 454, 483, 484, 485, 487, 494, 498-500; competition, 452, nonunion mills, 453, 455-56, 473 ff., 479, 484-85, 487, 499, South vs. North, 456, 462-63, 485, 501, 503; costs, labor, 452, 457, 482, 484, 492, 502, 505, 506, materials, 506; discharge, 460-61; employers, nonunion, wage policy, 490-91, 494-95, 498, yellow-dog contracts, 476; grievance procedure, 457 ff., arbitration by impartial chairman, 458 ff., 470, 483, 494, 496, 502; hours, 463, 470, nonunion, 476, 490; layoffs, 461-62; location, 450; machines, old vs. new, 455, 465, 477-78, 482, 502 ff.; NRA Code, 489, 491-94; Rehabilitation Program, 503-7, formula, 504-5; seniority, 461-62; strikes, 454, 467, 470-73, 480-81, 486, 487-88, 489-90, 498-500, (1921), 466, 471-73, sitdowns, 488, 499-500; unemployment, 453, 462, 483-84, 501; unions, history, early, 450-51, 464 ff., (1922-28), 473 ff., organizing efforts, 473 ff., 487-90, 494-95, in 1937, 498-500, *see also* Hosiery Workers, American Federation of; wages, earnings, 450, 451, 463, 475, 502, 506, nonunion employers' policy, 490-91, 494-95, 498, piece rates, standardization of, 455-57, rate-setting, economics of, 452 ff., under Rehabilitation Program, 504-5, uniform wage scale, 475, 478-79, 480 ff.; workers, nonunion, *see* unions, organizing efforts, preceding, women, 473
Hosiery (Full-Fashioned) Association, Inc., (nonunion), 488 ff.
Hosiery (Full-Fashioned) Manufacturers of America, Inc., 454 ff., 462-64, 482 ff., 496, 498, 502 ff.; formation, 454
Hosiery (Full-Fashioned) Manufacturers Association, Philadelphia, 469-73
Hosiery Manufacturers, National Association of, 456, 489
Hosiery Workers, American Federation of (American Federation of Full-Fashioned Hosiery Workers until 1933), 17, 450-507, 782; formation, 465-66; Local 706 (Branch One), 466, 470-78, 499, 501; membership, 473, 477, 483; organizing efforts, 473 ff., 487-90, 494-95, 498-500; policy, 465, 474-75, 480 ff.; *see also* Hosiery, Rehabilitation Program; Textile Workers Union of America; Textile Workers of America, United
Hotel Association of New York, 924
Hotel and Restaurant Employees' International Alliance and Bartenders' International League of America, 16, 924-25, 960
Hotels and restaurants, 20, 924-25
Hours, standard work week, 30; *see also* Fair Labor Standards Act; separate industries

INDEX

Hours of Service Act of 1907, 365
Howard, Charles P., 12, 76, 79, 81, 100

ILLINOIS COAL OPERATORS' ASSOCIATION, 244 ff.
Illinois Compensation Act, 855
Impartial chairman, see Arbitration
Independent unions, 13
Industrial Conferences (1919, 1920), 903
Industrial unionism, 16, 23; see also AF of L vs. CIO; Craft vs. industrial unionism; Unions
Industries (principal) covered in this survey, Anthracite, 280-317, 876, 887; Automobiles, 571-630; Bituminous coal, 229-79, 876-77, 885-86; Book and job printing, 118-82, 879, 884-85; Building construction, 183-228, 880, 881-83; Chicago service trades, 806-68: Cleaning and dyeing, 806-7, 808-29, 867, Motion picture machine operators, 808, 830-48, 867, Musicians, 808, 848-66, 868; Electrical products, 744-805; Glass, 682-743, 890; Hosiery, 450-507; Men's clothing, 381-449; Newspapers, 31-117, 879, 883-84; Railroads, 318-80, 879-80, 887-88; Rubber products, 631-81; Steel, 508-70, 893-95; see also separate listings
Inland Boatmen's Union of the Pacific, 963
International News Service, 954
International unions, unaffiliated, 13, 964-65
Interstate Commerce Commission, 320, 322, 342, 348, 367, 370-72, 948
Iron, 7, 16, 21, 508, 875-76, 879; see also Steel
Iron Molders, National Union of, 891
Iron and steel construction, 898
Iron and Steel Industry, National Committee for the Organizing of, 903
Iron and Steel Institute, American, 508, 513, 527, 539, 544, 567
Iron, Steel and Tin Workers, Amalgamated Association of, 510-11, 516-17, 544, 874, 876, 893-95, 963; agreement with CIO, 517, 535
IWW, 637, 880, 890, 922

JEWELRY WORKERS' UNION, INTERNATIONAL, 960
Job security, Washington Job Protection Agreement (railroads), 369-70, 376, 379; see also separate industries, seniority, unemployment
Johnson, Hugh S., 791, 793-96
Jones and Laughlin Steel Corporation, 509, 525

Jurisdictional disputes, 9-12; automobiles, 579-87, 627; bituminous coal, 266-67; building construction, 183-84, 195 ff., 200-3, 224, 880, 882, 883; electrical products, 791 ff.; glass, 688, 692-93, 719 ff., 740; railroads, 332-33, 352 ff.; see also AF of L vs. CIO; other separate industries and unions

KELLY, HARVEY, 62, 63
Keystone Manufacturers Association, 500, 502
Kickback, 208, 210, 866
Knights of Labor, 3, 234-36, 286, 323, 395, 692-93, 806, 908; growth, 874-75; Trade Assembly 300, 719-21
Knights of St. Crispin, 874, 877-79

LABOR MOVEMENT, split in, 9-12; see also AF of L vs. CIO
Labor Relations Act, see National Labor Relations Act
Laborsaving devices, 195, 214, 421, 510, 610, 662-63, 677, 680, 898, 939; see also separate industries, technological changes
Ladies' Garment Workers' Union, International, 11, 905, 959
La Follette Act, 888
Lathers, International Union of Wood, Wire and Metal, 196, 960
Laundries, 20
Laundry and Dye House Drivers' Union, see Teamsters, Chauffeurs, Warehousemen and Helpers, Local 712
Laundry Workers' International Union, 814, 960
Layoffs, 29; see also separate industries, seniority
Leather Workers International Union, United, 960
Leiserson, William M., 165, 502, 732
Letter Carriers, Federated Rural, 960
Letter Carriers, National Association of, 960
Letter Carriers' Association, National Rural, 15, 964
Lewis, John L., 260, 265, 266, 271, 313, 521, 586, 626, 794, 905; steel campaign, 515 ff.; Taylor-Lewis agreement, 509, 522-24, 544, 549 ff.
Libbey-Owens-Ford Company, 720 ff., 730, 731, 734, 735, 739
Linotype, 79-80, 86, 99, 128, 896
Lithographers International Protective and Beneficial Association, 125, 960
Lithographing, 21, 119
"Little steel," attitude of, 546-47; companies comprising, 525; SWOC organizing campaign, 12, 525-27, 530-33, 563, 565; see also Steel

INDEX

Local Industrial Unions, 964
Local Trade and Federal Labor Unions, 962
Lockouts (and strikes), 26, 27; *see also* separate industries
Loggers' Association, Columbia Basin, 926
Longshoremen, 19, 938-40
Longshoremen's Association, International, 938, 940, 960
Longshoremen's Board, National, 939
Longshoremen's and Warehousemen's Union, International, 938-40, 963
Lumber, 6, 22, 925-26
Lumbermen's Industrial Relations Committee, 926
Lynch, James, 52, 53, 100, 128

McCabe, David A., cited, 364, 695, 697, 890, 908
McCabe, Glen, 722, 725 ff.
McGrady, Edward F., 796 ff., 802
Machine tools, 21
Machinists, 928-30
Machinists, International Association of, 15, 16, 18, 332, 579, 897, 928-32, 960
Mailers, 39-40, 42, 80, 85, 125, 139; labor cost, 36; wage rates, 73; *see also* Typographical Union, International
Maintenance of Way Employees, Brotherhood of, 332, 960
Manning of machines, 94-96, 160, 164-66, 896
Manufacturers, National Association of, 899
Manufacturers' Association, Philadelphia, (clothing), 404
Manufacturers of Pressed and Blown Glassware, National Association of, 691, 694-95, 700, 701
Marble, Stone and Slate Polishers, Rubbers and Sawyers, Tile and Marble Setters' Helpers and Terrazzo Helpers, International Association of, 196, 960
Marine Cooks' and Stewards' Association, National, 935-36, 963
Marine Engineers' Beneficial Association, National, 937, 963
Marine Firemen, Oilers, Watertenders and Wipers' Association, Pacific Coast, 935, 964
Marine and Shipbuilding Workers of America, Industrial Union of, 932-33, 963
Maritime Commission, United States, 937
Maritime industry, 934-40; agreements, 936 ff., Pacific Coast, 938-39; grievance settlement, 937; hiring halls, 937; strikes, 935, 936, 937, 939; structure, 934-35

Maritime Labor Board, 935, 938
Maritime Union of America, National, 936-37, 963
Martin, Homer, 584-87; *see also* Automobile Workers of America (UAW-AF of L)
Mass production industries, 6 ff., 10 ff., 16, 24, 27 ff.; nonunionism in, 899, 905-7; *see also* Automobiles; Electrical products; Glass; Rubber; Steel
Master Cleaners' and Dyers' Association, *see* Cleaning and Dyeing Plant Owners' Association of Chicago
Master Mechanics and Foremen of Navy Yards and Naval Stations, National Association of, 960
Masters, Mates and Pilots of America, National Organization, 937, 960
Meat Cutters and Butcher Workmen of North America, Amalgamated, 16, 922-23, 960
Meat processing and distribution, 922-24; agreements, 923-24, coverage by, 20
Mechanics Educational Society of America, 580, 583
"Membership" agreements, 24
Membership maintenance clause, union, 25, 931
Men's clothing industry, 381-449; agreements, coverage by, 20, established principles, 414-16, 420-22, Hart, Schaffner and Marx, 406 ff., 415; arbitration, Hart, Schaffner and Marx system, 406-12, 426-27, decline in importance, 413-14, impartial machinery, 417-19, 448; checkoff, 398, 416; closed shop, 408, 415, 420; collective bargaining, benefits of, 444-47, early history, 406 ff.; competition, 391-93, 430, 448, regulation of, 436 ff.; contract system, 390-91, 421, 437-41, 447-48, registration of contractors, 416, 438, 440; costs, labor, 389, 412-13, 423, 431, 446, equalization under Stabilization Plan, 436-43, materials, 389, production, 389-90; discharge, 412, 416, 418-19, 420, 444; employers, 402-5, 446-47, 448, *see also* union-management cooperation, following; grievance adjustment, 406 ff., 416 ff., 448; hours, 412, 415, 435, 445-46; location, 384-85; negotiation, 414 ff.; open shop, 385, 410, 411; preferential shop, 408, 415, 420; price control, Stabilization Plan, 438-41, effects, 441-43; production, 383 ff., decline of, 406, 431-32, 448, demand, 385-86, processes, 386-87, seasonality, 386, small producers, 387-89, 403, 449; restriction, of output, 416, 421-22, 432-33, 446, of over-

time, 416, 446; seniority, 416, 420; Stabilization Plan, Amalgamated Clothing Workers', 382, 436-43; strikes (and lockouts), 381, 409, 411, Curlee, 402, 432, International Tailoring Company, 402, 432, 1910 strike, 406-7, 1920 lockout, 398, 400, 402, 405, 411, protection from, 415, 422, 444, 446; technological changes, 387, 421, 445; unemployment, 392, 429, 432, insurance, 401, 445, seasonal, 386, 448; union, label, 401, leadership, 399, 401, 448, *see also* Hillman, Sidney; union-management cooperation, 381, 402, 424, 431-43, 446; wages, determination of, 414, 415, 422-30, 432, 437 ff., differentials, 392, 423, 436, dismissal wage, 401, earnings, 384, 412, 428-30, 441, 445-46, piece-rate basis, 394, 413, 421, 424-26, 429, 439, 440, 446, trends, 411-12, 428-30; work sharing (equal division of work), 412, 416, 420-21, 445; workers, 384, 393 ff., 412, 444-46, women, 394, 412, 429; working conditions, 400, 406, 441, 445, 447; *see also* Clothing Workers, Amalgamated

Mercantile trade, 20, 940-42

Merchant Marine Institute, American, 936

Metal mining, smelting and fabrication, 20, 21, 942-45

Metal trades, 21, 897-98, 904

Metal Trades Association, National, 589, 599, 897-98, 904, 929

Metal Trades Council, AF of L (Metal Trades Department), 748, 900-1, 932 ff., 943, 948

Metal Workers' International Association, Sheet, 15, 196, 332, 960

Millinery, 21, 916-18

Millinery Stabilization Commission, 916-17

Mine, Mill and Smelter Workers, International Union of, 11, 942 ff., 963

Mine Workers of America, International Union Progressive, 267, 273, 960

Mine Workers of America, United, 11, 25; District 50, 913; formation, 235-36, 876; membership, 15, 905, 963; and NRA, 269-71, 515; organizing activities, 260, 263-64, 288 ff., 515 ff.; recognition in anthracite, 297, 887; steel campaign, 271, 515 ff., 535-37, 542, 564; *see also* Anthracite and Bituminous coal, 289-317, 235-279, *passim*

Mining Department, AF of L, 901

Mining and quarrying, 20; *see also* Anthracite; Bituminous coal; Metal mining, smelting and fabrication; Mine Workers of America, United

Miscellaneous workers, *see* separate industries

Mitchell, John, 288, 290, 293, 886

Molders' Union of North America, International, 579, 896, 960

Mollie Maguires, 285

Motion picture machine operators, Chicago, 808, 830-48, 867; agreements, 833 ff., coverage by, 20, 832; apprenticeship, 835-37, licenses issued, table 6, 835; arbitration, 833; chains vs. "the indies," 830-32, 838, 841-42, 845-46; closed shop, 834-38; costs, labor, 844-46; employers' associations, 831-32; hours, 833-34, 844; motion picture theatres: characteristics, 830-31, continuous operation, 844-45, 846, 848, 867, cost pattern variation, 844-46, change to sound movies, 838-40; strikes (and lockouts), 839, 841-42, 846; unemployment, 844; union control of labor supply: 832, 834-42, 847-48, closed-membership policy, 837-38, initiation fee, 837, licensing, 835-37, 842, permits to nonmembers, 837, 840, 842-43, two-man rule, 837, 839-42, 846; union membership, 832, 835; unionism, "here and now," 843, 847, 867; wages, 833-34, 843-46; *see also* Stage Employees and Moving Picture Machine Operators, Local 110

Murray, Philip, 515, 517, 519, 521, 523, 530, 538, 546, 568-69, 586, 599, 626

Murray Plan, industry council, 568-70

Musicians, American Federation of, 849 ff., 859, 865, 960; Local 10, Chicago, 848-68; bargaining structure, 849 ff.; dues, 850, 859, 866; membership, 849; placement agency, 855, 863; "union law," 851-52, penalties for violation, 861-62

Musicians, Chicago, 808, 848-66, 868; agreements, 851 ff., "union law," 851-52; closed shop, 857, 858-59, 861, 862, 867; contractor system, 852-56, 863, 868, "trade agreement" vs. "contract," 852-53; discharge, 854; employers, 848-49, 852-53; hours, 857-58; job classification, 852-53, 865-66; negotiation, 851-56; nonunion, "standby" fees, 858-59; radio broadcasting, influence of, 863-65; transfer rules, 859-60; unemployment, 865-66; wages, earnings, 856-58, scales, 850, 856-58, 861, 863

Mutual Network, 852

NATIONAL ASSOCIATION OF BUILDERS' EXCHANGES, 206

National Association of Manufacturers, 899

INDEX 979

National Broadcasting Company, 852
National Civic Federation, 290, 900
National defense, 24, 28, 747, 930-31, 932; and steel, 510, 533, 568-70
National Defense Mediation Board, 25, 26, 274-75, 931, 932, 934, 945
National Industrial Recovery Act [Section 7(a), NIRA, NRA], 5 ff., 81, 109, 269, 489, 581, 590, 613, 638, 688, 750, 774, 791, 901, 910, 942, 947, 956; administrative machinery, 7-8; invalidation, effect of, 8, 82, 271, 405, 436, 495, 582, 751, 814; *see also* Clothing Workers, Amalgamated; Mine Workers, United; separate industries
National Labor Board, 7, 8, 489, 513; Wolman Award, 492-93; *see also* National Labor Relations Board
National Labor Relations Act (Wagner), 8-9, 47, 110, 112, 204, 518, 526, 544, 547, 588, 593, 595, 626, 627, 688-89, 710, 901; Supreme Court validation, 8, 524, 564, 641, 796, 910, 911
National Labor Relations Board (NLRB), 8-9, 112, 140, 172, 447, 500, 518, 521, 533, 546, 587, 652, 679, 752, 763, 776, 794 ff., 939, 948, 953, 954; elections: 24, 173, 175, 728, 913, 921, 931, 933, 944, 945, 954, 955, in electrical products, 747, 751-52, 760, 794-95, 797, in rubber, 643, 654, 655, 656, 658, in steel, 525, 526, 530, 532, 533, 540
National Mediation Board, (railroads), 8, 318, 330, 339, 341, 342-43, 344, 362, 366, 374; accomplishments, 358-59; constitution and role, 357-58
National unions, unaffiliated, 13, 964-65
National War Labor Board, World War I, 4, 409, 637, 749, 901-2; World War II, 25
Needle trades, 18, 25, 29, 900; *see also* Men's clothing; Women's clothing
Negotiation of agreements, 25-26; *see also* separate industries, negotiation
Negroes, 518, 849, 925
New Deal, effect of, 3-30, 489, 518, 519, 568, 631, 917, 924, 950; in glass, 687, 688, 714, 717-18, 722; *see also* National Labor Relations Act; NRA
New York State Labor Relations Board, 946, 951
New York Telephone Company, 953
Newlands Act, 325-26
Newspaper Guild, American, 85, 108-17; agreements, 113 ff.; employment security, 115-16; freedom of press issue, 112-13; jurisdiction, 108-9; membership, 963; organization, 109, 113-14; union status, 113-14
Newspaper Publishers Association, American (ANPA), 43 ff., 50 ff., 68, 69, 92, 104, 883; and American Newspaper Guild, 110, 114; arbitration agreements with ITU, 51-66, 129, 884; membership, 44-45; Open-Shop Department, 46-47, 69; printing schools, 69; Special Standing Committee, 45-46, 50 ff.
Newspapers (daily), 31-117, 879, 883-84; agreements: coverage by, 21, 113, editorial and commercial, 111-12, mechanical departments, 65 ff.; apprenticeship, 68-70, training, 69-70, 90, 102; arbitration, 31, 50-64, 105, 111-12, 879, 883-85, achievements of, 63-64, Code of Procedure, 54-55, 60, 63, problems, 60-63; chains, 33-34, 39, 100; characteristics, 32-39, 103-4; circulation, 34 ff.; closed shop, 65 ff., 102; collective bargaining: birth of ITU, 47-48, early history, 47 ff., operative forces, 105, results, 101 ff., unsettled problems, 106-7; competency standards, *see* priority, following; consolidations, 35, 104; costs, labor, 35-37, 102, 104, 106-7, production, 35-37, 104, 106-7; discharge, 85-94, 102, 115-16; dismissal pay, 115-16, 117; editorial and commercial departments, 16, 21, 108-17, *see also* Newspaper Guild, American; employment, 32, 40, 70, 104; foremen, rules affecting, 67-68; grievance settlement, 50-64, 111-12, *see also* arbitration, preceding; hiring, 85-94; hours, 65, 79-84, 101, 115, five-day week, 81-83, 115; layoffs, 116, *see also* overtime, priority, following; manning requirements, 94-96; mechanical departments, 31-107; one-newspaper cities, 34-35, 103; open-shop, ANPA Open-Shop Department, 46-47, 69, editorial and commercial, 1-12-13; overtime, 66, 83-84, 115; prices, subscription, 37; priority (seniority), 86, 88-92, 93, competency, 90-92, superannuate scales, 92; production, requirements, 33, trends, 33-35, *see also* costs, preceding; publisher organizations, 43 ff., 49, *see also* Newspaper Publishers Association, American; reproduction (reset) requirement, 98-101; revenue, 37-39; size, 32; strikes (and lockouts), 46, 50, 63, 70, 102, 111, 112, 884, international law governing, 42, 52; substitutes, control of, 86, 92-94, phalanxing, 93; technological changes, 95, 96, 100, 103; transfers, 96-98, 106, 116; unemployment, 70, 83, 92, 95, 96, 104, 109; union shop (Guild shop), 110, 112, 113-14;

unions, 39 ff., editorial and commercial, 108-11, government and functions, 41-43, 109-11, internationals, dominance of, 42-43, international law, 42, 53, 54, 56-57, 106, jurisdictions, 39-40, 108-9, status, 65 ff., 113, *see also* Newspaper Guild, American; Printing Pressmen; Typographical Union; vacations, 84-85, 115, 117; wages, 70-79, 114-15, differentials, 75-78, earnings, 32, 71-75, 114-15, settlement, 47, 48, 65, 74-79, 106-7; work sharing, 92, 104, *see also* hours, five-day week, preceding; workers, 32-33, 108-9, nonunion, 66; working conditions, 65-66, 101, 109

Nonunion workers, *see* Unorganized workers; separate industries

Norris-La Guardia Anti-Injunction Act, 4-5

OFFICE OF PRICE ADMINISTRATION, 569
Office of Production Management, 569-70, 626
Office and Professional Workers of America, United, 945-46, 963
Office work, 16, 945-46; New York Credit Clearing House contract, 945
Offset printing, 103, 119, 123; *see also* Lithographing
Oil industry, *see* Petroleum
Oil Workers International Union, 947, 963
Open shop, 24, ANPA Open-Shop Department, 46-47, 69; early campaign, 898-900, 904; movement in the 1920's, 57, 884, 889, 903, 904, 905; UTA Open Shop Division, 131, 885; *see also* separate industries
Optical Workers Coordinating Committee, 964
Orchestral Association, Chicago, 852
Overtime, *see* separate industries
Owens-Illinois Glass Company, 686 ff., 689, 696-97, 709, 714, 717

PACIFIC AMERICAN SHIPOWNERS' ASSOCIATION, 936
Pacific Coast Association of Pulp and Paper Manufacturers, 927
Pacific Coast District Council, 933
Pacific Northwest Rate Coordinating Bureau, 949
Packinghouse Workers Organizing Committee, 923, 964
Painters, Decorators and Paperhangers of America, Brotherhood of, 196, 960
Paper, Novelty and Toy Workers International Union, United, 964

Paper Makers, International Brotherhood of, 927, 928, 960
Paper and pulp, 18, 21, 23, 927-28; Joint Relations Board, Pacific Coast, 927
Part-time work, *see* Work sharing
Pattern Makers' League of North America, 18, 579, 930, 961
Pattern making, 930
Paving Cutters' Union of the United States of America and Canada, 196, 964
Petroleum Labor Policy Board, 947
Petroleum production, 22, 946-48
Philadelphia Storage Battery Company (Philco), 746-47, 781, 782-90, 802 ff.
Philco Radio and Television Company, 788
Photo-Engravers' Union of North America, International, *see* Engravers' Union of North America, International Photo-
Piece rates, uniform, 23; *see also* separate industries
Pinchot, Gifford, 301; coal settlement (1923), 300, 310
Pittsburgh Plate Glass Company, 721 ff., 731 ff.
Plasterers' and Cement Finishers' International Association of the United States and Canada, Operative, 15, 196, 961
Plumb Plan League, 327, 334, 335
Plumbers and Steam Fitters of the United States and Canada, United Association of Journeymen, 196, 961
Pocketbook and Novelty Workers Union, International Ladies' Handbag, 961
Polishers, Buffers, Platers and Helpers International Union, Metal, 18, 961
Porters, Brotherhood of Sleeping Car, 961
Post Office Clerks, United National Association of, 964
Post Office and Railway Mail Laborers, National Association of, 961
Postal Employees, National Alliance of, 964
Postal Supervisors, National Association of, 965
Postal Telegraph Cable Company, 953, 954
Postmasters of the United States, National Association of, 964
Potters, National Brotherhood of Operative, 890, 908-11, 961
Potters Association, United States, 890, 909, 910
Pottery, 908-11; agreements, "Square Deal" clause, 909; size, 908; wages, 890, 909
Powder and High Explosive Workers of America, United, 961
Power, electric, 955
Prefabrication, 190-92

INDEX 981

Preferential shop, 14, 24-25, 273, 494, 595, 939, 941, 950; defined, 24; glass, 689, 712, 728, 731, 735, 740; men's clothing, 408, 415, 420; rubber, 645, 666
Press, freedom of, 112-13
Presses, automatic, 124, 158-59; manning of, 94-96, 160, 164-66
Printers, Die Stampers and Engravers' Union of North America, International Plate, 961
Printers' League of America, 130-33, 135, 143 ff., 150, 152, 166
Printers' National Association, 126, 136, 138, 181
Printing Pressmen and Assistants' Union of North America, International, 39-107, *passim*, 125-72, *passim*, 884; membership, 15, 125, 961; Research Division, 181; Technical Trade School, 102, 168; *see also* Book and job printing; Newspapers
Printing trades, 3, 21, 25, 879, 883-85; *see also* Book and job printing; Newspapers
Priority, *see* Seniority; Book and job printing; Newspapers
Professional workers, 20, 945-46
Promotions, 29, 116, 352-53, 461-62, 554-55, 647, 712-13, 734, 906; *see also* Seniority; separate industries
Public utilities, 19, 948-55; *see also* Railroads
Public Works Administration, 186, 210
Pulp, Sulphite, and Paper Mill Workers, International Brotherhood of, 133, 927, 928, 961
Pulp industry, *see* Paper and pulp

QUARRYING, 20
Quickies, 584, 591-92, 937

RADIO, broadcasting, 109, 848-49, 852, 856-66, *passim*; manufacturing, 16, 781-801, 804; operators (ship), 937-38; stations, network vs. local, 865, newspaper-owned, 38; *see also* Electrical, Radio and Machine Workers of America; Philco; RCA
Railroad Adjustment Board, National, 330, 357, 360-64, 374; appraisal of, 363-64
Railroad Employees' Retirement Insurance Act (1937), 368, 371-72
Railroad Labor Board, 328-29
Railroad Signalmen of America, Brotherhood of, 332, 965
Railroad Trainmen, Brotherhood of, 323, 332, 342, 354-56, 526, 965

Railroad Transportation Act, Emergency (1933), amendments, 368, 369
Railroads, 3, 18, 318-80, 879-80, 887-88; agreements: 343-44, Chicago Joint Agreement, 333, 353-55, Cleveland Compact, 333, 354, coverage by, 18, 19, 344-45, Railway Administration agreements, 327, Washington Job Protection Agreement, 340, 368, 369-70, 376, 379, yellow-dog contracts, forbidden, 330, 368; arbitration, 324 ff., 358, 887-88, *see also* Railroad Adjustment Board; closed shop, illegal, 25, 330, 356-57; and coal mining, 232-33, 281, 284; "Committee of Six," 372-73, 380, *see also* Transportation Act of 1940; company unions, 329 ff., 368, Texas and New Orleans case, 330; competition, 320-21, 378; consolidation, 368-71, 378-79; costs, labor, 376, 377; decline in business, 319 ff., 365, 372; discharge (and hiring), *see* seniority, following; disputes: settlement of, 327 ff., 336, 357 ff., re agreement, 357-59 (National Mediation Board, 330, 357-59, 374), under agreement, 357, 360-64 (National Railroad Adjustment Board, 330, 357, 360, 361-64), under government operation, 327, *see also* Railroad Labor Board; Railway Labor Act; employment, 319 ff., types of, 322-23, volume of, 321-22, 375, *see also* unemployment, following; financial condition, 319-21, 375; government operation, 326 ff.; hours, 325, 327, 345 ff., 365, 366, not worked, 348-50; negotiation, 319, 337 ff.; overtime, 326, 345, 346-47, 350; rehabilitation program, 372-73, 380; retirement, 371-72; seniority, 322, 327, 344, 351-56, 362, 376, 879, vs. work sharing, 355-56, 376; strikes, 324, 329, 373-75; technological changes, 320, 321, 378; unemployment, 322, 365-66, 375, 376, Railroad Unemployment Insurance Act (1938), 368, 371-72, *see also* Washington Job Protection Agreement, preceding; union-management cooperation, 366, 380, 907; unions, 323-25, 332 ff., early history, 323-26, 887-88, industrial vs. craft, 324-25, 333, jurisdiction, 332-33, legislative gains, 318, 335, 365, 368 ff., objectives, 334-35, program, 364 ff., structure, 336-37; vacations, 345; wages, basis of payment, 345 ff., constructive allowances, 346, 347, 350, daily and monthly guarantees, 347-48, earnings, 350-51, (1932-41), 340-43, 375-77, payment for hours not worked, 348-50, settle-

982 INDEX

ment of, 327, 328, 340-43, 357; work sharing, 342, 355-56, 376; *see also* National Mediation Board; Railway Labor Act; separate unions; Transportation Acts, 1920, 1940
Railway Carmen of America, Brotherhood of, *see* Carmen of America, Brotherhood of Railway
Railway Conductors of America, Order of, *see* Conductors of America, Order of Railway
Railway Employees' Department, AF of L, 333, 339, 366, 367, 901
Railway Employees' Retirement Act, 340
Railway Labor Act, 4, 318, 328 ff., 342, 344, 357, 368, 373; amendments (1934), 330-31, 337, 360, 368, 369, (1936), 359
Railway Labor Executives' Association, 333 ff., 339, 340, 341, 366 ff., 901
Railway Mail Association, 961
Railway and Motor Coach Employees of America, Amalgamated Association of Street, Electric, 950-52, 961
Railway and Steamship Clerks, Brotherhood of, *see* Clerks, Brotherhood of Railway and Steamship
Railway Union, American, 324-25, 333
RCA Manufacturing Company, 746-47, 781, 786, 787, 788, 790-802; contract, UER&MWA, 796 ff.; management training course, 799
Recognition, union, 24-25; *see also* separate industries, closed shop, preferential shop, union shop
Reconstruction Finance Corporation, 186, 372
Rehiring, *see* Hiring
Republic Steel Corporation, 509, 525 ff.; v. *NLRB,* 531; *see also* Steel
Restaurants, 20, 924-25
Retail, Wholesale and Department Store Employees of America, United, 940-41, 964
Retail Clerks' International Protective Association, *see* Clerks' International Protective Association
Retailing, *see* Mercantile trade
Reuther, Walter, 584, 627; Plan, 569
Rochester Printing Crafts Association, 174-76
Roofers, Damp and Waterproof Workers' Association, United Slate, Tile and Composition, 196, 961
Roosevelt, Franklin D., 7, 340-43, 371, 373, 515, 519, 526, 544, 581
Rubber products, 6, 9, 12, 16, 24, 631-81; agreements, 24, 644 ff., coverage by, 22, 641-43, Firestone, 653, 654, General Tire and Rubber, 666-67, Goodrich, 654, 655, Goodyear, 658, Seiberling, 665-66, U. S. Rubber, 643; checkoff, 645; closed shop, 645; company unions, 637 ff., 650, 652, 656; competition, 634-35; costs, labor, 635, 677, 680, materials, 634-35; decentralization, 633, 664-65, 678-79; discharge, 667-68; employers, attitude, 637 ff. 652 ff., 656, 676-78, 680-81, "Big Four," 633 ff., "Big Three" (Akron), 638, grievance machinery, 672-74, profits, 634, 680-81, welfare activities, 637, *see also* Firestone, Goodrich, Goodyear, U. S. Rubber; employment, 634-35, 658; grievances, settlement, 648, 669-74, types, 674-75; hours, 659, 661-63; location, 632-33, at Akron, 649; negotiation, 668-69; overtime, 646; preferential shop, 645, 666; production, 631 ff., processes, 636; seniority, 638, 647-48, 657, 659-61, 675, 681; size and structure, 632 ff.; speed-up, 661-63; strikes, 637, 666, 676, decline in number, 642, Firestone, 641, Goodyear, 640, 649, 656-58, sitdowns, 640, 641, 642, 649-52, 656, 657; technological changes, 635, 662-63, 666, 677; transfers, 647, 650, 659, 661; union shop, 642, 645; unions, 637, 638 ff., 658 ff., grievance machinery, 669-72, organizing problems, 639-41, 643-44, 678-80, *see also* Rubber Workers of America, United; vacations, 647; wages, cost-of-living adjustment, 645, 646, differentials, 645, 663-65, 677, 680, earnings, 635-37, grievances, table, 675, rates, 633, 638, 645-46, settlement of, 645 ff., 665-67; work sharing, 648, 657, 659; workers, 635-37, nonunion, 650, 655, 678 ff., women, 636, 646, 647, 674; working conditions, 675
Rubber Workers of America, United, 641-81, *passim;* dues, 653, per capita tax, 679-80; strength, 641-44, 964

SAILORS' UNION OF THE PACIFIC, 888-89, 935-36
Sanitary Potters Association, 910
Sanitary ware, 908, 910, 911
Sawmill and Timber Workers' Union, 926
Schechter, A.L.A., Poultry Corp., et al., v. *United States,* 8
Scrap iron, 260
Scrip, payment of wages, 243, 270, 287
Seafarers' International Union of North America, 936, 937, 961
Seamen's Union, International, 888-90, 935-36
Seniority, 29-30; *see also* separate industries

Index

Service trades, 3, 19, 20, 806-7; *see also* Chicago Service Trades
Seven-hour day in coal, 274, 279, 307
Share-the-work movement, *see* Work sharing
Sheep Shearers' Union of North America, 961
Sherman Anti-Trust Act, 440-41, 694, 918; *see also* Anti-Trust Division
Shipbuilding, 12, 21, 25, 932-34; regional contracts, 933-34
Shipbuilding Stabilization Conference, 933
Shipowners' Association of the Pacific Coast, 936, 888-89, 939
Shoe Workers of America, United, 914-15, 964
Shoes, 29, 872, 877-79, 883, 914-15; agreement coverage, 21; arbitration, 878-79, 883; Knights of St. Crispin, 874, 877-79
Sickness benefits, 401
Siderographers, International Association of, 961
Sitdown strikes, 712, 753, 760, 787, 937; automobiles, 571, 591 ff.; hosiery, 488, 499-500; rubber, 640, 641, 642, 649-52, 656, 657
Six-day week, 857, 925
Six-hour day, 242, 646, 662
Smelting, 20, 942 ff.
Social Security Act, 376, 401
Socialists, 400, 401, 584, 900
Southern Wage Conference, 274-75
Southwestern Interstate Field, 262
Special Delivery Messengers, National Association of, 961
Speed-up, 590, 612, 623-24, 661-63
Spinners Union, International, 18, 961
Squires, B. M., 822-25
Stage Employees and Moving Picture Machine Operators of the United States and Canada, International Alliance of Theatrical, 832, 842-43, 846, 961; Local 110, 832-48
State, County and Municipal Employees, American Federation of, 961
State, County and Municipal Workers of America, 964
Steel, 8, 16, 190, 192, 508-70, 893-95; ability rating, 554-55; agreements, 21, 515, 524-25, 528, 547, Bethlehem, 533, Inland Steel, 532, Jones and Laughlin, 525, Republic, 533, SWOC total, 542, U. S. Steel-SWOC, 1937 (Carnegie-Illinois, "Taylor-Lewis"): 509, 522-24, 544, 549 ff., formula, 522-23, (1941), 560 ff.; arbitration, 557, 559, 560, 561; captive mines, 25, 26, 269, 275, 515-16; checkoff, 534, 540, 542, 563; closed shop, opposition to, 25, 545-46, 563; company unions, 7, 9, 511, 512 ff., 524, 543-44, 558, 563, advantages, 513-14, disadvantages, 514-15, SWOC capture of, 520-22, 524; costs, labor, 508, 567; discharge, 559, 562, *see also* seniority, following; employers, 509, 525, attitudes: of large contract companies, 544-45, of Little Steel, 546-47, of small contract companies, 545-46, organization, 547 ff., policies, 542 ff., *see also* Little Steel; United States Steel Corporation (Big Steel); employment, 509, 510, 527-28; grievance settlement, 513, 531, 538, 548, 549, 556-60, 561, 562, 566, steps in, 556-57; hours, 510, 522, 549, 561, 566; job security, 554-55, 562, rights of service men, 560; layoffs, *see* seniority, following; location, 509, 551; national defense, 510, 530, 533, 568-70; negotiation, 549, 566; overtime, 510, 520, 560; production, defense, 509, 568-70, effect of, 510, 568-70; seniority, 528, 549, 554-55, 559, 562, 566, 570; size, 509; strikes, 515, 559, Homestead, 511, 895, Jones and Laughlin, 525, SWOC-Little Steel, 526-27, 531-33, 542, 565; technological changes, 510, 511, 529, 542-43, 565, 567-68; transfers, 568; unemployment, 528, technological, 510, 568; union-management cooperation, 546; union shop, 530, 534, 540, 542; unions, organizing drives, 510 ff., 894-95, 903, by UMW, SWOC, 515-70, *passim*, status, 534, 555-56, 558, 562-63, *see also* Iron, Steel and Tin Workers; National Committee for the Organizing of the Iron and Steel Industry; Steel Workers Organizing Committee; vacations, 513-14, 560-61; wages, cost-of-living proposal, 521, differentials, 551, rate structure, 551-52, rates, 510, 520-23, 533-34, 551, 560, settlement of, 553-54, 561-62; work sharing, 554; workers, 518, nonunion, 546, 558, number, 508; *see also* Iron; Steel construction
Steel (and iron) construction, 898
Steel Labor Relations Board, National, 544
Steel Mediation Board, Federal, 526
Steel Workers Organizing Committee (SWOC), 515-70, 649; accomplishments, 534, 541-42, 563 ff.; agreements, 509, 524-25, 528, 532-33, 547, total, 542, U. S. Steel (1937), 509, 522-24, 544, 549 ff., (1941), 560 ff.; to be autonomous union, 535-36, 565; dues, 14, 537, 542; financial control,

537-38; leadership, 535, 536-37, 540-41; objectives, 538-39; organization methods, 519; strength, 14, 16, 534, 541-42, 964; strikes, 525, 526-27, 531-33, 542, 565; structure, 534 ff.; Wage and Policy Conventions, 535, 537, 542, 552; *see also* Steel

Stereotypers' and Electrotypers' Union, International, 32, 36, 39 ff., 56 ff., 69, 71, 73, 80 ff.; manning requirements, 94 ff.; membership, 962; *see also* Book and job printing; Newspapers

Stone and Allied Products Workers of America, United, 964

Stonecutters' Association of North America, Journeymen, 196, 962

Stove Founders' National Defense Association, 891-93, 896

Stove industry, 890-93

Stove Mounters International Union, 962

Street, Electric Railway and Motor Coach Employees of America, Amalgamated Association of, 950-52, 961

Street railway and bus transportation, 19, 950-52

Strikebreakers, 48, 231, 278, 324, 402, 477, 593, 599, 601, 715, 793-95; Byrnes Law, 47

Strikes, 25, 26, 27; early, 871-80, *passim;* in defense industries, 25, 26, 199, 275, 931, 932, 934, 945; *see also* separate industries

Subcontracting, *see* Building construction

Sweatshops, 381, 391, 395, 441, 444, 914

Switchmen's Union of North America, 332, 962

TAILORS, independent, *see* Cleaning and Dyeing (Chicago)

Taylor-Lewis agreement, *see* Steel Workers Organizing Committee-U. S. Steel agreement (1937)

Teachers, American Federation of, 962

Teamsters, Chauffeurs, Warehousemen and Helpers of America, International Brotherhood of, 15, 196, 920, 949-50, 951, 962, Local 712, 814 ff.

Technological changes, *see* separate industries

Telegraph industry, 953-54

Telegraphers, Order of Railroad, 332, 954, 962

Telegraphers' Union, Commercial, 938, 954, 962

Telephone industry, 952-53

Telephone and Telegraph Company, American, 863-64, 952, 953

Telephone Workers, National Federation of, 953, 965

Temporary National Economic Committee, 183, 185, 189, 195, 205, 209, 212, 223, 226, 716

Ten-hour day, 871, 872, 873

Texas and New Orleans Railroad case, 4, 330

Textile Workers of America, United, 11, 451, 465-66, 470, 473, 497, 499, 956-57, 962; *see also* Textile Workers Union of America; Hosiery Workers, American Federation of

Textile Workers' Organizing Committee, 436, 499, 956

Textile Workers Union of America, 465, 957, 964

Textiles, 8, 12, 18, 21-22, 955-57; *see also* Men's clothing; Hosiery

Theatre Owners of Illinois, Allied, 832, 841

Thirty-five-hour week in coal, 274, 279, 307

Thirty-hour week, 223, 242

Thirty-six-hour week, 439, 445, 640, 662, 773, 787

Tile Contractors' Association of America, 227

Time studies, use of, 623, 629, 663, 666-67, 768-69, 786, 804

Tires and tubes, 614, 631 ff.; *see also* Rubber products

Tobacco Workers' International Union, 962

Trade unions, *see* Unions

Train Dispatchers' Association, American, 332, 965

Transfers, *see* separate industries, seniority, transfers

Transport Workers Union of America, 950-51, 964

Transportation, 19, 888-90, 948-52; intercity, 19, 951-52; urban, 19, 950-51; *see also* Railroads

Transportation, Federal Coordinator of, 345, 350 ff., 369, 380

Transportation Act of 1920, 328, 329, 360; (1940), 319, 370-71, 373

Trucking, 19, 948-50

Trucking Association, American, 949

Typesetting, first machine, 49; threat of offset method, 125

Typographical Union, International, 11, 15, 39-108, *passim*, 125-82, 883-85; early history, 47 ff., 126 ff., 883-85; formation, 47-48; membership, 965; reproduction (reset) requirement, 63, 98-101; *see also* Book and job printing; Newspapers

Typothetae of America, United, 122 ff., 128 ff., 154, 884-85; Closed Shop Division, 126, 131-33, 885; Open Shop Division, 131, 885

INDEX

UNAFFILIATED NATIONAL AND INTERNATIONAL UNIONS, 13, 964-65
Unemployment, effect of, 3-4, 873, 877, 907; *see also* separate industries; Technological changes
Unemployment insurance, 366, 368, 371-72, 401, 427, 445, 759, 822
Union label, *see* separate industries, unions
Union-management cooperation, 546, 900, 917; Amalgamated Clothing Workers, 381, 431-43, 446; electrical products, 746; 778-80; hosiery, 503-7; railroads, 366, 380, 907; *see also* other separate industries
Union membership, 5-7, 13-16; (1941), Appendix C: 958-65, AF of L, 958-62, CIO, 962-64, unaffiliated nationals and internationals, 964-65; in Canada, 6, 13; dues-paying, 14-15; gains, during World War, 901-2, (1937-41), 12 ff.; postwar losses, 903 ff.; problem of estimating, 14-15; total, 13; *see also* separate unions
Union shop, 24-25; anthracite, 299, 300, 307-8; automobiles, 595-96; bituminous coal, 273, 275; defined, 24; electrical products, 745, 747, 783, 786, 789; newspapers, 46, Guild Shop, 110, 112, 113-14; rubber, 642, 645; steel, 530, 534, 540, 542
Union status, 24-25; *see also* Closed, Preferential, Union shop; separate industries and unions
Unions, company, *see* Company unions; craft vs. industrial, 9 ff., 23, *see also* AF of L vs. CIO, separate industries; independent, 13; in mass production industries, 6 ff., 10 ff., 16, 24, 744, 905, *see also* Automobiles, Glass, Electrical products, Rubber, Steel
United Licensed Officers of the United States of America, 937-38
United Mine Workers of America, *see* Mine Workers of America, United
United Press, 954
United States Rubber Company, 633 ff., 643, 644, 649, 676, 679; *see also* Rubber products
United States Steel Corporation, 12, 508 ff., 515, 520 ff., 534, 544, 549 ff., 889, 903; agreements, *see* Steel, SWOC; cement producer, 912; formation of, 895
Unorganized workers, 3-4, 9 ff.; *see also* separate industries, nonunion workers, unions, organizing efforts
Unskilled workers, 12, 16, 628, 635, 769, 914, 924; glass, 684, 688, 718, 730, 739, 741; printing trades, 121, 124, 134 ff., 150, 178; rates in bituminous coal, 255, 257
Utility Workers Organizing Committee, 955, 964

VACATIONS, *see* separate industries
Vegetable growing and processing, 921-22

WAGE-HOUR ACT, *see* Fair Labor Standards Act
Wages, differentials, 23; earnings, 28; skilled vs. unskilled, 28; sliding scale, iron industry, 875-76; *see also* separate industries
Wagner, Robert F., 7, 490
Wagner Act, *see* National Labor Relations Act
Wall Paper Craftsmen and Workers of North America, United, 962
War Labor Board, National, World War I, II; *see* National War Labor Board
Waste in Industry, Committee on, 403
Water transportation, 19, 888-90
Waterfront Employers Association of the Pacific Coast, 938-39
Weavers' Protective Association, American Wire, 962
Western Union Telegraph Company, 953-54
Westinghouse Electric and Manufacturing Company, 746, 760-81, 801 ff.; East Pittsburgh works, 761-72, 801-2, Works Joint Conference Committee plan, 761 ff., 768, 773-74; East Springfield plant, 746, 772-81, 802, 805; union-management cooperation, 778 ff.
Wilson, Woodrow, 248, 903
Window Glass Cutters' League, *see* Glass Cutters' League of America, Window
Wolman, Leo, cited, 6, 74, 902 ff.
Wolman Award, 492-93
Women workers, *see* separate industries, workers, women
Women's clothing, 900; agreements, coverage by, 18, 22
Wood Carvers' Association of North America, International, 15, 962
Woodworkers of America, International, 926, 964
Work Projects Administration, WPA (Works Progress Administration), 186-87, 528, 659, 739, 803
Work sharing, 29-30; *see also* separate industries
Working conditions, *see* separate industries
Workingmen's Benevolent Association, 283 ff., 876, 887
World War I, 901 ff., 906, 932; legisla-

tion during, 4, 327, 901-2; postwar union decline, 3, 903 ff.; prices and cost of living, 75, 255, 411, 632; union gains during, 3, 326-27, 637, 748, 901-3, 946; *see also* National War Labor **Board**

YELLOW-DOG CONTRACTS, 325, 330, 368, 402, 403, 476, 904, 906

Youngstown Sheet and Tube Company, 509, 513-14, 525 ff., 530-31, 533, 546

American Labor: From Conspiracy to Collective Bargaining

AN ARNO PRESS/NEW YORK TIMES COLLECTION

SERIES I

Abbott, Edith.
Women in Industry. 1913.

Aveling, Edward B. and Eleanor M. Aveling.
Working Class Movement in America. 1891.

Beard, Mary.
The American Labor Movement. 1939.

Blankenhorn, Heber.
The Strike for Union. 1924.

Blum, Solomon.
Labor Economics. 1925.

Brandeis, Louis D. and Josephine Goldmark.
Women in Industry. 1907. New introduction by Leon Stein and Philip Taft.

Brooks, John Graham.
American Syndicalism. 1913.

Butler, Elizabeth Beardsley.
Women and the Trades. 1909.

Byington, Margaret Frances.
Homestead: The Household of A Mill Town. 1910.

Carroll, Mollie Ray.
Labor and Politics. 1923.

Coleman, McAlister.
Men and Coal. 1943.

Coleman, J. Walter.
The Molly Maguire Riots: Industrial Conflict in the Pennsylvania Coal Region. 1936.

Commons, John R.
Industrial Goodwill. 1919.

Commons, John R.
Industrial Government. 1921.

Dacus, Joseph A.
Annals of the Great Strikes. 1877.

Dealtry, William.
The Laborer: A Remedy for his Wrongs. 1869.

Douglas, Paul H., Curtis N. Hitchcock and Willard E. Atkins, editors.
The Worker in Modern Economic Society. 1923.

Eastman, Crystal.
Work Accidents and the Law. 1910.

Ely, Richard T.
The Labor Movement in America. 1890. New Introduction by Leon Stein and Philip Taft.

Feldman, Herman.
Problems in Labor Relations. 1937.

Fitch, John Andrew.
The Steel Worker. 1910.

Furniss, Edgar S. and Laurence Guild.
Labor Problems. 1925.

Gladden, Washington.
Working People and Their Employers. 1885.

Gompers, Samuel.
Labor and the Common Welfare. 1919.

Hardman, J. B. S., editor.
American Labor Dynamics. 1928.

Higgins, George G.
Voluntarism in Organized Labor, 1930-40. 1944.

Hiller, Ernest T.
The Strike. 1928.

Hollander, Jacob S. and George E. Barnett.
Studies in American Trade Unionism. 1906. New Introduction by Leon Stein and Philip Taft.

Jelley, Symmes M.
The Voice of Labor. 1888.

Jones, Mary.
Autobiography of Mother Jones. 1925.

Kelley, Florence.
Some Ethical Gains Through Legislation. 1905.

LaFollette, Robert M., editor.
The Making of America: Labor. 1906.

Lane, Winthrop D.
Civil War in West Virginia. 1921.

Lauck, W. Jett and Edgar Sydenstricker.
Conditions of Labor in American Industries. 1917.

Leiserson, William M.
Adjusting Immigrant and Industry. 1924.

Lescohier, Don D.
Knights of St. Crispin. 1910.

Levinson, Edward.
I Break Strikes. The Technique of Pearl L. Bergoff. 1935.

Lloyd, Henry Demarest.
Men, The Workers. Compiled by Anne Whithington and Caroline Stallbohen. 1909. New Introduction by Leon Stein and Philip Taft.

Lorwin, Louis (Louis Levine).
The Women's Garment Workers. 1924.

Markham, Edwin, Ben B. Lindsay and George Creel.
Children in Bondage. 1914.

Marot, Helen.
American Labor Unions. 1914.

Mason, Alpheus T.
Organized Labor and the Law. 1925.

Newcomb, Simon.
A Plain Man's Talk on the Labor Question. 1886. New Introduction by Leon Stein and Philip Taft.

Price, George Moses.
The Modern Factory: Safety, Sanitation and Welfare. 1914.

Randall, John Herman Jr.
Problem of Group Responsibility to Society. 1922.

Rubinow, I. M.
Social Insurance. 1913.

Saposs, David, editor.
Readings in Trade Unionism. 1926.

Slichter, Sumner H.
Union Policies and Industrial Management. 1941.

Socialist Publishing Society.
The Accused and the Accusers. 1887.

Stein, Leon and Philip Taft, editors.
The Pullman Strike. 1894-1913. New Introduction by the editors.

Stein, Leon and Philip Taft, editors.
Religion, Reform, and Revolution: Labor Panaceas in the Nineteenth Century. 1969. New Introduction by the editors.

Stein, Leon and Philip Taft, editors.
Wages, Hours, and Strikes: Labor Panaceas in the Twentieth Century. 1969. New introduction by the editors.

Swinton, John.
A Momentous Question: The Respective Attitudes of Labor and Capital. 1895. New Introduction by Leon Stein and Philip Taft.

Tannenbaum, Frank.
The Labor Movement. 1921.

Tead, Ordway.
Instincts in Industry. 1918.

Vorse, Mary Heaton.
Labor's New Millions. 1938.

Witte, Edwin Emil.
The Government in Labor Disputes. 1932.

Wright, Carroll D.
The Working Girls of Boston. 1889.

Wyckoff, Veitrees J.
Wage Policies of Labor Organizations in a Period of Industrial Depression. 1926.

Yellen, Samuel.
American Labor Struggles. 1936.

SERIES II

Allen, Henry J.
The Party of the Third Part: The Story of the Kansas Industrial Relations Court. 1921. *Including* The Kansas Court of Industrial Relations Law (1920) by Samuel Gompers.

Baker, Ray Stannard.
The New Industrial Unrest. 1920.

Barnett, George E. & David A. McCabe.
Mediation, Investigation and Arbitration in Industrial Disputes. 1916.

Barns, William E., editor.
The Labor Problem. 1886.

Bing, Alexander M.
War-Time Strikes and Their Adjustment. 1921.

Brooks, Robert R. R.
When Labor Organizes. 1937.

Calkins, Clinch.
Spy Overhead: The Story of Industrial Espionage. 1937.

Cooke, Morris Llewellyn & Philip Murray.
Organized Labor and Production. 1940.

Creamer, Daniel & Charles W. Coulter.
Labor and the Shut-Down of the Amoskeag Textile Mills. 1939.

Glocker, Theodore W.
The Government of American Trade Unions. 1913.

Gompers, Samuel.
Labor and the Employer. 1920.

Grant, Luke.
The National Erectors' Association and the International Association of Bridge and Structural Ironworkers. 1915.

Haber, William.
Industrial Relations in the Building Industry. 1930.

Henry, Alice.
Women and the Labor Movement. 1923.

Herbst, Alma.
The Negro in the Slaughtering and Meat-Packing Industry in Chicago. 1932.

[Hicks, Obediah.]
Life of Richard F. Trevellick. 1896.

Hillquit, Morris, Samuel Gompers & Max J. Hayes.
The Double Edge of Labor's Sword: Discussion and Testimony on Socialism and Trade-Unionism Before the Commission on Industrial Relations. 1914. New Introduction by Leon Stein and Philip Taft.

Jensen, Vernon H.
Lumber and Labor. 1945.

Kampelman, Max M.
The Communist Party vs. the C.I.O. 1957.

Kingsbury, Susan M., editor.
Labor Laws and Their Enforcement. By Charles E. Persons, Mabel Parton, Mabelle Moses & Three "Fellows." 1911.

McCabe, David A.
The Standard Rate in American Trade Unions. 1912.

Mangold, George Benjamin.
Labor Argument in the American Protective Tariff Discussion. 1908.

Millis, Harry A., editor.
How Collective Bargaining Works. 1942.

Montgomery, Royal E.
Industrial Relations in the Chicago Building Trades. 1927.

Oneal, James.
The Workers in American History. 3rd edition, 1912.

Palmer, Gladys L.
Union Tactics and Economic Change: A Case Study of Three Philadelphia Textile Unions. 1932.

Penny, Virginia.
How Women Can Make Money: Married or Single, In all Branches of the Arts and Sciences, Professions, Trades, Agricultural and Mechanical Pursuits. 1870. New Introduction by Leon Stein and Philip Taft.

Penny, Virginia.
Think and Act: A Series of Articles Pertaining to Men and Women, Work and Wages. 1869.

Pickering, John.
The Working Man's Political Economy. 1847.

Ryan, John A.
A Living Wage. 1906.

Savage, Marion Dutton.
Industrial Unionism in America. 1922.

Simkhovitch, Mary Kingsbury.
The City Worker's World in America. 1917.

Spero, Sterling Denhard.
The Labor Movement in a Government Industry: A Study of Employee Organization in the Postal Service. 1927.

Stein, Leon and Philip Taft, editors.
Labor Politics: Collected Pamphlets. 2 vols. 1836-1932. New Introduction by the editors.

Stein, Leon and Philip Taft, editors.
The Management of Workers: Selected Arguments. 1917-1956. New Introduction by the editors.

Stein, Leon and Philip Taft, editors.
Massacre at Ludlow: Four Reports. 1914-1915. New Introduction by the editors.

Stein, Leon and Philip Taft, editors.
Workers Speak: Self-Portraits. 1902-1906. New Introduction by the editors.

Stolberg, Benjamin.
The Story of the CIO. 1938.

Taylor, Paul S.
The Sailors' Union of the Pacific. 1923.

U.S. Commission on Industrial Relations.
Efficiency Systems and Labor. 1916. New Introduction by Leon Stein and Philip Taft.

Walker, Charles Rumford.
American City: A Rank-and-File History. 1937.

Walling, William English.
American Labor and American Democracy. 1926.

Williams, Whiting.
What's on the Worker's Mind: By One Who Put on Overalls to Find Out. 1920.

Wolman, Leo.
The Boycott in American Trade Unions. 1916.

Ziskind, David.
One Thousand Strikes of Government Employees. 1940.

HD
6508
T9
1971

HD 6508
.T9

1971

HD   Twentieth Century
6508   Fund.
T9
1971 How collective
        bargaining works.